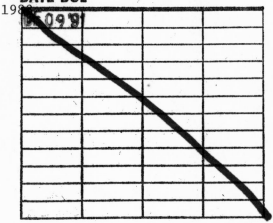

SUPER CHIEF

The Chief Justice in his robes (*Courtesy of the United States Supreme Court*)

SUPER CHIEF

EARL WARREN AND HIS SUPREME COURT —
A JUDICIAL BIOGRAPHY

by Bernard Schwartz

UNABRIDGED EDITION

New York University Press
NEW YORK AND LONDON
1983

Library of Congress Cataloging in Publication Data

Schwartz, Bernard, 1923–
   Super Chief, Earl Warren and his Supreme Court.

  Bibliography: p.
  Includes index.
  1. Warren, Earl, 1891–1974. 2. Judges—United
States—Biography. I. Title.
KF8745.W3S37 1983   347.73'2634 [B]   82-18868
ISBN 0-8147-7825-9   347-3073534 [B]

Manufactured in the United States of America

Clothbound editions of New York University Press books are Smyth-
sewn and printed on permanent and durable acid-free paper.
10 9 8 7 6 5 4 3 2

for Aileen ... let me count the ways

To those who served with him, Earl Warren will always be the Super Chief.

—*William J. Brennan, Jr.*
Associate Justice, United States Supreme Court

CONTENTS

Sources and Acknowledgments   xi

1. The New Chief Justice   I
2. The Court, the Brethren, "and Company"   25
3. Warren and the Brown Case   72
4. 1953–1954 Terms: Feeling His Way   128
5. 1954–1955 Terms: Moving toward Activism   169
6. 1956 Term: "B.B.D. and W."   204
7. The Elephant and the Mouse   253
8. 1957–1958 Terms: Little Rock, Expatriation et al   289
9. 1959–1960 Terms: The Shifting Balance   336
10. 1960–1961 Terms: Changing Guard and Changing Law   389
11. 1962 Term: A Deceptive Calm   445
12. 1963 Term: Days of Drums and Days of Law   493
13. 1964 Term: Television, Civil Rights, and Privacy   543
14. 1965 Term: Miranda, Discrimination, and First Amendment   586
15. 1966 Term: Warren and the "New" Black   629

16. 1967 Term: Abortive Retirement   680

17. 1968 Term: The Final Term   723

    Abbreviations Used in Notes   773

    Notes   775

    Bibliography   831

    Table of Cases   835

    Index   841

Illustrations appear as a group following page 466

SOURCES AND ACKNOWLEDGMENTS

This book is based upon both documentary and oral sources. The documentary sources are of two kinds: (1) the conference lists and notes and the docket books of the Justices. The votes on granting certiorari or hearing an appeal, which were normally not made public in the Warren Court, are taken from them. The conferences themselves, at which cases are discussed and the votes taken on decisions, are, of course, completely private—attended only by the Justices themselves. The secrecy of the conference is, indeed, one of the great continuing Court traditions. I have tried to reconstruct the conferences in most of the cases discussed, including all the important cases decided by the Warren Court. The conference discussions which are given in conversational form are reconstructed from notes made by at least one Justice who was present, including, but not limited to, the notes of Justices Felix Frankfurter, Harold H. Burton, Tom C. Clark, and John M. Harlan; (2) the correspondence, notes, diaries, memoranda, and draft opinions of members of the Warren Court, including, but not limited to, the papers of the same Justices and Justices Hugo L. Black and William O. Douglas. The documents used and their locations are identified in the notes, except where they were made available upon a confidential basis. In the latter case, I have tried to identify the documents, usually by title and date, in the text. I have personally examined every document to which reference is made. Most of them have never been published.

I have been afforded generous access to the papers of the Justices and am pleased to acknowledge the help given by the Manuscript Division, Library of Congress, for the papers of Justices Black, Frankfurter, Douglas, and Burton; by Professor Roy M. Mersky, University of Texas Law School, for the papers of Justice Clark; by the Mudd Manuscript Library, Princeton University, for the papers of Justice Harlan and permission to quote from them; and by the Harvard Law Library, for the papers of Justice Frankfurter and permission to quote from them. The Earl Warren Oral History Project at the University of California at Berkeley was also of great help and I gratefully acknowledge its permission to quote from its interviews. I should also thank David L. Snyder of the California State Archives for his assistance in my research in the Earl Warren papers there. In addition, I wish to acknowledge the help given me by the Oral History Research Office at Columbia University, as well as the Herbert Hoover, Franklin D. Roosevelt, Harry S. Truman, John F. Kennedy, and Lyndon B. Johnson Presidential Libraries for access to their materials relating to Earl Warren, and the National Archives for documents on the Warren Commission.

The oral sources were personal interviews. I interviewed some thirty former law clerks of Chief Justice Warren (including at least one from each Court term during the Warren years), as well as clerks of other Justices. Chief Justice Warren E. Burger and all the living members of the Warren Court, except Justice Thurgood Marshall, spoke with me. I also met with Judge Earl Warren, Jr., and former California Governor Edmund G. (Pat) Brown, others who knew Earl Warren, as well as Mrs. Margaret McHugh, his executive secretary. I should also acknowledge the help given me, on different aspects of this work, by Mrs. Alan Barth, Howard H. Callaway, Fred W. Friendly, Dr. Oscar Mann, Clark R. Mollenhoff, Dean Norman Redlich, Richard H. Rodda, Alden Whitman, and Judge Charles E. Wyzanski, as well as by Professor Julius J. Marke and the New York University Law Library staff and my untiring secretary, Mrs. Barbara Ortiz.

Every statement which is not otherwise identified was made to me personally. I have tried to identify the statements made to me by different people, except where they were made upon a confidential basis. In the latter case, I have given the position of the person involved, but not his name. This book could not have been written without the cooperation of those who shared their time and experience so generously with me. Nor could it have been undertaken without the generous support of Dean Redlich and the New York University School of Law, as well as help for incidental research expenses by the Charles Ulrick and Josephine Bay Foundation (through Mrs. Raymonde Paul).

I.

THE NEW CHIEF JUSTICE

The Attorney General read the coded cable with some satisfaction. Sent from Stockholm August 3, 1953, the message stated: THANKS FOR MESSAGE STOP HAVE BEEN REFRESHED BY TRIP STOP LOOKING FORWARD TO RETURN TO MY WORK EARL WARREN.

This was the message Attorney General Herbert Brownell had hoped to receive and he sent a return cable to Governor Warren, c/o the United States Embassy in Stockholm: WE ARE BOTH GRATIFIED TO RECEIVE YOUR CABLE.[1]

Earl Warren had been Governor of California since the beginning of 1943. He was now in 1953 in the middle of his third term—a record for the chief executive of the then second largest state. After overwhelming electoral victories, he was inevitably considered for national office. He had run for Vice-President in 1948, but the Dewey-Warren ticket had lost to President Truman, one of the greatest political upsets in American history. In 1952, he had campaigned to head the ticket himself, but Eisenhower's victory appeared to close the White House to him for the next eight years. Warren had already decided not to run for a fourth term as Governor. Thus his public career appeared at an end, unless he obtained a position in the new Administration.

In early December, 1952, a month after the election, Governor Warren was reading in bed in the Executive Mansion in Sacramento. It was 7 A.M., California time, when the telephone rang. It was the

Capitol switchboard operator saying that the President-elect was on the phone. Eisenhower said, "I am back here selecting my Cabinet, and I wanted to tell you I won't have a place for you on it." He went on to inform Warren that he had seriously considered him for Attorney General, but that he had decided to appoint Brownell, who had been his campaign manager.

"But I want you to know," Eisenhower went on, "that I intend to offer you the first vacancy on the Supreme Court." "That is very generous of you," Warren replied. "That is my personal commitment to you," the President-elect concluded.[2]

After his inauguration, President Eisenhower appointed Warren as one of the American delegates to the coronation of Queen Elizabeth II. Following the ceremony on June 2, 1953, Warren and his family planned to tour Scandinavia. But first the Governor had to fly back to Sacramento to close out the legislative session and act on the bills awaiting his signature. He felt that he had to do this personally because the Lieutenant Governor had signed a bill he opposed while he was in London. He feared similar action if he remained away.[3]

On his way back to Europe, Warren stopped in Washington and met Brownell at the latter's invitation for lunch at the Statler Hotel. The Attorney General told the Governor that the President wanted to appoint him as Solicitor General. It had been some time since Warren had actively practiced law, and Brownell said that the President believed that service as Solicitor General would be valuable prior to membership in the Supreme Court. Warren said that he would think it over and let Brownell know. They arranged a code message that Warren could send while he was abroad, and the cable Warren sent from Stockholm was in the code agreed upon to tell the Attorney General he had accepted. Brownell says, "I was enthusiastic about the idea of [Warren's] becoming Solicitor General," and sent the return cable to show how both he and the President felt about the acceptance.[4]

The Attorney General's pleasure was understandable. But it is more difficult to understand the other side of the equation, that is, why Warren would leave the California Governorship for what was after all only the third highest position in the Department of Justice. Later Warren wrote that he accepted because the Solicitor General "position is probably the most prestigious one in America in the practice of law. To be the principal lawyer for the United States Government in its most important litigation presents a challenge of enormous proportions."[5]

Despite the prestige of the Solicitor General position in legal circles, the move from Governor of California to Government counsel before the Supreme Court would have to be considered a step down for Warren. That he was willing to accept the lesser post confirms the strength of Eisenhower's commitment to put Warren on the Court. If the Governor agreed to serve as the new Solicitor General, the *quid pro quo* was the obligation to appoint him to the first Court vacancy.

Soon after Warren returned to Sacramento from his Scandinavian trip, he held a news conference. This was on September 3. He announced at it that he would not seek a fourth term as Governor, but declined to answer questions about his future plans. The next day, a front-page *New York Times* story quoted a "White House source" as saying that, if he wanted it, Warren could have the first vacant seat on the Supreme Court.[6] The Governor himself was beginning to make preparations for the move to Washington as Solicitor General.

Warren's prospects were changed when Chief Justice Fred M. Vinson died quite unexpectedly of a heart attack only a few days later, on September 8, 1953. Vinson's death posed a problem for the President. Eisenhower had made a commitment to appoint Warren to the first Supreme Court opening. But neither the President nor anyone else expected, nor had grounds to expect, that the vacancy would occur in the Court's central chair. Vinson was only sixty-three, in apparent good health, and came from a notably long-lived family.

Did the Eisenhower commitment to Warren apply to the Chief Justiceship? The President himself doubted that it did. In his memoirs, Eisenhower wrote that "neither he [Warren] nor I was thinking of the special post of chief justice, nor was I definitely committed to any appointment."[7] Yet Eisenhower had made the offer as a "personal commitment" to the Governor, and Warren had considered it as such. His acceptance of the proposal that he become Solicitor General can be explained on no other basis.

Eisenhower says that, "I gave serious thought to the possibility of appointing John Foster Dulles."[8] The President spoke to the Secretary of State, but the latter said that he did not have any interest in any position other than that which he currently held. The Attorney

General met with Eisenhower to discuss whether any member of the Court should be appointed Chief Justice. Brownell says that he considered recommending Justice Robert H. Jackson, but decided not to because of Jackson's active role in favor of President Roosevelt's "Court-packing" plan in 1937, as well as his bitter public dispute with Justice Hugo L. Black.[9]

Jackson's appointment was actually never a serious possibility, because the President and his aides felt that the first Republican Administration in twenty years could hardly appoint a Democrat to head the Supreme Court. The only Republican then on the Court was Justice Harold H. Burton. But Brownell states that "Burton's health was not of the best, and this factor militated against" his selection.[10] Even in perfect health, however, Burton scarcely had the leadership ability to make the President consider him seriously.

That meant that the appointment would have to go to someone not on the Court. But would that someone be Warren? Public speculation certainly focused on the California Governor. The day after Vinson's death, the *New York Times* reported that it was commonly accepted on the West Coast that Warren would succeed the Chief Justice. His political enemies, the report said, would be just as happy to get him out of the state as his friends would be to see him receive the appointment.[11] Justice William O. Douglas confirms what was widely rumored at the time—that Vice-President Richard M. Nixon called on Eisenhower to urge him to name Warren. According to Douglas, "Nixon went to Ike saying something like, 'You must get Warren out of California. He has control of the Republican Party machinery and we can't do business with him.' "[12]

Warren's own feelings on the matter had been conveyed to the President, when, at a White House breakfast, Eisenhower found himself seated next to Representative William S. Mailliard, who had been Governor Warren's travel secretary until he was elected to Congress. The President asked Mailliard, "Do you think that [Warren] would really want to be [on the court], after his years as Attorney General, Governor and all of this? Wouldn't it be pretty rarefied for him?"

Mailliard says he answered, "Yes, I frankly think he'd be very likely to be bored to death" as an Associate Justice. But Mailliard went on to say, "My answer would be emphatically different if we were talking about the Chief Justiceship. He could run the place. . . . The

Court would have decorum and dignity and it would be well-managed."[13] But Eisenhower was reluctant to appoint the California Governor to head the Court. Brownell says, "It was clear to me," from his discussions with the President on filling Vinson's seat, "that President Eisenhower did not feel that his prior discussions with Governor Warren had related to a vacancy in the post of Chief Justice, but that he had had in mind an Associate Justiceship in his original call to Governor Warren about a 'first vacancy.' "[14]

At this point the President asked the Attorney General to fly to California to put his view to Warren and see whether he agreed. At the time, the Governor was deer hunting with his sons on an isolated island off the Santa Barbara coast. The island had no telephone and, on Friday, September 25, Warren received a radio message asking him to telephone Brownell in Washington. The Governor had an airplane take him to the mainland and he called the Attorney General. The two arranged to meet two days later at McClellan Air Force Base, ten miles from Sacramento.

Brownell arrived at the base in a military plane at 8 A.M. Warren was waiting in a room set aside for the purpose, where they were able to talk in private. The press reported a week later that the conference had lasted three hours. Warren himself later wrote that the meeting took an hour,[15] while Brownell says that "we conferred about an hour and a half."[16]

The Attorney General told the Governor of the President's interpretation of the commitment, saying he felt it applied only to an ordinary vacancy in the Supreme Court. He then asked if they could "defer the commitment." If so, Warren could have any Cabinet position he chose. "Name your own," he was told.

Warren firmly rejected the suggestion. He said that he was not interested in any Cabinet post and could not afford to take one. He also insisted that this was the first vacancy. As Brownell recalls it, "Warren took the position that he was ready to accept the chief justiceship that was offered to him by the President, that he did feel that he had a commitment for the next vacancy, and that this *was* the next vacancy."[17]

Whether the Governor went further and threatened to accuse the President of reneging on his commitment is not known. But the threat was not necessary. The Attorney General gave in and said that the President would want his nominee to accept an interim appointment and be in Washington to start the new Court term a week later on Monday, October 5. Warren said that it was "a helluva way" to leave a state administration of eleven years. But he had already made arrangements to resign the Governorship to become Solicitor General, and he was prepared to leave immediately for the opening of the Court session.

Both Brownell and Warren later denied that there was any attempt to persuade the Governor that the President's commitment did not extend to the Chief Justiceship. In his memoirs, Warren went so far as to deny that anything "was said about my becoming Chief Justice."[18] Yet Brownell concedes that Warren did say that he felt that *this* was the next vacancy and he was, therefore, ready to accept Vinson's seat.[19] Warren would scarcely have made the statement except in response to a different interpretation of the commitment by Brownell.

The version of the Warren–Brownell meeting that has been relied upon here is based upon what Warren told his son, Earl, Jr. at the time, and the account he later gave a member of the Supreme Court.

Merrill H. Small, who served from 1945 to 1953 as Warren's executive secretary, also said that he got the impression from the Governor that he had insisted to Brownell on being named Chief Justice. Small stated in 1972, "I wrote in the *Sacramento Bee* of June 7, 1970, that he held out for the highest job . . . and nothing was said by him about it then or since."[20]

In addition, Chief Justice Arthur T. Vanderbilt of New Jersey, who was considered by the President for Vinson's seat, told his biographer, Eugene C. Gerhart, that Brownell tried to get Warren not to demand fulfillment by Eisenhower of his post-election promise. When Brownell was unsuccessful, Vanderbilt said, he "had to cave in." When Brownell flew out to meet Warren, Vanderbilt told Alfred Clapp, his colleague on the New Jersey Supreme Court, "They haven't got a Chinaman's chance of getting him to give up such a commitment."[21]

On Brownell's return to Washington, he invited six selected reporters to his home for "background information" and "leaked" the news that Warren would be appointed. The story was widely reported the next day.[22] When the President announced at his September 30 news conference that he was nominating Warren to be the fourteenth Chief Justice, be began by saying, "I could start off, I think, by confirming something that is certainly by no means news any more."[23]

Warren received a phone call telling of his appointment as he was finishing breakfast in the Governor's Mansion in Sacramento.[24] He immediately wired his appreciation to the President for "your designation of me to be Chief Justice of the Supreme Court."[25] Warren made a common error here in referring to his new office. By October 3, when he sent in his letter of resignation as California Governor, Warren had the title straight. He was to become "Chief Justice of the United States." He would not only preside over the Supreme Court, but also head the federal judicial system. For his additional duties, he would be paid $500 more than the eight Associate Justices. His new salary would be $25,500. As Governor he had received $25,000.

The Warren family had grown accustomed to the Governor's habit of sitting up in bed reading, often well into the night. During the 1953 Labor Day weekend, when Chief Justice Vinson died, Warren was reading Albert J. Beveridge's classic *Life of John Marshall*.[26] When, a month later, President Eisenhower appointed Warren to succeed Vinson, no one expected the new Chief Justice to rank with Marshall himself in the judicial pantheon. There was no hint of greatness in the first phase of Warren's career. An honest, hard-working, and vigorous law-enforcement officer, there was little to distinguish Warren from his peers. Even in his later role as Governor of California, nothing foreshadowed his performance as Chief Justice. Although he had evolved from the tough-minded prosecutor, who had been the partisan Republican state chairman during the 1936 Presidential campaign, to the "nonpartisan" Governor who appealed equally to Democratic and Republican voters, Warren's outstanding feature remained the image of bland competence that he projected. "Earl Warren is honest, likable, and clean," wrote John Gunther in 1947. Gunther listed his outstanding characteristics as "decency, stability, sincerity, and lack of genuine intellectual distinction. . . . he will never set the world on fire or even make it smoke."[27]

The early Earl Warren was more than most a product of his upbringing and surroundings. He was born on March 19, 1891, in Los Angeles, but his family moved to Bakersfield five years later. He lived in that California town, where his father worked on the Southern Pacific Railroad, until he started college in 1908.

The Bakersfield in which Warren grew up still had more than a few vestiges of the American frontier. Bakersfield then, wrote novelist Irving Stone in a campaign biography of the California Governor, "was a wide-open town in the wild and wooly tradition of the West, with as little law and order as any place in the United States. The cowboys came in on weekends dressed in their boots and spurs and flamboyant shirts and rode their horses into the saloons. The gambling houses ran twenty-four hours a day."[28] Of a population of seven thousand, it was estimated that five hundred were prostitutes. Warren personally recalled the shootout in which the singer Lawrence Tibbett's father, who was the sheriff, and uncle, the city marshall, were killed by outlaws.

The Bakersfield environment made an indelible impression. It left Warren with a lifelong antipathy toward gambling, drunkenness, and vice. "I saw conditions," he was to write in his memoirs, "in many of the homes where the breadwinner had lost his earnings at the gaming tables."[29] He also saw the same men spending more than they could afford in the local saloons and brothels. Warren's later attitude in cases involving gambling, pornography, and public drunkenness—seemingly so inconsistent with his normal judicial posture—can most effectively be explained in terms of the almost physical repugnance he felt toward them since his Bakersfield days.

The other feelings acquired in Bakersfield remained with him. "I witnessed," he recalled, "crime and vice of all kinds countenanced by corrupt government," and the "effect on the people of a community."[30] The result was a zeal in cases involving corruption by public officials that characterized his career, both as a prosecutor and on the bench.

In addition, it was at Bakersfield that Warren acquired his first experience with the conditions that faced the working man in an economy still largely dominated by laissez-faire. While he was in high school, he worked summers, usually for the railroad. The job he remembered most was that of "call boy" for the Southern Pacific, with the task of rounding up the train crews. The job gave him first-hand contact with the saloons, gambling tables, and the so-called "Jap Alley"—the red-light district. But it also exposed him to the worker's plight in the days before laws protecting the rights of labor.

His work, Warren later wrote, was "meaningful because I was dealing with people as they worked for a great corporation that dominated the economic and political life of the community. I saw that power exercised and the hardship that followed in its wake."[31] When he was Chief Justice, Warren used to tell his law clerks how his railroad experience affected him. "He told us," one of them recalls, "that he felt that the jobs used up the men and when they were no longer valuable, cast them aside. He supposed that was the first time he'd thought of the human cost of building the railroads and the country."[32] The Chief Justice's later efforts to protect workers in employer's liability cases, and his strong disagreements with Justice Felix Frankfurter over the matter,[33] can be traced directly to his days as a railroad call boy.

But turn-of-the-century Bakersfield also had a more baneful effect. The young Warren was inevitably affected by the xenophobic attitude that prevailed toward the large group of Chinese and other Orientals whom the railroad had imported as cheap labor. The Bakersfield city directory at the time listed all those who lived at the different addresses in the community. Whites and blacks were listed by name, but for houses where an Oriental was living, all it said was "Oriental," followed by the address.[34] Growing up in a town where Orientals did not count enough even to have their names listed had its inescapable influence.

Warren's professional career had begun in 1920, when he became a deputy on the staff of Ezra Decoto, the District Attorney of Alameda County, across the Bay from San Francisco. Before then, he had obtained undergraduate and law degrees from the University of California at Berkeley, served in the Army during World War I, and worked briefly in law practice and as a legislative aide. Warren later said, "I thought I would work in the district attorney's office for about a year and a half and at the end of that time I would go into private practice to become a great trial lawyer. So I . . . ended up by remaining eighteen years."[35]

By 1923, Warren had become the chief deputy in the D.A.'s office. When Decoto resigned in 1925, Warren became District Attorney. He held that position until 1938. In later years, critics constantly charged that Warren had very little legal experience. Those dissatisfied with the decisions of the Warren Court used to say that they were only what could be expected from a tribunal not headed by a real lawyer. But the charge was misplaced. In terms of legal practice, Warren had more experience than any member of the Court to which he was appointed. He had headed one of the biggest law offices in California for thirteen years and then served as his state's highest legal officer for four more before becoming Governor.

Alameda County, with its almost half-million population, was the third largest county in California. Almost as big as Rhode Island, it contained the industrial and commercial centers along the Bay, as well as large agricultural areas. The District Attorney's office there had one of the busiest law practices in the state. "In 1925," Warren recalled, "bootlegging, rumrunning, and hijacking were in full swing, and, of course, a county like ours had its share of lawbreakers."[36] Through the D.A.'s office in the old Alameda County Courthouse, a dilapidated wooden structure in Oakland, came the whole gamut of criminal cases—from organized crimes such as bootlegging, gambling, vice, dope, protection rackets, gang warfare, and government corruption to individual crimes of passion, as well as assaults, robbery, and murder.

From the time he became District Attorney, Warren's staff would call him "Chief." Since this was also the common way he was referred to on the Supreme Court, that was his designation during most of his career. He was the chief of the D.A.'s office in fact as well as name. According to Oscar Jahnsen, the office's chief investigator, in "every major case in Alameda county Earl Warren associated himself in the trial."[37] Warren personally appeared in court in many cases. In fact, he probably had more trial experience than most men appointed to the Supreme Court. Willard W. Shea, the first Public Defender of Alameda County, later referred to the record in Warren's most controversial trial and said, "if you flip pages rapidly and pick out the ones where Warren himself is doing either the examining or the cross-examining, it will give you considerable insight into his marvellous ability as a trial lawyer."[38]

When the Alameda County Charter was written in 1927, it was District Attorney Warren who insisted that it provide for a Public Defender. When Shea was appointed to the office, the two men worked out an agreement. "Willard," Warren said, "I know that you don't want to keep guilty men out of jail any more than I want to put innocent ones in. Therefore, I will make an agreement with you:

if at any time you are convinced that we have indicted an innocent man, just come and tell me so. I will then show you my files on the case. If after looking over my material you are still convinced that the man is innocent, I will release him."[39]

Shea recalled that he would average six such calls a year and the agreement was exercised in about two of them. The other times, Shea would come into the D.A.'s office and exclaim, "You are giving my client a rough time, and I think that such and such should be done." Warren would say with a little smile, "Willard, you know our agreement: are you prepared to tell me that this man is innocent?" Shea would exclaim, "Oh, go to hell!" and leave the office.[40]

But his relationship with Shea does not mean that Warren was not an effective prosecutor. According to former California Governor Edmund G. (Pat) Brown, Warren "was a tough prosecutor—hard as nails. He would really go after people."[41] His office had a far higher conviction rate than other district attorneys in the state. To be sure, defendants were not granted all the rights to which the Warren Court was later to hold they were entitled. But Warren was certainly more fair than most district attorneys in the era of the third degree and other abusive practices. His chief investigator, Oscar Jahnsen, quotes Warren as saying, "Be fair to everyone, even if they are breaking the law. Intelligence and proper handling can get confessions quicker than force. . . . Get the facts and then proceed, but get the facts honestly, and do not color them. If they are there, you will get them; if not, you don't want them."[42]

Warren was strict, for that time, on the taking of confessions. Unless he was convinced a confession was voluntary, he would not allow it to be used. He also strongly disapproved of unauthorized eavesdropping. Bakersfield Police Chief Robert B. Powers tells how, after Warren's own father was brutally murdered in 1938, a murder which was never solved, incidentally, a San Quentin prisoner, who had been in Bakersfield at the time, came under suspicion. "I wanted to put a stool pigeon in the cell with him," Chief Powers recalls, "and wire the cell for sound with a dictaphone." Powers spoke about it to Oscar Jahnsen, chief investigator in the D.A.'s office, who simply replied, "I don't think Earl Warren would go for that." Powers persisted, however, and said, "Well, check with him. It's a possibility. It's his father." Then, as Powers remembered it, "Oscar apparently checked with Warren, and Warren's answer was, 'I don't believe in dictaphones.' Period. And he wouldn't permit it or assist us in doing this. Even though his father was killed, this was something he didn't do." [43] So the taping was never done and the murder has remained an unsolved mystery to this day.

In 1931, Raymond Moley, soon to become famous as a member of Franklin D. Roosevelt's Brain Trust, made a survey of district attorneys. Among the offices he visited was that of Earl Warren. "After my survey," he wrote, "I declared without hesitation that Warren was the best district attorney in the United States." [44]

But the young prosecutor was, in many ways, still an orthodox Republican of the 1920s. He condemned the National Industrial Recovery Act as "the first major effort to change by stealth . . . the greatest free government of all time into a totalitarian state wherein men are but the pawns of a dictator." [45] In a radio talk, he denounced Upton Sinclair's program, when the writer was the Democratic candidate for Governor, as "a foreign philosophy of government, half Socialistic and half Communistic" and warned that it "means chaos to California." [46]

Warren's hostility to what he called "extreme radicalism" was more than mere political oratory. A young lawyer in the D.A.'s office recalled how he was working at his desk on a brief, with open lawbooks spread out, one morning in February, 1935. Warren came bursting in, flushed with indignation. "Throw 'em away," he said, slamming the books shut, "Forget 'em. They're no good now. Contracts don't mean anything any more." Warren had just gotten word of the Supreme Court's decision upholding President Roosevelt's action lowering the gold content of the dollar. [47]

But Warren also gave signs that he was already broadening his perspectives. Mention has been made of his efforts to protect defendants against coerced confessions and eavesdropping—most unusual for district attorneys of the day. Even more unusual at the time was that he conducted his office in a wholly nonpartisan fashion. According to Moley's 1931 survey, Warren was "the most . . . politically independent district attorney in the United States." [48] In 1928, when Warren led the Alameda County Republican campaign for Herbert Hoover, one of the deputies in his office was a prominent campaigner for Al Smith. A local politician complained. "The District Attorney's office is nonpartisan," replied Warren. "If Frank Coakley thinks Al Smith should be elected, he has every right to devote his spare time to the Democratic candidate."[49]

Just as significant was the statement on civil liberties Warren made during his last year as Alameda County Prosecutor. Robert W. Kenny, a leading California Democrat, then a Superior Court judge, asked for the statement at a luncheon meeting. According to Kenny's unpublished memoirs, Warren wrote, in a handwritten letter, that "he believed there was a grave danger of losing our civil liberties in the United States just as they had been lost in other countries. He referred to Mayor Hague's suppression of free speech in Jersey City and declared that he was unalterably opposed to any species of vigilantism."

Warren stressed the need for the majority to fight for the civil rights of minorities, "no matter how violently they disagree with their views. I believe that the American concept of civil rights should include not only an observance of our Constitutional Bill of Rights, but also the absence of arbitrary action by government in every field and the existence of a spirit of fair play on the part of public officials toward all."[50]

"What's more," Kenny writes, "Warren didn't just stop by sending me the letter. He incorporated most of it in a speech a few days later. That really shook people up."[51]

"Civil rights, in the context of that period," Kenny recalled, "meant the rights of labor to most people. . . . Warren, I think, went beyond this. He was saying that the Bill of Rights was an essential—if not the essential—part of the Constitution and, as Attorney General, he would see that it wasn't violated."[52] Warren expressed this view at a time when the Bill of Rights was still, in Sir Henry Maine's characterization, "a certain number of amendments on comparatively unimportant points"[53] and the Supreme Court held that its provisions were not binding on the states[54]—a situation that would be corrected in due time by the Warren Court.

When Kenny received Warren's statement, he writes, "I was delighted with this and announced my support of Warren for Attorney General."[55] The support of Democrats like Kenny enabled Warren to win both the Democratic and Republican nominations under California's cross-filing system (an unusual but not unheard-of feat) when he ran for Attorney General in 1938.

Kenny later described his own attempt to defeat Governor Warren for re-election in 1946, by quipping, "I saved him from oblivion in 1938, and then had the bad judgment to run against him and end in oblivion myself."[56] It was Kenny, too, who, when confronted with the campaign picture of Governor Warren and his family, including his six photogenic children, made the irreverent response, "Is this an election or a fertility contest?"[57]

Soon after he had been appointed District Attorney in 1925, Warren married Swedish-born Nina Palmquist Myers, whom he had met at a swimming party a few years earlier. By 1935, when Warren was in his last term as Alameda District Attorney, they had had their six children—giving Warren what rival politicians used to term his "unbeatable family." The importance of Nina and the family to Warren and his career cannot be overstated. If, as Justice Potter Stewart says, Chief Justice Warren looked at cases in terms of "those eternal, rather bromidic, platitudes," such as home, family, and country, it was only that they were "platitudes in which he sincerely believed." Warren's own home and family life furnished the foundation for his scale of values throughout his professional life. If there was something of the Babbitt in this, it was also, as Stewart puts it, "a great source of strength, that he did have these foundations on which his thinking rested, regardless of whether you agreed with him."

Warren was elected California Attorney General in 1938. Though he was most effective in the state's highest legal position, having modernized its then-antiquated office and having used it to continue his fight against organized crime, Warren's tenure as Attorney General is now remembered primarily because of his role in the Japanese evacuation in early 1942. "No one person," according to Carey McWilliams, editor of *The Nation* for many years, "had more to do with bringing about the removal of the West Coast Japanese during World War II—citizens and aliens alike; men, women, and children—than Mr. Warren."[58] A few weeks after Pearl Harbor, Warren declared that "the Japanese situation as it exists in this state today may well be the Achilles heel of the entire civilian defense effort."[59] In February, 1942, testifying before a House committee that came to California to investigate the situation, Warren said, "We believe that when we are dealing with the Caucasian race we have methods that will test the loyalty of them. . . . But when we deal with the Japanese we are in an entirely different field and we cannot form any opinion that we believe to be sound."[60] The next year, Warren, by then Governor, asserted at the Governors' conference in Columbus, Ohio, "If the Japs are released no one will be able to tell a saboteur from any other Jap."[61]

Of course, these statements were indefensible. Today, we agree with the title of a 1945 *Harper's* article which characterized the Japanese evacuation as "Our Worst Wartime Mistake."[62] Certain things should, however, be said in explanation, if not exoneration. It would perhaps have been too much to expect a different attitude from a man who grew up where Orientals were non-persons whose names were not even listed in the city directory. In this respect, as McWilliams put it in an interview, Warren "was entrapped to a certain extent by . . . a kind of political environment out of which he came in California."[63] Like most California politicians, Warren was active in the anti-Oriental Native Sons of the Golden West. Not long before Pearl Harbor, he spoke to its members, saying, "It is at such times that we most need loyal and patriotic organizations like the Native Sons. . . . This is your order and mine."[64] He remained active in the order throughout his years as Governor, despite its actions in urging exclusion of those of Japanese ancestry from citizenship.

Then, too, we should not forget the situation on the West Coast at the beginning of 1942. The panic which met the Japanese attack on Pearl Harbor had an almost Alice-in-Wonderland quality. "After Pearl Harbor," said former Los Angeles Mayor Fletcher Bowron, "everything was in a state of confusion. We kept getting reports of Japanese spying and sabotage. . . . There were reports they were in touch with the Japanese fleet . . . and we didn't have any way to tell who were loyal and who weren't."[65]

There were no actual cases of Japanese sabotage, but that did not prevent the mushrooming of anti-Japanese alarm. Tom C. Clark, who was on the West Coast as a Department of Justice representative at the time, later recalled how "the papers had big headlines, 'Los Angeles Bombed' and 'L.A. Raided,' but it was pure hysteria." Clark asserted, "I think that you have to live it to understand the feeling Californians had about the people of Japanese descent after Peal Harbor."[66]

Thus if Warren advocated the removal of the Japanese, he was hardly alone. In McWilliams' phrase, "the sad truth of the matter is that you could count on the fingers of two hands the number of so-called public personages in California who opposed mass evacuation of the Japanese."[67] Virtually every politician, labor leader, and newspaper, even Walter Lippmann, supported the evacuation. Lieutenant General John L. DeWitt, commanding general of the Western Defense Command, strongly recommended removal, asserting, "A Jap's a Jap. They are a dangerous element, whether loyal or not."[68] One of Warren's closest associates at the time stresses the military recommendation. "Remember," he says, "we were civilians. We weren't about to contradict a three-star general."[69]

"I have made a lot of mistakes in my life," Tom Clark, then a Justice of the Warren Court, told a San Diego newspaper on a 1966 visit. "But [one] that I acknowledge publicly . . . is my part in the evacuation of the Japanese from California in 1942."[70] Warren never made a similar public acknowledgment during his lifetime. At the end of 1944, he called a meeting as Governor of the state's Law Enforcement Advisory Committee to discuss the return of the Japanese to California. Robert B. Powers, then State Coordinator of Law Enforcement, prepared a resolution condemning the evacuation. As Powers later recalled it, the Governor objected. "No," Warren said, "This won't do, Bob: this sentence that you've got in here, that this was an 'improper thing' to do in the first place. We agree on that now, but none of us raised a voice against it when it happened."[71]

Years later, when he was Chief Justice, Warren was having lunch with his law clerks. He began teasing one of them about the way voting rights were being violated in his Southern state. The clerk, not feeling at all responsible for the violations, thought the Chief was riding him too hard. "Wait a minute," he retorted. "What was the name of the guy in California who put all the Japanese in concentration camps during World War II?"

At this there was a dead silence at the table. The other two clerks looked on in horror, as though they expected the offending clerk to be fired on the spot. Instead, Warren soon began to laugh and said, "Well, I get your point. But that was a clear and present danger. We really thought their fleets were going to land in California and I didn't think I had any choice."

In his 1962 James Madison lecture, *The Bill of Rights and the Military,*[72] the Chief Justice also went out of his way to defend the Supreme Court decisions upholding the 1942 measures against the Japanese. Some of his intimates think that Warren may have chosen the topic to find an occasion to state in public that, in the context of the situation on the West Coast at the time, he was not as wrong as people now thought in what he had done.

In his posthumously published memoirs, Warren finally did concede, "I have since deeply regretted the removal order and my own testimony advocating it, because it was not in keeping with our American concept of freedom and the rights of citizens. . . . It was wrong to react so impulsively, without positive evidence of disloyalty, even though we felt we had a good motive in the security of our state."[73] This was the only public expression of regret by Warren over his role in the Japanese evacuation. But former Justice Arthur J. Goldberg recalls that Warren once told him, when they were speaking of the Japanese evacuation, "You know, in retrospect, that's one of the worst things I ever did."

The Warren who sat on the Supreme Court was, of course, altogether another person than the Attorney General who had advocated removal of the Japanese. But the Warren who was elected Governor in 1942 was also a different man than the conservative Mr. District Attorney of ten years earlier. "I've always felt," states former California Governor Brown, "that Warren grew from the days that he was a prosecutor and Attorney General, where he was primarily interested in law enforcement."[74]

In those days, says Brown, Warren did not "evidence any great liberalism. As he stayed in the Governor's office and saw the need and the plight of people, I think he gradually changed. And I would say that I as a Democrat and he as a Republican thought pretty much alike."[75] It was Warren's performance as Governor that led to President Truman's famous characterization in 1948: "He's a Democrat and doesn't know it." When told of this, Warren smilingly replied, "Yes, but with a small 'd.' "[76]

According to Brown, Warren was "the best Governor that California ever had."[77] As Governor, Warren advocated the most far-reaching liberal program since the days of Hiram Johnson. A number of his measures were ahead of even the advanced political thinking of the day. In January, 1945, he urged enactment of a comprehensive state system of health insurance, to be financed by a payroll tax shared equally by employers and employees. The California Medical Association branded the proposal "socialized medicine, Communist inspired" and, with the help of a multimillion dollar campaign, were able to defeat it. Warren also sponsored a bill to set up a Fair Employment Commission—the first state bill outlawing racial and sexual discrimination in employment. Once again, as Warren later wrote, "My suggestion died aborning. . . . It died from the same kind of pressures."[78] Though Warren continued to push both measures, he could never get them enacted.

But Warren was a Governor who won most of the political battles he fought. He reorganized the state government and secured major reforming legislation—notably measures for a modern hospital system, improving the state's prisons and its correction system, providing an extensive highway building program, and improving old-age pensions and unemployment benefits. Warren proved an effective administrator. Despite a broad expansion of state programs, he was able to balance the budget and secure significant tax reductions.

Former Governor Brown's estimate of Warren as the best Governor his state ever had has been mentioned. "He felt the people of the state were in his care and he cared for them," Brown has said. "Earl Warren faced the problems of social responsibility and growth and met them head on."[79] Growth was, indeed, a prime Warren concern. "Gentlemen, we have to plan for a whole new city of ten thousand people every Monday morning,"[80] he used to tell his Governor's Council. In his later years, the Chief Justice used to recall proudly that, during his years as Governor, his state had been able to absorb five million new arrivals "without any confusion or discord whatsoever."[81]

Even his political opponents could not help being impressed by Warren's performance. Democrat Robert W. Kenny, who ran against Warren in 1946, tells how, on a visit to the White House, he was asked by President Roosevelt, "What kind of a fellow is your . . . Governor?" "Well, Mr. President," Kenny says he replied, "I'm just a California booster. Everything we have out there is better than it is anywhere else. Even our Republicans are better than they are anywhere else."[82]

Certainly, the California voters agreed with this estimate. Not only was Warren only the second Governor to be reelected in his state, he was the first to be elected to three terms. Warren literally swamped his opponents in his three gubernatorial races. He won both the Republican and Democratic primaries in 1946, and came close to doing the same thing in 1942 against Governor Culbert L. Olson and in 1950 against James Roosevelt.

It was during the 1950 election that Mrs. Eleanor Roosevelt came to California to campaign for her son. Congressman William S. Mailliard, Warren's travel secretary at the time, remembers that the Governor's staff was upset at the visit. They were concerned about how "to deal with this kind of thing, a legend . . . out there campaigning for her son." Mailliard recalls saying, "The only way you can deal with her is to absolutely brush it off. If you react, well by God, she's going to become a very important factor in this campaign."

But the Governor just laughed and said, "Well, I'll tell you what I'll do. I'm just going to issue a statement when we get there, 'Well, you wouldn't expect a mother not to be for her son, would you?' "[83]

Warren's impressive record, both in the State House and at the polls, inevitably brought him national attention. After his 1946 re-election sweep, he was definitely considered of Presidential timber. Just before the 1948 Republican Convention, *Time* characterized the California Governor as "the best campaigner yet on the newest communications medium. . . . His big square-cut Scandinavian face was etched handsomely on the screen; he was relaxed, direct and confident."[84]

But Warren had to settle for second place on the 1948 Republican ticket. Why he was willing to be Thomas E. Dewey's running mate has never been clear. Merrill H. Small, his executive secretary, was alone with Warren just after he received the Vice-Presidential nomination. According to Small, "He turned to me, and he said, 'Pop, I had to do it. I had to do it. If I hadn't taken it this time, they'd never consider me for anything again!' "[85]

Unlike most others, Warren soon realized that he was heading for his first electoral defeat. From the beginning, Warren was dismayed by Dewey's virtual do-nothing campaign. Earl Warren, Jr., recalls his father talking to Dewey on the phone many times during the campaign. "I can remember Dad saying, 'But Tom, you've got to go out and talk to the people.' 'Tom, you've got to tell them something.' 'Tom, you've got to talk about the issues.' "[86]

Well before the election, Warren knew that the Dewey–Warren ticket would lose. A former member of his staff said, "He told us we were going to be licked. He said, 'Truman's gotten through to the

people.' " When Warren was asked by reporters just after the election, "What happened?" he grinned and replied, "Mr. Truman just got too many votes."[87]

In 1952, Warren was again unsuccessful in his attempt to secure the Presidential nomination. His one hope was a deadlock between the two frontrunners, General Dwight D. Eisenhower and Senator Robert A. Taft, with Warren chosen as a compromise candidate. But the California Governor himself ensured that a deadlock would not develop by his support of the Eisenhower position on the seating of challenged pro-Taft delegates. Herbert Brownell, Eisenhower's campaign manager, believed that if the challenged delegates were allowed to vote on their own seating, they would win the vote and give Taft a majority. Because of this, Brownell says, "I . . . drafted the so-called 'fair play amendment' to the rules of the Republican convention which had the effect of disallowing the right of any contested delegate to vote on the confirmation of his seating."[88]

It would have been to Warren's advantage to oppose the amendment, or at least to split the California delegation's votes between the Eisenhower and Taft forces. But he firmly stuck with the position that it was only fair that those whose seats were being contested should not vote on the issue. So against his immediate interest, he urged the California delegates to vote for the Eisenhower proposal. "You people have to go back to California," he told the California caucus. "You have an obligation, and it seems to me that you have to discharge that obligation in a way that satisfies your conscience."[89] A delegate who was there says that Warren "made it very plain that this was the way he felt, and he didn't see how we could vote to seat the Taft delegation. Which might have brought about a deadlock, which would have meant that he would have walked right down the center."[90]

At the Governor's urging, the California delegation did cast all of its seventy votes for the "fair play" amendment. That ensured passage of the amendment, which in turn ensured Eisenhower's nomination. In his memoirs, Eisenhower denied that his appointment of Warren as Chief Justice was "the payment of a personal political debt, supposedly incurred at the time of my nomination. The truth was that I owed Governor Warren nothing."[91] The former President stressed that at the Convention Warren had refused to throw his seventy Cal-

ifornia votes to him and that it was Minnesota's switch from Harold Stassen (whose convention floor manager was Warren E. Burger) that supplied the necessary votes for his nomination. But Eisenhower forgot that it was the Governor's support of the "fair play" amendment that gave him the disputed delegates—effectively ending Taft's chances for the nomination and Warren's as well.[92]

The 1952 campaign also saw what Warren considered his "betrayal" by Richard M. Nixon. The then-Senator had, like all the California delegates, signed a pledge to support the Governor at the Convention. Despite this, Nixon worked, both in and outside the delegation, to obtain support for Eisenhower. Nixon joined the Warren campaign train in Denver, on July 4, the night before it was due in Chicago for the Convention. The train was in a festive mood, as the delegates had been celebrating in orange baseball caps, with the letter "W." Nixon and his supporters went through the train, shaking hands, and whispering that Warren did not have a chance and they should jump on the Eisenhower bandwagon.

Warren was infuriated. "A delegate cannot break his pledge and still be a man of honor," he was quoted in the press the next day. "People of honor keep their word; people of dishonor don't."[93] He felt that Nixon had dishonored his written pledge. Warren never forgave Nixon. From that time, he had an almost visceral repugnance toward his fellow Californian. "It all started with the '52 campaign," says former Governor Brown, "when . . . Nixon was on the Warren delegation. He went back and made a deal to support Eisenhower. And he got the vice-presidency as a result of that. But Warren never forgave him; he thought he double-crossed him."[94]

For the rest of his life, says his son, Earl, Jr., Warren "just detested Richard Nixon with an abiding passion." Brown recalls Warren's calling Nixon "a crook and a thief. He told *me* that; he's told me that Tricky Dick—that's what he used to call him—he didn't like him at all."[95] Nixon was one of only two persons whom Warren termed an "evil man" (the other was William B. Keck, the right-wing California oil magnate).[96]

After he lost the 1952 nomination, Warren's public career appeared over. He had decided that he would not run again for Governor of California and had begun to consider possibilities outside government. All this changed with Chief Justice Vinson's death. Now Warren was suddenly set to become the new Chief Justice of the United States.

Congress was not then in session, and the President wanted Warren to be in the Court's center seat when the October 1953 term opened. Therefore, the new Chief Justice received a recess or interim appointment, dated October 2, to remain in effect only until he could be confirmed by the Senate. If the Senate voted against him, the appointment would lapse. Against everyone's expectation, confirmation proved anything but routine. The new Chairman of the Senate Judiciary Committee, William Langer of North Dakota, delayed the nomination for weeks—not because he had anything against Warren, but as a protest against the lack of patronage for his state. Although it had not been the practice to have the F.B.I. investigate Supreme Court appointees, the Senate Committee wanted a check made. The F.B.I. agreed and made the first field investigation of any nominee for Chief Justice.

"I know of nothing," Justice Felix Frankfurter wrote a close friend, "that has made me more morally outraged . . . than the fact that . . . a man whom the President of the United States has named as the Chief Justice and who has been discharging that office for four months with true regard to its highest standards . . . should have to have his confirmation held up until some cops report whether or not he is a security risk or otherwise not qualified for the Chief Justiceship."[97]

Warren himself declined an invitation to appear at a subcommittee hearing, but a range of anti-Warren testimony, particularly by right-wing extremists, was heard. This brought on a storm of protest from supporters of the nomination, from the President down. Approval of the nomination by the Judiciary Committee (by a vote of twelve to three) soon followed, and the Senate voted to confirm, by voice vote without dissent, on March 1, 1954. "One must hope," a *New York Times* editorial commented, "that this kind of circus . . . will not play Washington again."[98]

In the meantime, the new Chief Justice had come to Washington, under his interim appointment, on Sunday, October 4, 1953, to be present for the opening of the new Supreme Court term. He was met at the airport by Vice-President Nixon, Attorney General Brownell, and other dignitaries, as well as the Clerk and Marshal of the Court. The latter drove him to the Statler Hotel.[99]

The next day was the opening day of the October 1953 Term. The ornate courtroom in the Marble Palace was crowded with dignitaries, including President and Mrs. Eisenhower and Vice-President and-Mrs. Nixon. Mrs. Warren, wearing a red hat and orchid, sat in the box in the front of and to the left of the bench, between the Vice-President and Mrs. Nixon. It was the first time that the Eisenhowers and Mrs. Warren had ever been in the Court building.

Precisely at noon, the Marshal pounded his gavel. The red velour curtains behind the bench parted, and the eight Justices filed in in order of seniority, led by Justice Hugo L. Black. Warren, in accordance with the tradition, made up the rear. The Justices took their seats, but the center chair remained vacant, while Warren proceeded to a seat behind the Clerk, at the right of the Court.

The Marshal intoned the time-honored cry that begins each Supreme Court session: "Oyez! Oyez! Oyez! All persons having business before the Honorable, the Supreme Court of the United States, are admonished to draw near and give their attention, for the Court is now sitting. God save the United States and this Honorable Court!"

Justice Black read a statement on the death of Chief Justice Vinson. Then the Clerk read the commission of the President appointing Warren as Chief Justice. The next order of business was the Judicial Oath. Warren had previously taken the Constitutional Oath, administered according to custom by the senior Associate Justice, in the conference room behind the bench, with only the other Court members present. That oath was the one prescribed in the Constitution for all federal officers. Warren had sworn "that I will support and defend the Constitution of the United States against all enemies, foreign and domestic; that I will bear true faith and allegiance to the same."

Though this oath was all that the Constitution demanded, tradition also required the taking of the Judicial Oath in open court. As the new Chief Justice stood up to have that oath administered by the Clerk of the Court, he was tall and impressive. An inch over six feet, he was broad-shouldered, and held his two-hundred-pound body erect. His fjord-blue eyes and fair complexion were signs of his Scandinavian ancestry. He gave an impression of bigness, even larger than his physical size. A former official tells of visiting him in his spacious gubernatorial office: "He himself was a man as big as the room, in a sense. He had a large body—he fitted into that spaciousness and, you know, the sense of California: large!" [100]

As he stood in his judicial robe, Warren looked the picture of a model Chief Justice as he swore the Judicial Oath:

"I, Earl Warren, do solemnly swear that I will administer justice without respect to persons, and do equal right to the poor and to the rich, and that I will faithfully and impartially discharge and perform all the duties incumbent upon me as Chief Justice of the United States according to the best of my abilities and understanding, agreeably to the Constitution and Laws of the United States.

"So help me God."

But the new Chief Justice was so much the judicial novice that he did not even have a robe of his own for the swearing-in ceremony. He had brought along an old robe that he had used in academic ceremonies in California. Told that it was not appropriate, he borrowed a spare that was hurriedly found in the Court's robing room. Surprisingly, it was too long even for his tall frame, and he tripped over it as he stepped up to the raised bench to take his place in the Chief Justice's seat after he had taken the Judicial Oath. Because of this, he later wrote, "I suppose it could be said that I literally stumbled onto the bench." [101]

There was, however, to be little stumbling as he took over his role as head of the Court. After an inevitable initial period of feeling his way, Warren was to lead the Court as effectively as any Chief Justice in our history.

2.

THE COURT, THE BRETHREN, "AND COMPANY"

William Howard Taft, the only man who was both President and Chief Justice, once said that the Supreme Court was his idea of what heaven must be like.[1] Earl Warren never went as far as that. Still, there is little doubt that, from the beginning, he found his new judicial position congenial. When the California Governor was appointed to the high Court's central chair, his friends worried about how he would adjust to his austere new surroundings,[2] which required a quantum change in Warren's way of life. In California, Warren had run a government staffed by thousands; he had had a mansion, limousines and motorcycle escorts, a personal airplane—all on call at the snap of his fingers. Now all this executive panoply was gone. The total Court payroll contained fewer than two thousand names, and the Chief Justice's staff a mere handful.

Warren later recalled that the change from Governor to Chief Justice "was a painful transition."[3] Some years earlier, he described his reaction on his arrival at what Justice Robert H. Jackson liked to call the marble mausoleum.[4] "I remember well the day of my arrival at the Court. . . . I walked into the Supreme Court Building, and was ushered into the chambers of the Chief Justice by the marshal. There I was met by Mrs. McHugh, who had been the secretary of my predecessor, Chief Justice Vinson, and who incidentally is still there in the same capacity with me. There were also there awaiting me two very elderly messengers . . . and there were three young law clerks recently out of law school, [one] of whom the Chief Justice had appointed but had not yet seen. That was my staff. Can you imagine the shock after the miltiple secretariat and staff I had been accustomed to?"[5]

But Warren soon recognized that, if the Court did not possess panoply, it certainly did possess power, and in the exercise of power Warren was at home. "The Supreme Court," wrote Alexis de-Tocqueville in 1835, "is placed higher than any known tribunal. . . . The peace, the prosperity, and the very existence of the Union are vested in the hands of the seven Federal judges."[6]

The U.S. Supreme Court is emphatically more than a law court, in the ordinary sense of that term. Before his elevation to the supreme bench, Benjamin N. Cardozo was for many years a distinguished member and chief of New York's highest court. With the perspective gained from judicial service in both Albany and Washington, Cardozo could note a basic difference between the highest courts of state and nation. The New York Court of Appeals, he said, "is a great common law court; its problems are lawyers' problems. But the Supreme Court is occupied chiefly with statutory construction—which no man can make interesting—and with politics."[7] Of course, as Justice Jackson once pointed out, in this statement, the word "politics" is used in no sense of partisanship but in the sense of policy making.[8]

When Cardozo came to Washington, he left what was then the greatest common-law court in the land; it dealt essentially with the questions of private law that are the preoccupation and delectation of most lawyers. The Court to which he came was not, and has not been since the time of Chief Justice John Marshall, the usual type of law court. Public, not private, law is the stuff of Supreme Court litigation. Elevation to that tribunal requires the judge to make the adjustment from preoccupation with the restricted, however novel, problems of private litigation to the most exacting demands of judicial statesmanship.

It is precisely that the Supreme Court *is* more than the usual law court that makes its work of vital significance to more than a relatively small number of jurists. To the Supreme Court alone, in the last analysis, is assigned the function of guarding the ark of the Constitution. The Constitution itself is not a self-executing document. The *ought* laid down in 1787 must run the gantlet of judicial interpretation before it attains the practical status of an *is*. The Constitution, to paraphrase a famous statement by Chief Justice Charles Evans Hughes,[9] must, in practice, be what the Supreme Court Justices say it is. Or, as Bishop Hoadly observed in 1717, "whoever hath an absolute authority to interpret written . . . laws; it is he who is truly the lawgiver to all intents and purposes and not the person who wrote . . . them." [10]

Another famous de Tocqueville statement is that "Scarcely any political question arises in the United States that is not resolved sooner or later into a judicial question." [11] From this point of view, the highest Court is primarily a political institution. Since its decrees mark the boundaries between the great departments of government, and since it is upon its actions that depend the proper functioning of federalism and the scope to be given to the rights of the individual, a judge on such a tribunal has an opportunity to leave his imprint upon the life of the nation as no mere master of the common law possibly could.

The Supreme Court's present physical setting matches the splendor of its constitutional role, and whatever purely architectural criticisms may be directed at the present Court building, it cannot be denied that it is one of the most imposing structures in Washington. Its design is modelled on a classical Greek temple, and is intended as a shrine to the majesty of the law. Its physical scale is truly impressive. Both longer and wider than a football field, it is four stories high, and is constructed almost entirely of marble. At the main entrance are sixteen huge Corinthian columns, topped by a pediment; in its center, Liberty Enthroned, holding the scales of justice, guarded by Order and Authority on either side.

The interior of the Court building is as impressive as its exterior. As a Smithsonian pamphlet describes it, "Six kinds of marble, three domestic and three foreign, along with thousands of feet of clear-grained white oak, give the building a feeling of polished, dust-free smoothness. Openwork gates, elevator doors, even the firehose cupboards are of gleaming bronze. Two spiral marble staircases, self-supporting marvels of engineering, soar from garage to the top floor, five levels up. For security's sake, these are unused—but only the Vatican and the Paris Opera can boast similar ones." The new building also has abundant office space, both for Justices' chambers and Court staff, and a magnificent courtroom—as well as ample amenities, including a mini-gymnasium and basketball court on the top floor, which Court personnel like to call "the highest court in the land."

When Justice Harlan F. Stone had visited the new Court building in the mid-1930s, he had written to his sons, "It is a very grand affair, but I confess that I returned from my visit with a feeling akin to dismay. The place is almost bombastically pretentious, and thus it seems to me wholly inappropriate for a quiet group of old boys such as the Supreme Court of the United States."[12] When the Court was preparing to move into the new edifice, one of the Justices sardonically asked, "What are we supposed to do, ride in on nine elephants?"

But traditions give way slowly at the Supreme Court. There are still spittoons behind the bench for each Justice, pewter julep cups (now used for their drinking water), and not long ago, there were quill pens at counsel tables. After the Court formally moved in 1936 from their cramped quarters in the old Senate Chamber into the new building, most of the Justices resented the change and declined to use the handsome new suites provided for them. With Chief Justice Hughes, they continued to work in their homes, as they had been accustomed to do. One result of this was that Hugo L. Black, the first "new" Justice to occupy chambers in the building, and at that time the junior member of the Court, got his pick and was able to choose a splendid corner suite, which he kept for the remaining thirty-four years of his life (instead of the least desirable space normally left to the junior Justice).

By the time Warren became Chief Justice in 1953, Black had risen in seniority to become the senior Associate Justice. He and all the other Justices also had years of the judicial experience which the new Chief lacked. Even the most junior, Sherman Minton, had served on the Court four years and, before then, had been a judge on the U.S. Court of Appeals for the Seventh Circuit. Moreover at least four of the Justices—Black, Felix Frankfurter, William O. Douglas, and Robert H. Jackson—could run intellectual rings around the new

Chief. But, as was soon to be apparent, Warren's forte was not so much intellect as it was leadership.

The Court he came to head is itself an institution in which it is most difficult for a Chief Justice to assert a *formal* leadership role. While it may be the custom to designate the high Court by the name of its Chief, one who looks only to the bare legal powers of the Chief Justice will find it hard to understand this underscoring of his preeminence. Aside from his designation as Chief of the Court and the attribution of a slightly higher salary, his position is not superior to that of his colleagues—and certainly is not legally superior. In Justice Tom C. Clark's words in a 1956 article, "The Chief Justice has no more authority than other members of the court." [13]

Understandably, the Justices themselves have always been sensitive to claims that the Chief Justice has greater power than the others. "It is vitally important," asserted Justice Frankfurter in a 1956 letter to Justice Harold H. Burton, "to remember what Holmes said about the office: 'Of course, the position of the Chief Justice differs from that of the other Justices only on the administrative side.' He is not the head of a Department; not even a quarterback." [14] Two years later, Frankfurter wrote Justice William J. Brennan "that any encouragement in a Chief Justice that he is the boss . . . must be rigorously resisted. . . . I, for my part, will discharge what I regard as a post of trusteeship, not least in keeping the Chief Justice in his place, as long as I am around." [15]

The Chief Justiceship should not, however, be approached only in a formalistic sense. Starting with Marshall, the greatest of the Chief Justices have known how to make the most of the extralegal potential inherent in their position. The Chief Justice may be only *primus inter pares;* but he is *primus.* Somebody has to preside over a body of nine, and it is the Chief who does preside, both in open court and in the even more important work of deciding cases in the conference chamber. It is the Chief Justice who directs the business of the Court. He controls the discussion in conference; his is the prerogative to call and discuss cases before the other Justices speak.

In addition, it has become settled by custom that it is for the Chief Justice to assign the writing of Court opinions. This function has been called the most important that pertains to the office of Chief. In discharging it, a great Chief Justice is similar to a general deploying his army. It is he who determines what use will be made of the

Court's personnel; his employment of the assigning power will both influence the growth of the law and his own relations with his colleagues.

A Justice who served with Warren told the author that the Chief used his assigning power with three ends in view:

1. So far as possible, opinions should be assigned evenly, with each Justice having his fair share to write. When one of the Justices started to issue a number of dissents, Warren wryly observed to his law clerks, "He'll still have to do his share of majority opinions."

2. The Chief Justice should not vote in order to control the assignment of opinions. Before and after Warren, the Chief would sometimes try to vote with the majority, so that he, rather than the senior Justice voting that way, could assign the opinion. So far as those who served with him recall, Warren would not do this.

3. The Justices should be generalists. Warren would try to assign them cases in all the different fields of law, rather than have them specialize in particular fields.

All the Justices emphasize Warren's fairness in assigning opinions. Justice Potter Stewart has been quoted as exclaiming, "I got shitty opinions from Earl Warren for ten years,"[16] but the Justice says he never made the statement, and an analysis of his opinions shows that he was, indeed, given his share of important opinions during the Warren years. The same was true of the other Justices on the Warren Court.

Warren himself speedily discovered the potential in the office of Chief Justice. In doing so, he used to the full the attributes that had made him a success in his pre-judicial career. The primary assets of a successful Governor are after all that he must be a leader, able to guide men toward attainment of his program, and must be capable of working effectively with men whom he cannot coerce, such as members of the Legislature, whose cooperation is essential. He must be an effective conciliator of diverse viewpoints, never letting intra-party strife destroy the essential unity of purpose needed for political success. He must be able to administer, capable of controlling all the different facets of the modern executive branch. Above all, he is more likely to be a success if he projects a reputation for fairness and integrity and has an aura of competence and prestige.

All these attributes were possessed by Governor Warren, and they gave him his outstanding political successes in California. Those became the same attributes that enabled him successfully to make the transition from the executive mansion to the high Court.

Frankfurter once compared a great Chief Justice's manner of presiding over the Court with Toscanini leading an orchestra.[17] And Warren brought more authority, more *bravura*, to the Chief Justiceship than had been the case for years. The Justices who sat with him have all stressed that Warren may not have been an intellectual like Frankfurter, but then, as Justice Potter Stewart puts it, "he never pretended to be one." More important, says Stewart, he possessed "instinctive qualities of leadership." When Stewart was asked about claims that Justice Black was the intellectual leader of the Court, he replied, "If Black was the intellectual leader, Warren was the *leader* leader." According to Stewart, Warren "didn't lead by his intellect and he didn't greatly appeal to others' intellects; that wasn't his style. But he was an instinctive leader whom you respected and for whom you had affection, and . . . , as the presiding member of our conference, he was just ideal."

Of course, the Supreme Court is a collegiate institution, whose collegiate nature is underscored by the custom the Justices have had of calling each other "Brethren." But the Brethren can only be guided, not directed. As Justice Frankfurter stated in a letter to Chief Justice Fred M. Vinson, "good feeling in the Court, as in a family, is produced by accommodation, not by authority—whether the authority of a parent or a vote."[18]

The Court "family" is composed of nine individuals, who constantly bear out James Bryce's truism that "judges are only men."[19] "To be sure," Frankfurter once wrote Justice Stanley Reed, "the Court is an institution, but individuals, with all their diversities of endowment, experience and outlook determine its actions. The history of the Supreme Court is not the history of an abstraction, but the analysis of individuals acting as a Court who make decisions and lay down doctrines."[20]

In many ways, the individual Justices operate, as some of them have said, like "nine separate law firms." Plainly Warren was not going to be able to deal with the Brethren in the way he had directed matters as Governor. "I think," Justice Stewart affirms, "he came to realize very early, certainly long before I came here [1958], that this group of nine rather prima donnaish people could not be led, could not be told, in the way the Governor of California can tell a subordinate, do this or do that."

What Stewart says is true of any Supreme Court, but it was particularly true of the Justices on the Court when Warren was appointed. The Court in the mid-1940s was characterized by Yale Law Professor Fred Rodell as "the most brilliant and able collection of Justices who ever graced the high bench together."[21] The stars of that Court were Black, Frankfurter, Douglas, and Jackson—four of the greatest judges ever to serve on the highest bench, brilliant jurists, each possessed of a peculiarly forceful personality. In addition, Black and Douglas, on the one side, and Frankfurter and Jackson, on the other, represented polar views on the proper role of the Court in enforcing the Constitution. Their doctrinal differences, fueled by increasing personal animosity, erupted into the most bitter feud in Supreme Court history. All four were still serving when Warren was elevated to Olympus. The Brethren he was called upon to lead were perhaps the most unbrotherly in the Court's annals.

The senior among them was Hugo Lafayette Black, who was sixty-seven years old and had been on the Court sixteen years. By then, the furor that had surrounded his appointment because of the disclosure that he had once been a member of the Ku Klux Klan seemed an echo from another world. "At every session of the Court," a *New York Times* editorial had thundered, after Black's Klan membership had been revealed, "the presence on the bench of a justice who has worn the white robe of the Ku Klux Klan will stand as a living symbol of the fact that here the cause of liberalism was unwittingly betrayed."[22] But by 1953, Black himself was the recognized leader of the Court's liberal wing.

Black never forgot his origins in a backward Alabama rural county. Half a century later, he described a new law clerk from Harvard as "tops in his class though he came from a God-forsaken place—worse than Clay County."[23] His Alabama drawl and his gentle manners masked an inner firmness found in few men. "Many who know him," wrote Anthony Lewis when Black turned seventy-five, "would agree with the one-time law clerk who called him 'the most powerful man I have ever met.'"[24] Though of only middling height and slight build, Black always amazed people by his physical vitality. He is quoted in *The Dictionary of Biographical Quotation* as saying, "When I was forty my doctor advised me that a man in his forties shouldn't play tennis. I heeded his advice carefully and could hardly wait until I reached fifty to start again."[25]

His competitive devotion to tennis became legend. Until he was eighty-three, he continued to play several sets every day on the private court of his landmark federal house in the Old Town section of the Washington suburb of Alexandria. In envy, retired Justice Minton, who had been an athlete in his youth, wrote Black in 1964, "The Chief calls me up once in a while and gives me a report on you and your tennis game. What a man! I can barely get around on crutches."[26]

Black brought the same competitive intensity to his judicial work. According to his closest colleague, William O. Douglas, "Hugo Black was fiercely intent on every point of law he presented."[27] Black was as much a compulsive winner in the courtroom as on the tennis court. "You can't just disagree with him," acidly commented his great Court rival, Justice Jackson, to *New York Times* columnist Arthur Krock, "You must go to war with him if you disagree."[28] The resulting war, despite disclaimers by the Justices, led to deeply felt personal bitterness.

After Frankfurter had retired, Black wrote him that "Our differences, which have been many, have rarely been over the ultimate end desired, but rather have related to the means that were most likely to achieve the end we both envisioned."[29] An agreeable sentiment, to be sure, but the differences between these two Justices *were* critical and, on Frankfurter's side at least, became increasingly acrimonious as time went on. The year before Warren's appointment, Frankfurter had, for example, written to Justice Jackson, his closest colleague, that Black "represents discontinuity in the law and a stick-in-the-mud like me is concerned with decent continuity."[30] Three years later Frankfurter was expressing a stronger opinion in a letter to Justice Harold H. Burton (which the latter labeled *Confidential* in his own handwriting), asserting, with regard to Black, "I've never known anyone who more steadily reads for confirmation of his views and not for disinterested enlightenment."[31] Similarly, in a letter to Justice Stanley Reed, Frankfurter, after referring to "some untenable notions in Hugo's head," asserted, "I put it to you: do you think that any amount of relevant or irrelevant discussion could shake Hugo loose from his conclusion? He has reached a conclusion and is not at all bothered about arguments which can be exposed. You might as well ask him to climb a greased telephone-pole as to change his conclusion."[32]

In 1958, the American Bar Association invited the Justices and their wives to attend the A.B.A. annual meeting in Los Angeles as guests of the Association. "I almost puked," wrote Frankfurter to Justice John M. Harlan in an undated handwritten letter, "when I heard Hugo say that if it would be good for the Court, he'll go. Gosh! For nearly twenty years I have heard his condemnation of the ABA and his contempt for their views. And now he puts on that noble act. The truth of course is, I have not a particle of doubt, that this will afford a pleasant trip for his young wife. He is not the only old Benedict I know who is more eager to please his new bride than ever he was his first wife. . . . I have little doubt that Hugo now believes that it 'will help the Court,' for he has infinite capacity—beyond anyone I've known—for self-deception."[33]

And we see the same denigrating attitude on Frankfurter's part toward Black's work as a judge. It was to Black that he referred when he wrote to Harlan, "I beg of you not to allow yourself to go in for heartbreaks by operating under the illusion that everybody has the same belief in the processes of law that guide you. There is all the difference in the world between starting with a result and clothing it in some appropriate verbal garb, and starting with a problem and letting it lead you where it will."[34] Another time, Frankfurter was heard dressing down one of his law clerks in a Court corridor. "That's the worst argument I ever heard! You sound just like Hugo Black!"

" 'Oh, Democracy,' " confided Frankfurter to his diary, "what flapdoodle is delivered in thy name.' Not the less so because it was all said in Black's irascible and snarling tone of voice."[35] His reaction to a Black opinion, he wrote Harlan in 1961, was to refer to a comment by Justice Oliver Wendell Holmes, "On far less provocation, he pithily disposed of writings by colleagues with, 'It makes me puke.' "[36] A striking indication of the attitude toward Black held by the Frankfurter wing of the Court is to be found in the following undated note on Frankfurter's Supreme Court stationary:

"He is a
demagogue
         Shay." [Shay was Sherman Minton's nickname]

Beneath this written comment, Frankfurter penned in, "Minton J. passed me this note after Black J. made one of his inflammatory outbursts at Conference."[37]

Black's differences with Frankfurter were primarily intellectual, though they degenerated at times into something more. "I thought Felix was going to hit me today, he got so mad," Black once said after a heated conference dispute. "But," he went on, "he'll get over it."[38] Such an underlying tolerant attitude did not exist, however, in the relations between Black and Justice Robert H. Jackson. These two became as bitter personal antagonists as ever sat together on the Supreme Court. Jackson had been convinced that Black had frustrated his long ambition to become Chief Justice by intervening with President Truman after Chief Justice Stone's death in 1946. A widely circulated column quoted the President as saying, "Black says he will resign if I make Jackson Chief Justice and tell the reasons why. Jackson says the same about Black."[39] Some time later Frankfurter wrote a close friend, quoting "a most reliable witness," that Truman had planned to appoint Jackson until he was "threatened with resignations" from the Court.[40] Jackson, then chief American prosecutor at the Nuremberg trials, held a well-publicized press conference, in which he ventilated his dispute with Black. Then he wrote bitterly to Frankfurter, "Black is now rid of the Chief. . . . Now if he can have it understood that he has a veto over the promotion of any Associate, he would have things about where he wants them."[41]

Justice Burton noted in his diary on October 10, 1946, his surprise that Black and Jackson exchanged "Good mornings" and even "joined in a brief discussion" at that morning's conference. "I mention this," he wrote, "because of the popular idea . . . that they could not speak to each other." Burton did, however, observe, "These were the first instances of their speaking to each other that I have seen this fall."[42]

The bitterness between these two Justices continued until Jackson's death in 1954. Not long before, Jackson sent Frankfurter a note in which, referring to Black, he declared, "I simply give up understanding our colleague and begin to think he is a case for a psychiatrist."[43] Black, on the other side, wrote a former law clerk that a copy of the *Macon Telegraph* had been sent him that contained an editorial entitled, "Jackson is an Unmitigated Ass." On the same page, Black went on, "appeared an article by John Temple Graves on the same subject. I have nothing but sympathy for John Temple."[44]

It seems fortunate in retrospective that Jackson was to serve only one more year after the new Chief Justice's appointment, since Warren could scarcely have been as effective a Chief as he was in a Court racked by the Black–Jackson feud. In personal terms, however, Jackson's sudden death at the age of sixty-two only underscored his personal failure as a Justice. One of the most gifted men ever to serve on the Court, Jackson harbored ambitions to be President or, at the least, to occupy the Court's central chair. His lack of success in this regard poisoned his whole outlook and made him, in his last years on the bench, increasingly embittered.

Jackson was termed by Frankfurter "by long odds the most literarily gifted member on the Court."[45] As a stylist and phrase-maker, Jackson can only be compared with Holmes. It was Jackson who aphorized the reality of the Supreme Court's position: "There is no doubt that if there were a super-Supreme Court, a substantial proportion of our reversals of state courts would also be reversed. We are not final because we are infallible, but we are infallible only because we are final."[46]

Jackson's sardonic attitude toward the Brethren surfaced in both his opinions and private comments. "The black hole of Columbia"[47] was the way he came to call the Court. Frankfurter's diary tells of Jackson's taking him off into a corner at the wedding of Dean Acheson's daughter and saying, "Do you feel as depressed as I do after these Saturday [Court] Conferences?"[48] "Congratulations," Jackson wrote Frankfurter another time, "on your absence from today's session. Only if you have been caught playing the piano in a whorehouse can you appreciate today's level of my self respect."[49]

The same attitude is apparent in some doggerel dashed off by Jackson, "With apology to Kip":

Come you back to Mandalay
Where the flying judges play
And the fog comes up like thunder
From the Bench decision day.

Come you back to Mandalay
And hear what the judges say
As they talk as brave as thunder
And then run the other way.[50]

Jackson's difficulty in getting along with some of the other Justices, which in its extreme form culminated in the feud with Black, stemmed, in large part, from an inner feeling of insecurity on his part. Few would have sensed this in a man of Jackson's patrician bearing, whose manners and way of life bespoke the upstate New York squire, transplanted to the Hickory Hill estate that was later to be owned by John and then Robert Kennedy. But Jackson had earned his position through a lucrative practice; he had come from a poor family and had only had one year of education at a second-rate law school. He never got over a sense of inferiority in the face of graduates of the great national law schools, particularly Harvard and Yale— a factor that doubtless contributed to his bitterness at those he felt had kept him from the highest judicial office. Once he was invited to sit as a judge in the moot court competition at Harvard Law School. He expressed reservations about accepting to Frankfurter, who dealt with the matter in the following mock opinion:

In the Matter of the I.Q.)
)
of Robert H. Jackson   )

FRANKFURTER, Circuit Justice:

The motion—such it is in effect—to declare Brother JACKSON disqualified to sit in the case of *N.B.C. and C.B.S. v. F.C.C.*, within the Ames jurisdiction boils down to the claim that the skill or learning of undergraduate law students will so undermine the understanding or disinterestedness of Mr. Justice JACKSON's judicial powers that, hereafter, he will not be able to hear with an open mind and judge with impartiality a future proceeding in the jurisdiction of the Supreme Court of the United States between the same parties raising the same issues.

While objectors ought not to be precluded from offering proof as to these moral and intellectual disabilities of the aforesaid JACKSON, I do not feel warranted in taking judicial notice of such disabilities. The motion must therefore be dismissed, without prejudice to an effort to raise them by an appropriate procedure.

So ordered.[51]

If Black's great personal antagonist on the Court was Jackson, his great intellectual adversary was Frankfurter. Few Justices have been of greater interest both to the public and to Court specialists than Felix Frankfurter. In large measure, that has been true because his career posed something of a puzzle. Before his appointment to the bench, he was known for his interest in libertarian causes. He was also closely connected in the public mind with the New Deal, and it was generally expected that, once on the Court, he would continue along a liberal path. Yet, if one thing is certain, it is that it is risky to make predictions in advance of how new appointees will behave after they don the robe. "One of the things," Frankfurter once said, "that laymen, even lawyers, do not always understand is indicated by the question you hear so often: 'Does a man become any different when he puts on a gown? I say, 'If he is any good, he does.' "[52] Frankfurter himself seemed an altogether different man as a Justice than he had been off the bench. From academic eminence behind the New Deal to leader of the conservative Court cabal—that was the way press and public tended to tag Justice Frankfurter.

Frankfurter, wrote Dean Acheson after the Justice's death, was "universally called . . . 'the little judge.' "[53] Small, feisty, endowed with what Judge Learned Hand termed "a superabundant vitality,"[54] Frankfurter was insatiable in his curiosity and love of gossip. Arthur M. Schlesinger, Jr., writes that he gave "off sparks like an overcharged electric battery. He loved people, loved conversation, loved influence, loved life."[55]

In a *New York Times* article, Anthony Lewis characterized Frankfurter as "an eighteenth-century man in the range of his interests."[56] He was an intensely social person. "How I chafe against the pressures of this job," he once complained to legal historian Charles Warren, "in that it deprives me of the most coveted pleasure in life, namely, converse with civilized and cultivated people."[57] To make up for the deprivation, Frankfurter became an inveterate letter writer. The Frankfurter papers contain correspondence with an amazingly diverse group of people—ranging from leading judges, lawyers, and law professors, to political leaders like Franklin D. Roosevelt and Winston Churchill, and philosophers and scientists like John Dewey, Alfred North Whitehead, and Albert Einstein.

"A policeman's lot" Frankfurter once complained to a federal judge, "is not the only one that's not a happy one."[58] Frankfurter found it most trying to be a judge. He wrote to Justice Harlan that Harlan was mistaken "if it appeared to you that the work on the Court rolls off my back like water on a duck's. The fact of the matter is that, as often as not, I have broken nights when problems touching the conduct of our business are on my mind."[59]

Frankfurter's difficulties stemmed in large part from the fact that, as he affirmed to Justice Charles E. Whittaker, "I have an incorrigibly academic mind."[60] The ex-professor always remained the professor on the bench. "If all this sounds to you professorial," he concluded a learned letter to Jackson, "please remember that I am a professor unashamed."[61] Frankfurter continued to have the professorial love of argument for its own sake. As Dean Acheson stated it, Frankfurter "liked nothing better than to win an argument, and by unfair means if possible."[62] He was willing to argue any subject, ever ready to play the pedant with attorneys and Brethren alike. "It is no news to you," he wrote Judge Charles Wyzanski, "that disputation is one of my great pleasures."[63] At Court conferences, says Justice Potter Stewart, "Felix, if he was really interesed in a case, would speak for fifty minutes, no more or less, because that was the length of the lecture at the Harvard Law School."

Of course, Stewart exaggerates—but not by that much. One thing the Justices who served with Frankfurter recall is his tendency to treat the conference as another Harvard seminar, in which he would lecture at great length to demonstrate his professorial erudition. "We all know," reads a 1954 *Memorandum to Mr. Justice Frankfurter,* signed "Wm. O. Douglas," "what a great burden your long discourses are. So I am not complaining. But I do register a protest at your degradation of the Conference and its deliberations."[64]

Frankfurter also treated oral argument as the equivalent of a Harvard Law School class, with himself displaying the professor's mastery of the Socratic method. All commentators refer to his "heckling from the bench" that so distressed lawyers who were unprepared for it.[65] Above all, he could never shed the professorial need to get in the last word, whether in conference or repartee from the bench. About the only time he failed to do so occurred when a lawyer from the Midwest arguing his case did not answer a series of Frankfurter questions to the Justice's satisfaction. His patience exhausted, Frankfurter testily asked, "Counsel, before you go any further, I want to know how did you get to this Court?" The answer came back, "I came on the Pennsylvania Railroad." For once, the normally irrepressible Justice was speechless.[66]

In both his judicial and personal life, Frankfurter always contended that (as he once noted to Black) "I 'have a romantic belief in Reason.' "[67] Some years earlier, he had sent to Jackson, "Some Reflections of an Unashamed Professor," in which he wrote, "You see, my dear Bob, one drawback of a professor is that he does believe in reason and profoundly believes that the mode by which results are reached is as important—maybe more important—in the evolution of society as the result itself." Having said this, however, Frankfurter concluded with a disclaimer, "But no sooner have I said that than I am wondering whether I do not claim too much for professors!"[68]

Certainly Frankfurter claimed too much for himself when he stressed only his belief in reason. The truth was that the professed man of reason was really, as Anthony Lewis pointed out, a man of emotion, at times even of passion. Lewis quotes a friend, who called the Justice "a passionate person, who has given up the other passions of his life for this one—the institution of the Court."[69]

To Frankfurter, the law was almost an object of religious worship—and the Supreme Court its holy of holies. "Of all earthly institutions," Frankfurter wrote in a 1946 note to Justice Frank Murphy, "this Court comes nearest to having, for me, sacred aspects."[70] If Frankfurter saw himself as the priestly keeper of the shrine, he looked on Black and his supporters, notably Justice Douglas, as false prophets defiling hallowed ground.

The issue between Frankfurter, on the one side, and Black, on the other, was more basic than the differences engendered by personal antipathies. At the core, there was a fundamental disagreement over the proper role of the judge in constitutional cases. The division is of importance to an understanding of the Warren Court because, during the first years of the new Chief Justice, the Court was sharply split between the Black and Frankfurter polar views. In simplified terms, the division was between judicial activism and judicial self-restraint. The rule of restraint had been the handiwork of one of the seminal figures of American law—Justice Holmes. It was Holmes who, in large part, furnished the jurisprudential foundation for twentieth-century constitutional law.

The Holmes philosopher's stone was "the conviction that our constitutional system rests upon tolerance and that its greatest enemy is the Absolute." [71] It was not at all the judicial function to strike down laws with which the judge disagreed. "There is nothing I more deprecate" asserted Holmes in a 1921 dissent, "than the use of the Fourteenth Amendment . . . to prevent the making of social experiments that an important part of the community desires . . . even though the experiments may seem futile or even noxious to me." [72] Not the judge but the legislator was to have the primary say on the policy considerations behind a regulatory measure. The judge's business, wrote Holmes in 1910 to his noted English correspondent, Sir Frederick Pollock, was to enforce even "laws that I believe to embody economic mistakes." [73]

By the 1940s, the Holmes approach of judicial self-restraint had become established doctrine. By then, the at-first lonely voice had become the new dispensation, which had now written itself into our law. [74] But the issues confronting the Supreme Court had also begun to change over the years, and judges like Black had come to feel that even the Holmes canon could not suffice as the "be all and end all" of judicial review. Black was willing to follow the rule of restraint in the economic area. But he believed that the protection of personal liberties imposed on the Court more active enforcement obligations. When a law allegedly infringed upon the personal rights guaranteed by the Bill of Rights, Black refused to defer to the legislative judgment that the law was necessary.

Black's view on the matter was well expressed in a 1962 letter. Replying to the question of whether the Court should defer to congressional judgment on constitutional issues, Black asserted, "The question just does not make sense to me. This is because if the Court must 'defer' to the legislative judgment about whether a statute is constitutional, then the Court must yield its responsibility to another body that does not possess that responsibility. If, as I think, the judiciary is vested with the supreme constitutional power and responsibility to pass on the validity of legislation, then I think it cannot 'defer' to the legislative judgment 'without abdicating its own responsibility. . . .' " To Black, constitutional decisions should not depend upon any deference doctrine, but only "on the Court's honest judgment" on constitutionality. "I think it is the business and the supreme responsibility of the Court to hold a law unconstitutional if it believes that the law is unconstitutional, without 'deference' to anybody or any institution. In short, as to this phase of the discussion, I believe it is the duty of the Court to show 'deference' to the Constitution only." [75]

To Frankfurter, this was constitutional heresy. In the first place, it violated the Holmes canon, which, to the judge who tried most to be a conscious Holmes disciple, had become the only orthodox doctrine. For Black, the restraint doctrine may no longer have been an appropriate response to the new constitutional issues presented to the Court. Frankfurter, on the contrary, whose attitude toward Holmes smacked as much of hagiography as agreement, remained wholly true to the approach of the mentor whom he called "My Master." As he wrote soon after his retirement, "You have a right to deem my attitude toward Holmes close to idolatry, certainly to reverence." [76] To Frankfurter, the Holmes canon remained *the* judicial polestar throughout his career on the Court.

Frankfurter's constant references to Holmes, particularly during conference discussion, tended to grate upon the Brethren. And he well knew it. In a letter to Justice Reed, Frankfurter compared his colleagues' attitude to that of "the Athenians [who] got sick and tired of hearing about Aristides 'the just'—so they banished him!" Similarly, he went on, "some of his successors get sick and tired of hearing about Holmes and his genius. I know that—but it's a state of mind I can't understand. I belong to the *Ecclesiastes* school. 'Let us praise famous men.' " [77]

But it was more than reverence for "the Master" who, as Frankfurter wrote to Justice Whittaker, "was the originating mind which transformed legal thinking between the time that he came to the bar and . . . our own day," [78] that made Frankfurter disagree so strongly with the Black activist approach. To Frankfurter, Black's refusal to defer to the legislative judgment did violence to the basic presuppositions of representative democracy. The essential condition, Frankfurter asserted to Black in 1943 was that judges do "not write their private notions of policy into the Constitution . . . merely translate their private convictions into decisions and call it the law and the Constitution." [79]

To Frankfurter, restraint was the proper posture for a nonrepresentative judiciary, regardless of the nature of the asserted interests in particular cases. In all cases, Frankfurter felt, "Humanity is not the test of constitutionality." On the contrary, as he once wrote Justice Murphy, "a sensitive humanitarian who has taken the oath as a judge . . . does not yield to his compassion, or . . . think his compassion is the measure of law." [80]

If Frankfurter found it difficult to be a judge, it was primarily because his own intense nature inevitably conflicted with the complete detachment required by his judicial philosophy. Frankfurter's papers refer with pride to a handwritten note sent him by Reed after Frankfurter had read an opinion, from which Reed had dissented: "One thing you always do, better than most of us, vote your view of the law, without direction from your own wishes." [81]

The emotional trials presented by a rigorous employment of the Frankfurter judicial technique are perhaps best illustrated by the Justice's opinions on the constitutionality of a state law making it compulsory for school children to salute the flag. In *Minersville School District v. Gobitis,* [82] decided in 1940, Frankfurter delivered the opinion of the Court sustaining the flag-salute requirement, with Justice Harlan F. Stone alone dissenting. In a letter to Stone explaining his opinion, Frankfurter claimed that "nothing has weighed as much on my conscience, since I have come to this Court, as has this case." [83] Then, when only three years later, in *West Virginia Board of Education v. Barnette,* [84] the Court reversed itself and ruled the compulsory salute unconstitutional, Frankfurter stood his original ground and delivered a sharp dissent, which began with as intensely personal a statement as any contained in a judicial opinion: "One who belongs to the most vilified and persecuted minority in history is not likely to be insensible to the freedoms guaranteed by our Constitution. Were my purely personal attitude relevant I should wholeheartedly associate myself with the general libertarian views in the Court's opinion, representing as they do the thought and action of a lifetime." [85]

In his letter to Stone explaining his opinion upholding the flag salute, Frankfurter stressed the basic difficulty in such a case: "Here, also, we have an illustration of what the Greeks thousands of years ago recognized as a tragic issue, namely, the clash of rights, not the clash of wrongs. For resolving such clash we have no calculus." But, even in such a case, the individual preferences of the judge had to give way: "What weighs with me strongly in this case is my anxiety that, while we lean in the direction of the libertarian aspect, we do not exercise our judicial power unduly, and as though we ourselves were legislators by holding with too tight a rein the organs of popular government."[86]

For Black, the Frankfurter posture was—it is not too much to say—both an exercise in judicial hypocrisy as well as a refusal of judicial responsibility. To Black it was hypocritical because it enabled Frankfurter to pose as a liberal who was barred by proper notions of the judge's function from reaching the libertarian results that his personal inclinations favored. In his letter to Stone, Frankfurter had asserted "that all my bias and predisposition are in favor of giving the fullest elbow room to every variety of religious, political, and economic view."[87] Black felt that this was only a facade designed to justify a result that was really the most congenial to a former liberal who was now leader of the Court's conservative bloc.

Black, moreover, considered the Frankfurter approach a repudiation of the duty delegated to the judge by the Constitution. As Black saw it, abnegation in the end came down to abdication by the Court of its essential role. The Court's decision, he wrote in a 1962 letter, should "not depend at all, however, upon 'deference' to the Congress, but on the Court's honest judgment as to whether the law was within the competence of the Congress."[88] The decision on constitutionality had to be made on the judge's independent judgment; to "defer" to others meant a passing of the buck that the Constitution had placed squarely on the judge.

For Frankfurter, on the other hand, the Black activist approach was utterly inconsistent with the proper exercise of the judicial function. In a 1949 letter to Jackson, Frankfurter stressed the need for acting "within the proper confines of what is our business as judges and not giving ground for believing that the very thing we charge the other fellow with we are guilty of ourselves, namely, to translate political views into judicial decisions."[89] Black *was* constantly guilty, as Frankfurter indicated in a 1943 letter to him, of trying to "write [his] private notions of policy into the Constitution."[90] In an earlier letter, Frankfurter had told Black straight out that he considered him a Benthamite.[91] (Jeremy Bentham was, of course, the great reformer whose philippics against legal archaisms were the catalyst that led to the reform movements that so substantially changed Anglo-American law.) "But," said Frankfurter in the same letter, "as is so often true of a reformer who seeks to get rid of the accumulated abuses of the past Bentham at times threw out the baby with the bath. In his rigorous and candid desire to rid the law of many far-reaching abuses introduced by judges, he was not unnaturally propelled to the opposite extreme." Frankfurter regarded Black as a Benthamite with a vengeance, who used the bench to remake the law in his own image.

To be sure, Frankfurter recognized that judges inevitably have a share in law-making. As he wrote to Black, "the problem is not whether the judges make the law, but when and how and how much. Holmes put it in his highbrow way, that 'they can do so only interstitially; they are confined from molar to molecular motions.' I used to say to my students that legislatures make law wholesale, judges retail."[92] The trouble with Black, as Frankfurter saw it, was that he made law "wholesale," and in so doing, was thus acting more like a legislator than a judge. Frankfurter's view is well shown by an unpublished opinion that he wrote in 1943. Black had dissented from an opinion of the Court upholding an Interstate Commerce Commission order, which stressed that discretion in the given case had been "left to it [i.e., the Commission] rather than to courts."[93] Referring to Black's dissent in his diary, Frankfurter stated, "Black indulged in a harangue worthy of the cheapest soapbox orator." Among Frankfurter's papers there is a sarcastic concurring opinion in the case, apparently never circulated, which reads as follows:

SUPREME COURT OF THE UNITED STATES

No. 175—October Term, 1942

The Interstate Commerce Commission, the Baltimore and Ohio Railroad Company, et al., Appellants	)))))))))))	On Appeal from the District Court of the United States for the Northern District of Ohio.
vs.		
Inland Waterways Corporation, et al.		

Mr. Justice FRANKFURTER, concurring

I greatly sympathize with the essential purpose of my Brother (former Senator) Black's dissent. His roundabout and turgid legal phraseology is a *cri de coeur*. "Would I were back in the Senate," he means to say, "so that I could put on the statute books what really ought to be there. But here I am, cast by Fate into a den of judges devoid of the habits of legislators, simple fellows who feel that they must enforce the laws as Congress wrote them and not as they really should have been written, that the task which Congress has committed to the Interstate Commerce Commission should be left to that Commission even when it decides, as it did in this case, against the poor farmers of the Middle West."[94]

The very basic differences in approach to the judicial role made for substantial differences in result in important areas of constitutional law. This was particularly true of the position Black most forcefully advocated while on the Supreme Court: his absolutist view of the First Amendment. Black explained this absolutist position in a 1962 interview thus: "I learned a long time ago that there are affirmative and negative words. The beginning of the First Amendment is that 'Congress shall make no law.' I understand that it is rather old-fashioned and shows a slight naiveté to say that 'no law' means no law. It is one of the most amazing things about the ingeniousness of the times that strong arguments are made, which *almost* convince me, that it is very foolish of me to think 'no law' means no law. . . . But when I get down to the really basic reason why I believe that 'no law' means no law, I presume it could come to this, that I took an obligation to support and defend the Constitution as I understand it. And being a rather backward country fellow, I understand it to mean what the words say."[95]

The Black position on the First Amendment meant, "without deviation, without exception, without any ifs, buts, or whereases, that freedom of speech"[96] was protected from *any and all* governmental infringements. To Frankfurter, Black's absolutist approach had no legitimate place in constitutional jurisprudence. For Frankfurter, the only absolute was that there were no absolutes in law. "Lincoln for government and Holmes for law," he once wrote, "have taught me that the absolutists are the enemies of reason—that the fanatics in politics and the dogmatists in law, however sincere, are the mischief-makers."[97] In a 1957 letter to Warren, Frankfurter asserted, "We get into a lot of trouble by talking about the plain and unequivocal language of the First Amendment in its provision about 'abridging the freedom of speech.' . . . The Constitution after all is not a verbal marionette in which one takes the words with literalness."[98] Frankfurter's opinion on Black's First Amendment absolutism was pithily stated to Justice Harlan: "Black and Co. have gone mad on free speech!"[99] Rather more forthrightly, Frankfurter had written to Learned Hand in 1954: "Hugo is a self-righteous, self-deluded part fanatic, part demagogue."[100]

As we shall see in later chapters, Black himself did not follow his own absolutist approach in cases involving speech combined with conduct. Thus, when critics would confront him with the famous Holmes example of the man falsely shouting "Fire!" in a crowded theater,[101] Black would reply, "That is a wonderful aphorism about shouting 'fire' in a crowded theater. But you do not have to shout 'fire' to get arrested. If a person creates a disorder in a theater, they would get him there not because of *what* he hollered but because he *hollered*."[102] Similarly, Black considered picketing to be more than mere speech. "Picketing," he asserted in a 1965 dissent, "though it may be utilized to communicate ideas, is not speech, and therefore is not of itself protected by the First Amendment."[103] In the last years of the Warren Court, Black was to apply the same approach to uphold governmental restrictions upon "sit-ins" and comparable civil-rights protests.

Frankfurter felt that Black's decisions in these cases demonstrated the untenability of his rival's whole First Amendment posture. In a dialogue circulated to the Brethren in 1960, he satirized the absolutist approach to speech:

A DIALOGUE
(With Apologies To Gertrude Stein)

L(ibertarian) L(ads):
    Speech is speech is speech.
F(rivolous) F(rankfurter):
    Crying-fire-in-theatre is speech is speech
      is not "speech."
    Libel is speech is speech is not "speech."
    Picketing is speech is speech is not "speech."
    Pornographic film is speech is speech is not "speech."
                                            —Anonymous[104]

Frankfurter may have been right in his rejection of constitutional absolutes, even where freedom of speech was concerned. Many writers have pointed to the legal impossibility of applying the First Amendment literally: the Holmes example of falsely shouting "fire!" in a theater is simply the most obvious example of speech that can

be controlled. Yet it cannot be denied that Black's absolutist advocacy was a prime mover in the First Amendment jurisprudence of
the past forty years. The absolutist view may not have been accepted;
but the "firstness" of the First Amendment has been firmly established. In a 1941 dissent, Black declared, "the guaranties of the First
Amendment [are] the foundation upon which our governmental
structure rests and without which it could not continue to endure as
conceived and planned."[105] If today, as he stated in the same opinion, "[f]reedom to speak and to write about public questions . . . is
the heart"[106] of the constitutional scheme, that has in large part been
due to the consistent Black evangelism on the matter.

As it turned out, it was Black, rather than Frankfurter, who was
more in tune with contemporary constitutional needs. History has
vindicated the Black approach, for it has helped protect personal liberties in an era of encroaching public power. No matter how he tried
to clothe his opinions with the Holmes mantle, there was an element
of shabbiness in the results reached by Frankfurter in too many cases.
After Frankfurter delivered his opinion upholding the compulsory
flag salute, he was talking about the opinion over cocktails at Hyde
Park. Mrs. Eleanor Roosevelt, in her impulsive way, declared that,
regardless of the Justice's learning and legal skills, there was something wrong with an opinion that forced little children to salute a
flag when such a ceremony was repugnant to their conscience.[107]

In the end, it was Black, not Frankfurter, who best served the
Court and the nation. With all his intellect and legal talents, Frankfurter's judicial career remained a lost opportunity. As far as constitutional law was concerned, he may well have had more influence as
a law professor than as a Supreme Court Justice.[108] There is no doubt
that Frankfurter expected to be the intellectual leader of the Court,
as he had been of the Harvard law faculty. As it turned out, the
leadership role was performed first by his great rival, Black, and then
by the new Chief Justice.

Indeed, if impact on the law is a hallmark of the outstanding judge,
few occupants of the bench have been more outstanding than Black.
It was Black who led the Court to tilt the Constitution in favor of
individual rights and liberties and who was, before Warren, the intellectual leader in what Justice Abe Fortas once termed "the most
profound and pervasive revolution ever achieved by substantially
peaceful means."[109] Even where Black's views have not been adopted

literally, they have tended to prevail in a more general, modified form. Nor has his impact been limited to the Black positions which the Court has accepted. It is found in the totality of today's judicial awareness of the Bill of Rights and the law's new-found sensitivity to liberty and equality.

More than anything, Black brought to the highest Court a moral fervor rarely seen on the bench. A famous passage by Holmes has it that the blackletter judge will be replaced by the man of statistics and the master of economics.[110] Black was emphatically a judge who still followed the blackletter approach in dealing with the constitutional text. "That Constitution," he said, "is my legal bible. . . . I cherish every word of it from the first to the last."[111] The eminent jurist with his dog-eared copy of the Constitution in his right coat pocket became a part of contemporary folklore. In protecting the sanctity of the organic word, Black displayed all the passion of the Old Testament prophet in the face of the graven idols. His ardor may have detracted from the image of the "judicial." But if Black did not bring to constitutional issues that "cold neutrality" of which Edmund Burke speaks,[112] his zeal may have been precisely what was needed in the Supreme Court. Anything less might have been inadequate to make the Bill of Rights the vital center of our constitutional law.

As Holmes once emphasized, theory is the most important part of the law, as the architect is the most important man in the building of a house.[113] The differences between Black and Frankfurter may have been differences in legal theory, but they had important practical consequences as well. It is no exaggeration to say that the early history of the Warren Court turned upon the reception by the new Chief Justice of the competing theories. While Warren was feeling his way in his unfamiliar judicial role, the two rival Justices remained the key intellectual figures on the Court. During his first few years, we will see, Warren hesitated between the antagonistic Black and Frankfurter approaches. Not until the 1956 Term, did Warren finally make the choice. When he did, it was to reject the philosophy of judicial restraint and join hands with Black. From then on, it was Warren who was to lead the Court, with Black as a principal ally, in rewriting so much of the corpus of constitutional law.

Before Warren's appointment, Black's chief supporter on the Court had been William O. Douglas. "If any student of the modern Supreme Court took an association test," wrote Black's son in his book about his father, "the word 'Black' would probably evoke the response 'Douglas' and vice versa."[114] Black himself recognized this. Declining a 1958 invitation to write an article about Douglas, Black wrote, "You perhaps know without my stating it that I have the very highest regard for Justice Douglas as a friend and as a member of this Court. In fact, our views are so nearly the same that it would be almost like self praise for me to write what I feel about his judicial career."[115]

Douglas reciprocated the Black feeling. Immediately after Chief Justice Vinson's death, he sent Black a handwritten note. "I wish Eisenhower would make you *Chief Justice*. It would be the smartest thing he could do *politically* and the best possible appointment on the merits. But I do not think he's smart enough to do it."[116]

Douglas had expressed a similar view when Chief Justice Hughes had retired in 1941. After Justice Harlan F. Stone received the appointment, Douglas, then on one of his cross-country trips, sent Black a June 22, 1941, written note: "I am sorry that it did not go to you. I thought you *deserved it*. And I know it would strengthen the Court greatly if you were the Chief." Douglas had no doubt who had blocked the Black appointment. " 'Felix has done it again' and there is no question in my mind that he was responsible."[117]

Douglas felt as warmly toward Black as he did toward any of the Brethren. But there never existed the warm personal relations between them that there were to be between Black and Warren, or even between Black and Justice Harlan, who, despite their legal disagreements, became friends. Douglas was the kind of individual who found it most difficult to maintain a close personal relationship. To outside observers, Douglas seemed the personification of the last frontier— the down-to-earth Westerner whose granite-hewed physique always seemed out of place in Parnassus. More than that, Douglas was the Court's Horatio Alger, whose early life was a struggle against polio and poverty. Told that he would never walk, he became a noted sportsman. Riding east on a freight car to enroll at Columbia Law School, with six cents in his pocket, he became an eminent law professor, chairman of the Securities and Exchange Commission, and at the age of forty a Supreme Court Justice.

But the real Douglas was different from his public image. Douglas was the quintessential loner, who personified the lover of humanity who did not like people. No one on the Court, neither among the Brethren or the law clerks, was really close to the strapping Westerner. The clerks particularly describe Douglas as the coldest of the Justices. It was an event when Douglas stopped to say "hello" in the Court corridors. His severity toward his own clerks became legend. At times, his behavior toward them was downright mean. Once, when a major university wanted to invite Douglas to speak, it asked one of Warren's clerks, a recent graduate, to make the necessary approach. The clerk arranged an appointment and proudly introduced the president of the student body, who started to tell the Justice what they wanted. At this, Douglas broke in, "Why are you bothering me with that? Talk to my agent; the fee is $3,000, and he'll handle it."

Douglas was noted for his lack of consideration; the feelings of others normally did not enter into his conduct. In 1954, Douglas began his publicized hikes along the Chesapeake and Ohio Canal. Each year thereafter, the hike became a minor social event, with the vigorous Justice leading a large group of Washingtonians along the pathway. At the end of the hike, full of mud in his lumber jacket and hiking boots, Douglas would seek refreshment. One year, he went tramping up to an elegant inn near the canal and was indignant when he was refused service and asked to leave. The incident attracted attention and was written up in the papers. Characteristically, Warren took his clerks to lunch the next Saturday at the same inn, saying it would be amusing to be welcomed there after Bill Douglas had been turned away in his muddy boots.

On the bench, as in his personal life, Douglas was a maverick, who went his own way regardless of the feelings of the Brethren. "Bill's headstrongness sometimes cannot be coped with," wrote Douglas' second wife to Black one summer.[118] Douglas would stick to his own views, quick to state his own way of deciding in concurrence or dissent. It made little difference whether he carried a majority or stood alone. He would rarely stoop to lobbying for his position and seemed more interested in making his own stand public than in working to get it accepted. As one law clerk put it, "Douglas was just as happy signing a one-man dissent as picking up four more votes."

There is no doubt that Douglas had a brilliant mind, but he was erratic. He could whip up opinions faster than any of the Brethren and did almost all the work himself, relying less on his clerks than any other Justice. But his opinions were too often unpolished, as though he lacked the interest for the sustained work involved in transforming first drafts into finished products. Lack of interest in the Court's work was, indeed, apparent in Douglas' very attitude as a judge. During oral arguments, Douglas seemed to spend most of his time writing letters. You could tell he was writing letters because, every once in a while, he would lift his head from his scribbling and very ostentatiously lick an envelope from side to side and seal it. At the same time, every now and then he would lift his head and direct an acute question to counsel. As one of the Brethren put it, "Bill could listen with one ear." Though Warren came to appreciate Douglas' supporting votes for his own positions, he always felt that the peripatetic Justice spent too much time writing books and doing things that were not related to the Court.

From the beginning, Douglas supported Black in his judicial differences with Frankfurter. During Douglas' first three terms, the two did not vote apart in a single case. In his book on the Court, Fred Rodell noted that "the phrase, 'Black and Douglas dissenting,' . . . has become as common . . . as 'Holmes and Brandeis dissenting,' thirty-odd years ago." [119] Inevitably, therefore, Douglas, like Black, soon became an object of Frankfurter's animosity. To Frankfurter, Black and Douglas were both, as he termed them in a letter to Justice Harlan, "self-righteous do-gooders." [120] When he read over a 1957 draft dissent by Justice Clark, which referred to a statement by Douglas on liability for negligence, Frankfurter wrote in the margin, "Brennan has his work cut out for him to teach Douglas . . . what 'negligence' is." [121] A little earlier, Frankfurter had received a letter from Judge Learned Hand, a close friend, which declared, "Black and Douglas are frankly not judges at all: 'to such favor will my lady come.' I am getting a bit obsessed about this step by step invasion of other folks duties by these conceited, wilful, obstinate, self-satisfied men, wholly without humility, moderation, or background." [122] Frankfurter then wrote Hand comparing Black and Douglas to the Justices who had invalidated the regulatory measures of the early New Deal. "If I gave you a bill of particulars of what I have lived through in these now nearly twenty years, even you with all your knowledge and discernment would realize that you don't know nuthin'. 'I could unto you a tale unfold' that would shock you, hardened character that you are." The "judicial process" illustrated by the Black-Douglas activism in cases involving personal rights, Frankfurter went on, "would have warranted Cardozo to say about these civil liberties cases, as he said about cases involving economic issues in his time, 'This is not a court of law.' Those are the words he used to me with tears in his eyes, adding, 'Why didn't you let me stay in Albany?' "[123]

In 1957 Frankfurter prepared a memorandum suggesting improvements in the Court's operation. At the end of a printed draft, he wrote, "These don't solve Ct's basic probs, of course. Unjudicious, unlearned, arrogant, power-thrilled do-gooders today's threat."[124] There can be little doubt to which of the Brethren Frankfurter was referring. Douglas, Frankfurter wrote Hand in 1954, "is the most cynical, shamelessly immoral character I've ever known."[125] A few years later, in a written note to Justice Harlan, Frankfurter declared, "I give up trying to understand W.O.D. . . . . I can understand his occasional resort to unvarnished unscrupulosities."[126] And, during World War II, Frankfurter's diary used to call Black, Douglas, and the Justices who voted with them "the Axis."[127] Strong stuff. Douglas, for his part, displayed a similar antipathy which seemed personal toward Frankfurter. In his *Autobiography,* Douglas termed Frankfurter a "prevaricator." Of Frankfurter's close relationship with President Roosevelt, Douglas says that it took years "before it dawned on Roosevelt that his 'friend' had chameleonlike qualities—no one told him; he found it out for himself. And the realization of it was shattering."[128] To Douglas, Frankfurter "was a real conservative who embraced old precedents under the guise of bowing to 'the law,' but who actually chose the old precedents because he liked them better."[129]

Douglas would use every opportunity to "needle" Frankfurter. In conference, Justice Stewart recalls, "after Felix spoke, in the order of seniority, then it was Bill Douglas' turn, and often, I remember, Bill was absolutely devastating after one of those fifty minute lectures. Bill would say, in a quiet voice, 'When I came into this conference, I agreed with the conclusion that Felix has just announced; but he's just talked me out of it'—which used to drive Felix Frankfurter crazy."

Underneath the raillery, however, there was a real personal antagonism. "Today at Conference," reads a biting Douglas memorandum to Frankfurter, "I asked you a question. . . . An answer was refused rather insolently. This was so far as I recall the first time one member of the Conference refused to answer another member on a matter of Court business."[130] Toward the end, Douglas and Frankfurter were scarcely on speaking terms.[131] Once when Professor Rodell visited the Court to see Douglas, he found the Justices in conference. After Douglas had been informed that Rodell was there, he sent out the following note: "That little S.O.B. knows you're here and he's filibustering."

If Frankfurter could refer to Douglas as "unlearned," Douglas felt that the ex-Harvard law professor had never shed the professorial habit of pontificating and demonstrating his erudition. Douglas sent a 1961 *Memorandum to the Conference* in which he referred to "the long law-review-article-opinion" circulated by Frankfurter in a case, and declared, "We have tended more and more to write a law-review-type of opinion. They plague the Bar and the Bench. They are so long they are meaningless. They are filled with trivia and non-essentials. . . . We should aim for brevity, not for professorial dissertations."[132]

The Douglas–Frankfurter animosity was fueled by Douglas' continuing political ambitions. "What jolts one in the Diaries," reads Joseph P. Lash's introduction to Frankfurter's diaries, "is that Frankfurter should have been so harshly critical of fellow Justices . . . for their nonjudicial activities [particularly] Douglas's interest in elective office."[133] On July 2, 1940, Douglas had sent Frankfurter a handwritten note "Enroute to Texas," headed *"Personal and Confidential."* Douglas wrote, "There is considerable talk in Washington about putting me on the ticket." He said that he discounted such talk. "But it is sufficiently active to be disturbing." It was disturbing "because I want none of it. I want to stay where I am." He was writing "to ask you, should the matter come your way, to scotch it." Douglas concluded, "I am MOST serious about this—probably more serious than the possibilities justify."[134]

To Frankfurter, this was a case where his Brother did protest too much. When Douglas was again mentioned in 1943 as a possible candidate, Frankfurter asked Justice Frank Murphy whether "it doesn't shock you to have this Court made a jumping-off place for politics." Murphy answered, "Well, I don't like it." To which Frankfurter declared, "it's much more than a matter of not liking. When a priest enters a monastery, he must leave—or ought to leave—all sorts of worldly desires behind him. And this Court has no excuse for being unless it's a monastery."[135] As late as 1954, former Justice Owen J. Roberts could write Frankfurter of the need "to keep people like Douglas from making the Court the stepping stone to the presidency."[136]

Douglas was seriously considered by Presidents Roosevelt and Truman for both elective and appointive offices. Roosevelt informed the 1944 Democratic Convention that he "would be glad to run" with either "Harry Truman or Bill Douglas," and Truman asked Douglas to run for Vice-President with him in 1948. Douglas turned down the offer, telling the President that he preferred to remain on the Court—though it is probable that the widespread expectation of a Truman defeat played a part in the refusal.[137]

Douglas also refused presidential offers of high executive positions. In 1946, Truman asked him to become Secretary of the Interior, but Douglas declined.[138] According to his *Autobiography,* however, Douglas did tell Truman "that there was one way he could get me into the Cabinet if he was anxious to have me. He asked me what that was and then I told him: Secretary of State."[139]

An important post had been offered five years earlier by President Roosevelt. Before he appointed Justice James F. Byrnes as director of the war mobilization effort, Roosevelt asked Douglas to accept a comparable position as director of war production. In a July 23, 1941, handwritten letter, marked *"Personal* and *Confidential,"* Douglas informed Black, "I received a telephone call from the President. He wants to see me. . . . I do not know what he has in mind. He said over the telephone that he needed me in a 'more active' job." Douglas said that he hoped to see Black after his talk with the President. "I do not want to leave the Court . . . ," he went on. "I want nothing but the opportunity to slug away along side of you for the next 30 years."[140]

Nothing came of this particular Presidential initiative, which was for Douglas to become, in Douglas' words "top guy in the defense work."[141] Douglas turned the job down, but what was of particular interest here was Douglas' apparent belief that F.D.R.'s offer was part of some Frankfurter-engineered stratagem. "I am quite sure," a September 8 letter to Black asserts, "that F.F. has inspired this offer—at least that he has been influential. It has come to me 'straight' that he thinks I am the ugly man. If he could get me there & you back in the Senate I am sure he would be happier."[142]

The remaining four Justices during Warren's first term as Chief Justice—Reed, Clark, Burton, and Minton—did not begin to compare, either in ability or personality, with Black, Frankfurter, Douglas, and Jackson, and with the exception of Clark, they did not play a particularly important role in the Warren Court. By the time the new Chief had become his own man and had assumed actual as well as titular leadership, all but Clark would have retired.

Three of the four—Clark, Burton, and Minton—had been appointed by President Truman; Reed, like the four already discussed, had been appointed by President Roosevelt. Stanley Reed had had a successful practice in his home state of Kentucky, when he was brought to Washington as a government lawyer by the Hoover Administration. Staying on with the new President, Reed became Solicitor General and argued the first important New Deal cases in the Supreme Court. His reward was his appointment to the second Court seat filled by Roosevelt.

With the exception of James F. Byrnes, who remained on the Court for only a short period, Reed was the most conservative of the Roosevelt-appointed Justices as well as the least intellectually gifted of them. He was a solid, plodding worker, who considered law in the traditional terms that had prevailed before the Court was recast by eight Roosevelt appointments. More than any other of the New Deal Brethren, Reed voted to uphold federal power, whether directed against property or personal rights. "How sure I was . . . ," reads a handwritten note from Reed to Frankfurter, "in the innocent days when law to a country lawyer seemed automatic—no two sides to any legal issue." [143] Reed tended throughout his judicial tenure to view often complex issues in simplistic terms.

Perhaps the most difficult questions faced by the Vinson Court were those presented by the loyalty program instituted in 1947 by President Truman. In another note to Frankfurter, Reed stated, "We will never agree on the loyalty investigations because we are not looking in the same direction." Reed recognized that "those who disagree with me, they say that the 'trials' are unfair, therefore unconstitutional because one is not confronted with his accusers." His own position, Reed said, was much simpler: "that a negative conclusion means nothing more, constitutionally, than a similar inquiry by me as to say—a law clerk." To Reed, giving the Loyalty Review Board power to decide loyalty cases, "on the evidence, including hearsay, before them," was "the only way to conduct affairs." [144]

The first Justice to be appointed by Truman was Harold H. Burton, then a Senator from Ohio, who had become a friend of the President as a member of the famous Truman Committee which investigated defense contracts during World War II. Burton's path to the high bench had followed the traditional pattern of practice as a local leader of the Bar, a political career (state legislator, Mayor of Cleveland, U.S. Senator), then elevation to the Court. In appearance, he has been compared to a small, neat version of a village storekeeper.[145] His biographer concedes that "Burton, an average justice, was not a bright, witty intellectual like a Frankfurter or a Black."[146] Yet, if he was quiet and unassuming, he was also hardworking. Frankfurter wrote Burton in 1947 that he had known every Justice since 1906, and "it is on that basis that I can say to you what I have said behind your back, that this court never had a Justice who was harder working or more conscientious."[147]

Burton, like the other Truman-appointed Justices, was usually to be found in the Frankfurter wing of the Court. Fully appreciative of his modest abilities, Burton was most deferential toward the ex-professor. Praise from the celebrated Harvard scholar led Burton to write, "I feel as though you have awarded me a mythical grade 'A' in your course on Constitutional Law, of which I may be proud."[148]

Truman's second Court appointee, Tom C. Clark, had started his legal career as a prosecutor, moved on to the Department of Justice, where he had worked with Warren while supervising the Japanese evacuation from the West Coast, and then been raised to Attorney General when Truman became President. Clark remained the glad-handing politician, whose flamboyant bowtie (worn even under the judicial robe) gave him a perpetual sophomoric appearance. Clark continued to flaunt his Texas background—his normal way of signifying agreement to an opinion was to write "Okey." "The duck was delicious," Clark wrote Warren in 1955. "It was big enough to be from Texas."[149] The Brethren, on their side, constantly teased Clark about his state. In 1959, Justice Harlan sent Clark a postcard from Australia: "Some of their sheep stations are nearly the size of the Sovereign State of Texas."[150]

It is said that, when Justice Murphy died, President Truman asked his Attorney General to suggest three names for the vacant seat. At which Clark is supposed to have replied, "Clark, Clark, Clark." Truman himself was quoted as saying that "Tom Clark was my biggest mistake. No question about it." According to the former President, "it isn't so much that he's a *bad* man. It's just that he's such a dumb son of a bitch. He's about the dumbest man I think I've ever run across."[151]

To one familiar with Clark's work, the Truman comment is ludicrous. Clark may not have been the intellectual equal of his more brilliant Brethren, but he developed into a more competent judge than any of the other Truman appointees. In fact, Clark has been the most underrated Justice in recent Supreme Court history. An examination of his Court files at the University of Texas reveals him as anything but dumb. The many drafts of opinions in his own handwriting belie the picture painted in Rodell's book on the Court of a Justice who, "more than any of his brethren, . . . depends on his young fresh-from-law-school assistants to outline and even write his opinions for him."[152]

Under Chief Justice Vinson, Clark almost always followed the conservative pro-Government Vinson position. In the Warren Court, Clark slowly came under the influence of his new Chief. This, in turn, made the Texan receptive to points of view that he might cavalierly have rejected during his early Court years. In the end, Clark became a crucial Warren supporter in a number of important cases. As we shall see in Chapter 10, it was Clark who played the key role in 1961 in *Mapp v. Ohio,* certainly one of the seminal cases decided while Warren was Chief Justice.

Sherman Minton, the last Truman-appointed Justice, had also been a personal friend of the President. Like Truman and Burton, Minton had been a midwestern Senator, elected from Indiana. During his one term, he was a strong Roosevelt supporter and served as Democratic whip. This probably cost him re-election, but F.D.R. consoled him with a seat on the U.S. Court of Appeals for the Seventh Circuit, where he served without distinction for eight years before being named to the high bench.

Minton was square-faced, with the build of a heavyweight boxer, and characterized by the saltiness of his tongue. He may have been the last Justice to use the spittoon provided for him behind the bench, which always upset the fastidious Burton next to him. Minton himself was the worst of the Truman appointees; by any standard he ranks near the bottom on any list of Justices. Yet his fellows considered the earthy Hoosier most congenial to work with. "Minton," wrote Frankfurter to a close friend, "will not go down in history as a great jurist, but he was a delightful colleague." Then he plaintively asked, "Why are most lawyers dull company?" [153]

During the three years he served on the Warren Court, Minton was most strongly influenced by Frankfurter. Like the other Truman appointees, he was flattered by the attention of the Court's leading intellectual. Once at least, Minton made an uncharacteristic riposte to the former professor. In a 1951 case, Frankfurter's agonizing over a decision led him to issue a separate opinion which he labelled, "Mr. Justice Frankfurter, dubitante." [154] At this, Minton sent the following "My dear Felix" letter: "I think you are slipping! I always thought you were a person who sometimes *fortasse errat,* but never *dubitante.*" [155]

"Alone among Government agencies," wrote Anthony Lewis in the *New York Times,* "the court seems to have escaped Parkinson's Law. The work is still done by nine men, assisted by eighteen young law clerks. Nothing is delegated to committees or ghost-writers or task forces." [156]

The only professional help Supreme Court Justices receive is that provided by their law clerks. The work of these clerks plays a very important and substantial part in the functioning of the Court. In a 1979 speech, Justice William J. Brennan referred to his opinions on the Court as "opinions that came from the Brennan chambers over the past 23 years. I say from the 'Brennan chambers' because, as Bentham said, the 'Law is not the work of judge alone but of judge and company.' The company in this case consisted of the 65 law clerks who have been associated with me on the Court." [157]

Ideally, the law clerk performs the functions of an associate in a law firm, i.e., research for senior members and assisting them generally in the firm's work. But the role of the clerks at the Supreme Court has greatly depended upon the tasks assigned them by their individual Justices. Inevitably the responsibility of the clerk has varied in adverse ratio to the caliber of the Justice. It may be doubted that the great Justices such as Holmes or Brandeis used their clerks as more than research assistants. More run-of-the-mill Justices have given their clerks a larger share of responsibility, including, in some cases, the writing of most opinions. The system was described a few years ago as out of control, with the clerks amok and virtually exercising the roles of junior (and, in some cases, even senior) Justices.[158] Complaints of this sort against the clerks' roles were common during the Warren years. A noted 1957 article in *U.S. News & World Report* by William H. Rehnquist, who clerked for Justice Jackson just before Warren's appointment and was himself to be named to the Court in 1971, was entitled, "Who Writes Decisions of the Supreme Court?"[159] Rehnquist stated that the Justices were delegating substantial responsibility to their clerks, who "unconsciously" slanted materials to accord with their own views. The result, Rehnquist argued, was that the "liberal" point of view of the vast majority of the clerks had become the philosophy espoused by the Warren Court. The Rehnquist thesis had been stated earlier, in satirical extreme, by Justice Jackson: "A suspicion has grown at the bar that the law clerks . . . constitute a kind of junior court which decides the fate of the certiorari petitions. This idea of the law clerks' influence gave rise to a lawyer's waggish statement that the Senate no longer need bother about confirmation of justices but ought to confirm the appointment of law clerks."[160] Not only wags stated that view: in 1958, Senator Stennis of Mississippi urged that law clerks should be confirmed by the Senate because of their rising importance and influence.[161]

A reply to Rehnquist was made, largely under Frankfurter's instigation, by Alexander M. Bickel, a former Frankfurter clerk, who had become a leading constitutional scholar. In a 1958 article in the *New York Times*, Bickel asserted that "the law clerks are in no respect any kind of a kitchen cabinet." Their job is only to "generally assist their respective Justices in researching the law books and other sources for materials relevant to the decision of cases before the Court." They also "go over drafts of opinions and may suggest changes."[162]

In the Warren Court, the truth varied between the Rehnquist and Bickel pictures. Douglas was noted for making practically no use of his law clerks. The practice of the other Justices differed. Some more or less abdicated their judicial functions, with almost everything put out in their names, including their correspondence, written by their clerks. Others, like Frankfurter, would do much of the work, including reading of certiorari petitions (what Frankfurter once called "the damned certs."), themselves. Yet even they would usually base their memoranda and opinions on drafts prepared by their clerks, though gone over and revised by themselves.

"As the years passed," says Douglas in his *Autobiography,* "it became more and more evident that the law clerks were drafting opinions."[163] Even the better Justices have made more extensive use of
their law clerks than outside observers have realized. Frankfurter can
be taken as an example. Particularly in his later years, he would have
his clerks draft not only opinions, but also memoranda. At the beginning of each term, Frankfurter used to send the Brethren a memo
suggesting improvements in Court procedure, always beginning with
the word "Greetings." Yet these "Greetings" memoranda, which
seemed so personal a product, were based upon drafts by Frankfurter's clerks.[164] The same was true of other Frankfurter products. During the 1960 Term, for example, Frankfurter circulated a memorandum, which he apparently thought so highly of that he had it
published in 1965 in the *Harvard Law Review* under his own name,[165]
the published version stating that it was "prepared with the help of
my law clerk, John D. French." Frankfurter's papers, however, show
that the memo was actually *written* by the clerk. Not only that; it
was French, not the Justice, who went over the *Harvard Law Review*
proofs.

Some of Frankfurter's best known opinions, too, notably his now-
famous dissent in the 1962 case of *Baker v. Carr,*[166] were drafted almost entirely by his clerks. In the 1960 case of *Elkins v. United States,*[167]
Frankfurter dissented in an opinion based almost verbatim on a draft
by one of his clerks. He then circulated a satiric dialogue criticizing
the Court's decision, entitled "Doctor and Student"[168] (in apparent
imitation of the classic sixteenth-century work by Christopher St.
Germain).[169] A Frankfurter letter[170] indicates that "both . . . the form
and substance of Doctor and Student" were the product of another
law clerk. The clerk in question, Anthony G. Amsterdam, was excep-
tionally able and the Justice relied on him extensively. Once he sent
back an Amsterdam-prepared draft, with minor corrections in his own
hand, with the comment, "If you approve of my revisions send to
printer and duly circulate."[171] To an outside observer, this may seem
an egregious reversal of the proper roles of Justice and clerk—almost
as though the law clerk system itself was being turned bottom-side
up.

Frankfurter himself characteristically expressed doubts about the
working of the law clerk system. "I wonder," he wrote Justice Harlan
in 1957, "how many who are reversing out of hand in these cases have

read the record and not relied merely on the memoranda of their law clerks. And, since my curiosity is very alert this morning, I wonder how many of the law clerks have read the whole record in these cases." [172] In a written note to Harlan a few years later, Frankfurter referred to those who "have mind all made up on basis of law clerk's bench memos, as I see the C.J. reading those bench memos." [173]

When Warren first came to the Supreme Court, he found on the staff awaiting him three law clerks appointed a short time earlier by Chief Justice Vinson, one of whom Vinson had not even seen before he died. As one of them recalls, Warren "didn't quite know what to make of us." Warren's relationship with his first clerks tended to be rather distant. Even after conferences of the Brethren, he did not follow the normal practice of summarizing the proceedings for his clerks. "We would go down to Justice Burton's," the same clerk says, "to find out what happened because he never told us what happened at the conference, even the results, during that year."

All this changed in later years. Warren then would meet with his clerks after conference sessions and describe for them in graphic detail what had happened. He would be entirely candid and often quite vivid in his characterizations of the Brethren's conduct. In addition, as the years went by, Warren developed a warm relationship with his clerks, treating them almost as surrogate sons during their year with him. He was wholly informal with them. Once he received a gift of a bottle of rare aged French cognac. He called in his clerks before one of their Saturday lunches and said, "Let's have a drink and unwind a bit before we go out." Then, according to one of the clerks, "he got this superb cognac and just picked up the water tumblers you have to clear your throat with and poured the cognac into these water tumblers and I was probably drinking the most valuable cognac I've ever had in my life out of a water tumbler."

By the end of the 1950s Warren had developed the practice of taking his clerks to lunch on Saturdays. He would sit and chat with them for hours about the work of the Court and other subjects, usually ending up with reminiscences about his political career. He always remained the avid sports enthusiast and would often break up the lunch sessions by saying, "Boys, let's go to the ball game." The group would then repair to Griffith Stadium for a baseball or football game. The Saturday lunches would most often be at the University Club. Warren's membership there has been criticized because the club had no black members.[174] However, Tyrone Brown, himself a black who was Warren's clerk in the 1967 Term, remembers that "the first couple of times that we went there he particularly enjoyed taking me over there with the group for lunch to, in a way, kind of desegregate the place."

Starting in 1961, the custom developed for the clerks, present and former, to give a Saturday dinner each year in honor of the Chief Justice. The next morning the Warrens would reciprocate with a brunch for the clerks and their wives at the swank Congressional Country Club. The clerks' dinner was a black-tie affair, exclusively for the Chief and the clerks, many of whom came from different parts of the country. Guests were invited to the pre-dinner cocktails, and, during their presidencies, both John F. Kennedy and Lyndon B. Johnson were invited and made brief appearances.

The first clerks' dinner was at the Metropolitan Club, noted as a stuffy place which closed at midnight. As the clerk who helped organize the affair recalls, "We were so offended that they would kick out the Chief Justice because they were closing, we decided never to go back there." Another thing that distressed the clerks was the fact that, when President Kennedy came during cocktails and asked for a beer, there was none available. The dinner was subsequently held at the Lawyers Club, and then at one of the large hotels. The one outsider who ever joined the clerks for dinner was Thurgood Marshall, then Solicitor General, who apparently did not realize that he had been invited only for cocktails. He went in and joined the dinner as, in the words of one clerk, "we couldn't figure out how to get rid of him."

To understand how Chief Justice Warren used his law clerks, one must understand how the Supreme Court operates. The Justices sit from October to late June or early July, in annual sessions called terms, with each term designated by the year in which it begins. Cases come to the Court from the U.S. Courts of Appeals and the highest state courts either by appeals or petitions for writs of certiorari. The Justices have discretion in deciding whether to take an appeal or grant certiorari (or cert, as it is usually called in the Court). Each year the Justices decide to hear only a fraction of the cases presented to them. Thus, in the 1953 Term, Warren's first, they heard only 170 cases out of 1,201 presented. In the 1968 Term, Warren's last, of 3,117 cases presented, the Justices heard only 257 cases. The normal proportion was that stated in a 1955 Frankfurter query to Minton, "wouldn't you gladly settle for one in ten—such is my proportion— in granting petitions for certiorari?"[175] By an unwritten rule, the Justices agree to take a case when at least four of the nine vote to do so.

If fewer than the required four vote to grant cert or take an appeal, the case in question is over, and the decision of the lower court becomes the final decision. When the Court agrees to take a case, it is scheduled for both written and oral argument. Written briefs are filed by the opposing lawyers, and they then appear for oral argument. The arguments are presented publicly in the ornate courtroom. Each side usually has half an hour, and the time limit is strictly observed. Once a lawyer was arguing his case in the last half hour before noon. He was reading to the Justices from his notes and did not notice the red light go on at his lectern, signalling that his time had expired. Finally, he looked up. The bench was empty; the Justices had quietly risen, gathering their black robes, and gone to lunch.

Oral arguments before the Court are often dramatic events, participated in by the leaders of the American Bar. The Justices are rarely passive participants, but instead use the occasion to question the attorneys closely on any aspect of the case that interests them. Justices frequently interrupt with questions. Frankfurter, in particular, was in the habit of treating the argument, even more than he did the conference, as something of a law-school seminar, with himself the professor conducting a Socratic dialogue for the edification of the unlearned. "Some of us," writes Douglas in his *Autobiography*, "would often squirm at Frankfurter's seemingly endless questions that took the advocate round and round and round."[176] Yet, when Frankfurter did pepper counsel with questions, Douglas and Black would usually ask questions on the other side, making it even more difficult for the lawyer caught between them. Warren usually tried to keep aloof from this intra-bench squabbling. There is no doubt, however, that the incessant questioning, especially by Frankfurter, riled the Chief Justice. One day in 1957, Frankfurter interrupted Warren and reworded some questions that the Chief was putting to a lawyer. Warren flushed and began to shout, "Let him answer my question! He is confused enough as it is." Frankfurter grew pale behind his spectacles and cut back, "confused by Justice Frankfurter, I presume."[177]

After oral argument, the Justices then discuss the cases argued at a conference session which is totally private and which is attended only by them. When Warren became Chief Justice, these conferences were held on Saturdays. As has been said, the privacy of the conference is one of the most cherished traditions at the Court. In addition to the conference discussion, ideas are exchanged through memoranda. Such a memo sent to all the Justices is usually called a *Memorandum to the Conference*.

After the vote is taken at the conference, the case is assigned by the Chief, if he is in the majority, to one of the Justices for the writing of an opinion of the Court. If the Chief is not in the majority, the senior majority Justice assigns the opinion. Justices who disagree with the majority decision are free to write or join dissenting opinions. If they agree with the result, but differ on the reasoning, they can submit concurring opinions. Opinions are usually issued in the name of individual Justices. Sometimes per curiam opinions are issued in the name of the Court as a whole.

The last stage is the public announcement of decisions and the opinions filed by the Justices. The custom when Warren joined the Court was to have decisions announced on Mondays; hence, the press characterization of "decision Mondays." Normally, the Justices would read only a summary of their opinions, especially when they were long. But some would insist on reading every word, no matter how much time it took. On June 17, 1963, Clark was droning through his lengthy Court opinion in the case involving the constitutionality of Bible reading in public schools. Douglas, who could stand it no longer, passed Black a plaintive note: "Is he going to read all of it? He told me he was only going to say a few words—he is on p. 20 now—58 more to go— Perhaps we need an anti-filibuster rule as badly as some say the Senate does."[178]

Warren, like the other Brethren, used his law clerks to screen the cert petitions and appeals filed with the Court—an important delegation of authority. The clerks would divide the petitions among themselves and prepare cert memos on all the cases that would summarize the facts and issues and *recommend* how Warren should vote on whether the Court should hear the cases. Warren stressed that the cert memos should be brief. One clerk tells how he wrote a few twenty-page memos on what he thought were important cases. Warren called him in and said, "I just read your memos . . . and I don't think you need twenty pages to convince me that those are cert worthy cases. I hope you can be a little bit more brief in the future, because I have to wade through an awful lot of these memos for each conference."[179]

In addition to the ordinary cert memos, the Chief Justice's clerks were primarily responsible for the so-called Miscellaneous Docket, largely made up of the *in forma pauperis* (or I.F.P.) petitions. These were the petitions for Supreme Court review filed by people who did not have attorneys and were too poor to pay the normal $100 filing fee. Each year the Court received an increasing number of I.F.P. petitions. During the Warren years they came to constitute the major part of the review petitions received by the Court. A 1959 *New York Times* article noted that the number of cases on the docket for that year's term (2,062) set a record. The big increase, the article said, came in the typewritten and handwritten papers filed by indigent prisoners (from 891 to 1,006).[180] By Warren's last term, in 1968–1969, the number of I.F.P. petitions had grown to 1,829, out of a total of 3,117.

Most of the I.F.P. petitions were drawn up by uneducated, sometimes barely literate, convicts claiming violations of their constitutional rights. They were, more often than not, handwritten on scraps of paper, frequently illegible and even incomprehensible. The petition filed in the famous case of *Gideon v. Wainwright*,[181] which led to the 1963 decision affirming the right to court-appointed counsel in criminal cases, was written by Clarence Gideon himself in pencil, on lined sheets of paper, in schoolboy-style printed script. Only a minute minority of the I.F.P. petitions have any merit, but a few have served as catalysts for key Court decisions, notably in the *Gideon* case itself.

The Chief Justice's office was primarily responsible for the I.F.P. petitions and, on them, the Warren clerks served, in effect, as law clerks to the entire Court. Only one copy of an I.F.P. petition had to be filed, instead of the forty ordinarily required. It was the Warren clerks' job to sift through what one of them terms "that handwritten garbage," to see which, if any, among the mass filed, had any merit. It was time-consuming work, since many of the petitions were lengthy and difficult to decipher. Yet Warren insisted that his clerks look with care at each of them. In a memorandum explaining to his clerks how they should handle the I.F.P. docket, Warren stressed that, "inasmuch as the I.F.P. petitioners generally do not have counsel, it is necessary for you to be their counsel, in a sense." [182]

Warren's clerks would write a short memo on the I.F.P. petitions that was sent to each Justice. Since this was before the photocopying machine, they were typed in originals and carbon copies. They were called "flimsies," because eleven copies were made on very thin paper, and the junior Justices, who received the last copies, often had difficulty reading them. If the clerk who handled the petition thought it had any merit, the petition itself would be circulated. Each Justice could call up any petition, but this was rarely done and so, in practice, the Warren clerks were the Supreme Court on I.F.P. petitions.

As far as Warren and most of the Justices were concerned, this was also true of the handling of ordinary cert petitions and appeals. With some exceptions (notably in the chambers of Justices Frankfurter and Brennan), *the* work on the petitions was done by the clerks. In the vast majority of cases, the Justices' knowledge of the petitions and the cases they presented was based on their clerks' cert memos, and they would normally vote in accordance with the memos' recommendations. This was as true of Warren as of most of the others. The Chief would take his pile of cert memos and petitions home every night and go over them carefully. He would, however, rarely discuss any of them with the clerks and would usually follow their recommendations. Sheer volume, if nothing else, made this the normal practice.

After the Court voted to hear a case, one of Warren's clerks (typically the one who had worked on the cert petition) would prepare a bench memo. This would contain a more detailed analysis of the facts and issues, as well as recommendations for decision. Though lengthier than the cert memos, Warren stressed that they also should be as brief as possible. The bench memos were intended to aid the Chief during the oral argument and conference that followed. Before each conference, Warren would summarize the bench memos in important cases in a page dictated to Margaret McHugh, his executive secretary. In lesser cases, he would write a few lines at the top of the bench memo to help him in the conference.

After the conference vote and assignment of opinions, Warren would discuss any opinion he had assigned to himself with the law clerk selected to draft the opinion, normally the clerk who had written the bench memo on the case. Warren would usually outline verbally (though in important cases he would dictate the outline to Mrs. McHugh) the way he wanted the opinion drafted. Most of the time, the outline would summarize the facts and how the main points should be decided. The Chief would rarely go into particulars on the legal theories involved in the case. The clerk was left with a great deal of discretion on the details of the opinion, particularly the reasoning and research supporting the decision.

Warren would normally go over the draft opinion with the clerk who had written it. Particularly where he was dissatisfied with a section, he would discuss it in some detail. He would make stylistic changes, often adding or substituting straightforward phrases typical of his manner of presentation. "He had a penchant," one of his clerks recalls, "for Anglo-Saxon words over Latin words and he didn't like foreign phrases thrown in if there was a good American word that would do."

Warren never pretended to be a scholar interested in research and legal minutiae. These he left to his clerks, as well as the extensive footnotes which are part of the panoply of the well-crafted judicial opinion. One year the clerks snickered with delight when they ran across a learned law-review article, analyzing an important Warren opinion, in which the author saw great significance in the order in which Warren cited cases in the footnotes. The clerks knew that was utterly foolish, because nobody (and certainly not the Chief) had paid any attention to it.

In considering the role of Warren's law clerks, we should bear in mind that, as the Chief constantly stressed to them, they were not "unguided missiles." Warren had been making important decisions throughout his career and, by the time he arrived at the Court, decision-making was second-nature to him. He had an open mind and was amenable to persuasion; but he never agonized over decisions the way some of the others did. What is more, he never delegated his decision power to any one; he would make up his own mind, and, once made up, he would stubbornly hold to his decision. As Justice Byron White recalls it, Warren "was quite willing to listen to people at length . . . but, when he made up his mind, it was like the sun went down, and he was very firm, very firm about it." The clerks never had any doubt about who was the judge in the Warren chambers.

Yet, even with that admitted, the domain of the law clerks was wide enough to give them tremendous influence. In particular, the job of screening the filed petitions to determine which should be heard was performed primarily by the clerks. In 1960, Frankfurter expressed qualms about this delegation of the task of screening petitions on the part of the Justices, asserting in a letter to Justice Potter Stewart, "The appraisal and appreciation of a record as a basis for exercising our discretionary jurisdiction is, I do not have to tell you, so dependent on a seasoned and disciplined professional judgment that I do not believe that lads—most of them fresh out of law school and with their present tendentiousness—should have any routine share in the process of disemboweling a record, however acute and stimulating their power of reasoning may be and however tentative and advisory their memos on what is reported in the record and what is relevant to our taking a case may be." Frankfurter was particularly disturbed by the role of the Chief's clerks in reviewing the I.F.P. petitions. Referring to the flimsy prepared in a recent case, he wrote Stewart, "it is a striking illustration of which I have found many over the years, Term after Term, of the slanted way in which, through compassionate feelings and inexperienced predispositions, these Miscellaneous cases are reported to us on the strength of which, so predominantly, action is taken by the court." [183]

Some years earlier, Frankfurter had circulated a memorandum on in forma pauperis petitions. Alluding to the flimsies prepared on them by the Chief Justice's clerks, he stated, "Normally that was the only knowledge that the Court had of this growing number of cases and on such knowledge alone, with relatively few exceptions, they were disposed of. Of course, on occasions, I believe they were rare, individual Justices had their interest aroused in particular cases. . . . It is, however, accurate to say that in few instances was the kind of examination made of these *in forma* records that is made as a matter of course of the cases having printed records and briefs." [184]

When Warren came on to the Court in 1953, most of the clerks were chosen from the Harvard and Yale Law Schools. The reason was that stated by Frankfurter. "If you want to get good groceries in Washington you go to Magruder's, or in New York to Park and Tilford, or in Boston to S.S. Pierce. If you wanted to get a lot of first-class lawyers, you went to the Harvard Law School." [185] Of course this meant that the clerks tended to have similar backgrounds and points of view, though it should also be said that the views were those inculcated by the nation's best law schools.

At the beginning of his Court tenure, when Warren was largely under the influence of Frankfurter, it was the latter who helped choose the clerks for Warren. During his first three terms, six of Warren's nine clerks were from either Harvard or Yale. In a few years, after the relationship between the Chief and Frankfurter cooled, Warren set up his own system of selecting clerks. Thus for a few years, he relied on recommendations from different law professors in whose judgment he had some particular confidence. Then, in 1962, he asked two of his former clerks, Murray H. Bring (now a senior partner at a leading Washington law firm) and William H. Dempsey (now President of the Association of American Railroads) to act as a committee of two to recommend the clerks he should select. The two would screen the applications sent to Warren each year. They made a particular effort to choose clerks from all over the country. The result was a far wider geographical dispersion among the Warren clerks, with a large number coming from the leading California law schools. After 1957, only one Warren clerk was a Harvard graduate. By then Warren had the definite feeling that Harvard was still Frankfurter's home base and that it was producing "little Frankfurters"—the last thing he wanted after his break with the former Harvard professor. It is significant that Warren also feared that Harvard clerks might pose some security problem in his chambers, since they might talk to their old professors, and it would ultimately get back to Frankfurter himself.

Warren's successor, Chief Justice Warren E. Burger, has been criticized for being excessively security conscious, so far as his law clerks were concerned. Court critics have quoted with glee from a Burger memorandum on confidentiality that stressed "the private nature of everything that transpires in the Chambers of the Justice" and the need to avoid "the possibility of unfavorable information being 'leaked' to other Justices."[186] Warren had basically the same attitude about his clerks. He constantly stressed that they were *his* clerks, not the Court's, and that what went on in his chambers was not to be revealed outside, not even to the other Justices or their clerks. Warren felt personally betrayed when one of his 1956 Term clerks went to work as a clerk for Frankfurter the next year. And, after the early Warren–Frankfurter relationship had begun to change, the Chief became very concerned about what he saw as Frankfurter's attempts to subvert his clerks. As one clerk recalls it, "we were enjoined from falling under that sway and he as much as said, 'I know you're all quite young fellows from law school and here's this great professor, but don't let him sell you any beans.' And it took the form of a mild paranoia about contacts between his law clerks and Frankfurter, or even Frankfurter's law clerks." For his part Frankfurter was, of course, also well aware of the Warren attitude. One time during the 1957 Term, Frankfurter asked one of the Warren clerks to come into his office, "unless, of course, I've been quarantined."

But we are getting ahead of our story. Before there could be any falling-out between Warren and Frankfurter, the Chief Justice had to familiarize himself with his new judicial role. Then he would be able to choose between the competing Black and Frankfurter philosophies. Before that happened, however, Warren had to lead the Court to one of its historic decisions. At the top of the judicial agenda when the new Chief arrived was the constitutional issue of segregation in public schools. The Vinson Court had not been able to decide the explosive issue. Now, with Vinson's death, it was left as his successor's principal legal legacy.

3.

WARREN AND THE
BROWN CASE

"This is the first indication that I have ever had that there is a God."

This caustic comment to two former law clerks was Frankfurter's reaction to Chief Justice Vinson's death in September 1953, just before reargument was scheduled in the *Brown* school segregation case.[1] Had Vinson presided over the Court that decided the *Brown* case, the result would have been a divided decision. In a May 20, 1954, letter to his colleague Stanley Reed, three days after the unanimous *Brown* decision was announced, Frankfurter wrote, "I have no doubt that if the *Segregation* cases had reached decision last Term there would have been four dissenters—Vinson, Reed, Jackson and Clark—and certainly several opinions for the majority view. That would have been catastrophic."[2]

Vinson, notably gregarious and good natured, had grown increasingly irritable during his last Court term. According to a close associate, "he was distressed over the Court's inability to find a strong, unified position on such an important case."[3] But Vinson was as much a cause, as a critic, of the *Brown* fragmentation. Throughout his career, he had been known for his skill at smoothing ruffled feathers. But his hearty bonhomie was not enough to enable Vinson to restore peace to the splintered Supreme Court. The Justices looked down on him as the possessor of a second-class mind. Even Reed,

the least intellectually gifted of the Roosevelt appointees, could dismiss the dour-faced Chief, in a comment to Frankfurter, as "just like me, except that he is less well-educated."[4] Frankfurter himself could characterize Vinson in his diary as "confident and easy-going and sure and shallow. . . . he seems to me to have the confident air of a man who does not see the complexities of problems and blithely hits the obvious points."[5]

Phillip Elman, who had clerked for Frankfurter and was one of the most knowledgeable Court watchers, wrote to the Justice about "the C.J." from the Solicitor General's Office: "What a mean little despot he is. Has there ever been a member of the Court who was deficient in *so* many respects as a man and as a judge. Even that s.o.b. McReynolds, despite his defects of character, stands by comparison as a towering figure and powerful intellect. . . . this man is a pygmy, morally and mentally. And so uncouth."[6]

When Vinson supported Tom Clark's appointment, Washington wags said it was because he wanted someone on his Court who knew less law than he did.[7] By the time the *Brown* case came before the Court, the Brethren were openly to display their contempt for their Chief. As a clerk during the 1952 Term recalls it, several of Vinson's colleagues "would discuss in his presence the view that the Chief's job should rotate annually and . . . made no bones about regarding him—correctly—as their intellectual inferior."[8]

Such a Chief Justice could scarcely be expected to lead the gifted prima donnas who then sat on the Court. If anything the division among the Brethren intensified and, all too often, degenerated into personal animosity during Vinson's tenure. By the time Warren was appointed, the Court had become the most severely fractured Supreme Court in history.

To be sure, judicial rancor did not turn into sweetness and light because Warren was elevated to the central chair. The antipathy between Jackson and Frankfurter, on the one side, and Black and Douglas, on the other, continued as strong as ever. But the Chief Justice plays a crucial role in the temper of the Court. A great Chief presiding over the Court can be compared to a great conductor leading an orchestra. He, too, strikes the pitch, as it were, and sets the tone for the entire performance.

When the Court first discussed the potentially explosive school segregation cases at its conference of December 13, 1952, Vinson sounded what can most charitably be described as an uncertain trumpet, instead of the clarion needed to deal with the issue that had become an incubus on American society.

By this time of course it had already become a constitutional cliché that the Fourteenth Amendment had not succeeded in securing equality for blacks. This was true, in large part, because of Supreme Court decisions, particularly that in the 1896 case of *Plessy v. Ferguson*.[9] Homer Adolph Plessy, one-eighth black, had been arrested while riding on a train out of New Orleans for refusing to move from a "white" car to a "colored" coach. The conductor had acted under a Louisiana law that required railroads "to provide equal but separate accommodations for the white and colored races," and the Supreme Court had rejected the contention that this law violated the Fourteenth Amendment's guaranty of equal protection of the laws. On the contrary, racial segregation alone was held not unconstitutional.

Upon the "separate but equal" doctrine approved by the Court was built a whole subsequent structure of racial discrimination. Jim Crow replaced equal protection, and legally enforced segregation became the dominant feature in Southern life.

All of this appeared lost on Vinson as he tried to set the tone for the December 13, 1952, conference, when the Brethren first discussed the *Brown* case, and several other cases that had come to the Court concerning segregation. Vinson's opening words in this particular conference indicated that he for one was not ready to overrule *Plessy v. Ferguson*. There was a whole "body of law back of us on separate but equal," he declared. Nor had the accepted law been questioned by Congress. "However [we] construe it," he said, "Congress did not pass a statute deterring and ordering *no* segregation." On the contrary, Congress itself had provided for segregation in the nation's capital. "I don't see," Vinson affirmed, "how we can get away from the long established acceptance in the District [of Columbia]. For 90 years, there have been segregated schools in this city." Of course, Vinson went on, "it would be better if [Congress] would act." But, even on congressional power, Vinson asserted a restrictive view. As recorded in Burton's notes of the conference,[10] Vinson stated the following opinion on congressional authority: "May act for DC— probably *not* for the States." If Congress could not end segregation outside Washington, even under its express power to enforce the

Fourteenth Amendment, it is difficult to see how the Court could interpret the amendment to ban segregation without any Congressional action.

With these views, Vinson could scarcely be expected to lead the conference to overrule the *Plessy* case. Instead, Vinson indicated in fact that he was leaning toward affirming the lower-court decisions— which meant a vote in favor of upholding the constitutionality of segregation.[11] Toward the end of his presentation Vinson stressed the seriousness of the race-relations problem in the South and the need for time to resolve it. In earlier cases, he said, the Court had dealt with individual Negro plaintiffs; but the situation became entirely different when large numbers were involved. The greater the number of Negroes in any community, he stated, the graver the problem. "We can't close our eyes to the seriousness [of the problem] in various parts of the U.S. We face the complete abolition of the public school system in the South."

But 1952 was not 1896. Even if he desired it, Vinson could hardly expect to lead the Court to a ringing reaffirmation of *Plessy v. Ferguson*. Despite Vinson's statement, the majority of the conference was in favor of striking down school segregation. But the Justices were sharply divided, with perhaps only five of them tilting toward repudiating the *Plessy* case. Unfortunately, from the point of view of the divisive effect of such a split decision, the Southern members of the Court, aside from Black (considered an apostate in his region), indicated that they would dissent from any overruling of the separate-but-equal doctrine.

No one was more troubled about the prospect of a fragmented decision than Frankfurter. More than any of the Brethren, he was concerned not only with results in cases, but with the manner in which those results were reached. To his detractors, in fact, he seemed to place all his emphasis on method and procedure, rather than on justice. "There was," as Richard Kluger puts it, "something very nearly masochistic in his frequent insistence that he could not reach judgments on the bench which he would readily have favored as an unrobed private citizen."[12] When, for example, he supplied the necessary fifth vote in 1947 to uphold the electrocution for the second time of Willie Francis, after a first attempt at electrocution had failed because of a mechanical defect, Frankfurter went out of the way to note his personal opposition to the death penalty.[13] If he had voted against the electrocution, he wrote to Harlan, "I would be enforcing my private view rather than that consensus of society's opinion."[14]

To the leading apostle of judicial restraint, the constitutionality of segregation presented a painful problem. His notes, written to clarify his own mind while the *Brown* case was pending, show that his own attitude to segregation was one of abhorrence. Yet was he more justified in imposing his personal views here than he would have been if he had voted against the death penalty for Willie Francis? In the December 1952 conference, to which reference has already been made, Frankfurter had indicated a clear willingness to strike down segregation but only in the District of Columbia. It was, he said, *"intolerable that the Government should permit segregation in D.C. life."* As far as the states were concerned, Frankfurter stated a more ambiguous position. He was clear that the Fourteenth Amendment did not limit the Court to consideration of only the physical facilities provided by the states for blacks. It was "arbitrary to say that 'equal rights' means physical things." On the other hand, he could not say that the framers of the amendment had meant to abolish segregation. If that was true, "we can't say that the Court has long misread the Constitution. What justifies us in saying that what *was* equal in 1868 is not equal *now?*"

Frankfurter suggested that counsel should be required to clarify the points raised by him: "Ask counsel to demonstrate what it is that justifies saying segregation is all wrong." Above all, Frankfurter concluded, let us avoid "going into the merits now." A "further maturing process would be desirable." To obtain it, the cases should be set for reargument later in the term.

Frankfurter was actually not being entirely candid in those comments of his at the conference. Far from being in doubt about segregation in the states, he had concluded early in his consideration of the *Brown* case that segregation should now be stricken down. According to William T. Coleman, who had been the first black clerk at the Supreme Court when he clerked for Frankfurter during the 1948 Term, there was never any doubt about Frankfurter's *Brown* vote. "From the day the cases were taken," Coleman told an interviewer, "it was clear how he was going to vote. . . . I know . . . that he was for ending segregation from the start."[15]

But the *Brown* case was more difficult for Frankfurter than Coleman indicates. The foundation of Frankfurter's judicial philosophy was the difference between desirability and constitutionality. As he wrote in a memorandum while *Brown* was pending, "However passionately any of us may hold egalitarian views, however fiercely any of us may believe that such a policy of segregation as undoubtedly expresses the tenacious conviction of Southern States is both unjust and shortsighted, he travels outside his judicial authority if for this private reason alone he declares unconstitutional the policy of segregation." [16]

The more he agonized over the matter, however, the more Frankfurter was coming to the conclusion that a vote against segregation had become the proper judicial posture. In written notes headed *Segregation*, designed to help his thinking on *Brown*, he recognized that "Stare decisis means respect for decisions," but it did not bar "reexamination of [the] reasoning and principles on which [they were] based." He then noted that segregation was a "legacy of history—to what extent is past perpetuated in Const[itution]?" The answer depends on an evolving conception of both society and law. "Society keeps changing or rots through stagnation. Human needs gradually emerge into consciousness . . . and assert themselves with such impact that they become absorbed into the existing framework of law." [17]

As Frankfurter saw it, "The equality of laws enshrined in the Constitution is not a fixed formula defined with finality at a particular time. It does not reflect as a congealed formulation the social arrangement and beliefs of a particular epoch." Instead, "It is addressed to the changes wrought by time and . . . must respond to transformation of views as well as to that of outward circumstances. The effect of the change in men's feelings of what is right and just is equally relevant in determining whether discrimination denies the equal protection of the laws." [18]

By the time of the December 1952 conference, Frankfurter had come to see that segregation had become a constitutional, as well as a moral, abomination. Four other Justices—Black, Douglas, Burton, and Minton—had clearly indicated at the conference that, in Minton's words, "classification by race is *not reasonable* [and] segregation [is] per se unconstitutional." With Frankfurter's vote, that made five votes in favor of striking down segregation. The other four Justices—Vinson, Reed, Jackson, and Clark—were, according to Frankfurter's already-quoted letter to Reed,[19] ready to dissent from any such ruling.[20]

More than any other Justice, Frankfurter was of the opinion that such a close vote, as he wrote in his letter to Reed, "would have been disastrous." With the Court as divided as it was and the lack of leadership from Vinson on a subject of such importance, the only tactic that appeared at all promising was delay. The longer the Court's decision could be postponed, the more chance there was that the majority to end segregation could be increased. At the December 1952 conference Frankfurter sought to have the cases set for reargument, and he stated that March was a possible date. As time went on, however, and discussion among the Justices indicated no shifts in position, Frankfurter realized that, for what he had called at the conference "further maturing process" to have any effect, an even longer delay was necessary. Thus Frankfurter began to work to have the cases set for reargument during the next term that would begin in October 1953.

To secure so long a postponement Frankfurter would have to devise a plausible pretext, which would convince both the Court and the country that more than stalling for time was involved. Two factors made it easier to persuade the Brethren. The first was that the Justices had not taken any vote on the segregation issue. Burton's diary entry on the December 1952 conference records, "We discussed the segregation cases thus disclosing the trend but no even tentative vote was taken."[21] The same was true in the later conferences discussing the matter. As Frankfurter put it after a conference toward the term's end, "no vote had actually been taken throughout the term." Just as important was the fact that, in Frankfurter's words at the time, "no one on the Court was pushing it."[22] Certainly Vinson was not eager to force a vote that he was going to lose; nor were most of the majority Justices satisfied with the divided decision that would have come in the spring of 1953.

According to Alexander Bickel, one of his 1952–1953 clerks, Frankfurter returned from a conference toward the end of May 1953 in a euphoric state: "He said it looked as if we could hold off a decision that term . . . . and that if we could get together some questions for discussion at a reargument, the case would be held over until the new term."[23]

With Bickel's help, Frankfurter formulated five questions "to which the attention of counsel on the reargument of the cases should be directed." They were sent to the other Justices in a *Memorandum for the Conference* of May 27, 1953.[24] At a conference on May 29, a majority agreed to put all the questions, with only minor changes from the Frankfurter draft. On June 8, the Court ordered the segregation cases restored to the docket for reargument in the next term, and the parties were asked to discuss "the following questions insofar as they are relevant to the respective cases":

1. What evidence is there that the Congress which submitted and the State legislatures and conventions which ratified the Fourteenth Amendment contemplated or did not contemplate, understood or did not understand, that it would abolish segregation in public schools?

2. If neither the Congress in submitting nor the States in ratifying the Fourteenth Amendment understood that compliance with it would require the immediate abolition of segregation in public schools, was it nevertheless the understanding of the framers of the Amendment.

(a) that future Congresses might, in the exercise of their power under section 5 of the Amendment, abolish such segregation, or

(b) that it would be within the judicial power, in light of future conditions, to construe the Amendment as abolishing such segregation of its own force?

3. On the assumption that the answers to questions 2(a) and (b) do not dispose of the issue, is it within the judicial power, in construing the Amendment, to abolish segregation in public schools?

4. Assuming it is decided that segregation in public schools violates the Fourteenth Amendment

(a) would a decree necessarily follow providing that, within the limits set by normal geographic school districting, Negro children should forthwith be admitted to schools of their choice, or

(b) may this Court, in the exercise of its equity powers, permit an effective gradual adjustment to be brought about from existing segregated systems to a system not based on color distinctions?

5. On the assumption on which questions 4(a) and (b) are based, and assuming further that this Court will exercise its equity powers to the end described in question 4(b),

(a) should this Court formulate detailed decrees in this case;

(b) if so what specific issues should the decrees reach;

(c) should this Court appoint a special master to hear evidence with a view to recommending specific terms for such decrees;

(d) should this Court remand to the courts of first instance with directions to frame decrees in this case and if so what general directions should the decrees of this Court include and what procedures should the courts of first instance follow in arriving at the specific terms of more detailed decrees? [25]

In addition, in accordance with the suggestion of both Frankfurter and Jackson, the U.S. Attorney General was invited to take part in the oral argument before the Court (no such invitation had been extended for the first argument in December 1952) and to file a new brief.

The five questions have been reprinted verbatim because they are necessary for an understanding of the Justices' reaction to them at the May 29 conference. On July 21, 1954, Frankfurter wrote to his close friend Judge Learned Hand that he would one day tell him the story of how *Brown* was decided. "But I will tell you that if the 'great libertarians' had had their way we would have been in the soup." [26]

A document in the Black papers makes plain what induced the Frankfurter comment. Black had felt strongly that details of the Court's decision process should not be made public except to the extent revealed in the published opinions. Just before his death in 1971, Black asked his son to burn his conference notes and other private Court papers. Although the request was honored, there were inevitably revealing documents that were overlooked. One of these was Black's copy of the Frankfurter May 27 memorandum with the draft questions. On the back of his copy, Black pencilled in his reaction to the proposed questions. He then crossed out what he had written. It was probably thought by his son or whoever went over this portion of Black's papers that this made the comments illegible. Despite that, a Xeroxed copy of this paper brings out the underlying writing in a manner that makes it relatively easy to read the words Black had written.

Black's pencilled comments indicate that he opposed the submission of questions to the parties. "I am willing," Black wrote, "to have [questions] 4 and 5 submitted to the parties—but believe 1, 2 and 3 should not be—There are too many reasons for my objections to set them out. In the main however, I think asking 1, 2 and 3 would bring floods of historical contentions on the specific points we asked about which woud dilute the arguments along broader lines—I doubt if it would be possible to isolate the framers' views about segregation in the primary schools—Although willing to acquiesce as to questions 4 and 5 I still rather doubt the wisdom of submitting any questions." [27]

At the May 29 conference, which considered the questions, Black expressed the view stated in his pencilled comments. Black's position was supported by Douglas, who also said that he preferred that none of the questions be submitted, but would be willing to go along with questions 4 and 5, though not 1, 2, and 3. Black and Douglas stood alone at the conference. Vinson said that he "would like [questions] 1, 2, and 3—not 4 and 5." The six other Justices voted in favor of all five questions, though Clark urged that the Court say that it was led to ask the questions about remedy because the government raised them.[28] The Clark suggestion was rejected because, as Frankfurter stated, "We ought to assume full responsibility for questions we put to counsel" and because the objections which the parties would have to the questions about remedy "ought not to be resolved into resentment against the Government for bringing up this matter in the first place, or to raise the thought that we are responsive to the Government's lead."[29]

If Black and Douglas had had their way, *none* of the questions would have been put to the parties, or, at most, only questions 4 and 5. Since questions 1, 2, and 3 were the *only* questions that related to the merits of the segregation issue, that would have left the order for reargument a transparent delaying device. Under those circumstances, it is probable that the Justices would not have voted for reargument and a delayed decision. That would have meant a June 1953 decision that would have been so closely divided as to justify Frankfurter's phrase that "we would have been in the soup."[30]

Black, one of the "great libertarians" to whom Frankfurter had referred, also opposed another essential item of what Frankfurter called "the single package"[31]—the invitation to the U.S. Attorney General to take part in the oral reargument. In a *Memorandum to the Conference,* Black wrote, "I think we should amend our order in the segregation cases and eliminate the paragraph which invites the Attorney General to argue." He asserted that "political uses . . . are being made of our permission to the Attorney General to argue" and declared, "I know of no way to prevent it . . . except to change our order."[32]

Frankfurter led the Court to reject Black's attempt to eliminate the invitation to the Attorney General. "The reason for having the Government appear," Frankfurter told the Brethren, "was not a matter of tactics or 'public-relations.'" He stressed "the point which Bob Jackson made very early in our deliberations, that the new

[Eisenhower] Administration, unlike the old, may have the responsibility of carrying out a decision full of perplexities; it should therefore be asked to face that responsibility as part of our process of adjudication."[33]

A month before he died, Chief Justice Vinson performed his last act in the *Brown* case. The government had delayed acting in the case. Philip Elman, who played the major role in writing the government brief, wrote to Frankfurter in July, 1953, "the fact is that as of now the Government of the United States of America has done almost nothing in response to the Court's invitation."[34] But now the government was ready to move. Its first step was to seek more time to prepare its case. Acting on the government's request, Vinson, on August 4, postponed the reargument until December 7. The Chief's action was taken on his own authority—a circumstance that miffed at least one of the Brethren. Frankfurter wrote Black that he had learned of the postponement only from reading of it in the *New York Times* and that he was "curious to know how that postponement was authorized. I don't mind the C.J. assuming authority from the rest of us for minor adjustments in the Calendar. But I should suppose that in the light of the history of these cases the C.J. would not act on his own."[35]

By the time the *Brown* case was reargued on December 7–9, Vinson's seat had been taken by Warren. Neophyte that he was, the new Chief Justice was to play the crucial role in fashioning the unanimous *Brown* decision. It is not too much to say, indeed, that Frankfurter's Fabian strategy was ultimately justified by Warren's leadership in disposing of the segregation issue. As Burton wrote in his diary just before the Court handed down its unanimous *Brown* decision, "This would have been impossible a year ago. . . . However the postponement then was with the hope of a better result later."[36]

During his first months on the bench, the new Chief Justice had to proceed cautiously, while he felt his way in learning how the Court operated. By December, when the segregation reargument took place, Warren was ready to play a more positive part. At the reargument itself, however, on Monday, Tuesday, and Wednesday, December 7, 8 and 9, 1953, the Chief said little. The Justices, especially Frankfurter and Jackson, peppered counsel with questions, but Warren intervened in the argument only three times. The first occurred during the presentation, on the first day of argument, by Thurgood Marshall, counsel for the National Association for the Advancement of Colored People. Marshall had floundered in his argument by trying to survey the prior Court decisions on racial classifications, instead of dealing with the key question that the Court had asked the parties to cover on the reargument: in the absence of Congressional action over so many years, "is it within the judicial power . . . to abolish segregation in public schools?" Warren interposed, "I would like to have you discuss the question of power because I believe that is the question the Court asked you to discuss." "The power?" Marshall asked. "Yes, the power," affirmed the Chief.[37]

On the third day of argument, the Delaware Attorney General, arguing the last segregation case on the docket, discussed the historical evidence to show that a decision against segregation would be contrary to the intent of the framers of the Fourteenth Amendment. Warren interrupted, "General, may I ask you what is the situation in Delaware today as of this moment?"[38] This brought the argument down to earth, and the Delaware counsel then gave the Court statistics to show how many blacks were attending the different schools in the districts involved.

The third Warren intervention illustrated the new Chief's impatience with some of the Justices' emphasis on technical requirements to avoid Court decisions. The Kansas Attorney General had confirmed that the Topeka Board of Education had instituted a program to abandon segregation as early as practicable. If that was true, interposed Black and Frankfurter, was there any justiciable controversy? Warren then broke into the argument: "I think when both parties to the action feel there is a controversy, and invited the Attorney General to be here and answer these questions, I, for one, would like to hear the argument."[39]

The Chief's interventions in the reargument typified what would become the Warren approach during oral argument: trying to bring the discussion down to the core facts and issue and impatience with attempts to avoid decision by technical requirements. But Warren's participation contributed little to the substance of the arguments.

The same was not true when the Justices met that Saturday, December 12, for this their first conference on the segregation case under the new Chief Justice. Until then, his Brethren had found a bluff, convivial colleague, who disarmed them with his friendliness and lack of pretension. Now they were to learn that he was a born leader, whose political talents were to prove as useful in the Judicial Palace as they had been in the State House.

The conference room itself was a large rectangular chamber at the rear of the Court building, behind the courtroom. One of the longer walls had two windows facing Second Street. The other, with a door in the middle, was covered with bookshelves. On one of the shorter walls was a fireplace, and above it a Gilbert Stuart portrait of Chief Justice John Marshall in his robes. In the center of the room was an ornate crystal chandelier, and at the end was a table around which the Justices sat, with the Chief Justice at the head and the others ranged in order of seniority, with the most senior opposite the Chief, the next at the Chief's right, the next at the senior Associate's right, and so on.

The December 12 *Brown* conference set the tone both for disposition of the segregation issue and for the entire tenure of the Warren Court. All the Justices were present except Black, who had to be away because his sister-in-law was near death in Alabama. In terms of Warren's leadership, Black's absence was fortunate. It meant that the new Chief's conduct of his first important conference did not have to take place under the abrasive eye of the Court's senior, who had actually presided at the first conferences after Warren took his Court seat.

Warren opened the conference[40] by proposing that the Brethren discuss the cases informally without taking any votes. The Justices agreed to this plan. Reed said that he favored the idea of delaying the vote; even if there were differences, it would help them to fix the issues. Frankfurter, citing the example of Benjamin Franklin at the Constitutional Convention, declared "we don't yet know what we should do," but should probe all the constitutional issues through as many discussions as necessary. The others concurred, though Burton stressed that "we should decide at this term."

Delay in voting until the issues had been thrashed out by discussion was just the plan to appeal to an experienced political leader. Certainly, as Warren put it to an interviewer a year after the *Brown* decision, "The fact that we did not polarize ourselves at the beginning gave us more of an opportunity to come out unanimously on it than if we had done otherwise."[41] That same year, Frankfurter pointed out that the *Brown* case was the only one which he could recall "in which we postponed a vote after argument for further study. The exception is significant. Who will deny that this maturing process in the segregation cases fully vindicated itself?"[42]

Warren's plan to talk about the issues as long as necessary without any vote led to what Frankfurter called "a reconnoitering discussion, without thought of a vote."[43] That discussion, at the December 12 conference, was made easier by a step that Frankfurter had taken after the *Brown* case had come to the Court. Early in the previous term, Frankfurter had given Alexander Bickel, then one of his law clerks, the job of doing intensive research on the original intent of the framers of the Fourteenth Amendment. Bickel's work, based on months of plowing through the musty, near century-old folio volumes of the *Congressional Globe*, was finished late in the summer of 1953. His lengthy memorandum, carefully revised by both the Justice and Bickel himself, was printed and sent to the other Justices just before the *Brown* reargument in early December. Frankfurter's covering *Memorandum for the Conference* summarized the result of Bickel's labors: "The [Bickel] memorandum indicates that the legislative history of the Amendment is, in a word, inconclusive."[44] The Thirty-ninth Congress, which voted to submit the amendment, with its guaranty of equal protection, to the states for ratification, did not indicate an intent to have it either outlaw or not outlaw segregation in public schools.

The conclusion that the legislative history of the Fourteenth Amendment was "inconclusive" on school segregation was significant enough to be repeated as the first important point in the Court's unanimous *Brown* opinion.[45]

It meant that those who argued that the framers of the amendment had intended not to abolish segregation, had misread the legislative history. At the beginning of the December 1952 conference, Chief Justice Vinson had asserted that it was "hard to get away from that contemporary interpretation of the amendments." If there was no such clear interpretation, the Justices were not foreclosed by any supposed intent in favor of segregation of those who wrote the amendment.

Before the December 12 conference, Warren had been careful not to give any indication of his own views on the constitutionality of segregation. Nor did his few interventions in the oral reargument earlier in the week suggest where he stood on the issue. His first words at the conference, however, after his proposal for discussion without any vote had been accepted, revealed his position and furnished a clear lead for the Court.

"I can't escape the feeling," Warren declared, "that no matter how much the Court wants to avoid it, it must now face the issue. The Court has finally arrived at the place where it *must* determine whether segregation is allowable in public schools." Of course, there was legitimate concern over whether the Court was called upon to reverse the older cases and lines of reasoning. "But the more I've read and heard and thought, the more I've come to conclude that the basis of segregation and 'separate but equal' rests upon a concept of the inherent inferiority of the colored race. I don't see how *Plessy* and the cases following it can be sustained on any other theory. If we are to sustain segregation, we also must do it upon that basis."

Warren then asserted that "if the argument proved anything, it proved that that basis was not justified." More than that, he went on, "I don't see how in this day and age we can set any group apart from the rest and say that they are not entitled to exactly the same treatment as all others. To do so would be contrary to the Thirteenth, Fourteenth, and Fifteenth Amendments. They were intended to make the slaves equal with all others. Personally, I can't see how today we can justify segregation based solely on race."

Having indicated his opinion on the constitutional issue, Warren interposed some cautionary words. "It would be unfortunate," he said, "if we had to take precipitous action that would inflame more than necessary. The condition in the different states should be carefully considered by the Court." He thought the enforcement problem would be less difficult in Kansas and Delaware. After all, they were not much different ethnically from California, with its 520,000 Negroes, 120,000 Japanese, and 100,000 Chinese. "But it's not the same in the Deep South. It will take all the wisdom of this Court to dispose of the matter with a minimum of emotion and strife. How we do it is important."

To sum up, the Chief concluded his presentation, "my instincts and feelings lead me to say that, in these cases, we should abolish the practice of segregation in the public schools—but in a tolerant way."

His opening statement was a masterly illustration of the Warren method of leading the conference. According to Justice Abe Fortas, "it was Warren's great gift that, in presenting the case and discussing the case, he proceeded immediately and very calmly and graciously, to the ultimate values involved—the ultimate constitutional values, the ultimate human values." Warren's *Brown* presentation clearly stated the question before the Court in terms of the moral issue of racial inferiority. Segregation, he told the Brethren, could be justified only by belief in the inherent inferiority of blacks and, if we follow *Plessy,* we have to do it upon that basis. Warren's words went straight to the ultimate human values involved. In the face of such an approach, traditional legal arguments seemed inappropriate, almost pettifoggery. To quote Fortas again, "opposition based on the hemstitching and embroidery of the law appeared petty in terms of Warren's basic value approach."

Warren's presentation put the proponents of *Plessy* in the awkward position of appearing to subscribe to racist doctrine. Reed, who spoke most strongly in support of *Plessy,* felt compelled to assert that he was not making "the argument that the Negro is an inferior race. Of course there is no inferior race, though they may be handicapped by lack of opportunity." Reed did not, however, suggest any other ground upon which the Court might rely to justify segregation now. The gap here was particularly apparent, since Reed went out of his way to "recognize that this is a dynamic Constitution and what was correct in *Plessy* might not be correct now." He also conceded that, under *Plessy,* "equal protection has not been satisfactory. The result has been less facilities for Negroes."

But Warren was not engaged in gaining debating points against Reed and any of the others who might still oppose the overruling of *Plessy.* Warren knew that with the four Justices—Black, Douglas, Burton, and Minton—who had indicated at the conference a year earlier that they were in favor of striking down school segregation, he had at least five votes. But for him to gain only a sharply split decision would scarcely be a ringing victory. He tailored his presentation thus to mollify those who might be persuaded to join the evolving majority. By stating the matter in terms of the moral issue of racial inferiority, he placed those who might still lean toward *Plessy* on the defensive. Then he reached out to them by his stress on the need to proceed "in a tolerant way."

He recognized and regretted that precedents would have to be overturned, but noted that that was necessary if the Court was not to rely on outdated racist theory. His moral tone did not contain any accusations against the South (that would certainly have raised the hackles of Reed and Clark, the two Southern members present), but said only that segregation was no longer justifiable "in this day and age."

Warren also sought to assuage Southern sensibilities by stressing the need for caution in effectuating the Court's decision. In particular he emphasized that *how* segregation was abolished was important. Unlike states like California, the Deep South had a very real problem, which should be carefully considered. Wisdom and understanding were called for if the decision was to produce "a minimum of emotion and strife." Warren was firm in his position that the Court should abolish school segregation. His clear lead on the overriding issue set the theme for the Court's decision—a matter of crucial importance given the uncertainties with which some of the Justices (notably Clark and Jackson) may have still been plagued. But the Chief indicated that the ultimate decision should take account of conditions in the different states. The Court should be flexible in how it framed its decree. Implicit was recognition that, as Burton summarized it in the margin next to his conference notes, the decree "could go long way in time."

When Warren completed his opening statement, he probably supposed that he had five, or at most six, votes to abolish segregation. That, at any rate, was the reasonable assumption, based upon the Court's discussion the year before. Yet the views expressed after Warren spoke indicated that there had been some movement among the Brethren. Douglas, Burton, and Minton repeated their strong views against segregation. Frankfurter again delivered an ambiguous statement, but from all we know (and probably, because of their close relationship at the time, from all Warren knew) the Justice had concluded the year before to vote against segregation.[46] But Clark and Jackson, who had expressed reluctance to overturn segregation the previous year, now suggested that they might be willing to support the new Chief's position.

Clark, who had supported Vinson at the December 1952 conference, pointed out how difficult the issue was for one who was closer to the race problem than anyone on the Court except Black. Nevertheless, Clark said he was willing to agree to a decision against segregation, but "it must be done carefully or it will do more harm than good." Above all, there "must be no *fiat* or anything that looks like a fiat." Clark indicated that he was not enthusiastic about an antisegregation decision, "but will go along as said before, provided relief is carefully worked out . . . in such a way that will permit different handling in different places."

Jackson, like Clark, had expressed unwillingness to overrule segregation at the conference a year earlier. He had deprecated the N.A.A.C.P. brief as sociology not law and asserted that, under legal tests, "I would have to say [segregation] *is* constitutional. . . . We can't ease this situation by putting children together." Now Jackson, too, revealed a change in view. The segregation issue, he said, was largely "a question of politics." This "for me personally is not a problem, but it is difficult to make it other than a political decision. . . . I don't know how to justify the abolition of segregation as a judicial act. Our problem is to make a judicial decision out of a political conclusion"—to find "a judicial basis for a congenial political conclusion." The implication was that he would support a properly written decision striking down segregation. "As a political decision, I can go along with it."

The conference discussion showed Warren that he could count on five, and probably six, solid votes to end segregation, and could secure two more votes, if an opinion could be written that would satisfy Clark and Jackson. That left Reed, who alone still supported the *Plessy* doctrine. But even Reed had conceded that *Plessy* should not be followed merely because it was a precedent. He had also recognized that, in practice, *Plessy* had not produced anything like equal facilities for blacks and had had difficulty in meeting Warren's claim that to affirm *Plessy* meant to affirm black inferiority.

Warren now devoted all his efforts to eliminate the danger of dissenting and concurring opinions. The main thing, he knew, was to avoid polarizing those who had not indicated whole-hearted agreement with his own forthright view. The last thing he wanted was a candid concurrence by Jackson, a learned separate opinion by Frank-furter—much less the Southern breach in Court unity that would be worked by a dissent by Reed.

In a 1959 memorandum, Frankfurter summarized the Court's han-dling of the *Brown* case after what he termed the "reconnoitering discussion" at the December 12 conference. "We then took several weeks to reflect on the views that were expressed, more in the spirit of inquiry than as conclusions, and there followed two further Con-ference discussions, weeks apart, before we finally came to a Court decision."[47] Warren later recalled that the Brethren agreed "to talk it over, from week to week, dealing with different aspects of it—in groups, over lunches, in conference. It was too important to hurry it."[48]

Warren's instinct for effective leadership was demonstrated by the way in which he acted after the December 12 conference. He moved on two levels to secure agreement to a single, unanimous opinion: the personal level and the conference level. During the months fol-lowing the December conference, Warren had frequent lunches with several of his colleagues. Most often, the luncheon group consisted of the Chief, Reed, Burton, and Minton. The three worked on Reed to induce him to go along with the majority. Among those who strongly favored striking down segregation, Burton and Minton were the two most congenial to Reed and the most likely to influence his vote, particularly by stressing the baneful effects of a split decision.

Warren also had many individual meetings with his colleagues. Burton's diary notes several such sessions at which he discussed the segregation case with the Chief. From all we know about Warren, he was most effective when he was able to operate in a one-on-one setting. That was the way he had been able to accomplish things back in California. The result in *Brown* showed that he had not lost any of his persuasive powers in the Marble Palace.

On January 16, 1954, Warren presided over his second *Brown* con-ference. For the January conference the Chief had developed the sec-ond prong of his *Brown* strategy, which he had revealed to Burton a month earlier. It was, in Burton's words, a "plan to try [to] direct discussion of segregation cases toward the decree—as providing now the best chance of unanimity in that phase."[49]

S. Sidney Ulmer, a political scientist who also used Burton's diary in writing about the *Brown* decision, concluded that the conference plan disclosed to Burton "reveals poor judgment on Warren's part since the subsequent processes by which a decree was produced proved to be much more complicated and difficult than the processes leading to the initial decision."[50] This comment misconceives the Warren strategy. Far from revealing poor judgment, the plan remains a striking illustration of the instinctive leadership that Warren displayed throughout his career. Continued discussion of the *decision* itself would only polarize potential concurrers and dissenters, solidifying their intention to write separate opinions. By concentrating instead on the *remedy*, all the Brethren would work on the assumption that the decision itself would strike down segregation. They would endeavor jointly to work out a decree that would best effectuate such a decision. Those who, like Reed, found it most difficult to accept a decision abolishing segregation, would grow accustomed to what might at first have seemed too radical a step.

At any rate, the second *Brown* conference under Warren was devoted to the question of remedy. The Chief led off the session along the lines he had indicated to Burton. And he did so by setting the remedial theme in the manner most calculated to appeal to Reed, Clark, and even Black, who feared the effects of ordering the South to admit the black plaintiffs *immediately* into white schools. Above all, the Southerners wanted a flexible decree that, as Clark had stated at the December 12 conference, "will permit different handling in different places."

In addition the Chief sought to reassure Frankfurter and, to a lesser extent, Jackson, who feared that for the Supreme Court itself to order relief in the individual school districts would bog the Brethren down in a political quagmire. On the day before the January 16 conference, Frankfurter had circulated a five-page memorandum devoted to "considerations [which] have arisen within me in regard to the fashioning of a decree." In it, he categorically asserted, "The one thing one can feel confidently is that this Court cannot do it directly."[51]

Warren's opening statement at the January 16 conference was aimed, first of all, at Frankfurter. The Court, he said, should be "as little involved in administration as we can. We should turn to the district courts for enforcement. But we ought not to turn them loose without guidance of what paths are open to them." Warren then addressed himself to the Southerners' concern. The Chief stressed that the enforcement problem was not the same in the different cases before them. Kansas would present no difficulty, he said. In Delaware, there would likewise be no trouble and, in the District of Columbia, it could also be done quickly. The South was another matter. As Frankfurter's notes tell us, Warren expressed "lot of concern for S.C. and Va."

Black, who had been absent at the conference a month earlier, spoke next. The Alabaman wanted the Court to do as little as possible in enforcement. "Leave it to the district courts," he urged, "let them work it out." "Would you give them any framework?" Warren interjected. "I don't see how you could do it," came back the reply, "we should leave it up to the district courts."

Reed also felt that the Court should lay down only general enforcement principles. But, unlike Black, he thought the Court must say a few things. Above all, it must ensure that enforcement was "not a rush job. The time they give, the opportunities to adjust, these are the greatest palliatives to an awful thing that you can do." By his remarks, Reed indicated that he was just beginning to feel that the "awful thing" of desegregation was becoming palatable, if enough time for adjustment was given.

The notes we have of the January 16 conference were taken by Frankfurter.[52] They do not contain any summary of his own statement. Presumably, he repeated the position in his January 15 memorandum that the Court should not enforce desegregation directly. He may also have repeated a suggestion that he made in the memorandum—that a master should be appointed, either by the Supreme Court or the district court, to determine the facts and propose decrees in each of the cases before the Court. Douglas agreed that the use of a master was a possible solution, since it would be difficult for the Court to decide anything concrete on enforcement. Douglas stressed that any decree should reflect generosity, as well as flexibility.

Jackson's statement showed the difficulty he still felt. If it was only a matter of personal right, there was no answer to the N.A.A.C.P. claim that the black plaintiffs were entitled to immediate admission to desegregated schools. "If what we're doing is to uproot social policy, what business is it of ours?" Jackson did not attempt to resolve the dilemma. Instead, he suggested that the Court needed more time to consider the remedial issue. As Frankfurter's notes quoted him, "let's have a reargument on terms of a decree!!"

Jackson's suggestion for reargument on the terms of the decree was supported by Clark and Black, and ultimately adopted by the Court. Burton and Minton restated the need for the Court itself not to perform the enforcement function. Burton said that "our contribution is to decentralize" enforcement and Minton that he was "not given to throwing the Court's weight around."

The conference closed with a strong statement by Black on the need for flexibility in enforcement. The worst thing would be for the Court to try to resolve everything at once by its decree. "If necessary, let us have 700 suits" to work out the process. "Vagueness is not going to hurt." What was most needed was time. That was why Black had no objection to reargument. "Let it simmer. . . . Let it take time. It can't take too long." In the Deep South "any man who would come in [in support] would be dead politically forever. . . . In Alabama most liberals are praying for delay." Black concluded the conference by warning the Brethren that enforcement would give rise to a "storm over this Court."

At his second *Brown* conference, Warren had stated his basic approach in the manner calculated to appeal to those in doubt: delegation of the decree power (to meet Frankfurter's fear of embroiling the Court directly in the enforcement process) and flexibility (to meet the fears of the Southerners over immediate desegregation). The discussion indicated a consensus that was in accord with the Chief's own position. The Southerners' alarm at precipitate action had led even the strongest proponents of overruling *Plessy* to concede the need for flexibility and time to work out the desegregation process.

The general agreement on Jackson's suggestion for a reargument on the terms of the decree now made Warren's task of securing a unanimous opinion outlawing segregation less difficult. Frankfurter and Clark would find it easier to agree, once it was clear that the Court itself would not immediately decree an end to segregation. Jackson and Reed might, it is true, prove more difficult to convince. But they, too, could be persuaded more readily, now that all had agreed to flexibility in enforcement and postponed the specifics on the remedial question to a later day.

After the January 16 session, there was one other conference discussion, several weeks later, before the Court took a vote on the matter. We do not know any details about the later conference or when the vote was taken. In his posthumously published memoirs, Warren states that the Court voted in February and that the vote was unanimous against the separate-but-equal doctrine.[53] In interviews during his lifetime, Warren had indicated that the vote came in March. The question of the exact date is less important than that of how the vote went. Despite Warren's statement in his memoirs, it is probable that the vote was eight to one, with Reed voting to follow the *Plessy* case.

That Reed did vote to uphold segregation is indicated by his working on the draft of a dissent during February, asserting that segregation by itself did not violate equal protection.[54] In addition, there are indications that Reed persisted in standing alone until the end of April. Warren continued to work on him to change his vote, both at luncheon meetings and in private sessions. Then, toward the end, the Chief put it to Reed directly: "Stan, you're all by yourself in this now. You've got to decide whether it's really the best thing for the country."[55] As described by Reed's law clerk, who was present at the meeting, Warren was typically restrained in his approach. "Throughout the Chief Justice was quite low-key and very sensitive to the problems that the decision would present to the South. He empathized with Justice Reed's concern. But he was quite firm on the Court's need for unanimity on a matter of this sensitivity."[56]

During this period, Jackson was working on a draft concurrence that was sketched out in a memorandum in mid-February. Writing Judge Learned Hand about *Brown* in 1958, Frankfurter stated, "The fact of the matter is that Bob Jackson tried his hand at a justification for leaving the matter to §5 of Art. XIV, 'The Congress shall have powers to enforce, etc.' and he finally gave up."[57] Jackson might well have persisted in trying to explain his vote in a separate opinion. But fate intervened on March 30, when he was hospitalized by a serious heart attack. His weakened condition prevented Jackson from doing the work required for a worthwhile opinion.

Rumors also persist that Frankfurter prepared a concurring opinion, or even a dissent, in *Brown*. The leading biography of John W. Davis, the famous lawyer who had argued the segregation case for South Carolina, asserts that Frankfurter was "the last holdout" in

Brown and indicated that he would join Warren's opinion only on May 12, five days before the decision was rendered.[58] But, if Frankfurter prepared any separate opinion, no one (not even his law clerks) ever saw it.[59] A recent biography of Warren, quotes an eminent federal judge, Charles E. Wyzanski, as telling the author that he "was lunching with Frankfurter in his chambers when the Justice showed me—without letting me read them—the galley proofs of his and Jackson's separate opinions in *Brown*."[60] According to Wyzanski, however, "Justice Frankfurter, on May 25, 1954, showed me lying on his table some printed galleys relevant to *Brown v. Board of Education*. I did not examine those galleys. I do not know whether they were drafts of separate opinions, or drafts of proposed opinions of the court, or merely intra-court memoranda."[61]

The stories about Frankfurter's being ready to file a separate concurrence or dissent in *Brown* are almost certainly without foundation. If anyone worked for a unified Court to strike down segregation, it was Frankfurter. Under Chief Justice Vinson, it had been he who had induced the postponement that enabled the decision to be made under Warren's leadership. Frankfurter, too, cooperated closely with the new Chief in securing Court unanimity. It is true that, more than any other Justice, Frankfurter was wont to give vent to separate reservations even to opinions with which he generally agreed. As he wrote to Justice John Harlan "I do not rate unanimity as high as perhaps all the rest of my brethren do. Indeed, I don't rate it very high except in circumstances like those in the Segregation Cases."[62] Aware as he was of the need for the Court to speak with one voice, it was most unlikely that Frankfurter would dilute the effect of the unanimous decision by expressing his separate view.

At the conference that took the vote to strike down segregation, it was agreed that the opinion should be written by the Chief Justice.[63] The writing of the *Brown* opinion was done under conditions of even greater secrecy than usual. The extreme secrecy was extended to the entire deliberative process in the segregation case. Thus, the covering note to Frankfurter's January 15, 1954, memorandum on the fashioning of a decree stated at the end: "I need hardly add that the typewriting was done under conditions of strictest security."[64] The Justices also took steps to ensure that the way they voted would not leak out. No record of actions taken in *Brown* was written in the docket book that was kept by each Justice and was available to his clerks.[65] Warren tells us that, at the conference at which the opinion was assigned, "the importance of secrecy was discussed. We agreed that only my law clerks should be involved, and that any writing between my office and those of the other Justices would be delivered to the Justices personally. This practice was followed throughout and this was the only time it was required in my years on the Court."[66]

In late April Burton wrote in his diary, "After lunch the Chief Justice and [I] took a walk around the Capitol then went to his chambers where he uttered his preliminary thoughts as to author segregation cases."[67] After he had gotten Burton's reaction, the Chief was ready to begin the drafting process.

By then Warren had secured Reed's agreement to a unanimous decision. Reed still thought, as he wrote to Frankfurter, that "there were many considerations that pointed to a dissent." But, he went on, "they did not add up to a balance against the Court's opinion. . . . the factors looking toward a fair treatment for Negroes are more important than the weight of history."[68]

At the end of April, Warren called in the three clerks he had inherited from Vinson and told them the decision of the Court, as well as the fact that it was unanimous. He enjoined them to the strictest secrecy, saying that he had not told anyone outside the Justices what the decision was—not even his wife. The Chief then divided up the drafting job: Earl Pollock was to work on the opinion in the state cases; William Oliver was to have the primary responsibility for the case involving segregation in the District of Columbia; Richard Flynn helped on both opinions, particularly in fleshing them out with footnote citations.

The Chief then spoke to Pollock alone about the drafting of the *Brown* opinion. Warren had prepared an outline that served as the basis for the draft. It summarized the question presented in a manner that clearly indicated how the Chief wanted it answered. It also contained some language that Warren wanted in the opinion. In particular, it included what was to become the most famous sentence of the *Brown* opinion. As Warren first drafted it, the sentence read, "To separate them from others of similar age and qualifications solely because of their race puts the mark of inferiority not only upon their status in the community but also upon their hearts and minds in a way that is unlikely ever to be erased."[69] Frankfurter suggested changing "puts the mark of inferiority" to "generates a feeling of inferiority."[70] But the sentence in the final version was essentially the one Warren had originally written.

Concern with the impact of segregation upon the "hearts and minds" of black children was typical of the Warren approach. In the case of segregation, it had roots in Warren's contact with Edgar Patterson, his black driver while he was Governor of California. Patterson later recalled how he used to talk to the Governor about his early years. Warren would ask, "Tell me about how you felt when you were a little kid, going to school. And then I used to tell him about some of the things that happened in New Orleans, the way black kids felt." Patterson thought that the *Brown* opinion "almost quoted the ideas that he and I used to talk about on feelings . . . things that he picked up as he was asking questions about how the black man felt, how the black kid felt." Just before Warren's death, Patterson visited him in Georgetown University Hospital and told him his *Brown* decision "seemed to be based on our discussion of my early school life in New Orleans." Warren laughed and indicated that many other factors had entered into the decision.[71]

When Warren gave Pollock the job of preparing the *Brown* draft, he stressed two things: the opinion should be as brief as possible, and it was to be written in understandable English and avoid legalisms. The Chief said he wanted an opinion that could be understood by the layman. This is confirmed by Warren's May 7 memorandum transmitting the draft opinion to the Justices. The draft, wrote the Chief, was "prepared on the theory that the opinions should be short, readable by the lay public, non-rhetorical, unemotional and, above all, non-accusatory."[72]

When Pollock received the go-ahead from the Chief, he worked on the draft for about twenty-four hours—straight through without sleep. The draft prepared by Pollock from Warren's outline was basically the opinion read by the Chief on May 17. There were some minor changes. Thus, on May 5, three days before the draft opinion was delivered to the other Brethren, Burton noted in his diary, "In AM conferred with Chief Justice. . . . He then read to me and we discussed the draft of a memo. to the conference and the text of an opinion in 4 state segregation cases. I agreed with his handling of it and made a couple of suggestions." Burton also made "a few minor suggestions" on May 8 after he read the printed draft. Burton's changes were, as he said, very minor. The Warren draft noted that pre–Civil War "education of Negroes was forbidden by law in most Southern States." Burton proposed changing the words at the end to "some states." The first footnote of the draft summarized the facts of the state cases, identifying them only by the states involved. Burton suggested adding the titles of the four cases.[73]

Frankfurter also suggested a few changes. The most important of them has already been noted. The rest were cosmetic in character. Their nature can be gathered from a few examples. The draft stated that education must be considered "in the light of its present place in American life." Frankfurter proposed adding "development and its" before "present" and "throughout the Nation" after "life." The draft stressed "the importance of education to our society." Frankfurter suggested "instead of 'society' 'democracy.'" The final version read "to our democratic society."[74]

Clark made a few comparable stylistic changes. Like Burton, he toned down the draft assertion that "education of Negroes was forbidden by law in most Southern States" to "in some states." And the statement that "public education had already received wide acceptance in the North" was changed to "had already advanced further in the North."[75]

Jackson proposed two additions when Warren delivered the opinion to him in the hospital. The Chief declined to accept one because he felt it could be interpreted as applicable to segregation in general, and Warren wanted the opinion to be narrowly limited to school segregation. The Chief was, however, willing to add a sentence stressing that "Negroes have achieved outstanding success in the arts and sciences as well as in the business and professional world."[76]

While Pollock worked on the text of the *Brown* opinion, another clerk, Richard Flynn, added the footnotes—including the soon-to-be notorious footnote 11. Flynn also helped the third clerk, William Oliver, draft the opinion in *Bolling v. Sharpe*,[77] the case involving school segregation in the District of Columbia. In his May 7 memo transmitting the *Brown* and *Bolling* drafts, Warren stated that "It seemed to me there should be two opinions—one for the state cases and another for the District of Columbia case."[78] *Brown* and the other state cases were decided under the Equal Protection Clause of the Fourteenth Amendment. Yet that amendment is binding only upon the states, not the Federal Government. The latter is bound by the Fifth Amendment, which contains a Due Process Clause, but no requirement of equal protection. Obviously, the Court would not decide that the states could not have segregated schools, while the District of Columbia could. The problem was how to reach the result in terms of due process, rather than equal protection, analysis. Oliver, with Flynn's help, worked out the legal theory. Their draft incorporating it was, however, not accepted in its original form.

The draft[79] asserted the view that racial discrimination might be considered so arbitrary as to constitute a denial of due process. In support, the draft referred to "analogous situations in the field of education" where the Court "has applied similar reasoning." There was a deprivation "of the liberty protected by the Due Process Clause when the children are prohibited from pursuing certain courses, or from attending private schools or foreign-language schools. Such prohibitions were found to be unreasonable, and unrelated to any legitimate governmental objective. Just as a government may not impose arbitrary restrictions on the parent's right to educate his child, the government must not impose arbitrary restraints on access to the education which government itself provides." The draft then declared, "We have no hesitation in concluding that segregation of children in the public schools is a far greater restriction on their liberty than were the restrictions in the school cases discussed above."

The problem was that, for legal support, the draft cited four cases decided in the 1920s, particularly *Meyer v. Nebraska*[80] and *Pierce v. Society of Sisters*,[81] in which the Court had ruled violative of due process state laws prohibiting teaching of foreign languages in schools and requiring parents to send their children to public schools. The opinions had been written by Justice James C. McReynolds, whose legal reasoning had become anathema to the Justices appointed by President Roosevelt. One or more of them persuaded Warren to drop his reliance on the McReynolds opinions. Douglas later stated in an interview that though he didn't know for sure, "I think that Black said something to Warren about those cites."[82] Black had been the strongest opponent of the McReynolds-era due process approach, under which the Court had invalidated numerous regulatory laws. Black was always sensitive about reliance upon, or even citation of, the pre–New Deal judicial philosophy, and seized every occasion to oppose what he termed the "natural law due process philosophy which many later opinions repudiated."[83] Warren yielded on the issue and eliminated the objectionable references.

After Warren had carefully gone over the draft opinions, they were typed. The typed *Brown* draft, composed of nine legal size pages, was titled "MEMORANDUM ON THE STATE CASES."[84] The draft in *Bolling v. Sharpe,* four typed pages, was titled, "MEMORANDUM ON THE DISTRICT OF COLUMBIA CASE."[85] The draft opinions were then delivered personally to the Brethren on Saturday, May 8. Burton's diary entry for that date notes, "In AM the Chief Justice brought his draft of the segregation cases memoranda. These were in accord with our conversations."[86] Warren himself took the printed drafts to the Justices who were in their chambers. His clerks brought copies to the others. Black's copy was brought to him on the tennis court at his home in Alexandria, Minton's at his Washington apartment.

After Burton received the draft opinions from the Chief, "I read them and wrote him my enthusiastic approval—with a few minor suggestions. He has done, I believe, a magnificent job that may win a unanimous court."[87] Approvals also came in from Frankfurter and Clark (who had suggested the stylistic changes already noted in the typed draft), as well as Black, Douglas, and Minton, who may also have made a few minor changes. Reed, too, gave his approval, although he would have preferred the *Brown* opinion to be based upon a due process rather than an equal protection violation. Yet, even if, as Reed wrote to Frankfurter, " 'due process' seemed a better ground to me," he recognized that "there really isn't much difference. Equal protection comes close in this situation."[88]

Warren personally delivered the draft opinions to Jackson's hospital room. While he might have preferred a more elegant style, Jackson found nothing glaringly unacceptable in the Warren product and gave his approval.[89]

On May 12, Burton visited Warren and discussed some judicial business. "The Chief Justice also read to me his latest revision (slight) of the draft in Segregation Cases. It looks like a unanimous opinion—a major accomplishment for his leadership."[90] The revised printed opinions were then personally circulated by Warren the next day.

Saturday, May 15, was a conference day. At lunch, the Brethren were entertained by Burton, with a large salmon provided by Secretary of the Interior Douglas McKay. Just before, Burton wrote, the "conference finally approved Segregation opinions and instructions for delivery Monday—no previous notice being given to office staffs etc so as to avoid leaks. Most of us—including me—handed back the circulated print to C.J. to avoid possible leaks."[91]

Monday, May 17, 1954. Noon. Tense expectancy pervaded the crowded courtroom. The chamber itself is by far the most ornate room in the building, with walls of ivory-veined marble and twenty-four stately side columns of sienna marble. Behind the Justices' mahogany bench and plush green leather chairs, the wall is hung with dark red velour, complemented by a mammoth wine-red rug. Above the columns on the east and west walls are carved two marble panels depicting processions of historical lawgivers. Of the eighteen figures on the panels only one is famous as a judge, and he is the one American represented: John Marshall.

The great lawgivers in other systems have been mighty monarchs, of the type of Hammurabi and Justinian, divinely inspired prophets like Moses, philosophers such as Confucius, or scholars like Hugo Grotius or Blackstone. We in the United States have certainly had our share of the last two types of lawgiver—particularly among the men who drew up constitutions during and after the Revolution. Yet it is not a Jefferson or a Madison who is depicted as *the* American lawgiver, but the great Chief Justice who established the role of the Supreme Court as the authoritative expounder of the Constitution. Since Marshall's time, the Supreme Court's role as primary lawgiver has never been more strikingly illustrated than on "decision Monday" (all decisions were announced on Mondays at that time), May 17, 1954.

At noon precisely, the curtain behind the bench parted and, led by the Chief Justice, the Brethren filed to their places. "As we Justices marched into the courtroom on that day," Warren later recalled, "there was a tenseness that I have not seen equaled before or since."[92] For weeks before the *Brown* decision was announced, the courtroom had been jammed; anticipation mounted as the weeks passed.[93] Now, to the acute Court watcher, there were definite signs that the day would not be a quiet one. For one thing, several of the Justices' wives were present (including Mrs. Warren and Virginia, the eldest

Warren daughter), something that rarely happened except on historic Court occasions. Even more significant was Jackson's presence. Early that morning Warren had gone to the hospital to show Jackson a copy of the final opinion. Then, says Warren, the ailing Justice "to my alarm insisted on attending the Court that day in order to demonstrate our solidarity."[94]

Warren had advised his law clerks to be in the courtroom that morning. They had also realized from their intensive work on the final proofs that weekend that announcement of the decision was imminent. Frankfurter had also told his clerks that *Brown* was coming down. The other Justices' clerks had not been informed in advance, but they all sensed that this was to be more than the usual decision day. On his way to the robing room, Clark had stopped to say to the clerks, "I think you boys ought to be in the courtroom today."[95]

Surprisingly, the air of expectancy was absent from the Supreme Court press room. The reporters were told before the Court convened that it looked like a quiet day. Their expectation appeared borne out by the routine business that occupied the first part of the Court session. First, there was the admission of 118 attorneys to the Supreme Court Bar. Then three unimportant opinions were read by Clark and Douglas.

By now, fifty minutes of the Court session had passed. The reporters did not bother going upstairs to hear the routine opinions being delivered. But then, as they sat in the press room over their coffee, Banning E. Whittington, the Court's press officer, started putting on his coat and announced, "Reading of the segregation decisions is about to begin in the courtroom." Whittington led a fast-moving exodus as the reporters dashed up the long flight of marble steps just as the Chief Justice began reading in his booming bass. It was then 12:52 P.M.

"I have for announcement" said Warren, "the judgment and opinion of the Court in No. 1—*Oliver Brown et al. v. Board of Education of Topeka.*" Then, in a firm, colorless tone, he read the opinion in the state segregation cases. First, the background of the cases was given. Plaintiff Negroes sought admission to public schools on a nonsegregated basis. They had been denied relief on the basis of the *Plessy* "separate but equal" doctrine. They contended that segregated schools were not "equal" and could not be made "equal" and, by their very nature, deprived plaintiffs of the equal protection of the laws. The Chief then summarized the reargument and concluded (following the Bickel–Frankfurter memorandum) that the legislative history of the Fourteenth Amendment was, at best, inconclusive. He also stressed the changed position in the society of both public education and the Negro.

The opinion next went into the origin of the separate-but-equal doctrine and the cases which had applied it. Here, unlike those cases, the lower courts had found that the Negro and white schools had been or were being equalized as to buildings, curricula, teacher qualifications and other "tangible" factors. The decision, therefore, could not turn on comparing merely these tangible factors: "We must look instead to the effect of segregation itself on public education."[96]

In approaching this problem, the Court could not "turn the clock back to 1868 when the Amendment was adopted, or even to 1896 when *Plessy v. Ferguson* was written. We must consider public education in light of its full development and its present place in American life throughout the Nation."[97] Then, in what for Warren was eloquent language, the Chief affirmed that, "Today, education is perhaps the most important function of state and local governments. . . . It is required in the performance of our most basic public responsibilities, even service in the armed forces. It is the very foundation of good citizenship. Today it is a principal instrument in awakening the child to cultural values, in preparing him for later professional training, and in helping him to adjust normally to his environment. In these days, it is doubtful that any child may reasonably be expected to succeed in life if he is denied the opportunity of an education. Such an opportunity, where the state has undertaken to provide it, is a right which must be made available to all on equal terms."[98]

This brought the opinion to the crucial question: "Does segregation of children in public schools solely on the basis of race, even though the physical facilities and other 'tangible' factors may be equal, deprive the children of the minority group of equal educational opportunities?"[99]

Until then, with the opinion two-thirds finished, Warren had not indicated the outcome of the decision. Now, in the next sentence, he did. Answering the critical question, he asserted: "We believe that it does."[100]

The opinion reviewed earlier cases which had held that, in colleges and universities, segregated schools could not provide equal educational opportunities. The same was true for children in public schools. "To separate them from others of similar age and qualifications solely because of their race generates a feeling of inferiority as to their status in the community that may affect their hearts and minds in a way unlikely ever to be undone." [101] This was the final version of the soaring sentence Warren had put in his original outline; it stated the baneful impact of segregation on black children better than a whole shelf of learned sociological tomes.

Plessy v. Ferguson had said that the assumption that segregation supposed colored inferiority was fallacious. Warren now declared that segregation did mean the inferiority of the Negro group. "Whatever may have been the extent of psychological knowledge at the time of *Plessy v. Ferguson,* this finding is amply supported by modern authority. Any language in *Plessy v. Ferguson* contrary to this finding is rejected." [102] This statement was supported by footnote 11 of the opinion,[103] which listed seven works by social scientists and was to become the most famous note in a Supreme Court opinion.

The Chief Justice then stated the Court's far-reaching conclusion: "We conclude"—here Warren departed from the printed text to insert the word "unanimously"—"that in the field of public education the doctrine of 'separate but equal' has no place. Separate educational facilities are inherently unequal." [104] Warren later recalled that, "When the word 'unanimously' was spoken, a wave of emotion swept the room; no words or intentional movement, yet a distinct emotional manifestation that defies description." [105] Other observers agree that, as Warren pronounced the word, barely suppressed astonishment swept around the courtroom.[106] Until then, neither the press nor the public had any idea that the man from California had achieved a unanimous decision.

The *Brown* opinion concluded with the holding that plaintiffs "and others similarly situated" had been deprived of equal protection by the segregation complained of. But it did not decree any relief. Instead, the Jackson suggestion at the January 16 conference was followed. "Because these are class actions, because of the wide applicability of this decision, the formulation of decrees in these cases presents problems of considerable complexity." [107] This decision dealt only with "the constitutionality of segregation in public education.

We have now announced that such segregation is a denial of the equal protection of the laws." [108] The question of appropriate relief was still before the Court. "In order that we may have the full assistance of the parties in formulating decrees," [109] the Court was scheduling further argument on the matter for the next Court term, beginning in October 1954. The U.S. Attorney General was again invited to participate. So were the Attorneys General of other states with segregated schools.

Almost never before, wrote Arthur Krock the next day in the *New York Times,* had "the high tribunal disposed so simply and briefly of an issue of such magnitude." [110] The *Brown* opinion was strikingly short for an opinion of such consequence: only ten pages in the *United States Reports,* in which Supreme Court opinions are printed. The second segregation opinion, that in *Bolling v. Sharpe,* [111] was even shorter, disposing of District of Columbia segregation in six paragraphs. The *Bolling* decision flowed naturally from that announced in *Brown.* "In view of our decision that the Constitution prohibits the states from maintaining racially segregated public schools," Warren declared, "it would be unthinkable that the same Constitution would impose a lesser duty on the Federal Government." [112] It is true that the District of Columbia presented a somewhat different legal problem, since the Fifth Amendment, applicable in the District, does not contain an Equal Protection Clause, as does the Fourteenth Amendment, which applies only to the states. But equal protection and due process both stem from the American ideal of fairness. Discrimination may be so unjustifiable as to be violative of due process and that is true of school segregation in the nation's capital. "Segregation in public education is not reasonably related to any proper governmental objective, and thus it imposes on Negro children of the District of Columbia a burden that constitutes an arbitrary deprivation of their liberty in violation of the Due Process Clause." [113]

When Warren concluded the *Bolling* opinion, it was 1:20 P.M. It had taken only twenty-eight minutes for the Chief Justice to read both opinions. After Warren finished, everyone in the courtroom looked to Reed to see what the courtly Southerner was going to do. Reed, who had had tears in his eyes during the opinion reading, now filed out silently with the Brethren. Despite Warren's use of the word "unanimously," it was hard for many to grasp that neither Reed nor any of the other Justices had filed a separate opinion. For weeks thereafter people would call the clerk's office and ask to see the dissenting opinion.[114]

The Court's unanimity came as a complete surprise both to Court watchers and the public. As Arthur Krock, the senior *New York Times* columnist wrote, the unanimity was "remarkable because dissents on this basic proposition were generally expected, a familiar prophecy having been that there would be nine opinions written and a close division among the Justices on the central finding."[115] For the unexpected unanimity, Warren deserved the major credit.

Discussing the *Brown* unanimity himself later, Warren said with a characteristic generosity of spirit that the real credit should go to the three Southern Justices.[116] "Don't thank me," he said to a California friend who visited him in his chambers, "I'm not the one. You should see what those . . . fellows from the southern states had to take from their constituencies. It was absolutely slaughter. They stood right up and did it anyway because they thought it was right."[117] Reed, in particular came to believe that the *Brown* decision was wholly right. He told one of his clerks that "if it was not the most important decision in the history of the Court, it was very close."[118]

In the *New York Times* of May 18, 1954, James Reston analyzed *Brown* in a column headed, "A Sociological Decision." According to Reston, the Court had relied "more on the social scientists than on legal precedents. . . . The Court's opinion read more like an expert paper on sociology than a Supreme Court opinion."[119]

The Reston characterization was based upon the fact that the *Brown* opinion rested, not so much on legal reasoning, as on the conclusion (initially stated by Warren at his first *Brown* conference) that segregation denoted Negro inferiority and also that it lessened the motivation to learn. Whatever may have been the extent of psychological knowledge at the time of *Plessy,* Warren's opinion asserted, these conclusions were "amply supported by modern authority." This assertion was backed by a footnote—the celebrated footnote 11, which has become the most controversial note in Supreme Court history.

Footnote 11 listed seven works by social scientists, starting with an article by Kenneth B. Clark and concluding with the massive two-volume study by Gunnar Myrdal, *An American Dilemma.*[120] Supporters and critics of the Court alike have assumed, like Reston, that footnote 11 means that the *Brown* decision was based on the work of the social scientists cited. As Kenneth Clark, the first mentioned in the footnote, summarized it, "the Court . . . appeared to rely on the findings of social scientists in the 1954 decision."[121] A plethora of learned commentary followed, analyzing in amazing detail the works cited, the significance of the order of citation, and the fact that other relevant writings were not cited—as well as the whole subject of using the methods and products of social science in deciding controversial legal issues. Even supporters of the decision have shown how vulnerable the studies and tests relied upon in most of the cited works really were.

Those who have focused intensively, however, upon the controversial footnote have acted out of less than complete understanding of the manner in which Supreme Court opinions are prepared. Warren himself of course always stressed it was the decision, not the citations, that was important. "It was only a note, after all," he declared to an interviewer,[122] and in fact Warren left the citations in opinions in the normal run of affairs to his law clerks. To him they were the minutiae of legal scholarship. In the main they could be left to others.

In the *Brown* case, the fleshing out of the opinion with footnotes had been left primarily to one of Warren's clerks, Richard Flynn, who had been responsible for footnote 11. As Flynn recalls it, there was no specific method in the organization of the note or in the listing of the cited works. The clerks had been working on the case all year and had constantly received materials from the Library of Congress on the segregation issue that they tried to read in preparation for the decision. When it came time to cite supporting authority, the works listed (particularly those by Myrdal and Clark) were, to Flynn, the "obvious" things to list. When asked if there was any method in the way he organized the note, he answered, "I don't recall any, that's just the way it fell."

It has been said that footnote 11 provoked concern among several Justices, particularly in the gratuitous citation of the Myrdal work, which had, in the decade since its publication, become a red flag to the white South.[123] In 1971, Clark, then retired from the Court, told an interviewer, "I questioned the Chief's going with Myrdal in that opinion. I told him—and Hugo Black did, too—that it wouldn't go down well in the South. And he didn't need it."[124]

Clark's recollection was not accurate. Over the years, he may have come to feel that, in view of the storm in the South caused by the Myrdal citation, he should have said something at the time—which may, years later, have become a blurred recollection that he and Black had expressed concern at the time. If Black and Clark had objected to the Myrdal reference, it would, in all likelihood, have been taken out. The citation was just not important enough to Warren to withstand even a mild indication of concern by any of the Brethren.

Clark did suggest one correction in footnote 11, that was speedily accepted by the Chief—which indicates that the same thing would have happened if Clark had asked for the Myrdal to be removed. In the draft of the *Brown* opinion that was originally delivered to the Justices, the footnote began with the citation: "Clark, Effect of Prejudice and Discrimination on Personality Development (Midcentury White House Conference on Children and Youth, 1950)." [125] Justice Clark objected that this did not sufficiently identify the Clark who had written the article cited. He did not want people, particularly in his own South, to think that the Court was citing an anti-segregation article that he—Tom Clark—had authored. He, therefore, asked that the citation be changed to "K.B. Clark," so that no one would confuse the Justice with the author. In the final opinion, the name of the first author cited appears with initials, as Justice Clark had suggested—the only author in the footnote not identified solely by last name.

In the interest of completeness with regard to a note that has been magnified by commentators out of all proportion to the importance placed upon it by the members of the *Brown* Court, it should be pointed out that there were two other changes in footnote 11, as it appeared in the original draft opinion. The first was its renumbering: it was footnote 10 in the original draft and received its present number after a new footnote 10 was inserted to support the finding by the lower court on the baneful effects of segregated schools. In addition, the original draft listed six works. The second work cited in the final footnote version, Witmer and Kotinsky, *Personality in the Making*, [126] was added in a later draft. The clerks who worked on the opinion think the omission of this book was a typographical error that was caught in the intensive proofreading before the draft was printed.

There is an undated note, written on a Supreme Court memo pad in Frankfurter's handwriting, that reads, "It is not fair to say that the

South has always denied Negroes 'this constitutional right.' It was NOT a constitutional right till May 17/54." [127] The more restrained critics of the *Brown* decision have been disturbed by what they claim is its inadequacy in explaining its vindication of the new right. They allege a lack of legal craftsmanship in the Warren opinion that has tended to deprive it of the respect to which it would otherwise be entitled. They point to the opinion's laconic nature, its failure to rely upon legal precedent, and its literary weakness, as compared with those produced by past masters of the judical art, such as Marshall, Holmes, or Cardozo.

It may be unfortunate that the *Brown* opinion was not written by a Marshall or a Cardozo. Great cases deserve nothing less than opinions by the consummate giants of legal craftsmanship. But the criticism brings to mind a comment of Warren E. Burger, shortly after he succeeded Warren as Chief Justice. Seated before the fire at the elegant Elizabethan manor where international conferences are held in Ditchley, Oxfordshire, rolling a glass of fine liqueur in his hand, the new Chief was distressed by critics who contended that he did not have the qualifications of a Cardozo. "Who is there today who does?" he wryly asked.

The same can be asked of those who have urged that *Brown* deserved a Holmes or a Cardozo for its creator. One can go further and wonder whether those virtuosos of the opinion could possibly have secured the unanimous decision that was the Warren forte. If we take the *Brown* opinion as it is written, it certainly ranks as one of the great opinions of judicial history—plainly in the tradition of Chief Justice Marshall's seminal 1819 dictum that the Court must never forget that it is a *Constitution* it is expounding.[128] Perhaps the *Brown* opinion did not demonstrate as well as it might have that the mere fact of segregation denies educational equality. But *Brown* is so clearly right in its conclusion in this respect that one wonders whether additional labor in spelling out the obvious would really have been worthwhile. Considerations of *elegantia juris* and judicial craftsmanship are largely irrelevant to the truism that segregation was intended to keep blacks in a status of inferiority.[129]

Almost three decades after the *Brown* case, it has become apparent that the criticisms of the Court's performance there have lost their relevancy. What is plain is that *Brown* has taken its place in the very forefront of the pantheon of historic decisions. In the light of what Justice Arthur J. Goldberg has termed the American commitment to equality[130] and its part in helping to fulfill the commitment, *Brown* will occupy a paramount position long after the contemporary criticisms will have ceased to have any more continuing significance than those voiced against the great decisions of the Marshall Court at the very outset of the nation's constitutional development.

To be sure, those whose ox had been gored could scarcely appreciate the greatness of the *Brown* decision. On the contrary, as Black had predicted at the January 16 conference, the *Brown* decision gave rise to a "storm over this Court." To the white South, May 17 became known as "Black Monday"; the decision rang through the Old Confederacy (to use a Jefferson phrase) "like a fire bell in the night."[131] After *Brown*, the Court began to receive the "hate mail" that was to become a feature of the Warren years. Warren himself states that when out of curiosity, in July 1954, he asked to see the accumulated mail on the case, he was surprised that there were only between six and seven hundred letters.[132] But the mail was soon to increase both in volume and intensity. By 1956, the *New York Times* could report that "old timers here say they have never seen anything to match in bitterness and vulgarity the mail that has come to members of the Supreme Court since [*Brown*]."[133]

Surprisingly perhaps, the first Southern reactions to the desegregation decision were somewhat muted. That may explain the small number of letters that Warren found. Of course, there were the shrill cries of the extreme white-supremacists, such as Senator James O. Eastland of Mississippi, who defiantly declared that the South "will not abide by or obey this legislative decision by a political court."[134] Generally speaking, however, even in the South, the immediate reaction was more temperate. A *Louisville Courier–Journal* editorial summarized the moderate approach: "The Supreme Court's ruling is not itself a revolution. It is rather acceptance of a process that has been going on a long time—people everywhere could well match the court's moderation and caution."[135] What was necessary, the Governor of Virginia urged, was "cool heads, calm study, and sound judgment."[136] It is a time, said the *Atlanta Constitution*, "for Georgia to think clearly. Our best minds must be put to work, not to destroy, but to arrive at constructive conclusions."[137]

Warren and the Brethren were heartened by the initial response. Even before the *Brown* decision, on May 5, Warren had written

Frankfurter about a *Washington Post* article indicating that Virginia would receive "even the most drastic decision calmly" that "this is a splendid and encouraging article"[138] During the summer, Frankfurter and Warren exchanged letters. Frankfurter jubilantly informed the Chief that a candidate for the Tennessee governorship, "who ran on a strong segregation ticket," had received less than five percent of the vote. He also remarked that he had been telephoned by former Justice James F. Byrnes, now Governor of South Carolina, who had indicated that he was taking a moderate attitude.[139] Warren replied that Byrnes "was certainly conciliatory but I cannot escape the thought that he could have been much more helpful, had he been as restrained in recent years."[140] To which Frankfurter wrote, "I quite agree with you that Jimmie Byrnes has shown more good sense after the event than before it."[141] Just before the new Court term opened, however, Warren noted a change in attitude. He sent Frankfurter an "article concerning the proposed disbarment of two attorneys for seeking to register some negro children in a segregated school. I call your attention to the statement of Jimmy Byrnes concerning the isolated instances in the border states and inviting 'far more serious ones' in the deep South."[142] Still, Warren typically asserted about the situation in the South in another letter, "I cannot believe it is as bad as [some] believe it to be."[143]

If the first Southern reaction was not as extreme as some had feared, that was true, in large part, because the *Brown* decision invalidating school segregation did not make any provision for enforcement. As the *Atlanta Constitution* pointed out in a May 18 editorial, "The court decision does not mean that Negro and white children will go to school together this fall. The court itself provides for a 'cooling-off' period. Not until next autumn will it even begin to hear arguments . . . . on how to implement the ruling."[144] Although the May 17 decision settled the issue of constitutionality, the Supreme Court still had another round to go in the *Brown* litigation. The situation was summarized in the *New York Times* account of the *Brown* decision: "when it returns in October for the 1954–1955 term [the Court] will hear rearguments then on the question of how and when the practice it outlawed today may finally be ended."[145]

The earliest date on which the reargument on the *Brown* decree could take place was in October 1954, when the new term would begin. During July, however, Frankfurter wrote Warren that since, in "some of the States segregation is exploited as a political issue . . . I suppose there will be no difficulty in hurdling the distorting opportunities of a Fall election and hearing the case after the election is wholly behind us."[146] Warren replied, "I agree with you that it would be sound judgment to place the cases on the calendar shortly after the fast approaching 'sound and fury.' "[147]

This would probably have meant scheduling the reargument in late November or December. Once again, however, the reargument had to be postponed—this time because of the death of Jackson, who suffered a fatal second heart attack in October, soon after the Court began the new term. Action on the *Brown* decree now had to be delayed until after a new Justice was appointed and confirmed. There is some irony in the fact that Jackson's successor was to be John Marshall Harlan, grandson of the Justice of the same name who had delivered the *Plessy v. Ferguson* dissent. Harlan, nominated by the President on November 8, was confirmed in late March, 1955, and the *Brown* reargument had to wait for him. It was finally scheduled for April 11, 1955.

Before the reargument, briefs were submitted both by the parties and the U.S. Attorney General, as well as by six segregating states, in response to the invitation at the end of the *Brown* opinion. The U.S. brief stressed that the Court should be flexible and let the district courts oversee the enforcement process, though it ought definitely to insist upon "an immediate and substantial start" toward desegregation. Anthony Lewis, then *New York Times* Supreme Court reporter, writes that he saw an insertion in President Eisenhower's handwriting on a draft copy of the government's brief. The insertion stressed that the Court should also consider and meet with understanding and good will the psychological and emotional problems of those who would have to comply with the decision.[148]

Eisenhower had expressed a similar view on desegregation to Warren himself. While the *Brown* decision was pending, the Chief Justice had been invited to a White House dinner. The President had, with remarkable obtuseness, seated Warren near John W. Davis, the lawyer who led the case in support of segregation. During the dinner, Eisenhower told Warren at length what a great man Davis was. Then, after dinner, taking Warren by the arm as they were walking to be served coffee, the President said, speaking of the South, "These are not bad people. All they are concerned about is to see that their sweet little girls are not required to sit in school alongside some big black bucks."[149]

The reargument on the terms of the *Brown* decree took place, as scheduled, on April 11, 1955, and lasted for thirteen hours spread over four days. This time, Warren took a more active part in the argument itself. As in the earlier reargument in December 1953, the Chief intervened several times to stress practical points. He interrupted the Kansas Attorney General to ask when the schools opened in Topeka and when the "determining as to where a child shall go is made," saying, "I think generally what the Court would be interested in knowing would be in the event there is a remand to the district court, if it might be said when it gets there, that it was too late for next year."[150] Then, when N.A.A.C.P. counsel asserted that the Court's decision applied to all Negro school children, even those not parties: "our research will show that they can intervene any time before judgment and merely show that they are within the class involved." At this, the Chief interposed: "Mr. Marshall, are your authorities on that subject in your brief?" Marshall had to admit they were not. "Would you furnish them to us?" came back Warren.[151]

But the most dramatic Warren intervention came when S. Emory Rogers led off the Southern case (in place of John W. Davis, who had died a few weeks earlier). Rogers, a short, florid scion of the plantation district involved, asserted, in answer to the *Brown* opinion statement that the clock could not be turned back to 1868, when the Fourteenth Amendment was adopted, or 1896, when *Plessy* was decided, "I do not believe that . . . we can push the clock forward abruptly to 2015 or 2045." He then asked for an "open decree"—one that sent the cases back without instructions specifying when and how the schools had to be desegregated. Then came the sharpest exchange of the reargument, which started with Warren's question:

"Is your request for an open decree predicated upon the assumption that your school district will immediately undertake to conform to the opinion of this Court of last year to the decree, or is it on the basis—"

The Chief could not finish the question. Rogers interrupted: "Mr. Chief Justice, to say we will conform depends on the decree handed down. I am frank to tell you, right now in our district I do not think that we will send—the white people of the district will send their children to the Negro schools. It would be unfair to tell the Court that we are going to do that. I do not think it is. But I do think that something can be worked out. We hope so." [152]

To Warren this was legal heresy. The parties did not "work out something" with Supreme Court decrees; they obeyed them. [153] Warren looked down on the Southern attorney: "It is not a question of attitude, it is a question of conforming to the decree. Is there any basis upon which we can assume that there will be an immediate attempt to comply with the decree of this Court, whatever it may be?"

Rogers replied that the question of compliance should be left to the lower court. Warren insisted on the question of compliance, "But you are not willing to say here that there would be an honest attempt to conform to this decree, if we did leave it to the district court?"

"No, I am not," answered Rogers. And, raising his forefinger toward the bench, he declared, "Let us get the word 'honest' out of there."

"No," countered the Chief, by now quite flushed, "leave it in."

The Southerner was not repressed, "No," he came back, "because I would have to tell you that right now we would not conform—we would not send our white children to the Negro schools." [154]

It looked for a moment as though Warren, bristling at the attorney's presumption, might take strong measures. "We thought he might charge Rogers with contempt," recalled Virginia Attorney General J. Lindsay Almond. [155] But Warren was able to keep his temper under control. The exchange was cut short by the Chief Justice's steely "Thank you." Still, Warren was plainly angry at the Rogers argument. When Robert McCormick Figg, Rogers' co-counsel, resumed the argument, Warren mused that he was thinking of Rogers' assertion that "these attitudes that he relies on could not be changed until 2015 or 2045. I wonder if the decision of May 17 last year would be of much value to these people if they waited until 2045 for that change in the attitude of these people." [156]

Later on, Warren came back to the Rogers contretemps: "I understood from Mr. Rogers that your school district there and your people, because of your attitude, would not permit white and colored children to go to school together, notwithstanding the opinion of this Court. Now when it comes to remanding this to the court below, do you not believe that it is essential for us to take into consideration, since it is a court of equity, whether there is an attempt to comply or an attempt at frustration?" Figg replied that, if the lower court were given the primary enforcement role, "it would advance public acceptance;" if not, "it would retard public acceptance." Warren then indicated that an "open decree," which simply sent the cases back to the lower courts without specifying when and how school desegregation was to be accomplished, might not be enough, asking, "Do you not think that it might be of some value to the court below to have some guidance as to the manner in which progress can be expected?" [157]

Warren had been shaken by the exchange with Rogers. But the Southern attorney's near-defiance must have confirmed him in the conclusion he had previously come to on enforcement. The Chief's attitude toward a decree was summarized in a conversation with one of Reed's clerks, who had delivered that Justice's file on desegregation for the Chief to work with during the summer of 1954. The clerk reported the substance of the conversation in a memo to Reed. Warren's inclination, it said, "was to send the cases back to the trial court for the entry of appropriate decrees." This would both allow more time for compliance and allow for local variations. The Chief stressed "that reasonable attempts to start the integration process is all the Court can expect in view of the scope of the problem, and that an order to immediately admit all negroes in white schools would be an absurdity because impossible to obey in many areas." [158]

Before Warren left that summer to go to California he received a letter from Frankfurter which sought to "think out loud about the *Segregation* decree. I suppose that the most important problem is to fashion appropriate provisions against evasion." The letter reaffirmed Warren's thinking on the need for the details of decrees to be left to lower courts. "I am," Frankfurter wrote, "of course, not assuming that in our decree we shall set forth with detailed particularity how Virginia, let us say, ought to go about reshaping its present school facilities or augmenting them. While all my thinking on this business is tentative I assume the contrary; I assume that the utmost we shall be doing is merely to define . . . the standards by which decrees will be locally spelled out in detail." [159]

During the summer, Warren had assigned six law clerks to do intensive research on desegregation and to make recommendations for the Court's decree. Their research report of eighty-one printed pages was circulated by the Chief in November 1954, and their recommendations on April 10, 1955, the day before the reargument.[160] The clerks recommended: (1) "that the cases should be remanded to the District Courts for supervision of the execution of the decree;" (2) "that this Court should formulate a simple decree;" and (3) the Court should provide guides to the lower courts. On his copy, Frankfurter wrote, next to the third recommendation, "It will make for endless litigation if we don't." The clerks proposed that any guides to the lower courts "should not be included in the decree itself, but rather in a separate opinion." Next to this Frankfurter wrote, "Why? I don't agree." As it turned out, the second *Brown* opinion was to be closer to the clerks' recommendation than the Frankfurter objection.

On the last day of the reargument, Frankfurter sent a "Dear Brethren" letter in which he stressed that "how we do what we do in the *Segregation* cases may be as important as what we do,"[161] and a memorandum in which he backed away from his earlier suggestion that a master be appointed. Now he said that two principal alternatives were open to the Court: (1) a "bare bones" decree permanently enjoining exclusion of the named plaintiffs and others within the defined class; or (2) a "more flexible decree which would take due . . . account of considerations relevant to the fashioning of a decree in equity" including "what are loosely called 'attitudes' as well as physical financial and administrative conditions." Frankfurter preferred the second alternative, which meant laying down "some kind of standards" that would give the lower courts "guides to which they are entitled . . . and yet not serve as the mere imposition of a distant will." The criteria should be "not too loose to invite evasion, yet with enough 'give' to leave room for variant local problems." Again the Justice stressed that the Court must not operate as "a super-school board."[162]

Burton also prepared a handwritten memorandum for the conference held on April 16 to consider the *Brown* decree. That memo, too, underlined the conviction that "neither this Court nor the District Courts should act as school boards" and urged that there should be "the allowance of time for the enforcement of the decree." Burton warned against putting anything in the order that would be futile. "It is better to get limited results which are ordered and let them serve as examples than to order something which will not be carried out." [163]

The Frankfurter and Burton memos stated views that were approved by most of the Brethren, including the Chief Justice. This was made apparent at the conference on the *Brown* decree which met on the Saturday following the oral reargument, April 16, 1955. In a 1956 memorandum, Justice Harlan says, "Very shortly after coming to the Court I heard it said by more than one of my brethren that in implementing the segregation decision of May 17, 1954, we should scrupulously adhere to traditional notions as to the powers and functions of this Court." [164] The same theme was repeated by most of the Justices at the conference, starting with the Chief himself.

Warren opened the discussion [165] in his easy way by indicating that he was open to as long a discussion as necessary. "I haven't reached a fixed opinion, and maybe we ought to talk this over the way we did in the main cases last year." To lead the discussion, however, he said, "I'm clear there are some things we should and should not do." First, on the things the Court should *not* do: (1) "we should not appoint a master or indicate to the court below that it should do so—though, of course, that court has that power;" (2) "we should not fix any date for completion of desegregation, nor suggest to the lower court that it should—though, no doubt, in some cases it could;" (3) "we should not *require* the court below to call for a [desegregation] plan—it is perfectly feasible for a lower court to do so, but we should not require it;" and (4) "I would not make any procedural requirements—this is a court of equity" and should follow traditional limitations upon such a court's powers.

Warren next turned to "what appeals to me," outlining the things the Court *should* do in its enforcement decision. First, he asked, "should we give guidance in an opinion or formal decree?" His answer was, "I think there should be an opinion with factors for the courts below to take into account rather than a formal decree." Second, "the opinion ought to give them some guidance. It would make it much easier and would be rather cruel to shift it back to them and let them flounder." Warren concluded by indicating the "ground rules" to guide the lower courts: (1) these are class actions; thus enforcement may be had not merely by the named plaintiffs; (2) the courts are entitled to take into consideration physical facts and financial problems—"but I wouldn't suggest psychological and sociological attitudes;" and (3) the courts must consider whether there has been any initiation of movement toward desegregation and its progress. Above all, Warren concluded, "Give District Courts as much latitude as we can but also as much support as we can."

Warren's presentation, like that at his first *Brown* conference, was masterly. It stated the main lines of what became the Court's enforcement decision. First of all, the Chief rejected proposals that had been discussed in the Court: appointment of a master, fixing of a date for completion of desegregation, requiring specific desegregation plans from defendant school districts, and imposing of procedural requirements—all of which were also rejected by the Court's decision. Then he emphasized the point he had made in the January 16, 1954, conference—that the Court should furnish guidance to the lower courts. The guidance should be in an opinion listing the factors to be taken into account, rather than a formal decree. This apparently was Warren's own idea. It took the law clerks' recommendation for an opinion, as well as a decree, one step further and was the method adopted in the *Brown* enforcement decision. The opinion-not-decree approach had the advantage of less formal precision and hence greater flexibility. Flexibility in enforcement was also the keynote of the "ground rules" Warren suggested to guide the enforcement process.

Once again, Warren's presentation set the theme both for the conference and the decision. With one exception, the Brethren indicated agreement with the Warren approach. The exception was Black. "I differ from your views," he told the Chief. "How to say and do as little as possible is my present desire. I was brought up in an atmosphere against federal officials, which is rooted in the race question. . . . . The South would never be a willing party to Negroes and whites going to school together. There's no more chance to enforce this in the deep South than Prohibition in New York City. Nothing is more important than that this Court should not issue what it cannot enforce." Black said he would render a decree limited to the individual plaintiffs. "We should move gradually and make it as narrow as possible." At best, there would be only "glacial movement" toward desegregation. "It is futile to think that in these cases we can settle segregation in the South."

The newcomer to the Court, Harlan, indicated that he was deeply impressed by what Black said on the difficulties in the South. The other Southern Justices, however, took a more optimistic attitude. Reed expressed the "firm belief" that a considerable group in the South was "willing to give sympathetic consideration" to the enforcement problem. Clark thought there would not be "too much trouble in Texas."

Several of the Justices emphasized how important it was for the Court to remain unanimous in the enforcement decision. One of these, fortunately, was Black. He said, "If humanly possible, I will do everything possible to achieve a unanimous result." Despite his different views, he ultimately went along with the *Brown II* decision and opinion.

Once again the conference agreed that the unanimous opinion should be written by the Chief Justice. Warren stressed to his clerks that the opinion should be as short as possible and cover the main points he had made at the conference: that enforcement be flexible, under accepted equity principles, and that it take into account various factors to be briefly listed to serve as "ground rules" for the lower courts.

The draft was speedily written in accordance with Warren's guide. It was shown in early May to individual Justices for their comments and suggestions. Burton's diary for May 11 notes: "Returned the Chief Justice's draft of segregation case memorandum with suggestions (Already submitted . . . suggestions from Black, Reed, Frankfurter and Clark)."[166] On May 25, Warren brought Burton a revised draft that was circulated the next day. The memorandum transmitting the draft noted that "minor changes, largely stylistic, have been made to conform to suggestions of several members of the Court." It also suggested that "if agreeable, we will discuss it at the Conference tomorrow."[167] The conference on May 27 considered the proposed *Brown II* opinion in detail. The one discordant note was a suggestion by Frankfurter (made privately a few days earlier to some of the Brethren) that the opinion should be an unsigned per curiam. The Court voted eight-to-one that the opinion should be by the Chief Justice, as originally decided. The Conference also agreed that the decision should be announced on May 31.

The conference made three changes in the draft *Brown II* opinion.[168] Two were minor. The draft referred to the "newly defined constitutional principles" laid down in *Brown I*. The words "newly defined" were omitted. Similarly, the draft stated that, in fashioning and executing decrees, the lower courts "will be guided by general equitable principles" and the conference deleted "general."

The third change was more substantial. The draft stated that the district courts were to enter such orders and decrees as to ensure the nondiscriminatory admission to public schools of "the plaintiffs and those similarly situated in their respective school districts who may within such time as may be fixed by the District Courts become parties to these cases." This wording would have converted *Brown* into a virtual class action, allowing not only the actual parties, but also those similarly situated, to obtain the relief ordered. At the April 16 conference, Warren had stated the view that "these are class actions and not only the named plaintiffs" would come within whatever decree was issued. Though several Justices agreed, Black and Douglas were opposed and insisted that relief should be restricted to the named plaintiffs only. Their opposition prevailed at the May 27 conference, and the final version ordered the district courts to enter such decrees as were necessary to admit to public schools "the parties to these cases."

The *Brown II* opinion was delivered by the Chief Justice, in a packed courtroom, on Tuesday, May 31, 1955—the last day of the 1954 Term. The reading this time took only ten minutes; the opinion consisted of just seven paragraphs. Commentators have noted that it did not contain the words "segregation" or "desegregation." Instead, Warren started by stating that the opinions of May 17, 1954, declared "the fundamental principle that racial discrimination in public education is unconstitutional." All legal provisions "requiring or permitting such discrimination must yield to this principle."[169] The question now was the manner in which relief was to be accorded.

The opinion went on to acknowledge the "informative and helpful" presentations on reargument. The problem was that "of the complexities arising from the transition to a system of public education freed of racial discrimination." Then, covering one of the essential points made in the Justices' discussions, Warren eschewed any super school-board role for the Court. The primary responsibility "for elucidating, assessing, and solving these problems" was in the school authorities. But the courts would have to consider whether actions of the authorities constituted good faith implementation. The "courts which originally heard these cases can best perform this judicial appraisal,"[170] and the cases were remanded to them for enforcement.

In fashioning enforcement decrees, Warren went on, the courts would be guided by equitable principles. They should balance the plaintiffs' interest in admission to the schools "as soon as practicable on a nondiscriminatory basis" with "the public interest in the elimination of such obstacles in a systematic and effective manner." Then there was a sentence Warren insisted upon because of his acrimonious exchange with Emory Rogers at the reargument: "But it should go without saying that the validity of these constitutional principles cannot be allowed to yield simply because of disagreement with them."[171]

While the courts should give due weight to public and private considerations, they "will require that the defendants make a prompt and reasonable start toward full compliance with our May 17, 1954, ruling." Once that start has been made, additional time may be necessary. In determining whether such time is needed, "the courts may consider problems related to administration, arising from the physical condition of the school plant, the school transportation system, personnel, revision of school districts and attendance areas into compact units to achieve a system of determining admission to the public schools on a nonracial basis, and revision of local laws and regulations which may be necessary in solving the foregoing problems."[172]

Then, instead of a decree, the opinion ended by reversing the judgments denying plaintiffs relief and remanding the cases "to the District Courts to take such proceedings and enter such orders and decrees consistent with this opinion as are necessary and proper to admit to public schools on a racially nondiscriminatory basis with all deliberate speed the parties to these cases."[173]

Then Warren concluded with the traditional formula, "It is so ordered."[174]

When the *Brown II* opinion declared that the lower courts were to ensure that blacks were admitted to schools on a nondiscriminatory basis "with all deliberate speed," it led to learned controversy on the origins of that phrase—itself so untypical of the normal Warren mode of expression. The phrase itself comes from Justice Oliver Wendell

Holmes. But it was used before him by the British poet Francis Thompson in an 1893 poem, *The Hound of Heaven*. After a newspaper account credited Frankfurter with suggesting the term in *Brown II*, several correspondents wrote asking whether he had gotten it from Thompson. The Justice replied, pointing out that "the phrase has a legal lineage older than Thompson's use of it. In a letter dated March 7, 1909, Mr. Justice Holmes wrote to his friend, Sir Frederick Pollock, 'in your chancery's delightful phrase, with all deliberate speed.' . . . Again, in his opinion in *Virginia* v. *West Virginia*, 222 U.S. 17, 20, he stated, 'in the language of the English Chancery, with all deliberate speed.' "[175]

Frankfurter wrote other correspondents that "I have made the most assiduous search to find Holmes's authority for saying this was a Chancery phrase"—but "all to no avail."[176] Nor has anyone else succeeded in tracing it to its alleged English legal derivation. "Yet," as Frankfurter insisted, "it cannot be that Holmes pulled it out of the air."[177]

But, if we remain uncertain where Holmes obtained the phrase, what is certain is that Frankfurter got it from Holmes and the *Brown II* opinion got it from Frankfurter. As early as January 1954, in a memorandum to the Brethren dealing with the enforcement problem, Frankfurter had written that "the court does its duty if it decrees measures that reverse the direction of the unconstitutional policy so as to uproot it 'with all deliberate speed.' *Virginia* v. *West Virginia*, 222 U.S. 17, 20."[178] Then, after he had read the *Law Clerks' Recommendations For Segregation Decree*, which the Justices received the day before the *Brown II* reargument, Frankfurter wrote at the top of his copy, "Va v W Va"[179]—showing that he was still thinking of the *Brown* decree in terms of the Holmes phrase.

A few days earlier, Frankfurter had tried his hand at the drafting of an actual decree. On April 7, he went over a typed draft of a proposed decree. The relevant part read, "On remand, the defendant school districts shall submit proposals for compliance to the appropriate lower courts." Frankfurter changed this, in his own handwriting, to, "On remand, the defendant school districts shall be required to submit w/all approp. speed proposals for compliance to the respective lower courts." He also added, "Decrees in conformity with this decree shall be prepared and issued forthwith by the lower courts."

The draft was retyped and gone over by the Justice the next day. This time, he crossed out the sentence requiring the school districts to submit "with all appropriate speed" proposals for compliance. And he changed the next sentence to read, "Decrees in conformity with this decree on the basis of detailed findings shall be issued by the appropriate lower courts with all deliberate speed, after due hearing on the relevant issues." This was the way Frankfurter's proposed decree read in its final typed form on April 14, just two days before the conference that met to consider the *Brown* enforcement question.[180]

Though Warren persuaded the conference that the Court should issue only an opinion, without any formal decree, he did retain the "all deliberate speed" language that Frankfurter had suggested—though, according to a 1958 Frankfurter letter, the phrase "was used, without credit (against my protest)."[181] The phrase was used in the Chief's opinion, not to instruct the lower courts when to issue decrees, but to guide them on when plaintiffs should be admitted to schools. This was a better use of the phrase, which was intended to indicate that desegregation was to move ahead but not be bound by any rigid schedule. Warren himself explained the use of the phrase in a statement he made after his retirement. It was used "because we realized that under our federal system there were so many blocks preventing an immediate solution of the thing in reality that the best we could look for would be a progression of action—and to keep it going, in a proper manner, we adopted that phrase."[182]

Black is said to have protested against the "all deliberate speed" language in the *Brown II* opinion. His son says that he tried to get the Court to abandon the phrase, and quotes him as saying, "It tells the enemies of the decision that for the present the status quo will do and gives them time to contrive devices to stall off segregation."[183] This Black statement is inconsistent with what he said at the April 16, 1955, conference on the *Brown* enforcement question. The Alabaman then had indicated that the Court should not try to settle the segregation issue too rapidly. If it attempted to do so, its decree "would be like Prohibition." Black, in fact, was the one Justice who predicted that the movement toward desegregation in the South would, at best, be only "glacial."

Warren, too, came to believe that it had been a mistake to qualify desegregation enforcement by the "all deliberate speed" language. In part, this was true because of the deteriorating relationship between the Chief and Frankfurter. In his later years, Warren concluded that he had been sold a bill of goods when Frankfurter induced him to use the phrase. It would have been better, he came to believe, to have ordered desegregation forthwith. By then, however, Black's prediction of the "glacial" pace of desegregation had proved, if anything, overoptimistic. The Justices had, to be sure, not expected enthusiastic compliance by the South. But the extent of opposition was something that had not been foreseen. Looking back, Warren, at least, felt that much of the defiance could have been avoided if the South had not been led to believe that "deliberate speed" would countenance indefinite delay. When a comparable problem arose in 1964 in connection with enforcement of the "one man–one vote" principle in legislative apportionments, the Chief did not hesitate to urge immediate enforcement, regardless of the problems in individual states in adapting to the new rule.

The bitterness of the South's reaction to the *Brown* decisions is, of course, now a matter of history. The obloquy directed at the Warren Court, the hatred of the Chief Justice culminating in the "Impeach Earl Warren" campaign—all had their origins in the desegregation decisions. The South resorted to every device, including pressure and intimidation, to block integration. As *The Oxford History of the American People* summarized it a decade after *Brown*, "In the lower South, the Supreme Court's decision was to all intents and purposes nullified and has remained so for ten years; John C. Calhoun would have been delighted!" [184]

The South even revived the doctrine of "interposition" relied on by Pre–Civil War Southern statesmen such as Calhoun. Soon after the *Brown II* decision, so-called resolutions of "interposition" were passed by several Southern legislatures. They asserted that the *Brown* decisions were "null, void and of no force or effect." [185] In light of this, the resolutions went on, the states declared their firm intention to take all appropriate measures against this "illegal encroachment upon the rights of her people."

What disturbed Warren in all this, more than the hate campaign, was the fact that the Court stood alone, unsupported by the President and Congress in the desegregation fight. Warren particularly resented the failure of the White House to speak out. "I still believe," wrote the retired Chief Justice in his *Memoirs*, "that much of our racial strife could have been avoided if President Eisenhower had at least observed . . . that it should be the duty of every good citizen to help rectify more than eighty years of wrongdoing by honoring that decision." [186]

Instead of urging support for the Court, Warren complained, Eisenhower "never stated that he thought the decision was right until after he left the White House"—and then only in a tepid way in his memoirs. [187] While in the highest office, Eisenhower refused to say whether he agreed with the *Brown* decision. "I think it makes no difference whether or not I endorse it," he ingenuously told a 1956 press conference. [188] Two years later, he was asked by a reporter whether it was true that he had told friends that he wished the Court had never handed down the *Brown* decision. The President replied that he might have "said something about slower." But he denied emphatically ever having said that he wished the Court had not decided as it did. [189]

All the same, during Eisenhower's presidency, stories continued to emerge from the White House that the President disagreed with the desegregation decisions. Warren always believed that Eisenhower resented *Brown*. The coolness that developed between the Chief Justice and the President who had appointed him stemmed directly from the Supreme Court decision. In Warren's pithy summary, "the *Brown* case was decided, and with it went our cordial relations." [190] After the decision, there were few meetings between the two that went beyond a formal "Good evening, Mr. President" and "Good evening, Mr. Chief Justice." On Warren's side, as Robert J. Donovan pointed out in a 1959 article, the estrangement came because of what the Chief "considered the failure of the President to take clear-cut and forceful action to give effect to the school-segregation decisions." [191] Warren used to tell his clerks that, if he were in the White House, he would take positive action to implement the Court's decisions in the school segregation cases. [192]

Warren had been careful to limit the first *Brown* opinion to desegregation in schools. But the decision necessarily had a broader impact. In *Bolling v. Sharpe*, [193] the District of Columbia school segregation case, the Court had declared, "In view of our decision that the Constitution prohibits the states from maintaining racially segregated schools, it would be unthinkable that the same Constitution would impose a lesser duty on the Federal Government." [194] It would similarly be unthinkable that the same Constitution would prohibit segregation in schools and impose a lesser duty on other public institutions.

Soon after the first *Brown* decision, the U.S. Court of Appeals for the Fourth Circuit was presented with the question of whether Baltimore could continue to segregate its public beaches. The court held that *Brown* required a negative answer. If segregation in schools generates a feeling of inferiority in Negroes, the same must be true, said the court, of segregation in recreational facilities.[195] In November 1955, the Supreme Court unanimously affirmed this decision without opinion.[196] At the same time, it unanimously reversed a decision upholding a segregated municipal golf course in Atlanta, citing in support only its decision in the Baltimore case.[197]

In 1956, the Court affirmed a decision striking down the segregated bus system in Montgomery, Alabama.[198] After the conference, Warren told his law clerks that they were going to affirm summarily, without hearing oral argument. He said they were going to cite three cases: *Brown* and the Baltimore and Atlanta cases of the previous year. The clerk who drafted the opinion recalls that, since he had no further guidance, he took the prudent course and simply followed the Chief literally. That is the way the per curiam opinion in the Montgomery bus case appears in the *United States Reports*—stating merely that the decision below is affirmed and citing only the three cases, without explaining what the Court was doing and the reasoning behind its decision.

The clerk involved says, "I thought at the time that it was a pretty casual way for the Court to advance a major proposition of constitutional law and still do." Legal scholars have voiced a similar criticism of the Court's failure to explain its extension of *Brown* to public facilities outside the field of education. The criticisms, however, are again beside the point. Was there a need for explanations once the *Brown* opinion—with the broad sweep of its language striking down separation of the races—had been written?

In the years after *Brown*, the Court ruled segregation invalid in all public buildings,[199] housing,[200] transportation,[201] and recreational[202] and eating facilities.[203] The Court, following Warren's lead, said as little as possible, but continued to strike down every segregation law challenged before it. By 1963, an opinion could declare categorically:

"it is no longer open to question that a State may not constitutionally require segregation of public facilities."[204]

Warren used to recall that, when he first arrived, the Supreme Court had a separate washroom for Negroes. One of the first things he did was to change the discrimination that was taking place right in the Court building itself. By the end of Warren's tenure, the Court had virtually rooted out racial discrimination from American law.

In other areas of the law, the new Chief moved more slowly. In his early terms, Warren, more often than not, was to be found with the conservative wing among the Brethren. A student of the Court, Glendon Schubert, wrote that in his first term Warren was "primarily a collectivist with strong authoritarian leanings" who showed "a trained incapacity to oppose the government in criminal cases."[205] The Court's neophyte was still "feeling my way," which meant "going along with the others"[206]—at least for a few years.

4.

1953—1954 TERMS: FEELING HIS WAY

On April 2, 1954, soon after Warren became Chief Justice, goose-quill pens were again placed on counsel tables in the Supreme Court chamber.[1] These had been provided from the Court's first session on February 1, 1790, until 1946, when the prewar supply ran out. Court traditionalists could rejoice that the disruption caused by World War II was finally over.

Things change slowly, if at all, at the Supreme Court. When Warren came to the Court, the page boys still wore knickers and double-breasted jackets, and counsel appeared in cutaway coats. The Justices and Court staff, except for menial employees, had always been white. In 1947, the law clerks wanted to give a Christmas party, inviting black employees. When Chief Justice Vinson discovered this, he brought the matter up before the conference. At least one of the Brethren, Reed, said that he would not attend if the blacks were invited. When he was told that that would place the Court in a "terrible position . . . after all the noble utterances of the Court publicly against racial discrimination," Reed said, "This is purely a private matter and I can do what I please in regard to private parties." Frankfurter interjected, "the very fact that we have been sitting here for nearly an hour discussing the right to hold the party makes it difficult to regard it as purely private. The Court is entangled no matter what way you look at it."[2] The proposed Christmas party was quietly shelved.

But even the most conservative institution must make some adaptations to changing conditions. After the ringing affirmation of racial equality in its *Brown* decision, the Court could no more continue the color line than it could maintain its separate white and black washrooms. In July 1954, the Court secured its first black page.[3] A month later, Frankfurter wrote to Warren, "It will interest you as much as it did me that the significance of the appointment of a Negro page should be noted abroad,"[4] and he enclosed a clipping on the matter from a London periodical. During Warren's tenure, the Court color line was further breached with the hiring of a number of black secretaries and law clerks (the first of the latter had been named by Frankfurter in the 1948 Term). Then, with Thurgood Marshall's appointment as a Justice in 1967, the Court itself became integrated.

Nor could the goose quills withstand the slowly changing order. Early in the 1961 Term, the pens and pewter inkwells for counsel were replaced by pencils.[5] A few years earlier, the Court clerk finally acquired a typewriter for docket entries. For over a century and a half, they had been entered in longhand. Then, in the 1963 Term, the Court pages ended a tradition of almost two centuries when they donned long trousers and single-breasted jackets. Four years earlier, the Court had given way on the annual party. At the end of 1959, the *New York Times* reported that "one of the last institutions holding out against the Christmas party succumbed last week," as the Court held its first such affair.[6] This time, there was no question of whether the entire staff should be invited. Five of the Justices (Black, Frankfurter, Douglas, Brennan, and Stewart) were there. The others were not in Washington during the holiday recess.

Other changes in the way the Court operated were made by the new Chief Justice. In June 1955, the Court announced a modification in its work schedule. The Court had been hearing cases Monday through Friday, with the weekly conference on Saturday. Warren changed this to a five-day week, with the conference on Friday. To balance this, he persuaded the Brethren to start Court sessions at 10 A.M., instead of the traditional noon.[7]

In June 1958, "decision Mondays" came to an end. Under the Chief's prodding, the Court began to deliver decisions when they were ready, rather than only on Mondays. Even outside the Court, not all considered the alteration a sign of progress. The *New York Times* reported that newspaper men had always admired the Court precisely because of its refusal to arrange its work for the convenience of the press.[8]

A more important Warren innovation was aimed at the one great defect of the Supreme Court's ornate courtroom. The chamber is a particularly handsome room, whose overpowering dignity befits the highest bench in the land. The room itself is as big as a basketball court, but there is not an acoustic in the place. Early in 1954, as the *New York Times* reported it, "Chief Justice Warren has come up with an astonishing idea. He thinks the members of the Court should be able to hear each other and be heard by lawyers . . . [so] the new Chief Justice has had the place wired for sound."[9] Microphones were placed before each Justice, and a tape recorder installed to take down oral arguments.

Frankfurter characteristically opposed the new sound system, insisting it would make the Brethren too conscious of the audience. Frankfurter could of course be contentious whenever alterations in the Court's procedure were proposed. In 1947, Chief Justice Vinson had proposed a change in the order of procedure on opinion day, so that admissions to the Supreme Court Bar would be the first order of business, with reading of opinions to follow. Vinson had acted as a courtesy to Senators and Congressmen, who had complained of having to wait for the completion of the opinions before presenting their constituents for admission. According to Frankfurter's diary, "When it came to my turn I spoke somewhat at length on the importance of not breaking with a tradition that is as old as the Court, that tradition, particularly in this disordered world, which is a fragile fabric, should be adhered to as one of the great social forces of justice unless change is called for in the interest of the administration of justice. . . . I asked the Conference to think twice and thrice before disobeying the injunction, 'Remove not the ancient landmarks of thy Fathers.' "[10]

When Vinson later announced that the change would be adopted, since a majority had supported it, Frankfurter wrote the Chief a strong protest headed, "This is a letter from a friend," which asserted that the Court should not "change its arrangements by a mere majority vote against the strong feeling of the minority."[11] The Frankfurter tendency to make a major issue out of such a minor change made it difficult for his less pesky colleagues. In 1956, Clark was asked by the Chief Justice to solicit funds for the United Givers Fund. The easygoing Texan readily assented and was met by a bristling Frankfurter letter, which asserted that it was "wholly wrong" to suggest the percentage of salary to be contributed. "Such a suggestion cannot but have some coercive influence and I think it is entirely wrong to exact such an influence." [12]

To Frankfurter, the prominence given to the admission of attorneys by the Vinson procedure change may have seemed misplaced. Others, too, have considered the personal admission a waste of time. Warren did not share these sentiments. He always stressed the importance of the admission ceremony. He used to say that the average lawyer would never have any opportunity to argue a case before the Supreme Court. The only experience he would ever have with the Court would be his admission to the Court Bar and he would consider that the pinnacle of his career. As Chief Justice, Warren said, he had the obligation to make that person feel accepted by the Court. That was why he would take the time personally to greet every applicant. "Every newly admitted attorney," reported *Newsweek* in 1955, "gets a smile" from the Chief Justice. [13] Warren always thought that the admission ceremony was one of the most important means by which he could help humanize the Court's operations.

The new Chief Justice displayed the same personal attitude toward everyone at the Court. He began by trying to meet everyone in the building. "I'm Earl Warren," he would say in his booming voice, as he shook hands with everyone, including the guards and plumbers. "When he says 'good morning,' he does it as if he hadn't seen you for a year," said one Justice. [14] His unpretentious manner and willingness to learn soon ingratiated him with his colleagues. At the beginning of the term, while the Brethren were deciding which of several hundred cases to hear, Warren would keep them informed of World Series developments by having notes passed into the conference room. [15]

There are those who assert that Warren's friendliness and unpretentiousness were only to project a favorable public image. He may, within a few weeks, have learned everybody's name, from the watchmen on up, and always have had time for a short chat and hearty laugh. [16] But this, they say, was second nature to the seasoned politician and did not reflect the inner persona, which was basically cold. The same was said of Warren's enthusiasm for sports. "I've always felt at least," says a former law clerk, "that spectator sport activities were kind of a shield, a way to be public without being personal."

It is, to be sure, always difficult to determine whether the public person and the private person are the same, or even similar—particularly where the former is part of a political image. "No one," a friend of Warren once said, "really knows this man." An early biography quotes a member of Warren's gubernatorial staff: "All day long we used to hear that booming voice, that belly laugh, that loud, 'How *are* you?' But sometimes in the evening when I worked late, I'd see him sitting in his office alone, his back to the door, his head bowed, and on that wall above him a sad, brooding picture of Lincoln. That's the Earl Warren few of us ever saw and none of us ever knew."[17]

Most of those who knew Warren, however, reject the alleged dichotomy between the public and private person. According to one of his former law clerks, Francis X. Beytagh, now Dean of the Toledo College of Law, "The Chief was a wholly consistent person, whether in public or in private, a quality rare among prominent public figures."[18] Beytagh stresses that Warren "knew the names of all the messengers around the Court, and all the secretaries personally, and he cared about them, he cared about the families of those people."

"How do you know he really cared?" Beytagh was asked, "Wasn't this just something he did because of his political background—he would know names, he would ask, but it wouldn't affect him personally?"

Beytagh replied that there was no way one could *really* know about such things, but "my impression is that he did care," based on incidents over the years that showed concern for others. One in particular stuck in Beytagh's mind. "I remember one guy that had been his messenger for years, and he said, 'God, you know, what an awful thing, one of his sons was killed in Vietnam.' And there was no reason he would have mentioned it to me except he was legitimately concerned about it."

Justice Potter Stewart tells how Warren would come to his chambers "to watch the World Series because . . . my secretary had the only television set in the building. He'd come in and say, 'Don't tell

Mrs. McHugh [Warren's executive secretary] where I am.' . . . He was like a little boy playing hooky." Certainly those who knew Warren best never doubted that his enthusiasm for sports was wholly genuine. Benno Schmidt, one of his clerks who is now a Columbia law professor, tells how he was playing on a hockey team and the Chief "knew nothing about hockey, but when he heard that I was playing he was very interested, and Mondays he would ask me how the game went on Saturday night . . . and he started watching hockey on television about that time, and he would ask me about it, when he didn't understand this or that aspect of it. So he was very, very interested in sports." Each year the law clerks would play the guards on the basketball court on the top floor of the Court building. The Chief, says Schmidt, "was a one-man rooting section for the clerks in that—we would always get crushed by the guards, but he would come up and watch the game and cheer and have a good time." [19] Those who knew him say that Warren was as unhappy as any Washingtonian when the Senators baseball team left Washington for Texas.

According to *Newsweek,* the Justices particularly liked the new Chief's calm and his vigor in pushing improvements in the Court's operation, such as the five-day week.[20] Aside from the few such innovations, however, Warren proceeded slowly in asserting his leadership role. Warren himself was the first to recognize that he was a judicial novice. The change from Governor to Chief Justice, he states in his memoirs, was made even more difficult "by my long absence from the courtroom." [21] Before he could establish himself as Chief in fact as well as name, he first had to familiarize himself with judicial work and the Court's procedure, as well as establish his own doctrinal underpinnings in the law.

Warren was a big enough person to seek help from the Brethren, while he familiarized himself with the way the Court operated. He sought the counsel of both Frankfurter and Black. In August 1954, Warren wrote to Frankfurter that he had "had an opportunity to do considerable reading. . . . I have also been reading all your decisions on 'Due Process.' Perhaps you will remember you gave them to me some time ago at my request. I am still endeavoring to orient myself in that field." [22]

While Warren was "still endeavoring to orient" himself, he asked

Black, as senior Justice, to preside at the first few conferences of the 1953 Term. Black's conference lists[23] indicate that he presided for the Chief at the first conferences of the term—those of October 10, 17, and 24, 1953. His work received the commendation of at least one of the Brethren. A handwritten note from Frankfurter told Black "how admirably I thought you conducted the proceedings. You stated, and stated well, the cases that should have been put to the Conference for discussion and guided the talk as talk should be guided—by a gentle but firm, or firm but gentle rein."[24]

Not only did Black preside at the first conferences. He also exercised one of the major prerogatives of a Chief Justice: that of assigning opinions. Black's conference lists state that he assigned opinions during the conferences over which he presided—including the first opinion assigned to the new Chief himself. That opinion was assigned at the October 17 conference, and delivered on November 9, only a month after Warren arrived at the Court, in *Voris v. Eikel*.[25] The case itself was a simple workmen's compensation case, where the lower courts had denied compensation to an injured longshoreman because he had not notified the employer of his injury as required by the statute. The short and simple Warren opinion reversed on the ground that it was enough for the worker to notify the foreman who was his immediate supervisor. The basic principle, said Warren, was that "this Act must be liberally construed . . . and in a way which avoids harsh and incongruous results."[26]

The opinion in *Voris v. Eikel* foreshadowed the typical Warren approach in cases involving what he was to consider his particular "constituency" while he was on the Court. "I often thought to myself," says Justice Potter Stewart, "that, if the Chief Justice can see some issue that involves widows or orphans or the underprivileged, that he's going to come down on that side." Warren would, whenever possible, go out of his way to protect minorities, individual workers, and institutions, such as the family, in which he strongly believed.

One case, early on, however, ran counter to this, and Warren himself once told Edward Bennett Williams that if there was any vote he had cast as Chief Justice that he could change, this would be it.[27] It was his deciding vote in *Irvine v. California*,[28] argued in his second month on the Court. This case arose after police officers secretly entered Irvine's house and installed a hidden microphone in the bedroom. Officers at a nearby listening post recorded incriminating conversations that were used to secure a conviction for bookmaking. Warren cast the fifth vote to sustain this conviction. Despite the patent police illegality, the bare majority held the case to be governed by *Wolf v. Colorado*,[29] which had ruled that the use of illegally obtained evidence to secure a conviction in a state court did not violate the U.S. Constitution.

According to Douglas, who dissented, "The search and seizure conducted in this case smack of the police state, not the free America the Bill of Rights envisaged."[30] The police conduct was so offensive that even Frankfurter, apostle of judicial restraint that he was, could not go along with the majority. At the conference on December 5, 1953, Clark had said that he was prepared to overrule *Wolf v. Colorado,* but unless he was in a majority, he would vote the other way—i.e., to apply *Wolf.* Clark did in fact finally write a concurring opinion agreeing with the majority result. On December 29, 1953, Frankfurter wrote Clark that *Irvine* and *Wolf* were different cases. "The controlling circumstance in this case . . . ," Frankfurter stated, "is that there was conduct by the police in obtaining this evidence which went way beyond merely not having a search warrant for the assailed evidence." *Irvine* involved more than a mere application of *Wolf,* since the *Irvine* evidence had been obtained through such extreme police methods. "I know," Frankfurter's letter concluded, "there are some Catholics who are more Catholic than the Pope. You do not have to be more *Wolfish* than *Wolf.*"[31]

Students of the Supreme Court have long been puzzled over Warren's position in *Irvine.* A few years later, he would certainly have voted the other way. At the *Irvine* Conference, however, Warren's presentation showed that he still saw such a case from the viewpoint of the district attorney he had been. "There's no doubt," he began, "but that petitioner's rights were infringed." Warren then referred to the *Wolf* case and also to *Rochin v. California*[32] a case in which the police had forcibly used a stomach pump to extract narcotics that the defendant had swallowed. *Rochin* decided that evidence obtained by so outrageous a method that shocks the conscience may *not* be used in a state criminal trial. The question, as Warren saw it, was, "Shall we rely on *Wolf,* or does the conduct rise to the indecency of *Rochin?*" "In cases of this kind," Warren went on, "we must consider whether the state encourages this kind of conduct. Here, it has slipped in. In California, we do not permit wiretapping at all. The California statute okay's dictaphones only when okayed by the police. Hence, it does not outrage my sense of decency and I'd affirm."[33] It is interesting here that Warren displayed, as he did throughout his judicial career, an almost proprietary interest in California law. He was always sensitive to challenges to California laws and procedures. In 1965, the California indeterminate sentencing law, which had been passed as part of Warren's gubernatorial program, was challenged before the Supreme Court.[34] At the cert conference, Justice John Harlan, who came from New York, voted to grant certiorari. Warren bristled. "You wouldn't have voted that way, John, if it had been a New York law."

In any event, at the *Irvine* conference, Black passed, but Frankfurter and Douglas urged that the ruling in *Rochin* should be followed. Burton said that what the police did would have been all right had it been done in an office, but not in a home, and that he also would vote to reverse. From Warren's point of view, however, the most important conference statement was that made by Jackson. Referring to the hidden microphone, Jackson asserted that "the fact they kept it for a month is bad—also their breaking in. But is this any worse than other cases we've okayed here?" In some ways, Jackson went on, "this offends me worse than *Rochin:* I don't want people breaking into my house. But we have said a state may adopt its own rule of evidence; so we must concede that the state has some latitude." The police action here may have been "officious," but it is "doubtful" that it violated due process.[35]

Since Reed, Clark, and Minton went along with Warren and Jackson, there were five votes for affirmance, and because Warren had been impressed with Jackson's presentation, he assigned the opinion to him. At the beginning of February 1954, Jackson circulated an opinion for the Court affirming the California conviction. Clark, however, refused to join it and wrote his separate concurring opinion to which reference has been made. Jackson's opinion thus was delivered on February 8 as that of a plurality. The other four Justices dissented, with separate dissenting opinions by Black, Frankfurter (joined by Burton, to whom Frankfurter had written "to tell you what comfort it gives me to have you share the views I've expressed in *Irvine*."),[36] and Douglas.

In later years Warren told his law clerks that the *Irvine* case "really bothered" him. After all, even Jackson's written opinion, which the new Chief joined, conceded that few police measures had come to the Court's attention "that more flagrantly, deliberately, and persistently violated the fundamental principle declared by the Fourth Amendment." Indeed, asserted Jackson, "that officers of the law would break and enter a home, secrete such a device, even in a bedroom and listen to the conversation of the occupants for over a month would be almost incredible if it were not admitted."[37]

Though Warren went along with the majority decision, he and Jackson went out of their way to state that, if the police had willfully violated the Fourth Amendment, their conduct constituted a federal crime. The clerk of the Court was "directed to forward a copy of the record in this case, together with a copy of this opinion, for attention of the Attorney General of the United States."

Warren told his law clerks that nothing ever came of the forwarding of the record and opinion to Attorney General Herbert Brownell, that no investigation was ever instituted by the Department of Justice. "I don't know how the Chief found that out," says one of the clerks, "but I assume he may just have asked Brownell what had come of it. And I think that case was a kind of symbol for the Chief."[38]

To Warren, the *Irvine* case and the Department of Justice's nonaction must have been a revelation. Following the doctrine of judicial restraint, he had distinguished between what belongs to the courts and what belongs to the Executive. Although there had been a Fourth Amendment violation, it was not for the courts to reverse the state conviction because evidence secured by the violation had been introduced. The remedy for the violation was not with the judicial, but with the law-enforcement branch. As a district attorney and Attorney General, Warren had vigorously prosecuted violations. He felt confident that the Department of Justice would do the same when the illegal police actions in *Irvine* were brought to the Attorney General's attention. The failure of the Department of Justice to do anything showed him that his confidence was misplaced.

From this point of view, *Irvine* had a crucial effect on Warren's thinking. His natural tendency as a former prosecutor may have been to adopt the judicial restraint approach in criminal law cases. But, if that meant in practice that constitutional rights would remain unenforced, he had to consider the need for a more activist role. The same was true whenever the political branches failed to vindicate constitutional rights or curb constitutional abuses. In such cases, Warren believed, with Black and Douglas, that judicial restraint relegated the violated constitutional provisions to the status of paper principles. As Warren put it in an interview just after he retired as Chief Justice, either the Court itself would act to enforce the constitutional guaranties involved in these cases, "or we let them go and sweep them under the rug, only to leave them for future generations."[39] During the rest of his first Court term, two other cases gave him the opportunity to demonstrate his protective inclination.

The first was *Hernandez v. Texas*,[40] where Warren could show that his concern for minorities was not limited to discrimination against blacks. Hernandez had appealed his murder conviction on the ground that persons of Mexican descent were systematically excluded from jury service in Jackson County, Texas.

To Warren, *Hernandez* presented a simple case. At the conference on January 16, 1954, Warren said that, while there was no right to racial proportional representation on juries, the evidence was that Texas had completely disqualified a section of the population solely because of their national origin. This the state could not do consistently with the Fourteenth Amendment's requirement of equal protection.[41] On May 3, two weeks before the school segregation decisions were announced, Warren delivered a short opinion, based upon a draft by Richard Flynn, his law clerk who worked on the case and who happened to have lived in that particular part of Texas, which reversed the conviction. Warren rejected the contention "that there are only two classes—white and Negro—within the contemplation of the Fourteenth Amendment."[42] Instead, said Warren, the amendment "is not directed solely against discrimination due to a 'two-class theory'—that is, based upon differences between 'white' and Negro.'"[43]

The *Hernandez* decision was the first to strike down discrimination not directed at blacks. The *Hernandez* Court was unanimous, but two of the Justices almost did not join their Brethren. Clark thought the opinion presented an unfair picture of his native Texas and was prepared to dissent. He persuaded Minton to follow him, but then decided to join the majority. He informed Warren of this in a short note on April 29: "While Shay and I think that your facts—as related—set up a 'straw man' we have decided not to dissent on the factual basis. You have covered the law in the field so well that we go along with you." [44]

Frankfurter had also expressed concern about two aspects of the *Hernandez* opinion. At the end of April, he had written to Warren saying, "Of course, I am for your result," but objecting to his discussion of the "two-class" theory, on the ground that it was not limited to "ensuring an undiscriminating jury system. Is it not highly undesirable to make such generalized pronouncements prior to the disposition of the Segregation Cases?" [45] Frankfurter also opposed reference in the opinion to discriminations against Mexicans other than exclusions from the jury, such as segregated toilets, as well as school segregation and exclusion from a restaurant. Warren did not change the opinion, despite Frankfurter's characterization of his first objection as "particularly important."

According to Justice Stewart, "Warren's great strength was his simple belief in the things which we now laugh at—motherhood, marriage, family, flag, and the like." Near the top in the Warren hierarchy of values was the family. To Warren, the Court's proposed decision in another case during his first term threatened the very institution of the family in our society. The case in question was *Alton v. Alton,* [46] where the issue was the constitutionality of the Virgin Islands Divorce Law. The law authorized divorces where the plaintiff had spent six weeks in the islands. The lower courts had ruled the statute unconstitutional on the ground that the Constitution makes domicile a prerequisite to divorce jurisdiction, and that it was unreasonable to infer domiciliary intent from six weeks' residence.

The *Alton* case was argued on April 7, 1954. The session was dominated by Frankfurter's questioning of Abe Fortas, which was so persistent that Fortas, who argued in favor of the divorce, was never able to present his argument. So harassing was the questioning that, as time ran out, Warren intervened and gave Fortas additional time. But the same thing happened again, and Fortas finally gave up trying to complete his argument.

In the last chapter, Warren's first conference on *Brown v. Board of Education* [47] was used to illustrate what Fortas himself noted after he had served on the Warren Court—that the Chief would present cases in terms of ultimate moral values. The *Alton* conference on April 12 [48] is another striking example. Warren began his presentation by asserting, "The very conception of the place of the family in our civilization, and our constitutional system in placing domestic relations within the control of the states, in effect subjects each state to some regard for the interests of other states in the marital relations of their citizens. No state is free to do what it pleases in dissolving the marriage of citizens of another state." Instead, for a valid divorce, there must be domicile in the divorcing state.

"Consensual divorce," Warren asserted "giving any state the right to dissolve the marriage status when that state had no relation whatever to the marriage status except giving the divorce, is inadmissible under our constitutional scheme. And of course the Virgin Islands legislation is, in effect, legislation to authorize consensual divorce, because the six-week residence, if both parties agree, . . . is merely a formality for getting a divorce. My conscience won't permit me to have this Court decide that one of the territories can disregard the interests of all the states by issuing consensual divorces."

Except for Frankfurter, none of the Brethren supported the Warren position. Black expressed his typically literal view of the Constitution: "There is nothing in the Constitution to prohibit this legislation, and we're not authorized to write anything into the Constitution to prohibit it. That's all there is to it and I don't think we have a right to amend the Constitution of the United States." Reed, Burton, Clark, and Minton thought that the statute established a reasonable prima facie presumption of domicile.

Frankfurter strongly backed Warren. He started with a jibe at his great rival: "I could understand Black, that each state can abrogate the marriage without regard to any tosh about domicile and that's that." Frankfurter conceded that domicile was not necessary to most lawsuits. "Domicile isn't necessary to recover the purchase price of a second hand automobile that Mrs. Alton sold to Mr. Alton if she sues him in Nevada and he puts in a general appearance. Why not in these instances and why in divorce? For the simple reason that release from marriage isn't a suit for a note or a bill of sale."

Frankfurter then referred directly to Warren's emphasis on marriage and the family. "What the Chief says about marriage being the basis of society . . . has consequences in life and in law which differentiates it from the sale of a second hand car. That difference is what underlies the concept of domicile, which simply means that before a state can divorce two people, who seek an escape outside the state in which they really live and propose to live, one of the parties must have some relation of substance, some relation that has some aspect of permanence, to the divorcing state."

One can understand how Frankfurter would get on the Brethren's nerves by his tendency to play the professor expounding elementary law to a freshman law class. On the other side, one can sympathize with his sometimes tart reaction to the remarks of the lesser intellects in the conference room. Several of them insisted that this was simply a case of the legislature determining the requisites of domicile and what satisfies them on the matter. When Minton repeated that view, Frankfurter notes, "I discourteously interrupted to say I thought it was a little late, in view of *Marbury v. Madison,* to say that judicial review is barred by legislative action."

The conference indicated a strong majority in favor of upholding the challenged divorce law. A seven-page printed opinion for the Court was circulated on April 24 by Clark, which stated, "The elementary question is the reasonableness of presuming domiciliary intent from six weeks' residence. We disagree with the courts below and hold the presumption a reasonable exercise of the legislative authority of the Virgin Islands Assembly."[49]

When Frankfurter received a copy of an April 29 letter from Reed to Clark saying, "I have decided to go along with your opinion," he wrote, "Do you suppose that those whom you respect most of those who sat here would have allowed such 'phony' stuff to go out?"[50]

Not only were all the Brethren except Warren and Frankfurter in favor of upholding the challenged divorce law. Warren's law clerks recall that they disagreed with the Chief more on this case than on any other during the 1953 Term. But Warren, according to Justice Stewart, could be "very stubborn. Once he had made up his mind, you could not get him to change it. He would stick to it regardless of facts and arguments." Particularly in a case like this, Warren was prepared to fight for his position, and he wrote a strong memorandum of dissent.[51] From its language and the fact that his clerks do not recall working on it, we can assume that this dissent was drafted by Warren himself. "Instinctively," Warren's draft asserted, "I feel this territorial statute constitutes a fraud on all the states. It is an attempt to disregard the institution of marriage as it is established, protected and preserved by each state for its own citizens." This case "brings us as close to the line of consensual divorces as it is possible to be without actually being there." If this law is upheld, the Court would be compelled to uphold any consensual divorce law. Even if, as some believe, "we will eventually arrive at that situation . . . , it seems to me that the Federal Government should not force it on the states through territorial law and a decision of this Court."

Warren then stressed that "marriage is our basic social institution. It is inherent in our civilization as well as in our colonial and national life. True, it is not mentioned specifically in the Constitution, but neither have many other problems that have been considered by this Court to be governed by the Constitution. I have no doubt it was considered as being ingrained in American life by all of the makers of the Constitution."

The draft dissent went on to "doubt if at any time since the adoption of the Constitution any state would have been admitted to the Union if its provisional government had authorized consensual divorces for citizens of other states." It follows, wrote Warren, "that domicile must, therefore, be inherent in the divorce laws of every state." Without domicile, no state can have divorce jurisdiction. "Domicile can be acquired in six weeks or six days or six hours where there is an intention to do so, but six hours can make no prima facie case of domicile without the all-essential element of intent. This statute clearly attempts to accomplish this purpose . . . by making mere physical presence for the statutory period a prima facie domicile without any evidence of intent." This constituted "an intrusion on the judicial function" and "also fails to respect the interests of other states of the Union." Warren concluded, "I would affirm the judgment of the court below."

As it turned out, the new Chief Justice was saved from the embarrassment of having to dissent against an overwhelming majority by the fact that Mr. Alton secured a divorce in Connecticut, where he was domiciled, before the Supreme Court decision could be announced. This rendered the case moot. As Frankfurter wrote Warren, "the changed aspect of Alton v. Alton" meant that the case should be "thrown out by us."[52] And, on June 1, 1954, the Supreme Court issued a brief order dismissing the case. The Clark opinion of the Court and the Warren dissent were consequently never delivered; neither the division in the Court nor Warren's stubborn defense of the family, in the face of strong opposition from virtually all of those around him, was made public.

The story is told at the Supreme Court that Justice James C. McReynolds was once late to conference. Chief Justice Charles Evans Hughes told a messenger, "Go tell him we're waiting." The testy McReynolds sent word back: "Go tell the C.J. I don't work for him."

The Justices had an entirely different attitude toward Chief Justice Warren. As a Justice remembers it, the Brethren soon developed the practice of gathering in the conference room before the Chief arrived and rising to their feet as he entered. Then after they went through their formal ritual of exchanging handshakes, Warren would take his seat at the head of the table and call out, in his cheerful tone, "Hey-ho, let's get going." He would then go down the cases on the conference agenda. His job as Chief was essentially that of presenting the issues involved before opening the floor to discussion by the others.

Justice Stewart recalls that "always, after stating the case, he would very clearly and unambiguously state his position." Then, hesitating, Stewart modified his statement: "I said always, but there would be an exception every now and then. About one in a hundred cases, there would be some tax case in which there would be some conflict in the circuits, and . . . he would say, 'Look, our duty is to resolve this conflict. I'm not a tax lawyer. I'll go whichever way you want to go on this, just go with the majority and get this conflict resolved . . . I just have no view on this one.' "

Even in those cases, says Stewart, "I often thought to myself he only does that when he can't see something involving these eternal, rather bromidic, platitudes in which he sincerely believed." It should be stressed, as Stewart recognizes, that "they were not platitudes for him: the family or the underprivileged or the widows or the orphans. . . . With him it wasn't cant and you very soon realized that it wasn't."

The indecisiveness in Warren's conference presentations in the tax cases, where his protective instinct for the weak and underprivileged did not come into play, was displayed most infrequently. Normally, in presenting cases at conference, the Chief Justice was not hesitant in stating his own opinion before opening the cases for discussion.

Describing Warren's role at the conference, Justice Byron White says that "he would state his position and he usually had his mind made up. He usually had a pretty firm view of the case."

Justice William J. Brennan, talking to a reporter after Warren had retired, said, "It is incredible how efficiently the Chief would conduct the Friday conferences, leading the discussion of every case on the agenda, with a knowledge of each case at his fingertips."[53] All the Justices who served with him lay stress on Warren's ability to lead the conference. Warren's predecessors had been notably inept in their conduct of conferences. According to Frankfurter's diary, Chief Justice Vinson presented cases in a shallow way. He "blithely hits the obvious points . . . disposing of each case rather briefly, by choosing, as it were, to float merely on the surface of the problems raised by the cases."[54] Chief Justice Harlan F. Stone, on the other hand, says Frankfurter, had "the habit . . . of carrying on a running debate with any justice who expresses views different from his."[55]

Justice Stewart confirms that he heard that "Stone's problem was that, at a conference, he himself always insisted upon having the last word, and that's not the way you preside—always arguing with the person that had spoken." The result, Stewart heard, was, not a discussion, but "a free-for-all." Warren's conduct of the conference was entirely different. He would rarely contradict the Brethren at the conference, and he would make sure that each of them had his full say—even Frankfurter, whose tendency to treat the session as a Harvard seminar would grate on the Chief just as much as it did on the others. Warren, according to Justice White, "never felt he had to get the last word in."

Above all, Warren possessed the ability to present cases in a manner that set the tone for the conference discussion. He would state the issues in cases in a deceptively simple way, which would get to the heart of the matter, stripped of legal technicalities, and, where possible, relate the issues to the ultimate values that concerned him. This technique was used from the beginning of his judicial tenure. As Stewart summarizes it, "he was an instinctive leader whom you respected and . . ., as the presiding member of our conference, he was just ideal."

Warren's ability to present cases at the conference, as soon as he took over the presiding role, may be seen from Clark's conference notes in five cases during Warren's first term.[56] None of the cases was of any great importance. Instead, they enable us to see how Warren conducted the conference in comparatively run-of-the-mill cases, free of the pressures under which, according to the Oliver Wendell Holmes aphorism, "Great cases like hard cases make bad law."[57]

In *Howell Chevrolet Company v. National Labor Relations Board*,[58], the Board had acted against a large Chevrolet dealer in California, which claimed as a defense that its business did not "affect commerce," as required by the Wagner Act. At the November 14, 1953, conference on the case, Warren's statement was incisive and to the point: "This is not a corner grocery case, as was argued. The method of operation puts them in the stream of commerce. I'd sustain the Board." And all agreed except Douglas, who subsequently dissented, without opinion.

The other cases saw the same type of Warren presentation. *Wilko v. Swan*[59] involved the issue of whether an agreement to arbitrate a future controversy was a waiver of the right to sue under the Securities Act. Warren's conference statement on October 24 said, "As I see it, we have to reconcile the arbitration statute with the Securities Act. I'd say they could not waive their statutory rights [under the Securities Act] and I'd reverse."

United States v. New Britain[60] presented the question of the relative priority of federal and municipal liens on the proceeds of a mortgage foreclosure sale of property to which the liens attached. At the October 24 conference, Warren stated, "If this were an insolvency case, the United States would have priority, but this is not such a case. If Congress wanted it to have priority, then it would have said so. The prior in time, prior in right theory should govern." All agreed except Douglas. And when, on February 1, 1954, Minton delivered the Court's opinion based on the Chief's statement, there was no dissent.

In *United States v. Binghamton Construction Company*,[61] the issue was whether the schedule of minimum wage rates in a government construction contract was a "representation" or "warranty" that the contractor would not have to pay more, even if the prevailing wage rates in the area were higher. Warren started the December 5 conference discussion by saying, "the only point in it is that the Government is a guarantor according to respondent. The Government disclaimed responsibility on its announcement of the minimum scale. Respondent had no right to rely on it." All agreed and Warren himself delivered a unanimous opinion on March 8 in favor of the government. The winning counsel in the case, incidentally, was Warren E. Burger, who was to succeed Warren as Chief Justice fifteen years later. This was the first case argued by Assistant Attorney General Burger in the Supreme Court.

Of the 1953 Term cases under discussion for which we have Clark's notes, the most interesting was *Public Utilities Commission of California v. United Air Lines.*[62] The case was argued on November 12 and 13, 1953, a month after Warren arrived at the Court. United had argued that it was not subject to the California commission's jurisdiction on rates charged for transportation between the California mainland and Catalina Island. United contended that the federal Civil Aeronautics Board had exclusive authority over these rates. At the November 14 conference, Warren urged, "the state should be permitted to proceed. There's nothing to show the state is going to do all the horribles pictured by United. They should proceed through the administrative process." Except for Reed and Douglas, the others agreed. Douglas thought the case was peculiarly appropriate for declaratory judgment, and wrote a dissent, joined by Reed, to that effect. The case was decided on November 30 by a short per curiam, on the authority of a decision requiring exhaustion of administrative remedies. Warren apparently thought better of participating in a case involving a California agency whose members he had appointed as Governor. The report of the case states (not entirely accurately in view of his conference participation), "The CHIEF JUSTICE took no part in the consideration or decision of this case."[63]

So from the start the new Chief Justice showed a clear ability to lead the conference. Even so, he was anything but an activist in the first of his Court terms. During that time, he was largely under the influence of Frankfurter and, more often than not, followed the latter's position of judicial restraint. Much of the early history of the Warren Court can, indeed, be presented in terms of the relationship between Warren and Frankfurter.

When Warren became Chief Justice, he was assiduously courted by Frankfurter, who sought to win the new Chief to his own judicial philosophy. At first, the courtship appeared successful. Within a few years, however, the Chief Justice became a vigorous adherent of judicial activism, rejecting the Frankfurter posture. The altered Warren approach was accompanied by increasing personal recrimination between the Chief and his rejected mentor, which culminated in unprecedented acrimonious exchanges in open court.

According to Justice Stewart, Frankfurter "was as fickle as a high school girl. I understand . . . that, when Earl Warren first came to the Court as Chief Justice, Felix was going around Washington saying, 'This is the greatest Chief Justice since John Marshall and maybe greater.' And by the time I got here [1958], Felix Frankfurter had very much been disenchanted by the Chief Justice."

Stewart's account is not overdrawn. At the beginning, Frankfurter's appraisal of the new Chief was glowing. A few days after Chief Justice Vinson's death, Frankfurter wrote, "What is most needed in a Chief Justice is what the Germans call *ein Tonangeber*—a tone-giver: one who by his example generates in the others complete dedication to the work of the Court."[64] Soon after Chief Justice Warren had been sworn in, Frankfurter indicated that the Court had found its *Tonangeber*.

Oliver Gates, the son of an English friend, had inquired about the new Chief. "You ask," Frankfurter wrote back less than a month after Warren's appointment, "whether I 'like' him. The short answer is I do and I am sure you would. But I shall detain you longer to answer your other question: What do I 'think of him?'"

Frankfurter's answer conceded that the new Chief "has not had an eminent legal career, but he might well have had had he not been deflected from the practice of the law into public life. He brings to his work that largeness of experience and breadth of outlook which may well make him a very good Chief Justice provided he has some other qualities which, from what I have seen, I believe he has."

Frankfurter then went into the qualities needed by a Chief Justice:

First and foremost, complete absorption in the work of the Court is demanded. That is not as easy to attain as you might think, because this is a very foolish and distracting town. Secondly, he must have great industry because, as you might infer from what you observed when you were here, for about nine months of the year it is a steady grind. Further, he must have the capacity to learn, he must be alert to the range and complexities of the problems that come before this Court. Under our constitutional system almost any question may be made to take the form of a legal controversy for settlement in this Court. One more requisite: you doubtless have observed the different ways in which people listen. Intent, open-minded, patient listening is a surprisingly rare faculty even of judges. The new Chief Justice has it, I believe, to a rare degree.

The Frankfurter letter concluded with a warm estimate: "The up-shot of it all is that I like him as a human being. He is agreeable without being a back-slapper; he is informal but has native dignity. Perhaps I ought to add that his interest in baseball is as great but as sensible as yours. For the reasons that I have indicated I also think he will turn out to be a very good Chief Justice." [65]

When C. C. Burlingham, an eminent New York lawyer and a close confidant, also asked Frankfurter his opinion of the new Chief Justice, Frankfurter replied with a copy of his letter to Oliver Gates. Early in 1954, Frankfurter wrote Burlingham, "the Chief Justice . . . has been discharging that office for four months with true regard to its highest standards." [66] Some months later, writing Burlingham about Warren's speech to the American Bar Association, Frankfurter declared, "he did not mouth the usual Bar Association emptiness or worse. He said things that much needed to be said and you can be sure of one thing: he spoke his own words and not some ghost's." [67] Frankfurter's early attitude toward the new Chief was summed up in an April 1954 letter written to Jackson, on a problem before the Court: "E.W. . . . showed the understanding that comes from caring for the real responsibility that that problem implies. What a pleasure to do business with him." [68]

In 1947, John Gunther had asserted that Earl Warren had "little intellectual background, little coherent philosophy." [69] As soon as he took his place on the bench, however, Warren was faced with a choice that would have to be made between the antagonistic judicial philosophies of Black and Frankfurter. In simplified terms, the Black–Frankfurter division was between judicial activism and judicial self-restraint. Black was willing to follow the rule of restraint only in the economic area. But he felt that the Bill of Rights provisions protecting personal liberties imposed on the Court more active enforcement obligations. To Frankfurter, judicial restraint was the proper posture for a nonrepresentative judiciary, regardless of the nature of the asserted interests in specific cases.

To Black and Frankfurter, Warren's accession presented an opportunity to acquire a crucial convert. As Professor Fred Rodell put it, "both Frankfurter and Black badly wanted him on their side and recruited him, from conference sessions, to Court corridors, to chats in chambers."[70] The situation was graphically described in *Time* after Warren retired: in his early years the new Chief Justice was "a large, powerful sphere of iron drawn between two magnetic poles."[71] At first, he was drawn toward Frankfurter. As time went on, however, Warren, more a man of action than reflection, found Black's activist posture preferable.

Frankfurter, in particular, made a massive effort to cultivate the new Chief Justice. He bombarded Warren with notes, memoranda, articles, and even texts intended to inculcate the Frankfurter view. On October 8, 1953, for example, only three days after Warren was sworn in, Frankfurter sent him an article on "the day-to-day work of a Chief Justice."[72] A few days later, Frankfurter, writing that "a remark of yours the other afternoon encourages me to send you some more literature,"[73] sent Warren his 1927 volume, *The Business of the Supreme Court*,[74] as well as his later articles surveying the conduct of the Court's business.

Frankfurter continued to send Warren materials in his effort to influence the new Chief. "Since you are short of reading matter," began a typical note (with unintended irony) from Frankfurter to Warren, "I am sending you this."[75] In January 1954, Frankfurter wrote the Chief, "Time has a nasty way of racing and May will be here before we'll know it,"[76] and enclosed materials to help Warren in preparing the report that the Chief Justice customarily delivered on the work of the Court at the May meeting of the American Law Institute. Frankfurter also sent Warren all of his opinions on due process, materials on the Commerce Clause which he hoped would be "helpful as direction for dealing with specific cases as they arise,"[77] and a decision of the English Court of Criminal Appeal to help Warren on his opinion in a case on admissibility of testimony by a woman against her former husband.[78]

Warren was hardly the type to labor over most of the mass of materials sent him. Frankfurter himself may have been aware of this. "I have not been left unaware," he once wrote the Chief, "that from time to time you have been rather puzzled by what you deem my technicalities, in the derogatory sense of the term."[79] Another time, Frankfurter ended a long letter to Warren on a case, "concerned with technicalities in the true sense of the word," with the wry comment,

"You will, I hope, at the worst be only bored by this discussion and forgive me for inflicting it on you."[80] Despite this, Warren could not help but be impressed by the personal efforts to win him over by the intellectual leader of the Vinson Court.

What is plain is that, while Warren was, as he put it in a 1954 letter to Frankfurter, "still endeavoring to orient myself"[81] in the judicial role, the personal relationship between the Chief and the Justice was close. When Warren first came to Washington, he intended to buy a house. Frankfurter and his wife helped in the house-hunting. Once, when he called Warren's attention to a house out on Massachusetts Avenue, Frankfurter stressed that his wife, who had told him about the house, "has never been inside it and, therefore, does not go bail for it."[82] As it turned out, Warren was unable to find a suitable house. He settled on a comfortable seven-room apartment in the Sheraton–Park Apartment Annex, where the Warrens lived until the Chief Justice's death.[83]

During Warren's early Court years, the relationship between him and Frankfurter was close enough for Frankfurter to suggest a "thoughtlet" for Warren to include in his first address as Chief Justice.[84] Warren accepted the suggestion warmly, writing on the speech manuscript, "The thought you gave me Friday fitted nicely into my manuscript. It appears on the last page."[85] Frankfurter similarly helped Warren on an address on Justice Louis D. Brandeis,[86] advised the Chief on whether President Eisenhower should be sworn in for his second term on a Sunday,[87] and spoke to the Ambassador of Israel about Warren's contemplated visit to that country "on a scholarly non-political occasion."[88]

As late as 1959, Frankfurter gave Warren this kind of help. At the top of a manuscript headed *Notes for Moscow,* Frankfurter penned in, "Written by F.F. for the C.J. for his remarks at American Exhibition in Moscow. After he read it, he said, 'If you don't mind, I'll take this straight, without changing a comma.' August 5, 1959."[89] By that date, however, the relations between the two men had begun to deteriorate. In a note attached to the manuscript, Frankfurter directed his secretary to see that it was appropriately filed and closed with a sarcastic "Unghostilly yours, FF."[90]

Five years earlier, Frankfurter had written Warren that, in the Chief's first speech to the American Bar Association, "you said important things that needed to be said. Unlike the usual palaver at Bar Associations, your utterance was wholly free from self-righteous complacency. . . . Finally, a man spoke, the man himself, not a ghost."[91] At the end of the 1953 Term, Frankfurter ended a letter on the segregation decree, "I hope you will be going to your beloved California before very long. I cannot close without saying again what a happy year this has been for me and I am sure for all the others."[92]

Frankfurter's feelings toward Warren reflected the influence that he had exercised during the new Chief Justice's first term. While Warren was still feeling his way in his judicial role, he was, more often than not, to be found in the Frankfurter wing of the Court. Thus, during Warren's first term, he and Black disagreed in twenty-two cases.[93] "When the generation of 1980 receives from us the Bill of Rights," Warren wrote in a 1955 *Fortune* article, "the document will not have . . . the same meaning it had when we received it from our fathers."[94] During Warren's first terms, the Bill of Rights was not being interpreted differently than it had been under his predecessor.

The initial hesitation of the judicial novice may have tended Warren toward the passive approach embodied in the Frankfurter judicial posture. In addition, as we have observed in the *Irvine* case,[95] it took some time for the new Chief Justice to free himself from his prosecutorial background. One observer went so far as to assert that, in his first term, Warren's record was that of "primarily a collectivist with strong authoritarian leanings" whose experience as a prosecutor showed "a trained incapacity to oppose the government in criminal cases."[96] The most striking of these criminal cases was of course *Irvine* itself, discussed near the beginning of this chapter.

Even more incongruous, in terms of Warren's later libertarian cast, was his action in *Barsky v. Board of Regents*,[97] decided in April 1954. Warren there joined a six-to-three decision which upheld the six-month suspension of a physician's license because he had been convicted of a misdemeanor for failing to produce papers of the Joint Anti-Fascist Refugee Committee, of which he was chairman, before the House Un-American Activities Committee. Here, too, as in *Irvine v. California*, Frankfurter had refused to join the majority. Judicial abnegation, in his view, did not require judicial abdication in the face of what his dissent termed "destruction of a man's professional life on grounds having no possible relation to fitness, intellectual or moral, to pursue his profession."[98]

In the main, however, during his first terms, Warren tended to follow the Frankfurter approach. He joined in another decision upholding a statute allowing illegally seized evidence in a state gambling prosecution;[99] delivered the opinion in a case sustaining, as against a double jeopardy claim, a conviction on both substantive counts and a conspiracy to commit them;[100] joined a Frankfurter opinion refusing to overturn the deportation of an alien who had been a member of the Communist party;[101] wrote the opinion upholding the Federal Lobbying Act against First Amendment attacks;[102] and concurred in a decision upholding an immunity statute against Fifth Amendment assertions.[103]

During his first two terms, even when Warren rejected the governmental claims, he tended to follow the Frankfurter approach of avoiding wide-ranging constitutional issues wherever possible. In *International Longshoreman's Union v. Boyd*,[104] decided in March 1954, a union sued to enjoin the Immigration and Naturalization Service from interpreting the relevant statute so as to treat aliens domiciled in the continental United States, who were returning from temporary work in Alaska, as if they were aliens entering the United States for the first time. Frankfurter wrote an opinion for the Court that dismissed the suit, on the ground that, until the I.N.S. applied its interpretation to a specific alien, there was no concrete case as required for proper exercise of the judicial function. On March 4, Warren wrote Frankfurter, "I agree."[105] On February 2, Douglas had also signified his agreement.[106] On March 6, however, in a note headed "3:20 AM," Douglas wrote to Frankfurter, "I am going with Hugo in the *Boyd* case."[107] When the decision was announced, Black, joined by Douglas, delivered a dissent.

An even more striking illustration of Warren's early willingness to avoid constitutional issues was presented in the 1955 case of *Peters v. Hobby*.[108] Peters had been removed by the Loyalty Review Board from his position as special consultant to a federal agency on the ground that "there is a reasonable doubt as to Dr. Peters' loyalty to the Government of the United States." Peters claimed that the denial of opportunity to confront and cross-examine his accusers violated his constitutional right to due process. The Loyalty Review Board had been set up under a presidential order giving it authority to review dismissals in loyalty cases. The order provided that "cases may be referred to the Board either by the employing department or agency, or by the officer or employer concerned." In this case, the Board had taken the case on its own motion, acting to conduct a "post-audit" of the agency's determination in Peters' favor.

During the argument, on April 19, 1955, Warren intervened to question closely Warren E. Burger, arguing for the government. Burger had argued that no punishment was involved in the loyalty proceeding. The Chief interjected; "If a man, in addition to dismissal, is barred from public employment for three years, isn't that punishment?" Burger replied, "Not in the constitutional sense." At which Warren asked, "Suppose he were barred for life?" [109]

The exchange is of interest both because it shows the differing approaches of Warren and his successor as Chief Justice and because it foreshadows Warren's position on the issues raised a few years later in the Expatriation Cases. Warren also got Burger to concede the secrecy of loyalty proceedings even as against the Supreme Court. "Mr. Burger," asked the Chief, "did I understand you to say that if the petitioner comes to the Court on the merits, all the information available to the Board would be in the record?" "No sir," came back the reply. The record, said Burger, was only the record of the evidence taken by the Board. "But," said Warren, "that would be only the testimony of the petitioner's witnesses." "That's right." Burger explained that he did not wish to give the Court the impression that it could have access to the secret information used by the Loyalty Review Board. "That would take an order of the President." [110]

Obviously irritated, the Chief Justice sarcastically concluded, "Then it seems to me we would accomplish nothing by having the petitioner bear the cost of printing his own evidence." [111]

At the argument, Thurman Arnold, appearing for Peters, declared that he wanted to win on the constitutional right to confront and cross-examine. At this, Justice Frankfurter interposed, "The question is not whether you want to win on that ground or not. This Court reaches constitutional issues last, not first." [112]

At the conference on April 23, [113] Warren noted that the case raised the constitutional issue, but urged that the Court should not decide it. There was, said Warren, a clear violation of the President's order that could not stand. If a majority of the Court wanted to reverse on procedural grounds, they could do so, reserving the constitutional point. Black and Douglas argued that the Court should reverse on the constitutional issue, but the other Justices who spoke in favor of reversal—Frankfurter, Clark, and Harlan—agreed with the Warren approach. Frankfurter, like Warren, stressed the procedural point on which the case could turn without reaching the constitutional issue. He repeated the point he had made at the argument—that counsel could not confer jurisdiction to review the constitutional issue. There was ultra vires action here, and the case should be decided on that ground. Frankfurter further developed his view in a memorandum, written "just after argument," which stressed the "cardinal rule controlling constitutional adjudication, that it should not reach a question of constitutional law unless absolutely necessary to decision." The basis on which the case should be decided was the lack "of authority in the [Loyalty Review] Board to 'review' on its own motion cases determined favorably to the employee by an agency board." [114]

On May 26, Warren circulated an opinion of the Court that was delivered on June 6. It followed the Frankfurter memo's approach, holding that, under the presidential order establishing it, the Loyalty Review Board had no authority to reopen the case on its own motion after Peters had twice been cleared by the loyalty board of the agency in which he was employed. To justify his approach, Warren relied specifically on the rule that "this Court has declined to anticipate a question of constitutional law in advance of the necessity of deciding it." [115] The Warren opinion toned down some of Frankfurter's language—eliminating, for example, the statement in Frankfurter's memo that "the [President's] order cannot be so read [i.e., to give the Loyalty Review Board the claimed power]—certainly not to bring about so harsh a result in a domain which is so disregardful of what ordinarily are basic requirements of due process."

Black and Douglas wrote separate opinions urging that the President's order did give the Board review authority and that, therefore, the constitutional issue must be reached. On it, they both strongly urged that the loyalty procedure's failure to afford full opportunity to confront and cross-examine violated Peters' constitutional rights.

At the April 23 conference, Reed, Burton, and Minton voted to affirm. Minton later agreed to join the Warren opinion, making it the opinion of a majority of the Court. Reed, joined by Burton, delivered a dissent asserting that the Board's review authority had "undoubtedly" been authorized by the President. On June 1, Frankfurter wrote Reed, "I think your 'undoubtedly' is almost as humorous as Brother Douglas' suggestion that since the Attorney General now speaks for the President and asserts the President's power in the past, the Court must say 'Aye, aye Sir.' 'You and I know,' if I may quote an FDR-ism, that in all the cases in which the validity of a regulation is in issue before this Court the Attorney General assures us that the regulation is a valid exercise of power." [116]

Earlier, Douglas had sent a handwritten note to Black: "I hope we can work it out so that *Peters* does not go off on the narrow ground of the Regulations. . . . A decision on the merits would be a wonderfully healthy thing. A decision on the regulations would, I fear, be tantamount to a victory for the Government. For their system of the Faceless Informer would continue." [117]

Arthur Krock complained in the *New York Times* that the *Peters* decision was an "obvious surprise," since it was based on an issue never raised by the lawyers on either side. [118] In fact, Thurman Arnold had been asked, during the argument, "Do you say that the Review Board did not have authority to review the case?" He answered, "No, we are not raising that question." [119] But the opinion of the Court was consistent with the Warren posture in his early Court years. Even an informed observer could say then that "Warren . . . had moved directly into former Chief Justice Vinson's position of moderate conservatism." [120] To Frankfurter, it must have seemed safe to assume that he had gained a critical convert for his judicial posture.

There was, to be sure, one area in which Warren did not follow the Frankfurter approach, even in his first years on the Court. In cases involving claims of racial discrimination, the new Chief adopted an activist posture from the beginning. In the last chapter, we saw how Warren led the Court in summarily extending the *Brown* principle against segregation to cases outside the field of education. In two other cases presenting racial issues during Warren's early years, Frankfurter persuaded the Brethren to avoid a decision over the new Chief's strong opposition.

In a commemorative article in the *American Bar Association Journal* on Warren's death, William O. Douglas wrote that, though the Chief

Justice would be remembered most for his opinions in the *Brown* school segregation case[121] and *Reynolds v. Sims,*[122] the 1964 reapportionment case, "in many ways the lesser cases mirrored the philosophy of the man. [A cemetery in] Sioux City refused burial of an Indian . . . because it had been reserved 'for Caucasians only.' The petition for certiorari aroused deep feelings in Earl Warren, and he voted to take the case. He did not write a word in the case but he was quite upset when the majority disposed of it on a rather technical ground."[123]

The action of the cemetery in refusing to bury the Indian, because the contract for the burial lot restricted "burial privileges . . . only to members of the Caucasian race," was plainly an act of racial discrimination. The deceased's wife had claimed in her action for damages that the restrictive provision violated the Fourteenth Amendment's guaranty of equal protection. The difficulty was that the amendment applies only to discriminatory acts by a state, and the cemetery in question was operated by a private company.

In the leading case on the subject—*Shelley v. Kraemer,*[124] decided in 1948—the Court had held that a racially restrictive clause in a private contract did not violate the Fourteenth Amendment, since it involved private, not state, action. However, if a state court issued an injunction to enforce the restriction, equal protection would be denied, since the court's decree would constitute state action. Was the same true when a state court relied upon the contract restriction as a defense to an action for damages?

The conference on November 13, 1954,[125] showed that the Brethren—temporarily reduced to eight by Jackson's death—were sharply divided on this question. In presenting the case, Warren conceded that the issue was "not entirely clear." As he saw it, however, "this woman who makes this contract does not have to go give up this contract if a clause is illegal." Yet, even if the theory of the clause's illegality was not sustained, "plaintiff may be entitled to damages for the manner in which the contract was broken." Although he recognized the broad implications in such a decision, the Chief said that he would vote to reverse.

Black and Douglas were also in favor of reversal. Black said that there was a cause of action and the only defense was the discriminatory clause. For the Court to uphold the defense was the same, in effect, as for it to enforce the clause in favor of the cemetery. Douglas asserted a similar view, saying that if the cemetery had come to court to prevent burial, "we would not put the court's force behind it and this is the same thing." Clark made a fourth for reversal, emphasizing also that the cemetery "can't go into court to keep him out"; the like result should be reached where "here they took the law into their own hands."

The other Justices voted to affirm. Reed said that, though he was bothered "by the way this was done," that was not the issue. The issue, as Reed saw it, was, "Can a private cemetery company select the race it will bury?" Frankfurter, like Warren, noted the broad implications of the case: "We can't decide this case without deciding a lot of others. If you reverse this, you reverse the *Civil Rights Case*"— i.e., the 1883 decision that the Fourteenth Amendment applied only to state action.[126] The real question, Frankfurter asserted, was, "Does the Fourteenth amount to an F.E.P.C.?"[127] A reversal would convert the amendment into a wholesale prohibition against all discrimination, even that committed entirely by private individuals. Burton and Minton agreed with the Reed—Frankfurter view. They emphasized that the cemetery did not contract to bury the deceased, saying they could not see how refusing to enforce a contract that they did not make would violate the Constitution.

When the Justices divide equally, the practice in the Supreme Court is to affirm the decision of the lower court without any opinions. On November 15, the Court announced that it was affirming in *Rice v. Sioux City Memorial Park Cemetery*[128] by an evenly divided Court. No indication was given regarding the grounds of the division or the way the Justices had voted. After Justice John Harlan took his place as Jackson's successor at the end of March 1955, the plaintiff filed a petition for a rehearing before a full Court.

The conference that considered the petition refused to deny the rehearing, though Clark, Burton and (according to a letter from Burton to Frankfurter)[129] "several others" were in favor of the denial. Frankfurter then circulated a memorandum[130] that suggested that, instead of setting the case down for reargument, the Court should dismiss the writ of certiorari as improvidently granted—i.e., certiorari should never have been granted. Frankfurter relied on an Iowa statute passed after the case had begun which provided that any cemetery contract permitting racial discrimination was null and void. The statute provided, however, that it would not "affect the rights of any parties to any pending litigation." "Accordingly," said Frankfurter, "any adjudication on the merits by this Court would be merely an adjudication of this single case." Had that been the case when certiorari was sought, the Court would have voted not to hear the case, and the same should be true "even at this late date."

The solution proposed by Frankfurter was, as Douglas characterized it in his already-quoted article, "rather technical." It masked the real basis for his proposal, stated frankly in another portion of the memo: "There can hardly be any doubt that so far as a claim under the 14th Amendment is concerned, this Court will divide 5 to 4. It seems to me highly undesirable to stir the embers of racial discrimination by a division of 5 to 4 in this Court, on which ever side the division falls, and particularly at this time. Nor does it make any difference that the division may be a division on what constitutes 'state action.' The fact that will matter in the present heated state of opinion is a division."

Warren and Black opposed avoiding the constitutional issue, as Frankfurter suggested. On May 4, Black sent Frankfurter a handwritten note, "I cannot go along with your opinion. But I doubt if any good purpose would be served by a written dissent."[131] Black, however, reconsidered, and he wrote a dissent, joined by the Chief and Douglas, which declared that cert had been granted because serious questions were raised concerning a denial of equal protection: "Those questions remain undecided."[132] The draft of the dissent was sent to Frankfurter with Black's note: "This is the way the CJ and I finally agreed on."[133]

The other Justices, except for Harlan, who took no part in the case, went along with Frankfurter's proposal, with Clark voting to make a five-man majority despite his original vote to reverse at the November 13 conference.[134]

Another 1955 case where Warren would have seized the discrimination issue by the constitutional bit was *Naim v. Naim.*[135] The case arose out of an action in Virginia by a white woman to have her marriage to a Chinese man annulled on the ground that it violated the Virginia miscegenation statute. The parties had left Virginia to be married in North Carolina, concededly "for the purpose of evading the Virginia law which forbade their marriage." The Virginia Supreme Court ordered the annulment, rejecting the husband's claim that the statute violated the Fourteenth Amendment. The Virginia court relied on an 1883 case upholding an Alabama law prohibiting interracial cohabitation, as well as *Plessy v. Ferguson*,[136] asserting that the *Brown* school segregation decision[137] did not affect the issue here. The Virginia court also relied on the fact that "as recently as November 22, 1954," the Supreme Court had denied certiorari in a case in which a black had been convicted of violating Alabama's miscegenation law.[138] Warren, Black, and Douglas had voted to grant cert in that case, but they had failed to secure the necessary fourth vote.[139]

The *Naim* case came up to the Supreme Court on appeal from the Virginia decision. The Justices could either dismiss for want of any substantial federal question or note probable jurisdiction and set the case down for argument. Here, too, four votes were necessary for jurisdiction to be noted. At the conference on November 4, 1955, that considered the matter, Warren, Black, Reed, and Douglas were recorded in Burton's docket book as voting to note probable jurisdiction. Clark's docket book recorded only the first three as so voting, with the others noted as voting to dismiss.[140] The matter was not decided, since the case was held over for a week at Clark's request, so he could study it further.

During the November 4 conference, Frankfurter read a typed statement that urged the Court not to decide the case. Frankfurter stated that, even if the issue presented was "of a seriousness that cannot be rejected as frivolous, I candidly face the fact that what I call moral considerations far outweigh the technical considerations in noting jurisdiction. The moral considerations are, of course, those raised by the bearing of adjudicating this question to the Court's responsibility in not thwarting or seriously handicapping the enforcement of its decision in the segregation cases."

Frankfurter said he assumed there would be "serious division here on the merits." The prepared statement concluded with the assertion, "that to throw a decision of this Court . . . into the vortex of the present disquietude would . . . seriously, I believe very seriously, embarrass the carrying-out of the Court's decree of last May"—i.e., the decree in the *Brown* school segregation case.

Frankfurter added to his statement by pointing out that what he had said "assumes that the main issue in this case is presented on this record free from subsidiary or preliminary questions. Such is not my reading of the record. I believe the contrary is true."[141]

After the conference, Frankfurter worked with Clark on a per curiam opinion that would remand the case on technical grounds, without any consideration of the merits. Frankfurter suggested an order dismissing the appeal "for the reason that the record is inadequate." Clark rewrote this to note that the record was inadequate as to the "citizenship of the parties at the time of their marriage" and that the husband had failed "to raise questions here, such as full faith and credit, which might be dispositive." Clark concluded that, because the issue was not presented "in a clean cut and concrete form," the appeal had to be dismissed.[142]

Frankfurter wrote back, "Your proposal fills me with hope, confident hope, that my anxiety will soon be lifted." He indicated, however, that his "preference is for the shortest and least explicit formula, & so I would substitute for f.f.& c. [full faith and credit] its deletion, leaving the idea to some such generality [as] 'to raise all questions relevant to the disposition of the case.' "[143]

Clark adopted Frankfurter's suggestion and circulated the final draft of the per curiam. At the second conference on the case, on November 11, the Brethren voted seven-to-two to adopt the Frankfurter—Clark draft. It was issued as a per curiam opinion on November 14:

Per Curiam: The inadequacy of the record as to the relationship of the parties to the Commonwealth of Virginia at the time of their marriage in North Carolina and upon their return to Virginia, and the failure of the parties to bring here all questions relevant to the disposition of the case, prevents the constitutional issue of the validity of the Virginia statute on miscegenation tendered here being considered 'in clean-cut and concrete form, unclouded' by such problems. *Rescue Army v. Municipal Court,* 331 U.S. 549, 584. The judgment is vacated and the case remanded to the [Virginia] Supreme Court of Appeals in order that the case may be returned to the Circuit Court of the City of Portsmouth for action not inconsistent with this opinion.[144]

At the November 11 conference, the dissenting votes had been cast by Warren and Black. A dissenting statement was sent to Clark in Black's handwriting, which Clark appended at the end of his circulated per curiam: "Mr. Justice Black, being of the opinion that this record properly presents a question arising under the United States Constitution, would note jurisdiction and set the case for arguments on that question."[145]

The dissenting statement was withdrawn by Black, largely at Warren's urging. The Chief had felt strongly on the case. According to one of his law clerks, "he was furious. He thought that was a failure to take the Court's responsibility." But Warren thought it was generally wrong to file dissents from denials of certiorari or similar actions. He had the clerk work all night on the draft of a dissent, but in the morning thought better of it and decided to go no further on the dissent.

Countless students of constitutional law have puzzled over the enigmatic *Naim* opinion. But the majority, led by Frankfurter, was simply seeking a make-weight excuse to avoid dealing with the miscegenation issue so soon after the school segregation decisions. As a former Warren law clerk puts it, the reaction in the South would have been, " 'Well, you know, first blacks in the school room, and then the next thing they are going to be doing is sleeping with your daughters and marrying your daughters,' and so on, the mongrelization of the races. And so I think the Court back in 1955 . . . didn't want to deal with it right away, it wanted to build up to it." [146] A memo on the *Naim* case to Justice Burton by one of his law clerks took the same position: "In view of the difficulties engendered by the segregation cases it would be wise judicial policy to duck this question for a time." [147]

Warren simply refused to accept this point of view in a case involving racial discrimination. The clerk who worked on the projected dissent explains that the Chief "thought . . . that they really had to deal with the issue. It was too bad that it had come so soon, but we just couldn't have enforceable laws based on race and marriage. . . . He was very angry about that and thought they hadn't carried out their clear responsibility and that they had to deal with these things, however impolitic it may be."

Warren's anger was pungently expressed at the ultimate outcome of the *Naim* case. The Supreme Court had remanded to the Virginia court so that the case could be returned to the trial court to be reopened for clarification of the record. On remand, the Virginia court balked at complying with this mandate. It stated that "the record . . . was adequate for a decision of the issues presented," that the issues had been fully adjudicated, and that Virginia law contained no provision for sending the case back to the trial court to be reopened. "We therefore adhere to our decision . . . holding that the marriage of the parties to this cause was void." [148]

The Brethren saw fit to turn their cheek in the face of this rebuff by the Virginia court. Although the husband immediately took the case again to the Supreme Court, that tribunal issued only a two-sentence March 12, 1956, per curiam refusing to take action on the ground that the Virginia decision on the remand "leaves the case devoid of a properly presented federal question."[149]

Warren felt that the Supreme Court had exposed itself to the kind of response it had received and that it got no more than it deserved from Virginia. When the Virginia court announced that it was sticking to its prior decision, the Chief exclaimed in disgust, "That's what happens when you turn your ass to the grandstand!"

Among the cases decided by the Court, few must have interested the new Chief Justice more than those presenting the issue of whether professional sports were subject to the Sherman Anti-Trust Act. In the 1922 case of *Federal Base Ball Club v. National League*,[150] the Court had ruled in an opinion by Justice Holmes that professional baseball was not commerce and that thus a Sherman Act case alleging monopolistic practices could not be brought. By the time Warren was appointed Chief Justice, the Court had adopted a much broader conception of interstate commerce, and an attempt was made in the 1953 case of *Toolson v. New York Yankees*[151] to have the Court overrule the *Federal* case. The Court refused to do so, instead issuing a brief per-curiam opinion reaffirming the baseball exemption on "the authority of *Federal Base Ball Club*."[152]

Yet, though both *Federal* and *Toolson* ruled baseball exempt from the anti-trust law, there was a significant difference. In *Federal*, this ruling was based on constitutional grounds, since the holding that baseball was not commerce placed it beyond the reach of congressional power. In *Toolson*, the Court stated that the authority of *Federal Base Ball* was confirmed, "so far as that decision determines that Congress had no intention of including the business of baseball within the scope of the federal antitrust laws."[153]

The quoted passage was added to the *Toolson* opinion at Warren's urging. At the *Toolson* conference on October 17, 1953, the Chief had expressed reluctance to reaffirm *Federal*. He indicated finally that he was willing to do so, "but I would want to make it clear that Congress has the right to regulate baseball if and when it desires to do so."[154] When he read over the draft *Toolson* per curiam, he wrote

Black, its author, that, as far as congressional power was concerned, the draft "is not clear and might be misunderstood by others." Warren, therefore, suggested that the language quoted at the end of the last paragraph "be added to the end of the *Per Curiam.*"[155] In an October 24 *Memorandum for the Conference,*[156] Black did add the suggested passage.

Warren's lifelong interest in athletics led him to look coldly on exemptions of professional sports from the anti-trust law. The result, he believed, was to deprive employees of what had become big business of protections available to those who dealt with other large businesses. He was ultimately willing to go along with the *Toolson* decision continuing baseball's exemption, yet only, as he expressed it in a 1955 case, as "a narrow application of the rule of *stare decisis*"[157] and only with the express disclaimer that the Court was not holding that Congress did not have authority to regulate baseball.

But Warren was unwilling to extend baseball's exemption to other professional sports. He was given the opportunity to demonstrate this during his second year on the Court, when the government appealed the dismissal of an anti-trust action against the International Boxing Club and others engaged in the business of promoting professional championship boxing contests. The case was joined with a similar suit against the Shubert brothers, who produced theatrical shows and booked them in theaters operated by themselves and others throughout the country. The lower court had dismissed both actions on the authority of the *Toolson* and *Federal Base Ball* cases.

At the November 13, 1954, conference[158] on the *International Boxing*[159] and *Shubert*[160] cases, Warren began by indicating that he would vote to reverse in both cases. "We can't," he asserted, "extend *Toolson* or *Federal Base Ball* to these cases. I would leave it to Congress to extend [the exemptions] to other sports or entertainment. Holmes intended *Federal Base Ball* to extend only to baseball. *Hart v. Keith*[161] [where Holmes wrote the opinion in 1922] shows that he believed theaters could be within the Anti-Trust Act."

Warren said that he could concede that the legitimate stage and boxing exhibitions standing alone were local in character. But the other things involved—booking, distribution, and so forth—could bring them within "commerce." In actuality, Warren concluded, "Baseball is commerce, but the Court has relieved it on its facts."

Most of the Brethren followed the Chief's lead. Black noted that he had tried to confine the *Federal* case principle to baseball, saying that he thought it wrong to overturn it after thirty years. By now, it was "as though Congress had excepted baseball by name." Reed, Douglas, and Burton also agreed to reverse in both cases. Frankfurter and Clark had no difficulty in approving such a result in *Shubert*. But both thought that the *International Boxing* case presented more difficulty. Frankfurter asserted, "I find it difficult to imagine Congress exempting only baseball and leaving other sports in." At this Black interjected, "Congress would not have exempted any. It's the Court which did exempt baseball." Clark said, "I don't want to say that baseball is out merely on stare decisis. The stronger reason is that Congress thought sports ought not to be covered."

Minton alone voted to affirm in both cases, asserting the view that baseball was not commerce and that the same was true here. The theatrical productions and boxing matches were not commerce. The other things referred to were incidental: "the tail should not wag the dog."

Warren considered the *International Boxing* and *Shubert* cases important enough to assign the opinions to himself. On January 31, 1955, he delivered opinions of the Court reversing in both cases. The opinions followed the approach Warren had outlined at the November 13 conference, refusing to extend the anti-trust immunity recognized by the *Toolson* and *Federal Base Ball* cases beyond baseball. Frankfurter, who had expressed doubts about the boxing case, delivered a sharp dissent, which ironically declared "that this Court gave a preferred position to baseball because it is the great American sport." [162] Minton also dissented. Clark, who had indicated doubts at the conference about the boxing case, had been persuaded to join the Warren opinion.

Frankfurter felt strongly that there was no logical basis for holding that baseball was the only sport outside the scope of the Sherman Act. After Warren had shown him a copy of his draft opinion in the boxing case, Frankfurter wrote the Chief on the ruling that baseball alone was exempted: "Once the matter is argued it becomes hard sledding." No matter how much he considered it, Frankfurter said, "that still leaves me the worry whether we can differentiate baseball from other sports which, so far as the Sherman law is concerned, *i.e.,* the ingredients of interstate commerce, are indistinguishable." [163]

Frankfurter must have been pleased when he received a February

3, 1955, letter from noted federal Judge Jerome Frank: "I, too, can't differentiate boxing and baseball." Frank also sarcastically "queried whether local playing of baseball differed from the locally indulged conduct condemned by the Mann Act."[164]

The new Chief Justice likewise led the Court to its decision avoiding an important constitutional issue in *United States v. Guy W. Capps, Inc.*[165] The issue was the legal effect of an executive agreement. The provisions of a treaty, duly ratified by the Senate, override conflicting federal statutes. Is the same true of an executive agreement, entered into on the authority of the President alone?

In the *Capps* case, the government sued for damages on an alleged contract to import seed potatoes from Canada. The action was based on a claimed violation of an executive agreement with Canada that sought to regulate the import of Canadian potatoes. The court of appeals decided against the government in an opinion by Judge John J. Parker, whose nomination to the Supreme Court by President Hoover had been turned down by the Senate. Parker ruled that the executive agreement contravened the provisions of a federal statute that governed limitations on agricultural imports. In such a case, the executive agreement could not be given effect.[166]

The Supreme Court had never decided the constitutional issue disposed of by Parker. At the November 20, 1954, conference[167] Warren proposed that the issue should not be dealt with. Referring to the decision below against the government, the Chief said, "Let it stand." But he proposed reaching that result without deciding the constitutional question. Instead, he would prefer to have the case go on the grounds given by the district court, that neither a valid contract nor damages had been proved. Warren, too, stated that he would exonerate the defendants from damages, as there was no adequate proof of any contract violation or damages. All the others agreed, and on February 7, 1955, an opinion of the Court following the Chief's approach was delivered by Burton.

At least two of the Brethren indicated their views on the constitutional issue. Warren himself had stated at the conference that "the Government was entitled to make such agreements." He recognized that the relevant statute provided for imposing import limitations through the Tariff Commission, under the President's direction. But, he asserted, it "was not the only procedure allowable for the President. It contemplated other international agreements." Black also said, "If I had to reach this question, the Government had the right to make these agreements." Burton's opinion of the Court did not, however, touch even inferentially upon the executive agreement issue. As Frankfurter had stressed at the conference, the opinion was written to "allow no basis to quote us on the issue."

In *Capps*, Frankfurter explained in a later memorandum to the Brethren, "in order to avoid entanglement in the explosive issue . . . the whole Court exercised not a little astuteness to have the case go off on a different ground to such an extent that the fact that the power to make treaties and executive agreements was in issue was not even mentioned but was discreetly covered up by reference to 'other questions' which we said there was no occasion to consider." [168]

Warren's early adherence to the judicial restraint wing of the Court may also be seen by his position in *Regan v. New York*, [169] another case where he would have decided differently in later years. Regan was a New York City policeman called to testify before the grand jury. He signed a waiver of his immunity against prosecution as to matters he testified about. Section 903 of the New York City Charter provided that any city employee who refused to sign such a waiver should be dismissed. Before the grand jury, Regan refused to answer certain questions, claiming his Fifth Amendment privilege against self-incrimination. He was convicted for criminal contempt.

At the conference on January 8, 1955, [170] Warren noted that "section 903 provides for loss of job on refusal to testify [and] to waive immunity." In the Chief's view, "it is constitutional. It was not forced testimony, but merely that he can't hold his job if he refuses." Warren said he would vote to affirm. The others agreed, except Black and Douglas.

Frankfurter's law clerk had tried to persuade him that the inquiry had been one "designed to get" Regan and hence was "fundamentally unfair." Frankfurter wrote back that that was not the issue presented here. "To my mind," he asserted, "there is a great difference between asking a fellow to testify *to get him* and asking him to testify as a relevant witness in a general investigation." [171]

At the conference, Frankfurter supported Warren on the constitutional issue. He was, however, concerned, as he stated in a letter to Warren, [172] that the Court not indicate "that there exists the privilege against self-incrimination under the federal Constitution in a state proceeding." For the Court to do so would be for it to adopt the theory urged by Black in his famous 1947 dissent in *Adamson v. California* [173]—that the Fourteenth Amendment incorporates the entire Bill of Rights. That would make all the Bill of Rights provisions, such as the Fifth Amendment privilege against self-incrimination, binding upon the states. "I should think," Frankfurter declared in his letter to Warren, "the theory of the incorporation by reference of the Bill of Rights in the Fourteenth Amendment involves such monstrous results that Hugo has never faced up to them. Namely, it would mean that by the adoption of the Fourteenth Amendment the legal systems of many of the ratifying states would have been turned topsy-turvy. Specifically, it would mean of course that all the states that do not begin criminal prosecutions with indictments would have to do so and *Hurtado v. California,* 110 U.S. 516, would have to be thrown in the ash can. It would mean that every civil suit for $20 would require a trial by jury, etc., etc."

In January 1955, Frankfurter wrote Reed, to whom the *Regan* opinion had been assigned, in a similar vein. He started by apologizing for telling Reed how the opinion should be written. "Of course, the writer of the Court's opinion must write according to his style. But, he is, after all, not singing a solo, but leads the orchestra to wit, the Court." Frankfurter urged Reed not to cast any doubt on the settled constitutional rule that the Fifth Amendment was not binding on the states. "You have heard my song before and I am afraid you will hear it as long as we are on the Court together, but nothing but mischief comes from talk that a case does not call for, particularly where constitutional issues are involved." [174]

To emphasize his point, Frankfurter sent Reed a paragraph draft concurrence, stressing, "This case presents no problem under the Fifth Amendment. That Amendment does not apply to the States—a conclusion which this Court reached and has adhered to for over half a century after the fullest argument and the deepest deliberation." On the merits, the Frankfurter draft declared, "The short answer to petitioner's case is that Regan called under ordinary circumstances for testifying as a witness, had the duty of testifying like any other witness, and the due process clause does not prevent New York from subjecting him to the duties of an ordinary witness." [175] Frankfurter wrote to Reed that the draft was not to be published.

The opinion of the Court, delivered by Reed on April 25, 1955, did avoid the constitutional question. It held only that Regan could be punished for his refusal to testify, regardless of the effect of the waiver of immunity. Black, joined by Douglas, dissented on the ground that the Fifth Amendment, made binding on the states by the Fourteenth Amendment, was violated.

Warren, as indicated by his conference statement, felt no doubt on the constitutionality of the New York requirement that a policeman testify and waive immunity or lose his job. But he was troubled by the possibility that the city employee who lost his job for refusing to testify might later be prosecuted if, on a subsequent hearing, he should incriminate himself after claiming his privilege against self-incrimination. Warren discussed this difficulty with Frankfurter, who wrote to the Chief suggesting a way out of the dilemma: "there is a way of affirming the conviction and that is by indicating that while Regan could be compelled to testify, he had that duty after he resigned from the force only if he was assured immunity from prosecution on the basis of his testimony. I think an opinion could be written in which this conclusion is to be attributed to New York law namely that he is not to be prosecuted for giving his testimony and that the so-called waiver of the New York immunity statute held good only so long as Regan had the status of a policeman."[176]

Warren wrote a short concurring opinion along the lines suggested. He was joined by Clark. Surprisingly, Frankfurter himself did not join, stating only that he concurred in the result reached by the Court.

Not long after Warren's first Court term, retired Justice Owen J. Roberts wrote to Frankfurter, "It looks as if the new Chief Justice is making you fellows work overtime. Do you get one and a half times straight pay for such overtime [?]"[177] By the end of his first term, Warren had settled completely into his new judicial role. Though Warren had been in politics most of his life, wrote *New York Times* columnist James Reston, he "is now in love with the court."[178] The quiet, scholarly life on the bench, said Reston, had proved much more satisfactory to the new Chief than he had ever imagined. A *Newsweek* article quoted Warren: "To me, the Chief Justiceship of the United States is the most important job in the world."[179]

5.

1954 — 1955 TERMS: MOVING TOWARD ACTIVISM

"One has to look far these days," according to an article in the *New Republic* at the beginning of 1956, "to find a self-respecting newspaperman who would consider writing a political story without mentioning in the third or fourth paragraph that in the event General Eisenhower should choose retirement, Chief Justice Earl Warren will loom in the minds of many Republicans as their last best hope for 1956."[1]

If Warren thought that his removal to the Judicial Palace would end speculation about his political future, he was mistaken. Even before 1956, the political pundits had begun to consider whether Warren might make himself available for the next election. In February 1955, a *New York Times* article had asked whether Warren would be willing to run if Eisenhower did not. It pointed out that Warren seemed to have made an unusual number of speeches for a Chief Justice.[2]

Those who knew him say that Warren was distressed by such articles. He felt that the discussion of his possible candidacy would only interfere with his duties and hurt the Court.[3] To quiet the speculation, he made a public statement in April 1955 that he was not a candidate and asserted that his decision ruling out a 1956 race was "irrevocable."[4]

After his appointment, Warren had told his son, Earl, Jr., "You understand, this is absolutely the end of my political life." His April 1955 statement publicly reaffirmed this position. Yet, as Earl, Jr., put it, though Warren meant exactly what he said about not running, "it was hard for him to understand that other people didn't feel that way. He said so as plainly as he could, but politicians kept looking for meanings in his words that weren't there."[5] That was particularly the case after September 24, 1955, when President Eisenhower suffered his severe heart attack.

On the same day that the President was placed in an oxygen tent, the *New York Times* reported that "the private speculation in Washington was that if the President should, as the result of his illness, refuse to stand for re-election, a strong effort might be made to induce the Chief Justice of the United States, Earl Warren, to retire from the bench and re-enter public life."[6] Referring back to Warren's April statement, the *Times* commented that Eisenhower's heart attack had altered circumstances and that perhaps Warren's decision was now not "irrevocable."[7]

The political interest in Warren was based on the fact that, as Roscoe Drummond wrote in the *New York Herald Tribune*, "He is undoubtedly the party's best vote-getter, outside of Ike himself."[8] In his memoirs, Richard M. Nixon later asserted that the Gallup Poll "after Ike's heart attack showed me leading Earl Warren."[9] The facts simply do not bear this out, however. All the polls, including the Gallup, showed that Warren was preferred over Vice President Nixon by a wide margin by both Republican and independent voters and that he was the strongest candidate, next to Eisenhower, whom the Republicans could nominate.[10]

As the highest judicial officer, Warren properly felt that he could not personally make any further statement on the matter. But in a column by James Reston less than a week after Eisenhower's heart attack, the Chief Justice spoke indirectly. Reston said that Warren "is embarrassed by the speculation that has linked his name to the Presidency since the illness of President Eisenhower. . . . He stands on the statement he made last April. He said then that his decision was 'irrevocable' and there is reason for stating that he still feels that way."[11]

Roscoe Drummond's column had stated, "My best information is that President Eisenhower would cordially welcome Mr. Warren's nomination." [12] It is, however, doubtful that Eisenhower would have supported Warren for the Presidency. On December 14, 1955, James Hagerty, the President's press secretary, discussed Presidential prospects with Eisenhower. "Mr. President, what about Warren?" Hagerty asked. "Not a chance," Eisenhower snapped back, "and I'll tell you why. I know that the Chief Justice is very happy right where he is." Warren, said the President, "is dedicated to the Court. . . . I believe that is his life's work and I do not believe he will run." Eisenhower took Warren's disclaimer at face value. "He has a life-long job and I think he means it when he says he will not enter political life again." [13]

"Furthermore," declared Eisenhower during his conversation with Hagerty, "I do not think I would approve of a Chief Justice stepping down from the bench to run for office." [14] At a press conference early in 1956, the President repeated this theme. Asked about Warren as a candidate if he decided not to run, Eisenhower replied, "Now I just don't believe we ought to cross over. . . . We shouldn't get too great a confusion between politics and the Supreme Court." [15] According to James Reston, what the President meant was that Warren should not get into the race unless he first resigned from the Court. And, said Reston, "the chances of Mr. Warren's resigning from the court are about as good as the chances of the Washington Monument falling into the Potomac River." All of this, the *Times* columnist concluded, "leaves Mr. Warren where he wants to be: quietly and happily aloof in his big paneled suite in the high court building." [16]

On February 29, 1956, Eisenhower announced that he would run again. This ended the speculation about Warren's possible candidacy.

But if the Chief Justice was now completely removed from politics, that did not prevent the Warren Court itself from becoming a political issue. In February, 1956, Vice-President Nixon, during a political speech, stated that, "speaking for a unanimous Supreme Court, a great Republican Chief Justice, Earl Warren, has ordered an end to racial segregation in the nation's schools." [17] Warren resented this attempt to use the Court to gain political capital. In this, he was supported by most of the press. Thus, a *New York Times* editorial attacked Nixon for linking the segregation decision to the political campaign [18] and the leading *Times* pundit, Arthur Krock, saw Nixon's speech as a "blunder." [19]

Southern critics of the Court, on the other hand, saw in the Nixon remark a confirmation of their own views. In a speech on the floor, Senator Olin D. Johnston, of South Carolina, declared that Nixon was right and that the *Brown* decision was purely a political decision.[20] On March 11, ninety-six Southern members of the Senate and House joined in issuing a "manifesto" that condemned the Court for abuse of judicial power, contrary to established law, which encroached upon the rights constitutionally reserved to the states.[21]

According to James Hagerty's diary, during his December 1955 talk with Eisenhower about Warren as a possible candidate, the President said that Warren "wants to go down in history as a great Chief Justice, and he certainly is becoming one. He . . . is getting the Court back on its feet and back in respectable standing again."[22] If Eisenhower was accurately quoted, his statement to Hagerty probably was among the last laudatory comments he made about Warren as Chief Justice. The President was becoming disenchanted with the Court head he had appointed and, by 1957, was openly complaining to friends about the Chief Justice and the Court. Inevitably, his complaint was picked up by the press. On June 25, 1957 the President wrote to Warren that "I was told this morning that some enterprising reporter has a story that at a private party I severely criticized the Supreme Court, expressing anger. I have no doubt that in private conversation someone did hear me express amazement about one decision, but I have never even hinted at a feeling such as anger. To do so would imply not only that I knew the law but questioned motives. Neither of these things is true."[23]

Warren replied to the President's letter, "concerning the gossip column," on July 15. "It was considerate of you to write, but it was in no sense necessary. Those of us who have long been in the public service know that some columns are written in ignorance and others to deceive. Whatever the reason, if unfounded, they should be ignored."

Warren referred to "some of the articles about our recent opinions" and asserted that "the writers could not possibly have read them unless there was a deliberate purpose on their part to deceive." This was intended as a thrust at the President himself, who had been widely quoted as critical of Court decisions, particularly that in the *Brown* school segregation case.

"While in other positions," the Warren letter went on, "I could and did speak out to counteract such statements. Here we do not respond regardless of what is said. We must live with what we write and are contented to do so." Then, in another dig at Eisenhower, Warren asserted, "Some of the things which were written about the Court are as silly as those they have written about the purpose of your civil rights bill and your action in the Girard case." Warren's letter concluded, "I am sure the only thing for us to do in such instances is to tune out on them and trust to the future to vindicate our actions and intentions." Presumably, the Chief Justice meant this to apply as much to criticisms by Presidents as by newspapers.

Warren's letter was read to Attorney General Herbert Brownell. According to a note attached to the letter, "Mr. Brownell said he thought this was a very friendly letter and was glad to know about it."[24]

The White House desire to obtain Brownell's opinion about whether the Warren letter was "friendly" indicates that the relationship between the President and the Chief Justice had become sensitive. In July, 1958, when Justice Burton went to see the President about resigning from the Court, Eisenhower went out of his way to express dissatisfaction with "the decisions of the Chief Justice."[25] The next month the *American Mercury* declared that Warren was "Eisenhower's worst appointment."[26] By then, the President agreed with this assessment. When an interviewer later asked Eisenhower what was his biggest mistake, he replied heatedly, "The appointment of that S.O.B. Earl Warren."[27]

Warren affirmed in his memoirs, "I knew he had some such opinion." He based this statement upon a conversation he had with Eisenhower in 1965 while both were flying to London to attend Winston Churchill's funeral. The ex-President expressed disappointment that the Chief Justice had not turned out to be the "moderate" he had expected. Warren asked Eisenhower what decisions had led to his disapproval. "Oh, those Communist cases." "What Communist cases?" asked Warren. "All of them," was the reply.

Warren then "tried to explain that in the judging process we were obliged to judge Communists by the same rules that we applied to others." Eisenhower refused to accept this statement. Warren then asked, "What would you do with Communists in America?" Eisenhower answered, "I would kill the S.O.B.s!"[28]

Warren states that the cordial relations between the President and himself evaporated after the *Brown* decision.[29] In January, 1959, Robert J. Donovan wrote in the *New York Herald Tribune* that the relationship between the President and Chief Justice was "cold and distant and marred by disapproval on both sides." Donovan quoted Eisenhower as saying to friends, "I find it a little hard to follow some of the latest decisions" and said that, in talking of Warren and the Court, the President "wound up in a state of anger."[30]

On the day the Donovan story appeared, Eisenhower held a press conference and denounced the piece as "irresponsible reporting." "I have regarded the Chief Justice as my personal friend for years," said the President, "and I know of no personal rift of any kind." Warren issued a tart statement: "The story merits no comment. It is wholly without foundation."[31]

The denials were widely perceived as pro forma disclaimers demanded by Washington protocol. According to *Newsweek*, "no amount of denial could obscure the fact that Donovan was right. There was indeed a rift between the two men."[32] There was no doubt that Eisenhower strongly disapproved of many of the Warren Court's decisions and the trend toward judicial activism that became apparent during the 1955 and 1956 Terms. On his side, Warren told friends that the President was damaging the integration cause by not endorsing the *Brown* decision and by being indecisive ("wishy washy" was the term the Chief most often used) about the methods to enforce it.[33]

During the last years of Eisenhower's Administration, the relationship between the President and the Chief Justice deteriorated to a purely formal one. They would trade perfunctory greetings when protocol dictated that the Court or its head be invited to the White House. In addition, the two would exchange ceremonial correspondence, such as birthday greetings. Thus, each year on March 19, Eisenhower would write that he had been reminded that that day was the Chief Justice's birthday and "I did not want the day to pass without extending to you my felicitations and best wishes." Warren would then send back a handwritten note along the lines of, "It is almost a sin for one so preoccupied with matters of great importance to take time out for recognizing birth-days," though noting appreciation for the recognition. In his last year in the White House, on March 15, 1960, Eisenhower wrote the Chief Justice, "*This* year I congratulate myself on remembering, in advance of your anniversary, that March nineteenth is your birthday," and sending felicitations and best wishes.[34]

Warren's attitude toward President Eisenhower was shared by most of the Justices. Like the Chief, the Brethren resented Eisenhower's lack of support for the school segregation decisions, as well as indications of disapproval from the White House at other important decisions. Just after he retired from the Court, Minton wrote to Frankfurter, "the fact that the Court has not received support from sources it had a right to expect support has given the South a propaganda victory."[35] In his *Autobiography,* Douglas went further, saying, "Ike's ominous silence on our 1954 decision gave courage to the racists who decided to resist the decision ward by ward, precinct by precinct, town by town, and county by county."[36]

Some of the Justices had a very low opinion of the President. In November 1958, Frankfurter wrote to a close friend, "The other day the Court paid our annual visit to the President and I left him . . . with a feeling that he is a very good man wholly unqualified to be President of the United States. When I came here I said to Marion, 'Could one make a more devastating commentary on a President of the United States than to say that you are sorry for him?' "[37]

The unfavorable estimate of Eisenhower was not limited to the Democratic members of the Court. Potter Stewart, the second Republican Justice appointed by Eisenhower, states that, in his opinion, "Warren may be the only one [i.e., Court member] Ike had a personal part in choosing. For example, he never knew who I was. He always thought I was Whittaker."

In a collegiate body as small and closely knit as the Supreme Court, the departure of a Justice is always an event of consequence, particularly where he had become as established a part of the institution as Robert H. Jackson had been. Soon after the Court convened for the 1954 Term, Jackson suffered a second and this time fatal heart attack. Jackson's death played a part in the judicial development of Earl Warren. As pointed out in chapter 2, Warren could scarcely have been so effective a Chief Justice in a Court torn apart by the feud between Jackson and Black. In addition, as shown by his following of Jackson's lead in *Irvine v. California,*[38] Warren was greatly influenced when he first came to the Court by the urbane New Yorker. Jackson would have been a strong second to Frankfurter's efforts to win the new Chief to his judicial philosophy, supplying just the bonhomie that the waspish Frankfurter lacked.

Shortly after Jackson's death, on November 8, 1954, President Eisenhower nominated another New Yorker, John Marshall Harlan, to fill the vacancy. Harlan was the grandson of the Justice with the same name who had written the dissent in *Plessy v. Ferguson*.[39] As soon as he took his place on the bench, Harlan had taken a place in the Court's history, as the only descendant of a Justice to become one. The first Harlan had been a judicial maverick, who had been an outspoken dissenter. The second Harlan took a more cautious approach to the judicial function that reflected his background. Educated at Princeton, he had been a Rhodes Scholar and had had a successful career with a leading Wall Street law firm prior to his appointment in January 1954 to the U.S. Court of Appeals for the Second Circuit.

On the Supreme Court, Harlan, like Jackson, became a firm adherent of Frankfurter's judicial restraint philosophy. After Frankfurter's retirement, it was Harlan who came to be looked on as the conservative conscience of an ever more activist Court. But Harlan had none of the acerbity that made Frankfurter distasteful to some of his colleagues. Harlan looked like a Supreme Court Justice. Tall and erect, with sparse white hair, conservatively dressed in his London-tailored suits, with his grandfather's gold watch chain across the vest under his robe, he exuded the dignity associated with high judicial office. Yet underneath was a warm nature that enabled him to be close friends with those with whom he disagreed intellectually, notably Black. Visitors could often see the two Justices waiting patiently in line in the Court cafeteria. The two were a study in contrasts: the ramrod-straight patrician with his commanding presence and his slight, almost wispy colleague who always looked like the lively old Southern farmer.

If Harlan at the Bar had been known as a "lawyer's lawyer," on the Court he soon acquired the reputation of a "lawyer's judge." Soon after Harlan took his seat (he was confirmed by the Senate on March 17, 1955), Frankfurter wrote a friend that "Harlan both on the bench and in the Conference is as to the manner born."[40] The new Justice was plainly one of the best, if not the best, lawyer on the Court and, next to Frankfurter, the Justice most interested in the technical aspects of the Court's work. He became a sound, rather than brilliant, Justice, who could be relied on for learned opinions that thoroughly covered the subjects dealt with, though they degenerated at times into law review articles of the type Frankfurter too often wrote.

The term most frequently used to describe Harlan by those who knew him is "gentleman"—though some say that beneath the veneer was a bland grayness that permeated both his life and work. To the Brethren, Harlan always appeared the quintessential patrician, with his privileged upbringing and Wall Street background. "I hear 'mi lord,' " reads a note from Clark to Harlan, "that you have been under the weather. . . . Your Lordship should be more careful of your whiskey and your habits." [41]

It was soon after Harlan's appointment that the Chief Justice began to find his jurisprudential roots. When Harlan came to the Court in early 1955, Warren was still largely under the influence of Frankfurter. During the next year and a half, the Chief began to reject the philosophy of judicial restraint. Three cases decided in 1955, in which Warren changed his mind about the proper decision, illustrate his changing posture.

The first two cases were *Quinn v. United States* [42] and *Emspak v. United States*, [43] decided as companion cases involving refusals to answer questions concerning Communist membership before the House Committee on Un-American Activities. The *Emspak* case came to the Court during the 1953 Term. Emspak had based his refusals to answer on primarily "the first amendment, supplemented by the fifth." The lower courts had held that that was not enough to invoke the constitutional privilege against self-incrimination. The case was discussed in conference on January 16, 1954. [44]

Warren began his conference presentation by saying, "It gets down to the question whether he actually claimed his privilege." The Chief recognized that, "we should not indulge in technicalities." But here the defendant wanted "to eat this pie and have it. He did not want to testify and yet not look guilty. We should not condone that action." Warren said that he would vote to affirm.

The strongest statement the other way was made by Black, who spoke after the Chief. "We should not condone a committee," Black declared, "that indicates that claiming the privilege is wrong. We would be condoning the committee's actions if we affirm. The Fifth Amendment is not bad and to claim his privilege is not bad. I don't believe in being strict on this claim. Here it would be bad for this Court to erect technical barriers."

Except for Frankfurter and Douglas (who passed) the others indicated they would vote to affirm, though several expressed the wish, as Jackson put it, that Congressional "committees would manage their work better and not abuse their power." Warren assigned the majority opinion to Reed. His draft opinion not only refused to accept the Fifth Amendment claim, but also contained a strong rejection of the claim that the refusal to answer questions about Communist membership was protected by the First Amendment. This was an issue that had not been discussed at the conference and one that the Court had, until then, been careful not to decide.

Black, in particular, bristled at the Reed draft. On April 23, 1954, he wrote the Brethren, "Except by outright repeal I cannot readily conceive of a way to give less effective meaning to the First Amendment than Justice Reed does in the opinion he has circulated in this case." Black asked that the others "not go along with his opinion until its devastating effect on free speech and press can be pointed out in dissent."[45]

Black's objection led Jackson to suggest that Black move to have the case reargued. Black wanted Frankfurter to make the reargument motion, but he declined. At the bottom of the letter from Frankfurter to that effect, Black penned in, "I made the motion Saturday May 15—and it was carried, Reed & Minton voting against it."[46]

Emspak was then set for reargument in the 1954 Term. The Court also fixed argument the same day for the *Quinn* case, which came to the Court toward the end of the 1953 Term and presented a similar fact pattern. *Emspak* and *Quinn* were argued on April 4 and 5, 1955, and were discussed together in conference, on April 9, 1955.[47] The conference began with a dramatic announcement by the Chief Justice: "I have changed my mind from last year."

In his April 9 discussion, Warren first addressed the issue to which Black had so strenuously objected. The Chief's suggestion was simple: "Set aside the First Amendment issue." It was not necessary for decision and its resolution should be avoided. As far as the Un-American Activities Committee was concerned, Warren said, the Court should assume the validity of the Congressional resolution establishing it. In addition, the questions asked were pertinent. But "we can dispose of these cases on the slipshod method of the committee in questioning."

According to Warren, both defendants had clearly claimed their privilege. The committee, however, did not give a clear warning of the need to answer. "The committee must clarify the claim and the contempt issue. Any indication of the claim should be enough to make the committee alert," and they must then indicate "whether they denied it or not. Here, there was a lack of direction by the committee on their duty to answer the questions."

Black agreed that the Court should decide on other than First Amendment grounds. The "narrow grounds" suggested by Warren "would be enough." Reed, Clark, and Minton adhered to the view they had expressed at the conference. Harlan, who had taken Jackson's place, also voted for affirmance. But Douglas and Burton said that they agreed with the Chief. That converted the prior year's six-to-two vote for affirmance into a bare majority for reversal. Warren delivered the *Quinn* and *Emspak* opinions on May 23, 1955. His opinions for the Court stressed that a claim of the privilege did not require any special combination of words and that, under this test, defendants *had* claimed the privilege. Warren also relied on the point raised in his second conference discussion—that the committee had failed to give a fair apprisal of its ruling on the privilege claim and to direct the witnesses that they were required to answer.

Harlan specifically dissented on the second ground. Reed also wrote a dissent, joined by Minton. He did not, however, deal with the First Amendment issue, as he had done in his draft opinion of the Court the previous term. Clark, who had said that he agreed with Reed at the April 9 conference, joined the Warren opinions, giving the Chief a six-to-three majority.

The grounds upon which *Quinn* and *Emspak* were decided were of less importance than the indication they gave that the Chief Justice and a majority of the Brethren were now ready, as Black had urged at the first *Emspak* conference, "to draw a line on the powers of the committee . . . and keep judicial and legislative powers separate." As Frankfurter wrote to Harlan, "I thought and think it was right to charge these loose-mouthed, loose-mannered and loose-headed men on the Hill with a little more responsibility in the serious business of Congressional investigations. That's all the [*Quinn* and *Emspak*] requirement . . . gets down to."[48]

Toth v. Quarles,[49] decided November 7, 1955, was even more important in illustrating the Chief Justice's changing judicial philosophy. It will be recalled that when Eisenhower criticized the Court's decisions in cases involving Communists on the plane to Winston

Churchill's funeral, Warren asked him what he would do with Communists and the former President said, "I would kill the S.O.B.s." Warren replied, "Perhaps that could be done in the Army, but it could not be done through civilian courts."[50]

The line between civil and military power that is so fundamental under our Constitution was drawn, in large part, by decisions of the Warren Court starting with *Toth v. Quarles*. Toth was an ex-serviceman who had been honorably discharged. He was arrested and had to stand trial before a court-martial for a murder allegedly committed while he was an airman in Korea. He claimed that an ex-serviceman could not constitutionally be subjected to trial by court-martial even though section 3(a) of the Uniform Code of Military Justice had authorized such a trial for crimes punishable by imprisonment for more than five years committed while in service.

The *Toth* case first came before the Court in the 1954 Term. After oral argument on February 8 and 9, 1955, the case was considered in conference on February 12.[51] Warren led the discussion, indicating that he saw no difficulty in affirming court-martial power. In his view, "Congress made the reasonable choice of making the soldier subject to court-martial jurisdiction." The Chief referred to the first statute of the type at issue: an 1863 law that subjected ex-servicemen to military jurisdiction for frauds against the U.S. committed while in service. To Warren, this was "just an extension of the old fraud statute of 1863 which has been upheld for ninety years." Indeed, he urged, "it is less objectionable than the old fraud statute. It has a better test, [that of] serious offences."

Once again it was Black who made the strongest statement in favor of reversal. He asserted that courts-martial were "not in high regard. I would not extend court-martial power any further than we have to. I still believe in *Milligan*." The reference was to the classic 1866 decision drastically limiting court-martial jurisdiction over civilians.[52] Black said that the Court did not have to extend court-martial power here. "People should be tried before juries and Congress can so provide." Black also stated that he was "disturbed about trying civilians who happened to be attached to the Army"—thus anticipating the issue that was to be resolved in 1957 in *Reid v. Covert*,[53] one of the great cases decided by the Warren Court.

Though the Brethren were closely divided, four of the seven present agreed with Warren. Again, he assigned the majority opinion to Reed, who circulated a draft opinion of the Court on March 23. That opinion ultimately became the dissent that Reed wrote in the case. Black circulated a draft dissent on April 7; Frankfurter and Douglas joined. The Black dissent was similar to the final opinion of the Court in *Toth*—also written by Black.

Toth was a case in which the original dissenters felt strongly. The depth of their feeling can be seen from a draft dissent circulated by Frankfurter, joined by Douglas, that began, "This case has nothing to do with the War Powers, nor do the legal questions it raises bring into relevance General Sherman's assessment of war. Considering his compassionate nature, even his experience might not have prepared him for the iron aspect of peace furthered by the Court's attitude toward the Bill of Rights."[54]

The tentative dissenters used Harlan's confirmation in March to urge that such a significant case should be heard and decided by a full Court. They persuaded a majority on June 6 to schedule the case for reargument. The reargument was on October 13, early in the new 1955 Term. *Toth* was then considered at a second conference on October 15, 1955.[55]

Once again Warren told the Brethren that he had changed his mind and was now for reversal. "At the heart of the Constitution," declared the Chief, was the principle that "courts-martial were for discipline and that is all." The Government had contended that Congress could enact section 3(a) under the Constitution's Necessary and Proper Clause. Warren disagreed, saying the clause "does not apply to it and cover this, after service. It conflicts with the [Sixth] Amendment" right to jury trial. Nor did reversal mean that Toth and other ex-servicemen would remain unpunished for crimes committed while in service. "I have no doubt," said the Chief, "that Congress might provide for a civil trial. That is a way to punish him if Congress says so." The case, Warren concluded, was of "greatest importance for civil liberties. I don't believe section 3(a) is consistent with jury trial of civilians."

This time the conference discussion was brief. Only Reed, Burton, and Minton still voted to affirm. The others all agreed with Warren, who assigned the opinion to Black. His opinion of the Court, delivered November 7, was a recast version of the dissent he had prepared in April. Reed used the draft opinion of the Court that he had circulated in March as the basis for a dissent, joined by Burton and Minton, who also wrote a short dissent.

Frankfurter had asked Black to tone down some of the language in his opinion pertaining to jury trial. He particularly urged the deletion of a statement by Jefferson. His request in a letter of October 26 is worth quoting, because Frankfurter used language he might not have been willing to include in a public statement. Frankfurter wrote that he could not agree with everything Jefferson said.

To regard "trial by jury as the only anchor ever yet imagined by man, by which a government can be held to the principles of its Constitution," strikes me as a bit of humorless hyperbole. I cannot regard the jury, any more than any other political device—and the jury system is that—as the final word of wisdom or as indispensable to the free human spirit. It is for that reason that I do not regard it as an aspect of due process. I cannot for the life of me believe that the Constitution is less regnant in Baltimore, where, as a matter of long tradition, trial by jury is waived in all but two or three percent of the criminal cases, including capital, than it is here in Washington, or in Alabama, or in Massachusetts.[56]

Black took out the Jefferson quote from his opinion. But he refused to take out a reference to Macaulay, even though Frankfurter had asserted, "Macaulay was a great historian, but not the most accurate."[57]

To the public, the decisions that best indicated the changing nature of the Warren Court were those involving alleged Communists that former President Eisenhower had criticized on the plane to Churchill's funeral. In April, 1956, the Justices handed down two such decisions, which were sharply attacked by critics of the Court. In both cases, Warren played a key role in the decision process.

The first case was *Pennsylvania v. Nelson*,[58] which a *New York Times* article characterized as "perhaps the most controversial case of the present term."[59] Nelson, an acknowledged member of the Communist Party, had been convicted of violating the Pennsylvania Sedition Act, which prohibited the knowing advocacy of the overthrow of the U.S. Government by force and violence. The Pennsylvania Supreme Court had reversed the conviction on the ground that the Smith Act, passed by Congress in 1940, proscribed the same conduct and hence superseded the state law.

At the *Nelson* conference on November 18, 1955,[60] Warren began the discussion by stating that, as he saw it, the case was reduced to one issue: "Has the U.S. superseded this state act?" Warren said that he thought it had and had overturned it. He also said that he thought that there would be "no loss to the U.S. if these acts are stricken." The Chief concluded by saying that he would vote to affirm.

Black, Frankfurter, and Douglas stated their agreement with Warren, with Frankfurter saying that, though they did not have to decide it, he would probably disallow all local laws as to treason. Reed, Burton, Clark, and Minton voted to reverse. Reed declared that he would be glad to see supersession of the state law, but did not find it here. Clark said that both the state and federal laws could "live together" and it was necessary that they do so. As he saw it, it was a "question of policy: Shall we overturn the States, Congress, and the Department of Justice?" The ninth Justice, Harlan, stated that he was "not ready to vote."

The four-to-four stalemate became a six-to-three decision, when Harlan decided to go along with Warren's view and Clark, despite his conference statement the other way, also agreed to reversal. The Chief Justice himself delivered the *Nelson* opinion, which, following his conference approach, found the state sedition law superseded by the Smith Act. Reed, joined by Burton and Minton, dissented.

The *Nelson* decision was sharply criticized, both by Representative Howard Smith of Virginia, the original author of the Smith Act, and by others in Congress. At a Senate hearing, the decision was denounced by the new chairman of the Senate Judiciary Committee, James O. Eastland of Mississippi, who declared that the Court was composed of "politicians instead of lawyers." At the same hearing, Senator Joseph R. McCarthy of Wisconsin complained, "We made a mistake in confirming as Chief Justice a man who had no judicial experience and very little legal experience."[61] The Eisenhower Administration announced that it was backing a Senate bill to nullify *Nelson,* which provided that no federal statute preempted state jurisdiction unless it specifically asserted that intention.[62]

In *Slochower v. Board of Regents,*[63] the Court again had before it the New York City law that it had dealt with the previous term in the *Regan* case.[64] It required the dismissal of a city employee who utilized the Fifth Amendment privilege against self-incrimination to avoid answering a question relating to his official conduct. Slochower had invoked the privilege and refused to answer questions about Communist membership before a Senate committee. He was summarily discharged from his position on the faculty of Brooklyn College.

Warren had voted with Reed and Minton not to hear Slochower's appeal. However, when the case was discussed in conference on October 21, 1955,[65] the Chief left no doubt that, on the merits, he was for reversal. The New York law, he said, "placed an unwarranted burden on these people. The premise in the plea is one of guilt and this is violative of the Constitution. I would reverse."

After Warren spoke, there was a long discussion by the others, particularly between Frankfurter and Douglas on whether there was a constitutional right to government employment. Frankfurter declared that, though "oceans of ink had been spent on this, nothing says more than Holmes in the police case,[66] where he said there was no constitutional right to be a policeman." Douglas, on the other hand, asserted, "There is a constitutional right in this country for a citizen to have a job. There is a constitutional right to be a policeman or a lawyer. These measures should not be permitted to prevent it. It's tantamount to the old bill of attainder."

But it was Warren's conference statement that set the theme for the *Slochower* decision. The Chief's position, in essence, was that it was arbitrary and hence violative of due process for New York to presume guilt every time the Fifth Amendment privilege is invoked. This was the position adopted by Clark, who wrote the Court's opinion, as well as that which persuaded Harlan, who had said at the conference that the case could not be decided under the Fifth Amendment since he could not find a claim based on it in the record. As Frankfurter wrote Warren, "I have had what I believe was a searching talk with Tom, and my clear conviction is that he is anchored for reversal in *Slochower*. His ground is my ground for reversal, namely, due process. This hurdles John's difficulty, that the Fifth Amendment wasn't raised in the state court."[67] After he had read the draft *Slochower* opinion, Frankfurter sent Clark a penciled note: "'I think your Slochower will have very wholesome effect, without impairing the effective control by states of their servants, including teachers in public institutions and doing so by making state educational institutions unintimidated places."[68]

The Clark opinion in *Slochower* was accepted by all the Justices except Reed, Burton, and Minton. Reed delivered a dissent, joined by the other two, which expanded on the statement that he had made in conference, that his views were "well known" that it was "within the power of the city to do this. He has the right to claim the privilege or to keep his job"—but not both.

A case involving the Communist Party itself might have attracted more attention had Frankfurter not succeeded in persuading the Brethren to avoid deciding the constitutional issues involved. The case in question—*Communist Party v. Subversive Activities Control Board* [69]—arose out of an order of the Board that the Communist Party register with the Attorney General as a "Communist-action" organization as required by a federal statute. The statute not only required registration, but also imposed sanctions on organizations that the Board ordered to register, including loss of tax exemptions and labeling of mail or use of radio or television as "disseminated by a communist organization." In addition, organization members were prohibited from government or defense employment, from office or employment in unions, or from holding passports. The party challenged the constitutionality of the statute, claiming that the registration and sanctions violated the First and Fifth Amendments, as well as other constitutional provisions.

At conferences on the case on November 18, 1955, and March 8, 1956,[70] the Justices addressed themselves to the constitutional issues. Indeed, according to a Frankfurter memorandum "at conference we all agreed to pass upon the constitutional issues."[71] At both conferences, Warren argued the unconstitutionality of the statute. As he saw it, the law violated the First Amendment, as well as the Fifth Amendment's demand of due process and its privilege against self-incrimination. The statute, he said, drew no distinction between legal and illegal activities; it struck at political rights and imposed severe sanctions against peaceful activities. It was true, he went on, that individual party members were not parties in the case, but it was the sanctions that prevented them from being such. Hence, the claims of members, including the self-incrimination claims, could be raised. At the second conference, Warren explained that the Court must consider the overall purpose of the legislation. "Was what was intended merely registration? If it was registration alone: O.K. If registration plus sanctions, that's outlawry and that's bad." The Chief urged the Court to "reach the constitutionality of the Act." Perhaps registration alone could be sustained, but they should strike down all the law's sanctions.

The Brethren were closely divided on the constitutional issues. Black, Douglas, and Burton supported the view that the statute was unconstitutional, with Burton declaring that Congress "went overboard," since this was not really registration but "an attempt to abolish the Communist Party." Reed, Clark, and Minton voted to affirm. Minton expressed their view most forcefully, saying, "Congress has found what everyone around this table should admit: what the Communist Party is!" He also caustically observed, "I'd rather have a little of my liberty chipped away today than have it all taken away tomorrow." Harlan thought the discussion too far-ranging; he felt that only the registration requirement was before the Court and, by itself, could be upheld.[72] Frankfurter took a similar view.[73]

Frankfurter was, however, disturbed about the splintered decision that would result if the Court did deal with the constitutional merits. In a *Memorandum Re Communist Party Opinion* of March 21, 1956,[74] he wrote, "The concerns in which the issues of the case are imbedded and the diverse rhetoric to which these may give rise make the atmosphere which the opinion should generate of predominant importance. This would be so even if one did not anticipate dissenting views which in their tenor will not be preoccupied with spreading light and avoiding heat."

During the next two weeks, Frankfurter worked to avoid the divisive result that decision on the constitutional issues would produce. He seized on a motion, which the lower court had denied, to adduce additional evidence before the Board. The motion alleged that the additional evidence would show that the testimony of three key witnesses on which the Board had relied was false and that they were under charges of false swearing. Frankfurter urged that the case should be reversed and remanded to the Board to receive the additional evidence. "Since the case must be reversed on this ground," reads a Frankfurter "Dear Brethren" letter of April 2, "I have come to the conclusion, after considerable reflection and with great reluctance, that the case must now be disposed of exclusively on the ground without reaching the constitutional validity of this Act."[75]

Frankfurter persuaded the Justices to decide the case solely on the nonconstitutional ground and wrote a draft opinion that, he asserted, "speaks for itself."[76] The draft was essentially the same as the opinion Frankfurter delivered for the Court on April 30, with a few minor changes. The most interesting of them involved a passage in the draft that said that petitioner should be given leave to produce the evidence before the Board, and then stated, "We assume, of course, that the members of the Board, like members of other tribunals charged with the reconsideration of evidence, are 'men of conscience and intellectual discipline, capable of judging a particular controversy fairly on the basis of its own circumstances.' "[77]

In a handwritten note, Douglas asked for deletion of this sentence, asking "if it does not cast aspersions (by implication) on the Board. It sounds as if we thought they were a slippery lot who need watching."[78] In an April 16 *Memorandum for the Conference*,[79] Frankfurter took out the sentence. Of course, he wrote, "no such thought ever crossed my mind," but, "since the . . . sentence has caused confusion, I think that it is better stricken."

The apparent unanimity of the Court on Frankfurter's approach was broken when Clark circulated an April 17 memorandum that stated, "I am sorry to disagree with the proposal of Brother Frankfurter in this case." According to Clark, the Frankfurter approach was only a "subterfuge." "The disposition of this case, as proposed by Brother Frankfurter, is but another effort to shirk our plain responsibility to pass on constitutional questions involved in this suit." For the Court to send the case back to the Board, Clark asserted, would "cause a serious miscarriage of justice, frustrate the congressional purpose and at the most serious time in world history strike down for all practical purposes the most effective tool against world Communism."

Clark concluded his memo by asking, "Why should we go through with this shadow-boxing? As I remember, it was agreed that even if the case was reopened the same judgment would result. Why stoop to such insincerity or demagogism? We should therefore not disturb the holdings below."[80]

On April 19, Clark explained his reasons for disagreeing with the Frankfurter approach in detail in a more restrained memorandum.[81] When the Frankfurter approach continued to command a majority,

Clark issued a dissent, joined by Reed and Minton, asserting that the decision was based on a "pretext" to avoid "important constitutional issues."[82]

Of course, that is what the Frankfurter approach was and precisely what it was designed to be. In his March 21 memo, dealing with the constitutional merits, Frankfurter had referred to the perjury claim and asserted, "It would reduce the self-restraints regarding consideration of constitutional questions to absurdity to dispose of this case merely on this point."[83] And his April 2 "Dear Brethren" letter had candidly recognized that, after the Board considered the case on remand, "I have no doubt that . . . the Board will on the remaining evidence again reach the conclusion it has reached. Nor do I doubt that the Court of Appeals will promptly affirm such an order and that the case will be back here."[84] This is exactly what happened after the Supreme Court's decision, so that the case came back to the Court in the 1960 Term. But that was the whole point about the Frankfurter strategy: to avoid decision on the constitutional merits when the Court was sharply divided. When the constitutional questions were actually decided in 1961,[85] the issue of subversion had become defused of most of its politically explosive force.

Though Warren was starting, during the 1955 Term, to assume a more activist posture, cases like *Communist Party v. Subversive Activities Control Board* demonstrated that he was still willing to follow the Frankfurter approach in important cases. This is also shown by *Ullmann v. United States,*[86] where the Court upheld a federal statute requiring witnesses to testify in cases involving national security. In return, they were granted immunity from prosecution based on evidence compelled after the privilege against self-incrimination had been claimed. Though Douglas, joined by Black, delivered a strong dissent, the Chief Justice was willing to go along with Frankfurter's opinion of the Court, delivered on March 26, 1956.

Douglas' draft dissent had cited an article by a Southern writer. Black wrote questioning the citation. "I am not sure about citing Pittman now. He has gone to very wild extremes recently in connection with his attacks on this Court because of the segregation holding. In some speech I saw he made, he seemed to get great comfort out of calling attention to the fact that this Court had cited his article several times."[87] Douglas, of course, took out the offending citation.

The Douglas dissent stressed that while the challenged law granted immunity from *criminal* charges, there were other disabilities imposed in security cases—loss of jobs, passport eligibility, expulsion from unions—against which the law did not grant protection. After Douglas had raised this point at the conference discussion, Frankfurter said that "if petitioner felt that any sanctions imposed against him were 'criminal' in nature he could always raise this later." In a note to Frankfurter, one of the Brethren objected, "But we have precluded him from raising this later . . . because we have at least characterized loss of job, expulsion from labor unions, passport eligibility as noncriminal in nature."[88]

Frankfurter replied, "Don't be bothered by my hasty remark. I did not mean to open up any Pandora's box."[89] To meet the point, he added to his draft opinion, "since the Immunity Act protects a witness who is compelled to answer to the extent of his constitutional privilege he has, of course, the right to claim that a particular sanction is criminal in nature."[90]

Another aspect of the *Ullmann* opinion should be noted. Frankfurter went out of the way to reaffirm his position on a principal point of contention between himself and Black. The latter was the principal judicial advocate of the so-called "preferred position" theory, under which personal rights, such as the Fifth Amendment's privilege against self-incrimination, are elevated above mere economic rights. Frankfurter was a consistent opponent of this preferred position approach. In the *Ullman* opinion, he declared, "As no constitutional guarantee enjoys preference, so none should suffer subordination or deletion."[91] This statement in the draft opinion led Reed to write, "I do not see how you . . . can say 'As no constitutional guarantee enjoys preference. . . .'"[92]

Frankfurter replied in a three-page letter that contains the best statement of his rejection of the preferred position theory. The key portion of this unpublished letter deserves quotation, since the Black-Frankfurter difference has been of such great interest to students of the Supreme Court. "When one talks about 'preferred,' or 'preferred position,'" Frankfurter wrote, "one means preference of one thing over another. Please tell me what kind of sense it makes that one provision of the Constitution is to be 'preferred' over another. When is that true? When are two provisions of the Constitution in conflict so that one must be subordinated to the other?"

Then Frankfurter stated what to him was the principal defect of the preferred position approach. "The correlative of 'preference' is 'subordination,' and I know of no calculus to determine when one provision of the Constitution must yield to another, nor do I know any reason for doing so. Accommodating two provisions so as to give effect to both is something else again. I do not think there is a second-class citizenship among the different clauses inhabiting the Constitution."[93]

In *Gibson v. Lockheed Aircraft Service*,[94] decided early in 1956, Warren would not yield to Frankfurter's view. His persistent opposition converted a bare Frankfurter majority into a unanimous decision the other way. *Gibson* was a negligence case, in which Gibson had recovered damages for personal injuries. The court of appeals had reversed on the ground that four instructions to the jury requested by Lockheed should have been given. At the conference on December 9, 1955,[95] Warren spoke in favor of reversal, as did Black, Douglas, and Clark. In their view, the charge given by the trial judge was adequate.

Frankfurter, however, felt strongly that the time of the Supreme Court should not be spent on comparatively minor negligence cases. Their difference on this matter was, as we will see, to become a major source of contention between Frankfurter and Warren. Frankfurter urged that, even though the case had already been briefed and argued, the Court should dismiss on the ground that certiorari had been "improvidently granted."

Reed, Burton, Minton, and Harlan agreed with Frankfurter. As Harlan put it in a letter to Reed, the question presented "is not a cert-worthy question, and, for myself, I do not think we should pass on it, as we would have to do if we do not follow the 'improvidently granted' formula."[96]

In the same letter, Harlan referred to "the Chief's strong distaste for the 'improvidently granted' formula." Warren thought that it was wrong to follow that formula. If cert should not have been granted, the time to hold that way was when first dealing with the cert petition, not at the stage the *Gibson* case had reached. In the Chief's view, it only made the Court look ridiculous, after a case had been briefed and argued, for it to be dismissed on the ground that the Justices should not have taken it in the first place.

Black, Douglas, and Clark agreed with Warren. Clark wrote a dissent to the proposed per curiam dismissing as improvidently granted. During the next two months, Warren worked to persuade those on the other side that the case should not be dismissed. In February 1956, Harlan wrote to Clark, "In view of the strong objections which have been made to dismissing the writ in this case as 'improvidently granted,' I intend to withdraw my concurrence in F.F.'s proposed *per curiam,* and to vote to decide the case (although still believing that we should not have brought the case here in the first place). I understand that H.H.B. has already done likewise." Harlan suggested that a short per curiam reversing was all that was necessary, "for these purely factual questions are surely not worth writing about."[97]

In the next two weeks, Reed and Minton also agreed that the "improvidently granted" dismissal was not the proper result. On February 27, the Court issued a per curiam reversing, which stated only "that the charge as given by the trial court was both complete and correct."[98] Even Frankfurter did not dissent, contenting himself with a one-paragraph opinion concurring in the reversal, which reiterated his view that "the writ should be dismissed as improvidently granted even though full argument has been had."[99]

During the 1955 Term Warren increasingly demonstrated the concern for individual rights that was to become the hallmark of the Warren Court. In *Gonzales v. Landon,*[100] the lower court had ruled that Gonzales had lost his citizenship by remaining outside the United States to avoid military service in time of war. The court had found that the Government had proved his expatriation by a preponderance of the evidence presented. At the conference on the case on December 2, 1955,[101] Warren said that he would vote to reverse because the "judge did not measure up to the proper standard," which was the requirement "of clear, convincing, and unequivocal testimony." The others agreed and a per curiam was issued December 12, holding that the stricter standard urged by the Chief, rather than the less strict preponderance of the evidence standard for ordinary civil cases, governed expatriation proceedings.

Another case, *Cammer v. United States,*[102] involved an attorney whose client had been indicted by a grand jury for filing a false non-Communist affidavit. The attorney sent a questionnaire to the grand jury members who were federal employees, designed to learn whether they might be influenced by bias or fear to indict alleged Communists. He was found guilty of contempt under a statute permitting a federal court to punish as contempt "misbehavior of any of its officers in their official transactions." At the conference,[103] Warren stated that the statute was "not intended for lawyers, only for court attachés." In addition, he thought that contumacy had not been established; there was no contempt here, though the practice was wrong. The others agreed to reverse, except for Reed, who declared that "a lawyer is an officer of the court and subject to discipline of the court." Black wrote an opinion of the Court, delivered March 12, 1956. It reversed, following Warren's view that a lawyer was not a court "officer" within the meaning of the contempt statute. The decision was unanimous, since Reed concurred in what he said was the Court's "otherwise unique reading of the term 'officers of the court.' "[104]

Two cases decided in the 1955 Term show how the Chief Justice was moving away from his early tendency to favor the prosecution in criminal cases. The first case was *Michel v. Louisiana*,[105] decided on December 8, 1955. A black who had been sentenced to death for rape challenged his conviction on the ground that blacks had been systematically excluded from the grand jury that had indicted him. Counsel had been appointed only three days before the deadline under state law for filing a motion for challenging the grand jury. He did not, however, file the motion until after he received his formal notice of appointment, since he stated that he did not consider himself appointed until that time. It was then too late to meet the deadline.

At the *Michel* conference on November 11, 1955,[106] Warren made a strong statement in favor of reversal. "The record," he said, "is so clouded" that it was not clear that the lawyer was clearly appointed before the deadline. As Warren saw it, "the fact that he did not do anything shows that the court deprived him of counsel during this critical three-day period."

Only Black and Douglas agreed with the Chief. The others voted for affirmance. Clark wrote an opinion of the Court, stressing the point that he had made in the conference, that deference should be given to the "meticulous findings" of the state courts that counsel had been appointed in time to meet the deadline. A year or two earlier, Warren would have gone along with the majority in order to present a less divided Court. Now he concurred in separate dissents by Black and Douglas.

The Chief was, however, able to lead the Brethren during the term in one of the key criminal-law decisions of the Warren Court—that in *Griffin v. Illinois*.[107] Griffin had been convicted of armed robbery in an Illinois court. He filed a motion for a free transcript of the trial record, alleging that he was indigent and could not get adequate appellate review without the transcript. The motion was denied.

At the conference on December 9, 1955,[108] Warren pointed out that Illinois had provided for full appellate review in such a case. A defendant who could pay for a transcript should not be given an advantage over one who could not. "We cannot," declared the Chief, "have one rule for the rich and one for the poor." Hence, he would require the state to furnish the transcript. "The only thing that concerns me," Warren noted, "is that there [might be] a flood [of requests for trancripts] all over the country. Can we give it prospective effect only?"

Black agreed with Warren that the denial of the transcript motion should be reversed on equal protection grounds. He disagreed, however, with the notion that the decision should be prospective only and indicated he would vote against it. Frankfurter said he was "with Warren completely." He also felt it was important "to make it prospective." The problem was that "it would be shabby to say" that other defendants were barred because "they did not raise" the issue when they were convicted. They could not have done so because "we are adding something to due process."

Douglas and Clark also voted for reversal, as did Reed and Harlan, though, as we will see, later they changed their minds. Reed stated that he agreed with what had been said by Warren, though he doubted if it was necessary to make the decision prospective only. Harlan said that he would reverse on equal protection grounds. Only Burton and Minton voted to affirm at the conference. "Here we go again," asserted Minton, interfering with state criminal procedure. There was "no reason," he asserted, "for us to tell them" to furnish the transcript. The case presented, "not an inequality of the law," but an "inequality of riches."

The opinion of the Court was assigned to Black. He wrote a strong opinion following the Warren conference approach that went through three drafts before its final version. After the third draft was printed,

Harlan circulated a memorandum indicating doubts about the majority decision. Harlan suggested that relief should be denied on the ground that appellate review of the conviction could have been obtained without use of a stenographic transcript.[109] Black replied with his own memorandum "The opinion I circulated in this case," said Black, "is *not* based on the premise that a convicted defendant can *never* get full appellate review without a transcript. . . . My opinion *is* based on the premise that in *many* cases it is impossible for a defendant to get full appellate review without a transcript." Harlan was urging "the premise that the State is wrong in conceding here that these petitioners have been denied full appellate review because of their poverty. Taking this step in order to avoid the determination of a constitutional question is a higher price than I am willing to pay."[110]

Harlan then circulated another memorandum: "After much thought, I have decided to vote with the dissenters in this case."[111] He attached a dissenting opinion that he planned to file. Harlan stated his new position succinctly in a handwritten note to Frankfurter, "Sorry I can't convince you in *Griffin!* If I followed my heart, I'd be with you, but what you have decided seems to me wholly unsound!"[112]

Burton wrote a dissent that Minton joined. Harlan joined this dissent, in addition to filing his own dissenting opinion. The Burton dissent was also joined by Reed, despite his support of the Warren and Black position at the conference. Warren, Douglas, and Clark joined Black's opinion, but it became that of only a plurality when Frankfurter sent a memorandum stating that he planned to write a separate concurring opinion that would "limit the doctrine to situations like unto those of the present petitioners—to have the doctrine operate prospectively (by prospectively I mean with a definite cut-off date) and not retroactively."[113]

The *Griffin* decision was announced on April 28, 1956. The four dissenters stressed that "Mr. Justice Black's opinion is not limited to the future."[114] In accord with his conference statement, Black refused to make the decision prospective only. That was why Frankfurter wrote his separate concurrence, which stressed, as his memo had indicated, that the decision should speak only prospectively. At the conference, Warren had expressed a similar view. But he joined the

Black opinion to prevent the Court from appearing even more divided on the case.

As it turned out, *Griffin* was a watershed in the Warren Court's jurisprudence. In it, following the Chief's conference lead, the Court made its first broad pronouncement of economic equality in the criminal process. After *Griffin* the Warren Court appeared to agree with Bernard Shaw that "the worst of crimes is poverty," as it tried to equalize criminal law between those possessed of means and the less affluent. It was the *Griffin* approach that was to be the foundation of the landmark 1963 decision in *Gideon v. Wainwright*[115] requiring counsel to be appointed for indigent defendants.

There is a note in Frankfurter's papers indicating that Harlan changed his mind again after *Griffin* was decided. "I think that I may say without impropriety," wrote Harlan, "that I am glad that Griffin v. Illinois was decided as it was. . . . We needed a jolt." Harlan emphasized, however, that "We have not dealt with the problems of the old cases. I am glad, indeed, that you discussed the question in your opinion. We need a doctrine that will permit the right course to be shaped for the future uninfluenced by the fear of wholesale jail deliveries."[116]

During the 1955 Term, Warren was also starting to assert himself more forcefully in other areas, even where his views conflicted with those of most of the Brethren. *United States v. E. I. du Pont de Nemours & Co.*,[117] decided on the last day of the term, June 11, 1956, is a good illustration. The Government had brought suit under the Sherman Anti-Trust Act, charging du Pont with monopolizing the market for cellophane. The lower court had decided for du Pont. Its decision was based on the finding that cellophane was part of the market for flexible packaging materials and that competition from other packaging materials prevented du Pont from possessing monopoly powers in its sales of cellophane.

At the conference on October 14, 1955,[118] only seven Justices participated, since Clark and Harlan had disqualified themselves. Warren began the discussion by saying that the more he heard, the more he was concerned about the case. "The relevant market here," he declared, "is cellophane and *not* the flexible wrapping papers. I don't believe they are in direct competition with cellophane. I don't believe that market is really competitive in the normal sense." The Chief noted that whether du Pont had tried to dominate the market was not controlling: "intent is not necessary if [there is the] actual fact of monopoly." Nor could du Pont rely on its waterproof patents as a defense. It had gone beyond the economic power of the patents in dividing up the world on cellophane. "I don't say any of their actions were illegal, but in combination I say it is monopoly." Warren concluded that he would reverse and send the case back for the district court "to write a decree to protect public against this control over cellophane."

Black and Douglas agreed with the Chief, but Reed, Frankfurter, Burton, and Minton voted for affirmance. Reed, in particular, stressed that there was "nothing unreasonable here and size makes no difference." He was most concerned that reversal "would mean du Pont must divest itself of its plants and teach others their secret methods."

Early in 1956, Douglas wrote Warren reaffirming the view that there was an antitrust violation. He asserted, "That du Pont had monopoly power in cellophane is clear: (1) it could exclude competitors as it chose (2) it could raise or control the price of cellophane as it chose." Douglas went even further than the Chief in disposing of the claim that du Pont did not have monopoly power over the entire market for flexible packaging materials. According to Douglas, "duPont's monopoly to be illegal need not extend to the entire market. It is sufficient under §2 of the Sherman Act that the monopoly extend to 'any part' of interstate commerce. . . . It is therefore immaterial that duPont does not have a monopoly over the entire flexible package market."[119]

Warren did not accept this far-reaching Douglas approach. Reed delivered the majority opinion affirming the lower court on the question of relevant market. The Chief Justice wrote a dissent, joined by Black and Douglas, that followed the approach outlined by Warren in his conference statement—that the relevant market was that for cellophane and, "Since du Pont has the lion's share of that market, it must have monopoly power."

As was true during Warren's first terms, his leadership abilities were displayed as much in the chaff, as in the wheat, of the judicial mill. Some cases during the 1955 Term, now of interest only to Supreme

Court specialists, show how the Chief Justice continued to develop his ability to direct the conference. An illustrative case is *Mastro Plas-tics Corp. v. National Labor Relations Board*,[120] decided on February 27, 1956. The Taft–Hartley Act provided that no collective bargaining agreement could be terminated or modified unless sixty days notice was given before the agreement's expiration date. Any employees who engaged in a strike during the sixty-day period would lose their status as employees, which meant that they would also lose their protection under the Act. Did this bar apply where the strike during the period was intended as a protest against unfair labor practices of the employer?

A literal reading of the Taft–Hartley provision would require an affirmative answer. But that was not the way Warren proposed to read the statute in his presentation at the conference on the case in October, 1955.[121] "I wouldn't hold the strike against the union," the Chief stated at the outset of his discussion. "The purpose of Congress was to have them bargain freely. . . . The union can't bargain at the table if the employer can go out and destroy the union. That wouldn't bring peace." Nor was it realistic to say that the union's only remedy against unfair labor practices was to complain to the National Labor Relations Board. "The right to go before the Board," said Warren, "is an empty gesture" because it would involve "too long a delay."

Warren's refusal to follow the literal language of the statute set the tone for the Brethren. Reed, Douglas, Burton, and Clark agreed with the Chief, with Frankfurter, Minton, and Harlan indicating they would vote the other way. The importance of Warren's lead may be seen from the reaction of Black, normally as pro-labor as any of the Brethren. When Warren finished his conference presentation, Black declared, "I wish I could come out that way. But the language is so clear I couldn't read into it such an interpretation." Black conceded, "I might change, but, as of now, I can't get around the clear language. It's an outrageous situation to put the union in such a position, but it does."

As it turned out, Black ultimately joined the opinion of the Court, written by Burton, which followed Warren's conference approach. Frankfurter wrote a strong dissent, joined by Minton and Harlan. He was bitter over what he felt was the Court's rewriting of the statute. On February 14, 1956, he wrote Reed, who had strongly supported Warren at the conference, "If I did not have, . . . a cast-iron stomach, your attitude toward congressional legislation would give me ulcers." What the Court was doing was "nullifying a provision of Congress. Your compassionate heart says, 'The hell with it! We are not going to allow an employer who is guilty of [unfair] labor practices to get away with it.' It is not to be assumed that Congress intended this." [122]

Two weeks later, Frankfurter wrote Reed "that this is the first case since you and I have been here in which the Court said to Congress: 'We seriously dislike what you have done, therefore we will completely undo it.'" [123] In another letter, he told Reed, "If I weren't so cowardly, I would have written a three-line dissent in the *Mastro* case:

" 'If it takes 19 pages to explain why the obvious meaning of language is to be rejected, the necessity for such elaborateness certainly disproves the justification for not giving English words their English meaning.'

"If I write that kind of a dissent, will you join it? Or would you prefer this:

" 'If it takes 19 pages to reject the obvious meaning of the English language, it is better not to reject it.'" [124]

Warren's willingness to lead the Court in construing a statute liberally to reach what he considered an essentially fair result may also be seen in *Indian Towing Co. v. United States*, [125] decided November 21, 1955. The statute was the Federal Tort Claims Act of 1946. It imposes liability in tort upon the United States "in the same manner and to the same extent as a private individual in like circumstances." Plaintiffs sued the U.S. when a barge towed by them was damaged. They claimed the accident occurred because of the negligence of the Coast Guard, which had failed to keep a lighthouse in proper operation. The Government relied on an exemption in the Tort Claims Act for damages caused by performance of discretionary functions by U.S. officials.

Even before the oral argument on October 13, Frankfurter prepared a memorandum, circulated October 7, that stated, "the real question in the case before us is whether the negligent failure of the Coast Guard in its duty to maintain a lighthouse is within or without the Tort Claims Act." [126] But how could the failure be within the Act if it was within the Coast Guard's discretion to decide whether and where it would operate lighthouses?

At the October 15 conference,[127] Warren indicated a simple way out of the dilemma. As he saw it, "The discretionary act is putting the lighthouse where it is. After it was put there, liability attaches." In other words, there is a difference between the discretion to undertake a function such as providing lighthouse service and, once the discretion is exercised in the affirmative, the negligent operation of a particular lighthouse. The Government may possess discretionary authority to perform or not to perform certain functions; but that should not immunize it from liability where the functions are performed negligently in circumstances where a private person could be liable.

"Is there anything so distinctive about lighthouses," Warren asked at the conference, "that lifts it from [this rule of] liability?" He answered that there was "nothing unique" about them. "There were no private persons to carry on such service and so the Government took it over." He gave as an example of a comparable private service the operation of lights on a railroad bridge, where the railroad would be liable in similar circumstances. He noted that the Tort Claims Act contained an exemption from liability for damages caused by carriage of the mail. Yet, "if a mail sack was thrown through a store window, the U.S. would be liable."

"The question," Warren concluded his conference presentation, "is: shall we take the plain purpose of the Act or shall we limit it? Congress has made it very broad and it can narrow it if that is desirable."

Warren's statement pointed the way to the *Indian Towing* decision. A Frankfurter opinion for a bare majority of the Court held the U.S. liable on the theory outlined by the Chief. As soon as he received Frankfurter's draft, Warren sent back a handwritten note, on November 10, "I like your opinion in *Indian Towing* Company but out of courtesy to the other side will withhold formal agreement until the dissent is circulated."[128]

Even at this early stage of his career on the Court, as these cases show, Warren tended to use "fairness" as the polestar of his judicial approach. When he felt that fair play had not been observed, he did not hesitate to take a position, even though it meant a formal dissent. In *Parr v. United States*,[129] decided June 11, 1956, Parr had been indicted for income tax evasion in Corpus Christi, Texas. He obtained a transfer of the proceeding to Laredo, on the ground that he could not obtain a fair trial because of local prejudice against him in Corpus Christi. The Government was dissatisfied with the transfer, but the district court at Laredo refused to move the case elsewhere. The Government then obtained a new indictment at Austin and moved to dismiss the case in Laredo. The motion was granted in the lower courts.

At the *Parr* conference,[130] Warren stated, "I'd reverse." The decision below "lets the Government play ducks and drakes. They went out of their way to file in Corpus. Now they want to get out of it." That said, Warren, was "unfair." He stuck to this position even though a majority voted the other way. When the opinion of the Court was announced, Warren, joined by Black, Douglas, and Clark, delivered a sharp dissent.

At the end of 1955, Frankfurter wrote to Harlan about a case involving railroad liability for damages to eggs: "I now appreciate better than I ever did before what is meant by 'walking on eggs.' "[131] During his first terms on the Court, Warren must also have felt at times that he was "walking on eggs." By the end of the 1955 Term, however, he could reasonably conclude that he was, as Frankfurter put it in the same letter, "walking over those eggs with, I hope, less breakage."

During the 1955 Term, the Chief Justice began to join hands with Black and Douglas. Particularly toward the end of the term, Warren increasingly refused to go along with the Frankfurter philosophy of judicial restraint. In his *New York Times* review of the term, James Reston concluded that "Chief Justice Earl Warren has joined what some people call the liberal . . . wing of the nation's highest tribunal." As Reston saw it, the Court now contained "a 'liberal nucleus' of Chief Justice Warren and Justices Black and Douglas."[132] A *Times* editorial, entitled *Guardian of Liberty,* approved the new alignment: "the term . . . saw the court consistently restating the principles of liberty, dignity, and justice."[133]

Others, however, took a dimmer view both of the Court and its Chief Justice. Critics now directed their condemnations at the decisions that appeared to favor Communists and those charged with subversive activities. In a handwritten note to Black during the 1955 Term, Douglas asked, "Did you see the article in Newsweek . . . where he said there were two groups in the Court one desiring to go easy on Communists and the other not?"[134] To those who attacked the Court on Capitol Hill, there was no doubt to which group the Chief Justice belonged. "In [the Communists'] book," declared Senator Joseph R. McCarthy, "Earl Warren is a hero. I don't accuse him of being a Communist, but there is something radically wrong with him. . . . The court has sunk to a new low since Warren took over." [135]

Congressional criticism was to intensify over the years as the Warren Court continued to rewrite so much of our constitutional law. Looking back at the Warren years, Justice Byron White points out that, as far as relations with Congress are concerned, "Things have changed . . . for the better as far as I can see" under Chief Justice Warren E. Burger. As White recalls it, "Chief Justice Warren did have such a problem with the civil rights thing, and with prayers and with reapportionment. Congress was in such a terrible stew that his name was mud [there], which rubbed off on all of us. . . . The Chief was not a big popular fellow over there, so he was very reluctant . . . to ask for substantial things" for the Court's budget.

When Warren became Chief Justice, neither he nor any of the Justices had an official car at his disposal. One night, he had his secretary call for a limousine to attend a White House dinner. Mrs. Warren protested that it was a needless extravagance, but he insisted that it would not be appropriate for the Chief Justice to call on the President in a taxicab. When they were told the car had arrived, they were shocked to find that it was a station wagon, with large lettering: WASHINGTON NATIONAL AIRPORT. The driver said they had thought the rental was for the airport, and this car had been used in order to take care of the baggage. It was too late to make other arrangements (and, besides, they would have had to pay in any case), so they went to the White House in it.

The arrival of the Chief Justice in the airport wagon created quite a stir in official Washington. Soon thereafter, the Chairman of the Senate Appropriations Committee added an amendment to provide the Chief Justice with an official car to an appropriations bill. It passed without discussion. Except for the White House incident, Warren said, "I doubt that I would ever have had a government vehicle." [136]

One of the things Justice White remembers about Warren is "that he enjoyed so much going around on trips. To me and for most people going on a trip, making speeches, meeting people all the time is absolutely exhausting. But it seemed to refresh him and it was almost like an old fire horse getting out. . . . If he went on a trip somewhere like to Europe, even though he was on an official schedule, he would come back not exhausted, but fresher."

Warren had rarely been abroad before his Court appointment. But he more than made up for this after he became Chief Justice. It was the rare recess between terms that did not see the Chief and Mrs. Warren traveling abroad, usually on an official visit as head of the federal judiciary. As soon as the 1954 Term ended, in June 1955, the Warrens left to visit the Scandinavian countries, Germany, and Belgium. Warren was able to fulfill his lifelong ambition when he visited the northernmost part of Europe, "to see the midnight sun on the longest day of the year."

Warren was the characteristic American traveler, visiting all the sights that should be seen and responding in typical tourist fashion. The Brethren would be bombarded by picture post-cards that read like a catalogue of travel clichés. "We have spent several days," reads one card to Black, "at the Lakes of Killarney. They are lovely. Yesterday we went to Cork and Blarney Castle where we performed all the rites." [137] "Here we are," to quote another, "on the beautiful island of Elba. Why Napoleon ever fled from it, I will never understand." [138] Most of the cards were sent by Mrs. Warren, both to members of the family and the Justices. She also kept a journal as a record of their travels. It was a family joke that Warren had once said, "Of course Nina has to go along. If she didn't how would we know where we'd been?" [139]

Toward the end of Warren's judicial career, he was attacked by Congressional critics because the State Department had paid travel expenses and per diem for both himself and Mrs. Warren on the trips he took as part of the Government's program of sending distinguished Americans abroad. There were five such trips while Warren was Chief Justice. According to one Congressman in 1967, Warren was "loading himself on the taxpayer's back." [140] The State Department replied that it considered itself "fortunate" that someone of Warren's stature was willing to represent the United States abroad. [141]

Perhaps the most important official trip by the Chief Justice was made during the summer recess after the 1955 Term, when the Warrens visited India. Two of the Brethren discussed the visit in letters. "What do you think of the Chief's junket to India?" asked Harlan in a July 1956 letter to Frankfurter. "I can see why the President would want him to go—and no one could do a better job than he—but I do wish the Court could be left alone on these essentially political activities."[142]

"I have good reason," Frankfurter replied, "for knowing that it was not the President who asked the Chief to go to India. He was invited directly by the Indians for some judicial and academic occasions. I share the thought behind the anxiety which you express. I think it was quite right for him to accept the Indian invitation during the summer recess, but it should have been accepted without asking either the President or the Secretary of State whether it was agreeable to them. Thereby occasion was given for publicity which they naturally would want to exploit, or at least to give it a political innuendo, which it ought not to have."[143]

Warren confirmed the Frankfurter version in a note to Black: "My invitation to visit India was transmitted to me by Sec. Dulles who said he thought it would be helpful if I would accept."[144] A week later, Douglas wrote Black, "I was glad the Chief went to India. He'll make a lot of friends for us there."[145]

As it turned out, Warren's Indian trip developed into a triumphal good-will tour. As *Life* reported, "the color-sensitive Indians were reminded that he was the man who had pronounced the momentous decision banning racial segregation in U.S. public schools."[146] Warren received a rousing reception as the author of the *Brown* opinion, making, according to A. M. Rosenthal of the *New York Times,* a "deep impression on the Indian people."[147] But the impression made was far from one-sided. Gerald T. Dunne states that, "in terms of attitude and determination, the trip's "decisive influence . . . could be compared only with Woodrow Wilson's tumultuous European reception of 1919."[148] Warren himself described his India visit as "one of the most moving experiences of my life."[149] For the first time, he was able to appreciate the work of the Court in a comparative context. He returned with a broadened perspective, aware that the judicial protection of human rights was supported by a constituency that stretched far beyond American boundaries. The global image of the United States was directly related to the Supreme Court's role in enforcing constitutional guaranties against governmental infringements.

6.

1956 TERM: "B.B.D. AND W."

"What does this mean? Why hasn't this got a head?" Governor Warren asked Irving Stone, the writer, who had become a close friend. Stone was trying to introduce Warren to modern art, but, he says, "it didn't, couldn't make any sense" to the Governor. Finally, Warren said, "Irving, I don't understand what this is all about. It is outside my training." Asked whether Warren got to know any more about art as their friendship ripened, Stone laughed and said, "I think he left the subject alone."[1]

In most respects Earl Warren could have been a character out of Sinclair Lewis or Sherwood Anderson. Justice Potter Stewart's comments are worth requoting: "Warren's great strength was his simple belief in the things we now laugh at: motherhood, marriage, family, flag, and the like." These, according to Stewart, were the "eternal, rather bromidic, platitudes in which he sincerely believed." These were the foundation of Warren's jurisprudence, as they were of his way of life.

When we add to this Warren's bluff masculine bonhomie, his love of sports and the outdoors, and his lack of intellectual interests or pretensions, we end up with a typical representative of the Middle America of his day. Except for one thing—Warren's leadership abilities. As Stewart sees it, Warren may not have been an intellectual, but "he had instinctive qualities of leadership."

Even the most inspiring general must, however, have troops who are willing and able to follow his lead. Chief Justice Warren received his most capable lieutenant after Sherman Minton resigned in 1956.

In October of that year, President Eisenhower appointed William J. Brennan, Jr., to fill the vacancy. Brennan had been a judge in New Jersey for seven years, rising from the state trial court to its highest bench, before being elevated to the Supreme Court. He had more judicial experience than any other member of the Warren Court and was the only one of the Brethren to have served as a state judge. Eisenhower told Brennan that he greatly admired New Jersey Chief Justice Arthur T. Vanderbilt, on whose court Brennan was then serving. The President said he had been sorry that Vanderbilt's illness had prevented his being considered for appointment to the Supreme Court.

In fairly short order Eisenhower became as disenchanted with his newest appointee as with Warren himself. When Burton went to see the President in July 1958 about his resignation from the Court, Eisenhower complained about Brennan's decisions, as well as Warren's.[2] Brennan became a firm adherent of the activist philosophy and a principal ally of the Chief Justice.

Brennan had been Frankfurter's student at Harvard Law School and, on his appointment, his former professor wrote a friend, "It makes me feel like an old man to think of having a former student on the Court and, of course, it gives me great pleasure to find myself on the Court with a former student."[3] Yet, if Frankfurter expected the new Justice to continue his pupilage, he was soon disillusioned. After Brennan had joined Warren in the Court's activist wing, Frankfurter supposedly quipped, "I always encouraged my students to think for themselves, but Brennan goes too far!"[4]

After his appointment in October 1956, Brennan went to the Court to visit the Chief Justice. Warren escorted him to the Brethren's third-floor lounge. The room was dark and, when Warren switched on the lights, there sat the other Justices watching the opening game of the World Series on television. Warren then introduced their new colleague to the others. Thereupon one of the Justices called out, "Sit down so we can see the game!"

Brennan soon became Warren's closest colleague. The two were completely dissimilar in appearance: the new Justice was small and feisty—almost leprechaun-like in appearance. Yet he had the same hearty bluffness and ability to put people at ease that characterized the Chief. On a personal basis, Warren was more comfortable with Brennan than with any of the other Justices, and an intimacy developed between them of a type that never took place between Warren and Black or Warren and Douglas, however close the latters' views may have been to his. The Chief would turn to Brennan when he wanted to discuss a case or some other matter on which he wanted an exchange of views. The two would usually meet on Thursday, when Warren would come to Brennan's chambers to go over the cases that were to be discussed at the Friday conference.

Just after Brennan's appointment, Frankfurter wrote, "Someone who knows him well . . . made a fitting characterization in saying he is a man of ability and affability."[5] Brennan's twinkling eyes and unassuming manner masked a keen intelligence. He was probably the hardest worker among the Brethren. It was Brennan to whom the Chief was to assign the opinions in some of the most important cases decided by the Warren Court.

It was during the 1956 Term, that Warren became a wholehearted advocate of judicial activism, finally rejecting the Frankfurter philosophy of judicial restraint. The new Warren posture was demonstrated early in the term by his dissent in *Breithaupt v. Abram*,[6] where he rejected a crucial line in the Frankfurter jurisprudence—that between *Wolf v. Colorado*[7] and *Rochin v. California*.[8] In *Wolf*, the Frankfurter opinion for the Court refused to hold that the exclusionary rule (barring illegally obtained evidence in a criminal trial) was incorporated within the due process clause of the Fourteenth Amendment. Due process, in the Frankfurter view, protects only those principles that the Supreme Court once said were "so rooted in the traditions and conscience of our people as to be ranked as fundamental"[9]—what Frankfurter termed, in *Rochin*, "those canons of decency and fairness which express the notions of justice of English-speaking peoples."[10] In *Wolf*, Frankfurter had found that the rule excluding illegally obtained evidence was not a basic notion of justice.

But *Wolf* did not mean that use of illegally obtained evidence could never violate due process. As Frankfurter wrote in his initial memorandum on the *Rochin* case, in which the police had forcibly extracted narcotic pills with a stomach pump, "there are certain standards of civilized conduct below which the Due Process Clause bars a State from falling."[11] The line was drawn by *Rochin*. Use of evidence thus obtained was held contrary to due process: "This is conduct," declared the *Rochin* opinion, "that shocks the conscience."[12]

Under *Rochin,* state criminal law may not resort to methods that offend civilized standards. It may not be enough to invalidate a state conviction that evidence has been obtained illegally; but a different result is reached where the method used by the state is deemed repulsive. Frankfurter explained the difference in a 1958 letter to Justice Charles E. Whittaker: "a particular instance of hardship may be so offensive to fundamental notions of fairness that the due process clause may be invoked by the victim of such individual outrage. That is the essence of due process: a shock to the conscience in a particular case." [13]

Under Frankfurter's *Wolf–Rochin* test, *Breithaupt v. Abram* did not present a difficult case. After a highway accident involving Breithaupt's auto, he was taken to a hospital. A doctor withdrew a sample of blood with a hypodermic needle while Breithaupt was still unconscious. At his trial for manslaughter, the blood test was admitted into evidence. The Brethren voted six-to-three to grant certiorari, with Black, Reed, and Clark for denial. In a Clark opinion delivered February 25, 1957, the Court upheld Breithaupt's conviction, emphasizing that a blood test, taken by a skilled technician, contains nothing of the brutal type of police conduct involved in *Rochin.*

Warren rejected the Frankfurter notion that there was a valid line between *Wolf* and *Rochin.* Warren's view on this was indicated in a pithy comment to Alan Barth, the civil libertarian: "What's so bad about a stomach pump? I've had my stomach pumped lots of times." [14] To Warren, the *Rochin* stomach pump was no worse than the *Breithaupt* hypodermic. Both were unauthorized physical intrusions condemned by due process.

In *Breithaupt,* the Chief Justice acted on this view and filed a short but vigorous dissent, joined by Black and Douglas. As Warren saw it in his dissent, "Only personal reaction to the stomach pump and the blood test can distinguish them. To base the restriction which the Due Process Clause imposes on state criminal procedures upon such realities is to build on shifting sands." [15]

His *Breithaupt* dissent was Warren's overt declaration of intellectual independence from the Frankfurter conception of review power, as well as a repudiation of his own view in *Irvine v. California,* discussed in Chapter 4. After *Breithaupt,* the Chief voted with Black and Douglas in virtually all cases involving individual rights. What made the 1956 Term so significant, however, was not only that it saw the joining of hands by Warren with Black and Douglas, but that it saw, for the first time, a fluctuating Court majority in favor of the activist approach.

During the 1956 Term, Brennan also became a follower of the Black–Douglas approach. The result was a firm core of four in favor of the activist posture, made up, as *New York Times* pundit Arthur Krock put it, of the "meeting of minds of two brethren of New Deal origin and philosophy and two appointed by President Eisenhower."[16] *Time,* in typical fashion, termed the new bloc on the Warren Court, "B.B.D. and W."[17]—in paraphrase of the initials widely used to designate a noted advertising firm. Most important, the activist four, only one short of a majority, were not opposed by a coherent conservative combination. In the significant decisions toward the end of the term, the four were able to obtain the concurrence of one or more other Justices. Observers credited Warren with the crucial role by, in *Time*'s phrase, "using his considerable personal talents to work out majorities for the liberal view."[18] Warren's influence was particularly important in its impact on Clark. According to a Clark law clerk, "When he went into conference with an open mind, he would often be influenced by the arguments of the Chief."[19]

Public attention during the 1956 Term came most particularly to be focused on the decisions in cases that involved alleged Communists. At the term's very beginning on October 10, 1956, the Court dealt the government a blow in *Mesarosh v. United States,*[20] where five Communists had been convicted of violating the Smith Act. Two weeks before the case was scheduled for argument, the government had moved to remand the case to the trial court to determine whether Mazzei, a paid informer who had been the government's principal witness, had testified truthfully. The motion was based upon the government's belief that Mazzei had given false testimony in other proceedings. The Court denied the motion. Instead, it vacated the convictions and ordered the district court to grant defendants a new trial.

On November 5, the Chief Justice delivered an unusually strong opinion in which, in the words of one writer, he "lectured the representatives of the Justice Department as if they were errant school boys."[21] According to Warren, "Mazzei, by his testimony, has poisoned the water in this reservoir, and the reservoir cannot be cleansed without first draining it of all impurity. . . . there can be no other just result than to accord petitioners a new trial." [22]

Harlan, joined by Frankfurter and Burton, wrote a dissent urging that the government's motion should be granted, since it was the job of the trial court to determine whether false testimony had been given by Mazzei in this case. Harlan stated that the Court had treated the case as though the government had conceded the untrustworthiness of Mazzei's testimony. That was not the case. The government had only conceded that it believed Mazzei had testified falsely in other proceedings and that his testimony at the trial should be thoroughly investigated.

In an earlier letter to Frankfurter, Harlan said that this alleged misunderstanding led the Brethren to an erroneous result. "After all," Harlan asserted, "the unsatisfactory discussion at our last Conference stemmed from the initial mistaken premise that the Government had conceded Mazzei's perjury at the trial. Even though this error was exposed, the discussion never got back on the track, and the stump speeches we heard really reflected, I think, that original error." [23]

During the October 19 conference to consider the *Mesarosh* opinions, Frankfurter passed Harlan a note complimenting him on the footnotes in his dissent. Harlan returned it, with the comment, "YES, but how write a memo on dissent that doesn't offend the Chief?!" Frankfurter wrote under this that Harlan "refers to the C.J.'s very touchy complaints about Harlan's draft dissent in *Mesarosh*. . . . The Chief quite unfairly tried to argue against Harlan's account of the facts, instead of setting down in his opinion . . . his view of them." [24]

According to Frankfurter, the following statements were made at the *Mesarosh* conference:

"*Black, J.:* It's too bad this question has not come up in a different kind of case, for then I would agree that as to two of the defendants there should be an acquittal directed, and I will still go along if a majority of the Court is for that. But on the whole, I think it is desirable in this case not to do that but to order a new trial for all five defendants.

"*Reed, J.:* If this had been an ordinary case, I would think we should not dispose of the motion for a remand but hear the whole case on the merits. But in this case I think it is perhaps better to order a new trial for all the defendants.

"*Clark, J.:* You have brought this on yourselves by what you did in the *Communist Party case*. In that case you sent the case back to the Board. In this case you should send it back to the jury."

Frankfurter sent the above quotes to Reed with the comment:

"Equal Justice to All"

"Q.E.D."[25]

The most important 1956 Term subversion cases were not decided until the end of the term. In the interim between *Mesarosh* and those decisions, the Court dealt with the usual run of cases. Some were of importance; most were the chaff of the court calendar, significant more for what they tell us of the Brethren than for their contribution to the law.

Thus "I must have been off my trolley," reads a note passed by Black to Douglas at a conference on *Miller v. Arkansas*,[26] in 1956.[27] And, in another case, (*Hintopoulos v. Shaughnessy*)[28] Frankfurter wrote to Harlan on his copy of his draft opinion, to confirm the criticism of the Court he had expressed years ago, "for not indicating why it granted *cert.* when it did not appear obvious," then adding, "P.S. I know that sometimes this cannot be truthfully done!" Harlan replied, that he didn't "quite like to say we granted cert 'out of consideration for the milk of human kindness!' "[29] Frankfurter, again indicating his disapproval of his activist colleagues, wrote to Harlan about a Black opinion in a case under the Federal Tort Claims Act,[30] and said that he agreed with the thrust of the opinion. "And so I am joining it, despite the reflection that you or I would not have dealt with the matter in such a cavalier fashion."[31]

Frankfurter was now starting to join Warren and Brennan with Black and Douglas in his deprecatory comments. The changing Frankfurter attitude is shown by his comments about *Smith v. Sperling*.[32] The case was a technical one, involving the question of the proper alignment of the parties in a stockholder's suit. Smith had brought a stockholder's derivative suit in a federal court against Warner Brothers' Pictures, Inc., and some of its directors, alleging fraudulent wastage of Warner Brothers' assets for the benefit of one director's son-in-law. The lower court had realigned the corporation as party plaintiff, on the ground that the cause of action sought to be enforced was one that belonged to the corporation. It relied upon *Doctor v. Harrington*,[33] a 1905 Supreme Court decision which held that there should be such a realignment, unless the corporation was "antagonistic" to the stockholder. The difficulty with the lower court decision, from plaintiff's point of view, was that it meant a dismissal of the suit, since, with Warner Brothers as plaintiff, there was no diversity of citizenship, as required for suit in a federal court.

At the conference, Frankfurter said the case raised "more basic questions affecting federal jurisdiction and procedure than, if I may quote Hamlet, 'are dreamt of in our philosophy'—and by 'our' I mean all of us."[34] Frankfurter urged that *Doctor v. Harrington* should be followed and, since the corporation was not "antagonistic" to the stockholder within the meaning of that case, the decision below should be affirmed. He was supported by Burton, Clark, and Whittaker, (whose March, 1957, appointment will be discussed later in this chapter). Warren, Black, Douglas, and Brennan felt that it was enough for the corporation to remain aligned as defendant that it failed to take action against the alleged fraud. Non-suit, even if non-collusive, was, in their view, enough to justify such a result.

Harlan had been unable to decide at the conference. Frankfurter, however, worked hard to persuade him. A letter from Harlan to Warren informed the Chief that the Frankfurter effort was successful. "I stand persuaded," wrote Harlan at the end of the copy of this letter that he sent to Frankfurter. "Perhaps this will open the way for our new brother to choose this as his 'first.' "[35] But the putative majority soon evaporated. A Frankfurter letter of April 9 to Clark declared, "I can't withhold the fact that I am shocked." The reason, Frankfurter wrote, was a conversation Clark had had with Whittaker, "when he [Whittaker] was told that you had left him."[36]

There was now a bare majority for reversal. Douglas wrote an opinion of the Court following the approach taken by Warren, Black, Brennan, and himself at the conference. The now-minority decided not to have the new Justice write the dissent. Instead, Frankfurter filed a vigorous dissent, joined by Burton, Whittaker, and Harlan, who had voted after months of persuasive effort by Frankfurter. Frankfurter had written a long letter to Harlan as part of his wooing campaign. In it he summarized the "attitude of mind" disclosed by Warren, Black, Douglas, and Brennan during the conference discussion. The Frankfurter statement deserves quotation, since it shows how he was tending to lump the four together as the 1956 Term went on:

The Chief moved easily from Warner Brothers' "skullduggery" to satisfaction of the requirements of federal jurisdiction. Black, J., having at the bar suffered from removal by corporations of state litigation to the federal courts, now is glad to have corporations get theirs. Douglas, J., having concluded that every situation like the allegations in Warner Brothers . . . satisfies as a matter of "human nature," and therefore of law, the requirements of *Doctor v. Harrington*, less than an hour later is ready to overrule *Doctor v. Harrington* if that is necessary for the desired result. Brennan, J., gives reasons that make one stand on one's head, by suggesting that since under *Erie* [*Railroad Co. v. Tompkins*], a federal court is to be deemed merely another state court in enforcing a state cause of action, the barrier against finding ready access to a federal court erected by the fifty-year old doctrine might as well be swept away, to say nothing of the procedural advantages afforded by a suit in the federal courts, advantages that in fact do not exist.

Frankfurter closed his letter to Harlan, "It is because I happily know that you have the same kind of allegiance to law that I have felt free to send you this letter."[37]

As the 1956 Term proceeded, the Chief Justice was moving further away from the doctrine of judicial restraint. Though he had earlier been drawn to the Frankfurter position, Warren, always more a man of action than reflection, found himself increasingly drawn toward the activist posture. Now he was starting to hesitate before casting his vote against those who claimed that their personal rights had been violated. "I agree with deep regret," wrote Warren to Brennan, in joining a decision upholding the deportation of a Philippine national on the ground that he became an alien on the grant of independence to the Philippines.[38]

In *Blackburn v. Alabama,*[39] certiorari had been granted, as Frankfurter put it in a memorandum on the case, "to review the question whether a State conviction obtained from a person with defendant's mental history offended the Due Process Clause of the Fourteenth Amendment." In his memo, Frankfurter urged the Court not to consider the merits because this federal question had not been properly presented to the Alabama courts. "I feel very strongly about the merits," Frankfurter asserted. "To me they are rather shocking and I would reverse as a matter of course. But in pointing out the jurisdictional difficulty, I am not indulging in mere formalism."[40]

To Warren, "mere formalism" was *exactly* what was involved in Frankfurter's approach, but since the majority disagreed, the case was disposed of in accordance with the Frankfurter memo by a per curiam remanding to the Alabama court to state whether it had passed on a federal question. Warren joined Douglas and Brennan in a short dissent that stressed "Petitioner has made as strong a showing as possible that he signed the confession when he was insane."[41] That was all that mattered, since it alone required the conviction to be reversed.

Warren and Frankfurter also differed in *Radovich v. National Football League*,[42] which presented the question of whether professional football was subject to the anti-trust laws. Warren had been willing, in the 1953 *Toolson* case,[43] to reaffirm the 1922 decision upholding baseball's anti-trust exemption, provided that it was made clear that Congress had the right to remove the exemption if it chose. But he was unwilling to extend baseball's exemption to other professional sports and wrote the 1955 *International Boxing* opinion[44] refusing to hold professional boxing immune from anti-trust suits. Warren believed that professional sports had become big business and that those employed in athletics should be given the same protection possessed by others who dealt with large businesses.

Frankfurter had strongly disagreed with the *International Boxing* decision, doubting, as he had written Warren after seeing his draft *Boxing* opinion, "whether we can differentiate baseball from other sports which . . . are indistinguishable."[45] Frankfurter now sent a letter to Harlan and Brennan, who had come to the Court since the *Toolson* and *Boxing* decisions, to persuade them "that you have two more or less conflicting decisions of the Court and therefore do not have to make, as I rightly think, an untenable differentiation between football and baseball."[46]

Harlan and Brennan agreed that they were not bound by the *International Boxing* decision. Harlan wrote Brennan and Frankfurter that he had talked with Clark about the case and "he expressed a preference for holding Football is controlled by *Toulson* [sic]." Clark also "said that he would canvass other members of the Court to see whether he could obtain a 'Court' for that disposition."[47]

As it turned out, not only was Clark unable to obtain a majority for such a disposition; he allowed himself to be persuaded by Warren, who felt strongly that the *Boxing* decision should be followed. When he saw the Texan wavering in his direction, Warren assigned him the majority opinion—a method often used by Chief Justices to cement uncertain votes. Clark wrote an opinion of the Court that followed Warren's *International Boxing* approach and specifically limited the *Toolson* rule to baseball. Frankfurter dissented, perhaps protesting too much when he acknowledged how "conscious . . . I am of my limited competence in matters athletic."[48] Harlan and Brennan also dissented.

Frankfurter must have been delighted when he received this comment from Learned Hand, considered by many the greatest living judge: "You and your eight fellow saints at times push hard upon our insufficient dialectical equipment; for example, to the Lower Orders it seems difficult to distinguish between baseball and football. However, I remain as ever an obsequious sequent."[49]

Another case where Warren disagreed with Frankfurter, though he ultimately went along with his colleague's opinion, was *Achilli v. United States.*[50] It arose out of a prosecution under § 145(b) of the Internal Revenue Code, which made it a felony to attempt to evade income taxes by filing a false return. Achilli claimed that his offense was punishable also under § 3616(a), which made it a misdemeanor to file a false return with intent to evade a tax assessment. The Government contended that § 3616(a) did not apply to the income tax, but Achilli showed that income tax prosecutions had been brought under § 3616(a), as well as § 145(b).

The conference voted to affirm the decision below that § 145(b) had been intended by Congress as the exclusive provision for prosecuting evasions of the income tax. It also voted to have the holding announced in a brief per curiam. Frankfurter objected in a memorandum which stated that the decision "is to be justified and not merely to be dogmatically asserted." He said that he had drafted an opinion containing "a reasoned, detailed exposition of our conclusion."[51] Frankfurter's opinion went into the legislative history of the income tax legislation to show that Congress intended to withdraw the income tax from the reach of § 3616(a). The opinion failed to convince Douglas and Black, who had voted for reversal at the conference. They filed a dissent asserting that the decisive element was the fact that the Government had invoked § 3616(a) in 175 cases of alleged income tax evasion during the previous five years.

Warren was also troubled by the government's change in position. "As you know," he wrote Frankfurter, "I think it is rather shabby for the Government to repudiate in this Court for the first time its practice of picking and choosing as to whether defendants should be prosecuted for felony or misdemeanor for evasion of income tax." The Chief was, nevertheless, willing to go along with Frankfurter's opinion if he put in a paragraph showing that the government had prosecuted under both sections for income tax evasions during the last five years, after having previously taken the position that § 145(b) repealed § 3616(a)'s applicability to income tax evasions. Warren wanted the opinion to state, "This double shift of interpretation certainly does not strengthen its position, and in even slightly different circumstances might well lead to a different result."[52]

Frankfurter replied the same day, "I am very sorry, but I cannot bring myself to deem the Government reprehensible for its 'shift of position.' There is nothing unusual in my experience for a more thorough investigation on the part of lawyers to bring to light such matters when there is pressure for a more thorough investigation than had been had in the past." He refused to add the sentence on "shift of position" suggested by Warren, saying, "I cannot in good conscience reprimand the Government for something that is not reprehensible."[53] Frankfurter did, however, add the paragraph showing that the Government had prosecuted under both sections. Warren accepted this as adequate and acquiesced in the opinion.

One reason why Warren did not persist in his objections to the Frankfurter opinion is revealed in a Frankfurter *Memorandum for the Conference*. "I should like to think," Frankfurter wrote, "that as a rule I am about the last man on the Court to hurry the handing down of opinions. But *Achilli v. United States* presents a special situation. A number of convicted defendants are now out on bail who ought not, in view of the Court's decision, to be out on bail." Among those defendants was the notorious reputed leader of organized crime, Frank Costello. "It would not be pleasant," Frankfurter's memo asserted, "if Frank Costello, while at large, should become involved in another fracas. It is for this reason that it seems highly desirable for the *Achilli* case to come down next Monday."[54]

The *Achilli* decision did come down on the next Monday, May 27. A week later, the Court summarily affirmed Frank Costello's conviction on the authority of the *Achilli* decision.[55]

Before turning to the important decisions at the end of the 1956 Term, a word should be said about another personnel change among the Brethren. In the middle of the term, on February 25, 1957, Reed retired. The vacancy was filled a month later by the appointment of Charles E. Whittaker. The new Justice had grown up on a small farm in Kansas. He had quit high school at sixteen and had never gone to college. He began work in a Kansas City law firm as a messenger, office boy, and "bottle washer," going to an unaccredited law school at night. He eventually became a prosperous lawyer and was appointed a district judge by President Eisenhower in 1954. He was promoted to the U.S. Court of Appeals for the Eighth Circuit two years later.

In his memoirs, Eisenhower indicates that, after his disappointment with Warren, he decided to appoint only those with service on the bench to the Supreme Court. The President attributed the Chief Justice's unsatisfactory performance, in large part, to his lack of previous judicial experience.[56] The requirement of prior judicial service was criticized by Frankfurter, when he wrote to a federal judge, "all this talk about the desirability of 'judicial experience' and promotion from the lower federal bench derives from uncritical conceptions about the history, and work of the Court. It presupposes that because one cannot become a colonel unless he has been a major, one should not be put on this Court unless he has been on a lower Court."[57]

Whittaker's service on the Court bears out the Frankfurter criticism. All who worked with him concede that Whittaker was serious and hard working ("superconscientious," according to a Justice who served with him), but, with all that and his judicial experience, he may have been the worst Justice of the century. He had two fatal defects: lack of intellectual capacity and inability to reach decisions.

Whittaker, says one of the Brethren, "used to come out of our conference literally crying. You know Charlie had gone to night law school, and he began as an office boy and he'd been a farm boy and he had inside him an inferiority complex, which . . . showed and he'd say, 'Felix used words in there that I'd never heard of.' "

Early in the 1957 Term, Frankfurter circulated the following satirical opinion in a movie censorship case:

No. 372.—October Term, 1957.

Times Film Corporation, Petitioner, v. City of Chicago, Richard J. Daley and Timothy J. O'Connor.	))))))))

The Court of Appeals in this case sustained the censorship, under an Illinois statute, of a motion picture entitled, "The Game of Love." The theme of the film, so far as it has one, is the same as that in Benjamin Franklin's famous letter to his son, to the effect that the most easing way for an adolescent to learn the facts of life is under the tutelage of an older woman. A judgment that the manner in which this theme was conveyed by this film exceeded the bounds of free expression protected by the Fourteenth Amendment can only serve as confirmation of the saying, *"Honi soit qui mal y pense."*[58]

On November 6, 1957, Whittaker wrote back,

Dear Felix:

No. 372—Times Film Corporation,
   Petitioner v. City of Chicago,
   et al.

I join in your *per curiam* in this case.[59]

Frankfurter had to send Whittaker a written note explaining, "This was intended as a joke."[60]

In addition, Whittaker, more than any other Justice, found it difficult to make up his mind. Warren's "great strength," according to the Justice already quoted, was "not to have to agonize. That was Charlie Whittaker's great problem, you know. He was a very, very conscientious man and a fine man, but he just didn't have the power of decision." According to Douglas, "In Conference, Whittaker would take one position when the Chief or Black spoke, change his mind when Frankfurter spoke, and change back again when some other Justice spoke."[61] Then, after the conference, Whittaker would often agonize and agonize over decisions, swinging back and forth in key cases, which would make it most difficult for the Chief and the others.

After Frankfurter had sent him Alfred North Whitehead's *Symbolism,* Reed wrote, "I liked his phrase about the 'many problematic futures which will never dawn.' I am not so sure he is correct, however, in our work. They seem to dawn sooner or later."[62].

During the Warren years, the Supreme Court was confronted with problems entirely different from those presented to prior Courts. Among the problems that "dawned" in the Warren Court was that of the relation of obscenity to the First Amendment. Thus, referring to the question "whether obscenity is utterance within the area of protected speech and press," the opinion of the Court in *Roth v. United States*, decided June 24, 1957, states, "this is the first time the question has been squarely presented to this Court."[63]

Prior to the Court's decision in the *Roth* case, however, it had had to deal with *Butler v. Michigan*.[64] Butler had been convicted of violating Michigan's obscene literature statute that made it a crime to sell or distribute a book or other reading matter containing materials "tending to the corruption of the morals of youth." He made a broad attack on the law as a violation of freedom of speech, as well as a narrower one stressing the statute's prohibition of distribution to the general public on the basis of the undesirable influence upon youth. He also objected to the condemnation of the book involved because of isolated passages that appeared objectionable when divorced from the book as a whole. The Brethren had been closely divided on whether to take the case, with Warren, Black, Frankfurter, Douglas, and Clark voting, on February 2, 1956, to note probable jurisdiction, and Reed, Burton, Minton, and Harlan voting to dismiss for lack of jurisdiction. During the *Butler* argument on October 16, 1956, Warren had asked: "Does the statute say the criterion is 'obscene?'"

"No," counsel for Butler replied. "'containing' obscene."

"Without [that]," the Chief asked, "you would think the statute is all right?"

"Yes, provided the word 'containing' was . . . eliminated from the statute."[65]

At the October 19 *Butler* Conference[66] Warren was still troubled by this exchange. He said that he would vote to reverse on the ground that the court below "did not find the book as a whole obscene and that is necessary to sustain the statute. The state applied the statute to a man if it 'contained' [objectionable material]. That is bad." Black also spoke for reversal because the statute was unduly vague. Reed, too, voted to reverse. Although he felt the statute was not too vague, he questioned whether its "dominant purpose" did not violate the First Amendment. Douglas agreed with Reed. Brennan also thought the statute raised First Amendment issues. Burton and Clark said they would vote to affirm.

Frankfurter stated that, while he was generally in sympathy with what had been said, he would pass and not vote now. He noted that the *Roth* case, where certiorari had just been granted, would soon challenge the validity of the federal obscenity law. Harlan said he was inclined to reverse if the merits of the *Butler* statute were decided, but also felt that they should wait for the *Roth* case before dealing with that issue.

After the conference, Frankfurter circulated a memorandum, in which he stated, "The more I thought about this case the clearer it became that it should be decided on a narrow ground on which the whole Court, such is my strong hope, can agree."[67] Frankfurter wrote a draft opinion that struck down the Michigan law on the "narrow ground" that, in making it an offense to make available to the general public a book having a potentially deleterious influence upon youth, Michigan was reducing its adult population to reading only what is fit for children: "Surely this is to burn the house to roast the pig."[68] As Frankfurter explained the opinion in his memo, "I have tried to write as briefly as possible to avoid any intimation, even unintended, on the more or less contentious issues raised by other obscenity statutes."

The Frankfurter opinion convinced the Brethren who had wanted to decide the constitutional merits of obscenity laws, and it was issued on February 25, 1957, with no dissents. Brennan expressed the sentiments of those who originally voted on the broader issue, when he wrote asking Frankfurter to join him in the opinion. "I confess," Brennan wrote, "I originally thought this should have full dress treatment. It is probably wise, however, to hold that treatment until we are forced to it."[69]

The Court was "forced to" the "full dress treatment" when it decided the pending *Roth* case toward the end of the term. In *Roth,* the constitutionality of the federal criminal obscenity statute was clearly presented. The statute prohibited mailing material that was "obscene, lewd, lascivious, or filthy." Roth, who had been convicted for violating the statute, contended that it violated the First Amendment, as well as due process and the Tenth Amendment (since power to punish obscenity, he claimed, was in the states alone). The Court split sharply on whether to take the case. On January 14, 1957, certiorari had been granted, with Reed, Frankfurter, Burton, Clark, and Harlan voting to deny cert.

The *Roth* conference was held on April 26, 1957.[70] Warren indicated that he would vote to affirm Roth's conviction. "To reverse on the First Amendment," he said, "would go too far. The Federal Government must have a right to protect itself. The states and the Federal

Government both have it." It was not an exclusive state power: "The mail should not depend on state law." Warren expressed the opinion that the statute was not too vague. In his view "obscenity" and "filth" were sufficient terms.

Black and Douglas, of course, had no difficulty in such a case. Their absolutist view of the First Amendment, as they wrote in the dissent they filed in *Roth,* prohibited placing "any form of expression beyond the pale of the absolute prohibition of the First Amendment." They repeated this simple view at the *Roth* conference. Frankfurter supported Warren and voted for affirmance. Obscenity, he said, is an adequate phrase. "The Fourteenth Amendment is similarly vague and it's O.K. I don't propose to define it. We can't rest on a formula, such as 'clear and present danger.'" Burton, Clark, and Whittaker also spoke in favor of affirmance. Harlan indicated doubt on whether the federal government could act, saying that the states had "a wider field" here, since obscenity was a local problem.

Aside from Warren, the most important contribution to the *Roth* conference was made by Brennan. Speaking in favor of affirmance, he argued that the question of obscenity was a judicial question. The Court should restate it in terms of criminal law. "The test should be the 'dominant theme' test" and it was the place of the judge to apply it "before it goes to the jury."

What Brennan meant was made clear when the Chief assigned him the *Roth* opinion. Brennan's opinion of the Court, delivered June 24, 1957, asserted the important principle "that obscenity is not within the area of constitutionally protected speech or press." It also stated the test to determine whether particular material is obscene: "whether to the average person, applying contemporary community standards, the dominant theme of the material taken as a whole appeals to prurient interest."[71]

Warren wrote a short opinion, concurring in the result in *Roth.* He stressed "the social problem presented by obscenity" but cautioned that, "because broad language used here may eventually be applied to the arts and sciences and freedom of communication generally, I would limit our decision to the facts before us."[72] Despite his concurrence, however, Warren did not object to the *Roth* test as such. Soon after the case was decided, he told his son, Earl, Jr., that while he was not wholly satisfied with *Roth,* "It's the best we could do with what we had." Later, in a 1964 case, he declared, "For all the sound and fury that the Roth test has generated, it has not been proved unsound."[73]

Roth and its progeny generated not only "sound and fury" but also confusion. It is hard to disagree with the 1965 conclusion of a federal court summarizing the Warren Court's efforts to deal with obscenity: "a comparison of judicial reactions to recent *causes célèbres* suggests that the judiciary in our tormented modern civilization are also lost in a wilderness."[74]

Much of the confusion resulted from the fact that, in the field of obscenity, the Chief Justice did not play his usual leadership role. Warren was ambivalent in obscenity cases. He recognized the relationship of even the least deserving forms of expression to the First Amendment. At the same time, he could not overcome his personal abhorrence of pornography and what he called smut-peddlers.

The day after *Roth* was argued, Frankfurter wrote Warren, "I don't know whether you were as much in need of a whiff of fresh air after the obscenity arguments as I was."[75]

To Warren, more than "fresh air" was necessary to deal with material so foreign to his scale of values. If there was one matter on which his law clerks disagreed with the Chief, it was what they deemed his puritanism in obscenity cases. Once, when they were pressing the Chief on his views about pornography, his answer was, "You boys don't have any daughters yet." Warren found the sexual material that had become so widely available "unspeakable."[76] *Newsweek* quoted him telling a colleague, when he was shown a pornographic work, "If anyone showed that book to my daughters, I'd have strangled him with my own hands."[77]

Some observers have depicted the glee with which the Justices have viewed films that were exhibits in obscenity cases before them.[78] Warren's attitude was entirely different. "Do we have to read all of them to determine if they have social importance?" asked Warren plaintively as the argument began in a 1965 obscenity case. "I'm sure this Court doesn't want to read all the prurient material in the country."[79]

It was not until the 1966 *Ginzburg* case[80] indeed, that Warren could bring himself to read obscenity exhibits. Then, to put it mildly, he was shocked. "Do you realize what's in there?" he asked his clerk. "This stuff is terrible." The Chief would never personally view the films in obscenity cases. He would either send his clerks or rely on the report of one of the Justices. "It's all garbage," Warren used to tell his colleagues. "How can you know if you don't look at it?" asked one of the Brethren. "I *know* what that stuff is!" came back the firm answer. Unlike Warren, the other Justices would try to attend "movie day"—but not more "elevating" fare." After arranging a private 1967 screening of *The Last Frontier,* a Department of the Interior film, Douglas wrote: "You may be interested to know that one Justice appeared, no law clerks, no one from the Clerk's Office, no one from the Library, no one from the Marshal's office except Mrs. Allen and Mr. Lippitt, four from the labor force, and four secretaries. There was a total of 12 from the entire building."[81]

During the previous term, Warren, Black, and Douglas had dissented in the *du Pont* cellophane case. Now, in June, 1957, joined by Brennan, they were to make up the majority of a six-man Court in a more significant anti-trust case, involving du Pont's ownership of 23 percent of the stock of General Motors.[82] The *New York Times* called the case the "most important anti-trust case to come up in years."[83]

The government had brought an action against du Pont under section 7 of the Clayton Anti-Trust Act, which prohibited a corporation from acquiring stock of another company where the effect might be to "substantially lessen competition," or to restrain commerce, or tend to create a monopoly. It was alleged that du Pont had acquired a dominant position as a General Motors supplier because of its stock ownership. Du Pont argued that section 7 of the Clayton Act applied only to acquisition of the stock of a competing corporation in the same business and not to acquisition by a supplier of the stock of a customer—in other words, that the statute applied only to "horizontal" and not to "vertical" acquisitions. Before this case, the courts and the Federal Trade Commission had ruled that the statute did not apply to vertical acquisitions. Relying on this line of precedent, the lower court had dismissed the suit.

The Court that decided the second *du Pont* case was made up of six Justices. Three disqualified themselves: Clark because he had been Attorney General, Harlan because he had once represented du Pont, and Whittaker because the case had been argued before his appointment. The six who decided the case gathered in conference, together with Reed, who was to retire before the decision, on November 19, 1956.[84]

Warren began the discussion by pointing out that the Court did not have much latitude. It was a question of either sustaining the lower court or reversing for a further decree. The question, said the Chief, was "fairly simple": was the conclusion below clearly erroneous? "I don't see," Warren asserted, "how we can sustain that conclusion. When du Pont went into this it did so for the purpose of controlling a channel for the outlet of its products and it gave them control" of supplying General Motors. Under the statute, "you don't have to show they monopolized this; a tendency is enough." Warren concluded by saying, "there's hardly any way we can avoid saying that the facts don't tend to confirm" the lower court.

There was a sharp division among the others. Black and Douglas said they agreed with Warren, while Burton spoke in favor of affirmance. Frankfurter said that he was not prepared to vote, though he stated his view that, "it is not the law that 23 percent of stock is a clear violation" of the Clayton Act. Brennan, too, did not vote. He stressed that both companies had tried not to abuse their relationship. But he thought the stock purchase was *not* solely for investment and could not escape feeling that they had used it to strengthen their position as supplier.

Brennan also indicated that he was disturbed by the suggestion that the proper remedy was to make du Pont give up their investment. On November 21, Frankfurter wrote Brennan, "I should like you to know that I am wholly clear in support of the disinclination that you expressed at the Conference that divestiture is the remedy required for such violation as may be found in this case." Frankfurter then explained why he felt as he did on the question of remedy. "Practically speaking, to impose this kind of 'death sentence' on every violation of § 7 would place such a situation as we have before us on a parity with a flagrant violation. Even with my limited knowledge of the record I do not think it impertinent to say that I agree with what you said at Conference, that 'both of these corporations tried hard not to abuse their relationship.' "[85]

Brennan's disturbance at divestiture is of interest because he was to write the opinion ordering du Pont to give up its General Motors stock when the case came back to the Court on the question of remedy in 1961.[86] Yet, as Warren had pointed out, the remedial issue was not before the Court in the 1956 Term. The only question then was whether the vertical acquisition violated the Clayton Act. At the conference, those who had voted split on this issue, with Warren, Black, and Douglas voting in the affirmative, and Reed and Burton the other way.

Before the decision, Reed retired and Frankfurter definitely decided to vote to affirm. Brennan, on the other hand, moved toward reversal, largely under the influence of Warren's urging. Once again, Warren assigned the opinion to the newest majority member. On June 3, Brennan delivered the opinion of the Court holding section 7 of the Clayton Act applicable to such a vertical acquisition and du Pont's stock purchase violative of the statute. Burton wrote a long, learned dissent that Frankfurter joined. Ironically, this dissent, which was more widely praised than almost any other Burton opinion, had been drafted nearly in its entirety by one of his law clerks.[87]

Just before the *du Pont* decision was announced, Frankfurter suggested to Brennan and then to Warren, "withholding until the New York Exchange closes announcement of an opinion which there is good reason to believe would feverishly affect the market."[88] Brennan was agreeable, but the Chief said, "we should not treat that case different from others."[89] Later, Warren sent Frankfurter a pencilled note: "My concern re changing the order of reporting du Pont was that it might be pointed out we recognized we are injuring the economic structure. I suppose we will be critized at all events."[90]

Du Pont was the first case of major economic importance decided by the Warren Court. The decision was to serve as a basic precedent for what the *New York Times* called the "anti-big business bloc" in the Court.[91]

Had Harlan and Whittaker participated, the decision might have been different. While Brennan was reading from his opinion on June 3, Harlan passed Frankfurter a note: "Now that my lips are no longer sealed, if there was ever a more *superficial* understanding of a really impressive record, than Bill's opinion in du Pont—I would like to see it. I hardly recognize the case as I listen to him speak." Harlan asserted that, the opinion, "(between you and me) for me has been the most disillusioning blot in the Court's processes. And what Bill has done to Sec 7 of Clayton Act!"[92] Whittaker was strongly influenced by Frankfurter and Harlan. If he and Harlan had voted, the result could have been an equally divided Court. That would have meant an affirmance of the lower court decision.

The decisions toward the end of the 1956 Term emphasized individual rights, both in cases involving subversive activities and in criminal cases. This enabled critics to claim that the Warren Court was coddling not only Communists, but also criminals.

Two of the Court's criminal law decisions attracted particular critical attention—those in the *Mallory*[93] and *Jencks* cases.[94] In *Mallory*, a convicted rapist appealed on the ground that his confession to the police had been improperly admitted in evidence in his federal trial. He had been arrested and questioned for ten hours before being arraigned, even though the Federal Rules of Criminal Procedure required the police to take an arrested person before a magistrate for arraignment "without unnecessary delay." All the Brethren except Reed and Clark voted to take the case.

On the law, *Mallory* was not a difficult case. In 1943, the Court had decided in *McNabb v. United States*[95] that confessions secured while defendants were illegally detained in violation of the duty to arraign them could not be introduced in evidence. *Mallory* involved a simple application of the *McNabb* rule.

At the *Mallory* conference on April 5, 1957,[96] most of the Brethren, including Warren, spoke in favor of reversal under *McNabb*. Only Burton said he would affirm, though Harlan indicated he was leaning the same way. Frankfurter and Brennan played the greatest part in the discussion. Frankfurter said that the *McNabb* rule was probably not a due process demand (which meant that it was not required by the U.S. Constitution in state cases), but that it was binding in federal criminal trials. Under *McNabb*, the police might "make immediate inquiries of others, but not out of his own mouth. That could be [only] after arraignment." Brennan agreed, saying "before arrest, the police could inquire; after arrest, they had to go to a magistrate and the magistrate must warn him" of his rights.

As it turned out, *Mallory* was so plainly governed by *McNabb* that Burton and Harlan concurred in a unanimous decision. The opinion of the Court was delivered on June 24 by Frankfurter, who had also written the *McNabb* opinion. In the original draft, Frankfurter had written, "Exceptional circumstances may justify a brief delay between arrest and arraignment." Burton wrote, on June 17, that he and Harlan would join the opinion if the word "exceptional" were omitted.[97] Douglas objected to the omission, but finally agreed to go along with it.[98]

Some years later, Warren was on a Mediterranean trip with California Governor Edmund G. Brown. The two were talking, when Brown happened to criticize the *Mallory* decision. Warren bristled. "Have you read it?" he demanded. "Read it again! You would have voted the same way if you had been on the Court."

The second important criminal decision at the end of the 1956 Term was *Jencks v. United States*.[99] Jencks had been convicted of filing a false non-Communist affidavit with the National Labor Relations Board. Matusow and Ford, the government's principal witnesses, were Communist Party members paid by the F.B.I. to make reports about Communist activities. They made reports of activities by Jencks, about which they testified. Jencks claimed that the trial court had erred in denying his motions to direct the government to produce these reports to the court for inspection, with the court to make available to Jencks those reports that would be of use in cross-examining Matusow and Ford. He also alleged error in the instructions given to the jury on Communist membership and affiliation.

The Brethren discussed *Jencks* in conferences on October 19, November 2, November 30, 1956, and January 11, and March 22, 1957.[100] The fullest discussions took place at the first and last of these conferences. Warren began the first session by saying he would vote to reverse. He was for Jencks's right to examine the reports, "particularly when he says he has no recollection of anything in those reports." None of the others disputed that the reports should be made available. They differed, however, on whether the reports should be turned over to Jencks or screened by the trial judge to make available to Jencks only those portions that he determined were of value for cross-examination. Burton and Clark spoke in favor of the latter alternative, with Clark declaring that it was a "big mistake to open up these reports to opposing counsel." But, in his view, it was "O.K. to let the judge see them." Brennan agreed with Warren that the reports should be given to Jencks. The ordinary rule, he said, that allows attorneys to examine such statements in civil cases should apply to criminal cases as well. Brennan urged that "the statements should be made available to the parties. I don't like this examination by the judge only."

At the March 22 conference, these views were repeated. The principal statements of the opposing views were by Clark and Brennan. Clark stated that he could support disclosure to the judge. He was "willing to send it back for the judge to examine the reports in camera. This is as far as I could go. [Jencks] did not ask for more." Brennan declared that, on disclosure, he would go further. "If a witness admits he made a statement as to testimony which he's given, that is enough to let his counsel see the statement." Brennan said that "counsel should have access except for overriding public security." He concluded, "I would go beyond what was asked for in this trial. We should indicate what is right practice."

In *Jencks,* Warren allowed Brennan to serve as his spokesman. Though the Chief indicated at the outset of the first conference his view that the reports should be furnished to Jencks, thereafter the primary role in arguing for production was left to Brennan. Warren also assigned the opinion to the *Jencks* Court's junior member (Whittaker did not sit in the case). Brennan's draft dealt not only with the disclosure issue, but also with the instructions to the jury on Communist affiliation. Though Brennan found that the instructions were defective, Douglas objected that Brennan's definition of affiliation was too loose. In a May 9, 1957, memorandum, Douglas denied that a "person should be condemned merely because [his] positions coincide with the Communist position. . . . I think that the affiliation condemned would have to [be] an affiliation with an illegal subversive aim of the Communist Party."

Brennan was unable to reconcile the Douglas position on the affiliation instructions with those of others in the majority. To avoid a further division, Brennan limited the *Jencks* opinion to the issue of disclosure of the witnesses' statements, holding that such statements must be made available to criminal defendants. On May 22, Warren wrote Brennan, "I like your opinion in the [*Jencks*] case and am happy to join you." The opinion was also joined by Black, Douglas, and Frankfurter. Burton, joined by Harlan, concurred in reversal, but would have limited the holding to disclosure to the trial judge. He also went into the issue of the judge's instructions and found them erroneous. Frankfurter stated that though he joined the opinion of the Court, he agreed with Burton that the jury instructions were erroneous.

Clark delivered a strong dissent. The Clark dissent, asserting that the Court had given criminals "a Roman holiday for rummaging through confidential information as well as vital national secrets,"[101] was widely quoted by Court critics. President Eisenhower was said in an International News Service story to have "confided to a group of friends at a White House stag dinner . . . that he has 'never been as mad in my life' as he is at the recent Supreme Court decision opening secret FBI files to accused subversives." [102] The Justice Department was particularly outraged. Attorney General Herbert Brownell declared that *Jencks* had created "an emergency in law enforcement," and F.B.I. Director J. Edgar Hoover was quoted as saying that he would favor refusing to prosecute rather than open his files. [103]

The uproar over *Jencks* led Congress to pass a statute only three months after the decision, attempting to narrow its impact by spelling out the types of documents that might be demanded by criminal defendants. This was a rare rebuke to a Supreme Court decision, though as Brennan put it in an August 31 letter to Frankfurter, "I gather that the statute finally passed doesn't really destroy the principle of the decision."

The Brethren were disturbed over the controversy caused by their decision. On August 29, Frankfurter sent Brennan a handwritten note: "The fact is that I very largely blame myself for all the dust that the case has kicked up. I firmly believe that if I had not allowed my good colleagueship to suppress my good sense the rumpus would have been avoided. For if I had had my wisdom govern, I would have written a short concurrence with your opinion, sticking my pen into Tom's hot air and puncturing his balloon."

Had he done this, Frankfurter went on, "the upshot of it would have been that in order to have a Court opinion, you, like a sensible lad, would yourself have added the substance of this indirect refutation of Tom." As a result, *Jencks* "would have gained—or, rather—retained John's adherence, and Brownell & Co. . . . . would not have made themselves the enslaved tools of Edgar Hoover."

Brennan replied on August 31 that he agreed that Clark's dissent should have been answered specifically. "But the regrets should not be yours—rather wholly mine, because you suggested not once but several times that something be done to anticipate Tom's approach." Brennan hoped "that the hub-bub may not have done lasting harm . . . but I confess to considerable concern over the summer that I may have been the instrument (& in my first year!) for demeaning the standing of the court." [104]

Had the *Jencks* case not involved an alleged Communist, it would probably not have generated as much criticism. The same was true of the other controversial decisions toward the end of the 1956 Term.

In them, too, critics claimed that the Warren Court was handcuffing governmental efforts to protect itself against Communists and other subversives.

A month before *Jencks,* in the *Schware*[105] and *Konigsberg* cases,[106] the Court had rebuffed state efforts to keep alleged former Communists out of the legal profession. Schware had been denied admission to the New Mexico Bar on the ground that his membership in the Communist Party from 1932 to 1940, as well as a prior arrest on "suspicion of criminal syndicalism," showed that he lacked good moral character. Konigsberg had been refused admission to the California Bar because of his refusal to answer questions about his membership in the Communist Party and about his political affiliations and beliefs, as well as testimony that he had been a Communist Party member in 1941. The Brethren had been closely divided on whether to take Konigsberg's case, with Reed, Clark, Minton, and Harlan voting to deny at the certiorari conference on May 21, 1956.

At the January 18, 1957, conference,[107] Warren stated that he would vote to reverse in both cases. He started by discussing the *Konigsberg* case. In his view, nothing had been demonstrated against Konigsberg's moral character. "It was legal to be a Communist and vote and register as a Communist, as the Communist Party was then on the ballot." The Chief said that Schware's case was "even clearer." His arrest meant nothing; his army record during the war was good; and he had been characterized by "clean conduct" since his Communist membership.

All the others except Clark, who stressed that the Court "should not be glorified bar examiners," agreed that the Schware denial should be reversed. The common theme was, as Brennan stated in agreeing with Warren, that "it was legal to be a member at that time." Konigsberg's case presented more difficulty. Black, Douglas, Burton, and Brennan followed the Chief in voting for reversal. Warren and those who agreed with him treated *Konigsberg* as involving essentially the same issue as *Schware*—whether past Communist membership could be the basis of denial of admission to the Bar.

Those who favored reversal did not deal with the point stressed by California, that denial had been based on Konigsberg's refusal to answer questions. That point troubled some of the remaining Brethren, who voted to affirm. Reed said that California had a right to examine him. "He stood on his right" to refuse to answer, "but it interfered with the exam." Harlan agreed, saying that there was "no free speech problem, his convictions are a legitimate subject of inquiry. Konigsberg refused to cooperate in an area where the Bar had a right." Frankfurter thought that the federal question had not been properly considered below, and Clark tentatively agreed.

The conference indicated eight in favor of reversing in *Schware,* but only five for reversing in *Konigsberg.* Clark was persuaded to go along in *Schware,* and the decision on May 6, 1957, unanimously reversed on the ground that Schware's prior arrest and Communist membership were not enough to demonstrate want of moral character. The decision the same day in *Konigsberg* was five-to-three for reversal, since Reed had left the Court and the others stuck to their conference positions. The *Konigsberg* opinion by Black followed Warren's conference approach. It ignored Konigsberg's failure to answer and held that, as in *Schware,* past Communist membership alone would not support the finding that he did not have a good moral character. Harlan, in a dissent joined by Clark, stressed the refusal to answer and concluded that Konigsberg could be denied admission because of his obstruction of the investigation into his qualifications.

Harlan's draft dissent had stated, "For me it would at least be intelligible if the Court were to hold that the Committee's questions called for matter privileged under the First and Fourteenth Amendments." At this Black sent Harlan a written note: "I only had time to read the last paragraph of your Konigsberg dissent but note that you regret to find what we say is 'unintelligible'—What's the matter? Are our words too big or something?"[108] Harlan changed the offending word "intelligible" to "more understandable."

Frankfurter, who had written a friend that Konigsberg "was one of those good citizens who had more brains than sense,"[109] also dissented on the ground stated by him in conference, that it was not clear that the federal question had been passed on by the state court. Sherman Minton went even further. "Some time when you have the leisure," the retired Justice wrote Frankfurter, "tell me what the Federal question was in Schware v. New Mexico & Konigsberg v. Calif? . . . Does the Supreme Court know better what good moral character is than the State Courts?"[110]

To the public and press, the culmination of the 1956 Term came on June 17, 1957, when four decisions were handed down reversing a dismissal from the State Department on loyalty grounds, as well as convictions of Communist leaders under the Smith Act, and convictions for contempt of the House Committee on Un-American Activities and a state legislature investigating subversive activities. Critics of the Court promptly dubbed the day, "Red Monday."

The least controversial of the four decisions was that in *Service v. Dulles*, [111] because it was decided on a narrow ground. Service was a career foreign service officer whose loyalty and standing as a security risk were under investigation. After extensive hearings, the State Department Loyalty Board concluded that he was neither disloyal nor a security risk. The Deputy Under Secretary of State approved these findings. The Secretary of State, on the recommendation of the Loyalty Review Board, had then discharged Service. The Secretary had acted under a statute giving him authority "in his absolute discretion" to terminate employment whenever he deemed it necessary or advisable.

The extent of discretion vested in the Secretary by the statute troubled Warren. During the argument, in early April, 1957, the Chief Justice asked the attorney arguing for the government, "Do you read the words 'absolute discretion' as synonymous with 'absolute power'?" "Yes," was the reply.

"No distinction at all?" Warren persisted. "I cannot," came back the answer, "conceive of a case that would turn on a distinction between those two words." [112]

At the conference on April 5, [113] the Chief's presentation showed that the extent of discretion still gave him difficulty. The statute, he stated, "doesn't mean absolutely arbitrary action, [it] doesn't say at his pleasure. 'Absolute' means merely 'final.'" Warren indicated, however, that he was willing to reverse on the narrower ground that the Secretary had not properly exercised the discretion vested in him because he had acted on the recommendation of the Loyalty Review Board.

Black agreed on reversal, but said it should be on another ground, referring to the principle laid down in the 1954 *Accardi* case [114] that a government agency is bound by its own regulations. The *Accardi* principle was relevant here because State Department regulations provided that the Secretary could dismiss for loyalty or security reasons only after the Deputy Under Secretary, acting on the findings of the Department's Loyalty Board, had recommended dismissal. In this case, the Deputy Under Secretary had approved the Department

Board decision favorable to Service, so that the Secretary could not, consistently with the regulations, dismiss him. Harlan also stated that it was preferable to reverse on the *Accardi* ground. The others agreed, except for Burton and Whittaker, who indicated that they would affirm, and Clark, who said he would not participate "unless [the vote was] four-to-four."

Warren readily went along with the Black–Harlan approach as a means to avoid deciding the difficult questions of the extent and legality of the discretion delegated to the Secretary. He assigned the opinion to Harlan, who wrote so convincingly that Burton and Whittaker joined to make the decision unanimous, with Clark not taking part.

Although Service's dismissal was ruled invalid on the narrow *Accardi* principle, which did not affect the substantive power to dismiss on loyalty grounds, that hardly appeased those who attacked the Court as soft on communism. Even worse from their point of view was *Yates v. United States*,[115] where the decision reversed the Smith Act convictions of fourteen leaders of the Communist Party. Defendants had been prosecuted for conspiring to advocate and teach the overthrow of the government by force and violence and to organize the Communist Party for that purpose. Yates and the others raised broad challenges to the constitutionality of such Smith Act prosecutions, as well as narrower claims that the lower courts had misconstrued the act's provisions.

"It has not been established," the Chief began the October 12, 1956, conference,[116] "that the Communist Party is force and violence. The Government has not made clear proof of the purpose of the party." The government's case was "weak, not substantial. It is important that it be shown beyond a reasonable doubt," and that was not done here. Here, they "have proved only membership in the Communist Party, not unlawful conduct. The only overt acts were attendance at public meetings and nothing was shown there to prove advocacy of force and violence."

Warren stressed that defendants were prosecuted as individuals. "Every man in a party doesn't *ipso facto* subscribe to party dogmas." He expressed difficulty with the charge that defendants "organized" the party. "It's not clear," he said "what 'organizing' is. The editor of a paper by his editorials is not 'organizing.' " Warren also had difficulty with the charge of teaching and advocacy. That is not enough, he declared. It is a "question of incitement."

In addition, the Chief stressed what he called the "impregnating atmosphere" in which such Smith Act trials took place. "We find a Congressional committee releasing an F.B.I. report at a crucial time and a series of lurid articles." In the aggregate, Warren concluded, he would vote to reverse.

Black and Douglas also spoke for reversal. Black declared, "the Smith Act provides for political trials—what the First Amendment was supposed to prevent." He also thought that the sufficiency of the evidence presented depended on what had to be proved under the statute. "If you need to show only ideas, they proved that. If you need to show 'acts,' they didn't."

Reed, Burton, Clark, and Minton said they would vote to affirm. Reed stated that Congress could provide what it did and it was not necessary to prove incitement. "The Communist Party," he asserted, "now is established as an advocate of force and violence. It is plain that they so urge." Minton declared that he could not agree with Black that "the Smith Act is for political trials. It is to cope with a conspiracy hatched by a foreign government."

Frankfurter and Harlan passed because they were not ready to vote, though Frankfurter noted how gratified he was by the Chief Justice's stress on the trial atmosphere which "fouled the air of this trial," and Harlan said—significantly as it turned out—that, on the assumption that teaching incitement was necessary, the charge to the jury was inadequate.

Since the Court was so fragmented—four for affirmance, three for reversal, two not voting—Warren suggested that the case be put over for a few weeks. It was next discussed at a conference on November 2, after Minton had retired. Reed, Burton, and Clark again voted to affirm and Warren, Black, and Douglas to reverse. This time Frankfurter and Harlan were ready to vote, and they both voted to reverse on the ground that the instructions given the jury were confusing ("muddy," Harlan termed them) and inadequate. In particular, they urged that active incitement was necessary, and the judge's charge had not required that. This point had been raised by both Warren and Harlan at the first conference.

The vote now stood five-to-three for reversal. With the close division, Warren assigned the opinion to Harlan, in the hope that, written narrowly and technically, it would command as much support as possible. Harlan's opinion was based on inadequacies in the instructions to the jury, particularly the failure to charge that more than advocacy of forcible overthrow as an abstract principle was required. The opinion also limited the word "organize" to creation of a new organization, not to acts performed in carrying on activities of an existing organization.

By the time *Yates* was decided, Reed had left the Court. Only seven Justices participated in the decision. Harlan's opinion of the Court was agreed to by Warren, Frankfurter, and Burton, who had changed his vote after Reed's retirement and joined Harlan's opinion. Black and Douglas also voted to reverse, but went further in a separate opinion, arguing that the Smith Act violated the First Amendment. Clark alone dissented.

Burton's change of vote had been influenced by a memorandum from his law clerk that Harlan's opinion would not destroy the effectiveness of the Smith Act.[117] It is, however, hard to see how successful Smith Act prosecutions could be brought after *Yates*. Critics cried out that the Court had voted "in favor of advocating treason."[118] Overlooked was the fact that the opinion had been written by the conservative Harlan, and the decision was far narrower than it would have been if Warren had joined Black and Douglas.

The last two June 17 decisions—in *Watkins v. United States*[119] and *Sweezy v. New Hampshire*[120]—involved legislative investigatory power. Watkins was a United Automobile Workers organizer who had been convicted of contempt of Congress for refusing to answer questions before the House Un-American Activities Committee regarding people who were past members of the Communist Party after he had told of his own participation in Communist activities. Watkins had claimed that the questions were not relevant to the work of the committee. He had nevertheless been directed to answer. Sweezy, a state university professor, had been convicted of contempt for refusing to answer questions during a legislative investigation into subversive activities in New Hampshire. The questions related to his lectures, writings, and knowledge of the Progressive Party and its adherents. Sweezy, too, claimed that the questions were not pertinent to the subject under inqury. Both Watkins and Sweezy also raised broad constitutional claims, urging in particular, that the First Amendment barred the inquiries made of them.

All the Brethren agreed to hear the *Sweezy* case. In *Watkins,* only Reed and Minton had voted to deny certiorari (with Burton disqualifying himself, both at the cert conference and on the merits, because his nephew had been the government's chief trial counsel). Both cases were considered at length in conference on March 8, 1957.[121] Warren began the *Watkins* discussion by noting the difference between contempt procedures before Congress and before a court. The Chief set the theme for the decision by stressing two main points: (1) "the committee must show why it is relevant and can get it in this kind of case"; (2) they do not "have right to expose for purpose of exposure." Warren's presentation thus summarized the two principal grounds upon which his *Watkins* opinion was to be based: (1) the narrow ground of pertinency, in which all but Clark could join; and (2) a broad limitation of Congressional investigatory power into private affairs.

All but Clark agreed that Watkins' conviction should be reversed. Frankfurter said that, though he went along with most of Warren's presentation, "it is important how it is said." He also subscribed to the proposition that "the witness should have been given a chance to see the relevance. The burden is on the committee to show it." Harlan as well urged that the reversal should be on that narrow ground.

After the *Watkins* discussion, disposition of the *Sweezy* case was not difficult. Warren started by conceding state power in this area. Last year's *Nelson* case did not apply since there was no federal preemption, and the state could investigate as to security, sabotage, and state employees. But the state here had transgressed the limitations on investigatory power. This conclusion was easier than in *Watkins;* here they "wanted to make this man state what his opinions were." Warren concluded that he would "strike all the categories of questions."

All except Burton and Clark agreed that Sweezy's conviction should be reversed. Frankfurter, Harlan, and Brennan emphasized the unique position of education in our society. His "chief concern here," said Frankfurter, "was the special position of educational institutions and teachers. I don't mean a 'preferred' position. I'm not prepared to say that every question was bad." Frankfurter asserted, at a later point, that he could not think of a situation "where a teacher [could be] hailed before a committee to ask what you did lecture on." Harlan stated that while the "state has a legitimate interest to find out what is being taught in state schools, [it] can't put a block on teaching." Brennan declared that the *Sweezy* investigation was "all bad." In his view, the "classroom is a sanctuary. . . . In there is the first essential of preservation of purity."

The *Watkins* case graphically illustrates the importance of chance in Supreme Court decisions. Had the Court's personnnel not changed during the 1956 Term, Reed and Minton, who had both voted to deny cert, would almost certainly have voted with Clark for the government. Had Burton's nephew not been trial counsel, Burton would (as his vote in the *Sweezy* case shows) also have voted to affirm. Had the division gone that way, the four for affirmance might well have been able to persuade Frankfurter, who was dissatisfied with the broad scope of Warren's opinion of the Court, to join them.

Instead, with Minton and Reed gone and Burton disqualified, only Clark dissented in *Watkins*. Brennan, who had replaced Minton, readily joined Warren's opinion of the Court, writing the Chief on May 29, "I think this is splendid. I cannot make a single suggestion; and am delighted to join." Whittaker, confirmed after the argument and conference, did not participate.

Warren assigned the *Watkins* opinion to himself and circulated a draft on May 20. Except for Frankfurter, the other majority Justices joined the draft opinion without difficulty. Frankfurter, however, suggested important changes that were accepted by the Chief Justice.[122]

Many of the changes made by Frankfurter were stylistic. Thus, the draft referred to "an outrageous" contempt sentence imposed by Parliament. Frankfurter changed this to "humiliating and cruel." Similarly Frankfurter removed the words "the demagogue" that had been used to describe John Wilkes. And, where Warren wrote that congressional investigatory "power is very broad," Frankfurter deleted "very."

Frankfurter also rewrote the Warren summary of the holding in *Kilbourn v. Thompson*,[123] the 1881 case that had imposed the most important limitations on congressional investigatory authority. The draft read: "The Court held that this was a subject matter upon which the Congress could not legislate. The investigation, therefore, lacked a valid legislative purpose and the House had thereby exceeded its jurisdiction."

Frankfurter changed this to: "The Court found that the subject matter of the inquiry was 'in its nature clearly judicial' and therefore one in respect to which no valid legislation could be had. The House had thereby exceeded the limit of its own authority."

Frankfurter also worked with Warren on stylistic changes in what became the most famous passage in the *Watkins* opinion—that in which Warren expanded on his conference statement that the committee did not "have right to expose for purpose of exposure." The draft passage read: "We have no doubt that there is no congressional power to expose for the sake of exposure. Whatever may be the function of the Congress to inform the electorate on matters of the conduct of government, there is no power to expose where the effect is to abridge First Amendment liberties of private citizens."

Warren himself changed the second sentence of this passage on Frankfurter's draft copy to: "The public is of course entitled to be informed concerning the workings of its government." Frankfurter suggested that the rest read: "But there is no power to expose where the predominant result can only be an invasion of the private rights of individuals."

Toward the end of the draft, Frankfurter inserted the following, to emphasize that congressional investigatory power remained broad: "We are wholly mindful of the complexities of modern government and the ample scope that must be left to Congress as the sole repository of legislative power. Equally mindful are we of the indispensable function, in the due exercise of that power, of Congressional investigation."

But the most important changes made by Frankfurter in the *Watkins* draft dealt with Warren's handling of the First Amendment issue. At the March 8 conference, Frankfurter had said, "Don't begin with First Amendment. Begin with due process and stay with it." Now, when he read the *Watkins* draft, he saw that the proposed opinion contained many references to the First Amendment. He suggested deletion of virtually all of them. "In this case," Frankfurter wrote on his copy of the draft that he returned to Warren, "Watkins' refusals were not based on First Amendment and we do not have to adjudicate what the bearing of the First Amendment to Congressional inquiries is . . . and there is the further objection of trying to

fit restrictions upon legislative inquiries into the First Amendment—
some of us, at least, may find such restrictions from the functional
limits of investigations & not draw it from concept of 'freedom of
speech.' "

Frankfurter let stand the draft statement that investigations are
subject to the First Amendment. But he changed the sentence in the
same paragraph: "The First Amendment prohibits infringement of
the protected freedoms by law or by law-making" by substituting
"may be invoked against" for "prohibits."

Warren had referred to the "unequivocal language of" the First
Amendment. Frankfurter deleted the quoted part, writing, "unequivocal is a dangerous word—since we are deciding in obscenity cases
once more that First Amendment not an absolute, as well as in *Yates*.
I'd leave it out."

Frankfurter removed all other First Amendment references, saying,
"This on its face is not a First Amendment case." Where the draft
spoke of "application of the First Amendment to legislative inquiries," Frankfurter substituted, "protecting these rights from infringement by legislative inquiries. . . . I suggest this broader way of putting it because we ought to assert limits on unjustifiable inquiry even
tho some of us may not find an infringement of the First Amendment."

In a letter explaining his suggestions, Frankfurter stressed, *"Watkins is not a First Amendment case."* His changes, wrote the Justice,
were "vital lest witnesses before a congressional committee parrot-
like repeat the phrase, 'First Amendment, First Amendment.' . . .
They would . . . save us from future embarrassment and leave un-
impaired the constitutional power of congressional investigations."[124]

After he received the Frankfurter suggestions, Warren wrote, "Many
thanks for the thought and attention you gave to *Watkins* over the
weekend."[125] Though almost all his changes were accepted, Frankfurter was still dissatisfied with the *Watkins* opinions. In another letter, the Justice warned Warren, "I have not a particle of doubt that
were Black still in the Senate he would raise hell about this opinion.
There are other Blacks still in the Senate."[126] Frankfurter thought
that the *Watkins* opinion should be limited to the narrow holding
that congressional committees have the duty to demonstrate to wit-

nesses the relevance of the questions they are required to answer. Warren's opinion did reverse on the pertinency ground, but it was not limited to it. Instead, it contained a broad lecture against abuses by congressional investigations, and stressed the constitutional limitations upon legislative investigatory power. Frankfurter wrote a short concurrence, stressing that the limited pertinency point was the true basis of the Court's decision.

In *Sweezy*, Warren's opinion of the Court was also cast in sweeping terms, reversing the conviction on the ground that the New Hampshire investigation "was an invasion of petitioner's liberties in the areas of academic freedom and political expression."[127] Frankfurter, joined by Harlan, wrote an opinion, "concurring in the result."[128] Clark, joined by Burton, delivered a dissent.

Soon after *Watkins*, Frankfurter received a letter from retired Justice Minton, which asserted, "The Super Rip Van Winkle Thompson v. Kilbourn was not only revived but fortified by the 'due process limitation' on the resolution so as to make Congressional Investigations very difficult if not impossible."[129] Frankfurter did not go that far. But he was plainly displeased with the broadside Warren opinion that had gone far beyond the bare pertinency holding, which would have sufficed for the reversal of the contempt conviction. In April, 1958, after Frankfurter had cited *Watkins* in a draft opinion, Harlan wrote to him, "This is not a good time to highlight *Watkins*, although it is a controlling authority."[130] Frankfurter replied, referring to that "god-awful *Watkins* opinion," and saying, "If I had my way, I wouldn't cite *Watkins*. I did it out of deference to the sensibilities of those who sponsored it. I'd be glad to omit it. You know what I think of that opinion. That chicken was due to come home soon."[131]

Two other important decisions handed down at the end of the 1956 Term turned on the line between military and civil power that the Warren Court had started to draw in its 1955 decision in *Toth v. Quarles*.[132] The more important of the decisions was that in *Reid v. Covert*.[133] Two wives of American servicemen, residing on American bases in England and Japan, were convicted of murdering their husbands by courts-martial and sentenced to life imprisonment. The Uniform Code of Military Justice subjected to court-martial jurisdiction "all persons serving with . . . or accompanying the armed forces without the continental limits of the United States." The wives claimed that this provision was unconstitutional, since they were civilians who might not be tried in military courts.

Among themselves, the Brethren referred to *Reid v. Covert* as the Case of the Murdering Wives. The case had come before the Court during the previous term. It was first argued May 3, 1956, and discussed in conference on the following day.[134] Warren began by reaffirming the strong view he had ultimately taken in the *Toth* case. He pointed out that, under the Uniform Code provision, even children of servicemen were subjected to military trials. "I doubt," Warren asserted, "that these youngsters are part of the Army of the U.S. It's hard to believe that a housewife and youngsters—not in the field— in England and Tokyo are members of the armed forces for military justice. The fact that they use the PX means nothing. If they are, then the Army may try them. That's not in keeping with our traditions."

Black agreed, saying that the government could subject soldiers to military jurisdiction, but to subject others "stretches the Constitution." Reed, too, was inclined to to the view that "camp followers," as he put it, were not subject to military jurisdiction. Douglas and Frankfurter also doubted that civilians could be tried by military courts. Clark passed. Only Burton and Minton spoke in favor of affirming military jurisdiction. Minton said that it was hard to "get away from [In re] *Ross*"[135]—the 1891 case that upheld the trial of an American seaman by a consular court in Japan. "The Constitution," said Minton, "does not follow him *there*."

On May 14, Reed circulated a memorandum, which stated, "Further examination of the law and the records in *Reid v. Covert* . . . convinces me that my tentative votes in these cases were erroneous." He had now concluded that the Uniform Code provision was constitutional. "Accordingly, I wish to change my vote."[136]

The next day Frankfurter wrote Reed, "My ears could hardly believe it when I heard you vote as you did in the case of the murdering wives. I had not the slightest doubt . . . that in due course you would vote the way I was sure you would vote, and as you have now indicated." Reed had cited five cases to support his vote change. According to the Frankfurter letter, however, "the five cases which you cite . . . haven't a thing to do with our problem."[137]

After Reed switched, Clark and Harlan also decided to vote in favor of military jurisdiction. This made a majority for a decision against the wives. Warren, Black, Douglas, and Frankfurter refused to go along. Reed, the senior majority Justice, assigned the opinion to Clark. His draft opinion stressed the cases like *Ross* that had upheld congressional power to set up so-called "legislative" courts and consular courts to try certain crimes overseas.

After he had received the Clark draft, Frankfurter sent Harlan a written note: "I have just read Tom's opinion . . . and I'm appalled." Frankfurter conceded "that a respectable—that is a lawyer-like opinion" sustaining the Uniform Code provision could be written. "But not this farrago of irresponsible, uncritical admixture of far-reaching needlessly dangerous incongruities." Frankfurter wrote, "I cannot believe that this opinion will be allowed to go down with your concurrence—until it does!" [138]

Harlan did, however, concur, so that Clark spoke for five Justices when he announced the opinion on June 11, 1956, upholding court-martial jurisdiction over the wives. Warren, Black, and Douglas announced that they dissented, but that the late date had not given them time to prepare opinions. They said they would file dissenting opinions during the next term.

At the conference that discussed the case before the June 11 decision was announced, Warren had stated "that a decision by the Court raises questions that 'are complex' and that the problems involved 'require extensive research and reflection.' " [139] Frankfurter wrote the Chief that, if his statement were true, "conclusions in this case ought not to be pronounced until there has been adequate time for 'extensive research and reflection.' That rightly calls for a reservation of judgment." [140] Frankfurther had voted with the dissenters. But, when the June 11 decision was announced, he stated that he was reserving judgment until a later date.

Though the Court had announced its decision and opinion, those who disagreed were dissatisfied. Black prepared a dissent, as did Frankfurter, who delivered copies to Warren, Black, and Douglas. The Frankfurter memorandum accompanying the dissent stated, "There is, I think, a very good reason why it should not be known outside ourselves that such a dissent has been prepared. Therefore, I am seeing to it that this gets to you in person, for it is just as well that not even the law clerks know about this at the moment." [141]

In addition, the now-four dissenters worked to secure a rehearing in the case. Counsel for the wives had filed a petition for rehearing after the June 11 decision against them. It is the normal practice for losing counsel in the Supreme Court to file petitions for rehearings, but they are almost invariably denied. This time the situation was different. Douglas sent a note to Frankfurter that he liked his dissent. "I hear," Douglas also wrote, "the majority are having conferences on the petition for rehearing. So maybe trouble for them is brewing."[142]

Later in September, the dissenters circulated a *Memorandum on Reid v. Covert,* drafted by Black. The memo stated the issue broadly: "The issue in these cases is whether Congress can constitutionally authorize the military trial of civilians during times of peace for alleged crimes." Though the bare majority had answered this question in the affirmative, "study and reflection since the Court's decisions have strengthened our view that this Court's holdings in these cases have given the military authorities new powers not hitherto thought consistent with our scheme of government." The memo asserted, "We see no possible way to reconcile these holdings with our decision in *Toth v. Quarles.* . . . We think that either the *Toth* case should be expressly overruled or that the Court should now reverse its holdings in . . . *Covert.*"[143]

The four dissenters now worked to win over one or more majority Justice to join them in granting the rehearing petition. Warren and Frankfurter tried to convince Harlan, who had never been firmly in the opposition camp. They persuaded Harlan that the technique used in the *Brown* school segregation case should be employed again to clarify the difficult points here. Harlan was assigned the job of drawing up questions on which counsel would be asked to reargue the case.

There is a Frankfurter memorandum to Harlan which indicates that the questions on which the Court invited discussion on reargument were drawn up almost entirely by Frankfurter, though submitted to the Brethren as a Harlan draft.[144] The four questions proposed[145] related to the practical necessities requiring court-martial jurisdiction over civilian dependents; the historical evidence on such jurisdiction; the distinction, if any, between civilians employed by the armed forces and civilian dependents; and that between major crimes and petty offenses. Black suggested a fifth question: "If soldiers' wives can be constitutionally tried by court-martial for violations in foreign countries of United States laws, what constitutional provision forbids their subjection to court-martial for violations of the same laws committed within the United States?"[146] On Harlan's copy of the proposed questions, Frankfurter wrote, next to Black's suggestion, "a question should not be argumentative. This is and raises a question not now here."[147] Black's proposed question, which would have predetermined the merits in accordance with the views of the dissenters the previous term, was rejected.

On November 5, the Court granted the petition for rehearing. At the reargument, counsel were "invited to include among the issues to be discussed" the four questions drafted by Frankfurter and Harlan. Reed, Burton, and Clark voted to deny the rehearing, Minton having retired before the Court acted on the rehearing petition. Before the reargument on February 27, 1957, the former majority was weakened further by Reed's retirement.

At the reargument, Warren, in particular, was troubled by where the line could be drawn if the wives were held subject to court-martial jurisdiction. "General," he asked the Solicitor General, "while we're dealing with dependents, suppose this was a child, clearly a juvenile who committed a serious crime. Would you try the child before a court martial?"

At another point, the Chief asked, "Suppose she chose to live in an apartment down in the center of London, would she still have been subject to court martial?" Then, pushing the Solicitor General further, he raised the point covered by Black's suggested fifth question: What is "the difference between . . . dependents who are living on a cantonment in this country, say outside of Washington on the one hand, and dependents living outside of London on the other hand?"[148]

At the conference after reargument on March 1, 1957,[149] the Chief Justice began, "I come out the same as before. We can't apply *Ross* and we can't say this was a 'legislative court', as permitted" by some cases. The decision last June had relied on the Necessary and Proper Clause of Article I, but Warren said that he could not see that that clause "comes into the case." As the Chief saw it, "the simple question is whether Congress has the right to declare these dependents a part of the armed forces of the U.S. and are subject to court-martial.

This goes beyond anything; it's contrary to the history of the U.S. and England. Congress does not possess the power to declare them in the armed forces."

This time there was little discussion after Warren's forceful presentation. All except Burton and Clark agreed with the Chief that the wives might not be subjected to court-martial jurisdiction. Warren assigned the opinion to Black, who had written the *Toth* opinion.

On March 4, Clark wrote a long letter to Brennan, in which he pointed to what he deemed the serious consequences "in the event we repudiate my opinion of last June." Clark pointed to the difficulty of securing the new agreements with foreign countries that would be needed "if we strike down the application of the Code" to wives and civilians. "The only remaining alternative would be to let prosecutions proceed in the local courts of the foreign sovereign. This might be okey in England. But in France one is presumed to be guilty rather than innocent and in Spain local courts are certainly no protection whatever. Likewise in the Middle & Far East we would have great difficulty."

Clark wrote that it was not "possible to keep the civilian employees under the Code and let the wives out. . . . If we follow the *present interpretation* of *Toth* all civilians are out." Nor was it possible to "carve out the so-called lesser offenses. . . . ie take out murder but leave burglary etc under the Code." Clark also asserted that a decision for the wives would mean that "commanders could exercise no control over wives or civilians. . . . Even in traffic violations."

In conclusion, Clark urged, "we should hesitate to repudiate our opinion of last June—and more so the power of the Congress that has been exercised *unquestioned* for over 40 years. It will have a disastrous effect on our foreign relations with 63 countries—cause the NATO agreement to be scrapped to the extent of the force treaties and undermine the morale of our armed forces in these foreign installations."

When Brennan finished the letter, Clark wrote, "just throw it in the waste basket." Brennan was, however, troubled by what Clark had written. As late as May 14, he wrote Black that he was not "formally sending you a return" on his draft opinion. He asked Black "about lesser offenses, for example, simple breach of the peace, traffic violations, disorderly conduct, etc. Do you think dispositions of such offenses (which I would suppose are technically not 'crimes' within

Art. 3, § 2, and the Fifth and Sixth Amendments) are within the holdings of your opinion?" [150]

In the end, however, Brennan decided to go along with Black's opinion. Warren also joined the Black opinion, since it strongly supported the views he had expressed in conference. On May 27, the Chief wrote Black, "This is to confirm my verbal statement to you that I like your opinion . . . and am happy to join you." [151] A similar note had been sent on May 9 by Douglas, who added, "that's a fine opinion." [152]

As it turned out, though six of the eight Justices who sat (Whittaker had come to the Court after the reargument and conference) voted to invalidate the court-martial of the wives, the Black opinion was joined only by Warren, Douglas, and Brennan—one less than a majority. It became merely a plurality opinion because of the objections of Frankfurter and Harlan. On March 6, Frankfurter wrote Warren that he could not go along with Black, "whose conclusion of unconstitutionality has the farthest reach." Instead of Black's broad condemnation of court-martial jurisdiction, the opinion should follow the practice "of not deciding more than the Court has to." Frankfurter urged that the Court should invalidate only the courts-martial "in these capital cases." As he wrote to the Chief, "The sole thought in my mind is the impressive value to the Court should it invalidate these capital cases, at the same time leaving everybody as free as a bird to deal with other questions that are not now here when they do come here—both those who deem the considerations embodied in a Court opinion relevant to other civilians and other crimes and those who do not." [153]

On March 13, Frankfurter wrote Black (with a copy to Warren) that, if Black adhered to his opinion, "I will have to express my own views." [154] Frankfurter then wrote his own opinion, which, he explained in a "Dear Brethren" letter in April, "is restricted to a test of constitutionality of the confined problem that these two cases raise, namely, the power of Congress under Art. I to authorize prosecution by court-martial procedure of *capital* crimes by civilian wives accompanying their service husbands." [155]

Frankfurter also became disturbed at another aspect of Black's opinion. American court-martial jurisdiction over American servicemen and their dependents was authorized by executive agreements with Britain and Japan. Black went out of his way to hold that such agreements could not violate the wives' constitutional right not to be tried by military tribunals. Black asserted that no international agreement could confer power "free from the restraints of the Constitution."[156] This part of the opinion dealt with the relation between international agreements and constitutional limitations that was covered by the controversial Bricker Amendment then before Congress.

Frankfurter objected to what he called, in a letter to the Brethren of May 20, "dragging the Court into the Bricker Amendment controversy." For the opinion to speak on the issue "is a great disservice to Court and country." Frankfurter wrote,

I need not remind my brethren that the Bricker Amendment is one of the most contentious controversies in the Senate and a matter of the liveliest controversy between the Executive and the Senate. Any discussion of the treaty-making power is bound to fan the flames of this controversy. Since only a minority of the Court is discoursing on the subject, it will of course be argued in the Senate that no chances should be taken on such a precarious support of the Constitution and that the adoption of an Amendment is required. Alternatively, it will be urged that since a pronouncement has come from the Supreme Court supporting the Bricker Amendment, there is no reason why it should not be formally put into the Constitution. Can it be that the divisive influences abroad in this land are not serious enough without projecting this Court quite needlessly into this controversy?[157]

On June 5, shortly before the *Reid v. Covert* decision was announced, Frankfurter went so far as to send a *Memorandum for the Conference,* which he called "this petition for rehearing of mine," in which he wrote, "I ask for reconsideration of the retention of treaty discussion in Brother Black's opinion in the cases of the Murdering Wives."[158]

Though Frankfurter's petition was rejected by the conference, he was induced by the others not to write separately on the Bricker Amendment matter. On June 10, when Black delivered his opinion ruling invalid any court-martial jurisidction over civilian dependents, Frankfurter wrote an opinion, concurring in the result but only in capital cases, that did not refer to the Bricker Amendment issue. Harlan wrote a similar separate concurrence. Clark, joined by Burton, dissented, saying that his former opinion in the case was correct.

The result, wrote Sherman Minton to Frankfurter, was that, "all you succeeded in doing in Covert . . . was to turn out a couple of cold blooded murderers without the Court arriving upon any principle of law." The concurring opinions, the retired Justice went on, seem "strangely to have found some difference between Capital and other Crimes not to be found in the Constitution." [159]

In his June 5 "petition for rehearing" in *Reid v. Covert,* Frankfurter wrote that one of the reasons he was asking for reconsideration of the Black opinion's discussion of the Bricker Amendment issue was "the active agitation, of which my Brethren cannot be unmindful, that has been aroused by the case of Army Specialist 3/c Girard." [160]

Wilson v. Girard [161] was a potential *cause célèbre* that came to the Court at the very end of the 1956 Term. Girard was a serviceman who had shot and killed a Japanese woman while trying to frighten her off an Army range in Japan. Under an executive agreement with Japan, Girard had been turned over to the Japanese for trial. A federal court granted an injunction against his delivery to Japanese authorities. The government appealed directly to the Supreme Court, which granted certiorari on June 21, 1957—three days before the term was scheduled to end. Argument was scheduled for July 8.

Even before *Girard* came to the Court, some of the Brethren were concerned about it. In a June 12 letter, Frankfurter asked Warren, "Am I wrong in deeming high the probability that not many days will pass before the case of Private Specialist Girard will be here?" Since "such a sensational case . . . is, as it were, on its way here it surely is desirable that we do not have a recurrence of the Saboteur and the Rosenberg incidents, when members of the Court had to be brought back from far and near. And so, I am wondering whether it wouldn't be desirable to assure the continued presence of the majority of the Court members in anticipation of what seems to be a reasonably to be expected event." [162]

Warren acted to ensure that the Brethren would remain in Washington for the argument and decision. He succeeded with all except Douglas, who had left for Europe as soon as the last scheduled session of the term was held. Warren also sent the Justices a twenty-one page memorandum "on the *Girard* case which was prepared . . . by my law clerks. . . . It is necessarily fragmentary, but in view of the possibility that the Court will be asked on very short notice to decide whether or not to grant cert, I thought this might be helpful in bringing out the issues." [163]

According to a *Memorandum for the Conference* by Warren of June 20: "The Solicitor General was in to see me this morning for the purpose of filing this petition with us, and to express the belief of the Government that it is a matter of paramount importance in foreign relations, not only as between this country and Japan, but also as between it and all of the other nations with which it has similar agreements.

"It is believed by the President personally that if this country cannot legally waive jurisdiction in such matters that other nations will not waive as they have done in the vast majority of cases because, to do so, would demean them before the world." [164]

This memorandum indicates that counsel for one party had an *ex parte* meeting with the Chief Justice on a pending case. Not only did they meet, but they discussed the merits in a manner that was bound to be prejudicial. Solicitor General J. Lee Rankin not only gave his view of the "paramount importance" of the case to our relations with all countries having "status of force" agreements. He also told of the President's personal belief of the adverse consequences that would result from a decision against the government.

In view of the criticisms called forth by the June 1957 decisions, Warren thought it desirable to decide *Girard* in as low-key a manner as possible. He persuaded the others that the best approach would be a unanimous per curiam that would dispose of the legal issues briefly. The opinion was assigned to Brennan, who was helped by a four-page printed draft previously prepared by Frankfurter,[165] as well as draft per curiams by Clark and Burton.

Brennan's draft per curiam, circulated shortly afterwards, was basically the same as the final *Girard* opinion delivered on July 11. It relied on the principle that "a sovereign has exclusive jurisdiction to punish offenses against its laws committed within its borders." The United States had ceded jurisdiction to Japan under the executive agreement. "The issue for our decision is therefore narrowed to the question whether, upon the record before us, the Constitution or legislation subsequent to the Security Treaty prohibited the carrying out of this provision authorized by the Treaty for waiver of the qualified jurisdiction granted by Japan. We find no constitutional or statutory barrier to the provision as applied here." [166]

The original Brennan draft concluded with the sentence, "It is not within our province or responsibility to pass judgment upon the wisdom of the arrangement which, in the absence of encroachment upon Constitutional limitations, is exclusively for the determination of the Executive and Legislative branches." Harlan objected to the sentence in this form and said he would write something if it was not changed. After discussion with Harlan on July 11, the day the opinion was announced, the sentence was changed to: "In the absence of such encroachments, the wisdom of the arrangement is exclusively for the determination of the Executive and Legislative Branches."

On July 10, Clark sent Brennan a note, "Please add at the end of your opinion in *Girard* that 'Mr. Justice Clark concurred in the result.' "[167] Clark went further the next day and wrote a draft dissent[168] in part, objecting to making public an affidavit filed in the district court by Robert Dechert, general counsel of the Defense Department, which was printed as an appendix to Brennan's per curiam opinion.[169] Clark protested that the affidavit had been submitted under seal and its confidence should not be broken.

The last thing Warren wanted, of course, was to have the Court's unanimity broken by a separate concurrence, much less a dissent. He spoke to Clark the morning of July 11 and persuaded him that the point on which he objected was not important enough to sacrifice the need for the Court to speak with one voice in such a sensitive case. When *Girard* was announced later that day, the per curiam spoke for all the Justices who sat in the case.

When the 1956 Term ended, the Brethren were, in Emersons' phrase, "enclosed in a tumultuous privacy of storm." There was, first of all, the storm of controversy over the decisions at the end of the term, particularly those on June 17, 1957. And there was the rising storm within the Court caused by the growing split between the Chief Justice and Justice Frankfurter.

A *New York Times* editorial labeled June 17 "A Day for Freedom" and declared, "The Supreme Court has shown itself by far the most courageous of our three branches of Government in standing up for . . . basic principles."[170] But a growing chorus of excoriation seized upon "Red Monday" as a sign that, in the words of Senator James O. Eastland of Mississippi, "The Court is on the march. It is attempting to consolidate all governmental power into its own hands."[171] At a Senate hearing, there was the following seriocomic exchange between Eastland and Senator Joseph R. McCarthy:

Eastland: The Supreme Court seems to be issuing one Communist decision after another.

McCarthy: You're so right.

Eastland: What influence is there except that some Communist influence is working within the Court?

McCarthy: Either incompetence or the influence you mention.[172]

The most widely circulated extreme attack against Warren and the Court was in *Nine Men Against America: The Supreme Court and Its Assault on American Liberties*,[173] a book which served as the basis for the soon-to-be-launched campaign to impeach Warren. According to it, "on June 17, 1957, the Court really went to town—amid the cheers and hurrahs of the communist conspirators."[174] The book characterized the key "Red Monday" decisions as follows: In *Watkins*, "Chief Justice Warren . . . took away from congressional investigating committees their freedom of inquiry"; in *Sweezy* he "nailed down the clamp . . . on the rights of the states to protect their students against subversive teachers"; and *Yates* "makes it practically impossible to prosecute conspirators against America."[175]

The Georgia Legislature overwhelmingly passed a resolution asking for the impeachment of Warren and the Justices for "high crimes and misdemeanors."[176] A similar call was made by Senator Strom Thurmond of South Carolina,[177] and it was reported that a group of House members were laying plans to attempt an impeachment of the Justices.[178]

At the same time, it was widely circulated that the President was among the severest critics. Asked about this at a news conference on June 26, 1957, Eisenhower conceded that "possibly in their latest series of decisions there are some that each of us has very great trouble understanding." Nevertheless, the President called on the nation to respect the Supreme Court, which he termed, "one of the great stabilizing influences of this country."[179]

Even the Brethren who tended to disagree with the Warren bloc—what James Reston called "the core of this [new] majority . . . extremely sensitive to defense of civil liberties."[180]—resented what they felt were unjustified attacks upon the Court. Though he had chided Frankfurter earlier on some of the June decisions, retired Justice Minton wrote on August 28, 1957, "As I read the recent opinions of the Court I find them far from as pernicious as some publicists make them out. It was ever thus!"[181]

From his vacation home on Long Island Sound, Harlan sent Frankfurter a handwritten letter which noted that Edward S. Corwin, a leading constitutional scholar, "continues to refer to 'the binge of June 17, 1957.'" Harlan went on, "I'm afraid he's slipping. His letters to the Times . . . gave every indication that he doesn't bother to read S.C. opinions—at least understandingly." [182]

Some of the Justices resented even more restrained criticisms of their decisions. Anthony Lewis, then the *New York Times* Supreme Court reporter, wrote a 1961 article in *The Reporter* criticizing the way in which many of the 1956 Term opinions had been written. [183] He praised the opinions of Harlan and Frankfurter and asserted that those two Justices "regretted the character of some of the opinions they joined in 1957."

There exists a copy of the Lewis article with marginal notations in Black's handwriting, [184] which show how sensitive the Justice was to criticism by even so informed an observer as Anthony Lewis. When Lewis contrasted the Warren and Black opinions with Harlan's *Yates* opinion, which he called "a masterful piece of legal craftsmanship," Black wrote, "Is Mr. Lewis an expert on 'legal craftsmanship'? If so, admission into the mysteries of 'craftsmanship' depends neither on study time nor actual practice."

Discussing Black's *Konigsberg* opinion, Lewis wrote, "some thought Black had to distort the factual record of the case to reach his result." At which, Black inquired, "Who thought this? Does he? If so can he claim to be fair without offering proof from the record that 'the factual record' had been distorted?" Lewis went on to say that Black's *Konigsberg* performance "did not increase the confidence of Justices Frankfurter and Harlan in their colleague's impartiality of judgment." To this, Black responded, "How does he know what FF and Harlan thought about my 'impartiality of judgment'? Has he talked with them? And is he agreeing with them? If [so] why not say it and offer proof to support the charge?" And when Lewis wrote that, in *Sweezy,* Frankfurter wrote "a much more persuasive separate concurrence," Black asked, "persuasive to whom?"

Lewis ended his article by saying that even sympathetic Court observers "wish above all that the Justices [Black asked, "which Justices?"] could more often find an unemotional . . . lawyerlike course." Black replied to this, "Is this non lawyer an expert on what is 'lawyerlike'? Why use an ambiguous term that probably means a different thing even to every lawyer who thinks of it much less to a man who has never been a lawyer nor tried a case. . . . ?"

The Lewis article did point out that the Court was becoming increasingly polarized. Frankfurter may have joined many of the 1956 Term decisions. But he regretted the breadth of the opinions and felt that Warren, in particular, had failed to exercise proper restraint. It was the Chief's job to check his colleagues against over-expansive language, unwarranted by the actual cases. Instead, in Frankfurter's view, Warren had been as guilty as any of uttering unduly broad dicta. More and more, Frankfurter realized, his quondam disciple was moving away from him and taking with him a temporary majority of the Court.

Warren, on his side, was growing more and more disenchanted with his erstwhile mentor. He was coming to think of Frankfurter as a petty pedant who used judicial restraint to mask an unwillingness to have the Court perform its full constitutional function. As their approaches to the proper judicial role diverged, there was increasing friction between the two men. These found expression in unprecedented acerbic exchanges in the courtroom, as well as a deteriorating personal relationship that, at least on Frankfurter's side, degenerated into virtual enmity—both toward Warren and the other three in "B.B.D. and W." [185]

7.

THE ELEPHANT AND
THE MOUSE

The Chief Justice's face was flushed and his voice intense as he denounced Frankfurter's statement of a dissent. This is "not a proper statement of an opinion," he bristled, but is "a closing argument by the prosecutor to the jury." What Frankfurter had done was nothing less than "degrading this Court."

Warren's charge was made in the crowded courtroom on April 24, 1961. Black had finished reading the opinion of the Court in *Stewart v. United States*.[1] A bare majority had reversed a murder conviction because of improper questioning by the prosecution. Frankfurter then leaned forward and stated his disagreement. His tone was sharp as he attacked the majority opinion as an "indefensible example of judicial nit-picking" and "excessively finicky appellate review."[2]

The Chief Justice grew visibly angry as he listened. As soon as Frankfurter concluded, Warren declared: "I must say that although I did not file an opinion in this case, that was not the dissenting opinion that was filed. This is a lecture. This is a closing argument by the prosecutor to the jury. It is properly made perhaps in the conference room, but not in the courtroom. As I understand it, the purpose of reporting an opinion in the courtroom is to inform the public and is not for the purpose of degrading this Court. I assure you that, if any written opinion had said these things, I would have had much to say myself. But unfortunately the record will not show it."

When the Chief ended, Frankfurter lamely commented, "I'll leave it to the record."[3] Then the nine Justices stiffly stood up and filed out—an august impersonal presence.

Though unprecedented in its bitterness, the Warren outburst was only the climax of an increasing display of acrimony between the Chief Justice and Frankfurter. The first public exchange between the two occurred during oral argument in 1957, when Frankfurter interrupted and reworded a question that Warren was putting to counsel. Warren flushed and exclaimed, "Let him answer my question! He is confused enough as it is." Frankfurter paled behind his eyeglasses and retorted, "Confused by Justice Frankfurter, I presume."[4]

On June 30, 1958, the two were at it again. It was the last day of the 1957 Term, and Warren read a one-sentence per curiam opinion in *Caritativo v. California*[5] that affirmed a judgment upholding a state statute giving wardens power to determine if a condemned person was sane. Again Frankfurter did not simply read his dissent, but embellished it with strong language not in the published opinion. Indeed, as one of the Brethren at the session recalls, "It was a typical Frankfurter oral dissent. If there was any resemblance to the written opinion, it was purely coincidental."

The same Justice says that, as Frankfurter went on, Warren kept getting whiter and whiter, and finally, when Frankfurter finished, the Chief burst out, "Neither the judgment of this Court nor that of California is quite as savage as this dissent would indicate."[6] He then reviewed the procedural guarantees given in California to defendants who alleged insanity. As one observer put it, "It appeared that he had, temporarily, reverted to being Governor of California and was making a defense of that state's laws."[7] Warren concluded, "I merely make this statement because I don't believe this case is as bad as it might appear."[8]

According to the Justice who was present, their public dispute over the *Caritativo* case signaled "the final break" between Warren and Frankfurter. From then on their relationship deteriorated to the point publicly revealed by the *Stewart* contretemps. A month before the collision there, the differences between the two surfaced in what *Time* termed "a lightweight larceny case."[9] The case was *Milanovich v. United States*.[10] Mr. and Mrs. Milanovich drove three men to a naval base to steal some money. The wife was charged as an accessory to the theft and with receiving stolen property. She was convicted on both counts. The Court, in another five-to-four decision, held that she could not be convicted of both the theft and receipt of the loot. Justice Potter Stewart, who wrote the majority opinion, simply announced the result on March 20, 1961. He said the reasoning was in the printed opinion, and those interested could look there.

Frankfurter took fifteen minutes to state his dissent. As in the other cases, he did not read it verbatim, but extemporized on its theme, sharpening his language and heightening his criticism of the majority. His basic point was that the theft and receipt of the stolen money were "two clearly severed transactions." Frankfurter said he had found "not a single case" supporting the majority's "absolutely novel doctrine." "I know what the Court has said," Frankfurter remarked, "but I don't understand the meaning of it." Several times he asserted that the majority view simply made no sense.

Once again, the Chief was stung by Frankfurter's words. When the Justice finished, Warren looked tartly at his colleague, who sat immediately at his left, and announced, "Since so much has been said here that was not in any written opinion," he wanted to add a word. "It is hornbook law," said the Chief, "that a burglar can't be charged with both robbery and receiving the stolen property. It is therefore an anachronism to say that the actual robber here could be charged with but one offence, while the person who did not participate in the theft but later received some of the money could be convicted of both theft and receipt of the money."

Warren then turned to his left and murmured an invitation to Frankfurter to respond. "The Chief Justice urges me to comment on what he said," Frankfurter told the courtroom, "but of course I won't. I have another case." Frankfurter then went on to state the opinion in the next case.[11]

The public exchanges between Warren and Frankfurter culminated in what the *Washington Post* called "the interpolation of barbs into dissents [and] rebuttals from the center of the bench" in the *Milanovich* and *Stewart* cases.[12] When Warren was asked about the *Stewart* incident, which made front-page headlines, he smiled and said that even Justices were human and could lose their tempers occasionally.[13] Black took a different approach. "It's a grand fight," he declared at a June 15, 1961, dinner in his honor. "The Supreme Court does disagree. I hope it always will. It does have men who express their differences. I hope it always will have." [14]

Despite Warren's attempt to play down his public dispute with Frankfurter, both men felt strongly about the growing differences between them. In Frankfurter's papers,[15] there is a *Washington Post* editorial[16] about the *Milanovich* exchange, with marginal comments in the Justice's handwriting. The editorial referred to "the warmth of the discussion in the conference room in the *Milanovich* case." Next to this, Frankfurter wrote, "A baseless assumption—there was no 'warmth of discussion' at Conference on *Milanovich.*" The *Post* said that Stewart had announced the decision without reading his opinion because he "appear[ed] to have foreseen the situation, and to have deliberately avoided stirring any further irritation." To this, Frankfurter observed, "I don't know why Stewart merely announced his opinion, but it could not have been in anticipation of the Chief's wholly unconventional outburst."

The editorial remarked that, in presenting his dissent, Frankfurter "added a few biting words that were not in the text." Frankfurter objected, "I said nothing in my oral that was not within the scope of my written opinion. So my brethren have assured me." The *Post* also said that Frankfurter had "provoked Chief Justice Warren to offer a brief rebuttal as an explanation of why he stood with the majority." Frankfurter objected, "He gave a totally different reason than what was set forth in the Stewart opinion which he had joined."

The editorial concluded by noting, "The Justices are divided by conflicting views that run to the very core of constitutional law." Frankfurter replied, "*Milanovich* had nothing to do—NOTHING—with constitutional law or the 'conflicting views' on the Court regarding it."

Milanovich may have had nothing to do with the polarization among the Brethren on constitutional issues. But, along with the other courtroom incidents, it did dramatically demonstrate the corroded relationship between the Chief Justice and his erstwhile mentor.

Perhaps the personal, as well as the juristic, differences between the two were inevitable. Writing about the tiff on the bench in the *Stewart* case, *Time* commented, "Chief Justice Earl Warren has a notably thin skin, and waspish Justice Felix Frankfurter can get under an elephant's hide." [17] According to a Justice who served with both on the Court, "Felix was like a mouse, and Warren like an elephant, and they had the same effect upon each other."

The two were so dissimilar that there was almost no individual rapport between them. "They were so different in personality," says the same Justice, "in origin and experience and in the kind of people they were. Felix Frankfurter was, above all, an intellectual. For him, just the pleasure of argumentation took the place of what, for many people, they get out of bridge or tennis or golf, or something like that. It was a recreation for Felix and this sort of attitude the Chief Justice just couldn't understand. He had all his life been a peace-maker and, if you will, a compromiser and to get people working together—not to argue, to avoid confrontations, and Felix liked them, just recreationally, intellectually. . . . just to have the fun of arguing it. . . . And this was just the kind of approach and attitude that the Chief Justice didn't and couldn't understand. . . . They were really just uncongenial personalities as people."

Frankfurter's constant argumentation and disputation were things Warren simply could not comprehend. "All Frankfurter does is talk, talk, talk," Warren used to tell his colleagues. "He drives you crazy."

When Warren charged Frankfurter with "degrading this Court" by his corrosive comments, he was not engaging in mere hyperbole. The Chief believed that Frankfurter was using the bench as a forum to denigrate the Court—and that at a time when the Brethren were beleaguered by the crescendo of extreme criticism directed against the Court. To Warren, the oral delivery of opinions served an important function. "It was," a former law clerk recalls, "kind of to humanize the Court and one of the things that offended him was that he thought that Frankfurter took advantage of that and . . . took the occasion too frequently to deliver a lecture. He didn't deliver an opinion . . . in the Chief's view, but he took this as a kind of a public pedestal to lecture not only the public, but his colleagues on what the law ought to be."

Justice Stewart says that he had "admiration and respect for [Frankfurter] but he had dramatic shortcomings and one of them was his fickleness." When Warren first came to the Court, Stewart recalls, Frankfurter had praised him as "the greatest Chief Justice since John Marshall." But, "when I got here [1958] Felix Frankfurter had been very much disenchanted by the Chief Justice."

Much of Frankfurter's disenchantment stemmed from his failure to continue as the dominating influence over the Chief Justice. This was particularly true after Warren had staked out his own juristic road, diverging ever more sharply from that followed by his former preceptor. In Frankfurter's eyes, apostasy compounded the Chief's dereliction from the proper judicial path.

Without a doubt, there was no personal chemistry between the two men. Warren just could not understand Frankfurter, and the latter looked down on the Chief as one who felt, rather than thought, his way through difficult decisions. Warren was primarily what used to be thought of as a "man's man." "He had," Justice Byron White says, "a lot of those simple sort of virtues that automatically recommend him to at least other men."

Warren was exactly the sort of vigorous outdoorsman with whom Frankfurter felt least comfortable. As Stewart recalls it, Warren truly loved sports; "he followed the baseball teams and the football teams— which again just infuriated Felix Frankfurter." It was beyond Frankfurter's comprehension that grown men could spend untold hours in watching others chase inflated pigskins or swing at horsehide balls. Stewart tells of the time Warren "even took Frankfurter to one of his games. Frankfurter went just to please the Chief, but he didn't really enjoy it or know what was going on and know why anyone was interested in it."

In the best of circumstances, Frankfurter was difficult to get along with. With all his gifts, he had basic flaws that resulted in his being all too often, as Flaubert once put it, "like a hedgehog wounding itself with its own quills." Writing Brennan in 1957, Frankfurter remarked, "I suppose it is the professor in me that talks this way."[18] The former professor could never shed the habit of treating others as students in his Harvard seminars. His supercilious attitude would surface even in his dealings with his colleagues. "It is not pleasant," he once wrote Reed, "to tell you things that are not pleasant. But after all we are not children."[19] Another time, he told Brennan, in a letter criticizing the large number of railroad negligence cases decided that term, "I look forward, though grimly, to your piling up a score, at least before I say *'nunc dimittus.'* * (I suppose you know what that means.) But I am afraid I never did understand that 'negligence' means anything except 'negligence,' as you and I were taught it in first year Torts."[20]

Dean Acheson, a close friend of Frankfurter, said, "One needs to see, to hear . . . to realize what an obstreperous person this man is, to have one's arm numbed by his vise-like grip just above one's elbow, to feel the intensity of his nervous energy."[21] Frankfurter's intense love of argumentation for its own sake would lead him into disputes even against his own interest. An example is to be found in some of his dealings with Harlan. If there was *any* colleague to whom Frankfurter was close, it was Harlan. And, if there was anyone whom Harlan revered, it was his grandfather, the Justice of the same name who had delivered the *Plessy v. Ferguson*[22] dissent. Frankfurter for his part did not think highly of the first Harlan and made no bones about it. "The present fashion," he noted to a close friend in 1956, "to make old Harlan out a great judge is plumb silly."[23]

To Harlan himself Frankfurter remarked that Harlan I had not been the fighter for racial equality that people supposed. "You will probably recall that some time ago I expressed to you the belief that there is no evidence whatever that Harlan I thought that segregation was unconstitutional and that it was my hunch that he would have sustained segregation."[24] Frankfurter then expanded on this theme in several letters. Even though Harlan II expressed irritation, writing back, "I think you push things too far,"[25] Frankfurter persisted. "Duly mindful of all you say about *Plessy,* I am sorry to have to stand my ground." He went on to say, "whatever virtues may be attributed to Harlan I, no one, I submit, would credit—or charge—him with having been a close reasoner."[26] It is almost as though Frankfurter did not know where to stop when he was engaged in a course of action. He was a born lobbyist and would go out of his way to influence colleagues, law clerks, and even clerks' wives. No one, indeed, could match Frankfurter in his incessant attempts to curry favor in the Court. This was particularly true after Whittaker's appointment. As a law clerk said, "Frankfurter really went to work on Whittaker from day one and Whittaker was just overwhelmed by . . . the notion that this great intellect was actually complimenting him."

---

* Ironically, Frankfurter himself misspelled *dimittis* in this letter.

Frankfurter would write Whittaker such things as, "Were I to retire tomorrow, one of the most gratifying memories I would carry with me of my whole judicial life would be your behavior in *Yancy*. It was judicial behavior at its finest."[27] Or he would tell Whittaker, "No one on the Court more than you searches more consistently to reach results in cases solely on relevant judicial grounds,"[28] and "how gladdened I was by the clear-sightedness" that he displayed "so early in your days on the Court."[29]

Written to one of the weakest Justices in Supreme Court history, these comments were ludicrous. "It was," says the same clerk, "clear to everybody on the Court with the exception of Whittaker that he was being used by Frankfurter and that Frankfurter was ingratiating himself in order to secure Whittaker's vote."

Frankfurter would at times so overdo his attempts at ingratiation that his exertions would have the reverse effect. When Warren first came to the Court, Frankfurter bombarded him with a mass of notes, memoranda, articles, and even texts intended to inculcate the Frankfurter view. This was scarcely the method to win over one who was more a man of action than intellect. Warren's resentment at his colleague's overzealous efforts was one of the factors that turned the Chief away from Frankfurter.

Perhaps the best example of how Frankfurter's tendency to overdo things had the opposite result from that intended was his attempt to have Learned Hand appointed to the Supreme Court. Hand was the outstanding federal appellate judge in the country and the virtual unanimous choice of the legal profession for the next Supreme Court vacancy. Frankfurter outdid himself in his zealousness to have Hand promoted. In the end, however, Frankfurter's relentless efforts backfired. In his *Autobiography,* William O. Douglas tells how, in January 1943, President Roosevelt told him at a buffet dinner during a poker party, "Learned Hand is *not* going to be appointed." Douglas protested that Hand was a fine judge. "Perhaps so," FDR came back. "But this time Felix overplayed his hand." The President put down his fork and said to Douglas, "Do you know how many people asked me today to name Learned Hand? Twenty, and every one a messenger from Felix Frankfurter. And by golly, I won't do it."[30]

Francis Biddle, then FDR's Attorney General, told Hand, "If Felix hadn't pushed, pushed, pushed, you'd have had a better chance—if he hadn't been so importunate."[31] After FDR died, it was too late.

When Burton was nominated to the Court in 1945, Minton wrote to Frankfurter, President Truman "told me that he would have named Learned Hand but he was too old!"[32]

It may be, as Frankfurter said in his comments on the *Washington Post* editorial on the *Milanovich* case, that "there was no 'warmth of discussion' " at the conference on that case. There were, however, other conferences that saw heated exchanges between Frankfurter and Warren. Not surprisingly, Frankfurter's initial high opinion of the Chief Justice changed as the relations between the two began to deteriorate. According to one account, when Warren took exception in conference to a Frankfurter sermon, the furious Frankfurter retorted, "You're the worst Chief Justice this country has ever had."[33] The Justices who sat during the Warren years say that no such Frankfurter outburst occurred. But none denies that Frankfurter came to have a poor opinion of Warren. Once, during a heated conference session, Frankfurter was overheard screeching at the Chief, "Be a judge, god damn it, be a judge!" Use of the verb "screeching" is not an exaggeration. As one of the Brethren remembers it, once Frankfurter would "get going . . . his voice would rise to a pretty high decible content and pretty high on the scales."

There are ample indications too that Frankfurter's differences with the Chief Justice became increasingly personal. Certainly Warren would have had difficulty in agreeing with Frankfurter's self-characterization: "I . . . do not stick out for my own personal even if strongly felt views, and make every possible accommodation."[34] What Frankfurter termed "the natural distaste of talking about colleagues,"[35] did not prevent him from expressing strong derogatory views both about the Chief Justice and the work of the Warren Court. His words and actions after his split with Warren give substance to his assertion to Clark that, "I am not a fellow who is for peace by surrendering everything he believes. You remember the Latin poet who said: 'They made a devastation and called it peace.' "[36]

During Frankfurter's last Court years, his relations with the Chief Justice grew increasingly touchy. In a 1957 letter to retired Justice Minton, Frankurter described an incident "about my alleged misbehavior during the reading of an opinion." The following, said Frankfurter, were "the precise facts" in the matter: "The Chief read an opinion and, having finished it, started to read another one, when

Harold whispered to me, 'I have a dissent in that opinion.' I tried to pass on that remark to the Chief Justice, with the view of course of having him turn to Harold to state his dissent. Instead of doing that, the Chief rapped on his desk with his fist to suggest silence to me." The sequel was an "exchange of notes between the Chief and me."[37]

At the end of the 1956 Term, Frankfurter objected to the continuing of cases on the docket to the next term, terming it "dishonest nonsense."[38] At the beginning of the 1957 Term, he sent a memorandum to the Brethren "criticising our 'practice' of 'massing' important adjudications toward the end of the Term. It is said that 'massing important adjudications is bad for the Court, internally and externally. . . .' "[39] Chief Justice Warren replied in a memorandum declaring, "I submit that none of the controversy which the Court found itself in at the conclusion of last Term or any recent Term was due to 'massing' of important cases at the conclusion of the Term." Warren listed the cases decided the prior June "which were most controversial, with the dates of reargument and opinion, as well as the cases to be reargued this term, with similar dates," and asserted, "The dates on these cases would indicate that the number of opinions filed in June was not due to 'massing' at the end of the Term."[40] Frankfurter then wrote a memorandum, saying he was sorry to have given "the impression that we purposefully so conduct our business that we hand down numerous important opinions toward the end of the Term. . . . I was directing myself to the fact that for one reason or another, or for many reasons, it happens, as it did last Term, that a number of very important decisions fall to be handed down at, or near, adjournment day. I was referring to a condition, not a 'practice.' "[41]

Letters exchanged between Frankfurter and Warren in 1960 indicate how sensitive their relations had become. "The other day," Frankfurter wrote the Chief on April 13, "you asked me whether I would put on paper a remark I had made to the effect that the Court can dispose of a case according to justice. I do so now put it on paper: The Court can dispose of a case according to justice, on the assumption that the Court has jurisdiction, i.e., legal power to adjudicate. But it cannot dispense with the requirements of jurisdiction in order to do justice."[42] But Warren had only been engaging in banter with his testy colleague. "You should not have taken my remark seriously," the Chief replied on April 14, "It was intended as a mere pleasantry while we were all in idle conversation."[43]

In conference a year earlier, on May 15, 1959, Warren angrily accused Frankfurter of "deceiving" him in the opinion that the Justice had delivered on May 4 in *Frank v. Maryland*.[44] That case, which will be discussed in more detail in the next chapter, involved the constitutionality of an administrative inspection. In the conference discussion on March 6, Frankfurter had stressed that the only penalty for refusing inspection was a small fine. His *Frank* opinion did not mention the point. According to a note in Frankfurter's writing, "At Conference on Friday, May 15/59, the Chief in connection with a discussion of the controlling authority of *Frank v.* [*Maryland*], charged me with 'deceiving' him about that opinion because I had not included in the opinion what I had said when we originally considered the case, i.e., the smallness of fine.' "[45]

In a letter to Harlan, Frankfurter explained that his reference to the amount of the fine "was a makeweight, not a determinant." He rejected "the suggestion that fugitive remarks from the bench or at Conference bind one in determining how an opinion should be written."[46] But the merits of the controversy were less important than the fact that Warren could be provoked to an outburst against Frankfurter on such a minor matter.

"After I rebutted the Chief," the note in Frankfurter's writing concludes, "Harlan sent me, that is passed to me (I sit next to him) this note." Then, the following is written in Harlan's handwriting: "What the Chief said was utterly inexcusable—don't mistake me on that. But for your own health, you mustn't allow yourself to get sucked into that kind of stuff—if you don't mind my saying so."[47] A few days later, Harlan wrote Frankfurter, "The episode . . . should never have happened."[48]

Among the cases in which the disagreement between Warren and Frankfurter was first manifested were the Expatriation Cases to be discussed in the next chapter. The scene when they were decided, on March 31, 1958, was described by Anthony Lewis in the *New York Times:* "The Justices put their deep philosophic differences on vivid display Monday, in their written opinions and even more in their oral comments. Their remarks in the courtroom verged on the bitter, even waspish."[49] In delivering his majority opinion in one of the cases,[50] the Chief Justice justified the decision by referring to eighty-one instances in which the Court had determined that congressional action was unconstitutional.[51] Frankfurter interpolated a direct answer in stating his dissent. According to Lewis, "These 81 cases, he said, are nothing to boast about. He said bitingly that many of the decisions had since been overruled."[52]

A few months later, Frankfurter wrote to a former law clerk, "Wouldn't it be interesting to study the eighty-one or so cases to which the Chief Justice referred in which this Court invalidated congressional legislation, with a view to ascertaining the value of the Court's corrective power?"[53] By then, Frankfurter had come to realize that his early efforts to win over the new Chief Justice to his judicial philosophy had not succeeded. During his remaining four years on the Court, there would be constant conflict between the two that would culminate in Frankfurter's dissent in *Baker v. Carr*,[54] during his last term on the Court.

The differences between the Chief and the Justice were, of course, juristic, as well as personal. To Frankfurter, many of the eighty-one cases invalidating congressional action were based on an improper conception of judicial review. Warren's adherence to the Black–Douglas view of the judicial function was, for Frankfurter, the ultimate apostasy. The activist approach, he felt, was reviving the situation that prevailed earlier in the century when, as a famous dissent by Justice Louis D. Brandeis put it, the Court was exercising "the powers of a super-Legislature—not the performance of the constitutional function of judicial review."[55]

Referring to that period, Frankfurter wrote, in an unpublished 1954 paper, "It is nothing new even for lawyers to identify desire with constitutionality and to look to the Court to declare unconstitutional legislation that one does not like. Now the roles are reversed; the so-called liberals who threw their hats high in the air when Brandeis in a dissenting opinion said that the Court was not a third House of the Legislature now want the Court to strike down all legislation that touches civil liberties." They now assert "the view that the provisions of the Constitution dealing with individual liberties are absolutes in the sense that the Court is to enforce them 'irregardless' of any concern for the legislative judgment."[56]

A Lincoln anecdote about an Illinois jury has it that the jury foreman asked the judge if he could help him out with a question, and the judge said that he would be glad to give any help he could. "Well, judge," said the foreman, "the jury wanted to know: was that there you told them the law or just your notion?"[57]

Above all, Frankfurter felt, it was not for the judge to read his own "notion" into the Constitution.

His colleagues who were doing so were, to Frankfurter, performing more a legislative than a judicial function. Writing to Potter Stewart about a Brennan opinion, Frankfurter noted that, had its author "been Senator . . . , he wouldn't have to change a word in what he has written in a speech voting against the legislation or the weight of arguments, pro and con, for enacting these provisions. What in effect he is doing is to pass *de novo* judgment on the propriety or wisdom, or even fairness, of the legislation."[58]

Warren had rejected the Frankfurter philosophy of judicial restraint because he had come to feel that it thwarted effective performance of the Court's constitutional role. Judicial abnegation, in the Chief's view, meant all too often judicial abdication of the duty to enforce constitutional guarantees. "I believe," Warren declared in an interview on his retirement, "that this Court or any court should exercise the functions of the office to the limit of its responsibilities." Judicial restraint meant that, "for a long, long time we have been sweeping under the rug a great many problems basic to American life. We have failed to face up to them, and they have piled up on us, and now they are causing a great deal of dissension and controversy of all kinds." To Warren, it was the Court's job "to remedy those things eventually," regardless of the controversy involved.[59]

Warren not only thought that the Frankfurter restraint doctrine was not the proper judicial posture. He also believed that it inevitably involved hypocrisy on the part of the judge. Frankfurter rejected the notion that certain constitutional guarantees—notably those protecting personal rights—have a "preferred position" and hence should be actively enforced by the Court. His firm position was stated in the *Ullmann* case, discussed in chapter 5: "As no constitutional guaranty enjoys preference, so none should suffer subordination or deletion."[60]

But Frankfurter, too, had his own scale of values. When a value that he thought particularly important was at stake, he, no less than Warren or Black, was ready to scrutinize more closely to ensure that the cherished value was not impaired. Warren could see this directly in a letter Frankfurter sent him in 1957, which discussed the difference in approach between Black and Frankfurter on the Fourth Amendment's guaranty against unreasonable searches and seizures. "The fact of the matter," Frankfurter wrote, "is that from the time I came on the Court there has been a deep cleavage of view regarding the Fourth Amendment between Black and myself. On more than one occasion, he expressed hostility to the *Silverthorne* decision[61] and readiness to overrule it; and for him the *Weeks* decision[62] merely stands for a judicially created rule of evidence. For me, *Silverthorne* and *Weeks* are among the most important decisions of this Court in the domain of civil liberties."

To Black, the Fourth Amendment was not as important as other Bill of Rights guarantees, and he had never been as vigorous in enforcing it. To Frankfurter, as his letter to Warren declared, the Fourth Amendment "and the responsibility of this Court in relation to it [are] of as great importance as any aspect of civil liberties. To the extent that I am charged, not by you, with being 'a nut' on the subject of the 'knock at the door,' I am ready to plead guilty."[63]

Warren also thought that Frankfurter's vote and opinion in the 1957 case of *Rowoldt v. Perfetto*[64] showed that Frankfurter's restraint doctrine was often a facade to mask the fact that the Justice could be as human in his decision process as any of the Brethren. Rowoldt was an elderly Jewish alien who had come to this country in 1914 and had been ordered deported for past membership in the Communist Party. He testified that he had briefly been a Communist in 1935 and worked for a while in a Communist book store. At the conference on the case on October 18, 1957, the Court was sharply divided. "The Four"—as Frankfurter was now calling Warren, Black, Douglas, and Brennan in his conference notes[65]—were for reversal; Harlan, Burton, Clark, and Whittaker for affirmance. Frankfurter tipped the balance by voting for reversal, and Warren assigned him the opinion. It was delivered December 9 and held that, despite a statute making any Communist membership a ground for deportation, Rowoldt's relations to the Communist Party were not "the kind of meaningful association required . . . particularly in the case of an old man who has lived in this country for forty years."[66]

In a number of cases, Frankfurter had written opinions upholding deportation of aliens with Communist associations. When Warren met his law clerks after the *Rowoldt* conference, he told them that Frankfurter had provided the vote for the bare majority to reverse. The clerks expressed surprise because Frankfurter's action was so inconsistent with his previous decisions. At this, the Chief said, "Well, you know, I think Frankfurter is capable of a human instinct now and then. Frankfurter really obviously just felt sorry for this poor old immigrant." Warren also noted that Frankfurter and Rowoldt had similar backgrounds, saying, "I think Frankfurter may well have thought that there but for the grace of God go I."

Warren used to express irritation at Frankfurter's constant lecturing of the Justices that they were nothing but a group of "result-oriented judges," who did not have the courage to vote for a decision that was mandated by precedent, where they felt it was not the right decision. To Warren, a case such as *Rowoldt* demonstrated that Frankfurter could be as "result-oriented" as any of the Brethren.

The deteriorating relationship between Frankfurter and Warren stemmed from more than Warren's abandonment of the judicial restraint doctrine. Frankfurter objected just as much to Warren's conception of the Supreme Court as a virtual modern Court of Chancery—a residual "fountain of justice" to rectify individual instances of injustice, particularly where the victims suffered from racial, economic, or similar disabilities. "If the Chief Justice," Justice Stewart recalls, "can see some issue that involves widows or orphans or the underprivileged, then he's going to come down on that side."

A much-quoted statement by Anthony Lewis has it that "Earl Warren was the closest thing the United States has had to a Platonic Guardian, dispensing law from a throne without any sensed limits of power except what was seen as the good of society."[67] But Warren was more than the judicial counterpart of the Platonic philosopher-king. He consciously conceived of himself as a present-day Chancellor, whose job was to secure fairness and equity in individual cases, particularly where they involved his "constituency" of the poor or underprivileged.

To Frankfurter, this was to misconceive utterly the role of the highest Court. "I do not conceive," he wrote Brennan in 1957, "that it is my function to decide cases on my notions of justice and, if it were, I wouldn't be as confident as some others that I know exactly what justice requires in a particular case. . . . I envy those for whom the dictates of justice are spontaneously revealed."[68]

In particular, Frankfurter objected to the Court's exercise of jurisdiction to review the merits of what he considered essentially petty cases. "The old saw that hard cases make bad law," he noted to Justice Minton, "has its basis in experience. But I have long been of the view that petty cases are even more calculated to make bad law. The impact of a sordid little case is apt to be more vivid than the implications of the generalization to which the immediate case gives rise."[69] Frankfurter felt strongly about the need for the Court to limit its docket to what he called, in a 1956 letter to Warren, "cases that alone should take the Court's time and energy"[70]—those worthy of consideration by the nation's highest tribunal. Thus, he constantly stressed, as he wrote to Burton the same year, "the wisdom and need for denying certiorari in cases presenting largely factual issues."[71]

Frankfurter's antipathy toward Justices who sought only to give effect to their individualized conception of justice had previously been expressed in his deprecating attitude toward Justice Frank Murphy, who had been noted for voting with his heart rather than his head in cases involving racial minorities and the poor. "Justice tempered by Murphy" had been the way wags described his record on the Court. Frankfurter sarcastically called Murphy "St. Frank" in his correspondence.[72] "The short of the matter," he once wrote Justice Reed, "is that today you would no more heed Murphy's tripe than you would be seen naked at Dupont Circle at high noon tomorrow."[73]

Now Frankfurter feared that Warren was turning into a latter-day Murphy, in his emphasis only on fairness in the individual case. More specifically, Frankfurter grew increasingly uneasy at Warren's tendency to reconsider the merits in cases involving workers—whether in employment injury cases under workmen's compensation laws or the Federal Employers' Liability Act (giving railroad workers the right to sue for injuries on the job), or in cases involving other statutes protecting workers, such as the Fair Labor Standards Act. Characteristically, Warren's first opinion reversed on the facts a lower court injunction against enforcement of a workmen's compensation award, emphasizing that "This Act must be liberally construed in conformance with its purpose."[74] During the next few years, the Chief Justice led the Court in reviewing and reversing on the merits a growing number of employment injury cases. A table prepared by Frankfurter in February 1957, shows that Supreme Court "decisions relating to sufficiency of the evidence under the FELA" increased four-fold in the 1954–1956 Terms, as compared with the three terms before Warren became Chief Justice.[75]

In a number of cases during the 1954–1956 Terms, Frankfurter voted to dismiss petitions for certiorari as improvidently granted, without passing on the merits.[76] He did not, however, indicate why he dissented in those cases. Before he enlarged publicly on the considerations that led him to dissent, Frankfurter sent a four-page memorandum to Warren early in 1956, explaining his position.[77] The memorandum was occasioned by two Warren opinions[78] holding that clothes changing and showering by workers in a battery plant and knife-sharpening by workers in a meat-packing plant constituted "principal activity or activities," not "preliminary or postliminary" activities within the Fair Labor Standards Act and hence had to be paid for by employers under the Act. "My subconscious," Frankfurter wrote after he agreed to concur silently, "must have been busy with my returns yesterday afternoon to your two FLSA cases, for I woke up this morning, after a good night's sleep, with the conviction that I should tell you my intrinsic position regarding those two cases, lest I misconveyed my views by merely returning your opinions with a 'Yes.' I am keeping quiet and thereby joining your opinions, partly because I deem the occasion undesirable to set out what I think, and partly because I do not want to make inroads on my time on other Court work at hand."

Frankfurter wrote that it was vital that the Court not take cases that turned on appraisals of evidence regarding issues of fact.

It is for these reasons that I have consistently voted against taking cases under the Federal Employers Liability Act . . . , the Fair Labor Standards Act, and like legislation, however much I may have disagreed with the opinions of state or federal courts in particular cases and however confident I may be that I do not feel less compassionately toward a plaintiff who loses than do my brethren. Thinking in terms of this institution and "what it takes" for the Court to do the job that nobody else can do, I do not think the correction of an erroneous decision, after two courts have dealt with the matter . . . is the proper business of this Court, with due regard to those awfully difficult and delicate issues that are the business of this Court.

Addressing directly Warren's feeling that the overriding consideration was that justice be done in the individual case "and that one more case is not likely to appear an important weight to the burdens the Court cannot escape," Frankfurter asserted, "It isn't just one more case. What is the Scotch proverb about 'many a muckle makes a mickle'? Every additional case we take that we shouldn't take is bound to be an undue drain of time and energy that belong elsewhere." Frankfurter conceded that he had "no doubt some of the lower court decisions which we bring here were decided erroneously against an employee." But, he concluded, "this is not a court for the correction of errors."

Despite the Frankfurter memorandum, the Warren Court continued to review the merits in employment cases involving issues of fact. On February 29, 1957, Frankfurter delivered a more detailed dissent, "in view of the increasing number of these cases that have been brought here for review . . . and in view of the encouragement thereby given to continuing resort to this Court."[79] In this dissent Frankfurter publicly explained his position—though less effectively than in his memorandum to Warren.

"Tell me," wrote retired Justice Minton to Frankfurter in the summer of 1957, "has the Chief prevailed on you to give up your method of dismissing as improvidently granted?"[80] Frankfurter continued to disagree with the Court's grant of certiorari in F.E.L.A.-type cases. "I deem," he wrote Harlan, "the granting of certs on questions of evidence in a negligence case to raise frivolous issues."[81] "Such being my views," he wrote Harlan in another letter, "I shall continue, as the only effective way of voicing my view, to state that the writ in these damn cases should be dismissed as improvidently granted."[82] But Frankfurter did not attempt further to explain his views on the matter. In cases in 1959 and 1960, he stated only that, for the reasons set forth in his February 1957 dissent, he "is of the view that the writ of certiorari is improvidently granted."[83]

Frankfurter did, however, publicly dispute Warren on whether the Court should take such minor cases in a 1959 case in which the Court reinstated a $7,500 jury verdict for a widow on an insurance policy.[84] According to Anthony Lewis in the *New York Times,* the opinion of the Court by Chief Justice Warren "reviewed in human, almost folksy terms, the issues in the case." Frankfurter, Lewis went on, then "read his colleagues a lecture on the need to conserve the Court's time and energy by avoiding trivial cases."[85] Frankfurter declared (in a passage not contained in his printed dissenting opinion), "This is a case that should never have been here. It will set no precedents. It will guide no lawyers. It will guide no courts."[86]

Warren felt as strongly as Frankfurter about these cases. Perhaps, as a *New York Times* comment about a 1959 F.E.L.A. case put it, "An argument among Supreme Court justices in a case concerning grease on a railroad tie may not appear to be a very weighty matter."[87] The Chief Justice had, however, had personal experience, when both his father and he had worked for the Southern Pacific Railroad in his youth, of how devastating accidents could be. "He told us," one of his law clerks said, "that he felt that the jobs used up the men and when they were no longer valuable, cast them aside. He supposed that was the first time he thought of the human cost of . . . the railroads."[88]

When he became Chief Justice, Warren looked upon the Supreme Court as the last resort of the widows and orphans who had lost in F.E.L.A. cases, as well as cases like the 1959 insurance case. The Chief used to stress to his clerks how important it was that the Court should take some F.E.L.A. cases each year to make sure that everyone knew that the statute meant what it said.

The Brethren were sharply divided between the Warren and Frankfurter views on the cases involving workers. In an F.E.L.A. case decided at the end of 1959, there was a bare majority for a decision against the injured worker. Douglas dissented, joined by the Chief Justice, Black, and Brennan. When the decision was announced on December 14, some of the majority Justices delivered concurrences poking fun at the dissent. When Douglas read his dissent, he included extemporaneous comments not in his opinion. The gravity of the issues, he said, "belie the rather smart-alecky things that have been said."[89]

Warren and his supporters continued to vote to take these cases and, more often than not, reverse despite Frankfurter's insistence in a 1957 letter to Brennan, that they involved only "different assessments" of evidence—"a difference *not* to be resolved by the Supreme Court of the United States."[90] At times, the Chief and his allies would vote in favor of the worker even against overwhelming evidence. In an F.E.L.A. case during the 1962 Term, a railroad worker lost a finger while the undercarriage of a railway car was being installed. The evidence seemed to show so clearly that the worker had been negligent that all the law clerks recommended that certiorari should be denied. After the conference at which the Court voted to grant cert, Black jubilantly exclaimed to his clerks: "The Justices beat the law clerks again!"

Thus, as Frankfurter wrote in a 1960 letter to Minton, "The Court

. . . merrily goes on under some compulsion of finding negligence from the fact of injury in every FELA. case."[91] Presumably, he enjoyed Minton's earthy comment on the Court's actions in these cases: "There seems to be no end to the FELA. Cases. You all seem to have reached the position in the law of negligence where a railroad employee has an urgent call of nature the railroad company is negligent if the railroad company does not furnish him with a safe gondola car to crap in—to your credit you are still dissenting to this kind of law."[92]

Frankfurter remained deeply disturbed by what he felt was the misuse of the Court's jurisdiction in the F.E.L.A.-type cases. "The real truth of the matter," he wrote Harlan in 1957, "is that some of our brethren play ducks and drakes with the jurisdictional requirements when they want to reach a result because they are self-righteous do-gooders, unlike Holmes who spoke of himself 'as a judge whose first business is to see that the game is played according to the rules whether I like them or not.' "[93]

Another letter to Harlan a month earlier had been bitter: "I wonder how many of those who are reversing out of hand in these cases have read the record and not relied merely on the memoranda of their law clerks. And since my curiosity is very alert this morning, I wonder how many of the law clerks have read the whole record in these cases." The letter was signed, "Reasonably or unreasonably yours, whichever I appear to you to be."[94]

Perhaps the best summing up of the F.E.L.A. situation in the Court was contained in a 1958 letter to Frankfurter from Dean Acheson, who was then in London. Commenting on a decision of the House of Lords, Acheson wrly commented, "It struck me that their Lordships of the Judicial Committee had not heard of [Warren's] rule in the Supreme Court of the United States to the effect that in negligence cases the defendant always loses. This is not to be confused with Clark's rule that in criminal cases the defendant always loses. It also occurred to me that if Mr. Justice Frankfurter had been sitting in the Judicial Committee he would have held that the appeal was improperly granted."[95]

During this period, the relations between Warren and Frankfurter continued outwardly correct, if no longer cordial. "From one old, nineteenth century model to another," wrote the Chief on February

11, 1958, when both he and the Justice were ill, "I can say there are worse places than bed when the old crankshaft needs repair or carburetor adjustment." It was the first time either had been away from the Court since Warren's appointment and the only time the Chief missed a day in his sixteen years on the Court. Warren wrote that, because of a virus, "I, of course, cannot go to the White House dinner tonight, not only because of my own discomfiture, but because of the danger of contaminating those in attendance."[96]

Warren continued to write in the same tone during Frankfurter's remaining years. "This is the voice of conscience," a letter in August 1960 reads. "—the conscience of a vagabond jurist who has been enjoying himself by travelling through these spacious and beautiful states, while a few of his associates are in hot, humid Washington, 'tending to the store.' . . . I do hope that neither the weather nor the work has been too rough on you."[97] After Frankfurter's stroke, which forced his retirement, Warren's letters expressed suitable concern. "I do wish," he wrote in May 1962, shortly after the Justice's first stroke, "there was something we could do to help. . . . Our only feeling of frustration is that we do not know what to do." At a dinner the Chief was giving, "in honor of Byron and Charley . . . we will think of you and will raise a glass to your early and complete recovery."[98]

Frankfurter, on his side, displayed the same external amenity toward the Chief. Even when he wrote a long letter, in July 1958, complaining of the grant of bail by Douglas to reputed underworld leader Frank Costello, he was careful to close with a friendly salutation: "I hope you have been a lucky fisherman, if fishing be part of your vacation. Howsoever you are utilizing your vacation, I hope for a refreshing and very pleasant time."[99]

Beneath the outer proprieties, however, there was increasing bitterness between the two. It is harder to document this with regard to Warren. His life in politics had taught him to mask his private emotions by a bland exterior. Whatever "resentments [Warren] may have privately harbored," says Justice Stewart, "he kept them very much under control," though "they came out sometimes"—as seen by some of the incidents already recounted.

In addition, Warren would rarely commit his inner feelings to correspondence. Frankfurter, on the other hand, was of course less restrained in this regard. His papers clearly show how his initial high estimate of Warren changed as time went on. After the 1957 Term, in a letter to Harlan, Frankfurter wrote: "I am afraid his attitude towards the kind of problems that confront us are more like that of a fighting politician than that of a judicial statesman. I shudder to think what would have happened to the institution if he had been in Hughes's place at the time that F.D.R. threw down the gage of battle."[100]

Five years later, in 1963, Frankfurter, writing about the "present result-oriented jurisprudence" of the Warren Court, complained of the " 'shoddy' way, professionally speaking, they are turning out . . . cases." Then, turning to the Chief Justice, he referred to "T.R.'s remark when he was reproved for being too critical of William H. Taft. When he did so, one of his friends said, 'You are unfair to Taft, for you must agree that he "means well." ' 'Yes,' replied the Colonel, 'Big Bill means well but he means well feebly.' "[101]

Frankfurter's disparaging attitude also surfaced in connection with *United States v. Dege*,[102] decided on the last day of the 1959 Term. The Court, in an opinion by Frankfurter, held that a husband and wife could be prosecuted for conspiracy under a statute making it an offense for two persons to conspire. The opinion rejected the medieval theory regarding a wife "as a person whose legal personality is merged in that of the husband."[103] That the case troubled Frankfurter is shown by a note in his handwriting: "This is one of those cases in which opposite results may be reached through abstract reasoning."[104] Though *Dege* had been voted on at a conference October 23, 1959, Frankfurter did not circulate his opinion until almost the end of the term.

Warren was upset both by Frankfurter's delay and the merits. He thought that the decision made inroads into the marriage relationship and made up his mind to dissent. The Chief was particularly irritated by Frankfurter's statement that the answer to the venerable authority cited in support of the rule that the wife's personality was merged in the husband's "was definitively made long ago by Mr. Justice Holmes: 'It is revolting to have no better reason for a rule of law than that so it was laid down in the time of Henry IV. . . ,' "[105]

When Warren delivered his dissent in *Dege,* joined by Black and Whittaker, it contained the assertion, "The 'definitive answer' to the problem posed by this case is not to be found in a breezy aphorism from the collected papers of Mr. Justice Holmes."[106]

After the Chief had left for the summer recess, Frankfurter called in the Warren law clerk who had worked on the *Dege* dissent. "I hold you personally responsible for that," the Justice declared. "The Chief Justice never wrote the word 'aphorism' in his life!"

Frankfurter's now censorious attitude toward the Chief Justice extended to his work as Chairman of the Warren Commission, which investigated the assassination of President Kennedy. "What did you think of Kempton's summary and review of the Warren Report?" the now-retired Justice asked in October 1964, with apparent glee, about a critical commentary. "I had not realized how full of holes it was on the evidentiary side. . . . I wonder if Harrison would dare to write to the Chief Justice and say he would be glad to have him point out any inaccuracy of facts in the Kempton account. I am strongly tempted to do so myself, but I know what it is to have a coronary and I don't want to induce one in him."[107] In another 1964 letter, Frankfurter again criticized Warren's work on the Commission, asserting that the Chief Justice's questioning of Jack Ruby without an attorney violated the Supreme Court decisions regarding the right to counsel. "Warren is thin-skinned, but he certainly ought not to be allowed to escape the contrast between what he decides and what he does."[108]

Frankfurter's disparaging estimate extended to the work of the Warren Court as a whole, particularly of those Justices who agreed with the Chief's activist posture. "Some of my brethren—particularly the Chief and Bill Brennan—" Frankfurter wrote Harlan in October 1958, "are not only very imperceptive, but cockily so."[109] A month before, in another letter to Harlan, Frankfurter had written that Brennan had "too much ego in his cosmos."[110]

Reference has already been made to Frankfurter's 1963 characterization of the Court's performance as "shoddy." A few years earlier, in July, 1959, he had written to retired Justice Minton (whom he had once told that they were both "on the same, even though *un*crusading team"),[111] that "we always tried to see through a lawyer's eye. But at least there were professional standards that you and I shared and there was nonsense for which you and I didn't fall. Take a good look at the opinions in the *Sawyer* case[112] and you will know what I am talking about."[113]

Other Frankfurter comments confirm his low opinion of the Court as it moved increasingly away from his doctrine of judicial restraint.

In letters to fellow Justices, he characterized opinions of which he disapproved as a "soap-box dissent"[114] and "billingsgate . . . in a dissent."[115] Another time, he wrote Harlan about a Douglas-Black dissent from a decision denying state immunity from federal taxation, "Calhoun couldn't have done better."[116]

Frankfurter was, of course, an intensely social person. "How I chafe against the pressures of this job," he once complained to legal historian Charles Warren, "in that it deprives me of the most coveted pleasure in life, namely, converse with civilized and cultivated people."[117] To make up for the deprivation, the Justice had become an inveterate letter writer. Perhaps his most interesting correspondence was with Judge Learned Hand. Contained in the correspondence with Hand are numerous frank statements about Warren and the bench over which he presided. In the letters that have been preserved, Judge Hand was the more candid in his comments on the Warren Court. But there is enough in Frankfurter's letters (as well as the fact that he received Hand's denigrating appraisals without objection) to indicate that he agreed with Hand's views.

Hand did not share Frankfurter's early enthusiasm for the Chief Justice. To be sure, Hand approved of the *Brown* decision[118]—"Thank God," he wrote Frankfurter, "we have not another Dred Scott division"[119]—saying, "I did not see how, had I been called on to vote, I could have failed to concur."[120] But, after he read the opinion there, he asserted in a June 1954 letter that Warren "has, I should judge . . . a small capacity for verbal analysis. . . . What he says will not satisfy the 'eggheads'—at least it should not, if they are real eggheads, as few are."[121]

As time went on, Hand's opinion of the Chief Justice hardened. At the beginning of the 1956 Term, when Frankfurter still hoped to lead Warren along the path of judicial restraint, Hand wrote the Justice, "The more I get of your present Chief, the less I admire him. It is all very well to have a man at the top who is keenly aware of the dominant trends; but isn't it desirable to add a pinch or two to the dish of what we used to call 'law.' "[122] Then, recognizing Frankfurter's position as a Justice, Hand admonished, "Don't, for God's sake, if you answer, say anything about my comments on . . . 'that Dumb Swede.' "[123]

A year later, Hand wrote Frankfurter, "Apparently the Swede is at least 67½% pure loss."[124] Throughout the correspondence, Hand tended to refer to the Chief Justice in slighting terms, sarcastically calling him "the Pontifex Maximus"[125] or "Judex Maximus."[126] In 1959, he caustically wrote, "As to the 'Chief,' somebody is writing for him better than at the beginning, though the results are ———."[127]

Hand's critical attitude extended to the Supreme Court as a whole. "You and your eight fellow saints," he complained in 1957, "at times push hard upon our insufficient dialectical equipment."[128] Later that year, he wrote, "when I think of the whole lot—minus you and John[129]—I am not filled with joy."[130] Frankfurter apparently replied in a letter that (though not preserved) took an even dimmer view of his Brethren, just after the 1956 Term. This seems clear from Hand's statement in his next letter, "Your letter was more discouraging than I had expected."[131] Hand had just read the controversial decisions at the end of the 1956 Term. "Yes," he wrote, "I have read, or at least 'been over' the batch of your opinions and they are discouraging. . . . It is hard to expect that men will be able to restrain their impulse to impose their own solutions upon others. The longer I live, the more I tend to agree with Acton."[132] Then, summing up his opinion of the now-activist Court, "the nagging, frustrating sense of being in a group of either wilfully self-insistent or incompetent associates must be hard to bear."[133] In another letter about the same time, Hand declared, "a court that is in such everlasting disharmony certainly loses most of its moral authority."[134]

Hand, like Frankfurter, took a dim view of the activist members of the Court. "It must be damnable," he asserted, "to be one of a bunch that can never agree, and of whom four at any rate regard themselves as Teachers of the Four Fold Way and the Eight Fold Path."[135] In other letters, he referred to "those Harbingers of a Better World—Black, Douglas, Brennan and THE CHIEF"[136] and called the four "the Jesus Quartet,"[137] "the Jesus Choir,"[138] and "the Holy Ones."[139] "Oh," he declared in still another letter, "to have the inner certainties of those Great Four of your Colleagues!"[140]

In his letters to Frankfurter, Hand was particularly caustic in his comments about the two Justices he termed, "Hillbilly Hugo" and "Good Old Bill."[141] "Black and Douglas," he asserted, "are frankly not judges at all."[142] In another letter, Hand commented, "I was flattered to read in a review by Edmond Cahn of a book by MR. JUSTICE DOUGLAS, that passionate defender of LIBERTY, to find myself bracketed with you as two termites, steadily devouring underpinnings of all free society: these being (as ought to be obvious to any but biased heretics) finally to be measured by five out of nine Peerless Champions of the Welfare of Democratic Society." [143]

Speaking of judges, Hand wrote another time, "Those whom I most dread . . . are the men who conceive it to be the chief part of their duty to keep this society in the path of righteousness and high endeavor." [144] Such judges, he observed in a 1955 letter, are filled "avec une folie de la grandeur. They are getting to believe that they are charged with remoulding this sorry scheme of things nearer to the heart's desire. If they keep on they will have their tail feathers clipped. True, the pendulum will swing back; but I don't want it to swing at all." [145]

Frankfurter's letters contain comparable derogatory comments. In a February 1958 letter, he referred to "the goulash of narrow minded prejudices of Earl & Black & Douglas & Douglas [sic]." [146] Writing Hand later in 1958 about his hope that Potter Stewart, then the new man on the Court, would be a good judge, Frankfurter stated, "I entertain a further hope about him. I do not believe that he will convince himself that the mere fact that he sits on this bench calls for arrogant confidence in his own wisdom and learning." [147] In 1959, he suggested his opinion of his activist Brethren, when he characterized Lord Denning as "the Black-Douglas-Brennan of the English judiciary [in] his addiction to *freie Rechtsfindung*." [148] In a letter about the same time to Harlan, Frankfurter had referred disparagingly to "the Lorelei voices of remaking the world according to one's own judicial heart's desire." [149]

Frankfurter's low opinion of another Justice was shown by his comment to Hand in a 1960 letter. "After all," he wrote, "you are not a bricklayer who is supposed to lay so many bricks per hour, according to scientific management. Quality is what matters in a judge. Leave maximum output to my Brother Tawm Clark." [150] In the same letter, there was another revealing remark about Stewart. "I have every expectation that he will turn out to be a judge, *i.e.*, not 'result-oriented.' . . . I also think, however, that he is concerned how he appears to the world outside and, more particularly, he doesn't want to appear to be lining up with John and me." [151]

After Hand had delivered the 1958 Holmes lectures at Harvard Law School, Frankfurter sent him a long letter expressing support for their "central theme"—a call for adherence to the doctrine of judicial restraint. "If the fates that rule over vitality are as kind to me as they have been to you and Dean Griswold asks me at eighty-six to deliver Holmes lectures, I should be tempted to bring concrete historic support to your views." Speaking of the Court before 1937, "your 'Four Horsemen' or 'Battalion of Death,' McReynolds & Co., one must in all fairness attribute to them the enforcement of their convictions. Indeed that was the trouble with them: they found their economic and social convictions in the Constitution. To a very considerable degree that cannot be said of many of their successors. If I gave you a bill of particulars of what I have lived through in these . . . years, even you with all your knowledge and discernment would realize that you don't know nuthin." [152]

Among the passages in the Frankfurter–Hand letters that have the greatest human interest are those in which Hand indicated that he was not sorry that he was not serving on the Warren Court. "I should find it a trying position," he wrote in 1958, "to be one of you NINE at the moment; and indeed I rather venture to believe that they are laying up trouble for themselves in the end." [153] Though he had for years "had the ambition to be on the Court," its decisions now made him "wonder whether I should have enjoyed myself." [154]

Yet Hand had to recognize that his disclaimer of earlier ambition was colored by the fact that the ambition had not been realized. "I will concede," he ended another 1958 letter criticizing the Court, "that for years I should have said that I wanted to be on your court as much as I wanted anything that could come from the outside. But now I ask myself whether it can be a paradise? I know, I know—the fox said, 'those grapes are sour anyway.' But yet, but yet, maybe they really were." [155]

Strong as the feelings between Frankfurter and Warren had become, they were mild compared to the hatred that was directed against the Chief Justice and the Brethren from outside the Court after the controversial decisions of the 1956 Term. Indeed, the fact that the Warren Court was now under virtual siege, with the growing volume of extreme attacks, was one of the things that turned Warren against Frankfurter. The Chief believed that the Justice was giving ammunition to the Court's enemies when he used the courtroom as a podium for his denigrating remarks.

Not that additional ammunition was needed after the Chief Justice led the Brethren to an increasingly activist stance. But it was more the results in the decisions than the change in judicial posture that really concerned the extreme critics. One of Warren's law clerks during the 1956 Term recalls that, toward the term's end, "the law clerks started kidding each other about the fact that we had the Communists before us in at least a dozen or more cases and they were winning every one. All those cases came down on different issues, but the one consistent thing about them was that, whatever position was being asserted in the various cases, the Communists prevailed."

The box-score in these cases was as obvious to the Court's critics. Senator Joseph R. McCarthy declared that "Warren has become a hero to the *Daily Worker*,"[156] a report of the Senate Internal Security Subcommittee attacked the Court as an instrument of Communist global conquest,[157] and the Texas American Legion asserted that the Court's decisions had "paralyzed" efforts to curb Communism.[158]

The Court's critics on Capitol Hill did not limit themselves to verbal abuse. They spearheaded a strong move in both Houses to curb the Justices by enacting the Jenner–Butler bill. It would have deprived the Supreme Court of jurisdiction in most security cases, as well as those involving Bar admissions. In his memoirs, Warren notes that "this legislation, evoking as it did the atmosphere of Cold War hysteria, came dangerously close to passing."[159]

That the Jenner–Butler bill did not pass was due primarily to the efforts of Lyndon B. Johnson, then Senate majority leader. The House had voted for the bill, and the Senate, which was debating the matter one night in August 1958, looked as though it, too, would pass the measure. The sponsors were calling for a vote. But the majority leader moved to adjourn, demanded a roll-call vote, and ostentatiously noted down the names of those who opposed him. The Senate voted to adjourn. By the next day, Johnson had gotten the votes to table the bill—though only by one vote.[160]

On December 9, 1958, the organizers of the John Birch Society met in Indianapolis and listened to founder Robert Welch read the society's *Blue Book*.[161] One of the first projects of the new society was a compaign to impeach Warren. The Birch attack was based upon the claim that the Chief Justice had voted "92 percent in favor of Communists"[162] and "sanctioned treason."[163] The American landscape soon blossomed with "Impeach Earl Warren" billboards, and Congressmen were deluged with letters urging impeachment.[164]

In 1961, Welch announced that the Birchers were conducting an essay contest on the "grounds for Chief Justice Warren's impeachment," because, Welch charged, Warren's decisions had helped the Communists.[165] The contest was won by a U.C.L.A. student, who received a $1,000 prize.[166] At a Boston meeting, radio commentator Fulton Lewis, Jr., said that the Birch Society was too moderate in merely urging impeachment. "I would lynch him," Lewis said.[167] A retired Marine colonel echoed the suggestion at a Los Angeles anti-Communist meeting.[168] Pamphlets calling for the Chief Justice's impeachment were even found widely distributed among the students of the Earl Warren High School in Downey, California.[169]

Warren's own attitude toward the John Birch campaign may be seen in the fact that just below his framed commission as Chief Justice of the United States, on his library wall, there hung the 1965 *New Yorker* cartoon showing an indignant caricature of *Whistler's Mother* frantically embroidering a sampler, "IMPEACH EARL WARREN." According to one of his sons, "It really breaks him up."[170] Warren himself laughingly told a Southern law clerk that, if he was fired by the Chief, he could go back home and run for Governor unopposed on both parties' tickets.

In his memoirs, Warren wrote that the impeachment drive "in my opinion . . . was a public relations stunt," and that "it was not difficult for me . . . to view those 'Impeach Earl Warren' billboards as ludicrous."[171] When Black sent Warren a postcard that had been sent to him containing the stamp, "This is a Republic, not a Democracy. Let's keep it that way by impeaching Earl Warren," the Chief wrote back, "If this is the worst they ever say about me, I will consider myself fortunate."[172]

Warren did concede that it "was not so easy, though, to convince my wife that the signs should provoke a smile."[173] Another time he confessed, "Sometimes it makes you cringe to see what people say and write."[174] Certainly, the Chief Justice would have had to be extremely thick-skinned not to be affected by incidents such as that which occurred when he was made an honorary member of the Association of the Bar of the City of New York on October 29, 1963. Shouting, "Impeach Earl Warren," a group picketing the event threw placards and leaflets at Warren and his wife, as they entered the building.[175] "It's a great thing," Warren commented, "that they can do this in this country whether they really believe in it or are being paid to do it."[176] But he was plainly ruffled by the episode.

Yet Warren was undoubtedly correct in his estimate of the artificiality of the John Birch campaign. In 1967, *The Atlantic* noted how many people were making a living from the "Impeach Earl Warren" campaign.[177] When Warren made his first public speech in the Deep South, at Georgia Tech in February 1963, his associates feared that there would be violent demonstrations. They were particularly disturbed after the so-called Alumni Committee to Combat Communism wired the Chief, "You should know that you are not welcome here" and gave wide distribution to a handbill, "let this unwelcome visitor speak to the empty hall he deserves, or attend and boo."

As it turned out, Southern hospitality overwhelmed whatever Southern hostility there was. There were a few "Impeach Earl Warren" signs. But the reception in Atlanta was friendly, despite the warnings. The Chief's address received a standing ovation from a packed audience of 3,600—four times the number, *Time* noted, who had been present for a talk two months earlier by Georgia Governor Carl Sanders.[178]

Warren displayed deeper resentment toward those he felt should have backed the Court against its critics than toward those like the Birchers, whom he considered a fringe group using him as a "whipping boy" to raise funds and call attention to their extremist program. In particular, the Chief Justice was irritated by the lack of support from the American Bar Association. "Throughout the years of the McCarthy era and the desegregation period," he complained after he retired, "the American Bar Association almost never had a kind word to say for the Court. On the contrary, it did much to discredit us."[179]

The A.B.A. got off on the wrong foot with Warren almost as soon as he became Chief Justice. Early in 1954, Harrison Tweed, one of the leaders of the American Bar, wrote to Frankfurter, "Bill Avery of Chicago, who is Chairman of the American Bar Association Committee on Legal Aid, and I had a pleasant talk with the C.J. He has promised to come to the Legal Aid luncheon at the time of the ABA meeting in Chicago next August. I was impressed by his virility and calmness as well as good nature. I thanked him for his willingness to speak." [180]

Warren had accepted the Tweed–Avery invitation with the impression that he would simply attend the luncheon, but not make a speech. When he arrived in Chicago for the A.B.A. convention, he saw his name listed on the program as a speaker. The Chief was furious. He called in Avery and, in the words of someone present at the meeting, Avery "got his tail chewed out, but good." Warren did attend the luncheon and make a few remarks. But, according to the same observer, "he did not get over being angry about it. He thought he'd been double-crossed. And he really was mad—mad as I've seen anybody who was not going to resort to physical violence."

During the next few years, various A.B.A. committees issued reports criticizing some of the Court's controversial decisions. On January 6, 1959, it was reported in the *New York Times* that Warren had resigned his A.B.A. membership. [181] The A.B.A. President was quoted as saying that Warren "advised me that he was doing so for personal reasons." [182] However, the *Times* said that the resignation had been motivated by a series of grievances about A.B.A. criticisms of the Court. [183] It noted particularly an occurrence a few months earlier when the A.B.A. had invited Warren to a dinner in honor of the Chief Justices of the states. The Conference of State Chief Justices had just adopted a resolution urging the Supreme Court to "put on the badge of 'judicial self-restraint' " and avoid exercising "essentially legislative powers." [184] At the A.B.A. dinner, the speaker, Chief Justice John R. Dethmers of Michigan, elaborated on the State Chief Justices' criticism of the Court. Warren himself says, "Dethmers . . . , a vitriolic fellow, gave the U.S. Supreme Court a lambasting the like of which I had never heard." [185] According to the *Times* story, Warren was annoyed enough by this episode to resign from the A.B.A.. [186]

This was not a correct chronology. The Chief Justice had actually sent in his resignation on September 3, 1957. The triggering incident had been the 1957 A.B.A. convention, held in London, in collaboration with the English Bar. As the highest American judicial officer, Warren was invited to lead the visitors. Frankfurter was the one Justice who had intimate knowledge of London, and Warren asked his advice on the invitation. "After giving the problem raised for you by the London shindig my best thought," Frankfurter replied, "I should like to express to you my strong hope that you will go." Frankfurter expressed reservations about "having you mill around with the thousands of the American Bar Association during their London stay. It somehow or other disturbs my feeling to have you a part of the ABA melee for a week." But Frankfurter did "think it is highly desirable that you should represent the Supreme Court on the one great occasion, namely, the meeting at Westminster Hall . . . in which you would respond, as it were, to the Address of the Lord Chancellor." [187]

Warren did accept the A.B.A. invitation. But then he learned that Vice-President Nixon was also going to be invited to the London meeting. Warren let it be known that if the Vice-President were asked, he would no longer attend. "If you let that fellow in, count me out," were the Chief's words to A.B.A. President David Maxwell, as reported by *Time*. [188] At any rate, the A.B.A. never extended the invitation to the Vice-President.

After the London meeting, Learned Hand commented to Frankfurter, who did not attend, "we Americans acquitted ourselves without discredit save for your Brother Clark, who spoke for an hour and a half!" [189] Clark, who attended the meeting with Warren and Harlan, sent Black a postcard: "London was gay and weather excellent. C.J. made a fine address with good reception." [190]

The fact that Warren was, as he said, "cordially treated by the English people, from Her Majesty the Queen and Sir Winston Churchill to the rank and file of the British Bar" [191] did not make up for what the Chief felt were deliberate affronts by the A.B.A. Symptomatic of Warren's relations with the A.B.A. was the *faux pas* that occurred at a session addressed by Prime Minister Harold Macmillan. The distinguished guests had decided to dress in formal morning dress or dark suits. But nobody had bothered to inform Warren, and he was conspicuous on the platform in a double-breasted brown suit and gray tie. The Chief was smiling and apparently unconcerned. But his son, Earl, Jr., recalls that he was mad as he could be about this when he returned. He was deeply offended by what he considered a slight on the dignity of his office. More than that, as he told one of the Brethren, he always felt that the A.B.A. leaders had intentionally neglected to tell him of their decision with regard to dress.

On the same day, the A.B.A. struck a more serious blow. The A.B.A. special Committee on Communism submitted its report to a session of the convention which neither Warren nor any of the other

Justices in London attended. To Warren, as he later described it, this report was a "publicity 'blockbuster.' . . . It told little about those matters; rather, it was a diatribe against the Supreme Court of the United States, charging it with aiding the Communist cause in fifteen recent cases."[192] The report proposed legislation which, in the words of the *New York Herald Tribune,* "would undo, if enacted, the legal effect of 15 Supreme Court decisions in the last 15 months."[193]

Warren tells of his indignant reaction when he learned of the filing of the report from a banner headline in the Paris edition of the *Herald Tribune,* "BAR ASSOCIATION TOLD HIGH COURT WEAKENS SECURITY AGAINST REDS."[194] In his memoirs, Warren asserted that the filing of the report "is indicative of the disservice the American Bar Association did to the Supreme Court, and I have no hesitancy in saying now that it was done designedly to besmirch the Court and to gain publicity for an otherwise rather unproductive convention."[195]

To Warren, submission of the report at the London meeting was a personal affront that was only aggravated when injury was added to insult by the approval early in 1959 by the A.B.A. House of Delegates (the association's legislative body) of a report urging Congress to revise the recent Court decisions affecting internal security.[196]

By then, the Chief Justice was no longer an A.B.A. member. When Warren returned from the London meeting, he flew to California for his forty-fifth college class reunion. "We had a whale of a time in Britain," he told the press there. Then he quietly sent in his letter of resignation to the A.B.A.[197] "I had concluded," Warren later said, "that I could no longer be a member of an organization of the legal profession which would ask me to lead fifteen thousand of its members overseas on a goodwill mission and then deliberately and trickily contrive to discredit the Supreme Court which I headed."[198]

Even the A.B.A. resignation involved a minor contretemps. Though Warren's resignation letter stated that he was leaving the association because of the London incident, the A.B.A. announced to the press a year later that the Chief Justice had been dropped from membership for "non-payment of dues." Warren, whose dues had been fully paid, was outraged. "Think what my grandchildren might think of me," he told Douglas, "if these lies went unanswered."[199] Warren wrote the A.B.A. President asking for a letter he could show his children proving "that their father had neither welched on his dues nor lied about his resignation." It was, however, not until 1970 that he received an A.B.A. letter stating unequivocally "the fact that your termination of membership in the American Bar Association came about solely from your voluntary resignation effective September 3, 1957."[200]

It is, however, erroneous to think of Warren only as embroiled in personal discord during this period. Except for his clashes with Frankfurter, his relations within the Court were warm, even with Frankfurter's closest ally, Harlan, with whom the Chief Justice was always on a cordial footing. However much he disagreed with Harlan's following in Frankfurter's juristic footsteps, Warren never let his disagreement go beyond the intellectual plane. When Harlan's eyesight began to deteriorate badly, the Chief went out of his way to help him as much as he could, in terms of case assignments and other ways. The strongest thing anyone heard Warren say about Harlan was when, after Frankfurter's retirement, Harlan began to write a number of dissents. "Well," the Chief told his clerks, "he'll have to do his share of the majority opinions, too." And there was a little smirk as he added that the Justices writing majority opinions "can't take potshots so often."

For a number of years after his appointment, the Chief Justice would take the Justices and their wives to the Army–Navy game in Philadelphia, as well as to other events. Just before Thanksgiving, the Brethren would receive a "Memorandum to All from Earl Warren," entitled "Re: Army–Navy Game." The logistics of the junket would be set out: e.g., which train car to take, that luncheon and dinner would be served on the journey, "and, of course, the usual liquid refreshments will be available both going and returning."[201] He and Mrs. Warren would give dinners for the Justices, though not at their Sheraton apartment, to which few outside the Chief's personal circle were invited. The Brethren would reciprocate by hospitality to the Warrens.

There was also the mutual exchange of birthday salutations and gifts—most often in fluid form. "If good old Chivas–Regal won't make a person feel young," wrote Warren in thanking Black for his birthday gift, "there is not much hope for him." For Warren's birthday on March 19, 1958, Black's wife wrote a panegyric, entitled *Hail to the Chief,* that began:

We stop the wheels of justice
From grinding on their way,
To wish our Chief the very best
On this his natal day.

We show cause to this august Court
Why we should have him cited
For great judicial wisdom
For all the wrong he's righted!"

Mrs. Black's opus ended:

That he deserves the very best
Is what we're all agreed,
That happiness will stay his way
'Tis ORDERED and DECREED.

The statements made herein are true
And all contain the facts.
A happy birthday to the Chief!
Is the RULING of the Blacks." [202]

Everyone who knew Warren stresses that he never set himself up as or pretended to be an intellectual in the Frankfurter sense. "I wish that I could speak to you in the words of a scholar," the Chief Justice told an audience in 1957, "but it has not fallen to my lot to be a scholar in life. I have been in public life for forty years. Since that time, I have been doing the urgent rather than the important. I was always jumping from one thing to another without the opportunity to explore any one thing to its roots." [203]

But, if Warren, as Stewart recalls, "didn't lead by his intellect and he didn't greatly appeal to others' intellects," he always tried to improve himself intellectually. The statement by Warren about not being a scholar was made at a seminar on Talmudic law that he attended at the Jewish Theological Seminary in September, 1957. Warren had long been acquainted with Dr. Louis Finkelstein, chancellor of the seminary, and expressed a desire to learn about the Talmud, with its emphasis on moral law. A weekend seminar was arranged, starting on Friday, September 13, and ending with a session on Sunday afternoon. The Chief Justice attended the meetings with scholars of the seminary, wearing the traditional skullcap at Sabbath eve services and during meals. At the end of the first day's session, Warren said that it showed how much of the common law could be traced to Judaic origins, particularly the protections against double jeopardy and self-incrimination.[204]

Warren had a surprise "classmate" the second day, when Harry S. Truman joined the seminar. The former President had been invited by the seminary for a luncheon session and explained his presence with one of his favorite jests, "I never turn down a free dinner." Yet, as the *New York Times* put it, "if the former President came to eat, he remained to praise." In impromptu remarks, Truman remarked that it was "wonderful" that the nation's Chief Justice "should renew his learning and inspiration" at the seminar. He called Warren "one of the truly great men of our time" and said that he was "very fond" of him.[205] This public commendation by a man Warren had come to admire must have helped make up for the chorus of denunciation that was now the constant accompaniment of the Warren Court.

8.

1957—1958 TERMS: LITTLE ROCK, EXPATRIATION, ET AL.

"I have never heard such an argument made in a court of justice before," the Chief Justice shouted at the attorney before the bench, "and I have tried many a case through many a year. I never heard a lawyer say that the statement of a Governor as to what was legal or illegal should control the action of any court."

Warren's angry comment was made in response to the statement of the lawyer for the School Board of Little Rock, Arkansas, "that if the Governor of any state says that a United States Supreme Court decision is not the law of the land, the people of that state . . . have a doubt in their mind and a right to have a doubt."[1]

The incident occurred during the August 28, 1958, argument of *Cooper v. Aaron*,[2] one of the most dramatic cases to come before the Warren Court—both because of the issues involved and the unprecedented way in which the Court dealt with it. As Warren himself later recalled, "There was but one event that greatly disturbed us during my tenure, and that was the . . . Little Rock case (*Cooper v. Aaron*) which gave Governor Faubus the national spotlight."[3]

The Little Rock case arose out of the continuing effort by Southern states to frustrate the *Brown* desegregation decision. In Arkansas, a constitutional amendment was passed that commanded the state to oppose "in every Constitutional manner the Un-constitutional desegregation decisions . . . of the United States Supreme Court." Despite this, the Little Rock School Board prepared a plan for gradual desegregation, with black children scheduled to enter Central High School in the school year beginning September 3, 1957. On September 2, Governor Orval Faubus dispatched Arkansas National Guard units to Central High and placed the school "off limits" to black students. On September 25, President Eisenhower sent federal troops to Little Rock, and they secured admission of the blacks to the school.

In February 1958, the School Board backed down on their desegregation plan and petitioned the district court for a postponement until "tempers had cooled." They alleged that because of extreme public hostility, engendered by the Governor and legislature, a sound educational program, with blacks in attendance, was impossible. On June 20, the district court granted a thirty-month delay.[4] The Court of Appeals for the Eighth Circuit reversed on August 18,[5] but stayed its order thirty days to permit the School Board to petition for certiorari.[6] The black students then filed a motion in the Supreme Court to stay the court of appeals postponement. The school term was scheduled to begin on September 2, and the opening of the 1958 Supreme Court Term was fixed for October 6. In order to have a decision in time to permit arrangements to be made for the 1958–1959 school year, Warren ordered the convening of a Special Term of the Court, which met to hear arguments on August 28.

It was during the argument on Thursday, August 28, that the attorney for the School Board, Richard C. Butler of Little Rock, received his dressing down from the Chief Justice. Butler was a courtly Southerner, normally self-possessed, with the calm assurance engendered by years of practice, but he blanched noticeably when Warren administered his reproof. The Arkansas attorney had urged that the board had done its best to obey the Court's decisions, but had been prevented by "social turmoil and other outward pressures." He asked for time for Little Rock "to work in a period of peace and harmony rather than turmoil and strife."

Warren kept asking the central question: "Can we defer a program of this kind because elements in a community will commit violence to prevent it from going into effect?"

Butler made the mistake of appealing to Warren's earlier career as a basis for understanding the Board's predicament: "Mr. Chief Justice, you have been Governor of a great state."

The Chief cut him off sharply: "But I have never tried to resolve any legal problem of this kind as Governor of my state. I thought that that was a matter for the courts, and I abided by the decision of the courts."[7]

At the end of the argument, the Court deferred decision on the motion to stay the court of appeals mandate, since it necessarily involved consideration of the merits. Argument on the merits was set for September 11, with the School Board ordered to file its petition for certiorari by September 8.

Just after the August 28 argument, the Arkansas legislature, called into special session, passed a number of prosegregation laws that gave the Governor power to close public schools facing integration and to transfer public school funds to private segregated schools. U.S. Attorney General William P. Rogers wrote the Little Rock School Board that the Department of Justice was ready to cooperate fully to prevent violence. The School Board, acting on Butler's advice, though against the wishes of Governor Faubus, then ordered the school term opening to be delayed until September 15.

Just before the second argument on September 11, Frankfurter wrote to Warren, "that the *Washington Post* was right the other day in its editorial, in characterizing the action of the School Board as courageous." Because the Board "showed a good deal of enterprise and courage to stand up against Faubus and Company," Frankfurter wanted "to suggest . . . the desirability of having you say, when Mr. Butler gets to his feet, that the Court takes note of the fact of the Board's vote not to open the schools until the 15th." Frankfurter said, "My own view has long been that the ultimate hope for the peaceful solution of the basic problem largely depends on winning the support of lawyers of the South for the overriding issue of obedience to the Court's decision. Therefore I think we should encourage every manifestation of fine conduct by a lawyer like Butler."[8]

Warren rejected Frankfurter's suggestion. He was not going out of his way to praise a lawyer who argued that Southern obstruction justified delay in implementation of black rights. The Chief's uncompromising attitude led Frankfurter to complain to Harlan: "I am bound to say that Butler's advice to his School Board was much wiser than the views which Bill Brennan tells me the Chief Justice expressed to you fellows at luncheon last Friday. Of course Faubus has been guilty of trickery, but the trickery was as much against the

School Board as against us. And in any event the fight is not between the Supreme Court and Faubus, tho apparently this is the way it lay in the C.J.'s mind. I am afraid his attitude towards the kind of problems that confront us are more like that of a fighting politician than that of a judicial statesman."[9]

At the argument on September 11, Warren and the Brethren were plainly disturbed by the Arkansas provisions designed to frustrate the *Brown* decision.[10] "Mr. Butler . . . ," the Chief Justice indignantly asked, "isn't it a fact that the State of Arkansas passed a constitutional amendment in defiance of the particular decision that the Court rendered, *Brown v. Board of Education,* and that it dedicated the State to oppose by every available method: 'The unconstitutional decision of *Brown v. Board of Education'?"* In addition, the Chief said, "the legislature in the meantime passes other laws to frustrate the rights of these individuals."

The others also pressed Butler on these measures. Black, in particular, questioned whether they did not provide for defiance of the Court, asking: "Does any of them provide for obedience to the Court's decree?"

Back came the answer, "Not in that language. No, sir." At which subdued laughter swept the courtroom.

But the Justices were not amused. Brennan asked whether the Arkansas actions did not violate the Supremacy Clause of the Constitution. Butler submitted that that was not true of the School Board, which was urging delay: "the School Board . . . is placed between the millstones . . . in a conflict between the State and the Federal Government."

Warren, however, stressed that "conceding absolute good faith to the Board" did not change the case. The Chief asked whether "the real issue before this Court is not just whether the School Board is frustrating the rights of these children, but whether the acts of any agency of the State of Arkansas are preventing them from exercising their constitutional rights, and whether it's the School Board or whether it's the Governor or whether it's the legislature, whether it's the militia, whatever agency of the State Government, if it did frustrate the rights of these children, it's a violation of the Constitution. Isn't that the issue that we have before us?"

The Chief Justice also pointed out the basic weakness in Butler's plea for the thirty-month delay. "Now," Warren said, "let us assume that at the end of the two years and a half, if you prevail, that the climate of opinion is as it is now. Would you be in asking for another two years and a half . . . ?"[11]

His questioning pointed to the firm stand taken by Warren at the conference that met as soon as the argument concluded. The Chief urged a decision upholding the court of appeals that would resoundingly reaffirm the duty of state officials to obey the law as laid down by the Supreme Court. All quickly agreed; indeed, the conference was concluded within thirty minutes. Burton's diary entry for September 11 noted, "decided to affirm to-morrow and hand down opinion later (by October 6). Frankfurter and Harlan to draft the order of to-morrow. Brennan to draft opinion for Court."[12]

Frankfurter and Harlan drafted a three-paragraph per curiam the same day. It was speedily approved and issued on September 12. It unanimously affirmed the court of appeals and dissolved that court's stay of its own order. Because "of the imminent commencement of the new school year," the decision was being promptly announced. "The expression of the views supporting our judgment will be prepared and announced in due course."[13]

Even before the opinion explaining it, the September 12 decision gave rise to a storm of Southern criticism. This time, President Eisenhower felt that he had to back the Court. The President issued a statement appealing for public support of the decision. "All of us know," it said, "that if an individual, a community or a state is going . . . to defy the rulings of the courts, then anarchy results." The force of the statement was somewhat dissipated by Eisenhower's reply to a reporter's question on whether the President had told friends that he wished the Court had never handed down the *Brown* decision. Eisenhower denied ever having suggested that. But he conceded that he might have said to friends that desegregation could be "slower"—[14] i.e., the very claim made by the Little Rock School Board.

In the Court itself, the apparent unanimity was threatened by Clark. The lanky Texan was troubled by the way in which the Brethren had handled the case. He wrote out a draft dissent in longhand on two pages of a memo pad of the American Bar Association Section of Judicial Administration, of which he was then Chairman. The draft began: "My action today in dissenting from the judgment of the Court is not to be construed in any respect whatsoever as a change of position from that taken in Brown etc. I adhere steadfastly to my vote there believing that every American citizen goes first class. Under our Constitution there is no steerage."

"However," the draft dissent went on, "as I understood *Brown* integration was not to be accomplished through push button action but rather by 'deliberate speed.'" The fact that there was "massive resistance" by some "gives us no excuse to in turn strip the latter of those procedural safeguards that are the right of all other litigants."

The Clark draft objected to the action Warren had taken to decide the case speedily in the August Special Term. "The case should be considered in its regular course, not by forced action. Of all tribunals this is one that should stick strictly to the rules. To do otherwise is to create the very situation that the Constitution prohibits, the existence of a preferred class."

As Clark saw it in his draft, "For all practical purposes it makes no difference whether the petitioners enter all integrated schools on Sept. 8th or October 6th the day we convene our next Term. But to strip from the respondent its right under the rules of the Court to the regular period for appeal means much in the administration of justice. 'Equal Justice under Law' requires at least that much. I would let the case take its regular course."[15]

For the Justice from Texas to have broken the unanimity in desegregation cases that had prevailed in the Warren Court could have had unfortunate consequences. Happily Clark did not go beyond venting his emotions in his written draft. It was never typed, much less circulated. Whether he discussed it with any of the Brethren is another matter. Other members of the *Cooper v. Aaron* Court did not remember hearing of Clark's intended dissent. If Clark did talk over the matter with Warren, there is no doubt that the Chief used all his persuasive powers to induce the Texan not to break the Court's unanimity in the face of what Warren later called "the great notoriety given Governor Faubus' obstructive conduct in the case."[16]

But the *Brown* tradition of the Court speaking with one voice in desegregation cases was in fact to be breached in the Little Rock case—and by Frankfurter, the Justice who, more than anyone except Warren, was responsible for obtaining the original unanimity in *Brown*. Even before the first argument in the Little Rock case, Frankfurter prepared a four-page printed memorandum which contained a strong rejection of the School Board's request for delay. "Whatever sophisticated explanations may be devised to justify such a request," Frankfurter wrote, "they cannot obscure the essential meaning that law should bow to force. To yield to such a claim would be to enthrone lawlessness, and lawlessness if not checked is the precursor of anarchy."[17] This memo contains most of the text of the concurring opinion that Frankfurter was to issue on October 6. Whether he intended to put out a separate concurrence when he prepared the memo cannot be determined. In circulating the memo to the Brethren, Frankfurter wrote that "I have prepared the enclosed memorandum for my own information."[18] But when he decided to concur separately, all he had to do in order to do so was make minor changes in his August 27 memo.

In the meantime, there was the task of preparing the Court's opinion. Even before the first argument on August 28, while Warren, Clark, and Brennan were on the train returning to Washington for the Special Term, the Chief asked Brennan to prepare a paper on the case. The opinion was formally assigned to Brennan at the September 11 conference and, according to the next day's entry in Burton's diary, "We are anxious that the Little Rock opinion come down by Oct. 6."[19]

Brennan got to work immediately and soon prepared a thirteen-legal-size-page typed memo to serve as the basis for a draft opinion. On September 17, he circulated a printed eighteen-page draft opinion of the Court delivered in his name. Before the opinion was finally approved, it went through five printed drafts.

Brennan's September 17 draft devoted its first eight pages to a detailed statement of the facts and prior history of the case. The remainder was divided into four parts. Part First (pages 9–11), as Brennan put it at the September 19 conference that discussed the draft, "proposed to restate elementary constitutional propositions drawing upon authority of Marshall, Taney and Hughes." To a student of the Court, this part is the most interesting portion of the draft, for it contains the first version of what became the most-quoted section of the eventual *Cooper v. Aaron* opinion. As originally drafted by Brennan, the key passage read:

This Court enunciated in the *Brown* case the fundamental proposition that racial segregation in public schools of the States is a denial of the equal protection of the law guaranteed by the Fourteenth Amendment. Since the School Board takes the position that the pronouncements and actions of the Governor and Legislature of Arkansas have spread doubt and confusion as to the significance of this decision under our federal system, it may be well to recall some elementary constitutional propositions which are no longer open to question.

Chief Justice Marshall declared the great constitutional truth over a century and a half ago in *Marbury v. Madison,* 1 Cranch 137, 177, that the Federal Constitution is "the fundamental and paramount law of the nation." Marshall also declared in that case the basic principle that the federal judiciary is supreme in the exposition of the Constitution: "It is emphatically the province and duty of the judicial department to say what the law is." *Ibid.* It follows from these principles that the interpretation of the Constitution enunciated by this Court in the *Brown* case is the supreme law of the land, and is made by Art. VI of the Constitution of binding effect on the States "any Thing in the Constitution or Laws of any State to the Contrary notwithstanding." All state legislators and executive and judicial officers are solemnly committed by oath taken pursuant to Art. VI, ¶ 3 "to support this Constitution" as so interpreted. Chief Justice Taney said that this requirement reflected the framers' "anxiety to preserve it [the Constitution] in full force, in all its powers, and to guard against resistance to or evasion of its authority, on the part of a State. . . ." *Ableman v. Booth,* 21 How. 506, 524.

Every state legislator and executive and judicial officer is thus solemnly bound not to war against the Constitution. He is obligated, rather, to obey its relevant commands as defined by this Court, and whatever his station, he may not consider himself free to act in his official capacity in a way at variance with those commands.[20]

This passage contained the substance of the basic principle of the Court's final opinion: that all officials are bound to obey the law as ultimately propounded by the Supreme Court. The changes made in later drafts, primarily by Brennan himself, were mainly stylistic.

Parts Second and Third of the Brennan draft were intended, in the Justice's words at the September 19 conference, "to deal with the questions of prompt and reasonable start and with all deliberate speed." Here, Brennan explained, "I have suggested that every school board must formulate a plan which provides specific dates both for the initiation and completion of the desegregation process." Part Fourth of the draft covered the School Board's argument that it was entitled to postponement because of the good faith it had exhibited. Brennan dealt with the argument in light of what he termed at the conference "the imperative nature of the Board's constitutional duty."

The Brennan draft was longer and looser than the Court's final opinion. But it covered all the essential points dealt with in the opinion, with most of the language finally used. The changes in the later drafts, also prepared by Brennan, involved a tightening of prolix passages, as well as alterations in language.

The Brethren met in conference on September 19 to discuss Brennan's draft. Warren suggested that Brennan's introductory material was "rather dry." Brennan agreed to compress the history of the case. Black suggested revising the key passage of Part First "to use the Marshall, Taney and Hughes quotes to greater effect." Brennan said he would work on that. As finally revised, the Brennan opinion here became one of the classic statements of the rule of law under the Constitution.

Black made another suggestion that proved less fortunate. He proposed "that after admonishing the states that they cannot evade the Constitution by schemes ingenious or ingenuous, a sentence should be added to the effect that the obligation applies to every school system maintained from the public purse." Brennan, therefore, added the sentence, "State support of segregated schools through any arrangement, management, funds, or property cannot be squared with the [Fourteenth] Amendment's command that no State shall deny to any person within its jurisdiction the equal protection of the laws." Critics were quick to point out that the issue of public support of private segregated schools had not been present in the case and that the Court was gratuitously prejudging an issue, in violation of its own taboo against advisory opinions.[21]

There was serious division on Parts Second and Third of the draft. Frankfurter and Burton disagreed with the way Brennan had formulated the duty of school authorities to bring about desegregation. Frankfurter questioned "whether the principles should be stated in such rigid terms." Brennan conceded, "I recognize a contradiction in the thought that the rights of the children are personal and the notion that their recognition may be delayed for some children so long as the start is made to enforce them for other children." Ultimately, the difference was resolved by eliminating Parts Second and Third from the opinion. It was also agreed that Brennan's Part Fourth, rejecting the Board's good-faith argument, should be moved to an earlier part of the opinion.

Both Black and Frankfurter suggested that "this is the kind of opinion which should close with two or three sentences highlighting for the public the true nature of the issues at stake." Brennan added the following paragraph to his next draft:

We are a people devoted to the ideal of equal justice under law. The Fourteenth Amendment gives concrete expression to that ideal. Whatever historical practice may be offered in justification of racial segregation, state support of segregated schools with public money and property cannot be squared with the Amendment's command that no State shall deny to any person within its jurisdiction the equal protection of the laws. The right of a student not to be segregated on racial grounds in schools maintained with public funds is indeed so fundamental and pervasive that it is embraced in the concept of due process of law. *Bolling v. Sharpe,* 347 U.S. 497. Public education, of course, is the primary responsibility of the States, but that responsibility must be discharged in obedience to the commands of the Constitution. Fidelity to the principle of equal justice under law made inescapable the decisions in the *Brown* case for a Court mindful of its high responsibility to expound the law of the Constitution. The members of this Court are one in steadfast adherence to the principles of the *Brown* decisions which we here unanimously and wholeheartedly reaffirm. Those principles, and the obedience of the States to them according to the command of the Constitution are indispensable for the protection of the freedoms guaranteed by the Constitution to all of us.[22]

This is substantially similar to the concluding paragraph of the final opinion, though to this writer it is stylistically superior. The one important change in the conclusion was made at Harlan's insistence. Harlan had prepared his own draft opinion in the case, consisting of twenty-five typed legal-size pages. Why he did this is not clear, but, on September 19, he gave copies to Frankfurter[23] and Clark. Harlan did not circulate the draft opinion to the other Justices. Instead, on September 23, the day before another conference on the case, Harlan sent the Brethren a "Suggested Substitute" for the last six pages of Brennan's draft.[24]

The differences between his and Harlan's draft, Brennan informed the conference, "are largely entirely verbal. His suggestions don't change the substance except in two respects." The first was to omit Brennan's statement that a state could not attempt to nullify *Brown* "whether accomplished ingeniously or ingenuously." Brennan refused to delete the language, saying, "Personally, I feel that is a vital statement very essential to the point we are making."

Harlan's suggested final pages also omitted reference to *Marbury v. Madison*[25] and Brennan's discussion of the Court's authoritative role as expounder of constitutional law. Again Brennan refused to change his draft. "That too I think," he said to the others, "is a very essential part of what I believe our opinion should contain."

The Brethren agreed to reject both Harlan suggestions, concluding correctly that they would have weakened the opinion. Harlan did, however, make another suggestion that was followed. Harlan's substitute pages contained the statement, "The basic decision in *Brown* was unanimously reached by a Court, composed of Justices of diversified geographical and other backgrounds, only after the case had been briefed and twice argued by lawyers of the highest skill and reputation, and the issues had been under deliberation for more than —— months. Since the first *Brown* opinion three new Justices have come to the Court. They are at one with the Justices still on the Court who participated in the original decision as to the inescapability of that decision."

Brennan opposed inclusion of such a statement. "I feel," he told the conference, "that any such reference to the three new members would be a grave mistake. It lends support to the notion that the Constitution has only the meaning that can command a majority of the Court as that majority may change with shifting membership. Whatever truth there may be in that idea, I think it would be fatal in this fight to provide ammunition from the mouth of this Court in support of it." Despite Brennan's objection, this Harlan suggestion was adopted.

Frankfurter had made another suggestion at the September 19 conference that was of crucial significance. As later described by Warren, Frankfurter, like Harlan, "called our attention to the fact that there had been a number of changes in the membership of the Court since *Brown v. Board of Education*. He suggested that in order to show we were all in favor of that decision, we should also say so in the Little Rock case, not in a *per curiam* or in an opinion signed by only one Justice, but by an opinion signed by the entire Court. I do not recall this ever having been done before. However, in light of the intense controversy over the issue and the great notoriety given Governor

Faubus' obstructive conduct in the case, we thought well of the suggestion, and it was done."[26] Only Douglas opposed Frankfurter's suggestion, saying that the Court had always issued opinions in the name of one Justice, and that should be done here also. Anyway, the suggestion carried, eight to one.

It was actually Harlan, rather than Frankfurter, who originally thought of the idea of a joint opinion by all the Justices. Harlan's draft opinion began: "The opinion of the Court, in which (naming each Justice) join, was announced by The Chief Justice." On the copy of the draft that Harlan had given him, Frankfurter changed the beginning to: "The combined views of (naming each Justice) constituting the opinion of the Court, was announced by The Chief Justice."[27]

The last of the printed drafts of the Little Rock opinion was circulated by Brennan on September 25, the day before the final conference on the case. Black, who had earlier indicated that the opinion's conclusion should contain more striking language, had similar qualms about the draft's beginning. Though it had been compressed in response to Warren's objection, it still started with a dull statement of facts. Just after the September 24 conference, Black gave Brennan a written suggestion for a dramatic beginning. The Black opening paragraph read:

As this case reaches us it involves questions of the highest importance to the maintenance of our federal system of government. It squarely presents a claim that there is no duty on state officials to obey federal court orders resting on this Court's deliberate and considered interpretation of the United States Constitution. Specifically it involves actions by the Governor, Legislature and other agencies of Arkansas, upon the premise that they are not bound by our holding in Brown v. Board of Education, 347 U.S. 483 that the Fourteenth Amendment forbids states to use their governmental powers to bar children from attending schools which are helped to run by public management, funds or other public property. We are urged to permit continued suspension of the Little Rock School Board's plan to do away with segregated public schools until state laws and efforts to upset and nullify our holding in *Brown* v. Board of Education have been further challenged and tested in the courts. We have concluded that these contentions call for clear answers here and now.[28]

This beginning was just what the opinion needed, and Brennan incorporated it verbatim into the draft that he circulated September

25. It was adopted as the final opening passage, with several stylistic changes recommended by Clark.²⁹ On September 26, the conference worked on a last draft that was circulated in final form and approved on Monday morning, September 29.

Later that day, the ornate courtroom was again a scene of quiet drama. There was an air of suppressed excitement, for it had been announced that the Little Rock opinion would be read, and it was rumored that this would be no ordinary opinion. Precisely at noon, the red velour curtains behind the bench parted and, led by Warren, the Justices filed in and took their places. They were all there with the exception of Douglas, who was once more travelling in the West. The Chief Justice began by announcing that all nine members of the Court had written the opinion. He looked at each of the Justices present as he pronounced their names, one after another, as joint authors.³⁰

In a steady voice, Warren read the opinion, starting with the opening suggested by Black. The central theme was the duty of all officials to obey the law as interpreted by the Supreme Court. The Chief's tone was firm as he declared "the basic principle that the federal judiciary is supreme in the exposition of the law of the Constitution and that principle [is] a permanent and indispensable feature of our constitutional system."³¹ *Brown* was reaffirmed as the basic decision on segregation. In a ringing voice, Warren concluded that obedience of the states to the principles announced in *Brown* "are indispensable for the protection of the freedoms guaranteed by our fundamental charter for all of us. Our constitutional ideal of equal justice under law is thus made a living truth."³²

The *Cooper v. Aaron* opinion fills sixteen pages in the *United States Reports*. The *New York Times* commented on its "clear and simple language, understandable even to the most fanatic segregationist."³³ The chief credit for this must go to Brennan, who justified the Chief's reliance on him for the most important opinion since *Brown*.

At the end of his reading, the Chief Justice announced, "The Special Term is now adjourned." The Brethren filed out in their usual stilted manner. The session had taken forty-five minutes.

As far as the press and the public knew, the Court had spoken through the one opinion in the Little Rock case, with the unprecedented opinion in the joint names of all the Justices dramatically emphasizing the unanimity of the decision. Yet the *Brown* tradition of speaking with one voice in desegregation cases was shortly to be broken. The Brethren knew this before the Court opinion was announced, for at the September 26 conference which worked on the final draft, according to Burton's diary, "Justice Frankfurter agrees to join it but he intends to file also a separate opinion. The Conference could not dissuade him from writing separately but he agreed not to file his separate opinion until a week or so after the Court opinion is filed."[34]

On September 29, after the morning conference that approved the final opinion, Burton wrote, "Nothing was said about any separate opinions to follow, but we expect one to [be] filed by Frankfurter, who joins the Court's opinion but wants to say something more. We were unable to dissuade him but did succeed in getting him not to announce it from the bench today."[35]

Frankfurter circulated his concurring opinion on October 3. Warren states in his memoirs that Frankfurter's announcement to the Brethren that he would file a separate opinion "caused quite a sensation on the Court."[36] This was an understatement. Warren, Black, and Brennan were furious. Warren, in particular, felt that such an opinion, which added nothing of substance to the opinion read September 29, could only detract from the force of the joint opinion. By now, his relations with Frankfurter had become too touchy for Warren personally to influence the Justice not to issue the opinion. But the Chief did ask others to talk to Frankfurter. A 1963 letter from Frankfurter to Black notes that, "when I wrote my separate opinion in *Cooper v. Aaron* and told my brethren why I was doing so, it was you who told me that . . . the Chief asked you to try to persuade me not to file a separate opinion."[37]

Neither Black nor anyone else was able to persuade Frankfurter to withdraw his opinion, and he issued it as a concurrence on October 6—the first day of the new 1958 Term.[38] Why he, who had fought so hard for the *Brown* unanimity, should have spoken separately has never been clear. The reason he gave the Brethren was pompously professorial. As one of them recalls it, Frankfurter told the conference that respect for law in the South depended on the Southern lawyers and that the leading ones were his former students, so that it was necessary for him to write personally to persuade them.

Frankfurter confirmed this in a letter a month later to one of his closest friends: "Why did I write and publish the concurring opinion? I should think anybody reading the two opinions would find the answer. My opinion, by its content and its atmosphere, was directed to a particular audience, to wit: the lawyers and the law professors of the South, and that is an audience which I was in a peculiarly qualified position to address in view of my rather extensive association, by virtue of my twenty-five years at the Harvard Law School, with a good many Southern lawyers and law professors."[39]

At the first conference of the new term, on October 6, the Brethren discussed Frankfurter's separate opinion. Black and Brennan insisted that, if Frankfurter persisted in filing the opinion, they would issue the following statement:

"Mr. Justice Black and Mr. Justice Brennan believe that the joint opinion of all the Justices handed down on September 29, 1958 adequately expresses the view of the Court, and they stand by that opinion as delivered. They desire that it be fully understood that the concurring opinion filed this day by Mr. Justice Frankfurter must not be accepted as any dilution or interpretation of the views expressed in the Court's joint opinion."[40]

Warren disapproved of Frankfurter's opinion as strongly as Black and Brennan. But he felt that it would be unwise to issue still another opinion, particularly one that would make public the animosity toward the Frankfurter opinion. The others agreed with the Chief, but they were unable to persuade Black and Brennan. They persisted in refusing to remain silent if Frankfurter went ahead, until Harlan passed around the following satirical opinion:

MR. JUSTICE HARLAN concurring in part, expressing a *dubitante* in part, and dissenting in part.

I concur in the Court's opinion, filed September 29, 1958, in which I have already concurred. I doubt the wisdom of my Brother FRANKFURTER filing his separate opinion, but since I am unable to find any material difference between that opinion and the Court's opinion—and am confirmed in my reading of the former by my Brother FRANKFURTER's express reaffirmation of the latter—I am content to leave his course of action to his own good judgment. I dissent from the action of my Brethren in filing their separate opinion, believing that it is always a mistake to make a mountain out of a molehill. *Requiescat in pace.*[41]

Harlan's droll draft defused the conference tension. Though Frankfurter filed his opinion later that day, Black and Brennan withdrew their statement.

The post-*Brown* unanimity in cases involving racial questions had also almost been broken in *National Association for the Advancement of Colored People v. Alabama.*[42] The June 30, 1958, decision there struck down an order requiring the N.A.A.C.P. to turn over to the Alabama attorney general the names and addresses of its members in the state. All the Justices had voted to grant certiorari and, at the conference on January 17, all agreed with the merits of the holding that Alabama had invalidly infringed the First Amendment rights of N.A.A.C.P. members. Clark, however, indicated some weeks later that he felt compelled to dissent, as he told Frankfurter, "on the ground that the State's interests have not been adequately put to us."[43] Warren and the Brethren worked on Clark to persuade him to withdraw the dissent. Their view was expressed in a letter from Frankfurter only five days before the decision was announced. For Clark to dissent as he planned, Frankfurter wrote, "doesn't seem to me a good enough starting point for a break in the unanimity of the Court in what is, after all, part of the whole Segregation controversy. The sky is none too bright anyhow. The mere fact that you are dissenting . . . would be blown up out of all proportion to what you yourself would subscribe to."[44] The arguments of Frankfurter and the others prevailed. At the last minute, Clark decided not to dissent, and the *N.A.A.C.P.* decision was unanimous.

As first drafted, Harlan's opinion of the Court was based on Alabama's asserted violation of freedom of speech. Frankfurter objected. In a letter to Harlan, he urged that the liberty protected by the Fourteenth Amendment "includes my right to belong to any organization I please. . . . To say that such right of association is an ingredient of a person's 'liberty' of which he cannot be deprived or in the exercise of which he cannot be limited, unless for a fairly statable justification of state control, seems to me a much more accurate and persuasive way of stating what is involved in the N.A.A.C.P. case, what would be involved if it were the American Philosophic Society, than to build up elaborate argumentation that somehow or other what Alabama has done affects free speech."[45] Harlan and the others accepted the Frankfurter approach and the *N.A.A.C.P.* case stands as the first decision holding that there is a constitutional right to organize and join an association for advancement of beliefs and ideas.

On May 23, Harlan circulated a memorandum, in which he wrote, "Unless there is objection, I propose to add at the appropriate spot in the opinion, the following sentence: 'We cannot blink the fact that strong local sentiment exists against the cause which petitioner espouses.' "[46] Frankfurter again took exception, saying, "I *much* prefer it be not added. . . . It seems to me to stir feelings needlessly—no matter how true the statement."[47] Frankfurter's remonstrance prevailed, and the offending sentence was not included.

As the *N.A.A.C.P.* case shows, Frankfurter still played a creative role in the Court's decision process. More and more, however, Frankfurter's remaining Court years were characterized by a continuing deterioration in relations with the Chief Justice and his supporters. Warren saw in Frankfurter's persistence in issuing the separate *Cooper v. Aaron* opinion a confirmation of an increasingly negative attitude. Until Frankfurter's retirement in 1962, the Chief displayed what even some of his law clerks characterized as "a mild paranoia" about Frankfurter. Warren was, for instance, most insistent that there be a minimum of contacts between his clerks and Frankfurter, or even Frankfurter's clerks. It was more than a quip when Frankfurter asked one of Warren's clerks to come to his office, unless, of course, he was "quarantined."

According to a Frankfurter letter, in one case during the 1957 Term, Warren assigned the opinion to Frankfurter and then wrote his own superseding opinion over Frankfurter's objection, even though the two opinions were essentially similar. Explaining to Brennan why he was not joining Warren's opinion, Frankfurter wrote:

The Chief assigned the writing of the *Nishikawa* opinion to me. He himself has told me that his view and mine are very close together. In so far as they are not, I should suppose that the ordinary course of judicial administration is to ask the fellow who wrote the opinion for the Court to make whatever accommodations others may desire. It does seem odd that the fellow to whom an opinion was assigned and wrote it four months ago should throw his opinion in the wastebasket for another formulation that is deemed to be substantially the same. The Chief Justice, I should suppose, is the last person who should cause the ordinary course of procedure to stand on its head. But even if remotely there is a suggestion of deference to the fact that it is the Chief Justice's opinion which others have to join, then I put it to you, with the depth of my conviction, that any encouragement in a Chief Justice that he is the boss—that he differs from the other members of the Court in matters other than administrative—must be rigorously resisted.[48]

Frankfurter's relations with the other activist Brethren had become equally touchy. "Unfortunately," Frankfurter wrote Harlan in 1958, "not a little aspect of the work of the Court represents what I must call an unfraternal attitude in the unjustified attribution of motives and conduct that sometimes finds lodgment."[49] But Frankfurter was as guilty of this sort of thing as the colleagues against whom he directed his complaint.

The sensitive relations between Frankfurter and his activist colleagues even extended to Brennan, with whom virtually all the Brethren found it easy to get along. Frankfurter prepared a draft dissent in a 1958 case that involved the application of a technical administrative law doctrine.[50] The draft asserted that the Court's use of the doctrine "makes of it a feckless ritual" and made the administrative process "constitute, as it were, a paper ballet."[51] Brennan, who had authored the majority opinion, wrote Frankfurter asking him to reconsider the characterizations. If he did not, Brennan said, he would add to the opinion: "Our reading of the *Far East*[52] and *Cunard* cases[53] is said in dissent to make a 'feckless ritual' of the administrative process and to make the Board's proceedings in this case a 'paper ballet'. It seems to us that an opposite reading would make a 'feckless ritual' of the judicial process. . . ."[54]

Frankfurter replied, "Matching candor with candor, let me say that I am rather surprised that 'feckless ritual' and 'paper ballet' should be offending phrases. . . . 'Feckless' only means 'futile' and I do in all good conscience think that your exposition of 'primary jurisdiction' makes of it a futile ritual. . . . As for 'paper ballet,' that seemed to me so lighthearted that I thought it might even amuse you."[55] Frankfurter did, however, take out the offending words.

At times, the touchiness between Frankfurter and the activist Justices had its humorous aspects. One day in 1960, during argument, Frankfurter put a series of sharp questions to counsel, only to have Douglas intervene each time with a helpful answer. "I thought you were arguing this case," Frankfurter snapped at the lawyer. "I am," counsel replied, "but I can use all the help I can get."[56]

Anthony Lewis used this incident to illustrate the point that frequently the Justices' "deep philosophical differences come to the surface and there may be bristling exchanges."[57] Another case where the differences between Frankfurter and Douglas led to acerbic exchanges was *Lambert v. California*.[58] But, this time, the exchanges were private and reflected the personal, more than the philosophic, differences between the two.

At issue in *Lambert* was a Los Angeles requirement of registration with the police for every person who had been convicted "of an offense punishable as a felony" in California. At the conference on October 22, 1957,[59] Warren led off by saying he would vote to reverse the conviction for failing to register, since as he saw it, the law was vague and arbitrary. All the Brethren agreed and the opinion was assigned by the Chief to Douglas, who circulated a draft November 8 following Warren's approach. "For the average person," the draft's key passage read, "the words 'punishable as a felony' are the equivalent of Arabic script or a formula written in mathematical symbols. . . . We conclude that the statutory standard 'punishable as a felony' is a snare for the average man and therefore too vague to pass the requirements of Due Process."

During the next few days, Douglas began to receive objections to the draft. Clark wrote that, if the reversal was to be on the ground that "punishable as a felony" was too vague, he could not join the opinion. "It would wreck a host of state statutes . . . and would cast a shadow on many old and well-established common law rules." Clark suggested an alternate ground: "actual notice is an essential element in prosecutive actions for failure to register, but would we not be on sounder ground if we held that and no more?" Frankfurter and Harlan, among others, also now objected to the "vagueness" approach.

On November 21, Douglas sent around a *Memorandum to the Conference* noting that his draft, "which stated the views expressed at Conference did not commend itself to a majority of the Brethren." At the conference that considered the draft, only Douglas himself and Black voted in favor of the draft.[60] Douglas, therefore, wrote that he was now circulating a rewritten opinion that, as suggested by Clark, reversed on the ground that due process was violated when the registration requirement was applied to a person who had no actual knowledge of the duty to register. Douglas secured a majority for his new draft and delivered it as the opinion of the Court on December 16, 1957.

But the new opinion caused a split in the unanimity expressed at the October 22 conference. Four Justices dissented. Burton's dissent said only that defendant's constitutional rights were not violated.

Frankfurter, joined by Harlan and Whittaker, delivered a character-istically more elaborate dissent. He stated that both federal and state statute-books were "thick with provisions" that made acts or nonac-tion criminal even though the persons convicted "had no awareness of what the law required or that what they did was wrongdoing." Frankfurter asserted that "a whole volume of the United States Re-ports would be required to document in detail the legislation in this country that would fall or be impaired"[61] under the majority deci-sion.

After Frankfurter's oral delivery of his dissent on December 16, Douglas sent him a handwritten note asking for "a citation of the statutes that would fall because of *Lambert*."[62] Frankfurter replied the same day, "You ask me for ordinances just like the Los Angeles or-dinance. I have no doubt that there are such. But that isn't the game I am playing." He also wrote that, when he had earlier objected to the "vagueness" ground, "In response, you said to me that to go on the other ground—the ground of want of notice—would cut too deeply into the criminal law."

Douglas sent Frankfurter another note on December 16, saying, "I am afraid you misunderstood what I said earlier about Lambert when it was in process of being discussed at the table." Douglas went on to say, "The reason that I asked you for some statute which would run afoul of Lambert other than the ordinance involved in Lambert was your statement on the bench that it would make a dissent much, much too long to list the statutes which would fall as a result of Lambert." Douglas stated that "a fairly exhaustive search in this of-fice" had not turned up other statutes with the same defect. The Douglas letter concluded, "In view of the fact that you had found so many that would suffer from the same infirmity, I thought you might be willing to disclose their identity—at least the identity of a single one."

Frankfurter answered this with another December 16 note: "I stand on what I wrote in my earlier letter. I may have misunderstood what you wanted to convey, but I would go to the stake for the accuracy of my statement that the words that I quoted as having been spoken by you you spoke."

Douglas then dispatched still another December 16 letter. It began, "Nobody in this office wants you to go through the ordeal by fire—especially at Christmas time." "However," Douglas wrote, "the purpose of the exchange is not to ascertain who said what, but to get from you that one citation that would fall because of the Lambert decision."

"I, too," this last December 16 letter by Douglas concluded, "would go to the stake for the accuracy of my quotation of what you said from the bench, i.e., that it would make a dissent much, much too long to list the statutes which would fall as a result of Lambert. To be more specific, you stated from the bench the list would fill a volume. So when we ask just for one, we are not asking for very much out of that long tabulation."

Even this did not end the judicial tempest in a teapot. Frankfurter wrote back the next day, "Of course you are accurate in indicating what I said from the bench in *Lambert*. . . . I stand on what I said there. The whole point of my dissent is that many statutes should fall if the reasoning in *Lambert* governed other instances, but my forecast is that they won't. I am sorry that what I wrote is opaque."

Douglas then sent the following note later on December 17: "I guess my writing must be the opaque one. For all I wanted was a citation of one statute that would fall if the reasoning in *Lambert* were followed."

Mercifully, that ended the exchange, as Frankfurter did not see fit to answer again.

Among the noteworthy decisions during the 1957 Term were those in two Passport Cases—even though they avoided the constitutional issues that had been presented. The cases were *Kent v. Dulles*[63] and *Dayton v. Dulles*.[64] Rockwell Kent, the well-known artist, was denied a passport because he was a Communist, after he had refused to submit an affidavit on Communist membership, as required by the relevant regulations. Dayton, a physicist, was refused a passport on the ground that he was going abroad to engage in activities that would advance the Communist cause. Dayton had been given a hearing by the State Department, but the decision was based not only on the evidence presented, but also on a confidential file that Dayton was not allowed to examine. The lower courts had upheld the passport denials.

Both cases raised broad constitutional issues. Kent challenged the power given to the Secretary of State to issue passports without any standards limiting his discretion to grant or deny. Dayton claimed that the hearing accorded him did not satisfy due process. These claims raised key constitutional questions that the Court had never decided.

The Passport Cases were discussed in conference on April 18, 1958.[65] Warren began the session by dealing with the *Dayton* case first. "We must decide," he said, "whether the Secretary has power to prevent travel by a citizen on grounds [that it is] detrimental to foreign relations of the U.S. on confidential evidence only. All the findings were based on confidential information." The Chief felt that the Secretary had no power to deny on that basis. As far as *Kent* was concerned, "The Solicitor General admits the right to travel is a constitutional one. There is no express Congressional grant to the Secretary, but the Solicitor General claims it is implicit." As Warren saw it, "Congress never has given the Secretary the right to deny a passport on substantive grounds. If we said Congress did give him the power, then I'd reverse as unconstitutional."

Frankfurter noted that the "passport is an old tool for moving in this world." He referred to the London *Economist* which, each week, printed a quotation from its issue a century earlier. The previous week, it had a quote from 1858 on passports. Black, Douglas, and Brennan approved the Chief's view that there was no delegation to deny on the substantive grounds relied on here. The same four, as well as Whittaker, agreed that there was no power to decide on the basis of confidential information alone. Frankfurter indicated that he would go along with reversal. Burton, Clark, and Harlan voted to affirm. Harlan asserted that it was "inconceivable that Congress has no power to give the Secretary the power."

Warren assigned the opinions to Douglas, who wrote a far-reaching *Dayton* opinion which held that the passport could not be denied on the basis of confidential information; due process required disclosure of all the facts upon which the government relied. Whittaker now changed his vote. Frankfurter, who continued to vote for reversal, refused to join the Douglas opinion, since he thought it went too far. Frankfurter was necessary for a majority, so Douglas gave way. On June 13, Douglas circulated a memorandum that stated, "There are only four for the opinion in this case as last circulated— namely the Chief Justice, Justice Black, Justice Brennan, and myself. Since we are in the minority and since this is a constitutional issue, we have decided to defer to the majority of the Court and accordingly not to reach the constitutional question."[66] Douglas was, therefore, striking out the constitutional holding. Instead, the *Dayton* opinion indicated that a majority had decided not to reach the constitutional issue and was reversing on the same ground as in the *Kent* case.

That ground, as it was announced in the *Kent* opinion on June 16, 1958, was essentially that stated by Warren at the April 18 conference—that Congress had not given the Secretary of State the power to deny passports on substantive grounds such as that relied on here. Clark wrote a strong dissent, joined by Burton, Harlan, and Whittaker. Harlan prepared a separate dissent in *Kent,* which stated, "I think there was no constitutional bar to requiring the affidavits involved in this case, and refusing passports to petitioners because of their failure to file the affidavits with the Secretary of State." [67] When Frankfurter wrote Harlan, "I'm a little baffled that you reach constitutional issues . . . in *Kent* and abstain therefrom in *Dayton*," [68] Harlan withdrew his separate dissent.

Clark had written an even stronger *Dayton* dissent on the due process issue, which he withdrew after Douglas had eliminated the constitutional holding from his Court opinion. Clark's original *Dayton* dissent contained language such as, "Such 'freedom' sounds wondrously like the pitch of tyranny to me. I have been far too long in the conflicting, adjusting, necessarily accommodating world of men, to contribute to the sort of Pyrrhic achievement reached for by the Court today." [69] As delivered, the Clark dissent contained only a short paragraph stating that, since the majority did not consider the constitutional issues, "I would affirm on the question of authority without reaching any constitutional issue." [70]

Clark's feelings about the cases were strong enough to induce him to telephone the Director of the F.B.I., J. Edgar Hoover, on June 5, asking for something Hoover had said on the importance of passport control. [71] Hoover replied in a "Dear Tom" letter, delivered by special messenger and signed, "Edgar." Hoover noted that he had given congressional testimony on the matter, but only in executive session. He did, however, refer Clark to a passage in his book, *Masters of Deceit,* that referred "to passports and other false documents used by Russian espionage agents." [72] Clark's *Kent* dissent contained a footnote reference to the Hoover book, "For a comprehensive story of Communism in America indicating the necessity for passport control." [73]

Another case that had been held over from the previous term appeared likely to give rise to an important Smith Act decision. The case in question—*Scales v. United States*[74]—arose out of a conviction under the so-called Membership Clause of the Smith Act making membership in an organization such as the Communist Party a crime. At the conference on October 15, 1956,[75] Warren said that, while he would vote to reverse, the case "can be disposed of on this indictment without reaching the constitutional question and we should do so." Warren referred to the Internal Security Act of 1950, which required registration of Communists and provided that membership alone would not violate any criminal statute. He said that this provision had qualified the Smith Act so as to bar prosecution under that Act's Membership Clause. "Congress in 1950 made its choice whether it would have registration or make membership an offense. They chose registration." Though "the Government says that mere membership is enough," the Chief concluded, "we need not go into the constitutional issue."

At the conference, a majority agreed with Warren's approach, with Burton and Clark voting to affirm. As time went on, however, the Brethren began to feel that the constitutionality of the Membership Clause would have to be decided. At a conference in March, 1957, four expressed themselves in favor of constitutionality and two against. Warren did not vote, since he still found it unnecessary to go beyond the view he had expressed at the October conference. Frankfurter wrote Warren pointing out an important objection to having the decision come down in accordance with the vote: "we are faced with the fact that we have only a Court of seven. (Brennan didn't hear the cases, and of course, Whittaker wasn't here.) That raises the question whether we should pass on such an issue of constitutionality as is raised by the relevant provision of § 2 of the Smith Act by less than a full Court. If the constitutionality of the Act is to be sustained, such a decision should at least have a majority of the whole Court in its support."[76]

In order to meet the objection, the Court, on June 3, 1957, scheduled the case for reargument in the 1957 Term, when a full Court could hear the case.[77] Before the case could be reargued, however, on October 14, the government confessed error because F.B.I. reports of two witnesses had not been turned over to defendant in violation of the rule laid down in the *Jencks* case.[78] The conviction was reversed because of the *Jencks* violation without any need for decision on the Membership Clause's constitutionality.

Apart from *Cooper v. Aaron,* the most important cases decided in 1958 were the two so-called Expatriation Cases—*Perez v. Brownell*[79] and *Trop v. Dulles.*[80] While the Little Rock case, with all its drama, presented no difficulty on the law, the legal issue in the Expatriation Cases was as troublesome as any that came before the Warren Court.

The government claimed Perez had lost his citizenship by voting in a foreign election. Trop, it was urged, had lost his citizenship because he had been convicted by court-martial of desertion from the Army in wartime. In both cases, Congress had provided for loss of citizenship for the acts done. Could Congress constitutionally provide for forfeiture of citizenship in these cases?

The Expatriation Cases had come to the Court during the 1956 Term. All the Justices had voted to grant certiorari in *Perez* and all except Burton and Clark (with Whittaker not sitting) in *Trop.* The cases were first argued on May 1, 1957. At the conference after the argument, on May 4,[81] Warren spoke strongly for reversal of the decisions in favor of the government. "Congress," he said, "has the right to provide for denationalization when he makes the claim to dual citizenship"—but not otherwise. The Chief asserted that citizenship by birth could come to an end only by "renunciation." Congress could not provide "a punishment of banishment" for desertion. "Congress can't impose it as punishment." If it does, "he has the right to a jury trial. I doubt if a court-martial would be enough."

The others were sharply divided. Black spoke most strongly in support of Warren, saying he had "never thought there is any constitutional power to strip a man of what's given for life." Frankfurter led the opposition. To him, the key issue was that of the proper judicial posture. "The ultimate determinant," he said, "is not what we find in the Constitution, but our conception of what is the job of the judge." For Frankfurter, the governing doctrine was that of deference to the legislative judgment.

Frankfurter expanded on his views in this respect in a letter on the cases that he sent Harlan a few days after the conference. The crucial question, he wrote, was "who is to judge" on denationalization, "Is it the Court or Congress? Indeed, more accurately, must not the Court put on the sackcloth and ashes of deferring humility in order to determine whether the judgment that Congress exercise, judged as it must be under the Due Process Clause, is so outside the limits of a supportable judgment by those who have the primary duty of judgment as to constitute that disregard of reason which we call an arbitrary judgment[?]"[82]

At the May 4, conference, Black, Douglas, Harlan, and Brennan supported Warren and voted to reverse in both cases. Frankfurter, Burton, Clark, and Whittaker voted the other way. On May 8, Warren assigned the opinions to himself. On June 5, he circulated draft opinions of the Court delivered in his name for both cases.[83] The principal opinion was prepared for the *Perez* case. It consisted of eighteen printed pages. The Warren draft rejected the government's contention of "a broad power in Congress, implied from the very fact of national sovereignty, to make loss of nationality follow from acts which Congress may reasonably think constitute an unwarranted participation in the sovereign affairs of a foreign nation or which are inconsistent with the gravest obligations of American citizenship. We do not believe the decisions of this Court sustain the exercise of any such broad implied power."

Warren's *Perez* draft recognized only "a power of Congress to declare citizenship forfeit contrary to the will of the citizen no broader than is necessary to prevent the acquisition of dual nationality." It concluded, "that whatever implied power there may be in Congress to regulate citizenship does not warrant . . . the statutory provisions involved in this case."

Warren's draft opinion of the Court in *Trop* was shorter, consisting of six printed pages. It stated that what had been said in the *Perez* draft "is largely dispositive" of the constitutional issue here. "We hold here . . . as we did there . . . that Congress has no power to prescribe loss of citizenship as the consequence of conduct inconsistent with fundamental obligations of citizenship. The Fourteenth Amendment leaves no authority in Congress to decide who among United States citizens are deserving of continued citizenship, no matter what their shortcomings may be."

Legally speaking, the Warren draft opinions were not impressive. The principal draft—that in *Perez*—did not really explain why the denationalization was beyond the power of Congress. It analyzed prior cases that had upheld voluntary renunciations of citizenship and then asserted, without supporting reasoning or authority, that

Congress could not provide for involuntary expatriation in this case. "Finding no power in Congress to take away citizenship for the acts described by" the statute, the opinion reversed. The *Trop* draft, as we saw, was based upon "what we have said in *Perez*."

The essential weakness of Warren's *Perez* draft was pointed out in a law clerk's memorandum analyzing the draft for one of the Justices: "This much is clear: if this case is to be reversed, the Court *must* meet the argument that there is an independent power, and it is best met squarely and frankly."

When Frankfurter received his copy of Warren's *Perez* draft, he wrote on the first page: "All power is, in Madison's phrase, of an encroaching nature. Judicial power is not immune against this human weakness, also must be on guard against this and not the less so, since the only restraint against it is self-restraint."[84] Frankfurter apparently liked what he wrote. The passage was used in the different drafts he wrote in the Expatriation Cases and appears in the *Trop* dissent that the Justice finally issued.

Two days after he had received the Warren draft, Frankfurter sent around a memorandum in which he wrote, "I regret to find myself unable to agree with it." He said that he would prepare a dissent. However, he noted, "The issues at stake are too far-reaching and the subject matter calls for too extensive an investigation, let alone the time necessary for writing an adequate opinion, that I shall not attempt the preparation of such an opinion before the Term closes. I shall content myself with noting my inability to agree and the promise of filing an opinion at the next Term of Court."[85]

Other Justices also had misgivings about the cases. Even those in the bare majority were not wholly satisfied with the decisions and the draft opinions. In these circumstances, it was natural for the Brethren to agree to hold the cases for the next term. On June 24, the Court issued an order setting the cases for reargument in October.[86]

In a letter a year later, Frankfurter explained why the reargument in *Perez* and *Trop* was scheduled: "There are situations when the feeling of a Brother that he needs the summer, as it were, to work on setting forth his views in a case should delay handing down a decision. Such a situation was presented by the *Expatriation Cases* at the end of last Term. . . . The problems there were new, difficult and of far-reaching import in our national life. More than that, not only was the Court closely divided, but within the narrow majority there were those who had doubts and uncertainties. Nothing could have been more appropriate to the circumstances of that situation than to set the cases down for reargument."[87]

The reargument of the Expatriation Cases took place October 28, 1957. At the conference the next day,[88] the Chief Justice restated his position that Congress had power to denationalize "only where there is a voluntary abandonment of citizenship." What Congress had done here, Warren went on "is to make loss of citizenship a punishment. It doesn't have that power—no power to add to any punishment loss of citizenship. It makes no difference whether it's by a jury or administrative procedure."

Most of the others adhered to the stands they had taken the prior term. But there were important shifts. Harlan said that he had found it "very difficult to vote" in these cases. Though he had voted originally to reverse, he was at present for affirmance in both cases. Brennan also changed his vote. He was voting to affirm in *Perez,* though he was still for reversal in *Trop.* Whittaker stuck to his vote to affirm in *Perez,* but had changed his mind and voted to reverse in *Trop.*

The October 29 conference left Warren with his bare majority in *Trop.* The only difference was that, since Harlan and Whittaker had switched positions, the vote for reversal was now Warren, Black, Douglas, Brennan, and Whittaker, with the remaining four voting to affirm. In *Perez,* however, the decision had changed. Because Harlan and Brennan had altered their votes, there was now a six-to-three decision for affirmance, with only Warren, Black, and Douglas still for reversal.

Frankfurter, now senior majority Justice in *Perez,* assigned the opinion to himself and soon prepared a draft essentially similar to his final opinion in the case. During the next month Whittaker again switched his vote in *Trop.* Frankfurter now had a bare majority and circulated his *Trop* opinion as the opinion of the Court.

Because of the changed votes, Warren had to recirculate his *Perez* and *Trop* opinions as dissents. But he did more than simply reissue them in dissenting form. They were now thoroughly redrafted by Jon Newman, the Warren law clerk primarily responsible for the Expatriation Cases during the 1957 Term, who is now a federal appellate judge. Newman was aware of the deficiencies in the original *Perez* draft and worked out a broad theory to support Warren's decision that denationalization for voting in a foreign election was unconstitutional. The theory was one of the want of any such power in a government such as ours because it severs the citizen relationship that is of the essence in our polity. "The power to denationalize," asserted Warren's new *Perez* draft, "is not within the letter or the spirit of the powers with which our Government was endowed."[89]

Warren's *Trop* opinion was also completely redrafted to accord with the theory the Chief had expressed at the October 29 conference: that loss of citizenship was a punishment that Congress had no power to impose. The redraft was expanded to assert that taking away citizenship for Trop's desertion was to impose cruel and unusual punishment—a point that had been mentioned, though expressly left open, in Warren's June 1957 *Trop* draft. Warren himself inserted into the new draft a statement that, "The basic concept underlying the Eighth Amendment is nothing less than the dignity of man. . . . The Amendment must draw its meaning from the evolving standards of decency that mark the progress of a maturing society."

Warren's new *Trop* draft went beyond the Constitution and relied also on the "cardinal principles" underlying the basic document. "No nation claiming adherence to a civilized system of law founded on democratic principles need arrogate to itself the power to punish its citizens by rendering them stateless." This sentence is not contained in Warren's published *Trop* opinion.

The Chief's new *Trop* draft, circulated as a dissent March 14, 1958, concluded with a ringing affirmation of the superiority of civil over military power:

Finally, wholly apart from the question of whether citizenship can ever be divested, either as punishment or otherwise, I deny that any power to denationalize may constitutionally be exercised by the military authorities. If the priceless right of citizenship is ever to be forfeited in a trial, it should be in a civilian court of justice, where all Bill of Rights protections guard the fairness of the outcome. Military courts are to try soldiers for military crimes and impose punishments that do not encroach on purely civilian rights. Who is worthy of continued enjoyment of citizenship is not the constitutional concern of the Army. Its business is to fight wars. . . . Far from keeping the military authorities within their proper bounds, this statute gives them the last word on the right to be a citizen—a right which is, or should be, peculiarly under civilian authorities and courts. Nothing in the language, history or any known purposes of our Constitution lends the slightest support to military control over the basic right of United States citizenship.

This passage was absent from the *Trop* opinion that Warren delivered. It is unfortunate that it was omitted. One of the particular things Warren was able to accomplish was to lead the Court in limiting military jurisdiction over civilians. The Warren Court opinions on the subject were not, however, delivered by the Chief Justice. It would have been of great significance if he had been able, in his own name, to pronounce the passage on "keeping the military authorities within their proper bounds" contained in his March 14 *Trop* draft dissent.

After Warren circulated his *Trop* dissent, Whittaker once more changed his vote and joined the Chief's opinion. This again made a bare majority for reversal. But Warren had to recirculate his *Trop* opinion as that of a plurality (Warren, Black, Douglas, and Whittaker), since Brennan wrote him on March 12, "I have tried over the past week, without success, to mesh our two opinions in *Trop*. Because I am not of the view that Congress is wholly without power to provide for expatriation of citizens in proper cases, and because my approach makes unnecessary a discussion whether expatriation as punishment violates the Eighth Amendment, I have concluded I should file my own opinion."

When Warren delivered the *Trop* opinion on March 31, it was joined by Black, Douglas, and Whittaker. Brennan concurred in the reversal, but not the opinion. He issued a separate opinion justifying the result on due process grounds.

The *Perez* opinion was announced by Frankfurter as an opinion of the Court on March 31. It was supported by a bare majority (Frankfurter, Burton, Clark, Harlan, and Brennan), for Whittaker had written Frankfurter March 5 and switched his vote here also. He later joined the Warren dissent.

In his March 12 note to Warren, Brennan had indicated that he also planned to issue a separate concurrence in *Perez* "because I cannot join . . . Felix's opinion." Frankfurter, however, was able to make revisions which met Brennan's objections, and the separate *Perez* concurrence was withdrawn. As Brennan explained it in a March 21 letter to Frankfurter, he now joined the majority *Perez* opinion because it made clear that "expatriation, as a means of regulating such conduct of American citizens, is reasonably calculated to effect the ends which Congress seeks to achieve, namely the avoidance of embarrassment to our foreign affairs by the voting of American citizens in foreign elections."[90]

Brennan did suggest one important change in the *Perez* opinion. Frankfurter had written that the sole inquiry for the Court was whether Congress might have reasonably concluded that there was a relevant connection between its foreign affairs power and its legislative action. Frankfurter's opinion then stated, "Once that relationship is satisfactorily established the concern of this Court ceases. We have reached the limit of our power—a limit which this Court, as the guardian of the division of power, must scrupulously respect."

In his March 21 letter, Brennan urged the deletion of the quoted passage, saying, "I am not at all clear whether due process considerations may not limit congressional power even when the consequence of expatriation may be thought reasonably calculated to achieve a congressional purpose. At least I think that consideration may be involved when and if expatriation for draft evasion or as a consequence of Smith Act convictions reaches us." The sentences were deleted by Frankfurter and do not appear in his final *Perez* opinion.

On March 31, 1958, when the *Perez* decision was announced, Frankfurter, as usual, did not read the opinion, but instead stated his oral version of it. After the Justice had finished, Warren, miffed once again by the Frankfurter practice, prefaced the delivery of his dissent with the remark that his opinion was directed at the printed opinion of the Court, not the oral opinion of Mr. Justice Frankfurter. At this, Frankfurter wrote on a memo pad, "Does he mean my oral was more persuasive?"[91]

During the 1957 Term, Burton had become increasingly ill with Parkinson's disease. Though he had hoped to serve one more term, he followed his doctor's orders and planned to retire soon after his seventieth birthday on June 22, 1958, when he became eligible for a pension. Burton informed Warren of his decision on April 30.[92] The Chief, who had grown fond of Burton, expressed his regret and the hope that the Justice could wait at least until September 30.[93] On

July 17, Burton, accompanied by Attorney General William P. Rogers, went to see the President to submit a notice of retirement to take effect October 13—the opening day of the new 1958 Term.

The conversation at the White House was devoted primarily to the question of Burton's successor. Eisenhower said that, because of his dissatisfaction with Warren and Brennan, the Attorney General should be "most careful" in the selection. The President said he had chosen Warren because of his years of legal practice as well as his service as Governor. But now, he intimated, he wanted someone with judicial experience. The only name mentioned was Potter Stewart, a Republican from Ohio, then a judge of the Court of Appeals for the Sixth Circuit. Eisenhower cautioned Rogers "to be espcially careful" because "Stewart's age is 43 and therefore he would have a very long service." He was most interested in ensuring "a conservative attitude" in the new Justice.[94]

The President did appoint Stewart, and Burton's successor took his seat on October 14. Except for Douglas, Stewart was the youngest Court appointee in over a century. His youth and handsome appearance added an unusual touch to the highest bench, showing that it need not always be composed of nine old men. Stewart came from a distinguished legal family. He had attended Hotchkiss and Yale, taken a post-graduate year at Cambridge, England, and been an honors graduate of Yale Law School. He had been active in municipal politics in Cincinnati, with two terms on the City Council. Eisenhower had appointed him to the federal court of appeals in 1954, four years before elevating him to the Supreme Court.

Anyone who meets Stewart is surprised by his vigor and clearly expressed views. They contrast sharply with his public image as an indecisive "swing man," without clearly defined conceptions. What is true of Stewart is that he never acted on the basis of a comprehensive judicial philosophy, such as that which guided Black or Frankfurter. When asked whether he was a "liberal" like Black or a "conservative" like Frankfurter, he answered, "I am a lawyer." He went on, "I have some difficulty understanding what those terms mean even in the field of political life. . . . And I find it impossible to know what they mean when they are carried over to judicial work."[95]

At times, Stewart's aptness for the pungent phrase, apparent to anyone who engaged him in private conversation, broke through the robe's restraint. Most people have heard of his famous statement, in a 1964 case about hard-core pornography, when he said he would not attempt to define it. "But I know it when I see it."[96] Stewart would often make such pointed remarks, though infrequently on the bench. Another example occurred during the argument in 1961 of an anti-trust case involving the Brown Shoe Company. Brown's attorney argued that all men's shoes did not compete for sales with all other men's shoes; thus, dress shoes did not compete for sales with casual shoes. The Solicitor General responded that they did, pointing to the example of Brown's President, who had come to court to testify wearing dress shoes one day and casual shoes the next. Stewart grinned and declared, "Maybe it was direct examination one day and cross-examination the next."[97]

Stewart still fondly remembers his first meeting with Warren. "When I first arrived here," he recalls, "the train from Cincinnati—we took the train in those days—arrived at the Union Station something like 6:30 in the morning. The Chief Justice was not an early riser. In fact, he often used to come in almost out of breath in the morning and go on the Court two minutes later. But there he was at the station to meet me and my wife and my children, at the Union Station at 6:30 in the morning."

Stewart also tells how, on his first Sunday in Washington, when he was in town alone, Warren took him to see the Washington Redskins play the Cleveland Browns, "knowing I was from Ohio, though I was never sure if he thought I was from Cleveland or Cincinnati"—which, to an Ohioan of course, makes all the difference in the world. The Chief, Stewart recollects, was not always accurate about names and places. Once when a large group of lawyers from Ohio was being sponsored for admission by a Senator from that state, Warren greeted them by telling them how happy he was to welcome lawyers from "Justice Stewart Potter's state." Similarly, in a 1965 oral argument, the Chief Justice told counsel to answer the question put by "Mr. Justice Goldwater," when he meant Justice Arthur J. Goldberg.

Writing to Judge Learned Hand about his new colleague, Frankfurter said, "My own feeling is that he suffers at present, and will for some time to come, from what I call an intellectual traffic jam. He terrifically feels the burden of the work. I also think, however, that he is concerned how he appears to the world outside and, more particularly, he doesn't want to appear to be lining up with John and me. (This is not merely my own suspicion. John is confident this is true.)"[98]

Despite this assessment, during the 1958 Term, Stewart sided with Frankfurter in a number of important cases, and his vote was crucial in moving a bare majority temporarily away from Warren to the Frankfurter approach on judicial review. One case where Stewart's ballot proved decisive was *Bartkus v. Illinois*.[99] Before Stewart's arrival, the Brethren had been unable to muster a majority for decision in that case.

Bartkus had been prosecuted in a federal court for robbery of a federally insured savings and loan association. The jury returned a verdict of acquittal. He was indicted for the same robbery less than three weeks later by Illinois. The indictment charged a violation of the state robbery statute. This time he was convicted and sentenced to life imprisonment. He claimed that the state conviction violated the constitutional prohibition against double jeopardy. The state courts rejected his claim.

The *Bartkus* case first came before the Supreme Court during the 1957 Term. At a conference on November 22, 1957, the Justices divided four-to-four (Frankfurter, Burton, Clark, and Harlan voting for affirmance and Warren, Black, Douglas, and Whittaker for reversal—with Brennan not participating). On January 6, 1958, the Court announced that it was affirming in *Bartkus* by an equally divided Court.[100] On May 26, however, a petition for rehearing was granted.[101] The January 6 judgment was vacated and the case set for reargument during the 1958 Term.

At the conference after the *Bartkus* reargument,[102] Warren spoke strongly in favor of reversal. "The Fourteenth Amendment," he urged, "bars a retrial after the federal acquittal." He pointed out that a 1956 case[103] prohibited the use of illegally obtained evidence when offered by federal to state officers. "These crimes are the same," the Chief stressed.

Black took a different approach in supporting reversal. He stated the view that the Court could apply the Fifth Amendment, which contains the constitutional prohibition against double jeopardy, "to the states. It doesn't say twice put in jeopardy by the same government, but for the same offense." Hence, said Black, "when the 'feds' do what was done here, we have a direct violation of the Fifth Amendment or it is so shocking to the conscience that we can't take it under the Fourteenth."

Frankfurter led the case for affirmance. "Both criminal justice and federalism," he said, "are involved here." To him, the case was a simple one. "The same act is a transgression against two sovereigns" and each may prosecute separately.

The vote at the conference was inconclusive. Frankfurter, Clark, and Harlan were still firm for affirmance, and Warren, Black, and Douglas for reversal. Frankfurter had tried the previous term to induce Whittaker to join the vote for affirmance.[104] Whittaker had refused, explaining, in a letter just after the prior term's four-to-four conference vote, that, "after a trial in a federal court resulting in acquittal, to permit a second trial and a conviction in a state court upon precisely the same issues seems quite unfair. . . . All of this 'shocks (my) conscience' and, in my view, constitutes a denial of due process."[105] By the October 1958 conference, however, Frankfurter was able to persuade Whittaker to change his vote to affirmance.

Brennan, however, now voted for reversal. At the conference, Warren had made the point that the case for reversal was "compounded by the federal officers' acts" in participating in the subsequent Illinois conviction. To Brennan, this became the crucial factor. As described by a contemporary observer, a "hot feud" developed between Brennan and Frankfurter as to whether the state conviction was, in fact, the result of a prosecution by federal officials using the state courts. Brennan believed that the second prosecution, though in form by the state, was in essence a federal prosecution and thus barred by the Constitution. As Brennan explained it, in a letter to Frankfurter, "You will remember how vigorously I balk at the extent to which the Federal Government made use of Illinois officials to effect Bartkus' conviction."[106]

With Whittaker's switch and Brennan's vote, the Brethren were still divided four-to-four, since Stewart said at the conference that he was not yet able to make up his mind. Soon afterwards, Frankfurter circulated a memorandum rejecting what he called Brennan's "surprising" approach. Frankfurter urged that the state was only "exercising its independent constitutional powers although it had evidentiary help and, if you please, encouragement from federal officials—a help and encouragement, to repeat, the desirability of which has been preached from the house tops for most of my professional life."[107]

Brennan replied by a memorandum which began "Brother Frankfurter not too delicately implies that my circulated dissent misrepresents the record." Brennan repeated his view, "that even though the state by 'its free will' decided to prosecute, if that prosecution is instigated by the federal government and the state case prepared and guided by federal authorities this is enough to void the state conviction. Such a situation, for all practical purposes, is one in which federal resources, federal power, and federal energies are utilized to put an accused twice in jeopardy for the same criminal conduct. I think it clear that that degree of federal participation was present in this case."[108]

Both the Frankfurter and Brennan memos were designed to persuade Stewart. A few days after the Brennan memo, Stewart made up his mind and joined Frankfurter. That made a bare majority for affirmance, and the decision was so announced, with Frankfurter delivering the opinion of the Court on March 30. Black, joined by Warren and Douglas, dissented on the ground that a state conviction after a federal acquittal violated due process. Brennan wrote a separate dissent, which Warren and Douglas also joined, based on his view that the federal officials had played the crucial role in the second prosecution.

Stewart also cast the determinative votes in two decisions involving legislative investigations that appeared inconsistent with the 1957 *Sweezy*[109] and *Watkins*[110] decisions. The first was in *Uphaus v. Wyman*.[111] Like the *Sweezy* case it involved a legislative investigation into subversive activities in New Hampshire. Uphaus was director of an organization that ran a discussion program at a summer camp in the state. It was alleged that he and some of the speakers were associated with "Communist front" movements. He was convicted of contempt for refusing to comply with a subpoena directing him to turn over the names of the camp's guests. He claimed that the Smith Act had precluded exertion of the state's investigatory power and that his First Amendment rights were violated.

At the conference on November 21, 1958,[112] Warren started by rejecting the preemption claim. "I don't," he said, "put much stock in preemption under *Nelson*.[113] It's one thing for us to be exclusive in the criminal field; but, for other purposes, the state would have legitimate legislative action." But, the Chief went on, he was for reversal because he believed there was an invasion of this area "without the state showing an interest endangered or being subverted. It would deter people from freely speaking."

Once again, the Brethren were sharply divided. Black, Douglas, and Brennan supported Warren. Douglas said that this was really like the 1958 *N.A.A.C.P.* case: [114] "there was no criminal here; they put a citizen [on the stand] and want to know with whom he associates." Frankfurter, once more leading those for affirmance, agreed that "*Nelson* is out," but asserted that "New Hampshire can be jittery about having [subversive] organizations in the state and can ask threshold questions and find out who is there and get their correspondence." Clark, Harlan, Whittaker, and Stewart agreed with Frankfurter. On June 8, 1959, Clark delivered the opinion for the five-man majority. Brennan dissented for the other four.

Frankfurter had concurred in the *Watkins* and *Sweezy* cases. But he saw *Uphaus* in terms of the need for judicial restraint in the face of legislative action, and this led him to oppose Warren's approach in deciding the case. Frankfurter explained his position in a letter to Brennan about the case:

I know that you agree that we are not a court of error and appeal and, still less, a *nisi prius* court. But we weigh differently the respect to be accorded to the determination of a State under the Fourteenth Amendment—for it is the State as a whole that you are denying the power—in exercising a judgment regarding the purposes for which a legislative investigation is conducted. When I consider the vast appropriations that the Congress of the United States votes each year to Edgar Hoover for the scrutiny of so-called 'front organizations,' when I consider that dear old wooly-headed Henry Wallace was made a cat's paw in his Progressive Party candidacy of avowed communists like Lee Pressman & Co., when I consider that Bill Douglas took it as a matter of course in one of his opinions that Congress could deny the right of naturalization to Communists as such, when I consider a lot of other things that I might enumerate, I cannot find it within what I deem my allowable scope of judicial review to conclude the Legislature of New Hampshire must first prove that an enterprise that is in effect run as an inn is a communist affiliation before it can make the inquiry now before us.

Frankfurter also added a personal disclaimer: "Need I add another word, namely, that there isn't a man on the Court who personally disapproves more than I do of the activities of all the Un-American Committees, of all the Smith Act prosecutions, of the Attorney General's list, etc., etc." [115]

The second case on legislative investigatory power was *Barenblatt v. United States.*[116] The lower court had affirmed a conviction for contempt of Congress for refusal to answer certain questions before a subcommittee of the House Committee on Un-American Activities. The questions inquired into whether Barenblatt, a college teacher, was or ever had been a Communist. He claimed that, under the *Watkins* decision, his conviction should be reversed because the House rule delineating the committee's jurisdiction was too vague and the pertinency of the questions had not been demonstrated.

At the conference after the *Barenblatt* argument on November 21, 1958, Warren had no doubt that the case was governed by *Watkins.* He said it was "unnecessary to say the resolution is void." The case could be decided on the pertinency issue. According to the Chief, "he sufficiently raised the question that there be pointed out to him the pertinency and, not having it, *Watkins* requires reversal." Warren also stated, "I don't think the resolution pertained to education."

At this conference, too, Frankfurter led the opposition. He said he thought the procedural requirements were satisfied here: "the ingredients of notice and pertinency were provided."

At the certiorari conference on April 4, 1958, the Brethren had been equally split—with Warren, Black, Douglas, and Brennan voting to grant and Frankfurter, Clark, Harlan, and Whittaker to deny. While a cert vote does not necessarily determine the vote on the merits, it often foreshadows that vote, and it did so in *Barenblatt.* So once more Stewart's vote was decisive, and once more he voted with Frankfurter. That again made a bare majority for affirmance. The decision was announced June 8, with the opinion of the Court by Harlan. Black, joined by Warren and Douglas, delivered a dissent. Brennan also dissented.

Another case where Frankfurter was able to secure a bare majority against those whom he now referred to as "The Four"[117] was *Frank v. Maryland.*[118] Frank was convicted of refusing entry to his house by a health inspector, who had evidence of rodent infestation there. The municipal code provided for forfeiture of $20 for any such refusal, and Frank was fined that amount. He claimed that, since the inspector did not have any warrant, his refusal was justified. There is no doubt that, under the Fourth and Fourteenth Amendments, the police may not normally enter a house without a warrant. Did the warrant requirement apply to administrative inspections as well as police searches?

At the *Frank* conference on March 6, 1959,[119] Warren spoke for affirmance, saying that the ordinance seemed reasonable even if the refusal was made criminal, so long as it did not "involve a jail sentence or excessive fine. If it's a question of putting in jail, I'd [feel] differently." Black stated that he did not know if they could draw a distinction based on the amount of the fine, but he would concur in the result. Frankfurter spoke strongly in support of affirmance. According to him, there was no illegal entry and the amount of the fine was important in deciding reasonableness. Other Justices stressed the long history of such inspections without warrants. Whittaker said that "the Fourteenth Amendment did not destroy history for the states" and Stewart observed, "if it was allowed in the Colonies and after, that's persuasive."

The Brethren had been closely divided on whether to take the *Frank* appeal, Warren, Black, Douglas, Brennan, and Stewart voting to note probable jurisdiction and Frankfurter, Clark, Harlan, and Whittaker to dismiss. At the March 6 conference, however, all but Douglas agreed to affirm. Frankfurter was assigned the opinion on March 9. The draft he circulated on April 7 and recirculated on April 14 was essentially the same as the final opinion that he delivered. The opinion was largely an analysis of historical materials. Clark wrote Frankfurter, "Okey. But. I still don't like . . . the emphasis on the 'long and consistent history of state practices,' etc." Frankfurter wrote back, on the bottom of the letter, "I know, I know, dear Tom. But the long history is essential, really is, for Frank—and we might as well not try to escape the truth that 'history' is sometimes controlling & sometimes not."[120]

Brennan sent around a one-paragraph concurrence on April 16 stressing that the Court was not retreating from the proposition that the "Due Process Clause of the Fourteenth Amendment enjoins upon the States the guarantees of privacy embodied in the Fourth Amendment." Since Frankfurter's "opinion demonstrates to me that enforcement of the demand made upon appellant does not amount to enforcing an unreasonable search, I concur."[121]

Later that day, Frankfurter wrote Brennan asking him to withdraw his opinion, saying that it "makes for confusion of thought." Brennan did withdraw his concurrence, but only because, on April 23, he wrote Douglas that the dissent Douglas had circulated had "persuaded me to the result you reach." The Douglas dissent was an eloquent assertion of the need to hold administrative inspections, as well as police searches, to the warrant requirement of the Fourth Amendment. When the *Frank* decision was announced, on May 4, Warren and Black, as well as Brennan, had joined the Douglas dissent. At one point, the Douglas opinion had persuaded Whittaker as well, and it looked as though it would be the opinion of a bare majority. At the conference on April 27, however, when the final vote on the case was taken, Whittaker switched again and Frankfurter delivered his opinion for a five-man Court.

Warren had sent his written agreement to Frankfurter's opinion on April 14. On April 24, however, according to a letter from Frankfurter to Harlan, "after the bell had rung for Conference, the Chief came into my room and said, 'I am sorry I am going to leave you in *Frank* and go with Bill's opinion.' "[122] Warren had voted with Frankfurter only because of the latter's emphasis at the conference that the small fine imposed was determinative. When he read Frankfurter's opinion, he saw that there was no mention of the smallness of the fine. Hence, the *Frank* holding would be applicable to cases where a harsher penalty for refusing entry to an inspector, even a jail sentence, could be imposed. Warren felt that Frankfurter had deceived him on the point and, as seen in the last chapter, accused the Justice of doing so in a conference on May 17, 1959.

The *Baltimore Sun,* commenting on the *Frank* opinion, noted that Frankfurter, in his oral delivery, "speaks of the action in this matter of 'The Maryland Supreme Court.' But there is no Maryland Supreme Court. Maryland's supreme court is the Court of Appeals."

Simon E. Sobeloff, then a judge of the U.S. Court of Appeals in Baltimore, sent Frankfurter the *Sun* statement, referring to it as "petty cavilling over the name of Maryland's highest court." Sobeloff wrote that he was reminded of Cardinal Gibbons' story about Papal infallibility, "I can tell you," Gibbons said, "that when I came to Rome to receive the red hat, His Holiness' greeting was, 'How do you do Jibbons?' " Gibbons went on, "His making me a Cardinal illustrates his infallibility in official Church action; his mispronunciation of my name shows that he was liable, in other matters, to human errors."[123]

Frankfurter's view did not, however, prevail in all the close 1958 Term cases. In *Vitarelli v. Seaton,*[124] Vitarelli had been dismissed in 1954 from his position in the Department of the Interior for security reasons. Under the relevant regulations, certain procedures had to be followed in security dismissals. They had not been in this case, but the government claimed that this had been corrected by a 1956 letter from the Secretary dismissing Vitarelli without reasons, since, in the case of such a dismissal, the regulations providing the procedural protections did not apply.

Warren started the *Vitarelli* conference on April 3, 1959, by saying, "they chose to dismiss for security reasons and did it unlawfully. Then they sought to remedy the defects in the act of 1956. I agree with petitioner that this was not intended to be new, but only a correction of the 1954 discharge." Warren concluded that Vitarelli should be reinstated.

All the Brethren agreed that the 1954 discharge was invalid because of the failure to follow the procedures prescribed by the regulations. Frankfurter, however, urged that he was validly fired "as of 1956."

The certiorari vote had been five-to-three (with Burton, Clark, and Whittaker against granting cert, and Frankfurter not voting). The vote on the merits was even closer, with a bare majority supporting Warren. The difference in result, as compared with the other cases just discussed, occurred because Harlan voted with "The Four," instead of with the Frankfurter bloc. Harlan was assigned the opinion and delivered it on June 1 along the lines indicated by Warren at the conference. Frankfurter dissented, joined by Clark, Whittaker, and Stewart, on the ground that, though the 1954 dismissal was illegal, that in 1956 was valid.

Again Frankfurter felt that the majority had gone beyond the proper role of judicial review. He wrote Harlan of the decision, "So to treat governmental action would seem to me a clear abuse of power by the judiciary in failing to respect what the Government has patently done and was entitled to do. Not even Seventeenth Century pleading turned on such empty dialectic." [125]

A week after the *Vitarelli* decision, retired Justice Minton wrote Frankfurter, "Of course you know if I were still there Harlan would have written for the minority in Vitarelli. John did a lot of wandering around Robin Hood's bar to reach his strange result." [126]

Not all the cases during the 1958 Term led to sharp divisions in the Court. Nor were Warren and Frankfurter always on opposite sides in those in which the Brethren were closely divided. *Scull v. Virginia* [127] was decided by a unanimous Court, although it involved a conviction for contempt for refusal to answer questions in a legislative investigation. Unlike the investigations in cases like *Watkins*[128] and *Barenblatt*,[129] the *Scull* investigation was not aimed at alleged subversive activities. The bill setting up the *Scull* investigating committee was part of a package passed in Virginia to resist desegregation after the *Brown* decision. It authorized the committee to investigate organizations connected with litigation relating to racial activities and whether they were violating laws prohibiting barratry, champerty, and maintenance. Scull had helped organize a group advocating orderly integration. He had refused to answer thirty-one questions relating to his group, such as whether other organizations like the N.A.A.C.P. had worked with it, and his connection with any lawsuits involving integration.

At the *Scull* conference on November 23, 1958, Warren took the broad ground that the Virginia "package of laws was designed to intimidate people." This was, he asserted, an "invasion of privacy without a showing of state interest." Most of the others agreed with the Chief on this. Even Stewart said that the session had been called by the Governor to pass laws to continue segregation and "that's an unconstitutional purpose."

Though the vote on the certiorari petition had been close (with Frankfurter, Burton, Harlan, and Whittaker voting to deny), at the November 23 conference only Clark and Whittaker spoke against reversal. It was, however, decided to confine the opinion to the narrow ground that Scull had not been informed of the questions' pertinence to the subject of inquiry. When Harlan prepared such an opinion, Clark and Whittaker agreed to join and the decision announced May 4 was unanimous.

United States v. Shirey,[130] on the contrary, was another five-to-four decision. But, in it, Warren and Frankfurter were on the same side. Shirey had been charged with unlawfully offering a Congressman to contribute $1,000 a year to the Republican Party for the Congressman's use of influence to procure Shirey a position as postmaster. The lower court dismissed the indictment.

At the conference on January 23, 1959, the Chief Justice spoke forcefully in favor of reversal. "The purpose of the statute," he said, "is to prevent people from wielding influence to get office. Here money was offered to get the postmastership and that was what Congress was trying to stop." Warren always took a strict approach in cases involving corruption. His attitude on them went back to his days as district attorney in California, where he could see the baneful effect of corrupt officials in government. Shirey had argued that, for the crime to be committed, the thing of value had to be paid to the person who was to use his influence to procure the office. At the conference, Warren dismissed the "thing of value argument [as] merely semantics."

Frankfurter strongly supported Warren's position. The conference vote was six-to-three for reversal. The Chief assigned the opinion to Harlan. In working on the opinion, Harlan concluded that the vote for reversal had been erroneous. On February 17, he circulated a memorandum "setting forth my reasons for now believing that the case should be affirmed."[131] Douglas also switched his vote after receiving this memo. There were now five for affirmance, and Harlan drafted an opinion of the Court so holding. On February 18, Frankfurter sent around a "Dear Brethren" letter stating that he would write a dissent.[132] Before the decision was announced on April 20, Douglas again changed his vote. Frankfurter's opinion was issued as the opinion of the Court and Harlan's as a dissent.

Frankfurter had written Brennan that government counsel in *Shirey* "is a very nice man, but I thought the Government's brief in this case and his argument were just lousy."[133] He had gone further and stated in his draft opinion that the government made "an inept or incompetent argument" and failed "to make an appropriate argument."[134] Brennan wrote back "that my personal regard for the fine young man who argued the case . . . underlies my feeling that the comments are neither necessary nor justified."[135] Frankfurter did delete the passage, though he told Brennan, "I cannot agree that it is not justified."[136]

In other 1958 Term criminal cases, Warren followed his now-usual approach of vindicating defendant's rights. *Spano v. New York*[137] arose out of a murder conviction based upon a confession made after eight hours of intensive police interrogation. Spano had surrendered voluntarily to the District Attorney, where his attorney had left him in police custody after cautioning him to answer no questions. At the conference May 1, 1959,[138] the Chief urged reversal. "When one surrenders to the D.A.," he said, "with instructions not to talk and they know he has such from a lawyer, they can't query him for hours until they get a confession. In the totality of this picture, due process was denied."

Though, here too, the Court had been divided on the certiorari petition (with Warren, Black, Douglas, and Brennan voting to grant and Clark, Harlan, Whittaker, and Stewart to deny—with Frankfurter out sick), at the conference on the merits the vote to reverse was unanimous. Warren delivered the decision July 22. The opinion was untypically eloquent and led Clark to write the Chief, on joining, "You've got even hard-hearted me to crying." [139]

Another criminal case in which Warren led the Court to a decision reversing a conviction was *Smith v. United States*. [140] The Fifth Amendment requires capital cases to be prosecuted by indictment. A federal law made kidnapping a capital offense except where the victim was liberated unharmed. Smith was prosecuted by information, rather than indictment, for kidnapping. Though the victim was not harmed, the information did not allege that fact. At the January 23, 1959, conference Warren declared that, "as pleaded in this information, the kidnapping is a capital offense. Therefore, he must be indicted. There's more to it than whether he can be executed. An indictment gives other protections. If they want less than a capital charge, they should allege the man was released unhurt." Referring to the court of appeals cases on the matter, the Chief said, "the consensus is that, if an information is used, it must allege that the victim was released unharmed."

At the conference, doubts were expressed by Clark, Harlan, Whittaker, and Stewart, but they said they would not dissent if the case went the way Warren recommended. When the opinion reversing the conviction was announced by Warren on June 8, however, Clark, joined by Harlan and Stewart, did dissent.

Warren also persuaded the Court to reverse a conviction—this time by a court-martial—in *Lee v. Madigan*. [141] Lee, while serving with the Army, was convicted by a court-martial in California of conspiracy to commit murder. The offense occurred in 1949. The Articles of War provided that no person should be tried by court-martial for murder committed within the United States in time of peace. Was 1949, when the crime was committed, "in time of peace?" The government relied on the fact that the war with Germany was not officially terminated by congressional resolution and presidential proclamation until 1951, and the war with Japan not until 1952, the effective date of the Japanese Peace Treaty.

Warren urged reversal at the December 12, 1958, conference. "Is this 'in time of peace'?" he asked. "The crime was 1949. I think we should construe the words favorably to civil trials when we're not actually at war. More than an armistice existed then." The government's statutory construction, the Chief concluded, was "wholly untenable."

Black, Douglas, Brennan, and Stewart supported Warren. Clark, Harlan, and Whittaker voted the other way urging that legally, as Clark put it, "we're still at war." Frankfurter did not participate. When the decision was announced on January 12, 1959, six joined the majority for reversal, with only Clark and Harlan in dissent. The opinion was by Douglas. Once again Warren had not taken the opportunity to speak in a case limiting military jurisdiction, although it was one of the subjects about which he felt strongly.

Warren would normally follow his approach of construing criminal statutes strictly in favor of defendants even where the majority would not go along. *Brown v. United States* [142] arose out of a summary conviction for contempt. Rule 42(b) of the Federal Rules of Criminal Procedure provides for prosecution of criminal contempts on notice, with reasonable time for preparing a defense, and other procedural protections. Rule 42(a) provides for summary punishment of contempts committed in the presence of the court. Brown had refused to answer questions before a grand jury. He persisted even though a federal judge accorded him immunity against prosecution. He was then brought to the courtroom and refused to answer the same questions put by the judge. He was held in criminal contempt and sentenced to fifteen months' imprisonment.

Warren's view at the October 17, 1958, conference [143] was that the government was seeking to get around the procedural protections of Rule 42(b) by transforming a contempt committed before the grand jury into one committed in the presence of the court. "The Government," the Chief declared, "is cutting corners and ought to be held rigidly to proper procedures. The contempt was complete in the grand jury room. They can't parlay 42(b) procedures into a 42(a) [case]."

Only Black, Douglas, and Brennan supported Warren's view. Stewart delivered the opinion of the Court affirming on March 9,

1959. Warren felt strongly enough about the government's "cutting corners" to write a dissent expanding on his conference statement, even though it meant a fragmented Court, with the Chief Justice speaking for a four-man minority.

Other 1958 Term cases illustrate the Chief Justice's concern with fairness and protection of those unorganized in corporations, unions, and the like. In *Atlantic Refining Co. v. Public Service Commission,*[144] the Federal Power Commission had tried to condition a license to sell natural gas upon a fixed maximum price. After the company threatened that, unless the license was issued without conditions, it would not sell its gas interstate, the Commission issued an unconditional license. The lower court had vacated the FPC order. At the May 22, 1959, conference,[145] Warren said, "If we don't affirm, there's no way to protect the interest of consumers, which was the primary purpose of the statute." The Brethren all agreed, and a unanimous decision affirming was issued June 22.

Northwestern States Portland Cement Co. v. Minnesota[146] involved the validity of a Minnesota tax on the income from sales of cement in the state of an Iowa corporation that manufactured the cement at its Iowa plant. There are few subjects in constitutional law more technically complicated than that of state taxation of interstate commerce. To Warren, however, the question was essentially one of fairness. As he stated at the October 17, 1958, conference,[147] "a fair tax on commerce derived from state activity is not prohibited by the Commerce Clause when it is a net income tax also payable by intrastate business. We don't have an overlap here with the home state." A majority agreed and, on February 24, 1959, the Court announced its decision upholding the tax, with Whittaker, Frankfurter, and Stewart dissenting.

In another case involving the states and interstate commerce—*Bibb v. Navajo Freight Lines*[148]—Warren indicated that he would defer to the legislative judgment on an Illinois law requiring all trucks, including interstate vehicles, to have certain types of rear fender mudguards. "It's difficult," the Chief said at the April 3, 1959, conference, "to second-guess legislatures and it might be best to let it stand." Interestingly, there was a reversal of roles here, and Frankfurter urged a broader reviewing role. "Even if it is a safety measure," he stated, "when a burden on interstate commerce is alleged, I think we can go behind it. With every presumption in its favor, does this outweigh the demonstrated interference with every truck coming into Illinois from other states?" Though the conference discussion had inclined toward the view that the state law was, as Douglas put it, not "without a rational basis," Frankfurter ultimately persuaded Warren and the others that the Court should strike it down as imposing an undue burden on interstate commerce. On May 25, 1959, Douglas announced a unanimous decision invalidating the Illinois statute.

In 1958 Warren confided to a reporter that he came occasionally to the old Supreme Court chamber in the Capitol, where Court sessions had been held before the Brethren moved into their Marble Palace in 1936. He used to commune silently with his predecessors, the Chief Justice said. Warren recalled the first time he came to the Supreme Court. That was on January 3, 1932, when District Attorney Warren argued his first case before the Court in defense of Alameda County in a case brought against it by the Central Pacific Railway.[149] The argument happened to be the last heard by Justice Oliver Wendell Holmes. After it, Holmes casually announced, "I won't be here tomorrow" and he left the Court for good. Warren said his friends accused him of driving Holmes from the bench. They used to tease him, "one look at you and he said, 'I quit.' "[150]

9.

1959—1960 TERMS:
THE SHIFTING BALANCE

The Chief Justice was livid at the crowded cocktail party. "You are a liar!" he roared at Earl Mazo, who had just written a favorable biography of Richard M. Nixon.[1] Warren charged that the book was a "dishonest account" written in order to promote Nixon's presidential candidacy. For over twenty minutes, Warren lashed out at the writer, becoming so intense at times that bystanders feared that he might resort to physical violence.[2]

Earl Warren may have projected a kindly, smiling public picture, whose outstanding characteristic was its blandness. The outer image was, however, deceiving. The Justices who served with him all reject the blandness notion. "He was rock-hard, . . ." says Justice Byron White. "He was very firm, very firm." According to another Justice, "he was a person who had deep-seated and permanent resentments of people and dislikes of people and stubbornly so." He normally could keep his feelings under control—"it was hard to rile him," White recalls. But the Chief Justice was quick to take umbrage when he was dealt with in ways that he considered unfair or reflected on the dignity of the Court or his office. His temper would then show, as in the incidents described in chapter 7. Certainly, they bear out Frankfurter's assertion that "Warren is thin-skinned."

Yet, even Warren's feelings toward Frankfurter, the extreme Court critics, or the American Bar Association were mild compared to his repugnance toward Richard Nixon. "There's no question," affirms a Warren law clerk, "that the one person whom I think above all else the Chief held in absolute contempt was Richard Nixon." Everyone who knew Warren agrees on this. Warren's antipathy was undoubtedly triggered by what he felt was Nixon's treachery at the 1952 Republican Convention. But he also began to perceive Nixon's character earlier than did most people. Years before Watergate, Warren felt that Nixon had fatal moral flaws. Nixon, Warren used to say, "is interested in only two things—money and power."

Even with regard to Nixon, however, Warren was usually able to check his emotions in public. The one great exception, to which we have just referred, occurred in July 1959 at a cocktail party celebrating the twenty-fifth wedding anniversary of Barnet Nover, Washington correspondent for the *Denver Post.* It was there that Warren had his encounter with Earl Mazo. The affair drew a top-level crowd—Senators, Congressmen, high officials, and four of the Brethren, including the Chief Justice. Near the bar, Warren saw a reporter he knew, Clark R. Mollenhoff of the *Des Moines Register,* and stopped to exchange greetings. Mollenhoff saw Mazo standing nearby and, as he describes it, "was innocently, or naively, in the process of making what I believed was a routine introduction of Chief Justice Warren to Earl Mazo."

"I was surprised and even a little stunned," says Mollenhoff, "at the fury of Warren's speedy and aggressive reaction."[3] The Chief Justice launched into a tirade against the Nixon biographer. "You are a damned liar!" Warren exploded. "It's a dishonest account to promote the Presidential candidacy of Nixon. . . . I don't care what you write about Nixon as long as you don't try to build him up over my body." As he ended his harangue, Warren held up clenched fists, with wrists together as though he was handcuffed. "You people are persecuting me because you know I can't strike back."[4]

In his posthumously published memoirs, Warren referred to the story "I had called Mr. Mazo a damned liar. This . . . was not true. . . . I was taught better manners than that."[5] But Clark Mollenhoff, whose article about the incident received wide circulation at the time, affirms that the episode happened as published,[6] and one of Warren's law clerks confirms the Mollenhoff account. Warren told him further that Mazo's book "is nothing but a whitewash of Nixon," and, when "he came up to me and asked me if I'd read the book, I got very irritated at him." Warren also "said there were a lot of things I would have liked to have told the son of a bitch, but I didn't think I could do it."

Compared with his antipathy toward Nixon, Warren's feelings toward others with whom he had differences were relatively mild. In the Court, he may have disliked Frankfurter, but there was nothing of the almost tangible aversion he felt for the then-Vice-President. Frankfurter now had three terms left, before he retired in August 1962. During them, the Court was sharply split between the Warren and Frankfurter approaches. In an article in July 1959, Anthony Lewis described the "growing" conflict between what he called the two "polar positions." According to Lewis, "the deep feelings on each side led to sharp intellectual dispute, to mutual suspicion, occasionally to overstatement by majority and dissenters."[7]

In the meantime, the business of the Court, like that of the country, was growing. "Certs," wrote Harlan to Warren, "are pouring in by the bucketful."[8] Lewis noted that the number of cases on the docket (2,062) set a record. The biggest increase was in the *in forma pauperis* petitions—the typewritten and handwritten petitions filed by indigent prisoners (from 891 to 1,006).[9] The Brethren differed over their ability to handle the caseload. Stewart, at a *Yale Law Journal* dinner, said that the work load had become too heavy to permit "ideal" reflective deliberation. Douglas, in a talk at Cornell Law School, asserted that it was a "myth" that the Court was overworked.[10]

During the 1959 Term, with the Court divided between Warren, Black, Douglas, and Brennan, on the one side, and Frankfurter, Clark, Harlan, and Whittaker, on the other, Stewart's remained the key vote. During his second term the new Justice was becoming something of a "swing man." After Stewart had given the Warren wing the victory in *Elkins v. United States*[11] and he wrote the opinion of the Court, Frankfurter, who delivered a strong dissent, sent Judge Learned Hand the opinion, "in the hope that you will lift some of the darkness with which this latest performance of Stewart leaves me."[12]

Despite his *Elkins* vote, Stewart remained closer to the Frankfurter than to the Warren conception of the Court's function. As Judge Hand put it, in expressing satisfaction with the new Justice, "He really does not believe himself vested with authority to direct the fate of 200,000,000 people through the 1st, 5th, and 14th Amendments."[13] Yet that did not mean that Stewart would not vote with the Warren wing when he felt that the individual case justified the decision favored by them. One should recall his answer to the question of whether he was a "liberal" like Black or a "conservative" like Frankfurter: "I am a lawyer."[14] Stewart approached cases on their individual facts and issues, without trying to fit them into the gestalt of a consistent philosophy.

In important cases during the 1959 Term, where his action was crucial, Stewart tilted the decision toward the Frankfurter wing. The most significant was *Abel v. United States.*[15] At issue was the conviction for espionage of the notorious Russian spy, Colonel Rudolf Ivanovich Abel. The F.B.I. had evidence that Abel was a spy, but, instead of arresting him, they had notified the Immigration and Naturalization Service that he was an alien illegally in the country. The head of the I.N.S. New York office issued an arrest warrant. F.B.I. agents went with I.N.S. agents to Abel's hotel. The F.B.I. men entered his room and interrogated him to see if he would "cooperate." When they were unable to get him to "cooperate" regarding his espionage, they signaled the I.N.S. agents (who had waited outside) to come in and arrest Abel. After the arrest, a search was made of the room and incriminating evidence found which was introduced in Abel's espionage trial.

Abel claimed in the Supreme Court that the administrative warrant by which he was arrested was invalid, since it did not satisfy the requirements for "warrants" under the Fourth Amendment. Hence, the evidence seized in the search incident to his arrest was inadmissible. The difficulty was that his counsel had not raised the constitutional claim in the lower courts. In addition, Abel claimed that the F.B.I. had used the arrest power of the I.N.S. to circumvent the more stringent requirements of the Fourth Amendment—that the administrative warrant had been a sham used for the sole purpose of gathering evidence in a criminal case.

Six of the Brethren had voted to grant certiorari in *Abel*—with Clark, Whittaker, and the Chief Justice for denial. Despite his vote against cert, Warren took the strongest stand of any of the Brethren against the administrative arrest at the *Abel* conference on November 13, 1959. He asserted that the "administrative warrant does not give any of the protections of a criminal warrant." In his opinion, the I.N.S. warrant was unconstitutional. The Chief was supported only by Black.

Warren also stated that he accepted the findings that there was no subterfuge. The F.B.I., in his view, had probable cause to arrest for espionage or failure to report to the Attorney General, as was required for aliens. He said that he would "permit a search of his person and effects for weapons," but would not allow use of the evidence for a criminal case.

The Justices were closely divided at the conference. Black, Douglas, and Brennan, like Warren, were inclined toward reversal. The others felt that, in Clark's words, "if we accept the finding that the arrest was in good faith," the arrest and search were legal.

At a second conference on the case, Warren said he now thought that "the administrative warrant point was waived below." This explains why he did not persist in his assertion at the November 13 conference that the administrative arrest was unconstitutional. The others agreed that, as Harlan put it on the warrant's validity, "it's out of the case." Harlan and Stewart stated, however, that they thought the provision for an administrative warrant was constitutional.

On the other issues in the case, Warren said, "I still think you can't rely on it [the administrative warrant] to make a general search of a man's home and effects for evidence of a crime. They had probable cause to arrest for espionage, but that wasn't what was attempted. If it had been, I'd have no trouble with the case."

Frankfurter, leading the case for affirmance, rejected the claim that the I.N.S. action "was a sham." This was not a case "where abdication of the I.N.S. to the F.B.I. was proved." As Clark said, in supporting Frankfurter, "For me it is clear that the I.N.S. was fully empowered to do what they did after checking their own records and finding nothing of an Abel." If that was true, the evidence was validly seized. The Frankfurter bloc's view was succinctly stated by Whittaker: "The reasons which allow the use of stuff found incidental to a criminal arrest should also apply to a search incidental to the use of an administrative arrest."

On March 28, 1960, Frankfurter delivered the opinion of the Court in *Abel* for a bare majority. His opinion (drafted by one of his clerks on the basis of an outline prepared by the Justice) was essentially an elaboration of the views expressed in conference by those voting for affirmance. Douglas, joined by Black, and Brennan, joined by War-ren, Black, and Douglas, wrote strong dissents.

Another case during the 1959 Term where Stewart's deciding vote was in favor of the Frankfurter position was *Parker v. Ellis*.[16] Parker had been convicted of forging a check in Texas, after what Warren, in his dissent in the case, called a "sham" trial conducted "in flagrant disregard of his constitutional right to assistance of counsel." He sought habeas corpus in a federal court. The lower courts denied the writ. Certiorari was granted, but, before the Supreme Court could hear the case, Parker was released from prison. The state claimed that this made the case moot and that the Court was now without juris-diction to deal with his claim.

The case presented a good illustration of the difference between the Frankfurter and Warren approaches to technical issues. Strictly speaking, habeas corpus is available only to secure release from cus-tody. When custody has ended, the basis for habeas corpus jurisdic-tion has ended. To Warren, such a technical approach improperly exalted form over substance. At the *Parker v. Ellis* conference on Jan-uary 22, 1960, the Chief started by expressing indignation at the un-fairness of Parker's trial. "The trial," he charged, "was manifestly un-fair. Throughout there was a taking advantage of accused's lack of experience and ineptitude." Warren asserted that, "even under *Betts v. Brady*[17] [the 1942 case holding that, in a non-capital state case, lack of counsel does not violate due process unless, in the circumstances of the case, it prevents the accused from having a "fair trial."] it's reviewable." On the main issue, the Chief declared, "the case is not moot since the man suffers disabilities and he has no way of getting relief." Though Parker was out of jail, he still had the conviction on his record and the various disabilities, such as voting disqualification, that it entailed.

Frankfurter took the view that "this is an inescapably moot case. This is a jurisdictional question—mootness is a matter of power." The others divided as they had in *Abel*—except for Brennan, who voted with Frankfurter, saying "the case is moot, not because he hasn't suffered disabilities, but because he's no longer in custody."

On April 21, however, Brennan wrote Frankfurter that he had de-cided to change his vote and join the dissent Warren had drafted. Frankfurter replied the same day, "I laid a wager with myself that you would join the dissent in *Parker v. Ellis,* so your note does not surprise me."[18] The final vote was thus five to four in favor of Frankfurter's position, with Stewart again casting the deciding vote. The decision was announced in a per curiam May 16, 1960. Warren wrote a sharp dissent for himself, Black, Douglas, and Brennan.

Stewart's vote was also determinative in *Flemming v. Nestor,*[19] where a bare majority again voted for Frankfurter's approach. Nestor was an alien who had been deported for having been a member of the Communist Party. His social security old-age payments were then terminated under a federal statute providing that no payments should be made to any person so deported. The lower court held the statute unconstitutional as a deprivation without due process of an accrued property right.

At the February 26, 1960, conference,[20] Warren stated that Nestor had a constitutionally protected interest. He "had paid [social security taxes] twenty-three years and had 'rights' in the benefits which matured before his deportation. These were forfeited, not to further the objectives of the program, but because he committed a deportable offense. This is not a regulation, but punishment. It's a bill of attainder," i.e., a legislative infliction of punishment without any judicial trial. Black, Douglas, and Brennan supported Warren, with Black asserting that this was a "bill of attainder in its classical sense." Once again Frankfurter led the other side and, with Stewart voting with Clark, Harlan, and Whittaker, obtained the majority.

On June 20, Harlan delivered the opinion for the five voting to uphold the statute. It followed the Frankfurter restraint doctrine, saying that Congress had a rational basis for enacting the provision and the Court could not inquire into congressional motives to determine whether there was a punitive intent behind the law. Black, Douglas, and Brennan, joined by Warren and Douglas, wrote dissents contending that the law did impose punishment and was consequently a prohibited bill of attainder.

A fourth case during the 1959 Term where Stewart's action—this time by disqualifying himself—was decisive in making the Frankfurter view prevail was *Eaton v. Price.*[21] Taylor had refused to allow housing inspectors to enter his house in Dayton, Ohio, unless they had a search warrant. He was prosecuted under a law making it a crime, punishable by a fine of $200 and imprisonment for thirty days, to refuse to admit inspectors. Since he was not able to make bond of $1,000, he was committed to jail to await trial. His lawyer, Eaton, sought habeas corpus against Price, the Dayton Chief of Police. The Ohio Supreme Court affirmed a denial of the writ.

On June 8, 1959, the Court, in a per curiam memorandum opinion, noted probable jurisdiction and set the case for argument the next term.[22] Brennan issued a short opinion explaining that, since four had voted to note probable jurisdiction of the appeal from the Ohio court, the case would be heard and decided. Brennan pointed out that the practice was the same as on certiorari petitions—i.e., the case would be taken if four voted in favor. Frankfurter, joined by Clark, Harlan, and Whittaker, also issued a short opinion asserting that the case was "controlled by, and should be affirmed on the authority of, *Frank v. Maryland*,"[23] decided only a month earlier.[24] Clark explained in a separate opinion how the validity of the administrative inspection at issue in *Eaton* had been settled by the *Frank* decision.

Douglas, who had dissented in *Frank*, had prepared a dissent to be used if, as Frankfurter, Clark, Harlan, and Whittaker had vigorously urged in conference on May 15, 1959, the Court had decided summarily to affirm on the authority of *Frank*. The Douglas draft asserted that the Court's action "justifies the worst fears of those who believe that the *Frank* case sanctioned a grave and serious dilution in the privacy of every homeowner." Some may have thought, the draft dissent went on, that the *Frank* decision was restricted "to a modest fine." Douglas declared, "That distinction now proves illusory. The holding today means that the citizen who insists on a search warrant as a condition of the health inspector's admission to his home can now go to jail."[25]

Douglas did not have to issue his dissent, since Stewart disqualified himself because his father had been on the Ohio Supreme Court which had denied habeas corpus. This meant a four-to-four division on whether to affirm summarily.

After the *Eaton* case was argued, the Brethren met in conference on April 22, 1960, to decide the merits. The opposing views were presented by the Chief Justice and Frankfurter. Warren said, "This case is not *Frank*, where the ordinance required: 1) that the officers have cause to believe [i.e., that there was a violation on the premises], which is not so as to the Ohio ordinance; and 2) only a $20 fine there and here a $200 fine, or thirty days in jail or both."

Frankfurter disagreed. The case, he urged, "is controlled by *Frank* and the differences are not constitutional differences. The problem, as I see it, is in the context of the big cities. I shudder at the thought of what we'd impose on millions of people if we provide that inspections were not permitted without a showing of probable cause."

With Stewart not voting, the others voted as they had in *Frank* and at the May 15, 1959, conference. That meant a four-to-four division that, in turn, meant a per curiam announcing that the judgment was "affirmed by an equally divided Court."[26] The announcement was made on June 27, 1960, the last day of the 1959 Term. The uniform practice when the Court is equally divided is simply to announce the judgment of affirmance without any opinions. This time, however, Brennan issued a thirteen-page dissent, joined by the Chief Justice, Black, and Douglas, explaining why they voted for reversal.

Brennan published his opinion despite two June 22 letters from Frankfurter attempting to dissuade him. "One can be, I believe," Frankfurter asserted, "dogmatic in saying that the settled practice of the Court of withholding any expression on the merits by a member of the Court, when there is an affirmance by necessity—when the Court is evenly divided as to result—has never been departed from. . . . I am clear . . . that there is not a case in the books in which a division on an entire case led to expounding any view on either side."[27]

The four dissenters broke the uniform practice and issued their opinion because they felt that *Eaton* showed how dangerous *Frank* was as a precedent. Warren, in particular, believed that Frankfurter had deceived him by stressing, at the original *Frank* conference, that only a small fine was involved in *Frank,* and then not mentioning that point at all in his *Frank* opinion. We saw in chapter 7 how Warren had accused Frankfurter of such deception at the May 15, 1959, conference that decided to hear the *Eaton* case. His personal irritation on the matter, together with his belief that *Frank* had been wrongly decided, led the Chief to acquiesce in the unprecedented *Eaton* dissent.

Stewart's vote gave Warren and his supporters the bare majority in one of the most important cases decided during the term—*Elkins v. United States.*[28] Elkins had been convicted in a federal court of wiretapping. The evidence against him consisted of recordings seized in his home by state police officers acting without a warrant. The lower courts refused to suppress the evidence, relying on the so-called "silver platter doctrine." That doctrine, followed since the 1914 *Weeks* case,[29] allowed federal judicial use of evidence seized in violation of the Constitution by state officers.

All the Brethren voted to grant certiorari in *Elkins*. At the conference on the merits in April 1960, the Chief Justice began by stating categorically, "I would abolish the silver platter case. We don't have to reach the Constitution or the *Wolf* case," i.e., the 1949 decision holding that a state conviction does not violate due process because illegally seized evidence was introduced at the trial.[30] Instead, said Warren, "We can *McNabb* this. Our supervisory power to fashion rules of the game is enough." The Chief was referring to the 1943 *McNabb* case,[31] under which the Supreme Court can use its supervisory power over the federal courts to ensure proper standards of procedure and evidence, though not required by the Constitution.

Warren went on to say that he "wouldn't let the state standard of illegality govern, however. I would apply the federal standard of legality and apply it without regard to whether the state has an exclusionary rule. Then, too, the Government here proceeded on the assumption of an illegal search."

Black, Douglas, and Brennan were with the Chief for reversal. Frankfurter, Clark, Harlan, and Whittaker were against changing the "silver platter" rule. This time, however, Stewart was for reversal. For him, the crucial factor was that "this is a federal crime," and the federal standard should prevail.

Warren assigned the opinion to Stewart. His opinion of the Court, announced June 27, 1960, followed the approach outlined by Warren at the conference, overruling the "silver platter" doctrine, but doing so under the Court's supervisory power over the federal courts, rather than as a constitutional requirement. Stewart's draft opinion had touched on the question of whether the *Weeks* rule was demanded by the Fourth Amendment. On May 23, Brennan wrote Stewart that his treatment might be read "as a square dictum that Congress could change the exclusionary rule as to federal seizures under the Fourth Amendment." This, he said, was the view indicated by "Hugo and Tom, at least." Stewart replied in a May 31 note that a new draft "eliminates all discussion of what the Constitution might or might not require in this general area."

Before the *Elkins* opinion was issued, Frankfurter prepared a *Memorandum to the Majority in the Silver Platter Cases* in the names of the four minority Justices. It disclaimed any intention of "inviting a reversal of the vote as such. We merely seek to raise the appropriateness of reaching the merits of the evidentiary issue on which decision turns in the way in which it is proposed to reach it, namely, by reversing out of hand a course of adjudications in this Court that began with a unanimous decision more than forty-six years ago." The memo urged that "the fashioning of such a new rule in light of the judicial history of the old rule [is] peculiarly a fit subject for consideration by the highly experienced, well-balanced Committee on Criminal Rules which the Chief Justice" had just appointed.[32]

When the majority declined to change its decision, Frankfurter issued an unusually vigorous dissent for the minority Justices. A draft, in the handwriting of one of Frankfurter's law clerks, indicates that the dissent was almost entirely the clerk's work.[33]

Two days after the *Elkins* decision was announced, Judge Henry J. Friendly wrote Frankfurter that, "Having just read Elkins. . . . I can now better understand some of the reservations you expressed about your latest colleague. A more conceptualistic approach I have never seen."[34] Frankfurter himself circulated *A Dialogue*, patterned on the sixteenth-century legal classic, *Doctor and Student*,[35] in which he said, "I am much more puzzled by the opinion . . . than I was disappointed by the result."

"Why then," *Student* asked, "do you boggle over the *Elkins* case?" Frankfurter as *Doctor* replied, "just as in most instances a case is an offspring, so it may also become an ancestor. . . . It projects itself into the future."[36] This proved true with regard to *Elkins*. The decision there foreshadowed the decision a year later in *Mapp v. Ohio*[37]—one of the Warren Court's seminal decisions.

Stewart also joined the Warren wing of the Court in *Talley v. California*,[38] but his vote there was not decisive, since Harlan ultimately also voted with the Chief, making the final decision six-to-three. Talley had been convicted of violating a Los Angeles ordinance that prohibited distribution of handbills which did not contain the names and addresses of the persons who prepared, distributed, or sponsored them. The Brethren were sharply divided at the certiorari conference on June 29, 1959, with Warren, Black, Douglas, and Brennan voting to grant cert and the rest to deny.

At the conference on the merits on January 15, 1960,[39] the Chief Justice led the case for reversal and Frankfurter for affirmance. To Warren, "This is a shotgun attack on pamphlets. There's no showing of necessity for such a broad ordinance." To Frankfurter, on the other hand, "We're trying too hard to make the states justify what they've done." Frankfurter noted that forty states had legislation on political advocacy. As he saw it, "that cuts into free expression more deeply than this. If that cutting is all right, I can't believe this is not."

Though he had voted to deny cert, Stewart voted with Warren, Black, Douglas, and Brennan to make a bare majority for reversal. Frankfurter distributed a memorandum advising that he would write a dissent. He could not, he wrote, "agree to an opinion which does not differentiate the invalidation of this legislation against anonymity from the great body of enactments requiring disclosure in a field that so deeply touches the protection of free discussion of public matters as against 'the fear of reprisal' etc. in the exercise of the voting franchise in political elections."[40]

When Clark wrote back that he would prepare a dissent,[41] Frankfurter decided not to go ahead with his own, despite a memorandum from his law clerk that "Clark's opinion seems to contain an awful lot of question begging, and to do quite poorly what it does."[42] On January 18, Harlan circulated a "Dear Brethren" letter letting the conference know that he had switched his vote. When Black announced the decision of the Court for reversal on March 7, 1960, it was joined by five other Justices.

Another change in the voting pattern gave the Warren bloc the decision in the 1960 Court-Martial Cases.[43] In *Reid v. Covert*[44]—the 1957 Case of the Murdering Wives discussed in chapter 6—the Court had held that wives accompanying servicemen overseas might not be tried for murder by court-martial. The 1960 cases began where *Reid v. Covert* left off. They involved the validity of court-martial convictions of the wife of a soldier stationed in Germany for manslaughter, a noncapital offense, of a civilian employee of the Army in France for murder, and of a similar employee in Morocco for larceny, a noncapital offense—i.e., the cases not covered directly by *Reid v. Covert*. The Brethren all voted to grant certiorari in the three cases.

Surprisingly, in view of his strong stand against military jurisdiction in *Reid v. Covert,* Warren compromised in his presentation at the October 23, 1959, conference[45] on the merits of the convictions. He stated the view that wives were not subject to court-martial, but that civilians presented a different case. "I think," Warren said, "the nature of the work civilians do may have a bearing on whether they are in the military forces. I think a builder of communications lines is doing more important work than the ordinary G.I. On the other hand, an auditor overseas is not doing anything not done in the Pentagon."

This time it was Black who led the case against military jurisdiction. Black said he was against the government in all the cases. These civilians, he urged, were not in the armed forces and could not be subjected to courts-martial. "Nor can I distinguish based on whether it's a capital or noncapital offense."

Frankfurter, on the other side, began with the bromidic caution: "Anything that brings an Act of Congress in jeopardy is terribly important. Here we sit in judgment on Congress." Frankfurter persisted in the distinction he had drawn in his *Reid v. Covert* concurrence. "The Necessary and Proper Clause," he stated, "applies to justify trial of noncapital cases by court-martial, but not capital cases." Stewart and Whittaker expressed another view. They agreed with Black that there was no valid distinction between capital and noncapital offenses. But they thought the case of the employee was different from that of the dependent. In their view, Congress had power to subject civilian employees abroad to courts-martial, but not civilian dependents.

As explained by Clark, in a memorandum, the conference voted that, under § 2(11) of the Uniform Code of Military Justice:

"First, that there shall be no prosecution of dependents thereunder.

"Second, that there shall be no prosecution of any capital offenses under it.

"Third, that employees of the armed services may be prosecuted in non-capital cases; and

"Fourth, that decision on the remainder is withheld."

Clark asserted that, "as I see it today, the 'speed limit' doctrine that first clipped Article 211 in *Reid v. Covert,* has now crashed into it and in the resulting wreck one category (dependents) of the Section is found dead, another (employees) mutilated beyond recognition, and the remainder (contractors and their employees) knocked up into the air." Clark concluded, "I am constrained to say that such a theory is not in keeping with the principles of sound constitutional interpretation, as I understand it. This leads me to apply the principles of *Reid v. Covert* to all prosecutions under Article 2(11)."[46]

Ultimately Warren, Douglas, Brennan, and Black agreed with Clark. That made a bare majority for invalidating court-martial jurisdiction in all three cases. Clark delivered the opinion of the Court on January 18, 1960, though he acknowledged in a written note to Black, "the gist of the holding is all yours, developed at Bethesda Naval Hosp. that night—For this I am grateful to you."[47] Frankfurter, joined by Harlan, and Whittaker, joined by Stewart, wrote dissents along the lines they expressed at the conference. Frankfurter had previously indicated his view of Clark's opinion in a note to Harlan: "I have now read the *Kinsella* and to me it is just rubbish. If this becomes the opinion of the Court, everything that Henry Hart says about the growing professional disrespect for the Court's work—its quality and its results—will be more than justified."[48]

The sharp split in the cases discussed reflected the polar division between the Warren and Frankfurter wings of the Court, as well as the personal differences between their leaders. "Frequently," as Anthony Lewis described it in a *New York Times* article, "their deep philosophical differences come to the surface and there may be bristling exchanges"[49] such as those between Frankfurter and Warren described at the beginning of chapter 7. The depth of feeling, wrote Lewis, was sometimes made clear even in the reading of opinions. Lewis referred to one decision day in 1959 when Frankfurter and Black, "elaborating on the written opinions in their oral statements, exchanged acid comments on each other's words. The audience felt the emotions involved."[50]

In April 1960, Frankfurter wrote Stewart, who delivered the majority opinion in *Wolfe v. North Carolina*,[51] of the "billingsgate"[52] in Chief Justice Warren's dissent in the case. And it was during the 1959 Term that one of Frankfurter's law clerks wrote him, in a comment about a Black opinion, "With regard to anything bad you've ever said to me about Black, you win, that is really the end."[53]

Even in so fragmented a Court, however, not every decision was reached by a closely divided vote. In a number of cases, the Chief Justice was able to lead the Brethren to adopt his view by a substantial majority. This was particularly true in cases with racial implications. In *Bates v. Little Rock*,[54] the Court had before it an ordinance requiring organizations in the city to pay license taxes, though exempting charitable organizations, and requiring all organizations to submit membership lists. Little Rock had secured a conviction against the local branch of the National Association for the Advancement of Colored People for its refusal to submit the list of its members. At the conference on November 20, 1959,[55] Warren said that the case "presents four questions: 1) does this encroach on liberties? Yes; 2) Is it a legitimate ordinance? It is; 3) Is it enough to allow the encroachment? Sometimes; 4) But is it necessary here? I can't believe it was. I don't think the names are essential to accomplishing the purpose of the ordinance." And in accordance with Warren's view, the Brethren unanimously struck down the ordinance in a decision announced February 23, 1960.

A unanimous decision was likewise handed down in *Thompson v. Louisville*,[56] which the Brethren referred to among themselves as the "Case of Shuffling Sam." Sam Thompson had been convicted of disorderly conduct and fined $20. He had been in a cafe shuffling his feet in time to the music for half an hour when he was arrested. Warren had no doubt about the case at the conference on January 15, 1960.[57] As he saw it, "There's not a shred of evidence of the violation of the ordinance and a conviction without evidence is a violation of due process. There's not a shred of relevant legal evidence." On March 21, Black delivered an opinion for all the Justices reversing Thompson's conviction because there was no evidence in the record to support it.

Warren was also able to secure a large majority for his view in *Smith v. California*.[58] Smith owned a bookstore in Los Angeles. He was convicted of violating an ordinance making it unlawful for any bookseller to have an obscene book in his possession. As interpreted by the California courts, the offense consisted solely of the possession of the book, without any requirement of scienter—i.e., knowledge of the obscene character of the book. At the December 18, 1959, conference,[59] Warren conceded that the book in question was probably obscene. "But," he said, "the ordinance is bad for failure to require the element of scienter." All agreed that the ordinance was bad, except Harlan. On December 14, 1959, Brennan issued an opinion of the Court reversing, as Warren had urged, on the scienter ground. Harlan announced a dissent.

At the conference, Black and Douglas had urged that the scienter ground was too narrow. Black said, "If I thought books could be censored, I'd think this case hard to distinguish from narcotics. So I'd reverse on the ground the Constitution doesn't allow censorship of any book." Douglas commented, "I don't think this is obscene by my standard or Lady Chatterley's. So I can go for reversal on either ground."

Douglas was referring to the decision the previous term striking down New York's attempt to ban the film, *Lady Chatterley's Lover,* as obscene.[60] That decision had led Sherman Minton to write Frankfurter that he would have voted the other way in the case. "Adultery," the retired Justice asserted, "has been outlawed since Moses brought the tablets down from the Mountain. . . . To say that this policy cannot be carried out by N.Y. preventing the teaching of adultery as a way of life because the Constitution makes teaching adultery something protected by it seems ridiculous to me—I suppose a gangster school set up to teach crime would be protected!"[61]

When *Smith v. California* was decided, Black and Douglas each wrote separate concurrences expounding on their view that the Constitution prohibited all restrictions on obscenity. Frankfurter felt he, too, had to write a separate concurring opinion rejecting the Black–Douglas absolutist view of the First Amendment.

In *Hannah v. Larche,*[62] the Chief Justice was able to secure a majority for his view, though the decision there was marked by a split in the normally united Warren wing of the Court. Larche had been summoned to appear at a hearing of the U.S. Civil Rights Commission into alleged civil rights violations in Shreveport, Louisiana. He sued to enjoin the hearing on the ground that the Commission's rules of procedure did not give witnesses the rights of apprisal of any charges against them, confrontation, and cross-examination. The lower court had granted the injunction.

Warren led the conference on January 22, 1960, by speaking in favor of reversal. "Congress may investigate," he said, "and, in essence, that's this case even if it's by a commission." The Chief noted that the Commission was only investigating, not adjudicating anyone's rights. There was, as he saw it, "no deprivation yet of any constitutional rights. We're asked to decide that per se the Commission is bad. We'd have a different case if the Commission had acted against someone." Warren concluded by stressing that the Commission "is not an adjudicatory body." Any exposure involved in its hearing, he commented, "is incidental."

All agreed except Black and Douglas. Black declared that, though the Commission was validly established, it "can't authorize trials prohibited by the Bill of Rights and that's what this is." To Douglas, "this is a new engine of government to perform the functions of a grand jury and I don't think we can play [with] due process so loosely as to allow the Government to do this."

Warren delivered the June 20, 1960, opinion of the Court, which followed his conference approach. Douglas, joined by Black, issued a dissent. Frankfurter wrote another separate concurrence that added little to Warren's opinion. The Chief tried unsuccessfully to dissuade Frankfurter from issuing his opinion. Frankfurter wrote Harlan that he did not "propose to be inhibited" in his separate expression "out of deference to temperamental suspiciousness which attributes sinister motives to innocent conduct." He was issuing his concurrence as a means of "dealing with the inadequacies of . . . the Chief's own opinion."[63]

Warren's irritation at Frankfurter's propensity to speak separately in cases where he agreed with the decision had been even greater in *United Steelworkers of America v. United States*,[64] which had come up near the beginning of the 1959 Term. The government sought an injunction under the Taft-Hartley Act against an industry-wide steel strike. The union, whose argument was presented by Arthur J. Goldberg, soon to be a Justice himself, urged that the strike did not present a peril to the national health or safety, as required by the statute.

At the conference on November 3, 1959,[65] Warren said that he thought that there was "nothing in the constitutional point." The findings and evidence on "national safety" were sufficient, with "safety being at least national defense. Given the findings on safety, the court has no discretion."

All except Douglas agreed that there was ample support for the injunction on the ground that the strike imperiled national safety. The Justices decided to dispose of the case by a short per curiam, which Warren assigned to Brennan. A draft was circulated the next day. Frankfurter returned his copy with numerous written suggestions.[66] Brennan had begun his draft by referring to "the commendably cooperative attitude of the parties to this litigation, and the expeditious consideration of it by the lower courts," which made it "possible for this most important case to be argued before this Court . . . only 14 days after it was originally filed in the District Court." Frankfurter wrote Brennan, "I'm against this ¶. My test for praise is that the opposite conduct would have been at least neutral if not equally OK. I see nothing here for praise of the A.G. and nothing that would not have been subject to criticism if Goldberg had unsuccessfully tried dilatory tactics. The case necessitated prompt [action]. It's the kind of thing that is done everyday in English courts. I'm against taffy."

Frankfurter made numerous stylistic changes and also objected to what he termed the "rebutting opinion" Brennan had written. Instead he urged "letting the Court's opinion march affirmatively—*i.e.* state the issues, the Court's position on them and leave rebuttal of losing party's position for the end, usually succinctly tho impressively stated."

Brennan may have resented Frankfurter's still playing the professor, but he adopted most of the suggestions. He also added the concluding paragraph of the opinion, after Frankfurter had noted, at the draft's end, "This is too weak or meagre for my taste. . . . I shall be surprised if this will be adequate as answer to WOD's blast!"

But Douglas' dissent was not the only deviation from the Court's unity. Even though Brennan had revised his draft to meet most of Frankfurter's points, Frankfurter circulated a November 5 memorandum in which he said that he might find it "necessary to add a separate concurrence." The reason, he said, was, "that a single Court statement on important constitutional issues and other aspects of public law is bound to smother differences that in the interest of candor and of the best interest of the Court ought to be expressed."[67] On the same day, Harlan sent a "Dear Brethren" letter indicating "my intention to amplify my concurrence in a separate opinion to be filed as soon as practicable."[68]

When the Steel Case per curiam was issued on November 7, in addition to the Douglas dissent, there was an announcement by Frankfurter (and Harlan as well) that, though they joined the Court's opinion, they also intended to file "an amplification of our views." Their separate concurrence was issued December 7. It said little, if anything, that had not been said in Brennan's per curiam.

The Chief Justice thought that Frankfurter's desire to have his own say only detracted from the dignity of the Court and gave critics an impression of division even where the Justices were almost united. But Warren himself did not hesitate to speak out when he felt that the Court was denigrating one of the basic values in which he strongly believed. In *Wyatt v. United States*,[69] the Chief saw the Court's decision as one that weakened the family—the foundation of his hierarchy of values. Wyatt had been convicted of violating the Mann Act. He had married the woman he had transported for immoral purposes. She had, nevertheless, been ordered to testify for the prosecution. The Court had previously decided that a wife could not testify against her husband. Should a wife who was a victim of a Mann Act offense be treated as an exception?

Warren answered in the negative at the January 15, 1960, conference.[70] "I don't think," he declared, "we should break down the rule against a wife testifying against a husband. The marital institution should prevent compelling the wife to testify against her husband."

The majority, however, disagreed. On May 16, Harlan delivered an opinion reading in an exception in such a case to the rule prohibiting a wife's testimony. Warren felt strongly enough on the issue to write a sharp dissent, though he was joined only by Black and Douglas.

Warren could, however, be flexible in changing his views to meet objections where neither an issue of principle nor one of the values he considered basic was involved. *United States v. Durham Lumber Co.*[71] illustrates this point. The case was a technical bankruptcy case involving competing claims of the government and certain subcontractors. The subcontractors had done work on which money was owing from the bankrupt contractor. The U.S. assessed the contractor for uncollected withholding and unemployment insurance taxes. The money due the bankrupt contractor under the contract was in possession of the trustee in bankruptcy. Both the subcontractors and the government claimed priority in the money. The court of appeals had held that the government's tax lien did not have priority and that the subcontractors were entitled to payment of their claims under the contract before the government could satisfy its lien.

At the conference on October 23, 1959,[72] Warren disagreed with the lower court. He said that under the law of the state concerned, North Carolina, a trust for the subcontractors was created in the money owing under the contract, but it was not fixed at a given time. The federal lien was prior and, under the principle, "prior in time, prior in right," the Court should reverse.

A majority supported Warren, and he prepared an opinion of the Court reversing in accordance with his conference view. Brennan then circulated a dissent taking issue with the opinion's construction of state law, which differed from that taken by the court of appeals. In Brennan's interpretation, North Carolina law provided for a trust in favor of the subcontractors as soon as notice was received of the subcontractors' claim. Douglas, Stewart, and Whittaker joined Brennan's dissent. There was basic agreement between the Chief Justice and Brennan in the recognition by both that the state law was governing. However, since four of the seven espousing this view supported Brennan's reading of state law, Warren gave way and circulated an opinion acquiescing in the lower court's view of the governing state law. Brennan and those concurring in his draft dissent joined the Chief's new opinion and it was issued as the opinion of the Court, with Harlan and Black dissenting, on June 20, 1960.

During the 1959 Term, the Brethren decided *United States v. Raines*.[73] It was the first case decided under the Civil Rights Act of 1957—the first civil rights law enacted by Congress since Reconstruction. The government brought an action against the Board of Registrars of Terrell County, Georgia, charging they had discriminated against blacks who desired to register. The case was brought under a provision of the 1957 act authorizing actions to enjoin interferences with voting rights. The lower court ruled the statute unconstitutional on the ground that, though this case involved only official action, the statute on its face could be used to enjoin purely private action that was beyond the scope of the Fifteenth Amendment's prohibition of "state action."

All the Justices voted to hear the government's appeal. At the January 15, 1960, conference,[74] the Chief Justice spoke for reversal, saying that the lower court had decided without regard to the actual facts. "State action *was* present and the fact that the statute may be used against individuals is erroneous. You can't conjure up such horribles." Black went further, stating that he thought the Fifteenth Amendment's "enabling clause would permit Congress to extend it to individual action." Warren, however, urged that the decision be confined to the narrower ground he had stated. The others agreed, and the opinion was assigned to Brennan.

Brennan circulated a draft following Warren's conference approach that was substantially similar to the opinion delivered in the case. When he read the draft, Frankfurter wrote Harlan, "I wish I could think as well of what I write as does Bill Brennan of his opinions!"[75] Frankfurter then sent around a memorandum suggesting that the opinion should be drastically shortened and omit most of its reasoning. Brennan replied in a February 11 *Memorandum to the Conference* rejecting Frankfurter's approach, saying that he had made "no changes of substance." Brennan conceded, "I recognize (as some have pointed out) that the opinion has a certain negative cast to it in places. But I think that this is necessary. . . . To be sure, this is all apt to give the opinion a defensive tone." But Brennan said that he could not "reduce this tone while adhering to" the substance of the opinion.

The draft of Brennan's memo had concluded, "In this regard, Felix has written to me that 'The difference between Homer and other poets is that Homer knew what to omit,' but I am convinced that in this case, Homer has nodded." This passage was omitted from the printed memo circulated by Brennan.

At the conference, seven of the Brethren rejected Frankfurter's approach, and Brennan was able to deliver his draft much as he had written it on February 29, 1960. Stewart had suggested rearranging the order of the discussion in the opinion, feeling, as he put it in a written note to Brennan, that that would "make the opinion somewhat more positive." Brennan also rejected Stewart's advice. He did, however, accept Clark's suggestion that he add to the opinion a quote from a 1913 opinion by Chief Justice Edward D. White. In a February 18 letter, Clark wrote, "The use of C.J. White of Louisiana would be most helpful. The only CJ from South (deep)."[76]

Two other 1959 Term cases should also be mentioned. The first is *Schilling v. Rogers*,[77] where a bare majority held, on June 20, 1960, that the Attorney General's determination that Schilling was an enemy alien and, as such, not entitled to return of property seized during World War II was not subject to any judicial review. Brennan, joined by Warren, Black, and Douglas, wrote a strong dissent asserting that the decision was an unjustified departure from the basic principle subjecting administrative action to review by the courts. The dissenting view had commanded a majority until just before the decision was announced. Harlan had voted with the Warren four at the conference and was assigned the opinion. On June 9, he circulated a memorandum in which he said, "My work in preparing the opinion has satisfied me that the case should be affirmed."[78] Harlan submitted an opinion supporting his changed view that was adopted by the new majority as the opinion of the Court.

The second case, *Mackey v. Mendoza–Martinez,*[79] almost resulted in an important decision. Mendoza–Martinez sought a declaratory judgment that he was a U.S. citizen. The lower court had found that he had lost his citizenship by leaving the country to evade military service during World War II. The Supreme Court had remanded the case for reconsideration in light of the decision in *Trop v. Dulles,*[80] which, we saw in chapter 8, had ruled invalid the denationalization of a soldier for desertion. On remand, the lower court held that section 401(j), of the Nationality Act providing for loss of citizenship for leaving the country to avoid military service in wartime, was unconstitutional.

At the conference, on December 11, 1959, the vote was in favor of reversing. Stewart was assigned the task of writing the opinion by Frankfurter, the senior majority Justice. He circulated a draft opinion in January 1960 that won a bare majority, with Warren, Black, Douglas, and Brennan not joining. The draft stated that it was not necessary to decide if the foreign-affairs power could justify denationalization for the conduct in question. For Congress, in enacting the statute, was drawing on another broad and far-reaching power—the war power. The Stewart draft maintained that this case was quite different from *Trop,* since section 401(j) "does not represent an attempt to impose additional punishment upon one convicted of a civil or military offense. Quite to the contrary, it provides that expatriation will follow voluntary flight from this country only when the very purpose of such flight is to evade the duty of service in the armed forces."

The draft went on to say, "It is not for us to say Congress may not have considered expatriation a necessary practical deterrent against flight by draft evaders to a foreign land. . . . Furthermore, the withdrawal of citizenship from one who voluntarily leaves his country to evade military service in time of war or national emergency is far from unreasonable. . . . It is hardly an irrelevant exercise of constitutional power for the Nation to disown those who have disowned it by seeking to escape this ultimate duty of citizenship." Nor was this cruel and unusual punishment, because this was not punishment in its constitutional sense.

After reading Stewart's draft, Brennan circulated a memorandum pointing out that, unless Whittaker, who had joined the Stewart opinion, was repudiating his stand in joining Warren's *Trop* opinion, Stewart's opinion must be read as a very limited holding. Whittaker replied by a memorandum confirming that the tentative majority opinion was so limited. Later in January, Brennan circulated an opinion stating that all that had been decided was that section 401 (j) was constitutional as applied to the stipulated facts of this case.

There was disagreement on just how far the projected decision went, particularly in its impact upon the *Trop* case. The Brethren were so sharply divided on this that Warren resolved to avoid the matter by deciding without reaching the merits. A per curiam drafted by Douglas was announced April 18, remanding the case to the lower court on a narrow technical ground that had been suggested by the Chief.

Service on the Supreme Court must often seem a glorified version of the labors of Sisyphus. Chief Justice Warren once referred to the Court's job as "our always unfinished work."[81] The Court term would scarcely be finished when the cases for the new term would start coming in. The Brethren would leave Washington during the summer recess. Some, like Douglas and, increasingly, Warren, would spend the time in travel. During the 1960 recess, the Chief travelled no farther than to his home state. In 1959, however, Warren had visited Russia, Germany, and Scandinavia and, in 1961, had gone on a world tour. He remained popular as a representative of his country. J. Lee Rankin, then Solicitor General, later said, "When you travel, you realize this is the best-known American in the world. The new nations of Asia and Africa call him a saint—the greatest humanitarian in the Western Hemisphere since Abraham Lincoln."[82]

Back in the Marble Palace, the docket for the coming term would be growing apace as the certiorari petitions and appeals would begin to pile up. In an August 1960 letter, Warren expressed guilt at being "a vagabond jurist who has been enjoying himself by travelling"[83] while others were starting to go through the cert heap. But the vagabondage would end all too soon, and the Chief would come back before the new term to, in Frankfurter's phase, "work on what Holmes called 'the damned *certs.*' "[84]

Yet none of the Brethren, with the possible exception of Whittaker, would have given up the chance to continue his judicial work. Perhaps Warren exaggerated when he wrote, as the 1960 summer recess wore on, "Now as the boys would say 'I have had it' and am happy to return and get started on the summer accumulation of certs."[85] But, after they were no longer able to participate in the Court's work, all the Justices felt the way just-retired Sherman Minton expressed it, in an October 1957 letter: "When that first Monday in Oct rolls around I miss joining the Court. I feel sorta left out."[86]

In the Court itself, the 1960 Term saw a continued intensification of the deteriorating relations between Frankfurter and the Chief Justice and his supporters. It was during the term that the unprecedented acerbic exchanges described at the beginning of chapter 7, during the reading of opinions in the *Milanovich*[87] and *Stewart* cases,[88] occurred. Interestingly, Warren had not expressed himself that firmly against Frankfurter's position in those two cases. At the *Milanovich* conference on February 24, 1961, the Chief had spoken for reversal of convictions for both stealing and receiving stolen currency on the ground that "larceny and receiving are inconsistent. If you're guilty of one, you can't be of the other." Because of this, he said, "I think there must be a new trial." But he had not been as categorical as in other conference presentations. In *Stewart,* at the February 24, 1961, conference, he had been even less certain on whether there should be reversal because defendant had been asked an improper question. Warren asked, "Did it prejudice defendant in the eyes of the jury? I don't know whether it did or not." However, the government had conceded that the question, which was about defendant's previous failures to testify, could not be justified under the Court's prior decisions. This tilted the balance for Warren toward reversal. "When the Government comes that close to confessing error," he asserted, "It's pretty hard to go with the Government."

The Warren outbursts after Frankfurter stated his *Milanovich* and *Stewart* dissents had nothing to do with the differences between them on the merits. They were caused by Warren's increasing irritation at Frankfurter and what the Chief considered his denigration of his colleagues. Warren's feelings toward the Justice were demonstrated graphically at the November 11, 1960, conference on *Monroe v. Pape*.[89] On November 9, Frankfurter circulated a lengthy memorandum on the case. He wrote that "the far-reaching importance of this case" and "inadequacies in the presentation of the case" had led him to circulate the memo, which "is the result of weeks of investigation, discussion and formulation."[90] After all of Frankfurter's efforts with the memo, Warren began the November 11 conference, "I haven't read Felix's memo, but I have looked at his conclusion and disagree with it."[91]

During the conference, Harlan passed the following note to Frankfurter: "Are you surprised that some of your Brethren are able to reach 'firm' conclusions on your memo on 2 days study & reflection! P.S. And that one should be ready to decide *without* reading the memo!"[92]

Rogers v. Richmond[93] was another case involving a minor Frankfurter–Douglas contretemps. Douglas wrote a December 15, 1960, memorandum to Frankfurter making suggestions in the latter's draft opinion. The two then had several telephone conversations, but Douglas felt that several new Frankfurter drafts did not meet his points. In January 1961, Douglas circulated a *Memorandum to the Conference* on the matter, asking the conference to adopt his principal suggestion, saying, "I am making the suggestion to the Conference because I have exhausted my administrative remedies."[94]

Frankfurter bristled at this statement. As soon as he received the Douglas memo, he fired off his own memorandum which declared, "In the interest of intra-Court relationships, the closing paragraph of Brother Douglas's memorandum ought not go without comment." Douglas, Frankfurter wrote, "advises the Conference that he has exhausted his 'administrative remedies' in connection with the latest recirculation of my draft opinion in *Rogers v. Richmond*. If that implies that I have been inhospitable or have shown the slightest impatience with any suggestion that has come from any of my Brethren for the improvement of that opinion, I am bound to say that it is without foundation. . . . So far as I am aware, I have given not the slightest basis for thinking that all further 'administrative remedies' are deemed to be exhausted."[95]

At this, Douglas sent Frankfurter a written note the same day: "My reference to 'exhaustion of administrative remedies' was *an attempt at humor!* I regret that I offended you."[96] Douglas also circulated another *Memorandum to the Conference,* also on January 12, which stated, "As I told Brother Frankfurter, my reference to the exhaustion of my administrative remedies made in my earlier memorandum of this date, was an attempt merely at humor and I apologize for any offense that can be deduced from it."[97]

As in the previous term, Stewart's vote remained decisive in most of the close cases. Once again, his vote was not consistent with either the Warren or Frankfurter view. He tended, however, to vote somewhat more with the Frankfurter bloc, especially in the area of alleged subversive activities. The result was a further narrowing of some of the controversial 1957 decisions in that area.

The Stewart tendency to vote with the Frankfurter wing in cases involving attempts to deal with subversion was shown in *Wilkinson v. United States*[98] and *Braden v. United States.*[99] Both cases arose out of convictions for refusing to answer questions at a hearing in Atlanta, Georgia, of a House Committee on Un-American Activities subcommittee. The chairman had stated that the purpose of the hearing was to inquire into Communist infiltration into basic industries and Communist propaganda in the South. Wilkinson and Braden refused to answer questions relating to alleged Communist activity and membership. They claimed the committee was without authority to interrogate them because the purpose was to harass and expose them for opposing and criticizing the committee, and also that no proper foundation had been laid for the questions.

There had been a sharp division on whether to grant certiorari in the cases, with Warren, Black, Douglas, and Brennan voting to grant and the rest to deny. The same split prevailed at both the conference on November 18, 1960, and at the final votes in the cases. Warren began the conference by speaking for reversal of the convictions. He felt that these cases "go beyond *Barenblatt*" [100]—the 1959 decision limiting the 1957 *Watkins* case. [101] "This goes to the right to petition," the Chief declared. "The committee is interfering with that right. Even a Communist has that right and no harassment of that right can be justified on the score of the committee's authority to inquire into Communist propaganda. Merely to say, 'We believe you are a Communist' is too flimsy a basis to sanction it." The committee's purpose, Warren concluded, "was to degrade and expose and not investigate."

Warren was supported by Black, Douglas, and Brennan. Douglas specifically agreed with Warren's analysis: "The core of this case is the First Amendment right of petition. If it were simply a question, 'are you a Communist?' we would have a different case." Brennan urged that affirmance would repudiate "what was deemed by commentators to have been held in *Watkins*." At which Frankfurter acidly noted on his conference sheet, "so that what writers think is law controls power of Congress." [102]

Frankfurter and the others thought the cases were governed by *Barenblatt*. Frankfurter said "this reaches deeply into the relations between this Court and the Congress" and that he would affirm per curiam on the authority of *Barenblatt*. Stewart, whose vote for affirmance was decisive, stated, "I am satisfied there are no significant differences from *Barenblatt*." Stewart delivered the opinions of the Court affirming in both cases on February 27, 1961. Black and Douglas, joined by Warren, and Brennan issued dissents.

Stewart's vote was also decisive in giving the victory to the Frankfurter wing in two other cases that limited the decisions restricting governmental power over alleged subversive activities in the 1957 *Konigsberg* [103] and *Yates* cases. [104] In the 1957 *Konigsberg* case, the Court had reversed a refusal of admission to the California bar on character grounds based on past Communist Party membership. After the California Bar Committee held a new hearing, it again refused to admit Konigsberg on the ground that his refusals to answer questions relating to his Communist membership had obstructed a full investigation into his qualifications.

At the certiorari conference on March 7, 1960, Warren, Black, Frankfurter, Douglas, and Brennan voted to grant cert—the others to deny. At the conference on the merits, April 28, 1961, Warren again urged that Konigsberg should be admitted. As he saw it, "The so-called lack of candor theory hardly stands up on his record. In the hearings, there was never a word of bad character, but only good."

This time, however, only four voted for reversal. Frankfurter, who had dissented from the 1957 decision, now spoke for affirmance. He was joined by Clark and Harlan (who had also dissented in 1957), as well as Whittaker (who had not participated in the 1957 decision), and Stewart (who had come to the Court since then). The opinion was assigned to Stewart, who announced it on April 24, 1961.[105] It affirmed the refusal to admit Konigsberg, holding that California could deny admission on the ground it had given—i.e., because his refusal to answer obstructed its investigation into his qualifications. Black and Brennan wrote dissents, joined by Warren and Douglas.

Six weeks after *Konigsberg,* the Court decided *Scales v. United States.*[106] Scales had been convicted of violating the Membership Clause of the Smith Act, making it a crime to hold knowing membership in an organization that advocated overthrow of the government by force or violence. The case had first come to the Court in the 1956 Term, and the Court reversed in October 1957 because the rule of the *Jencks* case had been violated. There was a new trial, and Scales was again convicted. Argument was heard again in the Supreme Court during the 1958 Term. The case was set for reargument in the 1959 Term, but after the case of *Communist Party v. Control Board*[107] came up, the Brethren decided that the two cases should be argued together and put over the *Scales* case for reargument during the 1960 Term.

Clark dissented from the February 6, 1960, order resetting *Scales* for argument in the 1960 Term, which had been drafted by Frankfurter,[108] on the ground that the case had been before the Court too long already. Frankfurter had written Clark "as a friend" to induce Clark not to issue his dissent.[109] Clark replied, in a letter of February 8. "As you say," he wrote, "the Court's judgment, like wine, 'requires seasoning.' But when old wine becomes *too* old, it goes sour. And so in my view it is one thing to give a case 'due deliberation' and quite another to confine it to the 'deep freeze' to be fed up at such later times as suits the whimsey. . . . I take it that we should do not less than follow our admonishment in *Brown* to the lower courts of 'deliberate speed.' "[110]

At the conference after the *Scales* argument, on October 14, 1960, Warren stated that he would reverse under the *Yates* standard (referring to the *Yates* case discussed in chapter 6), on the ground that

Scales did not have the required active purpose to overthrow the government. Warren urged reversal on nonconstitutional grounds. He said that, without reading in the requirements of "specific intent" and "active" membership, the statute would be unconstitutional. If that were true, he went on, "the indictment was insufficient because it doesn't charge the elements the Government now reads in: intent and activity." However, "if we read them in, the evidence is insufficient." In addition, "prejudicial evidence was admitted in proofs of Party aims, without bringing home knowledge of or agreement with what other party members said."

Warren was supported by Black, Douglas, and Brennan. Frankfurter, Clark, Harlan, and Whittaker were for affirmance. Stewart was undecided, but leaning toward affirmance. Stewart ultimately voted with the Frankfurter bloc and, on June 5, 1961, Harlan delivered the opinion of the Court affirming the conviction. Harlan reconciled the decision with that in *Yates,* where he had also written the opinion, by finding that Scales had been an "active" member with full knowledge and intent to participate in the illegal advocacy of forcible overthrow. Black, Douglas, and Brennan, joined by Warren, issued dissents.

Another case where Stewart provided the fifth vote for upholding governmental power over allegedly subversive activities was *Communist Party v. Subversive Activities Control Board.*[111] At issue were the registration requirements of the Subversive Activities Control Act, under which the Board had ordered the Communist Party to register as a Communist-action organization. The statute imposed sanctions on organizations ordered to register, including loss of tax exemptions, labeling of mail and broadcasts as Communist disseminated, and prohibition of organization members from holding union positions, passports, and restrictions on their government or defense employment.

The case had first come before the Court in the 1955 Term. Largely at Frankfurter's urging, as seen in chapter 5, decision on the constitutionality of the registration requirement had been avoided when the case was remanded to hear evidence of perjured testimony. On remand, the Party was once more ordered to register. This order again came before the Supreme Court, which this time decided the constitutional issue.

All the Brethren voted to grant certiorari (except for Stewart who passed). At the conferences on the merits on October 14 and 21, 1960, Warren and the others repeated the views on constitutionality that they had expressed at the conferences on November 18, 1955, and March 8, 1956, when the case had previously been before them. At those conferences, the Chief Justice had come out strongly against the constitutionality of the registration requirement. At the 1960 conferences, Warren indicated that his view had not changed. He urged that this time the Court should reach the constitutional issues and invalidate the statute under the Fifth Amendment privilege against self-incrimination, as well as under the First Amendment and due process.

Black and Douglas repeated their support of the Warren view that they had stated in the 1955 Term conferences. Clark still believed that the registration requirement was valid. Frankfurter and Harlan, who had not voted on the merits in 1956, now voted the same way. The three Justices who had been appointed since the case was first before the Court tilted the balance. Brennan voted with Warren, but Whittaker and Stewart voted with Frankfurter, Clark, and Harlan. That made for a bare majority in favor of constitutionality.

On June 5, 1961, Frankfurter announced the decision that the registration requirement, standing alone, did not violate the First Amendment or bill of attainder prohibition. Frankfurter's lengthy opinion avoided the claims that the self-incrimination privilege was violated and that the statute's sanctions were invalid by holding that those claims were premature, since only the order of the Party to register was at issue. Black, Douglas, and Brennan, joined by Warren, issued dissents asserting that the First Amendment and self-incrimination privileges were violated. Warren also wrote a short dissent. As he explained in a *Memorandum for the Conference*, "I have decided to write a short dissening [sic] opinion on the non-constitutional issues in the . . . case."[112] Warren's opinion urged that the case should be decided on nonconstitutional questions of evidence and statutory interpretation. This was surprising in view of the Chief's strong conference statement that the constitutional issues "should be reached."

Stewart's vote again proved decisive in favor of the Frankfurter view in *Cafeteria Workers Union v. McElroy*.[113] Rachel Brawner was a

cook employed at a cafeteria on a naval base. The commanding officer withdrew her permission to enter the base on the ground that
she had failed to meet security requirements. Her union challenged
the withdrawal of her permit. The lower courts decided for the government. Six of the Brethren voted to grant certiorari, with Clark,
Harlan, and Whittaker for denial.

The *Cafeteria Workers* case was argued January 12, 1961. Counsel
for the government claimed that Mrs. Brawner had not suffered a
complete loss of employment, since she could work anywhere else
except the naval base. The assertion offended Warren's sense of fairness. "The same argument," the Chief declared, could be made in
other cases. Warren referred, as an example, to an earlier case where
an engineer lost his job at a defense plant because of loss of security
clearance: "He was merely excluded from this one plant. He could
go anywhere else in the world and practice his profession." When
the attorney referred to the factual distinction between the two cases,
Warren asked, "Isn't that a matter of degree rather than principle?"
At this point, Frankfurter turned to counsel and tartly interposed,
"Why do you fiddle around with these peripheral things? . . . why
don't you stick to [the] problem?"[114] Though ostensibly directed at
the attorney, it was clear who Frankfurter thought was getting the
discussion off the main issue.

At the conference on January 13, Warren started by saying he was
not reaching the constitutional question, but was for reversal on the
ground that there was no explicit authority to withdraw access to the
base. He also felt the relevant "regulations are neither adequate nor
controlling, since no notice of them is given."

Frankfurter led the discussion for affirmance. As he saw it, there
were "two distinctive issues: 1) Was any harm done in that life, etc.
[i.e., liberty, or property] were taken? And the answer is, 'of course';
2) But was there due process?" Here, too, his answer was affirmative.
In addition, Frankfurter saw no problem with the question of authority. "I would think there's inherent power in a place like this,
and ample materials confirm this."

Most of the others agreed with Frankfurter, when he said that they
had "to reach the constitutional question." On the merits, the voting
pattern of the other cases involving alleged subversion prevailed, with
Stewart again supplying the fifth vote for affirmance. He delivered
the opinion June 19, 1961, finding that there was authority to deny

access and that no hearing was demanded by due process because the case involved the government's own internal affairs, where summary decision was permissible. Brennan, joined by Warren, Black, and Douglas, issued a vigorous dissent.

Shelton v. Tucker[115] was the one subversion case during the term where Stewart voted with Warren and his supporters, giving them their only victory in the subversion area. An Arkansas statute compelled teachers to file affidavits listing all organizations to which they belonged during the preceding five years. Shelton, a Little Rock teacher and a member of the National Association for the Advancement of Colored People, refused to file an affidavit, and his contract was not renewed. He sued challenging the constitutionality of the affidavit requirement and lost in the state courts.

At the conference on November 11, 1960, Warren urged reversal. "The language of this statute," he said, "is just too broad. The rights of association of the school teachers are invaded. They have the right to inquire into membership in organizations bearing on fitness, such as professional organizations. But church, political parties, social organizations, as to membership and contributions, goes too far. On that narrow ground, and laying aside their motive on racial considerations, I would reverse." Moreover, the Chief pointed out, there was no provision in the statute making the information filed confidential.

Once again the vote was close, with Stewart joining Warren, Black, Douglas, and Brennan to make a bare majority for reversal. Stewart was assigned the opinion and, as delivered by him on December 12, 1960, it largely followed Warren's conference approach. At Frankfurter's urging, as Stewart wrote him, "in *Shelton* I've taken out references to First Amendment. Thanks for the good suggestion."[116] Frankfurter and Harlan, joined by Clark and Whittaker, issued *Shelton* dissents.

In the close 1960 Term cases not involving subversion, Stewart shifted between the Frankfurter and Warren positions. In two cases, his vote gave the decision to the Frankfurter wing. The first was *Times Film Corp. v. Chicago.*[117] At issue was a provision of the Chicago Municipal Code that required submission of all motion pictures for examination prior to public exhibition. Times Film Corp. applied for a permit to show a film, but refused to submit it for examination. The permit was denied because of the refusal to submit the film. Times then sued for an injunction, claiming that requiring submission of the film was, on its face, a prior restraint prohibited by the First Amendment. The court of appeals dismissed the complaint on the ground that no justiciable controversy was presented. It found that the case presented merely an abstract question of law, since neither the film nor evidence of its content was submitted.

At the conference on October 21, 1960, Warren indicated that he disagreed with the court of appeals. He thought there was a justiciable issue and said that he would send the case back for a trial. Black differed on disposition of the case. He felt "we had to decide the prior censorship issue" and urged that the ordinance was void on its face. Clark argued the other way. "If we reach the constitutional question," he stated, "there are some instances where the city can demand prior submission. This is too broad an attack for me." Harlan agreed, saying, "there may be circumstances where the state can't require prior submission," but that he could not go along with the "naked proposition" that submission could never be required.

The Brethren rejected Warren's suggestion that the case be remanded without consideration of the constitutional issue. But they split on the merits of that issue. A tentative majority was secured for affirmance, and Clark was assigned the opinion. He circulated a draft on November 2. A second draft, sent around November 7, was returned by Frankfurter with the written notation: "This . . . ought to satisfy all reasonable men, and that I like to think includes, FF."[118] Despite this, Warren sent around a memorandum: "As soon as it is possible for me to do so, I will prepare and circulate a dissent."[119]

Warren circulated his dissent on January 4, 1961, and it was soon joined by Black, Douglas, and Brennan. In the meantime, Clark's opinion secured a bare majority. Stewart wrote to Clark, "As you know, I agree with you in this case." He suggested, however, that language should be included, "emphasizing that not only freedom of speech, but also freedom from previous restraint, is not absolute."[120] Clark added the suggested language, for Stewart's vote was decisive in making the Clark opinion the opinion of the Court in the case.

In one of his last drafts, Clark added, toward the end of the opinion, "We, of course, are not holding that city officials may be granted the power to prevent the showing of any motion picture they deem unworthy of a license." Clark explained to his clerk, in a written memorandum, "I have taken this language largely from the dissent—but do *not quote* it. This would point it up to the close reader." [121]

Clark's opinion of the Court, delivered January 23, 1961, did no more than reject the broadside attack upon all motion-picture censorship made by Times Film Corp., saying that there is no constitutional right to exhibit any and all movies without prior submission. Warren, joined by Black, Douglas, and Brennan, issued his dissent protesting against the constitutional legitimation of censorship. Warren's strong antipathy toward obscenity gave way in the face of his view that "the decision presents a real danger of eventual censorship for every form of communication." [122]

The second nonsubversion case where Stewart's vote gave the decision to Frankfurter and his supporters was *Green v. United States*. [123] Green had been convicted of bank robbery. Before the sentencing, the judge asked, "Did you want to say something?" Green's attorney then made a statement asking for leniency. Green claimed that the judge's action violated the Federal Rule of Criminal Procedure requirement that, before imposing sentence, the trial judge "shall afford the defendant an opportunity to make a statement in his own behalf." The claim was rejected by the lower courts.

The vote on whether to grant certiorari foreshadowed the decision in the case, with the Chief Justice, Black, Douglas, and Brennan voting to grant and the others to deny. At the January 13, 1961, conference on the merits, Warren argued for reversal. "As to the allocution right," he said, "it seems to me the Rule means what it says and he may be heard in his own defense, whatever may be the case as to his counsel. This is even more important where he pleads guilty than where he goes to trial."

There was a bare majority for affirmance. When the decision was announced Feburary 27, Frankfurter spoke for himself, Clark, Harlan, and Whittaker. His opinion found that Green's right under the Rule was not violated, since the judge's question "may have been directed to the defendant and not to his counsel." [124] Black, joined by Warren, Douglas, and Brennan, dissented, saying that the judge was required to show that he had given defendant a personal opportunity to speak for himself, rather than through counsel. Stewart wrote a one-paragraph opinion joining in the affirmance, but stressing that the judge was required "to assure the defendant an express opportunity to speak for himself, in addition to anything that his lawyer may have to say." He would, however, "apply such a rule prospectively." [125] Stewart's vote thus gave the decision to the Frankfurter view, but the rule he stated for future application was closer to that expressed by Warren.

In two of the close nonsubversion cases during the 1960 Term, Stewart voted with Warren, rather than Frankfurter. The first was *Burton v. Wilmington Parking Authority*. [126] Burton had been refused service because he was black in a restaurant in an automobile parking building operated by the Wilmington Parking Authority, a city agency. The restaurant was run by a private company under a lease from the Authority. Burton sued the Authority, claiming that his rights under the Equal Protection Clause of the Fourteenth Amendment had been denied. The highest state court rejected the claim on the ground that, since the restaurant was acting in "a purely private capacity," the "state action" required for the equal protection guaranty to operate was lacking.

Warren began the February 24, 1961, conference by rejecting the notion that "state action" was not involved. He noted that the building in which the restaurant was located was built with tax monies, operated with tax exemption, and on land acquired through the state's power of eminent domain, as well as the fact that the project had been "designed as a single enterprise." As Warren saw it, "The very people who are paying for it can't be discriminated against."

Only Harlan supported the state court. "I can see no state action whatever," he declared. "There's not a hint of an effort on the part of the state to mask a discriminatory purpose. The state's interest in divesting itself was not in furtherance of a public purpose. Its only purpose was to raise money."

Black, Douglas, and Brennan agreed with Warren's position, as did Clark, who said, "It all adds up to that this is a public project which is a unit." Frankfurter, however, stated that he did not want to decide whether Fourteenth Amendment discrimination was proven because the Authority was aided by tax exemption and eminent domain. Stewart also indicated that he did not get to the argument on whether the restaurant's refusal was "state action." Instead he pointed out that the restaurant had acted under a state law allowing a restaurant owner to refuse to serve persons where that "would be offensive to the major part of his customers." Stewart said that the highest state court had construed this to authorize refusals to serve because of race. This made the statute violative of the Fourteenth Amendment and he "would reverse on that ground."

Though Stewart agreed with Warren that there should be reversal, he did not agree with the Chief's reasoning. However, Clark did and his vote made for a majority in favor of the decision that "state action" was present where racial discrimination was practiced by anyone who operated on public property. Clark delivered an opinion of the Court to that effect April 17, 1961. Stewart wrote a separate concurrence on the ground stated by him at the conference. Frankfurter had written Clark that he was with him on the merits: "The hungry public, waiting to hear where I stand on this case, won't of course know that on the merits I am with you, but you at least will know it."[127] Despite this, Frankfurter and Harlan, joined by Whittaker, dissented. They urged that the constitutional issue should be avoided by remanding the case to the state court for it to indicate whether it did interpret the statute in accordance with Stewart's view.

The second close nonsubversion case during the 1960 Term in which Stewart voted with Warren was *International Association of Machinists v. Street*.[128] That case gave the Brethren more trouble than any other during the term. Street sued to enjoin enforcement of a union shop agreement on the ground that his union dues were used to promote political causes with which he disagreed. In the 1956 *Hanson* case,[129] the Court had upheld a Railway Labor Act provision authorizing union shop agreements. Did the *Hanson* rule mean that the union should be free to spend the employee's money for political causes which he opposed? The Supreme Court of Georgia held that the statute was unconstitutional to the extent that it permitted such use of the union dues and enjoined enforcement of the union-shop agreement.

The *Street* case had come to the Court the previous term. The Brethren had decided the case then and an opinion of the Court had been prepared by Black, with Frankfurter and Harlan dissenting, holding that the Railway Labor Act provision was unconstitutional as applied in the case. It was then realized that, since the validity of a federal statute was at issue, the United States had a right to intervene, and the case was put over on June 20, 1960, for reargument, with notice to the government that the statute was in question.

Street was reargued on January 17 and 18, 1961, together with the related case of *Lathrop v. Donohue*,[130] which had come to the Court at the beginning of the 1960 Term. At issue in *Lathrop* was the constitutionality of the Wisconsin "integrated" Bar, under which every lawyer in the state had to enroll in the State Bar and pay dues to it. Lathrop brought an action attacking the integrated Bar on the ground that it used his dues money in opposition to legislation that he favored. The Wisconsin Supreme Court dismissed the complaint.

Warren had joined Black's *Street* opinion the previous term, but at the conference following the reargument,[131] he indicated that he no longer felt that the *Street* statute was invalid. "In the light of *Hanson*," he stated, "I can't say this statute is unconstitutional." Nor could he see any difference between this and the integrated Bar. "Lots of people," the Chief asserted, "have to pay dues, some of which goes to support ideas with which they disagree. People pay taxes that go to things they don't believe in." On the other hand, Warren expressed doubt about spending money for advancing the causes of political candidates.

The result of the conference discussion was inconclusive. Black would not change the view stated in his prior *Street* opinion. According to Frankfurter's sketchy notes, Black expressed "fierce view on absolutes—will not draw lines." Douglas and Stewart also continued to adhere to the Black opinion. Frankfurter and Harlan reiterated their contrary view of the previous year. No firm decision as to either case was reached at the conference. The indecision on *Street,* so different from the strong majority the prior year, was largely attributable to the *Lathrop* case, since some of the Justices were inclined to the view that the latter decision should be in favor of the Bar Association, while the former might still go against the union. Such a divergence in decisions seemed undesirable, and Warren took steps to avoid it.

At this point, the Chief did what he tended to do when the Court was confronted with a legal Gordian knot. He turned to his closest ally among the Brethren, Brennan, and assigned him the task of writing the opinions in the hope that he would come up with an acceptable compromise.

The Chief Justice himself helped Brennan in working out the compromise. On February 6, 1961, Warren sent Brennan a four-page memorandum on the cases, which, he said, contained "my views in capsule form." Warren wrote that, while the record showed that there were union expenditures "which appear to me to be within the Act; i.e., . . . the promotion of legislation 'directly affecting unions and union members . . .'", there were also "some expenditures that, to me, are clearly beyond the purposes of the Act; i.e., contributions and expenditures for political candidates." Warren noted that "Both sides would like to have the issue decided on broad constitutional grounds." But, he said, "the parties cannot rightfully force us into such a position." Under *Hanson,* the money could be collected by the union. Although Street was "not entitled to a determination that the statute is unconstitutional," there should be a remedy for the money "expended for unauthorized purposes." The Chief suggested a remedy like that available to taxpayers to compel municipal officers to restore sums spent for illegal purposes—"with the union member awarded those rights presently available to taxpayers." Warren concluded by stating that he thought "all the expenditures revealed by the record are permissible upon the above analysis and [I] would affirm the decision below."

In accordance with Warren's suggestions, Brennan prepared opinions under which *Street* was decided without reaching the constitutional question and *Lathrop* by passing merely on the constitutionality of the integrated Bar as such, without reaching the further constitutional question of the expenditures for political purposes. Brennan's opinion disposed of the *Street* case on the statutory ground that ultimately became the holding of the Court—that the statutory provision authorizing union shops did not give the union the power to use dues to support political causes opposed by the dues-paying member. Brennan's *Lathrop* draft decided on the grounds taken in the final decision there—that an integrated Bar, as such, did not unconstitutionally infringe on the attorney's freedom of association, while avoiding the constitutional claim that his free speech rights were violated by use of his dues for causes he opposed.

Before circulating his draft opinions, Brennan secured Warren and Clark's tentative agreement. After the opinions were circulated, Stewart expressed himself favorably. Frankfurter and Harlan circulated a dissent in *Street,* rejecting Brennan's statutory construction and adhering to their former position on the constitutional issue. Douglas said he continued to believe that the constitutional issue should be faced, but that he was willing to concur in the remedial aspect of Brennan's *Street* opinion. Black, however, could not be moved. His view continued to be that the constitutional questions had to be faced and that both the constitutional and remedial questions should be decided the way they had been by the Georgia court.

Whittaker had become the decisive vote on Brennan's statutory ground. On January 30, 1961, he had prepared a memorandum opinion reversing on the ground that Congress had not restricted "the historic use which such unions make of their funds, and that the privilege was within the constitutional power of Congress to grant." Then Whittaker circulated an opinion taking the opposite approach and agreeing with the constitutional and remedial holdings below. This Whittaker draft went even further than Black by overruling the *Hanson* decision.

There was comparable uncertainty on Brennan's *Lathrop* draft. Warren, Clark, and Stewart agreed with it. Black and Douglas believed that the constitutional issue was properly before the Court and should be decided in Lathrop's favor. Frankfurter, Harlan, and Whittaker agreed that the issue should be decided, but *against* Lathrop.

At this point, there was a majority against Brennan's statutory construction in *Street*. In *Lathrop*, the majority was against Brennan's view that the question of the constitutionality of the Bar's political expenditures was not ripe for decision.

The impasse continued into June. To break it, Brennan decided to revise drastically his draft opinions. He sent a memorandum on June 7 to Warren, Douglas, Clark, and Stewart explaining revised drafts that he had prepared. On *Street*, Brennan wrote, "My previous circulation avoided decision of the constitutional question on the view that the statute was not to be read to authorize the unions to use compelled dues, over a member's objection, for such purposes. I still prefer this disposition but five Members of the Court disagree with my construction. I have, therefore, prepared the enclosed alternative circulation which accepts the majority view of the meaning of the statute, reaches the constitutional question, and holds that the First Amendment rights of objecting employees are violated."

In *Lathrop*, the June 7 Brennan memo explained, "The previous circulation, relying on *Hanson*, found no merit in the constitutional claim that enforced payment of $15.00 annual dues abridged freedom of association. The claim that to the extent the dues were used to support views contrary to the plantiff's freedom of speech protected by the Fourteenth Amendment was violated was not reached on the ground that the record did not properly present it. Here again a majority of the Court disagree and believe that the question is presented and should be decided. I have, therefore, prepared the enclosed alternative draft which reaches the question and decides that Lathrop is entitled to a refund of such proportion of the $15.00 as was expended to support political activities of the Integrated Bar."

Brennan concluded that though he still preferred his earlier opinions, he proposed the revisions as alternatives, "with the hope they might succeed, where the earlier failed, in commanding a court."

Warren and Douglas agreed to join the new *Street* opinion, and it looked as though Black might also. Clark and Stewart, however, were unwilling to decide the constitutional question. At this point, the prospect was that an opinion holding the Railway Labor Act provision unconstitutional would command five votes—Brennan, Warren, Black, Douglas, and Whittaker. But there was no such prospect as to *Lathrop*. Because Whittaker took the view that the two cases might be distinguished, there were, at most, four votes for unconstitutionality in *Lathrop*.

There was the further possibility that, if pressed to decide the *Lathrop* constitutional question, Clark and Stewart might join in rejecting the constitutional claim, thus making five against it. They might then feel compelled to apply the same view to *Street* and might vote with Frankfurter and Harlan there. This would have produced a one-vote majority in *Street* against the union position and a one-vote majority in *Lathrop* in favor of the Bar Association.

The matter was again discussed in conference in mid-June, but there was no further movement. Well might Harlan write Frankfurter, "So much water is over the dam since writing first started in this case that your last circulation leads me to say 'Amen.' . . . [But] I gather the log jam . . . is not yet broken." [132]

After the conference, however, the Chief Justice served as a catalyst by talking to Brennan and expressing his unwillingness to join the revised opinions going on constitutional grounds. Whittaker was then persuaded, primarily by Clark and Stewart, to alter his views on the question of statutory construction. He agreed to join Brennan's original interpretation of the statute. Brennan circulated two June 13 *Memorandums to the Conference* saying that he was going back to his earlier drafts. There was now a majority of five for Brennan's *Street* draft. Warren, Clark, and Stewart joined Brennan's original *Lathrop* draft without reservation. Those four held the balance as to the other constitutional questions tendered in the case, since the other five were split three-to-two as to their disposition (with Frankfurter, Harlan, and Whittaker for the constitutionality of the Bar's political expenditures and Black and Douglas for striking them down).

The result was to reserve that question while upholding the constitutionality of Bar integration as such and affirming the judgment below.

The decisive appeal of Brennan's statutory ground in *Street* was that it left the ultimate resolution of the controversy over union dissenters in the hands of Congress. That was why it was accepted by Warren and why he ultimately refused to go along with Brennan's June 7 willingness to decide the constitutional question. Once it appeared that the constitutional question was going to be avoided in *Street,* there was a strong incentive to do the same in *Lathrop.* Above all, Warren and Brennan feared the decisions in favor of the Bar Association and against the union which might have resulted if the issues were pressed to constitutional decision. Such a divergence and the criticism to which it would have subjected the Court was, if at all possible, to be avoided.

Another important case where Warren and Frankfurter differed was *United States v. du Pont.*[133] Warren's view prevailed because Clark and Harlan, who usually went along with Frankfurter, disqualified themselves. The case was a continuation of the 1956 *du Pont* decision, which had ruled that the ownership of 23 percent of General Motors stock by du Pont was an anti-trust violation. The case was remanded to the district court to determine the proper remedy. The government recommended that du Pont be required to divest itself of the stock. The district court rejected the government's plan in favor of a less drastic remedy.

At the *du Pont* conference on February 24, 1961, Warren said that he would reverse. As he saw it, "The remedy ordered is inadequate. The judgment . . . isn't enough on what's needed to achieve a remedy for the violation." Warren said he thought the cases under the Sherman Act supported divestiture. "Latitude in how to do it," he recognized, "is there. But the only real relief is divestiture." The Chief concluded that he would "send it back to order divestiture within a period [of time]. Let them do it as they work, but start in a reasonable time."

Frankfurter, in opposition, stressed the need for restraint in reviewing the lower court. "The case turns for me," he declared, "on the answer to the question, 'what is [our] duty toward the decree of the district judge?' If there was no abuse of discretion, we have no business upsetting the decree." Stewart voiced the same view, saying, "our question is not the ideal decree, but whether there was an abuse of discretion. I can't see any and would affirm." The vote was four (Warren, Black, Douglas, and Brennan) to three (Frankfurter, Whittaker, and Stewart) for reversal. As they had done in the first *du Pont* case, Clark and Harlan disqualified themselves.

Warren assigned the opinion to Brennan, who had also delivered the opinion in the 1956 *du Pont* case. The opinion was issued May 22, 1961. Frankfurter announced a vigorous dissent, joined by Whittaker and Stewart. "We are asked, in essence," he said in a passage not in his printed dissent, "to enter Alice's Wonderland where proof is unnecessary and the governing rule of law is 'sentence first, verdict after.' "[134] Even Black conceded, in a May 18 letter to Brennan, that, "as a whole I think Felix has written as forceful a dissent as can be written against our view."

Of course, Warren and Frankfurter were not on opposite sides in every case of consequence during the 1960 Term. A case where the two worked together to secure a unanimous Court was *Gomillion v. Lightfoot*.[135] Lightfoot, a black resident of Tuskegee, challenged an Alabama law redefining Tuskegee's boundaries. The law altered the shape of the city from a square to what the Court termed "an uncouth twenty-eight-sided figure" that removed from Tuskegee almost all its black voters, but none of its white voters. The purpose, said the Court, was that of "fencing Negro citizens out of town so as to deprive them of their pre-existing municipal vote." The lower court dismissed the action, relying on the 1946 decision in *Colegrove v. Green*,[136] which had held that federal courts should not exercise jurisdiction over cases complaining of inequality in the apportionment of legislative districts. Six of the Brethren voted to grant certiorari, with Clark, Whittaker, and Stewart for denial.

At the conference on October 21, 1960, Warren had no doubt that the Court should reverse, saying, "We don't have to deal with the *Colegrove* line of cases." On this complaint, there was a clear constitutional violation. Frankfurter, who had written the *Colegrove* opinion, forcefully supported the Chief's view. "The state," he said, "seeks cover under the *Colegrove* line of cases." But this was a different case: "the statute passed here [may appear] an act narrowly dealing with redistricting, but, actually and demonstrably from objective manifestations, it is a function of separating black from white."

Warren chose Frankfurter to write the opinion. Though the conference vote had been unanimous for reversal, Douglas and Whittaker prepared separate concurring opinions. Both the Chief and Frankfurter worked to persuade them not to issue their concurrences. They succeeded with Douglas, who withdrew his separate opinion, after Frankfurter made a change in his discussion of *Colegrove*. Frankfurter wrote Warren that he was willing to make the change and said, "If this seems a helpful change to avoid his concurring opinion, you might care to put it to him."[137] Frankfurter also revised his draft, as he noted, "to meet Black J.'s desire for deletions regarding *Colegrove v. Green* with which he disagreed and still does."[138] Frankfurter wrote Black that he did this "with a view of avoiding what is avoidable"— i.e., a Black concurrence. Referring to his hope for a unanimous opinion, Frankfurter declared, "Nothing has been more persistently or strongly in my mind than this desideratum."[139]

But Whittaker persisted in his separate concurrence. The opinion of the Court announced by Frankfurter November 14, 1960, was joined by all except Whittaker, who concurred separately on the ground that the decision should be rested on the equal protection guaranty of the Fourteenth Amendment, rather than the prohibition against racial discrimination in voting of the Fifteenth Amendment.

Warren and Frankfurter also cooperated to avoid decision of an important constitutional issue in *Poe v. Ullman*.[140] A husband and wife and their doctor brought actions for declaratory judgments challenging the constitutionality of a Connecticut statute that prohibited use of contraceptive devices and giving medical advice on their use.

The complaints alleged that the state's attorney intended to prosecute violators, but, though the law had been on the books since 1879, there had never been any prosecutions to enforce it. The state court dismissed the complaints.

Warren began the March 3, 1961, conference by saying, "I don't see how we could declare this bad on its face, but, as applied, it seemed to me wholly bad." Despite this, the Chief indicated that he would vote for dismissal. "It seems to me now," he commented, "they're made as guinea pigs for an abstract principle. We don't want to decide a contrived litigation."

The Chief also said that the state court had not decided a number of questions and there was thus no proper record on which to decide the constitutional questions.

Frankfurter, Clark, Whittaker, and Brennan voted with Warren for dismissal. Black, Douglas, Harlan, and Stewart voted the other way. Black said he would affirm as far as the patient was concerned. But he thought the First Amendment would prohibit prosecution of the doctor. Douglas and Harlan thought the law unconstitutional on its face. Stewart met Warren's approach by saying, "I don't think this law is a dead letter when, as a practical matter, there's no [birth control] clinic in Connecticut."

Surprisingly perhaps, the most emotional conference statement was made by Harlan, normally the most reserved of the Brethren. He started by saying he thought the Court had no business dismissing these cases. "I can't say," he went on, "that this is a feigned business. This is a full adjudication, as I see it, in Connecticut." On the merits, Harlan declared, "I think the statute is egregiously unconstitutional on its face. The argument submerged the real constitutional question. The Due Process Clause has substantive content for me. The right to be let alone is embodied in due process. Despite the broad powers to legislate in the area of health, there are limits." Harlan concluded by asserting, "This is more offensive to the right to be let alone than anything possibly could be."

The conference vote remained the basis for the *Poe v. Ullman* decision. Frankfurter was assigned the majority opinion. His opinion, delivered June 19, 1961, dismissed the complaints on the ground that, since the Connecticut law had never been enforced, there was no real case but only a hypothetical one for adjudication by the Court. Warren, Clark (who had written, "Good riddance! Join me up."),[141] and

Whittaker joined Frankfurter's opinion. Brennan wrote a short concurrence, agreeing that the case was not yet ripe for adjudication. Black dissented, saying he believed the constitutional questions should be decided. Douglas and Harlan also wrote dissents urging that the cases should not be dismissed and, on the merits, finding that the law violated due process. Stewart joined them in dissenting from the dismissal of the appeals.

Warren himself wrote the opinion in *McGowan v. Maryland*,[142] where the First Amendment's guaranty of religious freedom was at issue. McGowan worked in a large discount department store in Maryland. She was convicted for selling a loose-leaf binder on Sunday in violation of the state's criminal statutes commonly known as Sunday Closing Laws or Blue Laws. She claimed that the laws violated the constitutional guaranty of separation of Church and State. The highest state court affirmed the conviction. All the Brethren voted to take the appeal.

At the conference on December 8, 1960, Warren spoke in favor of affirmance. According to the Chief, "a proper economic and social objective supports these laws." But, he asked, "have they a right to select a particular day?" He answered, "I think so and the fact that the day conforms to the usages and habits of most people doesn't make this an invasion of religious beliefs or a preference for particular ones."

Only Douglas disagreed. "None of these statutes," he asserted, "comport with the First Amendment. I think we're entitled to our religious scruples, but I don't see how we can make everyone else attune to them. I can't be required to goose-step because eighty or ninety percent goose-step."

Warren circulated a draft opinion of the Court upholding the Sunday Laws on March 9, 1961. It was substantially revised, largely to meet objections by Black who said that, while he agreed with the opinion, some changes would be required in order to satisfy him. In particular, Black objected to the Chief's statement of the test of a forbidden "establishment" of religion as state regulation that operated "predominantly" to support religion. In the revised draft, circulated May 2, the language of "predominant" effect was eliminated and the touchstone became whether legislation does or does not aid religion. To accord with this test, Warren omitted a passage acknowledging that Sunday-observance, when state-compelled, was, in practical fact, quite another phenomenon than state-compelled Tuesday-observance.

Black also objected to an assertion in the draft that it was relevant to the constitutionality of state regulation that the regulation was, historically, of long standing. Warren omitted this statement, as well as a qualification of Black's famous dictum in the 1947 *Everson* case that the First Amendment forbids government to "set up a church . . . pass laws which aid one religion, aid all religions, or prefer one religion over another."[143] Warren's first draft had said that this statement had to be read in the context of *Everson's* facts, but the qualification was deleted after Black protested.[144]

Warren delivered the *McGowan* opinion May 29, 1961, with only Douglas dissenting. Once again, however, Frankfurter would not let the opinion of the Court speak for him. He circulated a memorandum for the conference, which stated that "The problem raised in these cases is one that cuts so deep that it is hardly to be expected that any one opinion would express the views of all who concur in the result." Therefore, said Frankfurter, "I will find it necessary in due course to circulate a detailed separate opinion reaching the same basic result as that which the Chief Justice reaches."[145]

When Warren issued his *McGowan* opinion, Frankfurter put out a lengthy separate opinion, joined by Harlan. Warren had talked with Harlan, but failed to persuade him not to join Frankfurter's opinion, even though Harlan conceded, "No doubt some will find little difference between the course of your analysis and that of Felix's separate opinion."[146] A little earlier, Harlan had written Frankfurter "that the CJ's [opinion leaves] me so unsatisfied, that I have decided not to join [it]."[147]

There was much less difficulty in deciding another case on religious freedom, *Torcaso v. Watkins*.[148] Torcaso was appointed to the office of Notary Public by the Governor of Maryland, but he was refused a commission because he would not declare his belief in God as required by the state constitution. The highest Maryland court held that the requirement did not violate the First and Fourteenth Amendments.

At the *Torcaso* conference on April 28, 1961, the Chief urged reversal, "This law," he said, "requires all people to profess belief in God, whether they are doubters or atheists. The fact that we are a religious people can't mean that public office constitutionally must depend upon belief in God. It interferes with free exercise of religion."

All the Justices agreed that the Maryland requirement violated the First Amendment, though Clark and Stewart said that they would go on the basis of the amendment's Establishment, rather than its Free Exercise, Clause. Black delivered the opinion of the Court following Warren's approach on June 19. There were no dissents, though Frankfurter and Harlan stated that they only concurred in the result.

One of the things that had most concerned District Attorney Warren was corruption in government. He had always been vigorous in prosecuting corrupt public officials and went out of his way, in his 1957 *Watkins* opinion, to stress that the limitations laid down there did not apply to "the power of Congress to inquire into and publicize corruption, maladministration or inefficiency in agencies of the Government."[149] Feeling as he did, the Chief Justice took a strong view in *United States v. Mississippi Valley Generating Co.,*[150] popularly known as the Dixon–Yates Case. In 1954, President Eisenhower had ordered the Atomic Energy Commission to negotiate a contract with a company created as a subsidiary of two utility holding companies headed by Messrs. Dixon and Yates for the building of a huge power plant in Tennessee. Wenzell, a vice-president of First Boston Corp., worked part-time as a Bureau of the Budget consultant on the financing that would have to be undertaken under the proposed contract. He gave the sponsors an opinion letter on the cost of the financing that contained information for which First Boston was the source. After the contract was signed, First Boston became the financing agent for the project, though it later announced that it would not charge any fee.

At the time, the Dixon–Yates affair developed into a minor scandal, both because of Wenzell's role and President Eisenhower's alleged favoritism toward political cronies. In August 1954, Justice Minton had written Frankfurter, "My regard for the Senate has fallen almost as low as that for Ike. . . . Maybe he didn't order the Dixon–Yates Contract to be signed because Bobby Jones his golfing pal was in the Syndicate—but the fact is he ordered the Contract without bidding and Bobby was a beneficiary. Why did he order the Contract made??? I am sure he wouldn't give a Contract for money but I am not sure of that old army game of helping your pals."[151]

The A.E.C. ultimately canceled the contract because it found that the proposed plant was no longer needed. Dixon–Yates then sued the government for the sums it had spent in connection with the contract. The government claimed that the contract was unenforceable because of an illegal conflict of interest, since Wenzell, as an officer of First Boston, was "directly or indirectly" interested in the contract which he, as an agent of the government, had helped to negotiate. Section 434 of the Federal Criminal Code prohibited anyone "directly or indirectly" interested in a company from acting for the United States in transacting business with the company.

"I think section 434 is made to order for this situation," Warren declared at the conference on October 19, 1960. He noted that Wenzell worked out the financing of the money even though he was an officer of First Boston. "Whether it was a good contract or not," said the Chief, "is irrelevant. What is crucial is that Wenzell's advice to Dixon and the Government wound his firm up with the deal. It's unimportant, too, that they finally waived the fee. Wenzell was as much connected with Dixon–Yates as with First Boston."

Warren himself delivered the Dixon–Yates opinion January 9, 1961, with Harlan, Whittaker, and Stewart dissenting, holding for the government because of Wenzell's conflict of interest. The opinion stressed the purpose of section 434 "to insure honesty in the Government's business dealings" and traced its foundation to the Biblical admonition that no man may serve two masters.[152] At Frankfurter's suggestion, two sentences were deleted from the opinion that, as Frankfurter put it in a letter to the Chief, "are impliedly derogatory of 'the business community of which Wenzell is a part.'" Warren had referred to "the relaxed standards of the market place." Frankfurter objected to this, saying that, "considering the extent to which the federal regulatory agencies have for some time been under fire for less-than-fastidious standards (see *e.g.*, the Landis Report, just issued), backfire is invited." In addition, wrote the Justice, "I see no advantage in diverting to self-defense the business community from attention to the moral lesson which they are here given."[153]

Despite Warren's acceptance of his suggestion, Frankfurter wrote Harlan, "I should not have read, as I did, the Chief's opinion in *Yates–Dixon* on Christmas Day, for it was not calculated to enhance my good-will to him. . . . his crude, heavy-handed repetitive moralizing makes me feel like eating rancid butter. . . . I cannot help believing that E.W. has the bias of a sansculotte."[154]

Warren's attitude in the Dixon–Yates case should be compared with that in *Eastern Railroad Presidents Conference v. Noerr Motor Freight,* [155] another case in which improper conduct was alleged. Noerr, a Pennsylvania trucker, brought an anti-trust suit against an association of railroads, charging a conspiracy to restrain trade in the freight business. The charge was based on extensive publicity campaigns by which the railroads had attempted to influence legislation adverse to truckers. The lower courts held for the truckers, finding that the railroads had intended to destroy the truckers' goodwill and had used fraudulent material. Warren, Black, Harlan, Brennan, and Stewart voted to grant certiorari, with the others for denial.

"This was a ruthless campaign," Warren declared at the December 16, 1960, conference. "But I'm strongly impressed that the judgment was wrong. This is not an anti-trust case or conspiracy within those laws." Warren felt that the injunction below "raised First Amendment problems." The Chief conceded that, "at first I thought paragraph 4 [of the complaint], involving publication of false matter, might stand; but, since this was not an anti-trust violation, that fails also."

Despite the closeness of the cert vote, all agreed with Warren that, in light of the First Amendment implications, the Sherman Act should not be construed to reach these activities. "If we can put qualification of 'reasonableness' on the statute," said Frankfurter, "we certainly can put qualification of these means as outside the statute—an inherent limitation that Congress never meant to include either ends or means protected by the First Amendment."

Black delivered a unanimous opinion on February 20, 1961, holding that the railroads' activities did not violate the anti-trust laws. As he summarized it in a pencilled note to one of the Brethren, "Congress did not mean to take away your Constitutional right to get or to block legislation because thereby you'll be doing in your competitor."

Mention should also be made of two criminal law cases that were decided without dissent. The first was *Ferguson v. Georgia.* [156] Ferguson appealed a Georgia murder conviction. Georgia was then the only state retaining the common-law rule that a criminal defendant was incompetent to testify in his own behalf. Section 416 of the Georgia Criminal Code expressly barred criminal defendants from testifying, though section 415 did permit them to make any unsworn statement they chose. The trial court had permitted Ferguson to make such a statement, but had denied him the right to have his attorney question him to elicit the statement. Ferguson claimed that this violated his constitutional right to counsel. The Georgia Supreme Court affirmed the conviction. All the Justices voted to hear the appeal.

At the November 18, 1960, conference,[157] Warren referred to the Georgia law as "antiquated." The provision for defendant's incompetency, he noted, "is out of date throughout the country." The Chief also felt that Ferguson was "entitled to the protection and guidance of counsel throughout the trial. I would treat section 415 and section 416 as a package and would declare that both violated the Constitution."

Black stated that they did not have to reach section 416, since they could go on the violation of the right to counsel. "If they let him speak," Black said, "he's entitled to a lawyer to help guide him." Frankfurter agreed with Warren that both provisions should be stricken down. "This case," he asserted, "shows why one must have a philosophy of the Fourteenth [Amendment]. Is this due process? If its old, its 'due.'" Frankfurter referred to cases so holding. "The essence of law for me," he went on, "is continuity through change. But history here doesn't have its usual weight. Georgia is the only state still having this rule of incompetency and it's against the overwhelming tide."

Clark said, "if we go off on Hugo's theory, I'll vote to affirm." Harlan agreed, remarking, "I can't say the right to counsel extends to this."

Black adhered to his position, and all but Frankfurter and Clark went along with him in voting for reversal on the ground that section 415, as applied here, violated Ferguson's constitutional right to counsel. Brennan delivered the opinion of the Court March 27, 1961, going on the denial of counsel. Frankfurter and Clark issued concurring opinions, urging that both sections had to be considered and that both violated due process. Brennan explained in a letter to Frankfurter that "I found it impossible . . . to strike down 38–416, the validity of which the appellant did not raise, and thus be forced to hold that 38–415, which he did challenge, was constitutionally invulnerable. I am satisfied that the only way out is the way I've taken, leaving the problem of 38–416 to await its presentation in another case. Still better, I hope that the opinion will induce the Georgia

Legislature to repeal 38–416 which should have been done long ago."[158]

Brennan also wrote Clark, "if we strike down [section] 416 for a prisoner who did not offer himself as a witness, . . . every other prisoner now in Georgia jails might be entitled to a new trial even though he never offered himself as a witness."[159]

The second criminal law decision to be discussed is *Silverman v. United States*.[160] Though the decision was without dissent, there was actually a sharp division in the Court on the issues raised. Silverman had been convicted of gambling. The police had installed a "spike microphone" through the wall of the adjoining house to overhear incriminating conversations in Silverman's house. The lower court had ruled that admission of police testimony regarding these conversations had not violated the Fourth Amendment. The Brethren had split on whether to grant certiorari, with Warren, Frankfurter, Douglas, and Brennan voting to grant and the rest to deny.

In the 1928 *Olmstead* case,[161] the Court held, over the famous dissents of Holmes and Brandeis, that wiretapping did not violate the Fourth Amendment. Later cases explained that *Olmstead* authorized electronic eavesdropping where there was no physical trespass. At the December 9, 1960, *Silverman* conference, Warren stated that he thought that *Olmstead* should be overruled. He also said that the Court "could say this was a trespass if we had to. But that's equivocating."

The conference discussion indicated a close split on Warren's recommendation that *Olmstead* should be overruled. Frankfurter, Douglas, and Brennan said that they, too, were ready to vote to overrule *Olmstead*. Frankfurter made the longest statement in support of the Chief. He started by attempting to reconcile his support with his basic judicial philosophy. "We have to face up to stare decisis," he said, "and the role it plays in the thinking and acting of the Court. I accept the broad classification between constitutional and statutory interpretation. But respect for either cannot be cast into an absolute formula. Law is too complicated and elusive to allow absolutes. We are not bound as to constitutional but are as to statutory." *Olmstead* involved constitutional interpretation and Frankfurter asserted that his agreement that "we should overrule *Olmstead*" was not inconsistent with his general judicial posture.

As already seen, in cases involving the Fourth Amendment, there was a virtual reversal in judicial approaches as between Frankfurter and Black. Frankfurter, as he wrote in the April 19, 1957, letter to Warren quoted in chapter 7, was a "nut" on the subject of Fourth Amendment enforcement. Black, on the other hand, read the Fourth Amendment narrowly. In the *Silverman* conference, Black led the opposition to Warren's *Olmstead* proposal. "I'm not willing," he declared, "to overrule *Olmstead*. . . . I'm not persuaded *Olmstead* was wrong. The Fourth Amendment uses the word 'unreasonable,' so there's latitude."

Harlan remarked, "We can't say there's been indiscriminate lawlessness of officers since *Olmstead*." He felt the same after Frankfurter sent him *The Eavesdroppers*,[162] a book that detailed the abuses of wiretapping and other forms of electronic eavesdropping. "It leaves me still unpersuaded," he wrote Frankfurter "that we should overrule *Olmstead*."[163]

Since Clark and Whittaker also supported Black, Stewart's vote was once again decisive. He refused to overrule *Olmstead*. Instead, he was willing to vote for reversal on the second ground stated by Warren—that the unauthorized physical penetration of the "spike mike" into Silverman's house constituted a trespass. "I think it's important," said Stewart, "to have a test on whether there's a trespass."

The conference vote was five-to-four for reversal because of the unauthorized physical intrusion. Clark had doubted the trespass holding, saying, "we can't measure the wall either. The findings are not that there was a trespass, so the burden of proof was not carried." But the others who were against overruling *Olmstead* agreed that the conviction should be reversed because of the trespass, and Clark decided to go along. Black, the senior Justice in the majority, assigned the opinion to Stewart. He wrote an opinion reversing on the trespass ground. Warren and his supporters ultimately decided not to dissent on the *Olmstead* issue. When Stewart delivered the opinion on March 6, 1961, there were no dissents.

During the 1959 and 1960 Terms, the balance clearly shifted between the Warren and Frankfurter wings of the Court. As often as not, Frankfurter was able to secure a majority and, in the process, was able to modify some of the important decisions of the 1956 Term.

It is fair to say, however, that it was the Chief Justice who won the most important decisions during Frankfurter's last terms. This was particularly true, as we will now see, of two of the most significant cases decided by the Warren Court: *Mapp v. Ohio* [164] and *Baker v. Carr.* [165]

10.

1960—1961 TERMS: CHANGING GUARD AND CHANGING LAW

January 20, 1961, was one of the coldest days within Washington memory. The inauguration of John F. Kennedy, who braved the weather without hat or overcoat, soon became part of American legend. After the oath taking and presidential address came the inauguration parade. Later at about six o'clock that evening one of Warren's law clerks was walking up Pennsylvania Avenue. He recalls that the reviewing stand at the White House was by then empty except for the President, the Chief Justice, and Mrs. Warren.

The next day the clerk asked Warren, who was then almost seventy, "What were you doing up there in that reviewing box at six o'clock in that zero weather?"

The Chief looked as if he did not understand the question. "You know," he replied, "the President of the United States invited me and he hadn't left, so I couldn't go either."

The new President sent Warren a note of thanks "for the generous role you played in . . . the Inauguration ceremonies." Kennedy stressed "Your cheerful endurance" during both the inauguration and the parade.[1]

On the Saturday following the inauguration, there was a ceremonial swearing in by the Chief Justice of Kennedy's Cabinet in the Gold Room of the White House. One member of that Cabinet, Secretary of Labor Arthur J. Goldberg, and a member of the sub-Cabinet, Deputy Attorney General Byron R. White, were soon to become Warren's colleagues.

The Chief and the Brethren had been far from Kennedy enthusiasts before the 1960 election. Most of them shared the sentiment expressed in a letter by Frankfurter to Judge Learned Hand: "Am I wrong in assuming that you do not look forward to the coming election with great cheer? At least that is my state of mind. I [note] that the Washington correspondent for the *London Times* reports to his paper that Kennedy is a man of 'polished ruthlessness.' I wish I were sure about the polished part of it."[2]

Former California Governor Edmund G. Brown recalls that he was shooting ducks with Warren before the 1960 Democratic Convention. The two had wandered off from the rest of the party. Knowing they were completely alone, Brown asked, "Who should I be for for President?" Warren leaned over, looked around to see that no one was near by, and stealthily whispered, "Adlai Stevenson."

Yet Kennedy had just the type of youthful vigor that appealed to Warren. The Chief soon appreciated the President's efforts to infuse the nation with a new spirit. Then, too, Warren was bound to be predisposed in favor of a man who had defeated Richard Nixon. Their common feelings toward the defeated Republican candidate laid the foundation for what became a warm relationship. Just after the 1962 election, when Nixon had lost his bid for Governor of California, Kennedy and Warren were flying to Eleanor Roosevelt's funeral. "Say," said the President to Mary McGrory, a reporter who was on the plane, "that was a nice story you wrote about Nixon." Warren then showed Kennedy a batch of clippings on Nixon's defeat. "It would have been hard to say," McGrory recalls, "watching their faces, who had enjoyed the downfall more, the Chief Justice or the President of the United States. They had their heads together over the clipping and were laughing like schoolboys over the contents."[3]

Warren, always sensitive to the dignity of his office, was also favorably impressed by Kennedy's efforts to stress his personal appreciation to the Chief Justice and the Court. Soon after Kennedy was sworn in, on March 18, 1961, Warren's past and present law clerks gave a dinner for the Chief in honor of his seventieth birthday. The President was a surprise visitor, dropping by at the affair in the Metropolitan Club on his way to the Radio and Television Correspondents dinner. Warren was delighted and, in his letter of thanks, typically stressed that "the law clerks were thrilled to have an opportunity to meet you."[4]

A few days earlier, to underline his support for the judicial branch, the President had sent a warm greeting to the annual meeting of the United States Judicial Conference, over which the Chief Justice presided. Two years later, congratulating Warren on his birthday, Kennedy referred to his gratitude "for the dignity and wisdom of your judicial leadership in the past ten years. Although it is not possible for all of us to be your clerks, in a very real sense we are all your students."[5] This was just the sort of gesture that would turn Warren into a warm admirer of the President.

The new decade saw a changing of the guard in the Marble Palace as well as the White House, for after the 1961 Term a stroke forced Felix Frankfurter to retire. As we saw in the last chapter, Frankfurter's last terms saw a shifting majority between the Warren and Frankfurter wings of the Court. The balance had, however, started to swing back toward the Chief Justice with the seminal decisions in *Mapp v. Ohio*[6] and *Baker v. Carr.*[7] Loss of the latter decision was, indeed, a key factor in Justice Frankfurter's physical collapse, as he saw all but Harlan ultimately desert him.

According to a *New York Times* survey of the 1960 Term, the decision in *Mapp v. Ohio* was the "most far-reaching constitutional step of the term."[8] Former Justice Abe Fortas went even further. "To me," he said, "the most radical decision in recent times was Mapp against Ohio." *Mapp* deserves this characterization because it overruled the 1949 decision in *Wolf v. Colorado*[9]—one of the cornerstones of the Frankfurter juristic edifice. *Wolf* held of course that the exclusionary rule was not required by the U.S. Constitution in state criminal cases. The result was, in the words of Frankfurter's *Wolf* opinion, "that in a prosecution in a State court for a State crime the Fourteenth Amendment does not forbid the admission of evidence obtained by an unreasonable search and seizure."[10]

Dollree Mapp was the catalyst. She had been convicted of having obscene books and pictures. Police officers had had information that a wanted person was hiding in Mapp's Cleveland home and that "policy paraphernalia" were also hidden there. Mapp had refused to admit the police without a search warrant, but they forcibly opened her door, physically subdued her, searched the house and discovered what was claimed as obscene materials. For her part Mapp maintained that her conviction was invalid because the Ohio statute providing that "no person shall knowingly . . . have in his possession or under his control an obscene, lewd or lascivious book [or] . . . picture" violated the First Amendment. The Ohio Supreme Court had upheld the statute and had affirmed the conviction. When Mapp turned to the Supreme Court, all the Justices, except Frankfurter, voted to hear her appeal.

The memorandum by his law clerk to Clark[11] (as we will see, the key Justice in the case), recommending that he vote to take the appeal, confirmed that the "main point" presented was the constitutionality of the Ohio statute barring possession of obscene material. "I think," the clerk wrote, "it should fall under Smith v. California,"[12] discussed in chapter 9, and the memo from Harlan's Clerk similarly stated though more categorically, "This is an obscenity case."[13]

The briefs and arguments in the Supreme Court were devoted also to the First Amendment issue. Only the brief of the American Civil Liberties Union, appearing as amicus curiae, referred to *Wolf* and asked the Court to reexamine and overrule it, though without any argumentation to support the request.

At the March 31, 1961, conference after the argument, the discussion continued to be devoted almost entirely to the constitutionality of the Ohio obscenity statute. Warren set the theme by declaring that the law "cuts across First Amendment rights. It's too broad a statute to accomplish its purpose, and on that basis I'd reverse." All the others agreed that the conviction should be reversed on the First Amendment ground. As Stewart put it, "if this stuff isn't covered by the First and Fourteenth" Amendments, it was hard to see what would be.

The conference discussion and vote was summed up by Harlan in a letter to Clark: "I would have supposed that the Court would have little difficulty in agreeing (as indeed I thought the whole Court had) that a state prohibition against mere knowing possession of obscene material, without any requirement of a showing that such possession was with a purpose to disseminate the offensive matter, contravenes the Fourteenth Amendment, in that such a statute impermissibly deters freedom of belief and expression, if indeed it is not tantamount to an effort at 'thought control.' "[14]

In his conference discussion, Douglas had agreed with the reversal on the First Amendment. But significantly he also gave *Wolf* as an alternate ground for reversal and said that he was prepared to vote to overrule that case.[15] Warren and Brennan indicated that they would vote with Douglas on *Wolf,* but when there was no support on this from the others, the three agreed to go along with the reversal on First Amendment grounds. The opinion was assigned to Clark.

While Clark was working on the opinion, Douglas reconsidered his agreement to the First Amendment reversal. On April 3, he prepared a draft opinion that stated, "I would apply the Fourth Amendment with full force to the States, making the exclusionary rule part and parcel of the constitutional guarantee. *Wolf v. Colorado* should be modified to that extent. As so modified, it would remove the entire underpinning of this case. The evidence seized and used in evidence having been unconstitutionally obtained, the judgment of conviction should be set aside."

The Douglas opinion was never circulated because Clark had changed his mind just after the conference. On the elevator after leaving the conference room, the Texan turned to Black and Brennan and asked, "wouldn't this be a good case to apply the exclusionary rule and do what *Wolf* didn't do?"

Under questioning by the others, Clark confirmed that he was serious and that he had, indeed, shifted his ground to the Douglas position. Clark's switch made four Justices in favor of the *Wolf* overruling. The key was now Black who, if persuaded, would become the fifth vote. Black, as we have seen, tended to a restrained approach in Fourth Amendment cases. In his discussion with Brennan and Clark, however, the Alabaman showed willingness to agree to a decision overruling *Wolf* insofar as it did not require the states to apply the exclusionary rule, though he indicated that he still had difficulty in doing it on Fourth Amendment grounds alone.

Clark then circulated a draft *Mapp* opinion on April 22.[16] The Clark draft was substantially similar to the opinion of the Court that he delivered on June 19. But there were differences in emphasis. The draft spelled out more fully why "other means of protection" to safe-guard "the right to privacy," other than the exclusionary rule, were "worthless and futile." The draft asked, "How can we expect to de-fend 'the indefeasible right of personal security' by telling him who suffers its invasion to seek damages for 'the breaking of doors'?" The draft referred to an "aroused public opinion and internal police dis-cipline" as "equally without the deterrent value." According to the draft, "it appears hopelessly impractical to consider formulation of an effective body of public opinion as a remedy practicably available to those who suffer unconstitutional invasions of their privacy. They are in large measure criminal defendants, and more unlikely organizers of an effective and respectable public opinion would be difficult to find."

Clark's draft then declared, "We are then at another time for de-cision. . . . The question is whether there presently exists available to citizens of the non-exclusionary states any remedy which can be said to meet 'the minimal standards of Due Process.' One fails of discovery, and we are bound to require adherence to the constitu-tionally mandated rule of *Weeks*."—i.e., the exclusionary rule.

The draft, like the final opinion, quoted Cardozo's noted state-ment, "The criminal is to go free because the constable has blun-dered." It said that, even if, in some cases under the exclusionary rule, this would be the result, "the criminal will go free, if he must, but he will be freed by the law. Even Titus has rights." This appears superior to the version of this passage in the *Mapp* opinion.

The draft next declared, "To say that a government should be able to use unconstitutionally seized evidence because there is no funda-mental prohibition against its use of evidence seized unlawfully by private persons, is to ignore the experience of ages. What can destroy a government more quickly than its failure to observe its own laws, or worse, its disregard of the charter of its own existence?" This, too, seems stylistically better than the passage in the final opinion.

The Clark draft concluded with the following paragraph, omitted from the *Mapp* opinion, except for the last sentence:

Our cases show that the honest and real enjoyment of such rights is wholly determined by the aggregate strength of the available remedies and enforce-ment devices which an individual and his community are able to muster in their defense. In not one has the Court exhibited such a high degree of judicial self-abnegation as would be involved in our further hesitation to take a step made necessary by *Wolf* and promised by *Irvine*. In violations of what other right do we abide unfettered judicial employment of the fruits of official lawlessness? In none, save those of the "core of the Fourth Amendment." The ignoble but doubtless efficient route to conviction left open to the state tends by its very efficiency to destroy the entire system of constitutional restraints on which the liberties of the people rest. Having once recognized, as was done in *Wolf,* that the right is nothing less than constitutional in origin, we can no longer abstain from drawing upon the same source for its safeguard. No longer can we permit it to be revocable at the whim of every policeman who, in the name of law enforcement itself, chooses to suspend its enjoyment.

After he had read the draft, Brennan wrote Clark, "Of course you know I think this is just magnificent and wonderful. I have not joined anything since I came with greater pleasure." [17] Black sent a pencilled note, after receiving a revised draft, telling Clark that none of the statements made "raise insuperable barriers for me." Black went on, "Your discussion of 'privacy' is so limited that it does not justify a belief that you are using it as a synonym for the 4th Amendment."

Black's note did, however, question a statement in the Clark draft that the right embodied by the Fourth Amendment "is vouchsafed against the States by the Due Process Clause." Black wrote, "Since I do not have my 'fortress', a dictionary, handy I am not sure that the word 'vouchsafed' in connection with Due Process accurately describes that clause's application to the states." [18] Despite Black's doubt, the passage remained unchanged in Clark's opinion.

Though Black agreed to the *Mapp* opinion, he felt that he had to explain his vote in a separate concurrence. It stated that though, in his view, the Fourth Amendment alone did not bar illegally seized evidence, the Fourth, taken together with the Fifth Amendment's ban against self-incrimination, required the exclusionary rule. Douglas also concurred, basing his opinion on his April 3 draft. The Douglas opinion stated that, after the *Wolf* decision, there "was a storm of constitutional controversy." [19] On his copy, Frankfurter wrote in the margin, "I wonder in what Weather Bureau this 'storm' was recorded?" [20]

Warren, Douglas, Brennan, and even Black agreed without difficulty to Clark's changed approach in *Mapp*. To the others, however, the draft opinion of the Court reversing on the *Wolf* ground came as a complete surprise. Even today, says Stewart, "I remember how amazed I was when the Justice Clark circulation in *Mapp v. Ohio* hit my desk." After he had read the draft, Stewart wrote Clark, "As I am sure you anticipated, your proposed opinion in this case came as quite a surprise. In all honesty, I seriously question the wisdom of using this case as a vehicle to overrule an important doctrine so recently established and so consistently adhered to." According to Stewart, "the idea of overruling *Wolf* . . . was not even discussed at the Conference, where we all agreed, as I recollect it, that the judgment should be reversed on First Amendment grounds. If *Wolf* is to be reconsidered, I myself would much prefer to do so only in a case that required it, and only after argument of the case by competent counsel and a full Conference discussion."[21] Although Stewart ultimately voted with the majority for reversal of Mapp's conviction, he refused to join the Clark opinion overruling *Wolf,* issuing instead, a short concurrence saying that he would reverse because the Ohio statute was "not 'consistent with the rights of free thought and expression. . . .' "[22]

Harlan also wrote Clark about "my concern over your opinion in this case. . . . Your proposed overruling of *Wolf* is, I submit, both unnecessary and undesirable." As Harlan saw it, Clark's "course threatens a jail delivery of uncertain, but obviously serious, proportions." In addition, "Your opinion will, I predict, prompt much, and perhaps confusing, writing among the Brethren."

Harlan's letter contained a different version of the syllogism that he was to say in his dissent was "at the heart of the majority's opinion" in *Mapp:* "(a) *Wolf* held that the concepts (including, as *Wolf* was interpreted in *Elkins,* the standards) of the Fourth Amendment are carried to the States as part of the 'ordered liberty' assured by the Fourteenth Amendment; (b) the *Weeks* 'exclusionary' rule is part of the Fourth Amendment; and (c) it is therefore incongruous that the *Weeks* rule should not also follow into the States." Harlan declared, "I seriously question the validity of both the minor premise and conclusion of this reasoning."

At the end of his letter, Harlan appended in his own hand, "P.S. If you don't mind my saying so, your opinion comes perilously close to accepting 'incorporation' for the Fourth A., and will doubtless encourage the 'incorporation' enthusiasts."[23]

The foremost of the "incorporation enthusiasts" was, of course,

Black. The "incorporation" issue was one of the principal points of difference between Black and Frankfurter. Since his famous *Adamson* dissent[24] in 1947, Black had consistently urged that the Due Process Clause of the Fourteenth Amendment incorporates all the specific guarantees of the Bill of Rights and hence makes them binding upon the states. Frankfurter just as consistently opposed this view, contending that the Fourteenth Amendment did not incorporate the Bill of Rights verbatim, but only those guarantees that were so fundamental that they were, in Justice Benjamin Cardozo's famous 1937 phrase, "of the very essence of a scheme of ordered liberty."[25] Harlan and Clark (at least until *Mapp*) had been Frankfurter's principal supporters on the "incorporation" issue.

In a reply to Harlan's letter, Clark denied "that the opinion is a windfall to 'incorporation' enthusiasts. If it is, then *Wolf* brought it on."

Clark also gave a succinct explanation of his theory in *Mapp*: "if the right to privacy is really so basic as to be constitutional in rank and if it is really to be enforceable against the states (*Wolf*), then we cannot carve out of the bowels [of] that right the vital part, the stuff that gives it substance, the exclusion of evidence. It has long been recognized and honored as an integral part of the equivalent right against federal action."

Clark concluded his letter, "I hope that you will restudy the opinion, John, and find logic and reason in it."[26] Instead, Harlan circulated a strong dissent on May 31. It was joined by Frankfurter and Whittaker on June 2. This meant that, when the *Mapp* decision to overrule *Wolf* and impose the exclusionary rule in state criminal cases was announced on June 19, it was only by a bare majority, since Stewart had, as already seen, concurred in the vote for reversal only on the First Amendment ground.

Only four days before the *Mapp* decision came down, Black wrote to Clark saying, "I am disturbed by the sentence . . . in your opinion that 'Since the Fourth Amendment's *right of privacy* has been declared enforceable against the States through the Due Process Clause of the Fourteenth, it is enforceable against them by the same sanction of exclusion as is used against the Federal Government.' [Emphasis supplied]. This, I think, makes it necessary for me to say that my agreement to your opinion depends upon my understanding that you read *Wolf* as having held, and that we are holding here, that the Fourth Amendment *as a whole* is applicable to the States and not some imaginary and unknown fragment designated as the 'right of privacy.' "

Black said that his concurrence in Clark's opinion was based upon this understanding. "If I am wrong in this and your opinion means that the Fourth Amendment does not apply to the States *as a whole,* I am unwilling to agree to decide this crucial question in this case . . . In other words, I am agreeing to decide this question in this case and agreeing to yours as the opinion for the Court on the basis of my understanding that the holding and opinion mean that hereafter the Fourth Amendment, when applied either to the state or federal governments, is to be given equal scope and coverage in both instances. If this is not correct, I think the case should be set down for reargument as the dissenters suggest."[27]

Clark replied the same day that "the gist of the opinion is that *Wolf* held the entire Fourth Amendment to be carried over against the states through the Fourteenth, and therefore the exclusionary rule which *Weeks* applied to federal cases must likewise be made applicable to state prosecutions."[28] Apparently, this was enough for Black, and he did not withdraw his concurrence in the overruling of *Wolf.*

To Frankfurter, the *Mapp* decision was a serious defeat. The Justice's bitterness over what he deemed Clark's apostasy in *Mapp* is shown in a 1964 letter to Alexander Bickel, a former law clerk who had written that the basis of *Mapp* was "an empirical judgment." Frankfurter wrote that when "you will examine my file in the *Mapp* case, you will find not a hint or an indication of any such thing but quite on the contrary you will find that my dissent was originally the Court's opinion and became the dissent because the Hon. Tom C. Clark flopped, and he did so after writing me a warm note of concurrence adding, 'Only fiat could answer your opinion.' "[29]

The Justice's memory here was faulty. Frankfurter never wrote a dissent in *Mapp*—much less one that had originally been the Court's opinion. The Justice was confusing *Mapp* with *Baker v. Carr,* where, we will see later in this chapter, Clark did send the note of concurrence quoted by Frankfurter, only to switch his vote later. But the letter does show Frankfurter's strong feelings about Clark's change of position in the *Mapp* case.

The defeat Frankfurter suffered in the 1960 Term in *Mapp* was soon to be overshadowed by his loss in *Baker v. Carr*,[30] one of the most important cases decided by the Warren Court. Before we deal with *Baker v. Carr*, however, the other decisions during the 1961 Term—Frankfurter's last—in which the Justice participated should be discussed.

During the term, the Court's workload continued to increase. So heavy had it become, indeed, that the Justices did not make their annual visit to Capitol Hill to hear the January 1962 State of the Union address. It was reported that their failure to attend was caused by the pressure of the Court's business.[31] The Brethren did, however, find time to recess to join the celebration for Lieutenant Colonel John Glenn, the first American astronaut to orbit the globe.[32] Warren also tried to get away from Washington whenever possible. In the summer of 1961 he went on his world tour. A year later, he traveled to Israel and was a guest of Agnes Meyer (wife of the *Washington Post* publisher), along with Adlai Stevenson and columnist Drew Pearson, on a Mediterranean cruise, during which he visited President Tito of Yugoslavia on his island retreat of Brioni. Warren caused some anxiety when he went swimming in the Adriatic. "Tito," Pearson later remembered, "warned him to be careful about the sharks, but he kept on swimming just the same."

In the following Christmas recess, Warren went on a duck-hunting trip with California Governor Brown, who had been a friend since the Chief himself had been Governor. "We used to hunt once a year," Brown recalls, "We'd go up there on a Friday. . . . And Warren would always have his boys with him and four or five of his old close friends." According to Brown, the trips were "very, very pleasant. We talked about everything. We played poker afterwards. Earl Warren played a good game of poker and played it with intensity."[33]

Warren had gotten tremendous pleasure from Brown's decisive defeat of Richard Nixon a month earlier. As Chief Justice, Warren could, of course, no longer speak out on political issues. But he had come close to doing so in an October 1962 speech at a building dedication in Oakland, and his son, Earl, Jr., had served as Brown's campaign vice-chairman. Brown himself says that it was Warren's dislike of Nixon that led him to let his son take the campaign position, with its clear inference that Warren was for Brown.

While he was in California, Warren was interviewed by Richard H. Rodda, political editor of the *Sacramento Bee*. The Chief Justice refused to discuss politics until nearly the end of the interview, when he leaned forward and asked, "Now Dick, off the record, do you think Pat Brown can beat Nixon?"

"It will be close, but I think Brown will win," was the answer.

Warren beamed as he retorted, "I think he's going to beat the hell out of Nixon! I can just feel it. I can't get involved, of course. But Nixon has to be stopped." According to Rodda, "the expression on [Warren's] face as he savored a Brown victory was revealing."[34]

Except for their fundamental split in *Baker v. Carr,* there were no important disagreements over decisions between Warren and Frankfurter during the 1961 Term. In addition, their personal relations were less marked by friction than they had been in previous terms. It was almost as though they had a premonition that the term would be Frankfurter's last, making their dispute over the proper scope of judicial review only a matter of Court history.

Of course, all was not suddenly sweetness and light between the Chief and the Justice. The two differed during the conference discussion in *Hoyt v. Florida.*[35] Mrs. Hoyt had been convicted in a Florida court of murdering her husband with a baseball bat. The jury was selected under a statute permitting women to decline to serve on juries. She claimed that her trial before an all-male jury worked an unconstitutional exclusion of women from jury service. The Florida Supreme Court affirmed the conviction.

Warren spoke strongly in favor of reversal at the October 20, 1961, conference. "I would do this," he stated, "on the narrow ground that, in this case, this statute has been limited to ten [women] a year out of 223 eligibles. This is a particularly flagrant case where a woman needs the help of a woman."

Frankfurter took the opposite view, saying, "how can we say there has been a systematic exclusion here?" Warren was supported only by Black and Douglas, and they decided ultimately to go along with an affirmance. Harlan delivered the opinion, holding that the Florida exemption did not work an arbitrary exclusion of women from jury service. Warren and his supporters did not dissent, but they set the stage for future challenges to sexual classifications when they issued a one-paragraph concurrence stressing the need for a state to make "a good faith effort to have women perform jury duty without discrimination on the ground of sex." [36]

Another case where Warren disagreed with Frankfurter at the conference but ultimately went along with a decision following the Justice's view was *St. Regis Paper Co. v. United States.* [37] The Federal Trade Commission brought an action to enforce orders directing St. Regis to turn over copies of reports it had submitted to the Census Bureau and to impose a $100 a day penalty for each day of noncompliance. St. Regis contended that it could not lawfully be required to produce the reports because the Census Act made them confidential.

At the November 10, 1961, conference, the Chief Justice said that he "would hold that the census reports are privileged and would not find a waiver." He also thought that "the imposition of penalties went too far," relying on a prior case which held that penalties might not be imposed for noncompliance with substantially defective orders. A majority, led by Frankfurter, disagreed. Here, too, Warren went along with the opinion of the Court rejecting the claim of privilege, which was delivered by Clark on December 11. Black, joined by Whittaker and Stewart, dissented.

In the *Hoyt* and *St. Regis* cases, Warren did not feel strongly enough to fragment the Court further by dissenting. In *Lanza v. New York,* [38] he refused to remain silent at what he saw, in the words of his dissent, as "conduct . . . universally reproached." Lanza had been convicted for refusing to testify before a New York legislative committee. He claimed that the questions put to him had been based on a conversation he had had with his brother in the visitors' room of a prison that had been electronically intercepted by prison officials in violation of the Fourth Amendment. The highest New York court affirmed the conviction.

At the April 6, 1961, conference, Warren urged reversal, stating that there "was an unconstitutional invasion," and he could not say that the questions were separable from the illegal interception. Black, following his restrained approach in Fourth Amendment cases, said, "I can't say the Fourth is violated and can't go on how shocking it is." Frankfurter also argued for affirmance, remarking that he saw no intrusion into the lawyer-client relationship and "I can't say this is shocking anyway."

Warren was supported only by Douglas and Brennan. But the three persisted in voting for reversal. When Stewart's opinion of the Court for affirmance was announced June 4, Warren and Brennan, joined by Douglas, delivered dissents. Frankfurter had been incapacitated by then and took no part in the decision. But there was no doubt, in view of his conference statement, that he would have joined the majority decision.

During Frankfurter's last term, the Court also started to get cases arising out of civil disobedience against racial discrimination. *Garner v. Louisiana*[39] was the first of the "sit-in" cases to reach the Court. Garner and other black college students had taken seats at a Baton Rouge lunch counter and were asked to leave. When they refused, they were charged with breach of the peace. Their convictions were affirmed by the Louisiana Supreme Court. They claimed that there was no evidence to support the convictions, that the breach-of-the-peace statute was void for vagueness, and that use of the police and courts to enforce a state custom of segregation constituted "state action" in violation of the Fourteenth Amendment.

At the certiorari conference, all but Frankfurter, Clark, and Harlan had voted to grant cert. During oral argument on October 18, 1961, Warren indicated a narrow approach to the case. Referring to *Thompson v. Louisville*,[40] the "Case of Shuffling Sam" discussed in the last chapter, he asked, "Can't it be disposed of under that case?" In further questions, Warren stressed that the store owner had not expressly told the blacks to leave. "In some communities," said the Chief, "churches segregate. Suppose Negroes walked into such a church and the minister told them that their policy is not to have Negroes, but he does not ask them to leave. The police come in and arrest the Negroes who stayed to pray. Would that be different from this case?"[41] Warren also asked questions to show that the police did not fear violence in the case.

At the conference after the argument, Warren said that the case could be decided on the narrow *Thompson* ground that there was no evidence to support the disturbance of the peace conviction. Most of the others agreed. Frankfurter, however, argued that this case was not like *Thompson* because there were "inflammable ingredients in the setting" here which were completely lacking in the Case of Shuffling Sam.

Warren, supported by Douglas and Brennan, also stated a broader view on the basis of which the case could be decided. In a letter to

Harlan, Frankfurter denigrated this approach as "the extreme Warren–Douglas–Brennan constitutional views regarding sit-ins."[42] Warren urged that a "sit-in" was a form of speech protected by the First
Amendment that might not be prohibited by governmental action.
Moreover the police and judicial action here was "state action" enforcing segregation in restaurant facilities.

Frankfurter summarized the broader Warren approach in his letter
to Harlan as based on "the premise that continuing to remain in
what heretofore has been deemed to be 'private' premises after a request to leave is a form of constitutionally protected free speech."
Under Warren's view, "such a constitutionally protected right over-
balances any claim to an exercise of property rights in an irrationally
discriminatory way." To Frankfurter, "such a premise opens up appealing [sic] contentions against irrational choices in the conduct of
one's theretofore considered 'private' affairs in matters involving the
right of association, testamentary dispositions, etc., etc."

Frankfurter wrote that he was "compelled to deem ominous"[43]
Warren's broader basis for deciding *Garner*. But Harlan, normally
Frankfurter's staunchest ally, indicated that he would not follow
Frankfurter's view.[44] The Justice then worked to have the case decided on the narrow *Thompson* ground as the lesser evil. On December 4, Frankfurter wrote Warren, "For the very reason that this case
is only the beginning of a series of cases in which we shall be called
upon legally to unwind the tangled skein of sit-in situations, I deem
it important to reflect the desirable narrow ground of decision in a
narrowly written opinion expressing that ground. For me that means
not only deciding as little as possible but saying as little as possible
in deciding it."

Frankfurter indicated to the Chief that he was now willing to go
along with the view first stated by Warren in the conference. "In
short, the decision should rest on the principle applied in *Thompson*
v. *City of Louisville*. I share deeply the view expressed by you at our
original Conference discussion of these cases that they should be disposed of on the narrowest allowable grounds."

"In sum," Frankfurter concluded his letter to Warren, "I would
make of this a little case, precisely for the reason that we are all fully
conscious of the fact that it is just the beginning of a long story.
. . . If what we are deciding is that this is a *Thompson* case, then we
are deciding only that these people were convicted in want of evi-

dence, and the closer we stick to the shore of that controlling determination the less we needlessly borrow trouble of the future—the
needless trouble, in emotionally entangled situations, of needless discussion."[45]

Frankfurter's letter persuaded Warren to write an opinion reversing in *Garner* on the *Thompson* ground of want of evidence to support the convictions. When the opinion was delivered on December
11, there were no dissents. Had the decision been based on the broader
ground, there would have been a sharp division, and the majority
would probably have been against the Chief.

Black had been as disturbed as Frankfurter by the Warren attempt
to decide the broad constitutional issues involved in the sit-ins. This
marked the beginning of the split on civil-rights issues between the
Chief Justice and the senior Justice that was to intensify in the next
few years. "No one knows better than you," Frankfurter wrote Black
in February, 1962, "the views on the 'Negro question' I had and had
translated into action years before I came on the Court. My convictions regarding Negro constitutional rights have certainly not weakened since I came here. I am sure that you and I are in agreement
that it will not advance the cause of constitutional equality for Negroes for the Court to be taking short cuts, to discriminate as parti-
sans in favor of Negroes or even to appear to do so."[46]

During the 1961 Term, the Brethren again had difficulty with the
Mendoza–Martinez case,[47] which had originally come to the Court in
the 1959 Term. The issue was the constitutionality of section 401(j)
of the Nationality Act, under which an American lost his citizenship
for leaving the United States, in time of war or national emergency
declared by the President, to evade service in the armed forces. In
the last chapter, we saw that Stewart had written an opinion during
the 1959 Term for a tentative majority upholding the statute. But the
case had ultimately been remanded on a technical issue. The case
now came back for reargument in the 1961 Term.

Mendoza–Martinez was argued on the same day as *Rusk v. Cort*,[48]
which involved a similar statutory provision—section 349(a) (10) of
the Immigration and Nationality Act of 1952. Cort had left the country in 1951, soon after registering for the draft. He failed to report for
induction, but instead remained abroad, despite an indictment charging him with draft evasion. In 1959, he was denied a passport on the

ground that he had lost his citizenship. He brought an action to contest the ruling. The lower court held that section 349(a) (10) was unconstitutional. The *Mendoza–Martinez* lower court had reached a similar decision on the constitutionality of section 401(j) of the Nationality Act.

At the October 13, 1961, conference following the *Mendoza–Martinez* reargument and the *Cort* argument, the Brethren were closely divided. There was a tentative majority of five (Frankfurter, Clark, Harlan, Whittaker, and Stewart) for reversing the district courts and holding sections 401(j) and 349(a) (10) constitutional. The Court was also closely divided on whether the district court had jurisdiction, with Warren, Black, Douglas, Brennan, and Stewart voting for, and the others against. Stewart, the swing man on both issues, was assigned the opinions.

Stewart circulated a *Mendoza–Martinez* draft which held that there was jurisdiction and, on the constitutional merits, was the same as his 1960 draft discussed in the last chapter. Stewart found that section 401(j) was validly designed to the accomplishment of vital objectives under the war power and that, unlike the provision struck down in the 1958 *Trop* case,[49] section 401(j) did not impose punishment that would call the Eighth Amendment into play. Frankfurter, Clark, and Harlan quickly agreed to join the *Mendoza–Martinez* draft.

Stewart also prepared a *Cort* draft holding that section 349(a) (10) was constitutional on the strength of the discussion in the *Mendoza–Martinez* draft. But the *Cort* draft found that the presumption in section 349(a) (10) that absence from the United States, coupled with a failure to comply with the conscription law, was presumed to reflect a draft evasion purpose was unconstitutionally arbitrary.

Harlan indicated serious doubts about the *Cort* draft, though Brennan stated that he was prepared to accept it. Then Douglas circulated a dissent. According to it, expatriation statutes were unconstitutional for the reasons Douglas had stated in a dissent in the 1958 *Perez* case.[50] Douglas also added the argument that such statutes amounted to bills of attainder. Black quickly joined the Douglas dissent.

Whittaker now sent around a *Memorandum to the Conference* on *Mendoza–Martinez*, saying that he agreed with Stewart on the jurisdiction issue. On the merits, Whittaker adhered to the view stated in his 1958 *Perez* opinion that involuntary expatriation may not be used by Congress in pursuance of the war power. But Whittaker wrote that the statute could be sustained on the narrow ground of congressional power to anticipate a condition describable as an abnegation of allegiance and prescribe expatriation as a consequence regardless of subjective intent concerning retention or loss of citizenship.

Whittaker's memo indicated that Stewart's *Mendoza—Martinez* draft now commanded only a plurality (Frankfurter, Clark, Harlan, and Stewart) on the merits.

By now it was February 1962, four months after the October 10 and 11 argument in the cases. In mid-February, Harlan circulated a *Cort* opinion holding that section 349(a) (10) was constitutional, though disagreeing with Stewart on the presumption point and the issue of jurisdiction. Frankfurter and Clark joined Harlan's opinion.

Brennan, with Warren's approval, tried to ease the division by circulating an opinion stating his view (with which the Chief agreed) that sections 401(j) and 349(a) (10) were both unconstitutional. He urged, however, that the Court should refrain from deciding the constitutional issue.

At this point Whittaker became ill, which left the Court evenly divided on the constitutionality of section 401(j)—with Frankfurter, Clark, Harlan, and Stewart for constitutionality, and Warren, Black, Douglas, and Brennan against. With the Court so divided, it was decided to hold *Mendoza–Martinez* until the next term. On April 2, 1962, an order was issued restoring the case to the calendar for reargument.

Brennan, with the Chief Justice's support, attempted to resolve the *Cort* impasse by having the Court uphold the jurisdiction of the district court and vacate the judgment below and remand for consideration of the presumption point developed in Stewart's *Cort* draft opinion. However, Douglas refused to go along, saying he doubted the invalidity of the statutory presumption and felt compelled to comment on the constitutionality of expatriation as well, along the lines of his already-circulated draft dissent. This would have led to a four-to-four split in *Cort,* comparable to that in *Mendoza–Martinez.*

At this juncture, Warren and Brennan urged the Court to decide only the jurisdictional issue and to postpone determination of the constitutional question. This solution was accepted. On April 2, 1962, Stewart delivered an opinion of the Court holding that Cort could litigate his claim to citizenship by a declaratory judgment action in the district court. With respect to the other issues presented, the case was set for reargument with the *Mendoza–Martinez* case. Harlan, joined by Frankfurter and Clark, dissented, contending that the procedures set out in the Immigration Act provided Cort's only remedy in such a case.

As it turned out, Warren and Brennan's decision not to press for resolution of the constitutional issue ultimately resulted in the ruling that they favored. When the Court did decide the merits a year later, it held both section 401(j) and section 349(a) (10) unconstitutional by a bare majority.

Carnley v. Cochran,[51] which came before the Court just before Frankfurter retired, is of interest as a precursor of *Gideon v. Wainwright*[52]—the landmark 1963 case on the right to counsel. Carnley had been convicted by a Florida court of incest and indecent assault upon a child. He claimed the conviction was invalid because, though he could not afford a lawyer, he had not been given the assistance of counsel. The trial judge had not offered counsel to Carnley, but the state court held that he had waived counsel because it followed the rule that waiver would be presumed where the record showed only that a defendant did not have counsel. The certiorari vote was close, with Black, Frankfurter, Douglas, Brennan, and Stewart voting to grant, and the others for denial.

Before *Gideon v. Wainwright,* the leading case on the right to counsel was *Betts v. Brady,*[53] decided in 1942. Under it, the failure of a state to furnish counsel in a noncapital case did not automatically violate due process. Whether it did depended on the so-called "fair trial" test—i.e., whether, under all the circumstances, it was possible for the accused to obtain a fair trial, even without counsel. Carnley was illiterate and unfamiliar with legal procedure. He did not interpose a single objection during the trial and, as Brennan stated in his opinion of the Court, "there was no cross-examination worthy of the name."[54] Even under *Betts v. Brady,* Carnley's attorney argued, "denial of counsel to an illiterate defendant such as petitioner deprives him of" due process.

At the February 25, 1962, conference, the discussion centered as much on *Betts v. Brady* as on *Carnley* itself. Warren started the conference by saying that the Court could reverse either within *Betts v. Brady* or by overruling that case. The Chief did not indicate a preference. But Black, who had delivered the *Betts v. Brady* dissent, declared, "I'd meet *Betts* and overrule it." Frankfurter disagreed, saying that, though he would reverse because "this comes within *Betts v. Brady*," he opposed using the case to reconsider *Betts*. "I can't," he asserted, "imagine a worse case, a more unsavory case to overrule a long standing decision."

Douglas and Brennan strongly supported Black. Whittaker also said, "I am willing to overrule *Betts v. Brady*, but only prospectively." Clark, however, stated that he "would not overrule *Betts*, but would reverse as within *Betts*" and Stewart expressed a similar view. Harlan noted that he "would be happy to overrule *Betts* if I didn't have to do so on a constitutional basis." He observed that the argument urged against *Betts*—" 'you can't have a fair trial without a lawyer'—is a fiction if one remembers the quality of representation provided" indigent defendants. Harlan also said that he "would be able to reverse as within *Betts v. Brady*, but with my tongue in cheek." He would not vote to overrule *Betts*, saying, "I would never overrule *Betts v. Brady* except prospectively in any event."

The other Justices were evenly split on *Betts v. Brady*—four to overrule and four the other way, without the Chief's vote. Warren was reluctant to overrule an established precedent by only a bare majority. That was true even though he was in favor of discarding the *Betts v. Brady* rule. This was shown by the fact that his clerks were instructed at the beginning of the 1961 Term to look for a right-to-counsel case that would give the Court an opportunity to overrule *Betts v. Brady*. He voted against cert in *Carnley v. Cochran* because, like Frankfurter, he did not think it was a good case to serve as the overruling vehicle.

It is also erroneous to assume, from Frankfurter's conference comments, that he favored strict adherence to *Betts v. Brady*. While the Brethren were considering *Carnley*, Brennan sent Frankfurter a penciled note: "I think this would be the salutary course . . . [i.e.] overruling Betts and Brady." Frankfurter replied in pencil at the bottom of this note, "I think I'm prepared in view of the change of climate and of legislation to spell out my view of due process and overrule Betts and Brady, but prospectively as I did in Griffin." This comment shows that, if Frankfurter had remained on the Court, he would have gone along with the 1963 decision in *Gideon v. Wainwright*, a case that did not present the "unsavory" elements that disturbed Frankfurter in *Carnley v. Cochran*.

With the Court divided so sharply in *Carnley* on whether *Betts v. Brady* should be overruled, Warren once more turned to Brennan, assigning the opinion to him in the hope that he could resolve the conflict among the Brethren. According to a note from Black to Brennan, "you and Bill [Douglas] have not been able to get support for your desire to overrule it"—i.e., *Betts v. Brady*. Before *Carnley* was decided, Whittaker resigned and Frankfurter became incapacitated by a stroke. This gave Brennan the votes for a four-to-three decision overruling *Betts*. Warren and he decided, however, that it would be unwise to overrule by a bare majority of only a seven-man Court. Brennan drafted an opinion of the Court reversing Carnley's conviction within the *Betts v. Brady* rule.

The decision, announced April 30, 1962, was unanimous. Frankfurter did not participate in the decision, as he had been incapacitated before it came down. But in view of his conference position, there is no doubt that he would have voted with the Court.

Black delivered a separate concurrence stressing what he called *Betts v. Brady*'s "basic failure as a constitutional guide."[55] Though joining Brennan's opinion, Black declared that he would overrule *Betts* and hold that defendants were entitled to counsel in all criminal cases. Warren and Douglas joined both the Brennan and Black opinions.

Black wrote Brennan an undated pencilled note on seven Supreme Court memo-pad pages explaining why he was issuing his concurrence: "if some one does not say what I have written in this case two impressions will be left that I would regret: (1) That I no longer adhere to my dissent in Betts & Brady . . . & that challenges to it are no longer advisable; (2) That the right to a lawyer under state law, depends entirely upon a 'shock the conscience' due process concept."

He was issuing his opinion, Black wrote, "precisely to let it be known that I am still as much opposed to this stretching-contracting meaning of 'due process' as I have always been." Black conceded that the *Carnley* holding "is going a very long way towards indicating . . . that all particular facts and circumstances show a right to counsel." But he insisted that "from my viewpoint we get a wholly incomplete repudiation of Betts v. Brady if it is at the cost of leaving as the only standard . . . that of the accordion-like meaning of due process on which FF and his brethren rested in Betts, Rochin & other like cases."

Of course, Black's comments were aimed at the Frankfurter approach to due process which he had opposed for years. In another pencilled note to Brennan, Black declared, "I am at present completely persuaded that unless I write the accordion followers will cite Carnley as a plain holding that accepts that concept. . . . That philosophy, I think more & more leaves this country no bill of rights except as doled out by this Court."

"A historic term of the Supreme Court is drawing to a close," wrote Anthony Lewis in the *New York Times* on June 17, 1962. "It rates that adjective because of a single momentous decision—the decision in Baker v. Carr."[56] Warren himself confirmed this assessment when he wrote in his memoirs that *Baker v. Carr*[57] "was the most important case of my tenure on the Court."[58] In a broadcast interview on June 25, 1969, two days after he retired as Chief Justice, Warren declared, "I think the reapportionment, not only of State legislatures, but of representative government in this country is perhaps the most important issue we have had before the Supreme Court."[59]

Baker was a Tennessee voter who brought an action for a declaratory judgment that the 1901 law under which seats in the state legislature were apportioned violated the Fourteenth Amendment. He claimed that voters from urban areas had been denied equal protection "by virtue of the debasement of their votes," since a vote from the most populous county had only a fraction of the weight of one from the least populous county. The population ratio for the most and least populous districts was over nineteen-to-one.

Baker v. Carr presented two principal issues: the first of jurisdiction and the second of the merits of the constitutional claim. The lower court dismissed Baker's complaint, relying on the decision made by the Supreme Court in the 1946 case of *Colegrove v. Green*.[60] The decision in this latter case had dismissed an action challenging a legislative apportionment on the ground that, as Frankfurter put it in the *Colegrove* opinion, "the petitioners ask of this Court what is beyond its competence to grant." To decide otherwise, Frankfurter asserted, would embroil the Court in issues "of a peculiarly political nature . . . not meet for judicial determination." It was in *Colegrove* that Frankfurter made his oft-quoted statement: "Courts ought not to enter this political thicket."[61]

One of the things that has puzzled students of the Court was the concurrence of Justice Wiley Rutledge in the *Colegrove* decision. Normally Rutledge voted with Black, Douglas, and Murphy, all of whom dissented in *Colegrove*. Irving Brant, the journalist and Madison biographer, disturbed by Rutledge's vote, had asked him about it. Rutledge explained that, had he not voted as he did, he knew that Justice Robert H. Jackson (who did not participate in *Colegrove* because he was serving at the Nuremberg trials) would have voted with Frankfurter. The same was true of Chief Justice Harlan F. Stone, who died just before the decision was announced. Rutledge also said he had reason to believe that Stone's successor, Chief Justice Fred M. Vinson, would have voted the same way. If *Colegrove* had not been decided as it was, but was held over for reargument, instead of the four-to-three decision his way, Frankfurter would have prevailed with a full Court. A solid precedent in his favor would have been handed down. Therefore, Rutledge voted for a decision that would dispose of the case, but not be a barrier to a subsequent decision like *Baker v. Carr*. Irving Brant never told anyone of Rutledge's explanation until the decision in *Baker v. Carr,* which he felt was a full vindication of the Rutledge strategy.

At the end of his *Colegrove* opinion, Frankfurter added an appendix containing maps of four states that, according to Frankfurter, were "fair samples of prevailing gerrymanders."[62] One of the four was California, which Warren himself subsequently noted in his memoirs, "was one of the most malapportioned in the nation."[63] A major reason for this ironically had been then-Governor Warren's strong opposition to a 1948 reapportionment attempt. In his memoirs, Warren was to concede that his action then "was frankly a matter of political expediency."[64]

Warren's position on the Court was entirely different. "In California," he said after his retirement, "I went along with the thought that we should leave well enough alone. . . . But I saw the situation in a different light on the Court. There, you have a different responsibility to the entire country."[65] Warren used to tell his law clerks that his perspective on the problem had changed with his change from Governor to Chief Justice, and he had no hesitation in saying, "I was just wrong as Governor."[66]

On November 21, 1960, the Court decided to hear Baker's appeal, with Warren, Black, Douglas, and Brennan voting to note probable jurisdiction, and the remaining five voting the other way. At the conference following argument, on April 20, 1961, Warren showed how far he had moved from the position he had taken as California Governor. "I think," he declared, "the case ought to be reversed on the Solicitor-General's argument. But I think he was too cautious. I don't see why we should say merely that there is jurisdiction. I'd say the case stated a cause of action." Warren denied that *Colegrove* was "authority for the decision below." As he saw it, *Colegrove* did not really deny judicial jurisdiction, and later cases implied that there was jurisdiction. "I'd let the Court determine the remedy," the Chief concluded.

Warren was strongly supported by Black, Douglas, and Brennan, and was vigorously opposed by Frankfurter. According to one of the Brethren who was present, "Frankfurter unleashed a brilliant tour de force, speaking at considerable length, pulling down reports and reading from them, and powerfully arguing the correctness of *Colegrove*." Clark and Harlan agreed with Frankfurter. Whittaker had been uncharacteristically vigorous in questioning the claim of lack of jurisdiction during the argument. "If there is a clear constitutional right being violated . . .," Whittaker had interrupted counsel at one point, "is there not both power and a duty in the courts to enforce the constitutional right?"[67] At the conference, Whittaker disagreed with Frankfurter on the question of jurisdiction. However, since he thought that *Colegrove* should not be abandoned by only a bare majority, he was voting with Frankfurter.

With Whittaker's vote the conference was divided four-to-four. That put the matter up to Stewart, who felt unable to decide and wanted the case to go over. At his urging, the case was put over for reargument during the 1961 Term.

In his *Autobiography*, Douglas states that the conference vote on *Baker v. Carr* was five-to-four in favor of reversal, with Stewart, tentatively at least, one of the five.[68] So far as he implies that this was true of the first conference, his recollection was mistaken. The contemporary notes of those present indicate that Stewart did not vote. A Douglas *Memorandum to the Conference* also confirms this. According to it, "In *Baker v. Carr* last Term, JUSTICE STEWART was undecided in his view. Hence we put the case down for reargument and we have recently reheard it. This is as it should be. . . . When opinions have jelled, the case is handed down. When jelling is not finished, the case is held."[69]

After the April 20 conference, Frankfurter wrote Stewart, "I feel so strongly the gravity of the implications, particularly for the Court, that one disposition of this case rather than another involves." Frankfurter stated that, "to seize jurisdiction in this case is bound to stimulate litigation by doctrinaire 'liberals' and the politically ambitious. On the basis of your view, shared by several of us, that egalitarianism, however determined, in the electoral distribution of legislative representation is not a constitutionally protected right, hopes engendered by a favoring decision are bound to be disappointed."

In Frankfurter's view, "To open up these undetermined and indeterminate questions is bound, I cannot but deeply believe, to bring the Court in conflict with political forces and exacerbate political feeling widely throughout the Nation." If the Court decided there was jurisdiction in apportionment cases, Frankfurter warned, "clash and tension between Court and country and politicians will assert themselves within a far wider area than the Segregation cases have aroused."

Nor could the Court accept "the jaunty analogue that we were offered between progress in the acceptance of our Segregation decision and this reapportionment problem." According to Frankfurter, "there is all the difference in the world between asking courts to differentiate between black and white, and asking courts to make the appraisal of factors which [are] relevant to this problem."[70]

The *Baker v. Carr* reargument took place on October 9, 1961. A Justice who was there has characterized it as "unstimulating." The next day Frankfurter circulated a sixty-page memorandum.[71] In a covering memorandum, Frankfurter wrote, "I find it necessary to state in comprehensive detail the problem involved in this case, the disposition of which has such far-reaching implications for the well-being of the Court."[72] The lengthy memo had been drafted by Anthony G. Amsterdam, who had been one of Frankfurter's law clerks during the 1960 Term. Except for the addition of four opening pages and some minor changes, the Amsterdam memo was later to be published as Frankfurter's dissent in *Baker v. Carr*.

The only answer to the Frankfurter memorandum came from Brennan, who, circulated a *Memorandum to the Conference,* enclosing an eleven-page chart that was, he explained, "prepared from the Record to depict the variances in county representation among

[Tennessee] counties of the same relative population; and, . . . some contrasts. The latter highlight (1) disproportions in representation among counties of the same size, (2) disproportions in population among counties with the same representation, and (3) situations in which counties with populations 1/6 as small as other counties, have up to three times as much representation."

Brennan's memo asserted, "I should think that at the very least, the data show a picture which Tennessee should be required to justify if it is to avoid the conclusion that the 1901 Act applied to today's facts, is simple caprice." [73]

The Brennan chart helped convince some of the Brethren, notably Clark, of the gross disparities that existed under the Tennessee apportionment law. Clark appended the chart as a table to his *Baker v. Carr* concurrence, to show that "Tennessee's apportionment is a crazy quilt without rational basis." [74]

From the discussion and vote at the first conference, on April 20, 1961, it looked as though Stewart and Whittaker would be the key Justices in the case. Harlan, who had become Frankfurter's strongest ally among the Brethren, wrote Whittaker and Stewart after the reargument. He was writing, said Harlan, because, "Unless I am much mistaken, past events in this case plainly indicate that your votes will be determinative of its outcome." Harlan maintained, "that from the standpoint of the future of the Court the case involves implications whose importance is unmatched by those of any other case coming here in my time (and by those in few others in the history of the Court, not excluding the *Desegregation* case)." Harlan's letter asserted, "I believe that what we are being asked to do in this case threatens the preservation of . . . the independence of the Court."

"Let me be as concrete and frank as possible," Harlan wrote. "Today, state reapportionment is being espoused by a Democratic administration; the next time it may be supported (or opposed) by a Republican administration. Can it be that it will be only the cynics who may say that the outcome of a particular case was influenced by the political backgrounds or ideologies of the then members of the Court (even, I daresay, that the vote of a particular member, ostensibly contrary to his supposed political polarization, may have been prompted by a conscious or subconscious 'leaning-over-backwards')?"

"The only sure way of avoiding this," Harlan declared, "is to keep the gate to the [political] thicket tightly closed. Politics being what they are it seems to me that it would be almost naive to blink the dangers of this situation." Now, Harlan concluded, "the responsibility is entirely in our laps, and to me it would be a sad thing were we by our own act to plunge this institution into what would bid fair, as time goes on, to erode it[s] stature."[75]

Stewart had, however, made up his mind to vote for reversal before he had received Harlan's letter. The notion that the courts were without jurisdiction over apportionments even in the face of patent violations of the Equal Protection Clause had increasingly troubled him after the April 20 conference. At the end of April, he expressed his doubts to Frankfurter, referring to the hypothetical extreme case of an apportionment restricting voting to men six feet high. In a May 1 letter to Stewart, Frankfurter sought to answer "the legitimate fear of an abusive extension of a doctrine." He urged that the courts could deal with such extremes "as and when they arise" under "the Due Process Clause of the Fourteenth [which] affords, I think, the widest scope for dealing with arbitrary abuses, the correction of which does not open the door to more and greater difficulties than the difficulties to be remedied."[76]

In an October letter, Frankfurter again tried to allay Stewart's anxiety about hypothetical extremes. To affirm, wrote Frankfurter, would still leave room for the courts to act in future cases involving "circumstances different 'in kind.' . . . . Disallowing all Christian Scientists or Jews to vote, or to reduce votes in any county that has Christian Scientists or Jews, would present circumstances different 'in kind.' "[77]

The October 13 conference following reargument made known Stewart's decision to vote with the Warren wing of the Court. The Chief Justice limited his discussion to reaffirming that the district court had jurisdiction. "This is a violation of equal protection," he declared. "I don't think we have to decide the merits or the question of [whether this violates the guarantee of a] republican form of government. All we have to decide is that there is jurisdiction. We don't have to say that the state must give complete equality."

Warren rejected the claim that elections involved political questions beyond judicial competence. "We can't say," he asserted, "we must stay out of state elections, since Congress has put us in it in the referee provisions for inquiring into denial of the vote on racial grounds. All we need here is to say that this shows an arbitrary and capricious practice. I would reverse solely on power and leave the rest of the case and the form of the decree to the district court."

As at the first conference, the Chief was supported by Black, Douglas, and Brennan. "I still feel," stated Black, "as I did in my dissent in *Colegrove v. Green*.[78] I think *Colegrove* is a weak reed on which to hang the notion of a settled rule of law." Black discussed the classic 1849 case of *Luther v. Borden*,[79] where the Court refused to decide which of two competing governments was the legal government of Rhode Island. "I think *Luther* was right," Black declared. "Two factions claimed to be the state. It wasn't a dispute over a law passed by a state, but which was the state." He referred to another case that held that it was for Congress to decide whether a state had a republican form of government. "But it's different," he said, "when you attack a law that's not an attack on the state's form of government. Here it's simply a question of whether the law passed bears so unequally, capriciously, as to deny equal protection."

Douglas said that he thought the case was governed by the 1960 decision in *Gomillion v. Lightfoot*.[80] He did not see how, after *Gomillion*, the district court denial of jurisdiction could be affirmed. He noted that "the Equal Protection Clause was not designed just for Negroes" and asserted that, "the difficulties of the judiciary doing anything about it, great as they are, can't deter us from doing our job." Brennan stressed the conclusion he had drawn from the chart he had circulated. Whatever might be true in other cases, here the apportionment defied rational explanation, and it had to be reversed.

This time the case in opposition to reversal was stated primarily by Harlan. Frankfurter spoke briefly. "Ascertaining jurisdiction in this case," he stated, "is fraught with such consequences that, to me, are dangerous to our system that I'd stay out." He then asked, "What are the standards by which the remedy is to be fashioned?" and deferred to Harlan.

Harlan, usually the most restrained of the Brethren, argued with intense emotion, as he sought to show the undesirable results he expected to flow from a reversal in the case. Harlan also doubted that equal protection was violated. As he put it, "if a state is entitled to distribute its organs of government as it pleases, without subjecting itself to federal judicial supervision, then it may also provide the means whereby those organs are to be created. And even if you get over this and say there is an equal protection claim, I can't see, under our standards that a disparity between urban and rural [districts] offends."

Clark indicated that he, too, was firmly in accord with the Frankfurter view. "Even if there was jurisdiction," he said, "I wouldn't exercise it. But there are a dozen cases since 1932 where the Court has stayed out of this problem." Clark also pointed out that Baker had "failed to show [he] had exhausted other avenues to relief"—a point that was to be the one on which the Texan's ultimate vote in the case was to turn. Clark added that he agreed with Harlan on the results that would ensue from court intervention in these cases. He emphasized that what really was at stake here, at least in the South, was the whites' control of the power structure.

Whittaker again voted as he had at the April conference, saying that, though he disagreed with the Frankfurter view on jurisdiction, he was not prepared to vote that way, with the Court so closely divided. That made the vote once again four-to-four and left the matter up to Stewart, who, as the junior Justice, spoke last, since the Brethren, after the Chief's presentation, discuss cases in order of seniority.

Stewart started by telling how he, too, had been troubled by the problems that disturbed Frankfurter, Clark, and Harlan. He went on to say that he thought, as Brennan had stated, that this case presented a malapportionment so extreme it could not have a rational basis. In such a situation, Stewart declared, "the district court did have jurisdiction." Stewart thought the case did not involve "a so-called 'political question,' in the sense of a question which the Constitution precluded" the courts from answering. Nor, in his view, did the case raise "a republican form of government issue." Since he thought the district court had jurisdiction, Stewart said he would vote to reverse. That made the conference vote five-to-four for reversal.

However, Stewart went out of his way to emphasize two points. The first was that he would agree only to decide that the district court had jurisdiction. "I can't say," he said, "whether we can or can't frame appropriate relief. On the merits, I couldn't say that equal protection requires respresentation approximately commensurate with voting strength. So the state doesn't have to justify every departure from a one-man vote basis." The second point made by Stewart was the heavy burden of proof that any voter would have to meet to prevail on the merits. In his view, there was "the greatest burden of proof on a plaintiff to show an arbitrary and capricious system."

Baker v. Carr directly illustrates the importance of the Chief Justice's assigning power. Warren devoted much effort to the question of the opinion assignment. He considered Black and Douglas, because they had dissented in *Colegrove v. Green* and had consistently expressed disagreement with that case. But assigning the opinion to either of them might have lost Stewart's vote, and the Chief soon decided that the assignment had to go to either Brennan or Stewart. This was the kind of close case where the Chief would often turn to Brennan. In addition, Douglas had indicated to him that he would be unable to join a Stewart opinion because he could not go along with what Stewart had said about burden of proof. On the other hand, Black, who had discussed the matter several times with Stewart, told him that unless Stewart was selected to write the opinion, he might not be held by the majority. Black also felt that, if Stewart did write and Douglas did not join his opinion, then also Stewart might waver in his vote.

Warren conferred repeatedly on the matter, particularly with Black and Douglas. Then, on the second Monday after the conference, the Chief came to see Brennan early in the morning, and assigned the opinion to him.

Baker v. Carr also shows the importance of the "might have been" in Supreme Court jurisprudence. Black, Douglas, and Brennan, with Warren's support, wanted to go beyond the jurisdictional issue. They also wanted to decide the merits and hold that the Tennessee apportionment law violated the Equal Protection Clause. Their view was that, as Frankfurter summarized it in his October 13 letter to Stewart, "the Fourteenth Amendment . . . requires what Hugo called 'approximately fair' distribution or weight in votes."[81]

Stewart, however, would vote for reversal only if the decision was limited to the holding that the district court had jurisdiction to entertain Baker's complaint. Since Stewart's vote was then necessary for the bare majority in favor of reversal, Warren and the other three agreed that Brennan would limit his draft opinion to the jurisdictional issue.

Clark was to switch his vote and that made the majority for reversal, six. Clark then urged that the decision also reverse on the merits, but at that point Warren felt that the opinion of the Court should not be changed against Stewart's wishes. If Clark had been with the majority from the second conference vote, it is probable that *Baker v. Carr* would have decided the merits as well as the jurisdictional issue.

If that had happened, it would have meant a different rule of equality in apportionments than that ultimately enunciated in the 1964 case of *Reynolds v. Sims.*[82] At the time of *Baker v. Carr,* those who favored the requirement of what Black called "approximately fair" weight in votes were willing to apply that requirement to only one house of the legislature. Warren, in particular, was swayed by the situation in California where only the Assembly was apportioned by population, while the Senate represented counties equally, regardless of population. In his memoirs, he called this the "Federal System of Representation" because of its resemblance to that in the United States Constitution.[83] He had thought that the system worked well when he was Governor and was reluctant to strike it down completely even now.

Brennan finished his *Baker v. Carr* draft in January 1962. He sent a copy to Stewart, who phoned that he approved. Douglas states that "there was a broad Irish grin on [Brennan's] face when he told me that the fifth vote was secure."[84] On January 27, Brennan sent a memorandum to Warren, Black, and Douglas, enclosing his draft, "which Potter Stewart tells me entirely satisfies him." The memo said, "Potter now agrees with me that we should not pass on any issues except [those] actually requiring decision at this time." This meant that Stewart agreed that the subject of burden of proof, which he had stressed at the conference, would not be discussed in the opinion. Douglas, in his *Autobiography,* referred to "Brennan's long, scholarly but tedious opinion," with "its length being due to the exhaustive and detailed examination of precedents which he undertook."[85] To secure Stewart's agreement, Brennan had to deal at length with *Colegrove v. Green* and other cases in an attempt to show that they did not really stand in the way of the *Baker* decision.

Brennan's memo also explained why he had devoted so much space to the so-called "political question" issue: "after much thought, I believe that the full discussion of 'political question', and its bearing on apportionment suits, is required if we are effectively and finally to dispel the fog of another day produced by Felix's opinion in *Colegrove v. Green*."

The political question discussion led to objections by Douglas, who took exception to anything that seemed to approve the political question decisions which Brennan's opinion discussed. Douglas ultimately agreed to join, but said he would have to write separately on the political question doctrine, though not on standards of apportionment.

Black phoned Brennan at home to say that he was somewhat surprised that Stewart had joined. He thought the opinion was longer than he would have liked, but he could understand the reason and was happy to join. Warren said that he was wholly delighted with the opinion.

Though the Brennan opinion went through four printings, print 4 differed in no major way from print 1. The opinion was circulated to all the Justices on January 31. A few minutes after he received his copy, Frankfurter dropped into Clark's chambers to announce, "they've done just as I expected." Frankfurter told Clark that he was circulating his dissent without delay. He did so the next day. Since Frankfurter's dissent was substantially the same as his October 10 memorandum, Brennan had been prepared for it. He made only three changes in his majority opinion after the dissent was circulated. They noted the impropriety of discussing the remedy at this stage, rephrased the explanation of the meaning of "lack of jurisdiction," and added to the statement of the holding in the 1956 case of *Kidd v. McCanless*.[86]

On February 3, Clark wrote Frankfurter, "Your dissent is unanswerable, except by ukase."

Clark also wrote, "As you suggested by telephone, I will prepare something on failure to exhaust other remedies."[87] Not satisfied with leaving well enough alone when Clark had indicated agreement with his dissent, Frankfurter had tried to firm up Clark's vote by suggesting that he write separately to show that there were other remedies open to Tennessee voters. It was Clark's research into the question that ultimately led him to switch his vote.

Clark wrote the others that he was going to have to delay the decision because he was going to write something in dissent in addition to Frankfurter's opinion. Since Clark, the Chief Justice, and

Brennan were leaving for ten days to attend a judicial conference in Puerto Rico, this meant that the decision would not be announced until late February at the latest. "We leave for 'sunnier' climes . . .," Clark wrote, in his February 3 letter, "so I shall have to set the task aside until I return. In light of the waiting period Tennessee has already experienced I hope my delay will not too long deprive it of a constitutional form of government, *i.e.*, control by the 'city slickers.' "

While the three were away at the conference, Harlan wrote Stewart "I am trying my hand at a piece directed to the proposition that the kind of 'rights' asserted by the petitioners in this case are *not* assured by the federal Constitution—a thesis with which I once understood you to agree."

Harlan urged Stewart to delay his final vote in the case. "Feeling as strongly as I do about the shortsightedness and unwisdom of what is proposed to us, I hope you will not think it presumptuous of me to ask you to await (if your mind is still open) what I am writing (which will not be long), before casting what will be the decisive, and if I may say so, fateful vote in this case."[88]

Though Stewart answered Harlan that he always kept an open mind, he had sent his note of concurrence to Brennan on February 1. This meant that Brennan already had the five votes needed to make his draft the opinion of the Court when Harlan sent his letter to Stewart.

After Warren, Clark, and Brennan returned from Puerto Rico, there was a recirculation of Frankfurter's dissent, which noted that Clark and Harlan had joined it. At that time, Douglas did not know that Harlan and Clark were preparing dissents, and he thought this meant that the decision would be announced the following week. Douglas immediately circulated his own concurrence, which, contrary to his previous statement, did discuss standards of apportionment.

The Douglas discussion of that issue upset Stewart, who decided that he also would have to write separately. Brennan tried to dissuade him, but the most he could get from Stewart was an agreement to a private circulation to the majority first.

After he learned of Stewart's reaction to his draft concurrence, Douglas phoned Brennan to say he was willing to make any changes in his opinion that would keep Stewart from writing. Brennan suggested changes accepted by Douglas which eliminated the discussion of standards of apportionment. In the meantime, Stewart had sent a draft concurrence around to the majority. Brennan took the changed Douglas opinion to Stewart, who said that he found the changes significant, but would still go ahead with his own opinion.

Harlan had by then circulated his dissent. He had done so with Frankfurter's encouragement. "Do send your own hot shot into *Baker* v. *Carr*," Frankfurter had written him. "It would please me because it would add impact to the dissent." [89] Stewart now indicated that, as a result of Harlan's draft, he would change his opinion to state that on the merits, in other cases, he agreed with Harlan. Brennan was able to persuade Stewart not to do this. In all this, Brennan consulted with Warren and had his strong support. A law clerk says that the Chief was "Gibraltarlike in his support of Justice Brennan." Without Warren's backing, Douglas and Stewart could not have been persuaded to restrain their separate opinions.

In mid-February, Stewart sent his concurrence to all the Justices. Frankfurter also circulated another print of his dissent, which began, "Mr. Justice Frankfurter, whom Mr. Justice Clark, Mr. Justice Harlan and Mr. Justice Whittaker join, dissenting." The Brethren now waited for three weeks while Clark worked on his expected dissent. It was generally thought that Clark would say that Baker had not exhausted his other remedies and that, in any event, Congress was the proper place for federal redress.

While they were waiting, the Justices received a March 2 memorandum from Douglas. Douglas wrote, "I hope we can get No. 6— *Baker* v. *Carr* down March 19th. This is an election year. If the lower court is to have an opportunity to act, the case should be disposed of soon." Douglas said that otherwise the case would be decided so late "that we [would be] powerless to act. I am sure there is no one here who wants to produce that result. But we should not drift into that situation." [90]

The Douglas memo upset the others. Though no one was happy at Clark's delay, they thought he had the right not to be pressed while he made up his mind. But Clark was now to surprise everyone by changing his vote. Clark had concluded, in the words of a note he had jotted down while considering the case, "Here a minority by [sic] representatives ignores the needs and desires of the majority— and for their own selfish purpose hamper and oppress them—debar them from equal privileges and equal rights—that means the failure of our constitutional system."[91] Clark had decided that only a judicial remedy could redress that failure.

On March 7, Clark wrote Frankfurter: "Preparatory to writing my dissent in this case, along the line you suggested of pointing out the avenues that were open for the voters of Tennessee to bring about reapportionment despite its Assembly, I have carefully checked into the record. I am sorry to say that I cannot find any practical course that the people could take in bringing this about except through the Federal courts."

Clark stated that, "Having come to this conclusion I decided I would reconsider the whole case, and I am sorry to say that I shall have to ask you to permit me to withdraw from your dissent. I regret this, but in view of the fact that the voters of Tennessee have no other recourse I have concluded" to issue a concurring opinion, which was attached.

Clark sent a copy of this letter to Harlan with a note that he had sent it to Frankfurter, and saying "I am sorry that I cannot go along but it does not change the result anyway."[92]

The day before, on March 6, Clark had sent Brennan a typed copy of an opinion "concurring in part and dissenting in part." It concluded: "My difference with the majority, therefore, narrows down to this: I would decide the case on the merits. Instead of remanding it for the District Court to determine the merits and fashion the relief, I would do that here. There is not need to delay the merits of the case any further. Indeed, as I say, it seems to be decided *sub silentio* anyway. On the relief I would set that down for reargument at the opening of the next Term, October 1962."[93]

After he received Clark's draft, Brennan conferred with the Texan. He persuaded Clark to issue his opinion only as a concurrence and to remove the statement that it was a dissent in part, as well as passages such as that quoted which indicated direct dissent from the opinion of the Court. As issued, however, Clark's concurrence did state that he would have invalidated the Tennessee apportionment law on the merits. Clark had tried to persuade Brennan to change his opinion to strike down the Tennessee law. Brennan had refused, saying that he had given an undertaking to Stewart that he would not do so.

Needless to say, Clark's switch brought jubilation to the majority Justices. When the Chief Justice received Clark's concurring opinion, he called Brennan at home. During the first minutes of the call, Warren just laughed with joy. When he was able to get down to serious discussion, the Chief said that, in spite of the fact that Stewart was no longer indispensable, he also believed that the majority opinion should not be changed unless Stewart agreed. The next day, Stewart indicated to Brennan that he would not agree to any changes of importance. In a March 10 memorandum to Warren, Black, and Douglas, Brennan informed them that he and Stewart had discussed the changes requested by Clark. "Potter felt that if they were made it would be necessary for him to dissent from that much of the revised opinion. I therefore decided it was best not to press for the changes."

When Brennan announced the decision on March 26, the opinion of the Court was substantially that which Stewart had joined before Clark changed his vote. Douglas, Clark, and Stewart delivered their watered-down concurrences. Frankfurter and Harlan delivered impassioned dissents. Just before the decision Whittaker, who had joined Frankfurter's dissent, was hospitalized and he had to abstain. The final decision was, therefore, six-to-two for reversal on the issue of jurisdiction. While the opinions were being read, the Chief Justice wrote a note to Brennan. As originally written, it read, "It is a great day for the Irish." Before passing the note, Warren crossed out "Irish" and substituted "country."

Frankfurter's dissent in *Baker v. Carr* was a veritable *cri de coeur* evoked by the realization that the balance had now swung all but irretrievably away from the Justice's juristic philosophy. "What powerfully emerged for me this afternoon," Frankfurter wrote Harlan when the conference confirmed the *Baker v. Carr* decision, "is that men who so readily impose their will on the nation and the fifty states by exultingly overruling their most distinguished predecessors behave like subservient children when lectured by a martinet with a papa-knows-best-for-the best complacency."[94]

Frankfurter had written Stewart on October 13, 1961, on "feeling as deeply as I do about the evil genii to be released by the decision."[95] With the decision itself, Frankfurter was sure that the bottle had been uncorked which would land the courts in what he called (in a sentence that he added to his dissent just before it was issued) "the mathematical quagmire . . . into which this Court today catapults the lower courts of the country, without so much as adumbrating the basis for a legal calculus as a means of extraction." [96]

An eminent lower court judge, Henry J. Friendly of the U.S. Court of Appeals for the Second Circuit, confirmed this estimate when he wrote Frankfurter only two days after the decision, "The only common thread I can find in *Baker v. Carr* . . . is a desire to increase the problems of the lower courts. What the Baker case will do you have demonstrated so convincingly that no further comment is necessary." [97] To which Frankfurter replied, "Really, really! Neither John nor I have added to your troubles, and we did our damndest to save you from it in *Baker v. Carr*." [98]

Frankfurter's close friend, former Secretary of State Dean Acheson, was asked by President Kennedy a few days later what he thought of the *Baker v. Carr* decision. In a contemporaneous *Memorandum of Conversation with the President,* Acheson wrote, "I said that I thought the Court had taken on in the desegregation decisions about all the legislative and executive governmental work that it could handle for the time being, and it seemed to me unwise to pick out another task, the end of which no one could see." The President, however, supported the decision, saying "that the legislatures would never reform themselves and that he did not see how we were going to make any progress unless the Court intervened." [99] To this, Acheson replied like a true Frankfurter disciple. "I said, suppose it didn't? It did not seem to me that the injustice resulting from the over-representation of rural areas was one of the tyrannical impositions which drove a people to rebellion. It was a long way from fascism. I did not believe that every injustice had to be corrected at once." The President closed the conversation on the subject by remarking that "mine was one point of view"—though obviously not Kennedy's. [100]

Even more important was the fact that Kennedy went out of his way publicly to defend the Court's decision. "The right to fair representation and to have each vote count equally," the President declared at his next press conference, "is, it seems to me, basic to the successful operation of a democracy." The President's brother, Attorney General Robert F. Kennedy, called *Baker v. Carr* "a landmark in the development of representative government." [101]

Reaction to *Baker v. Carr* in the country was divided. A *New York Times* editorial on the decision was entitled, "A Gain for Majority

Rule."[102] The supporters of the decision noted its precedent-making character. "The historic decision," observed Anthony Lewis, "was a sharp departure from the court's traditional reluctance to get into questions of fairness in legislative districting."[103]

Critics of the Court too had another field day. Senator Richard B. Russell of Georgia, leader of the Southern Senators, declared that the decision "was another major assault on our constitutional system. . . . If the people really value their freedom, they will demand that the Congress curtail and limit the jurisdiction being exercised by" the Court.[104] *New York Times* columnist Arthur Krock, normally a restrained conservative, termed *Baker v. Carr* an example of the "Big Brother function of the court."[105]

Above all, however, the decision was a graphic demonstration of the Warren Court's willingness to make new law where it deemed that course was warranted. Commenting on *Baker v. Carr*, Anthony Lewis wrote that a lawyer had remarked that the decision "had been 'inevitable.' Then he added: 'But twenty years ago, or even ten, it would have been inconceivable.' From 'inconceivable' to 'inevitable' in a decade or two—so swiftly does the course of decision run."[106]

Yet even informed observers did not fully appreciate the quantum change made by *Baker v. Carr*. They stressed that all that had been decided was that Baker's complaint was within the jurisdiction of the district court. The Supreme Court had left unanswered the question of enforcement and that of what apportionment standards were required by the Constitution. Instead, it had remanded to the district court for it to answer these questions.

As acute a student of the Supreme Court as Professor Paul A. Freund, of the Harvard Law School, concluded from this that *Baker v. Carr* would not result in rapid political changes. He wrote that the issue would "simmer in the lower Federal courts for years."[107] In his opinion, the decision neither ruled out representation on the basis of geography, rather than population, nor did it affect malapportionment in congressional districting. A leading Republican, Representative Carl Curtis of Missouri, when asked how long it would be before *Baker v. Carr* had any real effect, answered, "What is the timetable for the glacier?"[108]

Those who looked at *Baker v. Carr* this way could not know that five of the Justices had been willing to strike down the Tennessee apportionment on the merits and that at least four of them were ready to lay down a constitutional standard of apportionment that required what Black had called "approximately fair" weight in votes. This meant essentially a "one person—one vote" standard. It is true that the Justices were not yet ready to impose the requirement on both houses of state legislatures. But, even as applied to the lower house, the result would be a drastic change in the makeup of state legislatures.

Baker v. Carr was the last important decision in which Frankfurter participated. Whether there was a cause and effect relationship between his defeat in that case and the Justice's physical collapse can, of course, never be known. But, soon after the decision, on April 6, 1962, the Justice's career came to a sudden and unexpected end. He was working in his chambers, when he abruptly slumped to his desk. Not long afterwards, Frankfurter was carried from the building, protesting that his shoes were being left behind.

On May 2, Warren wrote to the hospitalized Justice that he was pleased to receive a favorable doctors' report, "and I was delighted to learn also that you are maintaining your reputation of being an obedient patient. . . . There is no doubt in my mind but what your abstention for the remainder of the Term will contribute greatly to your complete recovery." [109]

But the hoped-for recovery did not take place. Three months and two more heart attacks later, Frankfurter made the decision that he would never be able to resume his judicial duties. "I am thus," he wrote the President on August 28, 1962, "left with no choice but to regard my period of active service on the Court as having run its course." [110] In the same letter, Frankfurter formally retired from active service as a Justice.

Just before Frankfurter's stroke, the Court had unexpectedly lost another member. In mid-March of 1962, Whittaker had entered Walter Reed Medical Center for a physical examination. The doctors told him that he was completely exhausted and that his life would be endangered if he resumed his Court duties. For Whittaker, the agonizing he had gone through in making decisions had been unbearable, particularly in view of the constant lobbying to which he was subjected, particularly by Frankfurter. Now the strain had proved too much. Whittaker had joined Frankfurter's draft dissent in *Baker v.*

Carr. But his vote had never been firm, and he was subjected to constant pressure from Frankfurter to prevent him from wavering. Whittaker's stress over *Baker v. Carr* was a major factor in the collapse that led to his retirement, effective April 1, 1962.

After he left the Court, Whittaker took a highly paid legal post with General Motors. He then delivered widely reported attacks upon the Court's decisions, notably in a 1964 speech before the American Bar Association. When he heard about Whittaker's criticism, Warren used to say, "Charlie never could make up his mind about decisions until he left the Court."

Whittaker's retirement gave President Kennedy the opportunity to fill his first Court vacancy. President Eisenhower had not asked Warren for advice on Court appointments, but his successor immediately consulted with the Chief Justice through his brother, Attorney General Robert F. Kennedy. The Attorney General had recommended Judge William H. Hastie, a former Frankfurter student, who had been appointed in 1949 as the first black federal appellate judge. As the President's brother tells it, "I went up and saw Warren about Hastie. He was violently opposed to having Hastie on the Court. . . . He said, 'He's not a liberal, and he'd be opposed to all the measures that we are interested in, and he would just be completely unsatisfactory.'" Douglas, an old friend of the Kennedys, had the same reaction. Hastie, he told Kennedy, would be "just one more vote for Frankfurter."[111] Robert Kennedy writes that Hastie was ultimately passed over because naming a black would have been "too obvious" politically. The President was also influenced by an analysis of Hastie's opinions by Assistant Attorney General Nicholas Katzenbach, who concluded that they were "competent and pedestrian." When he told the President, Katzenbach recalls, "I thought his opinions were rather pedestrian, this just killed him with President Kennedy."[112]

The Kennedys then thought of Paul Freund, Frankfurter's foremost Harvard disciple. Once again, Warren was opposed, feeling that Freund would only be one more addition to Frankfurter's supporters. The President now proposed appointing Byron R. White, the Deputy Attorney General, who had impressed the Kennedys by his management of the Department of Justice, especially by his personal trip to Montgomery, Alabama, to restore order during the Freedom

Riders protest in May 1961. In a confrontation with the Governor of Alabama, when the Governor sarcastically asked, "Where are all those Freedom Riders?" White drily replied that they were in the hospitals to which the Governor's men had sent them.[113]

On March 30, 1962, the White House telephone operators tracked down White travelling in the West. "Well Byron," the President said, "we've decided to go ahead on you." After White had agreed, Kennedy said, "All right, we'll go ahead." He then asked Arthur M. Schlesinger, Jr., then an assistant at the White House, to "write a statement right away explaining why I am choosing White." Schlesinger called the Attorney General, who emphasized, "Make the point that White was no mere professor or scholar but had actually seen 'life'—in the Navy, in private practice, in politics, even on the football field."[114] The statement issued by the President emphasized that White "has excelled in everything he has attempted—in his academic life, in his military service, in his career before the Bar, and in the federal government."[115]

The new Justice, who took his seat April 16, was certainly not the typical Supreme Court appointee. He was known to most Americans as "Whizzer"—the all-American back who became the National Football League rookie of the year in 1938. A Rhodes Scholar, White had first met John Kennedy while he was touring Europe between terms at Oxford. He then studied law at Yale. There was a five-year break for military service after his second year in law school. He served in the South Pacific and later recalled, "It was out there that I met Kennedy again, and one of the jobs I had to do was write the report on the accident when his boat was sunk."[116]

On graduation from law school after the war, White clerked for Chief Justice Fred M. Vinson (he was the first former law clerk to become a Justice himself) and renewed his friendship with Kennedy, then a freshman Congressman. After practicing law in his native Colorado for fifteen years, he became Chairman of the nationwide Citizens for Kennedy in 1960 and moved to Washington as the number-two man in Robert Kennedy's Justice Department.

Physically, White was most impressive. At six feet two and a muscular 190 pounds, he retained the constitution that had made him a star quarterback. He was the only one among the Brethren whose physique compared with that of the Chief Justice. Even as a Justice,

White retained his athletic competitiveness, never hesitating to take part in the clerks' basketball games in the gymnasium at the top of the Court building.

On the Court, White, like Stewart, has defied classification. He, too, tends to take a lawyerlike approach to individual cases, without trying to fit them into any over-all judicial philosophy. He remembers first meeting Warren when he was a member of the Advisory Committee on Civil Rules, to which the Chief Justice had appointed him in October 1960. After his appointment to the Court, White was never close to Warren. "I wasn't exactly in his circle," White recalls. Certainly White never became a member of the Warren Court's inner circle. He went his own way, voting against the Chief Justice as often as not.

After *Baker v. Carr,* the Court functioned without Frankfurter during the remainder of the 1961 Term. Though White took office on April 16, 1962, he did not participate in most of the remaining decisions, since he had taken his seat too late to hear the arguments or take part in the conferences in those cases. For most of the decisions after Frankfurter's stroke, then, the Court consisted of only seven Justices.

When the Court sits, the Chief Justice is in the center of the bench with the Brethren around him in order of seniority. The senior Associate Justice is on the Chief's right, the second senior on his left, the next senior on the senior Justice's right, and so on. When a Justice leaves the Court, those below in seniority move up in their places on the bench. When the Court first convened after Whittaker's retirement, Stewart, who had moved from the Chief Justice's far left to Whittaker's old seat at his far right, was scheduled to read the first opinion of the day. As always, he waited for a nod from the Chief to begin. But Warren looked toward Stewart's old chair to his left. It was vacant, and the Chief kept looking with growing puzzlement. Finally, Warren remembered, looked the other way, and nodded. Stewart, smiling broadly, then began reading his opinion.[117]

In none of the cases during the remainder of the term were there more than two dissents. Had Frankfurter been able to participate in the decisions, the division would have been closer, though his vote would not have been able to swing any of the cases away from the Chief Justice and his supporters.

Frankfurter differed with Warren in the conference discussion, though his stroke prevented him from participating in the decisions, in four cases decided during the latter part of the 1961 Term. The first was *Russell v. United States*,[118] which arose out of convictions for refusing to answer questions before the Senate investigating subcommittee headed by Senator Joseph R. McCarthy and a subcommittee of the House Committee on Un-American Activities. The defendants claimed that they had not been told why they had been summoned or why the questions were pertinent. They also challenged the grand jury that indicted them because it was composed of federal employees, as well as the indictment itself because it did not identify the subject under inquiry at the time of defendants' refusal to answer. The lower court had rejected these claims.

At the conference in mid-December 1961, Warren spoke for reversal. "There's nothing here to show a basis for bringing him in," the Chief declared. "I'd also reverse on the grand jury point, limited to the times and atmosphere of the day. McCarthy was riding high and a Government employee would be hard put to refuse to indict someone charged to be a communist."

Frankfurter had led the case for affirmance. "As to the jury point," he said, "even where the whole petit jury were Government employees in *Frazier* [*v. United States*, 1948],[119] it was sustained and in *Dennis* [*v. United States*, 1950],[120] we did the same. Surely we can't extend to the grand jury" any bar on federal employees. The other claims, Frankfurter argued, were ruled out by the *Barenblatt* (1959)[121] and *Wilkinson* (1961)[122] cases. Nothing in those cases, he asserted, "means that the witness must be told why he was summoned or why he's being asked the questions." As Frankfurter saw it, there was "no difference between a court witness and a witness before a committee."

The conference discussion showed that the Brethren were so sharply divided that they agreed to avoid decision on the main issues raised by defendants. Instead, it was decided to reverse because the indictment had not identified the subject of inquiry. Stewart delivered an opinion to that effect on May 21, 1962. The decision was five-to-two, with Harlan and Clark dissenting in a seven-man Court.

The second case decided after Frankfurter's stroke, where he and Warren had expressed differing conference views, was *Wood v. Georgia*.[123] Wood, the elected sheriff of a Georgia County, was in the midst of a campaign for reelection. A local grand jury was instructed by a state judge to investigate alleged sales of black votes. Wood issued a statement accusing the judge of race agitation and an attempt at judicial intimidation of black voters and compared the calling of the grand jury to the activities of the Ku Klux Klan. Because of the statement, Wood was convicted of contempt of court. The Georgia Supreme Court affirmed. Warren, Black, Douglas, and Brennan voted to grant certiorari, Frankfurter, Clark, Harlan, and Stewart to deny, with Whittaker passing.

Warren urged reversal at the March 30, 1962, conference. "This is controlled by *Bridges* and *Pennekamp*," said the Chief. He was referring to the 1941 case of *Bridges v. California* [124] and the 1946 case of *Pennekamp v. Florida*, [125] which had held that the First Amendment prohibits punishment for contempt by publication in the absence of a showing that the published statement presented a "clear and present danger" to the administration of justice. As Warren saw it, "he was a candidate for reelection and I see nothing he said outside the presence of the court that constituted a clear and present danger."

Here, too, Frankfurter stated the case the other way. Contempt of court was a subject on which the Justice had always felt deeply. He thought that a broad contempt power was essential to the proper administration of justice. "This isn't the case of a butcher or candlestick maker," he declared. A sheriff was an officer of the court. "Our law of contempt," Frankfurter asserted, "is rested on the summary power in judges to punish for misconduct in the presence of the court, or by officers of the court, or parties litigant."

The conference vote was five-to-three for reversal with Frankfurter, Clark, and Harlan voting the other way, and Whittaker not voting because he was hospitalized at the time. Warren delivered the opinion of the Court on June 25. It followed his conference approach. Harlan and Clark dissented. Frankfurter, who would have dissented even more strongly, was incapacitated and took no part in the decision. White also did not participate. The decision was five-to-two instead of the bare majority it would have been if Frankfurter and Whittaker (or probably even White, his successor) had participated in the final vote.

Warren's draft opinion in *Wood v. Georgia* had stated, near the end, "Moreover the voting problem in the County is a fact of common knowledge." In a June 21 letter, just before the decision was announced, Brennan wrote the Chief, "I wonder if that is wise since so much is stewing in the courts about the Georgia apportionment and unit systems and only last week we noted the unit system appeal." The reference was to the case of *Gray v. Sanders*,[126] which challenged Georgia's county-unit system and was to be decided during the following term. "I may be overstating it," wrote Brennan, "but I wonder if the sentence will be vulnerable to the suggestion that we are pre-judging the merits of the apportionment cases."

The offending sentence was taken out. Warren's draft had also contained language that Black and Brennan objected to as suggesting a "balancing" test, such as that which Frankfurter had consistently urged was appropriate even in First Amendment cases. After referring to Wood's claim that the exercise of contempt power had abridged his freedom of expression, the draft read, "In this situation the burden upon this Court is *to accommodate the conflicting state and personal interests and* to define the limitations upon the contempt power according to the terms of the Federal Constitution." The italicized words were deleted in the final opinion. The other "balancing" sentence that was removed by Warren stated, after the opinion noted that this was not a situation where an individual was on trial, "It is clear that very different interests, both to the judiciary and to society in general must be weighed in such a case."

The third 1961 Term case decided after Frankfurter's stroke, where he disagreed with Warren at the conference, was *Lynch v. Overholser*.[127] Lynch had been prosecuted for writing checks without funds to pay for them. A psychiatrist reported that he was of unsound mind. Lynch had pleaded not guilty, but, at the trial, sought to change the plea to guilty. The judge refused to allow the change of plea, on the basis of the report of mental illness. Lynch was then found not guilty because of insanity. The court ordered him confined to a mental hospital under a statute providing that, if a person is acquitted because of insanity, the court shall order him so confined. Lynch sought habeas corpus to secure his release from the hospital. The lower court denied the writ.

At the January 19, 1962, conference, Warren first remarked that "confinement for treatment is a good policy and can't contravene the Constitution." He did, however, state, "The procedure troubles me and isn't authorized by the statute. If it's all right, they still have to include a provision for notice of this. You can't convert a criminal trial into a civil commitment proceeding, transferring the burden of proof to him if he's to get out of the hospital." Warren concluded that he would vote for reversal, but said that he "wouldn't hit the constitutionality of the statute, but only that it can't be used this way."

Frankfurter spoke in opposition, saying that the Court "can't reverse on this record." As the Justice saw it, "the only issue he raises is that the defense was imposed upon him. The court refused to take his plea of guilty, which was interposed as a strategy. I say a court has inherent power, it needs no statute or rule, to refuse a plea of guilty."

Frankfurter was supported only by Clark, who wrote the dissent, since Frankfurter did not participate in the decision. The opinion of the Court was delivered May 21 by Harlan. It reversed on the ground that the statute did not apply to a defendant who maintained that he was mentally responsible when the offense was committed. Clark alone dissented, though he would have been joined by Frankfurter, and possibly by Whittaker, had they participated in the decision.

In *Goldblatt v. Hempstead*,[128] Warren and Frankfurter also took opposing conference views, though, in it, Frankfurter was so plainly right on the law that the Chief soon switched his position. Goldblatt owned a tract within the Town of Hempstead, on which he mined sand and gravel. The town had expanded around the excavation, and it was now located directly in a large residential area. The town naturally desired to stop further mining on the tract. Had it done so by taking the property, compensation would have had to be paid. Instead, the town promulgated an ordinance prohibiting any excavating below the water table and requiring refilling of any excavation below that level. Since Goldblatt's excavation was below the water table, the practical effect was to require the end of further mining. Goldblatt claimed that the ordinance deprived him of his property without due process. The state courts decided against him.

Warren began the January 19, 1962, conference by stressing the unfairness of what the town had done. "This is a taking of their property," he asserted. "There's no showing this is a nuisance. They've been prevented from mining this [land]."

Warren's reaction was typical in cases where he felt an individual had been treated unfairly. Fairness to the individual may not, however, be the only criterion, for it must be balanced against the public interest in such a case. Frankfurter pointed this out. He stated that even though Goldblatt "was following a perfectly legitimate enterprise, more people moved in. That made continuance of this thing a dangerous use of property." Frankfurter answered Warren's nuisance point by saying, "We don't have to decide if this is a nuisance, implying that only this may be prevented." Frankfurter pointed to the 1920 case of *Walls v. Midland Carbon Co.* [129] and concluded, it "controls for me. This is an allowable use of the police power."

Black also delivered an effective statement in support of the ordinance. "I can't say," he declared, "the Constitution forbids the city from stopping an enterprise which may be a menace to people. I don't see why it can't deny this use." It is true, Black conceded, that "it's difficult to draw a line between taking for a public use and barring some particular use." But that should not affect the result here. "This Court," Black noted, "has said that forbidding saloons and a gambling house is not unconstitutional" and the same should be true of the prohibition at issue.

Only Clark supported Warren, though Douglas did say he would reverse because he thought the requirement of filling the pit went too far. Warren and Clark yielded and agreed to go along with an affirmance. Douglas also was persuaded not to issue a partial dissent. The opinion of the Court, delivered by Clark on May 14, largely followed Frankfurter's conference approach, though the Justice himself could not participate in the decision.

Another case where Warren changed his position from his conference presentation was *Manuel Enterprises, Inc. v. Day.* [130] The Post Office had barred three magazines from the mails on the ground that they were obscene and nonmailable under the so-called Comstock Act. The magazines consisted largely of photographs of nude or near-nude male models. The publishers brought suit for injunctive relief which was denied by the lower court. Warren, Black, Douglas, Harlan, Brennan, and Stewart voted to grant certiorari, with Frankfurter, Clark, and Whittaker voting to deny.

To Warren, with his personal abhorrence of pornography and smut peddlers, the case was a simple one. At the March 2, 1962, conference, the Chief opened the discussion with a short statement for affirmance. As he saw it, "Congress has power to regulate the mail and to exclude obscenity. This is not censorship because they can distribute some other way, by express, truck, etc." Warren then asked, "Is this obscenity?" He felt it was. "On the showing made and the admissions, these appeal to prurient interest"—i.e., under the test laid down in the 1957 *Roth* case.[131] Warren also thought that "the procedure is as expeditious as a thing of this kind can be."

Once again Clark agreed with Warren. The others were hopelessly split, with Black and Douglas rejecting any Post Office power to exclude from the mails and Harlan and Stewart upholding the power to exclude obscene matter, but doubting that the magazines were obscene. Brennan stated still another view. He voted to reverse on the ground that there was no statutory authorization for the administrative proceeding and, even if there was, the Post Office procedure ran afoul of the limitations imposed where prior restraint is employed.

The case was not decided until June 25 and, even then, no opinion could be written for a majority of the seven Justices who participated in the decision. The opinion was assigned to Harlan, who circulated a draft finding that the magazines were not obscene under a test requiring both patent offensiveness and the "prurient interest" appeal demanded by the 1957 *Roth* case.

Brennan wrote Harlan on June 9 that he considered "your approach . . . as an effort to refine the *Roth* test." Brennan said, "I have no doubt that we must some day give further thought to the *Roth* test." But he thought it was still too soon to do so. "I lean to the idea that we ought let the widespread ferment continue a bit longer in legal periodicals and courts over the soundness and meaning of the *Roth* test before we re-examine it. I am particularly persuaded to that view, of course, by the fact that the Court is hopelessly divided in this area and there appears almost no prospect of an agreement of five of us upon anything."

Brennan also wrote that he had "some difficulty with the element 'patent offensiveness'. I have the reaction that this element would only serve to limit obscenity to 'hard core' pornography, . . . And I have trouble defining 'hard core', although no trouble at all recognizing it when I see it"—which anticipated Stewart's famous 1964 statement that, though he could not define hard-core pornography, "I know it when I see it."[132] Brennan wondered "whether the introduction of the element of 'patent offensiveness' would really be an improvement upon the *Roth* test, or only result in still further confusing an already confused subject."

Brennan concluded his letter by saying that he would write something along the lines stated by him at the conference. Harlan replied on June 11, writing, "Naturally I am disappointed that we seem to be so far apart on this case, but feeling as you do, I can understand why you are constrained to write separately. Indeed, I am not at all sure that separate writing is not the best way to inch along in this elusive field."

On June 25, Harlan announced the judgment of reversal and an opinion, joined by Stewart, based upon his draft opinion. Black announced only that he concurred in the judgment. Brennan issued a concurrence on the ground that Congress had not authorized the Postmaster General to close the mails to obscene matter, on his administrative determination alone. Warren was induced to join this opinion, which did not close the door to barring obscene matter from the mails, provided it was done through a judicial proceeding. Douglas also joined Brennan's opinion. Clark delivered a vigorous dissent which asserted that the decision "requires the United States Post Office to be the world's largest disseminator of smut." [133]

The most complicated case decided during the 1961 Term was *Brown Shoe Co. v. United States*.[134] There are those who think that Whittaker's physical collapse in March 1962 was caused by his inability to write the opinion in this case, even more than by his agonizing over *Baker v. Carr* and Frankfurter's harassment over his vote in that case. *Brown Shoe* was an involved antitrust case, with the elephantine trial record usually produced in such cases. It arose out of a suit by the government to enjoin a merger of two shoe companies on the ground that the merger violated the Clayton Act prohibition against corporate mergers "where in any line of commerce in any section of the country, the effect . . . may be substantially to lessen competition, or to tend to create a monopoly." The district court found that the lines of commerce involved were men's, women's, and children's shoes, that the "section of the country" for manufacturing was the entire country, while that for retailing was every city of ten thousand or more in which both companies had stores, and that the effect of the merger would be substantially to lessen competition and tend to create a monopoly in such areas. The district court held that the merger violated the Clayton Act and ordered Brown Shoe Co. to divest itself of its stock in the acquired corporation and to file within ninety days a plan for carrying the decreed divestiture into effect.

Warren began the *Brown Shoe* conference on December 9, 1961, by urging affirmance. "The judge did a pretty good job," he stated. "His findings may not have been up to the best standard, but they sufficed." Warren noted that this was a Clayton, not a Sherman Act case. "I don't think we have to be as tight as under the Sherman Act. The record showed that Brown was in the acquisition business and this added up to a substantial part" of the shoe business. Warren also specifically agreed with the findings on "lines of commerce," saying "I think men's, women's, and children's shoes was an adequate breakdown of lines of commerce."

During the argument on December 6, Harlan had questioned whether the Court had jurisdiction, since the Court could hear direct appeals from only *final* district court judgments in antitrust cases. He queried whether there was any final decree here, since the district court had not acted on a divestiture plan. At the conference, both Harlan and Frankfurter raised the issue. They said they had "serious trouble" on the jurisdictional problem. Clark said he had "some trouble with the jurisdictional point. I'd strain to take jurisdiction, however." On the merits, none of the Brethren doubted that the finding of a Clayton Act violation was supported by the record.

Warren assigned the opinion to Whittaker, but the Justice was overwhelmed by the complexity of the case. When Whittaker retired, Warren reassigned the opinion to himself and, with the substantial help of the Whittaker law clerk who had worked on the case, was able to issue a complicated fifty-page opinion affirming in line with his conference approach. Only Harlan, of the seven Justices who participated in the decision, dissented, on the jurisdictional ground urged by him in conference.

The two most interesting cases decided in the 1961 Term after Frankfurter became incapacitated were *Robinson v. California*[135] and *Engel v. Vitale*.[136] In neither did Warren play an important leadership role. Robinson was convicted of violating a California law making it a misdemeanor for a person to use or be addicted to the use of narcotics. Before the November 20, 1961, conference at which the Court decided to hear Robinson's appeal, Harlan had circulated a November 11 *Memorandum to the Conference* urging that probable jurisdiction should be noted, which stated, "To me, the punishing in this manner of the status of being a drug addict raises serious constitutional questions." This Harlan memo raised the issue on which the case was to be decided. Four of the Brethren (Douglas, Harlan, Brennan, and Stewart) voted to hear Robinson's appeal, with Warren, Black, Frankfurter, Clark, and Whittaker voting the other way.

At the *Robinson* conference on April 20, 1962, Warren spoke for reversal on another ground. "He was charged," the Chief noted, "with both use and addiction and we don't know which the jury went on." Warren also pointed out that " 'addict' in another statute has a definition which was not instructed or given here. This makes [such] instruction a constitutional requisite."

Black argued for affirmance. He said he had "no complaint against the instruction," and he could not "say the statute is unconstitutional on a vagueness ground." The others, however, focused on the issue raised by Harlan in his November 11 memo. Harlan now said that it was "hard to say that 'status' can't be reached criminally. Conventionally it had been dealt with that way." Douglas made the strongest statement the other way. To him, narcotics addiction was an illness. "To the extent one is a sick person," Douglas declared, "just being one can't be made a crime." Brennan and Stewart supported the Douglas position, while Clark and White spoke the other way.

The conference division was four for reversal, three for affirmance, and Harlan tilting that way. Warren agreed to go along with the Douglas—Brennan—Stewart view and assigned the opinion to Stewart, in the hope that he would write a moderate draft that would gain a majority. Stewart's draft reversed on the ground that it was cruel and unusual punishment for the state to imprison someone for narcotics addiction, which was an illness.

After he had read Stewart's draft, Clark sent Black a written note: "The Calif Narcotic Case—by Potter—is put on drug addiction being a disease etc—Are you going to write? If you are still for Aff—& want me to write something I will be glad to do so—" [137]

Black had, however, decided to join Stewart's opinion. Harlan did also, though he wrote a two-paragraph concurrence explaining his vote. When Stewart delivered the opinion of the Court on June 25, 1962—the last day of the 1961 Term—only Clark and White issued dissents.

Even though the 1961 Term included *Baker v. Carr*, which Warren himself termed "the most important case of my tenure on the Court," the most controversial decision during the term was that in another case on the last day of the term—*Engel v. Vitale*.[138] A board of education in New York directed that a short prayer be said aloud at the beginning of each school day. Parents of pupils brought an action challenging the constitutionality of the school prayer.

At the certiorari conference on December 4, 1961, all except Whittaker and Stewart voted to grant. "I can't agree to hear this case," Whittaker had uncharacteristically asserted. "I feel strongly, very deeply about this."[139] Warren, on the other hand, did not have strong feelings about the case. He could not get excited about the official prayer which to him seemed as venial as the pledge of allegiance recited each school day. Despite this, he asked some penetrating questions of the counsel for the school board at the April 3, 1962 argument. Warren wanted to know the reasons behind the school's adoption of the prayer. The attorney said that the school district was interested in promoting belief in the morals, ethics, and virtues traditional in American life. The transcript reads:

Mr. Chief Justice Warren: "You shy away from the use of the word religion."

Mr. Daiker: "I don't want the Court to be left with the impression that the purpose was to teach religion."

Mr. Chief Justice Warren: "I know you want to keep away from that."[140]

At the argument, we will see, Warren also answered what turned out to be the chief objection to a ruling of unconstitutionality.

At the April 6 conference, Warren left the leadership to Black, who, more than any Justice, had fought what he considered infringements upon the First Amendment's Establishment Clause. To Black, the official prayer was a patent violation of the clause. All agreed with him except Stewart and Whittaker (who passed).

Douglas, however, who had usually been with Black in past cases on separation between Church and State, was troubled by the case. He wrote Black about his difficulty only two weeks before the decision was announced. "If . . .," Douglas wrote, "we would strike down a New York requirement that public school teachers open each day with prayer, I think we could not consistently open each of our sessions with prayer. That's the kernel of my problem."

The answer to the Douglas objection had been given by Warren during the oral argument. Counsel for the school board had compared the prayer to the Supreme Court's opening invocation—"God

Save the United States and this Honorable Court." To which Warren replied, "I wonder whether it would make a difference if we were to require every litigant and lawyer who comes in here to say the same prayer your school district requires." [141]

When Black delivered the opinion of the Court, on June 25, holding the school prayer unconstitutional, only Stewart dissented, stressing the pervasiveness in government of practices such as the invocation opening the Supreme Court's sessions. Douglas issued a concurrence that went on the ground stated in his letter to Black: "I am inclined to reverse if we are prepared to disallow public property and public funds to be used to finance a religious exercise." To Douglas, the school prayer involved improper use of public funds, since, as he wrote in his concurrence, "the teacher who leads in prayer is on the public payroll." [142]

The decision in the school prayer case was met by a storm of protest. The mail attacking it was the largest in the Court's history. [143] Warren himself later wrote, "I vividly remember one bold newspaper headline, 'Court outlaws God.' Many religious leaders in this same spirit condemned the Court." [144] Church leaders, according to the *New York Times,* expressed "shock and regret." "The decision," proclaimed Cardinal McIntyre in Los Angeles, "is positively shocking and scandalizing to one of American blood and principles." [145] "It is like taking a star and stripe off the flag," complained a Methodist bishop in Georgia. [146] Billy Graham announced that he was "shocked and disappointed." "Followed to its logical conclusion," declared the well-known preacher, "prayers cannot be said in Congress, chaplains will be taken from the armed forces, and the President will not place his hand on the Bible when he takes the oath of office." [147]

The school prayer case soured Graham on the Warren Court. So much so that when it was announced in June, 1968, that the Chief Justice had submitted his resignation, the evangelist wrote President Johnson, "it is my prayer that you will give serious consideration to balancing the Court with a strong conservative as Chief Justice. I am convinced that many of the problems that have plagued America in the last few years are a direct result of some of the extreme rulings of the Court, especially in the field of criminology. I believe that our mutual friend, Governor John Connally would make an ideal and popular choice. He might not be popular with the extreme liberals and radicals who are already fighting you anyway but he would make a great Chief Justice."[148] On Capitol Hill, the Court's critics had another field day. "In strident language," according to the *New York Times* account of congressional reaction, members "questioned the justices' honesty and patriotism."[149] Predictably, the most extreme response came from Southern solons. "They put the Negroes in the schools, and now they've driven God out,"[150] declared Representative George W. Andrews of Alabama. Not to be outdone, Congressman Mendel Rivers of South Carolina asserted, "I know of nothing in my lifetime that could give more aid and comfort to Moscow than this bold, malicious, atheistic and sacrilegious twist by this unpredictable group of uncontrolled despots."[151] Not long after, efforts began in Congress to overturn the prayer decision, either by constitutional amendment or statutory limitation of the Court's jurisdiction—efforts that, though unsuccessful, have continued to this day.

Even after all the abuse they had taken during the past decade, Warren and the Justices were both surprised and pained by the reaction to their decision. "My father," Earl Warren, Jr., was quoted at the time, "is the most religious man I ever knew. And here he was being attacked as being against God."[152] Black, who normally ignored critics of his decisions, now wrote personally in answer to those who sent him letters finding fault with the decision.

Clark took the almost unprecedented step of publicly defending the decision in a San Francisco speech. "Here was a state-written prayer," he said, "circulated by the school district to state-employed teachers with instructions to have their pupils recite it." Clark then explained that the Constitution provides "that both state and Federal governments shall take no part respecting the establishment of religion. . . . 'No' means 'No.' That was all the Court decided."[153]

The most important defense of the prayer decision, however, came from President Kennedy. At the President's news conference on June 27, the first question asked was on *Engel v. Vitale*—itself an indication of the heat generated by the decision. Kennedy urged that the Court should be backed on the prayer issue. "I think," he declared, "that it is very important for us, if we're going to maintain our constitutional principle, that we support Supreme Court decisions." We must, he affirmed, "support the Constitution and the responsibility of the Supreme Court interpreting it which is theirs and given to them . . . by the Constitution."

Kennedy also remarked, somewhat impishly, that there was "a very easy remedy" for those who disapproved of the decision—"and that is to pray ourselves, and I would think it would be a welcome reminder to every American family that we can pray a good deal more at home and attend our churches with a good deal more fidelity, and we can make the true meaning of prayer much more important in the lives of all our children." [154]

Though Warren quickly grew to love his work—"To me, the Chief Justiceship of the United States is the most important job in the world," he was once quoted in *Newsweek* [155]—the Chief Justice was still an outdoors type who found the physical conditions of judicial work confining. As far as he could, he would go on hunting and fishing trips with friends from his California days. In Washington, he would try to walk as much as possible. He would normally start on foot on his way to the Court in the morning, being picked up by his official car only after he had walked a few miles. He would usually be joined on these walks by Clark, who lived near the Chief's apartment at the Sheraton–Park. The two used to talk over pending cases and these discussions helped to swing Clark from the Frankfurter to the Warren view in important cases, particularly *Baker v. Carr*.

Warren would also try to break the Court day by walks, taking a few turns around the building or, where he could, longer walks, such as the periodic jaunt to the Hotel Washington to get a haircut. At first, he would go on these excursions alone, but it soon became the practice for his law clerks to accompany him. During the 1961 Term, two of his clerks were over six feet tall. When they walked with the Chief, everyone thought they were bodyguards. It got to be a game with them, and if Warren was walking with someone else, in addition to them, the clerks would drop back a few steps and move out to the flanks, as though they really were bodyguards.

The story went around Washington that the Chief Justice had had F.B.I. agents assigned to him for protection. Yet there had been a time when extremist threats had led to F.B.I. security efforts on Warren's behalf. In November 1958, the press reported that the F.B.I. had been discreetly guarding Warren and Frankfurter because of threatening letters. [156]

By now, Earl Warren was one of the most famous men in the country. To the average person, however, his position made him still a remote figure, august and impersonal, in his judicial robes. Once, toward the end of the 1961 Term, while the Chief and his clerks were walking around the Court building, getting some exercise, a tourist bus stopped in front of the Court. All the tourists filed out to take pictures just as the Warren entourage started to walk in front of them. At this, the tour guide held up his hand and said, "Stop! Let's let this old man by before we take the pictures."

II.

1962 TERM: A DECEPTIVE CALM

Just before 10 A.M. on October 1, 1962, a long black limousine pulled into the basement of the Supreme Court building. The still youthful President and his boyish-looking brother, the Attorney General, stepped from the car. They exchanged handshakes with Perry Lippitt, the dignified Marshal of the Court, and were taken by elevator to the courtroom. As the Kennedys entered the ornate chamber, a gavel sounded and Lippitt announced, "The President of the United States."

The President and his brother walked to two chairs in front of the bench. Soon after they were seated, at precisely ten o'clock, the red velour drapes behind the bench parted as Lippitt banged his gavel again and proclaimed, "The Honorable, the Chief Justice and the Associate Justices of the Supreme Court of the United States." All, including the President, rose as eight Justices filed in through three openings in the draperies. Page boys, still in the traditional knickers, pulled back the chairs behind the bench, and the Justices stood silently as Lippitt recited the traditional intonation, ending with "God save the United States and this Honorable Court."

The Justices and the audience took their seats. The Chief Justice looked up, smiled, nodded to the President, and announced the retirement of Justice Frankfurter. He then stated that Arthur J. Goldberg had been appointed and confirmed as Frankfurter's successor.

He said that Goldberg had taken the Constitutional Oath in a private ceremony a few minutes earlier. The Clerk of the Court would now read Mr. Goldberg's commission and administer the Judicial Oath. The commission's archaic words were pronounced and Goldberg, with a hand on a Hebrew Bible, repeated the time-honored oath in a firm voice.

The Marshal escorted the new Justice to his seat at the far left of the bench. The President now abruptly rose, and Lippitt sounded his gavel again. Kennedy stepped forward on to the marble ledge in front of the bench so that he could shake Goldberg's hand. At this, the Justices all rose. This was the Court's only formal recognition that the President was in attendance. Nowhere else could the holder of the highest office go and receive so little recognition.

As the President and his brother left the courtroom, their footsteps echoing in the long corridor, the spectators took their seats and the Chief Justice said, "Admissions to the Bar." The October 1962 Court Term had begun.[1]

It was the first term of Warren's tenure that began without Frankfurter. For Warren, the Justice's retirement removed his strongest opponent from the Court. Frankfurter's successor was cast in a different mold. Goldberg immediately became one of Warren's strongest supporters. If anything, the new Justice even went beyond the Chief in his willingness to expand the frontiers of constitutional law. "How they must miss you!" wrote former Justice Minton to Frankfurter in 1964. "Mr. J. Goldberg is a walking Constitutional Convention! Wow what an activist he is!"[2]

The Kennedys had had no difficulty in choosing Goldberg for their second Court appointment. The President had called his brother and, as the latter wrote in a contemporaneous memorandum, "said that he had heard from Warren that Frankfurter was not going to return to the Court. We discussed who might replace him." They both stressed "the necessity of replacing Frankfurter with a Jew. The President said that . . . the various Jewish organizations would be upset if this appointment did not go to a person of the Jewish faith." Both Kennedys agreed that, "if a Jew was placed on the Court it should be Arthur Goldberg. . . . Finally, however, the President called and said he had talked to Arthur Goldberg and that Goldberg was anxious to get the appointment."[3]

When the President announced his choice, a *Chicago Daily News* article characterized Goldberg's success story as "almost too corny."[4] The last of eleven children of an immigrant Russian fruit peddler, Goldberg rose from one of the poorest sections of Chicago. He worked his way through Northwestern Law School, where he graduated first in his class. He developed a labor practice and became counsel to the AFL—CIO. He became a Kennedy supporter in early 1960 and was appointed Secretary of Labor when the new Administration took office. In that position, he became the Kennedys' trouble shooter. In fact, as Robert Kennedy wrote about his discussions with the President on the Court vacancy, "the only reservation about Arthur Goldberg was the fact that he was so valuable to the Administration and could handle labor and management in a way that could hardly be equalled by anyone else."[5]

Physically and emotionally Goldberg was the antithesis of the first Kennedy appointee. Where White was dispassionate and reserved, Goldberg was warm and ebullient. He was of average build, with wavy grey hair, and none of the athletic propensities of his colleague. Goldberg noted the contrast in a speech the winter after his appointment. "As a new brother," he said, "I think I should tell you some of the innermost secrets of the Supreme Court. The Court is sorely divided. There is one group that believes in an active judicial philosophy; Justices Black, Douglas, and White are addicted to physical exercise. The middle wing, which believes in moderate exercise, consists of the Chief Justice and Justices Clark and Brennan. And then there's the third group—Justices Harlan and Stewart and myself."[6]

Goldberg recalls that he first met Warren while he was still a labor lawyer, when he invited the Chief Justice to attend his family's Passover Seder. Warren always had an interest in Jewish law and participated without discomfiture in the ceremony. "That was wholly natural with him," according to Goldberg. "When he was California's Governor, he, as a good politician, probably wore a yarmulke more than I did." In fact, when Nina Warren later gave Goldberg's wife a list of the things she customarily packed for the Chief Justice, she included a yarmulke in the inventory.

Goldberg soon became Warren's firm ally on the Court. "There is nobody," Goldberg says, "I felt closer to than Warren." In fact, states the former Justice, "if you look at the Harvard Law Review annual rack-up of how we voted during my tenure, he and I voted together more than any other Justice, as I recall it."

To Frankfurter's successor, Warren's "great contribution" as Chief

Justice came only "after he got away from Felix's influence in the early years." Referring to Frankfurter's influence, Goldberg says, "on the whole, I do not regard it to be a good influence. Felix was a technician, but always was fearful that the Court would injure itself. This was his principal concern, always. Frankfurter wrote that the Court should not mandate reapportionment. He said that this would bring the Court into the political thicket, to the injury of the Court."

Goldberg, like Warren himself, did not share Frankfurter's concern. "Well," Goldberg declares, "it's not the function of a Supreme Court Justice to worry about the Court injuring itself. It's the sworn duty of a Supreme Court Justice to do justice under law and apply the Constitution."

When he made this statement, Goldberg noted that, "after he got away from [Frankfurter] and became his own man, Warren would have subscribed to what I have said immeasurably. He then decided to use his own conception of law, morality, and realism and did not worry about what critics said. . . . He just decided and followed the pattern of voicing and voting his genuine convictions."

If Warren and his supporters were delighted with the new Justice's accession, the same was not—could not be—true of his now-incapacitated predecessor. Soon after Goldberg took his seat, Frankfurter wrote sarcastically to his former law clerk, Alexander M. Bickel, "I see that Goldberg, the scholar, has made his debut too."[7] The next year, the retired Justice again wrote Bickel, "And so, the men who are overruling prior decisions of a Court which contained Holmes, Hughes, Brandeis and Cardozo are . . . such wholly inexperienced men as Goldberg . . . without familiarity with the jurisdiction or the jurisprudence of the Court either as practitioners or scholars or judges."[8] In a 1964 interview, Frankfurter again complained of Goldberg's appointment, saying, "Throughout the history of the Court, there's always been one scholar on the Court—at least one."[9]

Frankfurter's strongest supporter on the Court, Harlan, indicated he felt the same way about the retired Justice's successor. In a written note to Frankfurter in 1963, Harlan referred to an address delivered by Goldberg at the American Bar Association a week earlier. "The A.J.G. speech left me cold. Respect for the Court is not something that can be achieved by fiat, but must come from its own performance. Who knows that as well as you do?"[10]

With Goldberg in Frankfurter's seat, Warren now had a clear majority in most cases. The difference made by Frankfurter's replacement was shown early in the 1962 Term, when the Brethren were again presented with the *Mendoza–Martinez* case [11] and *Rusk v. Cort.* [12] The cases, as we have mentioned before, involved the constitutionality of section 401 (j) of the Nationality Act and section 349 (a) (10) of the Immigration and Nationality Act. Under them, loss of citizenship was imposed on Mendoza—Martinez and Cort for leaving the United States to evade military service in time of war or declared national emergency. During the previous term, the Court had been divided four-to-four on the constitutional issue, and the cases were scheduled for reargument (*Mendoza–Martinez* for the second time) in December, 1962.

At the reargument on December 4, counsel for the government argued that a rational nexus existed between the statutory provision and the war power. The Chief Justice interrupted to ask: "Isn't it as important to pay for a war as to fight in it. Suppose a man left the country to evade a million dollars in taxes during a war. Could Congress impose expatriation?"

The reply was that serving the country in time of war is a more important duty. Under further questioning by Warren, however, Government counsel was pressed into arguing the *reductio ad absurdum* that "Congress could take away nationality for nonpayment of taxes during war." [13]

During the December 7 conference, Warren briefly stated the issues and said that he was still for a decision of unconstitutionality. As he saw it, "you can't take citizenship away without an unequivocal act of expatriation." He also asserted, "you can't 'punish' this way."

All the Brethren then turned to the new Justice. Warren asked, "Well Arthur, how do you vote?" Goldberg said that he would vote to hold the denationalization provisions invalid and gave his reasons. The Goldberg vote made for a bare majority in favor of Warren's position. The opinion was assigned to Goldberg, and he delivered it on February 13, 1963, holding sections 401 (j) and 349 (a) (10) unconstitutional because they imposed "punishment" without affording the procedural safeguards that must attend a criminal prosecution. Stewart, joined by White, issued a dissent similar to the draft opinions of the Court he had circulated in *Mendoza–Martinez* in 1960 and 1961 and in *Cort* in 1961. Harlan, joined by Clark, also dissented. Had

Frankfurter still been on the Court, the decision would have been five-to-four in favor of constitutionality.

Frankfurter's replacement by Goldberg also changed the result in the other close decisions of the 1962 Term. Particularly striking in this respect was *National Association for the Advancement of Colored People v. Button,* [14] for the Court had "decided" it in accordance with Frankfurter's view just before his stroke. The N.A.A.C.P. had sued to restrain enforcement of a 1956 Virginia statute that amended the laws on improper solicitation of business by attorneys to include agents for an organization which retained a lawyer in connection with an action to which it was not a party and in which it had no pecuniary interest. As construed by the Virginia Supreme Court, the amendment included the NAACP's activities within the statutory ban on improper solicitation of legal business. The Virginia court had upheld the amendment.

The case was first argued on November 8, 1961. At the conference on November 10, Warren spoke in favor of reversal. As he saw it, "the statute is discriminatory in prohibiting this unless the organization has a financial interest. This turns history around, since barratry statutes were aimed at commercialization of litigation." The Chief asserted that the amendment's "purpose is to circumvent *Brown* [15] obviously."

Black, who next delivered a strong statement for reversal, also stressed that "this is but one of a number of laws passed as a package designed to thwart our *Brown* decision—a scheme to defeat the Court's order. Sooner or later, we will have to grapple with these problems in these terms." Black, however, indicated he'd be willing to go along with a reversal on a narrow ground, though he felt that "the state can't handicap or hobble those who seek to protect their constitutional rights by contributing their time and money as this was done."

Frankfurter led the case for affirmance. "I can't imagine a worse disservice," he declared, "than to continue being the guardians of Negroes." He argued that the statute was a valid exercise of the state's regulatory power over the legal profession. "There's no evidence here," Frankfurter asserted, "that this statute is aimed at Negroes as such."

The conference voted five-to-four to uphold the Virginia law. Frankfurter circulated an opinion of the Court affirming the Virginia court. Black wrote a dissent stressing that the statute's legislative history showed that it had been enacted with the racially discriminatory purpose of precluding effective litigation on behalf of civil rights. Though the *N.A.A.C.P.* case had thus been "decided" during the 1961 Term, before the decision could be announced, Whittaker retired and Frankfurter became incapacitated. The case was then set down for reargument in the 1962 Term.

With the Court so closely divided, the votes of White and Goldberg would be decisive. Just before the 1962 Term began, Brennan sent a lengthy memorandum to the two new Justices. It emphasized the vital role played by the N.A.A.C.P.'s legal staff in Virginia public school desegregation. Brennan had, however, concluded that a majority would not join an opinion such as that issued by Black the previous term. Brennan's memo pointed out that a reversal could be based on First Amendment principles of overbreadth and protected associational activities, and need not rely upon inferences of discriminatory intent drawn from the legislative history.

The *N.A.A.C.P.* case was reargued on October 9, 1962. At the October 12 conference following the reargument, Warren repeated the view he had stated the previous year. "I think people have the right to organize to protect their constitutional rights." The Chief again stressed the law's requirement of financial interest, stating, "Virginia not only broadens the laws of barratry, but also denies equal protection in the requirement for proof of no pecuniary interest." Warren said that the Court could reverse either "on equal protection or on vagueness and indefiniteness."

The new Justices indicated they also would vote for reversal. White did not think "Virginia can constitutionally prevent representation by members of its legal staff when the case has been solicited by the N.A.A.C.P." Goldberg said that there was "a substantial equal protection point here and we could reverse on that."

The most important conference statement was, however, made by Brennan, who repeated the views expressed in his memo to White and Goldberg. He persuaded the conference to vote to reverse on the First Amendment ground, with Clark, Harlan, and Stewart voting the other way. Once again the Chief Justice turned to Brennan in a close case and assigned the opinion to him.

Brennan circulated a draft opinion of the Court that quickly won the approval of Warren, Douglas, and Goldberg. But Black had serious questions, because the draft did not hold that the N.A.A.C.P. had a constitutional right to maintain a legal staff to assist non-indigent civil-rights litigants. Black thought that the opinion as drafted was an open invitation to Virginia to employ a narrow statute against the N.A.A.C.P.'s legal staff to accomplish the same purpose as the challenged statute. Brennan decided to accommodate Black's view. The majority opinion was rewritten to intimate strongly that the activities disclosed on the record were beyond the reach of state power however expressed.

The *N.A.A.C.P.* opinion was delivered on January 14, 1963. Harlan, joined by Clark and Stewart, dissented. White delivered a partial dissent. He agreed with the majority opinion on overbreadth, but asserted that a narrowly drawn statute could proscribe the day-to-day management and dictation of litigation strategy and conduct by the N.A.A.C.P. Had White expressed this view of the case earlier, the original Brennan draft might never have been revised to meet Black's objections.

Another case where Frankfurter's departure made a difference was *Gibson v. Florida Legislative Investigation Committee.*[16] The committee was set up by the Florida legislature to conduct an investigation of the Miami branch of the N.A.A.C.P. Gibson, president of the branch, was ordered to appear and bring with him records pertaining to members and contributors. At the committee hearing, the chairman said that the inquiry was into Communist infiltration into organizations, including the N.A.A.C.P. Gibson refused to produce the records. He also declined to consult his records to inform the committee which, if any, of fifty-two individually identified persons were members of the Miami branch. Gibson was adjudged in contempt and sentenced to six months imprisonment and a $1,200 fine. The Florida Supreme Court upheld the judgment.

Gibson also had been argued and considered in the 1961 Term. At the conference then, on December 8, 1961, the Chief Justice declared, "If this case stands, it overrules *N.A.A.C.P. v. Alabama*"[17]—the 1958 decision discussed in chapter 8. "Even under the balancing theory," Warren said, "the state has shown no adequate interest."

The Chief was backed by Black, Douglas, and Brennan. But Frankfurter and his supporters voted the other way. Clark spoke most strongly for affirmance. "There was an interest here of the state," he asserted. "There was a resolution of the N.A.A.C.P. saying that

Communists were trying to infiltrate them, also testimony by witnesses about colored people attending Communist meetings." Clark differentiated *N.A.A.C.P. v. Alabama,* saying, "I don't see that he was forced to reveal all the names." Harlan made the same point. "This wasn't," he noted, "an effort to get membership lists wholesale, but to limit them to refreshing of recollection in respect of [specific] names."

The conference vote was five-to-four, with Frankfurter, Clark, Harlan, Whittaker, and Stewart for affirmance, but again Whittaker's retirement and Frankfurter's collapse caused the case to be set for reargument in the 1962 Term. At the October 12, 1962, conference after the reargument, the Chief Justice and the others who had participated in the December 8, 1961, conference voted as they had the first time. White voted, as had Whittaker, for affirmance. But Goldberg voted with Warren to reverse. That made the decision five-to-four for reversal. Goldberg was assigned the opinion and delivered it March 25, 1962, holding that the committee had failed to show any substantial relationship between the N.A.A.C.P. and subversive or Communist activities. Harlan dissented, joined by Clark, Stewart, and White. If Frankfurter had cast the decisive vote, the decision would have been the other way.

Frankfurter's replacement by Goldberg also changed the result in *Wong Sun v. United States,*[18] a criminal case with a complicated fact pattern. Federal narcotics agents in San Francisco arrested Hom Way and found heroin in his possession. Way stated that he had bought heroin from "Blackie Toy," proprietor of a laundry on Leavenworth Street. At 6 A.M., agents went to a laundry on Leavenworth Street operated by James Wah Toy. They rang the bell and, when Toy appeared, showed their badges. Toy slammed the door and ran to the bedroom where his wife and child were sleeping. The agents broke open the door and followed Toy and arrested him. Toy denied selling narcotics, but said he knew a "Johnny," who had sold heroin and described the house where Johnny lived. The agents located the house, entered it, and found Johnny Yee in the bedroom, who showed them heroin in a drawer. Yee said that the heroin had been brought to him by Toy and another known as "Sea Dog."

Toy was questioned and said that "Sea Dog" was Wong Sun. He took some agents to Wong Sun's dwelling. They were allowed in by

Wong Sun's wife and found him, but no narcotics. Toy, Yee, and Wong Sun were arraigned and released on their own recognizance. Each was later interrogated at the Narcotics Bureau office. Toy and Wong Sun made incriminating statements, but refused to sign English written versions. Both Toy and Wong Sun were convicted of transporting and concealing heroin. The government's evidence consisted of (1) statements made by Toy at his arrest; (2) heroin surrendered by Yee; (3) Toy's unsigned statement; and (4) Wong Sun's similar statement. The evidence had been admitted over objections that it was inadmissible as "fruits" of unlawful arrests or of attendant searches. The court of appeals had held that the arrests were illegal because they were not based on "probable cause," but that the four items of proof were properly admitted because they were not the "fruits" of the illegal arrests.

The Chief Justice, Black, Douglas, Clark, and Brennan voted to grant certiorari, with Frankfurter, Harlan, Whittaker, and Stewart for denial. While the case was argued, Stewart suggested to Harlan that he would be prepared to dismiss as improvidently granted.[19] The conference that first considered the *Wong Sun* case took place on April 6, 1962. This was the last conference Frankfurter attended; later that day, he suffered his first stroke. To Warren, the case was a simple one. When his law clerks started to discuss the technical elements involved, the Chief interjected, "Now, wait a minute! This guy was a Chinaman in San Francisco, who was awakened six o'clock in the morning by a couple of guys in plainclothes. They say they're narcotics agents. He's scared, he slams the door shut, he runs back to his bedroom, standing next to his wife, who was asleep in one bed. His kid was asleep in another bed in the corner of the room. These guys start to ask him questions. And now you're gonna tell me that the statements he makes in those circumstances can be admitted in evidence against him. *You can't do that!*"

At the April 6 conference, Warren urged reversal saying that the lower "court was right when it found that the arrest was illegal, but wrong when it said that they could use this evidence." Frankfurter argued the other way. In his view, the arrests were lawful, since there was "probable cause" to make them. The conference vote was four-to-four. Warren, Douglas, and Brennan voted to reverse. Black also voted that way, though only tentatively. Frankfurter, Clark, Harlan, and Stewart voted to affirm. White, who took his seat on April 6, did not participate. Because of the close division and Frankfurter's absence during the remainder of the term, the case was set for reargument.

Wong Sun was reargued October 8 and 9, 1962. The conference discussion took place October 12. "The court of appeals," said Warren, "held that the arrest was illegal, but the statements are not the fruit of the poison tree. I think they are and would, reverse. Hom Way's identification of 'Blackie Toy' and Toy's flight added nothing. His statements were under the [influence] of the arrest. As to Wong Sun, breaking into his bedroom helps none and [his later] admission doesn't help." Black, saying "my tentative vote last year is not tentative now," also voted to reverse, as did Douglas and Brennan.

Clark led the argument the other way. "I think there was probable cause," the Texan declared, "and we shouldn't take the court of appeals determination, but decide it for ourselves. 'Probable cause' is not a mechanical test. The mere fact that an informant has not been tested does not mean that Way's testimony was not reliable. He was not a paid informer, it's true. But it's the reasonableness of the circumstances of the particular case which must be our guide. Here, Way had the stuff on him and the officers were surely entitled to find out where he got it. He incriminated himself in naming Toy." Harlan and Stewart agreed that there was probable cause, Harlan commenting on Way's identification of Toy as his heroin seller, "the facts of human life when one is caught red-handed with the goods are not that he would enmesh himself in more."

That left the decision once more up to the two new Justices. White voted to affirm. "I think," he stated, "there was probable cause. Here was an accomplice telling about another participant in the crime." Goldberg, however, voted with Warren. He thought that the statements made by Toy and Wong Sun were fruits of illegal arrests. "You can't distinguish," the junior Justice asserted, "between statements and tangible objects as fruits."

Had Frankfurter still been on the Court, the *Wong Sun* decision would have been five-to-four for affirmance. With Goldberg voting in his place, the vote was five-to-four to reverse. The opinion was assigned to Brennan. On December 3, 1962, he sent a draft opinion to the other four members of the majority, together with a memorandum explaining the draft. Brennan noted that the draft reached the result of reversal agreed upon at conference, "but detours some from the route agreed upon at conference."

Brennan wrote that he agreed that Toy's arrest was illegal, "and that his oral statements in the bedroom and the narcotics surrendered by Johnny Yee were inadmissible against him because fruits of the illegal arrest." Toy's incriminating statement, however, required a different approach. As to it, Brennan informed his four colleagues, "I do not reach the fruits question. Rather the enclosed holds that his confession was not sufficiently corroborated since the only source of corroboration, Wong Sun's unsigned confession, being the statement of a co-conspirator, made after the end of the conspiracy, does not fall within the hearsay exception for statements of co-conspirators."

At the end of his memo, Brennan summarized how his draft disposed of Wong Sun's conviction. "I cannot agree with the Court of Appeals," he wrote, "that probable cause and reasonable grounds were lacking for the arrest of Wong Sun. I therefore reach no fruits question as to his confession." Instead, Wong Sun's conviction was reversed by a different route, because "the trial court did not tell us whether he found sufficient corroboration in the narcotics surrendered by Yee or solely or in part in Toy's unsigned confession. Since the Toy confession would not be admissible even for purposes of corroboration against Wong Sun, I conclude that Wong Sun is entitled to a new trial on a record without the Toy confession."

Goldberg and Douglas quickly agreed to join Brennan's opinion, with Douglas doing so after the draft was changed to include a statement on the salutary effect of arrest warrant procedure. Black suggested other changes, particularly on the deference to be accorded the lower court on the legality of the arrests. When Brennan made these suggested changes, Black and Warren also joined. It was certain from the outset that Clark, Harlan, and Stewart would dissent. The majority, however, still had hopes that White would agree, as he delayed joining either the draft opinion of the Court or the dissent which Clark had circulated.

Then, on January 9, White unexpectedly circulated a stinging dissent. White differed with the opinion of the Court on the "probable cause" question, suggesting that the discovery of Toy could be explained only by the officers' possession of information as to his identity. White's dissent also argued that the test under which the Court held Toy's bedroom statements excludable "constitutes a major step toward excluding any post-arrest statements made in the presence of the police and goes far beyond any previous tests which this Court has applied to determine the voluntary nature of statements made while in custody." White was accusing the majority of unduly broadening the rule of the 1943 *McNabb*[20] and 1957 *Mallory* cases,[21] governing confessions made during an illegal police detention, and elevating it to a constitutional plane.

Brennan responded to White's draft dissent by revising his opinion to make it clear that exclusion of Toy's bedroom statements was based not merely on the illegality of the arrest, but on the circumstances in which they were made, which made it "unreasonable to infer that Toy's response was sufficiently an act of free will." White, however, withdrew his dissent only two days after it was circulated and it was never issued. When Brennan delivered the opinion of the Court on January 14, 1963, only Clark delivered a dissent, joined by Harlan, Stewart, and White.

There is an amusing footnote to Clark's *Wong Sun* dissent. In his first draft, circulated January 3, 1963, Clark chided the majority for its "total lack of acquaintanceship with the habits and practices of Chinatown," which would enable the officers to know about the identity of a person described as "Blackie Toy." Clark did not realize that Toy's laundry on Leavenworth Street was nowhere near Chinatown, but was instead on Russian Hill, in an area notable for the absence of Chinese residents. Brennan went to Clark's chambers, armed with a map, and pointed out the error in geography. Clark revised his dissent to point out only that the Toy arrest was "by officers familiar with San Francisco and the habits and practices of its Chinese–American inhabitants."

The remaining 1962 Term cases were all argued and decided after Goldberg had taken his seat. These cases illustrate the point already made—that, with Frankfurter's departure, Warren now had a solid majority.

The most important 1962 Term case was *Gideon v. Wainwright*.[22] The book, *Gideon's Trumpet*,[23] and the movie made from it have made Clarence Gideon and his case part of American folklore. But few people realize that the *Gideon* decision resulted directly from Warren's leadership. Even before the 1961 Term began, the Chief's new law clerks were instructed by one of the prior term's clerks, "Keep your eyes peeled for a right to counsel case. The Chief feels strongly that the Constitution requires a lawyer."

Gideon had been convicted in a Florida court of breaking and entering a poolroom with intent to commit a crime—a felony under Florida law. The trial judge refused Gideon's request for counsel, and he had to conduct his own defense. The highest Florida court affirmed. Gideon then sent a petition to the Supreme Court for certiorari. The petition was laboriously scrawled in pencil in schoolboy-type printing on lined sheets furnished by the Florida prison. Gideon's papers arrived at the Court January 8, 1962—one of nine in forma pauperis petitions in that morning's mail.

Gideon's petition claimed that he had been denied due process, because, "When at the time of the petitioners trial he ask the lower court for the aid of counsel, the court refused this aid. Petitioner told the court that this Court made decision to the effect that all citizens tried for a felony crime should have aid of counsel. The lower court ignored this plea." At the trial, when the court had denied his request for appointed counsel, Gideon had asserted, "The United States Supreme Court says I am entitled to be represented by counsel."[24]

Gideon was, to be sure, wrong in his assertion. The leading case then was *Betts v. Brady*,[25] where the Court had held in 1942 that an indigent defendant did not have a due process right to appointed counsel in a noncapital case unless he could show that, under the special circumstances of his case, he could not obtain a "fair trial" without a lawyer. Gideon's petition did not claim any such "special circumstances" and, as Lewis put it in his book, the petition was not the type that evoked the rare comment in the Clerk's Office, where the petitions were sorted, "Here's one that I'll bet will be granted." On the contrary, says Lewis, "In the Clerk's Office it had no ring of history to it."[26]

But Lewis and other Court watchers were unaware of two crucial facts. One was that, as we saw, Warren's law clerks had been instructed to find in the mass of I.F.P. petitions just such a right-to-counsel case. The second was that, in their discussions on the *Carnley* case,[27] then pending, the Justices had come close to overruling *Betts v. Brady*. Even Frankfurter indicated that he would overrule, though he thought that *Carnley* was not an appropriate case to do so.

These facts made the *Gideon* case the proverbial needle in the I.F.P. haystack. We saw in chapter 2 that the Chief Justice's law clerks had the special duty of scrutinizing the I.F.P. applications and preparing a memorandum (called a "flimsy," from the thin paper carbon copy sent to each Justice). When the Warren clerk who prepared the flimsy considered the case worthy of consideration, he attached the red envelope containing the original petition to his memo. This was done in Gideon's case and served as a red flag that this was a right-to-counsel case that might serve as a vehicle for overruling *Betts v. Brady*.

The *Gideon* certiorari conference took place June 1, 1962. At Warren's urging, the Court voted to grant cert, with only Clark for denial. Even the normally conservative Harlan had written at the end of his clerk's cert memo, "YES, I think the time has come when we should meet the Betts question head-on." [28] The order granting cert stated that counsel were requested to discuss the question, "Should this Court's holding in Betts v. Brady . . . be reconsidered?" The question had been suggested in a May 28 Harlan memorandum. [29] On June 18, Gideon sent another penciled petition: "I do desire the Court to appoint a competent attorney to represent me in this Court." At the conference on June 22 (the last of the 1961 Term) Warren suggested that Abe Fortas, soon to be appointed to the Court himself, should be assigned to represent Gideon. The Brethren all concurred. The Court Clerk put in a call to Fortas, locating him in Dallas, and Fortas said he would be happy to serve.

"If an obscure convict named Clarence Earl Gideon," declared Attorney General Robert F. Kennedy in a speech after the Supreme Court decision, "had not sat down in his prison cell with a pencil and paper to write a letter to the Supreme Court . . ., the vast machinery of American law would have gone on functioning undisturbed. But Gideon *did* write that letter . . . and the whole course of American legal history has been changed." [30]

Yet it was Warren more than anyone who was responsible for the *Gideon* decision. It was the Chief who wanted his clerks to find a case like *Gideon,* led the Justices in granting cert in the case, and suggested that Fortas be assigned to argue it. Those were the crucial steps that made the *Gideon* decision inevitable. The rest was anticlimax—though none but the Brethren were privy to that reality.

Gideon was argued on January 15, 1963. In his *Autobiography*, Douglas called the Fortas argument the best he had heard. [31] But the Fortas eloquence was only the battering of an open door. The Justices, including Clark and Harlan, who had not been willing to go that far the previous year in *Carnley,* had reached a consensus on overruling *Betts v. Brady.* Led by Warren, the January 18 conference quickly agreed that *Betts v. Brady's* time had come.

There was some discussion of how far to make the right to counsel extend. The Chief Justice asked, "Do we say abolish the distinction between capital and noncapital serious felonies—or what?" Warren said it was "better not to say [the right to counsel applies in] 'every criminal case,' if we don't have to here." In his view, "maybe it's best just to decide this case." At any rate, he noted, "I'd make it fully retroactive."

The conference voted unanimously to reverse Gideon's conviction and to overrule *Betts v. Brady.* They followed Warren's suggestion to limit the opinion to the case at hand, without addressing the question of how far the new right to assigned counsel extended. The Chief assigned the opinion to Black—a gesture particularly appreciated by the Brethren because Black had delivered the dissent in *Betts v. Brady.* When Black wrote the opinion, he simply based it on his previous dissent, and he was able to circulate a draft within two weeks. The decision was announced for a unanimous Court on March 18.

For Black, writing *Gideon* was particularly satisfying. With typical understatement, he wrote Edmond Cahn, the legal philosopher, "I did not find it wholly unpleasant to write the *Gideon* case overruling *Betts v. Brady.*"[32] A few weeks later, he told a friend, "When *Betts v. Brady* was decided, I never thought I'd live to see it overruled."[33]

To one interested in Warren, the *Gideon* case is a good illustration of his fairness in assigning opinions. He did not take the "big" cases for himself, except where, as in the *Brown* segregation case,[34] he thought it was important that the Court speak through the Chief Justice, or, as in *Reynolds v. Sims*[35] or *Miranda v. Arizona,*[36] he wanted to bear the brunt of the expected criticism. The Brethren all received their share of the important opinions, though he naturally gave more of them to those who were his supporters and would express themselves in the manner closest to his own views.

There is nothing inconsistent in this with the proper assignment of opinions. "I think it is very fair," concedes White, himself never one of the Warren inner circle, "for a Chief Justice to assign opinions to the people who (a) are on his side; (b) will do the job the way the Chief Justice would best like it done, and I think that's part of the prerogatives of the Chief Justice." The Chief Justice, as White sees it, might rightly assign an opinion to one Justice rather than another because "he felt that [the Justice] would more accurately or better reflect the sentiment that he would like to see reflected."

It is also erroneous to judge the fairness of opinion assignments by focusing only on the "stars" of the Court calendar. "Every year on this Court we get 'dogs' of cases," Stewart explains. These are the cases where "you knew, right from the moment you started to work on it, it would add nothing to the jurisprudence of the United States at all. You had to do the best you could, but it was a 'nothing' case, except extremely hard and arduous. Every term there are cases like that."

Stewart recalls Warren's fairness in assigning the "dogs" as well as the "stars." "I remember," he says, "the Chief Justice typically and invariably would take more than his share of those, you know. So that if you got assigned one, you wouldn't resent it. He got more than his share; you wouldn't feel you were just getting this stuff."

Two other criminal cases decided toward the end of the 1962 Term involved the new technologies of television and electronic recording. In *Rideau v. Louisiana*,[37] Rideau had been arrested after a bank robbery and murder and put in the Calcasieu Parish jail. The next day and two days following, the local television station broadcast an interview in the jail between Rideau and the sheriff, in which Rideau admitted the crimes. Rideau moved for a change of venue, claiming it would deprive him of due process to force him to trial in Calcasieu Parish after the broadcasts of his interview. The motion was denied. Rideau was tried in the parish, convicted of murder, and sentenced to death. The court had also denied another motion to excuse for cause two jury members who were deputy sheriffs. The highest state court affirmed the conviction.

At the May 3, 1963 conference Warren had no doubt that the conviction should be reversed. First of all, said the Chief, "he was entitled to a change of venue in light of the television, particularly since three persons [on the jury] said they saw it." Warren also felt that "having two deputy sheriffs on the jury is grounds itself for reversal." Except for Clark and Harlan, all agreed on reversal because of the broadcast. Stewart delivered the opinion of the Court on June 3, reversing on that ground. Clark, joined by Harlan, dissented. Clark's dissent is of interest because he was to write the opinion in *Estes v. Texas*[38] two years later striking down the televising of a criminal trial.

The second case in which a new technology played a part saw an unusual split between Warren and Black on the one side and Douglas, Brennan, and Goldberg on the other. The case was *Lopez v. United States*[39] and arose out of a conviction for attempted bribery of an internal revenue agent. Davis, the agent, had told Lopez that he would be liable for a cabaret tax. Lopez offered $420 if Davis would drop the case. Davis took the money and reported the incident to his superior. He was ordered to return with a pocket wire recorder, on which he recorded the giving of another bribe. Lopez claimed entrapment and also moved to suppress the recording. The motion was denied and he was found guilty. The conviction was affirmed by the court of appeals. The Brethren split sharply on whether to take the *Lopez* case, with Black, Douglas, Brennan, and Goldberg voting to grant cert and the other five to deny.

Warren, strongly supported by Black, spoke for affirmance at the January 18, 1963, conference. "We can't say," said the Chief, "that the evidence shows entrapment." In addition, he felt, "This is different from *Silverman* [*v. United States*,[40] the 1961 case of eavesdropping with a "spike mike," discussed in chapter 9]. The man knew this was an agent and he talked openly with him."

Black asserted, "Unless we would overrule *On Lee*, we must affirm." Black was referring to the 1952 *On Lee* case,[41] where a narcotics conviction was sustained even though it was based on statements made by the accused to a supposed friend, who was an undercover agent with a "Dick Tracy" wristwatch radio transmitter. Warren did not go as far as Black. He felt that this case was different from *On Lee*, which he said he disapproved. Here Davis had given full notice of his authority and he used the recorder to corroborate his report, which otherwise would be a matter of his word against Lopez.

Douglas, Brennan, and Goldberg would not, however, go along with Warren and Black. Brennan, in particular, declared that *On Lee* was wrong and should be overruled. In fact, he went further and urged that the 1928 *Olmstead* decision,[42] which had ruled that wiretapping did not violate the Fourth Amendment, should likewise be overruled.

The other Justices voted for affirmance. On May 27, 1963, Harlan announced the opinion of the Court, holding that no entrapment was shown and that the recording was properly admitted on the authority of *On Lee*. Warren delivered a concurrence, stressing that "the recording served . . . to protect the credibility of Davis against that of a man who wished to corrupt a public servant in the performance of his public trust."[43] The next day Clark wrote Harlan, "Bravo! On [with] Lee! I'm for it."[44]

Brennan, joined by Douglas and Goldberg, issued a dissent that argued at length for the overruling of *Olmstead*. After Brennan read his dissent, Black, who had voted with the majority, sent him a penciled note, "you marshalled better arguments for your view, I think, than the dissenters did in Olmstead."

Potentially, the most explosive case during the 1962 Term was *Alabama v. United States*.[45] When George C. Wallace was inaugurated as Governor of Alabama in January, 1963, he vowed, "from this Cradle of the Confederacy . . . I say, Segregation now! Segregation tomorrow! Segregation forever!" During his campaign, Wallace had promised to place himself in the doorway of any school ordered to admit blacks. Now black students were applying to the University of Alabama, and the new Governor took steps to block their entry. On April 25, Robert F. Kennedy personally went to the Alabama state capitol to demonstrate federal resolve in enforcement of federal court orders. A Justice who served with Warren recalls that the Attorney General's visit converted the Chief from hostility to admiration of the younger Kennedy. The trip was a gesture of Administration support for the Court's desegregation rulings such as the Justices had never received from President Eisenhower, as well as a demonstration of personal courage of the type Warren appreciated.

In May, a federal court ordered the University of Alabama to admit a black applicant. Recalling the need for military force to secure the admission of James Meredith to the state university at Oxford, Mississippi, in 1961, the federal authorities took measures to use federal troops if they were needed. Military units in Birmingham were alerted, and additional troops were stationed there. At this, Alabama filed a motion in the Supreme Court for leave to file a complaint (under the constitutional provision allowing states to sue directly in the highest Court) for an injunction ordering removal of the federal troops from the Birmingham area.

After Alabama's application was received, the Chief Justice asked

Brennan to prepare a memorandum to serve as the basis for conference discussion. The Brennan memo recommended rejection of the state's motion on several grounds: the case was not "ripe" for decision, lack of a justiciable controversy because only a political question was presented, and failure to state a cause of action. Warren and the others agreed that the state's application should be denied, but thought Brennan's memo dealt with issues, such as whether Alabama had stated a case, that were best avoided. The Chief asked Brennan to prepare a per curiam opinion to be written as narrowly as possible. According to a Warren memorandum "After the Conference adjourned yesterday, I learned that Bill Brennan had worked out a tentative per curiam. . . . It appeared to me to be along the lines indicated at the Conference. I, therefore, assigned the writing of it to him."[46]

Brennan circulated a draft stressing that "the steps taken at the direction of the President, the mere alerting and dispatch of troops in the manner alleged, because of events in Birmingham, do not give rise to an infringement of any legally protected rights of the plaintiffs." The failure of the state to allege an injury to its "legal" rights, as opposed to its political rights, was fatal to justiciability.

The Brennan draft provoked an immediate strong dissent from Douglas, who (we saw in the discussion of *Baker v. Carr*[47] in the last chapter) always took exception to anything which seemed to approve the doctrine that "political questions" were beyond judicial competence. The Douglas dissent was fatal to the Brennan draft, because all the Brethren agreed that unanimity was essential for such a *cause célèbre*. Goldberg also expressed the view that the Court should not disavow all judicial control over federal military action, urging that a reservation be made for such action in violation of law.

The Douglas and Goldberg objections led Brennan to change the ground of the per curiam to emphasize the prematurity of the state's motion. As each Justice went over the revised draft, Brennan's language was progressively pared, until all that was left was a terse statement of the "unripeness" of the state's application. When the per curiam was issued on May 27, 1963, it stated only that the President had "merely made ready to exercise" his authority to use troops and such "purely preparatory measures . . . afford no basis for the granting of any relief."[48] There is a draft in Harlan's writing indicating that the final version was suggested by him.[49]

Shortly after he had appointed his brother to head the Department of Justice, President Kennedy quipped, "I can't see that it's wrong to give him a little legal experience before he goes out to practice law."[50] During the 1962 Term, the Attorney General took the opportunity to argue the case of *Gray v. Sanders*[51] in the Supreme Court—the first and only time that the younger Kennedy appeared professionally in a courtroom. The case arose out of a suit to restrain the Georgia county-unit system, which counted the votes of each county as a unit and gave the election to the winner of a majority or plurality of the units. Though the system was heavily weighted in favor of low-population rural counties, it had survived four pre–*Baker v. Carr* challenges. Despite this, the lower court had held the system violative of the Equal Protection Clause.

On January 17, 1963, looking, as James E. Clayton of the *Washington Post* put it, "like a nervous and uncomfortable young bridegroom"[52] in morning coat and striped trousers, Robert Kennedy argued against the county-unit system. His mother, his wife, two sisters, his brother Senator Edward Kennedy, his sister-in-law the President's wife, and four of his children were in the courtroom. The Kennedys outnumbered the Justices.[53]

The case itself was a simple one for the Brethren. Except for Harlan, who had dissented in *Baker v. Carr,* they had no difficulty in following Warren's lead and voting to strike down the Georgia system. The opinion was assigned to Douglas, who used the occasion to urge the concept of voter equality that he, Warren, Black, and Brennan would have adopted had *Baker v. Carr* been decided on the merits. He went so far as to assert, in his opinion, that the Constitution's "conception of political equality . . . can mean only one thing—one person, one vote."[54] This language went too far for Stewart and Clark. When the opinion was delivered on March 18, 1963, they issued a concurrence stressing that the decision did not lay down "the basic ground rules implementing Baker v. Carr," but only held that, within a given constituency, the "one voter–one vote" rule must govern.

Harlan delivered a sharp dissent. Frankfurter felt even more strongly that the decision was wrong. "If you want a realization of what is going on," the incapacitated former Justice wrote Alexander Bickel on the day *Gray v. Sanders* was decided, "read the Court's opinion in the light of the dissent in the Georgia County case. Think of not even mentioning four cases in which that issue had already been decided the other way. But then, by this time you will have taken due note of the same 'shoddy' way, professionally speaking, they are turning out other cases."

Frankfurter urged Bickel and other Court critics to speak out against the course of decision during the 1962 Term. "I can assure you," the retired Justice wrote, "that explicit analysis and criticism of the way the Court is doing its business really gets under their skin, just as the praise of their constituencies, the so-called liberal journals and well-known liberal approvers only fortifies them in their present result-oriented jurisprudence."[55]

Once again the term's decision that gave rise to the greatest public reaction had to do with religious exercises in the public schools. At issue in *Abington School District v. Schempp*[56] was a state requirement for the reading of verses from the Bible at the opening of each school day. A three-judge district court held the requirement violative of the First Amendment. Black, Clark, Stewart, Harlan, and White voted to hear the appeal, with Warren, Douglas, and Brennan voting the other way.

The case was argued before a packed courtroom on February 27 and 28, 1963. As he had done in *Engel v. Vitale*[57] the previous term, Warren cut to the core of the case by his questions. He asked counsel for the school board whether there could be one hour's Bible reading. That might go too far was the reply, but reading a few verses was acceptable. At which Warren asked, "Is one hour . . . unconstitutional, but ten minutes all right?" The attorney said that it was a question of degree; it was a question of whether the school was attempting to teach religion or morality. "Is that not our question today?" came back the Chief Justice.[58]

But the comment that indicated which direction the decision would take was made by Harlan, after he had asked counsel to distinguish the decisions in cases like *Torcaso v. Watkins*[59] (1961), discussed in chapter 9, and *Engel v. Vitale*, the 1962 school prayer case discussed in the last chapter: "What these cases really present is the question whether we are going to reexamine the past cases."[60]

The March 1 conference revealed a consensus not to overrule *Engel*. But concern was expressed that *Engel* had not fully explored the history and development of the Establishment Clause as it bore upon

Warren making address as Presidential candidate, June 1952

Unless otherwise stated, all photos are reproduced,
courtesy of the United States Supreme Court

Warren receiving congratulations on reelection as Governor, 1946

Warren and Eisenhower and wives, 1953: first visit to White House as Chief Justice

Warren being robed for first time on Supreme Court, October 5, 1953

The 1953 Court meeting President Eisenhower at White House (National Archives)

Frankfurter and Black: the Court's two poles in the early Warren years

Brennan: Warren's chief lieutenant (New York University)

Douglas and Jackson: Black and Frankfurter's leading supporters

Harlan: Frankfurter's principal ally

Warren: a rare candid photo

Frankfurter: Warren's testy adversary

Black: he always thought he had led the judicial revolution during
the Warren years

Warren with the Kennedys: The Brethren visit the White House, November 20, 1963 (National Archives)

Warren and fellow commissioners present Warren Commission report to President Johnson

The Court in 1965 (minus Harlan): The Brethren in a rare informal pose

Warren, Douglas and Robert Frost at a park dedication

Douglas and wife, Cathy, on Supreme Court steps

Clark and Mitchell: the Texan and Nixon's Attorney General at bar association function (Institute of Judicial Administration)

The Court in Warren's final term

cases like those before the Court. Brennan in particular asked whether it could be demonstrated that the Founding Fathers meant to forbid some forms of religious activities and manifestations in public institutions while permitting other forms to survive.

On the Monday following the conference, Brennan indicated that he would write a separate concurring opinion that would explore the history, scrutinize the Court's prior decisions, and attempt to fashion some viable distinctions between offensive and permissible practices. That afternoon notice was received that the opinion had been assigned to Clark, who circulated a draft opinion of the Court on May 20. It followed the approach of *Engel v. Vitale,* though it was longer. It was during the reading by Clark of his *Schempp* opinion that Douglas passed the note to Black quoted in chapter 2, which complained that Clark was reading every word of his opinion and commented, "Perhaps we need an anti-filibuster rule as badly as some say the Senate does." [61]

On May 21, Brennan circulated the first print of his concurrence, seventy pages in length. In his memorandum transmitting the draft, Brennan stressed that he wished this to be his own opinion, expressing his own view of the case. For that reason he would join with him no other member of the Court. Except for Stewart, the others promptly joined Clark's opinion, though Douglas and Goldberg, with Harlan joining him, later issued separate concurrences.

There had been near-unanimity on the decision from the time of the March 1 conference. Almost until decision day, however, there was doubt about Stewart. For a time, he seemed on the verge of joining the Court, but on May 24, Stewart announced his intention of preparing a dissent. Only five days before the end of the term, the Stewart dissent was circulated. Its substance was essentially that of a memorandum that Stewart had sent around on April 10, though substantially shorter.

The Clark, Brennan, and Stewart opinions, as well as the short Douglas and Goldberg concurrences, were issued on June 17, the last day of the 1962 Term. The press stressed that the voices of a Protestant (Clark), Catholic (Brennan), and Jew (Goldberg) on the Court spoke up for the Church-state separation in the decision. [62]

The choice of Clark to deliver the opinion of the Court was another illustration of Warren's skill in assigning opinions. Clark was generally thought of as a "conservative," while Black, who had been the Court's spokesman in *Engel v. Vitale* the year before, was widely thought of as a "radical" Justice. The decision announced by Clark might be attacked less fiercely than the same decision by Black. Warren himself had gone out of his way on May 22 to write Clark on *Schempp,* "I like your opinion."

Compared with the reaction a year earlier to the school prayer decision, *Schempp* was received with relative calm. To be sure, there were the usual denunciations by the Court's critics on Capitol Hill. Representative Robert T. Ashmore of South Carolina introduced a bill to put the inscription, "In God We Trust," above the Supreme Court bench.[63] In a letter to the Capitol architect, Warren opposed the proposal and it never got out of committee.[64] The reaction of religious leaders who disagreed with the decision was more muted, perhaps because the decision had been widely expected.

The last day of the 1962 Term also saw the decision in *Sherbert v. Verner*[65]—a case involving the right to free exercise of religion. Sherbert was a Seventh-day Adventist who worked in a South Carolina textile mill. She became a Seventh-day Adventist in 1957. Two years later, when the mill shifted to a six-day week, she told her employer that her religious beliefs forbade her to work Saturdays. She was fired because of her failure to appear for Saturday work. Her claim for unemployment compensation was denied. The highest state court sustained the denial. Warren, Douglas, Brennan, Stewart, and Goldberg voted to take the appeal, with Black, Clark, Harlan, and White voting to dismiss.

The April 26, 1963, conference vote was seven-to-two to reverse, with Harlan and White for affirmance. But the division was closer than the vote indicated, as shown by what happened at the opinion-writing stage. Warren assigned the opinion to Brennan on April 30. On May 29, Brennan circulated his first *Sherbert* draft. It was based on the narrow premise that a distinction could be drawn between persons who became unemployed because the employer altered the work schedule to conflict with the exercise of religious beliefs (exactly this case) and workers who had been disqualified because of a religious conversion that might, under the state unemployment compensation law, be deemed a "personal circumstance" barring them from compensation.

The distinction drawn in Brennan's draft was too narrow for the others, except for Clark who agreed to join. Brennan circulated a second draft in which the decision was broadened. But certain reservations remained. These included the suggestion that the statute did not purport to disqualify all persons unemployed for personal reasons, as well as the suggestion that Sherbert's religious practices did not make her unemployable, as shown by the employment of other Sabbatarians in her community. In this form, with minor changes, the opinion proved acceptable to Warren, Black, Clark, and Goldberg.

On June 4, Stewart sent around a sharp concurring opinion that chided the Court for failing to reconcile a "head-on collision" between the Establishment Clause and the Free Exercise Clause of the First Amendment. Stewart asserted that the Court's decision was inconsistent with the 1961 decision upholding Sunday Blue Laws,[66] discussed in chapter 9. In a companion case to that decision, the Court had held that a Sunday Closing Law did not violate the free exercise rights of an orthodox Jewish butcher, who also did not work on Saturday.[67] Now, Stewart urged, the *Sherbert* opinion was effectively overruling that decision, though pretending to distinguish it.

Douglas circulated a milder concurrence the following day. On June 11 Harlan issued a dissent, and White joined him a day later.

Brennan made several changes in his opinion to deal with the points made in the Stewart, Douglas, and Harlan opinions. To answer Stewart's charge that the opinion required the "establishment" of Seventh-day Adventism in order to protect the church member's free exercise right, a paragraph was added to refute the notion that the state was being compelled to pay benefits on religious grounds. Brennan also added a new subsection "E. Religious Considerations in Public Welfare Programs," to Part V of his *Schempp* concurrence, carefully distinguishing between public welfare conditions designed to benefit churches and religions as such, and those designed merely to avoid invidious religious classifications. Despite Brennan's changes in this regard, however, Stewart continued to charge that the Court had "studiously ignored" the asserted conflict between the Establishment and Free Exercise Clauses.

Harlan's dissent stressed that South Carolina had not discriminated against Sherbert because of her religious beliefs, saying she was not "denied benefits *because* she was a Seventh-day Adventist."[68] To answer Harlan, Brennan made two changes in his opinion. The first sought to demonstrate that the state courts had singled out the Sabbatarian for harsher treatment than persons unable to work for other personal reasons. The second was a paragraph to show that the statute contained a built-in discrimination between the Saturday and Sunday worshipper, since the latter could be exempted from Sabbath work in times of emergency while the former could not. The many revisions made by Brennan carried the opinion to six drafts before it was delivered on June 17.

Brennan and Warren played key roles in important decisions expanding the scope of federal habeas corpus and other post-conviction remedies. The first was in *Fay v. Noia*.[69] It arose years after Noia had been convicted with two co-defendants of murder in New York. All three had confessed. Noia had not appealed his 1942 conviction, though his co-defendants had done so and lost. In 1956, the highest New York court ruled that the co-defendants' confessions had been coerced and they should be released. Since Noia's confession had been secured in the same circumstances, Noia also petitioned the New York courts for release. They held that they had no jurisdiction to reopen the case because he had not appealed his conviction. Noia then filed a petition in the federal district court for habeas corpus. That court denied the writ because the governing rule then was that a federal habeas corpus petition could be entertained only if a state prisoner had exhausted all state remedies. The court of appeals reversed. At the certiorari conference on May 14, 1962, all except Clark (with Frankfurter absent) voted to grant New York's cert petition.

Though *Fay v. Noia* made for a fundamental change in the relationship between federal and state courts, its significance was not appreciated by the press and public. When, on January 7, 1963, the Chief Justice called, "Number 84, Edward M. Fay, petitioner, versus Charles Noia," only twenty-one spectators were in the courtroom. But counsel and the Justices were well aware of the case's potential. William I. Siegel, the assistant district attorney who appeared for New York, began his argument, "New York is here in this Court seeking to reverse a decision of the Second Circuit Court of Appeals which we believe has seriously infringed the sovereignty of the State of New York."[70]

The Justices had been concerned with the *Fay v. Noia* problem before that case came before them. In *Darr v. Burford*,[71] decided in 1950, the Court had said that unless a person convicted in a state court not only took all available appeals in the state courts, but also petitioned the Supreme Court for certiorari, he could never challenge his conviction by federal habeas corpus. During the *Fay v. Noia* argument, Clark remarked that some of the earlier decisions had given the Court great difficulty. He said that many drafts of one opinion were exchanged before the decision was announced and they produced "more heat than light." Clark was referring to *Irvin v. Dowd,*[72] decided in 1961. To obtain the Stewart vote needed for a bare majority there, Brennan had not dealt squarely with the issue later faced in *Fay v. Noia.* This had led to a noted *Harvard Law Review* article by Professor Henry Hart in which he attacked the Court for evading the issue.[73]

On October 26, 1961, before *Fay v. Noia* reached the Court, Brennan delivered a lecture at the University of Utah in which he dealt with the *Fay v. Noia* issue and outlined the approach later taken in his opinion in the case.[74] The lecture prompted Harlan to circulate a lengthy *Memorandum to the Conference* on December 3, 1962, taking issue with the view Brennan had expressed. The memo was over-technical, legalistic, and a less effective presentation of Harlan's position than the dissenting opinion he eventually issued. Brennan sent around a reply memorandum on December 10, and the issue was joined in the Court even before the *Fay v. Noia* argument.

At the January 11, 1963, conference, Warren spoke for affirmance saying that imprisonment in violation of the Constitution had to be remediable by federal habeas corpus, regardless of whether state remedies had been exhausted. Only Harlan was firmly committed to the contrary view, as he had expressed it in his memorandum, but the discussion indicated that Clark and Stewart would probably dissent with him.

Warren assigned the opinion to Brennan on January 21. Ten days later Brennan sent around a draft opinion. It stated the rule that a person held in prison in violation of his constitutional rights could obtain federal habeas corpus, whenever he could demonstrate the violation.

The Brennan draft was soon joined by the other majority Justices. Only one change of significance was made in the opinion, in response to a February 1 letter from White, who wrote that, since the opinion "disposed of" the already-mentioned case of *Darr v. Burford,* "Perhaps we should say so expressly." The opinion was changed to include a passage expressly overruling *Darr v. Burford*. The decision was announced by Brennan on March 18. Harlan, joined by Clark and Stewart, and Clark read biting dissents.

Townsend v. Sain[75] was decided the same day as *Fay v. Noia*. Townsend had been convicted of murder in Illinois. He was a drug addict, who was under the influence of a heroin dose administered before his arrest. When he began to show withdrawal symptoms, he was injected with phenobarbital and scopolamine (both having the effect of "truth serums") and made a confession. His attorney objected to its admission on the ground of coercion, but his motion was denied. After the highest state court had affirmed the conviction, Townsend petitioned the federal district court for habeas corpus. The district court refused to hold a hearing and denied the writ on the basis of the state-court record. The court of appeals affirmed.

Townsend v. Sain first came to the Supreme Court in the 1960 Term. On March 3, 1961, the Brethren voted to grant certiorari, with Warren, Black, Douglas, Brennan, and Stewart voting to grant, and Clark, Harlan, and Whittaker to deny. The case was argued on February 19, 1962. At the conference on February 23, Warren urged reversal. "There's enough in this case," he declared "to indicate the drug induces, not only truth, but hallucinations." The Chief also said that the federal courts should do more than rely on the state-court record in such a case. "I don't think," he stated, "a look at the state-court proceedings was enough. I would remand for a hearing" in the district court.

The conference was closely divided. Black, Douglas, and Brennan voted with Warren to reverse. But Frankfurter, Clark, Harlan, Stewart, and Whittaker voted the other way. Frankfurter, the senior Justice in the bare majority, assigned the opinion to Clark on March 7, 1962. Before the case could be decided, however, Whittaker retired and Frankfurter became incapacitated. In consequence the case was set for reargument during the subsequent term.

Once again, Frankfurter's replacement by Goldberg altered the result. The conference after reargument took place on October 12, 1962. Warren restated the position he had taken at the first conference. "I'd reverse," he said, "but not with a finding here that his confession was coerced." The Chief stressed that there was "knowledge by the police that he'd taken heroin. He was kept until withdrawal set in, and given scopolamine or truth serum. I think he ought to have a hearing on what happened at the time and what the effect of that dosage would be."

The others who had been at the conference the previous term adhered to their positions. That meant a four-to-three vote for reversal when the turn of the new Justices came. White took the same stand for affirmance as his predecessor, Whittaker, saying, "it seems to me he's had all he can get by way of state relief." That left the decisive vote to Goldberg. Here, too, he voted differently than Frankfurter and changed the decision. Goldberg voted to remand for a hearing because, as he saw it, "on the uncontradicted evidence, no court has yet considered the effect of the drug."

Warren assigned *Townsend* to himself. As it turned out, the Chief's opinion of the Court was a companion piece to *Fay v. Noia* that set forth the standards governing evidentiary hearings in federal habeas corpus proceedings. Under it, the federal court in a habeas corpus proceeding must hold a full evidentiary hearing if the habeas applicant did not receive such a hearing in a state court.

Warren's *Townsend* opinion did not, however, start out that way. The original draft dealt almost entirely with the substantive issue of whether the confession had been coerced. It gave only cursory treatment to the procedural question of the right to introduce evidence in federal habeas corpus proceedings. Brennan sent Warren a memorandum in opinion form dealing with this question. The Chief then recirculated his majority opinion, but it contained only a few of the suggestions in Brennan's memo. Brennan discussed the matter with Warren and persuaded him to accept the remaining suggestions. Parts II through V of the final opinion in *Townsend v. Sain* were taken almost verbatim from Brennan's memorandum.

On February 7, 1963, Brennan had written the Chief with another suggestion for the *Townsend* opinion. Brennan stated that he had "strong misgivings" about a reference Warren's recirculation made to "the increasing volume of federal applications." Brennan wrote, "I think your reference will only be seized upon and be used against us by judges, both federal and state, and state prosecutors, who are bound to wail about both *Townsend* and *Fay v. Noia.*"

Despite Warren's deletion of the offending reference, *Fay v. Noia* and *Townsend v. Sain* did give rise to a wail of protest by state officials. Chief Justice J. Ed Livingston of Alabama charged that the

Supreme Court was remaking the Constitution and using the Four-teenth Amendment for the "systematic destruction of state sove-reignty."[76] Mississippi Senator James O. Eastland, Chairman of the Senate Judiciary Committee, introduced a bill to strip the Court of power to review cases involving, among other things, state criminal laws.[77] More far-reaching were the implications of a constitutional amendment sponsored by the Council of State Governments. It would have set up a "Court of the Union," composed of the state chief justices, with jurisdiction to review Supreme Court decisions.

In September 1963, seven of the Brethren made their way to San Francisco to join in the homage paid Warren by the California Bar Association on the tenth anniversay of his appointment as Chief Jus-tice. Warren used the occasion to answer the charge that the Court had gone too far in reversing state court decisions in criminal cases. In a September 25 speech, the Chief Justice stated that the Court would seldom challenge states' rights, if the state courts vigilantly protected individual rights. "Where the Supreme Court of a state is vigilant concerning constitutional rights," Warren asserted, "the Su-preme Court of the United States is equally vigilant in supporting its decisions."[78]

A word should also be said about *Sanders v. United States,*[79] which rounded out the 1962 Term's decisions on federal post-conviction remedies. Sanders had pleaded guilty to bank robbery in a federal court. He filed a motion to have his sentence vacated because he was denied counsel and coerced into entering a guilty plea. The district court denied the motion, finding that it was "completely refuted" by the record. Eight months later, Sanders filed a second motion to vacate on the ground that he was mentally incompetent during the trial because he was under the influence of narcotics administered to him in jail. The judge denied the second motion without any hear-ing. The court of appeals affirmed, stating that there was no reason why Sanders could not have asserted the new ground in his first motion. Sanders claimed in the Supreme Court that he was entitled to a hearing before his second motion was denied. All except Doug-las and Clark voted to grant certiorari.

At the March 1, 1963 conference, the vote was seven-to-two, with Black and White casting the minority votes, to affirm. The majority felt that the district judge had not abused his discretion in refusing to produce Sanders for an evidentiary hearing on his contention. But the majority was far from certain since both Warren and Douglas stated that their votes to affirm were cast *dubitante*.

Warren assigned the opinion to Douglas, who, like himself, had doubts about the majority position. As he worked on the case, Douglas found increasing difficulties in writing in support of the conference vote. At this point, Warren decided to reassign to Brennan, turning once again to him in a difficult case. In preparing the opinion, Brennan also became convinced that the conference vote was wrong and that the decision should be reversed. He notified the others of his conclusion in an April 2 *Memorandum to the Conference.* The memo noted the conference vote. "However," it went on, "of the seven votes to affirm (on the statutory ground that 'The motion and files and records of the case conclusively show that the prisoner is entitled to no relief'), the votes of the Chief and Bill Douglas were not firm. Bill was originally assigned the opinion but, after study, concluded that a reversal was necessary. The opinion was reassigned to me and I, too, find an affirmance cannot be sustained on this record."

Attached to Brennan's memo was a proposed majority opinion for reversal. The draft held that the principles governing hearings on federal habeas corpus petitions should apply to motions to vacate sentences such as that made by Sanders. The second motion could not be denied without hearing where a different ground was presented in it. The draft was quickly joined by a substantial majority, who, like Brennan himself, were soon convinced that the conference had erred. The Brennan opinion was issued as the opinion of the Court on April 29, 1963, with only Harlan and Clark dissenting. Somewhat curiously, White, who had been one of the conference voters for reversal, concurred in the result only.

The most important 1962 Term case affecting business was *United States v. Philadelphia National Bank,*[80] decided on the last day of the term. During the Kennedy Administration, the Justice Department sought for the first time to apply the anti-trust laws to banking. Another statute, the Bank Merger Act of 1960, made bank mergers subject to approval by the Comptroller of the Currency. That official approved a merger between Philadelphia's second and third largest banks. The approval was given despite the opposition of the Justice Department.

The day after the Comptroller approved the merger, the Justice Department filed an anti-trust suit to stop it. The complaint charged that the consolidation would violate section 1 of the Sherman Act (outlawing all combinations in restraint of trade) and section 7 of the Clayton Act (prohibiting a corporation from acquiring any stock or, if it is subject to Federal Trade Commission jurisdiction, any of the assets, of another company, where, "in any line of commerce in any section of the country, the effect of such acquisition may be substantially to lessen competition, or to tend to create a monopoly").

The district court had decided for the banks. The Supreme Court reversed, holding that the merger was prohibited by section 7 of the Clayton Act. In his dissent, Harlan asserted, "I suspect that no one will be more surprised than the Government to find that the Clayton Act has carried the day for its case in this Court."[81] This assertion was truer than even Harlan knew. The Justice Department had based its case almost entirely upon the claim of a Sherman Act section 1 violation. Indeed, when the case was being prepared, the Justice Department attorney who framed the complaint is said to have declared, toward the end of his work, "What the hell, let's throw in a section 7 count just for the hell of it."

Assistant Attorney General Lee Loevinger, who argued for the government on February 20, 1964, also based his argument entirely on section 1 of the Sherman Act. When Brennan referred to section 7 of the Clayton Act and asked, "why didn't you argue it?" Loevinger replied that he was willing to rely on the discussion in his brief.

"When the argument ended," wrote James E. Clayton of the *Washington Post,* "the case seemed much less important than it had at the start." That was true, according to Clayton, because the Clayton Act, under which merger cases are normally brought, seemed "out of the case, as the banks argued and as the Justice Department seemed close to admitting."[82] But both the parties and the press reckoned without knowing the feeling of the Justices, particularly Warren and Brennan, that the recent trend toward concentration in banking should be checked by the anti-trust laws.

Warren began the February 22, 1963, conference by advocating reversal. "The market," he said, "is commercial banks (the product) and the four-county area (the geographical area). These two have not had a natural, but a merger, growth. If they get to be number one, then [numbers] two and four will merge and a whole wave stifling competition will begin." Warren went on to state, "Banks are not relieved by the Bank Merger Act of 1960 from the antitrust laws. I think both section 7 of the Clayton and section 1 of the Sherman apply. This has all of the attributes of a stock, not an asset, acquisition."

It was Brennan, however, who made the strongest statement for reversal and who also showed why reliance should be placed on the Clayton, rather than the Sherman Act. Brennan stressed that the record showed nothing approaching a monopoly for the merging banks. Illegality had to be based on the structure of the market, not the behavior of the banks. In such a case, the history and interpretation of section 7 made its application here more appropriate than section 1. Brennan also pointed to a danger in a finding of a section 1 violation. Such a finding would open up the possibility of the Justice Department's proceeding against banks for mergers before 1950 (when section 7 was amended to include its present language). That would make an unduly large number of banks vulnerable to anti-trust actions and give the Justice Department too great a club over the financial markets.

Black and Douglas voted with Warren and Brennan to reverse under the Clayton Act. Clark also voted to reverse on section 7, but his comments indicated that he did so on the erroneous assumption that the merger transaction was technically a stock acquisition and hence within section 7. Goldberg rejected the Clayton Act basis, but also voted to reverse, relying on section 1 of the Sherman Act. Harlan and Stewart voted to affirm, and White disqualified himself because he had been Deputy Attorney General.

The conference vote was thus six-to-two to reverse. As Brennan put it, in a March 27 memorandum to Warren, Black, Douglas, and Clark, "We five voted at conference to turn this case on the application of § 7 of the Clayton Act and not reach the Sherman Act § 1 charge," though he noted that "Arthur . . . voted to reverse on the Sherman Act."

Warren again turned to Brennan and assigned him the task of working out a rationale upon which the Clayton Act violation could be found. Brennan prepared a draft opinion of the Court that interpreted congressional intent in section 7 to bar the "entire range of corporate amalgamations, from pure stock acquisitions to pure asset acquisitions." This included within section 7's prohibition "mergers, which fit neither category perfectly but lie somewhere between the two ends of the spectrum." The exception for corporations not subject to FTC jurisdiction was read to exclude only asset acquisitions when not accompanied by merger.

As far as the relevant market in the case was concerned, Brennan's draft said that the four-county Philadelphia area was the appropriate one. And Brennan laid down a far-reaching test of anti-competitive effect, saying, "Specifically, we think that a merger which produces a firm controlling an undue percentage share of the relevant market, and results in a significant increase in the concentration of firms in that market is so inherently likely to lessen competition substantially that it must be enjoined in the absence of evidence clearly showing that the merger is not likely to have such anticompetitive effects." [83]

Brennan sent his draft on March 27 to Warren, Black, Douglas, and Clark. Though Brennan indicated in his covering memorandum that, "the grounds on which I find the section applicable differ somewhat from the views that some of you have expressed," the draft evoked few comments. Instead, the Chief Justice, Black, and Douglas speedily joined the opinion and Clark intimated that he would also. The most important change made at the instance of another Justice was Black's suggestion that a reference to the appropriateness of a wide-ranging inquiry in other factual situations under section 7 be deleted.

Clark did not, however, formally join the opinion of the Court. Instead, on June 12, only five days before the end of the term, the Texan unexpectedly circulated a separate concurrence rejecting the position that section 7 applied to bank mergers, but finding rather that there was a violation of section 1. The Clark draft took an extreme position on mergers under the Sherman Act. Under it, a merger that eliminated a substantial competitor of the acquiring firm was to be considered a per se violation of section 1.

Warren and Brennan were both upset by the Clark draft, which would convert Brennan's opinion into that of a plurality only and dilute its effect as an anti-trust precedent. Clark was persuaded by them to withdraw his opinion and formally join the majority. When the opinion of the Court was issued on June 17, it spoke for five Justices. Harlan, joined by Stewart, dissented on the ground that section 7 did not reach bank mergers and that the Court had nullified the Bank Merger Act. Goldberg wrote a short memorandum stating that he thought a substantial Sherman Act question was presented.

In many ways, the most difficult problem in the 1962 Term was presented by the cases that arose out of the "sit-in" demonstrations that began in Greensboro, North Carolina, at the beginning of 1960. The idea spread rapidly, and blacks were soon sitting in at lunch counters in cities throughout the South. The demonstrators were met by arrests and convictions, which slowly worked their way up to the Supreme Court.

The Sit-In Cases raised the issue of whether a state could use its power to help a private store owner to discriminate against blacks. The difficulty arose from the fact that the Equal Protection Clause of the Fourteenth Amendment prohibits only discriminatory "state action." It does not reach purely private discrimination.[84] Of course, if state law requires segregation in eating facilities, the Fourteenth Amendment is plainly violated.[85] What happens, however, if the police act in aid of a store owner, who is following his private policy of discrimination? When the police answer the owner's call and arrest the sit-in demonstrators, is that not "state action" subject to the Equal Protection Clause? And when a state court convicts the demonstrators for trespassing or breach of the peace, is the state not acting to enforce the store owner's decision to discriminate?

The Sit-In Cases presented a legal Gordian knot because competing interests were at stake which are normally deemed worthy of the law's highest solicitude. In favor of permitting prosecution was the right of property, obviously violated when people came on private premises and remained there over the owner's protest. On the other side was the social interest against allowing state action that supports racial discrimination. If that social interest would normally weigh more heavily, it was balanced here by the social interest in public order. Should that interest be defeated by the prejudice of the property owner immediately victimized?

Six Sit-In Cases came to the Court during the 1962 Term. In *Peterson v. Greenville*,[86] ten black boys and girls went into an S. H. Kress store in Greenville, South Carolina, and sat down at the lunch counter. The manager asked them to leave. When they remained seated, they were arrested and convicted of unlawful trespass. A

Greenville city ordinance required racial separation in restaurants. The convictions were affirmed by the state supreme court.

There were similar cases from Durham, North Carolina, and Birmingham, Alabama, both of which also had restaurant segregation ordinances.[87] Another case involved sit-ins at the McCrory store in New Orleans, Louisiana. That city had no ordinance requiring segregated eating facilities, but the police chief and mayor had publicly announced that sit-in demonstrations would not be permitted.[88]

In the fifth case, Reverend F. L. Shuttlesworth and another black clergyman were convicted of inciting a violation of Birmingham's criminal trespass ordinance. They had asked for volunteers to participate in sit-in demonstrations.[89] The last case, *Griffin v. Maryland*[90] arose out of the conviction of black youths for entering Glen Echo, a privately owned amusement park near Washington and boarding a carousel, despite Glen Echo's policy to exclude blacks. The youths had been arrested by a private detective employed by the park, who had been deputized by the county sheriff and wore a deputy sheriff's badge when he made the arrests.

At the November 9, 1962, conference Warren urged that the Court avoid the broader constitutional issue. Instead he proposed that the cases be decided without dealing with the conflicting rights of the property owners and the demonstrators and the question of whether state enforcement of their trespass laws constituted state action in violation of the Equal Protection Clause.

The Chief briefly stated the narrower ground on which he would reverse in each of the six cases. First of all, he said that "taking up the South Carolina case first, the ordinance is before us and clearly constitutes unlawful state action." Warren urged that the same approach be followed in the Alabama and North Carolina cases. "In the Alabama case," he said, "there's also an ordinance and there was testimony of action based on the ordinance." The same was true in the North Carolina case.

In the Louisiana case, Warren said that the decision "should be reversed on . . . the statements of the mayor and chief of police." They had the same effect as an ordinance not permitting desegregated restaurant service. The Chief next turned to the *Shuttlesworth* case, where, he stated, "there's no evidence of counseling an unlawful act. Nothing he said told them to stay when they were told to get out." Finally, Warren suggested that the Glen Echo case could be decided on the basis of the South Carolina and Louisiana decisions.

The conference discussion, however, went far beyond Warren's narrow approach. The polar views on the underlying constitutional issue were stated by Black, on the one side, and Douglas, on the other. Black made an impassioned plea for protection of property rights. "If we decide there was no consent of the owner," he declared, "we must hold or assume that the storekeeper can choose his customers." Unlike the Chief, the Alabaman said, "I'm ready to meet the basic question on the merits. I'd say we have a system of private ownership of property and, if we're going to trim these down under constitutional provisions, I'd have to look closely to find if there's anything which says the owner can't tell people he doesn't want to get out. I see nothing in the Constitution which says this. Therefore, he can call the police to help protect that right. If that right is in the owner, the law must enforce his right."

Black noted that, "while there's a difference between a store and a home and the legislature may order me to let them in my store, although not my home, the Constitution, taken without legislation, doesn't prevent this. I have no difficulty in sustaining a state or federal law that merchants must serve everyone despite color. But when the state wants the owner to do it, the burden is on the state." Black did, however, indicate that he would reverse in *Shuttlesworth,* saying, "they don't produce evidence to prove the case."

Douglas disputed Black's approach. "If Black's views of the retail store are adopted," the lanky Westerner asserted, "we will have a new *Plessy v. Ferguson*[91] regime by private people enforced by the courts. I'd say retail stores can't discriminate and therefore state proceedings to help them are unconstitutional." Douglas went further and stated, "I would make the store owner a public utility and I'd overrule the *Civil Rights Cases*"[92]—which held, in 1883, that the reach of the Fourteenth Amendment was limited to "state action" and that a federal civil rights law prohibiting discrimination by private hotels and restaurants was unconstitutional. Douglas said that he would hold that such "supplementing legislation was constitutional."

Clark, Harlan, and Stewart expressed agreement with Black on the broader issue. But they and the others thought that, in Goldberg's words, "it's not necessary to go into the basic questions raised by Black and Douglas." And even Douglas had concluded his conference statement by saying, "I could probably follow an opinion embodying the Chief's views, though I would prefer to face the issue Hugo proposed—i.e., owner rights."

The consensus was to follow the Warren approach and avoid the broader issue raised by Black and Douglas. Brennan agreed with the Chief that the three cases in which there were ordinances requiring segregation were clear, saying "the existence of the ordinance forecloses choice." White stated that he "might take a per se rule on the ordinance"—that the mere existence of a segregating ordinance requires the reversal of sit-in convictions. Only Harlan indicated doubt in the ordinance cases. "I can't agree," he said, "that the mere existence of a segregation ordinance proves 'state action.' I would still permit proof that the choice indeed was the owner's. However, the existence of the ordinance is a highly relevant fact. When it's in the record, the burden shifts to the state."

The others also agreed with Warren that the Louisiana case should turn on the statements made by the police chief and mayor. As White put it, "we can't read the mayor's statement any other way" than as tantamount to state action. The consensus favored reversing the *Shuttlesworth* convictions as well. He would reverse, said Stewart, on a "combination of free speech and *Thompson* [*v. Louisville* [93]—the 1960 Case of Shuffling Sam discussed in chapter 9]. They were only advising them to exert their constitutional rights."

There was, however, indication of doubt on the *Griffin* case. White said, "I have trouble with Glen Echo as being consistent with the notion of the right of the owner." Harlan went further and stated, "I would affirm the Maryland case. I don't think there was any state policy of segregation that this officer was enforcing. The deputation of this man cannot be said to be an effort of the state to enforce segregation."

Warren assigned the sit-in opinions to himself. At the November 9 conference, Stewart had urged that "*Peterson* [the South Carolina case] is the leading case" and the Court should "write here." Warren followed this suggestion and circulated a four-page draft opinion on February 7, 1963, reversing the South Carolina convictions because of the Greenville restaurant segregation ordinance. The key portion of the Warren *Peterson* draft, as recirculated on April 3, was its last paragraph, which read as follows: "If the State has reserved a particular power to itself, an individual in exercising that power is necessarily acting as the delegate of the State. When the State has commanded a particular result, it has saved to itself the power to determine that result. Here the City of Greenville, an agency of the State, has provided by its segregation ordinance that the decision as to whether a restaurant facility is to be operated on an integrated basis is to be reserved to it. It has removed that decision from the sphere of private choice. It has thus effectively determined that a person owning, managing, or controlling an eating place is left with no choice of his own but must segregate his white and Negro patrons. The Kress manager, in deciding to exclude Negroes, did precisely what the city law required. Consequently these convictions cannot stand, even assuming, as respondent contends, that the manager would have acted as he did had there been no ordinance. Where a state agency passes a law compelling persons to discriminate against other persons because of race, such a palpable violation of the Fourteenth Amendment cannot be saved by attempting to separate the mental urges of the discriminators."

On May 16, Brennan circulated a revision of the *Peterson* opinion, drafted by himself and White, in discharge of an assignment made at conference that morning. The revised draft eliminated a paragraph that indicated "that action may sometimes be state action within the meaning of the Fourteenth Amendment even though not taken pursuant to, or in obedience to, the authentic command of the State. . . . The course of decision could not have been otherwise. One purpose of the restrictions of the Fourteenth Amendment was to proscribe certain action by those clothed with the power of state government." The Brennan–White revision also substituted the last two paragraphs of the final *Peterson* opinion for the passage quoted in the preceding paragraph. Though largely based on the Warren draft, the revision did state specifically that the convictions had the effect of enforcing the Greenville ordinance.

Warren prepared one-sentence per curiams in the Alabama and North Carolina cases, reversing and vacating the convictions in light of the *Peterson* decision. The Chief also circulated a six-page opinion in *Lombard v. Louisiana* on February 7, which reversed the convictions there because of the statements made by the mayor and police chief. The key passage of the Warren draft, recirculated April 3, was once more the concluding paragraph, which read: "In any event we hold that it need not be shown that the store manager acted in obedience to the policy promulgated by the city officials. A State, or a city, may act as authoritatively through its executive as through its legislative body. See *Ex parte Virginia*, 100 U.S. 339, 347. The New Orleans city officials here determined that the city would not permit Negroes to seek integrated service in restaurants. Consequently, the city must be treated exactly as if it had an ordinance prohibiting such conduct. We have just held in *Peterson v. City of Greenville, ante*, p. ——, that where an ordinance makes it unlawful for owners or managers of restaurants to seat whites and Negroes together, a refusal to seat them together will be attributed to the coercive effect of the city's policy of segregation without regard to the owner's or manager's motives. The manager's action in refusing to countenance such efforts was therefore state action. And we have no doubt that the State cannot itself or through its municipal agencies constitutionally prohibit Negroes, in the absence of disorder, from seeking desegregated service. *Garner v. Louisiana*, 368 U.S. 157, 174. Thus these convictions—for refusing to leave the restaurant at the request of the store manager commanded by state policy—cannot stand."

Again Brennan and White revised the draft, changing the last four sentences of this paragraph to their form in the published *Lombard* opinion. The revision stressed explicitly that the officials' statements had as much coercive effect as an ordinance and that they were directed to continuance of segregated restaurant service, not to preservation of public peace in a nondiscriminatory fashion.

Warren also prepared a short opinion reversing the *Shuttlesworth* convictions under the approach stated by him at the November conference, as well as a one-sentence per curiam vacating the Glen Echo convictions and remanding to the Maryland court in light of the *Peterson* and *Lombard* decisions. On May 18, Warren circulated the final drafts of the *Peterson, Lombard,* and *Shuttlesworth* opinions, as well as the Alabama and North Carolina per curiams. The Chief's *Memorandum to the Members of the Conference* noted that "Justices Brennan, Goldberg, White and Harlan have made certain revisions of the *Peterson, Lombard* and *Shuttlesworth* cases."

When Warren delivered the sit-in opinions on May 20, he spoke for all the Brethren except Harlan, who dissented in part, though accepting much of the Chief Justice's reasoning. Douglas wrote a separate concurrence, urging that public businesses such as restaurants, particularly since they operate under licenses, may not "manage that business on the basis of *apartheid*."

There had been danger earlier that the Court might be more fragmented. White had circulated separate concurring opinions, but had withdrawn them to work with Brennan in revising the Warren drafts. Clark had written to Warren on May 3 asking him to add "at the appropriate place," in the *Peterson* and North Carolina opinions, "Mr. Justice Clark concurs in the result." Clark also asked Warren to add to the Alabama opinion that "Mr. Justice Clark, concluding after an examination of the record that it is doubtful whether the action of the Court of Appeals of Alabama was based upon an independent and adequate state ground, would vacate and remand the judgment for determination of this question by that court."

In addition, Clark's letter requested the Chief to add to the *Shuttlesworth* opinion, "Mr. Justice Clark would reverse the conviction of Billups on *Thompson* v. *Louisville,* 362 U.S. 199 (1960), and, as to Shuttlesworth, would vacate and remand to the Court of Appeals of Alabama for further determination on State ground questions relating to issues bearing on the segregation ordinance."

Worse still, Clark informed Warren, "I am writing a short dissenting opinion in both No. 58, *Lombard* v. *Louisiana,* and No. 26, *Griffin* v. *Maryland.* These will be around shortly."

Clark did prepare dissents in the two cases. In *Lombard v. Louisiana,* he wrote, on the back of the last page of Warren's draft opinion of the Court: "Despite the fact that there was no segregation ordinance on the books of New Orleans, the Court reverses on the ground that the city officials had made policy announcements requesting the citizenry not to engage in sit-in demonstrations. The Court holds that 'it need not be shown that the store manager acted in obedience to the policy promulgated by the city officials.' Believing that this was a necessary element of the petitioner's defense, I dissent."

At the bottom of Warren's *Griffin v. Maryland* per curiam, Clark wrote, "Up until last year Glen Echo had been operated by its private owners as a segregated amusement park. This case arose prior to the integration policy presently followed at the Park. Believing on this record that the action taken against petitioners here was that of the owner of the park—not the state, which had no policy of segregation I would affirm."

Warren and the others worked on Clark to induce him not to issue his projected opinions. A Brennan letter to the Chief Justice on May 17 informed Warren that, after the *Peterson* revision, "Tom has said that he thinks he can join it, although he has not formally done so." In addition, Brennan noted, with regard to the *Lombard* revision, "Tom may join it but that's more doubtful than whether he'll join *Peterson*. He has trouble treating the Mayor's statement as the same thing as an ordinance." However, Brennan went on, "Byron and I made a slight revision of the first paragraph of the Mayor's statement . . . deleting something you had in your old draft to show that the Mayor was forbidding sit-ins regardless of the purpose or intent of the participants. There is some chance this may persuade Tom."

Clark was prevailed upon to withdraw his *Lombard* dissent and separate statements in the *Peterson*, Alabama, and North Carolina cases. The Glen Echo case was more difficult, since White and Harlan also had doubts about the reversal there. The problem was resolved by deciding to postpone *Griffin v. Maryland*. In his May 17 letter, Brennan informed Warren, "Tom seems willing to have *Griffin*—No. 26 go over for reargument and John is now strongly in favor of this." On May 20, when the other sit-in decisions were announced, the Court issued an order setting *Griffin* for reargument during the coming term.[94]

The 1963 sit-in decisions, as James E. Clayton wrote, were "completely satisfactory to no one except the thirty-one demonstrators whose convictions were reversed."[95] The difficult issues had been put off for at least another year. Yet, when those issues came before the Court during the next term, the situation in the country had changed. Just before the 1963 sit-in decisions, there were large-scale demonstrations in Birmingham. They ended when businessmen promised to desegregate some lunch counters. New Orleans also was desegregating its restaurants. Even Glen Echo, whose case the Court would hear once more in the coming term, had announced that blacks would be admitted. By the time the Justices would deal again with sit-ins, the pace of the civil-rights movement had started to bypass the practical relevancy of the issues at stake.

For Warren personally, the 1962 Term had been gratifying. Frankfurter's departure had removed the Chief's strongest adversary and given him a solid majority. More than that, the personal recrimination that had characterized Warren's relationship with Frankfurter was now a thing of the past. In an interview a few years later, Warren recalled that not a single voice had been raised in the Court conferences over a time period that corresponded to Frankfurter's retirement.[96]

Of course, there were still opposing views among the Justices. But Warren's principal opponent was now the courtly Harlan, who had neither the departed Justice's abrasive personality nor his leadership abilities. Harlan's voice calling for judicial restraint was but a faint echo of his mentor, and in Clayton's phrase, "was now heard in a symbolic wilderness without the assured support of Frankfurter and Whittaker."[97] The balance of power had definitely shifted to the Chief Justice.

From a historical perspective, the Warren victory was a victory for Black and Douglas in the battle they had waged in the pre-Warren years for a sweeping interpretation of the Bill of Rights. But the constitutional issues were now changing and, as they did, there began to develop a split between Black, on the one side, and Warren and his other supporters, on the other. In particular, the long-standing relationship between Black and Douglas began to come under increasing strain. In the Sit-In Cases, we saw how the two Justices expressed sharply divergent views. Soon after the sit-in decisions, on June 3, Douglas publicly censured a Black opinion in biting language reminiscent of that used in the Warren–Frankfurter exchanges recounted in chapter 7. Black had delivered an opinion in a complicated case upholding the Interior Secretary's power over disputed Western water rights. A reporter noted that Black took particular pride in his lengthy opinion.[98]

Douglas delivered a dissent sharply denouncing Black's opinion. "It will, I think," he declared, "be marked as the baldest attempt by judges in modern times to spin their own philosophy into the fabric of the law." He went on to assert that the decision "has made the dream of the federal bureaucracy come true." Then, departing from the text of his dissent, Douglas noted caustically that Black's opinion was fifty-two pages long. "The advantage of a long opinion such as the one Justice Black has filed," he sarcastically pointed out, "is that it is very difficult to see how it failed to reach the right result, because one gets lost in the words." In another gibe not contained in the written opinion, Douglas charged that Black's opinion "was more like a Congressional committee report rather than an opinion worthy of this Court."[99] Black's severest critics (and Douglas', too, for that matter) had never used harsher words.

To be sure, as we saw in chapter 2, Douglas was an abrasive person, with whom even his firmest allies found it difficult to get along. Once Douglas had asked the Court Clerk to do something that Warren thought was improper. "You shouldn't have done that, Bill," the Chief rebuked the Justice. At this, Douglas did not speak to Warren, except on the formal level, for the better part of two years.

Douglas' personal life added to the friction with his colleagues. The *New York Times* reported in June 1963 that there was a "cooling of relations" between Black and Douglas and said that it was aggravated by Black's disapproval of Douglas' third marriage.[100] Early in April, Mercedes Douglas announced that she would seek a divorce. After the term closed, Douglas married a woman recently graduated from college, with whom he had frequently been seen. There was widespread criticism of the divorce and remarriage. It was reported that one of the Brethren told Douglas, "one Justice, one divorce"— a paraphrase of Douglas' "one man, one vote" standard in the Georgia county-unit case.

Both Black and Warren were unfavorably impressed by Douglas' matrimonial activities. To Warren particularly, there was something unsavory about leaving a wife of many years for a girl young enough to be a Douglas granddaughter. That was something a decent person just did not do. The Chief Justice was particularly concerned that Douglas' peccadilloes might reflect unfavorably on the Court and furnish fuel to its extremist critics who accused it of fostering Godlessness and immorality.

Warren was not, however, one to display resentment toward Douglas' new wife. She tells how she approached Warren timidly at a reception soon after the marriage, afraid that he would brush her off. Instead, Warren put his arms around her and said warmly, "Welcome to the family."[101]

The end of the 1962 Term marked the close of Warren's tenth year as Chief Justice. The months that followed saw him the recipient of compliments and honors that helped make up for the abuse heaped upon him over his judicial years. Particularly satisfying was the recognition of his home state. In September, the Earl Warren Legal

Center at the University of California Law School was dedicated in Berkeley. The 1914 alumnus dug the first spadeful of earth. Seven of the Brethren looked on, as did the entire California Supreme Court.[102]

During the same week, the California Bar Association used its annual meeting in San Francisco to honor its most distinguished member. "How good it is to be home—'Right back where I started from,'" began his address in response. Typically, Warren stressed the achievements of California, "in the forefront of the struggle for improved judicial administration," its Supreme Court, and its State Bar.[103]

Earl Warren had grown immeasurably during the ten years that he sat in the high Court. The truth about Warren as Chief Justice is, as civil libertarian Alan Barth once expressed it, that he "grew prodigiously."[104] An article a few years earlier on *The Education of Earl Warren* had stated, "Only small men are incapable of change, unable to learn by their mistakes. It speaks well for the Chief Justice of the Supreme Court that from a racially biased Attorney General he has grown to be a world leader in the fight for universal brotherhood."[105]

During the 1962 Term, Warren delivered an address at the Jewish Theological Seminary in New York. "In civilized life," the speech began, "Law floats in a sea of Ethics. Each is indispensable." Without law, there could be no civilization. "Without ethical consciousness in most people lawlessness would be rampant." Warren urged the creation of a new profession of ethics counselor. "Is it fantastic to suggest," he asked, "that there is an urgent need in our troubled times for the development of the profession of the counselor in ethics, having the same relation to interpersonal conduct, beyond the Law, that the lawyer has to conduct that is subject to review in the courts?" The new profession of ethics counselor would build on "the glories" of Aristotle, Maimonides, St. Thomas Aquinas, and Spinoza, and yet be different from them "in its concern with concrete problems of conduct, and training people to help themselves and to help others solve concrete issues of personal behavior."[106]

The speech was unusual for a Chief Justice and was front-page news. Ten years earlier Warren would not even have dreamed of making such a speech. Outwardly, Warren may still have been the bluff Californian who had been a leading Presidential contender—with the same hearty manner. "But internally," as James E. Clayton reported, "Earl Warren was a different man now." [107] The Court decade had left its imprint on the once glad-handing politician.

Not that Warren did not occasionally have a longing for the political arena. "No one," he told an interviewer, "could have a background of such activities as I had without having a nostalgic feeling for it, particularly when there are exciting things going on in the country and in the world." [108] Clayton tells of an occasion when Warren almost let himself go in revealing how he sometimes felt. Did he ever wish, a reporter asked, he could defend the Court against its critics? The Chief's blue eyes lighted up and his huge hand slapped his desk. "Oh boy!" he said. "Sometimes it makes you cringe to see what other people write and say." Then he quickly retreated back into the quiet, detached shell that Justices wear in public. [109]

Soon after the 1962 Term ended, President Kennedy appointed Warren, together with Senator Mike Mansfield of Montana (with whom he would soon share the traumatic task of delivering the Capitol eulogies for the fallen President), to head the United States delegation to the coronation of Pope Paul VI. From Rome, Warren went on another of his extensive tours. In summer 1961 he had gone on a world tour, and this year his itinerary included Athens, Istanbul, Iran, Kenya, and Addis Ababa, where he met Emperor Haile Selassie [110] (the Chief was to reciprocate by entertaining the monarch when he visited Washington at the beginning of October, just before the 1963 Term). Warren ended his trip with a visit to the Soviet Union, during which he was received by Soviet leader Nikita Khrushchev at a Black Sea resort. [111]

Had he been in Washington that summer, Warren would certainly have opposed the inclination of the Court's newest member to undertake a special assignment for the President. In July, Kennedy had asked Goldberg to serve as final arbitrator of the issues in a then-pending railroad strike. [112] The Justice had agreed, and Kennedy proposed Goldberg to the parties. Although the railroads were willing to accept, the unions rejected the Justice as arbitrator, and the dispute was settled without Goldberg.

In proposing the Justice, Kennedy had stated that "use of a member of the High Court for additional duties should be reserved for extraordinary situations." [113] This the President asserted, was such a situation. Goldberg agreed and still believes that, in appropriate circumstances, it is not improper, as some have maintained, for a Justice to accept an assignment of this sort. "I think the Court's been too stuffy anyhow," says the former Justice. "The A.B.A. likes this and they don't like judges doing anything else, but, in Britain, when there is a matter of national importance, like the Profumo case, where Lord Denning headed the committee of inquiry, there's frequently a judge on a royal commission. And I see nothing wrong with that."

Goldberg did concede at the time that "most of the other Justices very clearly think that it is the wrong thing to do." [114] In July, Harlan sent a written note to retired Justice Frankfurter: "I'm relieved that the Unions saved Arthur Goldberg from that job which the President tried to hand him. I can't imagine a worse undertaking for a Supreme Court Justice." [115] Warren shared this latter sentiment and, had he not been abroad, would surely have tried to dissuade Goldberg. Yet, ironically, the Chief Justice was soon to accept a far more controversial presidential assignment.

The coming 1963 Term looked as though it would be a particularly happy one for the Chief Justice. The Court had followed his lead in every important case during the term that had just ended. There was every prospect that the term ahead would provide even more opportunities for the Justices to remake our law in the Warren image. Above all, the Court appeared to be in for a period of relative peace after the turbulent years of the previous decade. Of course, there was still the extremist fringe with its "Impeach Earl Warren" billboards. But the Chief was increasingly coming to be revered by most Americans.

In addition, the country and its institutions seemed poised for a new commitment to social justice in which the President would now work in tandem with the judiciary. For Warren personally, few things were more gratifying than the Kennedy support for the Court and the constant deference which the President displayed toward the Chief Justice—both the man and the office. Warren reciprocated with warm, almost fatherly, feelings toward the still young Chief Executive. Typically, in September 1963, Kennedy sent Warren a cordial congratulatory note "in recognition of the full decade you have served as Chief Justice. . . . I am personally delighted that during this week you will receive not only the acclaim of Californians, but also the respect and affection of all Americans whose common destiny you have so faithfully helped to shape throughout your public career." [116]

As it turned out, the appearances in the summer of 1963 were an illusion. As much so as the appearances fifty years earlier, when Justice Oliver Wendell Holmes said about the Supreme Court, "We are very quiet there, but it is the quiet of a storm centre." [117]

The summer of 1963 saw the culmination of the year's civil-rights demonstrations, when a quarter of a million black and white Americans participated in a "March on Washington," climaxed by Martin Luther King's "I have a dream" speech at the Lincoln Memorial.

In a written note to Frankfurter from his summer home on Long Island Sound, Harlan stated, "The March on Washington . . . leaves me pretty cold, appearing at this distance more of a Madison Avenue show than what one thinks of as a 'petition for the redress of grievances.' "

"But I must be wrong," Harlan went on, "for my two law clerks, both sober minded boys, assure me that it was a very moving affair." Harlan wrote his former colleague that he was concerned about the march's impact on the Brethren. "I hope it won't lead the Court into doing foolish things. [We open the Term with a series of sit-in cases, followed shortly by the reapportionment cases]." [118]

As it turned out, the Warren Court, too, in the summer of 1963, was only in "the quiet of a storm centre." For the Chief Justice himself, the days of law were shortly to give way to the days of drums.

12.

1963 TERM: DAYS OF DRUMS AND DAYS OF LAW

"Watch out for those wild Texans, Mr. President," admonished the Chief Justice. "They're a wild bunch."[1] The occasion was the annual White House reception for the Supreme Court on Wednesday, November 20, 1963. The Justices and their wives had joined President and Mrs. Kennedy for cocktails in their private living quarters on the second floor. Kennedy sat in his rocker nursing a daiquiri when Warren jokingly called from the sofa across the room. The President smiled.[2]

Two days later, the Chief Justice was presiding over the usual Friday conference. The Brethren had just returned from lunch in their dining room on the floor above. They were discussing the Reapportionment Cases—the most important to be decided in the 1963 Term.

Warren's executive secretary, Margaret McHugh, was then having her lunch. She was interrupted by a telephone call from Mrs. Warren, who said that she had just heard on television that President Kennedy had been shot. Mrs. McHugh decided that the Justices should be told at once. She gave a typewritten note to a page, who handed it to Goldberg, then the junior Justice who customarily answered the conference door. Even in such an emergency, Mrs.

McHugh did not feel justified in breaching the Court tradition that messages to the Justices in conference came only through the page boys. Goldberg passed the message to Warren, who read it aloud: "The President was shot while riding in a motorcade in Dallas. It is not known how badly he is injured."[3] Warren's voice broke as he read the note. Those at the session confirm the emotional impact of the news. "The old Chief," says Douglas, "read the message to us and then broke down and wept, tears running down his cheeks."[4]

Warren immediately adjourned the conference. He went to his chambers to listen to the radio. Most of the Justices and the Court staff then crowded into Stewart's chambers, which at the time had the only television set in the building.

Later, after the events of that day, the Chief Justice decided he should be at Andrews Air Force Base to meet the new President. Warren's car was being used by his wife and he had a law clerk drive him most of the way, until his driver met them near the base and took him to meet the presidential plane. There, Warren remembered, it was "a heartrending sight" to see the President's widow, still numb from shock, descending the ramp. "There was that brave girl," he told his wife, "with her husband's blood still on her, and there was nothing that I could do—*nothing.*"[5]

At 9 P.M. on the following evening, the Saturday evening, Warren received a call from Mrs. Kennedy asking if he would speak the next day at the Capitol rotunda ceremony for the fallen President. This was one assignment that the Chief performed without help from his law clerks. He worked on a draft that night, but found it impossible to write anything satisfactory.

Warren spent the next morning composing his tribute. At 11:20 A.M., his daughter came running into his study. "Daddy," she cried, "They just killed Oswald." The Chief was annoyed and said, "Oh, Dorothy, don't pay any attention to all those wild rumors." She replied, "But Daddy, I *saw* them do it." Warren rushed into her room in time to see a television replay of Jack Ruby shooting Lee Harvey Oswald.[6]

With difficulty, Warren completed his talk, which was typed by his wife just before they hurriedly left for the Capitol. The President's widow had chosen three speakers for the emotional ceremony: Senate Majority Leader Mike Mansfield, House Speaker John W. Mc-Cormack, and the Chief Justice. Warren spoke last and delivered an intensely emotional address. "It was like losing one of my own sons," Warren later said. "You know he was just a little older than my oldest boy."[7]

Warren's brief words in the Capitol were among the best he ever wrote. Standing beside the flag-draped casket, he spoke of the nation's shock. "We are saddened; we are stunned; we are perplexed." "What moved some misguided wretch to do this horrible deed," he went on, "may never be known to us, but we do know that such acts are commonly stimulated by forces of hatred and malevolence such as today are eating their way into the blood stream of American life. What a price we pay for this fanaticism!"[8]

On the afternoon of Friday, November 29, Warren was with Clark and Brennan in his chambers. Deputy Attorney General Nicholas Katzenbach and Solicitor General Archibald Cox were announced, and Clark and Brennan left. The visitors said that the new President had decided to set up a bipartisan blue ribbon commission to investigate the Kennedy assassination. President Johnson wanted Warren to serve as chairman. The Chief declined, urging the impropriety of a sitting member of the Court on a Presidential commission. Warren suggested other names, particularly retired Justice Reed.

After the presidential emissaries had left, Warren, Clark, and Brennan resumed their discussion in Clark's chambers. They were interrupted again by a call from "Miss Alice," Clark's secretary, that the White House was telephoning. It was Joseph Califano who asked Warren to see the President on an urgent matter. Warren had determined to say no to the President directly. But he succumbed to Johnson's personal plea.

The President based his appeal primarily on Warren's patriotism. He stressed the need to quiet the wild stories about the assassination, and for Warren to head the investigation, saying only he would have the public's confidence. He told Warren that the other members he planned to appoint would serve only if he accepted the chairmanship.

Warren repeated his reasons for refusing. Johnson replied, "You were a soldier in World War I, but there was nothing you could do in that uniform comparable to what you can do for your country in this hour of trouble." Johnson emphasized the seriousness of the rumors floating around the world. The situation was so grave it might lead to war, even a nuclear war. The President said he had just talked to Defense Secretary Robert McNamara, who had told him that forty million people could be killed in the first nuclear strike.

Johnson ended by referring again to Warren's World War I service. "Mr. Chief Justice, you were once in the Army weren't you. Well, as your Commander-in-Chief, I'm ordering you back into service."

Warren then gave way. "Mr. President," he said, "if the situation is that serious, my personal views do not count. I will do it." Observers noted that Warren left the Oval Office with tears in his eyes. When he returned to the Court building he was, a law clerk who met him recalls, "really shaken. He came back and said that he agreed to do it. He wasn't enthusiastic at all about it. He still thought it was a mistake, but he said, 'You know when somebody appeals to my patriotism that way, I don't know how I can say no.'"

Warren called a conference the next morning. He told the Brethren what had happened. He emphasized that the Court would not be involved at all in the Commission's activities and that his work as chairman would not interfere with his Court work. As far as possible, Warren tried to do both jobs during the 1963 Term. He presided at all the Court arguments and conferences and assigned the most important opinions—those in the Reapportionment Cases—to himself. At the same time, he headed all the Commission's meetings and was present at virtually all of its hearings.

"I don't know where he got the energy," says a Commission staff member. "We'd start a hearing at nine in the morning. He'd preside until a few minutes before ten, then leave for the Court. At 2:30 he'd come back and sit there well into the evening. At times he was presiding at the Commission and the Court for stretches of eight and ten hours. During those last weeks, when we were finishing the report, he'd work till one in the morning, then be the first to show up next day."[9]

The President's Commission on the Assassination of President Kennedy quickly became known as the Warren Commission. The popular name caught the reality of the Commission's work. "Warren really ran the show," recalls Norman Redlich, a key staff member, who is now Dean of the New York University School of Law. "This was the *Warren* Commission in every sense of the word. He knew that. He knew he would ultimately be responsible for it and I think it probably was very similar to the Court."

Redlich says that he was concerned at first about Warren's ability to lead the strong men who made up the Commission. "You know, you start with the assumption that Earl Warren is a good-natured, kindly man. But, in a crowd with John McCloy, Richard Russell, Allen Dulles, and John Sherman Cooper, I feared those people would be ahead of him. But this was simply not true. In terms of the brain power that he brought to bear on this investigation, Earl Warren was ahead of all of them."

Warren led the Commission much as he had grown accustomed to lead the Court. He was not concerned with the minutiae, leaving them to the staff. But it was he who made the decision on all the main issues—though usually after detailed consultation with J. Lee Rankin, the general counsel. Rankin, the former Solicitor General, had been selected after Warren's suggestion of Warren Olney, Director of the Administrative Office of the Federal Courts, with whom the Chief Justice had worked closely in California, had met opposition.

Warren, with Rankin's help, made the decision to have a staff composed of "senior" counsel, six well-known lawyers who would lend professional eminence to the Commission's work, as well as "junior" counsel—lawyers in their early thirties who would do the bulk of the work. Warren insisted, however, that all the staff members below Rankin have the same title of "assistant general counsel." He thought that, if there was a hierarchy of titles, it would enable those with the higher ones to use them for personal gain. Warren had strong feelings that no one should profit from the Commission's work. He was deeply offended when Congressman Gerald R. Ford, a Commission member, published a *Life* article purporting to tell the inside story of the Commission's work only a week after the Commission's report had been issued, and signed a contract for a book on the subject two weeks later. Warren felt that Ford had used his Commission position for financial gain.

Inevitably, some senior counsel lent more of their reputations than their time to the Commission's work. Most of the staff work was done by the junior counsel, closely supervised by Rankin and Warren.

This was graphically demonstrated on March 16, 1964, when the Commission heard the testimony of the doctors who had conducted the autopsy on the night of the assassination. Francis W. H. Adams, former Police Commissioner of New York City, had been appointed as a senior counsel and had been assigned to investigation of "the basic facts of the assassination." He had not, however, done any work on the inquiry, when he unexpectedly appeared at the hearing when the autopsy doctors testified. As the hearing was about to begin, the Chief Justice come over to Redlich and Arlen Specter and asked, "Who are we scheduled to hear today?" When told it was the autopsy doctors, Warren looked around, saw a face that was new to him, walked up to Adams and said, "Doctor, it's a pleasure to have you with us."

Warren personally made one of the Commission's most controversial decisions—to suppress the autopsy photographs. Warren viewed them and was badly shaken, saying later that "they were so horrible that I couldn't sleep well for nights." He refused to allow other Commission members or the staff to see them. Warren said that he decided that the Commission should not use the autopsy photos "in order to prevent them from getting into the hands of . . . sensation-mongers."[10] As Redlich remembers it, "The Chief Justice had great compassion for the Kennedy family. . . . He envisioned that these pictures would be out on the cover of *Life* magazine. And there would be the Kennedy family seeing the blown-off head. When he talked about this, he would get this very sickly look on his face as to what it would mean for the Kennedy family and he just would not have it."

During the questioning of the autopsy doctors, Warren asked what he considered the key question on the autopsy pictures:

The CHAIRMAN. . . . may I ask you this Commander; if we had the pictures here and you could look them over again and restate your opinion, would it cause you to change any of the testimony you have given here? Commander HUMES. To the best of my recollection Mr. Chief Justice, it would not.[11]

Critics have seized upon the suppression of the autopsy photos to support their charges of a Commission cover-up. But Warren himself never doubted that he had done the right thing. The answer given by the autopsy doctor only confirmed the Chief's view that the autopsy pictures would not really have added anything to the evidence before the Commission.

Two incidents illustrate Warren's approach to the kinds of problems that could arise in the Warren Commission type of investigation. The first arose out of the staff questioning of a male witness. The staff had received an F.B.I. report that he had had relations with a woman witness. Rankin told the staff that they would have to go into the matter, since she might have told him things while they were intimate. During the questioning, the witness testified about an affair between the woman and a diplomat.

The next day, Warren was livid. "Why did you ask about this?" he stormed at the staff. "It's her personal affair and could ruin the diplomat." You could see, a staff member recalls, that he felt it was "dirty." On Warren's insistence, the testimony about the affair was excised from the transcript.

The second incident involved Norman Redlich, who had been an active civil libertarian before his appointment to the Commission staff. He was strongly attacked by the radical right, led by radio commentator Fulton Lewis, Jr. Representative Ford urged that he be dismissed. In reply, Warren asked for a security clearance for *all* staff members. The Commission voted the clearance, but Ford still moved at a closed meeting on May 19, 1964, to fire Redlich. Warren countered that the Commission should hold a hearing, since it would violate elementary justice to act summarily. Warren later told one of the Brethren that he feared that Ford would agree to this hearing proposal, which would only have publicized the unfair accusations.

Instead, Ford came back with, "My motion is still on the floor." "But you don't have a second, Gerry," interjected Congressman Hale Boggs, another Commission member.

Ford then tried another tactic. He said that the Commission's work would soon be finished, and they should begin letting the staff go, starting with Redlich. Warren pointed out that nothing had yet been written on the Commission's report. "So how can we start reducing the staff?" At this, Ford dropped the matter.

At the time, Redlich hoped that the Commission would issue a special statement of support for him. In retrospect, however, he now feels that nothing really would have been gained by an effort by Warren to secure such a statement. "I look back at it now and think that

Warren handled it just right. He showed a combination of political 'savvy' and procedural due process."

As far as the substantive work of the Commission was concerned, Warren followed the same technique he used as Chief Justice—personally going over the lengthy Commission report that had been drafted by staff members.

There was a sentence in the draft report that Ruth Hyde Paine, with whom Marina Oswald had lived, was "not involved in any way in the assassination of President Kennedy." [12] Warren wanted the sentence deleted. "How would you feel," he asked Redlich, "about having something in there that said Norman Redlich had nothing to do with the assassination of President Kennedy? Would you want your children to read something like that? Here's a perfectly innocent woman. Why should we do that?"

Redlich and Rankin argued that Ruth Paine was not just a woman coming out of the blue. She had harbored Lee Harvey Oswald and his wife, the rifle had been in her garage, and Oswald had taken it from there the night before the shooting. Redlich urged that they owed it to Mrs. Paine to absolve her even though she had not been formally charged. Warren continued to grumble, but said finally, "Okay. You fellows have studied the record more intensely than I have and if that's the way you want to do it, go ahead and do it."

Warren was as responsible for the unanimous Commission report as he was for the unanimity of the *Brown* decision. [13] "One thing he had feared," his son Earl, Jr., recalled, "was dissent within the Commission. It would have been a horrible thing if they had not been able to reach a unanimous conclusion. The effect might have been to split the whole country." [14] Some of the Commission members had reservations. In particular, Senator Richard B. Russell objected to the categorical conclusion that Oswald was not involved in any conspiracy. "But Warren," Russell later said, "was determined he was going to have a unanimous report. I said it wouldn't be any trouble to put a little asterisk in the text and then down at the bottom of the page say, 'Senator Russell dissents to this finding as follows.' But Warren wouldn't hear of it. He finally took that part and rewrote it himself." [15] As issued, the report concluded unanimously, "The Commission has found no evidence that either Lee Harvey Oswald or

Jack Ruby was part of any conspiracy, domestic or foreign, to assassinate President Kennedy."[16]

Warren never had any doubt about the correctness of the Commission's conclusion that Oswald alone had shot Kennedy. He was amused by the wild conspiracy theories about the Commission, as well as about the assassination. "What possible set of circumstances," he asked, "could get Dick Russell and me to conspire on *anything*?"

From the perspective of a former prosecutor, he considered the evidence overwhelming. "If I were still a district attorney," Warren remarked at a Washington cocktail party, "and the Oswald case came into my jurisdiction, given the same evidence I could have gotten a conviction in two days and never heard about the case again."[17]

While the Chief Justice headed the Commission, the work of the Warren Court went on. Anthony Lewis summed up the 1963 Term as "one of extraordinary importance for Court and country. Not since 1954 . . . have any term's decisions so deeply affected American institutions."[18]

The Lewis characterization was justified primarily because of the Reapportionment Cases, which the Brethren had been discussing in conference on November 22, 1963, when they received the news that the President had been shot. The 1962 decision in *Baker v. Carr*[19] had avoided the question of the substantive standards of apportionment required by the Constitution. That was the question now to be decided in the 1964 Reapportionment Cases.

The cases included one involving a congressional apportionment and several challenging state legislative apportionments. The Justices had originally intended to decide the cases together. Since one of the state cases was not set for argument until the end of March 1964, this would have meant that the decisions would not be handed down until near the term's end. Black, who had been assigned the opinion in *Wesberry v. Sanders*,[20] the congressional case, thought that the decision there should be announced earlier. On January 31, 1964, Black sent around a *Memorandum for the Conference* on *Wesberry*, which noted, "Georgia, New York, and other States having congressional apportionment problems, will have elections this year. Our holding . . . will help clarify these problems. The Chief Justice tells me he will wait about writing the State apportionment cases until after other arguments on that question are heard in March. Under these circumstances I think it highly desirable that the congressional cases come down without waiting for the others and hope this can be done."

The others agreed to have the congressional case come down earlier. Black announced the decision February 17. His opinion invalidated a Georgia system under which there were substantial population disparities in that state's congressional districts. According to Black, the intent of the Framers was that, in choosing Congressmen, each citizen of a state must have an equal quantum of voting power.

Arthur Krock, the *New York Times* pundit, criticized the decision as capping a trend toward the assumption of a legislative function when Congress failed to act.[21] But his censure was mild compared to that expressed privately by Frankfurter. The ailing former Justice now had only a year to live. In his papers there is a handwritten draft letter. The first eleven lines are in Frankfurter's increasingly wavering script and the rest by another firmer hand.

"Not since——," Frankfurter wrote, "when the Supreme Court in effect denied to the US Government the power to levy income taxes[22] that Court has not rendered a decision so disruptive of the time-honored operations of our Government as it did a week ago last Monday in the Congressional districting case (*Wesberry v. Sanders*)." The retired Justice declared that "all the Black opinion consisted of" was an "ipse dixit." Frankfurter asserted that there was "no reasoning in the Black opinion except circular reasoning, the essence of which was that voting for the House of Representatives necessarily implied that 'people' must mean equal numbers of people in each district, although article one on which the whole case turns merely provides that the voters for Congressional representatives should have the qualifications which the State designs."[23]

At least one of the Brethren shared Frankfurter's doubts about the Court's current caliber. After the retired Justice had sent him memoranda written by Justice Jackson some years earlier, Harlan replied, in a written note on October 8, just after the 1963 Term had begun, "They both reflect qualities which are notably (and sadly) missing in the 1963 Court for the most part."

Wesberry v. Sanders was relatively easy for the Justices who had concluded at the time of *Baker v. Carr* that the Constitution commanded equality of population in lower House apportionments. But the same was not true of the state apportionments before the Court. That was the case because they involved challenges to both Houses of the legislature. Even those Justices who wanted to decide the merits in *Baker v. Carr* and apply a standard of equality of population to legislative apportionments were not willing to apply it to more than one House. Warren, in particular, was influenced by his experience in California, where only the Assembly was apportioned by population. Each California county was represented by one state senator, regardless of population. Warren had believed that the system worked fairly and he thought that the population requirement under *Baker v. Carr* should not extend to similar state senates.

The same belief was expressed during the conference discussions that followed the arguments in November 1963 of four of the state reapportionment cases. Led by the Chief Justice, most of the Brethren quickly decided that the lower House apportionments, which were not based on equality of population, were invalid. But neither Warren nor the others were willing to apply the population standard to both Houses of the state legislature.

That a majority of Justices changed their minds was a direct result of Warren's lead. The Chief Justice had assigned the opinions in the state cases to himself at the November 22 conference, just before the Brethren received word of Kennedy's assassination. As Warren started to work out his reasoning, he came to realize that his California experience should not be determinative.

"It can't be. It can't be," declared the Chief as he burst without ceremony into Brennan's chambers after he had begun work on the reapportionment opinions. Warren proceeded to tell the Justice that the equal population standard must apply to both Houses of a state legislature. Warren persuaded Brennan, and later Black, Douglas, and Goldberg of the correctness of his new position.

That Warren should have been the catalyst for across-the-board adoption of the equal population standard was ironic in view of his opposition to that standard when he was Governor of California. After his opinion in *Reynolds v. Sims*,[24] the principal 1964 reapportionment decision, was announced, *U.S. News & World Report* quoted from a 1948 speech by Governor Warren that had effectively killed a reapportionment effort in California. "I believe we should keep . . . our present system of legislative representation," Governor Warren had declared. He rejected the idea "of restricting the representation in the [state] senate to a strictly population basis" for "the same reason that the Founding Fathers of our country gave balanced representation to the states of the union—equal representation in one house and proportionate representation based on population in the other."[25]

After Warren had concluded that *Reynolds v. Sims* had to be decided by an equal-population standard applicable to both Houses, he was talking to Francis X. Beytagh, the law clerk working on the case. He began to laugh and remarked, "You know I gave a speech some years ago in Calfornia supporting our reapportionment system there." He said it was based on the federal principle that the Court was rejecting. "You know," he went on, "I never really thought very much about it then. As a political matter it seemed to me to be a sensible arrangement. But now, as a constitutional matter, with the point of view of the responsibilities of a Justice, I kind of got to look at it differently." Beytagh recalls that the Chief Justice was not at all troubled by the fact that he had taken an entirely different position as Governor. "I was just wrong as Governor," Warren later told another law clerk.

There were six state apportionment cases, involving the legislatures in Alabama,[26] Colorado,[27] Delaware,[28] Maryland,[29] New York,[30] and Virginia.[31] The first thing to be done was to choose the case in which to write the principal opinion. The normal Court practice is to have a longer opinion, which goes in detail into the issues and governing principles, in that case and then to have shorter opinions in the companion cases, applying what has been said in the principal opinion.

Beytagh recommended that *Reynolds v. Sims,* the Alabama case, should be chosen for the principal opinion because it presented more of the basic issues, unencumbered by side issues (such as the referendum involved in the Colorado case), than any of the other cases. In addition, the other cases had more complicated apportionment schemes, while Alabama was a good example of a state with a simple scheme that had become outdated by changes in population patterns. During the argument, counsel for Alabama said that the legislature should have been given more time to act. The Chief Justice broke in with, "How long should we have to wait?"[32] There had been no Alabama reapportionment since 1901.

Warren was troubled about choosing the Alabama case. He did not want it to appear that the Court was going out of its way to continue a vendetta against the Southern states. After he considered the matter, however, the Chief concluded that the issues were sufficiently remote from racial discrimination so that there was no valid reason to be concerned. Warren did not discuss the point with any of the Justices, not even Black who was from Alabama, and none of them raised any objection to the choice of *Reynolds v. Sims* as the principal case.

Beytagh remembers that he worked on the apportionment cases from the time the bench memos (prepared by the law clerks prior to oral argument) were written. When the opinions were being drafted, Beytagh spent most of his time on them. He worked on the basic draft through the winter months into the spring. He would meet with Warren at different times, often talking to him over the phone on weekends because of the Commission demands on the Chief's time. Once the phone rang at Beytagh's home. One of his young children answered and said, "There's a nice old man on the telephone." It turned out to be the Chief.

Warren prepared a memorandum for Beytagh that outlined what he wanted to say in the *Reynolds* opinion. He stressed the equal population standard as the rule for both Houses and the rejection of the federal analogy. Beytagh then went to work on the draft. At first, he tried to write as narrowly as possible. But he soon concluded that Warren wanted the kind of broad-brush opinion that was ultimately issued.

Perhaps the most noted passage in the *Reynolds* opinion is the statement, "Legislators represent people, not trees or acres. Legislators are elected by voters, not farms or cities or economic interests."[33] Beytagh recalls that, when Warren saw that language, "he got a kick out of it. He kind of laughed and he said that's not a bad way of expressing the whole notion."

The approach embodied in this famous *Reynolds v. Sims* passage had been indicated in a question asked by the Chief Justice at the March 31 argument on the Colorado case (weeks after he had concluded that the equal-population rule had to govern in both Houses of state legislatures): "Isn't the basic issue whether these appellants and all other people in the State of Colorado have proper representation, whether they are city people or farmers, liberals or conservatives, or whatever?"[34]

One of the things that concerned Warren was the question of remedies. The Chief referred to the "all deliberate speed" language of the second *Brown* case[35] and made it plain that he did not want any such language in the *Reynolds* opinion. Aside from a suggestion at the end of the opinion that, where an election was actually in progress, it might be appropriate for a court temporarily to stay its hand, there was a clear indication that no remedial delay would be allowed.

Even though Warren's *Reynolds v. Sims* opinion was more far-reaching than the conference discussion, it was quickly accepted by a majority. The same was true of the shorter opinions in the five companion cases. As a Justice who participated in the cases remembered it, "The opinions issuing from the chambers of the Chief Justice in those cases were joined without the slightest apparent hesitation or reservation by Justices Black, Douglas, Brennan, and Goldberg, and eventually secured the vote of Justice White as well."

White's hesitation was caused by difficulty with the companion case that arose in his home state of Colorado.[36] The voters in Colorado had approved an apportionment of the lower House on a population basis and the Senate on a combination of population and other factors. White and some of the other majority Justices questioned how the Court could intervene where the people had opted for other than a one person–one vote scheme in both Houses. Warren, however, convinced them that they could not leave the definition of constitutional rights to the voters. He made the point by quoting from an opinion in a fifth circuit school segregation case: "No plebiscite can legalize an unjust discrimination."[37]

Warren announced his *Reynolds v. Sims* opinion of the Court, as well as the opinions in the companion cases, on June 15, 1964. They struck down all six legislative apportionments, enunciating the rule that "the Equal Protection Clause requires that both houses of a state legislature be apportioned on a population basis." The "basic constitutional principle of representative government" was "equality of population among districts."[38]

Only Harlan dissented in *Reynolds v. Sims*. But, on the equal-population-for-both-Houses principle, the vote was really six-to-three. On March 18, Clark had written the Chief, "Must we necessarily decide 'the federal analogy' here? Since the representation in both houses indicates invidious discrimination here it looks as if we could merely decide that and go no further. I am not yet ready to join a holding striking down the federal analogy."[39]

Clark's attitude led him to issue a short concurrence refusing to reject the federal analogy. Stewart also refused to agree to the Court's equal-population rule which, he asserted in a dissent in the Colorado case, involved "the uncritical simplistic, and heavy-handed application of sixth-grade arithmetic."[40]

During the first conference on the cases, Clark had written Frankfurter, "As we sit here discussing reapportionment problems (JMH has the floor for the moment) I am reminded of you. This is not alone because of your masterful opinions in the field but for me because of your forceful, cogent presentations in our Conference."[41]

Harlan also wrote the retired Justice, telling of his "despondency that I no longer have you as an active colleague—this being particularly accented today by the constitutional convention into which the Court convened itself at the Conference today on the first reapportionment cases."[42]

Frankfurter, now in his last year, was even more uncomplimentary. "Go and read Harlan's dissent in *Reynolds v. Sims,* the Reapportionment cases," he told an interviewer, "and then read the Chief Justice's . . . and see the difference. . . . Harlan made mincemeat out of the Chief Justice's opinion."[43]

Former Secretary of State Dean Acheson was caustic. "The separation of powers," he wrote Frankfurter, "is getting a rude shaking up these days. Shall I advise LBJ to convene a Curia Regis to deal with the redistricting matter?"[44]

In his *New York Times* column, Arthur Krock criticized *Reynolds v. Sims* as an "expression of the philosophy that the Constitution implicitly provides for the correction of any social or political condition that a majority of the Court deems undesirable and endows the Court with power to take the functions of another branch of Government when that branch fails to act."[45] Krock's colleague, Anthony Lewis, on the other hand, characterized decision day in the Reapportionment Cases as "one of the great days in the Supreme Court's history" and asked, "Where would we be today if the Supreme Court had not been willing ten years ago to tackle the great moral issue of racial discrimination that Congress had so long avoided?"[46]

Warren never had doubts about the reapportionment decisions. He maintained that, if the "one person, one vote" principle had been laid down years earlier, many of the nation's legal sores would never have festered. "If *Baker v. Carr* had been in existence fifty years ago," he later insisted, "we would have saved ourselves acute racial troubles. Many of our problems would have been solved a long time ago if everyone had the right to vote, and his vote counted the same as everybody else's. Most of these problems could have been solved through the political process rather than through the courts. But as it was, the Court had to decide."[47]

The Chief Justice was well aware that *Reynolds v. Sims* was the political death warrant for undetermined numbers of rural legislators, whose seats would now be reapportioned out of existence. Soon after the decision, Warren flew to his home state to hunt with his sons and some old friends. One of them was asked to invite the Chief to go with some state senators on a trip to hunt quail. When Warren was asked if he wanted to drive down and join them, he looked incredulous. "All those *senators?*" he inquired in mock horror. "With *guns?*"[48]

Reynolds v. Sims and the other Reapportionment Cases may have been the most important cases of the 1963 Term. But the great battle of the term within the Court was not fought over them. That battle was fought over the 1964 Sit-In Cases—argued on the first day of the term and decided on the last. They were the subject of fierce debate during the entire term.

The Justices agreed to take four Sit-In Cases for the 1963 Term: *Bell v. Maryland,*[49] *Barr v. Columbia,*[50] *Bouie v. Columbia,*[51] and *Robinson v. Florida.*[52] All involved fact patterns basically similar to the prior year's Sit-In Cases. In each, blacks sat down in restaurants or lunch counters and refused to leave without being served. They were arrested and convicted of violating state trespass laws. An allied case also on the docket was *Griffin v. Maryland,*[53] held over from the previous term. It involved blacks who had refused to leave Glen Echo Amusement Park, and had been arrested by an employee who had been deputized as a sheriff.

On September 5, 1963, the Court received a brief from the Solicitor General arguing that the 1963 Term cases, like those the last term, could be disposed of on narrow grounds. The brief contended that reversal was required in *Bell, Griffin, Barr,* and *Bouie* because the statutes applied only to entry on land after notice not to enter, and the demonstrators had not been told to leave until after they had entered the premises. Reversal was required in *Robinson,* the brief argued, because the demonstrators had not been informed, as the

Florida statute required, of the reason why they were being told to leave. The Solicitor General did suggest in his brief, however, that if the Court should nevertheless desire to reach the broad issue, he would be prepared to make a full statement of the government's views "upon reargument."

The 1963 Term Sit-In cases were argued on October 13 and 14, 1963. At the conference that followed, on October 18, the Court rejected the Solicitor General's argument that all the cases should be disposed of on narrow grounds, considering it only a legalistic excuse to avoid decision. As Douglas stated, in a memorandum summarizing his conference presentation, "If these lawsuits arose in my home town of Yakima, Washington, there might be substance to the argument that the statutes on their face and/or as applied were void for vagueness. In other words, where Negroes freely come and go, where there is no background of segregation, it might well be a trap to convict a man for remaining when the only prohibition was for entering."

To follow such an approach here, said Douglas, would lose sight of the reality in the areas concerned. "But in the present cases the entering was designed as a means of challenging the law and if necessary bringing the judgments here for review. No one was caught off-guard; no vice of vague statutes is present; no innocent person is trapped; everyone knew what he was doing and the things he expected and wanted to happen, did happen."[54]

The conference did, however, agree to decide three of the cases without reaching the constitutional issue. The Court voted, five-to-four, to reverse the conviction in *Griffin* because of the participation of a deputy sheriff in the exclusion of the demonstrators; and it voted eight-to-one (with only Black the other way) to reverse the convictions in *Barr*, and seven-to-two (with Black and Harlan contra) to do the same in *Bouie*, on the lack of fair warning urged by the Solicitor General. Warren had urged reversal in these cases on the ground that, in them, police officers had directly participated in demanding that the demonstrators leave. As he saw it, this fact brought the cases within *Lombard v. Louisiana*,[55] decided the previous term.

Following Warren's lead, the conference then decided to reach the basic issue in both the *Bell* and *Robinson* cases. "Here," declared the Chief, "we should get to the 'raw' of the problem and reach the basic questions." On the constitutional merits, Warren spoke for reversal, urging that the convictions of the sit-in demonstrators violated the Fourteenth Amendment. "In the field of public accommodations," he stated, "the owner abandons private choice. If it's a private property, for private use, he can call on the state to throw people off." As an example, said Warren, "I think a church can limit admission to its own members, but if it allows all, it couldn't shut out Negroes." But the situation was different where public accommodations were concerned. In them, "as long as they behave themselves, the owner can't have police to help to throw them out. The state then unconstitutionally enforces discrimination." Warren thought the Court could reach that result "even . . . on the principle of *Marsh v. Alabama*[56] and certainly within the principle of *Shelley v. Kraemer*."[57] *Marsh* was the 1946 case that held that action by a company-owned town was "state action" within the reach of the Fourteenth Amendment. *Shelley* was the 1948 case that reached the same result with regard to the action of a state court enforcing a restrictive covenant on land.

The case the other way was again stated most strongly by Black. "I think," he said, "a state can have a law forcing desegregation. The Civil Rights Cases[58] [holding in 1883 that a federal civil rights law could not reach discrimination by privately operated restaurants and hotels] were wrong. But not so wrong that the Constitution must do what that case said Congress could not do."

Black emotionally declared that he could not believe that his "Pappy," who ran a general store in Alabama, did not have the right to decide whom he would or would not serve. The state laws could make "it lawful for the owner to ask him to leave. I don't think the Constitution forbids the owner of a store to keep people out." Black stated that he did not think that either *Marsh* or *Shelley* was relevant, but, if they were deemed controlling, "I would overrule them."

The view expressed by Black was one deeply held by him. In a 1963 letter to the Alabaman, Frankfurter had set forth "the essentials of what you told all of us twice at Conference—that you would never consent to any decision which held that the Constitution of the United States compelled you to do business with whom you did not want to do business, subject of course to two qualifications, that 'your' business was really wholly your own and neither in its origin nor in its maintenance drew directly or indirectly on State or Federal funds and because of that factor no racial discrimination was permissible, and secondly, provided a specific case does not violate the Due

Process Clause in its procedural aspects, that is, does not fall within your opinion and the direction of your opinion in the *Thompson* v. *Louisville* case, in the general direction you there indicated."[59] (*Thompson v. Louisville*[60] was the Case of Shuffling Sam discussed in chapter 9.)

The opposition to Black's view was once more stated most effectively by Douglas, though this time a strong statement was also made, as we have seen, by Warren, as well as by Brennan and Goldberg. Douglas summarized his conference presentation in a memorandum. Douglas urged a broad interpretation of "state action" under the Fourteenth Amendment: "A State expresses a policy whenever it acts through a prosecutor and a court—a policy no less clear than when it acts through its legislator."

Three extreme hypothetical cases were stated by Douglas. "Suppose a Negro enters a drug store to buy penicillin for his sick child and is arrested and convicted for 'entering' or for 'remaining.' Suppose a Negro is denied admission to a private hospital and is arrested and convicted for 'entering' and 'remaining.' Assume there is a State that has no statute requiring a common carrier to carry on-comers and a Negro is arrested and convicted for riding on one."

In these cases, as in the Sit-In Cases before them, Douglas had no doubts. As he saw it, "The question in the sit-in cases is, in other words, not whether there is state action but whether States, acting through their courts, can constitutionally put a racial cordon around businesses serving the public. If they can do it in the restaurant cases they can do it in drug stores, private hospitals and common carriers, interstate carriers apart. Property is in one case as sacrosanct as in the other. But the businesses involved in these cases are in this day and age as much affected with the public interest as were the innkeepers and common carriers of old."

Douglas noted that the Court's decision might have drastic effects upon congressional power to enact civil-rights legislation, since, "Apart from the Commerce Clause, Congress has no power to legislate in this field if there is no state action in the meaning of the Fourteenth Amendment." Douglas asserted that, "if we hold that this kind of discrimination is beyond the purview of the Fourteenth Amendment there is nothing for Congress to 'enforce' and the Civil Rights Cases are vindicated."

Douglas concluded by declaring, "An affirmance in these cases fastens apartheid tightly onto our society—a result incomprehensible in light of the purposes of the Fourteenth Amendment and the realities of our modern society."[61]

The conference vote in both the *Bell* and *Robinson* cases was five-to-four to affirm the convictions on the merits. Clark, Harlan, Stewart, and White voted with Black to make up the bare majority. Black assigned the opinions to himself. Warren also chose Black to write for the Court in the *Barr* and *Bouie* cases. It was not clear why he did so, since Black had voted in the minority to affirm those convictions. However, since Black agreed to write the opinions for reversal, the Chief probably considered it desirable to let one Justice handle all four cases.

There was a further discussion at a subsequent conference, which lasted the entire day. Goldberg made what a participant termed an "elaborate and moving" attack on the proposed affirmance. Goldberg went back to the position that the cases be disposed of on the narrow grounds originally suggested by the Solicitor General, but a majority rejected the proposal. At the first conference, the minority *Bell* and *Robinson* Justices had stressed the fact that President Kennedy had sent Congress a civil rights bill to prohibit racial discrimination in public accommodations. Warren and Brennan both expressed a fear that the *Bell* and *Robinson* affirmances might have a crippling effect on the prospects for congressional passage of the bill. In the heat of the conference discussion, several members of the minority asserted that they would do their utmost to delay the decisions as long as possible, in the hope that Congress would meanwhile have acted favorably on the bill or that some member of the majority might be led to change his vote. The suggestion of delay caused hard feeling at the October 18 conference.

At the second conference, after Goldberg's proposal to decide narrowly had been rejected, the minority Justices switched to a delaying tactic. Led by Warren and Brennan, they argued that the Court should not decide such an important issue without first hearing the views of the Solicitor General. After a sharp-tempered debate, this proposal was approved by a bare majority only because Stewart voted for it, despite his adherence to the Black view on the merits.

On November 18, the Court issued an order inviting the Solicitor General to file a brief "expressing the views of the United States" on "the broader constitutional issues." The underlying acrimony within the Court surfaced in the statement by Black, Clark, Harlan, and White at the end of the order that they were of the opinion that the invitation should not be issued. Their statement referred to the views of the "Department of Justice" rather than, like the majority, to those of the "United States." In an earlier draft, their particular reference had significantly been to the views of the "Kennedy Administration."

The Solicitor General had been given thirty days to submit his supplementary brief, but he requested and received an additional thirty days, so that the brief was not filed until January 17, 1964. This brief also urged reversal on rather limited grounds, and had no direct effect on the Court's decisions. But the brief did have an important indirect effect on the *Bell* and *Robinson* cases. During the research for the supplementary brief, the Solicitor General's staff discovered that a regulation required toilet segregation in Florida restaurants. Under the Court's decision during the previous term in *Peterson v. Greenville*,[62] this fact required reversal of the *Robinson* convictions. That was the result subsequently reached unanimously in an opinion written by Black.

Black had been planning to write his principal opinion for affirmance in the *Robinson* case. The Solicitor General's discovery now compelled him to do so in *Bell* instead. The Black draft opinion for affirmance in *Bell,* containing fifteen printed pages, was first sent to Clark, Harlan, Stewart, and White. After it was approved by them, it was circulated to all the Justices on March 12, 1964. Black's draft opinion of the Court was substantially the same as the *Bell* dissent that he eventually filed, except for two sections added to the dissent to meet the points made in the Brennan opinion, which became the opinion of the Court, and a concurrence filed by Goldberg.

There were, however, two interesting passages in Black's draft opinion of the Court that were deleted from the *Bell* dissent that he ultimately issued. The draft, like the Black dissent, found that private businesses did not become state agencies because they were licensed. "And," the draft went on to say, "the mere fact that a privately owned business serves a large segment of the public does not mean that it is constitutionally required to serve all. One of the most distinguishing characteristics of a privately owned business is that, in the absence of statutory or common-law regulations, it conducts its business according to its own judgment as to what is in its best interests. And it should not need to be said that common law or statutory ideas of a duty of 'public utilities' to serve the public are not of constitutional dimensions."

The draft also stated the basic holding of the majority who then voted for affirmance of the *Bell* convictions as follows: "We hold that the Fourteenth Amendment does not bar Maryland from enforcing its trespass laws so long as it does not do so with an evil eye and a prejudiced heart and hand. We do not believe that the Amendment was written or designed to interfere with a property owner's right to choose his social or business associates, so long as he does not run counter to a valid state or federal regulation. It would overturn the whole history of this country to take away a man's property or any part of it except by taking it for a public use and paying him just compensation as the law provides."[63] Both these passages were deleted in Black's final opinion.

On March 20, Douglas circulated a *Bell* dissent. Together with the draft, Douglas sent Warren a written note: "I have my dissent in the sit-ins—for your eyes only (and Bill and Arthur but not law clerks)." Similar notes were sent to Brennan and Goldberg.

On April 20, Goldberg, too, circulated a dissent, and the Chief Justice sent around his own dissent on May 7. Brennan joined all three, and the dissenters joined each other. The Douglas and Goldberg draft dissents need not be discussed here, since they were essentially the same as the *Bell* concurring opinions that they finally delivered. A word should, however, be said about Warren's draft dissent because the Chief withdrew the draft and did not publish any opinion of his own in the *Bell* case.

"In this and companion cases," Warren's draft dissent began, "the Court has interposed principles of privacy and the protection of property rights between Negro petitioners and the right to equal treatment in public places. Its decision will stand in sharp contrast to the traditional fate in this Court of narrow and technical arguments which are offered as the excuse for denying fundamental human rights. More important, unfortunately, will be the effect which the decision will have on the future development of basic American principles of equality."

According to Warren, the majority had "elevated to the status of constitutional protection a claimed property right which is at best the right to solicit the patronage of Negroes at a lunch counter if they stand up, but to deny it if they sit down. What possible purpose the State advances by enforcing and protecting such a narrow and impersonal right completely escapes me, lest it be the right to perpetuate a custom of systematic segregation in public eating facilities. That this is a legitimate State objective cannot, of course, be argued."

The Chief's draft dissent indignantly referred to the policy of the luncheonette in one of the cases to sell food to blacks to take out, provided they did not sit at the lunch counter. This, wrote Warren, was asserting "a right to compel Negroes to stand up to buy their food solely for the reason that they were Negroes. The store might as well have offered to feed only Negroes who would crawl in on their hands and knees, or, as in other caste systems, who would purchase food under conditions that would not cause their shadow to fall on the food of whites. It saddens me deeply to think that this Court, which has so far advanced the notion of the equal dignity of all men before the law, would sanction the right so publicly to first shame and then punish one who merely seeks that which any white man takes for granted."

It ignored reality to say that only the property owner's private right was involved. As Warren saw it, the arrests of the sit-in demonstrators showed "that it is the policy of the State that is being enforced as well as that of the private entrepreneur. To say that the policy is merely 'private' ignores the fact that without the State it could not survive."

Warren's draft dissent concluded by asserting that "the important civil right of equal access to public places is a right which the Constitution forbids a State to deny in the name of private property. The Constitution can mean no less if it is to restore to the Negro, as the Civil War Amendments intended, that little bit of humanity which he loses each time a state-sanctioned inferior status is publicly thrust upon him. I cannot in conscience be a part of a return to a tradition which so belongs to the past."[64]

Warren and Brennan still very much feared the effect on Congress of the decision for affirmance. But the other dissenting Justices, Douglas and Goldberg, did not share their apprehension and the tentative majority, of course, sought a speedy decision. Black, in particular, expressed the view that the Court owed it to the nation to decide the sit-in issue as quickly as possible, and at the end of March, it looked as though he would get his wish.

While Clark and Goldberg had been judging a moot court together at a local law school, Clark stated to his colleague that the majority was "absolutely solid and indestructible." But as it turned out, the majority was not as solid as it then seemed. On April 13, Black circulated brief opinions for the Court in the *Robinson, Barr* and *Bouie* cases. Black's *Robinson* draft was for reversal on the basis of the toilet-segregation regulation already mentioned. But his *Barr* and *Bouie* opinions reached the result of rejecting the unfair-warning argument and affirmed the convictions.

Brennan sent a *Memorandum to the Conference* the next day in which he pointed out that "Hugo's result is contrary to the conference votes in which I joined." Brennan informed the conference that he would dissent in the *Barr* and *Bouie* cases on the basis of the original conference vote. Then, on April 18, Brennan began writing a dissent in *Bell* that relied on state laws prohibiting discrimination in public accommodations in Baltimore, where the *Bell* case arose, passed in 1962 and 1963 after the *Bell* convictions. Brennan concluded that these public accommodations laws required reversal of the *Bell* convictions. He relied on the common-law rule that repeal or other legislative nullification of a criminal statute had the effect of vacating convictions still pending under the statute.

Brennan circulated his *Bell* dissent based on these 1962 and 1963 state laws on April 27. At the same time, he sent around the dissent he said he would write in the *Barr* and *Bouie* cases.

According to a letter from Douglas to Clark, "When Bill Brennan first circulated his opinion for remand to the Maryland court, I asked him if he would have done the same thing if we had voted to reverse rather than to affirm. He said No. At least that was my understanding of the conversation." Douglas later referred to Brennan's "opinion in the Maryland case as involving purely matters of expediency and not principle," though he conceded that Brennan "said I had misunderstood him." [65]

On Wednesday, April 29, Black, looking toward a decision day the following Monday, May 4, circulated a fourth printing of his *Bell* majority opinion. It sought to answer the Brennan draft dissent in a lengthy footnote 40. The footnote stated that whether the 1962 and

1963 statutes required abatement of the prosecutions was a state question, "and for this reason our affirmance of these state convictions will, of course, not bar the Maryland court from considering that question and abating the convictions if it holds this result to be required or permitted by state law."

Black also argued that Brennan's approach would not really avoid the broader issue. His footnote asserted, "The dissent also argues that remand would enable this Court to avoid deciding the constitutional question presented. This argument is wholly without merit because we are compelled to decide the same question in *Barr v. City of Columbia* and *Bouie v. City of Columbia.*"

After he read Black's revised draft, Brennan notified the Alabaman that the cases could not come down on May 4, since he would have to revise his *Bell* dissent to meet Black's new points. In addition, he wanted to revise his dissent in *Barr* and *Bouie*. This necessitated at least a two-week delay, since the next decision day was scheduled for May 18. In the interim, on May 7, Warren circulated his draft dissent.

Brennan next circulated a revised dissent that covered the *Bell, Barr* and *Bouie* cases. To underline his point that the basic issue should not be decided because a decision on narrow grounds was compelled, Brennan began the draft by announcing that he no longer concurred in the Douglas and Goldberg draft dissents: "The constitutional question decided today should not have been reached, and I therefore join neither the Court nor my Brothers Douglas and Goldberg in their different resolutions to it."

The new Brennan draft contained strong language. Brennan referred to the congressional debate on Title II of the civil rights bill, which by then had degenerated into the longest filibuster in the Senate's history. "We of this Court," Brennan wrote, "are not so removed from the world around us that we can ignore the current debate over the constitutionality of Title II if enacted." Brennan then declared, "we cannot be blind to the fact that today's opposing opinions on the constitutional question decided will inevitably enter into and perhaps confuse that debate. My colleagues thus choose the most unfortunate time to commit the error of reaching out to decide the question. In doing so they unnecessarily create the risk of dealing the Court a 'self-inflicted wound'—because the issue should not have been decided at all."

At this time, it looked as though the sit-in decisions would be announced on May 18—ten years and a day after the first decision in *Brown v. Board of Education.*[66] On May 13, Brennan sent around a final version of his dissenting opinion. The sharp language and the references to the congressional debate had been deleted, and the opinion had been joined by the Chief Justice, who saw in Brennan's approach a way of avoiding what he considered the wrong decision on the merits, as well as by Goldberg—though not by Douglas, who still dissented on the merits.

Brennan now concluded that, despite his efforts, decision on the basic issue was all but inevitable. Because he wanted to state his view on that question, Brennan reinstated his concurrence with the other dissenters. At the end of the revised dissent, he noted, "Although I thus believe that the Court should not have reached the ultimate constitutional issue either in *Bell* or in the South Carolina cases [i.e., *Barr* and *Bouie*], I feel obliged, since the Court has done so, to express my position on that issue, and I therefore join the dissenting opinions of THE CHIEF JUSTICE and of my Brothers DOUGLAS and GOLDBERG."

Yet, even at this point, Warren and Brennan had not given up all hope of converting a member of the majority. Their attention focused on Stewart, who was reported by his law clerks to be seriously considering the Brennan opinion. Black also realized that Stewart might waver and conferred frequently with him. In addition, as Black planned to be out of town on what looked like the crucial conference day of Friday, May 15, he had appointed Stewart as "floor manager" of the majority Justices. Stewart wanted to discuss his doubts with White, who had been out of town, but returned on May 14. When Stewart went to see him that day, White reacted with a firm refusal to consider defecting from the Black opinion. This settled the matter for Stewart. When word of this was received by the dissenters, they now considered it certain that Black's opinion would come down Monday as the opinion of the Court.

At this point, Black softened his opinion to meet the minority's fear of the damaging effect on the civil-rights bill. A revised draft, circulated May 15, just before that morning's conference, began, "The case does not involve the constitutionality of any existing or proposed state or federal legislation requiring restaurant owners to serve people without regard to color."

The May 15 conference began, as usual, at 10 A.M. The formal handshakes exchanged by the Brethren at the beginning could not mask the underlying tension, as both the tentative majority and minority expected the sit-in cases to be decided the following Monday, with Black's *Bell* opinion issued as the opinion of the Court. But the anticipated scenario was not to be played. As soon as the discussion began, Clark asked that the cases again go over, since his present thinking was that Brennan's view was correct. Clark said he had reached that conclusion the night before upon reading the Brennan dissent, and that he had reported his change of heart to Black (who had decided to stay in town after all) just before the conference began. The rest of the conference discussion was brief and, according to one who was present, "exceedingly tense," with Black and Clark saying virtually nothing. The greatest outrage at Clark's changed position was expressed by Douglas, who said he would never join Brennan in his refusal to reach the "merits."

Clark's switch completely altered the Court's position in the *Bell* case. Assuming that Clark would adhere to his new position and that no other vote would change, the Court was at an impasse, with the Black opinion and the Brennan opinion each now commanding four votes, but neither of them having a majority.

Black now set to work on Clark to persuade him to rejoin the Black opinion. Black argued, relying on the 1937 case of *Helvering v. Davis*,[67] that when a majority wanted to reach the merits, the Court must do so. Rumors began to circulate that Clark had agreed to rejoin Black, but only on condition that the opinions not come down until the last day of the term. The rumors were, however, unfounded. Black had tried to push too hard and Clark, in exasperation, had told the Alabaman that if he really wanted a decision on the merits, Clark would give him one by joining the Warren–Douglas–Brennan–Goldberg view.

On May 27, Clark circulated a memorandum stating that, "As I advised Brother Black this morning, I am joining the opinion of Brother Brennan in these cases." Brennan then sent around a memorandum stating that he would not join the opinions of the Chief Justice, Goldberg, and Douglas.

Brennan also revised both his *Bell* and *Barr–Bouie* opinions, changing their form from that of a dissent and cutting each of them in half. The opinions could not command a majority without Douglas, but it was thought that they could be headed "Mr. Justice Brennan announced the judgment of the Court and delivered an opinion which the Chief Justice, Mr. Justice Clark and Mr. Justice Goldberg join," and could terminate with a sentence reading: "Since Mr. Justice Douglas would also reverse, the judgment . . . is *Reversed.*" Brennan prepared opinions in this form for circulation.

Before they could be circulated, they became the subject of a Douglas–Brennan memoranda duel. In answer to Clark's announcement, Douglas circulated a May 27 *Memorandum to the Conference,* which stated: "In No. 12—*Bell v. Maryland,* Brother Clark's decision to join Brother Brennan makes five votes for reversal. But I should make it unmistakably clear I would not reverse on any grounds but the ones I have written. In other words, on the issue presented by my Brother Brennan I join the group headed by my Brother Black, which, as I understand it, leaves the majority of the Court against the disposition which Brother Brennan has suggested."

The Douglas objection to having his vote joined with the Brennan four to produce a majority judgment of reversal was based primarily on his desire to have a decision on the merits (he was not dissuaded by the fact that the decision at this point would have been in favor of the Black view that he opposed). Douglas also contended that the Brennan disposition of *Bell* constituted not a "reversal" of the Maryland court's judgment but rather a "vacating" of the judgment and "remanding" of the case to that court for consideration of whether the state desired the affirmances to stand.

On May 28, Brennan sent around a *Memorandum to the Conference* which addressed itself to the latter contention, pointing out that in similar situations the Court had previously used as its operative order not "Vacated" but "Reversed." Brennan's memo went on to assert: "When questions of terminology are put aside, however, the reality remains that whether the term used is 'reversed' or 'vacated,' the state judgment is nullified and the case sent back to the state court for further proceedings. There would thus be five votes in *Bell* to nullify the state judgment and send the case back, although Brother Douglas would go further than four of us and rest this disposition upon his view of the constitutional merits."

The Douglas–Brennan exchange portended a deadlock not only over the Brennan opinion but even over the result, with Douglas challenging the assumption that his vote could be combined with the

Brennan four to produce, if not an opinion of the Court, at least a judgment of the Court. In another May 28 *Memorandum to the Conference,* Douglas asserted that only four Justices adhered to Brennan's view. "My vote is to reverse outright; and since the four who affirm have the same attitude as I do on my Brother Brennan's point, the mandate of this Court must be just the opposite of what my Brother Brennan intends to accomplish by changing 'vacate' to 'reverse.' "

At this point, Goldberg offered a "compromise" proposal. It involved no change in the ultimate disposition from that advocated by Brennan; yet it succeeded in getting Douglas to soften his position. The formula was contained in a memorandum circulated by Goldberg on May 28. "In view of the memoranda exchanged between Justices Douglas and Brennan and after consultation with the Chief Justice," Goldberg proposed that, instead of having Brennan announce the judgment of the Court, this would be done by a brief per curiam opinion that would state, "The judgment is reversed. The Chief Justice, Mr. Justice Clark and Mr. Justice Brennan would reverse for the reasons stated in Mr. Justice Brennan's opinion. Mr. Justice Douglas and Mr. Justice Goldberg would reverse for the reasons stated in their respective opinions."

Douglas agreed to the Goldberg formula. But that did not settle the matter. Black and the three Justices who still supported his *Bell* opinion refused to give in. To the per curiam statement as proposed by Goldberg stating that the judgment was reversed, they proposed to attach a "dissent" that opened with the statement, "Justices Black, Harlan, Stewart and White do not agree with the announcement that the judgment of the Court of Appeals of Maryland is 'reversed'; they believe that it would be more nearly accurate to characterize the result of the case as an 'affirmance' rather than a 'reversal.' "

The Black group's opinion based this assertion on the proposition that when a majority wanted to reach the constitutional merits, the Court must do so. Their opinion declared, "Since six members of the Court, constituting a majority and a quorum, have voted to reach and decide the constitutional question, and a majority of those so voting have voted to affirm the convictions, it is not accurate to announce, as the Court's *per curiam* opinion does, that the judgment of the Maryland court is 'reversed.' "

This opinion upset Warren and Brennan. The Chief, in particular, feared that, if it were issued, it would only hurt the Court's reputation. The depth of Warren and Brennan's feeling is shown by a short answer drafted June 4 by Brennan, after consultation with the Chief, as well as Clark, which read as follows: "The Chief Justice, Mr. Justice Clark and Mr. Justice Brennan deem too ill-becoming for comment the absurd proposition of our Brothers Black, Harlan, Stewart and White that their expression for a minority of four in support of an affirmance overrides the majority vote of five to reverse the judgment."

This draft was never circulated. Instead, at the conference the next day, June 5, Black and his supporters put forward a new proposal. This was that the Court should grant certiorari and call up for immediate argument—holding a special term for the purpose if necessary—some of the new cases involving sit-ins that had been docketed during the 1963 Term. Douglas indicated that he would support the proposal. That would give it five votes, and, as Brennan was heard remarking after the conference, "Five votes can do anything around here." The matter was not decided, however, because White asked for time to think it over. He was concerned about the effect such a grant of certiorari might have on the congressional debate.

But now another crucial switch was in the making. According to the June 8 letter from Douglas to Clark, the Texan had told Douglas the night before that he was going to write an opinion in *Bell* for reversal on the merits. On June 11, Clark circulated an opinion taking the anti-Black view on the merits. This Clark draft, written as a reversing opinion that could serve as an opinion of the Court in the *Bell* case, contained seventeen printed pages. It was divided into four sections: (1) The Facts; (2) The Factual Setting of the Claims; (3) Evolution of the "State Action" Doctrine; and (4) The Application of the Fourteenth Amendment.

Clark's draft stated, "The basic question on the merits is whether the convictions are proscribed by the Fourteenth Amendment." His answer was, "We have concluded that the State is involved to such a 'significant extent,' . . . that the case must be reversed."

A passage toward the end of the opinion summed up the reasoning supporting this conclusion:

In sum we believe that the character of the State's multifold involvement makes it responsible for the discrimination here. First, the customary usages to which public restaurants are devoted has become a 'kind of common law' within purview of the Fourteenth Amendment. Next, Maryland's statutes, licensing and regulatory authority inject it to a significant extent into the conduct of public restaurants. Third, the opening up of the property by the owner for use by the public generally circumscribes his rights of individual choice and especially here where the choice to discriminate is shown to be that of the customers rather than the owner. Fourth, the recognition of the right to private discrimination under such circumstances would be but to give vitality to a practice that is condemned by the Constitution, is prohibited to the States, and is against the national policy. And, finally, the use by the State of its trespass law gives substance, force and effect to a private discrimination that the Constitution prohibits the State from doing directly but which it accomplishes by indirection. It would to us seem strangely inconsistent to hold that although no legislature may authorize a court to prohibit Negroes the use of public restaurants for a moment that the owner through the use of the State's processes can prevent its use by Negroes forever.

Clark also sought to answer one of Black's principal arguments. "It is said that our conclusion will bring on violence and disrespect for law because parties, not being able to enforce their prejudices through legal channels, will resort to self-help. This, we believe, is an overstatement. Our conclusion . . . will act as a palliative against the increasing racial animosities that are encouraged by discrimination and are becoming more and more evident on our national scene. Unless this resurgence to the technique of the jungle is curbed we shall reap a whirlwind of discontent."[68]

Clark had shown his draft opinion to the Chief Justice before he circulated it. On June 10, Warren sent back a written note. "I have read the draft of your *Bell* opinion. It is a splendid job and if filed will without doubt be a classic. I would feel honored to join it."[69]

Despite the Chief's praise, Clark's opinion represented less a conversion on the merits than a tactic designed to secure a majority for Brennan's opinion avoiding the merits. Clark indicated that, while he was fully prepared to issue his opinion, he still felt that the Brennan disposition would be preferable.

If the Clark opinion was a strategic move, the strategy worked. On Monday, June 15, *Reynolds v. Sims*[70] and the other reapportionment decisions were announced. That evening Stewart telephoned Brennan to say that he was joining the Brennan opinion in the Sit-In Cases. Stewart told his law clerks that he had reflected on the bench that morning that if he could have done anything to stop the Reapportionment Cases from being decided as they were, he would have. He said that he felt the same way about the Clark opinion in the *Bell* case.

The next day, Brennan circulated a memorandum announcing that the Chief Justice had assigned him, in view of Stewart's decision, to circulate opinions for the Court in the *Bell, Barr* and *Bouie* cases. As it turned out in those cases, three Justices would express a view each way on the merits and three (Brennan, Clark, and Stewart) would express no view. The majority for the Brennan *Bell* opinion consisted of these three and also of Goldberg (who filed his own opinion on the merits and joined Douglas' opinion) and the Chief Justice (who now withdrew his opinion on the merits and joined Goldberg's).

The Court also had to dispose of *Griffin v. Maryland,* the Glen Echo case that had been held over from the previous term. Except for Black, Harlan, and White who dissented, the Justices agreed to a reversal on the ground voted on in the October 18, 1963 conference—that the participation of a deputy sheriff in the *Griffin* arrests required reversal of the convictions. Warren prepared a per curiam to that effect, stating, in a May 12, 1964 *Memorandum for the Conference,* "I have put it in this form rather than as an opinion of mine because of the broader dissenting opinions I have joined in *Bell.*" Then, on June 17, the Chief circulated the following *Memorandum for the Brethren:* "In view of the change of No. 12—*Bell* v. *Maryland*—I am recirculating, without change, as an opinion of the Court my per curiam in No. 6—*Griffin* v. *Maryland.*" Warren's *Griffin* opinion was issued as an opinion of the Court, together with the Brennan opinions in the other Sit-In Cases.

Brennan's now-majority opinions in the *Bell, Barr,* and *Bouie* cases were duly circulated, in essentially the same form as the previous Brennan dissents. Douglas and Black then incorporated in their respective opinions similar attacks on the Court for refusing to decide the basic question. On June 16, Douglas circulated a new draft that accused the Court of, among other things, "irresponsible judicial management of the foremost issue of our time" and "abdication of judicial authority." The final Douglas opinion eliminated these phrases, but was still unusually sharp.

Black, on the other hand, had his law clerks remove from his opinion anything that might impute discredit to the Court or any of its members. At a social gathering after the term had ended, he was heard to tell Brennan that, much as he disagreed with the result reached in the Sit-In Cases, he admired and was "proud of" Brennan for the way he had fought.

Douglas, however, remained bitter about Brennan's success in securing avoidance of a decision on the merits, even though that prevented the decision upholding the sit-in convictions that Douglas opposed. Brennan's law clerks felt that his resentment over the sit-in controversy led Douglas during the final week of the term to withdraw his concurrences with Brennan opinions in several unrelated cases. When the sit-in decisions were announced, on June 22, the last day of the term, Douglas was not on the bench. The task of announcing his opinion was split between Black and Goldberg, with Black reading the portion attacking the Court's failure to reach the merits and Goldberg stating the portion discussing the merits.

Warren, like Douglas, felt that the sit-in convictions involved discriminatory state action. Unlike the Justice, however, the Chief was not displeased by the way the *Bell* case was decided. Though his concurrence in Goldberg's opinion showed how he felt on the merits, Warren knew that a decision on the merits would have gone against his view. "You know as I recall," says one of his law clerks that year, "he certainly wasn't unhappy. He was happier that it was being put off for another day and perhaps forever than to have a majority decision going in the opposite direction."

As it turned out, the Court never did decide the constitutional issue that it avoided in *Bell*. Soon after the decision, on July 2, the Civil Rights Act of 1964 became part of the federal statute book. Its prohibition of racial discrimination in restaurants and other public accommodations elevated the goal of the sit-in demonstrators to the law of the land. The underlying issue that so sharply divided Black from his erstwhile Court allies thus became moot.

Warren's chairmanship of the commission on the Kennedy assassination had its unavoidable effect on his Court work. "Those of us who clerked that term," recalls Francis X. Beytagh, "were amazed at the stamina of a person his age. You know he was a tough, tough nut, and he told me he didn't want to appear to be slacking off on the work at the Court." The Chief told the Brethren the same thing at a conference he called to inform them he had agreed to head the Warren Commission. And he tried as best he could to do both jobs.

He also tried as much as possible to maintain his personal relations with his law clerks. He found time for his Saturday lunches with them and took them to at least one baseball game. Each Friday, after the Justices had finished their conference, he would still sit down with his clerks and go through in detail what had been decided at the conference and what he wanted them to do on those cases.

Yet inevitably Warren could not play the full leadership role in the Court's work that he did in other terms. The Chief had assigned the opinions in the Reapportionment Cases to himself before the Justices received word that the President had been shot. He told Beytagh afterwards, "I'm going to stick with that," and the reapportionment opinions were his major contribution to the 1964 Term. Though Warren wrote five other Court opinions and one short dissent, none of them can be characterized as major.

In the Reapportionment Cases, Warren not only wrote the opinions, he also led the Court to its decision requiring equal population in apportionments for both Houses of state legislatures. The Chief was also able to contribute substantially to the Sit-In Cases. He did not make the same contribution in the other cases decided during the term. Warren presided at the conferences, assigned the opinions, and read and criticized the drafts. But the major work was done by the others. For that reason, less attention can be devoted to the remaining 1963 Term cases, except for *New York Times Co. v. Sullivan,*[71] which made a major change in First Amendment law.

At the end of the 1963 Term, Anthony Lewis, in the *New York Times,* referred to "a new Supreme Court, exercising its great power in new ways, unabashed by that power, unafraid to intervene against strongly established forces in society in behalf of the individual." Summarizing the term Lewis wrote, "the general direction taken by the court was clear. In an urban society, marked by increasing governmental regulation of man's daily life, the Justices were protecting the integrity of the individual from official intrusion."[72]

In what Lewis termed the Court's "movement toward greater concern for the individual in a mass society,"[73] the term's criminal cases continued to play an important part. Yet there were differences on whether particular decisions did, in fact, make for constitutional progress. In *Jackson v. Denno*,[74] for example, Black asserted in dissent that the decision voted for by Warren and his supporters marked a "downgrading of trial by jury."

Jackson had been prosecuted for murder in New York. He claimed that a confession introduced in evidence was a product of coercion. Following New York practice, the trial judge submitted the issue of the voluntariness of the confession to the jury, along with the other issues in the case. The jury found Jackson guilty of murder.

In the 1953 case of *Stein v. New York*,[75] the Court had sustained the New York procedure under which the jury resolved disputed fact questions on voluntariness of confessions. At the December 13, 1963, conference, Warren spoke in favor of overruling *Stein*. He was supported by Black, Douglas, Brennan, Goldberg, and White, who asserted that "the *Stein* rule doesn't square with other cases." Clark, Harlan, and Stewart said that they would not overrule *Stein*, with Harlan stating that "it may be O.K. as a federal case to overrule but not under due process."

The opinion was assigned to White, who sent a revised draft around on February 20, 1964. The next day, Black wrote White that he was "writing you at once to tell you that I regret it will be impossible for me to agree with what you have written." Black objected to White's opening paragraph, which referred to the "fairness" of the New York procedure. To Black, this was a red flag which cautioned that the ghost of Frankfurter's notion of due process might still walk. "This word 'fairness,'" wrote Black, "used in its context implies that we are relying on the loose definition of 'due process' as meaning anything that is offensive to this Court's sense of decency or the basic principles of 'fundamental fairness in the English-speaking world.'"

Black objected even more strongly against striking down the New York procedure. Black had reconsidered his conference position and now felt that it was vital to have the jury decide the confession issue. "I think" his letter to White declared, "your opinion, if it should become that of the Court, is a long step backward—away from the safeguards our Constitution provides for fair trials in criminal cases. There might be more unfair things for a defendant than to have his guilt or innocence passed on by a jury on a confession admitted by the court as true while at the same time the jury is denied the benefit of evidence to show that the confession was in fact the result of coercion, intimidation, force or violence, but I cannot think of a worse procedure at the present." [76]

Despite a long letter from White on February 21 defending his opinion, Black prepared a dissent. So did Harlan, who was joined by Clark and Stewart. When White announced his opinion on June 22, 1964, invalidating the New York procedure and requiring the confession issue to be "determined in a proceeding separate and apart from the body trying guilt or innocence," he spoke for only five Justices.

There were other significant criminal cases, including *Escobedo v. Illinois*, [77] where a bare majority ruled (even though only three, Clark, Harlan, and Stewart had voted to deny certiorari) that the constitutional right to counsel attached as soon as the police focused upon the defendant as a particular suspect and were interrogating him at police headquarters, as well as *Malloy v. Hogan*, [78] which held that the privilege against self-incrimination is protected equally against state, as well as federal, action.

Another criminal decision led to a strong private reaction from a leading federal judge. The decision was rendered in *Massiah v. United States*. [79] After Massiah had been indicted for a drug violation and retained a lawyer, he was released on bail. He then spoke to a co-defendant in the latter's auto, which contained a hidden transmitter which allowed a federal agent to listen in. The Court held that the statements thus made, in the absence of counsel, might not be admitted at the trial without violating Massiah's Sixth Amendment right to counsel.

Though only Clark and Harlan had voted to deny certiorari, White issued dissent, joined by Clark and Harlan. Stewart voted with the majority and was assigned the opinion. The majority had voted to reverse on Sixth Amendment grounds, but Black wrote Stewart on April 11, 1964, that he felt "that the confession used against petitioner was obtained in a way that I believe violated his Fifth Amendment right not to be compelled to be a witness against himself," as well as his Sixth Amendment right. Black objected to Stewart's draft opinion and wrote, "I feel compelled to concur specially because your opinion, as I understand it, does not rely on these specific constitutional provisions but, rather, on the minority view expressed by Mr. Justice Frankfurter in *Watts v. Indiana,* 338 U.S. 49, which did not rest at all on these Bill of Rights safeguards but on his view that the Due Process Clause permits the Court to hold a court practice unconstitutional that offends 'the rudimentary requirements of a civilized order. . . .' " Black did not issue his special concurrence after Stewart wrote back on April 13 that he would delete the offending passage.

U.S. Court of Appeals Judge Henry J. Friendly was not so easily appeased. "I am really burned up at the opinion of your Court in *United States v. Massiah,*" he wrote Frankfurter (who hastened to send the letter to Harlan). Friendly asserted that, "to spell all of this out of the words of the Sixth Amendment that guarantee an accused the right 'to have the assistance of counsel for his defense' seems to me as wooden and unwarranted an interpretation of the Constitution as the economic decisions under the due process and equal protection clauses during the time when you had given me the privilege of serving Mr. Justice Brandeis. Doesn't the Court realize that placing such decisions on constitutional grounds projects it into details as to which it has no real competence and also precipitates a flood of habeas corpus applications from prisoners who will suddenly discover that not merely convictions after trial but pleas of guilty were procured by someone having talked to them after they had been indicted and been assigned counsel? And why is Stewart now rushing so hard to join the angels?"

At the bottom of his letter, Friendly wrote in, "Apparently the guiding principle now is 'Don't decide on anything *but* constitutional ground if such a ground exists.' "[80]

A 1963 Term case that should also be mentioned is *Hamilton v. Alabama,*[81] where the Court summarily reversed a contempt conviction of a black witness who refused to answer questions when she was addressed as "Mary," rather than "Miss Hamilton," the customary way white witnesses were addressed. To Warren such a case presented no problem, since it involved simple respect for human dignity, to which all regardless of race were entitled.

The day after the decision, Frankfurter wrote Harlan (who, with Clark and White, had voted to deny certiorari), "I am glad that there were three of you who thought Miss Hamilton's case was a silly case to take on certiorari, but once it was taken, I think I would have been against you on the merits. That is because I think the American habit of calling people by their first names when you hardly know a person is indignity and indefensible."

Frankfurter also included a "witticism" that he told Harlan to "tell . . . to Potter." "The wittiest condemnation of the practice is a witticism I heard the other day. Two men were talking about a third and one of the two mentioned the third by his first name. The first asked, 'Do you know Jim well?' The second fellow replied, 'I know him so well I even know his last name.' "[82]

Of the other noncriminal cases during the 1963 Term, a word should be said about *Banco Nacional de Cuba v. Sabbatino*,[83] before we give more detailed consideration to *New York Times Co. v. Sullivan*.[84] Banco Nacional, an instrumentality of the Cuban government, sued to recover payment for sugar sold by a Cuban company to an American buyer. The Cuban company's assets had been expropriated by the Cuban government because its stock was owned by U.S. residents. Banco Nacional relied upon the so-called "act of state" doctrine, which precludes the courts from inquiring into the validity of the public acts committed by a foreign country within its own territory. The lower court held that that doctrine was inapplicable when the questioned foreign act was in violation of international law. Finding the Cuban expropriation an invalid confiscation of American property, the court ruled that it did not give the plaintiff good title to the money owed for the sugar. All the Brethren except Stewart and White voted to grant certiorari.

During the oral argument on October 22, 1963, the Deputy Attorney General indicated that the Court was free to modify the act of state doctrine, though he urged it not to do so in this case. At the conference on October 25, 1963, Warren began his discussion by saying he was "with the Government in large part." The Chief said that he recognized the act-of-state doctrine "as positive law. But I don't agree that, whenever they say we shouldn't interfere, we can't." He would follow it "only to the extent that the Government's representation of embarrassment is a weighty factor."

Warren's restrained approach to the act of state doctrine did not commend itself to the others, who favored a rule of complete abnegation on the legality of foreign governments' acts within their own territories. The Chief yielded and went along with the majority. When

Harlan announced the opinion of the Court on March 23, 1964, that the validity of the Cuban expropriation decree could not be inquired into by the courts, only White delivered a dissent.

Apart from the Reapportionment Cases, the most important case decided during the 1963 Term was *New York Times Co. v. Sullivan*.[85] The key role in it was played, not by Warren, but by Brennan, though the Chief was, as always, supportive of Brennan's efforts. The case arose out of a libel action by the Montgomery, Alabama, police commissioner against four blacks and against the *New York Times*. The complaint alleged that Sullivan had been libeled by statements in a full-page advertisement that described alleged violations of black rights by the Montgomery police. The text appeared over the names of sixty-four persons, many widely known, and then there appeared the names of the four defendants, as individual Southern clergymen. Because the advertisement was placed by a responsible person, was signed by well-known persons, and seemed accurate, the *Times* published it without confirming its accuracy. It contained inaccuracies that would have been revealed by a check of the paper's own news files.

The state courts had ruled that the advertisement was libelous per se and had upheld a verdict in Sullivan's favor of half a million dollars. According to a federal judge, "The Supreme Court of the United States was confronted by a somewhat baffling problem insofar as the facts of the case were concerned. The jury had rendered a grotesquely huge verdict for $500,000, although there was no contention that the plaintiff had suffered any pecuniary loss. . . . If the verdict had stood, it does not seem unreasonable to suggest that there would have been a miscarriage of justice."[86] At the oral argument on January 6, 1964, counsel for the *Times* based his argument for reversal on the broadest possible ground. He characterized the Alabama judgment as a "hazard to the freedom of the press in a dimension not confronted since the early days of the Republic." When Brennan asked him whether the First Amendment gave the published article absolute protection, he replied that it did. In effect, counsel for the *Times* was asserting the absolutist view of the First Amendment that had been urged for years by Black and Douglas—that *all* libel suits by public officials based on statements concerning their official conduct were barred by the First Amendment.

Warren, Black, Douglas, Clark, Harlan, and Brennan voted to grant certiorari. At the January 10, 1964, conference the Chief Justice urged reversal, but not on the broad constitutional ground argued by counsel for the *Times*. Warren said he "would not go on the First Amendment giving complete immunity to the *Times*." Instead, he stressed that, "in this area of speech and press, where criticism is of official conduct, we ought to require a high degree of certainty that this involved the official. We must look more carefully to see if it was directed at the official or was in the area of fair comment." Here, Warren thought, the references to the police were really not libelous. Thus, the advertisement charged that the Montgomery police had "ringed" a black college campus. To the Chief, " 'ringed' the place with police is not libelous. It's really synonymous with deployment, which actually occurred." Warren concluded that a "test of fair comment might be forged" and the case should be decided under it.

Most of the others agreed, with even Douglas stating, "In the area of public affairs, the doctrine of fair comment is available to protect the *Times* and the other petitioners." Black, however, strongly differed. "If libel laws are valid when the press criticizes official conduct," he declared, "I'd find it hard to set this aside." But of course Black rejected *all* libel actions in such cases, saying, "If there's anything clear to me it is that in public affairs it was intended to foreclose any kind of proceedings which would deter full and open discussion. At least in the area of public affairs, the First Amendment permits any type of discussion, including false."

The case against the Black position was stated by Harlan. "The First Amendment," he maintained, "does not outlaw state libel laws in this field of public discussion." Instead, Harlan felt, the competing interests at stake must be balanced against each other. "This case presents a classic illustration of a First Amendment problem where the public interest in discussion has to be accommodated with the private right not to be defamed."

Harlan asserted that "we have to set down some constitutional standards to which state libel actions are subject." He urged adoption of two federal rules: "1) a high standard of proof across the board on all elements of the action; 2) while punitive damages are not constitutionally outlawed, they can't be assessed without proof of actual malice."

Clark agreed that the Court should "separate in matter of proof private libels from public affairs and put a much heavier burden on what it takes to tie something to a public official." Brennan summed up the basis on which the conference voted to reverse the verdict in Sullivan's favor. This was that the First Amendment should be interpreted to require "clear and convincing evidence" of every element of a cause of action for libel brought by a public official against a critic of his official conduct. In this case, evidence meeting this standard was lacking on such key elements as the defamatory nature of the advertisement and the "connection" between it and Sullivan. "None of these charges," Brennan asserted, "amount to this and we could reverse just on the ground this wasn't defamation."

The Chief Justice assigned the case to Brennan. In preparing his opinion the Justice did not confine himself to the narrow ground voted by the conference. The first draft of Brennan's opinion was based upon the rule, followed in a minority of states, that a libel action by a public official against a critic of his official conduct could not be sustained without a showing that the critic's statement was not merely false and defamatory, but was made with "actual malice." Under the Brennan draft, this rule was made a constitutional requirement. The draft then applied the "clear and convincing evidence" rationale stated by Brennan at the conference and held that such evidence was lacking with respect to the newly required element of malice, as well as the elements of defamation and "connection." The draft said nothing about whether the plaintiff could be given a new trial at which he might attempt to adduce the missing evidence.

The first Brennan draft was not circulated. It was revised in the Justice's chambers and the first circulated draft was sent around on February 6, 1964. It differed from the uncirculated draft by confining itself to the rule requiring malice and making no reference at all to the elements of defamation or connection that had been emphasized at the conference. The draft asserted that a reversal was required in any event because the state courts had not applied the rule requiring actual malice. Then, for the first time, it referred to the new-trial problem saying, "We think, moreover, that a new trial under the correct rule would not be warranted in this case since the evidence submitted was insufficient to establish actual malice." The draft then analyzed the evidence to demonstrate that insufficiency. The reference to "the evidence submitted" was designed to sidestep the critical question whether a new trial would still be barred if the plaintiff offered to submit additional evidence.

A second circulated draft was sent around by Brennan on February 17. The third print of Brennan's opinion retained the prior draft's treatment of the new-trial question, but differed from it because it found the evidence to be constitutionally insufficient not only on malice, but also on the connection between the advertisement and Sullivan. The prior draft had also been revised stylistically, which gave the opinion substantially its final form.

Notes of agreement with the Brennan draft were received on February 13 from the Chief Justice, on February 21 from White, and on February 28 from Clark. On February 25, however, Goldberg circulated a separate draft, in which he concurred "in the Court's opinion and judgment" but went on to say that a libel judgment based on criticism of a public official for his official conduct could not constitutionally be justified even *with* a showing of actual malice.

On February 26, Black also circulated a draft concurring in the judgment on the same ground as Goldberg. Black likewise sent Brennan a note: "You know of course that despite my position and what I write, I think you are doing a wonderful job in the *Times* case and however it finally comes out it is bound to be a very long step toward preserving the right to communicate ideas." Douglas immediately joined the Black opinion.

There were now three Justices who did not agree fully with the Brennan opinion. If that opinion was to have a majority, it could not lose more than one vote from the remaining Justices—Harlan and Stewart. The reaction of Harlan, in particular, was awaited with some anxiety by those who had joined Brennan.

A February 26 letter from Harlan showed the anxiety to have been justified. Harlan expressed agreement with Parts I and II of the opinion, which established the rule requiring a showing of malice. He did, however, suggest a footnote (added as footnote 23 of the final opinion) explicitly leaving open the question of how far down into the ranks of government employees the "public official" designation would extend for purposes of the decision's application.

"While I agree," Harlan's letter went on, "that there should not be a new trial, I would not feel able to join Part III of your opinion as presently written without writing something in addition by way of elaboration." Harlan offered a proposed revision of Part III that, if adopted by Brennan, would avoid such a separate opinion.

The Harlan revision dealt specifically with the question "whether we should leave the way open for a new trial or should terminate this litigation." It urged the latter course, relying on 28 U.S.C. § 2106, which authorizes a federal appellate court to "direct the entry of such appropriate judgment, decree, or order . . . as may be just under the circumstances." Harlan analyzed the evidence presented and found it insufficient to show malice or connection. His draft then stated that no new trial would be warranted "on the basis that respondent would be afforded an opportunity to adduce further and sufficient evidence."

The reasons given by Harlan were, as to the requirement of connection between the advertisement and Sullivan, that this had been a hotly contested issue at the trial and "we may reasonably assume therefore that he had no evidence of different and more substantial quality to offer," and, as to the malice requirement, that Alabama law required evidence of malice to establish punitive damages, and Sullivan accordingly had tried to prove malice, and had failed. Thus, the draft concluded, "the reasons favoring a retrial are unreal," and none could be had.

Though Brennan was not satisfied that Harlan's approach was preferable, he thought that he needed the support of the Justice and those who might follow him. Hence the Harlan revision was substantially incorporated in Part III of the fourth print of Brennan's opinion, which was circulated on February 28.

However, it was soon realized that there were major difficulties in the Harlan approach. Section 2106 of the Judicial Code had never been applied to a case from a state court, and its application to prevent the Alabama courts from allowing a new trial might exceed the constitutional limits of the Supreme Court's appellate jurisdiction. This was pointed out in a note from Black to Brennan. "I do not see," wrote the Alabaman "how John could possibly adhere to that position on more mature reflection. I can think of few things that would more violently clash with his ideas of 'federalism'. . . . Construing the statute as authorizing our Court to *overrule* state laws as to a right to a new trial would undoubtedly raise constitutional questions, some of which as I recall were discussed in the famous *cause célèbre, Cohens v. Virginia.*" [87]

Black repeated his criticism of the Harlan approach in another note. "I do think, however," Black also wrote, "that in getting him to agree to your opinion as it is you have done a great service to the freedoms of the First Amendment. For your opinion I believe will inevitably lead to a later holding that people have complete immunity from having to pay damages for criticism of Government or its officials in the performance of their public duties."

Brennan also questioned the Harlan draft's reliance on the absence of any evidence showing that Sullivan, as police commissioner, had actually participated in the alleged police misconduct. Harlan's draft had said that the belief of Sullivan's witnesses that the advertisement referred to him was based, "not on any evidence that he had in fact done so"—i.e., ordered or approved the police conduct, "but solely on the unsupported assumption" that he had.

Brennan asked Harlan what would happen if Sullivan now offered evidence to support the assumption. What if he produced witnesses to testify that Sullivan had participated personally and actively in the police activity, and that the witnesses had known this and because of such knowledge had associated the advertisement's allegations with Sullivan? Harlan conceded that, if such evidence was offered, he did not see how the state could be precluded from granting a new trial.

Because of the defects noted by Brennan, Harlan now withdrew his draft's proposal to expressly prohibit a new trial. In its place, he put forward an entirely different approach. Harlan now relied on the fact that, as Brennan had shown, a new trial upon additional evidence could not be absolutely prohibited. He also pointed out that reversal was required in any event because the Alabama courts had not applied the rule requiring actual malice. Therefore, Harlan said, there was no reason for the Court to concern itself at all with the sufficiency of the evidence submitted. In other words, Harlan now proposed that virtually all of Part II of the Brennan draft should be discarded. Under his approach, the opinion would merely propound the rule requiring a showing of malice, reverse for failure to apply the rule, and leave for another day all questions of how the rule should be applied to specific evidence.

Later the same day, Brennan wrote Harlan rejecting his new proposal. "I think," the Brennan letter stated, "we should retain the analysis of the constitutional insufficiency of the proofs of actual malice and connection even if this has the effect of 'chilling' the possibility of a new trial. I think we are justified in doing this on two counts: (a) the profession should be apprised now that we are going to examine evidence in this area as we have in others, and (b) because the analysis of the proofs to demonstrate their insufficiency will be both illustrative of how we do this and also informative to the parties in this case of a void in the proofs that would have to be filled if a new trial is had."

Brennan did, however, decide to eliminate from his opinion the explicit statements barring a new trial, and to say instead only that the proof presented was constitutionally insufficient. He would thus avoid any reference to the possibility of additional evidence being presented in a subsequent proceeding.

On the next day, March 3, Brennan circulated a fifth print of his opinion, which embodied this approach. Brennan explained this new draft in a March 3 *Memorandum to the Conference*. "My last circulation #4," it began, "stated at three places that, exercising our power under 28 U.S.C. § 2106—to require such further proceedings to be had as may be just under the circumstances—the respondent Sullivan was not to have a new trial. . . . All of these references have been deleted in the attached circulation." The reason given was that, "John Harlan and I have concluded after much discussion and thought that, even assuming constitutional power to deny a state the right to apply its new trial rules, it would not be wise to use this case as a vehicle for saying so for the first time." [88]

In essence, the new Brennan draft returned to his third print, except for the omission of any express reference to the possibility of a new trial. But Harlan indicated that he would not go along fully with the new draft. In his March 3 memo, Brennan informed the Brethren, "John also has misgivings whether the opinion should include any discussion of the sufficiency of the evidence. . . . He therefore has advised me that he is filing a short separate memorandum joining the opinion except for its discussion of the evidence."

On March 7, Harlan circulated the separate opinion. It stated, "that the Court's responsibility in cases of this kind does not end with the establishment of constitutional ground rules but includes also an obligation to scrutinize the record to ensure that such rules have not been defeated in the name of a jury verdict not supported by evidence of the convincing clarity which, with the Court, I believe the Constitution demands in this area."

"Nevertheless," Harlan went on, "I do not consider it appropriate for the Court to examine the constitutional sufficiency of the evidence at this stage, since the judgments stand already reversed on other grounds."

The Harlan opinion concluded by asserting, "The Court's anticipatory assessment of the evidence is an unprecedented step which in my opinion does disservice in the long run to the basic constitutional concerns out of which this litigation arose."[89]

In his March 3 memo, Brennan had rejected this Harlan approach, saying, "I am convinced, however, that the analysis of the evidence to show its insufficiency under the constitutional rule we lay down is essential to the opinion. Since Sullivan did undertake to prove actual malice as a predicate for punitive damages, we of necessity must demonstrate the insufficiency of his evidence under the constitutional test of actual malice."

"Moreover," the Brennan memo stated, "if Alabama should give Sullivan a new trial the parties should know that the evidence in this record will not support a judgment—that there is a large void to be filled. If we said nothing and we later overturned another judgment entered on this record, we might be rightly accused of having second thoughts because of the implication from our silence here that the application of the valid rule to this evidence would be sustained."

The question now was whether anyone would agree with Harlan. Warren and Stewart did not. Stewart sent Brennan a note of agreement with his opinion on March 3. The Chief Justice sent a written note soon thereafter: "I agree with you that III must remain in the opinion if I and II are to have any meaning." Warren wrote that, "Otherwise we will merely be going through a meaningless exercise. The case would be remanded, another improvisation would be devised and it would be back to us in a more difficult posture." It was, however, reported that Clark, who had agreed with Brennan's opinion a few days earlier, was now seriously attracted to the Harlan point of view. It was also feared that White might be wavering from his earlier agreement.

At this point, there was real doubt whether the entire Brennan opinion could command a majority. With the case in this posture, various suggestions were made for lining up a "Court" for the Brennan opinion by enlisting support from among the three Justices—Black, Douglas, and Goldberg—who disagreed with it only in thinking that it did not go far enough. Douglas, in a March 3 note, pointed out that he agreed with everything in the Brennan opinion except that portion of Part III stating that liability could constitutionally exist where actual malice was shown. Douglas offered to note his concurrence with Part III's holding that, the malice requirement having been established, the evidence presented was constitutionally insufficient. Under Douglas' proposal, there would be a majority for Part III, though a different one from that backing Part II. Goldberg made essentially the same proposal, suggesting that the opinion should note that all nine Justices agreed with Parts I and II up to the statement that liability could exist if malice was shown, that all Justices except Black, Douglas, and Goldberg agreed with that statement, and that all except Harlan and Clark agreed with the analysis of the evidence in Part III.

Black strongly disapproved of such a hybrid approach. He sent Brennan a pencilled note, "I think that under the definition you give malice the evidence (so far as I have read it) would prove malice." In effect, Black was saying that, if a finding of malice was sufficient to warrant liability despite the First Amendment, then in his view plaintiff's evidence here was sufficient to prove malice. Black rejected the Douglas–Goldberg approach. According to his note, "It will add to the idea which will likely be advanced that no one can actually tell what is decided."

On March 4, Brennan visited Clark to discuss the case, and was handed an uncirculated copy of a proposed Clark opinion. This opinion stated that Clark was joining "my Brother Harlan" in the view that "the question of the sufficiency of the evidence is not one for this Court at this stage of the proceeding." Clark said that, "Having demolished respondent's theory of the case, it appears to me that we should not go further."

The Clark draft went on to assert, "This action on the part of the Court is a departure from a long established—and, I dare say, never deviating—rule. While it may well be that the evidence of malice or reckless regard for truth is insufficient, still having been offered under the condemned standard the Court should not now measure the old record by a new standard not available at the trial here under scrutiny. In so doing it forecasts, for all practical purposes, the result of a new trial and thereby forecloses respondent's right to have a jury initially pass upon it. I would leave the state courts free to first determine whether the evidence on a retrial is sufficient."

The opinion that Clark showed to Brennan concluded as follows: "By prejudging the factual basis of the case the Court places an insurmountable task on respondent on remand. In so doing it departs from this Court's appellate character and thereby invades the province of Alabama's courts to initially pass upon the facts. And, unfortunately, by thus impuning [sic] the integrity of our dual federalism the Court fails to reflect that fairness which has always been the hallmark of our judicial processes."[90]

With Clark's vote thus apparently lost, Brennan and those who had joined his opinion agreed to adopt the hybrid approach suggested by Douglas and Goldberg. Douglas confirmed that he was still amenable to such an approach. He sent Brennan a note authorizing him to insert in his opinion the statement, "Mr. Justice Douglas, while believing that the evidence in question is constitutionally inadmissible because presence or absence of malice is immaterial, would agree that even by the lesser standard prescribed by this opinion the evidence is deficient." To defend the Brennan opinion's discussion of the evidence, a lengthy footnote attacking the Harlan–Clark view was prepared in Brennan's chambers.

In the meantime, White had come forward and suggested a different basis for justifying the review of the evidence. White's theory was that the Alabama court's failure to instruct that malice was required for an award of general damages did not itself warrant a reversal, since the verdict might have consisted wholly of punitive damages, for which malice *was* required under Alabama law. Therefore, White contended, the rule of law applied below was not *necessarily* erroneous in its failure to require a finding of malice. The evidence must consequently be reviewed to determine whether a justified finding of malice may have underlain the verdict.

White's approach appeared untenable to Brennan. In his view, the mere possibility of the verdict's having included an award of general damages, for which malice was *not* required, compelled the reversal. The White approach was, nevertheless, substantially incorporated in a sixth print of the Brennan opinion, circulated on March 4, in order to satisfy White and possibly attract Harlan. But Harlan adhered to his separate concurrence. The decision was now apparently settled—with the Douglas–Goldberg compromise serving as its basis.

The next morning, however, Clark, who only the afternoon before had unexpectedly produced his separate opinion, just as suddenly notified Brennan that he had decided to withdraw it. He said that he would join the Brennan opinion and go along with its analysis of the evidence if the justification for that analysis was expressed in terms of "effective judicial administration." Clark's suggestion was promptly incorporated in the seventh and final print of the Brennan opinion, circulated that afternoon: "Since respondent may seek a new trial, we deem that considerations of effective judicial administration require us to review the evidence in the present record to determine whether it could constitutionally support a judgment for respondent."[91]

The Chief Justice and White agreed to this. So also did Stewart, even though he said that, in his view, the entire battle had amounted only to quibbling. At the Conference on March 6, the opinion was approved for announcement the following Monday, with five votes behind it and only Harlan dissenting from Part III.

On Sunday evening, March 8, Harlan telephoned Brennan to tell him that he was withdrawing his separate opinion and joining Brennan's. Harlan notified the others of this in a letter sent March 9, just before the Brennan opinion was announced as the opinion of the Court.

For all the strain imposed by his dual role as Chief Justice and Chairman of the Warren Commission, the 1963 Term was essentially a satisfying one for Warren. He had seen his view prevail in the Reapportionment Cases and had helped prevent what he considered an ill-considered decision in the Sit-In Cases. Within the Court, the term saw the continued dominance of the Chief and his supporters. On no case of importance was Warren on the losing side. Just as important was the virtual elimination of personal friction among the Brethren. Gone was the backbiting and internal tension that had been so much a part of Court life a few years earlier. It is true that there was now coolness between Black and Douglas. But it was mild compared to the ill will that had existed between the polar blocs in Frankfurter's day.

Outside the Marble Palace, however, the hostility toward Warren and the Court continued—though even its intensity was abating. A *New York Times* article contrasted what it called the Chief Justice's "extraordinary reputation" abroad with the fact that, in his own country, he was a figure of controversy. The John Birch Society continued to sell "Warren Impeachment Packets" for one dollar, J. Edgar Hoover was reported to have called Warren and the Brethren "bleeding hearts," and former Justice Whittaker charged in an American Bar Association address that the Court was usurping the right of local self-government by its rulings expanding federal power.[92]

For the first time since Warren had become Chief Justice, the Court itself became a major issue in a presidential campaign. In a series of speeches after he had received the Republican nomination, Senator Barry Goldwater attacked the Warren Court as the governmental branch "least faithful to the constitutional tradition of limited government." He accused the Justices of sacrificing law and order "just to give criminals a sporting chance to go free" and charged that they were trying to achieve social goals through "illegal" means. The Republican nominee pledged to overturn the Court's criminal law decisions, saying that he would appoint as Justices only "seasoned men who will support the Constitution."[93]

During the summer following the 1963 Term, Congress passed a pay raise for federal judges of $7,500, but limited the Supreme Court Justices' increase to $4,500.[94] Well might a *New York Times* editorial characterize the difference as a "petty expression of Congressional resentment."[95]

13.

1964 TERM: TELEVISION, CIVIL RIGHTS, AND PRIVACY

After Fred W. Friendly had been appointed President of C.B.S. News, he met Earl Warren at a 1964 cocktail party. The Chief Justice wished Friendly well in his new job. In thanking the Chief, Friendly said he hoped he would still head C.B.S. News when they had television cameras on the moon and on the floor of the Supreme Court. Warren responded with a smile, "Good luck! You will have more luck with the former than the latter."[1]

Later that year, the Chief Justice turned down a C.B.S. request to televise the Supreme Court arguments in the Civil Rights Cases. Warren wrote that "the Court has had an inflexible rule to the effect that it will not permit photographs or broadcasting from the courtroom when it is in session." The Chief was sure that the Court "has no intention of changing that rule."[2]

Warren believed even more strongly that television had no legitimate place in a criminal trial. To allow televising of criminal proceedings, he declared in an unissued draft dissent in the 1965 case of *Estes v. Texas,*[3] means "allowing the courtroom to become a public spectacle and source of entertainment." Estes was a notorious swindler, whose trial and conviction in a Texas court was a national *cause célèbre.* Over Estes' objection, portions of the trial proceedings were televised. In the courtroom, twelve cameramen jostled for position, and bright lights and a tangle of wires and equipment, in *Time's* phrase, "turned the courtroom into a broadcast studio."[4] Despite this the Texas courts rejected Estes' claim that he was deprived of due process.

The Brethren were narrowly divided on whether to grant certiorari, with Warren, Douglas, Harlan, and Brennan voting to grant and the others to deny. They were as closely split throughout their consideration of the merits, though the lineup was not the same as on the cert vote. The April 2, 1965, conference after the oral argument began with a strong statement by the Chief Justice. "I think," he declared, "this violates due process. To stage a trial this way violates the decorum of the courtroom, and TV is not entitled to special treatment." Warren rejected any First Amendment claim the other way, saying he could "see no violation of [freedom of] speech or press. They may be in the courtroom, like the press, only as part of the public. The way this is set up bears on the question of fair trial." The Chief went far toward excluding television in all circumstances. "Here," he noted, "there was objection. But, even with the consent of the accused and his lawyers, I'd be against it."

Warren was supported by Douglas, Harlan, and Goldberg. "The constitutional standard," Douglas pointed out, "is a fair trial. Trial in a mob scene is not a fair trial." Here, Douglas referred to the 1936 case of *Brown v. Mississippi*,[5] where the Court had reversed convictions because of mob violence. He said, "that was a judgment not hinged to any particular specific." Douglas seconded the Chief in his objection to televised trials. "A trial," he observed, "is not a spectacle, whether he objected or not. This is the modern farce—putting the courtroom into a modern theatrical production."

Harlan said that the case "comes down to the concept of what is the right to a public trial. It doesn't mean for me that the public has the right to a public performance. This goes more deeply into the judicial process than just the right of the defendant." Goldberg asserted that "the shambles deprived defendant of a fair trial. In the present state of the art, this was an obtrusive intervention of the outside into this trial."

Clark, Stewart, and White opposed a flat ban on television in the courtroom. Clark stressed that the trial judge's finding that no prejudice had been shown was not clearly erroneous. The Texan had tried to avoid the constitutional issue by moving to dismiss the case as one in which cert had been improvidently granted. In a later memorandum, Clark noted, "not mustering any other votes for this disposition I then voted to affirm on the narrow basis of the facts, *i.e.*, the pre-trial televising of September 23–24 indicated no prejudice; the trial on the merits in October was telecast piecemeal—only picture, for the most part, without sound; the jury was sequestered and no prejudice was shown."[6]

Brennan was not as certain in his presentation. "What," he asked, "is the concept of a fair trial? Is there a court concept independent of the individual?" He pointed out that "technology may bring this into line within the courtroom." He then referred to the trial "as theatre or spectacle that's been part of our heritage," as well as to a "legislative inquisition," and asked about them, in light of this case. Brennan stressed that "this was no sham. The jury was sequestered. There's no suggestion that the witnesses, the judge, or others were affected in a way to hurt." Brennan conceded that, in such a case, "the totality [of circumstances] might knock it down," but said that was not the case here.

Black, who had spoken after Warren, indicated even greater doubt. As a starting point, he said, "I'm against television in courts. But this is a new thing that's working itself out." Black conceded that the case presented difficulties for his normal constitutional approach. "For me," he affirmed, "the test is, 'what is in the Constitution on which I can grasp as a handle?' On lawyers, confrontation, etc., I have no problem. I can't do this on how bad it is short of the *Brown* [*v. Mississippi*] test." Black concluded that "the case for me comes down to only a slight advance over what we've had before." He also noted that, "some day the technology may improve so as not to disturb the actual trial." But, even with the disturbance involved in Estes' trial, Black ultimately came down on the side of affirmance.

The *Estes* vote was for affirmance by a bare majority consisting of Black, Clark, Stewart, Brennan, and White. Black, as senior majority Justice, assigned the case to Stewart. A draft opinion of the Court was circulated on May 13. Except for its beginning and end, this draft was essentially like the dissent that Stewart eventually issued.

"In this case," Stewart's draft opinion of the Court began, "we deal with the claim that the introduction of newspaper photographers and television cameras into a state criminal trial, over the defendant's objection, is a violation of the Fourteenth Amendment. Limiting our decision to the specific record in this case, we reject that claim."

The Stewart draft found that, "On the record of this case, however, we cannot say that any violation of the Constitution occurred." It pointed (much as Stewart's final dissent does) to the facts that showed there was nothing to indicate that the conduct of anyone in the courtroom was influenced by the television. It then concluded with the following:

"We are thus presented with virtually an abstract question. We are asked to pronounce that the United States Constitution prohibits all television cameras and all still cameras from every courtroom in every State whenever a criminal trial is in progress. We are asked to enshrine Canon 35 of the American Bar Association into the Fourteenth Amendment, denying to the States or to individual trial judges any discretion whatever to conduct trials with cameras present, no matter how unobtrusive the cameras may be. We are asked to hold that it is impossible to have a constitutional trial where any part of the proceedings is televised or recorded on film. We are asked to hold that the Constitution absolutely bars television and cameras from every criminal courtroom, even if they have no impact upon the jury, no effect upon any witness, and no influence upon the conduct of the judge.

"However strong our personal views on the subject may be, we cannot find that requirement in the federal Constitution. The judgment is *Affirmed*."

Warren felt so strongly about the impact of television on courtroom dignity that, on May 21, he circulated a thirty-four page draft dissent, which Douglas quickly joined. Though similar in many ways to the concurring opinion that the Chief eventually put out in the case, there were some interesting passages in the draft that were never published. The draft dissent began:

The Court today has not faced up to the facts of this case and has given an unwarranted impression that the presence of television in no way affected the conduct of this criminal proceeding. No fair appraisal of the facts will support this conclusion. Nevertheless, by closing its eyes to the clear import of this record and accepting the trial judge's characterization of the trial, *ante,* pp. 6–8, the Court concludes 'there is no indication anywhere in the record of any disturbance whatever of the judicial proceedings,' *ante,* p. 10, and then proceeds to hold that this is neither the time nor the place to make a definitive appraisal of television in the courtroom. In these circumstances it is easy, of course, to arrive at some of the conclusions reached by the Court, but I do not believe that this approach should be unchallenged. In cases concerning rights under the Due Process Clause, it is this Court's duty to make an independent examination of the record in each case. *E.g., Watts v. Indiana,* 338 U.S. 49, 51; *Norris v. Alabama,* 294 U.S. 587, 590. Our Constitution insures for every criminal defendant a fair and impartial forum for the determination of the charges against him. Because today's decision— allowing the courtroom to become a public spectacle and source of entertainment—ignores this guarantee, I must dissent.

There then followed Parts I–III essentially as they are contained in Warren's *Estes* concurrence. In Part III of the concurrence, Warren refers to the kinds of commercials that were inserted when the trial proceedings were televised—"commercials for soft drinks, soups, eyedrops and seatcovers." The draft dissent went on to assert, "The commercials could just as easily have been for purgatives, cures for halitosis, detergents or beer."

In supporting his conclusion, Warren's draft dissent relied not only upon the list of American authorities cited in his concurrence, but also upon the unanimous condemnation of televising court proceedings "in England," with an appropriate footnote reference to *Halsbury's Laws of England.* Presumably one of the others objected to the Anglophile reference, and it was deleted from Warren's concurring opinion.

The draft dissent, like Warren's *Estes* concurrence, referred, in Part IV, to the fact that court proceedings are proper subjects for press coverage, making the point with the same quote from the 1947 case of *Craig v. Harney.*[7] Warren's draft, however, went on to conclude as follows:

But, '[t]he right to speak and publish does not carry with it the unrestrained right to gather information.' *Zemel v. Rusk,* 380 U.S.—. The television industry, like the other communications media, is free to send representatives to trials, and to report on those trials to its viewers. However, the right of the medium to attend trials is no greater than the right of other members of the public. Representatives of the communications media must conduct themselves with propriety if they desire to attend court functions. They are not free to bring to the courtroom whatever equipment serves their purpose. Just as an ordinary citizen might be told by the trial judge to refrain from using field glasses or a movie picture camera because of the distraction he is causing, representatives of press and broadcasting industries are subject to reasonable limitations when they attend court. The exclusion of television cameras is not only a reasonable limitation, but it is a necessary requirement for the proper conduct of judicial proceedings.

I would reverse.

On May 22, the day after Warren sent around his draft dissent, Goldberg circulated his own four-page dissent. "It is clear to me from the undisputed facts revealed by the record," the Goldberg draft declared, "that a calm judicial atmosphere was lacking at the trial of this case and that consequently the defendant was denied the fair trial guaranteed to him by the Constitution. I arrive at this conclusion from a consideration of the totality of the circumstances surrounding the trial."

Goldberg summarized the circumstances that led him to his conclusion and stated, "The potential for prejudice inherent in all the circumstances of this case was such that I am convinced that petitioner was denied that fair trial conducted with dignity in a calm and solemn judicial atmosphere which the Constitution guarantees him. The constitutional safegaurd [sic] of a fair trial protects not only against actual prejudice, but also against conduct that unduly tempts such prejudice. . . . In my view the manner in which petitioner's trial was conducted was not consistent with the standards of due process guaranteed him by the Constitution, and I would therefore reverse the judgment of the Supreme Court of Texas."

Harlan had also sent around a draft dissent on May 19. The draft was similar to the *Estes* concurrence that Harlan ultimately issued, except for the statement at the end, "I would reverse this conviction for that reason," instead of the statement of concurrence at the beginning and end of the opinion that Harlan actually issued.

Once again, however, the bare majority for affirmance in *Estes* did not hold and, once again, it was Clark who made the crucial shift to the Warren position. That the Chief himself played a key part in the Texan's switch cannot be doubted. As seen, Warren felt strongly about the baneful effect of television on court proceedings, and this was just the sort of thing he would talk over with Clark on their morning walks part of the way to the Court building.

On May 25, Clark circulated a *Memorandum to the Conference*[8] telling of his change in position. "After circulation of the opinions and dissents, along with my interim study," Clark informed the Brethren, "I became disturbed at what could result from our approval of this emasculation by TV of the trial of a case. My doubts increased as I envisioned use of the unfortunate format followed here in other trials which would not only jeopardize the fairness of them but would broadcast a bad image to the public of the judicial process."

The Clark memo stressed that the Sixth Amendment right to a public trial was granted only to the accused. "Nowhere does the Constitution say that the attendance of the public is mandatory or that that of the news media is required. The Founders spoke only of the benefit that must be accorded the accused. The presence of the public was made permissible so that Star Chamber methods might not result and the accused be unfairly condemned. It is even more certain that the news media were not in the mind of the Founders because there were few newspapers then and, of course, no radio or television." Clark denied "that First Amendment freedoms grant the news media an absolute 'right' to be present and to report trial proceedings."

"It appears to me," Clark's memo stated, "that the perils to a fair trial far outweigh the benefits that might accrue in the televising of the proceedings." Clark then enumerated the factors that made him conclude "simply that such an operation, at least in its present state, presents too many hazards to a fair trial." Clark's list is the most complete statement by a Supreme Court Justice of the undesirable elements that would be introduced by televising of trials and, for that reason, deserves quotation in full:

1. The quality of the testimony would be impaired because of the confusion of the witness caused by the knowledge of being televised; accuracy would be jeopardized; memories would fail because of stage fright; self-consciousness would be uppermost because of the knowledge that millions were watching every expression and gesture; and witnesses would evade appearance in order to avoid the attendant embarrassment and torture.

2. The intermittent selection by the telecaster of the parts of testimony to be telecast would not portray a fair image of the trial; a distorted picture of the case would result and our present problem in newspaper reporting

would be compounded. The entire proceedings could not be telecast from a profitable commercial standpoint; telecasting is expensive, particularly outside of the studio and video tape together with the clipping of it to show only the most publicly appealing parts of the trial would result.

3. The accused is placed in a helplessly precarious position. He unwillingly, despite his constitutional protections, becomes a victim of the continual glare of the close range lens of the camera revealing his most intimate and personal sensibilities. Such a psychological torture is reminiscent of the third degree. In addition, the accused must risk being mugged, lip read and otherwise overheard when in consultation over his defense with his lawyer at the counsel table.

4. The camera is an all powerful weapon. It may leave, intentionally or not, a distorted impression of the facts with consequent prejudgment of the witness that may be most damaging to the defense.

5. Many states do not sequester the juries in all felony cases and the additional hazard of jury misconduct in viewing the telecast would be present.

6. Witnesses placed under the rule would be able to view the telecast and contrary to the rule would be advantaged by the testimony of previous witnesses.

7. In case of a new trial or reversal being granted it would be impossible to secure a jury that had not witnessed the previous trial thus placing the fairness of the second trial in jeopardy.

8. Telecasting will lead inevitably to discrimination because the media will televise only the horrendous trials. As a result only the most sordid crimes will be telecast or possibly those that appeal to the prurient interest. This will but accumulate a wrongful store of public information as to the courts.

9. The judge and the jury's attention—as well as that of the lawyers—will be distracted from the serious work of the trial. In this case the court was interrupted time and time again on account of the presence of the television and radio media.

10. Commercials would degrade the judicial process, making the court a "prop" for some product of the sponsor and forcing the parties to become its actors and raise attendant connotations of some connection between the trial participants and the sponsor.

Two days later Clark circulated his formal opinion, which was headed, "MR. JUSTICE CLARK, reversing." This sixteen-page draft was almost the same as the opinion of the Court which he announced on June 7. The biggest difference was the statement in the draft at the beginning of Part VII, "The facts in this case demonstrate clearly the necessity for the adoption of a *per se* rule" (under which televising a trial would automatically violate due process)—a statement substantially watered down in the final opinion. The draft contained other passages that supported the statement of a per se rule, such as the following: "The introduction of television into petitioner's trial constituted a violation of due process regardless of whether there was a showing of isolatable prejudice." (omitted from the *Estes* opinion); "Such untoward circumstances are inherently bad and prejudice to the accused must be presumed." (changed, in the final opinion, to, "Such untoward circumstances as were found in those cases [four cited Supreme Court decisions] are inherently bad and prejudice to the accused must be presumed"); "In light of the inherent hazards to a fair trial that are presented by television in the courtroom I would hold that its use violated petitioner's right to due process." (the draft's concluding sentence, absent in the published opinion).

The Clark draft, like his memo, expressly denied any press right to a public trial. After referring to the public trial that the Sixth Amendment guarantees an accused, the draft read, "While the state and federal courts have differed over what spectators may be excluded from a criminal trial, . . . it is clear beyond question that no language in the First Amendment grants any of the news media such a privilege." This statement was deleted from the final opinion.

Like Warren's draft dissent, the Clark draft referred to the English, as well as the American, authorities on barring televising of trials. Once again, the reference was cut out. One wonders who the Anglophobe among the Brethren might have been.

Though, as seen, Warren had written a lengthy dissent that might easily have been converted into the opinion of the new majority (created by Clark's switch), the Chief assigned the *Estes* opinion to Clark. The Texan promptly circulated a revision of his own draft as the opinion of the Court, which was then issued on June 7. On the same day, Warren issued a revision of his draft dissent as a lengthy concurrence, joined by Douglas and Goldberg. Harlan also issued his draft dissent as a concurrence.

Stewart revised his draft opinion of the Court and issued it as a dissent, joined by the other members of the former majority, Black, Brennan, and White. Stewart's draft dissent, circulated June 1, had been intended as an answer to Clark's draft opinion. As such, it began, "If, as I apprehend, the Court today holds that any televising of a state criminal trial constitutes a *per se* violation of the Fourteenth

Amendment, I cannot agree." This sentence was taken out after Clark deleted the references to a per se violation from his opinion. Stewart also inserted a paragraph on the First Amendment toward the end of his dissent. This paragraph had been absent from his draft opinion of the Court and was put in to answer Clark's rejection (albeit weaker than his draft) of the First Amendment right of the press to be present in the courtroom.

On May 24, White, joined by Brennan, had circulated a draft concurrence, which stated that Stewart's then-opinion of the Court did not preclude a future decision that television could prove such a hazard to defendant's rights that it would be violative of due process without any showing of prejudice. On June 1, after Clark's switch, they issued this as a short dissent, stressing that the new opinion of the Court prevented a flexible approach to use of cameras in the courtroom.

Brennan also issued a separate short opinion emphasizing that, because of Harlan's concurrence, only four members of the majority held that televised trials would be invalid, regardless of the circumstances. In effect, Brennan was having it both ways, joining with White to condemn the majority's inflexible approach and then denying that a majority had really voted for it. Yet it was the Brennan approach that the Court was to follow in *Chandler v. Florida*,[9] a 1981 case holding that a state rule allowing television coverage of a criminal trial does not violate the Constitution. The *Chandler* opinion stressed that Harlan's *Estes* concurrence meant that a majority in *Estes* did not vote for a per se rule barring broadcast coverage under all circumstances.

On July 14, 1960, just after the Democratic Convention had adopted a far-reaching civil-rights plank, advocating a law prohibiting racial discrimination in public accommodations, Douglas sent Black a written note: "That was quite a civil rights plank put into the platform. I've been reading it; and its implications are so broad, it looks as if a constitutional amendment will be necessary."[10]

However, when, early in the 1964 Term, the public accommodation provisions of the Civil Rights Act of 1964 were challenged in the Supreme Court, neither Douglas nor any of the others had difficulty in holding the law valid. What gave the Justices more trouble was the effect of the 1964 statute on the new Sit-In Cases that had come before the Court. All had voted to grant certiorari near the end of the previous term in a case involving convictions under a state trespass law of black sit-in demonstrators at a McCrory lunch counter in Rock Hill, South Carolina. In addition two cases challenging the constitutionality of the Civil Rights Act's public accommodation provisions came up on direct appeal at the beginning of the 1964 Term. All the Brethren voted to hear those cases as well.

The Sit-In Case, *Hamm v. Rock Hill*,[11] was discussed in conference on October 16, 1964. Warren urged reversal because of the "abative effect of the Civil Rights Act." He referred to section 203 of the statute, which provided that no one should be punished for attempting to exercise any right or privilege secured by the statute. Warren noted that the state "admits McCrory is under the Act." He said that the case "could go on *Thompson* [*v. Louisville*,[12] the 1960 Case of Shuffling Sam, discussed in chapter 9], but there are 3,000 cases backed up." The last reference was to the large number of sit-in cases pending in the courts.

Black, speaking next, opposed the Warren approach. He asked, "How could the '64 law forgive crimes [committed] in '62 and '63?" Black said he also had doubts on "whether Congress abated. I do not think they did it and have doubts as to their power." Though he, too, would "share the pleasure of not having to pass on the 3,000," he would dissent from any decision following the Chief's approach.

Brennan rejected Black's constitutional suggestion and asserted "that Congress, having stepped in under the Commerce Clause, revoked all state laws." This, said Brennan, was "the rule of the Supremacy Clause." Goldberg also supported Warren. So did Douglas and Clark, though less firmly. Harlan, Stewart, and White, on the other hand, voted with Black for affirmance. Harlan noted that "this is not a federal crime." He rejected the notion of congressional abatement of such a state crime, saying, "If Congress did this, it would raise constitutional questions of a major order. It just can't do that. Practicalities have to bow to constitutional principle." Stewart said, "I doubt if the Civil Rights Act covers sit-ins. All it gives is the right to bring a law suit. It does not give [a right of] self-help."

Ultimately, Warren's view that the sit-in prosecutions were abated by the 1964 Civil Rights Act prevailed by a bare majority, with Douglas, Clark, Brennan, and Goldberg voting with the Chief. Clark had furnished the fifth vote for reversal on the abatement theory, and

Warren assigned him the opinion to cement his vote. Clark circulated a draft opinion of the Court on November 30, 1964. On December 2, Brennan sent Clark changes that covered virtually the entire opinion except for the statement of facts. The changes were adopted by Clark in substantially the form in which they were suggested.

Warren also assigned Clark the two cases on the constitutionality of the 1964 Civil Rights Act's prohibition of racial discrimination in restaurants, hotels, and other places of public accommodation. The Heart of Atlanta Motel in Atlanta and a restaurant operated by the McClung family in Birmingham brought actions challenging the Act. Because the 1883 *Civil Rights Cases*[13] had held that Congress could not enforce the Fourteenth Amendment against *private* hotels and restaurants, the 1964 statute was based on congressional power over commerce, rather than its power to enforce the Fourteenth Amendment. On that basis, the October 9, 1964, conference had no difficulty in voting to uphold the 1964 statute.

Several of the Brethren, particularly Douglas and Goldberg, wanted to go further and hold that the 1964 public accommodation provisions were valid under the congressional power to enforce the Fourteenth Amendment. The majority felt that such a ruling was unnecessary and voted to sustain the provisions under the commerce power alone. Clark wrote the *Heart of Atlanta*[14] and *McClung*[15] opinions on that basis. Douglas and Goldberg issued concurrences when the decisions were announced on December 14, 1964, stating that the statute could be upheld under the Fourteenth Amendment, even more than under the Commerce Clause. Black also issued a concurrence, but only to stress that the Court did not have to go beyond the Commerce Clause issue.

Clark's draft *Heart of Atlanta* opinion had gone further than the final opinion, by indicating that Congress could apply the statute to travellers on intrastate journeys in motels which also catered to interstate transients. In a November 25, 1964, letter Brennan asked Clark, "But what of the case of the motel which deals exclusively with intrastate customers? Should that question be expressly laid to one side or should we go all out and say that this must be such a rare motel that it is swept within the congressional power to deal generally with local activities having a substantial and harmful effect upon commerce?"

As Brennan saw it, "Your present treatment lends itself to the latter reading and I am fully content with it." Brennan wrote that he "had supposed that someone else, particularly John, might be concerned about it. If no one else is concerned perhaps we ought let sleeping dogs lie."[16]

Harlan, however, did not let the matter pass. He wrote Clark, "I don't see why we have to get into the 'transients' problem in the context of this case where there is no dispute that this motel did serve interstate travelers, and I would leave for another day the question of whether the Act can constitutionally be applied to motels serving only *intrastate* travelers."[17] The passage relating to transients was deleted in response to Harlan's letter.

Hamm v. Rock Hill enabled the Court to dispose of the sit-in problem without deciding the underlying constitutional question that had been avoided the two previous terms. But cases involving other civil-rights protest techniques now came before the Court. Yet the Brethren were also able to avoid most of the constitutional issues in them. That was true in *Abernathy v. Alabama*,[18] a case that arose out of the demonstrations by the Freedom Riders, who challenged segregation in Southern bus terminals and facilities. Reverend Ralph D. Abernathy, the civil-rights activist, led a group of Freedom Riders to the bus station in Montgomery, Alabama. They bought tickets and occupied seats at the lunch counter. A hostile crowd gathered, and the sheriff, fearing violence, arrested Abernathy and the other demonstrators. They were convicted of disturbing the peace. The convictions were affirmed by the Alabama appellate courts.

At the October 16, 1964, conference following oral argument in this case, Warren spoke for reversal. The 1960 case of *Boynton v. Virginia*[19] had outlawed segregation in the terminals as well as in the buses used in interstate transportation. Warren said this was a clear case under *Boynton,* since it gave Abernathy and the others the constitutional right to do what they were doing. They were not told to leave and were being served. Then the police arrested them. Warren thought the case was so clear that it could be decided on a per curiam.

Black and Douglas agreed, stressing that there was no valid order to leave. Harlan also said that "they must have some warning." He felt the Court "should not say that because these people have a right to eat that the police cannot forbid or order people not to eat," referring to a situation where there was actual mob violence. Harlan asserted that, "if the police had given notice and the state court convicted, I would have great trouble reversing," since the police concluded that otherwise "a riot will result." But Harlan conceded that there was "no such case here. Here there was a summary arrest and the reversal should go on [that] narrow ground. If it's broader, I might write something."

The others agreed, with Goldberg declaring that "one can in a peaceful way assert rights." Brennan alone said that "even if warning [had been] given, there could still be no conviction." But he said he would go along with the others. They all also agreed to a per curiam.

Warren summarized the conference result. They would reverse in a per curiam that should "just recite the facts and *Boynton*." The Brethren agreed to this. Warren thought they might also cite *Thompson v. Louisville* [20]—the 1960 Case of Shuffling Sam discussed in chapter 9. Stewart and Harlan objected. The decision was announced April 5, 1965 in a unanimous one-sentence per curiam, stating only that the judgments were reversed. White, who, as Deputy Attorney General, had been involved in the Freedom Rider problem, did not participate. Black had found out that his brother-in-law was involved in the case, and he, too, decided to be listed as not participating.

The Court also avoided the issue of how far civil-rights demonstrations could be curbed in the interest of public order in *Cameron v. Johnson*.[21] Individuals prosecuted for violating Mississippi's antipicketing statute brought a federal action to enjoin the law's enforcement on the ground that it was an unconstitutionally broad regulation of speech and was being used to discourage their civil-rights activities. The statute barred picketing or demonstrations that obstructed entrance to or exit from public property, and some of the plaintiffs had been prosecuted for blocking the entrance to a county courthouse during a civil-rights protest.

The majority decided not to deal with the merits, and Brennan was assigned the writing of a short per curiam. He wrote a one-line opinion, but Harlan suggested an expansion to the two-paragraph per curiam issued on June 7, 1965. The case was remanded for the district court to consider whether a statute that prohibited federal injunctions against state prosecutions, except in certain cases, was a bar here. Black, joined by Harlan (despite the fact that he had suggested the version of the per curiam that was issued) and Stewart, wrote a strong dissent accusing the Court of failure to deal with issues whose importance "Every person who has the slightest information about what is going on in this country can understand."[22]

It was harder to avoid the underlying constitutional issues in *Cox v. Louisiana*.[23] After students from Southern University, a black college, were arrested in a civil-rights protest in Baton Rouge, Reverend B. Elton Cox led 2,000 students in a protest demonstration. The group marched from the State Capitol to the courthouse, where they stood across the street, and sang, clapped, and listened to a speech by Cox. The police had told Cox to confine the demonstration to the other side of the street. When Cox asked the demonstrators to sit in at lunch counters, the sheriff deemed this "inflammatory" and ordered the demonstrators to disband. Cox did not do so, and he and the demonstrators only left after tear gas was used against them.

Cox was arrested and convicted for violating statutes prohibiting breach of the peace, obstructing public passages, and picketing or parading "in or near" a courthouse with intent to influence court personnel in performing their duties. The Louisiana breach-of-the-peace statute was a typically broad law of that type which did not define what constituted a "breach of the peace." The obstructing-public-passages law was narrower, but it exempted picketing and assembly by unions.

The Cox convictions posed a difficult problem for Warren. He believed that state power might not be used to restrain civil-rights demonstrations, even where they went as far as sit-ins on private property. But he also thought that government must have the power to maintain public order and ensure the proper functioning of public institutions, especially the courts upon whose dignified operation the very social order rested.

In his conference presentation on October 23, 1964, Warren showed his ambivalence. He started by stating that "the parade was in no sense illegal and the police, having undertaken to direct it, the mere congregation outside the courthouse was no offense. The conduct there—singing and speech-making—were not offenses. This was confirmed by the [Police] Chief when he said it was all right up to then." However, this picture was changed by what followed. Warren was "inclined to think that, when they were told to go and Cox said, 'don't move,' this was close to *Feiner* [*v. New York*]"[24]—a 1951 decision that upheld a breach of the peace conviction of a street speaker, where the police concluded that he was inciting his audience to riot. Warren said that, "in the context of the situation, with [Cox's] 'order' to go to the restaurants, the chance of a riot was really imminent. The tear gas was bad, but perhaps justified. So the breach of the peace [conviction] was okay." Warren reached the same result on the courthouse statute violation.

Warren was supported on the breach of the peace conviction by Clark and Harlan, with the latter admitting that there was "great force in the argument it embraces conduct not constitutionally reachable. But when the cops told them to move, it became a common-law breach, and the statute should be read that way."

The others, however, agreed with Black, who put the case against the breach-of-the-peace and obstruction-of-public-passages convictions. Black conceded that there was "ample evidence to convict under both [statutes] if they are valid." But he thought that both laws were invalid. "Even as written," Black said, "and certainly, as applied, they trouble me." He stated that "regulations of conduct tied up with speech are okay usually, but here [it] excepts labor unions. That picks out a certain kind of speech and permits it, but not [speech about] segregation or something we don't like." On the breach-of-the-peace statute, Black said that "mere stirring people up is an offense. Moreover a policeman without standards is allowed to tell me to move. . . . This is a perfect trap where the trigger can be pulled automatically when he says something the police don't want him to say. The rule that the statute must be narrow and precise applies here." Black did, however, state that the courthouse conviction was valid, unless the words in the statute "in or near" were too imprecise.

The conference consensus was that the breach-of-the-peace and obstructing-public-passages convictions should be reversed for the reasons stated by Black, while the courthouse convictions should be affirmed. Douglas, Brennan, and Stewart, disagreed with the courthouse decision, with Stewart saying, "The courthouse law is perfectly good, but I have trouble seeing intent to obstruct justice. It was to protest their [fellow students'] arrests."

Warren ultimately agreed with the Black conference approach and assigned the opinion to Goldberg. Goldberg wrote an opinion reversing the breach-of-the-peace and obstructing-passages convictions. This was readily joined by all except Black and Clark, who issued concurrences, and White, joined by Harlan, who concurred on the breach-of-peace conviction, but dissented from reversal of the conviction for obstruction of public passages.

Goldberg had voted with the majority to affirm the conviction for violating the courthouse picketing law. In working up the opinion, he changed his mind. He says that he was led to this by noticing in the record that there was a television show covering the demonstration. "And when I asked to see it, I found that the students were placed across the street by the sheriff. And since the statute was pretty vague on what was 'near' the courthouse, I said this was a form of entrapment and you could not convict the people."

Goldberg wrote a separate draft opinion on the courthouse conviction, based upon his changed view, that he circulated November 18. In an accompanying *Memorandum to the Conference,* he wrote, "At our conference, in discussing No. 49, I expressed the view that the picketing before the courthouse statute is constitutional. I adhere to this view in this circulation. However, a further study of the record has convinced me, contrary to my tentative view at the conference, that appellants' conviction under the statute cannot be sustained for the reasons stated in the attached circulation." The memo noted that Goldberg had conferred with Warren, who agreed that the Justice should proceed with the circulation, since the vote had been five-to-four for affirmance and Goldberg's switch made for a bare majority the other way.

Goldberg delivered both *Cox* opinions for the Court on January 18, 1965. The second opinion stressed that the courthouse statute itself was constitutional and could be applied to conduct like that in this case. The reversal was based on the fact that the police had told Cox and the others to confine their demonstration to the other side of the street. This was, in effect, permission for them to demonstrate there and they could not be convicted for doing so. Black, joined by White and Harlan, and Clark issued sharp dissents from the second *Cox* decision.

Two other civil-rights cases of interest were decided during the 1964 Term. The first was *McLaughlin v. Florida.*[25] It arose out of convictions for violating a Florida law making it a crime for a black and a white person who were not married habitually to occupy a room at night. All the Justices voted to hear the *McLaughlin* appeal, and they had no difficulty at all in voting for reversal. At the October 16 conference, Warren said that there was a clear violation of equal protection. All agreed and White delivered a unanimous opinion to that effect on December 7.

Just as easy was the decision in *Harman v. Forssenius*.[26] Virginia voters brought an action challenging the state law that required voters in federal elections either to pay a $1.50 poll tax or file a witnessed or notarized certificate of residence. They claimed that the law violated the Twenty-fourth Amendment, which prohibited poll taxes as a voting requirement in federal elections. The lower federal court had ruled the statute invalid.

Warren spoke for affirmance at the March 5, 1965 conference. "Is the decision justified under the Twenty-fourth Amendment?" he asked. His answer was, "This is an abridgement for me." The state had claimed that the payment of a poll tax was a reliable indication of continuing residence. Warren rejected this argument, saying, "The poll tax is not just a mere residence tool." There was a unanimous vote, after little discussion, in accord with the Chief's view. On April 27, Warren announced the opinion striking down the Virginia law.

Governmental power to deal with subversive activities, which had not come before the Court during the previous term, was at issue in *American Committee for Protection of Foreign Born v. Subversive Activities Control Board*.[27] The Board had ordered the Committee to register as a "Communist-front" organization, which was controlled by and gave "aid and support" to a Communist-action organization. The order was challenged as violative of the Committee's constitutional rights, but was sustained by the lower court.

At the December 11, 1964, conference, Warren recommended reversal, without consideration of the constitutional claims. The case, he said, came "down for me to a complete absence of proof that anyone in [the] organization had done anything except pursue lawful pursuits. Likewise, no control was proved—that is, that this was a stooge of the Communist Party. The 'aid' component should be construed to require aid and comfort to the objectives of the action organization." Warren thought the case "can be decided on the *De Jonge* case." He was referring to the 1937 decision in *De Jonge v. Oregon*,[28] which held that an individual could not be convicted of a crime for taking part in a peaceable meeting having a lawful purpose, although it was called under the auspices of the Communist Party. The Chief concluded that, "to avoid the constitutional questions, we ought to give this a limited construction."

The others, however, wanted to go into the constitutional issues. Black, Douglas, Brennan, and Goldberg voted to strike down the registration order on Fifth Amendment grounds. Warren, who had taken a position against the registration requirement in the conferences in the 1961 case of *Communist Party v. Subversive Activities Control Board,*[29] discussed in chapter 9, readily joined them. Warren assigned the majority opinion to Brennan, who prepared a full-scale opinion that he sent to the other members of the tentative majority in January 1965. This draft distinguished the 1961 *Communist Party* case on the ground that the First Amendment question presented here was different in nature and reversed on the self-incrimination privilege.

Brennan's memorandum accompanying the draft explained the opinion as follows: "You may recall that we five were in agreement at the Conference discussion that the registration orders should be invalidated on Fifth Amendment self-incrimination grounds. This is what I've attempted in the draft. However, this result leaves the orders standing as regards the determinations that the petitioners are Communist-front organizations. This is because I do not reach petitioners' First Amendment claims."

The Brennan memo noted that "although Bill and I, contrary to Hugo, found no merit in the First Amendment claims asserted in the *Communist Party* case, I, at least, think that there is much more to them in these Communist-front cases. The Chief did not reach them in the *Communist Party* case and, of course, Arthur did not participate. I would personally prefer, however, not to reach the First Amendment issues but recognize that Hugo may feel he has to in light of the position he took in *Communist Party*." Brennan concluded by expressing the "hope that whatever else might be said, the five of us will find it possible to agree upon an opinion along the line of the enclosed."

The hope was not to be realized. Prior to circulating his draft, Brennan secured tentative agreement from the Chief Justice, Black, Douglas, and Goldberg. After circulation, they speedily joined the opinion, and Clark prepared a dissent. Goldberg, however, soon began to express doubts and said he now wanted either to reach and reject the First Amendment arguments or to predicate the decision on statutory grounds (similar to those urged by Warren in his conference presentation) by finding that the organization could not be found a Communist front on the evidence before the Board.

Goldberg's defection meant that the Brennan draft no longer had a majority. After discussing the situation with Warren, Brennan prepared in its place a short per curiam remanding the case to the lower court on a technicality. On April 16, Brennan wrote Black, "The Chief, Tom, Potter, Arthur and I have agreed to dispose of the above according to the Per Curiam circulated on April 13th."

Brennan asked Black, "Have you decided what you'll do in light of the Per Curiam disposition?" Black issued a dissent when the per curiam was announced April 26, as did Douglas, joined by Harlan. The dissenters asserted that decision on the constitutional issue should not be frustrated by a technical excuse. White did not participate in the decision.

The merits were, however, forcefully dealt with under Warren's leadership in *United States v. Brown*.[30] A federal law made it a crime for a Communist to serve as a labor union officer. Brown's conviction for violating this law had been reversed by the federal court of appeals on the ground that the statute violated the First and Fifth Amendments. The certiorari vote was six-to-three, with Warren, Black, and Douglas voting to deny.

At the April 2, 1965, conference, Warren had no doubt that the statute was unconstitutional. The difficulty from his point of view was the 1950 precedent of *American Communications Association v. Douds*,[31] which had upheld a statute that conditioned the recognition of a union under the National Labor Relations Act upon the filing of non-Communist affidavits. Warren began his conference presentation by stating, "We don't have to overrule *Douds*, which wasn't a criminal case, but involved only access to the N.L.R.B." On the other hand, he said, "This is a criminal case and I think it a bill of attainder."

Warren had the support of a bare majority (Black, Douglas, Brennan, and Goldberg) for his position. He announced the opinion of the Court striking down the statute as a bill of attainder on June 7, the last day of the 1964 Term. White, joined by Clark, Harlan, and Stewart, dissented.

There were also two other cases during the term that dealt with governmental powers used primarily against alleged subversives. The first was *Zemel v. Rusk*.[32] After the United States broke relations with the Castro government, the State Department issued passports that were invalid for travel to Cuba. Zemel's request to have his passport validated for travel to Cuba as a tourist was denied. He brought an action for a declaratory judgment that the restriction on travel to Cuba was invalid. The Secretary of State contended that he was given the power to impose the restriction by the Passport Act of 1926, which gave the Secretary authority to issue passports, and the Immigration and Nationality Act of 1952, which gave the President authority to restrict travel abroad during a national emergency. Zemel argued that those statutes were unconstitutional. The lower court decided in favor of the government.

Warren began the March 5, 1965, conference discussion by asserting, "The President can't regulate travel. He must have Congressional authority. But the foreign affairs power allows Congress to paint with a broad brush. It has done so under the 1926 Act." The Chief felt that it was an "appropriate delegation." The power, in his view, was "like that under the Taft–Hartley law in the Steelworkers Case"—referring to the 1959 case of *United Steelworkers v. United States*[33] discussed in chapter 9. Warren also thought that, in view of his analysis, the Court did not have to reach the 1952 Act.

Black spoke the other way. He said he agreed "there's a right to regulate traffic." Like Warren, he said that Congress, not the President, had the power. But he disagreed with the Chief on the question of delegation. "I can't see," Black stated, "that the 1926 Act gives the President the power to regulate travel of this kind. We should require that to be explicit. Therefore this is within the Steel Seizure Case for me." Black's reference was to the famous 1952 case[34] that invalidated President Truman's order seizing the steel industry, on the ground that the President had no inherent power, in the absence of a congressional delegation, to order such a seizure. Black also said that he did not agree with the 1936 *Curtiss–Wright* case,[35] which had held that there were no constitutional limitations on delegations to the President relating to foreign affairs.

Douglas and Goldberg supported Black, but the others agreed with Warren. Brennan, in particular, supported the Chief on deciding only under the 1926 Passport Act, rather than the 1952 Immigration Act.

Brennan pointed out that, to uphold the restriction under the latter statute, it would be necessary to sustain a presidential declaration of national emergency issued some years earlier. As it was put in notes by Clark, summarizing this aspect of the conference discussion, "In this case the Conference seemed to agree . . . the opinion should be hinged on the 1927 [sic] Act—without use of 1952 . . . there is no necessity of an emergency being present or declared under the 1927 Act." [36]

The majority voted to affirm on the theory stated in an April 10 letter from Brennan to the Chief: "As I understand the consensus reached at conference, it was that the 1926 Act constitutionally authorized the Secretary of State to refuse to validate the passports of United States citizens for travel to Cuba, and that all of us wished to avoid the more serious statutory, and perhaps constitutional, questions which would arise in ruling on whether such travel was *prohibited.*" As Brennan recalled it, the conference agreed to consider only "the propriety of the passport restriction" without indicating whether any statutory provision "does or constitutionally can empower the Government to prevent or punish travel to restricted areas."

The Chief Justice had assigned the *Zemel* opinion to himself. When he circulated his draft on April 9, it was broader than the conference consensus. The issue for decision stated at the beginning of the Warren draft was "whether the Secretary of State is statutorily authorized to restrict the travel of United States citizens to Cuba by refusing to issue passports valid for that country, and, if he is, whether such restrictions are constitutionally permissible." The draft did not make it clear that the decision was only concerned with the refusal to validate passports for travel to Cuba and not the validity of prohibitions against travel to Cuba.

Brennan, in his April 10 letter, suggested that Warren change the statement of the issue to "whether the Secretary is statutorily authorized to *'refuse to validate the passports* of United States citizens for travel to Cuba, and, if he is, whether such statutory authority is constitutionally permissible.' "

Brennan also suggested revisions toward the end of the opinion that narrowed its breadth, avoiding any indication of whether the government could prevent or punish travel to Cuba. Brennan concluded his letter by stating, "In other words, our problem is only the constitutionality of an authority to refuse to *facilitate* travel to Cuba, not the constitutionality of a *prohibition,* punishable by criminal sanctions, against travel to Cuba. Since we do not reach the question whether travel is prohibited, it is inappropriate to decide whether it can be, and we are not to be understood to intimate any view upon that question."

Warren announced his *Zemel* opinion on May 3. It followed Brennan's suggestions and held that the Secretary of State's refusal to validate Zemel's passport for travel to Cuba was not unconstitutional. Black, Douglas, and Goldberg issued dissents.

Warren's *Zemel* draft had asserted "that the Executive possesses no inherent power to inhibit the travel of American citizens. . . . If, therefore, the Executive Department has authority to refuse to validate the passports of United States citizens for travel to Cuba, that authority must be found in some law enacted by Congress." An April 12 letter from Harlan objected, saying, "I am not prepared to hold that the President's power over foreign relations would not have supported what was done here." Harlan threatened "to write a separate concurrence . . . with a reservation on the 'inherent power' issue."[37] Harlan's objection led to the deletion of the offending passage.

The second case involving a governmental power used mainly against alleged subversives was *Lamont v. Postmaster General*.[38] A statute required the Post Office to detain mail from other countries which the Secretary of the Treasury had determined to be "communist political propaganda." The mail could be delivered only if the addressee specifically requested it. A copy of the *Peking Review* addressed to Lamont, a publisher of pamphlets, was detained. Lamont brought an action to enjoin enforcement of the law. The lower court dismissed his complaint.

At the April 30, 1965, conference, Warren urged that the law was invalid. "The statute," he declared, "on its face puts an impermissible burden on First Amendment rights. It's a direct infringement." Warren also thought the statute was "unconstitutionally vague. 'Propaganda' is determined by customs officers in their unlimited discretion."

Black, too, said the Court should reverse, but should "do it on First Amendment grounds, rather than vagueness." The others agreed with Black, with even Harlan saying that the case was so clear that the Court could almost decide by a per curiam "on the ground that no compelling interest was shown to override the admitted infringement of First Amendment rights."

Less than a month after the argument, on May 24, Douglas delivered a unanimous opinion striking down the statute as "an unconstitutional abridgement of the addressee's First Amendment rights." Brennan issued a concurrence saying that, though the First Amendment contained no specific guarantee of access to publications, one could be inferred since the Bill of Rights went beyond the specific guarantees to protect other fundamental rights as well. This Brennan approach, we will see, was to play an important part in the *Griswold* decision[39] at the end of the term.

These cases on governmental power to deal with subversive activities all had First Amendment implications and, indeed, the *Lamont* case was decided specifically on First Amendment grounds. However, the most important First Amendment case in the term was *Garrison v. Louisiana.*[40] Garrison was the New Orleans District Attorney. During a dispute with the criminal court judges, he issued a statement disparaging their judicial conduct. As a result, he was convicted of criminal defamation. The conviction was based upon his attribution of a large backlog of pending cases to the inefficiency, laziness, and excessive vacations of the judges and his accusation that the judges had hampered his efforts to enforce the vice laws. The state court rejected the claim that the Louisiana Criminal Defamation Law violated Garrison's freedom of expression.

The case was originally argued during the 1963 Term and, after the majority voted to reverse, the opinion was assigned to Brennan. His sixteen-page draft opinion held that criminal libel prosecutions such as that against Garrison violated the First Amendment: "criminal statutes punishing speech which merely censures government or government officials cannot survive the constitutional test. . . . Our Constitution flatly bars criminal prosecutions based on the mere criticism of public men for their public conduct."[41]

The Brennan draft's broadside approach was unable to secure a majority. Black and Douglas concurred in the reversal on their usual absolutist ground, rejecting any libel suit, criminal as well as civil, against a public official. Clark circulated a dissent, joined by Harlan, as did White. As summarized in a June 1964, letter from Harlan to Clark, White's draft opinion, "although upholding Louisiana's right to enforce its criminal libel laws, argues that this case be remanded because the conviction was not based on a finding that the false defamatory statements were made with 'reckless disregard' of their accuracy. According to that view, it is constitutionally permissible to punish reckless defamation but impermissible to punish defamation when . . . it is prompted by 'actual malice,' defined as 'hatred, ill will or a wanton desire to injure.' "[42]

Clark changed his draft dissent to deal with White's approach. White's position, the revised Clark draft asserted, "would hold invalid a more rigorous standard than one which it believes valid. Negligent misconduct, even when it amounts to recklessness, is not ordinarily thought to be a greater wrong and more deserving of punishment than the deliberate infliction of harm; negligence has traditionally been regarded as a fault which, if carried to the extreme of recklessness, might in some case *rise to* and be taken as *the equivalent* of actual malice. I cannot believe that the Constitution prevents a State from protecting its citizens against harm deliberately inflicted but not from harm occasioned by negligence. It seems obvious to me that our decision in the *Times* case[43] should not be so construed."[44]

The separate Black, Douglas, Clark–Harlan, and White opinions meant that there were only four (Warren, Stewart, Goldberg, and, of course, Brennan) for the position taken in Brennan's draft opinion. Late in the term, Stewart indicated that he was wavering. In these circumstances, the case was set for reargument during the 1964 Term.

The reargument was on October 19, 1964. At the October 23 conference, Warren urged a different approach. The Chief said the Court should "use the *Times* standard," and noted that "no actual malice was shown here." Warren also said that the Louisiana statute was "void on its face, since he's liable whether it's true or false if he's guilty of actual malice." He also thought "these remarks are not defamatory" and could not be the "subject of a prosecution."

Clark, Harlan, Brennan, and Stewart agreed that the *Times* standard should be applied. Brennan expanded on Warren's presentation. He said that the conviction could be reversed under *Times,* provided that the peculiar history of criminal libel did not require a different treatment. Brennan concluded that it did not and said that the statute was unconstitutional on its face because it did not meet the *Times* standard.

Black and Douglas persisted in the view expressed in their draft concurrences of the prior term. Douglas also asserted that they "couldn't apply the *Times* standard because I think there's plenty evidence of malice." Douglas thought "we have to go on the ground the statute's void on its face. This is seditious libel. It's out of step with the *Times* case, since it preserves the cause of action for libel." Goldberg said, "I agree with Bill Douglas," but indicated he would join an opinion along the lines indicated by Brennan.

Brennan circulated a new draft that held that the *Times* approach applied to criminal, as well as civil, libels. It found the Louisiana statute invalid because, contrary to the *Times* standard, it directed punishment for true statements made with malice and also punished false statements without requiring malice as defined in the *Times* case. The draft indicated that Garrison could not be retried under the statute because under the "vagueness" doctrine the statute was totally unavailable in the area of public libels.

Clark, Harlan, Stewart, and White objected to the latter approach. Because of this and because of the fact that the political situation in Louisiana now made it extremely unlikely that Garrison would be retried, Brennan omitted the portion of the draft that related to a possible retrial. In a memorandum to Clark, Harlan, Stewart, and White, Brennan noted that, "from what each of you has said to me . . . your difficulties with my *Garrison* v. *Louisiana* lie principally with my conclusion that Garrison may not be retried." Brennan wrote, "I have therefore revised my latest circulation as shown on the attached copy to propose that I delete the [offending] material."

Brennan also explained the disposition at the revised opinion's end: "I suggest the simple word 'Reversed' so as to leave it to the State to figure out, without instruction from us, whether or not to try Garrison again. I have sufficient confidence in the correctness of my view that I could not join in anything which said affirmatively that the State is at liberty to retry him." [45]

When Brennan delivered his opinion of the Court on November 23, 1964, there were no dissents. Only Black, Douglas, and Goldberg issued separate concurrences reiterating the view they had expressed in the *Times* case, that the First Amendment bars all libel proceedings, criminal or civil, based on criticisms of official conduct.

Freedman v. Maryland [46] was another First Amendment case decided during the 1964 Term. Freedman exhibited the film "Revenge at Daybreak" at his Baltimore theatre without first submitting it to the State Board of Censors as required by the Maryland motion picture censorship law. He was convicted of violating the law despite his contention that the statute unconstitutionally impaired freedom of expression. The highest state court affirmed. All the Brethren except Harlan voted to hear Freedman's appeal.

The vote was six-to-three to reverse (Clark, Harlan, and Stewart for affirmance) at the November 20, 1964, conference on the case. Black and Douglas predictably asserted their absolutist approach, denying that any censorship was consistent with the First Amendment. Brennan was assigned the case and he tried to write an opinion that would satisfy both the Chief Justice and Clark, who had written diametrically opposed opinions in the 1961 case of *Times Film Corp. v. Chicago,*[47] discussed in chapter 9. The Brennan opinion reversed on procedural grounds. It held the Maryland censorship invalid because it did not operate under adequate procedural safeguards which insured a prompt judicial decision on whether the film was protected by the First Amendment.

Brennan showed the first print of his opinion, before any circulation, to Warren and Clark. The Chief had no difficulty in concurring in the result but was troubled by the opinion. He thought it was inconsistent with his rejection of censorship in his *Times Film Corp.* dissent. Warren did, however, ultimately decide to join Brennan, doing so on the night before the *Freedman* decision was announced.

On December 21, 1964, Clark wrote Brennan, "I have read and reread your draft and doubt if I will be able to join it." Clark stated, "Your distinction with *Times Film* is unconvincing. The only difference is that we know that 'Revenge at Daybreak' does not violate the statutory standard of obscenity, while in *Times Film* we do not know the character of the film."

Clark objected in particular to a passage in which, he asserted, "You condemn all censorship, p. 6, which would strike down Chicago's program and hence overrule *Times Film*. What you do is place the Court in the censorship business."

Brennan toned down his animadversions against censorship. Some of the others called his attention to the difficulties that might follow from the draft's prohibition of any temporary restraint, even if provision were made for a prompt final determination. Under this approach, there could really be no effective way of preventing an exhibitor from showing an obscene film. Brennan changed his opinion to incorporate a passage permitting temporary restraints pending prompt judicial resolution. Clark then joined Brennan's opinion on February 22, 1965. Harlan, who had voted the other way at the conference, joined two days later, and Stewart, who had also voted for affirmance, agreed soon thereafter. When Brennan delivered the opinion on March 1, he spoke for a unanimous Court, with Douglas, joined by Black, issuing a short concurrence.

The First Amendment was also involved in *United States v. Seeger,*[48] though this time it was the amendment's guaranty of freedom of religion that was at issue. Seeger was convicted of having refused to submit to induction in the armed forces, after his claim to exemption as a conscientious objector was denied. The conscription statute exempted persons who by reason of their religious training and belief were opposed to war. The term "religious training and belief" was defined as "an individual's belief in a relation to a Supreme Being involving duties superior to those arising from any human relation, but [not including] essentially political, sociological, or philosophical views or a merely personal moral code."

Seeger declared he was opposed to war because of his "religious" belief, based on ethical thinkers like Plato and Spinoza, but would not admit to belief in God. The lower court held the statute invalid because it discriminated against persons who did not believe in a theistic God in favor of those who did. All the Justices voted to grant certiorari.

At the November 20, 1964 conference, the Chief Justice thought that Seeger came within the statute's exemption. He said that Seeger believed "in a guiding spirit and that's enough to give [him] the exemption. I don't know how to define 'Supreme Being' and judges perhaps ought not do so." He referred to the 1961 decision in *Torcaso v. Watkins,*[49] discussed in chapter 9, and questioned "whether *Torcaso* doesn't set a principle that religion encompasses all religions and thus 'Supreme Being' is discriminatory." On the other hand, Warren rejected the notion of selective opposition to war as a basis for exemption. "I don't think a man can say he's against war only with Russia, [he must be] against all war as a matter of conscience."

Black said, "the Government can compel everyone to go to war, whether [he is] for or against war. But it denies equal protection to separate conscientious objectors in the field of morality. If [the objection is] honest, conscientious, that's enough."

Douglas, on the contrary, stated, "I don't think, as a matter of power, government could require a man to bear arms if it's against his religious scruples. But that's not here. What's here is the classification." As Douglas saw it, "if conscience is linked to one or three or no Gods, they fall into the broad conception of religion."

Harlan and Stewart went along with Black's view. "I agree with Hugo," said Harlan, "about forcing everyone to fight and not give any exceptions. But when they do so, they can't pick and choose between religious beliefs." Stewart, too, thought that "Congress must exempt believers and nonbelievers alike."

As the discussion went on, the consensus was to follow Warren's view that Seeger came within the statutory exemption. Clark said, "I think we can get this under the statute. 'Supreme Being' under it means any religious belief and that's what he said here." Goldberg, who spoke last, declared, "The only difference between Seeger and Buddhism is that Seeger isn't a Buddhist. The statute doesn't say God. It goes more broadly."

The opinion was assigned to Clark, who circulated a draft in January 1965 that followed the conference consensus that the statute should be read to include Seeger within the exemption. Goldberg, however, circulated a concurrence in early February that held for Seeger on constitutional grounds. As explained in a February 5 Clark *Memorandum to the Conference,* "Brother Goldberg . . . says that Seeger has conceded in his brief that his belief was not based on relation to a 'Supreme Being.' " That being the case, according to the Goldberg draft, the issue was whether "Congress had the constitutional right to limit the exemption by choosing between religious beliefs which include a belief in *a* Deity and religious beliefs not based upon *a* faith *in God*."

Goldberg answered this question in the negative. The Goldberg draft asserted, "I cannot accept the Government's contention that a classification for military exemption based upon belief in a Supreme Being is a reasonable one, because Congress has only drawn 'a fair line. . . .' Were there no First Amendment, this argument might be tenable. But there is a First Amendment, and the least it means, in this context, is that Congress cannot draw a line on this 'continuum' which discriminates among religions and prefers some over others."[50]

Clark answered the Goldberg draft in a lengthy February 15 *Mem-*

orandum to the Conference. The memo asserted that Goldberg had written "upon what I conceive to be an entirely false premise"— namely, that the statute had to be read as choosing between "theistic and non-theistic beliefs." The memo summed up Clark's own interpretation: "In short, what I say is that any sincere belief which *fills, in the life of the objector,* the *same place as God fills* in the life of an *orthodox religionist* is entitled to exemption under the statute."

Most of the Justices, particularly Warren, wanted to avoid any opinion dealing with the underlying constitutional issues. Goldberg was persuaded to withdraw his separate opinion. When Clark announced the opinion on March 8, 1965, only Douglas issued a separate opinion. Douglas had originally written his concurrence as an answer to Goldberg. When it was first circulated on February 26, the Douglas draft began "If I read the statute as my Brother GOLDBERG reads it, I too would have difficulties." Although the Goldberg opinion was not issued, Douglas simply changed his first sentence and put out his opinion substantially as it was when he had aimed it at the Goldberg draft.

There were no important criminal law cases decided during the 1964 Term. Several should, however, be mentioned because of what they indicate about the Warren Court's operation at the time. The first is *Henry v. Mississippi.*[51] The case arose out of the conviction on a morals charge of Aaron Henry, a pharmacist of Clarksdale, Mississippi, who was a leader of the National Association for the Advancement of Colored People. Henry charged that he was the victim of a "diabolical plot" by the Clarksdale police chief and the county prosecutor. When the case came to the Supreme Court, a sentence in the Mississippi brief implied that Henry had previously indulged in homosexual acts.

At the October 13, 1964, oral argument, Warren was incensed. He turned to G. Garland Lyell, counsel for Mississippi. According to one reporter who was present, a red line of anger crept up the Chief's neck and his blue eyes grew frosty.[52] Warren indignantly declared that there was nothing in the record to justify the insinuation and called the sentence a device for "poisoning the mind of this Court and the public" against Henry. Lyell said he did not believe he or anyone could "poison the mind of this honorable Court," but he apologized and asked that the offending sentence be stricken. Warren unsmilingly said, "Very well." [53]

In the case itself, Henry claimed that evidence that was the fruit of an unlawful search had been improperly admitted. The state supreme court agreed that the evidence was tainted but refused to reverse, because Henry's counsel had failed to comply with the Mississippi requirement that an objection to illegal evidence be made at the time it was introduced.

The conference vote on October 16, 1964, was to dismiss certiorari as improvidently granted. Brennan circulated an October 20 *Memorandum to the Conference* saying, "I have decided that I cannot agree with the disposition of the above as improvidently granted and will in due course circulate a dissent."

Brennan drafted a dissent that began: "I can think of only two possible grounds to justify the Court's action in dismissing this writ as improvidently granted. First, the record might support a conclusion that the Mississippi Supreme Court's refusal to effectuate petitioner's federal claim rests on an independent and adequate nonfederal ground. Second, the record might support a finding that petitioner deliberately bypassed the orderly procedure of the Mississippi courts, and in so doing understandingly and knowingly forwent the privilege of seeking to vindicate his federal claim in the state courts. In my view, the record poses serious questions as to the adequacy of the nonfederal ground; also, the record plainly will not support a conclusion of deliberate bypassing. I therefore respectfully dissent from the dismissal of the writ."

Brennan's draft urged that the case should be remanded to the state court for a hearing to determine whether Henry knowingly waived his right to object to the illegal evidence. Brennan's opinion quickly secured the support of the Chief Justice, as well as of Douglas and Goldberg. Black then circulated an opinion for reversal on the ground that the conviction rested on evidence seized in violation of the U.S. Constitution. That meant that there was no majority for any disposition of the case, since the Court was now divided four-four-one.

With Warren's approval, Brennan recast his opinion as an opinion of the Court, in the hope that it would attract White, who had voted to dismiss the writ. After several changes in the Brennan draft, particularly insertion of a clear statement that a strategy choice by counsel would generally bind his client, White agreed to join. This gave the opinion its fifth vote, and it could be delivered by Brennan on January 18, 1965, as the opinion of the Court. Black issued his opinion as a dissent. Harlan, joined by Clark and Stewart, also dissented, saying that certiorari should be dismissed as improvidently granted.

In another criminal case, *Pointer v. Texas*,[54] the Court (after all but Brennan had voted to grant certiorari) unanimously held that the Sixth Amendment right of confrontation was binding in state, as well as federal, prosecutions. After Black had prepared an opinion of the Court, Warren wrote the Alabaman, on March 24, 1965, "I have read your opinion in the above case, and I agree with the result which you achieve, namely, that a defendant under the Sixth Amendment is entitled to confrontation of witnesses to the extent that right is accorded him in federal cases, but only to that extent." Warren, did, however, ask Black to put in a passage indicating that the decision "does not prevent introduction of dying declarations, or of testimony of a deceased witness who has been properly examined at a former trial."

But the Chief expressed a deeper concern drawn from his years as district attorney. His letter to Black stated that, "On the question of the reading of the testimony of a witness who has testified fully and been cross examined in a prior trial of the defendant, I would not like to see the existing law changed because in gangster trials particularly it might be an open invitation to dispose of an essential witness before a new trial could be had." Black inserted a sentence taking care of Warren's concern.

Another unanimous criminal decision was rendered in *Stanford v. Texas*.[55] Police had searched Stanford's San Antonio home under a search warrant issued by a county judge that authorized them to search for any books, papers, records, and the like which violated the so-called Texas Communist Control Law. They ransacked the house for over four hours and seized over three hundred books and pamphlets, numerous periodicals, and Stanford's private papers. The Texas court denied a motion to annul the warrant and order the return of the materials seized.

At the November 13, 1964, conference, all agreed with Warren's suggestion that they "reverse on the search warrant itself. This [is] in the nature of a general warrant." Black said, "This is a classical warrant of the kind the Fourth Amendment was designed to prevent." They all quickly joined a Stewart opinion vacating the search order that was announced on January 18, 1965.

Stewart had revised his draft so that it concluded with the statement that Stanford was protected against general warrants no less than the law two hundred years ago shielded John Entick—the individual protected in the classic 1765 case of *Entick v. Carrington* [56]— "from the messengers of the King." The change led Brennan to write Stewart on January 14, "I must express my personal gratitude that you revised the concluding sentence. . . . The Irish don't like the King."

Still another criminal case, *United States v. Gainey*, [57] gave the Court a great deal of difficulty. Gainey was convicted of violating the federal law prohibiting possession of an unregistered still and carrying on the business of a distiller there. The judge had instructed the jury that the statute authorized them to infer guilt from a defendant's unexplained presence at an illegal still. The court of appeals reversed on the ground that the connection between unexplained presence and the offenses of "possession" and "carrying on" was not close enough to satisfy due process.

The conference on October 16, 1964, voted to affirm. Warren, Black, Clark, Brennan, and Goldberg made up the majority. Harlan, Stewart, and White voted to reverse, while Douglas passed. Warren assigned the opinion to Brennan. He soon circulated a draft based on the 1943 decision in *Tot v. United States*, [58] which held that a statutory presumption violates due process where there is no rational connection between the fact proved and that presumed. The Chief Justice and Goldberg joined the Brennan opinion. Stewart circulated a dissent that accused the Brennan draft of confusing the activities of an illicit still with those more likely to be found at an Oriental bazaar. The dissent picked up the support of Douglas, Clark, and Harlan. In early January 1965, Black circulated a concurrence that found the statute and the jury charge to be an unconstitutional interference with the power of juries and courts to decide what facts were enough to convict. As Brennan summarized Black's approach in a January 5 letter to the Alabaman, "you had expressed yourself as believing, contrary to me, that the real issue was not *Tot* but the invasion by Congress of the judicial or jury functions." Black later expanded his draft to condemn the statute as also contrary to due process and the privilege against self-incrimination.

White now sent Brennan a memorandum saying that the *Tot* case was really nothing more than a no-evidence case flying under different colors. To apply *Tot* as Brennan had done, the White memo asserted, might seriously affect the use of circumstantial evidence as a basis for criminal convictions. White suggested that Brennan's opinion could be read as striking down the conviction, not because of the invalidity of the statute or instruction, but because the circumstantial evidence involved (mere presence) was not of a quality and quantity that would satisfy the standard the Court was propounding and applying to the case. As White saw it, this possible reading of the opinion had portentous significance for every criminal prosecution.

The opposition to Brennan's opinion now amounted to a majority. In consequence, the Justice sent a "Dear Chief" letter of January 8, "Byron has advised me that he will adhere to his conference vote to reverse in the above. Since Potter has a dissent in circulation which Bill Douglas, Tom Clark and John Harlan have joined, that means there are five votes to reverse. In the circumstances, the opinion which you assigned me will have to be reassigned."

The opinion for the new majority was assigned to Stewart, who circulated a revised version of his draft dissent as the opinion of the Court. Warren, Brennan, and Goldberg now joined the Stewart opinion. To get Brennan's vote, Stewart made several changes, particularly inclusion of the third paragraph of his opinion, which was written in Brennan's chambers. Instead of the paragraph's last sentence, Brennan had suggested a sentence to make it clear that all Congress had done in providing the statutory inference was to overrule decisions that presence alone was not enough to go to the jury: "The statute does no more than instruct the judge that there is no firm rule of law that precludes the submission of the question of guilt to the jury when the only evidence the government has adduced is that of the accused's presence at the site of the illicit still." This sentence was not adopted because Stewart felt that its point was already clear from what had been said in the opinion.

When Stewart delivered the *Gainey* opinion on March 1, 1965, he spoke for the entire Court except Black, who issued his draft concurrence as a dissent, and Douglas, who had changed his vote and also delivered a dissent.

In terms of legal impact, the most important 1964 Term case was *Griswold v. Connecticut* [59]—decided the last day of the term. At issue was a Connecticut law that prohibited use of contraceptive devices and the giving of medical advice in their use. Griswold was the director of the Planned Parenthood League and Dr. Buxton was the medical director of the League's New Haven Center. They gave advice to married persons on preventing conception and prescribed contraceptive devices for the wives. They were convicted of violating the birth control law. Their conviction was affirmed by the state's highest court. All the Brethren voted to hear the appeal from the state judgment.

In his statement at the April 2, 1965 conference, Warren indicated that, though he favored reversal, he had no clear theory upon which to base that result. "I can't say," the Chief stated, "it affects the First Amendment rights of doctors, nor that the state has no legitimate interest (that could apply to abortion laws). We can't balance, use equal protection, 'shocking' due process, or privacy." Warren did, however, say that reversal might be sustained "on a *Yick Wo* theory"—referring to the 1886 decision of *Yick Wo v. Hopkins,* [60] which held that a law might be invalidated, even though fair on its face, if it was administered in an arbitrary manner. Here, Warren said, they could go on the theory "that there is no prohibition on sales. They don't go after doctors as such, but only clinics." Warren said, however, that he preferred the idea that the act was not narrowly enough written. As he put it, "This is the most confidential relationship in our society. It has to be clear-cut and it isn't."

Griswold and Buxton had claimed that the Connecticut law violated their First Amendment right of association. Black, speaking next, rejected this claim. "The right of association," he stated, "is for me a right of assembly and the right of the husband and wife to assemble in bed is a new right of assembly for me." Black also said that he had a hard time saying the law was ambiguous enough to apply the overbreadth doctrine, "which for me is only applicable where the First

Amendment is involved. So I can't find why it isn't within state power to enact."

Douglas opposed Black's view, saying that the right of association was more than a right of assembly and that the case should be decided on that right. "We've said the right to travel is in radiation of the First Amendment, and so is this right of association. There's nothing more personal than this relationship and, if on the periphery, it's within First Amendment protection."

Only Stewart supported Black's view. He stated that he could not "find anything [against this law] in the First, Second, Fourth, Fifth, Ninth or other Amendments. So I'd have to affirm." The others agreed that the law should be ruled unconstitutional, but differed in their reasoning. Clark declared, "There's a right to marry, maintain a home, have a family. This is in an area where we have the right to be let alone." Goldberg said, "the state cannot regulate this relationship. There's no compelling state reason in that circumstance justifying the statute."

Warren assigned the opinion to Douglas, who had expressed the clearest theory upon which the Connecticut law might be invalidated. Douglas prepared a draft opinion of the Court of slightly over five printed pages. The draft based the decision on the First Amendment, likening the husband–wife relationship to the forms of association given First Amendment protection.

Most of the Douglas draft was used by him in his final opinion. There were, however, two key portions that were different. After the discussion of the cases on the right to educate one's children and the right to study in German, the draft read, "The family is an instruction unit as much as the school; and husband and wife are both teachers and pupils. And the family, together with its physician, is an instruction unit as much as a school is. To narrow, as does the Connecticut statute, discussion and advice on a problem as important as population and procreation is to introduce a dangerous state influence over the First Amendment right to disseminate knowledge."

The draft also had an entirely different ending that stressed the right of association. After declaring, as does the final Douglas opinion in *Griswold,* that the right of association is necessary to make the First Amendment guarantees meaningful, the Douglas draft concluded as follows:

The foregoing cases do not decide this case. But they place it in the proper frame of reference. Marriage does not fit precisely any of the categories of First Amendment rights. But it is a form of association as vital in the life of a man or woman as any other, and perhaps more so. We would, indeed, have difficulty protecting the intimacies of one's relations to NAACP and not the intimacies of one's marriage relation. Marriage is the essence of one form of the expression of love, admiration, and loyalty. To protect other forms of such expression and not this, the central one, would seem to us to be a travesty. We deal with a right of association older than the Bill of Rights—older than our political parties, older than our school system. It is a coming together for better or for worse, hopefully enduring, and intimate to the degree of being sacred. This association promotes a way of life, not causes; a harmony in living, not political faiths; a bilateral loyalty, not commercial or social projects. Yet it flourishes on the interchange of ideas. It is the main font of the population problem; and education of each spouse in the ramification of that problem, the health of the wife, and the well-being of the family, is central to family functioning. Those objects are the end products of free expression and these Acts intrude on them.

If the accessory statute can be enforced as it has been here, so can § 53-32 which also has criminal sanctions. The prospects of police with warrants searching the sacred precincts of marital bedrooms for telltale signs of the use of contraceptives is repulsive to the idea of privacy and of association that make up a goodly part of the penumbra of the Constitution and Bill of Rights. Cf. *Rochin v. California*, 342 U.S. 165. *Reversed.*

On April 23, Douglas showed a copy of his draft opinion to Brennan and asked for suggestions. The next morning Brennan sent Douglas a letter urging him to abandon his First Amendment approach. Brennan wrote that association under the First Amendment was not meant to protect grouping or coming together as such, but only to protect such activities where essential to fruitful advocacy. In Brennan's view, the "association" of married couples had nothing to do with the advocacy protected by the First Amendment.

To save as much of the Douglas draft as possible, Brennan suggested in his letter that the expansion of the First Amendment to include freedom of association be used as an analogy to justify a similar approach in the area of privacy. Privacy itself could be brought within the zone of constitutional protection by the approach stated in Brennan's concurrence in the already discussed case of *Lamont v. Postmaster General.*[61] Brennan there had stated that "the protection of the Bill of Rights goes beyond the specific guarantees to protect from congressional abridgement those equally fundamental personal rights necessary to make the express guarantees fully meaningful."[62]

Douglas adopted Brennan's suggested approach in his *Griswold* opinion, which stated, "specific guarantees in the Bill of Rights have penumbras, formed by emanations from those guarantees that help give them life and substance."[63] A constitutional right of privacy was included in these penumbras. The right of marital privacy—"older than the Bill of Rights—older than our political parties, older than our school system"[64]—was violated by the Connecticut law.

Brennan had intended to issue his own concurrence, but the adoption of his approach by Douglas made it awkward for him to do so. Instead, he joined the concurring opinion circulated by Goldberg, which elaborated the same basic ideas as the opinion of the Court, though at greater length.

Harlan and White issued separate concurring opinions rejecting the revised Douglas opinion's broadside approach. They urged instead that the law violated the Due Process Clause of the Fourteenth Amendment, not any "radiations" from the Bill of Rights. Black and Stewart prepared sharp dissents.

Warren felt that the Douglas approach was too broad. Like Harlan and White, he preferred to tie the decision to a specific constitutional provision. As late as June 3, he joined a recirculation of White's concurrence. But that would have made the Douglas opinion only that of a plurality, which would have left it uncertain just what the *Griswold* decision meant. When the decision was announced on June 7, the Chief had left White and joined the Goldberg concurrence, which specifically stated that it joined in the opinion, as well as the judgment, of the Court.

Just after it had ended, the 1964 Term was characterized in a *New York Times* article as the "most placid term in a decade."[65] That was true in large part because Warren had a solid majority in every case of consequence. The Chief did not issue a single dissent during the term. To be sure, he changed his vote in a few cases, but none dealt with an issue on which he felt strongly.

In one case, *Fortson v. Dorsey,*[66] the conference vote went against Warren on an issue of importance, but the opinion was ultimately written in a manner with which the Chief could agree. The case arose out of an action by Georgia voters challenging a 1962 law apportioning the Georgia Senate among the state's counties and providing for county-wide voting in seven multidistrict counties. The lower court held that the requirement of county-wide voting in the multidistrict counties violated the Equal Protection Clause.

At the December 11, 1964, conference, Warren and Black urged affirmance, but the others voted to reverse. The opinion was assigned to Brennan, who decided to write narrowly, pegging his opinion to the precise language used in Warren's landmark opinion the year before in *Reynolds v. Sims.*[67] This led Warren and then Black to join. The decision, announced January 18, 1965 (with Douglas now dissenting), was the first to uphold a state reapportionment scheme under the one person–one vote standard.

One reason the Brennan opinion attracted the support of almost the entire Court was the reservation in the last paragraph concerning multi-member constituencies which "operate to minimize or cancel out the voting strength of racial or political elements of the voting population." There had been some concern about this problem among the Justices, but Brennan showed that the record did not present the issue.

During 1965, Warren presided over two oath-taking ceremonies. The one that was especially gratifying was the admission to the Bar of his son, Earl, Jr., in November. The year itself had begun with the swearing in of Lyndon B. Johnson to the full term that he had won in his own right in the 1964 election. Johnson was the third President sworn in by Warren.

Warren had been delighted with Johnson's overwhelming electoral victory both as a voter and as Chief Justice. Senator Goldwater's extreme conservative positions were scarcely congenial to one who had been the leading liberal Republican of his day. And the Chief bitterly resented Goldwater's attacks on the Court during his campaign.

Yet, though Warren was pleased by the President's reelection, he never, as a colleague described it, "felt easy with L.B.J." That was true despite the fact that Warren agreed with Johnsons' principal policies, particularly in the areas of civil rights and social welfare. He also appreciated the President's constant efforts to emphasize the importance of the Court and its head.

During his White House tenure, Johnson always went out of his way to show his high regard for the Chief Justice. On Warren's seventy-fifth birthday, on March 19, 1966, the President sent him a congratulatory letter stating, "You are the fourteenth Chief Justice in the history of our nation. But not one of them will be remembered with the affection and respect that comes to you from a grateful country." [68]

Then Johnson, as Warren put it in a note of thanks, "arrived at our home laden like Santa Claus." The Warrens, wrote the Chief, "were surprised, to say the least." The President's gifts included the inevitable photograph, a copy of the *Oxford History of the American People,* and, in Warren's words, a "thirty year old 'Kings Favorite'! That is untouched and will remain so until the election night of 1968, when I will drink to your health and continued success." [69]

In 1967, the President wrote Warren, "I think you should know of a rather remarkable event. A member of the press has done you a good turn." Johnson informed the Chief that "your benefactor" in this "man-bites-dog story" was columnist Drew Pearson, who "has written me of your difficulties in finding a pool fit for winter dips. By coincidence, I happen to have one—warm, wet and absolutely snoop proof. I hope you will avail yourself of it."

The President concluded his note, "Bring your suit the first time and leave it on the peg. I will try to float free and join you from time to time." [70] Warren did use the White House pool and Johnson wrote him telling him how happy he was that he was doing so. [71]

A Johnson gesture that Warren particularly appreciated was the President's surprise visit to the annual dinner given by his law clerks to the Chief Justice on May 11, 1968. A White House memorandum to the President two days later informed him, "The Chief Justice could not have been more delighted by your visit on Saturday night. As he said several times later on that evening, he was so shaken that he forgot even to open your magnificent gift before you left." [72] On May 27, Mrs. Warren thanked Johnson for his gift of engraved silver cups. She expressed Warren's own delight at the Presidential recognition of the clerks, the Chief's own extended family, when she wrote, "The law clerks were completely overwhelmed by your appearance at the dinner they gave for the Chief Justice, and the next day when all of us were together for a brunch, they could talk of nothing else." [73]

Johnson also gave ample public indications of his esteem for the Chief Justice. At the 1966 White House reception for the federal judiciary, the President recalled that when Speaker Sam Rayburn dominated the House of Representatives, he considered the head of the table to be wherever Mr. Sam happened to sit. "Now," said the President, "wherever Warren sits is the head of the table." [74]

Among the Presidential photographs with which Johnson showered Warren were two in 1965 inscribed, "To the best Chief Justice" and "To my friend the great Chief Justice." And the inscription on the seventy-fifth birthday photograph was, "To the greatest Chief Justice of them all." [75]

Shortly after the 1964 Term ended, there was another change in the Court's membership. To the Court's junior Justice, his appointment to the high bench had been the crowning accomplishment in his life. Goldberg looked forward to service among the Brethren during the rest of his career. But he did not reckon on the crucial intervention of President Johnson.

In his memoirs, Johnson states, "I mentioned [to Goldberg] reports that he might step down from the Court and therefore might be available for another assignment. He told me these reports had substance." [76] According to Johnson, Goldberg told him that he was interested in a position having to do with foreign affairs.

When asked about this Johnson version, Goldberg's riposte was, "Well, everyone knows Lyndon Johnson!" Goldberg was dragooned by the President to serve as Adlai Stevenson's successor as Ambassador to the United Nations, much as Warren had been pressed by Johnson to chair the commission investigating the Kennedy assassination.

Johnson used the same approach on Goldberg that he had employed two years earlier on the Chief Justice. The President compared service at the U.N. to service in the Army. He called upon the Justice, as Goldberg told it, "to join in the greatest adventure of man's history—the effort to bring the rule of law to govern the relations between sovereign states. It is that or doom." After the President's entreaty, said Goldberg, "I have accepted, as one simply must." [77]

Goldberg recalls that when he told Warren he was leaving the Court, the Chief was "a little disturbed." But Warren soon called the Justice and apologized, telling him he understood his leaving. "It's the same thing like being drafted in the Army," said the Chief.

To fill the vacancy created by Goldberg's resignation from the Court on July 16, 1965, Johnson turned to Abe Fortas, a leader of the District of Columbia Bar who had argued the 1963 case of *Gideon v. Wainwright*.[78] Fortas was a close friend of the President and had been one of his closest advisers, even though he held no official position.

Fortas was one of the few Court appointees who had to be virtually drafted for his seat. Fortas had one of the most lucrative practices in Washington, and both he and his wife, also a partner in his law firm, were used to living on the income they made as lawyers. Douglas tells how the President asked him to speak to Fortas about the appointment. "I did so," says Douglas, "and received a firm refusal, as Abe's personal affairs would not permit him to leave law practice at that time."[79]

Much of the Fortas reluctance stemmed from his wife's strong opposition to his giving up practice. On August 1, 1965, Douglas wrote Black, "Abe Fortas' wife is very upset over Abe's appointment. It is apparently a very serious crisis."[80]

The President obtained Fortas' consent by the same pressure tactics that had succeeded with Warren and Goldberg. On July 28, he asked Fortas to help him with a Vietnam statement to the press. Just before the press conference, Johnson told Fortas, "Before announcing this statement, I am going to announce your appointment to the Court." Fortas objected. To which the President said, "This Vietnam statement that you approved says fifty thousand more boys are going to Vietnam—perhaps to die. No one is ever going to shoot at you on the Court. Tell me, how can I send them to battle and not send you to the Court?"[81]

Fortas, like Warren and Goldberg, had been given his marching orders and, like them, he acted like a good soldier and obeyed. As an additional inducement, Johnson told Fortas that he would make him Chief Justice, if the opportunity presented itself. This, at any rate, was what Warren later told one of the Brethren. Despite this, the news of the appointment stunned Fortas' wife, who was on a case at the Internal Revenue Service when the news reached her. "She refused to believe it," an I.R.S. official said. She indicated that she had no intention of giving up her practice, and she continued in his old law firm while her husband served on the Court.[82]

Abe Fortas himself was no ordinary junior Justice. He had one of the best minds of anyone appointed to the Supreme Court. "He's the lawyer's lawyer," said an attorney who worked with him, "the brain surgeon, the guy you call in when all else fails." Harlan, himself an outstanding legal craftsman, told his law clerks that he considered Fortas the most brilliant advocate to appear in his time.

Before his appointment, Fortas listed his business address in *Who's Who in the South and Southwest* as "c/o White House, 1600 Pennsylvania Avenue, Washington, D.C." He came to the Court with the celebrity and status of the President's close adviser. After John Kennedy's assassination, the first telephone call the new President made in Dallas was to Fortas.

His closeness to the President was, however, to prove a two-edged sword. James Shogan, in his book on Fortas,[83] entitled the chapter after his Court appointment, "On the Bench—and on Call." Fortas continued to give the President counsel from the sanctum of the Supreme Court. *Newsweek* reported that, even after the Court appointment, "the first person the President consults on anything is Abe Fortas" and that "few important Presidential problems are settled without an opinion from Mr. Justice Fortas."[84]

14.

1965 TERM: MIRANDA, DISCRIMINATION, AND FIRST AMENDMENT

"The Supreme Court," wrote Anthony Lewis in 1965, after the last argument he had heard as Supreme Court reporter of the *New York Times,* "is not only powerful, it is fascinating. People view it as a far-off abstraction. . . . But seeing it up close, one does not think in such generalities. For the Court is the least abstract of institutions. It is nine men, nine very human men, participating in a process that can be impressive or disturbing, grave or funny."[1]

The argument at which Lewis sat happened to be a humorous argument about a Palmolive Rapid–Shave television commercial. The commercial purported to show a razor shaving sandpaper with Rapid–Shave applied to it. The "sandpaper" was in fact a "mock-up" made of sand sprinkled on plexiglass. The Federal Trade Commission had found that the undisclosed use of the substitute was a deceptive misrepresentation. Colgate-Palmolive Co. appealed the Commission's order.

The case was a simple one for Warren and the Court. At the December 11, 1964, conference, the Chief stated simply, "There's no . . . problem here for me. Where they offer proof and it isn't proof, it's deceit." On April 5, 1965, Warren delivered a strong opinion affirming the Commission and denouncing the mock-up as a huckster's deceptive practice.[2]

But it was the argument, not the decision, that Lewis used to illustrate that the Justices were "nine very human men." The argument itself proceeded with anything but the gravity associated with Supreme Court sessions. The Brethren were full of jokes and the government counsel, Philip B. Heymann, finally remarked that he was "doing better as a comedian" than as a lawyer.

The members of the Warren Court were not only very human, they were also nine individuals, each with his personal manner of doing things. Former Justice Goldberg tells how, when he first came to the Court, the conference took a formal vote on whether the Justices should go to Capitol Hill for the State of the Union message. The motion to attend carried by only a bare majority and, despite the vote, Hugo Black and another Justice never did attend.

But the Alabaman was always an individualist, who would persist in doing things his own way. The ritual intonation that opens each Court session ends with, "God save the United States and this Honorable Court." One year a new member of the Court began bowing his head when those words were reached. The Justice beside him soon followed suit. It spread down the line until everyone bowed his head—except Black, who continued to look straight out at the audience.[3]

In summing up the Supreme Court's work in his valedictory article, Lewis stressed the difficulty of the Court's task. The issues that came before the Brethren, he pointed out, "are seldom black-and-white, and almost never easy." The difficulty of the Court's work, Lewis asserted, was insufficiently appreciated by either the Court's critics or its admirers. When the Court reversed a conviction, the decision was judged only in terms of the "poor downtrodden defendant" or the "vicious criminal threatening our peace."

Yet the criminal cases that come to the Court can rarely be dealt with in light of the individual attitude toward the particular defendant. Lewis illustrated the point by referring to "a typical criminal case that comes before the Court these days. A suspect has been arrested and brought to a local police station; he asks to see a lawyer, and the police say no; after questioning by a relay of officers he confesses.

Should the confession be admissible as evidence—or excluded because it resulted from the denial of counsel?"[4]

The Sixth Amendment guarantees the right to counsel in "all criminal prosecutions." But, as Lewis noted, "the Constitution does not answer the critical question: When does the right to counsel begin?"

Though Lewis published his article almost a year before *Miranda v. Arizona*[5] came to the Court, his illustrative case presented the same question posed in *Miranda*. The answer given in *Miranda* made that case the most important decided in the 1965 Term, as well as one of the most controversial to have come before the Warren Court.

Miranda had been convicted of kidnapping and rape in Arizona. He had been arrested and taken to an interrogation room, where he was questioned without being advised that he had a right to have an attorney present. After two hours, the police secured a confession that was admitted into evidence over Miranda's objection. The state supreme court affirmed the conviction.

The Justices all voted to grant certiorari to Miranda, though they were closely divided on the granting of cert in two companion cases. In *Vignera v. New York*,[6] Warren, Brennan, Stewart, White, and Fortas voted to grant, the others to deny. In *California v. Stewart*,[7] the vote was four (Warren, Black, Douglas, and Fortas) to grant, with the other five voting to deny.

Miranda and its companion cases were argued on February 28 and March 1 and 2, 1966. Warren's questions and comments during the argument foreshadowed the decision. After John J. Flynn, Miranda's counsel, had been pressed on whether the Fifth Amendment privilege against self-incrimination had been violated, the following colloquy occurred:

The Chief Justice: "Suppose the police had said 'we're your friends—you tell us everything and you can go home.' Is this a Fifth Amendment violation?"
Mr. Flynn: "It is an abdication of the Fifth Amendment right."
The Chief Justice: "Haven't we struck down such confessions?"[8]

At another point, Warren intimated that the case was no more difficult than *Gideon*.[9] "Don't most states," he asked, "require bringing before a magistrate, et cetera, and don't most states have clauses in their constitutions prohibiting self-incrimination? So this is not much different from *Gideon*."

One of the points for decision was when the proceeding "focused" on the defendant for purposes of his Fifth and Sixth Amendment rights—whether at the stage of police interrogation or only when an accusation was made. To Warren, the accusatory stage was reached with Miranda's arrest. "I didn't know," the Chief commented during the argument, "that we could arrest people in this country for investigation. Wouldn't you say it was accusatory when a man was locked in jail?" [10]

Warren also indicated that Miranda's right to consult counsel was not affected by whether or not he could pay for a lawyer. "When does the right to counsel attach?" the Chief asked, "Does inability to hire mean less generous treatment by the law?"

Last of all, the Chief Justice stressed the failure to advise Miranda of his rights—a focal point of the *Miranda* opinion. When counsel argued that the test was one of voluntariness of the confession, Warren came back with, "Wouldn't the best test be simply that the authorities must warn him?" Then the defendant could intelligently decide if he wanted to talk without counsel. "Do you agree," Warren asked, "that if a man says I would like to talk to a lawyer, the police should not interrogate?" [11]

According to former Justice Fortas, the *Miranda* decision "was entirely his"—i.e., Warren's. At the March 4, 1966, conference, Warren left no doubt where he stood. As at the argument, the Chief stressed that no warning had been given by the police. In such a case, the police must warn someone like Miranda of his right to silence, that anything he said could be used against him, that he could have a lawyer, and that he could have counsel appointed if he could not afford one. Warren said that such warnings had been given by his staff when he was district attorney. He placed particular emphasis upon the practice followed by the Federal Bureau of Investigation and explained how it worked. The "standard" F.B.I. warning covered the essential requirements Warren had posited. The F.B.I.'s record of effective law enforcement showed that requiring similar warnings in all police interrogations would not impose too great a burden. Another Justice who was present says, "the statement that the F.B.I. did it . . . was a swing factor. I believe that was a tremendously important factor, perhaps the critical factor in the *Miranda* vote."

Harlan led the presentation the other way. To him, Warren's approach meant an unwarranted extension of the Fifth Amendment. Harlan said that the privilege under it "is only a testimonial privilege. 'Compelling' means only coerced statements."

The conference was closely divided. Black, Douglas, Brennan, and Fortas supported Warren, though they were not united on the grounds for reversal. Thus, Douglas felt that the reversal should be based on the right to counsel and the interrogation by the police "without providing one." Black, on the other hand, said, "I think the focus is on the privilege against being a witness against himself. From the time government begins to move against a man, when they take him into custody, his rights attach. This . . . was inherently coercive and [they] can't make him be a witness against himself."

Brennan also urged that the decision should turn on the Fifth, rather than the Sixth, Amendment. His view, as he summarized it in a May 11 memorandum, was "that the extension of the privilege against the states by *Malloy v. Hogan* [12] [the 1964 decision mentioned in the last chapter] inevitably required that we consider whether police interrogation should be hedged about with procedural safeguards effective to secure the privilege as we defined it in *Malloy*, namely, 'The right of a person to remain silent unless he chooses to speak in the unfettered exercise of his own will.' "

Warren assigned *Miranda* to himself. He had a draft ready early in May. He sent Brennan a copy on May 9, writing, "This is not in circulation but I would appreciate your views." Brennan feared that the opinion was too rigid because it failed to leave room for legislatures to devise alternative procedures for safeguarding the Fifth Amendment privilege.

Brennan explained his concern in a May 11 "Dear Chief" memorandum: "We cannot prescribe rigid rules . . . we are justified in policing interrogation practices only to the extent required to prevent denial of the right against compelled self-incrimination as we defined that right in *Malloy*. I therefore do not think, as your draft seems to suggest, that there is only a single constitutionally required solution to the problems of testimonial compulsion inherent in custodial interrogation. I agree that, largely for the reasons you have stated, all four cases must be reversed for lack of any safeguards against denial of the right. I also agree that warnings and the help of counsel are appropriate. But should we not leave Congress and the States latitude to devise other means (if they can) which might also create an interrogation climate which has the similar effect of preventing the fettering of a person's own will?"

In response, Warren inserted in his opinion the second paragraph of Part III, which indicates that Congress and the states may devise alternative procedures to protect the Fifth Amendment privilege. Another important change was also made at Brennan's suggestion. As explained in his May 11 memo, "It goes to the basic thrust of the approach to be taken. In your very first sentence you state that the root problem is 'the *role* society must *assume,* consistent with the federal Constitution, in prosecuting individuals for crime.' I would suggest that the root issue is 'the *restraints* society must *observe,* consistent with the federal Constitution, in prosecuting individuals for crime.' "

In addition, other minor alterations were made in Warren's draft. The first paragraph was extended to make it plain that the case was concerned with procedures to assure that the individual was accorded his Fifth Amendment privilege. The paragraph at the end of the introductory material summarizing the holding was changed to define "custodial interrogation," to meet the suggestion in the Brennan memo, "Isn't it necessary to give a precise definition and show how it differs from the 'focus' concept of *Massiah* [13] and *Escobedo* [14] . . .?" The original paragraph concluded with the following sentence (omitted from the final opinion): "We are not here concerned with the right of a person to talk to the police, but with the circumstances under which the police may interrogate him when he is in their custody."

In the draft, after Warren referred to studies showing interrogation abuses, such as the third degree, he wrote, "In a series of cases decided by this Court long after these studies, Negro defendants were subjected to physical brutality—beatings, hanging, whipping— employed to extort confessions. In 1947, the President's Committee on Civil Rights probed further into police violence upon minority groups. The files of the Justice Department, in the words of the Committee, abounded 'with evidence of illegal official action in southern states.' "

Brennan's memo questioned this passage. "I wonder if it is appropriate in this context to turn police brutality into a racial problem. If anything characterizes the group this opinion concerns it is poverty more than race." The reference to blacks and the South was omitted.

Warren also deleted a statement that the Fifth Amendment "privilege is neither an historical relic nor a legal eunuch," as well as language stressing the indispensability of counsel to protect the privilege: "The presence of counsel at the interrogation may serve several significant subsidiary functions as well. He will prove a substantial restraint on the coercive police practices demonstrated in numerous cases. . . . Further, his presence as a third party to the proceedings can provide corroboration for the defendant as to precisely what transpired at the questioning and thus avoid the inevitable conflict of testimony between police and defendant which has plagued courts in cases involving the issue of voluntariness."

At a later point, the draft read, "Incommunicado interrogation, by contrast, does not necessarily afford the innocent an opportunity to clear themselves." The first two words were changed to "Custodial interrogation."

In the draft, the last full paragraph began, "We affirm. We will not presume that there have been warnings of the right to remain silent and the right to counsel at interrogation on a record that does not show that a person was advised of these rights." This was changed to stress the privilege against self-incrimination during custodial interrogation and the failure to give warnings or show "any effective alternative."

Apart from these changes, the opinion of the Court that the Chief Justice delivered in *Miranda* was essentially the same as the draft he had shown Brennan. After he had made the changes noted (particularly those suggested by Brennan), Warren circulated his opinion. It was speedily agreed to by Black, Douglas, Brennan, and Fortas and delivered as the opinion of the Court on June 13, 1966. But Clark, Harlan (joined by Stewart and White), and White (joined by Harlan and Stewart) delivered dissents. The dissents were notable for their sharp tone as they charged that the "Court's *per se* approach" would "have a corrosive effect on the criminal laws as an effective device to prevent crime." [15]

When he had read Harlan's dissent, Brennan prepared a short concurrence that began, "I join the Court's opinion in these cases and write merely to emphasize that the Court has not, as the dissents suggest, allowed no room for other systems that might as effectively safeguard against denial of the privilege." The draft concurrence then quoted the passage that Warren had inserted in his opinion at Brennan's suggestion, pointing out the power of Congress and the states to devise alternative procedures to protect the person being interrogated.

"It is certainly true," Brennan's concurrence went on, "as my Brother Harlan observes, that the rules we have found necessary in lieu of such creative action are not airtight safeguards against the possibility of prevarication by the police, as to whether warnings have been given or not, or whether waivers have been received. Through Federal Rule of Criminal Procedure 5(a) and the exercise of our supervisory authority over federal courts, the Court has found it possible to fashion a prophylactic rule designed to escape the 'evil potentialities' of a contest over such issues in federal criminal prosecutions. See *Mallory v. United States,* 354 U.S. 449, 456, 457. That avenue is not open to this Court in its review of convictions in state courts. But nothing we hold today prevents the States from devising and applying similar prophylactic means for avoiding the dangers of interrogation which at the same time eliminate the possibility of such contests of veracity between the police and the accused."

Brennan showed his draft concurrence to Warren. The Chief expressed concern at the prospect of a separate opinion by a member of the majority. He was also troubled by Brennan's implication that the required warnings need not be given if alternative safeguards were created. Though Brennan explained that the proposition was already embodied in the Court opinion and that the concurrence was being written solely for emphasis, Warren was not mollified. Brennan finally agreed neither to circulate nor issue the concurrence.

In his May 11 memorandum, Brennan declared that the *Miranda* opinion "will be one of the most important opinions of our time." *Miranda* also turned out to be the most controversial of the Warren Court's criminal-law decisions, and gave rise to anguished complaints from law-enforcement officers throughout the country. They denounced *Miranda* for putting, as Mayor Sam W. Yorty of Los Angeles said, "another set of handcuffs on the police department." [16] *Miranda* was condemned on Capitol Hill and became a major issue in Richard Nixon's presidential campaign.

The bitterness about *Miranda* was not confined to the Court's critics. The *Miranda* dissenters also thought that the decision was a disservice to both Court and country. Their strong feelings were shown when three of them almost refused to join an opinion of the Court which had only a bare majority with their support, just because it contained quotations from the *Miranda* opinion.

The incident referred to arose in *Schmerber v. California*,[17] which involved another aspect of the privilege against self-incrimination. Schmerber had been arrested at a hospital while receiving treatment for injuries suffered in an auto accident. At the direction of a police officer, a blood sample was taken from Schmerber, despite his objection. He was convicted of drunken driving, after the test result had been introduced in evidence. The California appellate court affirmed.

The *Schmerber* case was similar on its facts to the 1957 case of *Breithaupt v. Abram*,[18] discussed in chapter 6, where the Court upheld the use of a blood test, over Warren's dissent, joined by Black and Douglas. At the April 29, 1966, *Schmerber* conference, the three *Breithaupt* dissenters stated that their views had not changed. Warren declared, "I still believe in what I said in *Breithaupt*." If anything, the case was stronger in Schmerber's favor. Breithaupt "couldn't object there because he was unconscious" when the blood test was taken. "Here, he did object on the advice of counsel."

Black, Douglas, and Fortas voted with Warren for reversal. Clark, Harlan, Stewart, and White voted the other way. Harlan said, "I think the state can rest on its police power to require one to submit to a blood test, however it's put—so long as it's not arbitrary and applied by doctors and not mechanics." Stewart did, however, concede that the case was very close for him and, if it was a new matter, he would go the other way.

Brennan was at first undecided, but indicated that he, too, would vote to affirm. He said that a comprehensive opinion should be written limiting the scope of the Fifth Amendment. That, he felt, would soften the impact of the *Miranda* decision.

Clark was the senior Justice of the *Schmerber* majority. The Assignment List indicated that he had assigned the opinion to himself. Clark came to Brennan's chambers and said that there had been a mistake, as he had intended to assign the opinion to Brennan because he had been the swing vote and wanted a full opinion.

Even after he had prepared several drafts, Brennan was uncertain about his vote for affirmance. Indeed, he was still so in doubt that at one point he was prepared to recommend that the case should be put over to next term for reargument. Ultimately, Brennan decided to go forward with his opinion by emphasizing the Fifth Amendment privilege as a testimonial privilege that did not apply to the blood test evidence. Brennan's opinion also rejected Schmerber's Fourth Amendment claim, though it did emphasize the need for a search warrant in other cases.

As soon as Brennan circulated his opinion, Clark came back with: "A perfect job. Some of the boys might bolt on the *Miranda* references, and the search warrant requirement." None of the majority took issue with the search warrant requirement, but the references to *Miranda* did cause difficulty. Harlan, Stewart, and White said that they would not join the opinion because of its quotations from *Miranda*. Stewart also took issue with a sentence intimating that lie-detector tests were within the Fifth Amendment privilege.

Brennan declined to change his opinion. Even though the quotations from *Miranda* were unnecessary to the reasoning in the opinion, he refused to eliminate them. In large part, this was because he was the only Justice in the *Schmerber* majority who had joined the majority in *Miranda*. Harlan, Stewart and White also stood firm and stated that they would merely concur in the result without joining Brennan's opinion.

At the next to last conference of the term, Brennan said that he thought it foolish to announce an opinion that only one other Justice joined, when three other Justices concurred in the result. Harlan, Stewart, and White then changed their minds and said that they would join Brennan. They did so, and Stewart did not renew his objection to the lie detector dictum.

Brennan delivered the *Schmerber* opinion on June 13, 1966. Warren dissented, saying he was reiterating his *Breithaupt* dissent as the basis for reversing here. Black, Douglas, and Fortas also delivered dissents. Black's dissent led Brennan to modify his Fifth Amendment discussion. In particular, Black's draft caused Brennan to minimize his reliance on Wigmore's classic treatise on the law of evidence and to remove language suggesting that he was "balancing" the need for effective means of law enforcement against the guarantees of the Bill of Rights.

The focus of the civil-rights movement had started to shift from the courts to Congress. The emphasis during the 1965 Term reflected the shift, with the most important decisions dealing with congressional power to enforce the post–Civil War amendments to the Constitution. Before we deal with them, a word should be said about *Harper v. Virginia Board of Elections*,[19] where the Court finally ruled that poll taxes were prohibited by the Constitution. Harper had brought an action challenging the $1.50 poll tax that had to be paid as a precondition for voting in Virginia elections. The case did not appear the type that would present a problem to the Warren Court—except for one thing. That was the 1937 decision in *Breedlove v. Suttles*,[20] which had unanimously upheld state power to make poll tax payment a prerequisite to voting in state elections. The lower court had dismissed the complaint, deeming itself bound by *Breedlove*.

Warren had no doubt that the poll tax should be stricken down despite the *Breedlove* decision. He was supported by Douglas and Goldberg. But the others not only disagreed, they also decided that the constitutional claim was so insubstantial that the case should be decided without argument by a one-sentence per curiam: "The motion to affirm is granted and the judgment is affirmed."

Goldberg circulated a strong draft dissent on March 4, 1965, that was quickly joined by Warren and Douglas. Goldberg declared that he could not join "a holding by this Court that such poll taxes imposed upon citizens too poor to pay them are constitutional. With all deference, I dissent from this holding." The dissent asserted, "In practice the poll tax in Virginia and other States has resulted in making it burdensome and difficult for poor white people, as well as Negroes, to vote."

Goldberg then discussed the equal protection cases since *Breedlove*, stressing those, like *Reynolds v. Sims*,[21] that involved voting rights. He stated, "it must be concluded that no reasonable state interest is served by barring from voting those citizens who desire to vote but who lack the requisite funds." As the dissent saw it, "Providing an equal vote for poor and rich, weak and powerful alike, should be the 'central aim' of our voting system. . . . Just as 'there can be no equal justice where the kind of trial a man gets depends on the amount of money he has,' . . . so in voting cases, there can be no equal protection of the laws where a man's vote 'depends on the amount of money he has.' " If the Constitution means anything here, "it means that with respect to the fundamental right to vote, a reverse means test cannot be applied."

Goldberg's draft concluded with the affirmation, "A government is far less likely to mistreat any group of citizens and far more likely to respond to their needs when it is ultimately responsible to them through the ballot box. A government 'of the people' and 'by the people' is likely to be 'for the people.' . . . If the poor man is to be accorded his equal right to vote, which the Constitution guarantees, Virginia's poll tax cannot stand."

After he had read Goldberg's *Harper* draft dissent, Black circulated a *Memorandum for the Conference:* "Brother Goldberg's circulation persuades me that our line of decisions since *Breedlove* v. *Suttles* presents new arguments against the Breedlove poll tax holding that call for consideration by the Court after full hearings. For that reason I shall vote against summary decision by a *per curiam* opinion." [22]

Black's memo led the conference to decide against the summary affirmance. On March 8, 1965, they voted six-to-three (with Warren, Black, Douglas, Brennan, White, and Goldberg voting for) to hear Harper's appeal and set the case for argument during the coming 1965 Term.

Harper was argued on January 25 and 26, 1966. At the January 28 conference, Warren was more successful in securing a majority for his statement for reversal. The Chief said the Court should "do it on equal protection grounds rather than the First Amendment. This was a discrimination against the poor and Negroes as a matter of fact."

Black, whose memo had led the Court to reconsider its summary affirmance the previous term, now led the opposition. "This is a tax," he said, "and not necessarily a discrimination. I don't doubt Congress can get rid of this under section 2 [of the Fifteenth Amendment], but the Court can't. I don't think it comes within the classification [reached by] equal protection."

This time, however, the Chief had the votes. When Douglas announced the decision on March 23, 1966, striking down the poll tax as violative of equal protection, only Black, Harlan, and Stewart dissented. Fortas had circulated a short concurrence on March 21 that said, "I would emphasize that the Virginia poll tax is an impermissible attempt to impose a charge or penalty on the exercise of a fundamental right." This opinion was withdrawn the next day, and the Douglas opinion alone spoke for the majority.

As indicated, the most important 1965 Term civil-rights cases dealt with congressional power to enforce the post–Civil War amendments. The easiest for the Brethren was *South Carolina v. Katzenbach*.[23] It arose out of an original action in the Supreme Court by South Carolina challenging the Voting Rights Act of 1965. This was only the fifteenth time in its history that the Court was asked to take original jurisdiction of a case.

The Voting Rights Act was, in many ways, the most far-reaching of the civil-rights statutes passed during the 1960s. As summarized in Warren's *South Carolina* opinion, "The heart of the Act is a complex scheme of stringent remedies aimed at areas where voting discrimination has been most flagrant. . . . The first of the remedies, contained in § 4 (a), is the suspension of literacy tests and similar voting qualifications for a period of five years from the last occurrence of substantial voting discrimination. . . . The third remedy . . . is the assignment of federal examiners by the Attorney General to list qualified applicants who are thereafter entitled to vote in all elections. . . . Section 8 authorizes the appointment of federal poll watchers in places to which federal examiners have already been assigned."[24] The statutory remedies go into operation when it is determined by the Attorney General that a state or political subdivision maintained a "test or device" and the Director of the Census determines that less than 50 percent of its voting-age residents were registered or voted in the 1964 Presidental election.

In effect, the Voting Rights Act of 1965 provided for the supplanting of state election machinery by federal law and federal officials, where necessary to eliminate a pattern of voting rights violations. Yet, despite the far-reaching character of the 1965 law, the Justices had no difficulty in upholding it under the congressional authority to enforce the Fifteenth Amendment. Warren delivered a strong opinion on March 7, 1966, rejecting South Carolina's challenge. Black agreed with most of the Court's opinion, but disagreed with upholding a provision giving the Attorney General power to veto state voting practices. He filed a partial dissent.

Warren's draft opinion had discussed the statute's provision for suits to be brought only in the District of Columbia by noting the congressional desire to have such suits brought in a "neutral forum" to assure equal treatment of similarly situated areas. At a February 25, 1966, conference, it was pointed out that the judges of the Fourth and Fifth Circuits might be offended by such a statement. The reference was deleted from Warren's opinion.

Katzenbach v. Morgan,[25] another case under the Voting Rights Act, presented a harder problem. It arose out of a challenge to section 4 (e) of the 1965 statute, which provided that no person who had completed the sixth grade in an American-flag school (i.e., a school located within U.S. territory, such as Puerto Rico) in which the language of instruction was other than English, should be denied the right to vote because of his inability to read English. This provision gave the vote to many in New York's Puerto Rican community, who had previously been unable to pass the state's literacy test. Morgan, a New York resident, brought an action for a declaratory judgment that section 4 (e) was unconstitutional. The lower court decided in his favor.

The issue presented by *Katzenbach v. Morgan* was made difficult by the 1959 decision in *Lassiter v. Northampton Election Board,*[26] which had upheld a state English literacy test. If such a test does not violate the Fourteenth and Fifteenth Amendments how can Congress, in legislation enforcing the amendments, strike it down? Can Congress extend the substantive scope of the amendments to reach action that had been held by the Court not to contravene the amendments?

Harlan, in particular, was concerned by these questions at the April 22, 1966, conference. "This is Congress," he noted, "saying that it's a denial of equal protection to have an English literacy test for Spaniards. But Congress can't define the Equal Protection Clause. That's for us to say."

Stewart was also troubled. "Our question," he stated. "is whether the statute is 'appropriate' under section 5 of the Fourteenth Amendment. Is it, since the New York statute is not discriminatorily applied?" Stewart did say, however, "I might be persuaded."

Warren spoke in favor of section 4 (e), declaring, "I would reverse on the Equal Protection Clause. Congress may legislate against discriminations [in] voting under section 5 of the Fourteenth Amendment. Congress need make no findings of justification, as a rational basis appears."

Black argued the same way. "I would not say," he stated, "the New York statute is void on the face of the Fourteenth and Fifteenth Amendments themselves. But Congress has power to do something like this under both section 5 of the Fourteenth and section 2 of the Fifteenth. I would go on the enforcement of equal protection."

Douglas went even further. As he saw it, "the act of Congress makes it easier, but, apart from the act, I would think the [New York] statute invalid." Even without section 4 (e), Douglas said he would hold the English literacy requirement invalid as applied to a person literate in another language.

The conference decided to uphold section 4 (e). Harlan voted the other way, and Stewart was undecided, though he leaned toward Harlan's view. Warren asked Black if he would write the opinion. The Alabaman declined, saying that his views on the far-reaching scope of section 5 of the Fourteenth Amendment (giving Congress power to enforce the amendment) would not obtain a majority. The Chief then turned to Brennan and assigned the opinion to him.

Brennan prepared a draft that analogized the powers given Congress by section 5 of the Fourteenth Amendment to those given under the Necessary and Proper Clause of Article I, section 8. Section 4 (e) was upheld as "appropriate" enforcement legislation, since Congress could rationally conclude that the literacy requirement worked a discriminatory denial of the vote to large segments of the Puerto Rican community.

Brennan sent an uncirculated draft of his opinion to Black for his views. Black made several suggestions. The most significant was to eliminate the following footnote to the portion of the text which stated that *Lassiter v. Northamptom Election Board* "is inapposite":

This is not to suggest that *Lassiter* could not be distinguished on other grounds. It could be noted, for example, that we there sustained the North Carolina literacy statute on "its face"—not as applied to deny the vote to someone who was literate in a language other than English, who had received a measure of formal education in that language and who had access to sources of information printed in that language.

Black wrote that the footnote had the effect of blunting the opinion. Brennan eliminated the footnote and modified the text slightly to indicate that *Lassiter* dealt with the constitutionality of English literacy tests "in all circumstances."

The draft opinion was then circulated. Black made additional suggestions, most notably that the phrase "prohibit the enforcement of" be substituted for "nullify" or "invalidate" to describe the operative effect of section 4 (e). This would emphasize the distinction between the legislative and judicial functions. Black then joined the opinion, writing, on May 23, on the last page of the Brennan draft, "I am happy to agree to this historic opinion, which for the first time gives § 5 of the Fourteenth Amendment the full scope I think it was intended to have." Warren and Clark also joined.

White wrote expressing concern with that part of the opinion dealing with the argument that section 4 (e) worked an invidious discrimination. He thought that, in approving the distinction in section 4 (e) between American-flag and foreign schools, the Court would be understood as approving similar distinctions in state literacy laws, which he was not prepared to do.

Brennan rewrote the part of the opinion that White had criticized. Despite this, White said that he would wait until he saw Harlan's dissent, since he was still troubled by the proposition that under section 5 Congress could prohibit the enforcement of a state law that the judiciary was not prepared to invalidate as violative of the guarantees contained in section 1 of the Fourteenth Amendment.

At this point, Douglas sent Brennan a draft of a dissent. It took the view that section 4 (e) embodied an invidious discrimination, since it prohibited enforcement of the English literacy requirement only for those educated in American-flag schools, and not for those educated in schools beyond the territorial limits of the United States.

Douglas included a memorandum with his proposed dissent that suggested that the opinion should dispose of the invidious discrimination argument without a decision on the merits by holding that Morgan lacked the standing needed to bring the action. "It occurred to me," Douglas wrote "that on reflection you may not want to reach the question. If you do not reach it and merely reserve it, I'll join your opinion."

Brennan's reply to Douglas emphasized that section 4 (e) was a reform measure designed to eliminate barriers to the franchise, rather than a voter qualification statute granting or denying the right to vote. Brennan also wrote that Morgan did have standing, since he would be benefited by the invalidation of section 4 (e). Douglas then decided to issue a separate concurrence rather than file his dissent.

On June 2, Fortas sent a memorandum to Brennan and Douglas, in which he indicated disapproval of literacy tests. "I would," Fortas wrote, "extend Thurman Arnold's remark generally: that there is no evidence whatever that reading and writing have been of any assistance whatever to the people in Virginia. In my opinion, this is universal truth. In Puerto Rico, it was the illiterate people who were responsible for the election of Munoz–Marin. I think this proves my point. O'Dwyer said that 31 states have no literacy tests. I would like to make it unanimous. I am not suggesting that we do it right now, but I couldn't join . . . in approving—even lefthanded—the value of reading and writing."

The Fortas memo concluded, "I guess I will go along with Brother Brennan. At least, he has not indicated that he approves of reading and writing."

Harlan now circulated his dissent. After he read it, White decided to join the Brennan opinion. Brennan added footnote 10 to meet the dissent. Stewart still had not made up his mind. However, just prior to the June 10 conference, before the decision was announced, he decided to join Harlan's dissent. When Brennan delivered the opinion of the Court on June 13, he spoke for seven of the Brethren, with Harlan and Stewart dissenting.

Another far-reaching decision on congressional power to enforce the Fourteenth Amendment was rendered in *United States v. Guest*.[27] The case arose out of the indictment of Guest and five other men for criminal conspiracy in violation of section 241 of the Federal Criminal Code, originally enacted during the Reconstruction period. Section 241 made it a crime for "two or more persons [to] conspire to injure, oppress, threaten, or intimidate any citizen in the free exercise or enjoyment of any right or privilege secured to him by the Constitution or laws of the United States." The indictment charged that the defendants conspired to deprive blacks of their right to use of public facilities in Athens, Georgia, by, among other things, causing the arrest of blacks by false reports that the blacks had committed criminal acts. In addition, the indictment charged a conspiracy to deprive blacks of their constitutional right to travel to and from Georgia and within the state. The lower court had dismissed the indictment because defendants were private individuals, while the Fourteenth Amendment applied only to "state action." The 1883 *Civil Rights Cases*[28] had held invalid a federal law that attempted to bar wholly private discriminatory action and that decision had never been overruled.

At the *Guest* conference on November 12, 1965, there was a discussion of whether the indictment could reach Guest and the other defendants. Black felt strongly that it could. He said that section five of the Fourteenth Amendment gave Congress the power to prohibit Guest's discrimination on the basis of race. Black declared that he "would overrule the *Civil Rights Cases* if necessary."

Harlan took the opposite position. "I think," he stated, Congress "can restrain this only as to the right to travel. I can't see how under this statute [they] can otherwise reach the conduct of private persons under the Fourteenth Amendment." Harlan said that he "would not overrule the *Civil Rights Cases*."

The conference unanimously voted to reverse the dismissal of the indictment. But there was no uniformity on the ground of reversal. Seven of the Justices were unwilling to limit the reversal to that part of the indictment dealing with the right to travel. Harlan and Stewart voted to reverse *only* on the right to travel.

Warren assigned the opinion to Stewart. It is not clear why he did so. The Chief himself had first said that the indictment could be sustained on the right to travel charge. Perhaps he thought that Stewart, too, would broaden his approach and go beyond the right to travel while working out his opinion.

Stewart circulated a first draft on January 26, 1966, which held that the indictment could stand on the charge of depriving blacks of their right to use public facilities. Stewart relied on the allegation that defendants had caused the arrest of blacks by false reports of crimes. Stewart's theory was that this was broad enough to cover a charge of connivance by state agents in the false reports. That was enough to prevent dismissal of that branch of the indictment.

Stewart's draft referred to the argument that there was no equal protection right against wholly private action. Then, as in Stewart's final opinion, it read, "On its face, the argument is unexceptionable. The Equal Protection Clause speaks to the State or to those acting under the color of its authority." The draft next asserted, "And § 5 of the Fourteenth Amendment empowers Congress to effectuate and implement only those rights the Amendment itself confers."

In a later portion of the draft, Stewart referred to the cases holding "state action" present, even though the state involvement was not exclusive or direct. The draft went on, "It has also been suggested that a State can violate the Equal Protection Clause by abdication as well as by affirmative action, and the default or neglect of a State to accord the equal protection of the law to its inhabitants might be a predicate for congressional action under the Equal Protection Clause and § 5 of the Fourteenth Amendment."

Douglas and Clark immediately agreed to Stewart's draft. However, on February 4, Brennan sent a *Memorandum to the Conference* "to inform the Conference of some of my concerns with the position Potter has charted for the Court in this case." Brennan wrote, "My principal concern. . . . stems from the discussion in section II delimiting the scope of congressional power under § 5 of the Fourteenth Amendment. There are several critical ambiguities and I fear that the opinion could be read as putting undue limitations on the power of Congress to act in this area."

Stewart was touring in the Middle East when Brennan's memo was circulated. After he returned, Stewart sent a February 21 *Memorandum to the Conference* that stated, "My original circulation caused difficulties for Hugo and for Bill Brennan (perhaps for others too), and in re-reading that draft yesterday I completely understood why. Two passages in the original circulation, having to do with congressional *power,* simply did not belong there. They were at the most parenthetical asides—pure dicta—and could not but cause confusion. I have now deleted those passages."

The Stewart memo asserted that "this case does not involve any issue of congressional power under § 5 of the Fourteenth Amendment." But Brennan thought that, even with the deletions, the draft contained the implication that section 241 did not reach a private conspiracy to interfere with the right to equal utilization of public facilities.

Brennan discussed the matter with Stewart, who acknowledged that the implication was present. Brennan then asked, "If you're prepared to put the question of power to one side, why doesn't § 241 reach a private conspiracy to interfere with the right to equal utilization of state facilities?" When Stewart did not give a convincing answer, Brennan suggested that he delete the last four paragraphs of Part II of his draft.

Stewart was unwilling to do so, and Brennan decided to prepare an opinion dissenting from that aspect of Stewart's opinion dealing with the conspiracy to deprive blacks of the right to equal utilization of public facilities. On March 10, Brennan wrote Stewart, "You know how troubled I've been about pages 8 to 10 of your *Guest*. I finally decided to put my views on paper, as per the enclosed." Brennan recognized the changes Stewart had made, saying, "I appreciate . . . that you have expressly set aside the question of the scope of congressional power under § 5 of the Fourteenth Amendment."

Despite this, Brennan went on, he had written his own opinion. "I nevertheless read your circulation, and I think many others will also read it, as requiring proof of officer's participation to sustain a conviction. Thus, I've spelled out my reasons for construing § 241 as not requiring proof of official participation in the alleged private conspiracy. This, of course, means I have to reach the constitutional question."

Brennan's opinion took the position that section 241 did reach a private conspiracy to interfere with the exercise of the right to equal utilization and that, as so construed, section 241 was a proper exercise of congressional power to enforce the Fourteenth Amendment.

Before circulating his opinion, Brennan showed Warren a copy. The Chief told Brennan that the opinion required further consideration. As soon as Brennan circulated, Douglas decided to withdraw from Stewart's opinion and join Brennan's. He also said he would speak to Fortas to persuade him to join.

At this point, Warren became actively involved. He now thought it was important to have a majority of the Court subscribe to the view expressed in Brennan's dissent on the scope of congressional power under section 5 of the Fourteenth Amendment. The Chief had long discussions with Black and Clark. As a result, Clark circulated a separate opinion shortly before the March 28 conference preceding the announcement of the decision. In his opinion, Clark stated that, though he joined Stewart's opinion, he wanted to make it clear that there was no doubt that, under section 5 of the Fourteenth Amendment, Congress had the power to punish all conspiracies—with or without state action—that interfered with rights derived from that amendment.

At the March 28 conference, Fortas decided to join Clark's opinion. Black also joined. When he learned that Black and Fortas had joined Clark's opinion, Brennan changed his opinion to state that a majority of the Court now subscribed to the Brennan view on the scope of congressional power to enforce the Fourteenth Amendment—i.e., "that § 5 empowers Congress to enact laws punishing *all* conspiracies to interfere with the exercise of Fourteenth Amendment rights, whether or not state officers or others acting under the color of state law are implicated in the conspiracy." [29]

Since Warren also joined Brennan's opinion, six Justices supported the proposition that Congress had the power to reach private conspiracies under the Fourteenth Amendment. When the *Guest* opinions were announced on March 28, the majority thus effectively overruled the *Civil Rights Cases,* even though Stewart had amended his opinion expressly to disavow any intention to deal with the issue of congressional power. Stewart expressed his bewilderment at the turn of events since his initial circulation some three months earlier, which had made his opinion, though denominated "opinion of the Court," only that of a minority. Harlan, who had by this time written a dissent, added a footnote to his opinion characterizing the action of Clark, Black, and Fortas as "extraordinary." [30]

Brown v. Louisiana [31] was the 1965 Term's sit-in type case. As part of a campaign to integrate the public library in Clinton, Louisiana, Brown and four other black men went into its reading room. Brown asked for a book the library did not have. The librarian said she would request the book from the State Library and then asked the men to leave. They did not. Brown sat down and the others stood near him. Ten minutes later, the sheriff arrived and asked them to leave. When they still did not, he arrested them for not leaving a public building when asked by an officer. They were convicted of violating the Louisiana breach of the peace statute. The highest state court refused to hear their appeal. All the Brethren voted to grant certiorari.

The December 10, 1965, conference was closely divided. Warren had no doubt that the convictions should be reversed. As he saw it, there was "no evidence to show a breach of peace. Their conduct was not of that kind." Warren also thought "the judge was wrong in saying that this was not a case to prove segregation."

Douglas, Brennan, White, and Fortas supported Warren. White stated that, "apart from segregation, I can't suppose one may sit in a public building when told by the police to get out." But, White stressed, defendants' conduct had to be viewed "against a background of racial segregation." Fortas said that there was "just no evidence here of a violation of this statute showing an intent to breach the peace."

Black, Clark, Harlan, and Stewart voted the other way. "There's no question," Harlan affirmed, "that they went there to demonstrate against the segregated library. They stayed on and didn't go when told to." This had to be looked at, Harlan stressed, "in the context of a small library, attended by one old woman."

After the conference voted, five-to-four, to reverse, the opinion was assigned to Fortas. He circulated a draft opinion of the Court on December 30. The draft reversed the convictions because the evidence showed that no breach of the peace had been committed. Defendants could not constitutionally be convicted because they did not comply with an order to leave the library. They had the same right as whites to use the public facility and could not be convicted for engaging "in lawfully, constitutionally protected exercise of their fundamental rights" under the First Amendment.

Except for two changes, the Fortas draft was the same as his final *Brown* opinion. The first change was the omission of a sentence that appeared after the discussion of the Court's prior decisions striking down convictions under Louisiana's breach of the peace statute: "After these three decisions, we might reasonably expect the State of Louisiana no longer to tolerate use of its breach of the peace statute to punish persons engaged in orderly, peaceful, controlled civil rights demonstrations."

The final Fortas opinion also saw the deletion of a footnote about the decision on the breach of the peace statute in *Cox v. Louisiana*,[32] decided the previous term. The footnote was explained in a December 30 *Memorandum for the Brethren* that Fortas attached to his draft. "I have become concerned about the impact of language in the Court's opinion in *Cox v. Louisiana*. Perhaps *Cox* should be read as holding that the Louisiana breach-of-the-peace statute is unconstitutional on its face. MR. JUSTICE BLACK in his concurring and dissenting opinion so construed the Court's opinion."

Fortas was, however, disturbed about such an interpretation of *Cox*. His memo stated that, "If the Court is of the view that *Cox* held the Louisiana statute unconstitutional for all purposes, I think we should dispose of the present case on the basis of a short *per curiam*. I should regret this because I believe that there is a permissible and constitutional office for this kind of a breach-of-the-peace statute— and it would be difficult to distinguish the Louisiana statute from the statutes in a number of States."

That was why, Fortas indicated, he inserted the footnote on *Cox,* "which I hope is tactfully phrased," in his opinion. The footnote itself stated that *Cox* held the Louisiana statute "unconstitutional for vagueness and overbreadth. The Court's opinion was confined to the unconstitutionality of the statute as applied." The Fortas memo explained that, in the footnote, "I deal with *Cox* as holding essentially that the Louisiana breach-of-the-peace statute was unconstitutional *as applied* to the facts in *Cox.* I recommend this formula."

As it turned out, the Fortas opinion did not speak for a majority. Warren and Douglas joined. But Brennan was not prepared to hold that Brown's activity was constitutionally protected. He also thought that the Fortas attempt to confine *Cox* was untenable. Brennan discussed the matter with Fortas, saying that a declaration that a statute was unconstitutional for overbreadth could not, by the very nature of the vagueness doctrine, be reduced to a holding that the statute was unconstitutional "as applied" to the particular case. The judgment as to the statute's overbreadth must be predicated on possible or anticipated applications of the statute rather than the one at bar. Brennan indicated that he would join an opinion that rested reversal on the no-evidence ground alone. Fortas, however, changed his opinion only by deleting the footnote seeking to limit *Cox.* Fortas refused to eliminate that part of the opinion holding that the library protest was protected by the First Amendment. Brennan then announced that he would write separately and prepared a concurrence in the judgment, based on the overbreadth of the Louisiana breach of the peace statute.

White also wrote a separate opinion, concurring in the result, based on the lack of any evidence to support breach of the peace convictions. Black then circulated what one of the Justices called "his high-pitched dissent on 'law and order.'" Black's draft contained extreme language, particularly a statement accusing the majority of bias against the South. "There is," Black asserted, "simply no evidence in the record at all that petitioners were arrested because they were exercising the 'right to protest.' The Court concludes, nevertheless, apparently because the arrests were made in the Deep South that this was the *sole* reason for the arrests."

Brennan showed Fortas a copy of his concurrence prior to circulation, with the hope that he would adopt it. That would make a separate opinion unnecessary, and it would require Black to delete major portions of his dissent. Fortas again was unwilling to change his opinion. Brennan then circulated his separate concurrence.

Black modified his dissent to respond to Brennan's opinion and also toned down some of its stronger passages. Clark, Harlan, and Stewart joined Black's dissent.

On the eve of the announcement of the *Brown* decision Fortas informed Brennan that if he would join the Fortas opinion, White would also. Brennan refused. When Fortas delivered his opinion on February 23, he spoke for a plurality of three only. Brennan and White issued their separate concurrences. Black, joined by Clark, Harlan, and Stewart, read what was still an unusually sharp dissent.

Three school desegregation cases were disposed of summarily during the 1965 Term. In *Bradley v. Richmond School District*[33] and *Gilliam v. Hopewell School Board*,[34] the lower court had approved two school desegregation plans without hearing into the claim that faculty segregation rendered the plans inadequate. At the certiorari conference, the Justices decided, after a close vote, to reverse summarily in the *Richmond* case on the issue of faculty segregation, and to set down the *Hopewell* case for consideration on the issues raised by those challenging the plan. Brennan was assigned the per curiam.

Brennan circulated a draft per curiam, with a covering *Memorandum to the Conference*. The memo asked for guidance on two problems encountered in preparation of the draft: (1) Since there was some overlap between the *Richmond* and *Hopewell* cases and a decision on the common issue in the *Hopewell* case might make the proposed per curiam unnecessary, should the *Richmond* case also be set down for plenary consideration or at least held pending the decision in the *Hopewell* case? (2) Should the petitioners in the *Richmond* case be asked to respond to the representation in the school board's brief that the faculty had been desegregated since the court of appeals decision? At Harlan's request, the *Richmond* petitioners were asked to respond. Their response indicated that the board's representation on desegregation of the faculty was not true.

At the next conference on the cases, it was decided that both cases should be summarily vacated and remanded in the same per curiam. There was, however, no consensus on the ground of decision. Stewart rejected a per se approach that would have prohibited racial assignments of faculty under all circumstances. Black wanted the opinion to stress that desegregation must occur immediately, without further delay. Others expressed different views.

Brennan wrote an opinion, that granted cert and summarily vacated and remanded on the ground that the student desegregation plans could not be approved without a full inquiry into faculty segregation. There were minor suggestions from the other Justices. Black asked that the phrase "racial allocation of faculty" be substituted for "faculty segregation"—a suggestion that was accepted.

Douglas said that he would have preferred to include "additional, more general talk about the relevancy of faculty segregation to student segregation." But he stated that he would agree if Brennan thought the opinion circulated "is all that is feasible at the present time." Harlan wrote that he thought language should be added to "plainly indicate that there should be dealt with on remand what you have called the 'per se' aspect of the teacher-segregation question." Brennan told Harlan that such language was unnecessary, and Harlan agreed. The opinion was issued as a unanimous per curiam on November 15, 1965.

The same unanimity was not achieved in the third desegregation case, *Rogers v. Paul.*[35] Rogers and other blacks challenged a desegregation plan for the Fort Smith, Arkansas, high schools. The plan desegregated only one grade a year. The tenth, eleventh, and twelfth grades were still segregated, and petitioners were assigned to a black high school. Brennan again prepared a per curiam granting certiorari and vacating and remanding. The opinion ordered immediate transfer of petitioners to the white high school, as well as a prompt hearing on their claim of faculty segregation. Warren, Black, Douglas, Clark, and Stewart joined Brennan's per curiam.

Harlan informed Brennan that he could not go along with that part of the opinion stating "petitioners are entitled to immediate relief." He said that, unless Brennan modified it to indicate that petitioners were entitled to immediate transfers only because of the inadequacy of the curriculum at the black school, he would dissent. Brennan refused to make the change.

At the next conference Fortas urged that the case should be set down for argument and full consideration. He thought that the lower courts needed more guidance on plans for one grade-a-year desegregation and that the Court should adopt the desegregation guidelines issued by the Department of Health, Education, and Welfare.

Brennan disagreed. He said that it would be of little value for the

Court to adopt the H.E.W. guidelines, since they were constantly being reformulated. However, Clark and White agreed with Fortas. When the *Rogers* per curiam was issued on December 6, 1965, the three of them announced that they "would set the case down for argument and plenary consideration." Their statement was joined by Harlan, who had decided to do so rather than write the dissent he had threatened.

Warren was in dissent in one civil rights case, *Greenwood v. Peacock*.[36] The case arose out of state prosecutions of civil rights demonstrators for obstructing the streets of Greenwood, Mississippi. Peacock and the other defendants filed petitions to remove their cases to the federal district court under a statute providing for removal by a state defendant "who is denied or cannot enforce in the courts of such State a right under any law providing for the equal civil rights of citizens of the United States." Peacock and the others alleged that they were arrested because they were black or were helping blacks assert their civil rights, that they were innocent of the charges, and that they would be unable to obtain a fair trial in the state courts. The federal court of appeals held that these allegations stated a good case for removal.

The April 29, 1966, conference voted by a bare majority to reverse, with the Chief Justice, Douglas, Brennan, and Fortas voting the other way. Black, the senior majority Justice, assigned the opinion to Stewart. Brennan had said that he would write a dissent. After Stewart circulated his opinion, it was learned that Douglas had prepared a dissent. The first draft of the Douglas dissent stressed the untrustworthiness of Southern justice. It asserted, "We know from the flow of cases coming this way that there are many, many such harassment prosecutions in the South today—not only against Negroes but against whites as well who take up the cause of civil rights."

Warren found this Douglas language objectionable. So did Fortas, who circulated a short separate dissent stressing the role and responsibility of the Southern courts and judges in providing equal justice. Warren was considering joining the Fortas opinion. Brennan agreed with their objections, and in Douglas' absence, he drafted changes moderating the Douglas opinion. When the Chief and Fortas indicated that they would join the Douglas dissent if Brennan's changes were made, Douglas agreed and toned down his language.

The *Greenwood* opinion was announced by Stewart on the last day of the term. It held that defendants were not entitled to removal on their allegations. To hold otherwise, according to Stewart's opinion, would "permit the judges of the federal courts to put their brethren of the state judiciary on trial."[37] Douglas, joined by Warren, Brennan, and Fortas, delivered a dissent that, though toned down, was still critical of the majority's leaving Peacock and the other defendants to "local passions and prejudices."

Several significant First Amendment cases were decided during the 1965 Term. The easiest was *Mills v. Alabama.*[38] The *Birmingham Press–Herald* published an editorial on election day urging a vote for the mayor–council form of government. Mills, the editor, was prosecuted for violating a law making it a crime to do any electioneering or solicit votes on election day. The state court held that the law did not unconstitutionally abridge freedom of the press.

At the conference on April 22, 1966, all voted for reversal. Harlan felt that the reversal should be based on the vagueness of the statute. The others agreed with Warren, who said that the statute, "as applied violates the First Amendment." Black declared that there was "a straight, flat, open violation of the First Amendment" and delivered an opinion so holding on May 23. All joined except Harlan, who concurred on the ground that the statute did not give Mills fair notice that it reached his editorial.

More difficulty was presented by *Rosenblatt v. Baer.*[39] It arose out of a libel action by Baer, the appointed Supervisor of the Belknap County, New Hampshire, Recreation Area, a facility operated by the county. A column by Rosenblatt in a local paper discussed the operation of the Recreation Area, noted it was doing better that year despite worse weather conditions and asked, "What happened to all the money last year? and every other year?" Baer alleged that this falsely charged him with mismanagement or dishonesty. The jury awarded damages, and the New Hampshire Supreme Court affirmed.

Rosenblatt's certiorari petition reached the Court during the 1964 Term. Before the cert conference, Brennan sent around a *Memorandum to the Conference*, dated March 1965 (but which was sent around at the end of February), which noted that the crucial question was "whether respondent was a public official within the meaning of *Times–Garrison*"—referring both to *New York Times v. Sullivan*[40] and *Garrison v. Louisiana*,[41] the 1964 case discussed in the last chapter.

"My own view," Brennan informed the Brethren, "is that the nature of the public interest in free discussion, rather than the precise categorization of the function of the person defamed, should be determinative. On this reasoning, the category of public officials should include at least those persons whose conduct is a matter of public interest in a political context. To reach respondent's conduct, therefore, it is unnecessary to consider whether movie actors, football coaches, and others whose conduct may interest the public, fit within the *Times–Garrison* rationale."

To Brennan, Baer was definitely a public official, within *Times–Garrison*. "Clearly the public had an interest in respondent's discharge of his official duties. Moreover, his position was a [responsible] one, since he handled large sums of money and was apparently directly responsible to the governing body of the county. A formulation which included him could clearly avoid deciding whether all civil servants are public officials under the *New York Times* rule."

The Brennan memo stated, "Unless we deny certiorari, I think there are three courses open to us. First, we can set the case for plenary argument. . . . Second, we can remand for reconsideration in light of *Garrison*. . . . Third, we can dispose of the case in a short *per curiam*."

The suggested per curiam would conclude "that respondent was a public official; in so concluding, we can stress the fact that respondent was directly responsible to the governing body of the county and that his conduct in that position was a matter of the highest public concern." By following the third approach, Brennan wrote, "we can avoid expanding the public official concept in a manner which might prove unacceptable to some of the Brethren. For the reasons given, I would favor the third approach."

At the conference, a majority agreed to follow Brennan's third approach. The Justice prepared a two-page per curiam, which began, "The petition for certiorari is granted. The judgment is reversed." The per curiam said it accepted the assumption that Baer was a public official and, that being the case, "The jury instructions were plainly infirm under the *New York Times* standard."

Brennan's per curiam was circulated, and several Justices agreed to it. It looked as though the Court would go along with Brennan's summary disposition. But Harlan sent around a memorandum stating that he would deny certiorari since this was not a proper vehicle for establishing standards for determining who was a "public official." The Harlan memo said that, if certiorari were granted, he would set the case down for oral argument because he believed that such standards should only be established after full consideration.

Brennan answered Harlan with a March 2, 1965, *Memorandum to the Conference* that informed the Brethren: "In the light of John Harlan's proposed Memorandum in the above, I am withdrawing my proposed Per Curiam and will recommend at the conference that we grant certiorari and set the case down for argument." The Justices granted cert on March 15 and scheduled the case for argument during the following term, with counsel directed to argue the question whether Baer was a "public official" under the *Times* and *Garrison* decisions.

At the October 22, 1965, conference following the argument, Warren accepted the approach outlined by Brennan the previous term. "Was he a public official?" asked the Chief. "He was. Did the instructions conform to *New York Times?* No."

There was a solid vote for reversal, but the conference was unable to agree upon a ground of decision. Fortas, in particular, expressed concern with extending the *Times* doctrine without due regard for the privacy and reputation of the insignificant government employee. Because of the disagreement, the case was scheduled again at the next conference.

In the interim in mid-November, Brennan prepared a memorandum that stated the view taken in his final *Rosenblatt* opinion. The next conference did not resolve much, but Warren did assign the opinion to Brennan, who circulated a draft based on his memo.

Brennan explained the theory behind his draft opinion in a November 20 letter to Douglas. Brennan's letter asked, "is not reversal required under *Times* in any event for a reason which makes irrelevant a determination whether respondent was a 'public official?' As I discuss at pp. 3–4 of the draft, one of the theories on which the case went to the jury is flatly contradicted by our unanimous agreement in *Times* that libel cannot be made out where the statement involved is an 'impersonal attack' on government operations. This statement is surely as much an impersonal attack on the administration of the ski area as the attack on police administration in Montgomery in *Times*. Thus must not the judgment be reversed because an impermissible theory of liability was submitted to the jury, and might have been the basis of its verdict, whether or not we reach the 'public official' question?"

After he read Brennan's draft, Douglas circulated a memorandum urging that the writ of certiorari be dismissed as having been improvidently granted, because *New York Times* should not be applied "retroactively to this case." Baer's libel suit had been tried before the *Times* decision, and Douglas wrote that "factual building blocks more substantial than those offered by this truncated record" were needed to delimit the concept of the "public official." The Douglas memo also expressed fear that respondent would be unable, as a matter of state law, to obtain the new trial the majority assumed he could have. Douglas stated that he would have preferred the Court to focus on the "public" rather than the "official" nature of the defamed person's duties. Clark, Stewart, and Fortas, indicated that they would join in the dismissal recommended by Douglas.

Brennan responded to Douglas in his November 20 letter. He noted that the Douglas memo had asserted "that the draft announces a 'constitutional right to tell lies' even if it does reach the little man in government." Brennan wrote, "it was my intent, however, to leave the issue of the 'little man' open, and even to hint that he might not be reached. This is why I noted that the interests protected in *Times* included *both* free discussion of public issues *and* free discussion of persons in positions of responsibility for and influence on such issues; and that *both* were factors that would influence the 'public official' determination."

Brennan then gave examples of how he would apply his test:

While a night watchman might be an important figure in some clandestine conspiracy, he would not be among those within my suggested test, namely, among the "hierarchy of government employees who have, or appear to have, substantial responsibility for or control over the conduct of governmental affairs." The test is meant to suggest a "table of organization" hierarchy, which would focus on the expected functions of persons (including reputed powers behind the throne of the Col. House type), and not some special role they might suddenly be revealed to have by the very publication which is challenged as libellous. I would be surprised to see public discussion of the qualifications of candidates for janitorial, secretarial, or like positions. I would be not at all surprised to see discussion of the qualifications of a proposed Recreation Area manager, whether or not rumors of peculation were abroad. To me, this is a tenable, functional, important distinction.

After he read Brennan's letter, Douglas said that he would join Part II of Brennan's opinion, which avoided the question of whether Baer was a "public official." But Harlan now indicated that it was that part of the opinion that troubled him.

Brennan wrote Harlan on November 29 to explain Part II:

In essence, it attempts a distinction between an explicit defamatory statement levelled at a small group (the Cabinet are a bunch of crooks) and a statement impersonal on its face which extrinsic testimony may show hits at a group of public officials, large or small. In the former case this suggests that any member of the Cabinet on proofs meeting *New York Times'* malice standards may recover merely by identifying himself as such a member. In the latter case recovery would be allowed only if in addition the plantiff offers proofs supporting a finding that the statement was made of and concerning him.

As Brennan saw it, "There is no clear definition in this case as to who are the members of the group. There is no clear reference to the group. There is no clearly defamatory accusation. These missing elements, to me, indicate that the jury was given too much rein—more than is consistent with our holding in *New York Times*."

Harlan could not, however, be persuaded to join Brennan's opinion. He circulated a dissent from Part II. He had been persuaded to join Part III only after footnote 12 had been modified to remove the indication that *New York Times* would cover "public figures" who did not hold any governmental position. Harlan insisted that the note state expressly that the Court was intimating no view on that matter.

By this time, Black and Fortas had circulated dissents. Black disagreed with allowing the judge, in the first instance, to determine whether Baer was a "public official" and Fortas wanted dismissal as improvidently granted. At the same time, Warren and White joined Brennan's opinion without reservation.

At this point, the Brennan opinion had four votes for each of its two substantive parts—Warren, Douglas, Brennan, and White for Part II, and Warren, Harlan, Brennan, and White for Part III. Stewart now circulated what a member of the Court called "an intense and strongly worded dissent." Stewart protested that the Court was not giving sufficient recognition to the individual's interest in privacy.

To meet Stewart's criticism, Brennan inserted a paragraph referring to "the important social values which underlie the law of defamation." Stewart then changed his vote from a dissent to a concurrence, though he still issued a toned down version of his draft dissent as his separate concurrence. Stewart's vote now made a bare majority for each of the substantive parts of Brennan's opinion.

The situation was now complicated by Warren's reaction to the case of *Curtis Publishing Co. v. Butts.*[42] It involved a libel action against a magazine publisher by a famous football coach. The publisher claimed that it was protected by the *New York Times* decision. At its conference on Friday, February 18, 1966, the Court reached the certiorari petition in the *Butts* case. During the discussion, Warren became upset at the suggestion that a state university athletic director could be considered a "public official" within the meaning of *New York Times.* He was alarmed that *Rosenblatt v. Baer* could be used as support for that proposition. He wanted *Rosenblatt v. Baer* put over for a week, and threatened to withdraw his long-standing vote.

After the conference, Douglas spoke to the Chief Justice on the telephone and persuaded him that the *Butts* case would probably be covered by the "public figure" category reserved in footnote 12 in Brennan's *Rosenblatt v. Baer* opinion. Warren then decided to take his chances when the *Butts* petition was reconsidered and agreed that the *Rosenblatt v. Baer* decision could be announced on the following Monday.

But on Saturday morning, February 19, Clark sent Brennan a typewritten draft of an opinion that he proposed to file. He said that he would not file it if Brennan had strong objections. In his draft, Clark joined Harlan's dissent from Part II, and concurred in the result regarding Part III, though criticizing certain aspects of Brennan's discussion. Brennan vigorously opposed Clark's issuance of the opinion. He thought that it distorted the record and also objected that the late date precluded an effective reply. Accordingly, Clark withdrew his opinion and asked that his concurrence in the result should be noted. On that basis, Brennan delivered his *Rosenblatt v. Baer* opinion on March 21, 1966.

On the following Friday, the conference decided to ask the parties in the *Butts* case to address themselves to the decision in *Rosenblatt v. Baer.* The Justices expected that, by the time the additional papers were received, it would be too late to consider the case before the following term.

For Warren in particular, the most difficult First Amendment cases were the obscenity cases, for they brought into focus the conflict between his attachment to free expression and his abhorrence of pornography. Three important obscenity cases were decided during the 1965 Term. The first was *A Book Named "John Cleland's Memoirs of a Woman of Pleasure" v. Massachusetts.*[43] It arose out of a Massachusetts court finding that the Cleland book—popularly known as *Fanny Hill*—was obscene and not entitled to First Amendment protection. The second case was *Ginzburg v. United States,*[44] in which Ginzburg had been convicted of violating the federal obscenity statute by selling through the mails *Eros* (a hard-cover magazine with articles and photgraphs on "love, sex, and sexual relations").[45] *Liaison* (a newsletter on sex and sexual relations), and *The Housewife's Handbook on Selective Promiscuity* ("a sexual autobiography detailing with complete candor the author's sexual experiences from age 6 to 36").[46] The third case was *Mishkin v. New York,*[47] involving a state conviction for selling obscene books. The books Mishkin had sold were described by the Court as ones that "depict such deviations as sado-masochism, fetishism, and homosexuality. Many have covers with drawings of scantily clad women being whipped, beaten, tortured, or abused."[48]

In the *Fanny Hill* case, Black, Douglas, Harlan, Stewart, and Fortas voted to take the appeal. In *Ginzburg,* Black, Harlan, Stewart, and Goldberg voted to grant certiorari, with the others voting to deny. In *Mishkin,* the same four voted to hear the appeal, while the remaining five voted the other way.

In the decade since *Roth v. United States,*[49] discussed in chapter 6, it had been impossible to obtain any Court consensus on obscenity. The three 1965 Term cases proved no exception. They produced fourteen opinions. Warren and Fortas were the only Justices who did not write separately.

At the December 10, 1965, conference on the obscenity cases, Black and Douglas once again asserted their absolutist view of the First Amendment, urging that it protected obscene and nonobscene material alike. The majority, however, refused to repudiate the *Roth* holding that obscenity was beyond First Amendment protection. Consequently, the initial problem was to formulate a definition of obscenity for purposes of applying the *Roth* holding. The result was the statement of the threefold obscenity definition in the *Fanny Hill* opinion: "Under this definition . . . three elements must coalesce: it must be established that (a) the dominant theme of the material taken as a whole appeals to a prurient interest in sex; (b) the material is patently offensive because it affronts contemporary community standards relating to the description or representation of sexual matters; and (c) the material is utterly without redeeming social value."[50]

The opinions in all three cases had been assigned to Brennan. He circulated draft opinions in *Ginzburg* and *Mishkin* before he prepared his *Fanny Hill* opinion. The statement of the three criteria first appeared in the *Ginzburg* draft. At first it seemed that there would be no difficulty in obtaining a majority for that definition of obscenity. Warren and Fortas agreed to the draft without taking issue with the definition. Clark and White refused to commit themselves to *Ginzburg* or *Mishkin* until they saw *Fanny Hill* affirmed or disposed of without any holding that the book was not obscene. But there was no indication that they disagreed with the three-pronged definition then contained in the *Ginzburg* opinion.

At the conference, Warren, Clark, Harlan, Brennan, and White had voted to affirm in *Fanny Hill*. But Fortas expressed strong concern that an affirmance would give rise to a new wave of "book-burning" and tacitly conditioned his concurrence in *Ginzburg* and *Mishkin* upon a reversal in *Fanny Hill*. Brennan then decided to write an opinion to reverse in *Fanny Hill*. His opinion found that *Fanny Hill* was not obscene, since, even on the view of the court below, it possessed "a modicum of social value."[51] The decision was based on Brennan's three-pronged definition of obscenity.

Brennan persuaded the Chief to agree to his draft for reversal by telling him of Fortas' position and reminding him of his own dissenting opinion in the 1957 case of *Kingsley Books, Inc. v. Brown,*[52] where Warren had said that courts should not judge "the quality of art or literature. To do otherwise . . . savors too much of book burning."[53] Warren and Fortas joined the draft after it was circulated on February 2, 1966. As it turned out, they were the only Justices to join Brennan's *Fanny Hill* opinion.

The ground of decision chosen by Brennan for reversing in *Fanny Hill* made the definition of obscenity set forth in his *Ginzburg* draft critical—something he had not anticipated at the time the definition was formulated. White prepared a *Fanny Hill* dissent expressing an unwillingness to subscribe to the three-pronged definition, because it gave independent status to the redeeming social value criterion.

White told Brennan that this disagreement would preclude him from joining in *Ginzburg,* and he indicated that he would merely concur in the result in that case. Because of this, the statement of the definition of obscenity was moved to Brennan's *Fanny Hill* opinion. After all references to the three criteria were removed from the *Ginzburg* and *Mishkin* drafts, White said that he would join those opinions.

Though Clark had not yet indicated his position on Brennan's draft opinions, Warren and Brennan hoped that he would join in *Fanny Hill.* That would mean four Justices subscribing to Brennan's three-fold definition, since the Chief Justice and Fortas had already joined. Acting on that presumption, Stewart had circulated dissents in *Ginzburg* and *Mishkin.* But he now indicated that he would become the fifth in *Fanny Hill.* He said that he was prepared to join that part of Brennan's *Fanny Hill* opinion stating the definition of obscentiy because he thought it important to have a majority statement of the definition. To obtain Stewart's agreement, Brennan divided his *Fanny Hill* opinion into two parts. Stewart was noted as joining Part I, containing the obscenity definition. During this period, Warren tried to secure Clark's concurrence. This time, however, the Chief did not succeed in persuading the Texan. Not long before the obscenity decisions were announced, Clark informed the conference that he would concur in the result in *Ginzburg* and *Mishkin,* but would dissent in *Fanny Hill.* Clark circulated a dissent that discussed the sexual episodes described in *Fanny Hill.* This led to a March 15, 1966, *Memorandum to the Conference* from Douglas: "In view of Brother Clark's passion for detail, why don't we all chip in and buy him a copy of MY LIFE & LOVES, by FRANK HARRIS, published by Grove Press, Inc."

The Clark dissent took issue with Brennan's three-pronged definition of obscenity, objecting that requiring a book to be "utterly without redeeming social value" meant giving "the smut artist free rein to carry on his dirty business."[54] When he read Clark's dissent, Stewart withdrew his limited agreement in *Fanny Hill.* He had concurred in Part I of Brennan's opinion only for the purpose of obtaining a majority statement of the constitutional definition, and withdrew his concurrence now that it was clear that it would no longer achieve that result. When Brennan delivered his opinion in *Fanny Hill* on March 21, 1966, it had only the concurrences of the Chief Justice and Fortas. However the plurality believed that Brennan's obscenity definition would be the one followed by the lower courts since Black, Douglas, and Stewart indicated in their separate concurrences that they would go at least that far in delimiting the area of First Amendment protection.

In the *Ginzburg* case, a majority was obtained for Brennan's opinion. The vote at the December 10, 1965, conference was four (Warren, Clark, Brennan, and White) to affirm, and four (Black, Douglas, Harlan, and Stewart) to reverse. Fortas divided his vote among the publications *Ginzburg* had sold. He found *Liaison* obscene, and *Housewife's Handbook* not obscene because he thought it had therapeutic value. He said that he would probably join an opinion holding *Eros* obscene.

After the conference, Warren persuaded Fortas to join an opinion affirming Ginzburg's conviction based on a pandering approach. Though Ginzburg's pandering had not been discussed at the conference, a decision based on it fitted in directly with Warren's approach to obscenity. In his concurring opinion in the 1957 *Roth* case, Warren had stressed that defendants "were engaged in the commercial exploitation of the morbid and shameful craving for materials with prurient effect." And, in his previously mentioned *Kingsley Books* dissent, the Chief said, "It is the conduct of the individual that should be judged,"[55] not the quality of the books he sold.

To Warren, Ginzburg was marketing his materials with the representation that they were pornographic. They were mailed from Intercourse and Blue Ball, Pennsylvania, and Middlesex, New Jersey, and what the Court called the "leer of the sensualist"[56] permeated Ginzburg's advertising. Warren's approach here accepted the oft-voiced claim of the advertising industry that the image of a product becomes a part of the product itself.

Warren's pandering approach was accepted by Brennan. When he circulated a *Ginzburg* draft based on it, the Chief immediately indicated his willingness to join. Warren did suggest one modification. He did not want the doctrine limited to cases where the *sole* emphasis was on the sexually provocative aspect of the material. Brennan, supported by Fortas, insisted that the restriction imported by the word "sole" was necessary to prevent abuse of the pandering doctrine by the lower courts. Warren gave way on the point. Fortas made several suggestions that were accepted. They were directed toward making it clear that it was the objective conduct of Ginzburg in distributing the material, rather than his character or personal qualities, that was relevant. Fortas then said that he would join, though he did so formally only after the *Fanny Hill* opinion was circulated.

White and Clark at first indicated that they would not join Brennan's *Ginzburg* opinion, but would only concur in the result. They changed their mind after Brennan transferred the three-pronged definition of obscenity to the *Fanny Hill* opinion. Both then joined *Ginzburg*.

When Brennan announced his *Ginzburg* opinion on March 21, he could announce it as the opinion of the Court. For the first time in the decade since *Roth,* a majority (Brennan, Warren, Clark, White, and Fortas) was obtained on a full opinion that ruled on the alleged obscenity of material sold by a defendant.

While Brennan was announcing *Ginzburg,* Warren passed him the following note: "Because of the quizzical expression on the faces of some of the Sol. Gen's. staff I wonder how happy they are with *Ginzburg,* because you know it will cast quite a work burden on that office and on the US Attorneys."

In the *Mishkin* case, there was no doubt that defendant had also been engaged in pandering. But Brennan decided not to follow the *Ginzburg* approach in *Mishkin* because he felt that, even without regard to the manner in which the books were sold, they were beyond First Amendment protection. Accordingly, he wrote his *Mishkin* opinion to find the books obscene under straightforward application of the *Roth* test. He had to adjust *Roth's* prurient appeal criterion to the deviant groups reached by Mishkin's books. The Brennan opinion held that, when materials were aimed at a deviant group the criterion was met when there was prurient appeal to members of that group, even if not to the average person.

Brennan's approach here caused concern on the part of Fortas, who, with Black, Douglas, and Stewart, had voted at the conference to reverse the convictions. Fortas thought that it would be best not to tamper with the criterion. Instead, Fortas wanted to rely on the pandering approach, saying that Mishkin produced and distributed these publications for the announced purpose of appealing to his customers' prurient interest.

Brennan rejected the Fortas suggestion. But he did add a sentence that used *Ginzburg* to assert that Mishkin's "own evaluation of his material confirms such a finding"[57]—i.e., of prurient appeal. This met Fortas' approval, and he joined Brennan's opinion without insisting on his proposal. Clark and Harlan also joined and that made six Justices who supported the *Mishkin* opinion.

When Brennan had delivered the three obscenity opinions on March 21, 1966, Warren passed him another written note: "You have made a great contribution to the jurisprudence of our Court and your announcement was superb."

After the three obscenity decisions, the Justices decided whether to grant certiorari in two other obscenity cases, *Redrup v. New York*[58] and *Austin v. Kentucky*,[59] and whether to hear the appeal in a third, *Gent v. Arkansas*.[60] A majority at the conference on March 25, 1966, wanted to dispose of them summarily. But several were troubled by the prospect of affirming in *Gent,* or dismissing for want of a substantial federal question. White, for example, took the view that the "girlie" magazine in question was not obscene because it was not patently offensive. Before the next conference, Fortas circulated an April 13 *Memorandum to the Conference* that stated, "At Conference, I shared the apparently prevailing view that we should not at this time review obscenity cases in addition to those already decided. Further consideration has caused me to have serious misgivings as to my initial approach. . . . I no longer believe that we can appropriately rest on our laurels."

The Fortas memo suggested that *Redrup* and *Austin* should be taken to resolve the issue of scienter necessary for conviction in an obscenity case, and that *Gent* should be taken for the limited purpose of holding that the First Amendment prohibits the type of in rem proceedings involved there. Fortas wrote that he had come to the opinion that the obscenity exception to the First Amendment should be limited to those engaged in "a public tort—conscious and purposeful 'pandering' of such material."

At the conference on April 15, there were five votes for a grant of certiorari in *Redrup* and *Austin,* limited to the scienter question. It was more difficult to obtain a majority in *Gent.* After several conferences, the majority decided to take the *Gent* appeal, but limited to the question of whether the Arkansas obscenity law was invalid as a prior restraint on expression or because of vagueness. Black, Douglas, and Stewart dissented from the limitation on review.

Two 1965 Term cases were decided on governmental authority over subversive activities. We saw in the last chapter that a bare majority was prepared, in *American Committee for Protection of Foreign Born v. Subversive Activities Control Board*,[61] to invalidate a registration order of the Board as violative of the privilege against self-incrimination. However, after Goldberg had changed his vote, the case was disposed of on a technicality. Another Board registration order was challenged in *Albertson v. Subversive Activities Control Board*.[62] Albertson and several others were ordered by the Board to register as Communist Party members. The court of appeals rejected their challenge to the registration order. All the Justices (except White, who did not participate) voted to grant certiorari.

In the *American Committee* case, Warren had recommended reversal without consideration of the constitutional issues. This time, at the October 22, 1965, conference, the Chief spoke for reversal on the ground that the self-incrimination privilege had been violated. The government had relied on section 4 (f) of the statute, which provided that the fact of registration should not be received in evidence in any criminal prosecution. But Warren said that the Fifth Amendment violation was "not cured by section 4 (f)'s partial immunity." He also noted that, "here, unlike *Communist Party*, the privilege was asserted." His reference was to the 1961 case of *Communist Party v. Subversive Activities Control Board*,[63] discussed in chapter 9.

The conference voted unanimously to follow Warren's view and reverse on the Fifth Amendment claim. It was easier for all the Brethren to reach that result in *Albertson* than in *American Committee*, because the orders in it were orders to individuals, not to an organization, as had been the case in *American Committee*. For the Court to rule on the Fifth Amendment claim there would have meant overruling *United States v. White*,[64] a 1944 decision holding that the self-incrimination privilege did not apply to officers of an organization. There was no need in *Albertson* to deal with the *White* case.

Even Clark, who had prepared a strong dissent in *American Committee*, agreed at the conference to reversal "on self-incrimination grounds. *Counselman* would be all I need." The reference was to the 1892 case of *Counselman v. Hitchcock*,[65] which held that an immunity provision such as section 4 (f) was not enough to supplant the Fifth Amendment privilege. White, who had opposed reassertion of the *Counselman* principle in the *American Committee* case, did not participate in *Albertson*. So there was no opposition when Brennan circulated an *Albertson* draft opinion that relied on the *Counselman* case.

Despite his conference statement, Clark hesitated until the end before agreeing to Brennan's opinion. At the November 12, 1965, conference before the *Albertson* decision was announced, Clark finally said that he would join, though he would also issue a short concurrence pointing out that he had written to Congress while he was Attorney General expressing constitutional doubts about the registration requirement. In effect, as one of the Justices put it, Clark's *Albertson* opinion was addressed to Congress, saying, "I told you so."

The second 1965 Term subversion case was *Elfbrandt v. Russell*.[66] An Arizona statute required state employees to take an oath to support the Constitution and laws. The law provided for a perjury prosecution and discharge for anyone who took the oath and knowingly became a member of the Communist Party or any organization "having for one of its purposes the overthrow by force or violence of the government." Elfbrandt was a school teacher who refused to take the oath. She brought an action challenging the statutory oath requirement. The highest state court upheld the statute. Black, Douglas, Brennan, and Fortas voted to grant certiorari, while the others voted to deny.

Warren spoke for reversal at the February 25, 1966, conference. As he saw it, "They have singled state employees out on a basis not applicable to other people. I think it's vague also." In addition, the Chief was disturbed by "the absence of a hearing provision in this setting. If we assume that the state has the right to refuse jobs to Communists, it doesn't follow that [penalizing] the refusal to take an oath without a chance to explain why is constitutionally permissible." In such a case, the Court had to be especially careful to protect the individual. "They can't limit the right of association," Warren declared, "without turning square corners, procedurally and substantively."

The conference was closely divided, with only a bare majority for reversal. The opinion was assigned to Douglas. He delivered it on April 18, 1966, holding the oath invalid so far as it applied to passive members of organizations, who had no intent to further their illegal aims. White, joined by Clark, Harlan, and Stewart, dissented.

A word should also be said about *Burns v. Richardson*[67]—the term's apportionment case. Richardson was a Hawaii voter who brought an action to have that state's senate reapportionment plan declared invalid. The plan was based on the number of registered voters, rather than the total population of the state, and provided for multi-member senatorial districts. The lower court approved the use of registered voters as the measure of population, but declared the plan invalid because of the multi-member districts.

Warren began the February 25, 1966, conference by advocating reversal. He pointed out that this "is a special case" because of the Hawaiian demographic situation. "I think," the Chief declared, "registered voters is a satisfactory basis in this special situation—particularly because of the military problem, the problem as to transients. We don't have to say that it would be a proper basis in all circumstances. If it resulted in a gerrymander to discriminate, that would be something else." Warren further said, "I think multi-member districts are okay here, too."

The Court had approved the use of multi-member districts in *Fortson v. Dorsey*,[68] discussed in the last chapter. It also summarily affirmed in three 1965 Term cases involving such districts before it considered *Burns v. Richardson*. All the Justices thus had no difficulty in rejecting Richardson's challenge to the multi-districting feature of the Hawaii plan. This meant a reversal of the judgment below, though a majority agreed with Warren that the lower court was right on the use of the registered voter basis.

Black urged that the Court should come down immediately with an opinion approving the plan as a temporary measure and the best that could be expected under the circumstances. He suggested a very short opinion, and the opinion was assigned to Brennan, to be written on an expedited basis.

Brennan's circulated draft validated the Hawaii registered voter basis, because it produced a distribution of legislators not substantially different from that which would have resulted from a population base. The draft also dealt with the question of permissible population bases. Must gross population be used? Or may adult citizen population—those eligible to vote—be used? Brennan's opinion indicated that the states should be free to choose among these population bases, since each possessed a measure of rationality. The draft referred to the choices involved and left the decision to the states.

The others agreed that gross population was not the only permissible base—that a state could rationally exclude military, transients and the like from the population base. White, however, objected to the suggestion that states might properly choose a base, such as adult population, that would exclude children from the count. Since the record supported the conclusion that no improper divergence from a citizen population base had been shown, Brennan's opinion put aside the issue of other permissible types of population base and used state citizen population as a permissible population base.

Except for White's objection, Brennan's opinion was readily accepted and announced as the opinion of the Court on April 25, 1966. Black, however, had joined with reluctance. He wrote Brennan, "Unless someone else can write something that is persuasive enough to convince me that there is a better solution for this difficult Hawaiian problem, I am with you, and your good opinion puts a big burden on whoever attempts to prove you wrong."

In a speech just after the 1965 Term ended, Vice-President Hubert H. Humphrey declared that if President Eisenhower "had done nothing else other than appoint Warren Chief Justice, he would have earned a very important place in the history of the United States."[69] For Warren, the 1965–1966 Court year had been another satisfying one. March 1966 had seen his seventy-fifth birthday celebration—"the first birthday party I've had since I was a boy," the Chief commented—and with it an outpouring of tribute from the President down. During the same month, the World Association of Judges was formed in Geneva, with Warren named its Chairman. His bronze bust was unveiled at the National Lawyers Club in Washington and a *New York Times* article rated him "the greatest Chief Justice in the nation's history."[70]

To be sure, the acclaim did not drown out the Chief's extreme critics. Warren could scarcely attend any function without being met by "Impeach Earl Warren" pickets, who would shout and sometimes hurl their placards at Warren and his party. Alabama Governor George C. Wallace charged that the Court had destroyed the constitutional system and asserted that he was more qualified than Warren to serve as Chief Justice.[71]

The *New York Times* article already referred[72] to was entitled, "It Is the Earl Warren Court." The high bench was now emphatically the *Warren* Court and, without arrogance, he, as well as the others, knew it. During the 1965 Term, he led the Brethren in every important case to the decision he favored. He failed to do so only in the

Schmerber[73] and civil-rights removal cases,[74] which were hardly as significant as the term's other decisions. In particular, it was Warren who was primarily responsible for the decision in the term's great case, *Miranda v. Arizona*.[75]

Miranda, as much as anything, exemplified Warren's basic approach. Every so often in criminal cases, when counsel defending convictions would cite legal precedents, Warren would bend his bulk over the bench to ask, "Yes, yes—but were you fair?"[76] The fairness to which the Chief referred was no jurisprudential abstraction. It related to such things as methods of arrest, questioning of suspects, police conduct, and the like—matters that Warren still understood as intimately as when he himself was doing the prosecuting years earlier back in Alameda County, California. The *Miranda* decision was the ultimate embodiment of the Warren fairness approach.

15.

1966 TERM: WARREN AND THE "NEW" BLACK

"Look, Hugo, you can't unring a bell."

Black had just delivered a lecture in which he denied that the Chief Justice deserved the credit for the constitutional revolution worked by the Supreme Court. He told Warren that the press had distorted his statement. The Chief laughed and came back with the comment about the unringing of a bell.

Toward the end of Warren's Court tenure, a split had begun to develop between Black and the Chief Justice and his other supporters. In the 1966 Term, this converted the solid five-Justice core that the Chief had had since Goldberg replaced Frankfurter into a minority in several cases. Because of this, the term was not as successful for Warren. During it, he was in dissent more often than he had been at any time since Frankfurter's departure.

The split with Black was partly caused by personal differences. Mention has been made of the friction that had developed between Black and Douglas, exacerbated by Black's disapproval of his colleague's personal life. The 1966 Term saw strong exchanges between Black and Douglas, particularly, we will see, in the Georgia gubernatorial election case. Black also displayed a personal antipathy toward his newest colleague. He saw in Fortas a tendency to interpret due process as a broad guaranty of fairness and was particularly offended by his *Brown v. Louisiana* [1] opinion discussed in the last chapter. On his side, Fortas was hurt by the sharp attack in Black's draft *Brown* dissent. Black also denounced Fortas' draft opinion of the Court in the case of *Time, Inc. v. Hill.* [2] He told the others that it was the worst First Amendment opinion he had seen in a dozen years. [3]

Black did not have the same personal hostility toward Warren. But he did resent the acclaim which the Chief Justice received for leading what everyone looked on as the *Warren* Court. As Black saw it, the Court under Warren had only written into law the constitutional principles that he had been advocating for so many years. When Warren retired as Chief Justice, the Brethren prepared the traditional letter of farewell. The draft letter read: "For us it is a source of pride that we have had the opportunity to be members of the Warren Court." Black changed this to "the Court over which you have presided." [4]

Yet Black's movement away from Warren and his supporters was more than a matter of personalities. The Alabaman's fundamentalist approach to the Constitution did not permit him to adopt the expansive approach toward individual rights followed by some of the Justices. Black stood his constitutional ground where the rights asserted rested on specific provisions, such as the First Amendment or the Fifth Amendment privilege against self-incrimination. But when he could not find an express constitutional base, as in the right of privacy relied on by the *Griswold* decision [5] discussed in chapter 13, Black was unwilling to extend protection.

Black also refused to go along when rights that he recognized were being vindicated by direct action in ways he considered incompatible with the rule of law upon which all rights ultimately rested. The Sit-In Cases thus marked Black's constitutional divide. In the conflict of basic interests involved in them, Black came down on the side of property and the preservation of public order.

Warren was well aware of the changing Black posture and was more tolerant toward it than some of his colleagues. When others would complain to the Chief about Black's senility (Black turned eighty during the 1965 Term), Warren would chuckle and say, "No, Hugo just wants to be buried in Alabama."

In the 1964 case of *Bell v. Maryland,* [6] discussed in chapter 12, Black had secured a bare majority for his draft opinion affirming the sit-in convictions. Only at the last minute were Warren and his supporters able to obtain the votes to avoid such a decision on the merits. During the 1966 Term Black was again able to win five votes in *Adderley v. Florida.*[7] But this time the votes remained firm, and the Court affirmed the convictions of civil-rights demonstrators.

Adderley and other black college students had entered and remained on the grounds of the county jail in Tallahassee to demonstrate against the arrest of other students who had taken part in protests against segregation. The students had refused to leave after being ordered to do so by the sheriff, and they had been arrested and prosecuted for violating a state law prohibiting trespasses. Their convictions were affirmed.

The Supreme Court's certiorari vote anticipated the final division in *Adderley*, with Warren, Douglas, Brennan, and Fortas voting to grant and the others to deny. At the October 21, 1966, conference discussion, the Justices repeated the views they had expressed in the 1962 and 1963 Term Sit-In Cases. Warren led the case for reversal and Black that for affirmance. Once again Black had the conference votes, since Clark, Harlan, Stewart, and White supported him. In *Adderley,* as in the 1964 *Bell* case, Black wrote a draft opinion. This draft was, however, delivered as the opinion of the Court on November 14, 1966. Douglas, joined by Warren, Brennan, and Fortas, delivered a strong dissent.

The Black opinion alone spoke for the *Adderley* majority. Two of its members had almost written separately. Harlan did prepare a separate concurrence, but was persuaded to withdraw it and join the Black opinion. Clark joined, but only after Black took out the last sentence of his draft opinion, "And there is no right to 'demonstrate' which is constitutionally paramount to an owner's right to use his own property."

The majority view was criticized in a November 8, 1966, letter from Brennan to Douglas. "I had thought that our cases drastically limited the application of state statutes when one peacefully goes on *public* property to exercise First Amendment rights. . . . Hugo ignores the principle in his opinion and is very vulnerable on that score." Since this was a protest on public property, Brennan went on, it could not be treated as a trespass. "Since the record plainly shows, as you prove, that this was a legitimate protest enjoying First Amendment protection, the state was not at liberty to regard the conduct as a trespass, or any other violation of law."

Brennan feared that the Black opinion would have most undesirable effects. "Certainly, Hugo's opinion will have the most 'chilling effect' on legitimate protests on all forms of public property, parks, malls, etc. included." As Brennan saw it, "Hugo's opinion would support application of the trespass statute even to a demonstration on grounds outside a building which housed both the jail and the assembly chamber of a legislative body. . . . There are many buildings like that in the country and, if Hugo prevails, he's certainly effectively overruled *Edwards*." The reference was to *Edwards v. South Carolina*,[8] a 1963 case involving a civil-rights march around a State House.

Another civil-rights case where Black was able to secure a bare majority was *Walker v. Birmingham*.[9] The case arose out of the 1963 Easter protest demonstrations in Birmingham led by Martin Luther King. An ordinance prohibited street parades and demonstrations without a permit. The organizers of the 1963 demonstrations had tried unsuccessfully to obtain a permit. When the demonstrations began anyway, the city obtained an injunction prohibiting King and the other leaders, including Reverend Walker, from organizing street demonstrations without a permit. Despite the injunction, King and the others led protest marches. They were convicted of criminal contempt and jailed despite their claim that the injunction and the ordinance violated their First Amendment rights. The state supreme court affirmed. Certiorari was granted, with only Harlan and White voting to deny.

Warren urged reversal at the March 17, 1967, conference. As he saw it, "the ordinance is void on its face since it gives unfettered discretion to control First Amendment rights without standards." Nor did the injunction add anything to the case. "The injunction," Warren declared, "was simply a copy of the ordinance and I don't think [they] can bootstrap it by putting it in the form of an injunction."

Black spoke forcefully for affirmance, asserting that the demonstrators' motives did not excuse their violation of the injunction. Clark, Stewart, and White supported Black. But the conference voted five-to-four to reverse or vacate the convictions. The fifth vote was cast by Harlan, who said that defendants "should have had an opportunity to prove discriminatory application and I would remand for a hearing."

On March 20, however, Harlan circulated copies of a note he had sent to the Chief Justice, in which he asked that the case be listed for further discussion at the next conference. Harlan wrote, "I am not at rest on my vote and wish to give the matter more study before the case is assigned on the basis of my present vote, five to four to reverse or vacate, my vote being in the majority."

At the next conference, on March 24, Harlan switched and voted to affirm. That changed the decision to one for affirmance, and the majority opinion was assigned to Stewart. He circulated a draft that relied on the rule that it is not for the individuals enjoined to be the judges of an injunction's validity. They should try to have the injunction set aside by a higher court; but, until it is, they must obey it. The Stewart draft concluded with the statement: "Patience is a small price for the civilizing hand of the judicial process, which alone can give abiding meaning to constitutional freedom." In the next circulation "patience" was changed to "a modicum of patience," which was itself changed to "respect for judicial process" in the final *Walker* opinion.

Warren and Brennan were disturbed by Stewart's opinion, particularly by what they considered its sermonizing tone. The Chief asked Brennan to write the dissent. Brennan prepared a draft that began with strong language: "I expect that this decision reflects only sensitivity to today's transitory shift in political and social attitudes towards the civil rights movement. For under cover of pious preachments that the Negro exercise a 'modicum of patience,' the Court empties the Supremacy Clause of its primacy."

Brennan also referred to the background of the Birmingham demonstrations. As his draft put it, "These were the days before 'Black Power' and 'Long Hot Summer' became part of the jargon of the civil rights movement."

On June 6, while the Brennan draft was at the Court's print shop, Douglas circulated his own dissent. It took the same approach as Brennan, but, surprisingly for Douglas, used more moderate language. Brennan and Douglas then joined each other's opinions. Fortas sent a note to both that "It is seldom in this life that a person gets two for the price of one. Here I have the opportunity, which I hereby seize, to join each of you in his magnificent dissent."

Just after the term's last conference, on June 9, 1967, Warren told Brennan that he would join his dissent if the already-quoted introductory language and the references to "Black Power" and "Long

Hot Summer" were deleted. This was just the type of language that Warren felt had no place in a judicial opinion, and he joined Brennan as soon as the Justice agreed to remove the offending passages. Perhaps inconsistently, the Chief did not object to a reference to "Black Power" in the last paragraph of Brennan's opinion, but that may have been an oversight.

Warren also circulated his own dissent, which asserted, "I do not believe that giving this Court's seal to such a gross misuse of the judicial process is likely to lead to greater respect for the law." [10] The Chief wrote because he was upset about the decision. He thought that the symbol of Martin Luther King in jail for having engaged in activities clearly protected by the First Amendment was going to make people cynical about the courts and the law.

Brennan and Fortas joined the Warren dissent. Douglas did not. But that was not due to any disagreement with what the Chief wrote. Douglas failed to join simply because he had already left Washington for one of his extrajudicial jaunts, before Warren sent around his opinion.

The *Walker* decision upholding the contempt convictions was announced on June 12, 1967—the last day of the 1966 Term. Once more Black had secured a bare majority for his view that the social interest in law and order outweighed the right to direct action by civil-rights demonstrators.

Black also differed with Warren and was again able to secure a bare majority in *Fortson v. Morris*,[11] a case arising out of the 1966 Georgia gubernatorial election. But the case was notable, not because of the difference between Black and the Chief, but because of sharp exchanges between Black and Douglas.

No candidate for Governor received a majority in the Georgia election on November 8, 1966. In that situation, the state constitution provided that the Georgia Assembly should elect the Governor from the two persons having the highest number of votes. Before the Assembly could act, it was enjoined by a federal court on the ground that the method of election denied Georgia voters equal protection.

The case was argued as an emergency matter on December 5, 1966.

A conference was held immediately afterwards. Warren spoke in favor of affirmance. "Since Georgia chose an elective system by the people," he said, "that must be the way of choice. Here there is a taking away from the people and vesting it in the legislature. Therefore it is within the spirit of the unit-rule case"—i.e., *Gray v. Sanders,*[12] the case discussed in Chapter 11 that struck down the Georgia county-unit system.

Black led the argument the other way. *"Gray v. Sanders,"* he declared, "is inapplicable. That dealt with discrimination between individual voters, which was a denial of equal protection. The unit system operated to effect such a discrimination. But where a wholly proper election fails to produce a majority choice, the question becomes whether the Constitution limited the state's power to choose a Governor by a different method. The Constitution doesn't dictate that the Governor must be chosen by the people."

The conference vote was six-to-three to reverse, with Black, Clark, Harlan, Brennan, Stewart, and White casting the votes for reversal. The next day Black circulated a *Memorandum to the Conference* pointing out that, if the decision did not come down the following Monday, December 12, the next scheduled decision day would be January 9. "That," Black wrote, "is the very day upon which Georgia's General Assembly is required to meet to elect a Governor by its Constitution. It would seem to me that nothing short of an imperative necessity should cause this Court to hold in suspense a decision on the question of the Assembly's power to elect the Governor until the very date upon which the Assembly will meet to perform this duty."

Black's memo insisted that the decision be announced on December 12, even if it meant that the opinions would be issued later. Black noted, "There are valid objections to this disposition, particularly because of our Brother BRENNAN's strong hostility to this procedure. But in my view these objections are outweighed by the unfairness to Georgia in holding in suspense the question of its power if there is no other way to give Georgia an answer at a very early date."

Black stated that another method "to avoid keeping Georgia in this state of uncertainty" was to call a special session of the Court to announce the decision before the January 9 session. "This would, of course, be inconvenient to us in that it would require us to meet during our Christmas holiday recess. But I am of the opinion that this inconvenience to us is outweighed by the inconvenience to Georgia in compelling her to wait for our decision until the very day her Assembly is due to meet."

In a scrawled note to Brennan the same day, Black wrote, "I feel that the Court will be negligent in its duty if the case does not go down. A STATE is entitled to know what it can do and not left suspended in mid air."

On December 7, Douglas sent around a *Memorandum to the Conference,* strongly objecting to "Brother Black's memorandum urging that we get the opinions in this case down at the earliest possible moment." Douglas wrote that, if Black's proposal for decision by December 12 was adopted, there would not be enough time to write adequate opinions. Douglas noted that he had just circulated a draft dissent "and it is a very hurried afternoon job." Then, alluding to his reputation for facility in opinion writing, Douglas wrote, "Even I would like time to work further on it beyond this week."

"There is one possible advantage," the Douglas memo concluded, "in getting the opinions down quickly in cases like this—that is, it forecloses any possibility of any member of the Court changing his mind. But the issue is a close one in the minds of the Court, a five to four vote indicating the narrowest of margins by which we make the decision. And I think that in itself argues for a more deliberate slow speed rather than a deliberate fast one."

The Douglas memo evoked a waspish response from Black, who answered with his own December 7 *Memorandum for the Conference.* It asserted, "It is impossible for me to believe that it would take any member of this Court a whole month to write out his dissenting views, whether he does so at a 'deliberate slow speed' or at 'a deliberate fast one'." Black referred to the difficulties that delay would present to the state. "To keep the State in doubt as to whether the Assembly will elect or whether provision must be made for one or more new elections means that the whole government of the State of Georgia must be at a standstill. The old Governor will not know when he goes out or under what circumstances a new Governor can come in."

Black asserted, "Georgia should not be put in this unhappy predicament on the unsupported and, I believe, unsupportable assumption that it may take some member of this Court a month to write his views." Then the Alabaman took a sly dig at his quondam ally.

"Brother Douglas says he 'would like time to work further on it [his opinion] beyond this week.' But he does not say that he wants or needs an extra month, and it is inconceivable that he does, in view of his well-known speed in writing all his opinions."

The Black memo ended with unusually cutting language:

Finally, Brother Douglas' reason for saying we should wait a month is that some member of the present majority might change his mind and vote Brother Douglas' way—that is, to affirm. How long should Georgia be kept in ignorance of its constitutional power and have its machinery paralyzed on the hope that one of the present majority of five could be persuaded in some manner to reverse his vote? Members of this Court certainly are sufficiently mature to decide for themselves whether they need more time to announce their votes. Five have already indicated they need no more time by voting to reverse this case *now*. Whatever questionable reason there may be for waiting a few more days to announce this decision, Brother Douglas advances none whatsoever for keeping Georgia in doubt for an entire month.

Both the Douglas and Black memos referred to the division in the Court as five-to-four. Though the vote at the December 5 conference was six-to-three for affirmance, Brennan sent around a *Memorandum to the Conference* the next morning, which began, "I have changed my mind in *Fortson* v. *Morris, et al.* and vote to affirm." Brennan wrote that he would "be ready to come down Monday," but also planned "to file a dissent substantially as follows:

The Court asks the wrong question. The question is not whether Georgia may select a Governor at a legislative election. It is not the question because that is not Georgia policy. Georgia policy is to select a Governor by majority vote at a popular election, and if no candidate receives a majority vote, to choose a Governor from the two candidates receiving the largest number of votes. The question for our decision is thus the narrow one of the constitutionality of the method of making the choice from the two candidates. Plainly that method is unconstitutional, and would be whether an agency other than the legislature was designated to make the choice. In *Gray* v. *Sanders,* 372 U.S. 363, we held that a method which weighted some votes more heavily than others violated the Equal Protection Clause and that Georgia could not use that method to achieve its policy of selecting a Governor by majority vote at a popular election. The method by which a choice is made from the two candidates receiving the highest number of votes is constitutionally infirm for the same reason. The candidate receiving the lesser number of votes may be chosen under that method. This is thus an unconstitutional "way by which equality of voting power may be invaded," 373

U.S at 381. The voter who cast his ballot for the candidate receiving the highest number of votes is then not treated as equal to every other voter at the election. Only a method of choice which avoids that result will satisfy the Equal Protection Clause.

I respectfully dissent.

After Douglas modified his dissent to include much of what Brennan had written, Brennan decided not to issue his projected dissent and instead simply joined the Douglas opinion. It was also joined by Warren and Fortas. The latter circulated his own dissent on December 9, which Warren and Douglas likewise joined. But the decision did come down on December 12, as Black had urged. He delivered the opinion of the Court on that day reversing and upholding the election by the Georgia Assembly.

Black also supplied the decisive vote in *McCray v. Illinois*[13]—a criminal case in which Warren, Douglas, Brennan, and Fortas were again in the minority. McCray had been convicted for unlawful possession of narcotics. He had been arrested on information given by an informant, who had proved reliable in the past. The police refused to identify the informant at a hearing on McCray's motion to suppress evidence found on him. The state courts upheld the refusal.

At the January 13, 1967, conference, Warren advocated reversal. "I don't mean," he said, "that the police must disclose the informant in every case—certainly not if he acts on a tip to investigate and get evidence. But here there was no case without the testimony of the police about the informer." The Chief denied that "an arrest or search incident thereto [can] be supported without a warrant or disclosure of the informant's identity."

Black led the case the other way, emphasizing that Warren's home state had a law providing that disclosure of informants' identity would not be required. "I agree with California," Black declared. The Court divided five-to-four in favor of Black's view. As senior majority Justice, Black assigned the case to Stewart, who announced on March 20, 1967, the decision holding that the informant's identity did not have to be divulged. Douglas, joined by Warren, Brennan, and Fortas, delivered a dissent that asserted, "Unless [the informant] is produced, the Fourth Amendment is left to the tender mercies of the police."

Black's stand in *McCray* was not so much a manifestation of the "new" Justice Black as an application of the restricted approach to the Fourth Amendment that the Alabaman had always followed. That approach also determined Black's position in *Berger v. New York* [14]—another case where he differed with Warren, though this time it was the Chief's view that prevailed.

Berger tested New York's permissive eavesdrop statute. It authorized an ex parte order for eavesdropping on affirmation that there was reasonable ground to believe that evidence of crime might be thus secured. An order was obtained to install a recording device for sixty days in the office of a lawyer named Neyer. On the basis of leads gotten from this eavesdrop, a second order was issued permitting installation, for a like period, of a recording device in the office of one Steinman. Berger was convicted of a conspiracy to bribe a public officer on the basis of recordings made in the offices. The state courts affirmed the conviction, rejecting Berger's attack on the eavesdrop statute. Certiorari was granted by a vote of six-to-three, with Black, Harlan, and White for denial.

The vote at the April 17, 1967, postargument conference was the same, with Warren leading the case for reversal. The Chief declared, "This is a trespass to execute a general warrant—a twenty-four hour tap for sixty days, extended a further sixty days. I would strike the statute down."

Warren assigned the opinion to Brennan. However, when Clark asked the Chief for the case, the opinion was assigned to the Texan. Warren later apologized to Brennan, saying that he had forgotten that he had already assigned the case to him. Clark prepared a draft basing the decision that the New York law was unconstitutional upon an alleged absence of a requirement that "probable cause" be shown before an eavesdrop order could be issued. The statute did, however, require "reasonable ground to believe" that evidence of crime would be obtained. The Court had earlier interpreted the phrase as the equivalent of "probable cause." This was pointed out to Clark, and he abandoned this approach.

Clark's draft also went at length into the issue of whether probable cause was shown for the Steinman eavesdrop. It concluded that there was no probable cause because of the absence of any showing prior to the earlier Neyer eavesdrop that a "bug" in Steinman's office might turn up proof of crime.

Brennan pointed out to Clark that it was not shown that Berger had standing to attack the Neyer eavesdrop, and also that, if the Court found no probable cause under the particular facts, it would be hard pressed to justify reaching the validity of the statute. Clark eliminated the discussion, and the final opinion stated only that Berger "clearly has standing to challenge the statute" and went on to reach the question of the statute's validity.

Brennan had circulated a memorandum which demonstrated that the practice allowed by the statute failed to satisfy almost every one of the protections of the Fourth Amendment. Clark relied on the points made in this memo in his final opinion, delivered on June 12, 1967. Black, Harlan, and White issued separate dissents.

There were three other important Fourth Amendment cases during the 1966 Term, in which Warren and Black were on the same side. The first was *Warden v. Hayden.*[15] It arose out of Hayden's conviction for armed robbery. His cap, jacket, and trousers, found in a washing machine in his home after he was arrested, were admitted in evidence. The court of appeals held that the evidence was improperly admitted. It relied on the so-called "mere evidence" rule, under which search power might not be used to secure "mere evidence"— i.e., items of evidential value only—but solely instrumentalities or fruits of crimes. Six of the Brethren thought that they should take the occasion to reconsider the "mere evidence" rule and voted to grant certiorari. Douglas, Clark, and Fortas voted to deny.

Warren spoke for reversal at the April 14, 1967, conference, but said that he would not overrule the "mere evidence" rule. Black had no such doubt. "Under all the circumstances," he said, "this was reasonable. I don't understand the 'mere evidence' rule." Black noted that the classic 1765 case of *Entick v. Carrington*[16] involved search of "a man's papers to prove seditious libel." But, he said, "there's a difference between a man's documents and other things."

The conference vote was seven-to-two to reverse, with Douglas and Fortas for affirmance. The opinion was assigned to Brennan, at the same time that Warren had originally assigned the *Berger* opinion to him. Brennan prepared a draft justifying the search of Hayden's washing machine as a search to find weapons, for the protection of the police officers. Brennan intended to dispose of the "mere evidence" rule quickly by showing that the rule served none of the purposes of the Fourth Amendment. As the opinion evolved, however, it became a step by step historical analysis, showing how the rule developed and how the underlying property concepts on which it was founded were no longer valid.

Clark and Stewart quickly joined the opinion, with the latter telling Brennan it was a "fine job." White and Harlan, however, had objections. White said that not enough emphasis had been placed on the state's interest in effective law enforcement. Harlan sent Brennan a long letter on May 19 saying, "I do not think that it is necessary or wise to reach the question whether there are some items whose very nature precludes them from being the object of a reasonable search and seizure." Harlan thought the opinion should not reach the admissibility of "items which would be safeguarded from courtroom disclosure," as well as "items which by their nature preclude search and seizure" even apart from the "mere evidence" rule.

Harlan also indicated that the opinion did not adequately deal with the claim that the police had no lawful purpose in seizing mere evidence. Harlan stated that the nexus between the items seized and their usefulness in a particular arrest or conviction must be included in the opinion. "Under the facts of this case," Harlan wrote, "I see no real problem, for the clothes found matched the description of those worn by the robber and the police could reasonably believe that the items would aid in the identification of the culprit. I am thus of the opinion that a full-scale resolution of the purpose question need not be attempted, but I do think that something along that line must be included in the opinion."

Brennan revised his opinion to meet the White and Harlan objections. The draft was modified to leave open "whether there are items of evidential value whose very nature precludes them from being the object of a reasonable search and seizure." Brennan also added a paragraph expressly recognizing the state interest in proving crime and requiring that in any given case the nexus between that interest and the item seized be shown.

When he had read Brennan's revised draft, Harlan wrote back, "Your recirculated opinion meets my difficulties, and I am happy to join you." White also agreed to the opinion. Warren, however, thought that Brennan had gone too far in totally repudiating the "mere evidence" rule. The Chief joined a Fortas opinion concurring in the result because of an exception to the "mere evidence" rule for items "pertinent to identification" of a person being "hotly pursued."

Black had said that he could not agree with some of the views in Brennan's opinion, and he asked to be noted only as concurring in the result. Douglas dissented.

The other two Fourth Amendment cases were *Camara v. Municipal Court* [17] and *See v. Seattle* [18]—companion cases involving warrantless administrative inspections. The decisions in them must have been particularly satisfying to Warren because they overruled *Frank v. Maryland,* [19] the 1959 case discussed in chapter 8. Camara had been prosecuted for refusing to allow a health inspector to inspect his residence without a search warrant. See was convicted for refusing to allow a warrantless inspection of his commercial warehouse by a fire inspector.

Warren led the conference in voting to overrule *Frank* and hold that an administrative inspection, like a police search, was subject to the warrant requirement of the Fourth Amendment. The vote was six-to-three, with Clark, Harlan, and Stewart dissenting. In his conference presentation, Warren had no doubt that the Fourth Amendment protected Camara's home, but he said of See's warehouse, "This is a place of business and not a home." He was, however, willing to go along with White's opinions in the two cases, which treated residential and business premises alike for Fourth Amendment purposes.

Among the most difficult cases again were those presenting First Amendment issues. The first such case decided during the 1966 Term was *Time, Inc. v. Hill.* [20] It arose out of a story in *Life* magazine about a Broadway play, *The Desperate Hours,* which had been inspired by the experience of Hill and his family, who had been held hostage by escaped convicts. The play was fictionalized and had added scenes of violence for dramatic effect. The *Life* article portrayed the play as a reenactment of the Hills' experience, and it contained photographs of scenes acted in the home where the Hills had been held. Hill sued *Life's* publisher under a New York statute prohibiting invasions of privacy. The New York courts awarded Hill $30,000. The Supreme Court was closely divided on whether to hear the publisher's appeal, with Warren, Clark, Stewart, and Fortas voting to dismiss.

To the press, *Time, Inc. v. Hill* was newsworthy primarily because it marked Richard M. Nixon's debut before the Justices. Nixon, appearing for Hill, later said that he had prepared for the occasion by carefully reviewing every case under New York's privacy statute, enacted in 1903. His preparation did not, however, prevent him from slipping up on the law of his native California during the argument. Relying on a California case to support his position, Nixon referred to it as resting on the common law. Warren, himself a California lawyer, was quick to correct him, asking whether there was any common law in the state. Embarrassed, Nixon hesitated, then corrected himself, conceding that it was under the California Code.[21]

The Justices differed in their estimate of Nixon's presentation. Former Justice Fortas termed his performance "mediocre." But others disagree. One Justice says that he was "first-rate" during the original argument in April 1966. At lunch after the argument, the Brethren expressed surprise at how good he was. On the other hand, according to the same Justice, Nixon did not really seem to have his mind on the case during the October 1966 reargument, when he had taken time off from stumping for congressional candidates to appear before the Court.

Ironically, in view of his feelings toward his fellow Californian, Warren consistently voted for Nixon's position in the *Hill* case. In the first conference on the case on April 29, 1966, the Chief declared, "It's a fictionalization of these people's experience and false and, in that circumstance, there's no First Amendment problem. In this limited application, I see no threat to a free press." Black took the opposite position, saying "newspapers have the right to report and criticize plays. This is nothing but a statute prohibiting the press from publishing certain things."

The April 29 conference agreed with Warren and voted six-to-three to affirm the New York judgment, with Black, Douglas, and White voting for reversal. Warren assigned the case to Fortas, who circulated a sixteen-page draft opinion of the Court on June 8, 1966. The Fortas draft contained what one of the Brethren termed an "invective" against the press. After summarizing the case, Fortas declared, "The facts of this case are unavoidably distressing. Needless, heedless, wanton injury of the sort inflicted by *Life's* picture story is not an essential instrument of responsible journalism. Magazine writers and editors are not, by reason of their high office, relieved of the common obligation to avoid inflicting wanton and unnecessary injury. The prerogatives of the press—essential to our liberty—do not preclude reasonable care and thoughtfulness. They do not confer a license for pointless assault."

Fortas went on to discuss the right of privacy in as broad a statement as any ever made by a member of the highest Court:

There is, however, no doubt that a fundamental right of privacy exists, and that it is of constitutional stature. It is not just the right to a remedy against false accusation, provided, within limits, by the law of defamation; it is not only the right to be secure in one's person, house, papers and effects, except as permitted by law; it embraces the right to be free from coercion, however subtle, to incriminate oneself; it is different from, but akin to the right to select and freely to practice one's religion and the right to freedom of speech; it is more than the specific right to be secure against the Peeping Tom or the intrusion of electronic espionage devices and wiretapping. All of these are aspects of the right to privacy; but the right of privacy reaches beyond any of its specifics. It is, simply stated, the right to be let alone; to live one's life as one chooses, free from assault, intrusion or invasion except as they can be justified by the clear needs of community living under a government of law.

The Fortas draft then rejected the claim that the *Life* article was privileged as a newsworthy article because it was "a fictionalized version of the Hill incident, deliberately or heedlessly distorted beyond semblance of reality." Fortas concluded that, as applied to such an article, the New York statute was not "in fatal collision with the freedom of the press. The deliberate, callous invasion of the Hills' right to be let alone—this appropriation of a family's right not to be molested or to have its name exploited and its quiet existence invaded—cannot be defended on the ground that it is within the purview of a constitutional guarantee designed to protect the free exchange of ideas and opinions. This is exploitation, undertaken to titillate and excite, for commercial purposes. It was not a retelling of a news-worthy incident or of an event relating to a public figure. It was not such an account. It was not so designed. It was fiction: an invention, distorted and put to the uses of the promotion of Life magazine and of a play."

The Fortas draft led to a vigorous dissent by Douglas, joined by Black which asserted that the First Amendment immunized the press from damage suits. Harlan, on the other hand, circulated a concurrence which, as summarized in an October 17, 1966, memorandum circulated by Black, reached the majority result "on the basis of what he calls a 'weighing process' under which he found that Hill's 'right to privacy,' under the particular circumstances here, outweighed the public's interest in being informed of the particular subject dealt with in Life's news story.''

White also sent around a dissent saying that the state court, in affirming the award to Hill, had indicated that the New York right-to-privacy statute could be applied even to true news accounts if they were commercially exploited. Fortas prepared a revised draft, circulated June 14, which answered White by asserting that his version "is not a correct statement of New York law as we read it. If it were, we should be presented with an acute First Amendment problem. As we understand New York law, there must be deliberate, intentional pervasive fictionalization.''

On this interpretation, the revised Fortas draft stated that it affirmed the New York judgment. "Our conclusion follows from *New York Times v. Sullivan.*''[22] That was true because "the requirements for liability under the New York right-of-privacy statute as applied in this case are well within this test"—i.e., that of *New York Times v. Sullivan.*

But the difference between White and Fortas troubled some of the Justices sufficiently to lead Fortas himself on June 16 to propose an order, which was issued June 20, setting the case for reargument in the 1966 Term.[23] The order requested that counsel argue the meaning of the "fictionalization" standard applied by the New York courts.

On October 17, the day before the reargument, Black circulated a sixteen-page printed memorandum that bitterly attacked the Fortas opinion and the "weighing process" he thought was embodied in it. The memo's tone was sharp, but it reflected Black's strong feelings. The memo contains perhaps the most eloquent statement of Black's view and has not been published. It is, therefore, worthwhile to devote the space to some of its salient passages.

The Black memo started with an acerbic attack upon the "weighing process" that he asserted had been used by the Fortas opinion of the Court.

The use of the weighing process, which has here produced such divergent results, means simply to me that by legal legerdemain the First Amendment's promise of unequivocal press freedom, the freedom constitutionally promised, has been transmuted into a debased alloy—transmuted into a freedom which will vacillate and grow weaker or stronger as the Court personnel is shifted from time to time. This means that the scope of press freedom is not to be decided by what the Founders wrote, but by what a

Court majority thinks they should have written had they been writing now. I prefer to have the people's liberty measured by the constitutional language the Founders wrote rather than by new views of new judges as to what liberty it is safe for the people to have.

To Black, the majority approach meant a blatant usurpation of power by the judiciary.

For under its aegis judges are no longer to be limited to their recognized power to make binding *interpretations* of the Constitution. That power, won after bitter constitutional struggles, has apparently become too prosaic and unexciting. So the judiciary now confers upon the judiciary the more "elastic" and exciting power to decide, under its value-weighing process, just how much freedom the courts will permit the press to have. And in making this decision the Court is to have important leeway, it seems, in order to make the Constitution the people adopted more adaptable to what the Court deems to be modern needs. We, the judiciary, are no longer to be crippled and hobbled by the old admonition that "We must always remember it is a Constitution we are *expounding*," but we are to work under the exhilarating new slogan that "We must always remember that it is a Constitution we are *rewriting* to fit the times." I cannot join nor can I even acquiesce in this doctrine which I firmly believe to be a violation of the constitution itself.

Black was sarcastic about the Fortas panegyric of privacy. "Indeed a substantial part of the Court's opinion is devoted to rhapsodical descriptions of the great value of 'right to be let alone'." Black declared, "No one can deny that it is an exquisite thing to be let alone when one wants to be. But few people want all other people to let them alone forever." As Black saw it, "the very existence of Government negatives any claim that citizens have a general unconditional, unequivocal 'right to privacy' or 'to be let alone.' If every person carries with him an unconditional right to privacy or to be let alone, the burglars, rapists, robbers, murderers and other law violators would be completely immune from all government investigations, arrests, trials and punishments."

The Black argument here appears fanciful, but he asserted that it was the Fortas approach that was such. "But I think it approaches the fantastic for judges to attempt to create from these a general, all-embracing constitutional provision guaranteeing a general right to privacy. And I think it equally fantastic for judges to use these specific constitutional guarantees as an excuse to arrogate to themselves authority to create new and different alleged constitutional rights to be free from governmental control in all areas where judges believe modern conditions call for new constitutional rights."

The Black memo was particularly biting in its comments on the language in Fortas' proposed *Time v. Hill* opinion. It condemned "the Court's choice of inferences supposedly drawn from the evidence in the record and their stacatto-like repetition," and asserted, "This Court's repeated use of such sharp criticisms and invectives against Time's writers, researchers, and editors I think is completely unsupported by the record."

Black's conclusion was equally extreme: "After mature reflection I am unable to recall any prior case in this Court that offers a greater threat to freedom of speech and press than this one does, either in the tone and temper of the Court's opinion or in its resulting holding and judgment."

The scathing Black memo had its effect, for at the October 21, 1966, post-reargument conference, the Court changed its decision and voted seven-to-two for reversal, with only Warren and Fortas still voting for affirmance. Black, as senior majority Justice, assigned the new opinion of the Court to Brennan. Soon afterwards the highest New York court decided a privacy case involving Warren Spahn, the baseball player, that made it clear that truth was a complete defense in actions under the state's right-of-privacy statute based upon reports of newsworthy people or events.²⁴ That settled the issue on which White had differed from Fortas and on which the reargument had been ordered.

On December 1, Brennan circulated a draft opinion holding that the *New York Times v. Sullivan* standard must be applied to actions under the New York statute. In a case like *Hill*, plaintiff must show not only "fictionalization," but also "that the statements in the article were made with knowledge of their falsity or in reckless disregard of the truth."²⁵ The case was remanded to give the New York courts an opportunity to apply the statute in the constitutionally prescribed manner.

White immediately joined Brennan's opinion, "with a good deal of enthusiasm for the job you have done." On December 22, Fortas sent around a dissent that was more moderate in its language than his proposed opinion of the previous term. Warren joined Fortas, since he still felt that Hill's right of privacy should be protected against false press reports. Clark changed his October 21 conference vote and also joined.

On January 3, Harlan circulated a dissent taking the view that negligent, rather than knowing or reckless, fictionalization was all that should be required. The votes of Black and Douglas now became crucial. They agreed to concur in Brennan's opinion in order to preclude any retreat from the step toward their First Amendment position taken in *New York Times*. But they also issued concurrences that reaffirmed their absolutist views.

With the Court four for reversal and four the other way, Stewart's concurrence was necessary for Brennan's opinion to become that of the Court. Stewart had shown concern for the reputations of private individuals in his concurring opinion the previous term in *Rosenblatt v. Baer*.[26] To obtain Stewart's vote, Brennan added a paragraph expressly leaving open the rules to apply in libel actions by private individuals. In such actions, wrote Brennan, "the additional state interest in the protection of the individual against damage to his reputation would be involved," and Stewart's *Rosenblatt v. Baer* concurrence was cited.

This apparently convinced Stewart, who wrote Brennan the next day, "I think you have written a fine opinion, and I am glad to join it." On January 9, 1967, Brennan delivered his opinion for a bare majority setting aside the New York judgment. Fortas, joined by Warren and Clark, and Harlan issued their dissents.

Curtis Publishing Co. v. Butts[27] and *Associated Press v. Walker*[28] were decided as companion cases on application of *New York Times v. Sullivan*[29] to libel suits by "public figures" who were not government officials. Butts was a leading football coach who sued to recover damages for a *Saturday Evening Post* article that accused him of conspiring to "fix" a game. The defense was that the article was true. The jury returned a verdict for $60,000 in general damages and $3,000,000 in punitive damages. The trial court reduced the total to $460,000. The award was affirmed by the court of appeals. The petition for certiorari came before the Supreme Court while it was considering *Rosenblatt v. Baer*.[30] We saw in the last chapter that Warren was so upset at the suggestion during the cert conference that a football coach could be considered a "public official" under the *New York*

Times standard that he threatened to hold up the *Rosenblatt v. Baer* decision. He was dissuaded by Douglas, and consideration of *Butts* was delayed until the beginning of the 1966 Term. On October 10, 1966, certiorari was granted in *Butts*. The cert vote was eight-to-one, with only Clark voting to deny.

The companion case involved a libel action by Walker, a retired general, against the Associated Press for a news dispatch on a riot at the University of Mississippi during efforts to enforce a decree ordering enrollment of a black student. The dispatch stated that Walker had encouraged the rioters to use violence and had led a charge against federal marshals. The jury awarded $500,000 in damages, and the award was affirmed by the highest state court, which held that *New York Times* was inapplicable. The vote was unanimous to grant certiorari in *Walker,* and the case was set for argument with *Butts*.

At the February 12, 1967, conference, all voted to reverse in *Walker,* but there was little agreement on the grounds of decision. In *Butts*, the vote was four-to-four, with Harlan passing. Warren, Clark, Stewart, and Fortas voted to affirm the judgment for Butts. Stewart distinguished between privacy actions by newsworthy individuals and libel judgments by such people—the dividing line between his vote in *Time, Inc. v. Hill* [31] and that in *Butts*.

Warren's law clerks joked that the Chief's *Butts* vote was based upon his love of sports and that, to him, football coaches had a special status under the First Amendment. Warren now agreed that *New York Times* should apply to public figures as well as public officials. But he would not go along with Black, Douglas, Brennan, and White and hold that this required reversal in *Butts*. He insisted that the *Saturday Evening Post* had engaged in shoddy practices and that Butts ought to be vindicated.

Because Harlan had said that he wished to consider the matter further, *Butts* was put over to the next conference. At it, Harlan cast the deciding vote for affirmance. He was assigned the opinions in both *Butts* and *Walker* by the Chief Justice. On May 11, 1967, Harlan circulated one opinion for the two cases. With it, he sent *A Prefatory Note for the Conference,* which stated:

In preparing this opinion I have basically had in mind three things. *First,* to give effect to the dispositions voted by the majority at the Conference.

. . . *Second,* to avoid, so far as possible, the prospect that in future cases in this area we will find ourselves divided by the kind of conflicting views that have plagued us in the obscenity field. To this end I have tried to take into account the differences of viewpoints that have so far developed in the libel area among those of us who believe that the First and Fourteenth Amendments do not wholly prevent state libel actions. *Third,* to establish a constitutional rule for "public interest" libel cases that should be relatively easy to apply in most instances, yet not to put the state and lower federal courts in a straitjacket with respect to cases where the rule should not apply.

Harlan summarized the *Butts* holding: "With respect to the *Butts* case, the opinion reaches the conclusion that the judgment so far as it relates to *punitive* damages must be reversed, with the way being left open, however, for a new trial on that issue. . . . As regards *compensatory* damages the *Butts* judgment is affirmed."

In the Harlan draft opinion, the *New York Times* standard was applied to punitive damages. But it stated a special test for compensatory damages substantially similar to that stated in Harlan's published opinion. Under it, public figures who were not public officials could recover for libel on a showing less than that required by *New York Times.* They needed to show only "highly unreasonable conduct constituting an extreme departure from the standards . . . adhered to by responsible publishers." In addition, the state courts were to apply the test of responsibility on a sliding scale dependent upon the opportunity of the person libelled to rebut and the degree of potential harm reflected in the false statement on its face.

Brennan quickly circulated an opinion advocating full application of *New York Times* to public figures. Brennan critized what he called Harlan's "hodgepodge" standard for compensatory damages. White also circulated an opinion to the same effect. It asserted that the Harlan standard depended upon "conduct," and not state of mind. White and Brennan joined each other's opinions. Clark, Stewart, and Fortas joined Harlan's opinion.

On Thursday, June 1, Warren indicated to Brennan that he, too, was dissatisfied with Harlan's "hodgepodge" standard, although he was dead set against a reversal in *Butts.* Warren's apparent willingness to apply the *New York Times* standard now made it seem possible to secure a Court for that standard. Douglas agreed to file a statement, as he had in *Time v. Hill,* that he joined on the application of *New York Times* in order to make a majority on that point. Black, however, refused to go along, stating that he would not be privy to any judgment that, in result, treated *Butts* differently from *Walker.*

At conference the next day, Warren seemed to have changed his mind. He told Harlan that he had not had a full opportunity to study his opinion, but that it appeared that Harlan had gone a long way to satisfy his views. But, on the following Tuesday, June 6, the Chief informed Brennan that he was circulating an opinion adopting the *New York Times* test, but affirming in *Butts.*

Warren sent around an opinion that adopted the *New York Times* standard in Part I, reversed in *Walker* in Part II, and affirmed in *Butts* in Part III. The Chief then left town for two days to deliver a commencement address. While he was away, Black agreed to join Brennan's opinion, with his concurrence quoting directly from his statement in *Time v. Hill.*[32] Douglas joined Black's statement. This meant that there were now five for applying the *New York Times* standard to public figures.

But the Justices who had joined Harlan's opinion sought a way once again to win Warren's adherence to their standard. Fortas drafted an opinion for Warren to the effect that, while the Chief adhered to the *New York Times* standard, he viewed Harlan's test as merely an "embellishment" on *New York Times,* not as a substitute. Fortas phoned Warren at St. Mary's College, Emmetsburg, Maryland, where he was delivering the commencement address, to tell him of the opinion.

On June 7, Brennan sent Warren the following note, which led to the resolution of the *Butts* case: "In your absence I took the liberty of talking with Hugo and Bill about *Butts* and *Walker.* At their request, in order that everyone would know their view, I added the following statement at the foot of my opinion:

Mr. Justice Black, with whom Mr. Justice Douglas joins, concurring.

I concur in reversal of the judgment in No. 150, *The Associated Press v. Walker,* based on the grounds and reasons stated in Mr. Justice Brennan's opinion. I do this, however, as in *Time, Inc.* v. *Hill,* 385 U.S. 374, 398, in order for the Court to be able at this time to agree on an opinion in this important case based on the prevailing constitutional doctrine expressed in *New York Times Co.* v. *Sullivan,* 376 U.S. 254. Mr. Justice Brennan's opinion decides the case in accordance with this doctrine, to which the majority adhere. In agreeing to that opinion, I do not recede from any of the views I have previously expressed about the much wider press and speech freedoms I think the First and Fourteenth Amendments were designed to grant to the people of the Nation. See *e.g., New York Times Co.* v. *Sullivan,* 376 U.S. at 293 (concurring opinion); *Rosenblatt* v. *Baer,* 383 U.S. 75, 94 (concurring opinion).

"In these circumstances, my suggestion is that you might wish to substitute for Part I of your opinion the affirmative arguments in the opinions Byron and I have filed in favor of the application of the *New York Times* rule without commenting on John Harlan's proposed standard. I would suppose that without the majority for your test, reference to John's standard would be unnecessary. I could then withdraw my opinion in *Walker* and join you. You could then attach Hugo and Bill's statement to your opinion.

"All I would then have to file would be a paragraph in *Butts* dissenting from the *Butts* judgment. I understand that Hugo is preparing a couple of paragraphs for himself and Bill expressing their grounds of dissent from the affirmance of the *Butts* judgment."

When Warren returned, he rejected the Fortas substitute and accepted the approach stated in Brennan's note. The Chief quickly drafted an opinion drawing upon the discussions in both the Brennan and White drafts. Brennan and White then agreed to withdraw their own opinions in favor of joining Parts I and II of Warren's, though with a short statement of dissent from the affirmance in *Butts.* Black and Douglas agreed to a substitution of Parts I and II of Warren's opinion for Brennan's opinion in their short statement joining for purposes of a judgment based on *New York Times.*

When Harlan announced the judgments of the Court in *Butts* and *Walker* on June 12, he added a statement (which appears as a footnote in his published opinion) that a majority of the Court rested decision on grounds other than those stated in his opinion.[33]

As in the previous term, the First Amendment cases that gave the greatest difficulty were the obscenity cases. Once again, Warren played a minimal part in the resolution of these cases. In the last chapter, we saw that after it decided the 1965 Term's obscenity cases, the Court decided to hear three other obscenity cases. It granted certiorari in *Redrup v. New York*[34] and *Austin v. Kentucky,*[35] limited to the question of scienter. It voted to hear the appeal in *Gent v. Arkansas,*[36] limited to the question of whether the state obscenity law constituted an invalid prior restraint or was impermissibly vague. *Redrup* and

Austin involved convictions under state laws for selling paperback books and magazines found to be obscene. *Gent* involved a civil action to enjoin distribution of obscene magazines.

At the postargument conferences on October 14, 1966, there were at least five votes to reverse all three cases, but on a variety of grounds even greater than had existed in the 1965 Term. The opinions were assigned to Fortas, who had indicated that he was not satisfied with the test laid down in the 1957 *Roth* case,[37] as it had been applied in the *Ginzburg*[38] and *Mishkin*[39] cases discussed in the last chapter.

While Fortas was working on his opinion, it was reported that his view was that the *Roth* test and "pandering" were both necessary elements of a criminal prosecution. In other words, it was not enough that the material sold was obscene, but that in addition the selling had to amount to pandering. It was also rumored that, if Fortas could not secure a Court for his view, he was leaning toward joining Black and Douglas in their absolutist approach. Fortas was also heard to assert, with regard to *Gent,* that "book burning" should not be tolerated.

Fortas prepared opinions in *Redrup* and *Austin* that regarded the scienter requirement as identical to the mens rea requirement in the criminal law. Fortas even cited Blackstone for the proposition that "vicious will" was required. His draft in *Gent* indicated that any civil action to restrain obscenity would be invalid. It read the scienter requirement into this area as well, stating that the statute "stripped" the seller or publisher "of his right to a jury trial" at which scienter would have to be proved.

It soon became evident that a Court could not be obtained for either of the Fortas drafts. Stewart circulated an opinion concurring in the result in *Redrup* and *Austin* on the ground that the material was not obscene, but strongly disagreeing with the idea that the Court could impose a mens rea requirement through the Constitution. Black sent around a short opinion reaffirming his long espoused view and poking fun at the distinctions attempted by Fortas. Douglas wrote a similar opinion. It ended with an appendix devoted to an article by Reverend Howard Moody protesting obscenity regulation. It shocked some of the Brethren because it contained the sentence, "The dirtiest word in the English language is not 'fuck' or 'shit' in the mouth of a tragic shaman, but the word 'NIGGER' from the sneering lips of a Bull Connor."

Harlan then circulated three elaborate opinions. He concurred in *Redrup*, but dissented in the other two cases. He attacked the Fortas proposition that the propriety of the distribution of materials depended upon the means of distribution. Harlan pointed out that the 1959 opinion in *Smith v. California*,[40] discussed in chapter 8, indicated that unless the states were required to prove some mental element in obscenity prosecutions, there was a good chance that protected material would be suppressed. Harlan suggested what he termed "the middle course," that the defendant be allowed to assert as a defense that he reasonably dealt in obscene material without knowledge of its obscenity. Under his formulation, the test of scienter would vary with the importance of the person prosecuted. In the Harlan approach, Redrup, a mere clerk, stood in a different position from Austin, a bookseller who controlled the stock in his stores. Harlan would have required the state to prove that Redrup actually knew that what he was selling was obscene, while all that would have to be shown with respect to Austin was that he should have reasonably regarded the material as subject to condemnation.

In his *Gent* draft, Harlan would have upheld the Arkansas statute. He stressed the law's limitations: it allowed no injunction pendente lite; it required a prompt hearing; and the decree issued under it extended only to material in the county involved. Harlan acknowledged that there were many uncertainties in the statute, but he argued that Arkansas should be allowed to pass on these matters.

Brennan also prepared two draft opinions. He first showed them only to Fortas, but the others heard about his efforts and asked that they be circulated. Brennan's *Redrup–Austin* draft emphasized what he saw as the First Amendment basis of *Smith*—avoidance of self-censorship. Brennan pointed out that self-censorship is avoided entirely only when disseminators are relieved of the need to investigate or to guess about the contents of material. Brennan stated the scienter test as follows: "So long as the proof adduced is sufficient to support the conclusion of a judge or jury that, beyond a reasonable doubt, the defendant had no good-faith doubt that the material would be found obscene, the possibility of affecting the distribution of protected material is so minimal that it should be endured in light of the strong state interest in protecting citizens from salacious, socially worthless matter." Brennan also made the point that persons who had no part in policy decisions about the works prosecuted should be immune from prosecution. Brennan then analyzed the individual cases, concluding that scienter had been insufficiently proved in both the *Redrup* and *Austin* cases.

In his *Gent* draft, Brennan first summarized the Arkansas statute. He noted "that the structure of the Act was expressly designed to afford law enforcement officers procedures for controlling obscenity which would avoid suppressing or deterring the dissemination of constitutionally protected matter." He pointed out that the Act had a severability clause, which should lead the Court to give the Arkansas courts the first chance to interpret ambiguous provisions. Then followed a discussion of the Act's deficiencies; its definition of obscenity; the burden of proof imposed, pointing out that both the civil and criminal burdens should be the same or the civil finding could not be used to prove scienter; as well as the effect of the proceeding in a later criminal case.

At this point, Fortas circulated revised drafts in *Redrup* and *Austin*. He replaced his scienter discussion with a statement of the issue in First Amendment terms, eliminating most of the references to mens rea. Fortas stated that scienter might be proved from the material itself, where the defendant was shown to have actual knowledge of the material, and where he could not reasonably doubt it to be obscene.

Brennan wrote Fortas that he was satisfied with this revision and that it "would be a good basis so far as I am concerned for a Court disposition." Brennan noted, however, that he and Fortas were "still fairly far apart in *Gent*. I am reluctant to hold that the civil provisions cannot be allowed to stand. I prefer the disposition suggested in my memorandum . . . of seeing how far the Arkansas Supreme Court can save that procedure in light of the statute's severability clause. But, as I compare the memorandum and your recirculation, I expect our differences have deeper roots. That's not to say I am not prepared to continue the effort if you have a chance of getting a Court."

Fortas was dissatisfied with Brennan's response. He thought that the Justice should go along with him in *Gent*, since he had been willing to make what he considered a compromise of his position in *Redrup* and *Austin*. Fortas now decided to give up his compromise effort and returned to his original position in all three cases.

At this point, there was real danger of another display of disunity in the obscenity area. Six different opinions had been written in each of the cases, and more might be expected. At this juncture, it was suggested at the April 14, 1967, conference that the Court should agree to vacate the limitations on review in the three cases, and simply reverse them all on the ground that they all dealt with constitutionally protected matter. Stewart circulated a brief per curiam to that effect on April 18. It pointed out that none of the cases involved "a specific and limited state concern for juveniles," or "any suggestion of an assault upon individual privacy by publication in a manner so obtrusive as to make it impossible for an unwilling individual to avoid exposure to it,"[41] or any evidence of pandering. It then listed the legal positions of all the Justices except Harlan, and stated that under any of those positions the material involved was protected.

Some of the Justices, notably Brennan, hesitated to join the proposed per curiam because Stewart had noted in a footnote "that four members of the Court emphatically disagreed with the relevance of any such 'pandering' concept to the First Amendment." Stewart was prevailed upon to strike the comment, and all but Harlan and Clark joined.

Stewart announced his per curiam on May 8, 1967. Harlan, joined by Clark, issued a short dissent which pointed out that, because of the limitations on review, the obscenity of the material had not been briefed or argued. Harlan declared that "these dispositions do not reflect well on the process of the Court,"[42] and deferred expression of his views, since he felt that certiorari should be dismissed as improvidently granted.

The most difficult 1966 Term criminal decisions were those in what the Justices referred to as the Lineup Cases. There were three of them: *United States v. Wade*,[43] *Gilbert v. California*,[44] and *Stovall v. Denno*.[45] Wade had been indicted for bank robbery. Without any notice to his lawyer, he was placed in a lineup and identified as the robber. He was convicted despite his claim that the conduct of the lineup violated his privilege against self-incrimination and his right to counsel. The court of appeals reversed. All the Brethren voted to grant certiorari.

Gilbert had also been convicted after identification at a postindictment lineup without notice to his counsel. In addition, during an F.B.I. interrogation, he had given the agent handwriting exemplars. The state courts rejected his contention that they had been obtained in violation of his Fifth and Sixth Amendment rights. Gilbert had also attacked the taking of photographs from his apartment pursuant to a warrantless search. That claim was likewise rejected.

After Stovall's murder conviction, he sought federal habeas corpus because he had been compelled to submit to hospital-room identification by the victim's wife without counsel. The court of appeals decided against Stovall. Certiorari was granted in both the *Gilbert* and *Stovall* cases by a five-to-four vote, with Clark, Harlan, Stewart, and White voting to deny.

At the February 17, 1967, conference, Black took the strongest position in favor of the three defendants. "These cases," he asserted, "represent a violation of the right to counsel and the privilege against self-incrimination." Black asserted that, "as soon as you utilize a man's person to get evidence from him, or take him to a place to get someone else's evidence by having him act out a crime, you must give him a lawyer because you can't compel him to be a witness against himself."

Warren's conference statement did not go that far. He expressed the view that "you can't take voice or writing exemplars, dress [defendant] a certain way, or act out anything. Doing these things is the equivalent of interrogation and, therefore, *Miranda*[46] would apply." On the other hand, when he presented the cases, Warren said, "If none of these things were done and it was a pure line-up, counsel can be excluded."

After extensive discussion, which centered on the Fifth Amendment privilege, the conference was closely divided. The vote was five-to-four to reverse in *Wade* and affirm in *Gilbert* and *Stovall*. The bare majority consisted of Clark, Harlan, Brennan, Stewart, and White. Brennan had expressed the view (reflected the previous term in his *Schmerber v. California*[47] opinion) that no Fifth Amendment rights were violated by placing the suspect in a lineup and asking him to speak for identification. On considering the case after the conference, however, Brennan became convinced that the lineup was a "critical stage" requiring the presence of counsel under the Sixth Amendment. Brennan informed the conference in an April 17 *Memorandum to the Conference* that he had switched his votes and enclosed draft opinions that vacated the convictions in *Wade* and *Gilbert* and remanded for further proceedings.

Brennan's *Wade* draft rejected the Fifth Amendment claim, but held that Wade had a Sixth Amendment right to counsel at the lineup. As Brennan explained it in an April 24 memorandum to Warren, Black, Douglas, and Fortas, the draft's conclusion was "that the lineup was a critical stage of the prosecution at which Wade was as much entitled to the aid of counsel as at the trial itself." Brennan then stated a "fruits" rule for in-court indentification—i.e., that defendant had to show that the identification in the courtroom was the "fruits" of the lineup.

The *Gilbert* draft followed Brennan's *Schmerber* approach and held that the taking of the handwriting exemplars was valid. However, it vacated and remanded on the basis of *Wade* because of the lineup identification without counsel. Brennan's first *Gilbert* draft did not deal with the search-and-seizure issue. Later examination of the record convinced Brennan that there was conflict in the testimony of the police officers on the scope of the search, upon which the trial court made no findings. The next circulation of Brennan's *Gilbert* opinion, on April 28, relied on this to vacate certiorari as improvidently granted. As Brennan explained it in a *Memorandum to the Conference* accompanying the revised draft, "My reason for that disposition in *Gilbert* is that the factual record is so confused as to make it impossible to come to grips with the issue as I, at least, thought the record presented it."

Douglas circulated a dissent on the search and seizure claim that contained an appendix designed to show a lack of critical conflict in testimony. This led Brennan to add an appendix of his own to show the conflict. At the next conference, Warren indicated that he was disturbed by the issue. White stated that he thought the search invalid since an envelope, such as that which contained the seized photos, was a private enclosure like a suitcase or closet. Despite this, White joined Part III of Brennan's *Gilbert* opinion, dealing with the search-and-seizure issue. But Warren joined Douglas' dissent.

In *Stovall*, Brennan circulated a draft that refused to apply the *Wade* rule retroactively to Stovall's collateral attack on his identification. But Stovall had also claimed that the hospital identification violated due process, since he had been identified by himself rather than in a lineup. Brennan's draft remanded for a hearing on that claim in light of the fact that it had not been heard in the district court. Black sent around an opinion in *Stovall* that both attacked Brennan on the prospectivity point and said that there was no such abstract concept of "due process." Fortas asked that a sentence be added after the conclusion of Brennan's opinion ordering a new trial because of the unfair identification procedure.

Clark then stated that he would join the right to counsel discussion in *Wade* if *Stovall* was affirmed. Brennan recognized that the due process issue was a close one because of the emergency situation prevailing at the time of Stovall's identification, and he agreed to circulate an opinion affirming in *Stovall,* which found that, under the circumstances, "the usual police station lineup . . . was out of the question."[48]

The most important aspect of the decisions in the Lineup Cases was the holding in Brennan's *Wade* opinion that there was a Sixth Amendment right to counsel at the lineup. As already seen, Brennan circulated his draft to that effect on April 17. The next development was a meeting on April 21 of Stewart, Clark, Harlan, and White. What happened there was described in an April 24 Memorandum from Brennan to the other four Justices. Brennan wrote, "you may be interested in something Potter told me this morning. He, Tom, John and Byron had a meeting on Friday to exchange views. Potter tells me that the four of them agree with Part I and where I conclude that neither the lineup itself nor anything shown by the record that Wade was required to do in the lineup violated his privilege against self-incrimination."

"However," Brennan went on, "all four reject Part IV"—the part of Brennan's draft that extended the right to counsel to Wade. Brennan wrote, "Potter tells me that since this is a federal case, he would be willing to put the right to counsel on the basis of our supervisory power and that he believes Tom would do likewise. He is uncertain whether that would be acceptable to John and Byron, but does not rule out the possibility."

Brennan indicated in his memo to Warren, Black, Douglas, and Fortas that he was not willing to go along with Stewart's right-to-counsel approach. "I personally am convinced that the right to counsel should be declared a constitutional right for the reasons I have stated in the opinion. But apparently there can be a Court for that disposition only if you are of that view."

Douglas immediately sent back Brennan's memo with a written comment at the bottom: "I am [i.e., of your view]—but I'm not yet sure of the grounds."

Warren told Brennan that he agreed at least tentatively to join the Justice's *Wade* opinion in all respects. Fortas met with Brennan and objected to the extensive discussion in Brennan's draft of the things counsel might accomplish by his presence at a lineup. Fortas thought that the conclusion that the lineup was a "critical stage" requiring counsel was clear and the further discussion made the opinion appear defensive. Brennan pared down that portion of the opinion.

After he read the revised draft, Fortas sent Brennan a May 9 memorandum which asked, "Would you consider the elimination of your last section relating to the need for showing that the courtroom identification was the fruits of the lineup?" Fortas wrote, "I agree with your general proposition that courtroom identification should not be disallowed on the basis of improper lineup procedure unless the courtroom identification is the fruits of the lineup. But where the persons who identified the defendant at the improper lineup proffer the identification testimony in court, it seems to me inconsequential to find out whether they are willing to testify that they would have recognized the bum anyway."

The force of Fortas' suggestion was weakened when he added, "If you make this change, count me as joining. If you don't make the change, I'll join anyway." Brennan did not make the suggested change.

The Fortas memo also contained a postscript, reaffirming his agreement on the right to counsel. "P.S. Needless to say, on the central point I agree. I agree. I totally agree. This is critical stage. There is a right to counsel—Amendment V[sic], Amendment XIV. Federal. State."

On the same day, May 9, Douglas wrote Brennan formally joining the *Wade* opinion, except for Part I, which rejected Wade's Fifth Amendment claim. Also on May 9, Black circulated an opinion in *Wade* agreeing that there was a Sixth Amendment right to counsel at the lineup but dissenting from the view that this should affect the admissibility of the in-court identification.

This meant that getting a Court for Brennan's *Wade* reversal on the right-to-counsel ground now depended on obtaining the concurrences of Clark and the Chief Justice. Clark phoned Brennan on the night of June 1 that he would join him if certain changes were made in his *Wade* opinion. The next morning Clark met with Brennan and asked for the deletion of two pages about the various functions counsel could perform. Clark also conditioned his joinder in the *Wade* right to counsel discussion on an affirmance in *Stovall*. Brennan yielded on both these points.

But now Warren proved more difficult. At the February 17 conference, he had indicated the view that counsel might be excluded from a lineup that required defendant only to stand and be identified. The Chief still expressed difficulty with the right to counsel. What if, Warren asked, counsel was an obstructionist, or he was unavailable and his presence would require a delay in the identification? White circulated a dissent on the Sixth Amendment issue that mentioned these very problems. Brennan dealt with them by pointing out in a revised draft that no delay had been argued in *Wade* or *Gilbert*, leaving open the possibility of substitute counsel where delay might occur, and quoting the language in *Miranda* that it was not to be assumed that counsel would interfere with law enforcement.[49]

This did not, however, induce the Chief Justice to join in *Wade*. At the conference on June 2, Warren remained silent as Brennan outlined the complicated status of the cases, even though the Justice prefaced his remarks with, "assuming I have the Chief."

At the June 2 conference, Black strongly urged the Court to set the cases for reargument during the following term. Fortas then sent Brennan a note that he was revoking his agreement to join in *Wade*, and was writing separately in *Wade* and *Gilbert*. As it turned out, the Fortas opinions related solely to the issue of being compelled to appear in the lineup. Fortas thus still joined Brennan's Sixth Amendment discussion. But Fortas told Brennan he was still dissatisfied with the "fruits" discussion in *Wade*. Brennan mollified Fortas by framing the test as whether the in-court identification had an "independent source," deleting the word "fruits" and the statements recognizing the difficulty of applying the test.

On Monday, June 5, while Brennan was conferring with Warren on the *Butts* and *Walker* cases,[50] the Chief informed Brennan that he was going to join his opinion in *Wade* except for Part I, the Fifth Amendment privilege discussion, from which he dissented for the reasons expressed in Fortas' opinion, and his opinion in *Gilbert*, except for Part III, on the search and seizure issue, for the reasons expressed in Douglas' opinion.

There was now, a week before the decisions were announced, a fluctuating majority behind all the parts of Brennan's three opinions. At first, this appeared not true of Part III of *Wade*, which distinguished the lineup as a "critical stage" from preparatory steps such as fingerprinting, blood samples, clothing and hair analysis. White's opinion, joined by Harlan and Stewart, noted him as dissenting from Part III, which would have left only Warren and Clark behind Brennan on that part. This was apparently a mistake. When Brennan called this to White's attention, White circulated a new printing joining in Part III.

The Court was so fragmented on the different parts of Brennan's three opinions that Brennan circulated the following "score card":

June 6, 1967

MEMORANDUM TO THE CONFERENCE

The following is my score card on the *"lineup cases"* that I thought I'd circulate to be sure my count is accurate:

No. 334—*United States v. Wade*

Part I.

A Court made up of Tom, John, Potter, Byron and me; the dissenters are the Chief Justice, Hugo, Bill and Abe.

Part II.

A Court made up of the Chief Justice, Hugo, Bill, Tom, Abe and me; the dissenters are John, Potter and Byron.

Part III.

A Court made up of Bill, Tom, John, Potter, Byron and me; and I think also the Chief Justice and Abe (I say this because the Chief Justice is joining Abe's opinion and I see nothing in that opinion indicating that there is any dissent from Part III); the dissenter is Hugo.

Part IV.

A Court made up of the Chief Justice, Hugo, Bill, Tom, Abe and me; the dissenters are John, Potter and Byron.

Part V.

A court made up of the Chief Justice, Bill, Tom, Abe and me; the dissenters are Hugo, John, Potter and Byron.

No. 223—*Gilbert v. California*

Part I.

A Court made up of Tom, John, Potter, Byron and me; the dissenters are the Chief Justice, Hugo, Bill and Abe.

Part II.

A Court made up of the Chief Justice, Bill, Tom, John, Potter, Byron, Abe(?) and me; Hugo concurs separately.

Part III.

A Court made up of Tom, John, Potter, Byron, Abe(?) and me; dissenting in favor of Gilbert are the Chief Justice and Bill; dissenting against Gilbert is Hugo.

Part IV.

A Court made up of the Chief Justice, Bill, Tom, Abe and me; Hugo as to lineup identification only; the dissenters are John, Potter and Byron.

No. 254—*Stovall v. Denno*

A Court on both parts made up of the Chief Justice, Tom, John, Potter, Byron and me; the dissenters are Hugo, Bill and Abe.

W.J.B. Jr.

On June 12, the last day of the term, the results alone were announced along the lines of the Brennan "score card." According to one of the Justices, this made "the announcement smack of a colloquy from an Abbot and Costello movie."

There were two other criminal cases during the 1966 Term in which Black and Warren were on opposite sides. The first was *Giles v. Maryland*.[51] The Giles brothers were convicted of raping a teenage girl. Following the convictions, information came to light that reflected on the girl's sexual habits and her stability. The Giles brothers sought post-conviction relief, claiming that they had been denied due process because of the prosecution's suppression of this evidence and knowing use of perjured testimony. The post-conviction judge rejected the claims of bad faith suppression and knowing use of perjured testimony, but ordered a new trial because the information should have been disclosed to the defense. The highest state court reversed. Only Black and Clark voted against certiorari.

At the October 14, 1966, conference, the vote was six-to-three to reverse, with Black, Clark, and Stewart for affirmance. The majority was divided on the grounds of decision. Some wanted to reverse and order a new trial on the ground of suppression of evidence or use of knowingly perjured testimony, others because of insufficiency of the post-conviction hearing. Brennan, who was assigned the opinion, leaned toward the second approach, both because he thought that there was little evidence of knowing suppression or use of perjured testimony and because Harlan and White, who were critical votes, had advocated that approach.

The Supreme Court had requested Maryland to supply the material considered by the trial judge in imposing sentence on the Giles. While Brennan was preparing his opinion, the state filed two police reports with statements by the principal witnesses that conflicted with their trial testimony. Brennan circulated a draft stressing that the reports were potentially critical and remanding to the Maryland court for reconsideration in light of them.

Douglas and Fortas joined the Brennan draft opinion—though with reluctance. Douglas wrote "I rather thought that we should go further than merely remanding to the Maryland Court of Appeals to consider anew whether another hearing should be held in the Maryland court. But if that is the consensus of the Conference, I will go along." Douglas noted that he reserved the right to reconsider in light of whatever else was written. Fortas wrote, "I'm glad to join—although I don't entirely understand why you merely send this case back for another post-conviction hearing instead of for a new trial." Harlan, however, changed his conference vote and wrote a dissent asserting that it was conjecture to suppose either that the testimony at trial was false or that counsel did not see the police reports. This caused Brennan to send around a revised draft that contained a more detailed discussion of the record and the content of the police reports. In turn, Harlan revised his opinion with more detailed factual analysis of his own, seeking to explain away the discrepancies created by the police reports.

At this point, Warren joined the Brennan opinion. The balance now seemed to depend on White. Just before the Christmas recess, White circulated an opinion of his own rejecting the remand based on the police reports and remanding on the ground that the post-conviction hearing was inadequate.

Without White, there was no Court for the Brennan opinion. As it turned out, however, when it was announced on February 20, 1967, the opinion was supported only by a plurality of three (Brennan, Warren, and Douglas). In addition to White, Fortas wrote a separate concurrence advocating a new trial on the ground of suppression of evidence that "might be useful to the defense." Harlan, joined by Black, Clark, and Stewart, issued his dissent.

The remaining criminal case where Warren and Black differed was *Spencer v. Texas.*[52] This time it was Warren who was in dissent. Spencer had been indicted for murder with malice. The indictment alleged that he had previously been convicted of murder with malice—a fac-

tor that would entitle the jury to sentence him to death or life imprisonment under the Texas habitual-criminal statute. Without that
factor, the jury could fix the penalty at a prison term of not less than
two years. He was found guilty and sentenced to death. He claimed
that the use of his prior conviction violated due process. The conviction and sentence were affirmed by the highest state court. Warren,
Douglas, White, and Fortas voted to hear Spencer's appeal.

The October 21, 1966, conference vote on the Recidivist Case was
six-to-three for affirmance, with Douglas, Brennan, and Fortas voting to reverse. Harlan wrote an opinion upholding the Texas law,
stating that to hold the contrary would constitute an unjustifiable
encroachment upon state power to promulgate rules of evidence.

To Warren, Harlan's calling the Texas rule permitting prior crimes
to be revealed to the jury a mere "rule of evidence" was a play on
words. The Chief reconsidered his conference vote and wrote a persuasive dissent, joined by Fortas, Douglas, and Brennan. His law
clerks recall that they worked as hard on the *Spencer* dissent as on
anything during the term. Black, Clark, and White joined Harlan's
opinion. For some weeks, Stewart did not indicate which opinion he
would join. When Warren was told that Stewart was having a lot of
trouble deciding, Warren chuckled and said he was not surprised.
Ultimately, Stewart joined Harlan's opinion, and it was announced
as the opinion of the Court on January 23, 1967.

Black and Warren were also on opposite sides in *National Labor
Relations Board v. Allis–Chalmers Mfg. Co.*[53] Unions had imposed fines
on members who had crossed the picket lines during strikes at Allis–
Chalmers. The N.L.R.B. dismissed charges that the unions had committed unfair labor practices by acting to "restrain or coerce" employees in the exercise of their statutory right to "refrain from" con-
certed activities. The court of appeals reversed. The vote on the
certiorari petition was eight-to-one, with Douglas alone voting to
deny.

The March 17, 1967, conference voted to reverse by a bare majority,
consisting of Warren, Clark, Harlan, Brennan, and Fortas. The opinion was assigned to Brennan, who sent around a draft finding that
union imposition of reasonable fines upon members who declined to
honor a strike did not constitute an unfair labor practice. Brennan
conceded that section 8 (b) (1) of the Labor Act made it an unfair

labor practice for a union to restrain or coerce employees in the exercise of rights given by the statute. But he relied on a proviso that permitted a union to make its own rules with respect to acquisition and retention of membership.

Warren and Fortas immediately agreed to Brennan's draft. Harlan indicated, however, that he wanted to see the dissent before joining. Black circulated a dissent emphasizing employee freedom and relying on both the legislative history and what he termed the plain language of the statute. The dissent persuaded Harlan, who sent a note to Black, "You have converted me, and I would appreciate your joining me in your dissent." Harlan sent a copy with a note of apology to Brennan. The latter called Harlan and was told that nothing Brennan could do to the opinion could garner his vote.

It now looked as though Black's opinion would become the majority opinion. At the next conference, however, White indicated misgivings about Black's approach. He also expressed concern over Brennan's result if the fined members had no way of quitting the union or limiting their membership before a strike began. Clark had meanwhile been silent. When Brennan visited Clark, the Texan said that he thought he had joined Brennan's opinion long ago.

Brennan then called White for suggestions. White said that he thought that Brennan should take the dissenters' view of the scope of the section 8 (b) (1) proviso and point out the anomaly resulting from a ban solely on court enforcement. Two pages were added to Brennan's opinion to this effect. Other changes were made to show the "inherent imprecision" of the words "restrain or coerce" and to meet some statements in the dissent on the legislative debate.

White then informed Brennan that he would join, though with a short concurring statement. Brennan was thus able to announce his *Allis–Chalmers* opinion as the opinion of the Court on June 12, 1967. Black, joined by Douglas, Harlan, and Stewart, delivered his dissent the same day.

Black did, however, vote with Warren in several of the most important 1966 Term cases. Two of those cases gave the Chief Justice particular pleasure, for he not only led the Court to unanimous decisions, but also wrote precedent-breaking opinions in them. The first was *Bond v. Floyd*.[54] Bond, a black member of the Georgia House of Representatives, had been excluded from the House because of statements he had made sharply criticizing American policy in Vietnam and the discriminatory operation of the draft. The lower court rejected his challenge to the exclusion. With Clark and Stewart not voting, all the other Justices voted to hear Bond's appeal.

Until this case the Supreme Court had never overruled a state legislature on its decision to exclude a member. At the argument on November 10, 1966, Arthur K. Bolton, the Georgia Attorney General, asserted, "The House is the sole judge of qualifications." What if they imposed "an unconstitutional qualification?" he was asked.

Mr. Bolton: "Of course that's not good."

The Chief Justice: "Would that give us jurisdiction to determine the propriety of the rejection?"

Mr. Bolton: "Yes."

The Chief Justice: "Where is the dividing line?"

Mr. Bolton: "Whether constitutional rights were violated." [55]

Warren then asked what the situation would be if the legislature had excluded Bond because he was black. The Georgia lawyer conceded without hesitation that if the exclusion had been racially motivated, the federal court could step in and reverse it. This concession really destroyed the state's case. It would scarcely be logical to say that the federal courts had jurisdiction if the legislature excluded someone in violation of the constitutional right to racial equality, but not if the exclusion was for exercising equally basic First Amendment rights.

To Warren, the Bond exclusion had clear racial overtones. Bond was then one of the few black legislators in the South, and his case had symbolic importance throughout the country. The Chief strongly urged reversal. The others agreed, except for Clark and Stewart. (It is not clear from Clark's notes whether they voted to affirm or abstained). Warren assigned the opinion to himself, feeling that it was for the Chief Justice to speak in the first case setting aside a legislative refusal to seat a member.

Warren prepared a ten-page memorandum for Benno Schmidt, his law clerk, who had written the bench memo on the case and who was to work on the draft of the opinion. The memo set out the way in which the opinion was to be organized and contained a full statement of the crucial facts as well as an analysis in First Amendment terms. It concluded that, if Bond had been an ordinary citizen, what he had said could not have been the basis for any criminal penalty or any state-imposed disadvantage. There was strong language at the end about the need for the representatives of the people to have at least as broad a right of free expression as ordinary citizens. Warren thought that the Georgia Attorney General's concession made it unnecessary to go into the question of whether the legislature's exclusion presented a political question immune from judicial review.[56]

Warren's opinion, circulated at the end of November only three weeks after the argument, quickly won the agreement of all the Brethren, including Stewart and Clark, who sent the Chief his "Okey" on December 1. It was delivered as the opinion of the Court on December 5, 1966.

Warren also led the Justices to a unanimous decision in *Loving v. Virginia*,[57] where the Court finally struck down a state miscegenation law. Here, too, the decision was especially gratifying to Warren, who had protested unavailingly against the Court's avoidance of the issue in the 1955 *Naim* case[58] discussed in chapter 4. Loving was a white man who married a black woman. They were convicted of violating the Virginia law making it a crime for white and colored persons to intermarry. The highest state court affirmed. All the Justices voted to hear the appeal.

The Brethren agreed without dispute that the constitutional time had come for state miscegenation laws. Once again the Chief assigned the opinion to himself, thinking that he should take responsibility for a decision that would still offend Southerners. Virginia had argued that the statute was not discriminatory, since it applied equally to whites and blacks. Warren considered this argument nonsense. The law had been passed to ensure white supremacy, and the legislative history showed that. Warren told Benno Schmidt, who was drafting the opinion, to emphasize that point.[59] He wanted to make it clear that the statute was designed to stigmatize blacks. He insisted that the opinion contain a quotation from the Virginia trial judge that showed his racism: "Almighty God created the races white, black, yellow, malay and red, and he placed them on separate continents. And but for the interference with his arrangement there would be no cause for such marriages. The fact that he separated the races shows that he did not intend for the races to mix."[60]

When Warren read over the *Loving* draft, he saw that the 1923 case of *Meyer v. Nebraska*[61] was cited to show that there were fundamental freedoms connected with the family that the states could not restrict.

Warren chuckled and said that *Meyer* had been written by Justice James C. McReynolds back in the heyday of substantive due process. As such, it had been singled out by Black as an example of the "old" Court's acting without any basis in the constitutional text. Citing *Meyer,* said the Chief, would be like waving a red flag in front of Black. Despite this, he left the *Meyer* cite in, and Black let it pass.

Black's hackles were, however, raised by something else Warren put into the *Loving* opinion. The Chief wanted the draft to stress that the statute was dealing with a major aspect of the individual's life, that of whom to marry. As Schmidt recalls it, "Justice Black blew up because we were referring to the right to marry, which is nowhere mentioned in the Constitution. . . . So he sent back a statement indicating that he didn't want any sort of natural law notion creeping into the opinion."[62] Warren toned down the right to marry language, and Black withdrew his objection.

Some of the other Justices wanted more to be said about racial classifications. One in particular wanted to leave open the possibility of benign racial classifications to remedy past discriminations. Warren, however, did not want to anticipate the future on such questions, and he wanted the case decided without enunciating broad principles applicable to any and all racial classifications. The others ultimately went along, and Warren delivered his *Loving* opinion on June 12, 1967, with only Stewart issuing a short concurrence.

Warren also led the Court to decisions in close cases involving power over subversion and citizenship. In them, Black had no difficulty in joining the Chief to provide the necessary fifth vote.

Keyishian v. Board of Regents[63] arose out of New York's Feinberg Law, enacted to prevent state employment of "subversives." Under it, "utterance of any treasonable or seditious word or words or the doing of any treasonable or seditious act" was a ground for dismissal from the educational system. The law also disqualified from educational employment persons who advocated overthrow of government by force or unlawful means or joined any group so advocating. Teachers were required to sign a certificate that they were not members of the Communist Party. Keyishian, an instructor at the state university, refused to sign, and his teaching contract was not renewed. He brought a federal action, alleging that the law violated the Federal Constitution. The lower court upheld the law. The Justices voted eight-to-one to take Keyishian's appeal, with Stewart the sole vote against.

Warren urged reversal at the November 18, 1966, conference, saying, "Vague statutes can't be employed this way to do someone out of a job." The conference vote was five-to-four to reverse, with Warren, Black, Douglas, Brennan, and Fortas making up the bare majority. Fortas indicated, however, that his vote was not firm and that he was not certain which way he would ultimately vote. Brennan was assigned the opinion. The case was made difficult by the 1952 decision in *Adler v. Board of Education*,[64] which upheld the Feinberg Law. Brennan's opinion followed Warren's approach and struck down the law as unconstitutionally vague. It also showed how *Adler* had been undermined by more recent decisions, particularly the 1966 decision in *Elfbrandt v. Russell*,[65] discussed in the last chapter.

Black and Douglas quickly agreed to Brennan's opinion and Warren joined a week later. Over two weeks after Brennan's draft was circulated, Clark came out with a dissent that asserted, "the majority has by its broadside swept away one of our most precious rights, namely, the right of self-preservation."[66] Clark recognized that his draft was unusually sharp, for he wrote Brennan, "If you think I am too 'tough' on you, please advise what omissions or changes you would like." Brennan did not suggest any changes.

Clark's dissent was immediately joined by Harlan, Stewart, and White. Fortas was, however, outraged by the dissent and what he called its "McCarthyistic" tone. He decided definitely to join Brennan and write a concurrence to meet Clark's opinion. He was persuaded not to write separately, and Brennan was able to speak alone for the majority when he announced the decision on May 29, 1967.

The announcement by Brennan and Clark saw what an observer termed "some of the most impassioned oratory which followers of the Court had ever seen." Brennan charged that the Clark dissent "indulges in richly colored and impassioned hyperbole in assailing the majority decision." Clark replied that this reference to the dissent showed that it must have "hurt." After he stated his biting dissent, Clark smilingly turned to Brennan and was heard to say, "Well, I guess you got the best of that one."

The citizenship case where Warren and Black were joined to help make up the bare majority was *Afroyim v. Rusk*.[67] Afroyim was an American citizen who voted in an election in Israel. The State Department refused to renew his passport under a statute providing for loss of citizenship for voting in a foreign election.

For Warren, the *Afroyim* decision was another satisfying one, since it gave the Court the opportunity to overrule the 1958 decision in *Perez v. Brownell*,[68] discussed in chapter 8. Warren had strongly dissented there from a Frankfurter opinion upholding the statute.

At the February 24, 1967, conference, however, Warren sought only to distinguish *Afroyim* from *Perez* "In *Perez*," he said, "Mexico didn't allow foreigners to vote, but here Israel allowed it and, therefore, there's no problem of disrupting foreign relations." Black, on the other hand, urged that *Perez* be overruled, asserting that Congress had no power to take away citizenship. A bare majority, including Warren, ultimately agreed with Black. Though he had written the *Perez* dissent, Warren assigned the opinion overruling *Perez* to Black. The decision was announced May 29, 1967, with Harlan, joined by Clark, Stewart, and White, dissenting.

Mention should also be made of several other 1966 Term decisions that illustrate Warren in operation as Chief Justice. The first is *Baltimore & Ohio R. Co. v. United States*.[69] where Warren stepped in to ensure a speedy decision because of the public interest in an early announcement. The Interstate Commerce Commission issued an order approving the merger of the Pennsylvania Railroad and the New York Central Railroad. An action was brought by three small competing railroads adversely affected by the merger to enjoin enforcement of the I.C.C. order. The lower court denied an injunction, and the case was set for early argument in the Supreme Court.

The Court was most concerned with the plight of the small railroads, which the I.C.C. had said would be provided for by appropriate conditions *after* the merger was consummated. At the January 13, 1967, conference, Warren urged reversal. "We can't," he said, "let the merger go through without a decision of the I.C.C. on protection for the three lines. We can't say the I.C.C. has yet decided that the merger is in the public interest without that." The conference voted five-to-four to reverse, on the ground that the Commission should at least set conditions for protection of the small railroads prior to merger. Douglas would have gone further and invalidated the order because of the I.C.C.'s failure to support it by adequate findings. He was, however, willing to go along with the decision.

Brennan made the fifth vote, though he expressed concern about the involvement of the courts in such complex economic policy matters.

Soon after the conference, Fortas circulated a memorandum that relied on a Congressional policy in favor of mergers and found that the Commission's conclusion was reasonable. The majority opinion was assigned to Clark, who sent Brennan a first uncirculated draft limited to remand for establishment of protective conditions for the small railroads prior to the merger. Brennan suggested that Clark should alter his draft to stress that the public interest required consideration of the outcome of inclusion proceedings involving the small railroads. Clark circulated an opinion that briefly mentioned the point. Fortas prepared a dissent that was joined by Harlan, Stewart, and White.

Brennan thought that Clark's opinion was not adequate, and he sent around a concurrence showing at length that the I.C.C. could not fulfill its duty in determining whether the merger was consistent with the public interest without considering the effect of inclusion, or non-inclusion, of the objecting railroads in the merger. Clark asked Brennan whether he could use large parts of Brennan's draft in his majority opinion.

At this point, however, Warren became disturbed at the delay further rewriting would entail. He wanted the decision announced at the earliest possible moment and pressured Clark and Brennan to issue their opinions intact. They agreed and the decision was announced on March 27, 1967, less than three months after the argument—an unusually short time for decision in such a complex case.

The term's apportionment case was *Sailors v. Board of Education.*[70] Voters in a Michigan county brought an action claiming that the method by which the county board of education was chosen violated the "one man, one vote" principle. The lower court held that the Fourteenth Amendment was not violated. Warren spoke for affirmance at the April 21, 1967, conference. "We should," he said, "apply 'one man, one vote' insofar as the particular elected local body exercises legislative functions." As Warren saw it, the county board of education was not such a body. The others agreed, and Douglas announced a unanimous affirmance on May 22.

Warren's conference presentation also helped point the way to the decision in *In re Gault,* [71] which held that defendants in juvenile delinquency proceedings were entitled to most of the rights of adult criminal defendants. Gault, a fifteen-year old, had been committed as a juvenile delinquent to a state institution by an Arizona juvenile court for making indecent telephone calls. He sought habeas corpus, alleging that he had been denied the basic rights of criminal defendants. The state court rejected his claim, holding that due process requirements in juvenile proceedings were not the same as in criminal trials. All the Justices except Black, Clark, and Stewart voted to hear Gault's appeal.

The *Gault* case was argued on December 6, 1966. The decision was announced May 15, 1967. According to Fortas, who wrote the opinion, he had spent much of the summer between the 1965 and 1966 Terms working on what became the most important opinion he wrote while he was on the Court.

"Even if non-criminal," Warren had declared at the *Gault* conference, "the same due process must be provided." Minimally, said the Chief, there must be a lawyer, proper notice of the proceedings to the family, a fair warning of the charges, and confrontation. Warren was, however, dubious about requiring the privilege against self-incrimination in juvenile proceedings. Most of the others agreed that "the same due process" should be applied to juvenile, as to criminal, proceedings. But they wanted to go somewhat further than the Chief and follow Black's view that, "whether or not he's a juvenile, he's being restrained of his liberty. Thus, he's entitled to *all* the guarantees."

Fortas, in particular, urged that the Fifth Amendment privilege, as applied in the *Miranda* case,[72] should be fully applicable. He stressed that admissions made by juveniles tended to be unreliable, referring to a recent case before the District of Columbia Juvenile Court to show this. On December 10, 1966, just after the first conference on the case, Fortas circulated a *Memorandum to the Conference:* "This is the opinion of Judge Ketcham to which I referred at Conference in commenting upon the unreliability of confessions by juveniles." The Ketcham opinion was quoted in Fortas' *Gault* opinion to buttress the holding that the privilege against self-incrimination was as applicable in the case of juveniles as with respect to adults.

Aside from the self-incrimination point, the *Gault* opinion followed the approach Warren had outlined, holding that the other rights he had stated applied in juvenile proceedings. Only Harlan and Stewart dissented, though Black and White issued concurrences.

The last 1966 Term case to be discussed is *Dombrowski v. Eastland.*[73] The case arose out of subpoenas issued by the Senate Internal Security Subcommittee, chaired by Senator James O. Eastland, to obtain the records of the Southern Conference Educational Fund, of which Dombrowski was director. The documents had been seized in raids by the Louisiana state police on October 4, 1966, but the state courts later held the seizures illegal. Sourwine, the subcommittee counsel, was called about the raids by the counsel to a Louisiana committee investigating subversive activities. Then, as explained in an April 18, 1967, *Memorandum for the Conference* by Fortas, "Sourwine took a plane for Louisiana the next morning, October 5, at 8:20 a.m., taking with him blank subpoenas. These were filled out in Louisiana; Eastland was telephoned and approved their use, and the subpoenas were exchanged with the Louisiana committee for the hot documents. . . . *However,* the subpoenas were dated October 4, not October 5." The defense swore that the October 4 date was a typographical error. They were corroborated by the typist.

Dombrowki claimed that the date, as well as other facts alleged by him, showed a conspiracy by the Senate subcommittee and Louisiana officials to violate his Fourth Amendment rights. He sued Eastland and Sourwine for damages. As stated in the Fortas memo, his "theory is that the conspirators agreed that the raids would be conducted by arrests and search and that the documents so illegally obtained would immediately be taken over by, and under the umbrella of, the Senate Subcommittee."

The lower court upheld summary dismissal of the complaint on the ground that both defendants were insulated from suit by the doctrine of legislative immunity. The Brethren voted five-to-three, with Black not participating, to grant certiorari—Clark, Harlan, and White voting for denial.

At the February 24, 1967, conference, Warren said that he would "reverse as to both Eastland and Sourwine." It was, he stated, "a fact question whether respondents were acting in concert with state officials." The Chief's view was that, "if they did conspire, both are liable for acting outside the authority of legislative prerogative."

Clark disagreed. He said that the action against Eastland was "controlled by the Speech and Debate Clause." As a Senator, Eastland was completely immune from suit. Clark conceded that Sourwine was in a different situation. "On the Sourwine allegations of conspiracy," the Texan noted, "the appellants do raise conflicting fact questions. He doesn't have immunity."

The conference agreed with Warren, and it was decided to reverse with a short per curiam. Fortas drafted a per curiam of a little over a page on February 25, which was circulated two days later. The draft rejected the lower court's holding that Eastland and Sourwine were wholly insulated by legislative immunity.

We do not agree with this conclusion as it is broadly stated. Under the complaint herein, a case could be made out which would support petitioner's claim for damages. If the facts should show that respondents were participants with the state officials in a conspiracy to deprive the petitioners of their rights under the Fourth Amendment, the protection of the constitutional immunity would not be available to respondents. The constitutional immunity is available only with respect to the legislative functions of those claiming immunity. It does not protect acts, otherwise actionable, undertaken other than in the performance of their "legitimate legislative activity."

According to the draft per curiam, the lower court "did not consider whether . . . there were material issues of fact with respect to the existence of a conspiracy or concert of action between respondents and state officials which had as its object not 'legitimate legislative activity' but the illegal deprivation of petitioners' Fourth Amendments rights. Plainly such a conspiracy is not within the scope of legislative immunity."

On his copy of the February 27 *Memorandum to the Conference* transmitting the draft per curiam, Clark wrote, "I will dissent—I believe the immunity (Constitution) is broad enough to cover this. I would remand on Sourwine only—or say the facts not sufficient etc." [74]

Fortas revised his per curiam and sent around a new draft early in April. It was longer but still remanded with regard to both defendants. Fortas summarized the new draft in his April 18 memo, to which reference has been made: "My per curiam draft, dated April 4, vacates the judgment below and remands the case on the ground that there are disputed issues of material fact which entitled the petitioners to go to trial. The per curiam, I believe, avoids any statement of legal doctrine not contained in our decisions."

"The basic question, as I see it," Fortas wrote, "is whether this discrepancy in dates together with the general smell of the situation entitled petitioners to go to trial. . . . In view of the fact that this is a conspiracy case and that all of the specific facts have to be developed from the other side, it seemed to me that the petitioners were entitled to trial." This was true even though Fortas acknowledged, "On this record, petitioners' case is indeed feeble, and I regard the case as marginal."

Clark wrote at the top of his copy of the Fortas memo, "If this comes down—Note I would aff[irm] on CA opinion." [75] This was not a case where Warren wanted to hand down a decision rebuffing the Senate subcommittee unless the Court was united. Since Clark remained firm in his intention to dissent, the Chief and the others gave way.

Fortas prepared a new per curiam recognizing that Eastland as a Senator was fully protected by legislative immunity and affirming dismissal of the complaint against him. The immunity was held less absolute as applied to a legislative employee like Sourwine, and the case was remanded as to him to determine whether the complaint's allegation that he conspired to violate Dombrowski's Fourth Amendment rights was supported by the facts. Clark agreed to this disposition, and the per curiam was delivered for a unanimous Court on May 15, 1967.

From Warren's point of view, the 1966 Term had been the least successful since Frankfurter's retirement. Black's defection in close cases made it difficult for the Chief to lead the Court to the decisions he desired. The term saw more close divisions among the Brethren than had been the case for years. Brennan alone was assigned the opinion in eleven five-to-four cliffhangers during the term—a statistic that shows both how split the Court was and how Warren would turn to Brennan in the tough cases.

To be sure, the term had its satisfactions both on and off the bench. For Warren personally, the most gratifying was the swearing-in on December 16, 1966, of Earl Warren, Jr., as a Municipal Court judge in California. The Chief Justice flew to Sacramento to administer the oath. [76]

The Chief also enjoyed attending the opening game of the baseball season. As was true in other years, he was a guest in the box of Edward Bennett Williams. Warren had become a friend of the noted lawyer, who frequently extended hospitality to attend baseball and football games. At least one of the Brethren has questioned the propriety of the Chief Justice's closeness to a lawyer who might at any time have a case before the Court. A few of his law clerks were also concerned. But Warren himself was never bothered at being Williams' guest. To him, this was completely separate; this was baseball or football and had nothing to do with the work of the Court.

On the other hand, while Warren always insisted on respect for his office, he would rarely assert pretensions and prerogatives off the bench. "There's no question," says a former law clerk, "he was proud of the way he led the Court. He was also, however, the most humble person in power that I have ever known. . . . In personal relations there was no pomp, there was no ceremony about him." The clerk tells how he would go to ballgames with Warren and the ushers would recognize the Chief and ask him to come to the head of the line. "No," would be the reply. "I'll wait my turn here on the line." During the ten years that Warren was Governor of California, he once recalled, there were only two times that he had his police escort use their sirens.[77]

Yet, if the term was not as successful for Warren as previous terms, it is also true that none of the cases in which a majority disagreed with him was of great importance. The one possible exception may have been *Adderley v. Florida*[78]—the term's principal civil rights case. But the decision there was of little practical consequence, since the civil-rights movement had largely moved away from direct-action protests. In addition, cases during the next two terms would show that Warren was not as far from the "new" Black as people had supposed. The Chief, too, would draw constitutional lines beyond which speech might not be blended with action.

In his last two terms, however, Warren would once again have a normally solid majority to lead. June 12, 1967—the last day of the 1966 Term—not only saw the completion by Black of thirty years on the Court (only eight other Justices had served that long), but also the retirement of Clark. It is said that, when Chief Justice William Howard Taft died, President Hoover offered the Chief Justiceship to Charles Evans Hughes in the expectation that he would refuse it, since Charles Evans Hughes, Jr., was then Solicitor General. Instead, the son resigned so that his father could accept the highest judicial office.

In 1967 President Johnson wanted to appoint Ramsey Clark as Attorney General. But there was a problem similar to that which had confronted the Hughes family in 1930, since Ramsey was Justice Clark's son. This time, however, it was the father who made the sacrifice. The Justice sent the President a retirement letter, to take effect at the end of the 1966 Term. His son could then be sworn in as Attorney General.

Though Justice Clark had backed the Chief Justice in important cases, he could not be counted on as a consistent Warren supporter. In most of the cases during the 1965 and 1966 Terms where Warren and Black had been on opposite sides, Clark had voted with the Alabaman. Particularly in criminal cases, like *Miranda v. Arizona,*[79] and cases involving subversion, like *Keyishian v. Board of Regents,*[80] Clark would usually vote differently than Warren.

This was changed when Thurgood Marshall was appointed as Clark's successor. From the time he took his seat on October 2, 1967, Marshall became a firm vote for Warren. Marshall himself gave an equal protection dimension to the Horatio Alger legend. Great-grandson of a slave and son of a Pullman car steward, Marshall was the first black appointed to the highest Court. He had headed the N.A.A.C.P. Legal Defense Fund's staff for over twenty years and had been chief counsel in the *Brown* segregation case.[81]

Marshall had been appointed to the U.S. Court of Appeals for the Second Circuit in 1961 and had been named Solicitor General in 1965. When Marshall balked at the latter appointment, it is said that President Johnson had told him, "I want folks to walk down the hall at the Justice Department and look in the door and see a nigger sitting there."[82] The President elevated Marshall to the Supreme Court for the same reason. As Douglas put it in his *Autobiography,* "Marshall was named simply because he was black."[83]

Johnson called Warren in San Francisco to tell him of Marshall's appointment. Warren sent the President a written note to thank him for the call and tell him, "It was an excellent appointment. Few men come to the court with better experience or a sounder preparation for our work." Warren also noted that the appointment was in keeping with the policy of opening positions to all without regard to race. "All of us know Thurgood," Warren concluded, "and will welcome him to the court in the belief that he will make a real contribution."[84]

Warren's pleasure at the appointment was not necessarily induced by his new colleague's judicial ability. Henry J. Friendly, the outstanding judge on the Court of Appeals for the Second Circuit, had written Frankfurter in January 1962, "TM seems easily led. I do not have the feeling that he realizes the difficulties of his job and is burning the midnight oil in an effort to conquer them. . . . All this makes life fairly easy for him, save when he is confronted with a difference of opinion, and then he tosses a coin."[85] A month later Friendly wrote again, "I continue to be alarmed by Marshall's willingness to arrive at quick decisions on issues he does not understand."[86] The Friendly estimate was equally valid after Marshall's elevation to the high bench. Next to Whittaker, he was arguably the least able Justice to sit on the Warren Court. But, as Lyndon Johnson stressed, Marshall was not appointed because of his judicial prowess. On the Court the new Justice served as a judicial adjunct to the Chief. That gave Warren a solid majority again that all but nullified Black's apostasy. Except that is when Warren himself joined Black in trying to slow the onward rush of the constitutional revolution for which the Chief Justice, more than any person, had been responsible.

16.

1967 TERM:
ABORTIVE RETIREMENT

Saturday, June 1, 1968, was a gray day in Washington, with a downpour threatening at any moment. The Chief Justice was having lunch with one of his law clerks in a wooden booth in a small Pennsylvania Avenue restaurant not far from the Court. The conversation turned to politics, particularly the California primary. Warren leaned forward and said, "You know, I'm now persuaded that Bobby Kennedy's going to be elected President."

The Chief was asked what his basis was. "Well," Warren replied, "I read the reports in the papers this morning of the crowds that lined Kennedy's route from the airport to downtown Los Angeles. It persuades me that this man has something that's going to get him elected. I can remember when I was at the peak of popularity running for Governor following the same route from the airport and seeing no one on the streets."

Three days later, Senator Robert F. Kennedy was assassinated. Warren now felt that there was nothing to stop Richard M. Nixon from becoming President. Soon thereafter, the Chief called his law clerks into his chambers and told them that he was going to submit his retirement to the President.

On June 11, Fortas phoned the White House to ask for an appointment for Warren to see the President. Two days later James R. Jones, of the White House staff, wrote "Chief Justice Earl Warren met with the President at 9:20 a.m. today and departed the President's office at 9:40 a.m. He came down to say that because of age, he felt he should retire from the Court and he said he wanted President Johnson to appoint his successor, someone who felt as Justice Warren did."[1]

That same day, Warren wrote two retirement letters to the President. The first was a one-sentence formal note: "Pursuant to the provisions of 28 U.S.C. Section 371(b), I hereby advise you of my intention to retire as Chief Justice of the United States, effective at your pleasure."[2]

The second letter stated "my reason" for sending the first letter. "I want you to know," Warren wrote, "that it is not because of reasons of health or on account of any personal or associational problems, but solely because of age." The Chief noted that he was in good physical condition and still found his Court work satisfying. "The problem of age, however, is one that no man can combat and, therefore, eventually must bow to it. I have been continuously in the public service for more than fifty years. When I entered the public service, 150 million of our 200 million people were not yet born. I, therefore, conceive it to be my duty to give way to someone who will have more years ahead of him to cope with the problems which will come to the Court."[3]

Warren had been thinking about retirement for some time. He used to tell his law clerks that there should be a retirement age for the Court. He said it ought to be seventy, until he reached that age. He then thought it ought to be seventy-five. Yet he was now seventy-seven and, while he was in full possession of his faculties, he knew that this might not continue indefinitely. Just before his appointment as Chief Justice was announced, Warren had told his son, Earl, Jr., "If you ever see me slipping, tell me no matter how onerous it is. I don't ever want to get into that position." Now he would repeat this sentiment to his law clerks, saying that he did not want to get into a situation where he was not able to function effectively and nobody would dare to tell him that.

But, if Warren's age was a factor, the catalyst that led to his retirement letter was what he now considered the inevitability of a Nixon presidency. Soon after he saw the President, Warren called in a former law clerk and told him about the retirement, saying he wanted him to know about it before he read it in the newspapers. The Chief said that he thought that Nixon would be elected and anticipated that he would appoint Justices as far removed from the Warren Court philosophy as could be imagined. Certainly, he could not expect Nixon to appoint as the next Chief Justice, in his words to President Johnson as recorded in the Jones memo, "someone who felt as Justice Warren did."[4]

Warren's desire to have Johnson, rather than Nixon, appoint his successor may explain why the Chief sent his retirement letter when he did. It does not explain why he phrased the letter as he did. The federal statute on judicial retirement does not state what notice of retirement must be given to the President. There were no recent precedents, since Warren's two immediate predecessors, Fred M. Vinson and Harlan F. Stone, had both died in office. The Associate Justices who had resigned or retired in recent years had, it is true, given a specific date when they would step down. But Warren chose to do it differently. His retirement letter advised President Johnson of his intention to retire, "effective at your pleasure."[5]

According to a memorandum of the Deputy Attorney General, "the President indicated to the Attorney General that he wanted great care taken on the reply to the letter of retirement from the Chief Justice, the President indicating that he would like to accept the retirement in a manner to make it effective upon the qualification of Warren's successor, and to enable the retirement to be withdrawn if the successor does not qualify."[6]

In accordance with the President's wish, his June 26 letter of reply to Warren, drafted in the Attorney General's office, contained what the Deputy Attorney General's memo called the "key sentence": "With your agreement, I will accept your decision to retire effective at such time as a successor is qualified."[7]

Warren never adequately explained why he worded his retirement letter the way he did. At a press conference a few days after the President announced both the Chief Justice's retirement and his choice of Abe Fortas as his successor, Warren said only, "there always ought to be a Chief Justice of the United States." He referred to the Chief's administrative work and noted, "if I selected a particular day and the vacancy was not filled it would be a vacuum."[8]

In actuality, the result in such a case would be, not a vacuum, but the assumption of the position of Acting Chief Justice by the Senior

Associate Justice. At the time, that would have been Hugo Black, who was then in his eighties. Warren was concerned about Black's ability to function even as temporary head of the Court. At the same time, he wanted to avoid embarrassing the Alabaman publicly. He phrased his retirement letter as he did to make sure that Black would not become Acting Chief Justice, but without indicating that that was why he acted as he did.

The result was, however, to delay Warren's retirement for another year. At his press conference, Warren was asked what would happen if Fortas was not confirmed as his successor. "I neither expect nor hope that to be the fact," the Chief replied. But, "I am under oath to perform the duties of the office. And if the first of October rolls around and there is no successor, I suppose I would be obliged to act as Chief Justice."[9]

The comment proved prophetic. When October 1968 arrived, Warren was still in his seat at the center of the Court. Despite his retirement letter, the 1967 Term was not to be his last as Chief Justice.

During the 1967 Term, Warren and Black were to join in several decisions that were seen by some as retreats from the activist protection of individual rights which had been the hallmark of the Warren Court. Perhaps the most striking of these decisions was in *United States v. O'Brien*.[10] The case arose out of a draft-card burning on the steps of a Boston courthouse. O'Brien had acted to influence others to adopt his antiwar beliefs. He was convicted of violating a law making it a crime knowingly to destroy a draft registration certificate. The court of appeals reversed, holding that the law was an unconstitutional abridgement of freedom of speech. With Marshall not participating, all except Douglas voted to grant certiorari.

During the January 24, 1968, argument, O'Brien's counsel argued that the card burning was "symbolic speech." At this Warren broke in, "What cases do you have that equate the burning of the draft card to symbolic speech?" The Chief Justice also indicated that he was troubled by where the line could be drawn if the card burning was protected as "symbolic speech." "What," he asked, "if a soldier in Vietnam, in a crowd, broke his weapon? Would it be 'symbolic speech'?"[11]

At another point, Warren wanted to know, "Why do you think Congress passed this legislation?" Counsel's answer was, "The passage was an act of hysteria, not reflection." The Chief Justice then asked if there were any cases that stood for the principle that the motives of Congress supplied a basis for overruling a statute.[12]

Warren's questions suggested his view on the merits of the case. At the January 26 conference, he spoke for reversal. The others agreed, including Douglas who thought the case should be decided by a short per curiam. Warren took the case himself, so that he should bear the brunt of the expected criticism from the Court's normal constituency. He knew that such criticism would be forthcoming from the law clerks' almost unanimous sentiment against the decision. The clerks engaged in virtual guerrilla warfare against the decision and, while they could scarcely change the result, their lack of enthusiasm helped make the opinion a weak one.

Warren's draft opinion tried to avoid handling the case in traditional First Amendment terms. It was based upon classification of conduct in verbal and nonverbal categories. O'Brien's act was considered a nonverbal communicative act outside the amendment's protection. According to the draft, "an act unrelated to the employment of language or other inherently expressive symbols is not speech within the First Amendment if as a matter of fact the act has an immediate harmful impact not completely apart from any impact arising by virtue of the claimed communication itself."

The Warren draft's approach was similar to that urged by Black in the cases involving sit-ins and other civil-rights protests. The Alabaman was, of course, delighted and joined immediately. However, the others, particularly Harlan and Brennan, were disturbed. Harlan circulated a concurrence criticizing the Chief's approach. Brennan urged that the opinion should be redrafted in more traditional First Amendment terms. He tried to get Warren to accept the test that had been articulated in Brennan's opinion in the 1963 case of *N.A.A.C.P. v. Button:*[13] "only a compelling state interest in the regulation of a subject within the State's power to regulate can justify limiting First Amendment freedoms."[14] Brennan wanted Warren to recognize that the conduct involved did fall within First Amendment protection, but that the interest in regulating it was compelling.

Warren set his law clerk to work redrafting the opinion. The revised draft embodied much of the approach that Brennan had suggested. It recognized that the communicative element in O'Brien's conduct brought the First Amendment into play. But it found that the government had a *substantial* interest (not the *compelling* interest Brennan had urged was necessary) in assuring the continuing availability of draft cards which justified the law prohibiting their destruction. Except for Douglas, the Justices quickly joined the new circulation. When Warren announced the decision on May 27, 1968, Douglas issued a dissent challenging the constitutionality of a peacetime draft—an issue not previously raised in the case.[15]

Those who had charged Warren with imposing constitutional handcuffs upon the police must have been surprised by his opinion in *Terry v. Ohio*[16]—the Stop and Frisk Case. McFadden, a veteran detective, had seen Terry and another man in downtown Cleveland. He felt "they didn't look right" and observed them closely. After he saw them engage in repeated reconnaissance of a store window, he suspected them of "casing a job, a stick-up." He approached them, identified himself, and asked for their names. When they "mumbled something," McFadden grabbed Terry and patted down the outside of his clothing. He felt a pistol and removed it. Terry was convicted of carrying a concealed weapon. The state court rejected his claim that the gun had been obtained through an unlawful search and seizure. All the Justices voted to grant certiorari.

Once again, Warren indicated during the argument, on December 12, 1967, how he felt about the case. Turning to counsel arguing against the conviction, the Chief Justice said, "You are saying that unless a police officer has probable cause to arrest he cannot stop-and-frisk. Aren't there some circumstances when an officer confronts a person without having probable cause to believe that a crime has been committed, but with a fear that his safety is endangered?"[17]

At another point, Warren asked, "How far do you want us to go? I suppose you will agree that a police officer has a right to protect himself. Does the officer have the right to frisk a man to see if he has a weapon?"[18]

Warren began the December 15 conference by repeating that the detective did not have to have probable cause that a crime had been committed before he could stop Terry and frisk him. As he saw it, the key questions were, "Did the police officer have probable cause to believe his life was in danger?" Warren stated that the Court should give due weight to McFadden's experience, "having in mind a trained policeman may react different from an ordinary citizen." Warren also said that "people don't have to answer and may walk away." He wanted the decision to stress that point.

Black agreed that the Court "should use 'probable cause' and 'reasonable suspicion.'" He asked, "Does an officer have the right to interrogate people doing peculiar things? I don't know that this is forbidden by anything in the Constitution" Black stated that the police officer "further has the right to defend himself. I don't want anything said that the police can't make a guy stay until he answers or he stubbornly refuses."

Brennan advocated handling the "stop and frisk" issue in familiar Fourth Amendment terms. As he saw it, the authority of the police to stop and frisk and the limits on that authority should be stated in terms of probable cause—probable cause to investigate suspicious behavior and ask the person to give an account of himself, and probable cause to believe that the person might be armed and dangerous.

The conference voted unanimously to affirm the conviction on Brennan's "probable cause" approach. The Chief again assigned the opinion to himself, believing that, here too, he should receive the criticism that would come from many of the Court's normal supporters. In late January, 1968, Warren sent Brennan a typewritten draft opinion, asking for the Justice's comments. The draft focused primarily on the "frisk" issue, saying little about the question of a police officer's authority to approach and stop someone on the street. Warren asserted that frisking was essential to protect the lives of policemen as they engaged in routine investigations of suspicious persons. The need for a limited self-protective search was supported by statistics of police casualties attributable to guns and knives, the need for quick judgments, and the threat that the answer to a question might be a bullet.

The Warren draft stated, "We are not concerned here with the question whether Officer McFadden properly approached the . . . men in front of Zucker's store to ask them questions. Our inquiry must focus on the propriety of the search of petitioner for weapons." Warren's conclusion was that McFadden "had probable cause to initiate a limited search for weapons." That was true because, "if he had reasonable grounds to believe that his life was in danger, he was entitled to take reasonable measures to protect himself."

The Court's holding was summarized at the end of the Warren draft: "we merely hold today that where a police officer observes unusual conduct which leads him reasonably to conclude in light of his experience that criminal activity may be afoot; where in the course of investigating this behavior he identifies himself as a policeman and makes reasonable inquiries; and where his inquiries are met with evasive responses, which in the circumstances of the confrontation reasonably confirm his belief that the individuals involved may be armed and dangerous, he is entitled for the protection of himself and others in the area to conduct, without a warrant, a carefully limited search of the outer clothing of such persons in an attempt to discover weapons which might be used to assault him."

To Warren, this holding was a matter of common sense and, as such, not inconsistent with *Miranda*[19] and the other Warren Court decisions on the rights of criminal defendants. The *Terry*-type questioning in the street was an entirely different thing from the *Miranda*-type questioning in the station house. When the police were stopping to investigate and question a person on the street, they had to have the right to frisk so that they would not get shot or knifed. As the draft put it, "The initial inquiry must be whether the officer has reasonable grounds to believe that the person with whom he is dealing may be armed and dangerous to himself or others present, regardless of whether he is engaged in the criminal activity which the investigating officer suspects might be afoot."

Brennan replied to Warren's draft with a six legal-size page January 20 letter. Brennan wondered whether the opinion did not emphasize the "frisk" issue too much, while overlooking the question of the officer's authority to stop someone like Terry. Brennan wrote, "the emphasis is on probable cause to 'search' and the opinion does not deal with probable cause to 'seize.' I fully agree that 'probable cause' is the standard but I don't think in a case like this we get to probable cause for the 'search' until after we demonstrate that there was probable cause for the 'seizure,' that is, for the officer to stop the petitioner and require him to give an account of himself."

The Brennan letter stressed that the crucial holding was "that the Court is rejecting the extreme position that an officer may stop a citizen only if he has probable cause to arrest him." Brennan reaffirmed that "probable cause" was the proper standard and suggested that the opinion expressly reserve the question of what the rule of admissibility would be where the frisk turned up something other than a weapon. Brennan noted that, "when the question has to be answered," he might conclude that nonweapon evidence of crime should be excluded.

Brennan also urged Warren to develop in the text what "is for me a very important point"—namely, "[t]he position that courts may resort to the *exclusionary rule* only in criminal prosecutions where the prosecution offers illegally seized matter in evidence, and that police abuses of 'stop' and 'frisk' not followed by prosecutions are beyond judicial power to remedy." In addition, Brennan recommended that "something should be said to make clear that the 'stop' is not 'custodial detention' requiring the giving of the *Miranda* warnings," and that the opinion should "reserve the question of stops of motor vehicles and searches for weapons incident to such a stop."

On February 9, Warren circulated a printed *Terry* draft, As in the typewritten draft that he had sent Brennan, Warren still focused primarily on the frisk aspect of the case and said little about the officer's authority to stop Terry. As far as the authority to search Terry was concerned, Warren concluded that "Officer McFadden did not have probable cause to arrest petitioner for conspiracy to rob a store, but if he had probable cause to believe that his life was in danger, he was entitled to take reasonable measures to protect himself."

Warren's law clerks told the clerks of the other Justices that the Chief had instructed them to concentrate on the frisk aspect because he felt that only by limiting *frisks* could any practical controls be imposed on police conduct. In Warren's view, there was nothing to prevent a policeman from walking up to anyone he felt like confronting. If the Fourth Amendment was to be implemented, it would have to be by controlling interrogation (a factor not presented in *Terry*) or by controlling the frisk.

Once again Warren stressed the need to protect the police officer who was risking his life in the performance of his duty. If anything, his language now was stronger than in the typewritten version that had been shown to Brennan. "[A] police officer," the Warren circulated draft declared, "is not required to sacrifice his life on the altar of a doctrinaire judicial scholasticism which ignores the deadly realities of criminal investigation and law enforcement."

The circulated draft still retained the test of "probable cause." But Warren stated it in terms of an inquiry along a scale of reasonableness framed in terms of how intrusive the police officer had been. The less the intrusion, the less cause the officer would need to show a judge. In essence, Warren was adopting a balancing approach to probable cause, which he wrote was derived from the 1967 opinion in *Camara v. Municipal Court*,[20] discussed in the last chapter. The draft contended that this approach avoided the vagueness and uncertainty of framing the issue in terms of degrees of suspicion, and took a more realistic view of the variable nature of the street encounter. In effect, the draft was adopting a sliding scale of conduct. Under it, McFadden had acted "reasonably" on the facts and that brought his conduct within the Warren model of "probable cause."

Soon after he received Warren's circulated draft, Douglas sent the Chief a letter questioning his failure to deal with the "stop" issue. He suggested revisions to make explicit McFadden's justification for stopping Terry. The crucial Douglas revision, based on some of the Warren language, read as follows:

"Officer McFadden did not have probable cause to arrest petitioner for conspiracy to rob a store, but if he had probable cause to believe that a crime was in the making or about to be committed and that petitioner and his cohorts were implicated, he was entitled to confront them and detain them briefly to ask questions. Such action by an officer may uncover additional information that will create probable cause to arrest—but even if it does not, the likely result is that the officer's acts will frighten his suspects into abandoning a contemplated crime.

"While arresting persons who have already committed crimes is an important task of law enforcement, an equally if not more important function is crime prevention and deterence [sic] of would-be criminals. '[T]here is no war between the Constitution and common sense,' *Mapp v. Ohio,* 367 U.S. 643, 657, and it would be absurd if the Fourth Amendment required police officers to wait until they saw suspects actually commit such an overt act that would constitute a criminal [attempt] or disclose a criminal conspiracy before being able to stop and detain them for questioning. Effective crime prevention demands that the officer be empowered to intervene before the robber draws his revolver, the burglar breaks in a window, or the arsonist strikes a match.

"Similarly, the common sense of the Constitution requires that an officer be able to take reasonable steps to protect himself when his duty to investigate and prevent crimes leads him to confront persons whom he has probable cause to believe are armed and dangerous. In such circumstances a limited search for arms and other weapons is reasonable, for the police officer is not required to sacrifice his life on the altar of a doctrinaire judicial scholasticism."

On February 19 Black circulated a draft opinion, concurring in the result but taking issue with the idea that the Fourth Amendment protects "privacy." He also objected to Warren's balancing test saying that the issue for him was simply the reasonableness of Mc-Fadden's conduct. On February 20 Harlan wrote the Chief indicating that he too would file a separate opinion.

The next day, White circulated a draft of what became his short concurring opinion. White stated that, to him, the critical stage was the stop. Once that was justified, a brief detention for noncoercive questioning or for frisking was normally proper. The White draft indicated, however, that there might be cases where a frisk was not justified by the same facts as the stop. White's final version omitted that suggestion, looking instead only to the authority to detain briefly.

Harlan circulated a draft concurring opinion on February 27. Harlan, like White, emphasized the stop. But he went further, saying that the frisk was an automatic incident to the stop, relying on the analogy of the search-incident-to-arrest cases.

Most important of all, Harlan's draft was the first to reject probable cause as the standard, arguing instead for the "reasonable suspicion" formulation approved by the American Law Institute. Harlan argued that a stop and an arrest were different animals. Probable cause which was identified with arrests was a requirement for issuing warrants and was inappropriate to the street investigation situation. Moreover, probable cause for Harlan was troublesome because it involved notions of neutrality and objectivity which he claimed were neither obtainable nor desirable in this context. Rather stop and frisk questions came down to the officer's allegation that the defendant had acted in a manner that aroused suspicion, and the trial judge had to credit or reject that assertion as a matter of fact.

Harlan's draft urged a standard that would have called for suspicion of a particular crime under circumstances suggesting to a prudent police officer a substantial possibility that that crime had been or was about to be committed. In addition, he would have required the officer to establish the "forcible stop" as the only alternative available to deal effectively with the situation.

At this point, Brennan also intervened. "I've become acutely concerned," Brennan wrote Warren on March 14, 1968, "that the mere fact of our affirmance in *Terry* will be taken by the police all over the country as our license to them to carry on, indeed widely expand, present 'aggressive surveillance' techniques which the press tells us are being deliberately employed in Miami, Chicago, Detroit and other ghetto cities. This is happening, of course, in response to the 'crime in the streets' alarums being sounded in this election year in the Congress, the White House and every Governor's office."

By this time, Brennan, like Harlan, had concluded that trying to work out the problem in terms of probable cause had been a mistake. Brennan drafted a revised *Terry* opinion incorporating his new approach and sent it to Warren on March 14. His covering letter explained that he had tried to retain "much of your exposition," though "I have also suggested the omission of a great deal from your opinion," which included the weeding out of most of the Chief's pro-police rhetoric. Brennan also included what he termed "a rather extensively foot-noted memorandum stating my reasons for the conviction I've reached (contrary to my previous view) that we should not handle this question as a matter of 'probable cause' and the Warrant Clause, but as a matter of the Reasonableness Clause."

As this memo indicated, the Brennan revision abandoned the "probable cause" standard and substituted a test of the reasonableness of the police officer's conduct in the circumstances. It concluded that McFadden had acted reasonably in stopping Terry and frisking him for weapons. Brennan's approach was summarized in his March 14 letter to Warren: "from here on out, it becomes virtually unnecessary for the police to establish 'probable cause to *arrest*' to support weapons charges; an officer can move against anyone he *suspects* has a weapon and get a conviction if he 'frisks' him and finds one."

Warren told Brennan that he planned to rethink *Terry* as soon as he could find an opportunity to devote his undivided attention to the opinion for a sustained period. As it turned out, Warren could not find the time until the end of the 1967 Term's oral arguments in May. In the interim, several of the Justices, particularly Brennan and Stewart, began to think that the case should be set for reargument. They feared the effects of a potentially inflammatory opinion that might be taken by the police as a license for overaggressive tactics against racial minorities. But then, on May 31, Warren circulated a new *Terry* draft. It was, except for the first five introductory pages and the concluding paragraph, substantially the version that Brennan had prepared.

Stewart immediately agreed to the new *Terry* opinion, complimenting Warren on an "excellent job." So did Black, Brennan, Fortas, and Marshall. Harlan also agreed, withdrawing his draft concurrence and substituting a milder brief version. White joined as well, with a short concurrence. However, when Warren delivered the *Terry* opinion on June 10, 1968, he did not speak for a unanimous Court. At the last minute, Douglas suddenly wrote a dissent. The Douglas defection from the decision caught Warren completely by surprise. It came without warning and was inconsistent with Douglas' earlier contributions to the *Terry* draft. Douglas had also previously expressed his personal appreciation to Brennan for inducing Warren to abandon the probable cause approach because of the confusion that it was creating.

Douglas' behavior was not unusual for the idiosyncratic Westerner. In another case during the 1967 Term, *Zwickler v. Koota*,[21] Brennan had circulated a draft opinion holding that abstention by a federal court in a challenge to a state statute was not proper where the statute was attacked for overbreadth as repugnant to the First Amendment. Douglas wrote that "he could not agree more with each and every word in the opinion." Despite this, he intended to concur only in the result. The reason he gave was his strong objection to footnoted references in Brennan's draft to the American Law Institute. Brennan wrote his law clerk that Douglas "vehemently objects to any recognition whatever of the A.L.I. in our footnotes. He's suspicious of that organization from top to bottom and won't join anything that gives them any kudos for anything." Brennan ultimately gave in to the Douglas anti-A.L.I. bent and removed the tainted references. Douglas then joined the opinion with "three cheers and a hurrah."

In the *Terry* case itself Brennan may have been the author both of the Court's approach and most of the opinion. But he was troubled by what he called, in his March 14 letter to Warren, "our legitimating of frisks on the basis of suspicious circumstances." In his letter, Brennan pointed to "the terrible risk that police will conjure up 'suspicious circumstances,' and courts will credit their versions. It will not take much of this to aggravate the already white heat resentment of ghetto Negroes against the police—and the Court will become the scapegoat."

Warren and Black were joined in opposition to the Chief's usual supporters in *Powell v. Texas.*[22] Powell was convicted of violating a law making public drunkenness a crime. The Texas court rejected his claim that, since he was a chronic alcoholic, his conviction was invalid under the 1962 decision in *Robinson v. California,*[23] discussed in chapter 10, which held that narcotics addiction could not be made a crime. All the Justices except Warren and Black voted to take the case.

The Court voted five-to-four to reverse Powell's conviction. The majority was composed of Douglas, Brennan, Stewart, White, and Fortas. Both Warren and Black had urged affirmance, arguing that the case was different from *Robinson,* because it was not chronic alcoholism, but being drunk in public, that was made the crime. Warren and Black had both originally advocated a different approach than that taken in the *Robinson* conference. They now refused to extend *Robinson* to the extent sought by Powell.

However, the vote at the *Powell* conference was the other way by the bare majority. Douglas, the senior majority Justice, assigned the case to Fortas. He circulated a draft opinion of the Court on April 23, 1968, substantially similar to the dissent he ultimately delivered in the case. On April 30, Black sent around a strong draft dissent, which charged that "The Court thus significantly limits the States in their efforts to deal with a widespread and important social problem, and it does so by announcing a revolutionary doctrine of constitutional law that tightly restricts state power to deal with a wide variety of other harmful conduct."

In addition, Black claimed (in a passage toned down in his ultimate concurrence) that the majority was going beyond the proper limits of judicial power. "I will point out in this opinion," Black's draft dissent asserted, "that the Court relies on its own notions of the wisdom of this Texas law to erect a constitutional barrier the desirability of which is far from clear, and that the findings of fact so mechanically employed by the Court have no concrete meaning in terms of actual human behavior and therefore cannot be considered controlling on the constitutional question before us."

White had joined the tentative majority, but he had increasing doubts about the reversal of Powell's conviction. On May 8, he wrote Fortas that he had changed his vote. "I am with you part way but I am leaving you in other respects and in the result, the upshot being that I do not join your opinion or those on the other side either. I have been back and forth for weeks but it is more than likely that I am at rest, at least for now." The result was that White concurred in the decision to affirm, but wrote his own opinion to explain why he reached that result.

With White's switch, there was a majority for affirmance. Warren now assigned the case to Marshall. But he was concerned that the opinion should be done properly. He assigned one of his own law clerks to work with Marshall and his clerks on the opinion. Contrary to his usual practice, he also played a direct part in the drafting of another Justice's opinion. He and his clerk had several meetings with Marshall on how to write the opinion.

Marshall's opinion, distinguishing *Robinson* along the lines stated by Warren and Black at the conference, was delivered for a plurality of four on June 17, 1968. White, whose vote made the decision one to affirm, concurred in the result. Fortas, joined by Douglas, Brennan, and Stewart, recast his original majority opinion as a dissent.

Two other 1967 Term cases where Warren voted differently than his normal supporters (including Black this time) were *Marchetti v. United States*[24] and *Grosso v. United States*.[25] Even the Justices who were considered part of the Court's conservative wing voted against Warren in them, so that, in the end, the Chief had to dissent alone. Yet Warren's lone stand here may be attributed not to differences in legal doctrine but to his all but visceral abhorrence toward gambling. He saw *Marchetti* and *Grosso* as cases that involved not so much constitutional rights as a law designed to suppress gambling.

The federal wagering tax law required those in the business of accepting wagers to pay an annual $50 occupational tax, as well as an excise tax of ten percent on all wagers accepted. Those liable for the occupational tax had to register as professional gamblers with their local internal revenue district, which was to maintain a public list of all who registered and to provide copies to state and local prosecutors. Though the statute involved was ostensibly only a tax law, it was actually intended to place the gambler on the horns of a legal dilemma. If he were not to register, he would commit a federal offense. If he were to register, he would lay himself open to prosecution for violation of state antigambling laws.

But the Court had upheld the statute as within congressional taxing power in the 1953 case of *United States v. Kahriger*,[26] decided a few months before Warren became Chief Justice. Black and Douglas had dissented on the ground that the law violated the privilege against self-incrimination. Marchetti had been convicted of failure to register and pay the occupational tax, Grosso of failure to pay the excise tax. Their convictions had been affirmed on the authority of the *Kahriger* decision. The Supreme Court granted certiorari to consider whether *Kahriger* should be overruled in light of the 1965 decision in *Albertson v. Subversive Activities Control Board*,[27] discussed in chapter 14. *Albertson* had ruled that a registration requirement for Communists violated the Fifth Amendment privilege.

Despite the fact that he had led the conference to the *Albertson* decision, Warren voted to affirm Marchetti's conviction at the January 20, 1967, conference. But he was supported only by Clark, as the others voted, seven-to-two, to overrule *Kahriger* and reverse. In *Grosso*, the conference voted seven-to-two to affirm. Harlan was assigned both opinions.

Harlan circulated draft opinions in March, 1967. Part II of his *Marchetti* draft (Part I was a summary of the statutory provisions) started by rejecting the three bases on which *Kahriger* had been decided: (1) that Kahriger had lacked "standing to employ the privilege to challenge the constitutionality of the requirement to register"; (2) that he could have avoided self-incrimination "if only he elects to cease, or never to begin, gambling activities"; and (3) "that the wagering tax requirements are entirely prospective in their application." Harlan's conclusion was, "We are therefore unable to accept *Kahriger* . . . as affording any threshold block to the use of the Fifth Amendment privilege to excuse failures to register and to pay the occupational tax. And in light of the reach of the Fifth Amendment privilege against self-incrimination as reflected in the consistent course of decisions in this Court, it can hardly be maintained that these obligations are not otherwise within the privilege's protection."

Part III of Harlan's *Marchetti* draft asserted a balancing test for application of the Fifth Amendment privilege. Harlan based his approach here upon the premise that the privilege "is one of several instruments through which the Constitution was expected to reconcile the divergent interests of society and of the individual." The privilege "must for this purpose harmonize the individual's natural desire to find shelter in silence . . . with the urgent governmental need for accurate and timely information."

In the next part of his *Marchetti* draft, Harlan recognized the importance of the government need to collect revenue. But that was outweighed by the fact that, in the language of *Albertson,* wagering was "an area permeated with criminal statutes," and that those engaged in wagering were a group "inherently suspect of criminal activities." The Harlan draft concluded that, "In this context, neither the public importance of the information obtained nor the deference we must give to Congress' exercise of its taxing powers permits rejection of petitioner's claim of the constitutional privilege. . . . We must conclude that the registration and occupational tax requirements deny to petitioner his constitutional privilege against self-incrimination."

In his *Grosso* draft, on the other hand, Harlan pointed out that there was no statutory requirement, such as that which existed with respect to the occupational tax, for prosecutors to obtain lists of persons who had paid the excise tax. Applying the balancing test contained in his *Marchetti* draft, Harlan concluded that, in light of "the other public values at stake," and of the insubstantiality of the hazard of self-incrimination from payment of the tax, Grosso's constitutional rights had not been violated.

The *Grosso* draft recognized that the excise taxpayer was required to maintain extensive records, and to file each month Form 730, stating his name, address, registration number and gross amount of wagers accepted in the preceding month. But Harlan refused to reach the validity of the Form 730 requirement, reasoning that its filing was not a condition to satisfaction of the excise tax indebtedness, and that its consideration would raise serious questions on the continued validity of the so-called "required-records" doctrine laid down in the 1948 case of *Shapiro v. United States,*[28] under which records required to be kept by law are not protected by the Fifth Amendment privilege.

Soon after Harlan circulated his drafts, Douglas told the conference that he would circulate a concurring opinion in *Marchetti* and a dissent in *Grosso.* The Douglas opinions were circulated on March 23,

1967. In *Marchetti* Douglas wrote a one-page concurrence that rejected Harlan's balancing test. In *Grosso,* the Douglas dissent rejected the notion that the privilege must be interpreted in light of the other societal interests involved, and argued that payment of the excise tax would constitute a link in the chain of conviction for crime.

On the same day, Brennan wrote Harlan that he also could not join that part of *Marchetti* which applied a balancing test, though he would concur in the rest of the opinion. In addition, Brennan indicated that he could not agree in *Grosso,* and that he felt the constitutionality of Form 730 would have to be decided.

Harlan circulated revised drafts on March 30. In *Marchetti,* he stressed that, to violate the privilege, the danger of incrimination must not be insubstantial or remote. To support his balancing approach, Harlan quoted from Chief Justice John Marshall, that none of the Constitution's commands may be entirely disregarded. But Harlan now limited the weight to be given to public needs in the balancing process. He said that if the hazards of incrimination "prove to be substantial and real, no governmental purpose may override the constitutional privilege. Only if they are not are we permitted by the Constitution to measure and give effect to the other relevant public values."

In his *Grosso* revised draft, Harlan assumed that Grosso could not constitutionally be convicted for failing to file Form 730 and concluded that there was no violation of the privilege in requiring only payment of the tax.

Douglas quickly sent around a revised *Marchetti* concurrence asserting that the Harlan revision was still "but a less obvious statement of a 'balancing' approach to the privilege." On April 3, Brennan sent Douglas a note stating that he agreed with the Douglas *Marchetti* concurrence, but asking whether Douglas could not join all of Harlan's opinion except for the "balancing" section. "I think it might be helpful on this prickly problem," Brennan wrote, "if we would join as much as possible of what John has written."

Harlan now circulated new revised drafts. In *Marchetti,* he stressed even more his point that the hazard of incrimination had to be substantial. In *Grosso,* he eliminated the statement that, where the hazard was not substantial and real, other governmental purposes might be considered in interpreting the privilege.

At this point, Black sent a long note to Harlan reasserting his view that the Bill of Rights must not be balanced away. Black wrote that, while the power to tax might appear to overlap with the privilege, in actuality it did not. "There are hundreds of different ways to assess and collect taxes. There is only one way to protect a person from incriminating himself at all times and under all circumstances, and that is simply to do it."

Douglas now agreed to join all but the "balancing" section of Harlan's *Marchetti* opinion. Brennan and Black joined the Douglas concurrence refusing to join that section. Harlan sent Black an April 6 letter, with copies to Douglas and Brennan, that he had decided to delete the offending section entirely. It now looked as though Harlan would get a majority for his *Marchetti* opinion.

Though Brennan had, as seen, agreed to join *Marchetti,* he circulated his own dissent in *Grosso.* It affirmed the power of Congress to tax illegal activity, but asserted that the provisions involved in *Grosso* were controlled by *Albertson.*[29] Brennan argued that the excise tax requirement could not be separated from the supplementary requirements Congress saw fit to impose. In any case, he urged, there was a grave threat of incrimination from the mere payment of the excise tax since taxpayers had to identify themselves. Fortas joined the Brennan draft.

Warren had become increasingly concerned at the handling of *Marchetti* and *Grosso.* He was particularly disturbed at what he considered Harlan's scholastic attempt to avoid the constitutional issue in *Grosso.* But his disagreement with the majority was so fundamental that he now splintered the Court further. On April 5, he circulated an opinion dissenting in *Marchetti* and concurring in *Grosso,* though he rejected Harlan's refusal to face the Fifth Amendment question in the latter.

Warren's draft stressed "that these taxes are legitimate exercises of the power of the Federal Government to collect revenue. . . . This Court has consistently upheld Congress' power to levy excise taxes on the receipts of a variety of businesses, without regard to the legality of the business involved." In addition, Warren wrote, "the registration procedure adopted by Congress for the collection of taxes on gambling activities has been traditionally upheld as a reasonable incident to the taxing power. . . . Thus there can be no doubt but that the statutes imposing taxes on gambling activities fall within the taxing power of Congress."

The Chief's draft denied that "these otherwise legitimate exercises of the taxing power conflict with the privilege against compelled self-incrimination embodied in the Fifth Amendment." Warren answered the Fifth Amendment claim by relying on the analysis in the *Kahriger* case,[30] which "seems to me equally appropriate to these two cases. So long as the gambler voluntarily enters the activity with full knowledge of the tax and incident disclosures, I cannot see how the disclosures can be considered compelled within the meaning of the Fifth Amendment." Warren conceded "that these disclosures discourage gambling activities in States where the activity which is being taxed is illegal. But gambling is an activity which the Federal Government may tax and regulate or even prohibit in its interstate aspects; it is clearly not an activity around which there is any general constitutional protection."

The Warren draft distinguished *Albertson* because the registration there required "disclosure . . . of an activity which had been held constitutionally protected by this Court. Registration operated as a direct deterrent to a right of association protected by the First Amendment. The disclosures in these cases, on the other hand, pertain not to protected activity, such as speech or association, but to gambling."

Warren also distinguished *Marchetti* from *Albertson* on the ground that "here the disclosures serve a valid governmental interest—the collection of the taxes on gambling activities—whereas in *Albertson* the disclosures served no purposes other than to advance the aims of the criminal statutes in the area. The disclosures and the criminal statutes served the same purpose: to harass and eliminate the Communist Party."

As far as *Grosso* was concerned, Warren wrote, "I disagree with the Court's failure to confront the" self-incrimination issue. "I think it is unrealistic to separate the obligation to pay the excise tax and the obligation to make disclosures which the Government insists are essential for collection."

After Clark had read Warren's draft, he wrote Harlan, "I have decided to join the CJ," and he sent the Chief a formal joinder on April 6. Then, on May 1, the Court became further fragmented when White circulated an opinion which, like the Warren draft, dissented in *Marchetti* and concurred in the result in *Grosso*. White asserted that the Court had cast grave doubt on the viability of the required-records doctrine of the *Shapiro* case and argued that the government's concession that *Shapiro* was not involved should be disregarded. White also stated that "no sensible difference can be drawn" between the return required in these cases and the return required in the 1927 case of *United States v. Sullivan*,[31] where the Court held that a taxpayer could not refuse to file a return at all because it called for answers that the taxpayer was privileged from making. White called for a "thorough airing" of the difficulties presented by *Shapiro* and *Sullivan* through a reargument of *Marchetti* and *Grosso*.

The division in the Court at this point was summarized by Harlan in a May 2, 1967, letter to Black, the senior Justice in the majority: "The present posture of the votes in *Marchetti* and *Grosso* is as follows: Black, Douglas, Brennan and Fortas, JJ. are on my opinion in *Marchetti*. I am alone in the opinion I have circulated in *Grosso*. Douglas, J., has written for reversal, with you joining, as has Brennan, J., with Fortas, J., joining. The Chief Justice, joined by Clark, J., has written for affirmance of the judgment, as has White, J. I have not heard from Stewart, J., nor has he circulated separately in either of these cases."

In view of this division, Harlan decided to give up the chance of obtaining a Court for his *Marchetti* and *Grosso* drafts. "I am faced," he wrote in his letter to Black, "with the unusual experience of having to withdraw from the opinion which I prepared for the Court in this case, under your assignment." Harlan explained that, in preparing *Marchetti*, "I thought that, in view of the Government's disclaimer that *Shapiro v. United States* had anything to do with this case, the present case could be treated within the four corners of *Kahriger* which I continue to believe [was] wrongly decided."

Harlan noted, however, that "three members of the Court, the Chief Justice, joined by Justice Clark, and Justice White separately, have relied on *Shapiro*." This, Harlan thought, "would require adequate treatment of that case by the present majority. For myself, I do not think that this should be done without full-dress briefing and argument."

Harlan's letter informed Black, "I intend to propose at next Thursday's Conference that this case, and also No. 181, *Grosso v. United States*, be set for reargument next Term, as suggested by Brother White in his separate opinion." Harlan's letter concluded, "If the proposal for reargument carries, I should think that the parties in both *Marchetti* and *Grosso* should be asked to address themselves, among other things, to the applicability of *Shapiro,* and in *Grosso* to address themselves, in addition, to the question of whether payment of the excise tax can be made without disclosure of the activity to which the payment relates."

At the May 25 conference, Harlan did make his motion and it carried. The Court issued an order on June 12 setting *Marchetti* and *Grosso* for reargument in the 1967 Term.[32] Counsel were requested to argue the two points stated at the end of Harlan's letter to Black.

The reargument took place on October 10 and 11, 1967. In accordance with the reargument order, the principal questions dealt with by counsel were, whether an individual could pay the gambling excise tax without filing tax form 730—as Harlan had maintained in his *Grosso* draft—and whether the required-records doctrine was necessarily at stake—as White had maintained in his draft *Marchetti* dissent. Francis X. Beytagh, Jr., a former Warren law clerk who appeared for the government, demonstrated the correctness of the negative on both points.

In response, Harlan and White gave in on the two issues. The conference after the reargument voted seven-to-one (Warren voting against and Marshall not participating) to reverse in both *Marchetti* and *Grosso.* Harlan agreed to prepare new opinions in the two cases. His new drafts were based primarily upon the approach that had been followed in the *Albertson* case. The other majority members quickly joined the Harlan opinions. Brennan and Stewart, however, wrote concurrences. Brennan used material from his original *Grosso* dissent to emphasize the continuing validity of the *Sullivan* and *Shapiro* cases. Stewart said that, if the issue were a new one, he would agree with Warren, but felt himself bound by the *Albertson* case. When Harlan announced the decisions on January 29, 1968, Warren alone dissented. He delivered a shorter version of the opinion he had circulated the previous April.

Warren's dissents in the *Marchetti* and *Grosso* cases were, however, the rare exceptions during the 1967 Term. The Chief wrote a dissent in only one other case, and it involved a technical bankruptcy issue. In the term's other cases, Warren was able to lead the Court to the decisions he favored.

Two of those decisions were rendered in civil-rights cases. The first was *Jones v. Alfred H. Mayer Co.*[33] The company was selling homes in a housing development. It refused to sell a house to Jones because he was black. Jones sued for an injunction and damages, invoking federal-court jurisdiction to award relief "under any Act of Congress providing for the protection of civil rights." The lower courts dismissed the complaint on the ground that the civil-rights statutes did not reach purely private discrimination where no "state action" was involved.

Warren urged the conference to reverse. As he saw it, the concept of "state action" had been expanded sufficiently to cover this case. He referred to the 1946 case of *Marsh v. Alabama,*[34] where action by a company-owned town was ruled within the "state action" concept, because the private owner exercised governmental functions in running the town. To Warren, a housing development was, in effect, the equivalent of a municipality. The Chief said that he would "decide on the same theory we decided in *Marsh v. Alabama.* They have [governmental] power and are to take care of parks and streets, etc."

The Justices were willing to reverse on the *Marsh* ground—including Harlan and White who ultimately dissented. But Stewart argued for a new and far-reaching theory that would greatly extend federal power to protect civil rights. Just after the Civil War, Congress had enacted the Civil Rights Act of 1866, which was still part of the federal statute-book as 42 U.S.C. § 1982. It provided that "All citizens . . . shall have the same right, in every State and Territory, as is enjoyed by white citizens thereof to inherit, purchase, lease, sell, hold, and convey real and personal property."[35] Stewart urged that this statute would permit reversal, even if only private discrimination was involved.

At the argument on April 1, 1968, counsel for Jones had relied specifically on section 1982 and had argued that it was aimed at individual, as well as state, action. Stewart inquired whether the provision was not originally enacted under the Thirteenth Amendment, which contains no language limiting its operation to "state action." Counsel answered that it was so enacted. Stewart then asked, "If this law was valid under the Thirteenth Amendment, why do we bother with state action?"[36]

Stewart told the conference that he would go on a ground "much broader that *Marsh*," namely, that the defendant's refusal to sell because Jones was black violated section 1982. That statute, Stewart pointed out, "was enacted before the Fourteenth Amendment and under section 2 of the Thirteenth." Section 1982 was valid under the Thirteenth Amendment as a prohibition of the barriers to acquisition of property that were incidents of slavery before the Civil War. As such, section 1982 could reach private discrimination, since the Thirteenth Amendment, unlike the Fourteenth, contains no language limiting its operation to "state action." "Therefore," said Stewart, "I think this is a valid law operating against private people." Stewart asserted that, "even language in the *Civil Rights Cases*[37] supports this analysis." His reference was to the 1883 decision holding that laws protecting Fourteenth Amendment rights could reach only "state action."

Warren's first reaction to Stewart's approach was dubious. He said he would still prefer to decide on the *Marsh* theory. He noted that Congress was then passing the Civil Rights Act of 1968, which would prohibit housing discrimination. "Doing it that way," the Chief stated, "Congress can take care of it under the pending legislation."

Harlan and White were even stronger in their opposition to the Stewart approach. Harlan said that he "could perhaps go on the *Marsh* ground and *no other*." Indeed, Harlan went so far as to declare, "I don't think 1982 is a valid statute apart from 'state action.' "

The others, however, were willing to follow Stewart, agreeing with Black who said, "I would reverse on section 1982. I think the statute was passed by Congress to cover this." Warren also went along. He assigned the opinion to Stewart, who circulated a draft in the middle of May. Stewart announced the reversal and the new theory supporting it on June 17, 1968. Harlan, joined by White, issued a dissent that termed the decision "ill-considered and ill-advised."[38]

The second 1967 Term civil-rights case was *Green v. County School Board*.[39] Green brought an action against a segregated school system in a Virginia county. There were two schools in the county, one for whites and one for blacks. After the suit was brought, the school board adopted a "freedom of choice" plan, under which pupils could choose which of the two schools they would attend. In the three years in which the plan was in operation, no white child had chosen to attend the black school, and 85 percent of the black children still

attended the all-black school. The lower courts had upheld this freedom of choice plan. With Marshall not voting, all the other Justices
voted to grant certiorari.

As Warren saw it at the April 5, 1968, conference, "The only question is whether freedom of choice is violative of constitutional rights."
The Chief had no doubt that it was. "The purpose of *Brown*,"[40] Warren declared, "was to break down segregation and the school district
must have procedures that do that. So this is a problem of remedy,
nothing more. There are alternatives that will do it and they can't
ignore them for this one." Warren, however, thought that the Court
should not "make a per se rule of freedom of choice."

Brennan strongly supported the Chief. The board, he stated, "can't
maintain a segregated school system. This one does and, therefore,
since there are workable alternatives, this one can't be sustained."

The others agreed except for Black, who indicated that free choice
was the governing principle in school assignments throughout the
country, rather than only a Southern plan for formal compliance with
the desegregation requirement. Black alone voted to affirm, stressing
the sanctity of free choice. Warren chose Brennan to write the opinion, hoping that he would be able to win Black's concurrence. Both
the Chief and Brennan thought that the record of unanimous opinions in the sensitive area of school segregation had to be maintained.

Brennan chose the 1954 *Brown* opinion as his model. Like Warren
in it, he wanted the *Green* opinion to be "short, pungent, and to the
point."[41] Brennan's draft detailed in plain language the obligation of
those charged with implementing *Brown*. As Warren had done in
Brown, Brennan emphasized the "inferiority" of education in segregated schools: "The stigma of inferiority which attaches to Negro
children in a dual system originates with the State that creates and
maintains such a system. So long as the racial identity ingrained, as
in New Kent County, by years of discrimination remains in the system, the stigma of inferiority likewise remains." The draft was circulated on May 16, the eve of the fourteenth anniversary of the *Brown*
decision.

The Brennan draft was joined immediately by Marshall and, within
the next few days, by Stewart, Douglas, Fortas, and, on May 22, by
the Chief Justice. But there was resistance from Harlan and White.
At the May 17 conference, they indicated that they could not join
Brennan's opinion so long as it contained the *Brown*-type references

to "inferiority." They said that the references risked angering deseg-regation opponents further and rendering compliance even harder to obtain. White also said that in his view modern sociological and psy-chological data did not support the notion of stigma relied upon by the *Brown I* opinion and that, had he been on the Court in 1954, he would not have agreed with the opinion's famous footnote 11.[42] Both Harlan and White urged Brennan to avoid raising footnote 11's Myr-dal controversy[43] again and to leave the notion of stigma "implicit" in the opinion. Brennan said that he would consider their views, but that he had to consult with others in the majority.

Stewart and Fortas said that they would agree to any changes needed to obtain a Court for the basic result. Warren, however, was firmly opposed to having anyone "fooling around" with the *Brown* decisions. But the Chief did agree to go along with reasonable mod-ifications if they would produce a unanimous Court.

Brennan had not heard from Black since the April 5 conference, and he called on the Alabaman to find out what he was going to do. Black told him that he had been revising the Brennan draft so that he could join it. Brennan returned to his chambers and showed his law clerks Black's revisions. He was jubilant, for they left the sub-stance of the opinion virtually unchanged. Black had substituted the *Brown II*[44] quotation that now appears near the beginning of the opinion,[45] added several "state compelled" modifiers where appro-priate, included the reference to "zoning" in the mandate to the dis-trict court,[46] and added the equivocal introductory statement to the Civil Rights Commission quotation in footnote 5 that "we neither adopt nor refuse to adopt" the views therein.[47] Black also indicated agreement with Harlan and White about the deletions they had pro-posed.

Brennan adopted Black's changes verbatim, deleted the offending passages, and sent the revision to the printer. Brennan then called White to tell him of the changes. White told Brennan to join him "sight unseen."

Harlan was less willing to go along. He said that he was pleased to know of the changes, but had decided that the "tone" of the opin-ion was bothersome. He said that he was thinking of writing a con-curring opinion setting the proper tone. Brennan replied that that would be unfortunate, saying that unanimity was essential to the force of the decision. Warren, of course, felt the same way, and agreed to

Brennan's revised draft, even though he would have preferred the first version, with its stronger references to *Brown*.

Harlan now reconsidered his planned concurrence. At the May 24 conference, he announced that he would join the opinion and not write separately. Brennan was thus able to preface the delivery of his opinion on the following Monday, May 27, by the statement that it was for a unanimous Court.

When Warren joined the *Green* opinion, he wrote Brennan, "When this opinion is handed down, the traffic light will have changed from *Brown* to *Green*. Amen!" Perhaps the Chief Justice was overly optimistic. But, after the decision striking down "freedom of choice" plans was announced, Governor Lester Maddox of Georgia acknowledged it by ordering all state flags flown at half mast.

The term's obscenity case was *Ginsberg v. New York*.[48] Ginsberg, owner of a stationery store and lunch counter, had sold "girlie" magazines with nude photos to a sixteen-year old boy. He was convicted of violating a state law prohibiting the sale to minors under seventeen of materials defined to be obscene on the basis of appeal to them, even though they might not be obscene for adults. At the January 19, 1968, conference, the vote was five-to-four to affirm the conviction. Black and Douglas voted for reversal on their view that the First Amendment did not permit any prohibition of obscene material. Fortas also voted to reverse on the ground that mens rea in the criminal-law sense had not been shown. Stewart voted to vacate as moot. The opinion was assigned to Brennan.

The first thing that had to be resolved was the issue of mootness, on which Stewart had voted to vacate. Under the New York law, Ginsberg could have been sentenced to one year's imprisonment, or a $500 fine, or both. However, the trial judge suspended sentence. The 1943 case of *St. Pierre v. United States*[49] had held that a criminal case had become moot when the defendant had finished serving his sentence before direct review in the Supreme Court. On the last day of the 1966 Term, the Court had applied *St. Pierre* to dismiss appeals in two other cases involving convictions under the New York obscenity law. In those cases—*Jacobs v. New York*[50] and *Tannenbaum v. New York*[51]—the defendants had also received suspended sentences. The majority at the *Ginsberg* conference decided to overrule *Jacobs* and *Tannenbaum,* along with *St. Pierre.* Stewart alone resisted this approach.

Warren, in particular, was opposed to dismissal for mootness. It was the kind of technical approach that he considered an excuse for avoiding the constitutional merits, and he had vigorously dissented from the prior term's *Jacobs* and *Tannenbaum* decisions. During the 1967 Term, the mootness issue had also been presented in *Sibron v. New York* [52]—a companion case to the already-discussed case of *Terry v. Ohio* [53]—where the defendant had completed service of his six-month sentence long before his case was argued in the Supreme Court. Warren had circulated a *Sibron* opinion which contained a strong direct attack on the *Jacobs* and *Tannenbaum* decisions. Harlan had replied with a sharp draft dissent to the Chief's handling of the *Sibron* mootness issue.

Despite the fact that he had not expressed disagreement on mootness at the *Ginsberg* conference, Harlan felt that he had to follow his draft *Sibron* dissent. He told Brennan that he would not agree to the overruling of the *St. Pierre, Jacobs,* and *Tannenbaum* cases and that his continued adherence to the *Ginsberg* opinion would hinge on Brennan's ability to distinguish those cases. Research in Brennan's chambers disclosed that a New York statute provided for lunch counters like Ginsberg's to be licensed. New York was directed to advise the Court whether Ginsberg's license could be revoked because of his criminal conviction. New York's answer was affirmative. Brennan used this to dispose of the mootness issue in a footnote, which pointed out that, in *Jacobs* and *Tannenbaum,* comparable collateral consequences were not shown.[54] After he had read Brennan's treatment of the mootness issue, Harlan wrote back that it was "persuasive" and that the distinction of the prior cases was "compelling." Warren adopted Brennan's mootness approach in his *Sibron* opinion and Harlan withdrew his draft *Sibron* dissent.[55]

On the merits, Brennan decided to write as narrow a *Ginsberg* opinion as possible. He feared that, if he went beyond the issue of the facial validity of the New York law, the result would be the plethora of opinions that had marked most obscenity cases. The opening sentence of Brennan's draft narrowed the question presented to "the constitutionality on its face"[56] of the state statute.

Brennan's first *Ginsberg* draft was substantially different from his final opinion. Its essence was summarized in a March 4, 1968, letter from White to Brennan. "As I understand this skillful and subtle opinion," White wrote, "state infringement of First Amendment rights is justified by the overriding state interest in the welfare of children, expressed here by a not unreasonable assertion that the described material is harmful to the young." Brennan's draft emphasized that the invasion of First Amendment rights was not a significant one, given the state's interest in preventing access by children to obscene materials.

White's letter stated, "This is perhaps a less stringent burden on the State than we have insisted on when First Amendment rights are at stake. Am I right that this is a new rule, perhaps limited to the reading material of minors?" White preferred a different approach. "If you had taken the pure obscenity route, I suppose you would have pursued further the idea that obscenity is outside the area of First Amendment protection. Although these magazines were protected with respect to adults, they are not when sold to children because they appeal to prurient interest (as they do [not] with adults), because they are beyond community limits of candor for children (which they are not in the case of adults) and because they have no social value—indeed, they are harmful to children (which cannot be so rationally said with respect to adults)."

The White letter recognized that Brennan might have chosen a combined approach. "Perhaps you ride both horses in this case, that is, this junk is outside the First Amendment, but if it is not, it still may be kept from children because there is a sufficient reason to do so which overrides both the minor's right to read and the right of the publisher to disseminate. This is admirable eclecticism if it gets four other guys."

White concluded that he would "have preferred the 'outside' course if a choice must be made." Notwithstanding, he would probably join Brennan. "Since the more one stirs, the more this pot boils to no good end, I am not moved to write separately, at least not for now."

Brennan revised his *Ginsberg* draft to meet White's preference. He reworked the obscenity test of the 1954 *Roth* case[57] and the 1966 *Fanny Hill* case[58] to provide for a doctrine of "variable obscenity," which would reach material aimed at children, though not obscene to adults. Such material could be ruled "outside" the First Amendment, as White had suggested.

Warren, White, and Marshall quickly joined Brennan's revised *Ginsberg* draft, which was delivered as the opinion of the Court on April 22, 1968. Harlan decided to write a separate concurrence. Douglas wrote his typical dissent in an obscenity case. Black joined, writing Douglas on March 19, "I had thought about writing myself but I have written so much on the subject of obscenity that I think I shall simply rest on my agreement with you." Fortas also dissented. Stewart was the last to make up his mind. Until almost the end, he stuck to his guns on the mootness issue. Then he decided to issue a short concurrence.

United States v. Robel[59] was the 1967 Term's case involving subversive activities. In the 1961 case of *Communist Party v. Subversive Activities Control Board*,[60] discussed in chapter 9, the Court had upheld an order requiring the Communist Party to register under the Subversive Activities Control Act. That statute also made it unlawful for a member of an organization ordered to register "to engage in any employment in any defense facility." Robel was a Communist employed at a shipyard after the Secretary of Defense had designated it a "defense facility." He was indicted for violating the statutory prohibition. The district court upheld the statute by interpreting it as applying only to "active" members who had the specific intent of furthering the party's unlawful goals. Because the indictment failed to allege that Robel's membership was of that quality, the indictment was dismissed. The case went up on direct appeal to the Supreme Court.

At the conference on November 18, 1966, six Justices voted to affirm dismissal of the indictment, with Harlan and White voting to reverse and Clark not voting. But the majority were unable to settle on a ground for decision. They agreed that the district court construction could not be supported because the Court had previously held that a similar provision in the statute restricting the right to travel abroad could not be read to require "active" membership and specific intent. Brennan urged that the governmental interests supporting the exclusion of Communist-action organization members from defense facilities were more substantial than those supporting a limitation of the right to travel. Brennan said that Congress should be permitted to exclude all action group members from truly sensitive facilities. However, since the fundamental rights to employment and of political association were involved, the statute went too far in allowing the Secretary of Defense to designate virtually any plant as a defense facility. Warren, Black, and Douglas agreed with Brennan's analysis. But Stewart said that he did not agree that the delegation was defective.

Brennan suggested to the conference that he draft an opinion striking down the statutory provision on the ground that Congress improperly delegated power to restrict fundamental First and Fifth Amendment rights to the Secretary. On January 4, 1967, Brennan circulated a draft that invalidated the statute on the ground of improper delegation, but took pains to distinguish the doctrine against too-broad delegation as it had been used during the early days of the New Deal to strike down laws providing for economic regulation.

Brennan summarized the approach taken in his *Robel* draft in a May 28, 1967 letter to Warren. "You may remember," Brennan wrote, "that the approach taken in my circulation . . . was that the delegation of authority to the Secretary of Defense to designate 'defense facilities' violated constitutional standards of definiteness, particularly in light of its impact on the constitutionally protected right to hold specific private employment."

Warren agreed to join Brennan's opinion on January 5, and Black and Douglas also indicated that they were willing to go along. But Fortas objected to the idea of using the delegation doctrine and circulated his own opinion. It affirmed, partly on the ground stated by the district court and partly on the ground that Congress could not enact such a statute. Stewart wrote Brennan on January 5 that his opinion was "fine" and that he "would probably join." On January 20, however, Clark sent around a blistering dissent that changed Stewart's mind. He joined the Clark draft in mid-March, as did Harlan and White.

The four dissenters now decided to join that part of Fortas' opinion which rejected Brennan's delegation ground as a basis for decision. That meant that the Brennan rationale was rejected by a majority of the Court. In these circumstances, the Justices decided to put over *Robel* for reargument in the coming 1967 Term. At Brennan's suggestion, the June 5, 1967, order directing the reargument instructed counsel to brief and argue the delegation issue.

After the reargument on October 9, 1967, it was again plain that Brennan would not be able to secure a majority for his delegation approach. Warren was now concerned about securing a majority at all in a case striking down another statutory provision by which Congress had sought to deal with subversion. The Chief urged that the provision should be held invalid on the ground of overbreadth. He was able to secure four other votes for his position, including that of Stewart, who had joined Clark's draft dissent in the previous term. Brennan remained true to the approach taken in his quondam majority draft (which became his concurrence in the case). Harlan and White voted to reverse. Clark, who had written the tentative dissent before the case was set for reargument, was now off the Court and his replacement Marshall, who had been Solicitor General when the case was argued, did not participate. Stewart and Fortas agreed to join Warren's opinion, though Stewart agreed only when the citation of two overbreadth cases in which he dissented had been deleted from a footnote in the Chief's draft. Black had written on November 29, 1967, objecting to "statements . . . that say that the right to travel is protected by the Due Process Clause of the Fifth Amendment and by the First Amendment." Black threatened "to write a short, separate concurrence," but joined Warren's opinion when the offending statements were deleted.

Bruton v. United States[61] is a 1967 Term case that illustrates the give-and-take between the Justices as individuals. Bruton and Evans were tried jointly and convicted of armed postal robbery. A postal inspector had testified that Evans confessed to him that he and Bruton committed the robbery. The trial judge had instructed the jury that, although Evans' confession was competent evidence against Evans, it was inadmissible hearsay against Bruton and had to be disregarded in determining Bruton's guilt or innocence. The court of appeals affirmed, relying on the 1957 case of *Delli Paoli v. United States*,[62] where the Supreme Court had upheld the conviction of a defendant at a joint trial where the jury had been instructed that a codefendant's confession inculpating the defendant had to be disregarded in reaching the verdict concerning the defendant. With Marshall not participating, all but Harlan and Stewart voted to grant certiorari.

At the March 15, 1968, conference, Warren proposed that the Court should reverse Bruton's conviction but on nonconstitutional grounds. Instead, the decision would be limited to federal cases as an exercise of the Court's evidentiary "rulemaking" power. With Harlan and

White voting the other way (and Marshall not participating), the conference agreed to hold, as a rule of evidence, that hearsay confessions in joint trials were inadmissible unless references to codefendants were deleted.

Warren assigned the opinion to Brennan, who had dissented in *Delli Paoli*. Brennan circulated a three-part draft in mid-April. Part I (which eventually became the final *Bruton* opinion) found that admission of Evans' confession violated Bruton's right of cross-examination secured by the Confrontation Clause of the Sixth Amendment, since Evans' confession could not be tested by cross-examination. *Delli Paoli* was expressly overruled. Part II of Brennan's draft formulated an "effective deletion" rule: "Hereafter, in cases involving multiple defendants no extrajudicial confession is admissible unless all portions of that confession which implicate the declarant's co-defendants are effectively deleted." Part III stated that this deletion rule would "have prospective effect only." It also left open to the states application of the "harmless error" rule laid down in the 1967 case of *Chapman v. California*,[63] under which a conviction need not be reversed even for constitutional error if the error is "so unimportant and insignificant that [it] may . . . be deemed harmless, not requiring the automatic reversal of the conviction." According to Brennan's draft, "a harmless-error rule conforming to the [*Chapman*] standard . . . can satisfy constitutional requirements." In this federal case, however, the draft stated that a harmless-error rule would be unwise and found that the introduction of Evans' confession did not constitute harmless error.

In an April 17 *Memorandum for the Conference,* Black wrote that he agreed with the Brennan draft's confrontation section, but he opposed the notion that the Court had any "supervisory" authority to formulate the effective deletion rule. Though this was inconsistent with the position he had taken at the conference, Black now indicated that he would write a dissent on the matter. Black also objected to Part III, saying, it "appears to me to amount almost to overruling *Chapman v. California* and eliminating the power of courts to hold that error is harmless. This, I think, would be a drastic departure from the law as we have known it and takes a step which I think it wholly inadvisable for us to take."

Douglas informed Brennan that he preferred not to go beyond

confrontation, but would join Part II of the draft, if necessary. Douglas, too, objected to Part III, but only insofar as it accepted *Chapman* as applicable. Fortas also expressed dissatisfaction with Part III, saying that he did not like applying *Chapman* to this type of error. Fortas indicated that he agreed with the confrontation aspect of the opinion.

White, who had voted for affirmance at the conference, now suggested to Brennan that statements in the draft on the harmful effects of hearsay evidence should be modified to recognize that some admission of hearsay could be harmless. White said that he definitely agreed with Parts II and III of Brennan's draft, but that he was doubtful on the confrontation issue. Brennan pointed out that, in his 1964 opinion in *Jackson v. Denno*,[64] White had cited the Frankfurter dissent in the *Delli Paoli* case to show that the jury could not segregate improper evidence from that which it might consider. At this, White chuckled and said, "That was just in some footnote a law clerk had been able to sneak by me. You can't expect me to be bound by that."

White later called Brennan to tell him that he would definitely dissent on confrontation. He asked if Brennan would mind if he adopted the substance of Part II of Brennan's draft, if Brennan was not going to use it. Brennan said he had no objection, and White did use substantially Brennan's draft language to suggest the "effective deletion" rule, as well as refer to the harmless error point, at the end of his dissent.

By this time, Brennan had decided that the important thing was to obtain a firm majority for Part I of his draft. Brennan knew that he could count on Black, Douglas, and Fortas to support the confrontation holding. He felt that Warren would also concur, since he had indicated at conference that he was now convinced that he had been wrong in voting with the *Delli Paoli* majority. Brennan sent around a new draft that contained Part I only. Parts II and III had been dropped—to resurface in part, as noted, in White's dissent.

Brennan's majority proved less than firm, when Black sent the Justice a memorandum asking that he be noted as concurring in the result only, for the reasons stated in Frankfurter's dissent in *Delli Paoli*. When Black was asked why he had taken this position, which appeared inconsistent with views previously expressed by him, the

Alabaman testily replied, "I don't like opinions with so many footnotes citing authorities I didn't have time to read, as well as cases which I dissented in."

Stewart, who had not been heard from, now became the crucial vote, if Brennan's confrontation holding was to secure a majority of the eight-man Court. Stewart wrote a memorandum to Brennan saying that he "was disposed to concur" but would like to withhold a definite commitment until he had seen any other opinions that might be written. White finally circulated a draft dissent that ignored the confrontation issue and argued that reliable prejudicial evidence could be distinguished from unreliable prejudicial evidence, with only the former requiring exclusion. After he read the dissent, Stewart agreed to join Brennan's opinion, which now had a majority behind it. Stewart also added a two-paragraph concurrence to meet the White dissent.

The *Bruton* decision was cleared for announcement the following Monday at the conference on Friday, May 17, 1968. Black then told Brennan that he might decide to join the opinion after all. Brennan decided to encourage this by deleting some of the citations Black might have found objectionable, such as a law review note which criticized Black's opinion on the right of confrontation in the 1965 case of *Pointer v. Texas*.[65] Brennan rushed a new print of the opinion to Black's chambers, only to find that he had gone. On Saturday morning Black's law clerk called him at home and described the changes. But Black said that he did not now see any confrontation problem. After some discussion on the matter with his clerk, Black decided to stay with his decision to concur in the result only.

On May 20, with White, joined by Harlan, dissenting, Brennan delivered the opinion reversing Bruton's conviction on the ground that his right of confrontation (and that to cross-examine derived from it) had been violated. The discussion of whether the rule laid down was to be prospective only, which had been contained in Part III of Brennan's original draft, had been omitted.

But the issue had to be quickly faced, since there were over a dozen cases on the Supreme Court docket that called for disposition in light of *Bruton*. In his original Part III, Brennan had adopted a prospective rule. Faced with the actual cases to be decided, he now reconsidered his position and decided that the *Bruton* ruling had to be wholly retroactive because the risk of prejudice was too great. After going through all the cases presenting the *Bruton* issue, Brennan selected a federal habeas corpus case, *Robert v. Russell*,[66] as the vehicle for announcing the retroactivity ruling. He circulated a *Memorandum to the Conference* recommending that that case be chosen and that a per curiam should be issued summarily vacating the denial of the writ there under *Bruton*.[67] The others agreed and Brennan quickly prepared a per curiam holding that *Bruton* applied retroactively. It was issued on June 10, 1968.

At fifteen, Warren had played the clarinet in the Bakersfield town band. He became a charter member of Local 263 of the American Federation of Musicians and continued to retain his connection with the union. At the union's 1952 convention in Santa Barbara, California, Governor Warren was introduced as a "great liberal Republican of our time, a member of the musicians' union, and a clarinet player." Warren smilingly replied that the introduction should be amended to read, "a *former* clarinet player."[68] The union still kept Warren on its rolls as an honorary member after he moved to Washington. The connection led the Chief Justice to disqualify himself during the 1967 Term in *American Federation of Musicians v. Carroll*,[69] where the union had been sued for violating the Sherman Anti-Trust Act.

In the other cases worthy of note decided in the 1967 Term, however, Warren took an active part in leading the Brethren to decision. Thus, his conference presentation pointed the way in *Levy v. Louisiana*[70] to the first invalidation of a legal discrimination against illegitimate children. Levy sued on behalf of five illegitimate children to recover damages for the wrongful death of their mother. The action was brought against the doctor who had treated the mother under a state statute giving the "child or children" of the deceased the right to recover damages. The state court had dismissed, holding that "child" in the statute meant "legitimate child."

Warren indicated at the March 29, 1968, conference that the case was simple as far as he was concerned. "I can't see any interest," he declared, "that the state can have to exclude illegitimate children for the loss of their mother by a tortious act." The Chief said that he would "put this on equal protection." Black led the argument the other way. As he saw it, "This has been an acceptable classification for generations. It's bad state policy, but I can't say that it's not a rational one."

Warren's view won by six-to-three when the vote was taken. On May 20, 1968, Douglas delivered the opinion of the Court reversing on the approach Warren had stated. The basis of decision was stated in a passage in the draft Douglas circulated April 12, which was omitted from his final *Levy* opinion: "Here we are not concerned with alleged 'wrongdoers' but with people born out of wedlock who were not responsible for their conception or for their birth." Harlan, joined by Black and Stewart, issued a *Levy* dissent asserting that the decision was a "constitutional curiosity."

Another case where Warren's view prevailed was *Board of Education v. Allen.*[71] It arose out of a New York law requiring public school authorities to lend textbooks to all students including those attending private and parochial schools. A suit challenged the law as a violation of the prohibition against "an establishment of religion." The New York Court of Appeals upheld the law, saying that its purpose was to benefit all school children and that only books approved by the public school authorities could be loaned.

The Brethren considered the case at their April 26, 1968, conference. The Chief began the discussion by stating that he "would accept the construction of the Court of Appeals limiting the Act and would hold this is a welfare case for students and not a violation of establishment." Referring to the 1947 case of *Everson v. Board of Education,*[72] which had upheld free bus transportation for all school children, Warren said that this case was "like *Everson,* school lunches, health services type of grant."

The others agreed with the Chief except for Black, Douglas, and Fortas. Black declared, "I think when government begins to supply books to religious schools, it's a violation." Douglas sought to answer the *Everson*-type argument, saying, "There's nothing ideological about a school lunch or a bus. But it smacks of establishment when they get into textbooks."

"This is a tormenting case for me," Fortas avowed. "I come out for review on what may seem a picayune ground. The offensive part to me is that, in effect the parochial schools can designate the books. That to me is clearly an establishment of religion. The approval by the school board doesn't save it. The system is [one] of parochial schools picking out books which the state pays for."

Warren had wanted to write the *Allen* opinion himself and had had one of his law clerks do a great deal of work on the case. The case was, however, ultimately assigned to White, who announced the decision on June 10, 1968. White's opinion followed the approach outlined in the Chief's conference statement. Black, Douglas, and Fortas delivered separate dissents.

Warren also set the theme for decision in *King v. Smith*.[73] A class action had been brought challenging Alabama's so-called "substitute father" regulation, which denied welfare payments to the children of a mother who was living with a man other than the children's father. The lower court had found the regulation inconsistent with the Social Security Act and violative of the Equal Protection Clause.

At the April 26, 1968, conference, Douglas urged the Brethren to "put it on equal protection." Warren, however, stressed the nonconstitutional ground. He agreed that the "regulation has to go." But he said, "We don't have to do this on equal protection or due process, but on the statute and under the Supremacy Clause." The conference agreed and the Chief delivered an opinion on the last day of the term, June 17, 1968, striking down the regulation as inconsistent with the Social Security Act, with Douglas alone dissenting. Black, who had been uncertain about his vote, wrote a June 4 "Dear Chief" letter: "I have had some doubts about this case but your opinion has dissipated them."

Three 1967 Term criminal cases in which the Court followed Warren's lead, should also be mentioned. In *Witherspoon v. Illinois*,[74] Stewart's June 3, 1968, opinion of the Court ruled invalid a state statute excluding from murder juries those with conscientious scruples against or who opposed the death penalty. At the April 26 conference, Warren had argued that the statute should fall, where there was no "determination whether, notwithstanding their scruples, they can follow the instruction on law as given by the judge." Stewart's opinion essentially followed this approach.

The second criminal case was *Mathis v. United States*.[75] While Mathis was a prisoner in the Florida State Penitentiary, he was questioned by an Internal Revenue Service agent. The statements Mathis made in the interview were admitted in his trial for income tax fraud despite his claim that they were given without the warnings required by *Miranda v. Arizona*.[76] He was convicted, and the conviction was affirmed by the court of appeals. The vote at the certiorari conference was five-to-three to grant, with Harlan, Stewart, and White to deny, and Marshall not participating because he had been Solicitor General.

Warren had no doubt at the April 5, 1968, conference that the conviction should be reversed. "You can't distinguish," the Chief asserted, "between a police station and a prison cell. So there's a 'custodial' situation. But is this interrogation leading to prosecution? It's close, but I think so and would reverse." The conference voted with Warren. The opinion following his approach was delivered by Black on May 6, with White, joined by Harlan and Stewart, dissenting.

The last of the significant criminal cases was *Katz v. United States.*[77] The decision there must have given Warren special satisfaction because it effectively overruled the rationale of the 1928 case of *Olmstead v. United States,*[78] as the Chief had unsuccessfully urged in the 1961 case of *Silverman v. United States.*[79] Katz was convicted of interstate transmission by telephone of wagering information. F.B.I. agents had attached an electronic listening device to the outside of a public phone booth from which he had placed his calls. The court of appeals affirmed, rejecting the contention that the recording had violated the Fourth Amendment, because there was no physical entrance into the area occupied by Katz. The test applied was that of physical trespass upon which the *Olmstead* decision had been based. The Brethren were closely divided on whether to grant certiorari. Warren, Douglas, Brennan, and Fortas voted to grant on March 13, 1967; Black, Clark, Harlan, Stewart, and White voted to deny.

The first vote on the merits on October 20, 1967, reflected the cert division. With Clark no longer on the Court and his successor, Marshall, not participating, the Justices voted four-to-four. Harlan, Stewart, and White, however, eventually switched their votes. Stewart was assigned the opinion, which repudiated the physical trespass test and held that a person using a phone booth had a right to privacy protected by the Fourth Amendment. In joining Stewart's opinion on November 20, Warren wrote, "I believe that it will be a milestone decision." That was true because, as Harlan wrote in a concurrence, "today's decision must be recognized as overruling Olmstead."[80]

On November 30, 1967, Fortas wrote Stewart that he was joining the opinion. "However," he added, "I'd be happy if you would see fit to insert something reserving national security cases in which maybe the Constitution would permit electronic espionage on authorization by the President or the Attorney General. This is Byron

White's idea, and I think it would be well to adopt the suggestion."

Stewart responded by adding a footnote indicating that the question of national security cases was not presented by *Katz*.[81] This was enough for Fortas. But White issued a separate opinion asserting that warrantless electronic surveillance would be valid in national security cases. Douglas, joined by Brennan, answered this with a concurrence charging that White's opinion was "a wholly unwarranted green light" for the Executive in cases labeled "national security."[82] All the concurrences joined Stewart's *Katz* opinion. When it was delivered on December 18, 1967, only Black dissented.

Douglas once wrote that, while Chief Justice Warren would be remembered most for the major cases such as the *Brown* school segregation case,[83] "in many ways the lesser cases mirrored . . . the man."[84] During the 1967 Term, Warren the man was perhaps best shown in *Brooks v. Florida*.[85] Tyrone Brown, the law clerk who worked on the case, says that the case "will never be significant . . . but I think, for me at least, it revealed volumes about the character of the man."

The *Brooks* case arose out of a food riot by blacks in a Florida prison. Brooks and the others involved were stripped naked and placed in bare punishment cells which the Supreme Court described as "the windowless sweatbox . . . a barren cage with a hole in one corner into which he and his cell mates could defecate."[86] For two weeks, they were kept in these cells on a daily diet of twelve ounces of thin soup and eight ounces of water. Within minutes after Brooks was brought from the cell, he signed a confession. The confession was used to convict him of participating in the riot. The highest state court affirmed. Brooks filed an in forma pauperis petition for certiorari.

At the certiorari conference, the Justices voted eight-to-one, with Warren dissenting, not to take the case, feeling that it involved a matter of internal prison discipline in which the Court should not become involved. Warren was indignant at the decision to deny cert. He told Brown to work up a draft dissent. Brown prepared a number of drafts, but the Chief kept saying of each, "That's not strong enough. Doggone it! If those guys don't want to take this case, I want to be sure that every gruesome detail is recorded in those books up there [pointing to the Supreme Court Reports] for posterity."

Finally, Warren circulated an extremely sharp draft dissent on November 9, 1967, and, as Brown describes it, "just kind of sat in his office and waited."

In the next month, the Justices came in one by one and joined the dissent.[87] By the next conference on the case, the Chief had the votes of all, not only for the granting of cert, but for summary reversal. Warren had Brown draft a short per curiam to that effect, which was issued December 18, 1967.

When Warren presided over the Court on June 17, 1968—the final day of the 1967 Term—he expected it to be his last session as Chief Justice. But it did not turn out that way. Though he had, as seen at the beginning of this chapter, sent a June 13 retirement letter to President Johnson, it did not contain a retirement date. Instead, it was to become effective at the President's pleasure, which was interpreted by Johnson to mean as soon as Warren's successor took office. But now, as the 1967 Term ended, Johnson's nomination of a new Chief Justice was running into difficulties.

At a press conference a few days after Johnson announced Warren's retirement, a reporter asked, "Mr. Chief Justice, did you have any discussion with the President about a successor?" "No, I did not have," was Warren's reply.[88] Arthur J. Goldberg states that Warren telephoned him soon after he advised the President of his impending resignation and said that he recommended that Johnson appoint Goldberg as his successor. Those in the Court close to the Chief say that he laughed at the different names bruited about as possible presidential choices. The Chief said he knew that Johnson had always intended to name Fortas to head the Court. Warren did tell Brennan that he would personally want him as his successor, but he realized that that was not possible.

The President had made known his intention to nominate Fortas when he announced Warren's retirement letter. The White House expected the nomination to sail smoothly through the Senate—though a presidential aide later said that Johnson himself anticipated trouble.[89] In fact, the Fortas appointment ran into acrimonious opposition from the beginning. A core of Republican Senators, led by Senator Robert Griffin of Michigan, were ultimately able to defeat the nomination by a filibuster. But they had unexpected help from Fortas himself when he agreed to testify before the Senate Judiciary Committee—the first Chief Justice nominee ever to do so. His four days of testimony, starting on July 13, turned into an inquisition, which focused as much on the decisions of the Warren Court as on the nominee.

The dramatic high point of the grilling came when Senator Strom Thurmond of South Carolina shouted at Fortas, "Mallory—I want that name to ring in your ears! Mallory! Mallory, a man who raped a woman, admitted his guilt and the Supreme Court turned him loose on a technicality." For the first time in the hearings, according to a reporter, Fortas was visibly shaken[90]—and that even though the *Mallory* case[91] had been decided in 1957, eight years before Fortas was appointed to the Court.

Warren had hoped that Fortas would decline to testify, as he himself had done during his own 1954 confirmation hearings.[92] But the nominee had not consulted the Chief Justice in the matter.

On August 23, a month after the Senate committee finished its Fortas hearings, Warren took time off from vacationing in the West to address a luncheon of the Montana Supreme Court Justices. In it, he chided the Senate for not acting on the appointment. "I can assure you," he said, "that the delay is not because they want to retain *me*. If it's a choice of taking Abe Fortas or keeping me, they'll take Abe. But it looks like I'll be back to open the Supreme Court in October."[93]

Before the new Court term, the Fortas nomination had been withdrawn. In early September, it was revealed that the Justice had received a $15,000 fee for conducting a summer seminar at American University in Washington. The money had been raised by private donors who were described by Senator Thurmond as representing "a complex of business and financial holdings that scarcely could be extricated from anything touching upon the Court."[94] The rest was all but inevitable. Confirmation opponents staged a six-day Senate filibuster and, when a cloture motion failed decisively, Fortas wrote the President asking that his nomination be withdrawn to avoid "a continuation of the attacks upon the Court which have characterized the filibuster—attacks which have been sometimes extreme and entirely unrelated to responsible criticism."[95] On October 4, Johnson, "with deep regret," withdrew the nomination.[96]

By then, the 1968 Court Term was about to begin. The President called on the Chief to stay at his post, and Warren agreed. On October 10, Johnson released a statement that, "Under the circumstances, the foundations of government would be better served by the present Chief Justice remaining until emotionalism subsides, reason and fairness prevail." Warren, said the President, "has indicated his willingness to serve until his successor qualifies."[97]

The Johnson statement also revealed that the President would not "send another name to the Senate for this high office."[98] This meant that Warren's successor would be appointed by the new President who would take office at the beginning of 1969. More and more, it looked as though that would be Richard M. Nixon.

17.

1968 TERM: THE FINAL TERM

One of the most dramatic scenes of our history, according to Woodrow Wilson, was enacted when Andrew Jackson was sworn into the Presidency by John Marshall. "The two men," Wilson writes, "were at the antipodes from one another both in principle and in character; had no common insight into the institutions of the country which they served; represented one the statesmanship of will and the other the statesmanship of control."[1]

A modern counterpart took place on January 20, 1969, when Chief Justice Warren swore in Richard Nixon. The antagonists on either side of the podium were even more at the antipodes from one another than the President and Chief Justice of 1833. No one knows what Warren thought as he administered the oath to the one person toward whom he felt almost physical repulsion. But he told Herbert G. Klein just after the ceremony that he could not help feeling that, but for Nixon, he himself might have taken the Presidential oath in 1953.[2]

Warren had tried to retire during Lyndon Johnson's presidency, so that that President would be able, in the words of the June 13, 1968, White House memo on Warren's conversation with Johnson, "to appoint his successor, someone who felt as Justice Warren did."[3] That hope had been frustrated by the Senate failure to confirm Abe Fortas as Chief Justice. Now it was up to the new President to choose Warren's successor. The one thing that was clear was that, as an October 3, 1968, *Memorandum for the President* stated, "Nixon's views—

albeit exaggerated by campaign oratory and compromise—make it highly unlikely that he would pick a successor in the Warren tradition. His statements that recent court decisions 'aid the criminal,' his ambivalence on the exercise of desegregation powers, his commitment to protect big business against Federal bureaucracy, and his concern about judicial activism all seem to point to a conservative appointment."[4]

Warren had promised President Johnson that he would stay on. When the 1968 Term opened on October 7, Warren was still in the Court's center chair, with Fortas in his regular seat at the right end of the bench. But Warren's status at the beginning of the new term was unclear. The Republicans contended that Warren's retirement letter remained in effect and that his successor could now be chosen by the new President. The Democrats argued that his retirement letter was no longer effective and that he could stay on until he renewed his offer to retire. Warren himself had no legal doubts. He agreed with the view expressed in the October 3, 1968 memo to President Johnson, "that the resignation would still be effective upon qualification of a successor—that the exchange of correspondence with him runs with the office of the Presidency rather than to you individually."[5]

Warren told intimates that he now wanted to retire more than ever. Yet he was apprehensive that Nixon would immediately accept his resignation to create a vacancy that the new President could fill. That happening in mid-term would, he feared, disrupt the working of the Court. The situation was resolved by an informal agreement between the new President and the Chief Justice.

"Shortly after I was elected," writes Nixon, "I asked Bill Rogers to approach Chief Justice Warren and work out an understanding with regard to the timing of his resignation. Warren agreed to stay on until the end of the Court's session in June."[6] It was actually Warren's son-in-law, John Daly, the television newsman, who communicated Warren's concern to William P. Rogers during a game of golf, just after Nixon had chosen Rogers as Secretary of State. Rogers telephoned the President-elect, who told Rogers that "of course" the Chief Justice should continue to preside over the Court until the end of the 1968 Term, when his retirement would become effective.[7]

Rogers obtained Nixon's permission to call on Warren. Over lunch in the Chief's chambers, Rogers relayed Nixon's sentiments. Rogers reported that Warren was "most appreciative," both personally and on behalf of the Court. Rogers then arranged for Nixon to call Warren on December 4, 1968, when the President-elect personally asked the Chief Justice both to remain on the bench and to administer the oath of office on Inauguration Day. The next day, it was reported in the press that Warren had consented to Nixon's request to remain until the term's end, in order to prevent disruption of the Court's work.[8]

The case that received the most public attention during Warren's last term was *Powell v. McCormack*,[9] to be discussed later in this chapter. But the case that had the greatest impact on the law was *Shapiro v. Thompson*.[10] The Court there greatly expanded judicial review under the Equal Protection Clause—but only over the strong dissents of Warren and Black.

Thompson had applied to the Connecticut Welfare Department for assistance under the Program for Aid to Families with Dependent Children. Her application was denied because she had not lived in the state for a year as required by a Connecticut law. The Social Security Act required the Secretary of Health, Education, and Welfare to approve state A.F.D.C. plans. He was not to approve any plan that contained a residence requirement of more than one year. The lower court held the state residence requirement unconstitutional. Black, Stewart, White, and Fortas had voted to hear the state's appeal.

The case originally came before the Court during the 1967 Term. At the May 3, 1968, conference, the Chief Justice focused upon the Social Security Act in urging reversal. "Congress," he said, "allowed the one-year requirement." It permitted state statutes that "limited this particular kind of relief to residents of a year or more." To Warren, the Social Security Act was plainly within congressional power. "I can't see," he declared, "how I can say that the federal statute is unconstitutional."

The conference agreed with Warren, voting six-to-three to reverse and uphold the residence requirement. The Chief, Black, Harlan, Brennan, Stewart, and White made up the majority. Warren took the opinion himself and circulated a June 3 draft opinion of the Court. It relied entirely on the Social Security Act provision which, according to the draft, authorized the states to impose the one-year requirement. "In our view . . . ," the draft stated, "the relevant provisions of the Social Security Act place the appellees' constitutional challenges to durational residence requirements in a wholly different light [than that seen by the lower court] and require a reversal of the judgments below."

The draft typically accented the Chief's concern for the "plight of the poor." It conceded, "To the extent that the appellees have attempted to show that durational residence requirements impose hardships upon the poor of the Nation, they appeal to the right instincts of all men." Despite this, Warren asserted, "instinct cannot be our guide when we are asked to declare unconstitutional part of a statutory scheme enacted by Congress against the backdrop of the depression of the 1930s and preserved unchanged despite repeated and vigorous efforts to alter it."

Warren stressed the congressional purpose, saying that "Congress quite clearly believed that total elimination of durational residence requirements would be self-defeating because the prospect of a sudden influx of new residents might deter the States from significantly increasing categorical assistance benefits. We cannot ignore these legislative realities in assessing the validity of the congressional decision to authorize the durational residence requirements challenged in these cases."

The Warren draft rejected the claim that the residence requirement invalidly restricted the constitutional right to travel. Congress had the power under the Commerce Clause to authorize the states to impose the requirement. "Congress can specifically authorize the States to regulate what the Commerce Clause, by the force of its negative implications, would otherwise prohibit the States from regulating." Congress "has not acted to prohibit interstate movement by welfare recipients. Such individuals are still free to move from State to State and to establish residence wherever they please. . . . At most, Congress has authorized the States to act in a manner which imposes a burden of uncertain degree on the welfare recipient who chooses to travel interstate to establish a new residence."

The Chief's draft also rejected the contention that equal protection had been denied. It is important to note, in view of the different approach ultimately followed by the Court in the case, that Warren applied the "rational basis test" to the equal protection claim. He asserted that stricter review was required only "when the statutory classification is drawn along lines which are constitutionally imper-missible or 'suspect,' . . . or when the classification is invidious or wholly arbitrary." As Warren saw it, "there is nothing inherently sus-pect, arbitrary or invidious about the durational residence require-ments challenged in these cases to warrant the application of the stricter equal protection test advocated by appellees."

Thus, for Warren, "The question, stated quite simply, is whether the congressional authorization for durational residence requirements is rationally related to a legitimate legislative purpose. To state the question is to answer it." The legislative history showed that "Con-gress viewed the authorization for durational residence requirements as essential to securing state participation in that comprehensive scheme. We cannot say that the congressional judgment was unrea-sonable, and we hold, therefore, that the congressional authorization of durational residence requirements has the necessary rational basis to overcome an equal protection attack."

Douglas circulated a short dissent on June 5, 1968, and Harlan a brief concurrence on June 10. It had been decided by the dissenters that Fortas would prepare the principal dissent. He sent around his thirty-page draft on June 13. It concluded that "the durational resi-dence requirement is unconstitutional as an impermissible and unjus-tified burden on the right to travel. This is so whether the burden is imposed by state or by federal authority."

The Fortas draft also argued that the residence requirement vio-lated equal protection because "Congress and the States have dis-criminated 'between "rich" and "poor" as such.'" Referring to the lower court, Fortas noted that it "was unable to find a reasonable basis or purpose for the distinction between the two groups except the constitutionally impermissible purpose of deterring poor people from moving to the jurisdiction. This, they held, offends the Consti-tution. I agree."

At the May 3 conference, Brennan had indicated reservations about his vote supporting Warren. Fortas had sent him a typewritten copy of his dissent before it was circulated. Brennan wrote back on June 11, with copies to the conference, "I've studied your draft on the dissent and I've concluded that I can join your conclusion and about everything you say that relates to burden on the right to travel. I have a lot more difficulty, however, with affirming on the equal pro-tection ground. If the cases can be disposed of on the burden argument, is there any necessity to add the additional support of a denial of equal protection?"

Brennan's letter is of interest, since he was the ultimate author of the *Shapiro v. Thompson* opinion striking down the residence requirement on equal protection grounds. Notwithstanding the reservation he had expressed, Brennan telephoned Fortas to tell him that he was joining his opinion. At the next conference, on June 13, Stewart refused to cast a vote. With Brennan's switch, that made a four-to-four division. It was now almost the end of the term (at the June 7 conference, it had been decided that June 17 would be the term's last day), and it was decided to set the case for reargument in the 1968 Term.

At the conference after the reargument on October 25, 1968, Stewart indicated that he also was now in favor of affirmance. The new vote was five (Douglas, Brennan, Stewart, Fortas, and Marshall) to three (Warren, Black, and Harlan) to strike down the residence requirement, with White passing. Brennan was now assigned the opinion. Despite the closeness of the vote he wrote a broad opinion expanding the scope of judicial review in equal protection cases. Brennan's draft, circulated December 2, 1968, adopted the "compelling interest" test that he had unsuccessfully urged on Warren the year before in the *O'Brien* case,[11] discussed toward the beginning of the last chapter. Brennan wrote that, since the classification between new and old residents served to penalize the exercise of the fundamental right to interstate travel, it had to be justified by a compelling governmental interest. This extended the "compelling interest" standard to cases involving "fundamental rights," such as the right to travel. Warren, in his putative majority opinion of the previous June, had specifically refused to apply the "compelling interest" standard, holding instead that the traditional "rational basis" test was all that had to be met.

Brennan's draft opinion striking down the residence requirement under the "compelling interest" test won the speedy agreement of Douglas, Marshall, Fortas, and Stewart. But then Stewart had second thoughts. He spoke to Brennan and expressed hesitation about the "compelling interest" analysis. He said that the case should be decided on the traditional "rational basis" standard of equal protection.

Brennan prepared a memorandum to Stewart explaining why "compelling interest," rather than "rational basis" was the proper standard here. "Frankly," Brennan wrote, "I am uneasy about a flat statement that the waiting period requirement is invalid under a strict rationality test. I don't think the Court has ever struck down legislation under that test. And I am concerned that if we did so in this case we might invite a flood of challenges to ordinary economic or social legislation having no relation to the right to travel or any other underlying constitutional right."

Stewart had told Brennan that "we should reserve the compelling interest approach for cases involving the First Amendment or racial discrimination." Brennan answered this in the memo by asserting, "But the freedom of *interstate* movement is as fundamental as first amendment freedoms. Freedom of speech is at the core of our concept of a free society; freedom of interstate movement is at the core of our concept of a Federal *Union*. They are essentially the same kind of right—they provide the basis for our whole system of economic, social and political interchange. Furthermore, both are rights which are particularly vulnerable to restrictive legislation, since with each we cannot satisfactorily identify the group which may be chilled in the exercise of the right."

The Brennan memo also referred to "your fear that a compelling interest standard will endanger the validity of waiting period requirements for voting eligibility etc." Brennan wrote, "In my own view, there is no doubt that the state's interest in ensuring that its voters have adequate time in the community to acquaint themselves with local issues is compelling. I will certainly change footnote 24 to read: 'We imply no view of the validity of waiting period requirements for voting eligibility etc. Such requirements may very well promote compelling state interests.'" The footnote referred to became, in modified form, footnote 21 of the final Brennan opinion.

Even though Stewart then apparently represented the crucial fifth vote, Brennan decided not to send the memo, hoping instead that Stewart would again change his mind. The hope was realized when, a few days later, Stewart came in to tell Brennan that his insistence on the traditional equal protection standard had been mistaken. He now agreed that the compelling interest analysis was appropriate here because the right of interstate travel was a constitutional right.

Stewart indicated that he was willing to join Brennan's opinion if certain minor modifications were made. The most important was the deletion of the lengthy analysis in Brennan's draft of the sources of the right to travel. Stewart said that he thought it sufficed to cite his own opinion in the 1966 case of *United States v. Guest* [12] on the issue. Brennan readily agreed to the Stewart changes.

At this point, Black, who had been Warren's strongest supporter in the case until then, said that he too would join Brennan's opinion. Black had just remembered his own 1948 opinion in *Takahashi v. Fish and Game Commission*, [13] a case dealing with the right of Japanese aliens to fish in California. The case was not exactly in point, but it had broad language about the right of people to reside where they wished. Brennan inserted the appropriate language from *Takahashi* into his opinion. Black then joined Brennan's opinion.

In early January 1969, Harlan sent around a dissent, substantially similar to his final dissent in the case. After seeing the Harlan draft, White, who had passed at the October 25, 1968, conference and had not been heard from since, joined Brennan's opinion. Stewart suggested that he might write a short concurrence criticizing the Harlan opinion, since Harlan had commented critically on two Stewart opinions. On March 6, Stewart circulated a brief concurrence criticizing Harlan.

In the interim, Black had written Brennan to say that he would like his dissent noted. When his law clerks had informed him of his prior agreement to join Brennan's opinion, he did not remember it. Brennan made no attempt to get Black to change his mind. He simply deleted the reference to Black's *Takahashi* opinion that he had inserted in his draft.

The Chief Justice was now the only one who had not been heard from formally in the case. There is no doubt that he felt strongly on the residence-requirement issue. He looked at the issue from the perspective of a former Governor. As such, he favored waiting periods for nonresidents, feeling that they enabled the states to give more liberal benefits without fear of being swamped by destitute migrants. Warren recalled that, while he was Governor, his state program for the disabled had been dismantled by the legislature after too many disabled flocked to California. Warren was also particularly proud of the state university system that had been set up in California. Indeed, he regarded himself as its principal creator. He felt that a residence requirement was essential to maintain the excellence of that system.

Despite his strong feelings on the matter, Warren worked out a tentative compromise with Brennan to avoid the spectacle of a dissent by the Chief Justice in so important a case. Under it, Brennan would remove from his *Shapiro v. Thompson* opinion a paragraph that stated categorically that Congress could not authorize the states to impose residence requirements. In return, Warren would go along with Brennan's interpretation of the Social Security Act provision as not authorizing the states to impose one-year waiting periods. This would enable the Chief to concur.

Warren circulated an opinion, "concurring in the result" on March 25, 1969. "Left to my own independent judgment," it began, "I would interpret the legislative history differently than does the Court. I believe it indicates that in 402(b) Congress intended to authorize the States to impose durational residence requirements not exceeding one year." However, the Warren draft went on, the Court had read the statute as one that "did not intend to give to the States authority to impose residence requirements. Since any interpretation of the congressional intent does not emerge from the mass of legislative materials with compelling clarity, I am not disposed to pit my appraisal of these materials against that of so many members of the Court."

The Chief's draft concurrence stressed "what the Court does *not* hold. As I understand its opinion and its interpretation of the legislative materials, the power of Congress to impose or authorize the States to impose residence requirements is not an issue presented in the [case]. . . . Because I read the Court's opinion to leave open for resolution in an appropriate case the issue of congressional power to impose nationwide residence requirements, I concur in the result."

On the same day that Warren circulated his draft concurrence, Brennan sent around a new printing of his *Shapiro v. Thompson* opinion, with the paragraph on Congressional power left out. But the other majority Justices were unwilling to accept the compromise. On March 26, Fortas wrote Brennan, "This is now the department of utter confusion! Your opinion does *not* leave open the question of Congressional power. I would prefer reinstating the deleted material."

Stewart, White, and Harlan told Brennan that they thought his opinion clearly settled the issue of Congressional power. Douglas said that he would write a concurrence stating that he read the majority opinion as resolving that issue. He circulated a brief opinion containing the substance of Brennan's deleted paragraph. Several of the majority Justices indicated that they would join the Douglas draft.

This meant that the question of Congressional power would not be left open, as had been provided in the Warren-Brennan compromise. The Chief, therefore, withdrew his concurrence and, on March 28, Brennan reinserted the paragraph denying Congressional power to authorize the states to impose residence requirements.

Warren now circulated a dissent, which was an abbreviated version of the draft opinion of the Court he had prepared the previous June. It refused to accept the "compelling interest" approach upon which Brennan's majority opinion was based. Black joined the Warren opinion.

Warren's dissent held up the *Shapiro v. Thompson* decision another two weeks because it cited *Street v. New York*[14] to contrast the majority's avoidance of the constitutional issue there with what he called its "gratuitous" holding on Congressional power here.[15] This meant that *Shapiro* could not come down until *Street* was decided. Several of the Justices asked Warren to withdraw the reference to *Street*. Normally, the Chief would have readily acceded; but he felt strongly enough about *Shapiro* to refuse both requests made to him privately and at the conference. Ultimately, the *Shapiro v. Thompson* decision came down on April 21, 1968—the same day on which the *Street* decision was announced.

In *Shapiro v. Thompson,* Warren had joined with Black (as well as Harlan) to protest against what they considered an unwarranted extension of the Court's review power under the Equal Protection Clause. The Chief and the Alabaman had, of course, been the principal architects of the constitutional edifice erected by the Warren Court. But judicial revolutions, too, may devour their creators. Warren, like Black, had begun to take exception to the tendency of some of the Brethren to expand individual rights at the expense of essential societal interests.

A case in which those interests should clearly prevail, in the Chief's view, was *Street v. New York.*[16] Street was a black who heard a news report that civil rights leader James Meredith had been shot. He went to the street corner and burned an American flag. As it burned, he shouted, "We don't need no damn flag. . . . If they let that happen to Meredith, we don't need an American flag." He was convicted of violating a state law making it a misdemeanor publicly to desecrate the flag or cast contempt by words or acts upon it. The highest state court rejected Street's claim that his act was a protest protected by the First Amendment.

At the October 25, 1968, conference, Warren stated that he would affirm. "The only question is whether New York can punish public burning of the flag. I think the state can do so to prevent riots and the like. It's conduct and not speech or symbolic speech."

Black, of course, agreed, since the distinction between "conduct" and "speech" had been the basis upon which he had drawn the line in First Amendment cases since the first Sit-In Cases five years earlier. But the others decided to avoid the constitutionality of the flag-des-ecration law by following the approach put forward by Harlan. He urged that the decision of the state court "can't prevent us looking at the record and that puts the speech element of the incident into the case." Harlan stressed Street's words while he was burning the flag: "We can't say the conviction did not rest on verbal expression." The vote was six-to-three (Warren, Black, and White dissenting) to reverse in line with Harlan's view.

Harlan sent around a draft opinion of the Court on November 27. It found that Street's words were an essential element in his convic-tion and that "in light of all the circumstances, that conviction denied him rights of free expression assured against state infringement by the Fourteenth Amendment."

In his draft, Harlan had stated "that disrespect for our flag is to be deplored no less in these vexed times than in calmer periods of our history." This led Brennan to write on December 2, asking Harlan to "consider deletion of the sentence. . . . I must tell you in all candor I have no idea what this means and secondly, if I did, I still wouldn't like it." Despite this letter, Harlan did not remove the of-fending sentence from his opinion.

At the conference, Black had said, "I would be bothered if I thought [that], by the statute, he was punished for burning the flag and the speech." But he did not see the case that way. Instead, Black saw the conviction as resting entirely on the flag burning and, like Warren, he saw nothing in the Constitution to bar making flag burn-ing an offense. On December 4, Black circulated a short dissent. The draft was similar to Black's final dissent, except for a sharp introduc-tory paragraph.

"The Court's opinion in this case," the Black draft began, "is the result of what seems to me to be an extraordinary, gymnastic feat. It has struck down a law of the State of New York as a denial of the right of freedom of speech guaranteed by the Constitution of the United States without ever once mentioning the First Amendment." Black referred to the cases holding "that the Fourteenth Amendment makes the First Amendment enforceable against the States." The draft's opening paragraph concluded by noting, "But in the present case the Court's opinion is marked by a complete absence or intimation that the First Amendment has anything on earth to do with making freedom of speech, press, and religion free in this country. Whatever my position is in this case, I protest against the Court's silent revolution against this long-established constitutional doctrine."

Warren and White also circulated dissents, with the Chief protesting against the Court's avoidance "of the constitutionality of flag-burning prohibitions." Warren, like Black, was concerned that the decision, as his dissent put it, "encourages others to test in the streets the power of our States and National Government."[17]

Before the *Street* decision was announced by Harlan on April 21, 1969, there was another unexpected dissenter. At the conference, Fortas had agreed with Harlan, saying that the "speech element plays a substantial part." He prepared a concurrence which, as explained in a March 19, 1969, *Memorandum to the Conference,* expressly "stated . . . that the First Amendment does not preclude a State from enacting a statute making it a criminal offense publicly to mutilate, deface, or defile the flag."

Fortas' March 19 memo informed the Brethren, "I have again reviewed this case and I have decided that I will vote to affirm, withdrawing my concurring opinion. I have concluded that it is fair to say that the conviction was for the conduct of publicly burning the flag and not for the words used." Noting the affirmance of state power in his draft concurrence, Fortas wrote, "I have finally concluded that it is sensible to accept the realities of the facts: that appellant was arrested for publicly burning the flag and that the speech need not be considered part of the offense, but may be treated as merely part of the surrounding circumstances." The Fortas memo ended, "My apology to Brother HARLAN for inconstancy!"

It would, however, be erroneous to assume that, in his last term, Warren increasingly found himself in dissent. *Street* and *Shapiro* were the only important decisions in which the Chief Justice was not with the majority. Even though Warren dissented in two other cases and joined four other dissents, none of the cases involved was of more than minor consequence.

What is true is that, except for *Powell v. McCormack*,[18] Warren took none of the important opinions for himself. He regarded the *Powell* case as involving a matter of such political sensitivity, with its potential for confrontation between the Court and Congress, that he thought the Court should speak in it through the Chief Justice. But he told his law clerks that, since this was his last term, he wanted to retire gracefully and he felt that others should begin to deal with the Court's load.

Aside from *Powell v. McCormack*, the only controversial 1968 Term case in which Warren spoke for the Court was *Gregory v. Chicago*.[19] But he did so there only after the draft opinion of the Court could not command a majority. Dick Gregory, the black comedian, had led a march to protest the pace of desegregation in Chicago's schools. Though the demonstrators were orderly, a hostile crowd of onlookers was becoming increasingly unruly. The police demanded that the demonstrators disperse. When this command was not obeyed, they were arrested and convicted of violating a disorderly conduct ordinance. After the highest state court affirmed, the Brethren voted six-to-three (Black, Harlan, and Stewart against) to grant certiorari.

At the December 13, 1968, conference, Warren recommended reversal. As he saw it, "Gregory was not disorderly. The refusal to break up did not amount to disorderly conduct." The case was thus one in which there was "no evidence of disorderly conduct" and the conviction should be reversed under *Thompson v. Louisville*[20]—the 1960 Case of Shuffling Sam discussed in Chapter 9.

The others agreed. The opinion was assigned to Black, who soon circulated a draft. It began by asserting, "This is a strange but highly important case," and continued substantially along the lines of Black's final concurrence in the case. The Black draft was much broader than Warren's conference presentation. It struck down the Chicago ordinance for overbreadth and also contained a discussion of the distinction between "speech" and "conduct," which had given the Court difficulty since the first Sit-In Cases. On February 3, 1969, Harlan sent around a concurrence that declared, "it is particularly undesirable for us to intimate views upon matters with which we are not faced in the case at hand." Harlan stressed the principles under which "Constitutional adjudication should be as narrowly circumscribed as possible. . . . Adherence to these simple solid principles carries, in my view, better prospects for 'containing' judges than does any formula for a literalistic approach to constitutional interpretation."

Stewart and Fortas also circulated concurrences objecting to the breadth of Black's opinion. The Fortas draft stated, "I agree with all parts of the opinion that are relevant to the judgment, but I disagree, with profound respect, with some of the *obiter dicta.*"

Warren now sought to narrow the decision by circulating a two-page concurrence reversing on the simple ground that the convictions were devoid of evidentiary support. On February 27, the Chief's draft was recirculated, joined by Brennan, Fortas, and Marshall. It became the opinion of the Court when it was joined by Douglas and was issued as such on March 10, 1969.

During Warren's last term, the Court started to deal with cases arising out of protests against the Vietnam war. Two such cases are of interest. The first was *Tinker v. Des Moines School District.*[21] Several high school students wore black armbands to publicize their objections to the war. They were suspended from school under a regulation prohibiting wearing of black armbands on school facilities. They sought an injunction against the regulation which was denied by the lower courts. The Justices voted five-to-four to grant certiorari, with Black, Harlan, White, and Fortas for denial.

Warren advocated reversal at the November 15, 1968, conference, but only "on the narrow ground of equal protection." The record showed that the school authorities did not prohibit wearing of other political symbols, such as campaign buttons and even the Nazi Iron Cross. Because of this Warren said, "They have sought out a particular kind of conduct . . . here allowed wearing of Fascist crosses" and other symbols of political significance.

White, however, urged a broader approach. "If the authorities are empowered to maintain order," he stated, "they must be able to classify what disrupts communication among students. . . . But the state doesn't defend this on that ground, but on a physically disruptive ground of which there's no evidence." Except for Black and Harlan, who were for affirmance, the others agreed with Warren when he said that he "could go with Byron." Fortas, who wrote the opinion, said that "school authorities must control schools, but they must show some shred of justification in the sense of a prohibition necessary to carrying on school functions. But here no justification was shown."

Fortas delivered the opinion of the Court on February 24, 1969, invalidating the armband prohibition as a restriction of symbolic speech that was not justified by any evidence that it was necessary to prevent interferences with school work or disorder. Fortas' draft opinion had referred to the armbands as provoked by the Vietnam war. On January 7, Stewart wrote Fortas, "at the risk of appearing eccentric, I shall not join any opinion that speaks of what is going on in Vietnam as a 'war.' " Fortas made the necessary change so that the opinion referred to "the hostilities in Vietnam."

The second Vietnam protest case was *Gunn v. University Committee to End Vietnam War.*[22] It arose out of a protest by members of the committee at a Texas college speech by President Johnson. They were arrested and charged with violating a law making it a breach of the peace to use "loud and vociferous . . . language . . . in a manner calculated to disturb the person or persons present" in a public place. They brought an action for a declaratory judgment and injunction, which were granted on the ground that the statute was unconstitutionally broad. Black, Harlan, Stewart, and White voted to hear the *Gunn* appeal.

Warren urged affirmance at the conference. As he saw it, the statutory "language as construed is too broad. [There was] no riot except what was started by others. The conduct of the sheriff and the justice of the peace justified the injunction."

The Justices agreed with Warren and voted to strike down the law as an invalid interference with First Amendment rights. Fortas wrote an opinion of the Court, circulated March 14, 1969, that conceded, "It may be that Texas could punish persons under this statutory language for engaging in types of activity other than those that the First Amendment embraces—for disturbing those present at a chess tournament or a ladies sewing circle, for example, or a schoolroom or library, by 'loud and vociferous' shouting foreign to the surroundings and deliberately designed to disrupt the proceedings."

The case, however, involved, "activities in the First Amendment area." With regard to them, Fortas declared, the rule was different. "First Amendment rights cannot be delimited by a standard that is as broad as that of the Texas statute. Speech is not necessarily deprived of First Amendment protection solely because it is 'loud and vociferous' and because it is 'calculated to disturb the person or persons present.' Much conventional political debate falls within this vast category. Neither the decibels of the human voice nor the 'disturbance' of listeners at an otherwise appropriate rally in a public square set the limits of First Amendment rights."

Stewart and White circulated dissents. Stewart used strong language to support his contention that "the Court today has gone quite remarkably astray." Stewart asserted, "I cannot agree that this provision, as so construed, is unconstitutional on its face. Surely if recent history has taught us anything, it has taught us that noise is not necessarily speech—that sound and fury can as often stifle free expression as promote it." White wrote, "I am unaware of a constitutional right to disturb others by loud noises, whether the noise is speech or otherwise. The uninvited mouth is as obnoxious as the uninvited ear."

Fortas recirculated a final draft of his *Gunn* opinion on May 6. By then, however, Fortas was enveloped in the controversy that led to his forced resignation on May 14. His *Gunn* opinion of the Court was never delivered. Instead, on June 16, the case was set for reargument the following term.[23] Ultimately, on June 29, 1970, a year after Warren had retired, *Gunn* was decided, with an opinion by Stewart avoiding the constitutional issue.[24] The question of whether the volume of political speech can be controlled, which the Fortas *Gunn* opinion had answered with a resounding negative, remained unanswered.

Another case in which the Warren Court came close to handing down an important decision was *Maxwell v. Bishop,*[25] where the Justices nearly struck down the Arkansas death penalty law. Maxwell, a black, had been convicted of rape of a white woman. Arkansas law made the crime punishable by death, but gave the jury the right to impose life imprisonment. The trial was a unitary trial, with the same jury deciding the issues of guilt and punishment at the same time. The highest state court affirmed the conviction. Warren, Brennan, Stewart, White, Fortas, and Marshall voted to grant certiorari. The conference following the argument voted eight-to-one to reverse, with only Black for affirmance. The majority Justices expressed the view that the unitary trial and the lack of standards to guide the jury in sentencing violated due process.

On March 7, 1969, Harlan, who had voted for reversal on the unitary-trial issue, sent a "Dear Chief" letter: "I thought that I should advise you, and the other Brethren, that I am not at rest on my yesterday's vote to reverse this case on the basis of the 'split-trial' issue." Harlan wrote that, "In view of this, and the variety of views expressed upon the case at the Conference yesterday, you may wish to consider relisting the case for further discussion at the next Conference, before the case is assigned."

At the next conference, the vote remained the same. Warren, Douglas, and Brennan took the position that submission of the death penalty issue for a decision not based on pre-existing standards violated due process. The same three, as well as Fortas and Marshall, also thought that a bifurcated trial (with a *separate* hearing on sentencing) was constitutionally required. Harlan said that he had not completely made up his mind but that he also tended to believe that due process required a bifurcated trial.

White and Stewart wanted to dispose of the case under the rule laid down the previous term in *Witherspoon v. Illinois,*[26] discussed in the last chapter—i.e., that a conviction, must be reversed where those opposed to the death penalty are automatically excluded from the jury. White and Stewart urged the *Witherspoon* ground even though the issue had not been raised before the Court and certiorari had been granted limited to the bifurcation and standards questions. Black still voted to affirm.

Warren assigned the opinion to Douglas. He prepared a draft opinion of the Court at the end of March that reversed on both the bifurcation and standards grounds. The unitary trial, wrote Douglas, compelled defendant to forego his privilege against self-incrimination by taking the stand to make his case on punishment. As the draft explained, "This privilege against self-incrimination may be important. Yet if the defendant is to escape death, his testimony may be essential." The same was true, Douglas asserted, of defendant's right to testify. "Only by presenting his mitigating evidence may an accused make an impact on the jury's determination of the penalty. Yet he dare not exercise his right of allocution at the unitary trial, lest he suffer irreparable harm on the guilt issue. He thus purchases a fair trial on the issue of guilt at the cost of sacrificing his right to a fair trial on the issue of punishment."

The Douglas draft also stressed that, "Under Arkansas law those who should receive death and those who should not are undefined." Standards to guide the sentencing jury were constitutionally required. "Where there are no guidelines or relevant evidence," the Douglas draft declared, "one jury may decide that one defendant is not 'fit to live.' . . . because he is a black who raped a white woman, while another defendant is 'fit to live' because he is a white who raped a black. Or whatever the race of the defendant one jury may be seized by the spirit of the mob, while another, dealing with the same quality of offense, may be more reasoned and compassionate."

Brennan wrote to Douglas on April 1, 1969, suggesting that the bifurcation and standards issues be treated separately. "I think too that the standards discussion would be clearer if it was made plain that this is a separate and independent inquiry necessary to decision—that after demonstrating the unconstitutionality of the unitary trial, it is then required that the question be answered. Does due process require further that the jury be provided with standards governing their choice between life and death?"

Douglas followed Brennan's suggestion and revised his draft so that Part I dealt with bifurcation and Part II with standards. The opinion was then circulated and quickly joined by the Chief Justice and Brennan. On April 7, however, Fortas wrote Douglas that he could not join the section of the opinion requiring standards. "I continue to think that requiring standards is inadvisable and will be productive of results that I consider undesirable. The basic fact is that it is impossible, as far as I am concerned, to state standards which would justify capital punishment. . . . Further, I think that if standards are legislated, the result will be substantially to increase the number of cases of imposition of death penalty." Fortas circulated a short concurring opinion based on this view, which Marshall joined.

Douglas replied to Fortas with a tart April 8 letter: "Perhaps those who insist that there be standards before costs can be assessed, *Giaccio v. Pennsylvania,* 382 U.S. 399, [a decision Fortas had joined in 1966] can explain why standards are necessary for the assessment of costs but not for assessment of the death penalty. But that is a feat which surpasses my limited capacities."

The next day, Harlan wrote Douglas, "I am still of the view that the Arkansas judgment is not constitutionally infirm for want of 'standards' in the fixing of the death penalty. I therefore could not join Part II of your proposed opinion."

Harlan also wrote, "As to Part I, while I continue to think that in light of Arkansas procedures, as I presently understand them, a split trial on the issue of punishment was constitutionally required, I have not yet come to rest on the precise scope of what due process would require in this regard. Pending further research and consideration, I therefore cannot at this time say whether I would be able to join your Part I." Harlan indicated to Douglas that he was considering writing a separate opinion on the bifurcation issue.

Douglas now decided to abandon the discussion of standards. He circulated a new draft dealing only with the bifurcation requirement. Fortas withdrew his separate concurrence and joined Douglas. There were five votes for the Douglas opinion—Douglas, Warren, Brennan, Fortas, and Marshall. But Stewart and White, who had voted for reversal on the *Witherspoon* ground, were opposed to the bifurcation holding, Black still dissented, and Harlan, as shown by his April 9 letter, had not made up his mind.

Warren and Brennan, who had voted for reversal because of the lack of standards as well as bifurcation, refused to allow the decision to come down without discussion of the standards requirement. On May 14, Brennan circulated a concurrence arguing that "due process requires pre-existing standards for penalty determinations." Brennan stressed that standards were as necessary as bifurcation to protect defendant. "Without such standards, however, the separate penalty trial which the Court now requires could not conceivably afford a full and fair hearing for those faced with the possibility of a sentence of death. The convicted offender would be in the Kafkaesque situation of having his life at stake and not knowing which arguments will hurt him and which might save him."

Warren joined the Brennan concurrence by a May 23 letter and Douglas was also committed to join. But, here too, the Fortas resignation upset the decision for reversal that the Court had reached. Harlan now became the crucial vote on the Douglas opinion. But he was still unable to make up his mind. The law clerk whom Harlan had assigned to draft a concurrence had not begun work, and Harlan said that he had not yet had the chance to develop his thinking sufficiently to be willing to provide the fifth vote in such a crucial case.

He now preferred reargument. Douglas, unable to muster five votes for his opinion, decided that he could not issue it in these circumstances. He also pushed for reargument, as did Stewart. On May 26, 1969, the Court set the case for reargument in the following term.

But the Court that dealt with the case in the new 1969 Term was a different Court. With Warren and Fortas off the bench, two crucial votes for reversal on bifurcation were gone. On June 1, 1970, the Court issued a per curiam holding that the case should be remanded on the *Witherspoon* ground urged unsuccessfully the year before by Stewart and White, because a prospective juror had been removed after stating scruples about capital punishment.[27] Then, in the 1971 case of *McGautha v. California*,[28] the Burger Court held that a defendant's constitutional rights were not violated by the jury's imposition of the death penalty in the same unitary proceeding that determined the issue of guilt or by permitting the jury to impose the death penalty without governing standards.

Maxwell v. Bishop ended as a 1968 Term criminal-law landmark *manqué*. Warren was, however, able to lead the Court to an important criminal law decision in *Benton v. Maryland*.[29] Benton had been tried for burglary and larceny. The jury found him not guilty of larceny, but convicted him of burglary. The conviction was set aside because of improper jury selection. He was reindicted and charged again with both burglary and larceny. This time he was found guilty of both offenses. The highest state court rejected Benton's claim that the constitutional bar against double jeopardy had been violated. All the Brethren except Harlan voted to grant certiorari.

Palko v. Connecticut,[30] decided in 1937, had held that the Fifth Amendment's double jeopardy prohibition was not binding upon the states. At the *Benton* conference on March 28, 1969, the Chief Justice indicated that he disagreed with *Palko* and would be willing to overrule that decision. In *Benton* itself, it was, as Warren saw it, "wrong to retry him on larceny and to put the two together infected the whole trial. Since I apply double jeopardy to the states, that brings me to reverse both convictions."

Except for Harlan and Stewart, all agreed with the Chief. Marshall wrote the opinion overruling *Palko* and reversing. On May 6, Harlan sent Marshall a letter, "I feel sure that it will not surprise you to learn that I find it quite impossible to subscribe to your treatment of the

Palko case. I have not yet come to rest on whether I shall be in concurrence or in dissent." Ultimately Harlan issued a dissent that Stewart joined.

On May 7, Fortas circulated a draft concurrence that objected to the Marshall opinion's "language which makes it appear that in all instances where provisions of the Bill of Rights apply to the States as part of the Due Process Clause of the Fourteenth Amendment, the 'total gloss' of the federal provision is rigidly imported to bind the States." Fortas' resignation made it impossible for him to issue his concurrence. When the *Benton* opinion was delivered on June 23—the last day of Warren's last term—no one in the majority spoke against the Court's statement that the "federal double jeopardy standards" under the Fifth Amendment now applied to the states.

The Chief Justice was also able to secure the result he favored in other criminal cases. *Foster v. California*[31] arose out of a conviction for robbery. After Foster had been arrested, the victim viewed him in a lineup with two much shorter men, but was unsure whether he was the robber. Ten days later, the police arranged another lineup. Foster was the only one in the second lineup who had been in the first lineup. The victim identified Foster positively this time. The state courts upheld the conviction. Certiorari was granted by six-to-three, with Harlan, Stewart, and White to deny.

At the November 22, 1968, conference, Warren advocated reversal on the "totality of circumstances." "If they tried him only with the first lineup," he said, "I wouldn't say it was wrong." In addition, he thought that "the citizen who is conscientious about identification should be commended for his caution. But when they wait ten days and line him up with five strangers, that tips the scale. It's the same as saying, 'Here's the guy we want you to convict.' "

A bare majority agreed with the Chief. Fortas delivered the opinion reversing along the lines indicated by Warren. Black, who had declared at the conference that, "if we're going to say it was unfair, that adds to the Constitution," issued a dissent. White, Harlan, and Stewart also dissented.

Johnson v. Avery[32] was another criminal case where the Chief's lead was followed. Johnson, a prisoner in the Tennessee State Penitentiary, challenged a prison regulation barring inmates from assisting other prisoners in preparing "Writs or other legal matters." The court of appeals held that the regulation did not unlawfully conflict with the federal right of habeas corpus. The Supreme Court reversed, in an opinion by Fortas, after Warren had urged the November 15, 1968, conference to reverse. This was "too broad a prohibition," the Chief had declared. He was not proposing that the Court "set up a Legal Aid Bureau of prisoners or interfere with prison discipline." But, he said, "I can't see why a prisoner can't be a next friend to another prisoner."

Warren almost led the Court to a significant criminal law decision in *Frank v. United States*.[33] But a draft dissent by White led to a switch in the deciding vote and the case ultimately went the other way. Frank had been charged with criminal contempt for his violation of an injunction. He was convicted, but the court suspended sentence and placed him on probation for three years. The court of appeals affirmed. Certiorari was granted (only Harlan and Stewart voting to deny) to determine whether Frank was entitled to a jury trial.

The Supreme Court had previously held that jury trials were not constitutionally required in cases involving "petty" offenses[34]—where a penalty of no more than six months imprisonment could be imposed—or criminal contempts where no more than a six month sentence was imposed.[35] At the December 13, 1968, conference, Warren argued that this involved more than such a "petty" contempt, since the court had imposed control over Frank for three years. A bare majority (Warren, Black, Douglas, Fortas, and Marshall) accepted this approach and voted for reversal. Warren assigned the case to Marshall.

Marshall circulated a five-page draft opinion of the Court on January 7, 1969. The draft stated that the Court was reversing "because the right to trial by jury is so fundamental to our system of criminal justice." Marshall pointed out that, if Frank violated his probation terms, he could have been imprisoned for six months. "In the present case, petitioner has thus in effect been sentenced to a maximum term of three years probation, plus a possibility of six months in jail." The draft concluded that this was "in excess of the penalty which [prior cases] held was the maximum which could be imposed without according the right to a jury trial. Accordingly, petitioner was entitled to a trial by jury and it was error to deny him that right."

On January 21, White sent around a dissent that began, "The Court today, in an apparently narrow opinion, either abolishes the petty offense exception to the requirement of trial by jury in federal cases, or creates an irrational classification almost amounting to a denial of equal protection." According to White, the Court had reached a result which, he wrote, "is strange indeed. A man sentenced to three years probation, and the possibility of six months in jail should he violate probation, is entitled to a jury trial if he has been sentenced by a judge enjoying broad discretion because the judge has by his sentence showed that he considers the offense serious. But the same man, given the same sentence by the same judge under explicit federal statutes which all along authorized five years probation plus six months in jail as a maximum penalty for just that offense, is not entitled to a jury trial. The majority's result must embrace either this bizarre conclusion, or else must mean that the congressional authorization of five years probation for federal 'petty offenses' removes those crimes from the petty offense category, so that trials by jury are required by them. There is no justification for either result and I dissent."

White's draft dissent led Marshall to circulate a February 25 *Memorandum to the Conference* which informed the Brethren: "The original opinion by me . . . was effectively detonated by Byron's dissenting opinion. With his approval, I have redrafted it along the lines of his opinion."

After Marshall had prepared his new opinion of the Court affirming denial of jury trial, Warren sent him an April 3 note that, "I am not prepared to join your opinion as presently drafted because it is contrary to the way the case was decided in Conference." The Chief suggested that, "In the circumstances, I think it had better go over."

Warren's suggestion that *Frank* should be set for reargument was not accepted. Marshall delivered his new opinion as the opinion of the Court on May 19, 1969. By then, Fortas had resigned, so that the decision for affirmance was five-to-three. Warren delivered a sharp dissent, charging the Court with "an alarming expansion of the non-jury contempt power."[36]

An even more striking example of a case in which a draft dissent led to a changed decision was *O'Callahan v. Parker*.[37] O'Callahan was an Army sergeant who had been convicted by a court-martial of attempted rape committed in a Honolulu hotel room while he had been on leave and out of uniform. The conviction was upheld by the lower federal courts. Black, Douglas, Brennan, and Marshall voted to grant certiorari. The January 24, 1969, conference voted six-to-three to affirm, with Black, Douglas, and Marshall dissenting.

Harlan circulated a fourteen-page opinion of the Court on April 8, 1969, substantially similar to his ultimate dissent in the case. It rejected "petitioner's claim that courts-martial are without constitutional jurisdiction to try soldiers for 'purely civilian' offenses." The Harlan draft went out of its way to note "the fairness of military criminal procedure," saying that, "Whatever may have been the infirmities of 17th century English martial law, military personnel today are not summarily or arbitrarily treated, but enjoy a fair and enlightened system of criminal justice." Harlan's conclusion was, "The exercise of court-martial jurisdiction in the instant case is, thus, entirely consistent with the language of the Constitution and the standards hitherto enunciated by this Court."

Only two days after Harlan's draft was circulated, Douglas sent around an impassioned dissent, which began, "The Court's opinion leaves me aghast." At stake here, Douglas declared, were "the civil liberties of the citizen." The government had relied on a statutory provision which gave courts-martial jurisdiction to try "all conduct of a nature to bring discredit upon the armed forces." But Douglas asserted that, "one can search the Constitution and Bill of Rights in vain for making the glory and prestige of the armed services a reason for expanding their power."

The Douglas draft dissent pointed out that the state court could prosecute if the military were held without jurisdiction. "Can we say that Hawaii's scheme of civilian justice is too inadequate? Can we say there is in the present case an urgent national need to get the kind of hard-nosed justice which the military manufactures with ease?" Douglas stressed the difference between civil and military justice. "A civilian trial, in other words, is held in an atmosphere conducive to the protection of individual rights, while the military trial is marked by the age-old manifest destiny of retributive justice."

"While I have not decided," Douglas wrote, "what the precise constitutional line should be, I am clear that the crime to be under military jurisdiction must be service-connected." Otherwise, he maintained, the majority decision would include virtually all offenses committed by members of the armed forces. "It comes as a shock," Douglas concluded, "to learn that one on leave who (1) attends an anti-Vietnam rally or (2) testifies falsely on the probate of his mother's will or (3) attends a meeting of the 'socialist' study club or (4) joins a PTA resolution opposing the ABM system may be forced to an accounting by a court-martial."

Douglas' dissent was a tour-de-force, dashed off as soon as he had read Harlan's draft opinion of the Court. On April 11, Fortas, who had voted to affirm at the conference, wrote Harlan, "I am sorry to say that I cannot go along with your draft." In the next few weeks, Harlan lost his majority. On May 19, he wrote Douglas, "I thought I should let you know that in due course I shall turn my earlier opinion in this case, reflecting the original Conference majority vote, into a dissent." Douglas delivered a restrained version of his dissent as the *O'Callahan* opinion of the Court on June 2, 1969. Stewart and White joined Harlan in his dissent.

Two noteworthy Fourth Amendment cases were decided during the term. The first was *Kaufman v. United States*.[38] Kaufman had been convicted of armed robbery in a federal court. His only defense had been insanity. The conviction was affirmed. Kaufman then filed a motion to be released under a statute authorizing such a post-conviction proceeding where it was claimed that the sentence was imposed in violation of the Constitution. Kaufman claimed that the finding of sanity was based upon improper admission of illegally seized evidence. The lower courts had denied Kaufman's application, holding that he should have raised the Fourth Amendment issue in his appeal and that it was not cognizable in the post-conviction proceeding. Warren, Black, Douglas, and Brennan voted to grant certiorari.

At the November 22, 1968, conference, the vote (with Marshall not participating) was seven to reverse and one (Douglas) to dismiss certiorari as improvidently granted. Douglas said that he believed that Kaufman's underlying claim of unconstitutional search and seizure was frivolous. The seven who voted to reverse expressed two different theories. Warren and Brennan stated that Fourth Amendment claims should be no less cognizable in federal post-conviction proceedings than in federal habeas corpus proceedings involving state prisoners. Black and Harlan, on the other hand, thought that search and seizure claims should be available in post-conviction proceedings only in "special circumstances." They said that such circumstances were present here because Kaufman had written to his appellate counsel asking him to submit the illegal search and seizure claim and the letter had been forwarded to the court of appeals.

Brennan, who had been assigned the opinion, prepared a draft that rejected the "special circumstances" limitation and stated instead the broad rule that claims cognizable in federal habeas corpus proceedings were also cognizable in post-conviction proceedings. Brennan's draft was quickly joined by Warren, White, and Stewart, as well as by Douglas, though he said that he still would rather have seen the case dismissed.

Fortas then circulated a concurrence in which he joined Brennan's opinion but stated his own view that a prisoner would be guilty of a deliberate by-pass, and hence precluded from post-conviction relief, if he did not raise the search and seizure issue on the direct appeal from his conviction. Fortas believed Kaufman escaped this preclusion because of his letter to his appellate counsel attempting to raise the search issue. Fortas was, however, persuaded to agree to a compromise, under which he would withdraw his separate opinion, in return for which a footnote would be added to Brennan's draft stating that Kaufman's letter served to avoid any claim of "deliberate by-pass."

Now came Black with a ringing dissent. The Black draft, which was toned down in its final version, was circulated January 17, 1969. It contended that Kaufman was clearly guilty, that the illegally seized evidence was clearly reliable, and that the Court's opinion "insures that prisoners who are undoubtedly guilty will be set free" with no compensating "benefits in enforcing the Fourth Amendment."

After Black's draft was circulated, Stewart withdrew his agreement to join Brennan's opinion. Instead, he joined a brief dissent that Harlan filed. Douglas wrote Brennan on January 23 that, because Black had made such a *cause célèbre* out of the case, he would return to his original vote to dismiss. This meant that the lineup on *Kaufman* was now four-to-four, which, under the Court's established practice, would have resulted in an affirmance without opinion.

Nothing further happened in the case until a conference a few weeks later when it was announced that several other opinions which cited *Kaufman* were ready to be issued. Brennan then told the others that Douglas had indicated an intention to withdraw from his opinion. White argued that the case presented an important issue that should be decided promptly and not be postponed. Everyone around the table then turned to Douglas, but he sat motionless and said nothing. Warren asked Brennan to prepare to announce the case as an affirmance by an equally divided Court. Then, without prior warning, Douglas sent a brief note on March 3 that he was now willing to join Brennan's opinion: "after much vacillation and indecision on whether or not I should adhere to my original vote to dismiss as improvidently granted, I have decided to go along with you to give you a court."

Just as the opinion was ready to be issued, however, Fortas indicated his desire to write a concurrence on the "deliberate by-pass" issue. According to his law clerks, Brennan was annoyed that Fortas was reopening that issue after a compromise had been worked out. But it turned out that Fortas had not remembered the earlier compromise. When he was reminded of it by his law clerk, he sent a note to Brennan saying he was not an "Indian agreer" and did not issue any concurrence.

When Brennan announced the *Kaufman* decision on March 24, 1969, his opinion spoke for five of the eight Justices who sat in the case. Black and Harlan, joined by Stewart, delivered their dissents. Brennan was concerned about the effect of Black's pronouncing his "freeing the guilty" dissent in the crowded courtroom. He suggested that both he and Black refrain from reading their opinions. The Alabaman agreed and the *Kaufman* decision was scarcely noticed in the press. Douglas need not have worried about Black's dissent. The case turned out to be anything but a *cause célèbre*.

The second Fourth Amendment case decided in Warren's last term was *Alderman v. United States.*[39] It was important not so much for what it decided, but because the decision there led to what Warren later termed "a deliberate attempt to surreptitiously influence the action of [the Court]"[40]—an attempt made by the Nixon Administration through an emissary of the new Attorney General, John Mitchell.

The *Alderman* case arose out of a conviction for conspiracy to transmit murderous threats in interstate commerce. There were also companion cases involving espionage convictions of two Soviet agents.[41] In the Supreme Court, all three defendants alleged that they had been the subject of unlawful government wiretapping. The Court refused to accept the government's determination that no overheard conversation was arguably relevant to the prosecutions. The government then moved to have the transcripts subjected to in camera inspection by the trial judge, who would turn over to defendants only those materials relevant to their prosecutions.

On March 10, 1969, the Court, in an opinion by White, rejected the government's motion. It held that the prosecution should be required to turn over all conversations in which the accused played a part or which took place on their premises. There were then also over twenty other criminal cases in the Court raising the same issue, which were being held for action similar to that which would be taken in *Alderman*. They included prosecutions of the heavyweight champion, Cassius Clay,[42] and the Teamsters Union president, James R. Hoffa.[43] Two weeks after the *Alderman* decision, on March 24, these cases were dealt with in the same way, with the Government ordered to hand over the transcribed conversations to the defendants concerned.

On Wednesday afternoon, March 12, 1969, two days after the *Alderman* decision was announced, Brennan was working at his desk in his chambers, when he received a phone call from Jack C. Landau, the recently appointed Director of Public Information at the Department of Justice. Brennan had gotten to know Landau when he was working as a reporter for the Newhouse newspaper chain at the same time that the Justice's daughter-in-law was a Newhouse columnist. Brennan had later written a letter recommending Landau for a Niemann fellowship at Harvard Law School. In his phone call Landau told Brennan that he had to talk with him on a matter of utmost gravity. He asked if he could see the Justice and Brennan told him, "Of course, come on over." Brennan had no idea that Landau was then working for the Justice Department.

Within a short time, Landau arrived at the Court and was ushered into Brennan's chambers. He was very nervous, never sitting down; he paced up and down during the whole time he was with the Justice. He told Brennan that he was there on a mission from Attorney General Mitchell. He said that a real crisis for our relationships with foreign governments had been created by the *Alderman* decision because one of the tapes which the government would have to turn over was that of a conversation between Cassius Clay and a South

American Embassy. That, in turn, would disclose that not only that Embassy had its phones tapped, but that the F.B.I. had tapped the phones of every embassy in Washington. (Landau telephoned later that day to say that the Attorney General wanted the Justice to know that they only had forty-six embassies wiretapped). Landau told Brennan that the Attorney General was very concerned that disclosure of the embassy wiretapping would have most unfortunate consequences for our relations with foreign governments. He then asked Brennan what they could do about this situation.

"Well now," the Justice replied, "I'm not the one who can answer that. I'll call the Chief Justice." He phoned Warren, told him Landau was there, and asked if he might bring him in. The Chief told him to come right over and they went to the Chief Justice's chambers. At this point Landau became even more nervous; he was so upset that he was almost stuttering. Brennan and Landau informed Warren of what had happened. After the Chief had heard them out, he turned to Landau and told him that the Court might address such an application only if a petition for rehearing was filed. Despite the government's practice of not filing such petitions, they took Warren's advice and filed a petition for rehearing in the *Alderman* case, which was denied on March 24.

Just before he left, Landau told the Chief Justice that the Attorney General wanted him to know that he would do anything in his power to head off any congressional action that might lead to a curtailment of the Court's jurisdiction. Warren later said that he did not know why Landau made "this statement when there was nothing of the kind pending in the Congress."[44] In his *Autobiography,* however, Douglas writes that Landau's words were "a threat that something terrible would happen to the Court unless it changed its rulings in the Alderman case. This is the first instance in the memory of anyone connected with the Court in which the executive branch has made actual threats to the Court."[45]

When Landau left, Warren and Brennan discussed what the Chief termed in his memoirs "this outrageous attempt to influence a Court action."[46] They decided that the other Justices should be informed of what had happened. The Chief promptly convened a conference and Brennan and he told what had happened. There was no discussion. After Warren had finished, he asked Brennan if he had accurately reported what had transpired in his chambers. After Brennan affirmed that he had, the Chief announced, "The conference is adjourned."

After the conference, Warren and Brennan made contemporaneous memoranda of what had happened. So, it turned out, did Douglas. It was subsequently reported in the press in May, 1973, that Landau had called on Warren and Brennan in March, 1969, to convey the Attorney General's concern at the wiretap decision.[47] Neither the Chief nor the Justice would respond to press inquiries on the matter. But the inquiries led them to get out their memoranda on the incident. For the first time, they saw the Douglas memorandum. They were troubled to learn from it that Douglas had attributed the incident to a conspiratorial effort by Richard G. Kleindienst, whom Douglas had described as the then-Attorney General, to embarrass the Court. Neither Warren nor Brennan had ever suggested this. In his *Autobiography*, too, Douglas gave this version of what happened, attributing the incident to the fact that Kleindienst "wanted to give the Court as much trouble as possible."[48]

Among the cases during his last term in which Warren played a direct leadership role were the term's two Reapportionment Cases. *Kirkpatrick v. Preisler*[49] involved the Missouri Congressional redistricting plan, under which population variances ranged from 13,542 (3.13%) above the mathematical ideal of absolute equality to 12,260 (2.84%) below it. *Wells v. Rockefeller*[50] arose out of New York's Congressional districting law which divided the state into seven regions and divided each region into districts with equal population. The districts varied from 6.5 percent above to 6.6 percent below the state population mean. New York justified its scheme of equal districts only within each of the regions as a means to keep regions with distinct interests intact.

Warren began the January 17, 1969, conference by stating, "The sole question is whether the districts satisfy the *Sanders* test [laid down in the 1964 case of *Wesberry v. Sanders*,[51] discussed in chapter 12] of 'as close as practicable' " to population equality. "When it appears," said the Chief, "that there's a departure from the norm, the proponents must justify what was done." Here, Warren thought, neither state had met this burden and the Court should set aside both plans.

The vote was five-to-four to strike down both state plans. But there was a different five in each case. Fortas agreed that the New York scheme was unacceptable but thought that Missouri's plan came within the range of acceptable error. Marshall voted to invalidate the Missouri plan but not the New York plan. The Court scuttlebutt was that Marshall did not want to reverse the decision below written by Judge Leonard P. Moore, his colleague on the Second Circuit Court of Appeals. Marshall was also influenced by his law clerk, who asserted that it was proper to give recognition to regional interests as New York had done.

The cases were assigned to Brennan, who circulated opinions stressing that the equal-population requirement permitted only "unavoidable" population variances, with the states required to make "a good-faith effort to achieve precise mathematical equality." Both plans failed to meet this test. Brennan's opinion was quickly joined by Warren, Black, and Douglas. Fortas, however, notified Brennan that he would now concur separately in both cases rather than join either opinion.

Since Harlan, joined by Stewart, and White wrote dissents (in accordance with their conference votes), Marshall's vote became crucial, if the Brennan opinions were to have a majority. But Marshall, under strong pressure from his clerk, was balking and refused to join either opinion. Brennan spoke to Warren about the situation, and the Chief went to have a talk with Marshall. He convinced Marshall on the importance of defining the scope of the 1964 reapportionment decisions before new appointments to the Court were made that might well change the balance on reapportionment issues. Marshall joined Brennan's opinions immediately after his talk with Warren. The opinions themselves were delivered as the opinions of the Court on April 7, 1969.

The famous 1927 *Scopes* case[52] (headlined in the press as the "Great Monkey Trial") had discredited fundamentalist laws prohibiting the teaching of evolution. But laws such as those remained on the books in what H.L. Mencken had termed "the Bible belt." Indeed, it was not until the Warren Court's decision in *Epperson v. Arkansas*[53] that such laws were finally placed beyond the constitutional pale. Epperson, an Arkansas schoolteacher, brought an action challenging the state's anti-evolution statute. The highest state court upheld the law as "a valid exercise of the state's power to specify the curriculum in its public schools." Its opinion indicated that it was not clear whether the statute "prohibits any explanation of the theory of evolution or merely prohibits teaching that the theory is true."

None of the Brethren expressed any doubt at the October 18, 1968, conference that the state law was unconstitutional. Warren urged reversal on the ground that "the Act is too vague to stand. The Supreme Court of Arkansas opinion proves this. 'We can't say,' says the court, whether it goes to teaching or explanation.' " Warren also said that Arkansas had not shown a sufficient state interest to justify the law. "It had broad authority to fix curriculum, but a prohibition like this should have some reason related to the police power—[such as] morals or safety." The Chief indicated as well that "the overbreadth approach of *Butler v. Michigan* [54] [the 1957 case discussed in chapter 6] could work here." But, he concluded, "I tend toward vagueness as the safest basis."

Black stated, "If we go on vagueness ground, I can go along. I can't go on any ground that this statute is thought to be unreasonable or arbitrary, because that's not an acceptable constitutional standard. It was [Justice James C.] McReynolds' philosophy, which I utterly reject." Black also said, "There's no case or controversy here between this lady and the State of Arkansas."

Douglas agreed on the vagueness point. It had been argued that the Arkansas law violated the First Amendment's prohibition against an establishment of religion. But Douglas asserted, "I don't think establishment of religion is really in the case." He also thought "*Butler v. Michigan* would be a mistaken approach. I think the brightest of us are the young and the danger is we'd try to make them like us."

The others, however, wanted to go on the basis of the First Amendment. Stewart said, "we have to go on the basic issue of what the teacher can teach in the classroom under the cloak of the First Amendment. This to me is a simple violation of the First Amendment because it prohibits freedom of speech." Stewart issued a concurrence expressing this view.

The others agreed that the First Amendment had been violated. But they saw the violation in terms of the amendment's guaranty of religious freedom. "If it can't be decided on establishment," Harlan declared, "it can't be decided." Fortas, who wrote the *Epperson* opinion, said that he "would reverse on what to me is the narrowest ground—establishment of religion. I don't have trouble getting to that." The conference decided to go along with this approach. The Fortas opinion of the Court following it was issued November 12, 1968.

The Court was unable to resolve two cases presenting the issue of federal court abstention from interference in state criminal proceedings. The governing principle had developed that federal courts were not warranted in cutting short the normal adjudication of constitutional defenses in state criminal proceedings. An exception had been laid down in the 1965 case of *Dombrowski v. Pfister,*[55] where an injunction was granted against a state prosecution that was part of a plan to harass a civil-rights organization in the exercise of First Amendment rights.

In the two 1968 Term cases, it was claimed that *Dombrowski* authorized federal-court action to stop state prosecutions whenever they had a "chilling effect" on free expression. In *Younger v. Harris,*[56] Harris sought a federal injunction against a prosecution under the California Criminal Syndicalism Act on the ground that it inhibited him in the exercise of his rights of free speech and press. The lower court granted the injunction, holding that *Dombrowski* applied. In *Samuels v. Mackell,*[57] Samuels had been indicted on charges of violating the New York Criminal Anarchy Law. He brought a federal action for a declaratory judgment that the New York statute violated the First Amendment. The lower court dismissed the action.

At the *Younger v. Harris* conference, the vote was five-to-three to reverse, with Warren, Brennan and White voting the other way. The majority was, however, split. Black, Harlan, and Stewart wanted to use the case as a vehicle for cutting back on the *Dombrowski* decision, while Fortas and Marshall wanted a narrower opinion.

In *Samuels v. Mackell,* the conference vote was eight-to-nothing to affirm. The three *Younger* minority Justices thought that a distinction should be drawn between declaratory judgments and injunctions on grounds of comity. In this view a federal court could issue a declaratory judgment, but not an injunction, when there was a pending state prosecution. Douglas did not participate in either vote, because he had not heard argument in the cases. But, we will see, this did not stop him from later playing an active role in the two cases.

As senior majority Justice, Black assigned the opinions to himself. Toward the end of April 1969, Black circulated a *Younger* draft that would have returned the law to where it had stood prior to *Dom-browski*. In *Samuels*, Black took the position that no distinction should be made between injunctive and declaratory relief as far as federal court intervention in state prosecutions was concerned. Harlan and Stewart quickly joined these opinions. Douglas joined the *Samuels* draft and chose simply to concur in the result in *Younger*.

On April 29, Fortas wrote Black, "I am sorry to say that I cannot join your [*Younger*] opinion." Fortas noted that, when they had talked about the case, "I said that I would be happy to join a narrow opinion, but that I would not be able to join a general attack on *Dom-browski*." Fortas wrote that he had not yet decided whether to write separately "or merely concur in the result."

Brennan now circulated a concurrence that was intended to secure a majority instead of Black's opinion and save *Dombrowski* as good law. The Brennan draft dealt with both the *Younger* and *Samuels* cases. Its thesis was that, where no harassment was alleged, federal courts should not hear a claim that a state criminal statute had a chilling effect on the exercise of First Amendment rights, when the state had already returned a criminal indictment. This rationale disposed of both cases while preserving the essence of *Dombrowski* and without necessitating a decision on whether a distinction should be drawn between injunctive and declaratory relief.

Before Brennan was able to circulate his concurrence, Fortas resigned. That lessened the chances of securing a majority to support it. But Marshall and White quickly joined, and though Warren did not formally join, there was no doubt that he would. Brennan appeared to have his majority when Douglas also joined, but with the notation that he continued to concur in Black's opinion in *Samuels*.

At the term's last conference on June 13, nevertheless, Black refused to yield. He insisted that he still had the majority opinion in *Samuels*, since he had four of the eight possible votes. This argument ignored the fact that Brennan now had five votes on his opinion. But it drew attention to the fact that Douglas had concurred in both opinions. Stewart argued that the opinions were inconsistent and that it was logically impossible for Douglas to join both. After some discussion on this point, Douglas, obviously irritated, arose, turned toward Brennan, and said, "Take my name off your opinion."

This meant that no opinion had a majority, and the conference decided to set the cases for reargument in the coming 1969 Term.

The morning after the conference, however, Douglas' law clerk, at the urging of Brennan's clerks, made an impassioned plea to Douglas to reconsider his actions. He pointed out that to leave *Dombrowski* to the mercy of the Court without Warren and Fortas would surely be to destroy it. Douglas was persuaded and called Brennan to say that there might still be room for compromise. Brennan agreed and asked Warren to remove the cases from the order list. The Chief did so. But by this time White was having second thoughts about Brennan's opinion. He thought the Court needed to consider the issues raised by the cases more thoroughly and so he now favored reargument. As a result, the conference decision to order reargument was left unchanged. On June 16, 1969, the Court issued orders setting *Younger* and *Samuels* for reargument.[58] The cases were ultimately decided over a year later by the new Burger Court,[59] with Warren's place taken by Chief Justice Warren E. Burger and Fortas' by Justice Harry A. Blackmun. The Court then narrowed *Dombrowski* by holding that it did not upset the settled principle of federal abstention except where the complaint showed that the state prosecution was motivated by a bad faith intent to harass.

The culmination of Warren's last Court term was the decision in *Powell v. McCormack.*[60] The House of Representatives had voted overwhelmingly to exclude Congressman Adam Clayton Powell from his seat. Powell had just been reelected, but the House acted after a committee had reported that the controversial black legislator had abused his Congressional immunity and misused House funds. Powell brought an action against the Speaker, four Congressmen, and several employees of the House challenging the exclusion as violative of Article I, section 2, of the Constitution, which, he claimed, set forth the exclusive qualifications for House membership. The court of appeals affirmed dismissal of the suit, with the opinion written by Judge Warren E. Burger, soon to become Warren's successor. All the Justices voted to grant certiorari, except for Stewart and, surprisingly, Marshall. While the case was pending in the Supreme Court, Powell had again been reelected and seated in the new Congress, subject to a $25,000 fine. Defendants then filed a suggestion of mootness.

Warren was personally appalled by Powell's misconduct. He considered the flamboyant Congressman a disgrace both to his race and his office. But the law, as he saw it, was clear. Congress had asserted an unreviewable power to deny an elected Congressman his seat, even though he met all the qualifications for membership listed in the Constitution. "It was perfectly clear," Warren has been quoted on the case. "There was no other way to decide it. Anybody could see that."[61]

Warren wanted to have the case dealt with as soon as possible. The case was set for argument in February, 1969, but a request was made for postponement. According to a February 4 memorandum from the Chief to the Justices, "I have now heard from all of the Brethren in re the request to postpone argument in the above case, and the Court is so divided that there is no majority."

The Warren memo gave the vote as follows: "Justice Douglas prefers not to postpone the argument at all; Justices Brennan and Stewart would postpone the argument to March with the understanding the case would have to be heard at that time; Justices Black, White, and Marshall would agree to a postponement to April with the understanding that no further postponement would be granted; and Justices Harlan and Fortas would postpone without a time limitation."

Warren stated as his view, "I would prefer that the argument not be postponed beyond our March session." But he was willing to compromise. "However, in order to get a majority, I would be willing to let it go over to April provided it is definitely understood that it must be argued at that time."

The Brethren responded at once to Warren's memo. Later on February 4, the Chief was able to send around a *Memorandum to the Conference* stating, "Six of the Brethren have now voted to postpone the argument in No. 138—*Powell v. McCormack*—to the April session with the understanding that the case would have to be argued at that time. Accordingly, the case will be scheduled for our April session of arguments."

The argument took place on Monday, April 21, 1969. At the conference on the case, the Chief stated, "I would render a declaratory judgment that they must seat an elected Congressman who meets those qualifications specified in the Constitution." The defendants had argued that, since the Constitution gives the House authority to expel a member by a two-thirds vote and since the vote against Powell was by more than two-thirds, the action denying him his seat was a valid exercise of the expulsion power. Warren, however, stressed that the vote was on a resolution to exclude, not expel. As he saw it, "This is not a constitutional expulsion merely because two-thirds voted against him." Warren likewise said, "I also think Congress has no power to impose a fine on seating, but that issue is not here."

Warren had dealt with the mootness claim by stating, "I see nothing to the mootness argument in light of the salary claim"—i.e., if the exclusion was illegal, Powell had a valid claim to his congressional salary. Only Stewart disagreed on the mootness issue. On the merits, all the Brethren, including Stewart (who ultimately dissented on mootness), supported the Chief's approach. Fortas said that he had "worked out a theory that this was an expulsion," but that he would go along. Even Harlan, who might have been expected to demur on separation-of-powers grounds, declared that the counsel for the House's "basic argument is simply untenable."

As noted, Warren assigned the *Powell* opinion to himself, believing that, in such a case with its potential for direct conflict between Court and Congress, the Court should speak through the Chief Justice. There were those, indeed, who feared that the decision might be no more than an advisory opinion, since there was no practical machinery to force Congress to seat a member. Warren, however, had no doubts on the matter. The question of enforcement had never troubled him. From the *Brown* desegregation decision[62] to the Reapportionment Cases,[63] he had always felt that the Justices' duty was only to decide the cases before them as they thought the Constitution required. Warren's Court career was the living example of the old maxim: *Fiat justitia et ruant coeli* (Let justice be done though the heavens should fall).

But he did not expect the heavens to fall. Once, after the Court had ordered the release of an Army prisoner, one of his law clerks had asked him how they were going to make the Army do that. Warren just laughed and said, "Don't worry about it. They will do it." The clerk persisted and referred to the famous anecdote in which Andrew Jackson was reported to have said that Chief Justice John Marshall had made his decision, now let him enforce it.[64]

"Look," Warren said in reply, "you don't have to worry. If they don't do this, they've destroyed the whole republic, and they aren't going to do that. So you don't even have to worry about whether they are going to do it or not—*they're going to do it!*"

The *Powell* draft that Warren circulated in early June, 1969, was accepted by the Brethren, except for Stewart, who dissented, with relatively few changes. The draft stated that, "Consistent with these cases, the Speech or Debate Clause requires us to affirm the dismissal of petitioners' complaint as to those respondents who are also Congressmen." It was pointed out that the case could be decided against the employee defendants without reaching any question of the case against the Congressmen and the sentence was deleted.

In a letter of June 13, Black wrote that he could not agree to Warren's opinion because of the discussion of the relationship between declaratory judgments and injunctions. Black noted, "We are having a controversy in the Court requiring reargument next year because of a disagreement about the relationship between declaratory judgments and injunctions." Black was referring to the already-discussed cases of *Younger v. Harris* [65] and *Samuels v. Mackell.* [66] He asked Warren "to see if it is possible for you to eliminate the discussion. It seems to me that we will have enough controversy over that in *Samuels v. Mackell* and the related cases."

Warren did eliminate almost all of the discussion to which Black objected. Black then wrote, on June 13, "I am happy to agree with your excellent opinion." Black also asked Warren to cite the classic 1801 case of *Marbury v. Madison,* [67] along with *Baker v. Carr,* [68] at the end of the opinion. "If you disagree," Black noted, "that will be O.K. but *Marbury v. Madison* goes back much farther than our present Court." Needless to say, the Chief added the requested citation.

Warren announced the *Powell* decision invalidating the Congressional exclusion on June 16, 1969. It was his last important act as Chief Justice. A week later—on the last day of the term—he swore in his successor.

A month before the 1968 Term ended, Warren became involved in the controversy that led to Fortas' resignation. At the beginning of May, 1969, *Life* magazine published an article that detailed a financial arrangement between Fortas and a foundation created by financier Louis E. Wolfson. [69] Fortas had agreed to serve as a consultant to the foundation and had accepted a fee of $20,000 in January, 1966, when Wolfson was under investigation for fraud by the Securities and Exchange Commission. The money had been returned in December, 1966, after indictments had been returned against Wolfson.

The *Life* article, however, contained only a partial account of the dealings between Fortas and the Wolfson foundation. The Justice Department had secured information about the contract that made it far more damaging to the Justice. Attorney General Mitchell discussed the new material with the President on the morning of May 7. Later the same morning, the Attorney General's limousine drove around to the rear entrance of the Supreme Court and pulled into the basement garage. Mitchell was met by a marshal who escorted him to the Chief Justice's chambers. The Attorney General had made his unceremonious back entry to avoid being seen by the press.

The Warren–Mitchell meeting lasted less than thirty minutes, and the Attorney General did most of the talking.[70] He said later that he showed the Chief Justice "certain documents." From what Warren told the Brethren, this was a copy of the contract between Fortas and the foundation and the correspondence relating to it. The contract provided for an annual fee of $20,000 to be paid to Fortas for the rest of his life. After his death, the foundation would pay $20,000 a year to his wife.

Warren said nothing more than that he would take the matter under consideration. He also expressed appreciation to the Attorney General for his visit. The Chief then called a conference. When the Brethren had assembled, Fortas among them, Warren told of the contract that had been shown to him. Fortas then explained that he had paid back the money he had received. One of the Justices asked Warren why he had called the conference. "I thought that you should know all that I know about the matter," the Chief replied and adjourned the conference.

Warren brought no other pressure on Fortas. But only because he did not have to. Fortas relied on two principal advisers, William O. Douglas and Clark Clifford. Douglas had been lecturing in Brazil when the *Life* article had appeared. As soon as he returned, he sat up with Fortas two nights discussing the situation. Douglas urged Fortas to fight it out and not to resign. But Clifford persuaded him to step down and Fortas sent a letter of resignation to the President on May 13, effective the next day, as well as a letter of explanation to the Chief Justice.[71]

Had Fortas tried to heed Douglas' advice, there was no doubt that Warren would have done what he could to induce Fortas to leave the Court. The Chief had strict standards of right and wrong and looked upon Fortas' conduct as a "blot" on the Court.[72] "He can't stay," Warren told his executive secretary, Mrs. McHugh, at the time. As Richard Nixon later wrote, Warren felt that the contract with Wolfson's foundation "represented a serious threat to the reputation of the Court; he was convinced that Fortas had no choice but to step down."[73]

The Fortas imbroglio, as well as a milder controversy over the receipt by Douglas of a $12,000 a year fee from a foundation financed in large part by income from gambling, led Warren to urge restrictions on the outside activities of federal judges. Largely under the Chief's pressure, the Judicial Conference adopted strict rules of judicial conduct, including a code of ethics, rules requiring broad financial disclosure, and restraints on income from off-the-bench activities. The new rules did not apply to the Supreme Court, which alone has the power to prescribe rules for its members. Warren had told the Conference that the severe curbs on the lower federal judges would help him persuade the Supreme Court to go along with similar restrictions.[74]

It was reported in the press that the new rules were resented by many federal judges, who felt that the Chief had rammed them through the Judicial Conference.[75] But even a strong Chief Justice such as Warren could not accomplish the same in the Supreme Court, where the Chief is only the first among equals. At the June 13, 1969, conference, Warren moved that the Court formally adopt rules of conduct similar to those that now applied to the lower federal courts. The majority rejected the Chief's proposal and the conference decided to defer further consideration until the new 1969 Term—i.e., after Warren's retirement had finally taken effect. Under the new Chief Justice, the Brethren did nothing about the matter. Indeed, without Warren there, the Judicial Conference itself felt free, at the beginning of November, to suspend the new rules for lower court judges as too strict.[76]

The retiring Chief Justice had no illusions about the effect Richard Nixon's presidency could have upon the Court. Even more than Senator Goldwater in 1964, Nixon had made the Warren Court a major issue in the 1968 election. In fact, as one observer put it, Nixon had run against Warren and his Court as much as he had run against his

Democratic opponent, Senator Hubert H. Humphrey.[77] He accused the Court of "seriously weakening the peace forces and strengthening the criminal forces in our society." One of Nixon's principal pledges was that his Court appointees would be different. He promised to appoint only "strict constructionists," who would "interpret, not try to make laws."[78]

"During the entire campaign," Warren later wrote, "the principal issue was 'law and order.' It merely was an exercise in the rhetoric of accusation and recrimination which just increased divisiveness throughout the nation."[79] Now the architect of the anti-Court campaign was to choose the new Chief Justice, as well as a replacement for Fortas. Warren knew that Nixon would use the opportunity to try to remold the Court in his own, rather than in Warren's, image.

The Chief Justice was, however, far from pessimistic about the enduring impact of the Warren Court's work. He told a former law clerk that, though he thought that Nixon would appoint Justices as different in their views from Warren as possible, he remained philosophical about the matter. The Chief said that "the pendulum swings back and forth" and that, in due course, it would swing back the other way. Even with the Nixon appointments, he did not feel that the work of the Warren Court was going to be undermined.

During Warren's last months in office, both the Chief Justice and the President were careful to observe the outward amenities. Nixon not only formally requested Warren to administer the inaugural oath, but he also had the Chief swear in the new Cabinet and some eighty-one members of the White House staff.[80] Then, on April 23, 1969, the President honored the retiring Chief Justice and the Warren family at a sumptuous White House dinner. The guest list included the entire Court, most of the Cabinet, and virtually everyone who was anybody in Washington.

With what one writer terms "decorous insincerity,"[81] Nixon warmly toasted the Chief Justice and his years of distinguished public service. Warren replied in kind, stressing his appreciation of the President's warmth and saying, "I approach retirement with no malice in my heart toward anyone."

Public attention was now focused on selection of the new Chief Justice. Most observers were surprised by President Nixon's choice— Judge Warren E. Burger of the U.S. Court of Appeals for the District of Columbia. But not Warren. A book on the Supreme Court begins with a dramatic account of how, months before Burger's appointment, Warren suggested, during lunch with his law clerks, that they each write down on a piece of paper who they thought Nixon's nominee would be. The choices were sealed in an envelope. Warren had written, "Warren E. Burger" as the man Nixon would appoint.[82]

Warren's 1968 Term law clerks do not recall any such incident. They do, however, remember discussions with the Chief over who his successor would be. Warren indicated that he considered Burger at the top of the list of probable choices. He felt confirmed in this belief when he saw that Burger was the only lower court judge invited to the White House dinner in the retiring Chief Justice's honor.

On May 19, 1969, Nixon announced that he was, indeed, naming Burger as the new Chief Justice. Warren had not been consulted and had been informed "as a courtesy" only a few hours before the announcement. Eighteen days after the President had nominated him, Burger was confirmed overwhelmingly by the Senate.

June 23, 1969, was the final day of the term and Warren's last day as Chief Justice. Before the Court day began at 10 A.M., the Presidential Lincoln arrived at the basement entrance. Nixon got out and was escorted to the courtroom, where he sat silently for eighteen minutes, while the Warren Court announced its three final decisions. The Chief Justice then recognized the President. Clad in cutaway coat and striped trousers, which appeared ill-fitting on him no matter how carefully tailored, Nixon moved to the lawyer's lectern facing the long mahogany bench. This was his third appearance before the Brethren (the first two had been his 1965 and 1966 arguments in *Time, Inc. v. Hill*,[83] discussed in chapter 15) and the first time that a President had addressed the Court.

Nixon referred to his earlier appearances and said, looking back on them, "I can say Mr. Chief Justice, that there is only one ordeal which is more challenging than a presidential press conference and that is to appear before the Supreme Court." The remainder of the President's seven-minute talk was devoted to a laudatory review of Warren's career, which concluded, "this Nation owes a debt of gratitude to the Chief Justice of the United States for his example."[84]

The Chief Justice thanked the President for his "most generous" words, which "are greatly appreciated, I assure you." Warren next read Nixon a virtual lecture on the Court and its place in the constitutional order. He stressed the theme of continuity. "I might point out to you, because you might not have looked into the matter that it is a continuing body. . . . the Court develops consistently the eternal principles of our Constitution." The implication was that the Court and the principles laid down during his tenure would endure even Nixon's Presidency. "We serve only the public interest as we see it, guided only by the Constitution and our own consciences." So long as the Court was "manned by men . . . like those who sit today," the Chief had no fears. "So I leave in a happy vein, Mr. President, and I wish my successor all the happiness and success."[85]

The retiring Chief Justice then administered the oath of office to his successor. Everyone rose. Warren turned to the audience and said, "I present the new Chief Justice of the United States."

After the ceremony, Warren and Burger went into the conference room, where the clerk had left the necessary papers recording administration of the oath for their signatures. They were alone in the room, and Burger recalls that Warren had tears in his eyes as he commented that the President's remarks were very warm and generous.

At Warren's retirement, the controversy over him appeared to have died down. Even his long-term critics held their fire in the outpouring of encomia that greeted the Chief's stepping down. The high point came on June 29, with a national tribute on the steps of the Lincoln Memorial. The principal panegyrist was former Justice Arthur J. Goldberg, who hailed Warren as a "great emancipator of the law" whose achievement would long outlive any temporary criticism.[86] President Nixon had turned down an invitation to participate in the tribute. That was not unusual for Warren's political opponents. The year before California Governor Ronald Reagan had declined to attend the dedication of the Earl Warren Legal Center at Berkeley.[87]

Warren himself held a final news conference just after his successor had been sworn in. In reply to a reporter, the ex-Chief Justice said that he hoped that the decisions of the Warren Court would endure, "but I would not predict." He hoped his Court would be remembered as "the People's Court."

A reporter asked him to describe the major frustration of his Court years. Warren paused for a long moment, then broke into a wide smile, and replied that he could not think of any. "It has not been a frustrating experience," he said.[88]

Warren's years as the retired Chief Justice can be summarized briefly. Though the California press reported that he was househunting in the San Francisco area or Sacramento, he decided to retain his Washington apartment and remain in the capital. He was given a suite of chambers facing the Capitol and he appreciated the assignment by the new Chief Justice. He also had one law clerk to help him with his work.

But the work now was largely make-work. Warren would attend ceremonies and conferences, give speeches, and travel, often on behalf of the World Peace through Law movement. For one who had been active in government and the Court for his whole adult life, going through the motions of useful activity was scarcely an adequate substitute for the real thing. A former law clerk recalls that, one day, he came into the retired Chief's chambers and found him reading the *Congressional Record*. Warren laughed when he saw the visitor and said, "I'm not reading it all that carefully."

The one thing Warren seemed to enjoy in his retirement schedule was his talks to college and law students. He had an amazing empathy with young people. He was, it was well said, a hero to a generation that had lost the capacity for having heroes. To the young, he represented a person who had worked positively within the system and had succeeded in effecting changes for the good.

Warren was proud of his reputation with students. Once, after he had delivered a talk to hundreds of students in the basement lounge of Notre Dame Law School, he was responding to questions. A student in the back of the packed lounge began a question, "Some people have suggested that you'll go down in history with Marshall as one of the two greatest Chief Justices." Warren smiled broadly and interrupted, "Could you say that again—a little louder please? I'm having a little trouble hearing."[89]

The only controversial issue on which the retired Chief Justice took a public stance was the recommendation for a new court of appeals to screen out the cases which the Supreme Court would consider.

From the time of his appointment, Chief Justice Burger expressed concern over the Supreme Court's growing caseload. In mid-1971, Burger appointed a seven-member blue-ribbon committee, headed by Professor Paul A. Freund, to study the problem. On December 19, 1972, the Freund Committee recommended creation of a new National Court of Appeals to "screen all petitions for review now filed in the Supreme Court."[90] The proposed court was to exercise the Supreme Court's certiorari jurisdiction to determine which cases would be considered by the highest tribunal.

Warren reacted with uncharacteristic vehemence to the Freund Committee recommendation. After he read a November 5, 1972, article in the *Washington Star* describing the new court the committee would propose, Warren sent a letter to Peter D. Ehrenhaft, the one former Warren law clerk on the Freund panel. "To put it mildly," Warren wrote, "I was shocked to read in the Sunday Star that you and the committee of which you are a member are expected to advance a scuttling of the Supreme Court. I can think of few things which could throttle the Court to a greater extent in its avowed purpose of establishing 'Equal Justice under Law.' "[91]

On the same day Warren sent a memorandum to his former law clerks, enclosing copies of both the *Star* article and his letter to Ehrenhaft. The memo declared, "I consider this to be of tremendous importance—as a matter of fact, as important as the 50-member Court of the Union which was proposed as a Constitutional Amendment some years ago but aborted because of its absurdity. In my opinion, this is the same thing in a different disguise."

Warren's memo noted that, though "it is reported that one of my law clerks is involved in the recommendation, I want all of you to know that it was not through any collaboration with me or in any respect with my concurrence."[92]

Ehrenhaft wrote a conciliatory letter to the retired Chief, saying that neither he nor the other committee members "wants or proposes to scuttle" the Court.[93] "What we have tried to do is come up with some suggestions to relieve the Justices of what most of them feel is an increasingly oppressive work load." After the Freund Committee Report was published, Ehrenhaft sent a memorandum to the Warren law clerks that stated, "I hope that after reading the Report you will realize that our Group hoped only to aid the Court in discharging its historic role. No denigration of the institution was intended; no retreat from the principles of justice for all it so forcefully developed while we worked with the Chief was even considered."[94]

But Warren was not appeased. He looked on the Freund Report as a direct attack on the work of the Warren Court. His memo to his law clerks had asserted, "The news article is sketchy, but to me gives evidence of the real purpose behind it." To Warren, the proposal was but the latest version of the continuing efforts to curb the Supreme Court.

Warren had also been offended by the procedure adopted by the Freund panel. He objected to what he termed the "highly secretive" nature of the committee's work, citing its failure to hold public hearings. In particular, Warren felt affronted by the committee's failure to meet with him. The group did personally spend a day with each of the sitting Justices. But it decided that individual members only would meet with former Justices. Ehrenhaft was sent to talk to Warren and he spent a morning discussing the committee's work with the retired Chief. Understandably, Warren was miffed at the committee's treatment. To him it was a direct insult that denigrated the office he had held.

Warren condemned the Freund proposal in the bluntest public attacks delivered by him since his retirement. On May 1, 1973, the retired Chief delivered a Law Day speech that called the Freund report "naive" and "dangerous" and said that establishment of the new screening court would cause irreparable harm to the prestige, power, and functioning of the Supreme Court.[95]

Warren's opposition to the Freund proposal continued literally until the end of his life. Brennan, who saw Warren on his deathbed, recalls, "I last saw him only two hours before his death. He wouldn't talk with me about his health. He wanted an update on the status of the proposal to create a National Court of Appeals. He strongly opposed the proposal. Its adoption, he was convinced, threatened to shut the door of the Supreme Court to the poor, the friendless, the little man."[96]

Despite his resentment over the screening-court proposal, Warren's relations with his successor were not unfriendly. Warren appreciated the chambers assigned to him by the new Chief and Burger used to consult his predecessor about running the Court—often over

lunches in one or the other's chambers. Not long after Warren retired, Burger sent him a note, asking why he never joined the Brethren for lunch, writing that he and the others would welcome the
former Chief's presence. Warren replied that they might discuss
pending cases and his presence then would not be appropriate.

Toward the end of 1973 Warren came to see Burger and said that
he had not been able to arrange his annual medical examination at
Walter Reed Army Hospital. He had been informed that such services were no longer available to "retired officers." Warren, recalls
Burger, "was quite annoyed, to put it mildly." Another member of
the Warren Court says that Warren indignantly told him at lunch,
"What do you know, the bastards have kept me out of Walter Reed."

Burger states that he was no less annoyed than Warren, but immediately suggested that it was a bureaucratic error and that he would
call the Secretary of the Army. When he did, Secretary Howard H.
Callaway replied that it was obviously a mistake, since he alone had
the authority to define the people entitled to medical services. Cal-
loway later called back to advise that a routine bulletin had been
circulated stating that "retired officers" were no longer entitled to
medical examinations. The bulletin applied only to retired *military*
officers, but someone at Walter Reed had erroneously interpreted
this to include retired Justices. The Secretary said that it no more
affected Chief Justice Warren than it would a four or five-star general.

Callaway offered to call Warren and apologize. Burger suggested
that he write a letter first and make a telephone call afterwards when
the situation had cooled off. Burger was later told that the Secretary
had written his apologies to the retired Chief Justice and approved
his use of Walter Reed.

This incident was the basis for the story, published after Warren's
death, that President Nixon refused to grant authorization for the
retired Chief to be hospitalized at Walter Reed during his last illness.[97] After the Secretary of the Army's action, Warren could have
gone to the military hospital without White House permission. But
the retired Chief did not try to go to Walter Reed. His physician
there had retired a few years earlier. On the recommendation of a
California friend, Warren had been going to Dr. Oscar Mann, a private doctor affiliated with Georgetown University Hospital. When
he had to be hospitalized, he naturally went to the same hospital. If

Warren did try to get into Walter Reed, neither Dr. Mann nor the Chief's executive secretary, Mrs. McHugh, who would normally have handled the matter, was aware of it. Both assert that it was all but unthinkable that Warren would attempt to act in the matter without their knowledge.

Like Nemesis of Greek tragedy, the figure of Richard Nixon dominated Warren's last years. From the hybris of his 1972 electoral sweep, the Chief's old antagonist was sinking to his Watergate nadir. Warren saw the scandal enveloping the White House as a confirmation of all his doubts about his fellow Californian. When Nixon's so-called enemies list was made public, Warren used to joke that he had his own one-man enemy list.[98]

Warren followed the news about Watergate with an almost morbid fascination. A former law clerk remembers coming to see the retired Chief one morning during the height of the Watergate affair. Warren did not appear for an hour and his staff began to worry. They were about to call the Chief's apartment, when Warren came in and invited the visitor to his chambers. When asked whether he was feeling well in view of his late arrival, Warren grinned and said, "Oh no. That's not the problem. My problem is I get in late because I have to read everything about Watergate. I look at my watch and see it's already late. But I just can't pass any of this stuff up."

As the developing scandal began to reach into the Oval Office, Warren found it increasingly difficult to keep his views on the matter to himself. In his public speeches he began to condemn those in the Administration who had so dishonored the legal profession. In an April, 1974, address in New Orleans, he noted, "Altogether twenty-one people in and around the White House have been indicted, and sixteen of these were lawyers. . . . The inner sanctum of the White House has been tarnished, and the end of the debacle is not yet in sight."[99]

Yet Warren saw Watergate more as a vindication, than a condemnation, of the American system. He told college audiences that Watergate showed that "a humble night watchman" could start the disclosures which would ultimately unseat a President. "The great virtue of our government," he said at Morehouse College in Atlanta on May 21, 1974, "is that people can do something about it. . . . When they have made a mistake, they can rectify it."[100]

Warren had no doubt that the American people had made a mistake in electing Nixon to the highest office. Some months before he died, he expressed his feelings on the President with unusual frankness in an interview he gave to Alden Whitman of the *New York Times*.[101] The interview was to be off the record during Warren's lifetime, which accounts for the Chief's candor. Whitman spent an entire afternoon in the retired Chief Justice's chambers. Toward the end of the interview, Whitman asked the Chief what he felt about Nixon. Warren flushed and said, "Tricky is perhaps the most despicable President this nation has ever had. He was a cheat, a liar, and a crook," who had abused both the office and the people. He spoke about the terrible state the country was in because of Nixon. Whitman remarked, "You sound like a man who regrets having left."

Warren turned to his interviewer and said, "I know now. I felt the Presidency would elevate him and he would make the right choices. It didn't work out that way." Then, his face growing increasingly inflamed and his voice choking with emotion, Warren declared, "If I had ever known what was going to happen to this country and this Court, I *never* would have resigned. They would have had to carry me out of here on a plank!"[102]

In January 1974, Warren suffered a heart attack. He recovered within a week. But on March 19, he began his eighty-fifth year and his health was failing. At the end of May, he was again hospitalized. Then, on July 2, Warren was admitted to Georgetown University Hospital after a third heart attack that was to prove fatal. Warren's seventh floor room at Georgetown Hospital looked down on the Watergate apartments. And it was the scandal that started there that concerned him to the end. On Tuesday, July 9, Warren's physician reported his condition as "satisfactory." At about 5:30 that afternoon, the retired Chief was visited by Brennan, his closest associate on the Court. Brennan, more than any of the Justices, missed Warren. He used to refer to him as the "Super Chief"—a title that was soon adopted by those in the Court who were growing increasingly nostalgic about the Warren years.

Brennan found Warren alert and in good spirits. He had no idea that this would be the last time he would see the retired Chief. The next day Brennan told the Brethren of his visit and what had been said. Douglas in his *Autobiography* writes of the visit as being made by him.[103] But his account is based upon what he and the others had been told by Brennan.

When he saw Brennan, Warren was eager to talk and, above all, wanted to know what was happening in the *Nixon* case [104] then before the Court. The conference on that case had been held earlier that day and Brennan said that the Justices had decided unanimously against the President's claim that he could refuse to turn over crucial tapes to the district court.

"Thank God! Thank God! Thank God!" Warren declared with fervor. "If you don't do it this way Bill, it's the end of the country as we have known it."

Soon after Brennan left, Warren suffered a cardiac arrest. He died at 8:10 P.M., with his wife and youngest daughter at his bedside.

ABBREVIATIONS USED
IN NOTES

BOH:	Bancroft Library, University of California/Berkeley, Earl Warren Oral History Project
BRW:	Byron R. White
CEW:	Charles E. Whittaker
COH:	Benno Schmidt, Oral History Research Office, Columbia University (1977)
WOD:	William O. Douglas
EW:	Earl Warren
EW *Memoirs:*	*The Memoirs of Earl Warren* (1977)
FF:	Felix Frankfurter
FFH:	Felix Frankfurter Papers, Harvard Law School
FFLC:	Felix Frankfurter Papers, Library of Congress
FMV:	Fred M. Vinson
HHB:	Harold H. Burton
HHBD:	Harold H. Burton Diary
HHBLC:	Harold H. Burton Papers, Library of Congress
HLB:	Hugo L. Black
HLBLC:	Hugo L. Black Papers, Library of Congress
JMH:	John M. Harlan

JMHP:	John M. Harlan Papers, Mudd Manuscript Library, Princeton University
LBJ:	Lyndon B. Johnson
LH:	Learned Hand
RHJ:	Robert H. Jackson
NYT:	*New York Times*
PS:	Potter Stewart
SM:	Sherman Minton
SR:	Stanley Reed
TCC:	Tom C. Clark
TCCT:	Tom C. Clark Papers, Tarlton Law Library, University of Texas
WJB:	William J. Brennan

NOTES

1. THE NEW CHIEF JUSTICE

1. Brownell interview, BOH.
2. EW *Memoirs* 260.
3. Id. at 264.
4. Brownell interview, BOH.
5. EW *Memoirs* 269.
6. NYT, September 4, 1953, p. 1.
7. Eisenhower, *Mandate for Change 1953–1956: The White House Years* 228 (1963).
8. Id. at 227.
9. Brownell interview, BOH.
10. Ibid.
11. *NYT*, September 9, 1953, p. 25.
12. Douglas, *The Court Years 1939–1975: The Autobiography of William O. Douglas* 227 (1980).
13. Mailliard interview, BOH.
14. Brownell interview, BOH.
15. Pollack, *Earl Warren: The Judge Who Changed America* 155 (1979).
16. Brownell memorandum, BOH.
17. Brownell interview, BOH.
18. EW *Memoirs* 270.
19. Brownell interview, BOH.
20. Small interview, BOH.
21. Gerhart, *Arthur T. Vanderbilt: The Compleat Counsellor* 229–230 (1980).
22. E.g., NYT, September 29, 1953, p. 1.
23. Pollack, op. cit. supra note 15, at 157.
24. EW *Memoirs* 271.
25. Pollack, op. cit. supra note 15, at 158.
26. Weaver, *Warren: The Man, The Court, The Era* 190 (1967).

27. Gunther, *Inside U.S.A* 18, 20 (1947).

28. Stone, *Earl Warren: A Great American Story* 12 (1948).

29. EW *Memoirs* 31.

30. Id. at 31–32.

31. Id. at 30.

32. Katcher, *Earl Warren: A Political Biography* 21 (1967).

33. Discussed infra Chapter 7.

34. Earl Warren, Jr. interview, BOH.

35. Stone, op. cit. supra note 28, at 35.

36. EW *Memoirs* 72.

37. Jahnsen interview, BOH.

38. Shea interview, BOH.

39. Stone, op. cit. supra note 28, at 66.

40. Ibid.

41. Brown interview, BOH.

42. Stone, op. cit. supra note 28, at 73.

43. Powers interview, BOH.

44. Katcher, op. cit. supra note 32, at 63.

45. Weaver, op. cit. supra note 26, at 55.

46. Id. at 54, 60.

47. Id. at 54.

48. Id. at 44.

49. Stone, op. cit. supra note 28, at 65.

50. Kenny interview, Appendix I, BOH.

51. Katcher, op. cit. supra note 32, at 109.

52. Ibid.

53. Maine, *Popular Government* 243 (1886).

54. See Schwartz, *The Great Rights of Mankind: A History of the American Bill of Rights* 209–213 (1977).

55. Kenny interview, Appendix I, BOH.

56. Weaver, op. cit. supra note 26, at 149.

57. Pollack, op. cit. supra note 15, at 102.

58. McWilliams interview, BOH.

59. Weaver, op. cit. supra note 26, at 105.

60. Id. at 107.

61. Id. at 109.

62. Rostow, "Our Worst Wartime Mistake," *Harper's,* September 1945, p. 193.

63. McWilliams interview, BOH.

64. Earl Warren Papers, California State Archives.

65. Katcher, op. cit. supra note 32, at 141.

66. Clark interview, BOH.

67. McWilliams interview, BOH.

68. Weaver, op. cit. supra note 26, at 109.

69. Id. at 113.

70. Ibid.

71. Powers interview, BOH.

72. *The Great Rights* 87 (Cahn ed. 1963).

73. EW *Memoirs* 149.

74. Brown interview, BOH.

75. Ibid.

76. Weaver, op. cit. supra note 26, at 55; Pollack, op. cit. supra note 15, at 97.

77. Lewis, in 4 *The Justices of the United States Supreme Court 1789–1969*, 2728 (Friedman and Israel eds. 1969).

78. EW *Memoirs* 252.

79. Pollack, op. cit. supra note 15, at 105.

80. Weaver, op. cit. supra note 26, at 147.

81. Pollack, op. cit. supra note 15, at 105.

82. Kenny interview, BOH.

83. Mailliard interview, BOH.

84. *Time,* June 21, 1948, p. 23.

85. Small interview, BOH.

86. Earl Warren, Jr. interview, BOH.

87. Weaver, op. cit. supra note 26, at 158.

88. Brownell interview, BOH.

89. Mellon interview, BOH.

90. Ibid.

91. Eisenhower, op. cit. supra note 7, at 228.

92. See Weaver, op. cit. supra note 26, at 183.

93. Id. at 182.

94. Brown interview, BOH.

95. Ibid.

96. Earl Warren, Jr. interview, BOH.

97. FF–C. C. Burlingham, January 15, 1954. FFLC.

98. NYT, February 26, 1954, p. 18.

99. NYT, October 5, 1953, p. 1.

100. Zimmerman interview, BOH.

101. EW *Memoirs* 279.

2. THE COURT, THE BRETHREN, "AND COMPANY"

1. *Felix Frankfurter Reminisces* 86 (1960).

2. *Newsweek,* October 17, 1955, p. 36.

3. EW *Memoirs* 277.

4. RHJ–FF, August 6, 1949. FFLC.

5. 109 *Congressional Record* 19848 (1963).

6. 1 de Tocqueville, *Democracy in America* 156 (Bradley ed. 1954).

7. Quoted in Jackson, *The Supreme Court in the American System of Government* 54 (1955).

8. Ibid.

9. *2,000 Famous Legal Quotations* 197 (McNamara ed. 1967).

10. Id. at 260.

11. de Tocqueville, op. cit. supra note 6, at 290.

12. Mason, *Harlan Fiske Stone: Pillar of the Law* 406 (1956).

13. Quoted in Schwartz, *A Basic History of the U.S. Supreme Court* 172 (1968).

14. FF–HHB, January 31, 1956. FFLC.

15. FF–WJB, March 27, 1958. FFLC.

16. Woodward and Armstrong, *The Brethren: Inside the Supreme Court* 105 (1979).

17. Frankfurter, *Of Law and Men: Papers and Addresses of Felix Frankfurter* 133 (1956).

18. FF–FMV, n.d. FFLC.

19. 1 Bryce, *The American Commonwealth* 274 (1917).

20. FF–SR, April 13, 1939. FFLC.

21. Rodell, *Nine Men: A Political History of the Supreme Court from 1790 to 1955,* 284 (1955).

22. Quoted in *The Supreme Court under Earl Warren* 129 (Levy ed. 1972).

23. Dunne, *Hugo Black and the Judicial Revolution* 85 (1977).

24. Op. cit. supra note 22, at 135.

25. *The Dictionary of Biographical Quotation* 79 (Kenin and Winette eds. 1978).

26. SM–HLB, September 11, 1964. HLBLC.

27. Douglas, *Go East Young Man: The Early Years* 450 (1974).

28. Gerhart, *America's Advocate: Robert H. Jackson* 274 (1958).

29. HLB–FF, December 22, 1964.

30. FF–RHJ, January 19, 1952. FFLC.

31. FF–HHB, December 7, 1955. HHBLC.

32. FF–SR, December 21, 1954. FFLC.

33. FF–JMH, n.d. JMHP.

34. FF–JMH, February 22, 1956. FFH.

35. Lash, *From the Diaries of Felix Frankfurter* 283 (1974).

36. FF–JMH, May 19, 1961. FFLC.

37. FFLC (in Minton 1949–1954 folder).

38. Hugo Black, Jr., *My Father: A Remembrance* 234 (1975).

39. Gerhart, op. cit. supra note 28, at 260.

40. FF–C. C. Burlingham, October 27, 1954. FFLC.

41. RHJ–FF, June 19, 1946. FFH.

42. HHBD.

43. RHJ–FF, September 20, 195[?]. FFLC.

44. HLB–Jerome Cooper, 1946. *"Sincerely your friend": Letters of Mr. Justice Hugo L. Black to Jerome A. Cooper* (n.d.).

45. *"With Phil Kurland,"* n.d. FFLC.

46. Concurring, in Brown v. Allen, 344 U.S. 443, 540 (1953).

47. RHJ–FF, July 30, 1954. FFLC.

48. Lash, op. cit. supra note 35, at 173.

49. RHJ–FF, September 20, 1950. FFH.

50. FFLC.

51. FFLC.

52. Frankfurter, op. cit. supra note 17, at 133.

53. *Among Friends: Personal Letters of Dean Acheson* 280 (McLellan and Acheson eds. 1980).

54. Quoted in op. cit. supra note 22, at 127.

55. Quoted in Freedman, *Roosevelt and Frankfurter: Their Correspondence 1928–1945*, 8 (1967).

56. Op. cit. supra note 22, at 125.

57. FF–Charles Warren, April 28, 1943. FFLC.

58. FF–Joseph C. Hutcheson, April 25, 1938. FFLC.

59. FF–JMH, February 22, 1956. FFH.

60. FF–CEW, April 9, 1959. FFLC.

61. FF–RHJ, January 29, 1953. FFH.

62. Acheson, *Present at the Creation* 62 (1969).

63. FF–Charles Wyzanski, March 10, 1958. FFLC.

64. May 29, 1954. FFLC.

65. E.g., op. cit. supra note 22, at 126.

66. Warren, Address to State Bar of California, 109 *Congressional Record* 19849 (1963).

67. FF–HLB, n.d. HLBLC.

68. FF–RHJ, February 23, 1944. FFH.

69. Op. cit. supra note 22, at 126.

70. Lash, op. cit. supra note 35, at 264.

71. Frankfurter, "The Early Writings of O. W. Holmes, Jr.," 44 Harv. L. Rev. 717, 724 (1931).

72. Truax v. Corrigan, 257 U.S. 312, 344 (1921).

73. 1 *Holmes–Pollock Letters: The Correspondence of Mr. Justice Holmes and Sir Frederick Pollock, 1874–1932*, 167 (de Wolfe ed. 1961).

74. Compare Cardozo, *The Nature of the Judicial Process* 79 (1921).

75. HLB–Fred Rodell, September 5, 1962. HLBLC.

76. FF–Alexander Bickel, November 14, 1962. FFLC.

77. FF–SR, January 18, 1950. FFLC.

78. FF–CEW, April 3, 1961. FFH.

79. FF–HLB, November 13, 1943. FFH.

80. Lash, op. cit. supra note 35, at 85.

81. SR–FF, May 28, 1956. FFH.

82. 310 U.S. 586 (1940).

83. FF–Harlan F. Stone, May 27, 1940. FFH.

84. 319 U.S. 624 (1943).

85. Id. at 646.

86. Loc. cit. supra note 83.

87. Ibid.

88. Loc. cit. supra note 75.

89. FF–RHJ, December 1, 1949. FFLC.

90. FF–HLB, November 13, 1943. FFH.

91. FF–HLB, December 15, 1939. FFH.

92. Ibid.

93. Interstate Commerce Commission v. Inland Waterways Corp., 319 U.S. 671, 691 (1943).

94. FFH.

95. "Justice Black and First Amendment 'Absolutes:' A Public Interview," 37 N.Y.U. L. Rev. 549, 553 (1962).

96. Id. at 559.

97. FF–SR and HHB, February 23, 1955. FFH.

98. FF–EW, May 27, 1957. JMHP.

99. FF–JMH, May 19, 1961. FFH.

100. FF–LH, November 7, 1954, quoted in Hirsch, *The Enigma of Felix Frankfurter* 182 (1981).

101. Schenck v. United States, 249 U.S. 47, 52 (1919).

102. Supra note 95, at 558.

103. Dissenting, in Cox v. Louisiana, 379 U.S. 559, 578 (1965).

104. "Circulated October 25, 1960." FFH.

105. Dissenting, in Drivers Union v. Meadowmoor Co., 312 U.S. 287, 301 (1941).

106. Id. at 302.

107. Freedman, op. cit. supra note 55, at 701.

108. Compare Lash, op. cit. supra note 35, at 87.

109. Fortas, in *The Fourteenth Amendment Centennial Volume* 34 (Schwartz ed. 1970).

110. Holmes, "The Path of the Law," 10 Harv. L. Rev. 457, 469 (1897).

111. Dunne, op. cit. supra note 23, at 414.

112. 5 Burke, *Works* 67 (rev. ed. 1865).

113. Holmes, supra note 110, at 477.

114. Black, op. cit. supra note 38, at 239.

115. HLB–Alan Washburn, December 17, 1958. HLBLC.

116. WOD–HLB, September 12, 1953. HLBLC.

117. WOD–HLB, June 22, 1941. HLBLC.

118. Mercedes Douglas–HLB, June 29. HLBLC.

119. Rodell, op. cit. supra note 21, at 275.

120. FF–JMH, April 26, 1957. FFLC.

121. No. 844, Ringhiser v. Chesapeake & Ohio R. Co., Clark dissent, June 1957. FFLC.

122. LH–FF, March 28, 1956. FFLC.

123. FF–LH, September 13, 1958. FFLC.

124. Frankfurter, Greetings, October 5, 1957. FFH.

125. FF–LH, November 7, 1954. Quoted in Hirsch, *The Enigma of Felix Frankfurter* 182(1981).

126. FF–JMH, July 26, 1958. JMHP.

127. Lash, op. cit. supra note 35, at 176.

128. Douglas, op. cit. supra note 27, at 327.

129. Ibid.

130. WOD, Memorandum to Mr. Justice Frankfurter, May 29, 1954. HLBLC.

131. Lash, op. cit. supra note 35, at 78.

132. Douglas, Memorandum to the Conference, October 23, 1961. HLBLC.

133. Lash, op. cit. supra note 35, at 77.

134. WOD–FF, July 2, 1940. HLBLC.

135. Lash, op. cit. supra note 35, at 155.

136. Owen J. Roberts–FF, February 22, 1954. FFLC.

137. See Truman, 2 *Memoirs by Harry S. Truman: Years of Trial and Hope* 190 (1956).

138. Id. at 189.

139. Douglas, *The Court Years 1939–1975: The Autobiography of William O. Douglas* 288 (1980).

140. WOD–HLB, July 23. No year is given, but from its context it appears to have been written in 1941. HLBLC.

141. WOD–HLB, September 8, 1941. HLBLC.

142. Ibid.

143. SR–FF, nd. FFLC.

144. SR–FF, nd. FFLC.

145. Rodell, op. cit. supra note 21, at 310.

146. Berry, *Stability, Security, and Continuity: Mr. Justice Burton and Decision-Making in the Supreme Court 1945—1958,* vii (1978).

147. Id. at 89.

148. HHB–FF, April 29, 1964. FFH.

149. TCC–EW, October 24, 1955. TCCT.

150. JMH–TCC, Postcard, July 29, 1959. TCCT.

151. Miller, *Plain Speaking* 225–226 (1974).

152. Rodell, op. cit. supra note 21, at 312.

153. FF–C.C. Burlingham, September 8, 1956. FFLC.

154. Radio Corporation of America v. United States, 341 U.S. 412, 421 (1951).

155. SM–FF, May 25, 1951. FFLC.

156. NYT, April 21, 1962, p. 17.

157. Brennan, Address at Dean's Day, N.Y.U. Law School (1979).

158. Woodward and Armstrong, op. cit. supra note 16, passim.

159. *U.S. News & World Report,* December 13, 1957, p. 74.

160. Quoted in Clark, "Internal Operation of the United States Supreme Court," 43 J. Am. Jud. Soc. 45, 48 (1959).

161. NYT, May 1, 1958, p. 27.

162. Bickel, NYT Magazine, April 17, 1958, p. 16.

163. Douglas, op. cit. supra note 139, at 173.

164. FF–Paul, Mort, n.d., FFH.

165. Frankfurter, "Memorandum on the 'Incorporation' of the Bill of Rights into the Due Process Clause of the Fourteenth Amendment," 78 Harv. L. Rev. 746 (1965).

166. 369 U.S. 186 (1962).

167. 364 U.S. 206 (1960).

168. FFLC.

169. St. Germain, *Doctor and Student* (1532).

170. FF–Tony [Amsterdam], n.d. FFH.

171. No. 121, Paul Egan v. City of Aurora. FFH.

172. FF—JMH, March 26, 1957. FFLC.

173. FF—JMH, March 13, 1962. JMHP.

174. Woodward and Armstrong, op. cit. supra note 16, at 10.

175. FF—SM, September 19, 1955. FFH.

176. Douglas, op. cit. supra note 139, at 181.

177. *Time,* June 5, 1961, p. 17.

178. [WOD–HLB], June 17, 1963, HLBLC.

179. COH.

180. NYT, July 5, 1959, p. 33.

181. 372 U.S. 335 (1963).

182. Woodward and Armstrong, op. cit. supra note 16, at 33.

183. FF–PS, April 29, 1960. FFLC.

184. Memorandum of Mr. Justice Frankfurter on In Forma Pauperis Petitions, November 1, 1954. FFH.

185. Op. cit., supra note 1, at 249.

186. Woodward and Armstrong, op. cit. supra note 16, at 34–35.

3. WARREN AND THE BROWN CASE

1. Brown v. Board of Education, 347 U.S. 483 (1954).

2. FF–SR, May 20, 1954, FFH.

3. Quoted in Kluger, *Simple Justice: The History of Brown v. Board of Education and Black America's Struggle for Equality* 614 (1976).

4. Lash, *From the Diaries of Felix Frankfurter* 270 (1974).

5. Id. at 274.

6. Philip Elman–FF, September 3. FFLC.

7. Rodell, *Nine Men: A Political History of the Supreme Court from 1790 to 1955,* 311 (1955).

8. Kluger, op. cit. supra note 3, at 585.

9. 163 U.S. 537 (1896).

10. HHBLC.

11. Compare Kluger, op. cit. supra note 3, at 590.

12. Id. at 597.

13. Francis v. Resweber, 329 U.S. 459, 471 (1947).

14. FF–JMH, 1957. FFLC.

15. Kluger, op. cit. supra note 3, at 601.

16. FFLC. Kluger, op. cit. supra note 3, at 684.

17. FFH.

18. Ibid. This is an earlier draft than that quoted in Kluger, op. cit. supra note 3, at 685.

19. Loc. cit. supra note 2.

20. According to Burton, the vote would have been 6–3. See Kluger, op. cit. supra note 3, at 614. According to Douglas, the vote would have been 5–4 in favor of segregated schools. Douglas, *The Court Years 1939–1975: The Autobiography of William O. Douglas* 113 (1980).

21. HHBD, December 12, 1952.

22. See Kluger, op. cit. supra note 3, at 614.

23. Ibid.

24. FFLC.

25. Brown v. Board of Education, 345 U.S. 972 (1953).

26. FF–LH, July 21, 1954. FFLC. Kluger, op. cit. supra note 3, at 603, erroneously says this letter was written two years later.

27. HLBLC.

28. The May 29 conference reconstruction is based on sketchy Frankfurter notes which have not previously been used. FFH.

29. FF–TC, June 4, 1953. FFLC.

30. Loc. cit. supra note 26.

31. FF–Chief [Justice Vinson], June 8, 1953. FFLC.

32. June 13, 1953. HHBLC.

33. Loc. cit. supra note 31.

34. Philip Elman–FF, July 15, 1953. FFLC.

35. FF–HLB, August 8, 1953. HLBLC.

36. HHBD, May 8, 1954.

37. Briggs v. Elliott, Transcript of argument, p. 38 (December 7, 1953).

38. Gebhart v. Belton, Transcript of argument, p. 21 (December 9, 1953).

39. Brown v. Board of Education, Transcript of argument, p. 18 (December 8, 1953).

40. There are detailed notes on the conference by Burton, HHBLC, as well as sketchy ones by Frankfurter, FFLC. Quotations are from these notes.

41. Pollack, *Earl Warren: The Judge Who Changed America* 174 (1979).

42. FF, Memorandum for the Conference, September 16, 1955. FFH.

43. FF, Memorandum, September 29, 1959. FFH.

44. FF, Memorandum for the Conference, n.d. FFH.

45. 347 U.S. at 489.

46. According to Douglas, op. cit. supra note 20, at 114, FF spoke in favor of Plessy at the conference. This statement must be considered inaccurate from what we know of FF's views.

47. FF, Memorandum, September 20, 1959. FFH.

48. Kluger, op. cit. supra note 3, at 683.

49. HHBD, December 17, 1953.

50. Ulmer, "Earl Warren and the Brown Decision," 33 J. of Politics 689, 698 (1971).

51. FF, Memorandum, January 15, 1954. FFLC.

52. FFH. These notes have not been used by other writers on the Brown case.

53. EW Memoirs 285.

54. Kluger, op. cit. supra note 3, at 692.

55. Id. at 698.

56. Ibid. The clerk in question confirms this statement.

57. FF–LH, February 13, 1958. FFLC.

58. Harbaugh, *Lawyer's Lawyer: The Life of John W. Davis* 517 (1973).

59. See Kluger, op. cit. supra note 3, at 696.

60. Pollack, op. cit. supra note 41, at 174–175.

61. Charles Wyzanski–author, December 6, 1979.

62. FF–JMH, November 6, 1956. FFLC.

63. EW *Memoirs* 285.

64. FF, "Dear Brethren," January 15, 1954. HHBLC.

65. Kluger, op. cit. supra note 3, at 694.

66. EW Memoirs 285.
67. HHBD, April 20, 1954.
68. SR–FF, May 21, 1954. FFH.
69. EW, Memorandum on the State Cases, n.d. HHBLC.
70. FF, written notes. FFH.
71. Patterson interview, BOH.
72. EW, To the Members of the Court, May 7, 1954. TCCT.
73. HHB copy. HHBLC.
74. FF copy. FFH.
75. TCC copy. TCCT.
76. Kluger, op. cit., supra note 3, at 697.
77. 347 U.S. 497 (1954).
78. Loc. cit. supra note 72.
79. EW, Memorandum on the District of Columbia Case, n.d. TCCT.
80. 262 U.S. 390 (1923).
81. 281 U.S. 370 (1925).
82. See Hutchinson, "Unanimity and Desegregation: Decision-making in the Supreme Court, 1948–1958," 68 Geo. L. J. 1, 48 (1979).
83. Dissenting, in Griswold v. Connecticut, 381 U.S. 479, 516 (1965).
84. HHBLC.
85. TCCT.
86. HHBD, May 8, 1954.
87. Ibid.
88. SR–FF, May 21, 1954. FFH.
89. See Kluger, op. cit. supra note 3, at 697.
90. HHBD, May 12, 1954.
91. HHBD, May 15, 1954.
92. EW *Memoirs* 3.
93. Id. at 2.
94. Id. at 286.
95. See Kluger, op. cit. supra note 3, at 701.
96. 347 U.S. 15 492.
97. Ibid.
98. Id. at 493.
99. Ibid.
100. Ibid.
101. Id. at 494.
102. Id. at 494–495.
103. Id. at 494.
104. Id. at 495.
105. EW *Memoirs* 3.
106. Kluger, op. cit. supra note 3, at 707.
107. 347 U.S. at 495.
108. Ibid.
109. Ibid.
110. NYT, May 18, 1954, quoted in Kluger, op. cit. supra note 3, at 113.

111. Supra note 77.

112. 347 U.S. at 500.

113. Ibid.

114. EW *Memoirs* 3.

115. NYT, May 18, 1954, quoted in Kluger, op. cit. supra note 3, at 713.

116. EW *Memoirs* 4.

117. Scudder interview, BOH.

118. Kluger, op. cit. supra note 3, at 709.

119. NYT, May 18, 1954, quoted in Kluger, op. cit. supra note 3, at 711.

120. 347 U.S. at 494, n. 11.

121. Argument: The Oral Argument before the Supreme Court in Brown v. Board of Education of Topeka, 1952–55, XXXVII (Friedman ed. 1969).

122. Kluger, op. cit. supra note 3, at 706.

123. Ibid.

124. Ibid.

125. EW, Memorandum on the State Cases, May 7, 1954. HHBLC.

126. (1952). 347 U.S. at 494, n. 11.

127. HHBLC.

128. McCulloch v. Maryland, 4 Wheat. 315, 407 (U.S. 1819).

129. Compare Black, "The Lawfulness of the Segregation Decisions," 69 Yale L. J. 421, 429 (1960).

130. Goldberg, "Equality and Governmental Action," 39 N.Y.U. L. Rev. 205 (1964).

131. Quoted in Coit, *John C. Calhoun* 146 (1950).

132. EW *Memoirs* 302.

133. NYT, June 25, 1956, p. 11.

134. Kluger, op. cit. supra note 3, at 710.

135. NYT, May 18, 1954, p. 19.

136. Kluger, op. cit. supra note 3, at 711.

137. NYT, May 18, 1954, p. 19.

138. EW–FF, May 4, 1954. FFH.

139. FF–EW, August 18, 1954. FFLC.

140. EW–FF, August 6, 1954. FFLC.

141. FF–EW, August, 17, 1954. FFH.

142. EW–FF, September 27, 1954. FFLC.

143. EW–FF, August 6, 1954. FFLC.

144. NYT, May 18, 1954, p. 19.

145. Id. at 18.

146. FF–EW, July 21, 1954. FFLC.

147. EW–FF, August 6, 1954. FFLC.

148. Lewis, *Portrait of a Decade: The Second American Revolution* 29 (1964).

149. For a toned-down version of this incident see EW *Memoirs* 291.

150. Op. cit. supra note 121, at 353.

151. Id. at 527.

152. Id. at 412–413.

153. Kluger, op. cit. supra note 3, at 732.

154. Op. cit. supra note 121, at 414.

155. Kluger, op. cit. supra note 3, at 752.

156. Op. cit. supra note 121, at 419.

157. Id. at 423.

158. Kluger, op. cit. supra note 3, at 736.

159. FF–EW, July 5, 1954. FFH.

160. There are copies in FFLC and HHBLC.

161. FF–"Dear Brethren," April 14, 1955. FFLC.

162. FF, Memorandum on the Segregation Decree, April 14, 1955. FFLC.

163. HHB, Memorandum, n.d. HHBLC.

164. JMH, Memorandum for the Conference, Hood v. Board of Trustees, October, 1956. FFH.

165. Notes of the April 16 conference are in HHBLC and FFLC.

166. HHBD, May 11, 1955.

167. EW, Memorandum for the Conference, May 26, 1955. HHBLC.

168. See Hutchinson, op. cit. supra note 82, at 56.

169. Brown v. Board of Education, 349 U.S. 294, 298 (1955).

170. Id. at 299.

171. Id. at 300.

172. Id. at 300–301.

173. Id. at 301.

174. Ibid.

175. FF—Mr. Hennessy, September 8, 1958. FFLC.

176. FF—Mark de Wolfe Howe, May 5, 1958. FFLC.

177. FF—Paul A. Freund, July 22, 1958. FFLC.

178. FF, "Dear Brethren," January 15, 1954. HHBLC.

179. FFLC.

180. The FF drafts are in FFLC and FFH.

181. FF–Mark de Wolfe Howe, May 5, 1958. FFLC.

182. Kluger, op. cit. supra note 3, at 744.

183. Hugo Black, Jr., *My Father: A Remembrance* 209 (1975).

184. Morison, *The Oxford History of the American People* 1086 (1965).

185. See Schwartz, *A Basic History of the U.S. Supreme Court* 153 (1968).

186. EW *Memoirs* 211.

187. Ibid.

188. Kluger, op. cit. supra note 3, at 753.

189. NYT, September 13, 1958, p. 8.

190. EW *Memoirs* 292.

191. Katcher, *Earl Warren: A Political Biography* 401 (1967).

192. See Moody, 2 Hastings Const. LQ. 16 (1975).

193. Supra note 77.

194. 347 U.S. at 500.

195. Dawson v. Mayor, 220 F. 2d 386 (4th Cir. 1955).

196. Mayor v. Dawson, 350 U.S. 877 (1955).

197. Holmes v. Atlanta, 350 U.S. 879 (1955).

198. Gayle v. Browder, 352 U.S. 903 (1956).

199. Johnson v. Virginia, 373 U.S. 61 (1963).

200. New Orleans Park Improvement Assn. v. Detiege, 358 U.S. 54 (1958).

201. Loc. cit. supra note 198.

202. Watson v. Memphis, 373 U.S. 526 (1963).

203. Burton v. Wilmington Parking Authority, 365 U.S. 715 (1961).

204. Johnson v. Virginia, 373 U.S. 61, 62 (1963).

205. Schubert, *The Judicial Mind* 229 (1965).

206. See Pollack, op. cit. supra note 41, at 170.

4. 1953–1954 TERMS: FEELING HIS WAY

1. NYT, April 3, 1954, p. 9.

2. Lash, *From the Diaries of Felix Frankfurter* 334–336 (1974).

3. NYT, July 24, 1954, p. 14.

4. FF–EW, August 20, 1954. FFH.

5. NYT, November 6, 1961, p. 28.

6. NYT, December 28, 1959, p. 11.

7. NYT, June 7, 1955, p. 32.

8. NYT, June 16, 1958, p. 15.

9. NYT, November 14, 1954, p. 20.

10. Lash, op. cit. supra note 2, at 316.

11. FF–Chief Justice [Vinson], October 1947. FFLC.

12. FF–TCC, September 20, 1956. FFLC.

13. *Newsweek,* October 17, 1955, p. 36.

14. Ibid.

15. Ibid.

16. Kluger, *Simple Justice: The History of* Brown v. Board of Education *and Black America's Struggle for Equality* 667 (1976).

17. Weaver, *Warren: The Man, The Court, the Era* 348 (1967).

18. Beytagh, "Address," 64 Cal. L. Rev. 11 (1976).

19. COH.

20. *Newsweek,* October 17, 1955, p. 36.

21. EW *Memoirs* 276.

22. EW–FF, August 6, 1954. FFLC.

23. HLBLC.

24. FF–HLB, October 8, 1953. HLBLC.

25. 346 U.S. 328 (1953).

26. Id. at 333.

27. Williams, Address, 64 Cal. L. Rev. 8 (1976).

28. 347 U.S. 128 (1954).

29. 338 U.S. 25 (1949).

30. 347 U.S. at 149.

31. FF–TCC, December 29, 1953. FFLC.

32. 342 U.S. 165 (1952).

33. TCC conference notes. TCCT.

34. People v. Dorado, 381 U.S. 937 (1965).

35. Loc. cit. supra note 33.

36. FF–HHB, February 4, 1954. HHBLC.

37. 347 U.S. at 132.

38. COH.

39. *Time,* July 4, 1969, p. 63.

40. 347 U.S. 475 (1954).

41. FF notes. FFLC.

42. 347 U.S. at 477.

43. Id. at 478.

44. TCC–EW, April 29, 1954. TCCT.

45. FF–EW, April 29, 1954. FFH.

46. 347 U.S. 610 (1954).

47. 347 U.S. 483 (1954).

48. The conference quotations are from FF notes. FFH.

49. No. 531—October Term, 1953. Alton v. Alton [April—, 1954]. FFH.

50. SR–Tom [Clark], April 29, 1954. FFH.

51. No. 531—October Term, 1953. Sonia Harrup Alton v. David Elie Alton. Memorandum by Mr. Chief Justice Warren. FFH.

52. FF–Chief [Justice Warren], May 1, 1954. FFH.

53. NYT, July 10, 1974, p. 24.

54. Lash, op. cit. supra note 2, at 274, 283.

55. Id. at 152.

56. TCCT.

57. Dissenting, in Northern Securities Co. v. United States, 193 U.S. 197, 400 (1904).

58. 346 U.S. 482 (1953).

59. 346 U.S. 427 (1953).

60. 347 U.S. 81 (1954).

61. 347 U.S. 171 (1954).

62. 346 U.S. 402 (1953).

63. Ibid.

64. FF–C. C. Burlingham, September 12, 1953. FFLC.

65. FF–Master Oliver Gates, October 29, 1953. FFLC.

66. FF–C. C. Burlingham, February 15, 1954. FFLC.

67. FF–C. C. Burlingham, August 25, 1954. FFLC.

68. FF–RHJ, April 15, 1954. FFLC.

69. Gunther, *Inside U.S.A.* 18 (1947).

70. Quoted in Kathcer, *Earl Warren: A Political Biography* 61 (1967).

71. *Time,* July 14, 1969, p. 63.

72. FF–EW, October 8, 1953. FFLC.

73. FF–EW, October 12, 1953. FFLC.

74. Frankfurter and Landis, *The Business of the Supreme Court: A Study in the Federal Judicial System* (1927).

75. FF–EW, May 24, 1956. FFLC.

76. FF–EW, January 28, 1954. FFH.

77. FF–EW, April 1, 1954. FFH.

78. FF–EW, November 27, 1953. The Warren opinion was delivered in Pereira v. United States, 347 U.S. 1 (1954).

79. FF–Chief Justice [Warren], n.d. FFH.

80. FF–EW, March 26, 1955. FFLC.

81. EW–FF, August 6, 1954. FFLC.

82. FF–Chief Justice [Warren], February 19, 1954. FFH.

83. EW *Memoirs* 344.

84. FF–EW, June 4, 1954. FFLC.

85. Handwritten note, at top of EW Commencement Address, MacMurray College, June 6, 1954. FFLC.

86. FF–EW, November 9, 1956. FFLC.

87. FF–EW, January 10, 1957. FFLC.

88. FF–EW, May 9, 1958. FFLC.

89. Notes for Moscow, 1959. FFLC.

90. Note attached to ibid, FF–Elsie [Douglas], n.d.

91. FF–EW, August 20, 1954. FFH.

92. FF–EW, July 5, 1954. FFH.

93. Katcher, op. cit. supra note 70, at 336.

94. *The Public Papers of Chief Justice Earl Warren* 232 (Christman ed. 1959).

95. Supra note 27.

96. Schubert, *The Judicial Mind* 229 (1965).

97. 347 U.S. 442 (1954).

98. Id. at 470.

99. Salsburg v. Maryland, 346 U.S. 545 (1954).

100. Pereira v. United States, 347 U.S. 1 (1954).

101. Galvan v. Press, 347 U.S. 522 (1954).

102. United States v. Harriss, 347 U.S. 612 (1954).

103. Adams v. Maryland, 347 U.S. 179 (1954).

104. 347 U.S. 222 (1954).

105. EW–FF, March 4, 1954. FFH.

106. WOD–FF, February 2, 1954. FFH.

107. WOD–FF, March 6, 1954. FFH.

108. 349 U.S. 331 (1955).

109. 23 *U.S. Law Week* 3267 (1955).

110. Id. at 3268.

111. Ibid.

112. Id at 3266; NYT, June 7, 1955, p. 32.

113. HHB conference notes. HHBLC.

114. April, 1955. FFH.

115. 349 U.S. at 338.

116. FF–Stanley [Reed], June 1, 1955. FFH.

117. HLB–WOD, n.d. HLBLC.

118. NYT, June 7, 1955, p. 32.

119. Ibid.

120. Schubert, op. cit. supra note 96, at 119.

121. Brown v. Board of Education, 347 U.S. 483 (1954).
122. 377 U.S. 533 (1964).
123. Douglas, "As Chief Justice," 60 A.B.A.J. 1232, 1233 (1974).
124. 334 U.S. 1 (1948).
125. HHB conference notes. HHBLC.
126. Civil Rights Cases, 109 U.S. 3 (1883).
127. I.e., Fair Employment Practices Commission.
128. 348 U.S. 880 (1954).
129. HHB–FF, May 5, 1955. FFH.
130. FF, Memorandum for the Conference, Re No. 28, Rice v. Sioux City Memorial Park Cemetery, Inc. FFH.
131. HLB–FF, May 4, 1955. FFH.
132. 349 U.S. 80 (1955).
133. FFLC.
134. See Rice v. Sioux City Memorial Park Cemetery, 349 U.S. 70 (1955).
135. 350 U.S. 891 (1955).
136. 163 U.S. 537 (1896).
137. Brown v. Board of Education, 347 U.S. 483 (1954).
138. Jackson v. State, 348 U.S. 888 (1954).
139. See Hutchinson, *Unanimity and Desegregation: Decision-Making in the Supreme Court, 1948–1958*, 68 Geo. L.J. 1, 62 (1979).
140. See ibid.
141. See id. at 64–65. The Memorandum of Mr. Justice Frankfurter on Naim v. Naim is in FFLC.
142. TCC, Draft Opinions, Naim v. Naim. TCCT. See Hutchinson, supra note 139, at 65.
143. FF–TCC, n.d. TCCT. See Hutchinson, supra note 139, at 65.
144. Naim v. Naim, 350 U.S. 891 (1955).
145. TCCT. See Hutchinson, supra note 139, at 65–66.
146. COH.
147. See Hutchinson, supra note 139, at 63.
148. 90 S.E. 2d 849, 850 (Va. 1956).
149. 350 U.S. 985 (1956).
150. 259 U.S. 200 (1922).
151. 346 U.S. 356 (1953).
152. Id. at 357.
153. Ibid.
154. EW, Memorandum to Justice Black, October 23, 1953. HLBLC.
155. Ibid.
156. HLBLC.
157. United States v. Shubert, 348 U.S. 222, 230 (1955).
158. HHB conference notes. HHBLC.
159. United States v. International Boxing Club, 348 U.S. 236 (1955).
160. United States v. Shubert, 348 U.S. 222 (1955).
161. 262 U.S. 271 (1922).
162. 348 U.S. at 249.

163. FF–EW, January 5, 1955. FFLC.

164. Jerome Frank–FF, February 3, 1955. FFLC.

165. 348 U.S. 296 (1955).

166. 204 F.2d 655 (4th Cir. 1953).

167. HHB conference notes. HHBLC.

168. FF, Memorandum, May 20, 1957. FFLC.

169. 349 U.S. 55 (1955).

170. HHB conference notes. HHBLC.

171. Undated and unsigned written memos in Regan file. FFH.

172. FF–EW, November 19, 1954. FFH.

173. 332 U.S. 46, 68 (1947).

174. FF–SR, January 24, 1955. FFH.

175. Enclosed with ibid. No title, n.d. FFH.

176. FF–EW, February 26, 1955. FFH.

177. Owen J. Roberts–FF, September 30, 1954. FFLC.

178. NYT, September 29, 1955, p. 20.

179. *Newsweek*, October 17, 1955, p. 36.

5. 1954–1955 TERMS: MOVING TOWARD ACTIVISM

1. *New Republic*, January 23, 1956, p. 8.

2. NYT, January 27, 1955, section IV, p. 10.

3. NYT, September 29, 1955, p. 20.

4. NYT, April 16, 1955, p. 1.

5. Katcher, *Earl Warren: A Political Biography* 341 (1967).

6. Id. at 340.

7. Ibid.

8. Ibid.

9. Nixon, *RN: The Memoirs of Richard Nixon* 167 (1978).

10. NYT, September 29, 1955, p. 20.

11. Ibid.

12. Katcher, op. cit. supra note 5, at 340.

13. Hagerty Diary, December 14, 1955. Dwight D. Eisenhower Library.

14. Ibid.

15. NYT, January 26, 1956, p. 12.

16. Id. at 13.

17. NYT, February 14, 1956, p. 18.

18. NYT, February 16, 1956, p. 28.

19. Ibid.

20. NYT, March 2, 1956, p. 14.

21. NYT, March 12, 1956, p. 1.

22. Loc. cit. supra note 13.

23. Pollack, *Earl Warren: The Judge Who Changed America* 190 (1979).

24. EW–Dwight D. Eisenhower, July 15, 1957. Dwight D. Eisenhower Library.

25. HHB Diary, July 17, 1958. HHBLC.

26. *American Mercury*, August 1958, p. 5.

27. *New Republic,* May 9, 1981, p. 30.
28. EW *Memoirs* 5.
29. Id. at 292.
30. Katcher, op. cit. supra note 5, at 401.
31. Id. at 402.
32. *Newsweek,* February 29, 1959, p. 24.
33. Ibid.
34. The letters referred to are in the Dwight D. Eisenhower Library.
35. SM–FF, October 9, 1957. FFLC.
36. Douglas, *The Court Years 1939–1975: The Autobiography of William O. Douglas* 120 (1980).
37. FF–C. C. Burlingham, November 20, 1958. FFLC.
38. 347 U.S. 128 (1954).
39. 163 U.S. 537 (1896).
40. FF–C. C. Burlingham, April 24, 1955. FFLC.
41. TCC–JMH, September 12, TCCT.
42. 349 U.S. 155 (1955).
43. 349 U.S. 190 (1955).
44. HHB conference notes. HHBLC.
45. HLB–Justices (except for SR and RHJ), April 23, 1954. HLBLC.
46. FF–HLB, April 15, 1954. HLBLC.
47. HHB conference notes. HHBLC.
48. FF–JMH, June 2, 1955. FFLC.
49. 350 U.S. 11 (1955).
50. EW *Memoirs* 6.
51. HHB and TCC conference notes. HHBLC; TCCT.
52. Ex parte Milligan, 4 Wall. 2 (U.S. 1866).
53. 354 U.S. 1 (1957).
54. FF, draft dissent, March 1955. FFH.
55. HHB conference notes. HHBLC.
56. FF–HLB, October 26, 1955. FFH.
57. Ibid.
58. 350 U.S. 497 (1956).
59. NYT, May 6, 1956, section IV, p. 10.
60. HHB conference notes. HHBLC.
61. NYT, May 12, 1956, p. 6.
62. NYT, May 18, 1956, p. 17.
63. 350 U.S. 551 (1956).
64. Regan v. New York, 349 U.S. 58 (1955).
65. HHB and TCC conference notes. HHBLC; TCCT.
66. McAuliffe v. Mayor of New Bedford, 155 Mass. 216, 220 (1892).
67. FF–EW, March 13, 1956. FFH.
68. FF–TCC, n.d. TCCT.
69. 351 U.S. 115 (1956).
70. FF conference notes. FFH.
71. FF, Memorandum for the Conference, April 4, 1956. FFLC.

72. This is shown by JMH, Memorandum for the Conference, March 7, 1956. FFH.

73. As shown by FF, memorandum, March 21, 1956. FFLC.

74. FFH.

75. FF–Justices, April 2, 1956. FFH.

76. Ibid.

77. See WOD–FF, n.d. FFH.

78. Ibid.

79. FFH.

80. TCC, Memorandum to the Conference, April 17, 1956. TCCT.

81. TCC, Memorandum for the Conference, April 19, 1956. FFH.

82. 351 U.S. at 128.

83. FFH.

84. FFH.

85. Communist Party v. Control Board, 367 U.S. 1 (1961).

86. 350 U.S. 422 (1956).

87. HLB–WOD, March 6, 1956. HLBLC.

88. No names, n.d. FFH (in Ullman file).

89. FF writing, ibid.

90. See 350 U.S. at 431.

91. Id. at 428.

92. SR–FF, February 6, 1956. FFH.

93. FF–SR, February 7, 1956. FFH.

94. 350 U.S. 356 (1956).

95. HHB conference notes. HHBLC.

96. JMH–SR, December 13, 1955. FFH.

97. FF–TCC, February 9, 1956. FFH.

98. 350 U.S. at 357.

99. Ibid.

100. 350 U.S. 920 (1955).

101. HHB and TCC conference notes. HHBLC; TCCT.

102. 350 U.S. 399 (1956).

103. TCC conference notes. TCCT.

104. 350 U.S. at 408.

105. 350 U.S. 91 (1955).

106. HHB conference notes. HHBLC.

107. 351 U.S. 12 (1956).

108. HHB conference notes. HHBLC.

109. JMH, Memorandum for the Conference, in No. 95, Griffin and Crenshaw v. Illinois, n.d. March 6, 1956. FFH.

110. HLB, Memorandum In re Mr. Justice Harlan's Memorandum in No. 95, Griffin and Crenshaw v. Illinois, n.d. FFH.

111. JMH, Memorandum for the Conference, April 6, 1956. FFH.

112. JMH–FF, April 17, 1956. FFH.

113. FF, Memorandum for the Conference, February 11, 1956. HLBLC.

114. 351 U.S. at 29.

115. 372 U.S. 335 (1963).
116. No name or date, in JMH 1956 folder. FFLC.
117. 351 U.S. 377 (1956).
118. HHB conference notes. HHBLC.
119. WOD–EW, February 27, 1956. HLBLC.
120. 350 U.S. 270 (1956).
121. TCC conference notes. TCCT.
122. FF–SR, February 14, 1956. FFH.
123. FF–SR, February 28, 1956. FFH.
124. FF–SR, February 13, 1956. FFH.
125. 350 U.S. 61 (1955).
126. FF, Memorandum, Re No. 213, October 7, 1955. FFH.
127. HHB and TCC conference notes. HHBLC; TCCT.
128. EW–FF, "received Nov. 10" [1955]. FFH.
129. 351 U.S. 513 (1956).
130. TCC conference notes. TCCT.
131. FF–JMH, December 14, 1955. FFH.
132. NYT, June 15, 1956, p. 14.
133. NYT, June 17, 1956, section IV.
134. WOD–HLB, n.d. HLBLC.
135. NYT, June 27, 1956, p. 18.
136. EW *Memoirs* 347.
137. EW–HLB, August 8, 1957. HLBLC.
138. EW–HLB, July 26, 1966. HLBLC.
139. EW *Memoirs* 374.
140. *U.S. News & World Report*, June 12, 1967, p. 14.
141. *U.S. News & World Report*, July 17, 1967, p. 8.
142. JMH–FF, July 28 [1956]. FFH.
143. FF–JMH, July 31, 1956. FFH.
144. EW–HLB, August 15, 1956. HLBLC.
145. WOD–HLB, August 24, 1956. HLBLC.
146. Katcher, op. cit. supra note 5, at 356.
147. Id. at 357.
148. Dunne, *Hugo Black and the Judicial Revolution* 335 (1977).
149. *Saturday Review*, January 9, 1957, p. 34.

6. 1956 TERM: "B. B. D. and W."

1. Stone interview, BOH.
2. HHBD, May 17, 1958. HHBLC.
3. FF–George Wharton Pepper, October 19, 1956. FFLC.
4. Pollack, *Earl Warren: The Judge Who Changed America* 194 (1979).
5. Loc. cit. supra note 3.
6. 352 U.S. 432 (1957).
7. 338 U.S. 25 (1949).
8. 342 U.S. 165 (1952).

9. Snyder v. Massachusetts, 291 U.S. 97, 105 (1934).

10. Rochin v. California, 342 U.S. at 169.

11. FF, No. 83, Rochin v. California, "FF's initial memo" written at top, n.d. FFLC.

12. 342 U.S. at 172.

13. FF–CEW, March 5, 1958. FFLC.

14. Interview, Mrs. Alan Barth.

15. 352 U.S. at 442.

16. NYT, June 14, 1957, p. 24.

17. *Time*, July 1, 1957, p. 12.

18. Ibid.

19. Katcher, *Earl Warren: A Political Biography* 350 (1967).

20. 352 U.S. 1 (1956).

21. Pollack, op. cit. supra note 4, at 186.

22. 352 U.S. at 14, 9.

23. JMH–FF, October 4, 1956. FFH.

24. FF memorandum, October 19, 1956. FFH.

25. FF, with note in FF writing, "above was sent to Reed J. on October 20, 1956." FFH.

26. 352 U.S. 187 (1956).

27. HLB–WOD, December 14, 1956. HLBLC.

28. 353 U.S. 72 (1957).

29. JMH, United States v. Shaughnessy, draft opinion. FFH.

30. Rayonier, Inc. v. United States, 352 U.S. 315 (1957).

31. FF–JMH, January 25, 1957. FFH.

32. 354 U.S. 91 (1957).

33. 196 U.S. 579 (1905).

34. FF–JMH, March 29, 1957. FFH.

35. JMH–EW, April 1, 1957. FFH.

36. FF–TCC, April 9, 1957. FFH.

37. FF–JMH, March 30, 1957. FFH.

38. EW–WJB, May 23, 1957. The case involved was Rabang v. Boyd, 353 U.S. 427 (1957).

39. 354 U.S. 393 (1957).

40. FF memorandum, No. 426–*Blackburn v. Alabama*, n.d. FFH.

41. 354 U.S. at 393.

42. 352 U.S. 445 (1957).

43. Toolson v. New York Yankees, 346 U.S. 556 (1953).

44. United States v. International Boxing Club, 348 U.S. 236 (1955).

45. FF–EW, January 5, 1955. FFLC.

46. FF–JMH (cc: WJB), January 21, 1957. FFH.

47. JMH–WJB (cc: FF), February 1, 1957. FFH.

48. 352 U.S. at 455.

49. LH–FF, February 26, 1957. FFLC.

50. 353 U.S. 373 (1957).

51. FF, Memorandum for the Conference, May 15, 1957. FFH.

52. EW–FF, May 21, 1957. FFH.

53. FF–EW, May 21, 1957. FFH.

54. FF, Memorandum for the Conference, May 21, 1957. FFH.

55. Costello v. United States, 352 U.S. 1028 (1957).

56. Eisenhower, *Mandate for Change: The White House Years* 226–230 (1963).

57. FF–Charles Wyzanski, November 22, 1954. FFLC.

58. FFH.

59. FFH.

60. FF–CEW, n.d. FFH.

61. Douglas, *The Court Years 1939–1975: The Autobiography of William O. Douglas* 173 (1980).

62. SR–FF, n.d. FFLC.

63. 354 U.S. 476, 481 (1957).

64. 352 U.S. 380 (1957).

65. 25 *U.S. Law Week* 3117 (1956).

66. HHB conference notes. HHBLC.

67. FF, Memorandum for the Brethren, Re: No. 16, Butler v. Michigan, n.d. FFH.

68. 352 U.S. at 383.

69. WJB–FF, February 19, 1957. FFH.

70. HHB conference notes. HHBLC.

71. 354 U.S. at 489.

72. Id. at 494.

73. Dissenting, in Jacobellis v. Ohio, 378 U.S. 184, 200 (1964).

74. United States v. Klaw, 350 F.2d 155, 168 (2d Cir. 1965).

75. FF–EW, April 23, 1957. FFH.

76. Pollack, op cit. supra note 4, at 355.

77. Weaver, *Warren: The Man, The Court, The Era* 273 (1967).

78. Woodward and Armstrong, *The Brethren: Inside the Supreme Court* 198 (1979).

79. Weaver, op. cit. supra note 77, at 277.

80. Ginzburg v. United States, 383 U.S. 463 (1966).

81. WOD, Memorandum to the Conference, April 6, 1967. HLBLC.

82. United States v. Du Pont, 353 U.S. 586 (1957).

83. NYT, June 9, 1967, section IV, p. 7.

84. HHB and FF conference notes. HHBLC; FFH.

85. FF–WJB, November 21, 1956. FFLC.

86. United States v. Du Pont, 366 U.S. 316 (1961).

87. Berry, *Stability, Security and Continuity: Mr. Justice Burton and Decision-Making in the Supreme Court 1945–1958*, 233 (1978).

88. FF–EW, June 3, 1957. FFH.

89. FF writing at top of ibid.

90. EW–FF, n.d. FFH.

91. NYT, June 9, 1957, section IV, p. 7.

92. JMH–FF, June 3, 1957 [date in FF's writing]. FFLC.

93. Mallory v. United States, 354 U.S. 449 (1957).

94. Jencks v. United States, 353 U.S. 657 (1957).

95. 318 U.S. 332 (1943).
96. HHB conference notes. HHBLC.
97. HHB–FF, June 17, 1957. FFH.
98. FF writing at bottom of ibid.
99. Supra note 94.
100. HHB conference notes. HHBLC.
101. 353 U.S. at 681.
102. Katcher, op. cit. supra note 19, at 364.
103. Pollack, op. cit. supra note 4, at 189.
104. WJB–FF, August 31, 1957. FFH.
105. Schware v. Bar Examiners, 353 U.S. 232 (1957).
106. Konigsberg v. State Bar, 353 U.S. 252 (1957).
107. HHB conference notes. HHBLC.
108. HLB writing on JMH draft dissent, Konigsberg v. State Bar. JMHP.
109. FF–C. C. Burlingham, August 7, 1956. FFLC.
110. SM–FF, August 8, 1957. FFLC.
111. 354 U.S. 363 (1957).
112. 25 *U.S. Law Week* 3290 (1957).
113. HHB conference notes. HHBLC.
114. Accardi v. Shaughnessy, 347 U.S. 260 (1954).
115. Yates v. United States, 354 U.S. 298 (1957).
116. HHB and FF conference notes. HHBLC; FFLC.
117. Berry, op. cit. supra note 87, at 204.
118. Weaver, op. cit. supra note 77, at 288.
119. 354 U.S. 178 (1957).
120. 354 U.S. 234 (1957).
121. HHB conference notes. HHBLC. HHB took notes for both cases, though he disqualified himself in Watkins.
122. No. 261–October Term, 1956. John T. Watkins v. United States of America. Memorandum by THE CHIEF JUSTICE. FF copy, stamped May 20, 1957, with changes and comments in FF writing. FFLC.
123. 103 U.S. 168 (1881).
124. FF–EW, May 27, 1957. JMHP.
125. EW–FF, May 27, 1957. FFLC.
126. FF–EW, May 31, 1957. JMHP.
127. 354 U.S. at 250.
128. Id. at 255.
129. SM–FF, August 6, 1957. FFLC.
130. JMH–FF, April 23, 1958. FFH.
131. FF–JMH, April 23, 1958. FFH.
132. 350 U.S. 11 (1955).
133. 354 U.S. 1 (1957).
134. HHB conference notes. HHBLC.
135. 140 U.S. 453 (1891).
136. SR, Memorandum to the Conference, May 14, 1956. FFLC.
137. FF–SR, May 15, 1956. FFLC.

138. FF–JMH, May 26, 1956. FFLC.

139. FF–EW, June 8, 1956. FFH.

140. Ibid.

141. FF, Memorandum for the Chief Justice, Mr. Justice Black, Mr. Justice Douglas, September 19, 1956. FFH.

142. WOD–FF, September 20, 1956. FFH.

143. Memorandum by Mr. Justice Black, Re: No. 701, 1955 Term, Reid v. Covert, September 17, 1956 [3rd draft written at top]. FFLC.

144. FF–JMH, Memorandum, October 9, 1956. FFLC.

145. JMH, Memorandum for the Conference, Re: Nos. 701 and 713, October 10, 1956. FFH.

146. Typed at bottom of HLB copy of ibid. HLBLC.

147. JMHP.

148. 25 *U.S. Law Week* 3249–3251 (1957).

149. HHB conference notes. HHBLC.

150. WJB–HLB, May 14, 1957. HLBLC.

151. EW–HLB, May 27, 1957. HLBLC.

152. WOD–HLB, May 9, 1957. HLBLC.

153. FF–EW, March 6, 1957. FFH.

154. FF–HLB, March 13, 1957. FFLC.

155. FF–Justices, April 1957. FFH.

156. Compare 354 U.S. at 19.

157. FF–Justices, May 20, 1957. FFLC.

158. FF, Memorandum for the Conference, June 5, 1957. FFLC.

159. SM–FF, August 6, 1957. FFLC.

160. Loc. cit. supra note 158.

161. 354 U.S. 524 (1957).

162. FF–EW, June 12, 1957. FFH.

163. EW, Memorandum for the Conference, June 19, 1957. FFH.

164. EW, Memorandum for the Conference, June 20, 1957. FFH.

165. FF, Charles E. Wilson v. William S. Girard, Memorandum to the Conference, July, 1957. FFH.

166. 354 U.S. at 530.

167. TCC–WJB, July 10, 1957. TCCT.

168. TCCT.

169. 354 U.S. at 531.

170. NYT, June 18, 1957, p. 32.

171. NYT, June 25, 1957, p. 15.

172. Pollack, op. cit. supra note 4, at 187.

173. Gordon, *Nine Men Against America: The Supreme Court and Its Attack on American Liberties* (1958).

174. Id. at 128.

175. Id. at 128–130.

176. NYT, February 23, 1957, p. 1.

177. NYT, July 8, 1957, p. 15.

178. NYT, June 25, 1957, p. 15.

179. NYT, June 27, 1957, p. 10.

180. NYT, June 18, 1957, p. 23.

181. SM–FF, August 28, 1957. FFLC.

182. JMH–FF, July 24 [1957]. FFH.

183. Lewis, "A New Lineup on the Supreme Court," *The Reporter,* August 17, 1961, pp. 42–46.

184. HLBLC.

185. Loc. cit. supra note 17.

7. THE ELEPHANT AND THE MOUSE

1. 366 U.S. 1 (1961).

2. NYT, April 25, 1961, p. 1.

3. Id. at 27.

4. See NYT, March 21, 1961, p. 18.

5. 357 U.S. 549 (1958).

6. NYT, March 21, 1961, p. 18.

7. Katcher, *Earl Warren: A Political Biography* 391 (1967).

8. Loc. cit. supra note 6.

9. *Time,* May 5, 1961, p. 17.

10. 365 U.S. 551 (1961).

11. NYT, March 21, 1961, p. 18.

12. *Washington Post* editorial, March 22, 1961.

13. Weaver, *Warren: The Man, The Court, The Era* 256 (1967).

14. NYT, June 5, 1961, p. 10.

15. FFH.

16. March 22, 1961.

17. *Time,* May 5, 1961, p. 17.

18. FF–WJB, March 20, 1957. FFH.

19. FF–SR, January 12, 1952. FFLC.

20. FF–WJB, May 11, 1957. FFH.

21. Acheson, "Felix Frankfurter," 76 Harv. L. Rev. 14 (1962).

22. 163 U.S. 537 (1896).

23. FF–C.C. Burlingham, Thanksgiving 1956. FFLC.

24. FF–JMH, July 6, 1956. FFH.

25. JMH–FF, July 28 [1956]. FFH.

26. FF–JMH, July 31, 1956. FFH.

27. FF–CEW, May 5, 1960. FFLC. The case referred to was Yancy v. United States, 362 U.S. 389 (1960).

28. FF–CEW, March 24, 1960. FFLC.

29. FF–CEW, March 31, 1958. FFLC.

30. Douglas, *Go East Young Man, The Early Years: The Autobiography of William O. Douglas* 332 (1974).

31. Lash, *From the Diaries of Felix Frankfurter* 239 (1974).

32. SM–FF, January 20, 1962. FFLC.

33. Pollack, *Earl Warren: The Judge Who Changed America* 197 (1979).

34. FF–TCC, November 30, 1954. FFLC.

35. FF–JMH, April 3, 1957. FFLC.

36. FF–TCC, November 30, 1954, FFLC.

37. FF–SM, April 23, 1957. FFLC.

38. FF–JMH, June 11, 1957. FFLC.

39. EW, Memorandum to the Conference, October 7, 1959. FFLC.

40. Ibid.

41. FF, Memorandum for the Conference, October 7, 1959. FFLC.

42. FF–EW, April 13, 1960. FFLC.

43. EW–FF, April 14, 1960. FFLC.

44. 359 U.S. 360 (1959).

45. FFH.

46. FF–JMH, May 19, 1959. FFH.

47. Loc. cit. supra note 45.

48. JMH–FF, May 20, 1959. FFH.

49. NYT, April 3, 1958, p. 17.

50. Trop v. Dulles, 356 U.S. 86 (1958).

51. NYT, April 3, 1958, p. 17. This statement is not contained in Warren's printed opinion.

52. Ibid. This statement is not contained in Frankfurter's printed dissent.

53. FF–Alexander Bickel, July 7, 1958. FFLC.

54. 369 U.S. 186, 266 (1962).

55. Burns Baking Co. v. Bryan, 264 U.S. 504, 534 (1924).

56. FFH.

57. *Supreme Court and Supreme Law* 59 (Cahn ed. 1954).

58. FF–PS, February 28, 1962. FFLC.

59. *U.S. News & World Report,* July 15, 1969, p. 64.

60. Ullman v. United States, 350 U.S. 422, 428 (1956).

61. Silverthorne Lumber Co. v. United States, 251 U.S. 385 (1920).

62. Weeks v. United States, 232 U.S. 383 (1910).

63. FF–EW, April 19, 1957. FFH.

64. 355 U.S. 115 (1957).

65. FFLC.

66. 355 U.S. at 120.

67. Lewis, in 4 *The Justices of the United States Supreme Court 1789–1969,* 2726 (Friedman and Israel eds. 1969).

68. FF–WJB, April 10, 1957. FFLC.

69. FF–SM, January 25, 1950. FFLC.

70. FF–EW, January 26, 1956. FFLC.

71. FF–HHB, January 31, 1956. FFLC.

72. FF–LH, February 13, 1958. FFLC.

73. FF–SR, December 5, 1951. FFLC.

74. Voris v. Eikel, 346 U.S. 328, 333 (1953).

75. Ferguson v. Moore-McCormack Lines, 352 U.S. 521, 548–549 (1957) (dissent).

76. Id. at 526. The cases are cited, id. at 526, n. 3.

77. FF–EW, January 26, 1956. FFLC.

78. Steiner v. Mitchell, 350 U.S. 247 (1956); Mitchell v. King Packing Co., 350 U.S. 260 (1956).

79. Ferguson v. Moore-McCormack Lines, 352 U.S. 521, 526 (1957).

80. SM–FF, August 6, 1957. FFLC.

81. FF–JMH, February 23, 1957. FFLC.

82. FF–JMH, November 29, 1956. JMHP.

83. Harris v. Pennsylvania R. Co., 361 U.S 15, 16 (1959); Michalic v. Cleveland Tankers, 364 U.S. 325, 332 (1960).

84. Dick v. New York Life Ins. Co., 359 U.S. 437 (1959).

85. NYT, May 19, 1959, p. 1.

86. Ibid.

87. NYT, October 24, 1959, p. 20.

88. Katcher, op. cit. supra note 2, at 21.

89. NYT, December 15, 1959, p. 25. The case was Inman v. Baltimore & Ohio R. Co., 361 U.S. 138 (1959).

90. FF–WJB, May 11, 1957. FFLC.

91. FF–SM, February 1, 1960. FFLC.

92. SM–FF, August 6, 1957. FFLC.

93. FF–JMH, April 26, 1957. FFLC.

94. FF–JMH, March 26, 1957. FFLC.

95. Dean Acheson-FF, October 17, 1958. FFLC.

96. EW–FF, February 11, 1958. FFLC.

97. EW–FF, August 19, 1960. FFH.

98. EW–FF, May 2, 1962. FFLC.

99. FF–EW, July 28, 1958. FFLC.

100. FF–JMH, September 2, 1958. FFLC.

101. FF–Alexander Bickel, March 18, 1963. FFLC.

102. 364 U.S. 51 (1960).

103. Id. at 55.

104. No title, n.d. FFH.

105. 364 U.S. at 54.

106. Id. at 57.

107. FF–Alexander Bickel, October 8, 1964. FFLC.

108. FF–Alexander Bickel, June 8, 1964. FFLC.

109. FF–JMH, October 11, 1958. JMHP.

110. FF–JMH, September 12, 1958. JMHP.

111. FF–SM, May 28, 1954. FFLC.

112. In re Sawyer, 360 U.S. 622 (1960).

113. FF–SM, July 7, 1959. FFLC.

114. FF–JMH, June 4, 1958. FFLC. This letter was referring to the dissents in Beilan v. Board of Education, 357 U.S. 399 (1958), though it is not clear to which dissent FF was specifically referring.

115. FF–PS, April 4, 1960. FFLC.

116. FF–JMH, January 21, 1958. FFH.

117. FF–Charles Warren, April 28, 1943. FFLC.

118. Brown v. Board of Education, 347 U.S. 483 (1954).

119. LH–FF, September 25, 1957. FFLC.

120. LH–FF, February 26, 1956. FFLC.

121. LH–FF, June 5, 1954. FFLC.

122. LH–FF, October 25, 1956. FFLC.

123. Ibid.

124. LH–FF, June 27, 1957. FFLC.

125. LH–FF, February 26, 1957. FFLC.

126. LH–FF, April 22, 1958. FFLC.

127. LH–FF, July 21, 1959. FFLC.

128. LH–FF, February 26, 1957. FFLC.

129. I.e., JMH.

130. LH–FF, June 27, 1957. FFLC.

131. LH–FF, August 15, 1957. FFLC.

132. Ibid.

133. Ibid.

134. LH–FF, June 27, 1957. FFLC.

135. Ibid.

136. LH–FF, August 15, 1957. FFLC.

137. LH–FF, June 2, 1960. FFLC.

138. LH–FF, February 10, 1958. FFLC.

139. LH–FF, February 3, 1959. FFLC.

140. LH–FF, March 26, 1960. FFLC.

141. LH–FF, February 26, 1944. FFLC.

142. LH–FF, March 28, 1956. FFLC.

143. LH–FF, January 19, 1958. FFLC.

144. LH–FF, April 24, 1957. FFLC.

145. LH–FF, October 12, 1955. FFLC.

146. FF–LH, February 13, 1958. FFLC.

147. FF–LH, October 29, 1958. FFLC.

148. FF–LH, February 2, 1959. FFLC.

149. FF–JMH [December 1958]. JMHP.

150. FF–LH, July 10, 1960. FFLC.

151. Ibid.

152. FF–LH, February 13, 1958. FFLC.

153. LH–FF, July 10, 1958. FFLC.

154. LH–FF, August 15, 1957. FFLC.

155. LH–FF, October 9, 1958. FFLC.

156. Pollack, op. cit. supra note 33, at 187.

157. NYT, April 9, 1958, p. 24.

158. NYT, July 31, 1961, p. 13.

159. EW *Memoirs* 313.

160. Lewis, NYT *Book Review,* August 10, 1980, p. 1. See NYT, August 21, 1958, p. 14; NYT, August 24, 1958, p. 57.

161. See Weaver, op. cit. supra note 13, at 284.

162. NYT, March 31, 1961, p. 13.

163. Pollack, op. cit. supra note 33, at 189.

164. NYT, April 1, 1961, p. 1.

165. NYT, August 5, 1961, p. 1.

166. NYT, February 6, 1962, p. 17.

167. Katcher, op. cit. supra note 7, at 325.

168. NYT, December 17, 1961, p. 58.

169. NYT, May 1, 1963, p. 49.

170. Weaver, op. cit. supra note 13, at 283.

171. EW *Memoirs* 303.

172. EW–HLB, January 29, 1962. HLBLC.

173. EW *Memoirs* 305.

174. *U.S. News & World Report,* July 1, 1968, p. 11.

175. NYT, October 30, 1963, p. 1.

176. *U.S. News & World Report,* November 11, 1963, p. 24.

177. *The Atlantic,* April 1967, p. 118.

178. See *U.S. News & World Report,* February 25, 1963, p. 16; *Time,* February 22, 1963, p. 24.

179. EW *Memoirs* 321.

180. Harrison Tweed–FF, February 18, 1954. FFLC.

181. NYT, January 6, 1959, p. 23.

182. NYT, January 9, 1959, p. 17.

183. NYT, January 21, 1959, p. 44.

184. NYT, August 21, 1958, p. 1.

185. EW *Memoirs* 328.

186. NYT, January 21, 1959, p. 44.

187. FF–EW, November 8, 1956. FFH.

188. *Time,* July 13, 1959, p. 17.

189. LH–FF, September 13, 1957. FFLC.

190. TCC–HLB, n.d. HLBLC.

191. EW *Memoirs* 323–324.

192. Id. at 322.

193. Id. at 323.

194. Ibid.

195. Id. at 324.

196. NYT, February 25, 1959, p. 1.

197. Weaver, op. cit. supra note 13, at 284.

198. EW *Memoirs* 325.

199. Douglas, *The Court Years 1939–1975: The Autobiography of William O Douglas* 229 (1980).

200. EW *Memoirs* 328–330.

201. E.g., Memorandum to All from Earl Warren, November 23, 1954. HHBLC.

202. HLBLC.

203. Pollack, op. cit. supra note 33, at 193.

204. NYT, September 14, 1957, p. 1.

205. NYT, September 15, 1957, p. 65.

8. 1957–1958 TERMS: LITTLE ROCK, EXPATRIATION ET AL

1. NYT, August 29, 1958, pp. 10–11.
2. 358 U.S. 1 (1958).
3. EW *Memoirs* 298.
4. Aaron v. Cooper, 163 F. Supp. 13 (E.D. Ark. 1958).
5. 257 F.2d 33 (8th Cir. 1958).
6. 358 U.S. at 13–14.
7. Loc. cit. supra note 1.
8. FF–EW, September 11, 1958. FFLC.
9. FF–JMH, September 2, 1958. FFLC.
10. Brown v. Board of Education, 347 U.S. 483 (1954).
11. *54 Landmark Briefs and Arguments of the Supreme Court of the United States: Constitutional Law* 675–685 (Kurland and Casper eds. 1975).
12. HHBD, September 11, 1958. HHBLC.
13. 358 U.S. at 5, n.
14. NYT, September 13, 1958, p. 1, 8.
15. Cooper v. Aaron file, TCCT.
16. EW *Memoirs* 298.
17. FF, Memorandum by Mr. Justice Frankfurter on Little Rock, August 27, 1958. FFH.
18. FF–Justices, August 27, 1958. FFH.
19. HHBD, September 12, 1958. HHBLC.
20. WJB, No. 1—August Special Term, 1958. William G. Cooper et al. . . . . v. John Aaron, September 17, 1958. HHBLC.
21. Compare Peltason, *Fifty-Eight Lonely Men: Southern Federal Judges and School Desegregation* 191–192 (1961).
22. September 24 draft. HHBLC.
23. FFH.
24. FFLC; HHBLC.
25. 1 Cranch 137 (U.S. 1803).
26. EW *Memoirs* 298.
27. FFH.
28. Draft in HLB writing. HLBLC.
29. WJB draft opinion, with TCC written suggestions, September 25, 1958. TCCT.
30. NYT, September 30, 1958, p. 1.
31. 358 U.S. at 18.
32. Id. at 20.
33. NYT, September 30, 1958, p. 30.
34. HHBD, September 26, 1958. HHBLC.
35. Id. September 29, 1958.
36. EW *Memoirs* 298–299.
37. FF–HLB, May 7, 1963. FFLC.
38. 358 U.S. at 20.
39. FF–C.C. Burlingham, November 12, 1958. FFLC.

40. FFLC; HHBLC.
41. FFLC; HHBLC.
42. 357 U.S. 449 (1958).
43. FF–TCC, June 25, 1958. FFLC.
44. Ibid.
45. FF–JMH, April 24, 1958. FFLC.
46. JMH, Memorandum for the Conference, May 23, 1958. FFLC.
47. FF writing at bottom of ibid.
48. FF–WJB, March 27, 1958. FFLC.
49. FF–JMH, February 14, 1958. FFH.
50. Federal Maritime Board v. Isbrandtsen Co., 356 U.S. 481 (1958).
51. WJB–FF, April 29, 1958. FFH.
52. Far East Conference v. United States, 342 U.S. 570 (1952).
53. United States Navigation Co. v. Cunard Steamship Co., 284 U.S. 474 (1932).
54. WJB–FF, April 29, 1958. FFH.
55. FF–WJB, April 29, 1958. FFH.
56. NYT, June 11, 1961, section VI, p. 31.
57. Ibid.
58. 355 U.S. 225 (1957).
59. HHB conference notes. HHBLC.
60. WOD–FF, December 16, 1957. FFH.
61. 355 U.S. at 232.
62. The WOD–FF correspondence quoted from is in the Lambert v. California file. FFH.
63. 357 U.S. 116 (1958).
64. 357 U.S. 144 (1958).
65. TCC conference notes. TCCT.
66. WOD Memorandum to the Conference, June 13, 1958. TCCT.
67. JMH draft dissent, Kent v. Dulles. FFH.
68. FF writing at end of ibid.
69. HHB–TCC, June 13, 1958. TCCT.
70. 357 U.S. at 154.
71. J. Edgar Hoover–TCC, June 9, 1958. TCCT.
72. Ibid.
73. 357 U.S. at 140, n.2.
74. 355 U.S. 1 (1957).
75. HHB conference notes. HHBLC.
76. FF–EW, March 27, 1957. FFH.
77. 353 U.S. 979 (1957).
78. Jencks v. United States, 353 U.S. 657 (1957).
79. 356 U.S. 44 (1958).
80. 356 U.S. 86 (1958).
81. HHB conference notes. HHBLC.
82. FF–JMH, May 9, 1957. FFH.
83. These draft opinions are in FFLC; TCCT.

84. FFH.

85. FF, Memorandum for the Conference, Re: No. 572—Perez v. Brownell, June 7, 1957. FFH.

86. 354 U.S. 934, 935 (1957).

87. FF–HHB, TCC, JMH, WJB, CEW, June 25, 1958. FFLC.

88. HHB conference notes; FF conference list; TCC docket book. HHBLC; FFLC; TCCT.

89. The EW Perez and Trop drafts are in TCCT.

90. WJB–FF, March 21, 1958. FFH.

91. FFH.

92. HHB, April 30, 1958. HHBLC.

93. Berry, *Stability, Security, and Continuity: Mr. Justice Burton and Decision-Making in the Supreme Court 1945–1958*, 225 (1978).

94. HHBD, July 17, 1958. HHBLC.

95. Clayton, *The Making of Justice: The Supreme Court in Action* 217 (1964).

96. Jacobellis v. Ohio, 378 U.S. 184, 197 (1964).

97. Clayton, op. cit. supra note 95, at 218.

98. FF–LH, July 30, 1960. FFLC.

99. 359 U.S. 121 (1959).

100. 355 U.S. 281 (1958).

101. 356 U.S. 969 (1958).

102. TCC conference notes, TCCT.

103. Rea v. United States, 350 U.S. 214 (1956).

104. FF–CEW, November 25, 1957 and December 2, 1957. FFLC.

105. CEW–FF, November 29, 1957. FFLC.

106. WJB–FF, February 18, 1959. FFH.

107. FF, Memorandum for the Conference, January 30, 1959. FFH; TCCT.

108. WJB, Memorandum to the Conference, February 6, 1959. FFH; TCCT.

109. Sweezy v. New Hampshire, 354 U.S. 234 (1957).

110. Watkins v. United States, 354 U.S. 178 (1957).

111. 360 U.S. 72 (1959).

112. TCC conference notes. TCCT.

113. Pennsylvania v. Nelson, 350 U.S. 497 (1956).

114. N.A.A.C.P. v. Alabama, 357 U.S. 449 (1958).

115. FF–WJB, January 7, 1959. FFLC.

116. 360 U.S. 109 (1959).

117. E.g., FF conference list, March 7, 1958. FFLC.

118. 359 U.S. 360 (1959).

119. TCC conference notes. TCCT.

120. TCC–FF, April 13, 1959. TCCT.

121. TCCT.

122. FF–JMH, May 19, 1959. FFH.

123. Simon E. Sobeloff–FF, n.d. FFH. The *Baltimore Sun* statement was enclosed with ibid.

124. 359 U.S. 535 (1959).

125. FF–JMH, April 9, 1959. FFLC.

126. SM–FF, June 9, 1959. FFLC.

127. 359 U.S. 344 (1959).

128. Supra note 110.

129. Supra note 116.

130. 359 U.S. 255 (1959).

131. Quoted in JMH–FF, February 25, 1959. FFH.

132. FF–Justices, February 18, 1959. FFH.

133. FF–WJB, March 25, 1959. FFH.

134. Quoted in WJB–FF, March 24, 1959. FFH.

135. Ibid.

136. FF–WJB, March 25, 1959. FFH.

137. 360 U.S. 315 (1959).

138. TCC conference notes. TCCT.

139. TCC–EW, June 11, 1959. TCCT.

140. 360 U.S. 1 (1959).

141. 358 U.S. 228 (1959).

142. 359 U.S. 41 (1959).

143. TCC conference notes. TCCT.

144. 360 U.S. 378 (1959).

145. TCC conference notes. TCCT.

146. 358 U.S. 450 (1959).

147. TCC conference notes. TCCT.

148. 359 U.S. 520 (1959).

149. Central Pacific Ry. Co. v. Alameda County, 284 U.S. 463 (1932).

150. NYT, June 23, 1958, p. 12.

9. 1959–1960 TERMS: THE SHIFTING BALANCE

1. Mazo, *Richard Nixon: A Political and Personal Portrait* (1959).

2. NYT, July 1, 1959, p. 26; *Time,* July 13, 1959, p. 17; *Newsweek,* July 13, 1959, p. 20.

3. Clark R. Mollenhoff–author, March 7, 1979.

4. Supra note 2.

5. EW *Memoirs* 344.

6. Loc. cit. supra note 3.

7. NYT, July 5, 1959, p. 31.

8. JMH–EW, May 25, 1956. JMHP.

9. NYT, July 5, 1959, p. 33.

10. NYT, April 10, 1960, p. 41.

11. 364 U.S. 206 (1960).

12. FF–LH, July 30, 1960. FFLC.

13. LH–FF, November 1, 1958. FFLC.

14. Clayton, *The Making of Justice: The Supreme Court in Action* 217 (1964).

15. 362 U.S. 217 (1960).

16. 362 U.S. 574 (1960).

17. 316 U.S. 455 (1942).

18. FF–WJB, April 21, 1960. FFH.

19. 363 U.S. 603 (1960).

20. TCC conference notes. TCCT.

21. 364 U.S. 263 (1960).

22. 360 U.S. 246 (1959).

23. Id. at 248.

24. 359 U.S. 360 (1959).

25. Mr. Justice Douglas, dissenting, No. 699—October Term, 1958. Ohio ex rel. Eaton, Appellant, v. Price, Chief of Police [May, 1959].

26. 364 U.S. 263 (1960).

27. FF–WJB, June 22, 1960. FFH.

28. 364 U.S. 206 (1960).

29. Weeks v. United States, 232 U.S. 383 (1914).

30. Wolf v. Colorado, 338 U.S. 25 (1949).

31. McNabb v. United States, 318 U.S. 332 (1943).

32. See FF–Justices, April 12, 1960. FFH.

33. "PB's draft." FFH.

34. Henry J. Friendly–FF, June 29, 1960. FFLC.

35. St. Germain, *Doctor and Student* (1532).

36. FF, "A Dialogue." FFH.

37. 367 U.S. 643 (1961).

38. 362 U.S. 60 (1960).

39. TCC conference notes. TCCT.

40. FF, Memorandum for the Conference, Re: No. 154, Talley v. California, February 11, 1960. TCCT.

41. TCC–FF, written at bottom of ibid.

42. Mr. Justice: Re Talley, n.d. FFH.

43. Kinsella v. Singleton, 361 U.S. 234 (1960); Grisham v. Hagan, 361 U.S. 278 (1960); McElroy v. Guagliardo, 361 U.S. 281 (1960).

44. 354 U.S. 1 (1957).

45. TCC conference notes. TCCT.

46. TCC, Memorandum to the Conference, October 24, 1959. TCCT.

47. TCC–HLB, n.d. HLBLC.

48. FF–JMH, n.d. JMHP.

49. NYT, June 11, 1961, section VI, p. 31.

50. NYT, April 15, 1959, section IV, p. 7.

51. 364 U.S. 177 (1960).

52. FF–PS, April 4, 1960. FFLC.

53. Paul–Mr. Justice, Re Parke Davis, n.d. FFH.

54. 361 U.S. 516 (1960).

55. TCC conference notes. TCCT.

56. 362 U.S. 199 (1960).

57. TCC conference notes. TCCT.

58. 361 U.S. 147 (1959).

59. TCC conference notes. TCCT.

60. Kingsley International Pictures Corp. v. Regents. 360 U.S. 684 (1959).

61. SM–FF, July 7, 1959. FFLC.

62. 363 U.S. 420 (1960).

63. FF–JMH, June 7, 1960. FFH.

64. 361 U.S. 39 (1959).

65. JMH conference notes. JMHP.

66. FFH.

67. FF, Memorandum for the Conference, Re: Steel Case, November 5, 1959. FFLC.

68. JMH–Justices, November 5, 1959. FFLC.

69. 362 U.S. 525 (1960).

70. TCC conference notes. TCCT.

71. 363 U.S. 522 (1960).

72. TCC conference notes. TCCT.

73. 362 U.S. 17 (1960).

74. TCC conference notes. TCCT.

75. FF–JMH, February 1960. JMHP.

76. TCC–WJB, February 18, 1960. TCCT.

77. 363 U.S. 666 (1960).

78. JMH, Memorandum for the Conference, June 9, 1960. FFLC.

79. 362 U.S. 384 (1960).

80. 356 U.S. 86 (1958).

81. 380 U.S. VIII (1965).

82. EW *Memoirs* 374.

83. EW–FF, August 19, 1960. FFH.

84. FF–C. C. Burlingham, Thanksgiving 1956. FFLC.

85. Loc. cit. supra note 83.

86. SM–FF, October 15, 1957. FFLC.

87. Milanovich v. United States, 365 U.S. 551 (1961).

88. Stewart v. United States, 366 U.S. 1 (1961).

89. 365 U.S. 167 (1961).

90. FF, Memorandum for the Conference, November 9, 1960. TCCT.

91. FF conference list. FFLC.

92. JMH–FF [November 11, 1960]. FFH.

93. 365 U.S. 534 (1961).

94. WOD, Memorandum to the Conference, January 12, 1961. FFH.

95. FF, Memorandum for the Conference, January 12, 1961. FFH.

96. WOD–FF, January 12, 1961. FFH.

97. WOD, Memorandum to the Conference, January 12, 1961. FFH.

98. 365 U.S. 399 (1961).

99. 365 U.S. 431 (1961).

100. Barenblatt v. United States, 360 U.S. 109 (1959).

101. Watkins v. United States, 354 U.S. 178 (1957).

102. FF conference list. FFH.

103. Konigsberg v. State Bar, 366 U.S. 36 (1961).

104. Yates v. United States, 354 U.S. 298 (1957).

105. Konigsberg v. State Bar, 366 U.S. 36 (1961).

106. 367 U.S. 203 (1961).

107. 367 U.S. 1 (1961).

108. JMH–FF, February 4, 1960. FFH.

109. See FF–TCC, February 9, 1960. TCCT.

110. TCC–FF, February 8, 1960. TCCT.

111. Supra note 107.

112. EW, Memorandum for the Conference, May 10, 1961. FFH.

113. 367 U.S. 886 (1961).

114. 29 *U.S. Law Week* 3210 (1961).

115. 364 U.S. 479 (1960).

116. PS–FF, n.d. FFH.

117. 365 U.S. 43 (1961).

118. FFH.

119. EW, Memorandum for the Conference, November 2, 1960. TCCT.

120. PS–TCC, November 22, 1960. TCCT.

121. TCC, no title, n.d. TCCT.

122. 365 U.S. at 51.

123. 365 U.S. 301 (1961).

124. Id. at 304.

125. Id. at 306.

126. 365 U.S. 715 (1961).

127. FF–TCC, April 12, 1961. FFH.

128. 367 U.S. 740 (1961).

129. Railway Employes' Dept. v. Hanson, 351 U.S. 225 (1956).

130. 367 U.S. 820 (1961).

131. Among others, FF conference notes. FFH.

132. JMH–FF, June 15, 1961. FFH.

133. 366 U.S. 316 (1961).

134. *Washington Star* editorial, May 24, 1961. HLBLC.

135. 364 U.S. 339 (1960).

136. 328 U.S. 549 (1946).

137. FF–EW, November 10, 1960. FFH.

138. FF draft opinion, November 2, 1960. FFH.

139. FF–HLB, November 1, 1960. FFH.

140. 367 U.S. 497 (1961).

141. TCC–FF, June 6, 1961. FFH.

142. 366 U.S. 420 (1961).

143. Everson v. Board of Education, 330 U.S. 1, 15 (1947).

144. See Memorandum on the Changes in the Chief Justice's Sunday Law Opinions, n.d. FFH.

145. FF, Memorandum for the Conference, Re: Nos. 8, 11, 36, 67—Sunday Law Cases, March 10, 1961. FFH.

146. JMH–EW, May 26, 1961. FFH.

147. JMH–FF, May 26, 1961. FFH.

148. 367 U.S. 488 (1961).

149. Watkins v. United States, 354 U.S. 178, 200, n.33 (1957).

150. 364 U.S. 520 (1961).
151. SM–FF, August 25, 1954. FFLC.
152. 364 U.S. at 548–549.
153. FF–EW, January 5, 1961. FFLC.
154. FF–JMH, December 26, 1960. JMHP.
155. 365 U.S. 127 (1961).
156. 365 U.S. 570 (1961).
157. Among others, TCC conference notes. TCCT.
158. Quoted in WJB–TCC, March 2, 1961. TCCT.
159. Ibid.
160. 365 U.S. 505 (1961).
161. Olmstead v. United States, 277 U.S. 438 (1928).
162. Dash, Schwartz, and Knowlton, *The Eavesdroppers* (1959).
163. JMH–FF, January 18, 1961. FFH.
164. 367 U.S. 643 (1961).
165. 369 U.S. 186 (1962).

10. 1960–1961 TERMS: CHANGING GUARD AND CHANGING LAW

1. John F. Kennedy–EW, January 25, 1961. John F. Kennedy Library.
2. FF–LH, July 30, 1960. FFLC.
3. McGrory interview. John F. Kennedy Library.
4. EW–John F. Kennedy, March 20, 1961. John F. Kennedy Library.
5. John F. Kennedy–EW, March 23, 1963. John F. Kennedy Library.
6. 367 U.S. 643 (1961).
7. 369 U.S. 186 (1962).
8. NYT, June 25, 1961, p. 43.
9. 338 U.S. 25 (1949).
10. Id. at 33.
11. Memorandum to TCC, October 12, 1960. TCCT.
12. 361 U.S. 147 (1959).
13. October 19, 1960. JMHP.
14. JMH–TCC, May 1, 1961. TCCT.
15. See TCC–JMH, May 4, 1961. TCCT.
16. TCCT.
17. WJB–TCC, May 1, 1961. TCCT.
18. HLB–TCC, n.d. TCCT.
19. 367 U.S. at 670.
20. FFH.
21. PS–TCC, May 1, 1961. TCCT.
22. 367 U.S. at 672.
23. JMH–TCC, May 1, 1961. TCCT.
24. Adamson v. California, 332 U.S. 46, 68 (1947).
25. Palko v. Connecticut, 302 U.S. 319, 325 (1937).
26. TCC–JMH, May 4, 1961. TCCT.
27. HLB–TCC, June 15, 1961. TCCT.

28. TCC–HLB, June 15, 1961. TCCT.

29. FF–Alexander Bickel, October 8, 1964. FFLC.

30. Supra note 7.

31. NYT, January 12, 1962, p. 12.

32. NYT, February 27, 1962, p. 27.

33. Brown interview, BOH.

34. See Pollack, *Earl Warren: The Judge Who Changed America* 215 (1979).

35. 368 U.S. 57 (1961).

36. Id. at 69.

37. 368 U.S. 208 (1961).

38. 370 U.S. 139 (1962).

39. 368 U.S. 157 (1961).

40. 362 U.S. 199 (1960).

41. 30 *U.S. Law Week* 3127 (1961).

42. FF–JMH, December 1, 1961. FFH.

43. Ibid.

44. JMH–FF, December 4, 1961. JMHP.

45. FF–EW, December 4, 1961. FFH.

46. FF–HLB, February 19, 1962. FFH.

47. Kennedy v. Mendoza-Martinez, 369 U.S. 832 (1962).

48. 369 U.S. 367 (1962).

49. Trop v. Dulles, 356 U.S. 86 (1958).

50. Perez v. Brownell, 356 U.S. 44 (1958).

51. 369 U.S. 506 (1962).

52. 372 U.S. 335 (1963).

53. 316 U.S. 455 (1942).

54. 369 U.S. at 512.

55. Id. at 518.

56. NYT, June 17, 1962, section VI, p. 7.

57. 369 U.S. 186 (1962).

58. EW *Memoirs* 306.

59. EW interview, Morrie Landsberg, June 25, 1969. HLBLC.

60. 328 U.S. 549 (1946).

61. Id. at 556.

62. Id. at 555.

63. EW *Memoirs* 309.

64. Id. at 310.

65. Pollack, *Earl Warren: The Judge Who Changed America* 210 (1979).

66. COH.

67. 29 *U.S. Law Week* 3314 (1961).

68. Douglas, *The Court Years 1939–1975: The Autobiography of William O. Douglas* 135 (1980).

69. WOD, Memorandum to the Conference, October 23, 1961. HLBLC.

70. FF–PS, April 24, April 20, 1961. FFH.

71. FF, Memorandum of Mr. Justice Frankfurter on No. 6, Baker v. Carr, October 10, 1961. TCCT.

72. FF, Memorandum to the Conference, October 10, 1961. TCCT.

73. WJB, Memorandum to the Conference, October 12, 1961. FFH.

74. 369 U.S. at 254.

75. JMH–CEW and PS, October 11, 1961. FFLC.

76. FF–PS, May 1, 1961. FFLC.

77. FF–PS, October 13, 1961. FFH.

78. Supra note 60.

79. 7 How. 1 (U.S. 1849).

80. 364 U.S. 339 (1960).

81. Supra note 77.

82. 377 U.S. 533 (1964).

83. EW *Memoirs* 309.

84. Douglas, op. cit. supra note 68, at 136.

85. Ibid.

86. 352 U.S. 920 (1956).

87. TCC–FF, February 3, 1962. TCCT; FFH.

88. JMH–PS, February 8, 1962. FFH.

89. FF–JMH, February 2, 1962. JMHP.

90. WOD, Memorandum to the Conference, March 2, 1962. TCCT.

91. TCCT.

92. TCC–FF, March 7, 1962. FFH; TCCT.

93. No. 6—October Term, 1961. Charles W. Baker, et al., Appellants v. Joe C. Carr, et al. Mr. Justice Clark, concurring in part and dissenting in part. [March 1962]. TCCT. Brackets in original.

94. FF–JMH, March 5, 1962. JMHP.

95. Supra note 77.

96. 369 U.S. at 268.

97. Henry J. Friendly–FF, March 28, 1962. FFLC.

98. FF–Henry J. Friendly, March 30, 1962. FFLC.

99. Among Friends: Personal Letters of Dean Acheson 225 (McLellan and Acheson eds. 1980).

100. Ibid.

101. *Katcher, Earl Warren: A Political Biography* 429 (1967).

102. NYT, March 27, 1962, p. 36.

103. Id., p. 1.

104. NYT, March 28, 1962, p. 1.

105. NYT, March 29, 1962, p. 32.

106. NYT, June 17, 1962, section IV, p. 7.

107. Katcher, op. cit. supra note 101, at 430.

108. Ibid.

109. EW–FF, May 2, 1962. FFLC.

110. 371 U.S. xi (1962).

111. Schlesinger, *Robert Kennedy and His Times* 377 (1978).

112. Ibid.

113. Frank, *The Warren Court* 150 (1964).

114. Schlesinger, op. cit. supra note 111, at 378.

115. Frank, loc. cit. supra note 113.

116. Id. at 151.

117. NYT, April 3, 1962, p. 28.
118. 369 U.S. 749 (1962).
119. 335 U.S. 497 (1948).
120. 339 U.S. 162 (1950).
121. Barenblatt v. United States, 360 U.S. 109 (1959).
122. Wilkinson v. United States, 365 U.S. 399 (1961).
123. 370 U.S. 375 (1962).
124. 314 U.S. 252 (1941).
125. 328 U.S. 331 (1946).
126. 372 U.S. 368 (1963).
127. 369 U.S. 705 (1962).
128. 369 U.S. 590 (1962).
129. 254 U.S. 300 (1920).
130. 370 U.S. 478 (1962).
131. Roth v. United States, 354 U.S. 476 (1957).
132. Jacobellis v. Ohio, 378 U.S. 184, 197 (1964).
133. 370 U.S. at 519.
134. 370 U.S. 294 (1962).
135. 370 U.S. 660 (1962).
136. 370 U.S. 421 (1962).
137. TCCT.
138. Supra note 136.
139. FF conference list. FFLC.
140. 30 *U.S. Law Week* 3310 (1962).
141. Ibid.
142. 370 U.S. at 441.
143. NYT, June 29, 1962, p. 11.
144. EW *Memoirs* 315.
145. NYT, June 26, 1962, p. 17.
146. Weaver, *Warren: The Man, The Court, The Era* 260 (1967).
147. NYT, June 26, 1962, p. 17.
148. Billy Graham–LBJ, June 21, 1968. LBJ Library.
149. NYT, June 27, 1962, p. 1.
150. Weaver, op. cit. supra note 146, at 258.
151. Katcher, op. cit. supra note 107, at 423.
152. Id. at 424.
153. Ibid.
154. NYT, June 28, 1962, p. 12.
155. *Newsweek*, October 17, 1955, p. 36.
156. NYT, November 4, 1958, p. 17.

11. 1962 TERM: A DECEPTIVE CALM

1. See Clayton, *The Making of Justice: The Supreme Court in Action* 29–32 (1964).
2. SM–FF, October 22, 1964. FFLC.
3. Schlesinger, *Robert Kennedy and His Times* 379 (1978).

4. Clayton, op. cit. supra note 1, at 43.
5. Loc. cit. supra note 3.
6. Clayton, op. cit. supra note 1, at 159.
7. FF–Alexander Bickel, November 14, 1962. FFLC.
8. FF–Alexander Bickel, March 18, 1963. FFLC.
9. FF interview. John F. Kennedy Library.
10. JMH–FF, August 21, 1963. FFH.
11. Kennedy v. Mendoza-Martinez, 372 U.S. 144 (1963).
12. Ibid.
13. 31 *U.S. Law Week* 3191 (1962).
14. 371 U.S. 415 (1963).
15. Brown v. Board of Education, 347 U.S. 483 (1954).
16. 372 U.S. 539 (1963).
17. 357 U.S. 449 (1958).
18. 371 U.S. 471 (1963).
19. JMH note, n.d. JMHP.
20. McNabb v. United States, 318 U.S. 332 (1943).
21. Mallory v. United States, 354 U.S. 449 (1957).
22. 372 U.S. 335 (1963).
23. Lewis, *Gideon's Trumpet* (1964).
24. Id. at 7–8, 10.
25. 316 U.S. 445 (1942).
26. Lewis, op. cit. supra note 23, at 7.
27. Carnley v. Cochran, 369 U.S. 506 (1962).
28. JMHP.
29. JMH, Memorandum for the Conference, May 28, 1962. JMHP.
30. Quoted, Lewis, op. cit. supra note 23, jacket.
31. Douglas, *The Court Years 1939–1975: The Autobiography of William O. Douglas* 187 (1980).
32. HLB–Edmond Cahn, March 27, 1963. HLBLC.
33. Lewis, op. cit. supra note 23, at 192.
34. Brown v. Board of Education, 347 U.S. 483 (1954).
35. 377 U.S. 533 (1964).
36. 384 U.S. 436 (1966).
37. 373 U.S. 723 (1963).
38. 381 U.S. 532 (1965).
39. 373 U.S. 427 (1963).
40. 365 U.S. 505 (1961).
41. On Lee v. United States, 343 U.S. 747 (1952).
42. Olmstead v. United States, 277 U.S. 438 (1928).
43. 373 U.S. at 442.
44. TCC–JMH, May 28, 1963. TCCT. Brackets in original.
45. 373 U.S. 545 (1963).
46. EW, Memorandum for the Conference, May 21, 1963. JMHP.
47. 369 U.S. 186 (1962).
48. 373 U.S. at 545.

49. JMHP.

50. Schlesinger, op. cit. supra note 3, at 236.

51. 372 U.S. 368 (1963).

52. Clayton, op. cit. supra note 1, at 140.

53. Schlesinger, op. cit. supra note 3, at 399.

54. 372 U.S. at 381.

55. FF–Alexander Bickel, March 18, 1963. FFLC.

56. 374 U.S. 203 (1963).

57. 370 U.S. 421 (1962).

58. 31 *U.S. Law Week* 3278 (1963).

59. 367 U.S. 488 (1961).

60. Loc. cit. supra note 58.

61. [WOD–HLB], June 17, 1963. HLBLC.

62. NYT, June 18, 1963, p. 1.

63. NYT, June 26, 1963, p. 43.

64. NYT, November 13, 1963, p. 30.

65. 374 U.S. 398 (1963).

66. McGowan v. Maryland, 366 U.S. 420 (1961).

67. Gallagher v. Crown Kosher Market, 366 U.S. 617 (1961).

68. 374 U.S. at 420.

69. 372 U.S. 391 (1973).

70. Clayton, op. cit. supra note 1, at 124.

71. 339 U.S. 200 (1950).

72. 366 U.S. 717 (1961).

73. Hart, "Foreword: The Time Chart of the Justices," 73 Harv. L. Rev. 84 (1959).

74. Brennan, "Federal Habeas Corpus and State Prisoners: An Exercise in Federalism," 7 Utah L. Rev. 423 (1961).

75. 372 U.S. 293 (1963).

76. NYT, August 11, 1963, p. 49.

77. NYT, June 7, 1963, p. 16.

78. NYT, September 26, 1963, p. 29.

79. 373 U.S. 1 (1963).

80. 374 U.S. 321 (1963).

81. Id. at 373.

82. Clayton, op. cit. supra note 1, at 189.

83. 374 U.S. at 363.

84. Shelley v. Kraemer, 334 U.S. 1, 13 (1948).

85. United States v. Raines, 362 U.S. 17, 25 (1960).

86. 373 U.S. 244 (1963).

87. Avent v. North Carolina, 373 U.S. 244 (1963); Gober v. Birmingham, 373 U.S. 244 (1963).

88. Lombard v. Louisiana, 373 U.S. 267 (1963).

89. Shuttlesworth v. Birmingham, 373 U.S. 262 (1963).

90. 378 U.S. 130 (1964).

91. 163 U.S. 537 (1896).

92. 109 U.S. 3 (1883).

93. 362 U.S. 199 (1960).

94. 373 U.S. 920 (1963).

95. Clayton, op. cit. supra note 1, at 246.

96. Dunne, *Hugo Black and the Judicial Revolution* 372 (1977).

97. Clayton, op. cit. supra note 1.

98. Id. at 252.

99. Ibid.

100. Dunne, op. cit. supra note 96, at 380.

101. Simon, *Independent Journey: The Life of William O. Douglas* 376 (1980).

102. NYT, September 26, 1963, p. 29.

103. Ibid.

104. McWilliams, "The Education of Earl Warren," *The Nation,* October 12, 1974, p. 326.

105. Smith, "The Education of Earl Warren," *The Nation,* October 11, 1956, p. 208.

106. NYT, November 12, 1962, p. 1; Clayton, op. cit. supra note 1, at 95–98.

107. Id. at 99.

108. Id. at 100.

109. Id. at 100–101.

110. NYT, June 23, 1963, p. 2.

111. NYT, August 17, 1963, p. 17.

112. NYT, July 10, 1963, p. 1.

113. Id. at 16.

114. Frank, *The Warren Court* 166 (1964).

115. JMH–FF, July 10, 1963. FFH.

116. John F. Kennedy–EW, September 23, 1963. John F. Kennedy Library.

117. Holmes, *Collected Legal Papers* 292 (1921).

118. JMH–FF, August 31, 1963. FFLC. Brackets in original.

12. 1963 TERM: DAYS OF DRUMS AND DAYS OF LAW

1. Pollack, *Earl Warren: The Judge Who Changed America* 221 (1979).

2. EW *Memoirs* 352.

3. Id. at 351.

4. Douglas, *The Court Years 1939–1975: The Autobiography of William O. Douglas* 305 (1980).

5. Pollack, op. cit. supra note 1, at 222.

6. EW *Memoirs* 353.

7. Weaver, *Warren: The Man, The Court, The Era* 300 (1967).

8. EW *Memoirs* 353.

9. Weaver, op. cit. supra note 7, at 302.

10. EW *Memoirs* 371.

11. 2 Hearings before the President's Commission on the Assassination of President Kennedy 371–372 (1964).

12. Report of the Warren Commission on the Assassination of President Kennedy 266 (1964).

13. Brown v. Board of Education, 347 U.S. 483 (1954).

14. Katcher, *Earl Warren: A Political Biography* 462 (1967).
15. Pollack, op. cit. supra note 1, at 250.
16. Op. cit. supra note 12, at 41.
17. Weaver, op. cit. supra note 7, at 333; *Newsweek*, November 28, 1966.
18. NYT, June 20, 1964, p. 1.
19. 369 U.S. 186 (1962).
20. 376 U.S. 1 (1964).
21. NYT, February 20, 1964, p. 28.
22. Pollock v. Farmers' Loan & Trust Co., 157 U.S. 429 (1895).
23. FF–Philip B. Kurland, February 25, 1964. FFLC.
24. 377 U.S. 533 (1964).
25. *U.S. News & World Report*, July 6, 1964, p. 34.
26. Reynolds v. Sims, 377 U.S. 533 (1964).
27. Lucas v. Colorado General Assembly, 377 U.S. 713 (1964).
28. Roman v. Sincock, 377 U.S. 695 (1964).
29. Maryland Committee v. Tawes, 377 U.S. 656 (1964).
30. WMCA, Inc. v. Lomenzo, 377 U.S. 633 (1964).
31. Davis v. Mann, 377 U.S. 678 (1964).
32. 32 *U.S. Law Week* 3190 (1963).
33. 377 U.S. at 562.
34. 32 *U.S. Law Week* 3347 (1964).
35. Brown v. Board of Education, 349 U.S. 294, 301 (1955).
36. Lucas v. Colorado General Assembly, 377 U.S. 713 (1964).
37. Id. at 736, n. 29.
38. Id. at 567, 579.
39. TCC–EW, March 18, 1964. TCCT.
40. 377 U.S. at 750.
41. TCC–FF, n.d. FFLC.
42. JMH–FF, November 15 [1963]. FFH.
43. FF interview. John F. Kennedy Library.
44. Dean Acheson–FF, n.d. FFLC.
45. NYT, September 15, 1964, p. 36.
46. NYT, June 21, 1964, section IV, p. 3.
47. Pollack, op. cit. supra note 1, at 209.
48. Weaver, op. cit. supra note 7, at 249.
49. 378 U.S. 226 (1964).
50. 378 U.S. 153 (1964).
51. 378 U.S. 130 (1964).
52. 378 U.S. 153 (1964).
53. 378 U.S. 130 (1964).
54. WOD, Memorandum to the Conference, In Re: The Sit-In Cases Argued the Week of October 14, 1963, October 21, 1963.
55. 373 U.S. 267 (1963).
56. 326 U.S. 501 (1946).
57. 334 U.S. 1 (1948).
58. 109 U.S. 3 (1883).

59. FF–HLB, May 7, 1963. FFLC.

60. 362 U.S. 199 (1960).

61. Loc. cit. supra note 54.

62. 373 U.S. 244 (1963).

63. No. 12—October Term, 1963. Robert Mack Bell et al. v. State of Maryland. Black opinion of the Court. March 5, 1964. TCCT.

64. No. 9—October Term, 1963. Charles F. Barr et al., Petitioners v. City of Columbia. Mr. Chief Justice Warren, dissenting. [May, 1964]. Circulated: May 7, 1964. Brackets in original.

65. WOD–TCC, June 8, 1964. TCCT.

66. 347 U.S. 483 (1954).

67. 301 U.S. 619, 636–640 (1937).

68. No. 12—October Term, 1963. Robert Mack Bell et al., Petitioners v. State of Maryland. Mr. Justice Clark [June, 1964]. TCCT. Brackets in original.

69. EW–TCC, June 10, 1964. TCCT.

70. Supra note 24.

71. 376 U.S. 254 (1964).

72. NYT, June 29, 1964, p. 20.

73. Ibid.

74. 378 U.S. 368 (1964).

75. 346 U.S. 156 (1953).

76. HLB–BRW, February 21, 1964. TCCT.

77. 378 U.S. 478 (1964).

78. 378 U.S. 1 (1964).

79. 377 U.S. 201 (1964).

80. Henry J. Friendly–FF, May 28, 1964. FFLC.

81. 376 U.S. 650 (1964).

82. FF–JMH, March 31, 1964. FFH.

83. 376 U.S. 398 (1964).

84. Supra note 71.

85. Ibid.

86. Clark v. Pearson, 248 F. Supp. 188, 194 (D.D.C. 1965).

87. 6 Wheat. 264 (U.S. 1821).

88. WJB, Memorandum to the Conference, Re: Nos. 39 & 40—New York Times v. Sullivan and Abernathy v. Sullivan, March 3, 1964. TCCT.

89. Nos. 39 & 40—October Term, 1963, The New York Times Company, Petitier v. L.B. Sullivan, Ralph D. Abernathy v. L.B. Sullivan. Separate Memorandum of Mr. Justice Harlan, March 7, 1964. TCCT.

90. The New York Times Company, Petitioner v. L.B. Sullivan, Ralph D. Abernathy et al. v. L.B. Sullivan. Mr. Justice Clark [March, 1964]. TCCT. Brackets in original.

91. 376 U.S. at 284.

92. NYT, October 24, 1964, p. 16.

93. See Katcher, *Earl Warren: A Political Biography* 454–455 (1967).

94. NYT, August 4, 1964, p. 17.

95. NYT, August 9, 1964, section IV, p. 8.

13. 1964 TERM: TELEVISION, CIVIL RIGHTS, AND PRIVACY

1. Fred W. Friendly–author, February 14, 1980.
2. NYT, June 14, 1965, p. 38.
3. 381 U.S. 532 (1965).
4. *Time*, July 23, 1979, p. 76.
5. 297 U.S. 278 (1936).
6. TCC, Memorandum to the Conference Re: No. 256, Estes v. Texas, May 25, 1965.
7. 331 U.S. 367 (1947).
8. Supra note 6.
9. 449 U.S. 560 (1981).
10. WOD–HLB, n.d. HLBLC.
11. 379 U.S. 306 (1964).
12. 362 U.S. 199 (1960).
13. 109 U.S. 3 (1883).
14. Heart of Atlanta Motel v. United States, 379 U.S. 241 (1964).
15. Katzenbach v. McClung, 379 U.S. 294 (1964).
16. WJB–TCC, November 25, 1964. TCCT.
17. JMH–TCC, December 1, 1964. TCCT.
18. 380 U.S. 447 (1965).
19. 364 U.S. 454 (1960).
20. Supra note 12.
21. 381 U.S. 741 (1965).
22. Id. at 742.
23. 379 U.S. 536, 559 (1965).
24. 340 U.S. 315 (1951).
25. 379 U.S. 184 (1964).
26. 380 U.S. 528 (1965).
27. 380 U.S. 503 (1965).
28. 299 U.S. 353 (1937).
29. 367 U.S. 1 (1961).
30. 381 U.S. 437 (1965).
31. 339 U.S. 382 (1950).
32. 381 U.S. 1 (1965).
33. 361 U.S. 39 (1959).
34. Youngstown Sheet & Tube Co. v. Sawyer, 343 U.S. 579 (1952).
35. United States v. Curtiss-Wright Export Corp., 299 U.S. 304 (1936).
36. TCCT.
37. JMH–EW, April 12, 1965. JMHP.
38. 381 U.S. 301 (1965).
39. Griswold v. Connecticut, 381 U.S. 479 (1965).
40. 379 U.S. 64 (1964).
41. No. 400—October Term, 1963. Jim Garrison, Appellant v. State of Louisiana. WJB opinion of the Court [May, 1964]. Recirculated: 5–21–64. JMHP. Brackets in original.

42. JMH–TCC, June 12, 1964. TCCT.

43. New York Times Co. v. Sullivan, 376 U.S. 254 (1964).

44. Quoted loc. cit. supra note 42.

45. WJB, Memorandum to: Mr. Justice Clark, Mr. Justice Harlan, Mr. Justice Stewart, Mr. Justice White, November 19, 1964. TCCT.

46. 380 U.S. 51 (1965).

47. 365 U.S. 43 (1961).

48. 380 U.S. 163 (1965).

49. 367 U.S. 488 (1961).

50. Nos. 50, 51 and 29—October Term 1964. United States, Petitioner, v. Daniel Andrew Seeger. United States, Petitioner, v. Arno Sascha Jakobson. Forest Britt Peter, Petitioner, v. United States. Mr. Justice Goldberg, concurring [March, 1965.] Recirculated February 9, 1965. Brackets in original.

51. 379 U.S. 443 (1965).

52. Huston, *Pathway to Judgement: A Study of Earl Warren* 107 (1966).

53. Ibid.

54. 380 U.S. 400 (1965).

55. 379 U.S. 476 (1965).

56. 19 *Howell's State Trials* 1029 (1765).

57. 380 U.S. 63 (1965).

58. 319 U.S. 463 (1943).

59. 381 U.S. 479 (1965).

60. 118 U.S. 356 (1886).

61. Supra note 38.

62. 381 U.S. at 308.

63. Id. at 484.

64. Id. at 486.

65. NYT, June 14, 1965, p. 38.

66. 379 U.S. 433 (1965).

67. 377 U.S. 533 (1964).

68. LBJ–EW, March 19, 1966. LBJ Library.

69. EW–LBJ, April 6, 1966. LBJ Library.

70. LBJ–EW, November 8, 1967. LBJ Library.

71. LBJ–EW, November 22, 1967. LBJ Library.

72. Memorandum, For the President, From Jim Gaither, May 13, 1968. LBJ Library.

73. Nina E. Warren–LBJ, May 27 [1968]. LBJ Library.

74. Weaver, *Warren: The Man, The Court, The Era* 336 (1967).

75. Pollack, *Earl Warren: The Judge Who Changed America* 266 (1979).

76. LBJ, *The Vantage Point: Perspectives of the Presidency, 1963–1969* (1971).

77. Shogan, *A Question of Judgment: The Fortas Case and the Struggle for the Supreme Court* 107 (1972).

78. 372 U.S. 335 (1963).

79. Douglas, *The Court Years 1939–1975: The Autobiography of William O. Douglas* 318 (1980).

80. WOD–HLB, August 1, 1965. HLBLC.

81. Douglas, op. cit. supra note 79, at 319.

82. Shogan, op. cit. supra note 77, at 113.
83. Ibid.
84. Quoted ibid.

14. 1965 TERM: MIRANDA, DISCRIMINATION, AND FIRST AMENDMENT

1. NYT, January 17, 1965, section VI, p. 18.
2. Federal Trade Commission v. Colgate-Palmolive Co., 380 U.S. 374 (1965).
3. Supra note 1, at 58.
4. Id. at 18.
5. 384 U.S. 436 (1966).
6. Ibid.
7. Ibid.
8. 34 *U.S. Law Week* 3297 (1966).
9. Gideon v. Wainwright, 372 U.S. 335 (1973).
10. 34 *U.S. Law Week* at 3298–3299.
11. Id. at 3301.
12. 378 U.S. 1 (1964).
13. Massiah v. United States, 377 U.S. 201 (1964).
14. Escobedo v. Illinois, 378 U.S. 478 (1964).
15. 387 U.S. at 544, 543.
16. Weaver, *Warren: The Man, The Court, The Era* 234 (1967).
17. 384 U.S. 757 (1966).
18. 352 U.S. 432 (1957).
19. 383 U.S. 663 (1966).
20. 302 U.S. 277 (1937).
21. 377 U.S. 533 (1964).
22. HLB, Memorandum for the Conference, March 4, 1965. TCCT.
23. 383 U.S. 301 (1966).
24. Id. at 315–316.
25. 384 U.S. 641 (1966).
26. 360 U.S. 45 (1959).
27. 383 U.S. 745 (1966).
28. 109 U.S. 3 (1883).
29. 383 U.S. at 782.
30. Id. at 762, n. 1.
31. 383 U.S. 131 (1966).
32. 379 U.S. 536 (1965).
33. 382 U.S. 103 (1965).
34. Ibid.
35. 382 U.S. 198 (1965).
36. 384 U.S. 808 (1966).
37. Id. at 828.
38. 384 U.S. 214 (1966).
39. 383 U.S. 75 (1966).

40. 376 U.S. 254 (1964).
41. 379 U.S. 64 (1964).
42. 388 U.S. 130 (1967).
43. 383 U.S. 413 (1966).
44. 383 U.S. 463 (1966).
45. Id. at 466.
46. Ibid.
47. 383 U.S. 502 (1966).
48. Id. at 505.
49. 354 U.S. 476 (1957).
50. 383 U.S. at 418.
51. Id. at 420.
52. 354 U.S. 436 (1957).
53. Dissenting, id. at 446.
54. 383 U.S. at 441.
55. 354 U.S. at 446.
56. 383 U.S. at 468.
57. Id. at 510.
58. 384 U.S. 916 (1966).
59. Ibid.
60. 384 U.S. 937 (1966).
61. 380 U.S. 503 (1965).
62. 382 U.S. 70 (1965).
63. 367 U.S. 1 (1961).
64. 322 U.S. 694 (1944).
65. 142 U.S. 547 (1892).
66. 384 U.S. 11 (1966).
67. 384 U.S. 73 (1966).
68. 379 U.S. 433 (1965).
69. NYT, July 7, 1966, p. 22.
70. NYT, March 13, 1966, section VI, p. 30.
71. NYT, July 5, 1966, p. 18; September 24, 1966, p. 18.
72. Supra note 70.
73. Supra note 17.
74. Supra note 36.
75. Supra note 4.
76. Lewis, *Portrait of a Decade: The Second American Revolution* 139 (1964).

15. 1966 TERM: WARREN AND THE "NEW" BLACK

1. 383 U.S. 131 (1966).
2. 385 U.S. 374 (1967).
3. Shogan, *A Question of Judgment: The Fortas Case and the Struggle for the Supreme Court* 134 (1972).
4. "Dear Chief," June 23, 1969. Draft with changes in HLB writing. HLBLC.
5. Griswold v. Connecticut, 381 U.S. 479 (1965).

6. 378 U.S. 226 (1964).
7. 385 U.S. 39 (1966).
8. 372 U.S. 229 (1963).
9. 388 U.S. 307 (1967).
10. Id. at 330.
11. 385 U.S. 231 (1966).
12. 372 U.S. 368 (1963).
13. 386 U.S. 300 (1967).
14. 388 U.S. 41 (1967).
15. 387 U.S. 294 (1967).
16. 19 Howell's State Trials 1029 (1765).
17. 387 U.S. 523 (1967).
18. 387 U.S. 541 (1967).
19. 359 U.S. 360 (1959).
20. 385 U.S. 374 (1967).
21. Shogan, op. cit. supra note 3, at 127.
22. 376 U.S. 254 (1964).
23. 384 U.S. 995 (1966).
24. Spahn v. Julian Messner, Inc., 18 N.Y.2d 324 (1966).
25. 385 U.S. at 394.
26. 383 U.S. 75, 92 (1966).
27. 388 U.S. 130 (1967).
28. Ibid.
29. Supra note 22.
30. 383 U.S. 75 (1966).
31. Supra note 20.
32. 385 U.S. at 398.
33. 388 U.S. at 133.
34. 386 U.S. 767 (1967).
35. Ibid.
36. Ibid.
37. Roth v. United States, 354 U.S. 476 (1957).
38. Ginzburg v. United States, 383 U.S. 463 (1966).
39. Mishkin v. United States, 383 U.S. 502 (1966).
40. 361 U.S. 147 (1959).
41. 386 U.S. at 769.
42. Id. at 772.
43. 388 U.S. 218 (1967).
44. 388 U.S. 263 (1967).
45. 388 U.S. 293 (1967).
46. Miranda v. Arizona, 384 U.S. 436 (1966).
47. 384 U.S. 757 (1966).
48. 388 U.S. at 302.
49. 384 U.S. at 480.
50. Supra notes 27 and 28.
51. 386 U.S. 66 (1967).

52. 385 U.S. 554 (1967).

53. 388 U.S. 175 (1967).

54. 385 U.S. 116 (1966).

55. 35 *U.S. Law Week* 3171 (1966).

56. COH.

57. 388 U.S. 1 (1967).

58. Naim v. Naim, 350 U.S. 891 (1955).

59. COH.

60. 388 U.S. at 3.

61. 262 U.S. 390 (1923).

62. COH.

63. 385 U.S. 589 (1967).

64. 342 U.S. 485 (1952).

65. 384 U.S. 11 (1966).

66. This was omitted from the published dissent.

67. 387 U.S. 253 (1967).

68. 356 U.S. 44 (1958).

69. 386 U.S. 372 (1967).

70. 387 U.S. 105 (1967).

71. 387 U.S. 1 (1967).

72. Miranda v. Arizona, 384 U.S. 436 (1966).

73. 387 U.S. 82 (1967).

74. TCCT.

75. TCCT.

76. NYT, December 17, 1966, p. 19.

77. Hoerner, 2 Hastings Const. L.Q. 18 (1975).

78. Supra note 7.

79. 384 U.S. 436 (1966).

80. Supra note 63.

81. Brown v. Board of Education, 347 U.S. 483 (1954).

82. Woodward and Armstrong, *The Brethren: Inside the Supreme Court* 47 (1979).

83. Douglas, *The Court Years 1939–1975: The Autobiography of William O. Douglas* 251 (1980).

84. EW–LBJ, June 19, 1967. LBJ Library.

85. Henry J. Friendly–FF, January 9, 1962. FFLC.

86. Henry J. Friendly–FF, February 2, 1962. FFLC.

16. 1967 TERM: ABORTIVE RETIREMENT

1. Jones, Memorandum for the Record, June 13, 1968. LBJ Library.

2. EW–LBJ, June 13, 1968. LBJ Library.

3. White House Press Secretary, For Immediate Release, June 26, 1968. Text of Chief Justice Earl Warren's Letter to the President. LBJ Library.

4. Supra note 1.

5. Supra note 2.

6. Office of the Deputy Attorney General, Memorandum for Honorable Larry

Temple, Special Assistant to the President Re: The Fortas and Thornberry Nominations, December 20, 1968. LBJ Library.

7. Ibid.

8. *U.S. News & World Report*, July 15, 1968, p. 63.

9. Ibid.

10. 391 U.S. 367 (1968).

11. 36 *U.S. Law Week* 3302 (1968).

12. Id. at 3303.

13. 371 U.S. 415 (1963).

14. Id. at 438.

15. Though WOD had circulated a memorandum February 1, 1968, and recirculated it April 13, asking for "restoring the instant case to the calendar for reargument on the question of the constitutionality of a peacetime draft." JMHP.

16. 392 U.S. 1 (1968).

17. 36 *U.S. Law Week* 3248 (1967).

18. Ibid.

19. Miranda v. Arizona, 384 U.S. 436 (1966).

20. 387 U.S. 523 (1967).

21. 389 U.S. 241 (1967).

22. 392 U.S. 514 (1968).

23. 370 U.S. 660 (1962).

24. 390 U.S. 39 (1968).

25. 390 U.S. 62 (1968).

26. 345 U.S. 22 (1953).

27. 382 U.S. 70 (1965).

28. 335 U.S. 1 (1948).

29. Supra note 27.

30. Supra note 26.

31. 274 U.S. 259 (1927).

32. 388 U.S. 903 (1967).

33. 392 U.S. 409 (1968).

34. 326 U.S. 501 (1946).

35. 42 U.S.C. § 1982.

36. 36 *U.S. Law Week* 3385 (1968).

37. 109 U.S. 3 (1883).

38. 392 U.S. at 449.

39. 391 U.S. 430 (1968).

40. Brown v. Board of Education, 347 U.S. 483 (1954).

41. Compare EW–Justices, May 7, 1954. HHBLC.

42. 347 U.S. at 494, n. 11.

43. See Chapter 3 supra, pp. 106–107.

44. Brown v. Board of Education, 349 U.S. 294 (1955).

45. 391 U.S. at 436.

46. Id. at 442.

47. Id. at 440, n. 5.

48. 390 U.S. 629 (1968).

49. 319 U.S. 41 (1943).

50. 388 U.S. 431 (1967).

51. 388 U.S. 439 (1967).

52. 392 U.S. 40 (1968).

53. Supra note 16.

54. 390 U.S. at 633, n. 2.

55. 392 U.S. at 55–56.

56. 390 U.S. at 631.

57. Roth v. United States, 354 U.S. 476 (1957).

58. A Book Names "John Cleland's Memoirs of a Woman of Pleasure" v. Massachusetts, 383 U.S. 413 (1966).

59. 389 U.S. 258 (1967).

60. 367 U.S. 1 (1961).

61. 391 U.S. 123 (1968).

62. 352 U.S. 232 (1957).

63. 386 U.S. 18 (1967).

64. 378 U.S. 368 (1964).

65. 380 U.S. 400 (1965).

66. 392 U.S. 293 (1968).

67. WJB, Memorandum to the Conference, May 28, 1968. JMHP.

68. Pollack, *Earl Warren: The Judge Who Changed America* 24 (1979).

69. 391 U.S. 99 (1968).

70. 391 U.S. 68 (1968).

71. 392 U.S. 236 (1968).

72. 330 U.S. 1 (1947).

73. 392 U.S. 302 (1968).

74. 391 U.S. 510 (1968).

75. 391 U.S. 1 (1968).

76. 384 U.S. 436 (1966).

77. 389 U.S. 347 (1967).

78. 277 U.S. 438 (1928).

79. 365 U.S. 505 (1961).

80. 389 U.S. at 362, n.

81. Id. at 358, n. 23.

82. Id. at 359.

83. Brown v. Board of Education, 347 U.S. 483 (1954).

84. Douglas, As Chief Justice, 60 A.B.A.J. 1232, 1233 (1974).

85. 389 U.S. 413 (1967).

86. Id. at 414.

87. See HLB–EW, December 12, 1967; WJF–EW, December 12, 1967; Thurgood Marshall–EW, December 12, 1967; PS–EW, December 12, 1967; BRW–EW, December 12, 1967; Abe Fortas–EW, December 13, 1967; JMH–EW, December 13, 1967. JMHP.

88. *U.S. News & World Report,* July 15, 1968, p. 63.

89. Miller, *Lyndon: An Oral History* 484 (1980).

90. Shogan, *A Question of Judgment: The Fortas Case and the Struggle for the Supreme Court* 170 (1972).

91. Mallory v. United States, 354 U.S. 449 (1957).

92. Pollack, op. cit. supra note 68, at 280.

93. NYT, August 23, 1968, p. 12; Pollack, op. cit. supra note 68, at 281.

94. Shogan, op. cit. supra note 90, at 179.

95. Id. at 182.

96. Office of the White House Press Secretary, Statement by the President, October 10, 1968. LBJ Library.

97. Ibid.

98. Ibid.

17. 1968 TERM: THE FINAL TERM

1. Wilson, *Constitutional Government in the United States* 160 (1911).

2. Klein, *Making It Perfectly Clear* 1 (1980).

3. Supra Chapter 16, note 1.

4. Pierson, Memorandum for the President, October 3, 1968. LBJ Library.

5. Ibid.

6. Nixon, *RN: The Memoirs of Richard Nixon* 419 (1978).

7. See Mackenzie, "Nixon and Justice Warren: Rivalry to Reconciliation," *Washington Post*, July 11, 1974.

8. NYT, December 5, 1968, p. 1.

9. 395 U.S. 486 (1969).

10. 394 U.S. 618 (1969).

11. United States v. O'Brien, 391 U.S. 367 (1968).

12. 383 U.S. 745 (1966).

13. 334 U.S. 410 (1948).

14. 394 U.S. 576 (1969).

15. Id. at 653.

16. Supra note 14.

17. 394 U.S. at 605.

18. Supra note 9.

19. 394 U.S. 111 (1969).

20. 362 U.S. 199 (1960).

21. 393 U.S. 503 (1969).

22. 399 U.S. 383 (1970).

23. 395 U.S. 956 (1969).

24. Supra note 22.

25. 398 U.S. 262 (1970).

26. 391 U.S. 510 (1968).

27. 398 U.S. 262 (1970).

28. 402 U.S. 183 (1971).

29. 395 U.S. 784 (1969).

30. 302 U.S. 319 (1937).

31. 394 U.S. 440 (1969).

32. 393 U.S. 483 (1969).

33. 395 U.S. 147 (1969).

34. Schick v. United States, 195 U.S. 65 (1904).

35. Cheff v. Scknackenberg, 384 U.S. 373 (1966).

36. 395 U.S. at 152.

37. 395 U.S. 258 (1969).

38. 394 U.S. 217 (1969).

39. 394 U.S. 165 (1969).

40. EW *Memoirs* 337.

41. Ivanov v. United States, 394 U.S. 165 (1969); Butenko v. United States, 394 U.S. 165 (1969).

42. Clay v. United States, 394 U.S. 310 (1969).

43. Hoffa v. United States, 394 U.S. 310 (1969).

44. EW *Memoirs* 339.

45. Douglas, *The Court Years 1939–1975: The Autobiography of William O. Douglas* 259 (1980).

46. EW *Memoirs* 340.

47. NYT, May 17, 1973, p. 35.

48. Douglas, op. cit. supra note 45, at 260.

49. 394 U.S. 526 (1969).

50. 394 U.S. 542 (1969).

51. 376 U.S. 1 (1964).

52. See Schwartz, *The American Heritage History of the Law in America* 224 (1974).

53. 393 U.S. 97 (1968).

54. 352 U.S. 380 (1957).

55. 380 U.S. 479 (1965).

56. 401 U.S. 37 (1971).

57. 401 U.S. 66 (1971).

58. 395 U.S. 955 (1969); 395 U.S. 957 (1969).

59. Supra notes 56 and 57.

60. 395 U.S. 486 (1969).

61. Woodward and Armstrong, *The Brethren: Inside the Supreme Court* 25 (1979).

62. Brown v. Board of Education, 347 U.S. 483 (1954).

63. Reynolds v. Sims, 377 U.S. 533 (1964).

64. See Schwartz, *From Confederation to Nation: The American Constitution, 1835–1877,* 29 (1973).

65. Supra note 56.

66. Supra note 57.

67. 1 Cranch 137 (U.S. 1803).

68. 369 U.S. 186 (1962).

69. "Fortas of the Supreme Court: A Question of Ethics," *Life,* May 4, 1969.

70. Shogan, *A Question of Judgment: The Fortas Case and the Struggle for the Supreme Court* 248–249 (1972).

71. Douglas, op. cit. supra note 45, at 358–359.

72. Shogan, op. cit. supra note 70, at 249.

73. Nixon, *RN: The Memoirs of Richard Nixon* 420 (1978).

74. NYT, June 13, 1969, p. 1.

75. Ibid.

76. NYT, November 2, 1969.

77. Pollack, *Earl Warren: The Judge Who Changed America* 283 (1979).

78. Ibid.

79. Ibid.

80. NYT, January 22, 1969, p. 28; January 23, 1969, p. 22.

81. Pollack, op. cit. supra note 77, at 286.

82. Woodward and Armstrong, op. cit. supra note 61, at 10–11.

83. 385 U.S. 374 (1967).

84. 395 U.S. VII, X (1969).

85. Id. at X, XI.

86. NYT, June 30, 1969, p. 24.

87. NYT, January 3, 1968, p. 15.

88. NYT, June 23, 1969, p. 24.

89. See Pollack, op. cit. supra note 77, at 309.

90. Federal Judicial Center, Report of the Study Group on the Caseload of the Supreme Court (1972).

91. EW–Peter D. Ehrenhaft, November 8, 1972.

92. EW, Memorandum to My Law Clerks, November 8, 1972.

93. Peter D. Ehrenhaft–EW November 15, 1972.

94. Ehrenhaft, Memorandum to the Law Clerks of Chief Justice Warren, December 21, 1972.

95. Warren, 59 A.B.A.J. 724 (1973).

96. Brennan, "Chief Justice Warren," 88 Harv. L. Rev. 1, 4 (1974).

97. NYT, July 9, 1979, p. B4; Douglas, op. cit. supra note 45, at 239.

98. Pollack, op. cit. supra note 77, at 288.

99. Id. at 319–320.

100. Id. at 321.

101. See NYT, March 23, 1975, section IV, p. 6; Whitman, *Alden Whitman's Golden Oldies*, April, 1975, p. 82.

102. See Pollack, op. cit. supra note 77, at 333.

103. Douglas, op. cit. supra note 45, at 238.

104. United States v. Nixon, 418 U.S. 683 (1974).

BIBLIOGRAPHY

Acheson, Dean. *Present at the Creation.* New York: Norton 1969.

Berry, Mary. *Stability, Security and Continuity: Mr. Justice Burton and Decision-Making in the Supreme Court 1945–1958.* Westport, Connecticut: Greenwood Press, 1978.

Black, Hugo, Jr. *My Father: A Remembrance.* New York: Random House, 1975.

Bryce, James. *The American Commonwealth.* 2 vols. London and New York: Macmillan and Co., 1889.

Cahn, Edmond, ed. *Supreme Court and Supreme Law.* Bloomington: Indiana University Press, 1954.

Cardozo, Benjamin N. *The Nature of the Judicial Process.* New Haven: Yale University Press, 1921.

Christman, Henry, ed. *The Public Papers of Chief Justice Earl Warren.* New York: Simon & Schuster, 1959.

Clayton, James M. *The Making of Justice: The Supreme Court In Action.* New York: Dutton, 1964.

Douglas, William O. *The Court Years 1939–1975: The Autobiography of William O. Douglas.* New York: Random House, 1980.

Douglas, William O. *Go East Young Man: The Early Years.* New York: Random House, 1974.

Dunne, Gerald. *Hugo Black and the Judicial Revolution.* New York: Simon & Schuster, 1977.

Eisenhower, Dwight D. *Mandate for Change 1953–1956: The White House Years.* New York: Doubleday, 1956–61.

Frank, John P. *The Warren Court.* New York: Macmillan and Co., 1964.

Frankfurter, Felix. *Felix Frankfurter Reminisces.* New York: Doubleday, 1962.

Frankfurter, Felix. *Of Law and Men: Papers and Addresses of Felix Frankfurter.* New York: Harcourt Brace, 1956.

Frankfurter, Felix and James M. Landis. *The Business of the Supreme Court: A Study in the Federal Judicial System.* New York: Macmillan and Co., 1927.

Freedman, Max. *Roosevelt and Frankfurter: Their Correspondence 1928–1945*. Boston: Little, Brown & Company, 1967.

Friedman, Leon and Israel, Fred, eds. *The Justices of the United States Supreme Court 1789–1969: Their Lives and Major Opinions*. New York: Chelsea House, 1969.

Gerhart, Eugene. *America's Advocate: Robert H. Jackson*. Indianapolis: Bobbs-Merrill, 1958.

Gerhart, Eugene. *Arthur T. Vanderbilt, The Compleat Counsellor*. New York: Q Corp., 1980.

Gordon, Rosalie M. *Nine Men Against America, The Supreme Court and Its Attack on American Liberties*. New York: Adair Co., 1958.

Gunther, John. *Inside U.S.A.* New York and London: Harper & Brothers, 1947.

Harbaugh, William. *Lawyer's Lawyer: The Life of John W. Davis*. New York: Oxford University Press, 1973.

Hirsch, H.N. *The Enigma of Felix Frankfurter*. New York: Basic Books, 1981.

Huston, Luther. *Pathway to Judgment: A Study of Earl Warren*. Philadelphia: Chilton Books, 1966.

Jackson, Robert H. *The Supreme Court in the American System of Government*. Cambridge: Harvard University Press, 1955.

Johnson, Lyndon B. *The Vantage Point: Perspectives of the Presidency 1963–1969*. New York: Holt, 1971.

Katcher, Leo. *Earl Warren: A Political Biography*. New York: McGraw-Hill, 1967.

Klein, Herbert. *Making It Perfectly Clear*. New York: Doubleday, 1980.

Kluger, Richard. *Simple Justice: The History of Brown v. Board of Education and Black America's Struggle for Equality*. New York: Knopf, 1975.

Kurland, Phillip and Gerhard Casper, eds. *Landmark Briefs and Arguments of the Supreme Court of the United States: Constitutional Law*. Arlington, Virginia: University Publishers of America, 1977.

Lash, Joseph P. *From the Diaries of Felix Frankfurter*. New York: Norton, 1975.

Levy, Leonard W., ed. *The Supreme Court under Earl Warren*. New York: Quadrangle Books, 1972.

Lewis, Anthony. *Gideon's Trumpet*. New York: Random House, 1964.

Lewis, Anthony. *Portrait of a Decade: The Second American Revolution*. New York: Random House, 1964.

Mason, Alpheus T. *Harlan Fiske Stone: Pillar of the Law*. New York: Viking Press, 1956.

Mazo, Earl. *Richard Nixon, A Political and Personal Portrait*. New York: Harper, 1959.

McCloskey, Robert Green. *The Modern Supreme Court*. Cambridge: Harvard University Press, 1972.

McLellan, David S. and David C. Acheson, eds. *Among Friends: Personal Letters of Dean Acheson*. New York: Dodd, Mead, 1980.

Miller, Merle. *Lyndon: An Oral Biography*. New York: Ballantine, 1981.

Nixon, Richard M. *RN: The Memoirs of Richard Nixon*. New York: Warner, 1981.

Parrish, Michael E. *Felix Frankfurter and His Times: The Reform Years*. New York: Free Press, 1982.

Peltason, Jack. *Fifty-Eight Lonely Men: Southern Federal Judges and School Desegregation*. New York: Harcourt Brace & World, 1961.

Pollack, Jack Harrison. *Earl Warren: The Judge Who Changed America*. Englewood Cliffs, New Jersey: Prentice Hall, 1979.

Pusey, Merlo J. *Charles Evans Hughes*, 2 vols. New York: Macmillan and Co., 1951.

Rodell, Fred. *Nine Men: A Political History of the Supreme Court from 1790 to 1955*. New York: Random House, 1955.

Schlesinger, Arthur M. *Robert Kennedy and His Times*. Boston: Houghton Mifflin, 1978.

Schubert, Glendon. *The Judicial Mind*. Evanston, Illinois: Northwestern University Press, 1965.

Schwartz, Bernard. *A Basic History of the U.S. Supreme Court*. Princeton: D. Van Nostrand Company, 1968.

Schwartz, Bernard. *The Great Rights of Mankind: A History of the American Bill of Rights*. New York: Oxford University Press, 1977.

Schwartz, Bernard. *The Law in America: A History*. New York: McGraw-Hill, 1974.

Schwartz, Bernard. *The Reins of Power: A Constitutional History of the United States*. New York: Hill and Wang, 1963.

Schwartz, Bernard. *The Supreme Court: Constitutional Revolution in Retrospect*. New York: Ronald Press, 1957.

Shogan, Robert. *A Question of Judgment: The Fortas Case and the Struggle for the Supreme Court*. Indianapolis: Bobbs-Merrill, 1972.

Simon, James. *Independent Journey: The Life of William O. Douglas*. New York: Harper & Row, 1980.

Stone, Irving. *Earl Warren: A Great American Story*. New York: Prentice Hall, 1948.

Tocqueville, Alexis de. *Democracy in America*. New York: Vintage Books, 1954.

Truman, Harry S. *Years of Trial & Hope*. "Memoirs," vol. 2. Garden City, New York: Doubleday, 1956.

Umbreit, Kenneth Bernard. *Our Eleven Chief Justices*. New York: Harper & Brothers, 1938.

Warren, Charles. *The Supreme Court in United States History*, 3 vols. Boston: Little, Brown & Company, 1922.

Warren, Earl. *The Memoirs of Earl Warren*. New York: Doubleday, 1977.

Weaver, John D. *Warren: The Man, The Court, The Era*. Boston: Little, Brown & Company, 1967.

White, G. Edmund. *Earl Warren: A Public Life*. New York: Oxford University Press, 1982.

Woodward, Bob and Scott Armstrong. *The Brethren: Inside the Supreme Court*. New York: Simon & Schuster, 1979.

TABLE OF CASES

Aaron v. Cooper, 804

Abel v. United States, 339-341

Abernathy v. Alabama, 555

Abington School District v. Schempp, 65, 466-468, 469

Ableman v. Booth, 296

A Book Named "John Cleland's Memoirs of a Woman of Pleasure" v. Massachusetts, 618-622, 708, 827

Accardi v. Shaughnessy, 231, 232, 797

Achilli v. United States, 214-215

Adams v. Maryland, 789

Adamson v. California, 397, 811

Adderley v. Florida, 631-632, 677

Adler v. Board of Education, 670

Afroyim v. Rusk, 670-671

Alabama v. United States, 463-464

Albertson v. Subversive Activities Control Board, 624-625, 695, 696, 699, 701

Alderman v. United States, 749-751

Alton v. Alton, 139-142, 788

American Committee for Protection of Foreign Born v. Subversive Activities Control Board, 560-562, 624

American Communications Association v. Douds, 562

American Federation of Musicians v. Carroll, 715

Associated Press v. Walker, 648-652, 661

Atlantic Refining Co. v. Public Service Commission, 334

Austin v. Kentucky, 623, 652-656

Avent v. North Carolina, 816

Baker v. Carr, 61, 264, 388, 391, 398, 399, 400, 410-428, 430, 437, 439, 443, 464, 465, 501, 502, 503, 760, 813

Baltimore & Ohio R. Co. v. United States, 671-672

Banco Nacional de Cuba v. Sabbatino, 530

Barenblatt v. United States, 325-326, 362, 431, 809, 814

Barr v. Columbia, 508-509, 512, 516, 517, 518, 519, 524, 819

Barsky v. Board of Regents, 151

Bartkus v. Illinois, 322-324

Bates v. Little Rock, 350

Beilan v. Board of Education, 801

Bell v. Maryland, 508-525, 630, 819

Benton v. Maryland, 742-743

Berger v. New York, 639-640

Betts v. Brady, 341, 407-409, 458-460

Bibb v. Navajo Freight Line, 334

Blackburn v. Alabama, 212, 795

Board of Education v. Allen, 716

Bolling v. Sharpe, 98-100, 105, 125, 298

Bond v. Floyd, 666-668

Bouie v. Columbia, 508-509, 512, 516, 517, 518, 519, 524

Boynton v. Virginia, 555-556

Braden v. United States, 361-362

Bradley v. Richmond School District, 609

Breedlove v. Suttles, 596, 597

Breithaupt v. Abram, 206-207, 594, 595

Bridges v. California, 432

Briggs v. Elliott, 783

Brooks v. Florida, 719-720

Brown v. Board of Education, Chapter 3, 159, 242, 276, 289, 292, 295, 298, 299, 300, 301, 302, 405, 460, 500, 506, 518, 704-706, 759, 790, 801, 804, 815, 817, 818, 825, 826, 827, 829

Brown v. Louisiana, 606-609, 631

Brown v. Mississippi, 545

Brown v. United States, 333

Brown Shoe Co. v. United States, 437-438

Bruton v. United States, 711-715
Burns v. Richardson, 625-627
Burns Baking Co. v. Bryan, 800
Burton v. Wilmington Parking Authority, 370-371, 787
Butenko v. United States, 829
Butler v. Michigan, 218-219, 754, 796

Cafeteria Workers Union v. McElroy, 365-366
California v. Stewart, 588
Camara v. Municipal Court, 642, 689
Cameron v. Johnson, 556
Cammer v. United States, 191
Caritativo v. California, 254
Carnley v. Cochran, 407-410, 458, 815
Central Pacific Ry. Co. v. Alameda County, 807
Chandler v. Florida, 552
Chapman v. California, 712, 713
Cheff v. Schnackenberg, 829
Civil Rights Cases, 157, 481, 510, 554, 602-603, 606, 703
Clark v. Pearson, 819
Clay v. United States, 829
Cohens v. Virginia, 535
Colegrove v. Green, 377-378, 410-412, 416, 418, 419, 420
Communist Party v. Subversive Activities Control Board, 185-188, 363, 364-365, 561, 709, 793
Cooper v. Aaron, 289-303, 305, 804
Costello v. United States, 796
Counselman v. Hitchcock, 624
Cox v. Louisiana, 557-559, 607-608, 780
Craig v. Harney, 547
Curtis Publishing Co. v. Butts, 617, 648-652, 661

Darr v. Burford, 470, 471
Davis v. Mann, 818
Dawson v. Mayor, 786
Dayton v. Dulles, 309-311
De Jonge v. Oregon, 560
Delli Paoli v. United States, 711-713
Dennis v. United States, 431
Dick v. New York Life Ins. Co., 801
Doctor v. Harrington, 210-212
Dombrowski v. Eastland, 674-676
Dombrowski v. Pfister, 755-757
Drivers Union v. Meadowmoor Co., 780

Eastern Railroad Presidents Conference v. Noerr Motor Freight, 384
Eaton v. Price, 342-344, 808
Edwards v. South Carolina, 632
Egan v. City of Aurora, 781
Elfbrandt v. Russell, 625
Elkins v. United States, 61, 338, 344-346, 396
Emspak v. United States, 177-179

Engel v. Vitale, 438, 440-442, 466, 467
Entick v. Carrington, 575, 640
Epperson v. Arkansas, 753-756
Erie Railroad Co. v. Tompkins, 212
Escobedo v. Illinois, 528, 591, 822
Estes v. Texas, 462, 545-552
Everson v. Board of Education, 381, 810

Far East Conference v. United States, 306, 805
Fay v. Noia, 470-472, 473
Federal Base Ball Club v. National League, 162, 163, 164
Federal Maritime Board v. Isbrandtsen Co., 805
Federal Trade Commission v. Colgate-Palmolive Co., 822
Feiner v. New York, 557
Ferguson v. Georgia, 384-386
Ferguson v. Moore-McCormack Lines, 800, 801
Flemming v. Nestor, 342
Fortson v. Dorsey, 580-581, 626
Fortson v. Morris, 634-638
Foster v. California, 743
Francis v. Resweber, 782
Frank v. Maryland, 263, 326-328, 343-344, 642
Frank v. United States, 744-745
Frazier v. United States, 431
Freedman v. Maryland, 568-570

Gallagher v. Crown Kosher Market, 816
Galvan v. Press, 789
Garner v. Louisiana, 402-404, 484
Garrison v. Louisiana, 566-568, 612-613
Gault, In re, 672-673
Gayle v. Browder, 786
Gebhart v. Belton, 783
Gent v. Arkansas, 623, 652-656
Giaccio v. Pennsylvania, 740
Gibson v. Florida Legislative Investigation Committee, 452-453
Gibson v. Lockheed Aircraft Service, 190
Gideon v. Wainwright, 66, 195, 407, 457-460, 584, 822
Gilbert v. California, 656-663
Giles v. Maryland, 663-664
Gilliam v. Hopewell School Board, 609
Ginsberg v. New York, 706-709
Ginzburg v. United States, 618-622, 653, 824
Gober v. Birmingham, 816
Goldblatt v. Hempstead, 434-435
Gomillion v. Lightfoot, 377-378, 416
Gonzales v. Landon, 191
Gray v. Sanders, 433, 465, 635
Green v. County School Board, 703-706
Green v. United States, 369
Greenwood v. Peacock, 611
Gregory v. Chicago, 735-736

Griffin v. Illinois, 193-195, 793
Griffin v. Maryland, 480, 482, 485, 486, 508, 524
Grisham v. Hagan, 808
Griswold v. Connecticut, 566, 577-580, 630, 784, 820
Grosso v. United States, 694-701
Gunn v. University Committee to End Vietnam War, 737-738

Hamilton v. Alabama, 529
Hamm v. Rock Hill, 553, 555
Hannah v. Larche, 351-352
Harman v. Forssenius, 560
Harper v. Virginia Board of Education, 596-597
Harris v. Pennsylvania R. Co., 801
Hart v. Keith, 163
Heart of Atlanta Motel v. United States, 554, 820
Helvering v. Davis, 519
Henry v. Mississippi, 572-574
Hernandez v. Texas, 138-139
Hintopoulos v. Shaughnessy, 210
Hoffa v. United States, 829
Holmes v. Atlanta, 786
Howell Chevrolet Company v. National Labor Relations Board, 145
Hoyt v. Florida, 400-401
Hurtado v. California, 167

Indian Towing Co. v. United States, 198-199
Inman v. Baltimore & Ohio R. Co., 801
International Association of Machinists v. Street, 371-376
International Longshoreman's Union v. Boyd, 152
Interstate Commerce Commission v. Inland Waterways Corp., 45, 779
Irvin v. Dowd, 471
Irvine v. California, 134-137, 151, 175, 207
Ivanov v. United States, 829

Jackson v. Denno, 527, 713
Jackson v. State, 790
Jacobellis v. Ohio, 796, 806, 814
Jacobs v. New York, 706-707
Jencks v. United States, 225, 226-228, 229, 312, 796, 805
Johnson v. Avery, 743-744
Johnson v. Virginia, 786, 787
Jones v. Alfred H. Mayer Co., 702-703

Katz v. United States, 718-719
Katzenbach v. McClung, 554, 820
Katzenbach v. Morgan, 599-602
Kaufman v. United States, 747-749
Kennedy v. Mendoza-Martinez, 357-358, 404-407, 449, 812, 815
Kent v. Dulles, 309-311, 805
Keyishian v. Board of Regents, 669-670, 678

Kidd v. McCanless, 420
Kilbourn v. Thompson, 236, 239
King v. Smith, 717
Kingsley Books, Inc. v. Brown, 619
Kingsley International Pictures Corp. v. Regents, 808
Kinsella v. Singleton, 349, 808
Kirkpatrick v. Preisler, 752-753
Konigsberg v. State Bar, 229-230, 251, 362-363, 797, 809

Lambert v. California, 307-309, 805
Lamont v. Postmaster General, 565-566, 579
Lanza v. New York, 401
Lassiter v. Northampton Election Board, 599, 600
Lathrop v. Donohue, 372-376
Lee v. Madigan, 332-333
Levy v. Louisiana, 715-716
Lombard v. Louisiana, 483-486, 509, 816
Lopez v. United States, 462-463
Loving v. Virginia, 668-669
Lucas v. Colorado General Assembly, 818
Luther v. Borden, 416
Lynch v. Overholser, 433-434

McAuliffe v. Mayor of New Bedford, 792
McCray v. Illinois, 638
McCulloch v. Maryland, 785
McElroy v. Guagliardo, 808
McGautha v. California, 742
McGowan v. Maryland, 380-381, 816
McLaughlin v. Florida, 559-560
McNabb v. United States, 225, 345, 815
Mackey v. Mendoza-Martinez, 357-358
Mallory v. United States, 225-226, 593, 721, 796, 815, 828
Malloy v. Hogan, 528, 590
Manuel Enterprises, Inc. v. Day, 435-437
Mapp v. Ohio, 58, 346, 388, 391-398, 399, 689
Marbury v. Madison, 140, 296, 299, 760
Marchetti v. United States, 694-701
Marsh v. Alabama, 510, 702, 703
Maryland Committee v. Tawes, 818
Massiah v. United States, 528-529, 591, 822
Mastro Plastics Corp. v. National Labor Relations Board, 197
Mathis v. United States, 717-718
Maxwell v. Bishop, 738-742
Mayor v. Dawson, 786
Mesarosh v. United States, 208-209
Meyer v. Nebraska, 99, 668-669
Michalic v. Cleveland Tankers, 801
Michel v. Louisiana, 192
Milanovich v. United States, 254-256, 260, 359-360, 809
Miller v. Arkansas, 210
Milligan, Ex parte, 180, 792

Mills v. Alabama, 612
Minersville School District v. Gobitis, 43
Miranda v. Arizona, 460, 588-595, 628, 661, 673, 678, 687, 688, 717, 824, 825, 826
Mishkin v. New York, 618-623, 653, 824
Mitchell v. King Packing Co., 801
Monroe v. Pape, 360

Naim v. Naim, 158-162, 668, 790, 825
National Association for the Advancement of Colored People v. Alabama, 304-305, 452, 453, 806
National Association for the Advancement of Colored People v. Button, 450-452, 684
National Labor Relations Board v. Allis-Chalmers Mfg. Co., 665-666
New Orleans Park Improvement Assn. v. Detiege, 787
New York Times Co. v. Sullivan, 530, 531-541, 567-568, 612-616, 645-648, 650-652, 819, 821
Nishikawa v. Dulles, 305
Norris v. Alabama, 547
Northern Securities Co. v. United States, 788
Northwestern States Portland Cement Co. v. Minnesota, 334

O'Callahan v. Parker, 745-747
Olmstead v. United States, 386-387, 462, 463, 718, 811, 815
On Lee v. United States, 462, 463, 815

Palko v. Connecticut, 742, 743, 811
Parke Davis, Re, 808
Parker v. Ellis, 341-342
Parr v. United States, 199-200
Pennekamp v. Florida, 432
Pennsylvania v. Nelson, 182-183, 324, 325, 806
People v. Dorado, 787
Pereira v. United States, 789
Perez v. Brownell, 313-319, 671, 806, 812
Peters v. Hobby, 152-155
Peterson v. Greenville, 479-486
Pierce v. Society of Sisters, 99
Plessy v. Ferguson, 74-75, 87, 89, 103, 104, 112, 113, 159, 176, 259, 481
Poe v. Ullman, 378-380
Pointer v. Texas, 574
Pollock v. Farmers' Loan & Trust Co., 818
Powell v. McCormack, 725, 735, 757-760
Powell v. Texas, 693-694
Public Utilities Commission of California v. United Air Lines, 146

Quinn v. United States, 177-179

Rabang v. Boyd, 795
Radio Corporation of America v. United States, 781

Radovich v. National Football League, 213
Railway Employes' Dept. v. Hanson, 371, 373, 374, 810
Rayonier, Inc. v. United States, 795
Rea v. United States, 806
Redrup v. New York, 623, 652-656
Regan v. New York, 166-168, 183, 792
Reid v. Covert, 180, 239-247, 347-349, 798
Rescue Army v. Municipal Court, 160
Reynolds v. Sims, 419, 460, 503-508, 523, 581, 596, 818, 829
Rice v. Sioux City Memorial Park Cemetery, 156-158, 790
Rideau v. Louisiana, 461
Ringhiser v. Chesapeake & Ohio R. Co., 780
Robert v. Russell, 715
Robinson v. California, 438-439, 693, 694
Robinson v. Florida, 508, 512-513, 516
Rochin v. California, 135, 136, 206-207, 579, 795
Rogers v. Paul, 610-611
Rogers v. Richmond, 360
Roman v. Sincock, 818
Rosenblatt v. Baer, 612-617, 648
Ross, In re, 240, 241, 243
Roth v. United States, 218, 219-221, 436, 618, 622, 653, 708, 814, 824, 827
Rowoldt v. Perfetto, 266-267
Rusk v. Cort, 404-407, 449
Russell v. United States, 431

Sailors v. Board of Education, 672
St. Pierre v. United States, 706, 707
St. Regis Paper Co. v. United States, 401
Salsburg v. Maryland, 789
Samuels v. Mackell, 755-757, 760
Sanders v. United States, 474-475
Sawyer, In re, 275
Scales v. United States, 312, 363-364
Schenck v. United States, 780
Schick v. United States, 829
Schilling v. Rogers, 356-357
Schmerber v. California, 594-595, 628, 657, 658
Schware v. Bar Examiners, 229-230, 797
Scull v. Virginia, 329-330
See v. Seattle, 642
Service v. Dulles, 231
Shapiro v. Thompson, 725-732, 734
Shapiro v. United States, 696, 700, 701
Shelley v. Kraemer, 157, 510, 816
Shelton v. Tucker, 367
Sherbert v. Verner, 468-470
Shuttlesworth v. Birmingham, 480, 481, 484, 816
Sibron v. New York, 707
Silverman v. United States, 386-387, 462, 718
Silverthorne Lumber Co. v. United States, 266, 800
Slochower v. Board of Regents, 183-185

Smith v. California, 350-351, 392, 654
Smith v. Sperling, 210-211
Smith v. United States, 332
Snyder v. Massachusetts, 795
South Carolina v. Katzenbach, 598
Spahn v. Julian Messner, Inc., 824
Spano v. New York, 331-332
Spencer v. Texas, 664-665
Stanford v. Texas, 574-575
Stein v. New York, 527
Steiner v. Mitchell, 801
Stewart v. United States, 253-256, 359-360, 809
Stovall v. Denno, 656-663
Street v. New York, 732-734
Sweezy v. New Hampshire, 234-236, 239, 250, 324, 806

Takahashi v. Fish and Game Commission, 730
Talley v. California, 346-347, 808
Tannenbaum v. New York, 706-707
Terry v. Ohio, 685-692, 707
Thompson v. Louisville, 350, 402-404, 482, 485, 511, 553, 556, 735
Time, Inc. v. Hill, 630, 642-649
Times Film Corp. v. Chicago, 216-217, 367-369, 569
Tinker v. Des Moines School District, 736-737
Toolson v. New York Yankees, 162-163, 164, 213
Torcaso v. Watkins, 381-382, 466, 570
Tot v. United States, 575-576
Toth v. Quarles, 179-182, 239, 242, 244
Townsend v. Sain, 472-474
Trop v. Dulles, 313-318, 405, 806, 812
Truax v. Corrigan, 779

Ullmann v. United States, 188-189, 265, 800
United States v. Binghamton Construction Company, 145
United States v. Brown, 562
United States v. Curtiss-Wright Export Corp., 563, 820
United States v. Dege, 274
United States v. du Pont, 195-196, 222-224, 376-377, 796
United States v. Durham Lumber Co., 354-355
United States v. Gainey, 575-577
United States v. Guest, 602-606
United States v. Guy W. Capps, Inc., 165-166
United States v. Harriss, 789
United States v. International Boxing Club, 163-164, 213, 790, 795
United States v. Kahriger, 695, 700
United States v. Klaw, 796
United States v. Mississippi Valley Generating Co., 382-383
United States v. New Britain, 145
United States v. Nixon, 772, 830

United States v. O'Brien, 683-685, 728, 828
United States v. Philadelphia National Bank, 475-479
United States v. Raines, 355-356, 816
United States v. Robel, 709-711
United States v. Seeger, 570-572, 821
United States v. Shaughnessy, 795
United States v. Shirey, 330-331
United States v. Shubert, 163-164, 790
United States v. Sullivan, 700, 701
United States v. Wade, 656-663
United States v. White, 624
United States Navigation Co. v. Cunard Steamship Co., 306, 805
United Steelworkers of America v. United States, 352-353, 563
Uphaus v. Wyman, 324-325

Vignera v. New York, 588
Virginia v. West Virginia, 122
Virginia, Ex parte, 484
Vitarelli v. Seaton, 328-329
Voris v. Eikel, 134, 800

Walker v. Birmingham, 632-634
Walls v. Midland Carbon Co., 435
Warden v. Hayden, 640-642
Watkins v. United States, 234-239, 250, 324, 326, 362, 797, 806, 809, 810
Watson v. Memphis, 787
Watts v. Indiana, 529, 547
Weeks v. United States, 266, 345, 394, 396, 398, 800, 808
Wells v. Rockefeller, 752-753
Wesberry v. Sanders, 501-502, 752
West Virginia Board of Education v. Barnette, 43
Wilkinson v. United States, 361-362, 431, 814
Wilko v. Swan, 145
Wilson v. Girard, 247-249, 798
Witherspoon v. Illinois, 717, 739, 741, 742
WMCA, Inc. v. Lomenzo, 818
Wolf v. Colorado, 135, 206, 207, 345, 391, 393-398, 808
Wolfe v. North Carolina, 349
Wong Sun v. United States, 453-457
Wood v. Georgia, 431-433
Wyatt v. United States, 354

Yancy v. United States, 799
Yates v. United States, 232-234, 250, 251, 362, 364, 797, 809
Yick Wo v. Hopkins, 577
Younger v. Harris, 755-757, 760
Youngstown Sheet & Tube Co. v. Sawyer, 820

Zemel v. Rusk, 563-565
Zwickler v. Koota, 692

INDEX

Abel, Rudolf Ivanovich, 339-340
Abernathy, Ralph D., 555
Abortion, 577
Abstention, 692, 755-757
Acheson, Dean, 36, 38, 39, 259, 272, 425, 507
Act of state, 530
Adams, Francis, W. H., 498
Administrative arrests, 339-340
Aid to Families with Dependent Children, 725
Alameda County, 10
Alcoholics, 693-694
Aliens, 152, 212, 266, 339, 357, 730
"All deliberate speed," 121-123, 505
Allocution right, 369
Almond, J. Lindsay, 114
American Bar Association, 34, 148, 150, 282-286, 336, 428, 448, 546
American Civil Liberties Union, 392
American Federation of Musicians, 715
American Law Institute, 149, 690, 692
American Philosophic Society, 304
American University seminar, 721
Amsterdam, Anthony G., 61, 413
Anderson, Sherwood, 204
Andrews, George W., 442
Anti-evolution statute, 753-754
Anti-Fascist Refugee Committee, 151
Anti-trust, 162-164, 195-196, 213, 222-224, 376-377, 384, 437-438, 475-479
Apportionment, 124, 377-378, 410-427, 501-508, 625-627, 672, 752-753
Armband wearing, 736
Army, Secretary of the, 769
Arnold, Thurman, 153, 155, 601
Arraignment, 225

Articles of War, 332
Ashmore, Robert T., 468
Association, freedom of, 304, 367, 577-579
Association of American Railroads, 70
Association of the Bar, N.Y.C., 281
Atheists, 381
Atomic Energy Commission, 382
Attorney General (Ala.), 304
Attorney General (Cal.), 13-17
Attorney General (Del.), 83
Attorney General (Ga.), 667, 668
Attorney General (Kan.), 83, 113
Attorney General (U.S.), 1-4, 80, 81, 105, 112, 137, 173, 228, 291, 320, 325, 357, 425, 428, 429, 463, 465, 598, 625, 677-678, 682, 718, 749-752, 761
Attorney General (Va.), 114
Attorney solicitation, 450-452
Avery, William, 282-283

Bakersfield, 7-9
Balancing test, 409-410, 433, 527, 695-698
Bank Merger Act, 475-479
Bankruptcy, 354
Bar admission, 229-230, 362-363
Barth, Alan, 207, 489
Bench memos, 67-68, 505
Bentham, Jeremy, 44-45
Beveridge, Albert J., 7
Beytagh, Francis X., 132, 504-505, 526, 701
Bible reading, 65, 466
Bickel, Alexander M., 60, 78, 85, 103, 398, 448, 465, 466
Biddle, Francis, 260
Bifurcation, 738-742
Bill of attainder, 184, 342, 365, 405, 562

Black, Hugo L.
appointment, 28, 32
competitive intensity, 33
Frankfurter disagreements, 33-35, 37, 40, 73, 349
Jackson antagonism, 35, 73, 175
activism vs. restraint, 41-46, 148
Bill of Rights protection, 41, 49
First Amendment, 46-48, 220, 379, 531-532, 535-536, 539, 565, 618, 621, 645-648, 653
absolutist approach, 46-48, 220, 531-532, 653
picketing, 47
sit-ins, 47
Douglas, relations with, 49-50, 487-488, 541, 629, 634-638
Brown case, 77, 81, 84, 87, 91-93, 100, 107-108, 118-120
"all deliberate speed," 123
presiding at conference, 134
opinion assignments, 134
loyalty cases, 154-155
cemetery discrimination, 156-158
executive agreements, 166
Bill of Rights incorporation, 167, 396-397
self-incrimination, 168, 590, 595, 657, 695
Congressional committees, 179
courts-martial, 180-181, 240-246
preferred position, 189
free transcripts, 193-194
realignment, 211
obscenity, 220, 351, 618, 653, 709
Bar admission, 230
Smith Act, 233
Lewis criticism, 251-252
Fourth Amendment, 265-266, 387, 393, 639, 640, 748
worker protection, 271
Little Rock case, 297-303
denationalization, 313-314
double jeopardy, 322
bill of attainder, 342
"state action," 356, 510
censorship, 368
allocution rights, 369
union dues, 371, 374
apportionment, 378, 416, 418-419, 426, 501-502, 581
contraceptive prohibition, 379
religious establishment, 380-381, 440, 716
counsel, 385, 407-409, 460, 657
due process, 395, 409-410, 527, 529, 658, 669
sit-ins, 404, 481, 510-525
split with Warren, 404, 629-640
balancing test, 409-410, 433, 527, 698
regulation vs. taking, 435
narcotics addiction, 439
school prayer, 440, 442
jury trial, 527-528
confessions, 527

libel, 535-536, 539, 566, 650-651
television, 545
civil-rights protests, 553, 558, 631-632
commerce power, 554
passports, 563
conscientious objectors, 570
confrontation, 574
general warrant, 575
right of association, 577
individualism, 587
poll tax, 597
Congressional civil-rights power, 599, 603
Fortas antipathy, 629-630, 645-646
Georgia gubernatorial election, 634-638
informers, 638
mere evidence rule, 641
privacy, 645-648, 690
right to marry, 669
juvenile delinquency, 673
thirty years on Court, 677
Acting Chief Justice, 683
stop and frisk, 685
public drunkenness, 693
wagering tax, 697-698, 700
freedom of choice plan, 704-705
illegitimacy, 715
residence requirement, 730, 732
flag burning, 733-734
Black, Hugo, Jr., 50, 80, 123
Blackmun, Harry A., 757
Blood test, 207, 594
Blue Book, 281
Blue Laws, 380-381, 469
Boggs, Hale, 499
Bolton, Arthur K., 667
Bowron, Fletcher, 15
Brandeis, Louis D., 52, 59, 150, 264, 386, 448, 529
Brant, Irving, 411
Breach of peace, 557-558, 606-608
Brennan, William J.
certiorari petitions, 67
Warren as leader, 144
appointment, 205
description, 205-206
Warren relations, 205-206
realignment, 211
anti-trust, 213, 223-224, 476-478
obscenity, 218-220, 435-437, 618-623, 654-656, 707-709
arraignment, 225
witness reports, 226-228
legislative investigations, 235-236
Little Rock case, 292-303
expatriation, 314-319, 405
double jeopardy, 322-324
mootness, 341
exclusionary rule, 345, 393, 395

"state action," 356, 604-606
union dues, 372-377
integrated Bar, 372-377
ripeness, 380, 464
defendant testimony, 385-386
counsel, 407-409, 590
apportionment, 411-427, 581, 626-627, 753
poliltical questions, 419-420, 464
attorney solicitation, 451-452
illegal arrests and "fruits," 456-457
religious freedom, 467-470
habeas corpus, 470-475
sit-ins, 482-486, 512-525
libel, 531-541, 566-568, 612-617, 650-652
television, 545, 552
self-incrimination, 561, 590-593
passports, 564-565
fundamental rights, 566, 579-580
censorship, 569
illegal evidence waiver, 573
presumptions, 575-576
privacy, 579-580, 647-648
Congressional civil-rights power, 600-606
library protest, 608-609
desegregation, 609-611
civil-rights protests, 631-634
gubernatorial election, 637-638
mere evidence rule, 640-642
lineup, 657-663
railroad merger, 672
compelling interest test, 684, 728-732
stop and frisk, 686-692
freedom of choice plan, 704-706
moootness, 707
delegation, 709-711
codefendant confession, 712-715
harmless error, 712
effective deletion rule, 712-713
confrontation, 712-714
Warren choice as C.J., 720
residence requirement, 725-732
right to travel, 728-732
bifurcation and standards, 740-741
post-conviction proceedings, 748-749
Landau incident, 750-752
Warren deathbed visit, 768, 771-772
Bricker Amendment, 246-247
Bring, Murray H., 70
Brown, Edmund G. (Pat), 11, 17, 18, 21, 226, 390, 399-400
Brown, Tyrone, 63, 719-720
Brownell, Herbert, 1-2, 4-6, 20, 22-23, 137, 173, 228
Bryce, James, 31
Burger, Warren E., 21, 70, 109, 146, 153, 201, 757, 763-765, 767-769
Burke, Edmund, 49
Burlingham, C. C., 148

Burton, Harold H., 4, 29, 33, 35, 56, 57, 58, 62, 77, 82, 87, 88, 90, 93, 96-98, 100, 101, 116-117, 119, 136, 140, 154, 157, 159, 164, 166, 173, 179, 181, 183, 185, 186, 190, 193, 194, 196, 197, 205, 209, 211, 218, 219, 220, 223-227, 229, 233-236, 239, 240, 244, 246, 262, 266, 297, 310-314, 318, 319-320, 322, 329, 330
Business of the Supreme Court, 149
Bus transportation, 126, 716
Butler, Richard C., 290-292
Byrnes, James F., 55, 56, 111

Cahn, Edmond, 277
Calhoun, John C., 124, 276
Califano, Joseph, 495
California Bar Association, 489
California Criminal Syndicalism Act, 755
Callaway, Howard H., 769
Cardozo, Benjamin N., 26, 53, 109, 394, 448
Cemetery discrimination, 156-158
Censorship, 216, 368, 569
Census Bureau, 401
Churchill, Winston, 38, 173, 179-180, 284
Citizenship, 191, 313-319, 357-358, 404-406, 449, 670-671
Civil Aeronautics Board, 146
Civil Rights Act, 1866, 702
Civil Rights Act, 1957, 355
Civil Rights Act, 1964, 512, 517, 518, 525, 552-555
Civil Rights Act, 1968, 703
Civil Rights Commission, 352
Civil Rights, President's Committee on, 591
Civil-rights protests, 47, 402-404, 479-487, 492, 508-525, 552-559, 631-634, 735-736
Clapp, Alfred, 6
Clark, Kenneth B., 106-108
Clark, Ramsey, 677-678
Clark, Tom C., 15, 16, 29, 52, 56, 57-58, 65, 72, 73, 77, 81, 88, 89, 91, 98, 100, 102, 107-108, 119, 136, 138, 140, 141, 144, 154, 157, 159, 160, 164, 168, 178, 179, 183, 184, 187-188, 191, 192, 193, 194, 195, 197, 200, 207, 208, 209, 211, 213, 218, 219, 220, 222, 225-230, 233-236, 239, 240, 241, 244, 246, 249, 261, 266, 278, 284, 293-295, 298, 301, 304, 307, 310-314, 318, 322, 323, 326, 327, 329, 330, 332, 333, 338-340, 342, 343, 345, 347-349, 363-371, 374-379, 382, 385-387, 392-398, 405-408, 412, 414, 417, 419-424, 431, 432, 434-439, 442, 443, 447, 449, 454-457, 459-468, 471, 472, 474-478, 481, 485, 486, 495, 506, 507, 512, 513, 516, 519-524, 528-530, 534, 538-540, 544, 545, 548-555, 558, 559, 561, 564, 566-572, 574-576, 578, 592, 594, 595, 601, 604-607, 609-611, 615, 617, 619-625, 631, 632, 635, 639-642, 648-650, 656, 657, 659, 660-668, 670, 672-678, 695, 699, 700, 709-711
Clay, Cassius, 750
Clayton, James E., 465, 476, 486, 487, 489-490
Clayton Act, 222-224, 437-438, 476-478
Clifford, Clark, 761

Coakley, Frank, 12
Coast Guard, 198
Codefendant confession, 711-715
Coleman, William T., 76
Commerce power, 149, 162-163, 334, 511, 553-555, 726
Comptroller of the Currency, 475-476
Communist cases, 152, 173, 177-180, 182-188, 208, 225-226, 228-239, 266, 285, 309, 312, 361-365, 560-562, 624-625, 669-670, 709-711
Communist registration, 185-188, 364-365, 560-562, 624-625, 709
Compelling interest test, 684-685, 728-732
Comstock Act, 435
Conference of State Chief Justices, 283
Confessions, 11, 331, 457, 588-593
Conflict of interest, 382-383
Confrontation, 574, 712-714
Congressional investigations, 177-179, 234-239
Connally, John, 441
Conscription, 404-405, 570, 683-685
Contempt, 191, 236, 333, 432, 744-745
Contraceptive prohibition, 378-379, 577-580
Contrived litigation, 379
Cooper, John Sherman, 497
Corwin, Edward S., 251
Costello, Frank, 215, 273
Council of State Governments, 474
Counsel, 192, 331, 341, 385, 407-410, 456, 460, 528, 588-592, 657-663
County-unit system, 433, 465, 635
Courthouse picketing, 557-559
Courts-martial, 180-182, 240-245, 313, 317, 332, 347-349, 745-747
Cox, Archibald, 495
Cox, B. Elton, 557-559
Criminal libel, 566-568
Cross-examination, 153-154, 712-714
Cruel and unusual punishment, 317-318, 358
Curtis, Carl, 426

Daly, John, 724
Davis, John W., 94, 112, 113
Death penalty, 717, 738-742
Deceptive practices, 586-587
Dechert, Robert, 249
Declaratory judgment, 755-757
Decoto, Ezra, 9
Defendant testimony, 385-386
Defense, Secretary of, 709-710
Delegation, 563, 709-711
Dempsey, William H., 70
Denationalization, 313-316, 404-406, 449
Denning, Lord, 278, 491
Deportation, 152, 212, 266
Desegregation, Chapter 3, 289-303, 609-611
Desperate Hours, 642

Dethmers, John R., 283
Dewey, John, 38
Dewey, Thomas E., 1, 19
Dewitt, John L., 16
Divorce, 139-142
Dixon-Yates affair, 382-383
Doctor and Student, 61
Domicile, 139-143
Donovan, Robert J., 125, 174
Double jeopardy, 152, 288, 322-324, 742-743
Douglas, Mercedes, 51, 488
Douglas, William O.
    Frankfurter disagreements, 39, 52-55, 73, 306-309, 360-361
    Black, relations with, 49-50, 487-488, 541, 629, 634-638
    character, 50-52
    law clerks, 51, 60
    opinion writing, 51-52
    Eisenhower opinion, 50
    political ambitions, 54-55
    Brown case, 77, 81, 87, 88, 92, 100, 120
    loyalty cases, 154, 155
    cemetery discrimination, 156-158
    self-incrimination, 168
    government employment, 184
    immunity statute, 188-189
    anti-trust cases, 196
    realignment, 211
    First Amendment, 218, 362, 531, 565-566, 618, 621, 645-648, 653
    obscenity, 218-220, 351, 618, 653, 709
    Communist affiliation, 227
    worker protection, 271
    confidential information, 310
    inspections, 327-328, 343
    Court caseload, 338
    contraceptive prohibition, 379
    Church-State separation, 380, 716
    goose-step requirement, 379
    exclusionary rule, 393
    apportionment, 416, 418, 421-424, 465
    political questions, 420, 464
    narcotics addiction, 439
    school prayer, 440-441
    arrest warrants, 456
    voter equality, 465
    sit-ins, 481, 509-525
    "state action," 481
    personal life, 488
    libel, 531, 566, 615-617, 650
    television, 544
    conscientious objectors, 571
    right of association, 578-579
    privacy, 580
    counsel, 590

literacy test, 599-601
segregation, 610
Southern justice, 611-612
loyalty oath, 625
Georgia gubernatorial election, 634-638
I.C.C. findings, 671
Marshall appointment, 678
draft constitutionality, 685
stop and frisk, 689
American Law Institute, 692
balancing test, 697
illegitimacy, 716
bifurcation and standards, 739-742
courts-martial, 746-747
Landau incident, 751-752
Fortas adviser, 761
foundation fee, 762
Draft-card burning, 683-685
Drummond, Roscoe, 170
Due process, 99, 105, 133, 219, 225, 307, 310-311, 322-324, 327, 332, 350, 366, 385, 394, 395, 397, 409-410, 527, 529, 547, 580, 658-659, 669, 673, 711, 743
Dulles, Allen, 497
Dulles, John Foster, 3, 203
Dunne, Gerald T., 203

Eastland, James O., 110, 183, 249-250, 474, 674-676
Eavesdroppers, The, 387
Eavesdropping, 11, 386-387, 401, 639-640, 718-719
Effective deletion rule, 712-713
Ehrenhaft, Peter D., 767-768
Eighth Amendment, 317-318, 405
Einstein, Albert, 38
Eisenhower, Dwight D., 1-7, 20-23, 50, 112, 124-125, 150, 169-175, 179-180, 205, 216, 250, 290, 293, 320, 382, 428, 463, 627
Elman, Phillip, 73, 82
Employer's liability, 9, 268-269
Entick, John, 575
Equal protection, Chapter 3, 370, 410-427, 479-486, 501-508, 599-606, 635, 717, 725-732
Establishment of religion, 380-382, 440-443, 466-470
Ethics code, 762
Exclusionary rule, 206, 345, 391-398, 688
Executive agreements, 165-166
Exhaustion of administrative remedies, 146, 360-361
Expatriation, 313-319, 357-358, 404-406, 449

Fair Labor Standards Act, 268-269
Fair play amendment, 20-21
Fanny Hill, 618-622, 708
Faubus, Orval, 289-291, 294
Fay, Edward M., 470
Federal Bureau of Investigation, 22, 339-340, 443, 589
Federal Employers' Liability Act, 268-272
Federal Lobbying Act, 152

Federal Power Commission, 334
Federal Tort Claims Act, 198, 210
Federal Trade Commission, 476, 478, 586
Feinberg Law, 669-670
Fifteenth Amendment, 355, 378, 598, 599
Fifth Amendment, 152, 166-168, 177-179, 183-185, 322, 332, 528, 561, 588-595, 624, 630, 657-663, 695-701, 742
Figg, Robert McCormick, 114
Finkelstein, Louis, 287
First Amendment, 46-48, 152, 178-179, 185, 218-222, 237-238, 362, 367, 368, 379, 380-382, 384, 392-393, 431-432, 440, 450, 466-470, 531-541, 561-562, 565-571, 577-579, 607-608, 612-623, 630, 632, 642-656, 667, 683-685, 706-711, 729, 733-734, 737-738, 754-755
Flag burning, 732-734
Flag salute, 43, 48
Flaubert, Gustave, 258
Flynn, John J., 588
Flynn, Richard, 96, 98-99, 107, 138
Footnote 11, 98, 106-108, 705
Ford, Gerald R., 497, 499
Fortas, Abe, 48, 87, 139, 391, 459, 584-585, 588-590, 592, 594, 595, 597, 601-602, 605-612, 615, 616, 618-623, 625, 629-631, 633, 634, 638, 641, 643-649, 651, 653-655, 658-666, 670, 672-676, 682, 683, 693, 700, 704, 709-711, 714, 716-721, 723, 727-728, 731, 734, 736-745, 748, 749, 752-758, 760-763
Fourth Amendment, 135-137, 339, 345, 386-387, 391-398, 401, 462-463, 639-642, 674, 685-692, 718-719, 747-750
Francis, Willie, 75, 76
Frank, Jerome, 165
Frankfurter, Felix
Chief Justice, 29, 31, 305
Black disagreements, 33-35, 37, 40, 73, 275, 349
Court conferences, 39, 53, 261, 263
oral arguments, 39, 64-65
judicial restraint, 41-46, 75-76, 148, 159-161, 186-188, 325, 329, 342, 348, 377, 379
Holmes disciple, 42
flag-salute, 43, 48
mock opinions, 37, 45, 216
absolutist approach, 46-47, 351
Douglas disagreements, 52-55, 73, 275, 306-309, 360-361
law clerks, 60-62, 69-71, 340, 346
certiorari petitions, 60, 67
"Greetings" memoranda, 61
Brown case, 72, 76-82, 84-85, 88, 90-96, 98, 102, 103, 108, 115-117, 119, 120
death penalty, 76
stare decisis, 77, 386
"all deliberate speed," 122-124
Fourth Amendment, 135-136, 265-266, 387, 391-398
domicile, 140
early praise of Warren, 147-148, 150-151

cemetery discrimination, 157-158
miscegenation, 159-161
Bill of Rights incorporation, 167, 397
Eisenhower opinion, 175
Congressional committees, 179, 326
courts-martial, 181, 348
jury trial, 182
government employment, 184
Communist registration, 186-188, 364-365
immunity statute, 188-189
preferred position, 189-190, 265
anti-trust cases, 196
rewriting statutes, 197-198
lighthouse negligence, 198-199
"walking on eggs," 200
Brennan relations, 206, 211, 258, 265, 275, 306, 331, 353, 356, 362
exclusionary rule, 206
Warren disagreements, 206, 210-211, 252, Chapter 7, 291-292, 305, 319, 349, 352-354, 359-360, 366, 383, 400, 431-435, 487
realignment, 211
anti-trust, 213, 223, 377
prior judicial service, 216
obscenity, 218-221
arraignment, 225
legislative investigations, 235-239, 325-326
First Amendment, 237-238, 367, 384, 433
courts-martial, 241-245
Bricker Amendment, 246-247
Washington Post editorial, 256, 261
worker protection, 268-272
stroke, 273, 291, 409, 427
husband-wife conspiracy, 274
Little Rock case, 293-295, 297-303
separate opinions, 294-295, 302-303, 352-354, 381
joint opinion suggestion, 299-300
association, freedom of, 304
passports, 310-311
denationalization, 313-319, 406
double jeopardy, 322-324
inspections, 327-328, 344
security dismissals, 329
committee burden, 335
mootness, 341
Dialogue, 346
handbills, 347
"damned certs," 359
allocution right, 369
apportionment, 378, 410-427, 465, 502, 507
hypothetical case, 379
due process, 385, 527, 529
1960 election, 390
exclusionary rule, 391-398
women jury exclusion, 400

sit-ins, 402-404
counsel, 408-409, 458
retirement, 427
jury composition, 431
contempt, 432-433
regulation vs. taking, 434-435
lawyer regulation, 450-451
F.B.I. protection, 443
Goldberg estimate, 446-448
attorney solicitation, 450
first names, 529-530
Franklin, Benjamin, 84
Freedom of choice, 703-706
Freedom Riders, 428-429, 555-556
Free exercise of religion, 468-470, 570-572
French, John D., 61
Freund, Paul A., 426, 428, 767-768
Freund Committee, 767-768
Friendly, Fred W., 543
Friendly, Henry J., 346, 425, 529, 679
Fundamental rights, 684-685, 728-732

Gallup Poll, 170
Gambling, 8, 694-701
Gates, Oliver, 147
Georgetown University Hospital, 769, 771
Georgia gubernatorial election, 634-638
Gerhart, Eugene C., 6
Gibbons, Cardinal, 328
Gideon, Clarence Earl, 66, 456-460
Gideon's Trumpet, 457
Glenn, John, 399
Goldberg, Arthur J., 17, 109, 321, 352, 353, 390, 445-452, 455, 464, 467-469, 472, 473, 477, 481, 484, 490-491, 493, 494, 503, 506, 512-521, 524-525, 527, 534, 538-540, 544, 548, 551, 553, 554, 556, 558-559, 561-563, 567, 568, 571-573, 575, 576, 578, 580, 583-584, 587, 596-597, 618, 629, 720, 765
Golden West, Native Sons of the, 15
Goldwater, Barry, 321, 542, 581
Graham, Billy, 441
Grand jury, 333, 352, 421, 432
Graves, John Temple, 35
Gregory, Dick, 735
Griffin, Robert, 720
Griswold, Erwin, 279
Gunther, John, 7, 148

Habeas corpus, 470-475, 747-748
Habitual criminal, 664-665
Hagerty, James, 171, 172
Hand, Learned, 38, 47, 52, 53, 94, 214, 260-261, 276-279, 284, 321, 338, 390
Handbills, 346
Handwriting exemplars, 656
Hard-core pornography, 321, 436

Harlan, John M., 34, 38, 47, 50, 52, 53, 57, 61, 62, 95, 112, 117, 119, 136, 154, 157, 176-177, 179, 183, 184, 190, 191, 193-195, 197, 200, 202, 209, 210, 211-212, 213, 218, 219, 220, 222, 224, 225, 227, 229, 230, 233-235, 239-246, 249, 251, 259, 263, 266, 270, 272, 274, 275, 284, 286, 293, 298-300, 303, 304, 306, 308, 310, 311, 313, 314, 316, 318, 322, 323, 326-333, 338, 340, 345-347, 349, 352-357, 360, 363-367, 369-377, 379-385, 392, 396, 397, 400, 403, 405, 406, 408, 412, 414-417, 431, 432, 434-439, 447-451, 457, 459-469, 471, 472, 475, 476, 478, 481, 482, 484, 487, 491, 492, 502, 506, 507, 509, 512, 522, 524, 528-541, 544, 548, 551-556, 558, 559, 565-571, 574-576, 580, 585, 589-590, 592-595, 597, 599-603, 606, 607, 609-614, 616, 618, 619, 621, 631-633, 635, 639, 641, 644, 648-652, 654, 656, 657, 659, 662-666, 671-674, 684, 690-692, 695-707, 709-711, 714, 716-718, 725, 728, 730-737, 739-743, 746-749, 753, 755, 758, 759
Harmless error, 712
Hart, Henry, 349, 471
Harvard Law School, 37, 39, 48, 70, 303, 750
Hastie, William H., 428
Health, Education, and Welfare Department, 610-611
Henry, Aaron, 572-573
Heymann, Philip B., 587
Hoadly, Bishop, 27
Hoffa, James R., 750
Holmes, Oliver Wendell, 34, 36, 40-42, 46-48, 52, 59, 109, 122, 162, 163, 184, 274, 278, 335, 359, 386, 448, 492
Hoover, Herbert, 12, 165, 677
Hoover, J. Edgar, 228, 311, 541
Housing discrimination, 702-703
Hughes, Charles Evans, 27, 50, 143, 274, 295, 297, 448, 677
Hughes, Charles Evans, Jr., 677
Humphrey, Hubert H., 627, 763
Hypothetical case, 379

Illegitimacy, 715-716
Immigration and Nationality Act, 404
Immigration and Naturalization Service, 152, 339-340, 449, 563
Immunity statute, 152, 188-189
Impeachment, 250, 280-281, 491, 541, 627
Income tax evasion, 199, 214
Income tax fraud, 717
Informers, 208-209, 638
Inspections, 326-328, 342-344, 642
Integrated Bar, 372-377
Interior, Department of the, 222, 328
Interior, Secretary of the, 487
Internal Revenue Code, 214
Internal Revenue Service, 584, 717
Internal Security Act, 312

Interposition, 124
Interstate Commerce Commission, 45, 671

Jackson, Andrew, 723, 759
Jackson, Robert H., 4, 25, 28, 32, 33, 35-37, 39, 40, 60, 72, 73, 80, 82, 88, 89, 90, 92-95, 98, 104, 112, 136-137, 157, 175-176, 411, 502
Jahnsen, Oscar, 10, 11
"Jap Alley," 8
Japanese evacuation, 14-17, 57
Japanese Peace Treaty, 333
Jefferson, Thomas, 101, 110, 182
Jenner-Butler bill, 280
Jewish law, 287-288, 447
Jewish Theological Seminary, 287, 489
John Birch Society, 280-282, 541
Johnson, Hiram, 17
Johnson, Lyndon B., 63, 280, 495-496, 581-585, 677-682, 720-724, 737
Johnston, Olin D., 172
Joint Anti-Fascist Refugee Committee, 151
Jones, Bobby, 382
Jones, James R., 680
Judicial Conference, 391, 762
Jury discrimination, 138-139
Jury trial, 181-182, 400, 744-745
Justice, Department of, 291, 465, 475-477, 513, 591, 750
Juvenile delinquency, 672-673

Katzenbach, Nicholas, 428, 495
Keck, William B., 21
Kempton, Murray, 275
Kennedy, Edward M., 465
Kennedy, Jacqueline B., 493, 494
Kennedy, John F., 37, 63, 275, 389-391, 425, 428-429, 442, 445-446, 465, 490, 493-501, 512
Kennedy, Robert F., 37, 425, 428-429, 445-446, 459, 463, 465, 680
Kent, Rockwell, 309-311
Kenny, Robert W., 13-14, 18
Khrushchev, Nikita, 490
King, Martin Luther, 492, 632-634
Klein, Herbert G., 723
Kleindienst, Richard G., 752
Kluger, Richard, 75
Krock, Arthur, 33, 105, 106, 171, 208, 426, 502, 507

Lady Chatterley's Lover, 351
Landau, Jack C., 750-752
Landis Report, 383
Langer, William, 22
Lash, Joseph P., 54
Legislative apportionments, 124, 337-378, 410-427, 501-508, 625-627, 672, 752-753
Legislative exclusion, 666-668, 757-760
Legislative immunity, 674-676

Legislative investigations, 234-239, 452-453
Lewis, Anthony, 32, 38, 59, 112, 251-252, 263-264, 267, 270, 338, 349, 426, 458, 501, 507, 526-527, 586-688
Lewis, Fulton, Jr., 281, 499
Lewis, Sinclair, 204
Libel, 531-541, 566-568, 612-617, 648-652
Lie detectors, 595
Lien priority, 145, 354
Lincoln, Abraham, 264
Lineup, 656-663
Lippitt, Perry, 445
Lippmann, Walter, 16
Literacy test, 599-602
Livingston, J. Ed, 472
Loevinger, Lee, 476
Louisiana Criminal Defamation Law, 566
Loyalty cases, 56, 152-155, 230-232, 328-329
Loyalty oath, 625
Loyalty Review Board, 152-154
Lyell, G. Garland, 572

Macaulay, Thomas B., 182
Macmillan, Harold, 284
McCarthy, Joseph R., 183, 201, 249-250, 280, 431
McCloy, John J., 497
McCormack, John W., 494
McGrory, Mary, 390
McHugh, Margaret, 25, 68, 133, 493-494, 762, 770
McIntyre, Cardinal, 441
McKay, Douglas, 101
McNamara, Robert, 496
McReynolds, James C., 73, 99, 143, 279, 669, 754
McWilliams, Carey, 14, 15
Maddox, Lester, 706
Madison, James, 101, 315
Mailliard, William S., 4, 19
Maine, Sir Henry, 13
Mann, Oscar, 769-770
Mann Act, 165, 354
Mansfield, Mike, 490, 494
Marshall, John, 7, 26, 29, 101, 109, 295-297, 723, 759, 766
Marshall, Thurgood, 63, 83, 113, 129, 678-679, 694, 709, 711, 712, 718, 728, 741, 744-747, 753, 755-758
Maxwell, David, 284
Mazo, Earl, 336-337
Membership Clause, 312, 363-364
Mencken, H. L., 753
Meredith, James, 463, 732
Mere evidence rule, 640-642
Meyer, Agnes, 399
Minimum wages, 145
Minton, Sherman, 28, 33, 34-35, 56, 58-59, 77, 87, 88, 90, 93, 100, 136, 140, 141, 157, 175, 179, 181, 183, 184, 185, 186, 190, 191, 193, 194, 196, 197, 204, 218, 229, 230, 233-236, 239, 240, 246, 250, 261, 268, 271, 272, 275, 329, 351, 382, 446

Miscegenation, 158-162, 668-669
Mitchell, John, 749-751, 761
Moley, Raymond, 12
Mollenhoff, Clark R., 337
Moore, Leonard P., 753
Mootness, 341, 706-707
Murphy, Frank, 40, 54, 57, 268
Musicians' union, 715
Myrdal, Gunnar, 106-108, 705

Narcotics addiction, 438-439, 693
National Association for the Advancement of Colored People, 83, 92, 113, 304-305, 350, 367, 450-453, 572, 678
National Court of Appeals, 767-768
National Industrial Recovery Act, 12
National Labor Relations Act, 562, 665
National Labor Relations Board, 145, 197, 665
National Lawyers Club, 627
Nationality Act, 404, 449
Necessary and Proper Clause, 181, 243, 348, 600
Newman, Jon, 316
New York City Charter, 166
New York Criminal Anarchy Law, 755
Nine Men Against America, 250
Nixon, Richard M., 4, 21, 22, 23, 170, 171, 172, 284, 336-337, 390, 399-400, 593, 642-643, 680-682, 722-725, 761-765, 769-772
Non-Communist affidavit, 562
Nover, Barnet, 337

Obscenity, 217-222, 321, 350-351, 392, 435-437, 618-623, 652-656, 706-709
Oliver, William, 96, 98-99
Olney, Warren, 497
Olson, Culbert L., 19
Oswald, Lee Harvey, 494, 500, 501
Oswald, Marina, 500
Overbreadth, 577, 608, 692, 735
Oxford History of the American People, 582

Paine, Ruth Hyde, 500
Parker, John J., 165
Passport Act, 563-564
Passports, 309-311, 404, 563-565
Patent offensiveness, 436
Patterson, Edgar, 97
Paul VI, Pope, 490
Pearson, Drew, 399, 582
Pennsylvania Sedition Act, 182
Per se rule, 551-552, 592
Petty offenses, 744-745
Planned Parenthood League, 577
Plessy, Homer Adolph, 74
Police interrogation, 587-593
Political questions, 415-416, 419-420
Pollock, Earl, 96-98

Pollock, Sir Frederick, 41, 122
Poll tax, 560, 596-597
Pornography, 8, 217-222, 321, 350-351, 392, 435-437, 618-623
Post-conviction proceedings, 747-749
Postmaster General, 437
Post Office, 436-437, 565
Powell, Adam Clayton, 757-760
Powers, Robert B., 11, 16
Preemption, 183, 235
Preferred position, 189-190, 265
Presumptions, 405, 575-576
Primary jurisdiction, 306
Prisoner punishment, 719-720
Privacy, 330, 395, 397-398, 514, 577-580, 630, 642-648, 690
Public defender, 10
Public drunkenness, 693-694

Railroad merger, 671-672
Railway Labor Act, 371
Rankin, J. Lee, 248, 358, 497-499
Rational basis test, 727-728
Rayburn, Sam, 583
Reagan, Ronald, 765
Realignment, 210-211
Reapportionment, 124, 410-427, 492, 493, 496, 501-508, 526, 625-627, 752-753
Redlich, Norman, 496-500
"Red Monday," 230-239, 249-250
Reed, Stanley, 31, 33, 42, 43, 56, 72, 84, 88, 89, 90, 91, 92, 93, 94, 96, 100, 105, 119, 128, 136, 140, 154, 155, 157, 159, 164, 167, 178, 179, 181, 183, 184-186, 189-194, 196-198, 207, 209, 215, 217-219, 224, 225, 229, 230, 233-236, 240-243, 268, 495
Regulation vs. taking, 434-435
Rehnquist, William H., 60
Required records doctrine, 696, 699-701
Religious oath, 381-382
Residence requirement, 725-732
Reston, James, 106, 168, 170-171, 200, 250
Ripeness, 379-380
Rivers, Mendel, 442
Roberts, Owen J., 55, 168
Rodda, Richard H., 400
Rodell, Fred, 32, 52, 54, 58, 148
Rogers, S. Emory, 113-115, 121
Rogers, William P., 291, 320, 724-725
Roosevelt, Eleanor, 19, 48, 390
Roosevelt, Franklin D., 12, 18, 38, 53, 55, 56, 58, 155, 260, 274
Roosevelt, James, 19
Roosevelt, Theodore, 274
Rosenthal, A. M., 203
Ruby, Jack, 275, 494
Russell, Richard B., 426, 497, 500, 501
Rutledge, Wiley, 411

St. Germain, Christopher, 61
Sanders, Carl, 282
Schlesinger, Arthur M., Jr., 38, 429
Schmidt, Benno, 133, 667-669
School prayer, 440-443
School segregation, Chapter 3, 609-611, 703-706
Schubert, Glendon, 127
Scienter, 350-351, 654
Securities Act, 145
Security dismissals, 328-329
Segregation, Chapter 3, 139, 159, 463, 479-484, 506, 509-516, 555, 606-610, 631, 703-706
Selassie, Haile, 490
Self-incrimination, 152, 166-168, 177-179, 183-185, 288, 365, 528, 561, 588-595, 624, 630, 657-663, 694-701, 739
Seventh Day Adventists, 468-470
Shaw, Bernard, 195
Shea, Willard W., 10-11
Sherman Act, 195-196, 377, 384, 438, 476-478, 715
Shogan, James, 585
Shuttlesworth, F. L., 480
Siegel, William I., 470
Silver platter doctrine, 345
Sinclair, Upton, 12
Sit-ins, 47, 402-404, 479-487, 492, 508-526, 606-608, 630, 735
Sixth Amendment, 181, 574, 588-590, 657-663
Small, Merrill H., 6, 19
Smith, Al, 12
Smith, Howard, 183
Smith Act, 182-183, 208, 231-234, 312, 318, 325, 363
Sobeloff, Simon E., 328
Social security, 342
Social Security Act, 717, 725-726, 731
Solicitor General, 1-3, 6, 56, 63, 73, 248, 321, 358, 412, 509, 512-513, 622, 677, 678, 711, 718
Southern Conference Educational Fund, 674
Southern Pacific Railroad, 7, 271
Spahn, Warren, 647
Specter, Arlen, 498
Speech and Debate Clause, 674
Speech volume, 737-738
Spike microphone, 386
Standards, 738-742
Stare decisis, 77, 386
Stassen, Harold, 21
State, Secretary of, 55, 231, 309-310, 563-565
State action, 156-158, 355-356, 370-371, 481, 702
Stein, Gertrude, 47
Stennis, John, 60
Stevenson, Adlai, 390, 399, 583
Stewart, Potter, 14, 30, 31, 32, 39, 53, 69, 129, 132, 134, 139, 141, 143, 144, 175, 204, 255, 257, 258, 265, 273, 278, 320-325, 330-334, 338-349, 355-358, 361-372, 374, 375, 378-380, 383, 384, 387, 396, 397, 401, 404-408, 412-424, 430-432, 435-437, 439, 440, 441, 447, 451, 453, 454, 456, 461, 465, 467-469, 471, 472, 481, 494,

507, 512, 513, 518, 521, 522, 524, 528-530, 534, 538, 544-546, 551-553, 556, 558, 567-571, 574-578, 580, 588, 592, 594, 595, 597, 599, 600, 602-606, 609-611, 615-618, 620-623, 631-633, 635, 638, 641, 648-650, 653, 656, 657, 659, 662-673, 691, 692-694, 700-707, 709-711, 714, 717-719, 725, 728-731, 735-739, 741-743, 747-749, 753, 754-757, 759, 760
Stockholder's suit, 210
Stomach pump, 135, 207
Stone, Harlan F., 28, 35, 43, 50, 144, 411, 682
Stone, Irving, 8, 204
Stop and frisk, 685-692
Stuart, Gilbert, 84
Substitute father, 717
Subversive Activities Control Act, 364, 709
Sunday Closing Laws, 380-381, 469
Supreme Court
    swearing-in ceremony, 23-24, 445-446
    constitutional role, 26-27
    building, 27-28
    traditions, 28
    Chief Justice role, 29-31, 73
    opinion assignment, 29-30, 418
    collegiate nature, 31
    law clerks, 59-63
    operation, 63-65
    certiorari procedure, 63-64
    oral arguments, 64
    conferences (*see also* individual cases), 65
    decision Mondays, 65, 101, 129
    decision announcements, 65
    in forma pauperis cases, 66-67, 69, 338, 458
    conference room, 84
    courtroom quill pens, 128
    page boys, 129-130
    Christmas party, 129-130
    attorney admission, 130-131
    growing caseload, 338, 399
    seating order, 430
    nonjudicial assignments, 490-491
    principal and companion cases, 504
    pay raise, 542
    photos and broadcasting, 543
    Acting Chief Justice, 682-683
Symbolic speech, 683-685, 737

Taft, Robert A., 20, 21
Taft, William Howard, 25, 274, 677
Taft-Hartley Act, 197, 352, 563
Talmudic law, 287-288
Taney, Roger B., 295, 296, 297
Tariff Commission, 165
Television, 461, 543-552
Tenth Amendment, 219
Texas Communist Control Law, 574

Textbook law, 716-717
Thirteenth Amendment, 702-703
Thompson, Francis, 122
Thurmond, Strom, 250, 721
Tibbett, Lawrence, 8
Tito, 399
Tocqueville, Alexis de, 26, 27
Transcripts, 193-195
Travel, right to, 563-565, 711, 725-732
Treasury, Secretary of the, 565
Trespass, 386-387, 639, 718
Truman, Harry S., 1, 17, 19-20, 35, 55, 56-58, 288, 563
Tweed, Harrison, 282-283
Twenty-fourth Amendment, 560

Ulmer, S. Sidney, 90
Un-American Activities Committee, 151, 177-179, 233, 234, 325, 326, 361, 431
Unfair labor practices, 665
Uniform Code of Military Justice, 180-182, 239-241
Union dues, 372-377
Unitary trial, 738-742
United Givers Fund, 131

Vanderbilt, Arthur T., 6, 205
Variable obscenity, 708
Vinson, Fred M., 3, 7, 22, 31, 50, 58, 62, 71, 72-75, 78, 81, 82, 85, 88, 89, 95, 130, 144, 150, 411, 429, 682
Virgin Islands Divorce Law, 139
Voting Rights Act, 598

Wagering tax, 694-701
Wagner Act, 145
Wallace, George C., 463, 627
Walker, Wyatt Tee, 632
Walter Reed Army Hospital, 769-770
Warrants, 339-340
Warren, Charles, 38, 276
Warren, Dorothy, 494
Warren, Earl
    Chief Justice appointment, 1-7, 28
    Solicitor General offer, 1-3, 6
    Eisenhower, relations with, 2, 124-125, 172-174, 320
    early life, 7-9
    gambling, 8, 694-701
    pornography, 8, 218-222, 350, 435-437, 618-623
    corruption, 8, 330-331, 382-384
    worker protection, 8-9, 268-272
    Frankfurter disagreements, 9, 124, Chapter 7, 291-292, 305, 319, 336, 338, 344, 349, 352-354, 359-360, 366, 400, 431-435, 487
    army service, 9, 495-496
    district attorney, 9-14, 17, 137, 335, 382, 628
    eavesdropping, 11, 386-387, 401, 462-463, 639, 718
    father's murder, 11-12
    coerced confessions, 11

civil liberties statement, 13
Attorney General, 13-17, 137, 489
marriage, 14
family, 14, 139-143, 354
scale of values, 14, 87, 139-143, 354
Japanese evacuation, 14-17
Governor, 17-19, 411, 419, 503-504, 677, 715, 730
Vice-President nominee, 19
Presidential candidate, 20
Nixon antipathy, 21, 336-337, 643, 681-682, 723, 770-772
swearing-in, 23-24
opinion assignment, 30, 418, 460-461, 467-468
law clerks, 62-63, 65-71, 115-116, 126, 136-137, 391, 458-459, 526, 682, 649, 684
sports, 62, 132-133, 162-164, 213, 258, 443, 508, 526, 676-677
opinion writing, 68, 96-97, 526
Brown case, 82-111
conference leadership, 84-88, 117-118, 143-146
footnote 11, 98, 106-108
Brown II, 113-124
"all deliberate speed," 121-124, 505
Southern resistance, 124-125
reapportionment, 124, 377, 410-427, 465, 503-508, 541, 626, 752-753
Court changes, 129-130, 133
attorney admission, 131
friendliness, 131-132
first opinion, 134
workmen's compensation, 134, 268
jury discrimination, 138-139
family in society, 139-143
divorce, 139-143
early restraint, 146, 151-155, 188
house hunting, 150
cemetery discrimination, 156-158
miscegenation, 158-162, 668-669
anti-trust cases, 162-164, 195-196, 213, 223-224, 376-377, 384, 437-438, 476-478
executive agreements, 165-166
self-incrimination, 166-168, 183-185, 694-701
1956 election, 169-171
Southern criticism, 171-172, 250
Communist cases, 173, 177, 179, 182-188, 208, 226-239, 285, 312, 361-365, 560-562, 624-625, 670, 709-711
restraint abandonment, 177 et seq.
Congressional committees, 177-179
First Amendment, 178-179, 185, 237-238, 369, 384, 433, 643
civil vs. military power, 180-182, 240-245, 317-318, 348
preemption, 183, 235, 324
Communist registration, 185-186, 365, 560-562, 624
"improvidently granted" formula, 190-191

citizenship, 191, 313-319, 357, 405-407, 449, 670-671
"clear and convincing" standard, 191
contempt, 192, 333, 432-433, 744
counsel, 192, 331, 341, 407-409, 458-460
free transcripts, 193-195
labor cases, 197
lighthouse negligence, 199
fairness, 199-200, 334, 628
official car, 201
travels, 201-203, 358, 399, 490
modern art, 204
blood test, 207, 594
stomach pump, 207
"B.B.D. and W.," 208, 252
informers, 208-209
realignment, 211
deportation, 212, 266-267
government changed position, 214-215
obscenity, 218-222, 350, 435-437, 618-623, 652
arraignment, 225-226
Bar admission, 229-230, 362-363
legislative investigations, 235-239, 324-326, 330, 452
murdering wives case, 240-245
impeachment campaign, 250, 280-281, 491, 541, 627
Court as Chancery, 267
Holmes aphorism, 274-275
Warren Commission, 275, 495-501, 525-526, 541, 583
extreme critics, 280-282, 442
New Yorker, cartoon, 281
Southern visit, 282
A.B.A. relations, 282-286
hospitality to Justices, 286
Talmudic law, 287-288, 447
Little Rock case, 289-303
passports, 310, 311, 563-565
expatriation, 313-319, 357, 405-407, 449
double jeopardy, 322-324
inspections, 327-328, 343, 642
security dismissals, 329
confession without attorney, 331-332
first Supreme Court argument, 335
administrative arrests, 339-340
mootness, 341, 707
social security benefits, 342
silver platter doctrine, 345
exclusionary rule, 345, 393
handbills, 346
Shuffling Sam case, 350, 402, 482, 553, 556, 735
scienter, 350
investigation procedure, 351-352
Taft-Hartley injunction, 352
"state action," 355-356, 370, 510, 702
employment loss, 366
association, right of, 367
censorship, 368-369, 569
allocution right, 369

union dues, 372-377
integrated Bar, 372-377
apportionment, 377, 410-427, 465, 503-508, 581, 626, 672, 752-753
contraceptive prohibition, 379, 577
contrived litigation, 379
Sunday laws, 380-381
religious oath, 381-382
Dixon-Yates affair, 382-383
defendant testimony, 385
Kennedy inauguration, 389
hunting, 390, 399, 443, 508
women jury exclusion, 400
census reports, 401
sit-ins, 402-404, 480-486, 509-525, 541, 606
political questions, 415-416
jury composition, 431
regulation vs. taking, 434-435
exclusion from mails, 435-437
narcotics addiction, 438-439, 693
school prayer, 440-441
walks, 443
F.B.I. protection, 443
Goldberg estimate, 447-448
attorney solicitation, 450
illegal arrest and "fruits," 454-455
television, 461, 543-551
electronic recording, 462-463
R. F. Kennedy, attitude toward, 463
county-unit system, 465
Bible reading, 465
habeas corpus, 470-475
state courts, 474
Earl Warren Legal Center, 488-489, 765
law and ethics, 489
extrajudicial assignments, 490-491, 495-501
J. F. Kennedy, relations with, 491
Kennedy assassination, 493-495
autopsy photos, 498
act of state doctrine, 530
libel, 531-533, 567, 614, 648-652
civil-rights protests, 552-559, 606, 631-634, 735-736
poll tax, 560, 596-597
bill of attainder, 562
mail detention, 565
conscientious objectors, 570
confrontation, 574
general warrant, 574-575, 639
abortion, 577
Johnson, relations with, 581-583
Goldberg resignation, 583
deceptive practices, 586-587
confessions without counsel, 588-593
Voting Rights Act, 598
Congressional civil-rights power, 599, 603, 605
election day editorial, 612

loyalty oath, 625
75th birthday, 627
Black, split with, 629-640, 663-666, 676-677
informers, 638
mere evidence rule, 640-641
privacy, 643
lineup, 657-663, 743
habitual criminal, 664-665
legislative exclusion, 666-668, 757-760
right to marry, 669
employment of subversives, 670
railroad merger, 671-672
juvenile delinquency, 672-673
legislative immunity, 674-676
retirement letters, 681, 724
draft-card burning, 683-685
symbolic speech, 683-685
compelling interest test, 684-685, 728-732
stop and frisk, 685-692
public drunkenness, 693-694
freedom of choice plan, 704-706
overbreadth, 711
codefendant confessions, 711-712
musicians' union, 715
illegitimacy, 715-716
textbook law, 716
substitute father regulation, 717
death penalty, 717, 739
prison interrogation, 718
prisoner punishment, 719-720
Fortas as C.J., 720
Nixon inauguration, 723, 763
residence requirement, 725-732
rational basis test, 727-728
flag burning, 733-734
armband wearing, 736
speech volume, 737
double jeopardy, 742
petty offenses, 744
jury trial, 744-745
post-conviction proceedings, 747-749
Landau incident, 751-752
anti-evolution statute, 754
decision implementation, 759
Fortas resignation, 760-762
ethics code, 762
retirement, 764-767
law school speeches, 766
Freund Committee report, 767-768
relations with successor, 768-769
Walter Reed incident, 769-770
Watergate, 770-772
"Super Chief," 771
death, 772
Warren, Earl, Jr., 6, 19, 21, 170, 220, 284, 399, 442, 500, 581, 676, 681
Warren, Earl Legal Center, 488-489, 765

Warren, Nina P., 14, 23, 202, 389, 447, 493, 494, 582
Warren, Virginia, 101
Washington, march on, 492
Watergate, 337, 770-772
Welch, Robert, 280-281
Welfare, 717, 725-732
White, Byron R., 69, 144, 201, 258, 316, 336, 390, 428-430, 432, 447, 455-457, 460, 461, 468, 471, 473, 482-486, 506, 512, 513, 518, 527-530, 534, 540, 541, 544, 545, 551, 556, 559, 566-568, 573-576, 580, 588, 592, 594, 595, 597, 601, 602, 606, 616, 619, 621, 623-628, 631, 632, 635, 639, 641-645, 647, 650, 652, 657-659, 662-665, 670, 671-674, 690, 692-694, 699-705, 708-715, 717-719, 725, 728, 731, 733, 736-739, 741, 744, 745, 747-750, 753, 755-758
White, Edward D., 356
Whitehead, Alfred North, 38, 217
Whitman, Alden, 771
Whittaker, Charles E., 39, 42, 175, 207, 211, 215-217, 220, 222, 224, 259-260, 266, 308, 310, 311, 314, 318, 322, 323, 326-330, 332-334, 338, 339, 342, 343, 345, 349, 355, 358, 359, 363-365, 367, 369, 374-380, 383, 387, 405, 406, 408, 409, 412, 414, 417, 424, 427-428, 430, 432, 435, 437, 438, 440, 453, 454, 472, 473, 541, 679
Whittington, Banning E., 102
Who's Who in the South and Southwest, 585
Wilkes, John, 236
Williams, Edward Bennett, 134, 676-677
Wilson, Woodrow, 203, 723
Wiretapping, 344, 462, 750-752
Wolfson, Louis E., 760-762
Workmen's compensation, 134, 268
World Association of Judges, 627
World Peace Through Law, 766
Wyzanski, Charles E., 39, 95

Yorty, Sam W., 593